The Jerusalem Talmud

Second Order: Mo'ed

Tractates *Ta'aniot, Megillah, Ḥagigah* and *Mo'ed Qaṭan (Mašqin)*

Studia Judaica

Forschungen zur Wissenschaft des Judentums

Begründet von
Ernst Ludwig Ehrlich

Herausgegeben von
Günter Stemberger,
Charlotte Fonrobert und
Alexander Samely

Band 85

De Gruyter

The Jerusalem Talmud
תלמוד ירושלמי

Second Order: Mo'ed
סדר מועד
Tractates *Ta'aniot, Megillah, Ḥagigah* and *Mo'ed Qaṭan (Mašqin)*
מסכתות תעניות מגילה חגיגה ומועד קטן (משקין)

Edition, Translation, and Commentary

by

Heinrich W. Guggenheimer

De Gruyter

ISBN 978-3-11-068127-7
e-ISBN (PDF) 978-3-11-041289-5
e-ISBN (ePub) 978-3-11-041293-2

This volume is text- and page-identical with the hardback published in 2015.

Library of Congress Control Number: 2020943461

Bibliographic information published by the Deutsche Nationalbibliothek
The Deutsche Nationalbibliothek lists this publication in the
Deutsche Nationalbibliografie;
detailed bibliographic data are available on the Internet at http://dnb.dnb.de.

© 2020 Walter de Gruyter GmbH, Berlin/Boston

Printing and binding: CPI books GmbH, Leck

www.degruyter.com

This edition of the Talmud Yerushalmi is dedicated to the remembrance of my wife's illustrious ancestors

Rabbi Meïr bar Baruch of Rothenburg, Maharam
1215?-1293

Rabbi Jacob Weilla, Mahariw
Fifteenth Century, Rabbi of Erfurth

Rabbi Jacob Ettlinger, Arukh Laner
1798-1871, Chief Rabbi of Altona

Rabbi Dr. Marcus Horovitz
1844-1910, Rabbi of Frankfurt/Main

Preface

The present volume is the seventeenth and last in this series of the Jerusalem Talmud, the fourth in a four-volume edition, translation, and Commentary of the Second Order of this Talmud. The principles of the edition regarding text, vocalization, and Commentary have been spelled out in detail in the Introduction to the first volume. The text in this volume is based on the manuscript text of the Yerushalmi edited by J. Sussman for the Academy of the Hebrew Language, Jerusalem 2001. The text essentially represents an outline, to be fleshed out by a teacher's explanation. The translation should mirror this slant; it should not endow the text with literary qualities which the original does not possess. In particular, the translation is not intended to stand separate from the Commentary. In one respect the principles of edition have been changed from the previous volumes. Instead of occasionally remarking about questionable changes of the text by the corrector preparing the Venice *editio princeps,* in all cases where the corrector changed the text, the scribe's version is given in (parentheses), the corrector's in [brackets]. Naturally, the corrector rectifies spelling errors and omissions, mostly sentences left out because of homeoteleuton; but in many cases the corrector's additions are questionable, as indicated in the Commentary. The full text will permit every reader to form his own judgment. Translator's additions in the English text are put in {braces}.

As in the preceding volumes, for each paragraph the folio and line numbers of the Krotoschin edition are added. It should be remembered that these numbers may differ from the *editio princeps* by up to three lines. In the Tractates treated in the volume, Mishnah and Halakhah frequently differ widely in numbering. Adapting the headers to both Mishnah and Halakhah would not be satisfactory.

Biblical quotations are given with the masoretic accents, except for words which differ (usually by *plene* spelling) from the masoretic texts. Since the quotes are part of oral tradition, the deviations in spelling are examples of substandard spelling, rather than changes in the text.

Again, I wish to thank my wife, Dr. Eva Guggenheimer, who acted as critic, style editor, proof reader, and expert on the Latin and Greek vocabulary. Her own notes on some possible Latin and Greek etymologies are identified by (E. G.).

Contents

Introduction to Tractate Ta`aniot ... 1

Ta`aniot Chapter 1, מאימתי

Halakhah 1	3
Halakhah 2	18
Halakhah 3	22
Halakhah 4	29
Halakhah 5	34
Halakhah 6	35
Halakhah 7	42
Halakhah 8	44
Halakhah 9	45

Ta`aniot Chapter 2, סדר תעניות כיצד

Halakhah 1	46
Halakhah 2	57
Halakhah 3	66
Halakhah 4	68
Halakhah 5	70
Halakhah 6	71
Halakhah 7	73
Halakhah 8	74
Halakhah 9	75
Halakhah 10	75
Halakhah 11	76
Halakhah 12	77
Halakhah 13	81
Halakhah 14	87
Halakhah 15	89

Ta`aniot Chapter 3, סדר תעניות אילו

Halakhah 1	93
Halakhah 2	95
Halakhah 3	96
Halakhah 4	99

Halakhah 5	103
Halakhah 6	104
Halakhah 7	106
Halakhah 8	106
Halakhah 9	107
Halakhah 10	108
Halakhah 11	110
Halakhah 12	112
Halakhah 13	115
Halakhah 14	117

Ta`aniot Chapter 4 בשלשה פרקים

Halakhah 1	119
Halakhah 2	134
Halakhah 3	144
Halakhah 4	146
Halakhah 5	148
Halakhah 6	150
Halakhah 7	152
Halakhah 8	153
Halakhah 9	177
Halakhah 10	181
Halakhah 11	183

Introduction to Tractate Megillah	187

Megillah Chapter 1 מגילה נקראת

Halakhah 1	188
Halakhah 2	200
Halakhah 3	201
Halakhah 4	202
Halakhah 5	203
Halakhah 6	204
Halakhah 7	215
Halakhah 8	223
Halakhah 9	229
Halakhah 10	230
Halakhah 11	236
Halakhah 12	255

Halakhah 13	265
Halakhah 14	276

Megillah Chapter 2 הקורא את המגילה

Halakhah 1	286
Halakhah 2	289
Halakhah 3	292
Halakhah 4	298
Halakhah 5	303
Halakhah 6	304
Halakhah 7	304

Megillah Chapter 3 בני העיר

Halakhah 1	310
Halakhah 2	318
Halakhah 3	322
Halakhah 4	323
Halakhah 5	325
Halakhah 6	327
Halakhah 7	329
Halakhah 8	331

Megillah Chapter 4 הקורא עומד

Halakhah 1	337
Halakhah 2	349
Halakhah 3	351
Halakhah 4	353
Halakhah 5	358
Halakhah 6	361
Halakhah 7	362
Halakhah 8	364
Halakhah 9	365
Halakhah 10	366
Halakhah 11	368
Halakhah 12	370

Introduction to Tractate Ḥagigah — 375

Ḥagigah Chapter 1 הכל חייבין

Halakhah 1	376
Halakhah 2	388
Halakhah 3	394
Halakhah 4	396
Halakhah 5	398
Halakhah 6	400
Halakhah 7	402
Halakhah 8	405

Ḥagigah Chapter 2 אין דורשין

Halakhah 1	415
Halakhah 2	434
Halakhah 3	441
Halakhah 4	444
Halakhah 5	448
Halakhah 6	454
Halakhah 7	457

Ḥagigah Chapter 3 חומר בקודש

Halakhah 1	461
Halakhah 2	469
Halakhah 3	483
Halakhah 4	487
Halakhah 5	492
Halakhah 6	494
Halakhah 7	495
Halakhah 8	498

Introduction to Tractate Mo`ed Qaṭan (Mašqin)   503

Mo`ed Qaṭan (Mašqin) Chapter 1 משקין

Halakhah 1	504
Halakhah 2	509
Halakhah 3	515
Halakhah 4	517
Halakhah 5	520
Halakhah 6	524
Halakhah 7	525
Halakhah 8	529

Halakah 9	531
Halakhah 10	532

Mo`ed Qaṭan (Mašqin) Chapter 2 מי שהפך

Halakhah 1	535
Halakhah 2	538
Halakhah 3	540
Halakhah 4	543
Halakhah 5	545

Mo`ed Qaṭan (Mašqin) Chapter 3 ואילו מגלחין

Halakhah 1	548
Halakhah 2	561
Halakhah 3	563
Halakhah 4	564
Halakhah 5	567
Halakhah 6	597
Halakhah 7	598
Halakhah 8	612
Halakhah 9	617

Indices

Sigla	619
Index of Biblical quotations	619
Index of Talmudical quotations	
Babylonian Talmud	623
Parallel texts in Jerusalem Talmud	625
Mishnah	626
Tosephta	627
Midrashim	627
Author Index	627
Index of Greek, Latin, Arabic, and Hebrew Words	628
Subject Index	629

Introduction to Tractate Ta`aniot

As the title of the Tractate indicates, several kinds of fast days are discussed. The first topic is that of fast days in times of draught; therefore the Tractate starts with an extended discussion of prayers for rain in the rainy season. If the rains did not start come December, the rabbinic authorities are empowered to decree a series of fast days, if necessary of increasing severity. These fast days always are consecutive Monday-Thursday-Monday. On these special fast days the extended service is held in a public square, not in the synagogue; its details (together with general information on prayer and its efficacy) are given in Chapter 2. As an appendix to the description of the service in the times of the Mishnah, the service on the Temple Mount in the times of the Temple and the role of the participating delegations of priests and people is described, as also is the status of the Pharisaic (pre-rabbinic) "Scroll of Fasts" (i. e., a list of minor holidays on which fasting is forbidden). Chapter 3 enumerates calamities as consequence of which local fast days are organized. The song designated as hymn of thanks for Divine help in answer of any fast day is the "Great Hallel", *Pss.* 135-136. Chapter 4 takes up from Chapter 2 the topic the role of fasting priests and representatives of the public in the Temple prayer service, a feature of Pharisaic rules of the Temple service, removed from the sacrificial acts based on the Pentateuch but whose origins can be found in *Chronicles*. Halakhah 1 contains a lengthy section copied from *Berakhot* of which only the first paragraph is relevant to the topic of this Tractate. In connection with a discussion of biblically determined days on which fasts are forbidden there is mention of specific minor holidays of donations of wood to the Temple for which prophetic sanction is claimed. Of all the fast days of the current Jewish year only the 17th of Tammuz and the 9th of Av are mentioned. In the lengthy aggadic treatment of the destruction of the Temple and of Betar, there is a text which in the scribe's version asserts that the Messiah always will have to come in the future, whereas the Venice editor's text asserts that sometime in the future the Messiah will have come[1].

---

1. An echo of the original text may be found in the Medieval text *Zohar* (II,8a) which

Halakhah 2 also contains a note characterizing the Masoretic Text of the Bible of talmudic times as a scholarly edition. In order to end the Tractate on a happy note, the final Mishnah celebrates the evening following the Day of Atonement and the 15th of Av which were dedicated to match-making activities.

---

describes the permanent place of the Messiah, "bird's nest", in Paradise.

מאימתי פרק ראשון תעניות

(fol.63c) **משנה א**: מֵאֵימָתַי מַזְכִּירִין גְּבוּרוֹת גְּשָׁמִים רִבִּי אֱלִיעֶזֶר אוֹמֵר מִיּוֹם טוֹב הָרִאשׁוֹן שֶׁל חָג וְרִבִּי יְהוֹשֻׁעַ אוֹמֵר מִיּוֹם טוֹב הָאַחֲרוֹן. אָמַר רִבִּי יְהוֹשֻׁעַ הוֹאִיל וְאֵין הַגְּשָׁמִים סִימָן בְּרָכָה בֶּחָג לָמָּה הוּא מַזְכִּיר. אָמַר לוֹ רִבִּי אֱלִיעֶזֶר אַף הוּא אֵינוֹ אוֹמֵר אֶלָּא מַשִּׁיב הָרוּחַ וּמוֹרִיד הַגֶּשֶׁם בְּעוֹנָתוֹ. אָמְרוּ לוֹ אִם כֵּן לְעוֹלָם יְהֵא מַזְכִּיר:

Mishnah 1: From when does one mention the Power of rains[1]? Rebbi Eliezer says, from the first holiday of Tabernacles, but Rebbi Joshua says, from the concluding holiday[2]. Rebbi Joshua said, since rain during Tabernacles is not a sign[3] of blessing[4], why should he mention? Rebbi Eliezer said to him, he only says "He Who makes the wind blow and brings down the rain", in its appropriate time. They answered him, if that is so, one should always mention it[5].

1 In the second benediction of the *Amidah* which celebrates God's power in resurrecting the dead, during the rainy season in the winter one inserts the formula mentioned later celebrating God's power to bring or withhold rain.

2 The last holiday is the eighth day of Tabernacles which follows the seven days of dwelling in huts when one returns to dwell in houses.

3 Greek σημεῖον.

4 This also is Maimonides's version. In the Babli "a sign of curse", since rain (in Israel) during Tabernacles is a sign that Heaven is not interested in the Jews sitting in huts.

5 If the intent only is to refer to the winter months, the prayer could be said 12 months a year.

(63c line 47) **הלכה א**: מֵאֵימָתַי מַזְכִּירִין גְּבוּרוֹת גְּשָׁמִים כול'. טַעֲמֵיהּ דְּרִבִּי אֱלִיעֶזֶר. עַל יְדֵי שֶׁאַרְבַּעַת מִינָיו הַלָּלוּ גְדֵילִים עַל הַמַּיִם לְפִיכָךְ הֵן בָּאִין פְּרַקְלִיטִין לַמָּיִם. דָּבָר אַחֵר. בְּשָׁעָה שֶׁהָעֶבֶד מְשַׁמֵּשׁ אֶת רַבּוֹ כָּל־צוֹרְכּוֹ הוּא תוֹבֵעַ פַּרְסוֹ מִמֶּנּוּ. אָמַר לוֹ רִבִּי יְהוֹשֻׁעַ. וַהֲלֹא מִשָּׁעָה שֶׁהָעֶבֶד מְשַׁמֵּשׁ אֶת רַבּוֹ כָּל־צוֹרְכּוֹ וְרוּחַ רַבּוֹ נוֹחָה הֵימֶנּוּ הוּא תוֹבֵעַ [פַּרְנָסָתוֹ] מִמֶּנּוּ. דָּבָר אַחֵר. אֵין הָעֶבֶד תּוֹבֵעַ פְּרָסוֹ אֶלָּא סָמוּךְ לִפְרָסוֹ. תַּנֵּי. רִבִּי לִיעֶזֶר אוֹמֵר. מִשְּׁעַת נְטִילַת לוּלָב. רִבִּי יְהוֹשֻׁעַ אוֹמֵר. מִשְּׁעַת הַנִּיחוֹ. עַל דַּעְתֵּיהּ דְּהָדֵין בַּתְרָיָיא הִיא דַעְתֵּיהּ דְּרִבִּי לִיעֶזֶר קַדְמָיָיתָא הִיא דַּעְתֵּיהּ אַחֲרָייָתָא. מַחְלְפָה שִׁטָּתֵיהּ דְּרִבִּי יְהוֹשֻׁעַ. תַּמָּן הוּא אָמַר. מִיּוֹם טוֹב הָאַחֲרוֹן. וְהָכָא

הוּא אָמַר. מִשְׁעַת הַנִּיחוֹ. אָמַר רִבִּי מָנָא. שֶׁכָּל הַיּוֹם כָּשֵׁר לַלּוּלָב. וְיַזְכִּיר מִבְּעָרֶב. לֵית כָּל־עַמָּא תַּמָּן. וְיַזְכִּיר בַּשַּׁחֲרִית. אַף הוּא סָבוּר שֶׁמָּא הִזְכִּירוּ מִבְּעָרֶב וְהוּא הֲוֵי מַדְכַּר. מִכֵּיוָן דְּהוּא חֲמֵי לוֹן דְּלָא מַדְכְּרִין בְּקַדְמִיתָא וּמַדְכְּרִין בָּאַחֲרִיתָא. אַף הוּא יוֹדֵעַ שֶׁלֹּא הִזְכִּירוּ מִבְּעָרֶב. אָמַר לֵיהּ רִבִּי חִיָּיה בַּר מָרִיָּיא. הָכֵין הֲוָה רִבִּי יוֹנָה אָבוּךְ הֲוֵי בָהּ.

Halakhah 1: "From when does one mention the Power of rains," etc. The reason of Rebbi Eliezer, because these four kinds[6] grow on water, they become attorneys[7] for water. Another explanation, when the slave serves all his master's needs he asks for his reward from him. Rebbi Joshua said to him, is it not that when the slave has served all his master's needs and his master is satisfied with him[8] that he asks his [sustenance][9] from him? Another explanation. The slave asks for his reward only close to the time when his reward is due[10]. It was stated[11]: Rebbi Eliezer says, from the time one takes the *lulav*; Rebbi Joshua says, from the time he puts it down. In the opinion of the latter Tanna, the opinion of Rebbi Eliezer in the first is his opinion in the latter[12]. The argument of Rebbi Joshua is inverted. There, he says from the concluding holiday, but here he says, from the time he puts it down[13]. Rebbi Mana says, because the entire day is qualified to take the *lulav*[14]. Should he not mention in the evening[15]? Not everybody is there. Then he should mention it in the morning. He would think that maybe they mentioned in the evening and he will mention. Since he sees that they do not mention in the first {prayer} but mention in the later {prayer}, he understands that they did not mention in the evening[16]. Rebbi Ḥiyya bar Marius said to him, so was your father Rebbi Jonah arguing it.

6   The 4 kinds of plants to be waved on Tabernacles, cf. *Sukkah* Chapters 3-4. Babli 2b.

7   Greek παράκλητος.

8   In this case, by showing through the absence of rain that the service of the Jews is agreeable to Heaven.

9   Corrector's text, overwriting the scribe's which probably was פרס "reward".

10 In this version, R. Joshua would have preferred to start mentioning rain only at the presumed beginning of the rainy season.

11 Babli 2b.

12 The earlier opinion is that given in the Mishnah, the latter that of the *baraita*.

13 In the Mishnah he designates the eighth day of Tabernacles; his opinion in the *baraita* can be read as meaning that on the seventh day after morning prayers, when the *lulav* is no longer needed, one should start mentioning rain in his prayers.

14 While weaving the *lulav* during morning prayers is preferred, the obligation can be discharged during the entire day. As

a generally applicable rule, R. Joshua's statement in the *baraita* also refers to the eighth day.

15 Since the first prayer on the eighth day is the evening prayer, there seems to be no reason for R. Joshua to wait until the second prayer in the morning, which is the third after the start of the day.

16 For R. Joshua it would have been better to start mentioning rain in the evening prayer but this turns out to be not practicable.

(63c line 60) רִבִּי חַגַּיי בְּשֵׁם רִבִּי פְדָת. אָסוּר לְיָחִיד לְהַזְכִּיר עַד שֶׁיִּזְכּוֹר שְׁלוּחַ צִיבּוּר. רִבִּי סִימוֹן בְּשֵׁם רִבִּי יְהוֹשֻׁעַ בֶּן לֵוִי. בְּשָׁלוּחַ צִיבּוּר הַדָּבָר תָּלוּי. אָמַר רִבִּי מָנָא קוֹמֵי רִבִּי חַגַּי. מָה וּפְלִיג. אָמַר לֵיהּ. לֹא. דָּא דְאַתְּ אָמַר. בְּשָׁלוּחַ צִיבּוּר הַדָּבָר תָּלוּי. יָחִיד אִם רָצָה לְהַזְכִּיר מַזְכִּיר. טָל. וְדָא אַתְּ אָמַר. אָסוּר לְיָחִיד לְהַזְכִּיר עַד שֶׁיִּזְכּוֹר שְׁלוּחַ צִיבּוּר. בַּגְּשָׁם. קָמוּן לִצְלוֹתָא. כְּמִי שֶׁהִזְכִּיר שְׁלוּחַ צִיבּוּר.

Rebbi Ḥaggai in the name of Rebbi Pedat: It is forbidden for the individual to mention before the public reader mentions[17]. Rebbi Simon in the name of Rebbi Joshua ben Levi: Is the matter dependent on the public reader[18]? Rebbi Mana said before Rebbi Ḥaggai, do they disagree? He said to him: no. That which you are saying, is the matter dependent on the public reader? The individual if he wants to mention, he mentions dew[19]. But what you are saying is: it is forbidden for the individual to mention before the public reader mentions rain[20]. If they rise for prayer it is as if the public reader mentioned it[21].

17 At a place where there is public worship with a quorum of ten adults, no individual may recite his *Musaf-Amidah* before the reader in the synagogue starts. This version may be read to mean that the individual may not start mentioning rain unless he could have heard the mention in the repetition of the prayer by the reader.

18 He seems to hold that private prayers are not dependent on public worship even in places where organized synagogue worship is held regularly.

19 On the first day of Passover, when one stops mentioning rain after the morning prayers, every individual is free to mention dew in the benediction celebrating God's power but not obliged to do it (in the Galilean rite.) This conforms to Mishnah 2 which requires that one stop mentioning rain on Passover but does not require starting to mention dew.

20 In the fall, where Mishnah 2 requires that the mention of rain be initiated by the public reader of the second *Amidah* of the last holiday of Tabernacles.

21 The public is required to mention rain in their silent prayer whether or not the reader notified them.

(63c line 66) כְּשֵׁם שֶׁתְּחִיַּת הַמֵּתִים חַיִּים לָעוֹלָם. כָּךְ יְרִידַת גְּשָׁמִים חַיִּים לָעוֹלָם. רִבִּי חִייָה בַּר בָּא שָׁמַע לָהּ מִן הָדָא. יְחַיֵּינוּ מִיּוֹמָיִים בַּיּוֹם הַשְּׁלִישִׁי יְקִימֵנוּ וְנִחְיֶה לְפָנָיו. וְנֵדְעָה נִרְדְּפָה לָדַעַת אֶת־יְיָ כְּשַׁחַר נָכוֹן מֹצָאוֹ.

1-2 חייה בר בא | ב חייא בר אבא

[22]Just as the resurrection of the dead brings life to the world, so rains bring life to the world. Rebbi Ḥiyya bar Abba understood it from here: *He will resurrect us after two days, on the third day He will raise us up and we shall live before Him. We shall know, we shall pursue to know the Eternal, like morning His appearance is well based*[23].

כָּתוּב וַיֹּאמֶר אֵלִיָּהוּ הַתִּשְׁבִּי מִתּוֹשָׁבֵי גִלְעָד אֶל־אַחְאָב חַי־יְיָ אֱלֹהֵי יִשְׂרָאֵל אֲשֶׁר עָמַדְתִּי לְפָנָיו אִם־יִהְיֶה הַשָּׁנִים הָאֵלֶּה טַל וּמָטָר כִּי אִם־לְפִי דְבָרִי. רִבִּי בֶּרֶכְיָה אָמַר. רִבִּי יוֹסֵה וְרַבָּנִין. חַד אָמַר. בֵּין עַל הַטַּל בֵּין עַל הַמָּטָר נִשְׁמַע לוֹ. וְחוֹרָנָה אָמַר. עַל הַמָּטָר נִשְׁמַע לוֹ וְעַל הַטַּל לֹא נִשְׁמַע לוֹ. מָאן דְּאָמַר. עַל הַמָּטָר נִשְׁמַע לוֹ וְעַל הַטַּל לֹא נִשְׁמַע לוֹ. מִן הָדֵין קִרְייָא. לֵךְ הֵרָאֵה אֶל־אַחְאָב וְאֶתְּנָה מָטָר עַל־פְּנֵי הָאֲדָמָה. מָאן דְּאָמַר. בֵּין עַל הַטַּל בֵּין עַל הַמָּטָר נִשְׁמַע לוֹ. אֵיכָן הוּתַּר נִדְרוֹ שֶׁל טַל. אָמַר רִבִּי תַּנְחוּם אָדְרְעִייָא. סָבְרִין מֵימַר. נֶדֶר שֶׁהוּתַּר מִכְּלָלוֹ הוּתַּר כּוּלוֹ. אִית דְּבָעֵי מֵימַר. בִּבְנָהּ שֶׁלְּצָרְפִית. וַיִּקְרָא אֶל־יְיָ וַיֹּאמַר יְיָ אֱלֹהָי הֲגַם עַל־הָאַלְמָנָה אֲשֶׁר־אֲנִי מִתְגּוֹרֵר עִמָּהּ הֲרֵעוֹתָ לְהָמִית אֶת־בְּנָהּ: אָמַר רִבִּי יוּדָה בַּר פָּזִי. לְאֶחָד שֶׁגָּנַב נַרְתִּיקוֹ שֶׁלְּרוֹפֵא. אִם כְּשֶׁהוּא יוֹצֵא נִפְצַע בְּנוֹ. חָזַר אֶצְלוֹ וְאָמַר לוֹ. אֲדוֹנִי הָרוֹפֵא. רְפָא אֶת בְּנִי. אָמַר לוֹ. לֵךְ וְהַחֲזֵר אֶת הַנַּרְתִּיק שֶׁכָּל־מִינֵי רְפוּאוֹת נְתוּנִין בּוֹ וַאֲנִי מְרַפֵּא אֶת בִּנְךָ. כָּךְ אָמַר לוֹ הַקָּדוֹשׁ בָּרוּךְ הוּא לְאֵלִיָּהוּ. לֵךְ וְהַתֵּר נִדְרוֹ שֶׁלְּטַל שֶׁאֵין הַמֵּתִים חַיִּים אֶלָּא בְטָלִים. וַאֲנִי מְחַיֶּה בְּנָהּ שֶׁלְּצָרְפִית. וּמְנַיִין שֶׁאֵין הַמֵּתִים חַיִּים אֶלָּא בְטָלִים. [שֶׁנֶּאֱמַר] יִחְיוּ מֵתֶיךָ נְבֵילָתִי יְקוּמוּן הָקִיצוּ וְרַנְּנוּ שׁוֹכְנֵי עָפָר כִּי טַל אוֹרוֹת טַלֶּךָ וָאָרֶץ רְפָאִים תַּפִּיל: מָהוּ וָאָרֶץ רְפָאִים תַּפִּיל. אָמַר רִבִּי תַּנְחוּם אָדְרְעִייָא. וְאַרְעָא תַּפְקִידָה תְּפַלֵּט.

1 אלהי ישראל אשר עמדתי לפניו | ב - 2 יהיה | ב יש יוסה | ב יסה ורבנין | ב ורבנן 3 וחורנה | ב [החרנה] 4 דאמר | ב [דמר] הדין קרייא | ב הדא 5 על פני האדמה | ב [וגו׳] מאן דאמר | ב ומן דמר 6 תנחום אדרעיא | ב תנחומא אדרעיה 7 אלהיי | ב אלהי הגם האלמנה אשר אני מאגורר עמה הרעותה להמית את בנה | ב וגו׳ 9 ואמ׳ | ב אמ׳ 10 הנרתיק | ב הנרתק 11 חיים | ב חייו [שנאמר] | ב - 13 מהו וארץ רפאים תפיל | ב - 14 תפקידה | ב תפקידיה

It is written[24] *Elijah the Tisbite, from the inhabitants of Gilead, said to Ahab: By the Living Eternal One, the God of Israel, before Whom I stood, there will not be dew nor rain these years except by my word.* Rebbi Berekhia said, Rebbi Yose and the rabbis. One of them said, he was heard both for dew and for rain; the other one said, he was heard for rain but was not heard for dew[25], from[26]: *Go, appear before Ahab and I shall give rain on the face of the earth.* He who said, he was heard both for dew and for rain, where was the vow of dew dissolved? Rebbi Tanḥum from Edrei said, they are of the opinion that a vow that was dissolved partially is dissolved totally[27]. Some want to say, on the occasion of the son of the woman from Sarepta: *He called on the Eternal and said, o Eternal, my God, also the widow with whom I am dwelling You are doing evil to kill her son*[28]. Rebbi Judah ben Pazi said, about one who stole a doctor's bag[29]. When he left, his son was injured. He returned to him and said: Please, sir doctor, heal my son. He said to him: Go and return my bag because it is full of medicines, and I shall heal your son. So the Holy One, praise to Him, said to Elijah: Go and lift the vow of dew because the dead are resurrected only by dew, then I shall resurrect the son of the Sareptan. And from where that the dead will live only by dew? [30]*Your dead will live, the corpses will arise. Wake up and jubilate, those who dwell in dust! For a dew of light is Your dew,* וְאֶרֶץ רְפָאִים תַּפִּיל. What means וְאֶרֶץ רְפָאִים תַּפִּיל? Rebbi Tanḥum from Edrei said, "the earth will give up what is deposited in it.[31]"

רִבִּי יַעֲקֹב דִכְפַר חָנָן בְּשֵׁם רִבִּי שִׁמְעוֹן בֶּן לָקִישׁ. בְּשָׁעָה שֶׁעָשָׂה אַבְרָהָם זְקֵינָם אֶת רְצוֹנִי נִשְׁבַּעְתִּי לוֹ שֶׁאֵינִי מַזִּיז טַל מִבָּנָיו לְעוֹלָם. מַה טַעַם. נִשְׁבַּע י֯י֯ וְלֹא יִנָּחֵם אַתָּה־כֹהֵן לְעוֹלָם. וּכְתִיב תַּמָּן לְךָ טַל יַלְדוּתֶיךָ: אָמַר רִבִּי יוּדָה בַּר פָּזִי. בְּדַיְיתִיקִי נְתַתִּיו (לַאֲבִיהֶם) [לְאַבְרָהָם]. וְיִתֶּן־לְךָ הָאֱלֹהִים מִטַּל הַשָּׁמַיִם וגו׳. אָמַר רִבִּי שְׁמוּאֵל בַּר נַחְמָן. בְּשָׁעָה שֶׁיִּשְׂרָאֵל בָּאִין לִידֵי עֲבֵירוֹת מַעֲשִׂים רָעִים הַגְּשָׁמִים נֶעֱצָרִין וְהֵן מְבִיאִין לָהֶן זָקֵן אֶחָד כְּגוֹן רִבִּי יוֹסֵי הַגְּלִילִי וְהוּא מַפְגִּיעַ בַּעֲדָם וּמִיַּד הַגְּשָׁמִים יוֹרְדִין. אֲבָל הַטַּל אֵינוֹ יוֹרֵד בִּשְׁבִיל בִּירְיָיה. מַה טַעַם. אֲשֶׁר לֹא־יְקַוֶּה לְאִישׁ וְלֹא יְיַחֵל לִבְנֵי אָדָם:

1 ר׳ שמעון בן | **ב** ריש זקינים | **ב** זקיני את | **ב** - 2 מזיז | **ב** זז 2-3 נשבע . . . לעולם. וכת׳ תמן לך . . . ילדותיך | **ב** לך . . . ילדותיך. וכת׳ בתריה נשבע . . . ינחם 3 ( )|**ב** - | **ב** במתנה נתתיו לו 4 וגו׳ | **ב** - נחמני | **ב** נחמני 5 עבירות מעשים רעים | **ב** עבירה [ו]מעשים [רעים] והן | **ב** הן 6 ומיד הגשמים | **ב** והגשמים בשביל | **ב** בזכות 7 - | כְּטַל מֵאֵת י֯י֯ כִּרְבִיבִים עֲלֵי־עֵשֶׂב

[32]Rebbi Jacob from Kefar Ḥanan in the name of Rebbi Simeon ben Laqish: When Abraham their forefather did My will, I swore to him that I never shall remove dew from his descendants forever; what is the reason? *The Eternal swore and He will not change His intention, you are appointed forever*[33]. And it is written there[34], *you have the dew of your youth*. Rebbi Judah ben Pazi said, by a will[35] I gave it to Abraham: *God may give you from the dew of Heaven*[36]. Rebbi Samuel bar Naḥman said, when Israel comes to sin by their evil deeds the rains are arrested. They bring an old man like Rebbi Yose the

Galilean, he prays for them and immediately the rains come. But dew does not descend by the merit of any creature, what is the reason? *Which do not listen to anybody nor wait for humans*[37].

22 This and the following paragraphs are reproduced in *Berakhot* 5:2 (Notes 63-86); the origin is here. The theme is that God has to be praised for rain in the prayer for resurrection of the dead during the rainy season (Mishnah *Berakhot* 5:2, Note 62).

23 *Hos.* 6:2-3. The first verse of Hosea clearly speaks of resurrection, the second verse ends: *it* (knowing God) *will come like rain to us, like late rains which pour on the Land.* The verses are further discussed in *Sanhedrin* 11:8 (Note 117), Babli *Rosh Hashshanah* 31a, *Sanhedrin* 97a.

24 *1K.* 17:1.

25 In *Berakhot* the two statements were added by the corrector. Since these are the essence of the argument in the entire paragraph, the original omission in *Berakhot* shows that the text there is not original.

26 *1K.* 18:1. But dew is not mentioned. Since the sequel is a justification for the inclusion of praise for giving dew, it shows that including the sentence "Who brings down dew" in the prayer for resurrection is Galilean usage (unknown in Babylonia), as noted by I. Elbogen (*Der jüdische Gottesdienst in seiner geschichtlichen Entwicklung*, Chapter 2, §9).

27 A minority opinion of R. Aqiba (Mishnah *Nedarim* 9:6) that if in an earthly court part of a vow is annulled (because is was made under false intent), the entire vow is annulled. This is not the majority opinion and is not practice; therefore it does not imply Heavenly standards.

28 *1K.* 17:20.

29 Greek νάρθηξ, a plant (*Ferula communis*), word also used for "casket for unguents". Hesiod has Prometheus carry off the fire in the stalk of a νάρθηξ.

30 *Is.* 26:19.

31 R. Tanhum from Edrei explains the difficult phrase, *it will fell Netherworlds*, by reading תַּפִּיל in the sense of Mishnaic Hebrew "having a miscarriage": The Netherworld will expel what is in its belly. (Read totally differently in the Babli, *Ketubot* 111a,111b).

32 This paragraph explains the reasons of those who say that Elijah's prediction that there would be no dew never came true.

33 *Ps.* 110:4.

34 *Ps.* 110:3.

35 Greek διαθήκη.

36 *Gen.* 27:28. While this is Isaac's blessing for Jacob, later (28:4) it is called "Abraham's blessing".

37 *Micah* 5:6. The verse starts, *like dew from the Eternal, like light showers on grass.*

(63d line 20) רִבִּי זְעוּרָה בְשֵׁם רִבִּי חֲנִינָה. הָיָה עוֹמֵד בַּגֶּשֶׁם וְהִזְכִּיר שֶׁלְטָל אֵין מַחֲזִירִין אוֹתוֹ. בַּטָּל וְהִזְכִּיר שֶׁלְגֶּשֶׁם מַחֲזִירִין אוֹתוֹ. וְהָא תַנֵּי. בַּטָּל וּבָרוּחוֹת לֹא חִייְבוּ חֲכָמִים לְהַזְכִּיר. אִם רָצָה לְהַזְכִּיר מַזְכִּיר. לֹא דָמֵי הַהוּא דְמֵיקַל לַהוּא דְלָא מַצְלֵי וְלָא מֵיקַל. בַּגֶּשֶׁם וְהִזְכִּיר שֶׁלְטָל

אֵין מַחֲזִירִין אוֹתוֹ. וְהָא תַנֵּי. אִם לֹא שָׁאַל בְּבִרְכַּת הַשָּׁנִים. אוֹ שֶׁלֹּא הִזְכִּיר גְּבוּרוֹת גְּשָׁמִים בִּתְחִיַּית הַמֵּתִים. מַחֲזִירִין אוֹתוֹ. בָּהוּא דְּלָא אִדְכַּר לָא טַל וְלָא מָטָר.

1 חנינה | ב חנינא   2 והא תני | ב והתני   3 להוא | ב לההוא   4 והא תני | ב והתני   5 בהוא | ב בההוא

רִבִּי זְעוּרָה בְשֵׁם רַב חוּנָה. לֹא שָׁאַל בְּבִרְכַּת הַשָּׁנִים אוֹמְרָהּ בְּשׁוֹמֵעַ תְּפִילָּה. וְדִכְוָותָהּ. אִם לֹא הִזְכִּיר גְּבוּרוֹת גְּשָׁמִים בִּתְחִיַּית הַמֵּתִים אוֹמְרָהּ בְּשׁוֹמֵעַ תְּפִילָּה. מָה אִם שְׁאֵלָה שֶׁהִיא מְדוּחָק אוֹמְרָהּ בְּשׁוֹמֵעַ תְּפִילָּה. אַזְכָּרָה שֶׁהִיא מֵרְווַח לֹא כָּל־שֶׁכֵּן. וְהָא תַנֵּי. לֹא שָׁאַל בְּבִרְכַּת הַשָּׁנִים אוֹ שֶׁלֹּא הִזְכִּיר גְּבוּרוֹת גְּשָׁמִים בִּתְחִיַּית הַמֵּתִים מַחֲזִירִין אוֹתוֹ. אָמַר רִבִּי אַבָּא מָרִי אֲחוֹי דְרִבִּי יוֹסֵי. בְּשֶׁלֹּא אֲמָרָהּ בְּשׁוֹמֵעַ תְּפִילָּה.

1 זעורה | ב זעורא   לא | ב אם לא   3 הא תני | ב והתני   לא | ב אם לא   4 בתחיית המתים | ב בתחיית המתים   אב מרי | ב אבדימי

אִיכָן הוּא חוֹזֵר. יָבֹא כַּיי דְּאָמַר רִבִּי שִׁמְעוֹן בַּר בָּא בְשֵׁם רִבִּי יוֹחָנָן. בְּרֹאשׁ חוֹדֶשׁ אִם עָקַר אֶת רַגְלָיו חוֹזֵר לַכַּתְּחִילָּה. וְאִם לָאו חוֹזֵר לָעֲבוֹדָה. וְכָא אִם עָקַר אֶת רַגְלָיו חוֹזֵר לַכַּתְּחִילָּה. וְאִם לָאו חוֹזֵר לְשׁוֹמֵעַ תְּפִילָּה.

1 ייבו כיי דאמ' | ב כדמר   בא | ב ובא   2 וכא | ב אף הכא   3 לשומע תפילה | ב לעבודה בשומע תפילה

Rebbi Ze`ira in the name if Rebbi Ḥanina: When someone stood {praying} in the rainy season and mentioned dew one does not make him repeat. In the season of dew and he mentioned rain one makes him repeat. But is it not stated[38]: The Sages did not oblige one to mention dew and winds but if he wants to mention them, he may mention? One cannot compare one who takes it easy[39] to one who does not pray and does not take it easy[40]. "When he stood in the rainy season and mentioned dew one does not make him repeat." But is it not stated: If he did not ask for it in the benediction "for years"[41], or he did not mention the power of rains in "resurrection of the dead", one makes him repeat? That is about one who mentioned neither dew nor rain.

Rebbi Ze`ira in the name of Rav Huna: If he did not ask in the benediction "for years" he says it in "He Who hears prayer". If he did not mention the power of rains in "resurrection of the dead" he says it in "He Who hears prayer". If the request, made under duress[42], may be recited in "He Who hears prayer," the mention, made under easy circumstances, so much more! But is it not stated: If he did not ask in the benediction "for years" or that he did not mention the power of rains in "resurrection of the dead", one makes him repeat from the start[43]? Rebbi Abbamari[44] the brother of Rebbi Yose, said, if he did not say it in "He Who hears prayer"!

Where does he return to[45]? Just as Rebbi Simeon bar Abba said in the name of Rebbi Johanan: On the day of the New Moon[46], if he had moved his feet[47] he repeats from the start, otherwise from "Temple service". Here also, if he had moved his feet he repeats from the start[48].

38 Babli 3b.

39 And does not mention the dew which he needs, but mentions the rain out of season.

40 Who prays neither for dew, nor for rain, nor for winds, and therefore does not slight anything.

41 The ninth benediction where in winter one prays for rain, Mishnah *Berakhot* 5:2.

42 The request for rain is made only in the rainy season, "under duress" when rain is urgently needed. The mention of rain in the second benediction already starts "under easy circumstances" around the time of the fall equinox, some weeks before rain is needed. The benediction "He Who hears prayer" is the last of the middle benedictions, #15 (in Babylonia #16) on weekdays .

43 As a tannaitic statement, this has precedence over the statement of Rav Huna. How can Rav Huna present his statement about power of rains? [The Babli, *Berakhot* 29a, has the statement formulated here in the name of Rav Assi from the Yeshivah of Rav in Babylonia; the Babli mentions neither the statement of Rav Huna, Rav's student, nor the explanation of Rebbi Abbamari.]

44 Brother of the Amora R. Yose of the fourth generation. In the *Berakhot* text, the statement is attributed to R. Eudaimon, another brother of R. Yose. Neither of the two brothers is mentioned in the Babli.

45 If he forgot either prayer for or mention of rain, and realizes his omission at the end of the *Amidah*.

46 When the day has to be mentioned in "Temple service", the first of the last three benedictions; cf. *Berakhot* 4:1 Note 90.

47 During *Amidah* it is forbidden to move one's feet since the angels do not move their feet (*Berakhot* 1:1, Note 61). Hence, moving after prayer is the outward sign that prayer is finished.

48 Otherwise, he returns to "He Who hears prayer."

(63d line 35) בְּנֵי נְוֵה צָרְכוּן לְמֶיעֱבַד תַּעֲנִי בָּתַר פִּסְחָא. אֲתוֹן וּשְׁאָלוּן לְרִבִּי. אֲמַר לוֹן רִבִּי. לְכוּ וַעֲשׂוּ. וּבִלְבַד שֶׁלֹּא תָשֻׁנּוּ מִטְבִיעָהּ שֶׁלִּתְפִילָה. הֵיכָן הוּא אוֹמְרָהּ. רִבִּי יִרְמְיָה סָבַר מֵימַר. אוֹמְרָהּ בְּשׁוֹמֵעַ תְּפִילָה. אָמַר לֵיהּ רִבִּי יוֹסֵי. לֹא אָמַר רִבִּי זְעוּרָה בְשֵׁם רַב חוּנָה. לֹא שָׁאַל בְּבִרְכַּת הַשָּׁנִים אוֹ שֶׁלֹּא הִזְכִּיר גְּשָׁמִים בִּתְחִיַּת הַמֵּתִים אוֹמְרָהּ בְּשׁוֹמֵעַ תְּפִילָה. וַאֲמַר לוֹן רִבִּי. לְכוּ וַעֲשׂוּ. וּבִלְבַד שֶׁלֹּא תָשֻׁנּוּ מִטְבִיעָהּ שֶׁלִּתְפִילָה. עַל דַּעְתֵּיהּ דְּרִבִּי יוֹסֵי הֵיכָן הוּא אוֹמְרָהּ. בְּשֵׁשׁ שֶׁהוּא מוֹסִיף. עַד כְּדוֹן צִיבּוּר שֶׁיֵּשׁ לוֹ שֵׁשׁ. יָחִיד שֶׁאֵין לוֹ שֵׁשׁ. אָמַר רִבִּי חִינָּנָא. לֹא כֵן אָמַר רִבִּי זְעוּרָא בְשֵׁם רַב חוּנָה. יָחִיד תּוֹבֵעַ צְרָכָיו בְּשׁוֹמֵעַ תְּפִילָה. וְאִילּוּ צְרָכָיו הֵן.

1 בני נווה | ב בני נוה למיעבד | ב מיעבד תעני | ב תעניות ושאלון | ב שיילון   2 תשנו | ב תשנן היכן | ב איכן   3 זעורה | ב זעיר' לא | ב אם לא   4 אומרה | ב מחזירין אותו ואמ' | ב ומר   5 ר' | ב [ר'] על דעתיה דר' יוסי | ב [על דעתיה דר' יוסי] היכן | ב איכן   6 שש | ב שש [מניין]   7 חיננא | ב חנינא תובע | ב שואל

At Nineveh[49] they needed to make a fastday after Passover[50]. They came to ask Rebbi. He told them, go ahead and make one but do not change the form of prayer[51]. Where may he say it? Rebbi Jeremiah thought to say that he says it in "He Who hears prayer." Rebbi Yose said to him: Did not Rebbi Ze`ira say in the name of Rav Huna: If he did not ask in the benediction "for years", or that he failed to mention the power of rains in "resurrection of the dead", he says it at "He Who hears prayer"? But Rebbi said to them, go ahead and make one but do not change the form of prayer! According to the opinion of Rebbi Yose, where does one say it? In the six that he adds[52]. That works for the public which has six. A private person who does not have six, where? Rebbi Hinena said, did not Rebbi Ze`ira say in the name of Rav Huna[53], a private person asks for his personal needs in "He Who hears prayer," and these are his needs[54].

49 This is not Biblical Niniveh but Naveh in the center of the Bashan plateau, see *Demay* 2:1 (Note 99). (Eusebius mentions that the Jews call it Nineveh) On the Golan plain, one needs spring rains if the winter was relatively dry.
50 Babli 14b.
51 Since if one fasts for rain one must pray for rain in one's *Amidah*.
52 Six additional benedictions that the reader inserts in the public prayer of fast days for rain, as explained in Mishnah 2:2-10. Rebbi Yose implies that even a local fast for rain is a public fast.
53 In *Berakhot* 4:4 Note 212; Babli 31a.
54 Here ends the parallel in *Berakhot*. In the last two paragraphs, the omissions in the scribe's text of *Berakhot*, filled by the corrector as given in the readings, again show the originality of the text in *Ta`aniot*.

(63d line 44) תַּנֵּי. נִתְפַּלֵּל וְאֵינוֹ יוֹדֵעַ מַה הִזְכִּיר. אָמַר רִבִּי יוֹחָנָן. כָּל־שְׁלֹשִׁים יוֹם חֲזָקָה מַה שֶׁהוּא לָמוּד לְהַזְכִּיר (יַזְכִּיר) [הִזְכִּיר]. מִיכָּן וָהֵילָךְ מַה שֶׁצּוֹרֶךְ יַזְכִּיר. רִבִּי בָּא בְשֵׁם רִבִּי חוּנָה. שְׁנֵי יָמִים טוֹבִים שֶׁלְגָּלֻיּוֹת מַזְכִּיר בַּשַּׁחֲרִית וְאֵינוֹ מַזְכִּיר בְּמוּסָף. מִנְחָה בְשַׁחֲרִית וְעַרְבִית בְּמוּסָף. חֲנַנְיָה בֶּן אֲחֵי רִבִּי יְהוֹשֻׁעַ אוֹמֵר. בַּגּוֹלָה לָא נָהֲגוּ כֵן אֶלָּא עַד שִׁשִּׁים יוֹם בַּתְּקוּפָה. שְׁמוּאֵל אָמַר. הֲלָכָה כַחֲנַנְיָה בֶּן אֲחֵי רִבִּי יְהוֹשֻׁעַ. וְתַנֵּי כֵן. בַּמֶּה דְבָרִים אֲמוּרִים. בְּחוּצָה לָאָרֶץ. אֲבָל בְּאֶרֶץ יִשְׂרָאֵל הַכֹּל לְפִי הַזְּמָן הַכֹּל לְפִי הַמְּאוֹרַע. הָדָא דַתְּ אָמַר בְּגֶשֶׁם. אֲבָל בְּטַל אִם רָצָה לְהַזְכִּיר כָּל־יְמוֹת הַשָּׁנָה מַזְכִּיר.

It was stated: If he prayed but does not know what he mentioned, Rebbi Joḥanan said, all of thirty days there is a presumption that what he is used to he (would mention) [mentioned][55]. Rebbi Abba in the name of Rebbi Huna:

On the second holiday of the diaspora he mentions in the morning prayers but not in the *musaf* prayer[56]. Afternoon prayers like morning prayers and evening prayers like *musaf* prayers. Ḥananiah the son of Rebbi Joshua's brother[57] says, in the Diaspora[58] they did not have this custom, but until sixty days after equinox. Samuel said, practice follows Ḥananiah the son of Rebbi Joshua's brother[59]. And it was stated thus: When was this said? Outside of the Land. But in the Land of Israel, everything according to the season, everything according to the event[60]. That is, about rain. But dew, if he wants to mention the entire year he may mention it.

55 There is no difference in meaning between the texts of the (scribe) and the [corrector], even though the scribe's text seems more appropriate. Since it was stated in the paragraph before the last that the *Amidah* has to be repeated in whole or in part if the appropriate mention of or prayer for rain was omitted, the question arises what to do if the person does not know whether he recited the required text or not. Within thirty days one presumes that he has to repeat, after thirty days one presumes that he has not to repeat. Since prayers and prayer texts are purely rabbinic institutions, this must be accepted as rabbinic decree. The problem is not mentioned in the Babli; therefore it is accepted as universal practice.

56 In the Babli 4b this is quoted as opinion of the Galilee trained Rav (a little more in detail, that on the 8th day of Tabernacles one mentions rain only for *musaf* and on the 9th one starts with *musaf* and from there on one continues in all prayers), but rejected by the autochthonous Samuel.

57 His name, as was his father's, was Ḥananiah ben Ḥananiah; two generations of posthumous sons. One avoids the mention of this unlucky circumstance by circumlocution. He was one of Samuel's ancestors.

58 This may mean either Babylonian in general or Nahardea, presumed residence of King Jojachin, in particular. From the Babli 10a one understands that all of Iraq is included, from Nisibis to the Persian gulf.

59 Babli 10a.

60 The standard commentators emend the text, switching the places of inside and outside the Land. This switch is unjustified. It is stated that in Babylonia uniformly one starts praying for rain on the 20th of November, 60 days after the fall equinox, but in the Land of Israel the different dates for starting to pray for rain given in Mishnah 4 are matters of local need or local usage (denied in the Babli 10a).

(63d line 53) אָמַר רִבִּי יְהוֹשֻׁעַ הוֹאִיל וְאֵין הַגְּשָׁמִים סִימָן בְּרָכָה בֶּחָג לָמָּה הוּא מַזְכִּיר. אָמַר לוֹ רִבִּי אֱלִיעֶזֶר. אַף הוּא אֵינוֹ אוֹמֵר אֶלָּא מַשִּׁיב הָרוּחַ וּמוֹרִיד הַגֶּשֶׁם בְּעוֹנָתוֹ. בְּעוֹנָתָן הֵן חֲבִיבִין כִּתְחִיַּית הַמֵּתִים. אָמַר רִבִּי יוֹסֵה. וּתְמִיהּ אֲנָא. הֵידְ רַבָּנָן מְדַמֵּיי יְרִידַת גְּשָׁמִים לִתְחִיַּית הַמֵּתִים. וְלֹא דַמְייָא. בָּעֵי בַּר נַשָׁא יֵיחוּן מֵיתַייָא כָּל־אֵימַת. לָא בָעֵי בַּר נַשָׁא יֵיחוֹת מִיטְרָא כָּל־אֵימַת.

"Rebbi Joshua said, since rain during Tabernacles is not a sign[3] of blessing[4], why should he mention? Rebbi Eliezer said to him, he only says 'He Who makes the wind blow and brings down the rain', in its appropriate time." In its time it is desirable like the resurrection of the dead. Rebbi Yose said, I am wondering how the rabbis could compare rainfall to the resurrection of the dead, but they are not comparable. A person prays all the time for the dead to become alive. Does a person pray for rain to fall all the time[61]?

61 Since the last sentence of the last Mishnah in this Chapter notes that in Palestine summer rain is a curse.

(63d line 58) אָמְרוּ לוֹ אִם כֵּן לְעוֹלָם יְהֵא מַזְכִּיר: מַחְלָפָה שִׁיטָתֵיהּ דְּרִבִּי לִיעֶזֶר מַחְלָפָה שִׁיטָתֵיהּ דְּרִבִּי יְהוֹשֻׁעַ. דְּאִיתְפַּלְגוּן. רִבִּי לִיעֶזֶר אוֹמֵר. אִם אֵין יִשְׂרָאֵל עוֹשִׂין תְּשׁוּבָה אֵין נִגְאָלִים לְעוֹלָם. שֶׁנֶּאֱמַר. בְּשׁוּבָה וָנַחַת תִּוָּשֵׁעוּן. אָמַר לוֹ רִבִּי יְהוֹשֻׁעַ. וְכִי אִם יַעַמְדוּ יִשְׂרָאֵל וְלֹא יַעֲשׂוּ תְשׁוּבָה אֵינָן נִגְאָלִין לְעוֹלָם. אָמַר לוֹ רִבִּי אֱלִיעֶזֶר. הַקָּדוֹשׁ בָּרוּךְ הוּא מַעֲמִיד עֲלֵיהֶן מֶלֶךְ קָשֶׁה כְהָמָן וּמִיַּד הֵן עוֹשִׂין תְּשׁוּבָה וְהֵן נִגְאָלִין. מַה טַעַם. וְעֵת־צָרָה הִיא לְיַעֲקֹב וּמִמֶּנָּה יִוָּשֵׁעַ: אָמַר לוֹ רִבִּי יְהוֹשֻׁעַ. וְהָא כָתוּב חִנָּם נִמְכַּרְתֶּם וְלֹא בְכֶסֶף תִּגָּאֵלוּ: מָה עָבַד לָהּ רִבִּי לִיעֶזֶר. תְּשׁוּבָה. כְּמָה דְאַתְּ אָמַר. צְרוֹר־הַכֶּסֶף לָקַח בְּיָדוֹ וגו'. אָמַר לוֹ רִבִּי יְהוֹשֻׁעַ. וְהָא כָתוּב אֲנִי יי בְּעִתָּהּ אֲחִישֶׁנָּה: מָה עָבַד לָהּ רִבִּי לִיעֶזֶר. תְּשׁוּבָה. כְּמָה דַתְּ אָמַר. וְעַתָּה֙ יִשְׂרָאֵל֙ מָה יי אֱלֹהֶ֖יךָ שֹׁאֵ֣ל מֵעִמָּ֑ךְ כִּ֚י אִם־לְיִרְאָ֣ה וגו'. רִבִּי אֲחָא בְשֵׁם רִבִּי יְהוֹשֻׁעַ בֶּן לֵוִי. אִם זָכִיתֶם. אֲחִישֶׁנָּה. וְאִם לָאו. בְּעִתָּהּ. כֵּיוָן שֶׁאָמַר לוֹ רִבִּי יְהוֹשֻׁעַ. וַיָּרֶם יְמִינוֹ וּשְׂמֹאלוֹ֙ אֶל־הַשָּׁמַ֔יִם וַיִּשָּׁבַע֙ בְּחֵ֣י הָעוֹלָ֔ם כִּ֚י לְמוֹעֵ֣ד מוֹעֲדִ֔ים וָחֵ֑צִי וּכְכַלּ֛וֹת נַפֵּ֥ץ יַד־עַם־קֹ֖דֶשׁ תִּכְלֶ֥ינָה כָל־אֵֽלֶּה: אִיסְתַּלַּק רִבִּי לִיעֶזֶר.

"They said to him, if that is so, one should always mention it[62]." The argument of Rebbi Eliezer seems inverted; the argument of Rebbi Joshua seems inverted[63]. As they disagree: Rebbi Eliezer says, unless Israel repent they never will be redeemed, as it is said, *by repentance and satisfaction you will be helped*[64]. Rebbi Joshua said to him, if Israel would stay and never repent, would they never be redeemed? Rebbi Eliezer said to him, the Holy One, praise to Him, causes a hard king like Haman to rule over them and immediately they repent and are redeemed. What is the reason? *It is an evil time for Jacob and from it he will be helped*[65]. Rebbi Joshua said to him, but is it not written, *gratis you were sold and not by money you will be redeemed*[66]? How does Rebbi Eliezer deal with this? Repentance, as you are saying, *a bundle of money he took in his hand*[67], etc. Rebbi Joshua said to him, but is it not written, *in its time I shall quickly do it*[68]. How does Rebbi Eliezer deal with this? Repentance, as you are saying, *but now, Israel, what does the Eternal, your God, ask from you but to fear*[69] etc. Rebbi Aha in the name of Rebbi Joshua ben Levi: If you merit it, *I shall quickly do it*; if not, *in its time*[70]. When Rebbi Joshua said to him, *he lifted his right and his left arms to heaven and swore by the Eternally Living that in term, terms and a half, when he finished to smash the hand of the holy people, all this will finish*[71], Rebbi Eliezer withdrew[72].

62 Quote from the Mishnah, not quite correct. It is the objection of R. Eliezer to R. Joshua's statement.

63 The argument is not about the prayer text of the *Amidah* but about the doxology of the introductory benediction preceding to *Amidah*, "praise to You, Eternal, Redeemer of Israel". According to R. Eliezer, redemption uniquely depends on Israel's actions; therefore prayer for redemption either is unnecessary because all of Israel are repenting or it is useless because not all of Israel are repenting; the prayer text should be forbidden as vain invocation of the Name. According to R. Joshua the prayer is legitimate but one cannot understand why during the summer one should not mention God's power to give rain in its time just as one prays for redemption in its time.

64 *Is.* 30:15. The interpretation agrees with the interpretation in Targum Jonathan ben Uziel.

65 *Jer.* 30:7.

66 *Is.* 52:3. Not by money, but by repentance. The argument is switched between RR. Eliezer and Joshua in the Babli, *Sanhedrin* 97b.

67 *Prov.* 7:20. In the Babli, *Sanhedrin* 96b, the "bundle of money" is interpreted as referring to the pious people (whom God took away by death, since in *Prov.* Chapter 7 the adulteress is interpreted as apostle of apostasy.) If this interpretation is accepted here, R. Eliezer's argument is that for redemption it is not required that all of Israel rise to the status of pious people, but universal repentance is required nevertheless

68 *Is.* 60:22.

69 *Deut.* 10:12. Fear of God is repentance.

70 Babli *Sanhedrin* 98a.

71 *Dan.* 12:7. In the entire talmudic literature it is understood that the prophecies contained in Daniel have no relation with Maccabean times.

72 Since this prophecy is unconditional. Babli *Sanhedrin* 98a.

(63d line 72) מִתּוֹךְ חֲמִשָּׁה דְבָרִים נִגְאֲלוּ יִשְׂרָאֵל מִמִּצְרָיִם. [מִתּוֹךְ הַקֵּץ.] מִתּוֹךְ צָרָה. מִתּוֹךְ צְוָוחָה. מִתּוֹךְ זְכוּת אָבוֹת. מִתּוֹךְ תְּשׁוּבָה. מִתּוֹךְ הַקֵּץ. הָדָא הִיא דִכְתִיב וַיְהִי בַיָּמִים הָרַבִּים הָהֵם וַיָּמָת מֶלֶךְ מִצְרַיִם וַיֵּאָנְחוּ בְנֵי־יִשְׂרָאֵל מִן־הָעֲבֹדָה וַיִּזְעָקוּ מִתּוֹךְ צָרָה. וַיִּשְׁמַע אֱלֹהִים

אֶת־נַאֲקָתָם מִתּוֹךְ צְוָחָה. וַיִּזְכֹּר אֱלֹהִים אֶת־בְּרִיתוֹ מִתּוֹךְ זְכוּת אָבוֹת. וַיַּרְא אֱלֹהִים אֶת־בְּנֵי יִשְׂרָאֵל מִתּוֹךְ תְּשׁוּבָה. וַיֵּדַע אֱלֹהִים מִתּוֹךְ הַקֵּץ. וְכֵן הוּא אוֹמֵר בַּצַּר לְךָ מִתּוֹךְ צָרָה. וּמְצָאוּךָ כָּל הַדְּבָרִים הָאֵלֶּה בְּאַחֲרִית הַיָּמִים וְשַׁבְתָּ מִתּוֹךְ תְּשׁוּבָה. כִּי אֵל רַחוּם יְהוָה אֱלֹהֶיךָ מִתּוֹךְ רַחֲמִים. לֹא יַרְפְּךָ וְלֹא יַשְׁחִיתֶךָ וְלֹא יִשְׁכַּח אֶת־בְּרִית אֲבֹתֶיךָ מִתּוֹךְ זְכוּת אָבוֹת. וְכֵן הוּא אוֹמֵר וַיַּרְא בַּצַּר לָהֶם מִתּוֹךְ צָרָה. בְּשָׁמְעוֹ אֶת־רִנָּתָם מִתּוֹךְ צְוָחָה. וַיִּזְכֹּר לָהֶם בְּרִיתוֹ מִתּוֹךְ זְכוּת אָבוֹת. וַיִּנָּחֵם כְּרֹב חֲסָדָיו מִתּוֹךְ תְּשׁוּבָה. וַיִּתֵּן אוֹתָם לְרַחֲמִים מִתּוֹךְ רַחֲמִים.

Israel were redeemed from Egypt for five reasons. [Because of the term,][73] because of tribulation, because of entreaty, because of the merit of the Fathers, because of repentance, because of the term[74]. That is what is written[75], *it was in these important times that the Children of Israel were sighing at the work and crying,* because of tribulation; *and God heard their wailing,* because of entreaty; *and God remembered His Covenant,* because of the merit of the Fathers. *And God saw the children of Israel,* because of repentance[76], *and God knew,* because of the term. And so it says[77], *if you are in trouble,* because of tribulation; *and all these matters will find you in future times and you will repent,* because of repentance; *for the Eternal, your God, is a merciful power,* because of mercy; *He will not let you sink nor destroy you, nor will He forget your Fathers' Covenant,* because of the merit of the Fathers. And so it says[78], *He saw how they were in trouble,* because of tribulation; *when He heard their prayer,* because of entreaty; *and remembered for them His Covenant,* because of merit of the Fathers; *and consoled them in the abundance of His grace,* because of repentance; *and He had mercy with them,* because of mercy.

73 Corrector's addition, to be deleted.
74 The predetermined date for their rescue, *Gen.* 15:13.
75 *Ex.* 2:23-25.
76 Pseudo-Jonathan (*Ex.* 2:25) reads *saw* and *knew* as parallels, matters that only God knew or saw: The Eternal saw the pain of the servitude of the Children of Israel and their individual repentance was evident before Him, since no one knew of his neighbor's.
77 *Deut.* 4:30-31.
78 *Ps.* 106:44-46.

(64a line 7) חַד בַּר נָשׁ הֲוָה אִיחְטָא בְּלִישָׁנֵיהּ. אֲתָא לְגַבֵּי רִבִּי יוֹחָנָן וְשַׁלְחֵיהּ גַּבֵּי רִבִּי חֲנִינָה. אֲמַר לֵיהּ. אֵיזִיל תָּהֵי בָךְ וְלָעֵי בְּאוֹרָיְתָא. דִּכְתִיב מַרְפֵּא לָשׁוֹן עֵץ חַיִּים.

A person sinned with his tongue[79]. He came before Rebbi Joḥanan who sent him before Rebbi Ḥanina. The latter[80] told him, go, examine yourself, and study Torah, as it is written[81], *the tree of life*[82] *is healing for the tongue*.

79 He was used to gossip about other people, which is sinful behavior.
80 His instructions for repentance of gossipers are a matter of controversy between his sons in Babli *Arakhin* 15b.
81 *Prov.* 15:4.
82 Which customarily is identified with the Torah (*Prov.* 3:18.)

(64a line 9) אָמַר רִבִּי חֲנִינָה בְּרִיהּ דְּרִבִּי אַבָּהוּ. בְּסִפְרוֹ שֶׁלְּרִבִּי מֵאִיר מְצָאוּ כָּתוּב מַשָּׂא דּוּמָה. מַשָּׂא דּוּמִי. אֵלַי קוֹרֵא מִשֵּׂעִיר. אָמַר רִבִּי יוֹחָנָן. אֵלַי קוֹרֵא מִפְּנֵי שֵׂעִיר. אָמַר רִבִּי שִׁמְעוֹן בֶּן לָקִישׁ. אֵלַי מֵאֵיכָן נִזְדַּוֵּוג לִי. מִשֵּׂעִיר. אָמַר רִבִּי יְהוֹשֻׁעַ בֶּן לֵוִי. אִם יֹאמַר לְךָ אָדָם. אֵיכָן הוּא אֱלֹהֶיךָ. אֱמוֹר לוֹ. בְּכָרָךְ גָּדוֹל שֶׁבְּרוֹמִי. מַה טַעֲמָא. אֵלַי קוֹרֵא מִשֵּׂעִיר.

Rebbi Ḥanina ben Rebbi Abbahu said, in the book of Rebbi Meïr they found: *a saying about Duma*, "a saying about Domae[83], *to me He called from Seïr*[84]. Rebbi Joḥanan said, He called to me because of Seïr[85]. Rebbi Simeon ben Laqish said, from where was He inimical to me, from Seïr[86]. Rebbi Joshua ben Levi said, if a person asks you, where is your God? Tell him, in the great fortification[87] at Rome. What is the reason? *To me He called from Seïr*[88].

83 Reading רוֹמֵי "Romae".
84 *Is.* 21:11. Since *Seïr* is the place of Edom, and Edom is the code name for Rome, the prophecy about Duma is taken as a prophecy about Rome. This paragraph is the introduction to the next one, referring to the second half of the verse, reassuring the people that the night coming from Seïr (the oppression by Rome) will come to an end.
85 Because of the oppression by Rome, God is calling to His people even without their repentance.
86 This is the opposite of R. Joḥanan's interpretation. Because of the bad behavior of the People, Rome is an organ of divine retribution.
87 Since in his time, at the start of the military anarchy, Rome was not fortified, the reference must be to the seat of the Roman government. Greek χάραξ "palisades".
88 If this is the introduction to the next paragraph it means that in his time the most important Jewish diaspora was in Rome.

(64a line 14) תַּנֵּי רִבִּי שִׁמְעוֹן בֶּן יוֹחַי. בְּכָל־מָקוֹם שֶׁגָּלוּ יִשְׂרָאֵל גָּלַת הַשְּׁכִינָה עִמָּהֶן. גָּלוּ לְמִצְרַיִם וְגָלַת הַשְּׁכִינָה עִמָּהֶן. מַה טַעַם. הֲנִגְלֹה נִגְלֵיתִי לְבֵית אָבִיךָ בִּהְיוֹתָם בְּמִצְרַיִם לְבֵית פַּרְעֹה: גָּלוּ לְבָבֶל וְגָלַת שְׁכִינָה עִמָּהֶן. מַה טַעַם. לְמַעַנְכֶם שׁוּלַּחְתִּי בָבֶלָה. גָּלוּ לְמָדַי וְגָלַת הַשְּׁכִינָה

עִמָּהֶן. מַה טַעֲמָא. וְשִׂמְתִּי כִסְאִי בְעֵילָם. וְאֵין עֵילָם אֶלָּא מָדַי. כְּמָה דַתְּ אָמַר. וַאֲנִי בְּשׁוּשַׁן הַבִּירָה אֲשֶׁר בְּעֵילָם הַמְּדִינָה. גָּלוּ לְיָוָן וְגָלַת הַשְּׁכִינָה עִמָּהֶן. מַה טַעַם. וְעוֹרַרְתִּי בָנַיִךְ צִיּוֹן עַל־בָּנַיִךְ יָוָן. גָּלוּ לְרוֹמִי הַשְּׁכִינָה עִמָּהֶן. מַה טַעַם. אֵלַי קוֹרֵא מִשֵּׂעִיר שֹׁמֵר מַה־מִּלַּיְלָה. אָמְרוּ יִשְׂרָאֵל לִישַׁעְיָה. רַבֵּינוּ יְשַׁעְיָה. מַה יוֹצֵא לָנוּ מִתּוֹךְ הַלַּיְלָה הַזֶּה. אָמַר לָהֶן. הַמְתִּינוּ לִי עַד שֶׁנִּשְׁאַל. כֵּיוָן שֶׁשָּׁאַל חָזַר אֶצְלָן. אָמְרוּ לוֹ. שׁוֹמֵר מַה־מִּלֵּיל: מַה מֵילֵל שׁוֹמֵר הָעוֹלָמִים. אָמַר לָהֶן. אָמַר שׁוֹמֵר אָתָא בוֹקֶר וְגַם־לָיְלָה. אָמְרוּ לוֹ. וְגַם־לָיְלָה. אָמַר לָהֶן. לֹא כְּאַתֶּם סְבוּרִים. אֶלָּא בוֹקֶר לַצַּדִּיקִים וְלַיְלָה לָרְשָׁעִים. בּוֹקֶר לְיִשְׂרָאֵל וְלַיְלָה לְאוּמוֹת הָעוֹלָם. אֲמָרוּן לֵיהּ. אֵימַת. אֲמַר לוֹן. אֵימַת דְּאַתּוּן בָּעֵי הוּא בָעֵי. אִם־תִּבְעָיוּן בְּעָיוּ. אָמְרוּ לוֹ. מִי מְעַכֵּב. אָמַר לָהֶן. תְּשׁוּבָה. שׁוּבוּ אֵתָיוּ:

רִבִּי אָחָא בָשֵׁם רִבִּי תַנְחוּם בֵּירִבִּי חִיָּיה. אִילּוּ יִשְׂרָאֵל עוֹשִׂים תְּשׁוּבָה יוֹם אֶחָד מִיַּד הָיָה בֶן דָּוִד בָּא. מַה טַעַם. הַיּוֹם אִם־בְּקוֹלוֹ תִשְׁמָעוּ: אָמַר רִבִּי לֵוִי. אִילּוּ הָיוּ יִשְׂרָאֵל מְשַׁמְּרִין שַׁבָּת אַחַת כְּתִיקְנָהּ מִיַּד הָיָה בֶן דָּוִד בָּא. מַה טַעַם. וַיֹּאמֶר מֹשֶׁה אִכְלוּהוּ הַיּוֹם כִּי־שַׁבָּת הַיּוֹם לַיי וגו'. חַד יוֹם. וְאוֹמֵר. בְּשׁוּבָה וָנַחַת תִּוָּשֵׁעוּן. בְּשׁוּבָה וְנַיַּח תִּתְפָּרְקוּן.

[89]Rebbi Simeon ben Yoḥay stated: Every place to which Israel was exiled, the Divine Presence was exiled with them. They were exiled to Egypt and the Divine Presence was exiled with them. What is the reason? [90]*Was I not revealed to your Father's house when they were in Egypt, the house of Pharaoh?* They were exiled to Babylon and the Divine Presence was exiled with them. What is the reason? [91]*On your behalf I was sent to Babylon.* They were exiled to Media and the Divine Presence was exiled with them. What is the reason? *I installed My throne in Elam*[92], but Elam is nothing else but Media as you are saying, *when I was in the Capital city of Susa which is in the province of Elam*[93]. They were exiled to Ionia and the Divine Presence was exiled with them. What is the reason? *I shall awake your sons, Zion, over your sons, Ionia*[94]. They were exiled to Rome and the Divine Presence was exiled with them. What is the reason? [95]*He calls to me from Se`ir: watchman, what time is it in the night?* Israel said to Isaiah: our teacher Isaiah, what will lead us out from this night? He told them, wait until it will be asked. After he asked, he returned to them and they asked him, *watchman, what time is it in the night?* He said to them, *the watchman said, there comes morning and also night.* They said to him, *and also night*? He told them, not as you understand it. But "morning" for the just ones, and "night" for the evildoers. "Morning" for Israel and "night" for the peoples of the world. They asked him, when?

He said to them, any time you want, He wants: *if you desire to ask, ask*. They asked him, what obstructs? He told them, repentance: *repent, come*.

[96]Rebbi Aha in the name of Rebbi Tanhum ben Rebbi Hiyya: If Israel would repent on one day, David's son would immediately come. What is the reason? *Today, if you will listen to His voice*[97]. [98]Rebbi Levi said, if Israel would keep one Sabbath following its rules, David's son would immediately come. What is the reason? *Moses said, eat it today, for Sabbath is this day to the Eternal*[99], etc. One day. And it says, *by repentance and satisfaction you will be helped*[64]. By keeping the Sabbath and staying put you will be freed.

89 Babli 29a; *Mekhilta dR. Ismael Bo* Chap. 14; *Sifry Num.* 84, 161; *Ex. rabba* 15(17).
90 *1S.* 2:27.
91 *Is.* 43:14.
92 *Jer.* 49:38.
93 *Dan.* 8:2. The identification is erroneous.
94 *Sach.* 9:13.
95 *Is.* 21:11,12. The previous paragraph is the introduction to this sermon.
96 Slightly differently and in the name of R. Levi *Cant. rabba* 5(2); cf. Babli *Sanhedrin* 98a.
97 *Ps.* 95:7.
98 *Midrash Ps.* 95[3]; cf. Babli *Šabbat* 118b.
99 *Ex.* 16:25.

(fol. 63c) **משנה ב**: אֵין שׁוֹאֲלִין אֶת הַגְּשָׁמִים אֶלָּא סָמוּךְ לַגְּשָׁמִים. רִבִּי יְהוּדָה אוֹמֵר הָעוֹבֵר לִפְנֵי הַתֵּבָה בְּיוֹם טוֹב הָאַחֲרוֹן שֶׁל חָג הָאַחֲרוֹן מַזְכִּיר וְהָרִאשׁוֹן אֵינוֹ מַזְכִּיר. בְּיוֹם טוֹב הָרִאשׁוֹן שֶׁל פֶּסַח הָרִאשׁוֹן מַזְכִּיר וְהָאַחֲרוֹן אֵינוֹ מַזְכִּיר.

משנה ג: עַד אֵימָתַי שׁוֹאֲלִין. רִבִּי יְהוּדָה אוֹמֵר עַד שֶׁיַּעֲבוֹר הַפֶּסַח. רִבִּי מֵאִיר אוֹמֵר עַד שֶׁיֵּצֵא נִיסָן שֶׁנֶּאֱמַר וַיּוֹרֶד לָכֶם גֶּשֶׁם מוֹרֶה וּמַלְקוֹשׁ בָּרִאשׁוֹן:

Mishnah 2: One asks for rain[100] only close to the rainy period. Rebbi Jehudah says, the one who stands before the Ark on the last holiday of Tabernacles[101], the last one[102] mentions but the first one[103] does not mention. On the first day of Passover, the first one mentions but the last one does not mention.

Mishnah 3: Until when does one pray[104]? Rebbi Jehudah says, until Passover has passed; Rebbi Meïr says, until Nisan has passed, as it is said[105], *He will bring down for you rain, early rain and late rain, in the first {month}.*

100 In contrast to the mention of God's power to bring rain (Mishnah 1), which is recited in the part of the Amidah which is pure praise and recited daily, prayer asking for rain is different and part only of the weekday *Amidah*.

101 The Eighth day which is a separate holiday, where one does not sit in the *sukkah* and would not be importuned by rain. Since this is a holiday where nothing should be demanded from God, R. Jehudah must refer to the praise of God's power to bring rain, not prayer asking for rain.

102 The reader of the *musaf* service.

103 The reader of the morning service.

104 As explained in Note 101, R. Jehudah prescribes stopping the praise for rain at the start of the Passover festival; in Mishnah 2 he does not indicate a time for stopping the prayer.

105 *Joel* 2:23. Since it may happen that all winter rains are concentrated in Nisan, one should not stop praying in Nisan even though late spring rain is very infrequent in Israel.

(64a line 34) **הלכה ב**: אָמַר רִבִּי יוֹחָנָן. הֲלָכָה כְּרִבִּי יוּדָה שֶׁאָמַר מִשֵּׁם רִבִּי יוּדָה בֶּן בָּתִירָה. רִבִּי אָבוּן בְּשֵׁם רִבִּי יוֹחָנָן. טַעֲם דְּרִבִּי יוּדָה כְּדֵי שֶׁיֵּצְאוּ הַמּוֹעֲדוֹת בְּטָל. מִפְּנֵי שֶׁהַטַּל סִימָן יָפֶה לָעוֹלָם.

מַחְלְפָה שִׁיטָתֵיהּ דְּרִבִּי יוּדָה. תַּמָּן הוּא אָמַר. הָעוֹבֵר לִפְנֵי הַתֵּבָה בְּיוֹם טוֹב הָאַחֲרוֹן שֶׁל חָג. הָאַחֲרוֹן מַזְכִּיר וְהָרִאשׁוֹן אֵינוֹ מַזְכִּיר. וְהָכָא הוּא אָמַר הָכֵין. חָדָא בְּשֵׁם גַּרְמֵיהּ וְחָדָא בְּשֵׁם רִבִּי יוּדָה בֶּן בָּתִירָה. וְלָא יַדְעִין הֵיי דָא בְּשֵׁם גַּרְמֵיהּ וְהֵיידָא בְּשֵׁם רִבִּי יוּדָה בֶּן בָּתִירָה. מִן מָה דְאָמַר רִבִּי יוֹחָנָן. הֲלָכָה כְּרִבִּי יוּדָה שֶׁאָמַר מִשֵּׁם רִבִּי יוּדָה בֶּן בָּתִירָה. וְאָמַר רִבִּי אָבוּן בְּשֵׁם רִבִּי יוֹחָנָן. טַעֲם דְּרִבִּי יוּדָה כְּדֵי שֶׁיֵּצְאוּ הַמּוֹעֲדוֹת בְּטָל. מִפְּנֵי שֶׁהַטַּל סִימָן יָפֶה לָעוֹלָם. הָדָא אָמְרָה קַדְמָייָתָא בְּשֵׁם גַּרְמֵיהּ וְתִנְייָיתָא בְּשֵׁם רִבִּי יוּדָה בֶּן בָּתִירָה.

Rebbi Johanan said, practice follows Rebbi Jehudah who said in the name of Rebbi Jehudah ben Bathyra[106]. Rebbi Abun in the name of Rebbi Johanan: The reason of Rebbi Jehudah, that all holidays end with dew[107] since dew is a good sign[3] for the world.

The argument of Rebbi Jehudah seems inverted. There[108] he says, "the one who stands before the Ark on the last holiday of Tabernacles, the last one mentions but the first one does not mention;" and here[109] he says so? One {Mishnah} in his own name, the other one in the name of Rebbi Jehudah ben Bathyra. But we do not know which one in his own name and which one in the name of Rebbi Jehudah ben Bathyra. Since "Rebbi Joḥanan said, practice follows Rebbi Jehudah who said in the name of Rebbi Jehudah ben Bathyra, and Rebbi Abun said in the name of Rebbi Joḥanan: The reason of Rebbi Jehudah, that all holidays end with dew since dew is a good sign for the world," this implies that the first one is in his own name, the second one in the name of Rebbi Jehudah ben Bathyra[110].

106 Since R. Jehudah's statement in Mishnah 2 contradicts his statement in Mishnah 3, only one of them may be followed in practice. R. Joḥanan notes that the one which will be determined not to represent R. Jehudah's personal opinion will be actual practice.

107 Since in Mishnah 2 R. Jehudah holds that in all Passover prayers except the first two one mentions dew but not rain in the second benediction of the *Amidah*, R. Abun's statement must refer to Mishnah 2, since in Mishnah 3 R. Jehudah requires a mention of rain in all Passover prayers. This conforms to actual practice.

108 Mishnah 2.

109 Mishnah 3.

110 "First" here must refer to Mishnah 3, "second" to Mishnah 2. Only Mishnah 2 is practice. Babli 4b.

(64a line 44) בְּעוֹן קוֹמוֹי. אוֹ נֵימַר. כָּאן לְהַזְכִּיר כָּאן לִשְׁאֵלָה. אֲמַר לוֹן. הֲלָכָה מָקוֹם שֶׁמַּזְכִּירִין שׁוֹאֲלִין. אֲמַר רִבִּי יוֹסֵי לְרִבִּי חֲנַנְיָה אֲחוֹי דְּרַב הוֹשַׁעְיָה. נְהִיר אַתְּ כַּד הֲוִינָן קַיָּימִין קוֹמֵי חֲנוּתֵיהּ דְּרַב הוֹשַׁעְיָה חָבִיבָךְ. עָבַר רִבִּי זְעוּרָה וּשְׁאַלְנָן לֵיהּ וְאָמַר. עוֹד אֲנָא הִיא צְרִיכָה לִי. עָבַר רִבִּי יָסָא וּשְׁאַלְנָן לֵיהּ וְאָמַר. עוֹד אֲנָא הִיא צְרִיכָה לִי. וּבְסוֹפָה אַתְּ מְצָיֵית לֵיהּ וְאָמַר. לָא שַׁנְיָיא. הֲלָכָה מָקוֹם שֶׁמַּזְכִּירִין שׁוֹאֲלִין. רִבִּי חִייָה בַּר בָּא אֲתָא מִן צוֹר וְאָמַר מִן שְׁמֵיהּ דְּרִבִּי יוֹחָנָן. הֲלָכָה מָקוֹם שֶׁמַּזְכִּירִין שׁוֹאֲלִין. רִבִּי אָחָא דָּרַשׁ בְּבֵית מִדְרָשָׁא. רִבִּי יִרְמְיָה דָּרַשׁ בִּכְנִישְׁתָּא דְבוּלֵי. הֲלָכָה מָקוֹם שֶׁמַּזְכִּירִין שׁוֹאֲלִין. וְהָא תַנִּינָן [בִּשְׁלֹשָׁה] בְּמַרְחֶשְׁוָן שׁוֹאֲלִין אֶת הַגְּשָׁמִים. אֲמַר רִבִּי תַנְחוּם בַּר חִייָה. בִּשְׁעַת הַמִּקְדָּשׁ שָׁנֵי.

They asked before him[111], or might we say, here to mention and there to ask for[112]? He said to them, practice is that where one mentions one asks[113]. Rebbi Yose said to Rebbi Ḥanania the brother[114] of Rav Hoshaia, do you remember when we were standing in front of your uncle Rav Hoshaia's store, Rebbi Ze`ira passed by and we asked him, but he said, this[115] is still problematic for me; Rebbi Yasa passed by and we asked him, but he said, this is still problematic for me. But at the end you heard from him: there is no difference; where one mentions one asks. Rebbi Ḥiyya bar Abba came from Tyre and said in the name of Rebbi Joḥanan, practice is that where one mentions one asks. Rebbi Aḥa preached in the house of study, Rebbi

Jeremiah preached in the council synagogue, practice is that where one mentions one asks. But did we not state[116], "[on the third of][117] Marḥeshwan one asks for rain"? Rebbi Tanḥum bar Ḥiyya said, that was stated in Temple times[118].

111 R. Joḥanan.

112 One stops mentioning rain on the first day of Passover but continues to pray for rain all intermediate days of the holiday.

113 If one stops the praise for rain one also has to stop the prayer. From the following it is clear that for R. Joḥanan and his students this also applies to fall; one has to start praying for rain immediately in the night following the last day of Tabernacles. Accepted in the Babli 4b for dwellers in the Holy Land.

114 From the following it is obvious that one has to read "son of Rav Hoshaia's brother" (cf. Šabbat 1, Note 180).

115 The date when best to start praying for rain.

116 Mishnah 4.

117 The corrector's addition reproduces the start of Mishnah 4. It is possible that the scribe's text correctly gives the argument. The exact date of the start of the prayer for rain is in dispute, but all opinions concur that one only starts in the second month of the year, whereas R. Joḥanan requires starting during the first month, in the evening prayers of Tishre 23.

118 In Temple times one had to let people return safely from Jerusalem to their homes in Egypt, Palestine, or Syria. But after the destruction of the Temple everybody stayed at home and one is able to combine mention and prayer also in the fall.

(64a line 54) תַּנֵּי אָמַר רִבִּי יוּדָה. לְפִי שֶׁבָּעוֹלָם הַזֶּה הַתְּבוּאָה עוֹשָׂה לְשִׁשָּׁה חֳדָשִׁים וְהָאִילָן עוֹשֶׂה לִשְׁנַיִם עָשָׂר חוֹדֶשׁ. אֲבָל לֶעָתִיד לָבוֹא הַתְּבוּאָה עוֹשָׂה לְחוֹדֶשׁ אֶחָד וְהָאִילָן עוֹשֶׂה לִשְׁנֵי חֳדָשִׁים. מָה טַעֲמֵיהּ. לֶחֳדָשָׁיו יְבַכֵּר. רִבִּי יוֹסֵי אוֹמֵר. לְפִי שֶׁבָּעוֹלָם הַזֶּה הַתְּבוּאָה עוֹשָׂה לְשִׁשָּׁה חֳדָשִׁים וְהָאִילָן עוֹשֶׂה לִשְׁנַיִם עָשָׂר חוֹדֶשׁ. אֲבָל לֶעָתִיד לָבוֹא הַתְּבוּאָה עוֹשָׂה לַחֲמִשָּׁה עָשָׂר יוֹם וְהָאִילָן עוֹשֶׂה לְחוֹדֶשׁ אֶחָד. שֶׁכֵּן מָצָאנוּ שֶׁעָשְׂתָה הַתְּבוּאָה בִּימֵי יוֹאֵל לַחֲמִשָּׁה עָשָׂר יוֹם וְקָרַב הָעוֹמֶר מִמֶּנָּה. מָה טַעֲמֵיהּ. וּבְנֵי צִיּוֹן גִּילוּ וְשִׂמְחוּ בַּי"י אֱלֹהֵיכֶם כִּי־נָתַן לָכֶם אֶת־הַמּוֹרֶה לִצְדָקָה וַיּוֹרֶד לָכֶם גֶּשֶׁם יוֹרֶה וּמַלְקוֹשׁ בָּרִאשׁוֹן: מַה מְקַיֵּים רִבִּי יוֹסֵי טַעֲמֵיהּ דְּרִבִּי יוּדָה לֶחֳדָשָׁיו יְבַכֵּר. בְּכָל־חוֹדֶשׁ וָחוֹדֶשׁ יְהֵא מְבַכֵּר.

[119]It was stated: Rebbi Jehudah said, in the present world grain grows in six months and trees produce every twelve months, but in the future grain will grow in a month and trees will produce in two months. Rebbi Yose said, in the present world grain grows in six months and trees produce every twelve months, but in the future grain will grow in fifteen days and trees will produce

in a month, for so we find that grain grew in the days of Joel in fifteen days, and the '*Omer* was brought from it. What is the reason? *The people of Zion shall enjoy and be happy in the Eternal, your God, for He in truth gave you strong rain, early rain and late rain in the first {month}*[120]. How does Rebbi Yose satisfy Rebbi Jehudah's reason, *in its months it shall produce first fruits*? Every month it shall produce first fruits.

119 This is copied from *Šeqalim* 6:2, Notes 87-88.

120 Joel 2:23

(fol. 63c) **משנה ד**: בִּשְׁלֹשָׁה בְּמַרְחֶשְׁוָן שׁוֹאֲלִין אֶת הַגְּשָׁמִים. רַבָּן גַּמְלִיאֵל אוֹמֵר בְּשִׁבְעָה בוֹ חֲמִשָּׁה עָשָׂר יוֹם אַחַר הֶחָג. כְּדֵי שֶׁיַּגִּיעַ הָאַחֲרוֹן שֶׁבְּיִשְׂרָאֵל לִנְהַר פְּרָת

Mishnah 4: On the Third of Marḥeshwan[121] one prays for rain. Rabban Gamliel says on the Seventh of the month, fifteen days after Tabernacles, so that the last of the Jews may reach the river Euphrates[122].

121 The eighth Month of the year, counting from Nisan.

122 Then he is in Mesopotamia where rains start only at the end of November; he is not hindered by rains falling near the coast of the Mediterranean.

(64a line 64) **הלכה ג**: מַתְנִיתָא דְּרִבִּי מֵאִיר. דְּתַנֵּי. אֵי זֶהוּ זְמַנָּהּ שֶׁלְּרְבִיעָה. רִבִּי מֵאִיר אוֹמֵר. הַבְּכִירָה בִּשְׁלֹשָׁה וְהַבֵּינוֹנִית בְּשִׁבְעָה וְהָאֲפִילָה בְּשִׁבְעָה עָשָׂר. רִבִּי יוּדָה אוֹמֵר. הַבְּכִירָה בְּשִׁבְעָה וְהַבֵּינוֹנִית בְּשִׁבְעָה עָשָׂר וְהָאֲפִילָה בְּעֶשְׂרִים וּשְׁלֹשָׁה. רִבִּי יוֹסֵה אוֹמֵר. הַבְּכִירָה בְּשִׁבְעָה עָשָׂר וְהַבֵּינוֹנִית בְּעֶשְׂרִים וּשְׁלֹשָׁה וְהָאֲפִילָה בִּשְׁלֹשִׁים יוֹם. שֶׁכֵּן מָצָאנוּ שֶׁאֵין הַיְּחִידִים מַתְחִילִין לְהִתְעַנּוֹת אֶלָּא בְּרֹאשׁ חוֹדֶשׁ כִּסְלֵיו. אָמַר רִבִּי אַבָּמָרִי אָחוּי דְּרִבִּי יוֹסֵי. הַכֹּל מוֹדִים בְּשִׁבְעָה עָשָׂר שֶׁהוּא זְמַן כִּימָה לִשְׁקוֹעַ. שֶׁבּוֹ יָרַד מַבּוּל לָעוֹלָם. מַה טַעַם. בַּיּוֹם הַזֶּה נִבְקְעוּ כָּל־מַעְיְינוֹת תְּהוֹם רַבָּה. רִבִּי אַבָּא בַּר זְמִינָא רִבִּי לַעְזָר בְּשֵׁם רִבִּי הוֹשַׁעְיָה. הֲלָכָה כְּמִי שֶׁהוּא אוֹמֵר. בִּשְׁלֹשָׁה בְּמַרְחֶשְׁוָן שׁוֹאֲלִין אֶת הַגְּשָׁמִים. וְלָמָּה לֹא אָמַר. כְּרִבִּי מֵאִיר. אִית תַּנֵּיי תַּנֵּי וּמַחֲלָף.

Halakhah 3: The Mishnah is Rebbi Meïr's, as it was stated, [123]"what is the time of rainfall? Rebbi Meïr says, the early one on the Third, the average one on the Seventh, and the late one on the Seventeenth. Rebbi Jehudah says, the early one on the Seventh, the average on on the Seventeenth, and the late one on the Twenty-third. Rebbi Yose said, the early one on the Seventeenth,

HALAKHAH 3

the average one on the Twenty-third, and the late one on the Thirtieth day[124], since we find that particular people[125] only start to fast on the New Moon of Kislev." Rebbi Abbamari, the brother of Rebbi Yose, said: everybody agrees that the Seventeenth is the time for the pleiads to disappear[126], since on it the Deluge came over the world. What is the reason? *On this day all sources of the deep abyss were opened*[127]. Rebbi Abba bar Zamina, Rebbi Eleazar in the name of Rebbi Hoshaia: Practice follows him who says, "on the Third of Marḥeshwan one prays for rain"[128]. And why did he not say, following Rebbi Meïr? There are Tannaim who switch[129].

123 Babli 6a, *Nedarim* 63a; Tosephta 1:3.
124 The 30th day after the first of Marḥeshwan, which may be the first of Kislev.
125 The community leaders start to fast in a year of drought; Mishnah 5. In the Tosephta this is formulated as a statement of R. Yose, contradicting Mishnah 5.
126 Since the pleiads are visible only in summer. Cf. Babli *Berakhot* 59a. Babli *Roš Haššanah* 11b.
127 *Gen.* 7:11. In the verse, the date is "the 17th day of the Second Month."
128 Denied in the Babli, 6a.
129 The tradition of names here, in the Tosephta and the Babli is not beyond dispute.

(64a line 75) כַּמָּה גְשָׁמִים יֵרְדוּ וִיהֵא אָדָם צָרִיךְ לְבָרֵךְ. רִבִּי חִייָה בְשֵׁם רִבִּי יוֹחָנָן. כַּתְּחִילָּה כְּדֵי רְבִיעָה. וּבַסּוֹף כְּדֵי שֶׁיְּדוּחוּ פְּנֵי הַקַּרְקָמִיד. רִבִּי יַנַּאי בֵּירִבִּי יִשְׁמָעֵאל בְּשֵׁם רִבִּי שִׁמְעוֹן בֶּן לָקִישׁ. כַּתְּחִילָּה כְּדֵי רְבִיעָה. וּבַסּוֹף כְּדֵי שֶׁתִּשָּׁרֶה הַמְּגוּפָה. וְיֵשׁ מְגוּפָה נִשְׁרֵית. אֶלָּא רוֹאִין אוֹתָהּ כְּאִילּוּ הִיא שְׁרוּיָיה. רִבִּי יוֹסֵה בְשֵׁם רַב יְהוּדָה רִבִּי יוֹנָה רַב יְהוּדָה בְשֵׁם שְׁמוּאֵל. כַּתְּחִילָּה כְּדֵי רְבִיעָה. וּלְבַסּוֹף אֲפִילוּ כָּל־שֶׁהוּא. רִבִּי יוֹסֵה בְשֵׁם רִבִּי זְעוּרָה. לְהֶפְסֵק תַּעֲנִית נֶאֶמְרָה. רִבִּי חִזְקִיָּה וְרִבִּי נָחוּם וְרַב אָדָא בַּר אִיפּוּמָא הֲווֹן יְתִיבִין. אָמַר רִבִּי נָחוּם לְרַב אָדָא בַּר אִיפּוּמָא. לֹא מִסְתַּבְּרָא לִבְרָכָה נֶאֶמְרָה. אָמַר לֵיהּ. אִין. וְלָמָּה אָמַרְתְּ לֵיהּ אָכֵין. אָמַר לֵיהּ. דְּהוּא נְהִיג בְּשִׁיטַת רַבֵּיהּ. אָמַר רִבִּי מָנָא לְרַבִּי חִזְקִיָּה. מָנוּ רַבֵּיהּ. אָמַר לֵיהּ. רִבִּי זְעוּרָא. אָמַר לֵיהּ. [אַף] אֲנָן אָמְרִין. רִבִּי יוֹסֵה בְשֵׁם רִבִּי זְעוּרָה. לְהֶפְסֵק תַּעֲנִית נֶאֶמְרָה.

1 כמה | ב וכמה חייה | ב חייא   2 שידוחו פני הקרקמיד | ב שיודחו פניה ינאי | ב ינאי ביר' | ב בר   3 ובסוף | ב ולבסוף   4 יוסה | ב יוסי ר' | ב ור' רב | ב ורב   5 זעורה | ב זעירא להפסק | ב להפסיק   6 בר איכומא | ב ורב בימי יתיבין | ב יתבין בר איכומא | ב בר אבימי   7 אין | ב הין - | ב אמ'ר' חזקיה לרב אדא נר אבימי. לא מסתברא להפסיק תעניתא נאמ'. אמ' ליה. אין.   אכין | ב אין SR דהוא נהיג | ב   8 SR רביה | ב רבי מנו | ב מני   9 [אף] אנן | ב ואנן אמרין | ב אמרינן יוסה | ב יוסי זעורה | ב זעירא

How[130] much rain should fall that a man is required to recite a benediction? Rebbi Ḥiyya in the name of Rebbi Joḥanan: At the start[131], that it should fertilize, at the end that a brick should be soaked[132]. Rebbi Yannai ben Rebbi Ismael in the name of Rebbi Simeon ben Laqish: At the start, that it should fertilize, at the end that the seal of the amphora should be soaked. Is the seal ever soaked[133]? But it is as if it were soaked. Rebbi Yose in the name of Rav Jehudah, Rebbi Jonah, Rav Jehudah in the name of Samuel: At the start, that it should fertilize, at the end even a minimal amount. Rebbi Yose in the name of Rebbi Ze`ira: It was said for the interruption of fasting[134]. Rebbi Ḥizqiah, Rebbi Naḥum, and Rav Ada bar (Ikoma) <Abimi>[135] were sitting. Rebbi Naḥum said to Rav Ada bar (Ikoma) <Abimi>: Is it not reasonable that this was said for the benediction; he answered: Yes. [136]<Rebbi Ḥizqiah said to Rav Ada bar (Ikoma) <Abimi>: Is it not reasonable that this was said for the interruption of fasting; he answered: Yes.> He said to him, why did you say "yes" here? He said to him, because he follows the argumentation of his teacher. Rebbi Mana asked Rebbi Ḥizqiah, who is his teacher? He said to him, Rebbi Ze`ira. He said to him, so we are saying: Rebbi Yose in the name of Rebbi Ze`ira: It was said for the interruption of fasting.

130 The text almost to the end of the Halakhah also appears in *Berakhot* 9:3 (Notes 155-162,‏ב) and partially in *Gen. rabba* 13(16).

131 If in a year of drought a public fast was proclaimed and before the start of the fast it rained, everybody agrees that the fast is cancelled if the rain has agricultural use. (This is the only criterion known to the Babli, 25b.) If one started to fast, one interrupts the fast according to one of the criteria "at the end".

132 That a brick should become soft from the rain. The Arabic dictionary translates קרמיד by "(fired) brick, roof tile; plaster of Paris."

133 Are these statements only phrases which hide the fact that a fast for rain which has started is never interrupted? The fast will be interrupted for a real downpour.

134 Even though the question was asked about the benediction required by Mishnah *Berakhot* 9:3, the statements are about aborting a fast announced in a drought. The implication is that the benediction, or alternative prayer as described in the next paragraph, is required if the amount of initial rainfall is of agricultural significance.

135 The name <used in *Berakhot*> is to be adopted here also.

136 Added from ‏ב, needed but missing here because of homeoteleuton.

(64b line 10) רַב יְהוּדָה בַּר יְחֶזְקֵאל אָמַר. הָכֵין הֲוָה יְחֶזְקֵאל אַבָּא מְבָרֵךְ עַל יְרִידַת גְּשָׁמִים. יִתְגַּדַּל יִתְקַדַּשׁ יִתְבָּרַךְ יִתְרוֹמַם שְׁמָךְ מַלְכֵּינוּ עַל כָּל־טִיפָּה וְטִיפָּה שֶׁאַתְּ מוֹרִיד לָנוּ. שֶׁאַתְּ מַטְמִיעָן זוֹ מִזוֹ. [שֶׁנֶּאֱמַר] כִּי יְגָרַע נִטְפֵי־מָיִם יָזוֹקּוּ מָטָר לְאֵידוֹ. כְּמָה דְּאַתְּ אָמַר וְנִגְרַע מֵעֶרְכֶּךָ:

אָמַר רִבִּי יוּדָן אֲבוֹי דְרִבִּי מַתָּנְיָה. וְלֹא עוֹד אֶלָּא שֶׁהוּא מוֹרִידָן בְּמִידָה. [שֶׁנֶּאֱמַר] וּמַיִם תִּיכֶּן בְּמִידָה: רִבִּי יוֹסֵה בַּר יַעֲקֹב סָלַק מְבַקְּרָה לְרִבִּי יוּדָן מוּגְדְלַיָּא. עַד דְּהוּא תַּמָּן נְחַת מִיטְרָא. שְׁמַע קָלֵיהּ אָמַר. אֶלֶף אֲלָפִים אָנוּ חַיָּיבִין לְהוֹדוֹת לְשִׁמְךָ מַלְכֵּינוּ עַל כָּל־טִיפָּה וְטִיפָּה שֶׁאַתְּ מוֹרִיד לָנוּ. שֶׁאַתְּ גּוֹמֵל טוֹבָה לַחַיָּיבִים. אָמַר לֵיהּ. הָדָא מְנָן לָךְ. אָמַר לֵיהּ. הָכֵין הֲוָה רִבִּי סִימוֹן רִבִּי מְבָרֵךְ עַל יְרִידַת גְּשָׁמִים.

1 הכין הוה יחזקאל | **ב** - 2 יתקדש יתברך יתרומם | **ב** ויתקדש ויתברך ויתרומם 3 [ ] | **ב** - יזוק מטר לאידו | **ב** - 4 אבוי דר' מתניה | **ב** - 5 יוסה | **ב** יוסי מוגדליא | **ב** מגדליא 6 שמע | **ב** ושמע אלפים | **ב** אלפין וריבי ריבוון אנו | **ב** - 7 מנן | **ס** מנא 8 רבי | **ב** -

Rav Jehudah bar Ezechiel[137] said, so was my father Ezechiel used to recite for rainfall: May Your Name be magnified, sanctified, praised, and elevated, our King, for every drop that You bring down to us, and you make them refrain one from the other[138]. [As it is said,] *for He reduces water drippings; they combine as rain for a flood*[139], as one says, *the valuation will be reduced*[140]. Rebbi Yudan, the father of Rebbi Mattaniah, said, not only that, but He brings them down in measure, as it is said: *Water He determined by measure*[141]." Rebbi Yose bar Jacob went to visit Rebbi Yudan from Migdal. While he was there, rain started to come down and he heard his voice saying: Thousands of thousands we are obliged to thank Your Name, our King, for every drop that You bring down to us, for You do good things for the guilty ones. He said to him[142]: From where do you have this? He said to him: This is the benediction that Rebbi Simon recited for rainfall.

137 He is Rav Jehudah, frequently mentioned in both Talmudim.
138 Differently in the Babli 6b.
139 *Job* 36:27.
140 *Lev.* 27:18.
141 *Job* 28:25.
142 R. Yose bar Jacob to R. Yudan from Magdala.

(64b line 20) וְכַמָּה גְשָׁמִים יֵרְדוּ וִיהֵא בָהֶם כְּדֵי רְבִיעָה. מְלֹא כָלִי מַחֲזִיק שָׁלֹשׁ טְפָחִים. דִּבְרֵי רִבִּי מֵאִיר. רִבִּי יְהוּדָה אוֹמֵר. בַּתְּחִילָּה טֶפַח. וּבַשְּׁנִייָה טְפָחַיִם. וּבַשְּׁלִישִׁית שְׁלֹשָׁה טְפָחִים. תַּנֵי. רִבִּי שִׁמְעוֹן בֶּן אֶלְעָזָר אוֹמֵר. אֵין לָךְ טֶפַח שֶׁהוּא יוֹרֵד מִלְמַעְלָן שֶׁאֵין הָאָרֶץ מַעֲלָה טְפָחַיִים כְּנֶגְדּוֹ. וּמַה טַעַם. תְּהוֹם אֶל־תְּהוֹם קוֹרֵא לְקוֹל צִינּוֹרֶיךָ.

1 בהם | **ב** בהן 2 טפחים | **ב** שני טפחים 3 שאין הארץ | **ב** (S) עד שהארץ

How much rain should fall that it is considered fertilizing[143]? If it fills a vessel of three handbreadths, the words of Rebbi Meïr. Rebbi Yehudah says, the first rainfall one handbreadth, the second one two hand breadths, and the third one three handbreadths.   It has been stated[144]: Rebbi Simeon ben

Eleazar says, there is no handbreadth that falls from above that the earth does not raise two handbreadths towards it. What is the reason? *The deep calls to the deep by the sound of Your water spouts*[145].

143 The root רבע of רְבִיעָה may mean either "to lie down", as an Aramaism parallel to Hebrew רבץ, or it may have the same sexual connotation as the synonym שכב. Therefore רְבִיעָה either may be interpreted as the rain which "lies down" on the earth and moistens it for agricultural use or as "fertilizing".

There are two parallel traditions, both of Galilean origin. The text here is almost identical with Tosephta 1:4. In the Babli (25b) and the Yerushalmi source *Gen. rabba* 13(13), Rebbi Meïr is reported to require that the rains penetrate the depth of the penetration of the ploughshare (which is assumed to be three hand-breadths,) whereas R. Yehudah says that for dry earth, one handbreadth was enough, for average ground two handbreadths, and for well worked ground, three handbreadths. If these are two equivalent formulations, then the text here has to be interpreted in the light of the text in Babli/Midrash: Not that R. Meïr requires a rainfall of three handbreadths (10.8 inches) in one storm (or R. Yehudah rainfalls of 3.6, 7.2, 10.8 inches, respectively) but that the moisture has to penetrate the earth to the depth indicated. In that case, "dry earth" is simply the earth after the rainless summer months, average earth is the earth after the first winter storms, and well worked ground is the earth after an uninterrupted rain of seven days (the first, second, and third fertilizing periods in the language of Tosephta Taaniot 1:4). R. Simeon ben Eleazar seems to object to both R. Meïr and R. Yehudah because rain will make the ground water level rise by twice the amount of rain water; hence, moisture in the ground can come from below as well as from above. One must assume that in the Yerushalmi also the measurements are those of moist spots in the earth and not of rainfall in the modern sense.

144 Tosephta 1:4.

145 *Ps.* 42:8. Rashi explains in Babli Taanit that clouds also are called "deep". The Targum to *Ps.* reads: The upper abyss calls to the lower abyss by the sound of the sprinkling of your channels (Rashi *Ps.* in Romance: *tes canales.*)

(64b line 24) אָמַר רִבִּי לֵוִי. הַמַּיִם הָעֶלְיוֹנִים זְכָרִים וְהַתַּחְתּוֹנִים נְקֵבוֹת. מַה טַעַם. תִּפְתַּח־אֶרֶץ וְיִפְרוּ־יֶשַׁע. תִּפְתַּח־אָרֶץ. כִּנְקֵיבָה הַזֹּאת שֶׁהִיא פוֹתַחַת לִפְנֵי הַזָּכָר. וְיִפְרוּ־יֶשַׁע. זוֹ פְּרִיָּיה וְרִבְיָּיה. וּצְדָקָה תַצְמִיחַ. זוֹ יְרִידַת גְּשָׁמִים. אֲנִי יְהוָה בְּרָאתִיו: לְכָךְ בְּרָאתִיו. לְתִיקוּנוֹ וּלְיִישׁוּבוֹ שֶׁלְעוֹלָם. רִבִּי אָחָא. וְתַנֵּי לָהּ בְּשֵׁם רַבִּי שִׁמְעוֹן בֶּן גַּמְלִיאֵל. וְלָמָּה נִקְרָא שְׁמָהּ רְבִיעָה. שֶׁהִיא רוֹבַעַת אֶת הָאָרֶץ.

1 אמ' | ב ואמ' נקבות | ב נקיבות 1-2 תפתח ארץ ויפרו ישע | ב - 2 פרייה | ב פריה 3 תצמיח | ב תצמיח יחד אני | ב כי אני

Rebbi Levi said: The upper waters are male and the lower ones female. What is the reason? *The earth shall open, they shall bear fruit of help*[145]. *The earth shall open*, like a female who opens before a male; *they should bear fruit of help*, that is being fruitful and multiplying; *and justice shall sprout*, that is rainfall; *I, the Eternal, did create it,* for this purpose I created it, for the wellbeing of the world. Rebbi Aḥa stated it in the name of Rebbi Simeon ben Gamliel[146]: Why is it called "fertilizing"? Because it impregnates the earth.

145 The verse starts: *The heavens should pour down from high, and the skies should flow with justice,"* speaking of rain. The Babli has two contradictory sermons in this matter. Rav Jehudah is reported in 6b that rain is the earth's husband because in *Is.* 55:10 it is said that rain makes the earth give birth, while Rebbi Abbahu (there and *Berakhot* 59b) says that a benediction is recited only if "the bridegroom goes towards the bride," meaning that drops jump up from the earth towards the descending rain. [This is the traditional interpretation, given by Ashkenazic Rabbenu Gershom and North-African Rabbenu Ḥanan`el. Rashi, sensing the apparent contradiction to R. Levi's statement, has a prosaic interpretation, that on both sides of the street the gutters will spout water one towards the other.]

146 This is the end of Rebbi Simeon ben Eleazar's text in Tosephta 1:4. In the Babli 6b, this passage appears as a statement of the Amora Rebbi Abbahu. The statement also is quoted in *Ševi`it* 9:7 (Note 101), *Nedarim* 8:6 (Note 73).

(64b line 30) רִבִּי חֲנִינָה בָּרִיקָה בְשֵׁם רַב יְהוּדָה. שׁוֹרְשֵׁי חִיטָּה בּוֹקְעִין בָּאָרֶץ חֲמִשִּׁים אַמָּה. שָׁרְשֵׁי תְאֵינָה רַכִּין בּוֹקְעִין בַּצּוּר. אִם כֵּן מַה יַּעֲשׂוּ שָׁרְשֵׁי חָרוּב וְשָׁרְשֵׁי שִׁקְמָה. אָמַר רִבִּי חֲנִינָה. אַחַת לִשְׁלֹשִׁים יוֹם הַתְּהוֹם עוֹלֶה וּמַשְׁקֶה אוֹתָהּ. מַה טַעַם. אֲנִי יי נֹצְרָהּ לִרְגָעִים אַשְׁקֶנָּה. [תַּנֵּי. רִבִּי שִׁמְעוֹן בֶּן אֶלְעָזָר אוֹמֵר. מְלַמֵּד שֶׁאֵין הָאָרֶץ שׁוֹתָה אֶלָּא לְפִי חִיסּוּמָהּ.]

1 חנינה | **ב** חנינא   בריקה | **ב** בר יקא **ע** בר יסא   2 שרשי | **בע** שורשי (2)   רכין | **ע** רכים   יעשו | **ב** יעשה ושרשי | **ב** מה יעשו שורשי   חנינה | **ב** חנינא   3 התהום | **ב** תהום   אותה | **ב** אותו **ע** אותה   מה | **בע** ומה   4 שמעון | **ב** ישמעאל   מלמד | **ב** -   שאין | **ב** אין

[147]Rebbi Ḥanina bar Yaqqa in the name of Rav Jehudah[148]: The roots of wheat split the earth to a depth of three cubits. The soft roots of a fig tree split rock. If this is so, what do the roots of the carob or the roots of the sycamore do[149]? Rebbi Ḥanina[150] said, once every thirty days the abyss wells up and drenches them. What is the reason? *I, the Eternal, watch over it*[151] *and water it in*[152]." [It has been stated: Rebbi Simeon ben Eleazar says, the earth drinks only according to its hardness.[153]]

147 This paragraph also is copied in *Avodah zarah* 3:6, Notes 152-153. Like the entire series here it seems that the origin is in *Gen. rabba* 13.

148 In all readable sources of *Gen. rabba* "Rebbi Jehudah". In the Genizah fragment published by M. Sokoloff (Jerusalem 1982), ". . . bar `Iqa, R. Berekhia in the name of Rebbi Jehudah."

149 Which grow on hard soil unfit for agriculture.

150 In the *Gen. rabba* fragment: R. Levi.

151 The desirable vineyard.

152 *Is.* 27:3.

153 Corrector's addition from the parallel sources. In the ms. sources of *Gen. rabba* the name is as given here; in the Midrash prints R. Eleazar ben R. Simeon; in *Berakhot* R. Ismael ben Eleazar.

(64b line 37) תַּנֵּי. אִם הָיְתָה הַשָּׁנָה חֲסֵירָה נוֹתְנִין לָהּ חֶסְרוֹנָהּ. וְאִם לָאו הוֹלְכִין אַחַר סִידְרָהּ. דִּבְרֵי רַבָּן שִׁמְעוֹן בֶּן גַּמְלִיאֵל. רִבִּי אוֹמֵר. לְעוֹלָם הוֹלְכִין אַחַר סִידְרָהּ. אִם הָיְתָה הַשָּׁנָה מְעוּבֶּרֶת הוֹלְכִין אַחַר עִיבּוּרָהּ. מְחִלְפָה שִׁיטָתֵיהּ דְּרִבִּי. תַּמָּן הוּא אָמַר. אַחַר סִידְרָהּ. וְכָא הוּא אָמַר. אַחַר עִיבּוּרָהּ. רִבִּי זְעוּרָה רִבִּי יָסָא רִבִּי שְׁמוּאֵל בַּר רַב יִצְחָק מַטֵּי בָהּ בְּשֵׁם רִבִּי יוֹחָנָן. לַבָּסוֹף נִצְרְכָה.

[154]"If the year was deficient, one makes up for the deficiency[155]; otherwise one follows its order, the words of Rabban Simeon ben Gamliel. Rebbi says, one always follows its order. If the year was intercalary, one follows its intercalation." The argument of Rebbi seems inverted. There he says, one follows its order. And here he says, after its intercalation. Rebbi Ze`ira, Rebbi Yasa, Rebbi Samuel ben Rav Isaac brings it in the name of Rebbi Joḥanan, this was needed for the end[156].

154 Tosephta 1:2. There the name tradition is switched. From the Yerushalmi text, practice follows Rebbi.

155 If the lunar year makes the fall festivals early in the solar year, one waits with praying for rain until two weeks after the fall equinox, in order not to pray for unnatural acts of nature. Following Rebbi one starts early in Marheshwan, irrespective of the solar date.

156 The month after the intercalary, the second Adar, as well as the first two weeks of Nisan, always are a time to pray for rain. One stops only on the 15th of Nisan, irrespective of the solar date.

(fol. 63c) **משנה ה:** הִגִּיעַ שִׁבְעָה עָשָׂר בְּמַרְחֶשְׁוָן וְלֹא יָרְדוּ גְשָׁמִים הִתְחִילוּ הַיְחִידִים מִתְעַנִּין. אוֹכְלִין וְשׁוֹתִין מִשֶּׁחֲשֵׁיכָה וּמוּתָּרִין בִּמְלָאכָה וּבִרְחִיצָה וּבְסִיכָה וּבִנְעִילַת הַסַּנְדָּל וּבְתַשְׁמִישׁ הַמִּטָּה:

Mishnah 5: When the Seventeenth of Marḥeshwan arrived without rainfall, particular people[157] started to fast. They eat and drink while it is dark and are permitted work, washing, and anointing, and wearing sandals[158], and sexual intercourse.

157 As described in the Halakhah.

158 During daylight time when they were fasting. "Sandals" stand here for any leather shoes. Any of these fast-days are either Monday or Thursday. The Babli version is "started to fast three fast-days." The version in the *editio princeps* of the Yerushalmi and reproduced here, identical to Maimonides's autograph Mishnah, seems to imply that they were fasting every Monday and Thursday between Marḥeshwan 17 and Kislew 1.

(64b line 40) **הלכה ד:** אִילוּ הֵם הַיְחִידִים. אֵילוּ שֶׁהֵן מִתְמַנִּין פַּרְנָסִין עַל הַצִּיבּוּר. מִכֵּיוָן שֶׁהוּא מִתְמַנֶּה פַּרְנָס עַל הַצִּיבּוּר הוּא מִתְפַּלֵּל וְנַעֲנֶה. אֶלָּא מִכֵּיוָן שֶׁהוּא מִתְמַנֶּה פַּרְנָס עַל הַצִּיבּוּר וְנִמְצָא נֶאֱמָן כְּדַי הוּא מַצְלְיָיא וּמִתְעַנְיָיא.

Halakhah 4: These are the particular people, those who were appointed overseers[159] over the public. Because he was appointed overseer over the public he will be heard when he prays? But since he was appointed overseer over the public and found to be honest, he is worthy to pray and be heard.

159 The classical Arabic vocalization is פַּרְנָאס "village head". The Babli 10a/b admits only rabbis worthy to be appointed to public office.

(64b line 43) חַד בַּר נַשׁ הֲוָה מַפִּיק מַעְשְׂרוֹי כְּתִיקְנָן. אָמַר לֵיהּ רִבִּי מָנָא. קוּם אֱמוֹר בְּעַרְתִּי הַקּוֹדֶשׁ מִן־הַבַּיִת.

חַד בַּר נַשׁ אֲתָא גַּבֵּי חַד מִן קְרִיבוֹי דְרִבִּי יַנַּאי. אָמַר לֵיהּ. רִבִּי. זְכֵה עִימִּי. אָמַר לֵיהּ. וְלֹא הֲוָה לָאֲבוּךְ פְּרִיטִין. אָמַר לֵיהּ. לָא. אָמַר לֵיהּ. גַּבֵּי אִינּוּן מְפַקְדִין. אָמַר לֵיהּ. שְׁמָעִית עֲלֵיהוֹן דְּאִינּוּן [פֵּרְקוּן]. אָמַר לֵיהּ. כְּדַי אַתְּ מַצְלְיָיא וּמִתְעַנְיָיא.

A person was tithing following the rules[160]. Rebbi Mana said to him, stand up and say, *I removed the sancta from the house*[161].

A person came to a relative of Rebbi Yannai and said to him: Rabbi, acquire merit with me[162]. He said to him, did your father not have money[163]? He answered, no. He told him, it is deposited with me. He told him, I heard about it that it was [repayment[164]]. He said to him[165], you are worthy to pray and be heard.

160 Which not may people did.

161 *Deut.* 26:13. One has to explain that this happened during a prayer for rain, and R. Mana wanted him to recite the entire passage, ending with v. 15: *Look down from Your holy Place, from Heaven, and bless Your people Israel, and the Land which You gave us as You had sworn to our forefathers, a land flowing with milk and honey.*

162 By giving me alms.

163 And you are barred from taking alms.

164 It is not known what the original text of the scribe was. The *editio princeps* has סרקון, Arabic סרק "to steal". The beggar did not want to take the money, either following the *editio princeps* because his father stole it, or following the corrector's text in the ms. because it was not the father's money since it came to the hand of the holder as repayment of a loan. The second version is preferable. (Cf. *Peah* 8:9, *Šeqalim* 5:6 Note 99.)

165 Depending on the interpretation of the previous sentence, the pious party should be the leader in prayers for rain.

(64b line 48) אִיתְחֲמֵי לְרַבָּנָן. פְּלַן חַמָּרָא יַצְלֵי וּמֵיטְרָא נָחַת. שָׁלְחוּן רַבָּנָן וְאַייתוּנֵיהּ. אֲמָרוּן לֵיהּ. מָה אוּמָנָךְ. אֲמַר לוֹן. חַמָּר אֲנָא. אֲמָרוּן לֵיהּ. וּמַה טִיבוּ עֲבַדְתְּ. אֲמַר לוֹן. חַד זְמַן אוּגְרִית חַמְרִי לְחָדָא אִיתָּה. וַהֲוָת בַּכְיָה גּוֹ אִיסְרָטָה. וְאָמְרִית לָהּ. מַה לִיךְ. אָמְרָה לִי. בַּעֲלָהּ דְּהִיא אִיתְּתָא חֲבִישׁ וַאֲנָא בָעְיָא מֵיחְמֵי מַה מֵיעֲבַד וּמִפְנְיָנֵיהּ. וְזָבְנִית חַמְרִי וְיַבֵּית לָהּ טִימִיתֵיהּ. וְאָמְרִית לָהּ. הָא לִיךְ. פְּנֵי בַּעֲלִיךְ וְלָא תֶחְטֵיי. אָמְרִין לֵיהּ. כְּדַיי אַתְּ מַצְלָיָיא וּמִתְעֲנֵייָא.

אִיתְחֲמֵי לְרִבִּי אַבָּהוּ. פֶּנְטָקָקָה יַצְלֵי וַאֲתֵי מִיטְרָא. שְׁלַח רִבִּי אַבָּהוּ וְאַייתִיתֵיהּ. אֲמַר לֵיהּ. מָה אוּמָנָךְ. אֲמַר לֵיהּ. חָמֵשׁ עֲבֵירָן הַהוּא גוּבְרָא עָבִיד בְּכָל־יוֹם. מוֹגַר זַנְיָיתָא. מְשַׁפֵּר תֵיַיטְרוֹן. מָעִיל מָאנֵיהוֹן לְבָנֵי. מְטַפַּח וּמְרַקֵּד קֳדָמֵיהוֹן. וּמַקִּישׁ בְּבַבּוּלִייָא קֳדָמֵיהוֹן. אֲמַר לֵיהּ. וּמַה טִיבוּ עֲבַדְתְּ. אֲמַר לֵיהּ. חַד זְמַן הֲוָה הַהוּא גַּבְרָא מְשַׁפֵּר תֵיַיטְרוֹן. אֲתַת חָדָא אִיתָּא וְקָמַת לָהּ חוֹרֵי עַמּוּדָא. בַּכְיָא. וְאָמְרִית לָהּ. מַה לִיךְ. וְאָמְרָה לִי. בַּעֲלָהּ דְּהִיא אִיתְּתָא חֲבִישׁ וַאֲנָא בָעְיָא מֵיחְמֵי מַה מֵיעֲבַד וּמִפְנְיָנֵיהּ. וְזָבְנִית עֲרַסִי וּפְרוֹס עַרְסִי וְיַבֵּית לָהּ טִימִיתֵיהּ. וְאָמְרִית לָהּ. הָא לִיךְ. פְּנֵי בַּעֲלִיךְ וְלָא תֵיחְטֵיי. אֲמַר לֵיהּ. כְּדַיי אַתְּ מַצְלָייָא וּמִתְעֲנֵייָא.

It was seen by the rabbis[166], a certain donkey driver should pray[167] and rain will come. The rabbis sent and brought him. They asked him, what is your profession? He said, I am a donkey driver. They asked him, what good deed did you do? He told them, once I rented out my donkey to a certain woman, and she was crying on the road. I asked her, what is your problem? She said to me, this woman's husband is jailed and I have to see what to do to free him[168]. I sold my donkey, gave her its value[169] and told her, this is yours; free your husband and do not sin. They told him, you are worthy to pray and be heard.

It was seen by Rebbi Abbahu, Pantokaka[170] shall pray and rain will come. Rebbi Abbahu sent and brought him. He asked him, what is your profession? He told him, five sins this man commits every day. He rents out prostitutes[171], maintains the theater[172], brings their garments to the baths, claps his hands and dances before them, and plays cymbals[173] before them[174]. They asked him, what good deed did you do? He told them, once I was maintaining the theater, when a woman came and stood behind a pillar, crying. I asked her, what is your problem? She said to me, this woman's husband is jailed and I have to see what to do to free him. I sold my bed, and my bed-spread, gave her its value, and told her, this is yours; free your husband and do not sin. They told him, you are worthy to pray and be heard.

166 In a dream.
167 Be the reader in the services, described in Chapter 2, of a public fast for rain as described in Mishnah 6. This service contains parts reserved for the reader alone.
168 To bribe the jailer.
169 Greek τιμή.
170 Greek παντόκακος, "all bad".

171 Usually gentile slaves.
172 Greek θέατρον.
173 Greek βαβούλια (Liebermann.) The Hebrew word is misspelled in the *editio princeps* and all printed editions depending on it.
174 Either the customers of his bordello or the public in the theater.

(64b line 63) אִיתְחֲמֵי לְרַבָּנָן. חֲסִידָא דִכְפַר אִימִּי יַצְלֵי וּמִיטְרָא נָחַת. סַלְקוּן רַבָּנָן לְגַבֵּיהּ. אָמְרָה לוֹן בְּנֵי בֵיתֵיהּ. בְּטוּרָא הוּא יְהִיב. נַפְקוּן לְגַבֵּיהּ. אָמְרוֹן לֵיהּ. אֵישַׁר. וְלָא אַגִּיבוֹן. יָתַב מֵיכוּל וְלָא אָמַר לוֹן. אַתּוֹן כְּרֵיכִין. מִי עֲלַל עֲבַד חַד מוֹבַל דְּקִיסִין וִיהַב גּוּלְתָּא מְרוֹם מוּבְלָה. אֲעַל וַאֲמַר לִבְנֵי בֵיתֵיהּ. אִילֵּין רַבָּנָן הָכָא בָּעֵי נִצְלֵי וְיֵיחוֹת מִיטְרָא. וְאִין אֲנָא מַצְלֵי וּמִיטְרָא נָחַת גְּנַאי הוּא לוֹן. וְאִין לָא חִילוּל שֵׁם שָׁמַיִם הוּא. אֶלָּא אַיְתֵיי אֲנָא וְאַתְּ נִיסּוֹק וְנַצְלֵי. אִין נְחַת מִיטְרָא. אֲנַן אָמְרִין לוֹן. כְּבָר דְּעָבְדוֹן שְׁמַיָּא נִיסִּין. וְאִין לָא. אֲנַן אָמְרִין לוֹן. לֵית אֲנַן כְּדַיִּי מַצְלַיָּיא וּמִתְעַנְיָיא. וְסָלְקוּן וְצָלוּן וּנְחַת מִיטְרָא. נְחַת לְגַבּוֹן. אֲמַר לוֹן. לָמָּה אִיטְרְפוּן רַבָּנָן לְהָכָא יוֹמָא דֵין. אָמְרִין לֵיהּ. בָּעֵי תַּצְלֵי וְיֵיחוֹת מִיטְרָא. אֲמַר לוֹן. וְלִצְלוֹתִי אַתּוֹן צְרִיכִין. כְּבָר דְּעָבְדוּן שְׁמַיָּא נִיסִּין. אָמְרִין לֵיהּ. לָמָּה כַד הֲוֵיתָה בְּטוּרָא אֲמָרִינָן לָךְ. אַיְשַׁר. וְלָא אַגִּיבְתִּינוֹן.

אָמַר לוֹן. דַּהֲוֵינָא עָסִיק בְּפָעוּלָתִי. מַה הֲוֵינָה מַסְעָה דַעְתִּי מִן פְּעוּלָתִי. אָמְרִין לֵיהּ. לָמָּה כַד יָתַבְתְּ לְמֵיכוֹל לָא אֲמַרְתְּ לוֹן. אֵיתוֹן כְּרִיכִין. אָמַר לוֹן. דְּלָא הֲוָה גַבַּיי אֶלָּא פַּלְחִי. מַה הֲוֵינָא מֵימוֹר לְכוֹן בְּחַנְפִין. אָמְרִין לֵיהּ. לָמָּה כַד דַּאֲתֵית לְמֵיעוֹל יְהַבְתְּ גּוּלְתָּה מְרוֹם מוּבְלָה. אָמַר לוֹן. דְּלָא הֲוָת דִּידִי. שְׁאִילָה הֲוָת דְּנִצְלִי בָהּ. מַה הֲוֵינָא מְבַזְעָא יָתָהּ. אָמְרוֹן לֵיהּ. וְלָמָּה כַד הֲוֵוי אַתְּ בְּטוּרָא אִיתְּתָךְ לְבָשָׁה מָאנִין צָאִין. וְכַד דְּאַתְּ עָלִיל מִן טוּרָא הִיא לְבָשָׁה מָאנִין נְקִיִּין. אָמַר לוֹן. כַּד דַּאֲנָא הֲוֵי בְטוּרָא הִיא לְבָשָׁה מָאנִין צָאיִין דְּלָא יִתֵּן בַּר נַשׁ עִינוֹי עֲלָהּ. וְכַד דַּאֲנָא עָלִיל מִן טוּרָא הִיא לְבָשָׁה מָאנִין נְקִיִּין דְּלָא נִיתֵּן עֵינַיי בְּאִיתְּתָא אוּחְרִי. אָמְרוֹן לֵיהּ. יָאוּת אַתְּ מַצְלַיָּא וּמִתְעַנְיָיא.

[175]It was seen by the rabbis that the pious man of Kefar-Immi shall pray and rain will come. The rabbis went up to him. His house-companion[176] told them, he is working on the mountain. They went out to him. They said to him "much success" but he did not answer. He sat down to eat and did not invite them to partake. When he finished he made one load of firewood and put the coat on top of the load. He went and said to his house-companion, these rabbis here want us to pray that rain should fall. But if I shall be praying and rain would fall, it would be a shame for them, and if not it would be a desecration of the Name of Heaven. Therefore come, I and you shall go up and pray. If it will rain, we shall say to them, Heaven already did wonders; and if not, we shall say to them, we are not worthy to pray and be heard. They went up, prayed, and it rained. He descended to them and asked them, why did the rabbis trouble themselves here today? They said to him, we ask that you should pray that it rain. He answered them, do you need my prayer? Heaven already did wonders. They asked him, when you were on the mountain, we said to you "much success" but you did not answer us? He told them, I was occupied in my work and did not want to divert my thoughts from my work. They asked him, and when you sat down to eat, why did you not invite us to partake? He answered them, because I had with me only my portion. What could I say to you in flattery? They asked him, why when you finished you put the coat on top of the load? He told them, because it is not mine. It is borrowed so I could pray wearing it. Why should I denigrate it? They asked him, why while you were on the mountain your wife wore dirty clothing, but when you came from the mountain she wore clean clothing[177]? He told them, while I was on the mountain your wife wore dirty clothing so no

man should turn his eyes to her; but when I came from the mountain she wore clean clothing so I should not look at another's wife. They told him, it is correct that you should be heard when praying.

175 Like in the preceding paragraphs the pure Aramaic of the text shows that this is suggested text of sermons. A very similar story is told in the Babli 23a/b of Abba Ḥilkiah the son of Onias the circle-drawer, a mythical holy man from Hasmonean times.

176 His wife.
177 They took her dirty clothing as a sign that she was impure having her period and were taken aback noticing suddenly that she was pure without any purification.

(64c line 10) תַּנֵּי. מוּתָּר לוֹכַל עַד שֶׁיֵּיאוֹר הַמִּזְרָח. דִּבְרֵי רִבִּי. רַבָּן שִׁמְעוֹן בֶּן גַּמְלִיאֵל אוֹמֵר. עַד קְרִיאַת הַגֶּבֶר. מַה תַּלְמוּד לוֹמַר עַד קְרִיאַת הַגֶּבֶר. יָשַׁן וְעָמַד אָסוּר. בְּשֶׁלֹּא הִתְנָה. אֲבָל אִם הִתְנָה מוּתָּר.

It was stated[178]: "One is permitted to eat until the East is illuminated, the words of Rebbi. Rabban Simeon ben Gamliel says, until the cock calls[179]." What means "until the cock calls"? If he slept and awoke he is forbidden. That is, if he did not stipulate, but if he stipulated it is permitted.

178 Discussion of Mishnaiot 5 and 6, the daytime fasts. Parallel texts are Tosephta 1:6, Babli 12a/b. In the Babli sources the author is not Rabban Simeon ben Gamliel but R. Eleazar ben R. Simeon and no stipulation which allows eating after a night's sleep is accepted.
179 Approximately astronomical dawn.

(fol. 63c) **משנה ו**: הִגִּיעַ רֹאשׁ חֹדֶשׁ כִּסְלֵיו וְלֹא יָרְדוּ גְשָׁמִים בֵּית דִּין גּוֹזְרִין שָׁלֹשׁ תַּעֲנִיּוֹת עַל הַצִּיבּוּר. אוֹכְלִין וְשׁוֹתִין מִשֶּׁחֲשֵׁיכָה וּמוּתָּרִין בִּמְלָאכָה וּבִרְחִיצָה וּבְסִיכָה וּבִנְעִילַת הַסַּנְדָּל וּבְתַשְׁמִישׁ הַמִּטָּה:

Mishnah 6: If the New Moon of Kislev came without rainfall the Court decrees three public fast-days. They eat and drink while it is dark and are permitted work, washing, and anointing, and wearing sandals[158], and sexual intercourse.

(64c line 13) **הלכה ה**: אָמַר רִבִּי יוֹחָנָן. כָּל־תַּעֲנִית שֶׁבֵּית דִּין גּוֹזְרִין לְהַפְסִיק אֵין עוּבָּרוֹת וּמֵינִיקוֹת מִתְעַנּוֹת בָּם. אָמַר רִבִּי שְׁמוּאֵל בַּר רַב יִצְחָק. נִרְאִין דְּבָרִים בְּשֶׁגְּזָרוּ כְבָר שֶׁלֹּא לְהַפְסִיק. אֲבָל אִם גָּזְרוּ מִיַּד לְהַפְסִיק עוּבָּרוֹת וּמֵינִיקוֹת מִתְעַנּוֹת בָּם. וְתַנֵּי כֵן. עוּבָּרוֹת

וּמֵינִיקוֹת מִתְעַנּוֹת כְּדַרְכָּן בְּתִשְׁעָה בְּאָב [וּבְיוֹם הַכִּפּוּרִים] וּבְשָׁלֹשׁ תַּעֲנִיּוֹת הָרִאשׁוֹנוֹת וּבְשָׁלֹשׁ הַשְּׁנִיּוֹת. אֲבָל בְּשֶׁבַע הָאַחֲרוֹנוֹת אֵינָן מִתְעַנּוֹת בָּהֶן. אַף עַל פִּי כֵן אֵינָן מְנַהֲגוֹת עַצְמָן בְּתַפְנוּקִים אֶלָּא אוֹכְלוֹת וְשׁוֹתוֹת כְּדֵי קִיּוּם הַוָּלָד. לֹא בְשֶׁגָּזְרוּ כְבָר שֶׁלֹּא לְהַפְסִיק. אֲתָא רִבִּי בָּא בַּר זַבְדָּא רִבִּי יִצְחָק בַּר טַבְלַיי בְּשֵׁם רִבִּי יוֹחָנָן. וַאֲפִילוּ גָזְרוּ מִיַּד לְהַפְסִיק אֵין עוּבָרוֹת וּמֵינִיקוֹת מִתְעַנּוֹת בָּם.

Halakhah 5: Rebbi Joḥanan said, pregnant and nursing women do not fast on any fast-day for which the Court decides to interrupt[180]. Rebbi Samuel bar Rav Isaac said, this seems reasonable if they originally decided not to interrupt[181], but if they directly decided to interrupt, pregnant and nursing women have to fast. It was stated thus: "Pregnant and nursing women fast regularly on the Ninth of Av [and the Day of Atonement][182] and on the first and the second groups[183] of fast-days. But on the seven last ones they do not fast; nevertheless they should not spoil themselves but eat and drink for the necessities of the child." Does this not refer to the case that they decided originally not to interrupt[184]? Rebbi Abba bar Zavda, Rebbi Isaac bar Tevlai came in the name of Rebbi Joḥanan: Even if they directly decided to interrupt, pregnant and nursing women do not fast[185].

180 "Interrupt" means that one stops eating before sundown on the day preceding the fast; this refers to the three fast-days (Monday, Thursday, and Monday) mentioned in Mishnah 7 and the seven mentioned in Mishnah 8.
181 The fast-days mentioned in Mishnaiot 5, where it is understood that women do not fast, and Mishnah 6, where women are not mentioned. The fasting on these days essentially means missed lunch.
182 Corrector's addition; out of place since the *baraita* concerns rabbinic fast-days only.
183 Mentioned in Mishnaiot 6 and 7.
184 Since the *baraita* explicitly states that women have to fast on fast-days which as a matter of course start in the evening. Babli 14a.
185 Denied in the Babli.

(fol. 63c) **משנה ז**: עָבְרוּ אֵילּוּ וְלֹא נַעֲנוּ בֵּית דִּין גּוֹזְרִין עוֹד שָׁלֹשׁ תַּעֲנִיּוֹת עַל הַצִּבּוּר. אוֹכְלִין וְשׁוֹתִין מִבְּעוֹד יוֹם וַאֲסוּרִין בִּמְלָאכָה וּבִרְחִיצָה וּבְסִיכָה וּבִנְעִילַת הַסַּנְדָּל וּבְתַשְׁמִישׁ הַמִּטָּה וְנוֹעֲלִין אֶת הַמֶּרְחֲצָאוֹת.

Mishnah 7: If these passed without rainfall the Court decrees three supplementary public fast-days. They eat and drink while it is daylight and are forbidden work, washing, anointing, wearing sandals, and sexual intercourse[186]. In addition, one closes the bath houses[187].

186 Following the rules of the Day of Atonement.
187 The thermal baths.

(64c line 22) **הלכה ו**׃ רִבִּי זְעוּרָה בְשֵׁם רַב יִרְמְיָה. הָעוֹשֶׂה מְלָאכָה בְּתַעֲנִית צִיבּוּר כְּעוֹשֶׂה מְלָאכָה בְּיוֹם הַכִּיפּוּרִים. מַה טַעַם. קַדְּשׁוּ־צוֹם קִרְאוּ עֲצָרָה׃ וְהָא תַנֵּי. הַלַּיְלָה מוּתָּר וְהַיּוֹם אָסוּר. אָמַר רִבִּי זְעוּרָה. קִיְּימָהּ אַבָּא בַּר יִרְמְיָה. אִסְפוּ־עָם. מִשְׁעַת אֲסִיפַת עָם.

Halakhah 6: Rebbi Ze'ira in the name of Rav Jeremiah: He who does work on a public fast-day is like one who does work on the Day of Atonement. What is the reason? *Sanctify a fast-day, call an assembly*[188]. But was it not stated, the night is permitted but the day forbidden[189]? Rebbi Ze'ira said, Abba bar Jeremiah[190] confirmed it; *assemble the people*[191], at the time of the popular assembly.

188 *Joel* 2:15.
189 Babli 14a.
190 In the Babli 13b: Rav Jeremiah bar Abba.
191 *Joel* 2:16.

(64c line 26) נָשַׁיָּיא (דְנָהִיגָן) [דְנָהִיגִין] דְּלָא לְמֵיעֲבַד עוֹבְדָא בְּפוּקֵי שׁוּבְתָא אֵינוֹ מִנְהָג. עַד דְּיִתְפְּנֵי סִדְרָא מִנְהָג. בַּתְרַיָּיא וּבַחֲמִשְׁתָּא אֵינוֹ מִנְהָג. עַד דְּיִתְפְּנֵי תַעֲנִיתָא [מִנְהָג]. בְּיוֹמָא דַעֲרוּבְתָא אֵינוֹ מִנְהָג. מִן מִנְחָה וּלְעֵיל [מִנְהָג]. בְּיוֹמָא דְיַרְחָא מִנְהָג. אָמַר רִבִּי זְעוּרָה. נָשַׁיָּיא דְנָהִיגָן דְּלָא לְמִשְׁתַּיָּיא מִן דְּאָב עָלִיל מִנְהָג. שֶׁבּוֹ פָּסְקָה אֶבֶן שְׁתִיָּיה. מַה טַעְמָא כִּי־הַשְׁתוֹת יֵהָרֵסוּן.

אָמַר רִבִּי חִינְנָא. כָּל־הַדְּבָרִים מִנְהָג. אַיְין דְּשִׁיטִין הֲווּ בְמִגְדַּל צִבְעַיָּיא. אָתוּן וּשְׁאָלוּן לְרִבִּי חֲנַנְיָה חֲבֵרְהוֹן דְּרַבָּנִין. מָהוּ מֵיעֲבַד בְּהוֹן עֲבִידָא. אָמַר לְהֶן. מִכֵּיוָן שֶׁנָּהֲגוּ אֲבוֹתֵיכֶם בָּהֶם בְּאִיסוּר אַל תְּשַׁנּוּ מִנְהַג אֲבוֹתֵיכֶם נוּחֵי נֶפֶשׁ. רִבִּי לְעֶזֶר בְּשֵׁם רִבִּי אָבוּן. כָּל־דָּבָר שֶׁהוּא מוּתָּר וְהוּא טוֹעֶה בּוֹ בְאִסּוּר נִשְׁאָל וּמַתִּירִין לוֹ. וְכָל־דָּבָר שֶׁהוּא יוֹדֵעַ בּוֹ שֶׁהוּא מוּתָּר וְהוּא נוֹהֵג בּוֹ בְאִיסּוּר נִשְׁאָל וְאֵין מַתִּירִין לוֹ.

[192]If women use not to work after the end of the Sabbath, it is no {legitimate} usage; until the end of the *seder*[193] it is {legitimate} usage. On Monday and Thursday[194], it is no {legitimate} usage, to the end of the fast-day prayers it is [{legitimate} usage]. On the day of the willow twigs[195] it is not

{legitimate} usage, after afternoon prayers it is [{legitimate} usage]. On the day of the New Moon it is {legitimate} usage. Rebbi Ze`ira said, if women use not to weave[196] from the start of Av it is {legitimate} usage, for the *šetiah* stone stopped to exist[197]. What is the reason? *For the woofs will be torn down*[198].

Rebbi Ḥinena said, everything they made dependent on usage. There were acacia trees in Migdal Ṣevaya[199]. They came and asked Rebbi Ḥanania, the colleague of the rabbis, may one use them for work? He told them, since your ancestors used to treat them as forbidden, do not change the usage of your deceased ancestors. Rebbi Eleazar in the name of Rebbi Abun[200]. In any case which is permitted but in error he treats it as forbidden, if he asks they will permit him. But in any case where he knows that it is permitted but he has the usage to treat it as forbidden, if he asks they will not permit him[201].

192 This text is from *Pesahim* 4:1, Notes 28-37.
193 The additional prayer at the end of the evening service at the end of the Sabbath.
194 Which were common fast-days of the pious in Palestine (cf. L. Ginzberg, *Genizah Studies in Memory of Doctor Solomon Schechter*, vol. 1, p. 483, §6.)
195 The Seventh Day of Tabernacles. Since the following day is a holiday, it is appropriate that the preparations be finished by the time of the afternoon prayers.
196 Between the first and the tenth of Av.
197 The stone in the Holiest of Holies in the Temple.
198 *Ps.* 11:3. If read as *the foundations will be torn down* it is appropriate for the anniversary of the destruction of the Temple.
199 Since by a Galilean tradition the Tabernacle was built in the desert from perfect logs of acacia wood (*Mimosa nilotica L.*) cut for this purpose by Jacob and his sons when they travelled to Egypt [*Gen. rabba* 94(4).]
200 Even though all sources have R. Eleazar in the name of . . ., it must be . . . in the name of R. Eleazar.
201 Since he intentionally accepted an unnecessary stringency, it has the status of a vow.

(64c line 37) בִּרְחִיצָה. זְעוּרָה בַּר חָמָא יוֹסֵי בְּרֵיהּ דְּרִבִּי יְהוֹשֻׁעַ בֶּן לֵוִי בְּשֵׁם רִבִּי יְהוֹשֻׁעַ בֶּן לֵוִי. בְּתַעֲנִית צִיבּוּר מַרְחִיץ יָדָיו וּפָנָיו [וְרַגְלָיו] כְּדַרְכּוֹ. בְּתִשְׁעָה בְאָב מַרְחִיץ יָדָיו וּמַעֲבִירָן עַל פָּנָיו. בְּיוֹם הַכִּיפּוּרִים מַרְחִיץ יָדָיו וּמְקַנְּחָן בְּמַפָּה וּמַעֲבִיר אֶת הַמַּפָּה עַל פָּנָיו. רִבִּי יוֹנָה תָרֵי מַרְטוּטָה וִיהַב לָהּ תּוּתֵי כָדָהּ. וְהָא תַנֵּי. אֵין בֵּין תִּשְׁעָה בְאָב לְתַעֲנִית צִיבּוּר אֶלָּא אִיסּוּר מְלָאכָה. בְּמָקוֹם שֶׁנָּהֲגוּ. הָיָה הוֹלֵךְ אֵצֶל רַבּוֹ אוֹ אֵצֶל בִּתּוֹ וְעָבַר בַּיָּם אוֹ בַנָּהָר אֵינוֹ חוֹשֵׁשׁ. נִיטַנְּפוּ רַגְלָיו מַטְבִּילָן

HALAKHAH 6

בַּמַּיִם וְאֵינוֹ חוֹשֵׁשׁ. הוֹרֵי רִבִּי בָּא כָּהֵין תַּנָּיָיא. הוֹרֵי רִבִּי אָחָא בְּבָא מִן הַדֶּרֶךְ וְהָיוּ רַגְלָיו קִיהוֹת עָלָיו שֶׁמּוּתָּר לְהַרְחִיצָם בַּמַּיִם. תַּנֵּי. אָבֵל וּמְנוּדֶּה שֶׁהָיוּ מְהַלְּכִין בַּדֶּרֶךְ מוּתָּרִין בִּנְעִילַת סַנְדָּל. לִכְשֶׁיָּבוֹאוּ לָעִיר יַחֲלוֹצוּ. וְכֵן בְּתִשְׁעָה בְאָב וְכֵן בְּתַעֲנִית צִיבּוּר.

[202]"Washing". Ze`urah bar Ḥama, Yose the son of Rebbi Joshua ben Levi in the name of Rebbi Joshua ben Levi: On a public fast-day[201] one washes as usual his face, hands, and feet. On the Ninth of Av[202] one washes his hands and moves them over his face. On the day of Atonement one washes his hands, dries them with a towel, and moves the towel over his face. Rebbi Jonah moistened a rag and put it under the water pitcher[203]. But did we not state that there is no difference between a public fast and the Ninth of Av except the prohibition of work at places where they were used to it[204]? If somebody was going to his teacher, or to his daughter, and crossed a lake or a river he does not worry[205]. If his feet were dirtied he immerses them in water and does not worry. Rebbi Abba instructed following this Tanna. Rebbi Aḥa instructed that one who comes from the road and his feet are dulled, he may wash them in water. It was stated: A mourner and one in the ban[206] on a trip are permitted leather shoes. When they come to the town they shall take them off. The same applies to a public fast and the Ninth of Av[207].

200 The following texts are from *Yoma* 8:1, Notes 15-45.
201 A fast day called to pray for rain in a year of drought as described in the present Chapter.
202 The fast instituted to mourn the destruction of the Temple.
203 He soaked the rag before the start of the Day of Atonement, squeezed it and let it dry somewhat during the night so that the next morning it should be somewhat moist but not dripping.
204 There were places where the community had adopted the rule that one did not work on the Ninth of Av. Nowhere was this extended to all fast days in years of drought.
205 On a day where washing was rabbinically forbidden. *Yoma* Babli 77b, Tosephta 4:5.
206 Any weekday of the year the mourner and the person in the ban are forbidden to wear leather shoes. The person in the ban has to follow these rules if he ever wants to have the ban lifted. Babli *Mo`ed Qaṭan* 15b.
207 For everybody.

(64c line 48) בְּסִיכָה. כְּהָדָא דְתַנֵּי. בַּשַּׁבָּת בֵּין סִיכָה שֶׁהִיא שֶׁלְּתַעֲנוּג בֵּין סִיכָה שֶׁאֵינָהּ שֶׁלְּתַעֲנוּג מוּתָּר. בְּיוֹם הַכִּיפּוּרִים בֵּין סִיכָה שֶׁהִיא שֶׁלְּתַעֲנוּג בֵּין סִיכָה שֶׁאֵינָהּ שֶׁלְּתַעֲנוּג אָסוּר. בְּתִשְׁעָה בְאָב וּבְתַעֲנִית צִיבּוּר סִיכָה שֶׁהִיא שֶׁלְּתַעֲנוּג אָסוּר. שֶׁאֵינָהּ שֶׁלְּתַעֲנוּג מוּתָּר. וְהָא תַנֵּי.

שְׁוות סִיכָה לִשְׁתִיָּיה לְאִיסּוּר וּלְתַשְׁלוּמִין אֲבָל לֹא לְעוֹנֶשׁ. בְּיוֹם הַכִּיפּוּרִים לְאִיסּוּר אֲבָל לֹא לְעוֹנֶשׁ. וְהָא תַנֵּי. לֹא יְחַלְּלוּ. לְרַבּוֹת אֶת הַסָּךְ וְאֶת הַשּׁוֹתֶה. אָמַר רִבִּי יוֹחָנָן. לֵית כָּאן סָךְ. אָמַר רִבִּי אַבָּמְרִי. אִין לֵית כָּאן סָךְ לֵית כָּאן שׁוֹתֶה. דְּלֹ"כֵן דָּבָר שֶׁהוּא בָא מַחֲמַת שְׁנֵי לָאוִין מִצְטָרֵף.

מְנַיִין שֶׁהוּא מְחוּוָּר בַּעֲשֵׂה. רִבִּי לְעָזָר בְּשֵׁם רִבִּי סִימַיי. וְלֹא־נָתַתִּי מִמֶּנּוּ לְמֵת. מָה נָן קַייָמִין. אִם לְהָבִיא לוֹ אָרוֹן וְתַכְרִיכִין. דָּבָר שֶׁהוּא מוּתָּר לַחַי. לַחַי הוּא אָסוּר. לֹא כָל־שֶׁכֵּן לְמֵת. אֵי זֶהוּ דָבָר שֶׁהוּא מוּתָּר לַחַי וְאָסוּר לְמֵת. הֱוֵי אוֹמֵר. זוֹ סִיכָה.

[208]"Anointing." As it was stated: On the Sabbath both anointing for pleasure and anointing not for pleasure are permitted. On the Day of Atonement, both anointing for pleasure and anointing not for pleasure are forbidden. On the Ninth of Av and public fasts, anointing for pleasure is forbidden but anointing not for pleasure is permitted. But it was stated: Anointing is equal to drinking regarding prohibition and reparation but not punishment[209]. On the Day of Atonement regarding prohibition but not punishment[210] But was it not stated, *they shall not desecrate*[211], to include him who anoints or drinks? Rebbi Johanan said, there is no "anoints" there. Rebbi Abba Mari said, if there is no "anoints" there is no "drinks". For if it were not so, do matters combine which come from two different prohibitions[212]?

From where that there is a clear commandment[212]? Rebbi Eleazar in the name of Rebbi Simai: *Nor did I give from it to the dead*[213]. Where do we hold? If not to bring a casket or shrouds for him, would this be permitted for the living? Since this is forbidden for the living, therefore certainly for the dead. What is permitted to the living but forbidden to the dead? This implies that this is anointing[214].

208 This text is not only copied in *Yoma*, it is shortened from the main source *Ma`aser Šeni* 2:1 (Notes 28-35), and *Šabbat* 9, Notes 122-127.

209 Referring to illegal use of heave and dedicated food by non-Cohanim and its replacement by 5/4 of the value taken.

210 The only biblical prohibitions on the Day of Atonement are eating, drinking, and working. The other two, anointing and sexual relations, are rabbinic and not subject to biblical punishment.

211 Lev. 22:15. The verse refers to the non-Cohen who "eats" holy food in error. Babli *Niddah* 32a.

212 If the verse in *Lev.* is needed to subsume drinking under eating, it is incomprehensible that for inadvertently eating and

drinking together on the Day of Atonement one should be responsible only for one sacrifice since in that case, one infringes on two separate biblical prohibitions and should be liable for two separate sacrifices. Similarly, if one illegitimately ate and drank heave he should be liable for two separate fifths. Since in both cases the Mishnah treats eating and drinking together, the verse cannot express a separate status for drinking; the addition of anointing and drinking is rabbinic interpretation but not biblical law and there is no reason to exclude anointing.

212 This paragraph is copied from *Maʿaser Šeni*; there is no connection to the rules of fast-days.

While illegitimate use of heave oil for anointing is prohibited, it is mentioned in the framework of the farmer's declaration in the Temple, which is a positive commandment. Overstepping the prohibition of anointing when it is forbidden legally is overstepping a positive commandment not under the scope of biblical penal law.

213 *Deut.* 26:14.

214 Cf. *Sifry Deut.* 302. Second Tithe must be consumed; no other use is authorized..

(64c line 60) בִּנְעִילַת סַנְדָּל. תַּנֵּי. כָּל־אִילוּ שֶׁאָמְרוּ אֲסוּרִין בִּנְעִילַת סַנְדָּל. יָצָא לַדֶּרֶךְ נוֹעֵל. הִגִּיעַ לַכְּרַךְ חוֹלֵץ. וְכֵן בְּאָבֵל וְכֵן בִּמְנוּדֶּה. אִית תַּנָּיֵי תַנֵּי. יוֹצְאִין בְּאַנְפִּלְיָא בְּיוֹם הַכִּיפּוּרִים. וְאִית תַּנָּיֵי תַנֵּי. אֵין יוֹצְאִין. אָמַר רַב חִסְדָּא. מָאן דָּמַר. יוֹצְאִין. בְּאַנְפִּילְיָא שֶׁלְּבֶגֶד. מָאן דְּאָמַר. אֵין יוֹצְאִין. בְּאַמְפִּלְיָא שֶׁלְּעוֹר. רִבִּי יִצְחָק בַּר נַחְמָן סָלַק גַּבֵּי רִבִּי יְהוֹשֻׁעַ בֶּן לֵוִי בְּלֵילֵי צוֹמָא רַבָּא. נָפַק לְגַבֵּי לָבוּשׁ סוֹלְיָיסָה. אָמַר לֵיהּ. מָהוּ הָכֵין. אָמַר לֵיהּ. אִיסְתְּנִיס אֲנָא. רִבִּי יְהוֹשֻׁעַ בַּר נַחְמָן סָלַק גַּבֵּי רִבִּי יְהוֹשֻׁעַ בֶּן לֵוִי בְּלֵילֵי תַעֲנִיתָא. נָפַק לְגַבֵּהּ לָבוּשׁ סוֹלְיָיסָה. אָמַר לֵיהּ. מָהוּ הָכֵין. אָמַר לֵיהּ. אִיסְתְּנִיס אֲנִי. רִבִּי שַׁמַּי חֲמוּנֵיהּ נָפִיק לְבִישׁ סוּלְיָיסֵיהּ בְּלֵילֵי תַעֲנִיתָא. חַד תַּלְמִיד מִן דְּרִבִּי מָנָא הוֹרֵי לְחַד מִן קְרִיבוֹי דִנְשִׂיָּיא לְמִילְבּוֹשׁ סוֹלְיָיסֵיהּ. אָמַר לֵיהּ. מִן הָדָא. דְּרִבִּי יְהוֹשֻׁעַ בֶּן לֵוִי. דְּרִבִּי יְהוֹשֻׁעַ בֶּן לֵוִי אָמַר. אִיסְתְּנִיס אֲנִי.

"Wearing shoes". It was stated: In all cases where they said that one may not wear shoes, when he departs on a trip he puts them on, when he arrives at a walled city he takes them off; this includes the mourner and the person in the ban[215]. There are Tannaim who state, one goes in slippers[216] on the day of Atonement; and there are Tannaim who state, one does not. Rav Ḥisda said, he who said one goes, in textile slippers, and he who said one does not go, in leather slippers[217]. Rebbi Isaac bar Naḥman visited Rebbi Joshua ben Levi in the night of the Great Fast[218]; he came to him wearing laced shoes[219]. He asked him, what is this? He answered, I am asthenic[220]. Rebbi Samuel bar Naḥman visited Rebbi Joshua ben Levi in the night of a fast day[221]; he came to him wearing laced shoes. He asked him, what is this? He answered, I am asthenic. They saw Rebbi Shammai walking in the night of a fast day in laced shoes. A student of Rebbi Mana instructed a relative of the Patriarch to wear laced shoes[41]. He asked him, from where? From Rebbi Joshua ben Levi. For Rebbi Joshua ben Levi said, I am asthenic.

215 Babli *Mo`ed qatan* 15b. The Yerushalmi version is quoted by *Or zarua* §277.
216 Latin *impilia, -ium* (pl/) "felt slippers".
217 *Yebamot* 12:1, Note 35, Babli *Yebamot* 102b.
218 The day of Atonement.

219 A leather sole with a textile upper part held together by laces.
220 Greek ’ασθενής. Since the rules of not wearing leather shoes are rabbinic, they are waved for health reasons.
221 A rabbinic fast day.

(64c line 72) בְּתַשְׁמִישׁ הַמִּטָּה. אִיתָא חֲמֵי. בְּרְחִיצָה אָסוּר. בְּתַשְׁמִישׁ הַמִּטָּה לֹא כָּל־שֶׁכֵּן. תִּיפְתָּר בְּמָקוֹם שֶׁאֵין טוֹבְלִין אוֹ קוֹדֶם עַד שֶׁלֹּא הִתְקִין עֶזְרָא טְבִילָה לְבַעֲלֵי קְרָיִין. רִבִּי יַעֲקֹב בַּר אֲחָא רִבִּי אִימִּי בְשֵׁם רִבִּי יְהוֹשֻׁעַ בֶּן לֵוִי. אֵין קְרִי אֶלָּא מִתַּשְׁמִישׁ הַמִּטָּה. רַב חוּנָה אָמַר. אֲפִילוּ רָאָה עַצְמוֹ נִיאוֹת בַּחֲלוֹם. הֲוֺון בָּעֲיֵי מֵימַר. וּבִלְבַד מֵאִשָּׁה. רִבִּי יוֹנָה וְרִבִּי יוֹסֵה תְּרֵיהוֹן אָמְרִין. אֲפִילוּ מִדָּבָר אַחֵר. תַּמָּן תַּנִּינָן. יוֹם הַכִּפּוּרִים אָסוּר בַּאֲכִילָה וּבִשְׁתִיָּיה וּבְרְחִיצָה וּבְסִיכָה וּבִנְעִילַת הַסַּנְדָּל וּבְתַשְׁמִישׁ הַמִּטָּה. וְתַנֵּי עֲלָהּ. בַּעֲלֵי קְרָיִין טוֹבְלִין כְּדַרְכָּן בְּצִינְעָה בְּיוֹם הַכִּפּוּרִים. לֵית הֲדָא פְּלִיגָא עַל רִבִּי יְהוֹשֻׁעַ בֶּן לֵוִי. פָּתַר לָהּ בְּמִי שֶׁשִּׁימֵּשׁ מִיטָּתוֹ מִבְּעוֹד יוֹם וְשָׁכַח וְלֹא טָבַל. וְהָא תַנֵּי. מַעֲשֶׂה בְּרִבִּי יוֹסֵי בֶּן חֲלַפְתָּא שֶׁרָאוּ טוֹבֵל בְּצִינְעָה בְּיוֹם הַכִּפּוּרִים. אִית לָךְ מֵימַר עַל אוֹתוֹ הַגּוּף הַקָּדוֹשׁ בְּשׁוֹכֵחַ.

[222]"And sexual relations." Come and see, he is forbidden to wash, not so much more to have sexual relations[223]? Explain it that it was a place where one does not immerse oneself, or before Ezra instituted immersion for people having had an emission. [224]Rebbi Jacob bar Aḥa, Rebbi Yasa in the name of Rebbi Joshua ben Levi.: *Qeri* is only from sexual intercourse. Rav Huna said, even if he saw himself enjoying in his dream. They wanted to say, only from a woman. Rebbi Jonah and Rebbi Yose both say, even from something else. There, we did state: "On the Day of Atonement eating, drinking, washing, anointing, wearing shoes, and sexual relations, are forbidden"? And it was stated in that respect: Men with *qeri* immerse themselves secretly in their normal way on the day of Atonement[225]. Does this not contradict Rebbi Joshua ben Levi? Explain it if he had intercourse on the previous day and forgot and did not immerse himself. But it was stated: It happened that one

saw Rebbi Yose bar Ḥalaphta immersing himself secretly on Yom Kippur. Can you say about that holy body that he forgot[226]?

222 From here on there exists a much shortened version in an Ashkenazi ms. (A) published by J. Sussman, *Kobez al Yad* 12(22), 1994, pp. 43ff.

223 Since the Day of Atonement is a day of prayer and by an institution of Ezra prayer was forbidden after sexual relations before immersion in a *miqweh*, the prohibition of washing should imply the prohibition of sexual relations without the need to spell it out.

224 This text to the end of the paragraph is also from *Berakhot* 3:4 (Notes 167-168) which is the original source.

225 In Tosephta *Kippurim* 4:5 and Babli 88a the reading is: "Men with *qeri* (emission of semen) immerse themselves normally on Yom Kippur"; one speaks of a full immersion and "in secret" is not mentioned. The Tosephta is Babylonian formulation.

226 Hence, the interpretation of Rav Huna is incorrect and that of rabbis Yose (the Amora) and Jonah is correct.

Here ends the *Yoma* text.

(64d line 8) רִבִּי יוּדָה בַּר פָּזִי רִבִּי חָנִין בְּשֵׁם רִבִּי שְׁמוּאֵל בַּר רַב יִצְחָק. נֹחַ בִּכְנִיסָתוֹ לַתֵּיבָה נֶאֱסְרָה לוֹ תַשְׁמִישׁ הַמִּיטָה. מַה טַעַם. וּבָאתָ אֶל־הַתֵּיבָה אַתָּה וּבָנֶיךָ וְאִשְׁתְּךָ וּנְשֵׁי־בָנֶיךָ אִתָּךְ. וּבִיצִיאָתוֹ הוּתְּרָה לוֹ תַשְׁמִישׁ הַמִּיטָה. מַה טַעַם. צֵא מִן־הַתֵּיבָה אַתָּה וְאִשְׁתְּךָ וּבָנֶיךָ וּנְשֵׁי־בָנֶיךָ אִתָּךְ: אָמַר רִבִּי חִייָה בַר בָּא. לְמִשְׁפְּחוֹתֵיהֶם יָצְאוּ מִן־הַתֵּבָה: עַל יְדֵי שֶׁשִּׁימְּרוּ יַחֲסֵיהֶן זָכוּ לְהִינָּצֵל מִן הַתֵּיבָה. תֵּדַע לָךְ שֶׁהוּא כֵן. דְּתַנִינָן. חָם כֶּלֶב וְעוֹרֵב קִילְקְלוּ מַעֲשֵׂיהֶן. חָם יָצָא מְפוּחָם. כֶּלֶב יָצָא מְפוּרְסָם בְּתַשְׁמִישׁוּ. עוֹרֵב יָצָא מְשׁוּנֶּה מִן הַבְּרִיוֹת. אָמַר רִבִּי אָבוּן. כָּתוּב בְּחֶסֶר וּבְכָפָן גַּלְמוּד. בְּשָׁעָה שֶׁאַתְּ רוֹאֶה חִסָּרוֹן בָּא לָעוֹלָם עֲשֵׂה אִשְׁתְּךָ גַּלְמוּדָה. אָמַר רִבִּי לֵוִי. כָּתוּב וּלְיוֹסֵף יוּלַּד שְׁנֵי בָנִים. אֵימָתַי. בְּטֶרֶם תָּבוֹא שְׁנַת הָרָעָב. תַּנֵּי בְּשֵׁם רִבִּי יְהוּדָה. תְּאִיבֵי בָנִים מְשַׁמְּשִׁין מִיטוֹתֵיהֶן. אָמַר רִבִּי יוֹסֵי. וּבִלְבַד יוֹם שְׁטִבְלָה.

[227]Rebbi Jehudah bar Pazi, Rebbi Ḥanin in the name of Rebbi Samuel bar Rav Isaac: On his entrance to the Ark Noe was forbidden sexual relations. What is the reason? *You shall come into the Ark, you, your sons, your wife, and your sons' wives*[228]. On his exit sexual relations were permitted to him. What is the reason? *Leave the Ark, you, your wife, your sons, and your sons' wives with you*[229]. Rebbi Ḥiyya bar Abba said, *by their families they left the Ark*[230]; since they refrained from their relations they merited to be saved from the Deluge. You may know that it is so since we stated[231], Ham, the dog, and the raven misbehaved. Ham exited charcoal colored. The dog exited public in his relations. The raven exited different from the creatures. Rebbi Abun[232] said, it is written, *in want and hunger infertile*[233]. If you see that want comes

into the world make your wife infertile[234]. Rebbi Levi[235] said, *to Joseph were born two sons*[236], when? *Before the start of the year of famine.* It was stated in the name of Rebbi Jehudah[235]: those who desire to have children do have sexual relations. Rebbi Yose said, only on the day she immersed herself[237].

227 *Gen. rabba* 31(17), *Tanhuma Noah* 11, with different name traditions. Also in A the attributions are different.
228 *Gen.* 6:18.
229 *Gen.* 8:16.
230 *Gen.* 8:19.
231 Babli *Sanhedrin* 108b.
232 In *Gen. rabba* Abbin.
233 *Job* 30:3.

234 Formulated as a general prohibition Babli 11a, *Sanhedrin* 108b.
235 Babli 11a in the name of R. Simeon ben Laqish. Those who "desire children" are whose who yet have none.
236 *Gen.* 41:50.
237 A day of maximal probability of conception; Babli *Sotah* 27a.

(fol. 63c) **משנה ח**: עָבְרוּ אֵילוּ וְלֹא נַעֲנוּ בֵּית דִּין גּוֹזְרִין עוֹד שֶׁבַע שֶׁהֵן שְׁלֹשׁ עֶשְׂרֵה תַּעֲנִיּוֹת עַל הַצִּבּוּר. וּמֶה אֵילוּ יְתֵרוֹת עַל הָרִאשׁוֹנוֹת שֶׁבְּאֵילוּ מַתְרִיעִין וְנוֹעֲלִין אֶת הַחֲנוּיוֹת. בַּשֵּׁנִי מַטִּין עִם חֲשֵׁיכָה וּבַחֲמִישִׁי מוּתָּרִין מִפְּנֵי כְּבוֹד הַשַּׁבָּת.

Mishnah 8: If these passed without rainfall the Court decrees seven supplementary public fast-days[238] for a total of thirteen. Additional to the prior ones on these one blows horns and locks the stores. On Mondays one relaxes at nightfall[239]; on Thursdays they are permitted[240] because of the honor of the Sabbath.

238 On successive Mondays and Thursdays.
239 The grocer may open the store to sell food but not display his wares.

240 The seller of edibles may sell during the entire Thursday to provide food for the Sabbath.

(64d line 20) **הלכה ז**: רִבִּי יוּדָן בְּרֵיהּ דְּרִבִּי חָמָא דִּכְפַר תְּחָמִין. כְּבָתוּךְ אַרְבָּעִים שֶׁעָשָׂה מֹשֶׁה בָהָר. אָמַר רִבִּי יוֹסֵה. עַל שֵׁם שֶׁאֵין מַטְרִיחִין עַל הַצִּיבּוּר יוֹתֵר מִדַּאי. אָמַר רִבִּי חִייָה בַּר בָּא. שֶׁאִם הָיוּ שְׁנֵי דְבָרִים כְּגוֹן עֲצִירַת גְּשָׁמִים וְגוֹבַיי מַתְרִיעִין עֲלֵיהֶן. וְלָמָּה בָּאֵילֵין תַּרְתֵּין מִילַיָּא. אָמַר רִבִּי יוֹסֵי בֵּירִבִּי בּוּן. בָּאֵילֵין תַּרְתֵּין מִילַיָּא שִׁיעֲרַיָּיה רַבֵּיי.

Halakhah 7: Rebbi Yudan son of Rebbi Hama of Kefar Tehamin, like the forty which Moses spent on the Mountain[241]. Rebbi Yose said, because one does not excessively impose on the community²⁴². Rebbi Ḥiyya bar Abba said, for if there were two causes, for example a lack of rain and locusts, one blows for both²⁴³. And why for these two occasions²⁴⁴? Rebbi Yose ben Rebbi Abun said, for these two cause prices to increase.

241 On Sabbath one may not fast. This means that Monday and Thursday together represent a week of 6 days; every actual fast day represents three days, and 3×13=39, "like forty", approximately 40.

242 For him the number 13 is for a practical reason, not the symbolic one given by the aggadic preacher. Babli 14b as tannaitic statement, not unopposed.

243 If a swarm of locusts should appear in a dry winter, one combines prayers relative to both calamities and never exceeds the number of 13 public fasts even for multiple causes.

If this is an explanation of the previous statement, one has to read "Yasa", one of R. Ḥiyya's teachers, instead of "Yose", R. Ḥiyya's student's student's student.

244 These are mentioned explicitly to be combined.

(64d line 25) וּבַשֵׁנִי מַטִּין עִם חֲשֵׁיכָה. פּוֹתֵחַ אֶחָד וְנוֹעֵל אֶחָד. וּבַחֲמִישִׁי מוּתָּרִין מִפְּנֵי כְבוֹד הַשַּׁבָּת. מָה. פּוֹתֵחַ אֶחָד וְנוֹעֵל אֶחָד אוֹ פּוֹתֵחַ אֶת שְׁנֵיהֶם.

"On Mondays one relaxes at nightfall," he opens one wing and locks the other²⁴⁵. "On Thursdays they are permitted." How? He opens one wing and locks the other, or he opens both²⁴⁶?

245 The grocer opens his store but does not turn the shutter into a selling platform.

246 The store is open the entire day but whether one turns the shutter into a selling platform and displays one's wares is not decided and therefore depends on local custom.

(fol. 63c) **משנה ט**: עָבְרוּ אִילּוּ וְלֹא נַעֲנוּ מְמַעֲטִין בְּמַשָּׂא וּמַתָּן בְּבִנְיָן וּבִנְטִיעָה בָּאֵירוּסִין וּבַנִּישׂוּאִין וּבִשְׁאֵילַת שָׁלוֹם בֵּין אָדָם לַחֲבֵרוֹ כִּבְנֵי אָדָם הַנְּזוּפִין לַמָּקוֹם. הַיְחִידִים חוֹזְרִין וּמִתְעַנִּין עַד שֶׁיֵּצֵא נִיסָן. יָצָא נִיסָן וְיָרְדוּ גְשָׁמִים סִימָן קְלָלָה שֶׁנֶּאֱמַר הֲלוֹא קְצִיר חִטִּים הַיּוֹם.

Mishnah 9: If these passed without rainfall one decreases commercial activity, building, planting, preliminary and definitive marriage, and greetings between people, as persons reprimanded by the Omnipresent. Particular people[157] continue to fast up to the end of Nisan. If it rained after the end of Nisan it is a sign[3] of curse as it is said, *is today not harvest of wheat*[247]?

247 *1S.* 12:17, where Samuel invokes summer rain as a sign of Divine displeasure about the people's demand for a king.

(64d line 28) **הלכה ח**: אָמַר רִבִּי יְהוֹשֻׁעַ בֶּן לֵוִי. הָדָא דַתְּ אֲמַר בְּבִנְיָין שֶׁלְשִׂמְחָה. אֲבָל אִם הָיָה כּוֹתְלוֹ גּוֹהֶה סוֹתְרוֹ וּבוֹנֵיהוּ. שְׁמוּאֵל אָמַר. כּוֹתְלָא דְגָנָאי בֵּיהּ.

Halakhah 8: Rebbi Joshua ben Levi said, that is a building of enjoyment. But if his wall was inclined, he tears it down and rebuilds it[247]. Samuel said, the wall were he sleeps[248].

247 In a year of drought only buildings for happy occasions are forbidden. No opinion is indicated for building as investment or similar activity. Construction to avoid danger is obligatory.

248 He requires construction only if there is danger to life.

(64d line 30) רִבִּי בָּא בַּר כֹּהֵן אָמַר קוֹמֵי רִבִּי יָסָא רִבִּי אָחָא בְּשֵׁם רִבִּי יַעֲקֹב בַּר אִידִי. אָסוּר לְאָרֵס אִשָּׁה בְּעֶרֶב שַׁבָּת. הָדָא דְאַתְּ אֲמַר. שֶׁלֹּא לַעֲשׂוֹת סְעוּדַת אֵירוּסִין. הָא לְאָרֵס יְאָרֵס. שְׁמוּאֵל אָמַר. אֲפִילוּ בְתִשְׁעָה בְאָב יְאָרֵס. שֶׁלֹּא יְקַדְּמֶנּוּ אַחֵר. מַחֲלָפָה שִׁיטָתֵיהּ דִּשְׁמוּאֵל. תַּמָּן הוּא אָמַר. אֱלֹהִים | מוֹשִׁיב יְחִידִים | בָּיְתָה. בְּמֹאזְנַיִם לַעֲלוֹת הֵמָּה מֵהֶבֶל יַחַד: וְכָא הוּא אָמַר הָכֵין. אֶלָּא שֶׁלֹּא יְקַדְּמֶנּוּ אַחֵר בִּתְפִילָה. אֲפִילוּ כֵן לֹא קַיָּימָה.

[249]Rebbi Abba bar Cohen said before Rebbi Yose: Rebbi Aḥa in the name of Rebbi Jacob bar Idi: A man may not preliminarily marry on a Friday. That means, to make an engagement feast[250]. This implies that the preliminary marriage itself is permitted. Samuel says, even on the Ninth of Ab[251] a preliminary marriage is permitted, lest another forestall him. The argument of Samuel seems inverted. There[252], he says, *God puts singles in a house*; *To rise on scales; they all are of vapor!*[253] And here, he says so[254]? That means, that he should not forestall him in prayer. Even so, it would not be permanent.

249 The parallels are in *Ketubot* 1:1 (Notes 34-42), *Yom Tov* 5:2 (Notes 65ff.)
250 Since this would impinge on the Sabbath meal. It is in order to make the preliminary marriage on Friday and arrange the festive meal as Sabbath meal.
251 The anniversary of the destruction of both Temples.
252 A similar argument is in the Babli, *Mo`ed qatan* 18b.
253 *Ps.* 68:6; 62:10. This means that marriages are pre-ordained in Heaven. (*Lev.*

rabba 29(5).)

254 If marriages are pre-ordained, why should anybody be afraid that another man could snatch the bride pre-selected for him? Another man might by his prayer cause the Heavenly decree to be changed, but this would lead to the early death of one of the partners of the marriage. Babli *Sota* 2a, *Sanhedrin* 22a.

(64d line 36) (בִּשְׁאֵילַת שָׁלוֹם) [הֲלָכָה ט׳.] לֹא כֵן תַּנֵּי. אֵין שׁוֹאֲלִין בִּשְׁלוֹם חֲבֵירִים בְּתִשְׁעָה בְאָב. אֲבָל מֵשִׁיבִין אֶת הָהֶדְיוֹטוֹת בְּשָׂפָה רָפָה. לְיָמִים שֶׁבֵּנְתַיִים נִצְרְכָה.

(Greetings) [Halakhah 9:]²⁵⁵ Was it not stated²⁵⁶: "One does not greet fellows on the Ninth of Av, but one answers common people in a soft manner"²⁵⁷? It is needed for the days in between²⁵⁸.

255 Corrector's addition, to be deleted.

257 Greek 'ιδιώτης "individual", a term for the unlearned. One greats them in a weak voice, not to be impolite but hinting that greeting is undesirable on this day. "Fellow" is the appellation of a person careful (and therefore knowledgeable) in matters of tithes and impurity, cf. Introduction to Tractate Demay.

256 Tosephta 3:12.

The implication is that on a full fast day, from evening to evening, greeting is frowned upon. Then it should have been unnecessary to mention this in the Mishnah.

258 The Mishnah teaches to refrain from personal greetings all the days of a drought, not only on the Mondays and Thursdays of actual fasts.

(64d line 38) יָצָא נִיסָן הַגְּשָׁמִים סִימָן קְלָלָה. אָמַר רִבִּי יוֹסֵי בֵּירִבִּי בּוּן. וּבִלְבַד נִיסָן שֶׁלִּתְקוּפָה. אָמַר רִבִּי שְׁמוּאֵל בַּר רַב יִצְחָק. הָדָא דַתְּ אֲמַר. בְּשֶׁלֹּא יָרְדוּ לָהֶן גְּשָׁמִים מִכְּבָר. אֲבָל אִם יָרְדוּ לָהֶן גְּשָׁמִים מִכְּבָר סִימָן בְּרָכָה הֵן.

"After the end of Nisan it is a sign of curse." Rebbi Yose ben Rebbi Abun said, only after a Nisan of equinox²⁵⁹. Rebbi Samuel ben Rav Isaac said, this you are saying if it did not rain earlier²⁶⁰. But if it rained earlier it is a sign of blessing.

259 If the spring equinox was in Nisan. But if the month named "Nisan" really should have been the second Adar, one stops praying for rain only after the spring equinox, or if the equinox was in Adar, one has to stop fasting at the end of this month.

Since the calendar rules were promulgated by R. Yose, preceding R. Yose ben R. Abun, one may read the statement as a criticism of these rules which occasionally permit such a deviation. (But it must be remembered that the detailed rules which have come down to us were written up by authors who lived at least 600 years after R. Yose.)

260 When rain was really needed.

סדר תעניות כיצד פרק שני תעניות

(fol.64d) **משנה א**: סֵדֶר תַּעֲנִיּוֹת כֵּיצַד. מוֹצִיאִין אֶת הַתֵּיבָה לִרְחוֹבָהּ שֶׁל עִיר וְנוֹתְנִין אֵפֶר מִקְלֶה עַל גַּבֵּי הַתֵּיבָה וּבְרֹאשׁ הַנָּשִׂיא וּבְרֹאשׁ אַב בֵּית דִּין. וְכָל־אֶחָד וְאֶחָד נוֹטֵל וְנוֹתֵן בְּרֹאשׁוֹ. הַזָּקֵן שֶׁבָּהֶן אוֹמֵר לִפְנֵיהֶן דִּבְרֵי כִבּוּשִׁין. אַחֵינוּ לֹא נֶאֱמַר בְּאַנְשֵׁי נִינְוֵה וַיַּרְא הָאֱלֹהִים אֶת שַׂקָּם וְאֶת תַּעֲנִיתָם. אֶלָּא וַיַּרְא הָאֱלֹהִים אֶת מַעֲשֵׂיהֶם כִּי שָׁבוּ מִדַּרְכָּם הָרָעָה. וּבַקַּבָּלָה מָהוּ אוֹמֵר וְקִרְעוּ לְבַבְכֶם וְאַל־בִּגְדֵיכֶם וְשׁוּבוּ אֶל־ה׳ אֱלֹהֵיכֶם.

Mishnah 1: How is the order of the fast days? One removes the Ark[1] to the town plaza[2] and gives burnt ashes[3] on top of the Ark, and on the head of the Patriarch, and on the the head of the presiding judge; also each individual takes and puts on his head. The Elder among them gives an exhortatory sermon: Our brothers, it is not said about the people of Nineveh, God saw their sackcloth and their fasting, but *God saw their deeds that they repented their evil ways*[4], and what does it say in prophecy? *And tear your hearts and not your clothes, and return to the Eternal, your God*[5].

1 This statement confirms that in Mishnaic times the Ark containing the Torah scrolls was a movable chest, not part of the synagogue building. This is confirmed by the archeological evidence that in early Galilean synagogues the entrance was in the South. For prayers the Ark was moved from the storage room to the entrance; the reader stood before the Ark, and everybody was praying in the direction of Jerusalem, facing the Ark. In Amoraic times the Ark became part of the building in the South wall and the entrance was moved to the North.

2 The town square accommodating a maximum number of people.

3 The Mishnah explicitly excludes dust which is not ash.

4 *Jonah* 3:10.

5 *Joel* 2:13.

(65a line 29) סֵדֶר תַּעֲנִיּוֹת כֵּיצַד כול׳. אָמַר רְבִּי חִיָּיה בַּר בָּא. וְלָמָּה יוֹצְאִין לִרְחוֹבָהּ שֶׁלָּעִיר. לוֹמַר. חָשַׁבְנוּ כְּאִילּוּ גוֹלִים לְפָנֶיךָ. אָמַר רְבִּי יְהוֹשֻׁעַ בֶּן לֵוִי. לְפִי שֶׁנִּתְפַּלְּלוּ בְּצִינְעָה וְלֹא נַעֲנוּ לְפִיכָךְ יֵצְאוּ לַחוּץ וְיִתְפַּרְסְמוּ. אָמַר רְבִּי חִיָּיה בַּר בָּא. וְלָמָּה מוֹצִיאִין אֶת הַתֵּיבָה לִרְחוֹבָהּ שֶׁלָּעִיר. לוֹמַר. כְּלִי אֶחָד שֶׁלְּחֶמְדָּה שֶׁהָיָה לָנוּ גָּרְמוּ עֲווֹנוֹתֵינוּ שֶׁיִּתְבַּזֶּה. רְבִּי חוּנָה רַבָּה דְצִיפּוֹרִין אָמַר. אֲבוֹתֵינוּ חִפּוּ אוֹתוֹ זָהָב וְאָנוּ חִיפִּינוּ אוֹתוֹ אֵפֶר. אָמַר רְבִּי יַעֲקֹב דְּרוֹמַיָּא. וְלָמָּה תּוֹקְעִין בְּקַרְנוֹת. לוֹמַר. חָשַׁבְנוּ כְּאִילּוּ גוֹעִים כִּבְהֵמָה לְפָנֶיךָ. אָמַר רְבִּי לֵוִי. וְלָמָּה יוֹצְאִין בֵּין הַקְּבָרוֹת.

לוֹמַר. חָשְׁבֵינוּ כְּאִילוּ מֵתִים לְפָנֶיךָ. אָמַר רִבִּי תַנְחוּמָה. וְכוּלְהוֹן בָּהּ. אִם מִיתָה אָנוּ חַייָבִין הֲרֵי
מֵתִים. אִם גָּלוּת הֲרֵי גוֹלִים. אִם רָעָבוֹן הֲרֵי רְעֵבִים.

"How is the order of the fast days," etc. Rebbi Ḥiyya bar Abba said, why does one move to the town plaza? To say, we are considered as if exiled before You. Rebbi Joshua ben Levi said, because they prayed in privacy and were not answered; therefore they went public and were publicized. Rebbi Hiyya bar Abba said, why does one bring the Ark to the town plaza? To say that we had one precious vessel and our sins caused it to become debased. The Elder Rebbi Huna of Sepphoris said, our forefathers covered it with gold and we covered it with ashes. Rebbi Jacob the Southerner said, why does one blow horns? To say, we are considered as if bellowing like animals before You. Rebbi Levi said, and why does one visit graves? To say, we are considered like dead before You. Rebbi Tanhuma says, all of this is included. If we are guilty to die there are the dead, if exile there is exile, if hunger there is hunger[6].

6   All these texts are sermon concepts.   Babli 16a.

(65a line 38) וְנוֹתְנִין אֶפֶר מַקְלֶה עַל גַּבֵּי הַתֵּיבָה. עַל שֵׁם עִמּוֹ אָנֹכִי בְצָרָה. אָמַר רִבִּי זְעוּרָה. כָּל־זְמַן דַּהֲוֵינָא חָמֵי לוֹן עָבְדִין כֵּן הֲוָה גוּפִי רָעַד. בְּיוֹמוֹי דְּרִבִּי אִילָא הֲווֹן שָׁבְקִין אֲרוֹנָא וְעָלְלִין לוֹן. אָמַר לֵיהּ רִבִּי זְעוּרָה. לֹא כֵן תַּנֵּי. לֹא הָיוּ מִתְחַלְּפִין עָלֶיהָ כָּל־הַיּוֹם אֶלָּא אֶחָד הָיָה יוֹשֵׁב וּמְשַׁמְּרָהּ כָּל־הַיּוֹם.

רִבִּי יוּדָן בֵּירִבִּי מְנַשֶּׁה וְרִבִּי שְׁמוּאֵל בַּר נַחְמָן. חַד אָמַר. כְּדֵי לְהַזְכִּיר זְכוּתוֹ שֶׁלְּאַבְרָהָם. וְחוֹרָנָה אָמַר. כְּדֵי לְהַזְכִּיר זְכוּתוֹ שֶׁלְּיִצְחָק. מָאן דְּאָמַר. כְּדֵי לְהַזְכִּיר זְכוּתוֹ שֶׁלְּאַבְרָהָם. בֵּין עָפָר בֵּין אֶפֶר. עַל שֵׁם וְאָנֹכִי עָפָר וָאֵפֶר׃ מָאן דְּאָמַר. כְּדֵי לְהַזְכִּיר זְכוּתוֹ שֶׁלְּיִצְחָק. וּבִלְבַד אֶפֶר. רוֹאִין אֶפְרוֹ שֶׁלְּיִצְחָק כְּאִילוּ צָבוּר עַל גַּבֵּי הַמִּזְבֵּחַ. רִבִּי יוּדָה בַּר פָּזִי כַּד הֲוָה נָפֵק לְתַעֲנִיתָא הֲוָה אָמַר קוֹמֵיהוֹן. אָחֵינוּ. כָּל־מָאן דְּלָא מָטָא שִׁמְשָׁא לְגַבֵּיהּ יִסַּב עָפָר וְיִתֵּן גּוֹ רֵישֵׁיהּ.

"One gives burnt ashes[3] on top of the Ark." Because of *with him I am in trouble*[7]. Rebbi Zeˋira said, any time that I saw them doing this my body shuddered. In the days of Rebbi Ila they left the Ark standing and went away. Rebbi Zeˋira said to him, was it not stated: they should not take turns during the day but one person should sit there and watch it during the entire day[8]?

Rebbi Yudan ben Rebbi Menashe and Rebbi Samuel bar Nahman. One said, to mention the merit of Abraham; the other one said, to mention the merit of Isaac[9]. He who said, to mention the merit of Abraham, either ashes or dust, because of *I am dust and ashes*[10]. He who said, to mention the merit of Isaac, only ashes. One sees the ashes of Isaac as if his ashes were collected on the altar[11]. When Rebbi Judah bar Pazi went on a fast day; he said before them, our Brethren, anybody whom the beadle does not reach should take dust and put it on his head[12].

7 Ps. 91:15. Babli 15b.
8 One has to date the abolition of this ceremony to his days.
9 His willingness to be sacrificed on Mount Moriah.
10 Gen. 18:27. Cf. *Gen. rabba* 49(23), Babli 16a.
11 Since the only reason that he was not burned was the intervention of the angel, his merit is to have been burned.
12 The Mishnah requires that the synagogue personnel distribute ashes to everybody; but if the supply of ashes runs out one may substitute dust for ashes since according to one opinion the two are equivalent.

(65a line 49) וּבְרֹאשׁ הַנָּשִׂיא. אָמַר רִבִּי תַחְלִיפָא קַיְסָרְיָא. כְּדֵי לְפַרְסְמוֹ. לֹא דוֹמֶה הַמִּתְבַּזֶּה מֵעַצְמוֹ לַמִּתְבַּזֶּה מֵאַחֵר.

כָּתוּב יֵצֵא חָתָן מֵחֶדְרוֹ וְכַלָּה מֵחוּפָּתָהּ. יֵצֵא חָתָן מֵחֶדְרוֹ. זֶה אָרוֹן. וְכַלָּה מֵחוּפָּתָהּ. זֶה הַתּוֹרָה. דָּבָר אַחֵר. יֵצֵא חָתָן מֵחֶדְרוֹ. זֶה הַנָּשִׂיא. וְכַלָּה מֵחוּפָּתָהּ. אַב בֵּית דִּין. רִבִּי חֶלְבּוֹ אָמַר לְרִבִּי יוּדָן נְשִׂייָא. פּוּק עִימָּן וְצַעֲרָךְ עֲבַר. אָמַר רִבִּי יוֹסֵה. הָדָא אָמְרָה. אִילֵּין תַּעֲנִייָתָא דַּאֲנַן עָבְדִין לֵית אִינּוּן תַּעֲנִיִּין. דְּלֵית נְשִׂייָא עִמָּן.

"And on the head of the Patriarch." Rebbi Taḥlifa Caesarean said, to give it prominence. One cannot compare self-abasement with abasement by the hands of others[13].

It is written[14]: *May the bridegroom leave his room, and the bride her bridal chamber. May the bridegroom leave his room*, that is the Ark, *and the bride her bridal chamber*, that is the Torah[15]. Another word: *May the bridegroom leave his room*, that is the Patriarch, *and the bride her bridal chamber*, that is the presiding judge. Rebbi Ḥelbo said to Rebbi Yudan the Patriarch[16], come with us and your pain will be gone[17]. Rebbi Yose said, this implies that our fasts are no real fasts since the Patriarch is not with us[18].

13 Since the Mishnah requires that the ashes be applied by others.
14 Joel 2:16. Babli 15b/16a.
15 In A: the Torah scroll.
16 R. Judah II, Rebbi's grandson.
17 In A and the quote by R. Nissim

Gerondi *ad loc.*: will be effective.

18 Since the Patriarch resided in Sepphoris but the Academy was in Tiberias. The implication seems to be that other details of the Mishnah also do not have to be executed exactly as described.

(65a line 55) כָּתוּב אֶחָד אוֹמֵר אֶל־פְּנֵי הַכַּפֹּרֶת וְכָתוּב אַחֵר אוֹמֵר אֶל־פְּנֵי פָרוֹכֶת הַקּוֹדֶשׁ׃ רִבִּי אָחָא אָמַר. אִיתְפַּלְגוּן רִבִּי אַבָּהוּ וְרַבָּנָן. חַד אָמַר. חָטָא הַנָּשִׂיא הַגְּדוּלָּה בִּמְקוֹמָהּ. חָטָא הַצִּיבּוּר אֵין הַגְּדוּלָּה בִּמְקוֹמָהּ. וְחוֹרָנָה אָמַר. לְפִי שֶׁחָטְאוּ הַלָּמֵד וְהַמְלַמֵּד. לְפִיכָךְ יָצְאוּ לַחוּץ וְיִתְפַּרְסְמוּ. עַל שֵׁם וְהוֹצִיא אֶת־הַפָּר אֶל־מִחוּץ לַמַּחֲנֶה. תַּנֵּי חִזְקִיָּה. רֶמֶז. כָּל־מָקוֹם שֶׁיֵּשׁ מָשִׁיחַ יֵשׁ אָרוֹן. וְכָל־מָקוֹם שֶׁאֵין מָשִׁיחַ אֵין אָרוֹן. וְאַתְיָיא כַּיי דָמַר רִבִּי שְׁמוּאֵל בַּר יַנַּאי בְשֵׁם רִבִּי אָחָא. חֲמִשָּׁה דְבָרִים הָיָה הַמִּקְדָּשׁ הָאַחֲרוֹן חָסֵר מִן הָרִאשׁוֹן. וְאֵילּוּ הֵן. אֵשׁ וְאָרוֹן וְאוּרִים וְתוּמִּים וְשֶׁמֶן הַמִּשְׁחָה וְרוּחַ הַקּוֹדֶשׁ. עַל שֵׁם וְאֶרְצֶה־בּוֹ וְאֶכָּבְדָה. וְאֶכָּבֵד כָּתוּב חָסֵר ה"א. אֵילּוּ חֲמִשָּׁה דְבָרִים שֶׁהָיָה הַמִּקְדָּשׁ הָאַחֲרוֹן חָסֵר מִן הָרִאשׁוֹן.

One verse says, *in front of the cover*[19], but another verse says, *in front of the holy gobelin*[20]. Rebbi Aḥa said, Rebbi Abbahu and the rabbis disagree. One said, if the Patriarch sins, majesty remains in place. If the community sinned, majesty is not in place[21]. But the other one said, because teacher and student sinned, they have to go public and be noticed, following *and he shall remove the bull to outside the camp*[22]. Ḥizqiah stated: it is a hint. Anywhere there is an anointed one there is the Ark[23]. Anywhere there is no anointed one there is no Ark. This follows what Rebbi Samuel ben Aina said in the name of Rebbi Aḥa[24]: Five things was the last Temple missing which were in the first Temple, as it is written[25]: *I shall be pleased with it and I will be honored*. It is written *I will be honored*, without the letter *he*[26]. These are the five things which the last Temple was missing which were in the first Temple. They are: The {heavenly} fire, the Ark, Urim and Tummim, anointing oil[27], and the Holy Spirit.

19 *Lev.* 16:2. (But maybe *Lev.* 4:17 was intended.)
20 *Lev.* 4:6, the purification offering of the anointed High Priest.
21 In the Babli, *Zevaḥim* 41b, the idea is formulated so: If an individual revolts, the king's government is unchanged; if an entire country revolts, the king's government is abolished.
22 *Lev.* 4:21.
23 As long as anointed High Priests officiated in the Temple, the Ark was in the Holiest of Holies. In the Second Temple, whose High Priests were invested but not anointed, there was no Ark.
24 *Makkot* 2:7 (Notes 124-130), *Horaiot* 3:2, Babli *Yoma* 21b
25 *Hag.* 1:8.

26 *Ketib* וְאֶכְבָּד, *Qere* וְאִכָּבְדָה. Both spellings make sense. The missing ה is interpreted in the Alexandrian system of numeration as "5".

27 It is stated in *Ex.* 30:23 that only Moses himself could compound this oil and in v. 31 that it should be used for all subsequent generations. By tradition, Josia buried the oil flask together with the Ark of the Covenant in the Temple Mount (*2Chr.* 35:3) after the prophetess Hulda informed him of the imminent destruction of the Temple.

(65a line 66) דִּלְמָא. רִבִּי בָּא בַּר זַבְדָא וְרִבִּי תַנְחוּם בַּר עִילַאי וְרִבִּי יֹאשִׁיָה נָפְקוּן לְתַעֲנִיתָא. דָּרַשׁ רִבִּי בָּא בַּר זַבְדָא. נִשָּׂא לְבָבֵנוּ אֶל־כַּפָּיִם. וְאֶיפְשָׁר כֵּן. אִית בַּר נָשׁ דְּנָסַב לִיבֵּיהּ וְיָהַב גּוֹ יָדֵיהּ. אֶלָּא מָהוּ נִישָּׂא. נַשְׁוֵי לִיבֵּינָן לְכַף יָדֵינוּ. וְאַחַר כָּךְ אֶל־אֵל בַּשָּׁמָיִם. כָּךְ אִם יִהְיֶה הַשֶּׁרֶץ בְּיָדוֹ שֶׁלְאָדָם. אֲפִילוּ טוֹבֵל בְּמֵי שִׁילוֹחַ אוֹ בְּמֵי בְרֵאשִׁית אֵין לוֹ טַהֲרָה עוֹלָמִית. הִשְׁלִיחוֹ מִיָּדוֹ מִיָּד טָהֵר. דָּרַשׁ רִבִּי תַנְחוּם בַּר עִילַאי. וַיִּכָּנְעוּ שָׂרֵי־יִשְׂרָאֵל וְהַמֶּלֶךְ וַיֹּאמְרוּ צַדִּיק | יי וּבִרְאוֹת יי כִּי נִכְנְעוּ הָיָה דְבַר־יי אֶל־שְׁמַעְיָה | לֵאמֹר. נִתְעַנּוּ אֵין כָּתוּב כָּאן. אֶלָּא נִכְנָעוּ. לֹא אַשְׁחִיתֵם. דָּרַשׁ רִבִּי יֹאשִׁיָה. הִתְקוֹשְׁשׁוּ וָקוֹשּׁוּ. נִתְקוֹשֵׁשׁ גַּרְמָן עַד דְּלָא נְקוֹשֵׁשׁ חוֹרָנִין. בְּגִין דְּאִית הָכָא בְּנֵי נָשׁ דְּאָמְרִין עֲלַי לִישָׁן בִּישׁ גַּבֵּי רִבִּי יוֹחָנָן. אֶלָּא כָּל־עַמָּא לְדִינָא אָמְרִין. הֲוָה תַּמָּן רִבִּי חִיָּיה וְרִבִּי אִיסִי וְרִבִּי אִימִּי וְקָמוּן וְאָזְלוּן לוֹן.

Explanation[28]. Rebbi Abba bar Zavda, Rebbi Tanḥum bar Ilai, and Rebbi Joshia came to the fast. Rebbi Abba bar Zavda preached: *Let us lift our hearts on the palms*[29]. Is this possible? May a person take his heart and put it on his hand? So what means "let us lift"? Let us treat our hearts equal to our hands[30], and then *to God in Heaven*. So if somebody would hold a crawling animal[31] in his hand, even if he immerses himself in the waters of Siloam or of the ocean, he never can become pure[32]. But if he throws it[33] from his hand he immediately is pure. Rebbi Tanḥum bar Ilai preached: *The ministers of Israel and the King submitted and said, the Eternal is just. And when the Eternal saw that they submitted, the Eternal's word was to Shemaya as oracle*[34]. It is not written "their fast" but *they submitted, I shall not destroy them*. Rebbi Joshia preached: *Become improved and improve*[35], let us purify ourselves before we purify others[36]. Since here are people present who calumniate me before Rebbi Joḥanan. But every single one is called to justice. Attending were Rebbi Ḥiyya[37], Rebbi Issy[38], and Rebbi Immi. They got up and left[39].

28 Greek δήλωμα. A shortened version is in *Thr. rabba* 3(33).

29 *Thr.* 3:41.

30 Which one always washes to keep them clean.

31 A dead crawling animal as enumerated

in *Lev.* 11:29-30, as source of original impurity. Babli 16a.

32 In A one reads: even if he immerses himself in all oceans he never will be pure. If he throws it from his hands, even if he only immerses himself in the waters of the Siloam which are 1×1×2 cubits, he immediately is pure.

33 The dead crawling animal.

34 *2Chr.* 12:6-7.

35 *Zeph.* 2:1.

36 Babli *Sanhedrin* 18a,19a, *Bava batra* 60b, *Bava meṣi`a* 107b.

37 Bar Abba.

38 Usually he is called Yasa, in the Babli Assi.

39 What offended them in R. Joshia's sermon is everybody's guess; each commentator has his own opinion.

(65b line 3) אָמַר רִבִּי לְעָזָר. שְׁלֹשָׁה דְבָרִים מְבַטְּלִין אֶת הַגְּזֵירָה קָשָׁה. וְאֵילוּ הֵן. תְּפִילָה וּצְדָקָה וּתְשׁוּבָה. וּשְׁלָשְׁתָּן בְּפָסוּק אֶחָד. וְיִכָּנְעוּ עַמִּי אֲשֶׁר נִקְרָא־שְׁמִי עֲלֵיהֶם וְיִתְפַּלְלוּ. זוֹ תְפִילָה. וִיבַקְשׁוּ פָנָי. זוֹ צְדָקָה. כְּמָה דְאַתְּ אָמַר אֲנִי בְּצֶדֶק אֶחֱזֶה פָנֶיךָ. וְיָשׁוּבוּ מִדַּרְכֵיהֶם הָרָעִים. זוֹ תְשׁוּבָה. אִם עָשׂוּ כֵן מַה כָּתוּב תַּמָּן. וַאֲנִי אֶשְׁמַע מִן־הַשָּׁמַיִם וְאֶסְלַח לְחַטָּאתָם וְאֶרְפָּא אֶת־אַרְצָם:

רִבִּי חַגַּי דָּרַשׁ הֲדָא דְרִבִּי לְעָזָר כָּל־שָׁעָה בְּתַעֲנִיתָא. אָמַר רִבִּי לְעָזָר. סוֹף שַׁתָּא כְשַׁתָּא. מִן עֲפַר קַייְטָא לְסִיתוּא. נָפַח צָפוֹנָה יְצֵף לְבָנָיו. כָּל־שָׁנָה שֶׁאֵין מַתְרִיעִין עָלֶיהָ בָרִאשׁוֹנָה סוֹף שֶׁמַּתְרִיעִין עָלֶיהָ בְסוֹפָהּ. כָּל־שֶׁאֵינָהּ חָסָה עַל פֵּירוֹת חֲבֵירָתָהּ סוֹף שֶׁהִיא מְאַבֶּדֶת פֵּירוֹתֶיהָ. אָמַר רִבִּי אֲחָא. וְרוֹב הַיַּיִן מַחֲמִיץ. אִית הֲוָה סַבִּין בְּצִיפּוֹרִין. כַּד הֲוַת רְבִיעָתָא קַדְמִייתָא הֲווֹ מְרִיחִין בְּעַפְרָא וְיָדְעִין מֵימוֹר מֵימֵי שַׁתָּא.

[40]Rebbi Eleazar said, three things annul the harsh decree. They are: prayer, charity and repentance. All three are from one verse[41]: *My people, over whom My Name is called, will submit and pray,* this is prayer, *and desire my presence,* this is charity as you are saying, *by charity I shall see Your presence*[42]. *They will repent their evil ways,* this is repentance. When they act in this way, what is written there? *Then I shall hear in Heaven and forgive their sins and heal their land.*

Rebbi Ḥaggai always preached the following from Rebbi Eleazar. Rebbi Eleazar said, the end of the year is like the year. From the dust of summer to winter, if North wind blows[43] take care of your children. Any year for which no *shofar* was blown at the start, one will have to blow at the end[44]. Any which does not care for the produce of the preceding will at the end lose its produce[45]. Rebbi Aḥa said, and most of its wine will turn to vinegar. There were old men in Sepphoris who at the first rainy period[46] were smelling the dust and could tell the {amount of} rains of the year.

40 Tanḥuma Noah 8, Tanḥuma Buber Noah 13, *Gen. rabba* 44(15), *Eccl. rabba* 7(59). In a different context, *Sanhedrin* 10:2 (Notes 169-171). Differently, Babli *Roš Haššanah* 16b. The Tanḥuma text seems to be the source for Moses ben Kalonymos's poem וּנְתַנֶּה תּוֹקֶף.
41 *2Chr.* 7:14.
42 *Ps.* 17:15.
43 At a time when the West wind should bring rain.
44 If one fails to obey the religious commandment to blow the *shofar* on New Year's Day one will have to blow later as a call of calamity and emergency. Babli *Roš Haššanah* 16b.
45 If heave and tithes are not given according to the rules after the harvest of the preceding year, the yield of the following year is in jeopardy.
46 The text A reads: רְבִיעֲתָא קַדְמֵיָיתָא נַחְתָּה "when the first rains came down". The character of A makes it questionable whether this is text or a gloss.

(65c line 14) אָמַר רִבִּי לְעָזָר. הֲכָזֶה יִהְיֶה צוֹם אֶבְחָרֵהוּ אֶלָּא יוֹם עַנּוֹת אָדָם נַפְשׁוֹ. אֵין זֶה צוֹם שֶׁאֲנִי חָפֵץ בּוֹ. וְאֵי זֶהוּ צוֹם שֶׁאֲנִי חָפֵץ בּוֹ. הֲלוֹא זֶה צוֹם אֶבְחָרֵהוּ פַּתֵּחַ חַרְצוּבּוֹת רֶשַׁע הַתֵּר אֲגוּדּוֹת מוֹטָה. הֲלוֹא פָּרוֹשׂ לָרָעֵב לַחְמֶךָ וַעֲנִיִּים מְרוּדִים תָּבִיא בָיִת. מַה כְּתִיב בַּתְרֵיהּ אָז תִּקְרָא וְיֵי יַעֲנֶה וגו'.

אָמַר רִבִּי שִׁמְעוֹן בֶּן לָקִישׁ. כָּתוּב וְאֵיד יַעֲלֶה מִן־הָאָרֶץ. עָלָה שֶׁבֶר מִלְּמַטָּן מִיַּד הַגְּשָׁמִים יוֹרְדִין. אָמַר רִבִּי בֶּרֶכְיָה. כָּתוּב יַעֲרֹף כַּמָּטָר לִקְחִי. כְּפִי עוֹרְפִין לִתְשׁוּבָה מִיַּד הַגְּשָׁמִים יוֹרְדִין. רִבִּי בֶּרֶכְיָה עֲבַד תְּלַת עֶשְׂרֵה תַּעֲנִייָן וְלָא נְחַת מִיטְרָא. וּבְסוֹפָהּ אֲתָא גוֹבַיי. עָאַל וְאָמַר קוֹמֵיהוֹן. אֲחִינַן. חָמוּן מַה דַאֲנַן עָבְדִין. לָא דָא הִיא דִנְבִיָּיא מְקַנְתַּר לָן עַל־הָרַע כַּפַּיִם לְהֵיטִיב. מֵרִיעִין זֶה לָזֶה בְכַפֵּינוּ וּמְבַקְּשִׁין טוֹבָה. הַשַּׁר שׁוֹאֵל. אֵיכָן הוּא הַשּׁוֹחַד לִיקַח. וְהַשּׁוֹפֵט בַּשִּׁילוּם. שַׁלֵּם לִי וַאֲשַׁלֵּם לָךְ. וְהַגָּדוֹל דּוֹבֵר הַוַּת נַפְשׁוֹ הוּא וַיְעַבְּתוּהָ. עַבְדּוּהָ עָבְיָא. עַבְדּוּהָ קְלִיעָה דְחוֹבִין. וּמָן פָּסַק לָהּ. טוֹבָם כְּחֵדֶק. טָבָא דִּבְהוֹן כְּאִילֵּין חִידְקַיָּא. יָשָׁר מִמְּסוּכָה. יָשָׁר דִּבְהוֹן כְּאִילֵּין סוֹכַיָּיא. יוֹם מְצַפֶּיךָ פְּקֻדָּתְךָ בָאָה. יוֹם שֶׁצִּיפִינוּ לִרְוָוחָה בָא עָלֵינוּ גוֹבַיי. עַתָּה תִּהְיֶה מְבוּכָתָם: מִן גְּוָא דְאִינּוּן בַּיְיכָן. וּבָכוּן וּבָכוּן וּנְחַת מִיטְרָא.

Rebbi Eleazar said: *Is that a fast day which I would prefer,* that is *a day where a person deprives himself?* This is not a day to my liking. What is a day to my liking? *Is not this a day I would prefer, opening chains of evil, unbinding fetters of the yoke. Is it not breaking your bread for the hungry, and bring to the house the poor persecuted ones.* What is written after this? *Then you will call and the Eternal will answer,*[47] etc.

Rebbi Simeon ben Laqish said, it is written[48]: *and distress*[49] *rose from the earth*. If rupture rises from the earth, rain will fall immediately. Rebbi Berekhiah said, it is written[50]: *may my teaching drip like rain*, because if one confesses in repentance[51] rain will fall immediately. Rebbi Berekhiah made thirteen fast days but no rain fell; at the end locusts came. He went and said before them, our brethren, look at what we are doing. Is that not what the prophet needles us[52], *from evil hands to profit*, we damage one another with our hands and expect good things; *the noble asks* where is the bribe to be collected, *and the judge in payment*, pay me and I shall pay you, *the great one speaks lies from his soul and they will distort it*, they will turn it thick, they turned it into a plaiting of debts. And who can stop it? *Their best one is like thorns*, the best one among them is like thorns, *the straight one like a hedge of thorns*, the most upright among them is like those branches, *on the day to which they looked comes their due*, on the day which we expected relief locusts, *this shall be their consternation!* From the midst of their crying, and crying, and crying, there fell rain.

47 *Is.* 58:5,7,9. The spelling פרוש against masoretic פרס is confirmed by Babli *Bava batra* 9a and is not to be explained away (cf. *Mesoret Hashas Babli* 9a, Note 2.)
48 *Gen.* 2:6.
49 He identifies אֵד "fog" and אֵיד "dies ater". In *Gen. rabba* 13(15) the entire paragraph is attributed to R. Berekhiah.
50 *Deut.* 32:2.
51 The homily identifies ערף "to drip" (Accadic *arapu* "to be cloudy") with another root ערף (Arabic ערף "to know", אעתרף "to confess".)
52 *Micah* 7:3-4.

(65b line 30) אָמַר רִבִּי שִׁמְעוֹן בֶּן לָקִישׁ. תְּשׁוּבָה שֶׁלְּרַמָּיוּת עָשׂוּ אַנְשֵׁי נִינְוֵה. מֶה עָשׂוּ. רִבִּי חוּנָה בְשֵׁם רִבִּי שִׁמְעוֹן בֶּן חַלְפּוּתָא. הֶעֱמִידוּ עֲגָלִים מִבִּפְנִים וְאִמּוֹתֵיהֶם מִבַּחוּץ. סַיָּיחִים מִבִּפְנִים וְאִמּוֹתֵיהֶם מִבַּחוּץ. וַהֲווֹן אִילֵּין גָּעֵי מִן הָכָא וְאִילֵּין גָּעֵי מִן הָכָא. אָמְרִין. אִין לֵית מִתְרַחֵם עֲלֵינָן לִינָן מְרַחֲמִין עֲלֵיהוֹן. הָדָא הִיא דִכְתִיב מַה־נֶּאֶנְחָה בְהֵמָה נָבֹכוּ עֶדְרֵי בָקָר וגו׳. אָמַר רִבִּי אֲחָא. בַּעֲרָבְיָא עָבְדִין כֵּן. וַיִתְכַּסּוּ שַׂקִּים הָאָדָם וְהַבְּהֵמָה וְיִקְרְאוּ אֶל־אֱלֹהִים בְּחָזְקָה. מָהוּ בְּחָזְקָה. אָמַר רִבִּי שִׁמְעוֹן בֶּן חַלְפּוּתָא. חֲצִיפָה נָצַח לִכְשִׁירָא. כָּל־שֶׁכֵּן לְטוֹבָתוֹ שֶׁלְּעוֹלָם. וְיָשׁוּבוּ אִישׁ מִדַּרְכּוֹ הָרָעָה וּמִן־הֶחָמָס אֲשֶׁר בְּכַפֵּיהֶם: אָמַר רִבִּי יוֹחָנָן. מַה שֶּׁהָיָה בְכַף יְדֵיהֶם הֶחֱזִירוּ. מַה שֶּׁהָיָה בְשִׁידָה תֵּיבָה וּמִגְדָּל לֹא הֶחֱזִירוּ.

Rebbi Simeon ben Laqish said, the people of Nineveh repented in trickery. What did they do[53]? Rebbi Huna in the name of Rebbi Simeon ben Halfuta[54]:

They put calves inside and their mothers outside, foals inside and their mothers outside; these were mooing from one side and those mooing from the other side. They said, if He does not have mercy on us we shall not have mercy on them. That is what is written[55], *how the animals groan, are cattle herds confused*, etc. Rebbi Aḥa said, that is what they do in Arabia. *They should be covered by sack-cloth, humans and animals, and call on God in force*[56]. What means "in force"? Rebbi Simeon ben Halfuta said, the brash one wins over the proper one[57], so much more if it is for the good of the world. *Each man shall repent his evil ways and robbery in their hands.* Rebbi Joḥanan said, what they had in their hands they returned, what was in a chest, a trunk and a cupboard they did not return.

53 Babli 16a.
54 In A: R. Ḥanania in the name of Resh Laqish.
55 *Joel* 1:18.
56 *Jonah* 3:8.
57 Cf. Babli *Sanhedrin* 105a.

(65b line 40) כָּתוּב וְקִרְעוּ לְבַבְכֶם וְאַל־בִּגְדֵיכֶם וְשׁוּבוּ אֶל־יי אֱלֹהֵיכֶם כִּי־חַנּוּן וְרַחוּם הוּא. אָמַר רִבִּי יְהוֹשֻׁעַ בֶּן לֵוִי. אִם קְרַעְתֶּם לְבַבְכֶם בִּתְשׁוּבָה אֵין אַתֶּם קוֹרְעִין בְּגִדֵיכֶם לֹא עַל בְּנֵיכֶם וְלֹא עַל בְּנוֹתֵיכֶם אֶלָּא יי אֱלֹהֵיכֶם. לָמָּה. כִּי־חַנּוּן וְרַחוּם הוּא אֶרֶךְ אַפַּיִם וְרַב־חֶסֶד וְנִיחָם עַל־הָרָעָה: רִבִּי שְׁמוּאֵל בַּר נַחְמָן בְּשֵׁם רִבִּי יוֹנָתָן. אֶרֶךְ אַף אֵין כָּתוּב כָּאן אֶלָּא אֶרֶךְ אַפַּיִם. מַעֲרִיךְ רוּחוֹ עִם הַצַּדִּיקִים וּמַעֲרִיךְ רוּחוֹ עִם הָרְשָׁעִים. רִבִּי אָחָא רִבִּי תַּנְחוּם בְּרִבִּי חִייָה בְּשֵׁם רִבִּי יוֹחָנָן. אֶרֶךְ אַף אֵין כָּתוּב כָּאן אֶלָּא אֶרֶךְ אַפַּיִם. מַעֲרִיךְ רוּחוֹ עַד שֶׁלֹּא יִגְבֶּה. הִתְחִיל לִגְבּוֹת מַעֲרִיךְ רוּחוֹ וְגוֹבֶה. אָמַר רִבִּי חֲנִינָה. מַאן דְּאָמַר דְּרַחֲמָנָא וִוַתְרָן יִתְוַותְרוּן בְּנֵי מָעוֹי. אֶלָּא מַעֲרִיךְ רוּחֵיהּ וְגָבֵי דִידֵיהּ. אָמַר רִבִּי לֵוִי. מַהוּ אֶרֶךְ אַפַּיִם. רְחִיק רְגִיז. לְמֶלֶךְ שֶׁהָיוּ לוֹ שְׁנֵי לִגְיוֹנוֹת קָשִׁים. אָמַר הַמֶּלֶךְ. אִם דָּרִים הֵן עִימִּי בַּמְּדִינָה. עַכְשָׁיו בְּנֵי הַמְּדִינָה מַכְעִיסִים אוֹתִי וְהֵן עוֹמְדִין וּמְכַלִּין אוֹתָן. אֶלָּא הֲרֵינִי מְשַׁלְּחָן לְדֶרֶךְ רְחוֹקָה. שֶׁאִם הִכְעִיסוּ אוֹתִי בְּנֵי הַמְּדִינָה עַד שֶׁאֲנִי מְשַׁלֵּחַ אַחֲרֵיהֶם בְּנֵי הַמְּדִינָה מְפַיְּיסִין אוֹתִי וַאֲנִי מְקַבֵּל פִּיּוּסָן. [כָּךְ אָמַר הַקָּדוֹשׁ בָּרוּךְ הוּא. אַף וְחֵימָה מַלְאֲכֵי חַבָּלָה הֵן. הֲרֵי אֲנִי מְשַׁלְּחָן לְדֶרֶךְ רְחוֹקָה. שֶׁאִם מַכְעִיסִין אוֹתִי יִשְׂרָאֵל. עַד שֶׁאֲנִי מְשַׁלֵּחַ אֶצְלָן וּמְבִיאָן יִשְׂרָאֵל עוֹשִׂין תְּשׁוּבָה וַאֲנִי מְקַבֵּל תְּשׁוּבָתָן.] הֲדָא הוּא דִכְתִיב בָּאִים מֵאֶרֶץ מֶרְחָק מִקְצֵה הַשָּׁמַיִם וגו'. אָמַר רִבִּי יִצְחָק. וְלֹא עוֹד אֶלָּא שֶׁנָּעַל בִּפְנֵיהֶן. הֲדָא הוּא דִכְתִיב פָּתַח יי אֶת־אוֹצָרוֹ וַיּוֹצֵא אֶת־כְּלֵי זַעְמוֹ. עַד דּוּ פָּתַח עַד דּוּ טָרַד דּוּ רַחֲמוֹי קְרִיבִין. תַּנֵּי בְשֵׁם רִבִּי מֵאִיר. כִּי־הִנֵּה יי יֹצֵא מִמְּקוֹמוֹ. יוֹצֵא לוֹ מִמִּדַּת לְמִידָה. יוֹצֵא לוֹ מִמִּדַּת הַדִּין וּבָא לוֹ לְמִידַּת הָרַחֲמִים עַל יִשְׂרָאֵל.

It is written[58], *and tear your hearts instead of your garments and return to the Eternal, your God, for He is compassionate and merciful.* Rebbi Joshua ben Levi said, if you tear up your hearts in repentance you will not have to tear your garments about your sons or daughters[59], only about the Eternal, your God. Why? *For He is compassionate and merciful, slow in anger, full of love, and sorrow about evil.* [60]Rebbi Samuel bar Nahman in the name of Rebbi Jonathan: It is not written here "slow in one anger" but "slow in anger". He is slow in anger with the just ones, and slow in anger with the evil ones. Rebbi Aha, Rebbi Tanhum ben Rebbi Hiyya in the name of Rebbi Johanan: It is not written here "slow in one anger" but "slow in anger". He is slow in anger before he starts to collect. Once He starts to collect he is slow to complete His collection. [61]Rebbi Hanina said, anybody who says that the All-Merciful is indulgent, his intestines shall dissolve themselves; for He is forbearing and then collects His due. Rebbi Levi said, what means "forbearing"? He is far from being angry[61]. {A parable of} a king who had two violent legions. Said the king, if they dwell with me at the capital, if the people of the capital would anger me they would get up and decimate them. Therefore I shall send them to a faraway place. Then if the people of the capital would anger me, until I shall send for them the people of the capital will pacify me and I will accept their excuses. [So the Holy One, praise to Him, said, anger and rage are angels of destruction. Therefore I shall send them to a faraway place. Therefore if Israel would anger me, until I shall send for them and bring them, Israel will repent and I shall accept their repentance.][62] That is what is written[63], *they come from a far country, from the ends of heaven*[64], etc. Rebbi Isaac said, not only that but He locked them up. That is what is written[65], *the Eternal opened His storehouse and removed the vessels of his wrath.* By the time He opened and He took pains, His mercies take over. It was stated in the name of Rebbi Meïr: *For the Eternal left His place*[66], He went from mode to mode. He left the mode of judgement and came to the mode of mercy[67] for Israel.

58 *Joel* 2:13.
59 They will not die young.
60 Babli *Eruvin* 22a.
61 *Šeqalim* 5:2 Note 39, *Yom Tov* 3:9 Note 124; Babli *Bava qamma* 50a/b.
62 Corrector's addition; no source known for it.
63 *Is.* 13:5.
64 The verse continues: *The Eternal and the instruments of His rage, to destroy the earth.*
65 *Jer.* 50:25.

66 *Is.* 26:21.

67 The designation of the mode of judgment is the name *Elohim* "supreme power", referring to His rule of the forces of nature. The designation of the mode of mercy is *YHWH* "Eternal".

(65b line 64) כָּתוּב לֹא אִישׁ אֵל וִיכַזֵּב. רִבִּי שְׁמוּאֵל בַּר נַחְמָן וְרַבָּנָן. רִבִּי שְׁמוּאֵל בַּר נַחְמָן אֲמַר. הַקָּדוֹשׁ בָּרוּךְ הוּא אוֹמֵר לַעֲשׂוֹת טוֹבָה. לֹא אִישׁ אֵל וִיכַזֵּב. אוֹמֵר לַעֲשׂוֹת רָעָה. הַהוּא אָמַר וְלֹא יַעֲשֶׂה וְדִבֶּר וְלֹא יְקִימֶנָּה: וְרַבָּנָן אֲמְרֵי. לֹא אִישׁ הוּא שֶׁעֲשָׂה דְּבָרָיו שֶׁלֹּאֵל כְּאִילוּ אֵינָן. לָמָה יֶחֱרֶה אַפְּךָ בְּעַמֶּךָ. וּבֶן־אָדָם וְיִתְנֶחָם. לֹא בֶן עַמְרָם הוּא שֶׁעָשָׂה לָאֵל שֶׁיִּתְנָחָם. וַיִּנָּחֶם י"י עַל־הָרָעָה אֲשֶׁר דִּבֶּר לַעֲשׂוֹת לְעַמּוֹ.

It is written[68], *God is no human that He would lie.* Rebbi Samuel bar Nahman and the rabbis. Rebbi Samuel bar Nahman said, if the Holy One, praise to Him, says to give a benefit, *God is no human that He would lie.* If he said to make a detriment, *He would say but not do it, and speak but not keep it.* But the rabbis are saying, there is no man who could make God's words as if nonexistent. *Why should Your anger burn against Your people*[69]? *Or a human and He be sorrow.* Not the son of Amram who made God to have second thoughts: *the Eternal had second thoughts about the evil He had said to bring over His people*[70].

68 *Num.* 23:19. In this verse Balaam seems to proclaim an extreme doctrine of predestination which negates the possibility of effective repentance, against the homiletics described in the Halakhah. *Tanhuma Mas`e* 6.

69 *Ex.* 32:11. *Num. rabba* 23(8).

70 *Ex.* 32:14.

(65b line 69) אָמַר רִבִּי אַבָּהוּ. אִם יֹאמַר לְךָ אָדָם. אֵל אֲנִי. מְכַזֵּב הוּא. בֶּן אָדָם אֲנִי. סוֹפוֹ לִתְהוֹת בּוֹ. שֶׁאֲנִי עוֹלֶה לַשָּׁמַיִם. הַהוּא אָמַר וְלֹא יְקִימֶנָּה.

Rebbi Abbahu said, if a man says to you, I am a god, he lies. I am the Son of Man[71], at the end he will regret it. That I ascend to heaven, "this he says but cannot fulfill.[72]"

71 The expression, in imitation of Accadic *awelum*, "free man", by which Ezechiel was addressed by God as true prophet.

72 An imitation of *Num.* 23:19.

(65b line 70) רִבִּי אָחָא בְשֵׁם רַב. אֵין תַּעֲנִית עַכְשָׁיו. אָמַר רִבִּי יוֹסֵה. הָדָא אָמְרָה. אִילֵּין תַּעֲנִייָתָא דַאֲנַן עָבְדִין לֵית אִילֵּין. אָמַר לֵיהּ. כֵּן אָמַר רַב. כָּל־תַּעֲנִית שֶׁאֵינָהּ נַעֲשִׂית כְּתִיקְנָהּ עָלֶיהָ הַכָּתוּב אוֹמֵר נָתְנָה עָלַי בְּקוֹלָהּ עַל־כֵּן שְׂנֵאתִיהָ:

Rebbi Aḥa in the name of Rav: Today there is no fast-day[18]. Rebbi Yose said, does this mean that the fast-days which we are arranging are not those? He said to him, so says Rav: The verse says about any fast-day which does not follow its rules, *she was noisy around me, therefore I hated her*[72].

72 *Jer.* 12:8. Since in Babylonia, country of Rav's activity, there was no Patriarch, all that can be inferred from his statement is that in Babylonia, in his times amply supplied by water by a large system of canals between Tigris and Euphrates, no fasts in years of drought are authorized. Babli 16b.

(fol. 64d) **משנה ב**: עָמְדוּ בִתְפִילָּה מוֹרִידִין לִפְנֵי הַתֵּבָיה זָקֵן וְרָגִיל וְיֵשׁ לוֹ בָנִים וּבֵיתוֹ רֵיקָן כְּדֵי שֶׁיְּהֵא לִבּוֹ שָׁלֵם בַּתְּפִילָּה. וְאוֹמֵר לִפְנֵיהֶן עֶשְׂרִים וְאַרְבַּע בְּרָכוֹת שְׁמוֹנֶה עֶשְׂרֵה שֶׁבְּכָל־יוֹם וּמוֹסִיף עֲלֵיהֶן עוֹד שֵׁשׁ: אֵילוּ הֵן. זִכְרוֹנוֹת וְשׁוֹפָרוֹת. אֶל ה' בַּצָּרָתָה לִּי. אֶשָּׂא עֵינַי אֶל הֶהָרִים. מִמַּעֲמַקִּים קְרָאתִיךָ ה'. תְּפִלָּה לְעָנִי כִי יַעֲטֹף.

Mishnah 2: After they stood to pray they place before the Ark an old knowledgeable man who has children but his house is empty[73] so that his mind should be concentrated on prayer. He recites before them 24 benedictions, eighteen of the daily prayers and additional six. These are they, *Zikhronot* and *Shofarot*[74]. *To the Eternal in my straights*[75]. *I lifted my eyes to the Mountains*[76]. *From the depths I called on You, Eternal*[77]. *Prayer of the poor who is fainting*[78].

73 He has to be poor but must be knowledgeable enough to be able to recite all prayers without slowing down or interruption, and must have young children who are dependent on him.

74 The two additional benedictions in the *musaf* prayer of New Year's Day; each one accompanied by the blowing of the *shofar*.

The text of each addition is followed by an invocation and a doxology as spelled out in Mishnaiot 4-10.

75 *Ps.* 120.
76 *Ps.* 121.
77 *Ps.* 130.
78 *Ps.* 102.

(65b line 74) **הלכה ב**: תַּנֵּי. וְשָׁפַל בֶּרֶךְ וְנוֹחַ תִּשְׁחוֹרֶת וְרָגִיל בְּחָכְמָה וְרָגִיל בָּאֲגָדָה וְיֵשׁ לוֹ בַיִת וְשָׂדֶה. תַּנִּינָן וּבֵיתוֹ רֵיקָן. וְאַתְּ אָמַר הָכֵין. יֵשׁ לוֹ בָנִים וּבָנוֹת. אִם אֵין לָהֶן מַעֲבִירִין כָּל־מַה שֶׁיִּרְצוּ.

It was stated: "And modest, easy on youth, used to study, used to preaching and owner of house and field[79]." We have stated, "but his house is empty", and you are saying so[80]? If nobody is available one may place anybody one wants[81].

79 Babli 16a.
80 The Mishnah seems to imply that he is a renter and does not own anything.
81 Since usually nobody available fills all qualifications stated in Mishnah and *baraita*, the community organizer may appoint any person to be reader.

(65c line 2) וְלָמָּה שְׁמוֹנֶה עֶשְׂרֵה. אָמַר רִבִּי יְהוֹשֻׁעַ בֶּן לֵוִי. כְּנֶגֶד שְׁמוֹנֶה עֶשְׂרֵה מִזְמוֹרוֹת שֶׁכָּתוּב מֵרֹאשׁוֹ שֶׁלְּתִילִּים עַד יַעַנְךָ י"י בְּיוֹם צָרָה. אִם יֹאמַר לָךְ אָדָם תִּשְׁעָה עָשָׂר הֵן. אֱמוֹר לוֹ. לָמָּה רָגְשׁוּ לֵית הִיא מִינּוֹן. מִיכָּן אָמְרוּ. הַמִּתְפַּלֵּל וְאֵינוֹ נַעֲנֶה צָרִיךְ תַּעֲנִית. אָמַר רִבִּי מָנָא. רֶמֶז לְתַלְמִיד חָכָם הוּא. שֶׁאָדָם צָרִיךְ לוֹמַר לְרַבּוֹ. תִּשָּׁמַע תְּפִילָתָךְ.

1 אמ' ר' יהושע בן לוי | **ב** ר' יהושע בן לוי או' | R 2 אדם | **ב** - תשעה עשר | **ב** תשע עשרה   3 רגשו | **ב** רגשו גוים   היא | **ב** הוא

[82]And why eighteen? Rebbi Joshua ben Levi said, corresponding to the eighteen psalms that are written from the start of Psalms to *May the Eternal listen to you on the day of trouble*[83]. If somebody would say to you they are nineteen, tell him *Why are <the Gentiles> in upheaval*[84] is not in the count[85]. From here they said that one who prayed and was not answered needs to fast[86]. Rebbi Mana said, a hint that a Torah student must say to his teacher: May your prayers be answered[87].

82 The remainder of this Halakhah is parallel to Halakhah 4:3 in *Berakhot* (Notes 138-181,**ב**). The text is quoted at length in *Tanhuma Wayyera* and from there in midrashic literature. Babli *Berakhot* 28b
83 *Ps.* 20:2.
84 *Ps.* 2:1.

85 In most Talmudic sources Psalms 1 and 2 form one song. To compensate, *Ps.* 116 is split into two. Babli *Berakhot* 9b.
86 Since the "trouble" referred to in the Psalm is interpreted as fasting.
87 Since *Ps.* 20 is read as addressed to David.

(65c line 6) רִבִּי סִימוֹן בְּשֵׁם רִבִּי יְהוֹשֻׁעַ בֶּן לֵוִי. כְּנֶגֶד שְׁמוֹנֶה עֶשְׂרֵה חֻלְיוֹת שֶׁבְּשִׁזְרָה. שֶׁבְּשָׁעָה שֶׁאָדָם עוֹמֵד וּמִתְפַּלֵּל צָרִיךְ לָשׁוּחַ בְּכוּלָן. מַה טַעַם כָּל עַצְמוֹתַי | תֹּאמַרְנָה יי מִי כָמוֹךָ.

1 - **ב** | אמ'   בשם ר' יהושע בן לוי | **ב** - G א' | **ב**G חוליות | G חליות   2 אדם G אדן   בכולן G בכולם   יי מי כמוך G -

HALAKHAH 2

רִבִּי לֵוִי אָמַר. כְּנֶגֶד שְׁמוֹנָה עָשָׂר אַזְכָּרוֹת שֶׁכָּתוּב בְּהָבוּ לַיְיָ בְּנֵי אֵלִים. אָמַר רִבִּי חוּנָה. אִם יֹאמַר לְךָ אָדָם. שִׁבְעָה עָשָׂר הֵן. אֱמוֹר לוֹ. שֶׁלְּמִינִין כְּבָר קְבָעוּהָ חֲכָמִים בְּיַבְנֶה. הֵתִיב רִבִּי לְעָזָר בֵּירְבִּי יוֹסֵי קוֹמֵי רִבִּי יוֹסֵי. וְהָא כְתִיב אֵל־הַכָּבוֹד הִרְעִים. אָמַר לֵיהּ. וְהָתַנֵּי. כּוֹלֵל שֶׁלְּמִינִים וְשֶׁלְּפוֹשְׁעִים בְּמַכְנִיעַ זֵידִים. שֶׁלְּזְקֵינִים וְשֶׁלְּגֵּרִים בְּמִבְטָח לַצַּדִּיקִים. שֶׁלְּדָוִד בְּבוֹנֶה יְרוּשָׁלַ͏ִם. אִית לָךְ מְסַפְּקָא לְכָל־חָדָא וְחָדָא מִנְּהוֹן.

1 ר׳ לוי אמ׳ | **ב** אמ׳ ר׳ לוי עשר | G עס׳ | **ב** אזכרות | **ב** הזכרות חונה | G חי׳ | 2 אדם G | אדן שבעה עשר הן | **ב** שבע עשרה אינון G שבע עס׳ אמור G אמר שלמינים | G**ב** שלמיניו | G שלמינין קבעוה | G קבעו | 3 לעזר | **ב** G אלעזר יוסי G יוסה (2) | 4 שלמינים G שלמיניי ושלפושעים G ושלפושעין זידים G זידין שלזקינים | **ב** ושלזקינים ושלגרים G ושלגירין לצדיקים G לצדיקיו בבונה | G בבוני | 5 לכל G לכול וחדא | G וחדה מנהון | **ב** מינהון אדכרה G מינהן אזכרה

[88]Rebbi Simon in the name of Rebbi Joshua ben Levi[89]: corresponding to the eighteen bones in the spine since when a person prays he has to bend all of them bowing down. What is the reason? *All my bones shall say, Eternal, who is like You*[90]?

Rebbi Levi[91] said, corresponding to the eighteen Divine Names[92] written in *Give to the Eternal, sons of the mighty*[93]. Rebbi Huna said: If it were said that they are seventeen, tell him the one against sectarians the Sages fixed already at Jabneh[94]. Rebbi Eleazar ben Rebbi Yose objected before Rebbi Yose, but is it not written *the God of Glory thundered*[95]? He said to him: Has it not been stated: "He takes together the one against sectarians and sinners in 'He Who subdues offenders', the one for elders and proselytes in 'Assurance to the righteous', and the one for David in 'He Who builds Jerusalem.'[96]" Then you have enough to have <a Divine Name>[97] for each one of them.

88 Here starts an extensive Genizah text edited by Ginzberg in his *Yerushalmi Fragments*, New York 1909 (G).

89 While the name of R. Joshua ben Levi is missing in G and the parallel text **ב**, in the Babli *Berakhot* 28b the statement is ascribed to the school of R. Joshua ben Levi, whose great authority turns this haggadic statement into halakhic prescription.

90 *Ps.* 35:10.

91 In the Tosephta (*Berakhot* 3:25) this is a tannaitic text together with the later quote about composite benedictions; in the Babli (*loc. cit.*) it is attributed to the school of R. Samuel bar Nahman, and by implication to the latter's teacher, the first generation Amora R. Jonathan.

92 In biblical language, אזכרה is the part of a cereal sacrifice burned on the altar (*Lev.* 2:2). It is best explained from Accadic *zekrun* "pronounced name", since the part to be burned is taken ceremoniously in God's Name. The same explanation applies here; the word is used exclusively to refer to the Name YHWH.

93 *Ps.* 29.

94 Rebbi Huna's question is an attack against all who try to find a reason for the eighteen benedictions by pointing out that in the 500 years between the institution of formalized prayer by the Men of the Great Assembly and the Synhedrion of Rabban Gamliel, the Amidah prayer consisted of only 17 benedictions. Rebbi Huna's answer is that the eighteenth benediction also is an institution of the Synhedrion, the legal successor of the Great Assembly, and, therefore, all eighteen benedictions have the same status.

95 *Ps.* 29:3. This Divine name is not an *askara*.

96 This implies that the benediction containing the curse upon apostates and sectarians (i. e., Christians) was not newly introduced at Jabneh but that it was a modification of an old benediction directed at those who wantonly transgress the commandments of the Torah. Hence, the original number of benedictions instituted by the Great Assembly was 18. The Palestinian version had no separate benediction asking for the return of the Davidic rulers. The Babylonian version has no mention of the Davidic dynasty in the prayer for the rebuilding of Jerusalem; it is retained in today's Yemenite prayerbook. Current Ashkenazic and Sephardic versions combine the Palestinian prayer for Jerusalem and the Davidic dynasty in benediction 14, with the Babylonian one for the Davidic dynasty alone in benediction 15. Hence, Psalm 29 accommodates both the Galilean 18 benedictions based on the number of mentions of the Tetragrammaton, and the 19 of the Babylonian version, based on all invocations of the Deity in the Psalm.

97 Added from G and ב.

(65c line 15) רִבִּי חֲנַנְיָה בְּשֵׁם רִבִּי פִּינְחָס. כְּנֶגֶד שְׁמוֹנָה עָשָׂר פְּעָמִים שֶׁאָבוֹת כְּתוּבִין בַּתּוֹרָה אַבְרָהָם יִצְחָק יַעֲקֹב. אִם יֹאמַר לְךָ אָדָם. תִּשְׁעָה עָשָׂר הֵן. אֱמוֹר לוֹ. וְהִנֵּה יי נִצָּב עָלָיו וַיֹּאמַר לֵית הוּא מִינּוֹן. וְאִם לְךָ אָדָם. שִׁבְעָה עָשָׂר הֵן. אֱמוֹר. וְיִקְרָא בָהֶם שְׁמִי וְשֵׁם אֲבֹתַי אַבְרָהָם וְיִצְחָק מִינּוֹן הוּא.

1 חנניה | ב חנינא עשר | ב עשרה פעמים G פעמין | ב אדן G אדם 2 אדם G אדן | ב עשרה והנה G הנה ויאמר | G - 3 מינון G מן המנין ב מינהון ואם G ואם יומר אדם G אדן עשר | ב עשרה הוא | ב -

רִבִּי שְׁמוּאֵל בַּר נַחְמָן בְּשֵׁם רִבִּי יוֹנָתָן. כְּנֶגֶד שְׁמוֹנָה עָשָׂר צִיווּיִין שֶׁכָּתוּב בְּפָרָשַׁת מִשְׁכָּן שֵׁינִי. אָמַר רִבִּי חִייָה בַּר אָדָא. וּבִלְחוּד מִן וְאִתּוֹ אָהֳלִיאָב בֶּן־אֲחִיסָמָךְ לְמַטֵּה־דָן עַד סוֹפֵיהּ דְּסִיפְרָא.

1 בר G בר' נחמן | ב נחמני יונתן | ב יוחנן עשר | G עשרה ציווין | G ציוויין ב ציווין 2 חייה | ב חייא בר | G בר' אדא | ב ווא ובלחוד | ב ובלבד מן | G מין סופיה | G סופי דסיפרא | G דספרה

Rebbi Hanania in the name of Rebbi Phineas: Corresponding to the eighteen times the Patriarchs are mentioned together in the Torah, Abraham, Isaac, Jacob. If somebody will tell you that there are nineteen, tell him that *Behold, the Eternal was standing on it*[98] is not counted. If somebody will tell you that there are seventeen, tell him that *My name should be called over them, as well the names of my fathers Abraham and Isaac*[99] is counted.

Rebbi Samuel bar Naḥman in the name of Rebbi Jonathan: Corresponding to the eighteen times "commandment" is mentioned in the second description of the Tabernacle[100]. Rebbi Ḥiyya bar Ada said, only from *And with him Aholiab ben Aḥisamakh*[101] to the end of the book.

98 *Gen.* 23:13. In this verse Jacob is not mentioned by name.	the Tabernacle.
99 *Gen.* 48:16. Jacob's name is mentioned implicitly.	101 *Ex.* 38:32. From the start of the section, v. 21, there would be 19 times mention of *the Eternal commanded to Moses.*
100 The description of the actual building of	

(65c line 22) שֶׁבַע שֶׁלְשַׁבָּת מְנַיִין. אָמַר רִבִּי יִצְחָק. כְּנֶגֶד שִׁבְעָה קוֹלוֹת שֶׁכָּתוּב בְּהָבוּ לַיי בְּנֵי אֵלִים. אָמַר רִבִּי יוּדָן עַנְתּוֹנְדְּרַיָּא. כְּנֶגֶד שִׁבְעָה אַזְכָּרוֹת שֶׁכָּתוּב בְּמִזְמוֹר שִׁיר לְיוֹם הַשַׁבָּת:

1 שבע G | שיבע שלשבת G | שלבת מניין G | מניין 2 ענתונדריא G | ענתדריה ב ענתריא | ליום G | שליום

תֵּשַׁע שֶׁלְראֹשׁ הַשָׁנָה מְנַיִין. אָמַר רִבִּי בָּא קַרְתִּיגְנָא כְּנֶגֶד תֵּשַׁע אַזְכָּרוֹת שֶׁכָּתוּב בְּפָרָשַׁת חַנָּה. וְכָתוּב בְּסוֹפָהּ יי יָדִין אַפְסֵי־אָרֶץ.

1 תשע G | תישע מניין G | מניין בא | ב אבא קרתיגנא G | קורטיגנייא ב קרטיגניא תשע G | תיש׳

[102]The seven of Sabbath, from where? Rebbi Isaac said, corresponding to the seven *voices* written in *Give to the Eternal, sons of the mighty*[93]. Rebbi Yudan Antodraya said, corresponding to the seven Divine Names in *Psalm, Song for the Sabbath Day*[103].

Nine of New Year's Day, from where? Rebbi Abba from Carthage said: Corresponding to the nine Divine Names in Hanna's prayer; there it is written at the end: *The Eternal will judge the ends of the earth*[104].

102 These paragraphs about the number of benedictions in the *Amidah* of special days are simply copied from *Berakhot*; they have no relevance here since fasting is forbidden	on Sabbath and holidays. Babli *Berakhot* 29a.
	103 *Ps.* 92.
	104 *1Sam.* 2:10.

(65c line 27) עֶשְׂרִים וְאַרְבַּע שֶׁלְתַּעֲנִיּוֹת מְנַיִין. רִבִּי חֶלְבּוֹ וְרִבִּי שְׁמוּאֵל בַּר נַחְמָן תְּרֵיהוֹן אֲמָרִין. כְּנֶגֶד עֶשְׂרִים וְאַרְבָּעָה פְעָמִים שֶׁכָּתוּב בְּפָרָשַׁת שְׁלֹמֹה רִינָה תְפִילָה תַּחִינָה.

1 עשרים G | עשרין שלתעניות G | שלתענית מניין G | מניין 2 פעמים G | פעמין בפרשת | ב בפרשה של תפילה | ב ותפילה תחינה | ב ותחינה

רִבִּי זְעוּרָה בְּשֵׁם רִבִּי יִרְמְיָה. יָחִיד בְּתַעֲנִית צִיבּוּר צָרִיךְ לְהַזְכִּיר מֵעֵין הַמְאוֹרָע. וְהֵיכָן הוּא אוֹמְרָהּ. בֵּין גּוֹאֵל יִשְׂרָאֵל לְרוֹפֵא חוֹלִים. וּמָה הוּא אוֹמֵר. עֲנֵינוּ יי עֲנֵינוּ בָּעֵת וּבָעוֹנָה [הַזֹּאת] כִּי בְצָרָה גְדוֹלָה אֲנָחְנוּ. וְאַל תַּסְתֵּר פָּנֶיךָ מִמֶּנּוּ וְאַל תִּתְעַלַּם מִתְּחִינָתֵינוּ. כִּי אַתָּה יי אֵל חַנּוּן וְרַחוּם עוֹנֶה בְּעֵת צָרָה פּוֹדֶה וּמַצִּיל בְּכָל־עֵת צוּקָה. וַיִּצְעֲקוּ אֶל־יי בַּצַּר לָהֶם מִמְּצוּקוֹתֵיהֶם יוֹצִיאֵם. בָּרוּךְ אַתָּה יי הָעוֹנֶה בְּעֵת צָרָה. רִבִּי יַנַּאי בֵּירִבִּי יִשְׁמָעֵאל בְּשֵׁם רִבִּי שִׁמְעוֹן בֶּן לָקִישׁ. אֲפִילוּ יָחִיד שֶׁגָּזַר עַל עַצְמוֹ תַּעֲנִית צָרִיךְ לְהַזְכִּיר מֵעֵין הַמְאוֹרָע. וְאֵיכָן הוּא אוֹמְרָהּ. רִבִּי זְעוּרָה בְּשֵׁם רַב חוּנָה. אוֹמְרָהּ כְּלֵילֵי שַׁבָּת וְכְיוֹמוֹ. אָמַר רִבִּי מָנָא. וַאֲנָא דְלָא בְדִיקְתָּהּ אִין כְּהָדָא דְרַב יִרְמְיָה וְאִין כְּהָדָא דְרִבִּי יַנַּאי בֵּירִבִּי יִשְׁמָעֵאל. סָלְקִית לְסִדְרָא וּשְׁמָעִית רַב חוּנָה בְּשֵׁם רַב. אֲפִילוּ יָחִיד שֶׁגָּזַר עַל עַצְמוֹ תַּעֲנִית צָרִיךְ לְהַזְכִּיר מֵעֵין הַמְאוֹרָע. הָתִיב רִבִּי יוֹסֵה. וְהָא מַתְנִיתָה פְּלִיגָא. בְּכָל־יוֹם מִתְפַּלֵּל אָדָם שְׁמוֹנֶה עֶשְׂרֵה וּבְמוֹצָאֵי שַׁבָּת וּבְמוֹצָאֵי יוֹם הַכִּפּוּרִים וּבְמוֹצָאֵי תַעֲנִית צִיבּוּר. מִן מַה דְאָמַר רִבִּי יוֹסֵה. מַתְנִיתָה פְּלִיגָא. הֲוֵי אִיתְּתָבַת בֵּין גּוֹאֵל יִשְׂרָאֵל לְרוֹפֵא חוֹלִים.

1 זעורה | **ב** זעירא ר' | G רב' **ב** רב ציבור | G צבור והיכן | G ואיכן **ב** איכן   2 ומה הוא | G ומהוא **ב** ומהו   3 ואל | G **ב** אל מתחינתינו | G מתחנתינו אל חנון ורחום | G **ב** -   4 צוקה | G וצוקה **ב** מצוקה   5 העונה | **ב** עונה ינאי | G **ב** ינ"י ביר' **ב** בשם ר' בשם | G בשם דבית ר' ינ"י אומרה בשמיע תפילה. ר' יונה בש' ר' שמעון בן לקיש | G ר"ב **ב** רב   6 על עצמו תעניות | **ב** תענית על עצמו ואיכן | **ב** איכן זעורה | **ב** זעירא   7 חונה | G חנינה **ב** הונא אמרה | G אומר **ב** - כלילי שבת | **ב** כלילי שלשבת מנא | **ב** מני ואנא | **ב**G אנא בדיקתה | **ב** בדקתה כהדא | G כהדה דרב | G דר'   8 כהדא | G כהדה ינאי | G ינ"י ביר' ישמעאל | **ב** בשם ר' שמעון ושמעית | G ושמעת   9 יוסה | G יודה **ב** יוסי   10 פליגא | G פליגה אדם מתפלל אדם | G **ב** אדם מתפלל עשרה | G עשרה הכיפורים | G הכפורין   11 ציבור | G צבור דאמ' | G דמר יוסה | **ב** יוסי חווי | G חוי כן **ב** הוה

The twenty-four of fast days, from where? Rebbi Helbo and Rebbi Samuel bar Naḥman both say, corresponding to the twenty-four times that entreaty, prayer, and supplication are mentioned in Solomon's prayer[105].

Rebbi Ze`ira in the name of (Rebbi) <Rav>[106] Jeremiah, a private person has to mention the occasion on a public fast day. Where does he say it? Between "Redeemer of Israel" and "Healer of the sick.[107]" What does he say? "Answer us, Eternal, answer us in this time and season because we are in great trouble, do not hide Your presence from us, do not be oblivious to our supplications, because You, Eternal, will answer in time of trouble, redeem and save in any time of distress. *They cried to the Eternal in their trouble, He led them out from their distress*[108]. Praise to You, Eternal, Answering in times of trouble." Rebbi Yannai ben Rebbi Ismael in the name <of the House of Rebbi Yannai says: In "He Who hears prayer."[109] Rebbi Jonah>[110] in the name of (Rebbi Simeon ben Laqish) <Rav>[111]: Even an individual who decreed a fast day on himself has to mention the occasion. Where does he say it? Rebbi

Ze'ira in the name of Rav Huna: Similar to Friday night and Sabbath day[112]. Rebbi Mana said: I, who did not check whether one follows Rav Jeremiah or Rebbi Yannai the son of Rebbi Ismael, went to the study hall and I heard: "Rav Huna in the name of Rav: Even an individual who decreed a fast day on himself has to mention the occasion." Rebbi Yose objected that a *baraita* disagrees: Every day one prays eighteen benedictions, including the night after Sabbath and the nights after Yom Kippur and after Public Fasts. Since Rebbi Yose said, this *baraita* disagrees, it contradicts the statement: between "Redeemer of Israel" and "Healer of the sick.[113]"

---

105 *IK*. 8. Babli 29a.

106 Since Rebbi Jeremiah was a student of R. Ze'ira, the reading Rav of the parallel sources has to be accepted.

107 Between the Seventh and Eighth benedictions, as a separate benediction.

108 *Ps*. 107:6 conflated with v. 13.

109 The Fifteenth benediction, place of all personal additions to the weekday prayers.

110 Part of the text, added from G, missing here by scribal error because of homeoteleuton.

111 It is difficult to decide between the two readings since it is unusual that a very late Amora should quote directly an Amora of the first or second generation.

112 During every prayer he has to add the special prayer formulated for fast days.

113 Rebbi Mana's argument goes as follows: Since R. Yose stated that the *baraita* contradicts Rav, he takes the *baraita* to mean that a private person always recites 18 benedictions on weekdays, never 19, even on fast days. The additional days are mentioned to point out that insertions for a private person are always accommodated in an existing benediction, never as an additional one, in contrast to the opinion of R. Aqiba who states in *Berkahot* 5:2 that *Havdalah* Saturday nights is a separate benediction. In addition, it is stated that on those days when the additional *Ne`ilah* prayer is recited, the Day of Atonement and fast days for a severe draught, the *Ne`ilah* prayer does not replace the following night's prayer as discussed in Halakhah *Berakhot* 4:1. The Yerushalmi does not address the question what the reader says on a public fast day which is not a fast for rain; the Babli decides that the reader will recite ענינו as a separate benediction between "Redeemer of Israel" and "Healer of the sick." This decision does not go against R. Mani's argument.

(65c line 43) רִבִּי אָחָא בַּר יִצְחָק בְּשֵׁם רִבִּי חוֹנָה רוּבָּה דְּצִיפּוֹרִין. יָחִיד בְּתִשְׁעָה בָּאָב צָרִיךְ לְהַזְכִּיר מֵעֵין הַמְּאוֹרָע. וּמָהוּ אוֹמֵר. רַחֵם יי אֱלֹהֵינוּ בְּרַחֲמֶיךָ הָרַבִּים וּבַחֲסָדֶיךָ הַנֶּאֱמָנִים עָלֵינוּ וְאַל יִשְׂרָאֵל עַמָּךְ וְעַל יְרוּשָׁלַם עִירָךְ וְעַל צִיּוֹן מִשְׁכַּן כְּבוֹדָךְ. וְעַל הָעִיר הָאֲבֵילָה הֶחָרוּסָה הַשּׁוֹמֵמָה הַנְּתוּנָה בְּיַד זָרִים הָרְמוּסָה בְּכַף עָרִיצִים וִיבַלְּעוּהָ לִגְיוֹנוֹת וִיחַלְּלוּהָ עוֹבְדֵי פְסִילִים. כִּי

לְיִשְׂרָאֵל עַמְּךָ נְתַתָּהּ בְּאַהֲבָה לְנַחֲלָה וּלְזֶרַע יְשׁוּרוּן יְרוּשָׁה הוֹרַשְׁתָּהּ. כִּי בָאֵשׁ הֶחֱרַבְתָּהּ וּבָאֵשׁ אַתָּה עָתִיד לִבְנוֹתָהּ. כָּאָמוּר וַאֲנִי אֶהְיֶה־לָּהּ נְאֻם־יי חוֹמַת אֵשׁ סָבִיב וּלְכָבוֹד אֶהְיֶה בְתוֹכָהּ:

1 חונה | ב חייא רובה | בG - | 2 ומהו | G ומהוא ב מהו 3 ישראל עמך | ב עמך ישראל ירושלם G ירושלים ההרוסה | ב והחריבה והחרוסה 4 השוממה | G והשומימה ב והשממה בכף | ב ביד ויבלעוה | ב ויירשוה כי | G - ב ו 5 באהבה לנחלה | בG נחלה החרבתה | ב היצתה אתה | G את 6 לבנותה | S² לנחמה ולכבוד אהיה בתוכה | G -

רִבִּי אֲבָדוֹמָא דְצִיפּוֹרִין בָּעָא קוֹמֵי רִבִּי מָנָא. אֵיכָן הוּא אוֹמְרָהּ. אָמַר לֵיהּ. וַאֲדַיִין אַתְּ לְזוֹ. כֵּן אָמַר רַב יִרְמְיָה בְשֵׁם רַב. כָּל דָּבָר שֶׁהוּא לָבֹא אוֹמְרוֹ בָעֲבוֹדָה. כָּל דָּבָר שֶׁהוּא לְשֶׁעָבַר אוֹמְרוֹ בְהוֹדָיָה. מַתְנִיתָה אָמְרָה כֵן. נוֹתֵן הוֹדָיָה לְשֶׁעָבַר וְצוֹעֵק לֶעָתִיד לָבוֹא:

1 אבדומא | ב אבדימא בעא | G בעה הוא | ב - ליה | ב לו את | ב אין את 2 כן אמר רב ירמיה בשם רב | בG - כל | G וכל 3 בהודייה | G בהודיה ב בהודאה בהותיי' | G ומתניתה ב ומתניתא אמרה | G אמר כן | ב - הודייה | G הודיה ב הודאה לעתיד | G לעתיד

Rebbi Aha bar Isaac in the name of the older Rebbi Huna of Sepphoris: An individual must mention the occasion on the Ninth of Av. What does he say? "Have mercy, Eternal, our God, in Your great mercy and your trusted kindness, towards us, Your people Israel, Your city Jerusalem, Zion the dwelling place of Your glory, and on the mourning, destroyed, and desolate city that is given into the hand of strangers, trampled down by haughty peoples, that was raped by legions and desecrated by idol worshippers, when You had given her to Your people Israel in love as property, and let her be inherited by the seed of Yeshurun, for in fire You destroyed her and in fire You will build her in the future as it has been said: *But I shall be for her, says the Eternal, a wall of fire around, and Glory I shall be in her midst.*"[114]

Rebbi Eudaimon of Sepphoris asked before Rebbi Mana: Where does one say this? He said to him: You still do not understand? So says Rav Jeremiah in the name of Rav: Anything for the future one says in "Service"[115] and anything about the past one says in "Thanksgiving"[116]. The Mishnah says as much[117]: "One gives thanks for the past and cries about the future."

114 *Zach.* 2:9. This is the only talmudic text of this prayer, reproduced in R. Saadia's *siddur*. However all current prayer rites have another text, given by Maimonides.
115 The prayer for the restoration of the Temple service, benediction 16, Babylonian 17.
116 Benediction 17, Babylonian 18. However all known prayer manuals, starting with R. Saadia, treat this text as an alternative for the prayer for Jerusalem, benediction 14.
117 Mishnah *Berakhot* 9:5.

(65c line 55) אֵי זוֹ הִיא שֶׁבַע מֵעֵין שְׁמוֹנֶה עֶשְׂרֵה. רַב אָמַר. סוֹף כָּל־בְּרָכָה וּבְרָכָה. וּשְׁמוּאֵל אָמַר. רֹאשׁ כָּל־בְּרָכָה וּבְרָכָה. אִית תַּנָּיֵי תַנֵּי. שֶׁבַע מֵעֵין שְׁמוֹנֶה עֶשְׂרֵה. אִית תַּנָּיֵי תַנֵּי. שְׁמוֹנֶה עֶשְׂרֵה מֵעֵין שְׁמוֹנֶה עֶשְׂרֵה. מָאן דְּאָמַר. שֶׁבַע מֵעֵין שְׁמוֹנֶה עֶשְׂרֵה מְסַיֵּיעַ לִשְׁמוּאֵל. מָאן דְּאָמַר שְׁמוֹנֶה עֶשְׂרֵה מֵעֵין שְׁמוֹנֶה עֶשְׂרֵה מְסַיֵּיעַ לְרַב. רִבִּי זְעוּרָה שָׁלַח לְרִבִּי נָחוּם גַּבֵּי רִבִּי יַנַּאי בֵּירִבִּי יִשְׁמָעֵאל. אָמַר לֵיהּ. אֵי זוֹ הִיא שֶׁבַע מֵעֵין שְׁמוֹנֶה עֶשְׂרֵה דִּשְׁמוּאֵל. אָמַר לֵיהּ. הֲבִינֵנוּ רְצֵה תְשׁוּבָתֵינוּ סְלַח לָנוּ גוֹאֲלֵינוּ רְפָא חוֹלְיֵינוּ בָּרֵךְ שְׁנוֹתֵינוּ. אָמַר רִבִּי חַגַּיי. אִם הָיוּ יְמוֹת גְּשָׁמִים אוֹמֵר. גִּשְׁמֵי בְרָכָה. אִם הָיוּ טְלָלִים אוֹמֵר. טַלְלֵי בְרָכָה. כִּי מְפוּזָּרִים אַתָּה מְקַבֵּץ וְתוֹעִים עָלֶיךָ לִשְׁפּוֹט וְעַל הָרְשָׁעִים תָּשִׁית יָדֶךָ. וְיִשְׂמְחוּ כָּל־חוֹסֵי בָךְ בְּבִנְיַן עִירָךְ וּבְחִידּוּשׁ בֵּית מִקְדָּשֶׁךָ. כִּי טֶרֶם נִקְרָא אַתָּה תַעֲנֶה. כָּאָמוּר וְהָיָה טֶרֶם־יִקְרָאוּ וַאֲנִי אֶעֱנֶה עוֹד הֵם מְדַבְּרִים וַאֲנִי אֶשְׁמָע׃ בָּרוּךְ יי כִּי־שָׁמַע קוֹל תַּחֲנוּנָי. בָּרוּךְ אַתָּה יְיָ שׁוֹמֵעַ תְּפִילָּה. וְאוֹמֵר שָׁלֹשׁ בְּרָכוֹת רִאשׁוֹנוֹת וְשָׁלֹשׁ בְּרָכוֹת אַחֲרוֹנוֹת.

1 זו | G היא | G הוא ושמואל | G שמואל | 2 עשרה | G עסרה אית | ב ואית | 3 עשרה | G עס' (3) מאן | ב G מן דאמר | ב דמר מסייע | G מסיע מאן | G ומן ב ומאן | 4 עשרה | G עס' (2) זעורה | ב זעורא ינאי | G יניי | 5 זו | G זה - | ב מעין עשרה | G עס' | 6 חוליינו G חליינו ימות גשמים | G גשמין ב גשמים 7 טללי | ב בטללי | 8 הרשעים | G רשעים תשית | G תשוב בבניין | G בבנין ובחידוש | G ובחדוש 10 ברוך ... תחנוני | ב - | ראשונות G הראשונות 11 אחרונות | G האחרונות - | ב ואומר ברוך ...

[118] **What are "seven similar to eighteen"?** Rav says the end of each benediction and Samuel says the start of each benediction. Some formulate "seven similar to eighteen" and some formulate "eighteen similar to eighteen." He who says "seven similar to eighteen" supports Samuel, he who says "eighteen similar to eighteen" supports Rav. Rebbi Ze`ira sent Rebbi Nahum to Rebbi Yannai ben Rebbi Ismael and said to him: What are the "seven similar to eighteen" of Samuel? He said to him: "Give us understanding, have pleasure in our repentance, forgive us, redeem us, heal our sicknesses, bless our years; Rebbi Haggai said, in the rainy season one says: with blessed rains, in the season of dew one says: with blessed dew; for You gather in the dispersed, Yours it is to judge the misguided, put down Your hand on the wicked, but in You may rejoice all who hope for You to rebuild Your city, to renew Your Temple, because before we call You will answer as it is said: *It shall be before they call that I shall answer, they still shall be talking while I will listen*[119]. *Praised be the Eternal, Who certainly hears the voice of my supplications*[120]. Praise to You, Eternal, Who hears prayer." And he says the first three and the last three benedictions.

118 This paragraph is copied from *Berakhot* 4:3 where is its logical place; it has no relation with the topics discussed in *Ta`aniot*. The topic is a shortened form of

the *Amidah* available as private prayer for people who either are ignorant or are inhibited by the circumstances from reciting the entire prayer. The short form certainly is inadmissible if an addition for public or voluntary fast day is required.
119 *Is.* 65:24.
120 *Ps.* 28:6.

(fol. 64d) **משנה ג**: רִבִּי יְהוּדָה אוֹמֵר לֹא הָיָה צָרִיךְ לוֹמַר זִכְרוֹנוֹת וְשׁוֹפָרוֹת אֶלָּא אוֹמֵר תַּחְתֵּיהֶם רָעָב כִּי יִהְיֶה בָאָרֶץ דֶּבֶר כִּי יִהְיֶה וגו'. אֲשֶׁר הָיָה דְבַר ה' אֶל יִרְמְיָהוּ עַל דִּבְרֵי הַבַּצָּרוֹת. וְאוֹמֵר חוֹתְמֵיהֶם:

Mishnah 3: Rebbi Jehudah says, it was not necessary to recite *Zikhronot* and *Shofarot*[74], but he recites in their stead, *if famine will be in the land, if a plague will be in the land*[121], etc. *The Eternal's Word which was to Jeremiah in the matter of droughts*[122]. And he recites their conclusions[123],

121 *1K.* 8:37 ff.
122 *Jer.* 14:1 ff.
123 The final sentence, "He Who heard . . ."

and the following doxology as explained in Mishnaiot 4-10.

(65c line 69) **הלכה ג**: כָּל־הַבְּרָכוֹת אַחַר חִיתוּמֵיהֶן. וְאֵין אוֹמֵר [אַחַר] בְּרָכָה פָּסוּק. הָתִיב רִבִּי יִצְחָק בַּר אֶלְעָזָר קוֹמֵי רִבִּי יוֹסֵה. מִכֵּיוָן דּוּ אָמַר. אַחַר חוֹתְמוֹתֵיהֶן. וְיֹאמַר בְּרָכָה פָּסוּק. אָמְרִין. (חָכָם) [הָכֵין] הוּא הָדֵין (טַלְיָיא) [מְלַיָּא]. דְּהוּא סָבוּר. מָהוּ אַחַר חוֹתְמוֹתֵיהֶן. שֶׁאִם הָיָה עוֹמֵד בַּשַּׁחֲרִית וְהִזְכִּיר שֶׁלְּעַרְבִית וְחָזַר וְחָתַם בְּשֶׁלְּשַׁחֲרִית יָצָא. אָמַר רִבִּי אָחָא. כָּל־הַבְּרָכוֹת מֵעֵין חוֹתְמוֹתֵיהֶן. וְאִילֵּין דְּאָמְרִין אַהֲלֵי וְרוֹנִי יוֹשֶׁבֶת צִיּוֹן כִּי־גָדוֹל בְּקִרְבֵּךְ קְדוֹשׁ יִשְׂרָאֵל: אֵין בּוֹ מִשּׁוּם בְּרָכָה פָּסוּק.

1 חיתומיהן G חותמותיהון ואין | ב אין   2 בר | G ביר' ב בר' אלעזר | G לעזר קומי | ב קומוי מכיון | G מין כיון דו אמר | ב דתימר חותמותיהן | ב חיתומיהן ויאמר | G ויומר   3 חכם | G חכים ב חכימי הוא | ב - הדין | G איין דהוא | G דו סבור | ב סבר מהו | G מהוא   4 - | ב השכח וחזר | G חזר מעין Gב כעין   5 ואילין G ואלין כי גדול בקרבך קדוש ישראל | ב וגו'

[124]All benedictions after their seals; one does not say a verse as [after a] benediction[125]. Rebbi Isaac (bar) <ben Rebbi> Eleazar objected before Rebbi Yose: Because you say after their seals, one does not say a verse as benediction[126]? They said, (that young man is intelligent,) [so is the matter] because he thinks what is the meaning of "after their seals"? It is that when he was standing in the morning prayer and mentioned the text of evening prayers but he caught himself and finished with the text of morning prayers,

then he did his duty¹²⁷. Rebbi Aḥa said, all benedictions in the kind of their seals¹²⁸. But those who say: *Jubilate and sing, inhabitant of Zion, for great is in your midst the Holy One of Israel*¹²⁹ do not violate the rule that no benediction is a verse¹³⁰.

124 This text is from *Berakhot* 1:8 (Notes 281-285, ב). The corrector's addition and changes, given in brackets, are unsupported by the parallel sources and have to be deleted.

125 The "seal" of a longer benediction is the last sentence "Praise to You, Eternal, . ." It is stated that this seal is what makes the benediction valid and it cannot be a Biblical verse.

126 Since the two statements appear together in one *baraita*, there should be a logical connection between them but there seems to be none.

127 "They" are the members of R. Yose's Academy. They do not disagree with the rule which they state, but they note that the *baraita* does not deal with it; its correct interpretation is by R. Aḥa.

About the rule itself, there is disagreement between the Yerushalmi and the parallel Babli, *Berakhot* 12a, where it is stated: "If in the morning one started with 'Creator of light' and ended with 'Making evenings dark', he did not do his duty. If in the evening he starts with 'He Who makes evenings dark' and ends with 'Creator of light', he did not do his duty. But if he started with 'Creator of light' and ended with 'Making evenings dark', he did his duty. The principle is: Everything is determined by the seal." The Babli asserts that if in evening prayers one started out wrongly with the text appropriate for morning prayers then everything is O.K. if only the final doxology is correct. But the Yerushalmi speaks of one "who is standing in morning prayers and mentioned evening", i. e., he started out correctly, forgot himself in the middle, and remembered in time to close with the correct text. The principles of prayer texts were instituted by the Men of the Great Assembly. They determined the contents of the prayers but not, in general, their texts. (For the Amidah, a later Mishnah reports that Rebbi Eliezer holds that one who repeats the same text for more than 30 days cannot really be an honest supplicant). The question is whether, in addition to the contents, the Men of the Great Assembly only determined the "seals" (following the Babli) or also the introductory sentences (following this Yerushalmi, but incompatible with the poetic versions of the daily prayers known from Yerushalmi sources from the Cairo Genizah).

128 The language is difficult. R. Eleazar Askari in his Commentary to *Berakhot* explains that Rebbi Aḥa insists that only the "seal" counts and, therefore, the text preceding the "seal" is unimportant; the text of the seal cannot be a verse. R. Shelomo Cirillo and R. Moshe ben Habib in their Commentaries to *Berakhot* explain, on the contrary, that the seal must fit the text of the benediction just preceding and that this text cannot be a verse. In the Babli (*Pesaḥim*

104a) this principle is spelled out only for Havdalah.
129 *Is.* 12:6.
130 Ezra Fleischer (*Tarbiz* 41, p. 450) has published a Yerushalmi prayer text from the Cairo Genizah which uses this verse in the third benediction of the `Amidah. From what is left of the original Galilean practice it seems clear that the standard text of longer benedictions always ended with a Biblical verse just preceding the "seal". The text here states that the only acceptable place for a Biblical verse is before the "seal". Since the Mishnah prescribes benedictions on fast days whose text is a Biblical verse, what is prohibited is using a verse in the final doxology.

(fol. 64d) **משנה ד**: עַל הָרִאשׁוֹנָה הוּא אוֹמֵר מִי שֶׁעָנָה אֶת אַבְרָהָם אָבִינוּ בְּהַר הַמּוֹרִיָּה הוּא יַעֲנֶה אֶתְכֶם וְיִשְׁמַע בְּקוֹל צַעֲקַתְכֶם בַּיּוֹם הַזֶּה. בָּרוּךְ אַתָּה ה' גּוֹאֵל יִשְׂרָאֵל.

Mishnah 4: On the first he says[131]: "He Who answered our forefather Abraham on Mount Moriah, He may answer you and hear your vociferation today. Praise to You, Eternal, Redeemer of Israel."

131 The first additional benediction (either the text of *Shofarot* without its doxology or the text from *1K.* 8) is followed by the text of the Mishnah, to be answered with "Amen" by the congregation.

(65c line 76) **הלכה ד**: וְלֹא יִצְחָק נִגְאַל. מִכֵּיוָן שֶׁנִּגְאַל יִצְחָק כְּמִי שֶׁנִּגְאֲלוּ כָּל־יִשְׂרָאֵל. רִבִּי בֵּיבַי אַבָּא בְּשֵׁם רִבִּי יוֹחָנָן. אָמַר אַבְרָהָם לִפְנֵי הַקָּדוֹשׁ בָּרוּךְ הוּא. רִבּוֹן הָעוֹלָמִים. גָּלוּי וְיָדוּעַ לְפָנֶיךָ שֶׁבְּשָׁעָה שֶׁאָמַרְתָּ לִי לְהַעֲלוֹת אֶת יִצְחָק בְּנִי הָיָה לִי מַה לְהָשִׁיב וְלוֹמַר לְפָנֶיךָ. אֶתְמוֹל אָמַרְתָּ לִי כִּי בְיִצְחָק יִקָּרֵא לְךָ זָרַע וְעַכְשָׁיו אַתְּ אוֹמֵר וְהַעֲלֵהוּ שָׁם לְעוֹלָה. חַס וְשָׁלוֹם לֹא עָשִׂיתִי כֵן אֶלָּא כָּבַשְׁתִּי אֶת יִצְרִי וְעָשִׂיתִי רְצוֹנָךְ. כֵּן יְהִי רָצוֹן מִלְּפָנֶיךָ יי אֱלֹהָי. שֶׁבְּשָׁעָה שֶׁיִּהְיוּ בָנָיו שֶׁלְּיִצְחָק בָּנַי נִכְנָסִים לִידֵי צָרָה וְאֵין לָהֶם מִי יְלַמֵּד עֲלֵיהֶם סֵנֵיגוֹרְיָא אַתָּה תְהֵא מְלַמֵּד עֲלֵיהֶם סֵנֵיגוֹרְיָא. יי יִרְאֶה. אַתְּ נִזְכַּר לָהֶם עֲקֵידָתוֹ שֶׁלְּיִצְחָק אֲבִיהֶם וּמִתְמַלֵּא עֲלֵיהֶם רַחֲמִים. מַה כְּתִיב בַּתְרֵיהּ. וַיִּשָּׂא אַבְרָהָם אֶת־עֵינָיו וַיַּרְא וְהִנֵּה־אַיִל אַחֵר וגו'. מַהוּ אַחֵר. אָמַר רִבִּי יוּדָה בֵּירְבִּי סִימוֹן. אַחַר כָּל־הַדּוֹרוֹת עֲתִידִין בָּנֶיךָ לֵיאָחֵז בַּעֲוֹנוֹת וּלְהִסְתַּבֵּךְ בְּצָרוֹת וְסוֹפָן לְהִגָּאֵל בְּקַרְנָיו שֶׁלְּאַיִל הַזֶּה. [שֶׁנֶּאֱמַר] וַיי אֱלֹהִים בַּשּׁוֹפָר יִתְקָע וְהָלַךְ בְּסַעֲרוֹת תֵּימָן.

1 מכיון G | אלא מכיון כמי G | כמו אבא G | רובה 2 אברהם G | אבינו אברהם העולמים G | שעולמים 3 בני G | בני על גבי המזבח מה להשיב G | מלהשיב לפניך G | - אמרת G | אמרתה 4 חס G | וחס 5 שבשעה G | בשעה שיהיו G | שיהו בני G | - 6 נכנסים G | נכנסין סניגוריא | G סניגוריה (2) אתה תהא G | את תהי 7 את G | את תהי עקידתו שליצחק אביהם G | עקידת יצחק אביהן עליהם רחמים G | עליהון רחמין מה כת' בתריה G | כת' 8 וגו' | G נאחז בסבך בקרניו מהו G | מהוא אמ' ר' יודה ביר' סימון G | אר' יודן בר שלום אמ' הקב"ה לאבינו אברהם אבר' 9 בעונות G | בעוונות

ולהסתבד G | ונסבכין להיגאל G ליגאל G [שנא'] 10 הדה הוא דכת' G

Halakhah 4: [132]But was not Isaac redeemed[133]? Since Isaac was redeemed it is as if all of Israel was redeemed. Rebbi Bevai Abba[134] in the name of Rebbi Johanan: Abraham said before the Holy One, praise to Him: Master of the worlds, it is open and known before You that when You said to me to sacrifice my son Isaac I could have answered and said before You, yesterday You said to me, *for in Isaac will your descendants be named*[135], and now You are saying, *sacrifice him as elevation offering*[136]. Heaven forbid that I should have done this, to the contrary I suppressed my inclination and did Your will. So may it be Your pleasure, Eternal, my God, that when my son Isaac's descendants will be in trouble and nobody will speak in their defense[137], that You will speak in their defense. *The Eternal will see*[138]. You will remember for them the binding of Isaac and be filled with mercy for them. What is written afterwards? *Abraham lifted his eyes and saw a ram, after*[139], etc. What means "after"? Rebbi Judah ben Rebbi Simon[140] said, after all generations in the future your sons will be gripped by sins and involved in troubles but at the end they will be redeemed by the horns of this ram, [as it is said][141], *and the Eternal, God, will blow the horn and go in Southern storms*[142].

132 Cf. *Gen. rabba* 56(15), *Lev. rabba* 29(8), *Midrash Ps.* 29[1].
133 Since Mt. Moriah is invoked, it was Isaac who was in danger, not Abraham.
134 In G: The Elder R. Bevai.
135 *Gen.* 21:12.
136 *Gen.* 22:2.
137 Greek συνηγορία.

138 *Gen.* 22:14.
139 *Gen.* 22:13.
140 In G: R. Yudan bar Shalom said, the Holy One, praise to Him, said to Abraham: Abraham, after . . .
141 In G: This what is written.
142 *Zach.* 9:14.

(65d line 13) רִבִּי חוּנָה בְשֵׁם רִבִּי חִינְנָה בַּר יִצְחָק. כָּל־אוֹתוֹ הַיּוֹם הָיָה אַבְרָהָם רוֹאֶה אֶת הָאַיִל נֶאֱחָז בָּאִילָן זֶה וְנִיתּוֹר וְיוֹצֵא. נֶאֱחָז בַּחוֹרֶשׁ זֶה וְנִיתּוֹר וְיוֹצֵא. נֶאֱחָז בַּסְּבָךְ זֶה וְנִיתּוֹר וְיוֹצֵא. אָמַר לוֹ הַקָּדוֹשׁ בָּרוּךְ הוּא. אַבְרָהָם. כָּךְ עֲתִידִין בָּנֶיךָ נֶאֱחָזִים בָּעֲוֹנוֹת וּמִסְתַּבְּכִין בַּמַּלְכֻיּוֹת. מִבָּבֶל לְמָדַי. מִמָּדַי לְיָוָן. וּמִיָּוָן לֶאֱדוֹם. אָמַר לְפָנָיו. רִבּוֹן הָעוֹלָמִים. [וְיִהְיֶה] כֵן לְעוֹלָם. אָמַר לֵיהּ. וְסוֹפָן לְהִיגָּאֵל בְּקַרְנָיו שֶׁלָאַיִל הַזֶּה. וַיי אֱלֹהִים בַּשּׁוֹפָר יִתְקָע וְהָלַךְ בְּסַעֲרוֹת תֵּימָן.

Text of G

אָמַר ר' חֲנַנְיָה בְּרִבִּי יִצְחָק. כָּל־אוֹתוֹ הַיּוֹם הָיָה אָבִינוּ אַבְרָהָם רוֹאֶה אֶת הָאַיִל נֶאֱחָז בַּסְּבָךְ הַזֶּה וְנִיתּוֹר וְיוֹצֵא מִסְתַּבֵּךְ בַּחוֹרֶשׁ הַזֶּה וְנִיתּוֹר וְיוֹצֵא. כָּךְ עֲתִידִין בָּנֶיךָ נֶאֱחָזִים וּמִסְתַּבְּכִים

בְּמַלְכֻיּוֹת. אָמַר לְפָנָיו אֲנִ"י. רִבּוֹן הָעוֹלָמִים. וְכֵן לְעוֹלָם. אָמַר לֵיהּ לֹא. וְסוֹפָן לִיגָּאֵל בְּקַרְנָיו שֶׁלְאַיִל הַזֶּה. הֲדָה הִיא דִכְתִיב וַיי' עֲלֵיהֶם יֵרָאֶה.

[143] Rebbi Huna in the name of Rebbi Hinena bar Isaac. This entire day Abraham saw the ram being caught at one tree but freed and leaving, caught in that thicket but freed and leaving, caught in this underbrush but freed and leaving. The Holy One, praise to Him, said to him, Abraham. So in the future will your descendants be caught in sins and become entangled with governments: From Babylon to Media[144], from Media to Greece[145], from Greece to Edom[146]. He said before Him: Master of the worlds, [will this be] so forever? He said to him, at the end they will be redeemed by the horns of this ram: *and the Eternal, God, will blow the horn and go in Southern storms*[142].

Text of G

Rebbi Hanania ben Rebbi Isaac said: This entire day our father Abraham saw the ram being caught in this underbrush but freed and leaving, caught in this thicket but freed and leaving. The Holy One, praise to Him, said to Abraham: Abraham, so in the future your descendants will be caught and entangled with governments. Abraham our forefather said to him, Master of the worlds, will this go on forever? He said to him, no. At the end they will be redeemed by the horns of this ram. This is what is written, *The Eternal will appear over them*[142].

143 Cf. *Lev. rabba* 56(14).
144 The Persian Empire.
145 Alexander's Empire and its successors.
146 The Roman Empire.

(fol. 64d) **משנה ה**: עַל הַשְּׁנִיָּיה הוּא אוֹמֵר מִי שֶׁעָנָה אֶת אֲבוֹתֵינוּ עַל יַם סוּף הוּא יַעֲנֶה אֶתְכֶם וְיִשְׁמַע בְּקוֹל צַעֲקַתְכֶם הַיּוֹם הַזֶּה. בָּרוּךְ אַתָּה ה' זוֹכֵר הַנִּשְׁכָּחוֹת.

Mishnah 5: On the second he says[147]: "He Who answered our forefathers on the Reed Sea, He may answer you and hear your vociferation today. Praise to You, Eternal, Who remembers the forgotten.[148]"

147 The second additional benediction, with doxology appropriate for a recitation of *Zikhronot*.
148 Since Israel was like forgotten during the time of servitude in Egypt.

(65d line 20) **הלכה ה:** אַרְבַּע כִּיתִּים נַעֲשׂוּ אֲבוֹתֵינוּ עַל הַיָּם. אַחַת אוֹמֶרֶת. נְפוֹל לַיָּם. וְאַחַת אוֹמֶרֶת. נַחֲזוֹר לְמִצְרַיִם. וְאַחַת אוֹמֶרֶת. נַעֲשֶׂה עִמָּהֶן מִלְחָמָה. וְאַחַת אוֹמֶרֶת. נִצְוַוח כְּנֶגְדָּן. זוֹ שֶׁאָמְרָה. נְפוֹל לַיָּם. אָמַר לָהֶן מֹשֶׁה. הִתְיַצְּבוּ וּרְאוּ אֶת־יְשׁוּעַת יי וגו'. וְזוֹ שֶׁאָמְרָה. נַחֲזוֹר לְמִצְרַיִם. אָמַר לָהֶן מֹשֶׁה. כִּי אֲשֶׁר רְאִיתֶם אֶת־מִצְרַיִם הַיּוֹם הַזֶּה וגו'. וְזוֹ שֶׁאָמְרָה. נַעֲשֶׂה עִמָּהֶן מִלְחָמָה. אָמַר לָהֶן מֹשֶׁה. יי יִלָּחֵם לָכֶם. וְזוֹ שֶׁאָמְרָה. נִצְוַוח כְּנֶגְדָּן. אָמַר לָהֶן מֹשֶׁה. וְאַתֶּם תַּחֲרִישׁוּן:

1 כיתים G | כיתות נפול G ניפול | נפול G | 3 נפול G ניפול | וגו' G התייצבו G התיצבו | אשר יעשה לכם היום
4 הזה וגו' | לא תוספו

Halakhah 5: [149]Our forefathers formed four factions on the Sea. One said, let us fall into the Sea. And another said, let us return to Egypt. And another said, let us fight with them. And another said, let us shout against them. To the one who said, let us fall into the Sea, Moses said, *stay firm and see the help of the Eternal*[150], etc. And to the one who said, let us return to Egypt, Moses said, *for as you are seeing Egypt today*[150], etc. And to the one who said, l let us fight with them, Moses said, *the Eternal will fight for you*[151]. And to the one who said, let us shout against them, Moses said, *and you be silent*[151].

149 *Mekhilta dR. Ismael Bešallaḥ* (ed. Horovitz-Rabin p. 96); *dR. Simeon ben Iohai* 14:13 (ed. Epstein-Melamed p. 56). *Targum Pseudo-Jonathan* and *Fragmentary*

Targum Ex. 14:13.
150 *Ex.* 14:13.
151 *Ex.* 14:14.

(fol. 64d) **משנה ו:** עַל הַשְּׁלִישִׁית הוּא אוֹמֵר מִי שֶׁעָנָה אֶת יְהוֹשֻׁעַ בַּגִּלְגָּל הוּא יַעֲנֶה אֶתְכֶם וְיִשְׁמַע בְּקוֹל צַעֲקַתְכֶם הַיּוֹם הַזֶּה. בָּרוּךְ אַתָּה ה' שׁוֹמֵעַ תְּרוּעָה.

Mishnah 6: On the third he says[147]: "He Who answered Joshua at Gilgal He may answer you and hear your vociferation today. Praise to You, Eternal, Who hears the sound of the horn.

(65d line 27) **הלכה ו:** רִבִּי שִׁמְעוֹן בֶּן לָקִישׁ בְּשֵׁם רִבִּי יַנַּאי. שִׁיתּוּף הַקָּדוֹשׁ בָּרוּךְ הוּא שְׁמוֹ הַגָּדוֹל בְּיִשְׂרָאֵל. לְמֶלֶךְ שֶׁהָיָה לוֹ מַפְתֵּחַ שֶׁלְּפַלְמֶנְטָרִין קְטַנָּה. אָמַר הַמֶּלֶךְ. אִם אֲנִי מְנִיחָהּ כְּמוֹת שֶׁהִיא אֲבִידָה הִיא. אֶלָּא הֲרֵינִי עוֹשֶׂה לָהּ שַׁלְשֶׁלֶת. שֶׁאִם אָבְדָה. הַשַּׁלְשֶׁלֶת תְּהֵא מוֹכַחַת עָלֶיהָ. כָּךְ אָמַר הַקָּדוֹשׁ בָּרוּךְ הוּא. אִם מֵנִיחַ אֲנִי אֶת יִשְׂרָאֵל כְּמוֹת שֶׁהֵם נִבְלָעִין הֵן בֵּין הָאוּמוֹת. אֶלָּא הֲרֵי אֲנִי מְשַׁתֵּף שְׁמִי הַגָּדוֹל בָּהֶם וְהֵן חַיִּים. מַה טַעַם. וְיִשְׁמְעוּ הַכְּנַעֲנִי וְכָל יֹשְׁבֵי

הָאָרֶץ וְנָסַבּוּ עָלֵינוּ וְהִכְרִיתוּ אֶת־שְׁמֵינוּ מִן־הָאָרֶץ וּמַה־תַּעֲשֵׂה לְשִׁמְךָ הַגָּדוֹל׃ שֶׁהוּא מְשׁוּתָּף בָּנוּ. [מִיָּד] וַיֹּאמֶר יי אֶל־יְהוֹשֻׁעַ קוּם לָךְ. קֶם לָךְ הַהוּא דַּאֲדַכַּרְתְּ.

1 ינאי G | ייני 2 הגדול G | - G | 3 כמות G | אני כמות הריני G | הרי אני שלשלת G | שלשילת שאם G | ואם השלשלת תהא G | תהא השלשילת 4 שהם G | שהן בין G | בן 5 האומות G אומות העולם שמי G | את שמי בהם G | בהן חיים G | חייו מה טע' G | הדה הוא דכ' הכנעני G הכנענים 7 [מִיָּד] | SG -

רְבִּי יַנַּאי זְעֵירָא בְּשֵׁם אֲבָהָתֵיהּ. כָּל־מִי שֶׁאֵינוֹ כָשֵׁר כִּיהוֹשֻׁעַ שֶׁאִם יִפּוֹל עַל פָּנָיו וְיֹאמַר לוֹ הַקָּדוֹשׁ בָּרוּךְ הוּא קוּם לָךְ. אַל יִפּוֹל. {וּ}בִלְבַד יָחִיד עַל הַצִּיבּוּר.

1 ינאי זעירא G | ינני זעורה כיהושע G | כיהושוע 2 יפול G | יפל

Halakhah 6: Rebbi Simeon ben Laqish in the name of Rebbi Yannai: The Holy One, praise to Him, associated His great Name with Israel. {A parable} of a king who had the small key of a jewelry box[152]. The king said, if I leave it as it is, it is apt to be lost. Therefore I shall put in on a chain. Then if it were lost the key would prove where it is. So the Holy One, praise to Him, said, if I leave Israel as they are, they would be absorbed by the nations. Therefore I shall associate My great Name with them and they will survive. What is the reason? *The Canaanites and all inhabitants of the Land will hear, and encircle us, and eradicate our Name from the Land; then what would You do for Your great Name*[153]*?* [Immediately][154], *the Eternal said to Joshua, get up*[155]. Rise for what You mentioned.

The younger Rebbi Yannai in the name of his ancestors: Anybody who is not qualified like Joshua that in case he falls on his face the Eternal, praise to Him, will tell him, "get up", should not fall down. This applies to a single person {praying for} the community[156].

152 Explained as Greek διπλωματάριον.
153 *Jos.* 7:9.
154 Corrector's addition, to be deleted.
155 *Jos.* 7:10.
156 This paragraph belongs to the rules of prayer. On all days (except those of festive character) after the main *Amidah* said standing there follows a private penitentiary prayer said first falling down and then sitting up. Since prostration was part of the Temple service, one has to be careful not to imitate the details of Temple prostration. In addition, it is stated here that in contrast to the public Temple service, this prayer has to be private. It is authorized as public ceremony only for a genuine holy man praying for a community in distress. Since it is presumptuous for anybody to declare himself a holy man, the statement has to be read as a general prohibition to make the prostration into a public act. Babli *Megillah* 22b (in the name of R. Eleazar).

משנה ז: (65d line 37) עַל הָרְבִיעִית הוּא אוֹמֵר מִי שֶׁעָנָה אֶת שְׁמוּאֵל בַּמִּצְפָּה הוּא יַעֲנֶה אֶתְכֶם וְיִשְׁמַע בְּקוֹל צַעֲקַתְכֶם הַיּוֹם הַזֶּה. בָּרוּךְ אַתָּה ה' שׁוֹמֵעַ צְעָקָה.

Mishnah 7: On the fourth he says[147]: "He Who answered Samuel at Mispah may answer you and hear your vociferation today. Praise to You, Eternal, Who hears vociferation."

הלכה ז: (65d line 37) כָּתוּב וַיִּקָּבְצוּ הַמִּצְפָּתָה וַיִּשְׁאֲבוּ־מַיִם וַיִּשְׁפְּכוּ | לִפְנֵי יְיָ. וְכִי מַיִם שָׁפְכוּ. אֶלָּא מְלַמֵּד שֶׁשָּׁפְכוּ אֶת לִבָּם כַּמָּיִם. (וַיֹּאמְרוּ שָׁם) [וַיֹּאמֶר שְׁמוּאֵל] חָטָאנוּ לַיְיָ אָמַר רִבִּי שְׁמוּאֵל בַּר רַב יִצְחָק. לָבַשׁ שְׁמוּאֵל חֲלוּקָן שֶׁלְּכָל־יִשְׂרָאֵל. אָמַר לְפָנָיו. רִבּוֹן הָעוֹלָמִים. כְּלוּם אַתְּ דָּן אֶת הָאָדָם אֶלָּא עַל שֶׁהוּא אוֹמֵר לְפָנֶיךָ. לֹא חָטָאתִי. הִנְנִי נִשְׁפָּט אוֹתָךְ עַל־אוֹמְרֵךְ לֹא חָטָאתִי. וְאֵלּוּ אוֹמְרִין לְפָנֶיךָ חָטָאנוּ.

2 לבם | G ליבן   3 בר | G בר' ר' אמ' | G ואמ' העולמים | G העולמין   4 האדם | G האדן לפניך | G - הנני | G לא הנני   5 לפניך | G -

Halakhah 7: It is written[157]: *They assembled at Mispah, drew water, and poured it out before the Eternal.* Did they pour out water? But it teaches that they poured out their heart like water[158]. *(They said there)* [Samuel said] *we sinned before the Eternal*[159]. Rebbi Samuel bar Rav Isaac said, Samuel wore the robe of all of Israel[160]. He said before Him: Master of the worlds, do You not judge a person only if he says before You, "I did not sin"? *I shall sit in judgment over you because you said, I did not sin*[161]. But those said before You "we sinned".

157 1S. 7:6.

158 Since water libations are authorized only in the central Sanctuary on Tabernacles, this pouring out cannot refer to a sacral act. The explanation given here is found in *Targum Jonathan ad loc.*, *Midrash Sam.* 13[1], *Midrash Psalms* add. 119:77; quoted by Rashi *ad loc.* This has to be the original meaning of the verse, as noted by S. R. Driver (*Notes on the Hebrew Text and the Topography of the Books of Samuel*², Oxford 1913) following A. B. Ehrlich, (*Randglossen zur Hebräischen Bibel*, vol. 3): "LXX add ארצה, perhaps rightly: the water was poured out not as a libation (for which יִסְכוּ would have been said), but probably as a symbolic act implying a complete separation from sin: sin was to be cast away as water poured out upon the earth (2S. 14:4)."

159 The (scribe's text) is the MT; [the corrector's] is unsupported.

160 The verse does not mention any prayer of Samuel at this occasion; one has to explain why the Mishnah refers to Samuel and not the entire people. Wearing the robe of all of Israel means arguing for all of Israel.

161 *Jer.* 2:35.

(fol. 64d) **משנה ח**: עַל הַחֲמִישִׁית הוּא אוֹמֵר מִי שֶׁעָנָה אֶת אֵלִיָּהוּ בְּהַר הַכַּרְמֶל הוּא יַעֲנֶה אֶתְכֶם וְיִשְׁמַע בְּקוֹל צַעֲקַתְכֶם הַיּוֹם הַזֶּה. בָּרוּךְ אַתָּה ה' שׁוֹמֵעַ תְּפִילָה.

Mishnah 8: On the fifth he says[147]: "He Who answered Elijah on Mount Carmel may answer you and hear your vociferation today. Praise to You, Eternal, Who hears prayer.

(65d line 43) **הלכה ח**: כָּתוּב וַיְהִי | בַּעֲלוֹת הַמִּנְחָה וַיִּגַּשׁ אֵלִיָּהוּ הַנָּבִיא וַיֹּאמַר֘ יְיָ אֱלֹהֵ֣י אַבְרָהָם֘ יִצְחָק וְיִשְׂרָאֵל הַיּוֹם יִוָּדַע וגו'. וְאֵלִיָּהוּ מַקְרִיב בִּשְׁעַת אִיסּוּר הַבָּמוֹת. אָמַר רְבִּי שְׂמְלַאי. דִּיבִּירָא אָמַר לֵיהּ. וּבִדְבָרְךָ עָשִׂיתִי. וּבְדִיבּוּרְךָ עָשִׂיתִי. עֲנֵנִי יְיָ עֲנֵנִי. עֲנֵינִי בִּזְכוּתִי. עֲנֵינִי בִּזְכוּת תַּלְמִידִי.

1 המנחה G | המזבחה יי ... וישראל G | וגו'   2 היום יוודע G | וגו' עוד היום יודע כי אתה אלדים בישראל ואני עבדך הבמות G | במות דיבירא G | דבירה   3 ובדברך G | בדבריך ובדיבורך G | בדבירך   תלמידי G | תלמידים

Halakhah 8: It is written[162]: *At the approach of the afternoon sacrifice, Elijah the prophet stepped up and said, Eternal, God of Abraham, Isaac, and Israel, today may it be known <that You are God in Israel and I am Your servant.>*[163] And Elijah sacrifices when local altars are forbidden[164]? Rebbi Simlai said, the Word He said to him[165]: *I acted on Your saying.* I acted following Your Word. *Answer me, Eternal, Answer me*[166]. Answer me for my merit, answer me for the merit of my student <the students.>[167]

162 *1K.* 18:36.
163 Added from G.
164 Since the Temple was already built, all other altars became illegitimate. This doctrine was certainly held by the author of the books of Kings who nevertheless reports favorably on Elijah's action in repairing an abandoned High Place dedicated to the Eternal.
165 One must assume that he acted on direct Divine command.
166 *1K.* 18:37. Why a double invocation?
167 The reading of G, "students", is preferable since the singular would have to refer to Elisha who at that moment was not Elijah's student.

(fol. 64d) **משנה ט**: עַל הַשִּׁשִּׁית הוּא אוֹמֵר מִי שֶׁעָנָה אֶת יוֹנָה מִמְּעֵי הַדָּגָה הוּא יַעֲנֶה אֶתְכֶם וְיִשְׁמַע בְּקוֹל צַעֲקַתְכֶם הַיּוֹם הַזֶּה. בָּרוּךְ אַתָּה ה' הָעוֹנֶה בְּעֵת צָרָה.

Mishnah 9: On the sixth he says[147]: "He Who answered Jonah in the belly of the fish may answer you and hear your vociferation today. Praise to You, Eternal, Who answers in time of trouble.

(65d line 47) **הלכה ט**: כָּתוּב וַיֹּאמֶר קָרָאתִי מִצָּרָה לִי אֶל־יי וַיַּעֲנֵנִי. לָא צוּרְכָא דְּלָא דָוִד וּשְׁלֹמֹה וְאַחַר כָּךְ אֵלִיָּהוּ וְיוֹנָה. אֶלָּא בִּשְׁבִיל לַחְתּוֹם בִּמְרַחֵם עַל הָאָרֶץ.

1 אל G | ואל - | G וגו' | צורכא G | צורכה G | דוד G | דויד

Halakhah 9: It is written[168]: *He said, I called on the Eternal in my trouble and he answered me.* Would not David and Solomon have to precede Elijah and Jonah[169]? Only to conclude with "Who shows mercy for the Land."

168 *Jon.* 2:3. The verse referred to in the Mishnah.
169 Since the next Mishnah refers to David and Solomon, the sequence Abraham, Exodus, Joshua, Samuel, Elijah, Jonah, David and Solomon, is not chronological.

(fol. 64d) **משנה י**: עַל הַשְּׁבִיעִית הוּא אוֹמֵר מִי שֶׁעָנָה אֶת דָּוִד וְאֶת שְׁלֹמֹה בְּנוֹ בִּירוּשָׁלַיִם הוּא יַעֲנֶה אֶתְכֶם וְיִשְׁמַע בְּקוֹל צַעֲקַתְכֶם הַיּוֹם הַזֶּה. בָּרוּךְ אַתָּה ה' הַמְרַחֵם עַל הָאָרֶץ.

Mishnah 10: On the seventh he says[147]: "He Who answered David and Solomon in Jerusalem may answer you and hear your vociferation today. Praise to You, Eternal, Who shows mercy on the Land.

(65d line 49) **הלכה י**: עַל הַשְּׁבִיעִית. מִשּׁוּם סוּמָכוֹס אָמְרוּ. בָּרוּךְ מַשְׁפִּיל רָמִים. נִיחָא שְׁלֹמֹה. דִּכְתִיב בָּנֹה בָנִיתִי בֵּית זְבוּל לָךְ. דָּוִד לָמָּה. עַל יְדֵי שֶׁבִּיקֵּשׁ לַעֲמוֹד עַל מִנְיָנָן שֶׁלְּיִשְׂרָאֵל. אָמַר רִבִּי אַבָּהוּ כָּתוּב בְּקָרְאִי עֲנֵנִי | אֱלֹהֵי צִדְקִי בַּצַּר הִרְחַבְתָּ לִי. אָמַר דָּוִד לִפְנֵי הַקָּדוֹשׁ בָּרוּךְ הוּא. רִבּוֹן הָעוֹלָמִים. כָּל־צָרָה שֶׁהָיִיתִי נִכְנַס לָהּ אַתָּה הָיִיתָ מַרְחִיבָהּ לִי. נִכְנַסְתִּי לְצָרָתָהּ שֶׁלְּבַת שֶׁבַע וְנָתַתָּ לִי אֶת שְׁלֹמֹה. נִכְנַסְתִּי לְצָרָתָן שֶׁלְּיִשְׂרָאֵל וְנָתַתָּ לִי אֶת בֵּית הַמִּקְדָּשׁ.

1 משום G | משם G | סומכוס G | סומכס רמים G | רמין 2 לך G | לך וגו' | דוד G | דויד על ידי G | אלא מניינן G | מנינן 3 אבהו G | אבוהו בקראי G | בקוראי אלהי G | אלודי בצר הרחבת לי G | וגו' | דוד G | דויד 4 כל G | בכל לה G | בה לצרתה G | לצרתה 5 ונתת G | ונתתה נכנסתי G | ניכנסתי לצרתן G | בצרתן - | G הדה הוא דכת' ויאמר דויד זה הוא בית אלודים וזה מזבח לעולה לישראל

Halakhah 10: On the seventh? In the name of Symmachos they said, "praise to Him who humiliates the haughty.[170]" One understands Solomon as it is written[171]: *I was able to build a dwelling house for You*; why David? Rebbi Abbahu said, it is written[172]: *When I am calling, answer me, my true God; in straights You widened for me.* David said before the Holy One, praise to Him: Master of the worlds, in any straights which I was entering into[173] You widened for me. I entered the straights of Bat-Sheva and You gave me Solomon. I entered the troubles of Israel and You gave me the Temple.

¹⁷⁴<This is what is written¹⁷⁵: *David said, this is the Temple and this is the altar for Israel's elevation offerings.*>

170 Since there are only six additional benedictions, what is the seventh? The answer is given in Tosephta 1:10 which here is quoted only in part: "The seventh, Symmachos they said, "praise to Him who humiliates the haughty," this is the benediction about sectarians; i. e., a modified conclusion of one of the permanent benedictions; cf. Note 95. In the Babli 16b the modified daily benediction is the seventh, the prayer for redemption.

171 *1K.* 8:3.
172 *Ps.* 4:2.
173 Any trouble which he caused for himself, as the affair of Batseba and the census against which he was warned. The census resulted in David's buying of the Temple Mount, Arawna's threshing floor, as building plot for the Temple.
174 Added from G.
175 *1Chr.* 22:1.

(fol. 64d) **משנה יא:** מַעֲשֶׂה בִימֵי רַבִּי חֲלַפְתָּא וְרַבִּי חֲנַנְיָה בֶן תְּרַדְיוֹן שֶׁעָבַר אֶחָד לִפְנֵי הַתֵּבָה וְגָמַר אֶת כָּל־הַבְּרָכָה וְעָנוּ אַחֲרָיו אָמֵן. תִּקְעוּ הַכֹּהֲנִים תָּקָעוּ. מִי שֶׁעָנָה אֶת אַבְרָהָם אָבִינוּ בְּהַר הַמּוֹרִיָּה הוּא יַעֲנֶה אֶתְכֶם וְיִשְׁמַע בְּקוֹל צַעֲקַתְכֶם הַיּוֹם הַזֶּה. הָרִיעוּ בְּנֵי אַהֲרֹן הָרִיעוּ. מִי שֶׁעָנָה אֶת אֲבוֹתֵיכֶם עַל יַם סוּף הוּא יַעֲנֶה אֶתְכֶם וְיִשְׁמַע בְּקוֹל צַעֲקַתְכֶם הַיּוֹם הַזֶּה. וּכְשֶׁבָּא דָבָר אֵצֶל חֲכָמִים אָמְרוּ לֹא הָיוּ נוֹהֲגִין כֵּן אֶלָּא בְשַׁעַר הַמִּזְרָח.

Mishnah 11: It happened in the days of Rebbi Ḥalafta and Rebbi Ḥanania ben Teradion that somebody stood before the Ark¹⁷⁶ and finished the entire benediction and they answered after him Amen¹⁷⁷. "Blow, Cohanim", they blew. "He Who answered our forefather Abraham on Mount Moriah, He may answer you and hear your vociferation today." "Treble, Cohanim", they trebled. "He Who answered our forefathers on the Reed Sea, He may answer you and hear your vociferation today." When the case came before the Sages they said, this we only used to do at the Eastern gate¹⁷⁸.

176 The reader in the synagogue service
177 This also is the text of Maimonides's autograph Mishnah. In the Babli one reads: They did not answer Amen.
178 In the Babli one reads: At the Eastern gate on the Temple Mount. Maimonides reads: At the Eastern gates, and he explains that there were synagogue services both at the Eastern entrance to the Temple and the Eastern entrance to the Temple Mount.

The way it is described in the Yerushalmi Mishnah, the procedure was a hybrid between regular synagogue service, where every benediction by the reader is answered by "Amen", and Temple service where "Amen" never was used, and the Temple service where Cohanim blew trumpets and horns in straight or modulated sounds to accompany every public action. (According to the Babli 16b the order to the Cohanim was given not by the reader but by the beadle.) The objecting Sages decided that proceedings used only on the Temple Mount never should be imitated at other places.

(65d line 56) **הלכה יא**: תַּנֵּי: לֹא הָיוּ עוֹנִין אָמֵן בְּבֵית הַמִּקְדָּשׁ. וּמָה הָיוּ אוֹמְרִים. בָּרוּךְ שֵׁם כְּבוֹד מַלְכוּתוֹ לְעוֹלָם וָעֶד. וּמְנַיִין שֶׁלֹּא הָיוּ עוֹנִין אָמֵן בַּמִּקְדָּשׁ. תַּלְמוּד לוֹמַר קוּמוּ בָּרְכוּ אֶת־יְיָ אֱלֹהֵיכֶם מִן־הָעוֹלָם עַד־הָעוֹלָם. וּמְנַיִין עַל כָּל־בְּרָכָה וּבְרָכָה. תַּלְמוּד לוֹמַר וּמְרוֹמַם עַל־כָּל־בְּרָכָה וּתְהִלָּה:

1 עונין | G עונים   2 ומניין | G ומנין | במקדש | G בבית המקדש ת״ל | G - ברכו | G וברכו   5 אלהיכם | G אלודיכם   ומניין | G ומנין | - | G ויברכו שם כבודך

Halakhah 11: It was stated: "One does not answer 'Amen' in the Temple. What did they say? 'Praised be the glory of His Kingdom forever and ever.' And from where that one does not answer 'Amen' in the Temple? The verse says[179], *Arise, praise the Eternal, your God, forever and ever.* From where for every single benediction? The verse says, *and exalted over all praise and glory.*[180]"

179 *Neh.* 9:5.
180 Tosephta 1:11. Babli 16b, *Berakhot* 63a, *Sota* 40b; Yerushalmi *Berakhot* 9:7 (Notes 278-280).

(fol. 65a) **משנה יב**: שָׁלֹשׁ תַּעֲנִיּוֹת הָרִאשׁוֹנוֹת אַנְשֵׁי מִשְׁמָר מִתְעַנִּין וְלֹא מַשְׁלִימִין וְאַנְשֵׁי בֵית אָב לֹא הָיוּ מִתְעַנִּין. שָׁלֹשׁ שְׁנִיּוֹת אַנְשֵׁי מִשְׁמָר מִתְעַנִּין וּמַשְׁלִימִין וְאַנְשֵׁי בֵית אָב מִתְעַנִּין וְלֹא מַשְׁלִימִין. שֶׁבַע אַחֲרוֹנוֹת אֵילוּ וְאֵילוּ מִתְעַנִּין וּמַשְׁלִימִין, דִּבְרֵי רַבִּי יְהוֹשֻׁעַ. וַחֲכָמִים אוֹמְרִים שָׁלֹשׁ תַּעֲנִיּוֹת הָרִאשׁוֹנוֹת אֵילוּ וְאֵילוּ לֹא הָיוּ מִתְעַנִּין. שָׁלֹשׁ שְׁנִיּוֹת אַנְשֵׁי מִשְׁמָר מִתְעַנִּין וְלֹא מַשְׁלִימִין וְאַנְשֵׁי בֵית אָב לֹא הָיוּ מִתְעַנִּין. וְשֶׁבַע הָאַחֲרוֹנוֹת אַנְשֵׁי מִשְׁמָר מִתְעַנִּין וּמַשְׁלִימִין וְאַנְשֵׁי בֵית אָב מִתְעַנִּין וְלֹא מַשְׁלִימִין:

משנה יג: אַנְשֵׁי מִשְׁמָר מוּתָּרִים לִשְׁתּוֹת יַיִן בַּלֵּילוֹת אֲבָל לֹא בַיָּמִים. וְאַנְשֵׁי בֵית אָב לֹא בַיּוֹם וְלֹא בַלַּיְלָה. אַנְשֵׁי מִשְׁמָר וְאַנְשֵׁי מַעֲמָד אֲסוּרִין מִלְּסַפֵּר וּמִלְּכַבֵּס וּבַחֲמִישִׁי מוּתָּרִין מִפְּנֵי כְבוֹד הַשַּׁבָּת:

Mishnah 12: On the first three fast days, the people of the watch[181] fast but do not finish, but the people of the clan[182] do not fast. On the second three the people of the watch fast and finish, but the people of the clan fast and did not finish. On the last seven both fast and finish, the words of Rebbi Joshua. But the Sages say, on the first three fast days neither of them did fast. On the second three the people of the watch fast but do not finish, but the people of the clan do not fast. On the last seven the people of the watch fast and finish, but the people of the clan fast and do not finish.

Mishnah 13: The people of the watch are permitted to drink wine during nights but not during days[183]. The people of the clan neither by day nor by night. The people of the watch and those of the bystanders[184] are forbidden to shave and to wash their garments, but on Thursday they are permitted because of the honor of the Sabbath.

181 The priests were divided into 24 "watches", *1Chr.* 24. Each "watch" was serving in the Temple for one week, from the *musaf* sacrifice of the Sabbath to the morning sacrifice of the following Sabbath.

182 The watch was divided into seven clans; each of the clans was serving for one day of the week. However, if the members of the clan were too few to complete all required service, they could ask other members of the watch to come and help. Therefore the members of the clan whose day of work is the fast day cannot be ask to finish a fast since rabbinic fast days may not impinge on the biblically ordained Temple service. The remaining members of the watch who are on stand-by may be asked to fast as long as they are not called up for actual duty.

183 Priests on duty are forbidden wine and any intoxicating drink, *Lev.* 10:8-11. The priests on stand-by may drink in the evening since by morning the effects of the wine will have disappeared. The members of the clan who during the night also are occupied in Temple service, either on watch or to dispose of the remainders of the sacrifices of the previous day, may not drink alcohol during the entire period of their actual duty. Obviously this Mishnah spells out rules for the entire year, independent of fast days.

184 The Non-priests standing by at the time of offering of the public sacrifices as representatives of this public (Mishnah 4:2). In practice these are delegates of the district from which the watch serving during the week was drawn. They are forced to appear for duty in clean garments and well groomed by being forbidden these activities during their week of duty.

הלכה יב: (65d line 60) מִפְּנֵי מָה אַנְשֵׁי מַעֲמָד מוּתָּרִין לִשְׁתּוֹת מַיִם בַּלֵּילוֹת אֲבָל לֹא בַיָּמִים. שֶׁאִם תִּכְבַּד הָעֲבוֹדָה אַל אַנְשֵׁי מִשְׁמָר יִצְטָרְפוּ אַנְשֵׁי מַעֲמָד עִמָּהֶן. אַנְשֵׁי בֵית אָב לֹא בַיּוֹם וְלֹא בַלַּיְלָה. שֶׁהֵן תְּדִירִין בָּעֲבוֹדָה.

1 מעמד | G משמר   מים | G יין   2 משמר | G מעמד   יצטרפו | G יסטרפו   מעמד | G משמר

Halakhah 12: Why are the bystanders <men of the watch> permitted to drink water <wine> during the night but not during the day? For if the service would be too much for the men of the watch <bystanders> the bystanders <men of the watch> would join them[185]. "The people of the clan neither by day nor by night," since they are permanently in service[183].

185 The scribe's text clearly is completely off; the text of G has one major defect. The correct text obviously has to read: "Why are the men of the watch permitted to drink wine during the night but not during the day? For if the service would be too much for the men of the clan the men of the watch would join them."

(65d line 63) אַנְשֵׁי מִשְׁמָר וְאַנְשֵׁי מַעֲמָד אֲסוּרִין מִלְסַפֵּר וּמִלְכַבֵּס. בַּחֲמִישִׁי מוּתָּרִין מִפְּנֵי כְבוֹד הַשַּׁבָּת: הָא שְׁאָר כָּל־הַיָּמִים אֲסוּרִין. רִבִּי יוֹסֵה רִבִּי אַבָּהוּ בְשֵׁם רִבִּי יוֹחָנָן רִבִּי אָבוּן רִבִּי יָסָא בְשֵׁם חִזְקִיָּה. גָּזְרוּ עֲלֵיהֶן שֶׁלֹּא יִיכָּנְסוּ לְשַׁבָּתָן מְנוּוָלִין. תַּמָּן תַּנִּינָן. אֵילּוּ (מְכַבְּסִין) [מְגַלְחִין] בַּמּוֹעֵד, הַבָּא מִמְּדִינַת הַיָּם וּמִבֵּית הַשִּׁבְיָה וְהַיּוֹצֵא מִבֵּית הָאֲסוּרִין וְהַמְנוּדֶּה שֶׁהִתִּירוּ לוֹ חֲכָמִים. הָא שְׁאָר כָּל־בְּנֵי אָדָם אֲסוּרִין. אָמַר רִבִּי סִימוֹן. גָּזְרוּ עֲלֵיהֶם שֶׁלֹּא יִיכָּנְסוּ לָרֶגֶל מְנוּוָלִין.

2 הימים | G הימין   אבהו | G אבהוא   אבון | G בון   3 עליהן | G עליהם   לשבתן | G לשבת   - | G תני מנוולין   אילו | G אלו   [מגלחין] | G [מכבסין]   4 והיוצא... חכמים | G -   5 בני אדם | G אדן   עליהם | G עליהן   ייכנסו | G יכנסו

[185]"The people of the watch and those of the bystanders[184] are forbidden to shave[186] and to wash their garments, but on Thursday they are permitted because of the honor of the Sabbath." Therefore on all other days they are forbidden[187]? Rebbi Yose, Rebbi Abbahu in the name of Rebbi Joḥanan; Rebbi Abun, Rebbi Yasa in the name of Ḥizqiah: They decreed about them so they should not enter their week badly groomed. There[188], we have stated: "The following do (wash their garments) [shave][189] on the holiday[189]: He who comes from overseas, or from captivity, or who leaves the jail, or the excommunicated one from whom the Sages lifted {the excommunication.}" Therefore all other people are forbidden? Rebbi Simon said, they decreed about them so they should not enter the holiday badly groomed.

185 This paragraph is repeated at the start of *Mo'ed qatan* 3:1, with the places of *Ta'aniot* and *Mo'ed qatan* duly switched.
186 Groom their beards.
187 There seems to be no biblical or rabbinical reason for the prohibition.
188 Mishnah *Mo'ed qatan* 3:1.
189 The corrector's [text] is that of the Mishnah; also confirmed by G. The scribe's text is a lapse of the pen.

(65d line 70) תַּנֵּי. כָּל־מִי שֶׁהוּא מַכִּיר אַנְשֵׁי מִשְׁמָר שֶׁלּוֹ וְאַנְשֵׁי בֵית אָב שֶׁלּוֹ וְאֵינוֹ מִבָּתֵּי אָבוֹת קְבוּעִין אָסוּר כָּל־אוֹתוֹ הַיּוֹם. וְכָל־מִי שֶׁהוּא מַכִּיר אַנְשֵׁי מִשְׁמָר שֶׁלּוֹ וְאֵינוֹ מַכִּיר אַנְשֵׁי בֵית אָב שֶׁלּוֹ וְאֵינוֹ מִבָּתֵּי אָבוֹת קְבוּעִים אָסוּר כָּל־אוֹתָהּ הַשַּׁבָּת. וְכָל־מִי שֶׁאֵינוֹ מַכִּיר לֹא אַנְשֵׁי מִשְׁמָר שֶׁלּוֹ וְלֹא אַנְשֵׁי בֵית אָב שֶׁלּוֹ וְאֵינוֹ מִבָּתֵּי אָבוֹת קְבוּעִים. רִבִּי אוֹמֵר. אוֹמֵר אֲנִי שֶׁהוּא אָסוּר לְעוֹלָם. אֶלָּא שֶׁתַּקָּנָתוֹ קַלְקָלָתוֹ. שֶׁהוּא מוּתָּר בְּהֶסְפֵּד. כְּמָה דְּתֵימַר. קַלְקָלָתוֹ תִּיקָנָתוֹ שֶׁהוּא אָסוּר בְּהֶסְפֵּד. וְדִכְוָותָהּ. (תַּקָּנָתוֹ קַלְקָלָתוֹ) [קַלְקָלָתוֹ תַּקָּנָתוֹ] שֶׁיְּהֵא אָסוּר בִּמְלָאכָה.

1 ואינו G, ואנו | 2 קבועין G הקבוע' | 3 קבועים G הקבועין | 4 קבועים G הקבועין | 5 תקנתו G שתיקנתו שהוא G שיהא | שיהא G דתימר | דתמר G קלקלתו תיקנתו | תיקנתו קלקלתו שהוא G שיהא תיקנתו G [ותקנתו]

It was stated[190]: "Any one who knows the people of his watch and the people of his clan which is not[191] of the fixed clans, is forbidden this entire day. Any one who knows the people of his watch but not the people of his clan which is not[191] of the fixed clans, is forbidden this entire week. Any one who knows neither the people of his watch nor the people of his clan which is not[191] of the fixed clans: Rebbi says, I am saying that he is permanently forbidden, but his improvement is his detriment, in that he may deliver eulogies.[192]" As you are saying, his detriment is his improvement that he may not deliver eulogies, similarly is (his detriment his improvement) [his improvement his detriment] that he would be forbidden to work[193]?

190 Tosephta 2:2, Babli 17a.
191 Even though this is the text of both Yerushalmi sources, it seems clear that with all Tosephta and most Babli texts one has to delete this word.
192 This Tosephta presupposes that even after the destruction of the Temple it was known (and, as Genizah poems prove, up to the time of the first crusade it was publicly announced every Sabbath, ידיעות המכון לחקר השירה העברית vol. 5, pp. 111-112) which watch would serve were the Temple in existence. If a person has a tradition that his ancestors actually had been serving in the Temple as members of the clan whose day is fixed any time their watch is serving are subject to the restriction in the use of wine spelled out in the Mishnah and in addition have to treat the day as a holiday when they are forbidden work and mourning. Since the rebuilding of the Temple is expected to be sudden in a miraculous way, the Cohen has

to be ready to serve anytime at a moment's notice. If these data are unknown to the Cohen, logically he should be forbidden wine and work all his adult life. Since this is obviously a rabbinic restriction which is impossible to follow, the restriction must be waved and his detriment, that he does not know his place in the genealogy of priests, is his improvement in that he may work and drink wine any day where this is permitted to non-Cohanim.

193 The text of this sentence is thoroughly garbled in the scribe's, the corrector's, and G's versions but the meaning is clear as explained in the preceding Note.

(fol. 65a) **משנה י״ד**: כָּל־הַכָּתוּב בִּמְגִילָּה דִי לָא לְמִיסְפַּד לְפָנָיו אָסוּר לְאַחֲרָיו מוּתָר. רִבִּי יוֹסֵי אוֹמֵר לְפָנָיו וּלְאַחֲרָיו אָסוּר. דִי לָא לְהִתְעַנָּאָה לְפָנָיו וּלְאַחֲרָיו מוּתָר. רִבִּי יוֹסֵי אוֹמֵר לְפָנָיו אָסוּר לְאַחֲרָיו מוּתָר:

Mishnah 14: Anywhere it is written in the Scroll "not to deliver eulogies", before it is forbidden, afterwards is permitted. Rebbi Yose says, before and after are forbidden. "Not to fast", before and after it is permitted; Rebbi Yose says, before is forbidden, afterwards permitted[194].

194 The "Scroll" is the "Scroll of fasts", a late pre-Mishnah document mostly commemorating victories either of Maccabeans against Seleucids or revolutionaries against Romans, or Pharisees abolishing Sadducee usages. The entire discussion of *Megillat Ta`anit* is repeated in *Megillah* 1:6 (**מ**). "Before" and "after" refers to the days preceding and following these rabbinic (or traditional) festive days, which are treated as if biblical.

(66a line 2) **הלכה י״ג**: מַתְנִיתָהּ דְּרִבִּי מֵאִיר. דְּרִבִּי מֵאִיר אָמַר. דִי לָא לְמִיסְפַּד. אָסוּר לְהִתְעַנּוֹת. וּדְלָא לְהִתְעַנּוֹת. מוּתָּר בְּהֶסְפֵּד. וְדִי לָא סְתָם. כְּדִי לָא לְהִתְעַנְיָיא. אָמַר רִבִּי יוֹנָה. אִילֵּין יוֹמַיָּא דִי לָא לְמִיסְפַּד בְּהוֹן מִקְצָתָן דִי לָא לְהִתְעַנְיָיא בְּהוֹן. אָמַר רַבָּן שִׁמְעוֹן בֶּן גַּמְלִיאֵל. מַה תַּלְמוּד לוֹמַר בְּהוֹן שְׁנֵי פְעָמִים. אֶלָּא מְלַמֵּד שֶׁהַלַּיְלָה מוּתָּר וְהַיּוֹם אָסוּר. כְּהָדָא דְּתַנֵּי. לְהֶן אֵינָשׁ דִּייהֲוֵי עֲלוֹהִי יֵיסַר בְּצַלוֹ. אָמַר רִבִּי יוֹסֵי בֵּירִבִּי בּוּן. שֶׁהוּא צָרִיךְ לְהַזְכִּירָן מִבְּעָרֶב. וְאַתְיָא כַיי דְּאָמַר רִבִּי זְעוּרָה בְּשֵׁם רַב חוּנָה. אוֹמְרָהּ כְּלִילֵי שַׁבָּת וְכִיוֹמוֹ.

1 למיספד G | למספר   2 ודלא להתענות G | ודילא להתעניה מ ודילא להתענות כדי לא | G כלא להתעניא מ להתעניה להתעניא | G להתעניה   3 יומיא G | יומיה למיספד | G למספד מ להתענאה מקצתן | מקצתן מ ומקצתן G | ומקצתהון להתעניא | G להתעניה למיספד מ להתעניא | G אמ' רבן שמעון בן גמליאל | G רבן שמעון בן גמליאל או'   4 פעמים G | פעמין   כהדא G | כהדה   5 אינש G | אנשי   דיהוי | G דיהוו דיבעי | G ייסר בצלו | G אסר דצלו מ אסר בצלו   להזכירן מG | להזכיר   6 ואתייא G | ותייה כיי | מ כהיא דאמ' | G דמר

Halakhah 13: [194]*The Mishnah is Rebbi Meïr's, since Rebbi Meïr said, "not to eulogize" one is forbidden to fast, "not to fast" one is permitted to eulogize[195]. "Not to" unspecified[196] is as "not to fast." Rebbi Jonah said, "these are the days not to eulogize <fast> on them, and partially not to fast <eulogize> on them.[197]" Rabban Simeon ben Gamliel said, why does it say "on them" twice? To teach that the night is permitted but the day forbidden[198]. As it was stated[199], "therefore a person who takes it on himself has to forbid himself in prayer." Rebbi Yose ben Rebbi Abun said, that he must mention it on the preceding evening[200]. This comes following what Rebbi Ze`ira said in the name of Rav Huna: Similar to Friday night and Sabbath day[112].

194* This Halakhah and the next are repeated in *Megillah* 1:5 (מ).

195 "To eulogize", to eulogize a deceased person either on his funeral or on a formal occasion in his remembrance. Both are incompatible with a holiday spirit. In the Babli, the attribution to R. Meïr is affirmed in *Roš Haššanah* and denied in *Ta`anit* 18a.

196 A day mentioned in the Scroll without indication of any restriction.

197 The introductory statement to *Megillat Ta`anit*. All sources of *Megillat Ta`anit* support the version in *Megillah*, here given in <braces>, that days of fast are fewer than days of no eulogies.

198 No restrictions apply to the night of the day mentioned in the Scroll.

199 *Megillat Ta`anit*, end of Month of Adar.

200 If a person intends to fast on a day where this is prohibited by *Megillat Ta`anit*, he has to start in the evening and mention his fast in the prayer. Then he has to fast as a vow which is a biblical obligation which cannot be annulled by rabbinical festive days.

(66a line 10) מַתְנִיתָה אוֹ בְאַחַד עָשָׂר. כְּרַבִּי יוֹסֵי. אוּ בִשְׁנַיִם עָשָׂר. כְּרַבִּי מֵאִיר. וְקַשְׁיָא עַל דְּרַבִּי מֵאִיר. לָא כֵן תַּנֵּי. בִּתְרֵין עֲשַׂר בֵּיהּ יוֹם טִירְיוֹן. וְאָמַר רִבִּי יַעֲקֹב בַּר אָחָא. בָּטֵל יוֹם טִירְיוֹן. יוֹם שֶׁנֶּהֱרַג לוּלְיָינוּס וּפַפּוּס. יוֹם תְּלַת־עֲשַׂר בֵּיהּ יוֹם נִיקָנוֹר. מַהוּ יוֹם נִיקָנוֹר. שַׁלְטוֹן שֶׁלְּמַלְכוּת יָוָון עוֹבֵר לְאָלֶכְּסַנְדְּרִיָּאה וְרָאָה אֶת יְרוּשָׁלַם וְחֵירֵף וְגִידֵּף וְנִיאֵץ וְאָמַר. בְּשׁוּבִי בְשָׁלוֹם אֶתּוֹץ אֶת־הַמִּגְדָּל הַזֶּה. יָצָא אֵלָיו אֶחָד מִשֶּׁלְבֵּית חַשְׁמוֹנַי וְהָיָה הוֹרֵג בְּחַיָּילוֹתָיו עַד שֶׁהִגִּיעַ לְקֵירוּכִין שֶׁלּוֹ. וְכֵיוָן שֶׁהִגִּיעַ לַקֵּירוּכִין שֶׁלּוֹ קָטַע אֶת יָדוֹ וְחָתַךְ אֶת רֹאשׁוֹ וְתָחְבָּן בָּעֵץ וְכָתַב מִלְּמַטָּן. הַפֶּה שֶׁדִּיבֵּר בְּאַשְׁמָה וְהַיָּד שֶׁפָּשְׁטָה בְגַאֲוָה. וּתְלָיָין בְּקוֹנְטָס נֶגֶד יְרוּשָׁלַם. עַל דַּעְתֵּיהּ דְּרִבִּי מֵאִיר נִיחָא. בָּא (לוֹסֵר) [לֶאֱסֹר] לְפָנָיו. עַל דַּעְתֵּיהּ דְּרִבִּי יוֹסֵה מַה בָּא (לוֹסֵר) [לֶאֱסֹר]. לֵית לֵיהּ עַצְמוֹ אָסוּר מִפְּנֵי אַרְבָּעָה עָשָׂר. בָּא לְהוֹדִיעֲךָ שֶׁהוּא אָסוּר בְּהֶסְפֵּד. וַאֲפִילוּ עַל דְּרִבִּי מֵאִיר לֵית הִיא מַקְשְׁיָיא. לָא כֵן תַּנֵּי. בִּתְרֵין עֲשַׂר בֵּיהּ יוֹם טִירְיוֹן. וְאָמַר רִבִּי יַעֲקֹב בַּר אָחָא. בָּטֵל יוֹם טִירְיוֹן. יוֹם שֶׁנֶּהֱרַג לוּלְיָינוּס וּפַפּוּס. בְּאַרְבָּעַת־עֲשָׂר וּבַחֲמֵשֶׁת־עָשָׂר פּוּרַיָּא דִי לָא

HALAKHAH 13

לְמִיסְפַּד. בְּשִׁית־עֲשַׂר בֵּיהּ שְׁרִיּוּ לְמִבְנֵי שׁוּר יְרוּשָׁלַיִם דִּי לָא לְמִיסְפַּד. עַל דַּעְתֵּיהּ דְּרַבִּי מֵאִיר נִיחָא. בָּא לוֹסַר לְפָנָיו. עַל דַּעְתֵּיהּ דְּרַבִּי יוֹסֵה מַה בָּא לוֹסַר. לוֹסַר לְפָנָיו. לֵית לֵיהּ עַצְמוֹ אָסוּר מִפְּנֵי חֲמִשָּׁה עָשָׂר. בָּא לְהוֹדִיעֲךָ שֶׁהוּא אָסוּר בְּהֶסְפֵּד. וַאֲפִילוּ עַל דְּרַבִּי מֵאִיר לֵית הִיא מַקְשִׁיָיא. לֹא כֵן תַּנֵּי. בִּתְרֵין עָשָׂר בֵּיהּ יוֹם טִירְיוֹן. וְאָמַר רַבִּי יַעֲקֹב בַּר אַחָא. בָּטֵל יוֹם טִירְיוֹן. יוֹם שֶׁנֶּהֱרַג לוּלְיָינוֹס וּפַפּוֹס.]

1 יוסי G | יוסה וקשיא | וקשיה 2 לא G | ולא טיריון | טוריון G | ואמ' G | ומר 3 לוליינוס G | לוליינוס ופופוס G | ופפוס יום תלת G | בתלת ניקנור G | נקנור מהו G | מהוא 4 יוון מ | יון לאלכסמדריאה | G לאלכסמדריה ירושלם G | ירושלים וחירף G | וחרף וגידף וניאץ | מ | וניאץ וגידף 5 אחד | מ - משלבית חשמוני | מ משלחשמוניי 6 לקרוכין | לקונין לקרכין | לקורכין | לקרוכין קטע... חתך | G חתך | מ חתך... קטע ידו | מ ידו 7 מלמטן G | עליהן מלמטה והיד | G היד בקונטוס G | בקונטס ננד | G כנגד 8 ניחא G | ניחה בא | G בבא לוסר | G לו אסר (2) 9 לית | מ לפניו לית אסור | G מותר 10 מקשייא | מקשיה לא G ולא ואמ' | G ומר 11בארבעת | מ בארבעה פוריא | G פוריה די לא | G דלא 12 בשית G | בשתת שרייו G | שריו מ שרון למבני | מ למבנא למיספד G | למספד 13 ניחא G | ניחה בא | G בבא לוסר | G לו אסר (2) לית | G מ לאסר לפניו לית 14 היא מקשייא | G מקשיה לא G | ולא [...] | מ -

The Mishnah either follows Rebbi Yose on the eleventh or Rebbi Meïr on the twelfth[201]. But it is difficult for Rebbi Meïr. Was it not stated[202], "on the twelfth of it is Tirion[203] Day?" But Rebbi Jacob bar Aḥa said, Tirion Day was disestablished; the day when Julianus and Pappos were killed. "On the thirteenth of it is Nikanor Day[202]." What is Nikanor Day? [204]"A commander of the Greek government was passing by on his way to Alexandria when he saw Jerusalem, and insulted, vituperated, and blasphemed and said, *when I shall return in peace I shall destroy this tower*[205]. One of the dynasty of the Hasmoneans went out against him, killed his soldiers until he came to his car[206]. When he came to his car he hacked off his hand and cut off his head, stuck them on a piece of wood and wrote under it, the mouth which spoke in guilt and the hand stretched out in haughtiness, and hung it on a pole[207] outside Jerusalem." In Rebbi Meïr's opinion it is understandable, it comes to forbid the previous day[208]. What does it come to forbid for Rebbi Yose? To forbid the day before he does not need since itself it forbidden because of the fourteenth. It comes to inform you that eulogies are forbidden[209]. And also for Rebbi Meïr it is not difficult; was it not stated, "on the twelfth of it is Tirion Day?" But Rebbi Jacob bar Aḥa said, Tirion Day was disestablished; the day when Julianus and Pappos were killed[204]. "On the fourteenth and the fifteenth is Purim, not to eulogize. On the sixteenth they started to build the wall of Jerusalem[210], not to eulogize[202]." In Rebbi Meïr's opinion it is understandable, it comes to forbid the previous day. What does it come to forbid for Rebbi

Yose? To forbid the day before he does not need since itself is forbidden because of the fifteenth. It comes to inform you that eulogies are forbidden. [211][And also for Rebbi Meïr it is not difficult; was it not stated, "on the twelfth of it is Tirion Day?" But Rebbi Jacob bar Aḥa said, Tirion Day was disestablished; the day when Julianus and Pappos were killed.]

201 This and the following paragraph refer to Mishnah *Megillah* 1:5 where it is stated that even though if the Purim scroll cannot be read on the 14th, one reads it on one of the preceding days, this does not mean that the Purim celebration and the concurrent prohibition of fasting and public mourning are extended. Now *Megillat Ta`anit* for the month of Adar notes rabbinic festive days on the 12th and the 13th, Purim on 14th and 15th, and other holidays on 16th and 17th. Therefore the statement that one may fast and publicly mourn before the official Purim date certainly cannot apply to Adar 13th, and on first look also not to Adar 12th. Since the holiday on the 12th is rejected in the Halakhah, the Mishnah in *Megillah* may apply to Adar 12th for R. Meïr who does not extend the influence of rabbinic holidays to the preceding day, but only to Adar 11th for R. Yose following his opinion recorded here in Mishnah 14.

202 *Megillat Ta`anit, Adar*.

203 The name is טיריון in both occurrences in the Yerushalmi (the single טוריון in G may be disregarded); in *Megillat Ta`anit* it is טורייניס, in the Babli 18b טורייניס or טריניס.

Only the last reading can be interpreted as "Trajanus", and it is difficult to imagine that any happy occasion for Jews should be connected to this name. Also the *baraita* in *Megillat Ta`anit* makes it clear that one does not refer to an emperor since it states that after this Tirion had killed Julianus and Pappos in Laodicea for their being Jews there came an order from Rome and he was slain.

204 *1Maccabees* 7:19, *2Maccabees* 15:36.

205 An ironical quote of *Jud.* 8:9.

206 Latin *carruca*, Greek καρούχα. A travel wagon, not a fighting vehicle.

207 Greek κοντός.

208 The day preceding Purim.

209 Since R. Yose only forbids fasting on the day preceding a holiday.

210 According to the *baraita* in *Megillat Ta`anit*, the repair of the walls damaged by a Gentile army. There is no necessity to refer to the first war against the Romans.

211 Corrector's addition, probably to be deleted since missing in *Megillah*, even though it seems to be supported by G which ends here after two words.

(66a line 30) בְּשִׁבְעַת עָשָׂר בֵּיהּ קָמוּן עַמְמַיָּא עַל פְּלֵיטַת סָפְרַיָּא בִּמְדִינַת כַלְקִיס וּבֵית זְבָדִין וַהֲוָה פֶרְקָן. עַל דַּעֲתֵּיהּ דְּרִבִּי מֵאִיר נִיחָא. בָּא לוֹסַר עַצְמוֹ. עַל דַּעֲתֵּיהּ דְּרִבִּי יוֹסֵה מַה בָּא לוֹסַר. [לוֹסַר לְפָנָיו. לֵית לֵיהּ עַצְמוֹ אָסוּר.] אָמַר רִבִּי יוֹסֵה. כָּל־אִילֵּין מִילַּיָּא לָא מְסַיְּיעָן וְלָא תְבָרָן לָא עַל דְּרִבִּי מֵאִיר וְלָא עַל דְּרִבִּי יוֹסֵה. לֹא בָא אֶלָּא לִמְנוֹת יָמִים שֶׁנַּעֲשׂוּ בָהֶן נִסִּים לְיִשְׂרָאֵל.

תֵּדַע לָךְ שֶׁהוּא כֵן. דְּתַנִינָן. בְּרִישׁ יַרְחָא דְנִיסָן דִּיתָקַן תְּמִידָא דִּילָא לְמִיסְפַּד. בְּלֹא כֵן אֵינוּ אָסוּר מֵחֲמַת רֹאשׁ חוֹדֶשׁ. אֲבָל בַּשַּׁבָּתוֹת וּבְיָמִים טוֹבִים מִתְעַנִּין לִפְנֵיהֶן וּלְאַחֲרֵיהֶן. מָה רָאִיתָה לְהָקֵל בָּאֵילּוּ וּלְהַחֲמִיר בָּאֵילּוּ. שֶׁאֵילּוּ דִבְרֵי תוֹרָה וְאֵין דִּבְרֵי תוֹרָה צְרִיכֵין חִיזּוּק. וְאֵילּוּ דִבְרֵי סוֹפְרִים וְדִבְרֵי סוֹפְרִים צְרִיכֵין חִיזּוּק. הָדָא דַתְּ אָמַר. עַד שֶׁלֹּא בָטְלָה מְגִילַּת תַּעֲנִית. אֲבָל מִשֶּׁבָּטְלָה מְגִילַּת תַּעֲנִית בָּטְלוּ כָּל־אֵילּוּ. רִבִּי חֲנִינָה וְרִבִּי יוֹנָתָן תְּרֵיהוֹן אָמְרִין. בָּטְלָה מְגִילַּת תַּעֲנִית. רִבִּי בָא וְרִבִּי סִימוֹן תְּרֵיהוֹן אָמְרִין. בָּטְלָה מְגִילַּת תַּעֲנִית. רִבִּי יְהוֹשֻׁעַ בֶּן לֵוִי אָמַר. בָּטְלָה מְגִילַּת תַּעֲנִית. אָמַר רִבִּי יוֹחָנָן. אֶמֶשׁ הָיִיתִי שׁוֹנֶה מַעֲשֶׂה שֶׁגָּזְרוּ תַּעֲנִית בַּחֲנוּכָּה בְּלוֹד. וְאָמְרוּ עָלָיו עַל רִבִּי אֱלִיעֶזֶר שֶׁסִּיפֵּר וְעַל רִבִּי יְהוֹשֻׁעַ שֶׁרָחַץ. אָמַר לָהֶם רִבִּי יְהוֹשֻׁעַ. צְאוּ וְהִתְעַנּוּ עַל מַה שֶּׁהִתְעַנֵּיתֶם. וְאַתְּ אָמַר. בָּטְלָה מְגִילַּת תַּעֲנִית. אָמַר רִבִּי בָא. וַאֲפִילּוּ תֵימַר. בָּטְלָה מְגִילַּת תַּעֲנִית. חֲנוּכָּה וּפוּרִים לֹא בָטְלוּ.

1 ובשבעות | מ בשובעת ספרייא | מ ספרייא   2 לוסר | מ לאסור (2)   3 [....] | מ - | מ יוסה | מ יוסי מילייא | מ מיליא   5 דיתקן | מ דיתקם   8 סופרים | מ סופריו   דת | מ דאת   9 יונתן | מ יהושע בן לוי נ יוחנן   10 תריהון אמרין | מ אמרי   יהושע בן לוי | מ יונתן   שונה | מ יושב ושונה   13 ואפילו תימר | מ אע״ג דאת אמר

"On the seventeenth of it Gentiles attacked the remainder of the Sopherim at the city of Khalkis and Bet-Zabdin[212] and there was relief.[202]" In Rebbi Meïr's opinion it is understandable, it comes to forbid the {day} itself. What does it come to forbid for Rebbi Yose[213]? [The day before? Is not the day itself forbidden for him?][214] Rebbi Yose said, all these matters neither support nor contradict either Rebbi Meïr or Rebbi Yose; they only come to report the days on which miracles were done for Israel. You have to understand that this is so since we have stated[215]: "On the New Moon of Nisan the Daily Offering was settled, one may not eulogize." Without this is he not already forbidden because of the New Moon[216]? [217]"But on Sabbath and holidays one fasts before and after them. What is your reason to be lenient with these and restrictive with those? For these are words of the Torah, and words of the Torah do not need reinforcement. But those are words of the Sopherim[218], and words of the Sopherim need reinforcement." That is what you were saying, as long as *Megillat Ta`anit* was not abolished. But since *Megillat Ta`anit* was abolished, all these were abolished. Rebbi Ḥanina and Rebbi Jonathan both said, *Megillat Ta`anit* was abolished[219]. Rebbi Abba and Rebbi Simon both said, *Megillat Ta`anit* was abolished. Rebbi Joshua ben Levi said, *Megillat Ta`anit* was abolished. Rebbi Joḥanan said, yesterday I was repeating, [220]"it happened that in Lydda they decided on a fast-day on Ḥanukkah. They said about Rebbi Eliezer that he got a haircut, and about Rebbi Joshua that he took a {thermal} bath[221]. Rebbi Joshua said to them, go and fast because you fasted." And you are saying, *Megillat Ta`anit* was abolished? Rebbi Abba said, even if you are saying that *Megillat Ta`anit* was abolished, Hanukkah and Purim were not abolished[222].

212 Khalkis was a city near Tripolis (Lebanon) and Bet-Zavda probably was in Syria. The *baraita* in *Megillat Ta`anit* connects this with the persecution of the Pharisees by Alexander Yannai.

213 Since it is the day after the second day of Purim which for him automatically is forbidden.

214 Unsupported corrector's addition, to be deleted.

215 *Megillat Ta`anit, Nisan*. This does not refer to the start of regular sacrifices as described by *Lev.* 9, but to the acceptance as Temple practice that public offerings must be paid for by public taxes, against the Sadducee opinion that private donations may be solicited for these.

216 Which is a semi-holiday, only without work-related restrictions.

217 Tosephta 2:6, Babli 17b, Babli *Roš Haššanah* 19a.

218 The mention of *Sopherim* indicates that the principles of *Megillat Ta`anit* are part of Ezra's organization of post-exilic Judaism, even though the redaction of the Scroll belongs to the last generation before the destruction of the 2nd Temple.

219 First generation Amoraim. Babli *Roš Haššanah* 18b. From here on a similar text also is in *Nedarim* 8:1 (Notes 33-35,נ).

220 Tosephta 2:5, Babli *Roš Haššanah* 18b.

221 Forbidden on a later fast-day for rain, Mishnah 1:7.

222 Confirmed in the Babli *Roš Haššanah* 19b.

(66a line 47) מֵילֵיהוֹן דְּרַבָּנָן אָמְרֵי. בָּטְלָה מְגִילַת תַּעֲנִית. רִבִּי יוֹנָתָן צָיֵּים כָּל־עֲרוּבַת רֵישׁ שַׁתָּא. רִבִּי אָבוּן צָיֵּים כָּל־עֲרוּבַת שׁוּבָא. רִבִּי זְעוּרָה צָם תְּלַת מָאוָון צוֹמִין. וְאִית דְּאָמְרֵי. תְּשַׁע מָאוָון. וְלֹא חָשׁ לִמְגִילַת תַּעֲנִית. רִבִּי יַעֲקֹב בַּר אָחָא מְפַקֵּד לְסַפְרַיָּא. אִין אֲתַת אִיתָּא מִישְׁאֲלִינְכוֹן. אוֹמְרוּן לָהּ. בַּכֹּל מִתְעַנִּין. חוּץ מִשַּׁבָּתוֹת וְיָמִים טוֹבִים וְרָאשֵׁי חֳדָשִׁים וְחוּלוֹ שֶׁלְּמוֹעֵד וַחֲנוּכָה וּפוּרִים.

1 אמרי | מ אמרין   2 צומין | מ דצומין   3 לספריא | מ לספרייה   4 משאלינכון | מ משאלנכון אומרין | מ אימרין

The actions of the rabbis imply that *Megillat Ta`anit* was abolished. Rebbi Jonathan fasted every New Year's Day's eve. Rebbi Abun fasted every Sabbath eve[223]. Rebbi Ze`ira fasted 300 fasts, and some say 900, and disregarded *Megillat Ta`anit*[224]. Rebbi Jacob bar Aha commanded the schoolteachers, if a woman comes to ask you, tell her that one may fast any time except Sabbaths, holidays, New Moons, intermediate days of holidays, Hanukkah and Purim[225].

223 Even though Tosephta 2:6 states that one may fast on Fridays, it notes, as quote from *Megillat Ta`anit*, the dissenting opinion of R. Yose the Galilean who forbids. The problems of fasting on Friday are taken up in the last paragraph of this Chapter.

224 The Babli (*Bava Meṣia`* 85a) reports that he fasted in order to forget the teachings of his native Babylonia.

225 Only Purim and Hanukkah are rabbinic holidays in this list.

(66a line 53) **הלכה יד**: שִׁמְעוֹן בַּר בָּא אָמַר. אֲתָא עוֹבְדָא קוֹמֵי רִבִּי יוֹחָנָן וְהוֹרֵי כְּרִבִּי יוֹסֵה. וַהֲוָה רִבִּי לְעָזָר מִצְטַעֵר. אָמַר. שָׁבְקִין סְתָמָא וְעָבְדִין כְּיִחִידָיָא. אַשְׁכַּח תַּנֵּי לָהּ רִבִּי חִייָה בְשֵׁם רִבִּי מֵאִיר. כַּד שְׁמַע דְּתַנֵּי לָהּ רִבִּי חִייָה בְשֵׁם רִבִּי מֵאִיר אָמַר. יָאוּת סַבָּא יָדַע פִּרְקֵי גַרְמֵהּ. רִבִּי מָנָא בְעָא קוֹמֵי רִבִּי יוּדָן. לֹא כֵן אָמַר רִבִּי חִזְקִיָּה רִבִּי אַבָּהוּ בְשֵׁם רִבִּי לְעָזָר. כָּל־מָקוֹם שֶׁשָּׁנָה רִבִּי מַחֲלוֹקֶת וְחָזַר וְשָׁנָה סְתָם. הֲלָכָה כִסְתָם. אָמַר לֵיהּ. וְלֹא רִבִּי. דִּילְמָא חוֹרָן. מָה הֵן. אִין דְּאַשְׁכַּח רִבִּי מַתְנֵי מַחֲלוֹקֶת וְחָזַר וְשָׁנָה סְתָם. הֲלָכָה כִסְתָם. אָתָר דְּלָא אַשְׁכַּח רִבִּי מַתְנֵי מַחֲלוֹקֶת. אֶלָּא אֲחֵרִים שָׁנוּ מַחֲלוֹקֶת וְרִבִּי שָׁנָה סְתָם. כָּל־שֶׁכֵּן שֶׁתְּהֵא הֲלָכָה כִסְתָם. וַאֲתָא רִבִּי חִזְקִיָּה רִבִּי יַעֲקֹב בַּר אָחָא רִבִּי שִׁמְעוֹן בַּר בָּא בְשֵׁם רִבִּי לְעָזָר. וַאֲפִילוּ אֲחֵרִים שָׁנוּ מַחֲלוֹקֶת וְרִבִּי שָׁנָה סְתָם הֲלָכָה כִסְתָם. וְלָמָּה הוּא מוֹרֶה לָהּ כְּיִחִידָיָא. רִבִּי שְׁמוּאֵל בַּר יַנַּאי בְשֵׁם רִבִּי אָחָא. הָדָא דְאַתְּ אָמַר בְּשֶׁאֵין מַחֲלוֹקֶת אֵצֶל סְתָם. אֲבָל אִם יֵשׁ מַחֲלוֹקֶת אֵצֶל סְתָם לֹא בְדָא הֲלָכָה כִסְתָם. רִבִּי יוֹסֵי בֵּירִבִּי בּוּן בְּשֵׁם רִבִּי אָחָא. הָדָא דַתְּ אָמַר בְּיָחִיד אֵצֶל יָחִיד. אֲבָל בְּיָחִיד אֵצֶל חֲכָמִים לֹא בְדָא הֲלָכָה כִסְתָם.

1 יוסה | מ יוסי   2 אמ' | מ ואמ'   כיחידיא | מי כיחידייא   3 כד שמע | י כר' שמעון שמע לה   פרקי גרמה | מ פירקי גרמיה י פירקי גיטא   4 לא כן | י תמן   5 ולא | מ לא   אין | מ אן   6 מתני | מ -   7 ואתא | מ אתא   9 ינא | מ ינה

Halakhah 14: [226]Simeon bar Abba said, there came a case before Rebbi Johanan[227] and he instructed following Rebbi Yose. Rebbi Eleazar was sorry about this; he said, does one disregard the anonymous {Mishnah} and follow an isolated opinion[228]? He found that Rebbi Hiyya stated this in the name of Rebbi Meïr. When he understood that Rebbi Hiyya stated this in the name of Rebbi Meïr., he said, the old man[229] understands his chapters well. Rebbi Mana asked before Rebbi Yudan: Did not Rebbi Hizqiah, Rebbi Abbahu say in the name of Rebbi Eleazar, every place where Rebbi taught a disagreement and afterwards taught it anonymously, practice follows the anonymous statement. He said to him, and if not Rebbi, maybe somebody else. How is this? If it is found that Rebbi taught a disagreement and afterwards taught it anonymously, then practice follows the anonymous statement. In a case where Rebbi did not teach a disagreement but others taught it in disagreement and Rebbi taught it anonymously, certainly practice has to follow the anonymous text. There come Rebbi Ḥizqiah, Rebbi Jacob bar Aḥa, Rebbi Simeon bar Abba, in the name of Rebbi Eleazar, every place where Rebbi taught a disagreement and afterwards taught it anonymously, practice follows the anonymous statement. Why does he instruct here following the isolated opinion? Rebbi Samuel bar Ina in the name of Rebbi Aḥa: That is, if no disagreement is stated together with the anonymous opinion. But if a disagreement is stated together with the anonymous opinion, practice does not follow the anonymous opinion. Rebbi Yose ben Rebbi Abun in the name of Rebbi Aḥa: that is if an individual disagrees with an individual. But in the case of an individual following the {anonymous} Sages, practice does not follow the anonymous text[230].

226 This text is not only copied in *Megillah*, it exists in a slightly different text in *Yebamot* 4:11 (Notes 172-175).

227 Since the two texts are not identical, one cannot say that the instructions of R. Joḥanan reported here refer to the opinion of R. Yose in *Yebamot*. It was reported in the previous paragraph that R. Joḥanan was reluctant to declare *Megillat Ta`anit* as obsolete; here it is noted that he even endorsed the most restrictive version of the interpretations of the scroll. Since the following discussion is one about the principles of edition of Rebbi's Mishnah, the implication is that R. Joḥanan's objection is disregarded.

228 Since R. Joḥanan holds in general that the anonymous Mishnah is practice (*Menaḥot* 52b).

229 R. Joḥanan.

230 The Babli (*Yebamot* 42b, *Bava qamma* 102a, *Avodah zarah* 7a, *Niddah* 11b) formulates the rule in the name of R. Joḥanan: Disagreement followed by anonymous statement, practice follows the anonymous statement. Anonymous statement followed by disagreement, practice does not follow the anonymous statement.

(fol. 65a) **משנה טו**: אֵין גּוֹזְרִין תַּעֲנִית עַל הַצִּבּוּר בַּתְּחִלָּה בַּחֲמִישִׁי שֶׁלֹּא לְהַפְקִיעַ אֶת הַשְּׁעָרִים אֶלָּא שָׁלֹשׁ תַּעֲנִיּוֹת הָרִאשׁוֹנוֹת שֵׁנִי וַחֲמִישִׁי וְשֵׁנִי וְשָׁלֹשׁ שְׁנִיּוֹת שֵׁנִי וַחֲמִישִׁי וְשֵׁנִי וַחֲמִישִׁי. רִבִּי יוֹסֵי אוֹמֵר כְּשֵׁם שֶׁאֵין הָרִאשׁוֹנוֹת בַּחֲמִישִׁי כָּךְ לֹא שְׁנִיּוֹת. וְלֹא אַחֲרוֹנוֹת:

Mishnah 15: One does not decide about a public fast on Thursdays in order not to inflate prices[232], but the first three fast days on Monday, Thursday, and Monday, and the second three on Thursday, Monday, Thursday. Rebbi Yose says, just as the first one not on Thursdays so not the second ones. Nor the last ones[233].

232 If people suddenly have to buy provisions not only for the Sabbath but also for breaking the fast on Thursday, food stores might use the increased need to raise prices. The next week people also know of the need to buy extra food and they will do this earlier in the week when competition will keep the prices down.

233 As the Halakhah shows, this sentence is copied from the Babli version; it is not originally Yerushalmi.

(מוֹדֶה רִבִּי יוֹסֵה בְּשֶׁבַע הָאַחֲרוֹנוֹת.)

(Rebbi Yose agrees for the seven last ones.[234])

234 The sentence was deleted by the editor of the Venice edition and therefore is missing in the printed versions of the Yerushalmi. R. Yose agrees that by the time of the last fast days people already are used to preparing for the fast day well in advance. J. N. Epstein in *Tarbiz* 5, 1934, pp. 261-262.

(fol. 65a) **משנה טז**: אֵין גּוֹזְרִין תַּעֲנִית בְּרָאשֵׁי חֳדָשִׁים בַּחֲנוּכָּה וּבַפּוּרִים. וְאִם הִתְחִילוּ אֵין מַפְסִיקִין דִּבְרֵי רַבָּן גַּמְלִיאֵל. אָמַר רִבִּי מֵאִיר אַף עַל פִּי שֶׁאָמַר רַבָּן גַּמְלִיאֵל אֵין מַפְסִיקִין מוֹדֶה הוּא שֶׁאֵין מַשְׁלִימִין. וְכֵן תִּשְׁעָה בְאָב שֶׁחָל לִהְיוֹת בְּעֶרֶב שַׁבָּת:

Mishnah 16: One does not decide on a fast day[235] on a New Moon, on Ḥanukka, or Purim. If they started, they do not interrupt[236], the words of Rabban Gamliel. Rebbi Meïr said, even though Rabban Gamliel said that one does not interrupt, he agreed that one does not complete[237]. The same on a Ninth of Av which falls on a Friday[238].

235 To start a series of 3 or 7 fast days for rain, or an isolated fast day because of a public calamity.

236 Once the fast day on a New Moon or Ḥanukkah, etc., is not the first in the series, one does not interrupt the regular sequence of Mondays and Thursdays.

237 One stops fasting before nightfall.

238 So one does not start the Sabbath when hungry. In our computed calendar the Ninth of Av, which always falls on the same weekday as the first day of Passover, never falls on an Friday.

(66a line 68) **הלכה טו**: כַּמָּה הִיא הַתְחָלָה. רִבִּי בָּא אָמַר. אַחַת. רִבִּי יוֹסֵה אָמַר. שְׁתַּיִם. וְכֵן נְפַק עוֹבְדָא כְהָדָא דְּרִבִּי בָּא. וּבַמֶּה קוֹרִים. רִבִּי יוֹסֵה אָמַר. קוֹרִין בְּרָכוֹת וּקְלָלוֹת. אָמַר לֵיהּ רִבִּי מָנָא. בְּגִין מוֹדַעְתִּין דְּהוּא תַעֲנִיתָא וְרִבִיעִין עַל מֵעִיהוֹן. וְלֹא יָדְעִין דְּהִיא תַעֲנִיתָא. אָמַר לֵיהּ. לְהוֹדִיעָךְ שֶׁקּוֹרִין בְּרָכוֹת וּקְלָלוֹת. רִבִּי יוּדָן קַפּוֹדְקַיָּא אָמַר קוֹמֵי רִבִּי יוֹסֵה בְשֵׁם רִבִּי יוּדָה בַּר פָּזִי. קוֹרִין בְּרֹאשׁ חוֹדֶשׁ. קָם רִבִּי יוֹסֵה עִם רִבִּי יוּדָה בַּר פָּזִי. אָמַר לֵיהּ. אַתָּה שָׁמַעְתְּ מִן אָבוּךְ הָדָא מִילְתָא. אָמַר לֵיהּ. אַבָּא לֹא אָמַר כֵּן. אֶלָּא בְעֵינֵי טָב. עַל־יְדֵי דְאִינּוּן יָדְעִין דְּהִיא רֵישׁ יַרְחָא הֵן קוֹרִין בְּרֹאשׁ חוֹדֶשׁ. וּשְׁאָר כָּל־הַמְּקוֹמוֹת קוֹרִין בְּרָכוֹת וּקְלָלוֹת.

Halakhah 15: How much is "started"[239]? Rebbi Abba said, once. Rebbi Yose said, twice. It was acted on following Rebbi Abba[240]. And what does one read? Rebbi Yose said, one reads "blessings and curses.[241]" Rebbi Mana said to him, since they know it is a fast day they are falling on their bellies, do they not know that it is a fast day[242]? He said to him, to tell you that one reads "blessings and curses.[243]" Rebbi Yudan from Kappadokia said before Rebbi Yose in the name of Rebbi Jehudah bar Pazi, one reads about the New Moon[244]. Rebbi Yose met Rebbi Jehudah bar Pazi; he said to him, did you hear this from your father? He said to him, my father said this only about Eintab[245]. Since they know that it is the New Moon, they are reading about the New Moon. At all other places they are reading "blessings and curses."

239 How many times does one have to fast to continue fasting on a day of the New Moon?

240 This is binding precedent. The Babli 18b concurs. [However the Babli switches the attributions between RR. Aha and Yose (not Assi, impossible for chronological reasons, cf. Rabbinovicz, *Variae Lectiones*, ad loc. Note מ.)]

241 *Lev.* 26:3-46, the public Torah reading for all fast days for rain, even if such a fast is on a New Moon or Hanukkah which have their own fixed readings.

242 Usually called "falling on one's face", the penitentiary prayer following the Amidah, which is omitted on all festive days. But if the day of the New Moon, where usually the penitentiary prayer is omitted, is a fast day for rain, the penitentiary prayer is recited. Since therefore everybody knows that it is a fast day, why does one have to change the customary Torah reading?

243 Since the penitentiary prayer is incompatible with the reading for the New Moon, everybody expects to read the portion customary for the fast day.

244 *Num.* 28:11-15.

245 The permanent seat of the Calendar Court, which has to proclaim every New Moon in the absence of a computed calendar.

1) 66b line) תַּנֵּי. תִּשְׁעָה בְאָב שֶׁחָל לִהְיוֹת עֶרֶב שַׁבָּת אוֹכֵל אֲפִילוּ בֵּיצָה אַחַת וְשׁוֹתֶה אֲפִילוּ כוֹס אֶחָד. כְּדֵי שֶׁלֹּא יִיכָּנֵס לַשַּׁבָּת מְעוּנֶּה. דִּבְרֵי רִבִּי יוּדָה. רִבִּי יוֹסֵי אוֹמֵר. מִתְעַנֶּה וּמַשְׁלִים. רִבִּי זְעוּרָה בְשֵׁם רַב יְהוּדָה רִבִּי בָּא בְשֵׁם רִבִּי אִימִּי בַּר יְחֶזְקֵאל בְּשֵׁם רַב. הֲלָכָה כְּמִי שֶׁהוּא אוֹמֵר. מִתְעַנֶּה וּמַשְׁלִים. וְלָמָּה לֹא אָמַר. הֲלָכָה כְּרִבִּי יוֹסֵה. אִית תַּנָּיֵי תַנֵּי וּמַחֲלַף דִּבְרֵי חֲכָמִים. רִבִּי זְעוּרָה בְשֵׁם רַב חוּנָה. וַאֲפִילוּ יָחִיד שֶׁגָּזַר עַל עַצְמוֹ תַעֲנִית בְּעֶרֶב שַׁבָּת מִתְעַנֶּה וּמַשְׁלִים. כָּהֲדָא רִבִּי בִּיבִי הֲוָה יְתִיב קוֹמֵי רִבִּי יָסָא. בָּעָה מֵילַף מִינֵּיהּ הָדֵין עוֹבָדָא. אֲמַר לֵיהּ. נִימְטֵי בַיְיתָא צִיבְחַר. אֲמַר לֵיהּ. רוּמְשָׁא הוּא. אֲמַר לֵיהּ. אִית בְּתַעֲנָה. אֲמַר לֵיהּ. אִית גַּבִּי תּוֹרְמוֹסִין. אֲמַר לֵיהּ. וּמַשְׁלִימִין כְּרִבִּי יוֹסֵי.

It was stated[246]: "On a Ninth of Av which falls on a Friday he eats even an egg and drinks even a cup full[247], in order not to enter the Sabbath being deprived, the words of Rebbi Jehudah. Rebbi Yose says, he fasts and finishes.[248]" Rebbi Ze`ira in the name of Rav Jehudah, Rebbi Immi bar Ezechiel[249] in the name of Rav: Practice follows him who says, he fasts and finishes. Why does he not say, practice follows Rebbi Yose? There are Tannaim who switch the names of the sages. Rebbi Ze`ira in the name of Rav Huna: Even an individual who decided for himself to fast on a Friday fasts and finishes. As the following: Rebbi Bevai was sitting before Rebbi Yasa; he wanted to learn from him this matter[250]. He said, let me go home a little bit. He said to him, it is afternoon. He answered, I am fasting. He said to him, I have lupines with me. He answered, and one finishes following Rebbi Yose[251].

246 Tosephta 2:7; Babli *Eruvin* 41a.
247 He breaks the fasts shortly before sundown.
248 He fasts until it certainly is the Sabbath since the obligation is to eat a festive meal on the Sabbath and this is not infringed on if he stays fasting into the Sabbath.
249 The brother of Rav Jehudah, ordained in Palestine. In the Babli he is called Rammi bar Ezechiel.
250 He fasted on a Friday in order to receive instructions from his teacher on how ro proceed.

251 First R. Bevai asked whether he could go home and break the fast before sundown. This was denied, but R. Yasa said, he had some lupines, (Greek θέρμος) animal feed which is turned into human food by extended cooking. Since the lupines would not be edible before nightfall, R. Bevai concluded that he was told that practice is to keep fasting into the Sabbath.

סדר תעניות האילו פרק שלישי תעניות

(fol.66b) **משנה א**: סֵדֶר תַּעֲנִיּוֹת הָאֵילוּ הָאָמוּר בִּרְבִיעָה הָרִאשׁוֹנָה. אֲבָל צְמָחִים שֶׁשָּׁנוּ מַתְרִיעִין עֲלֵיהֶן מִיָּד. וְכֵן שֶׁפָּסְקוּ גְשָׁמִים מִגֶּשֶׁם לְגֶשֶׁם אַרְבָּעִים יוֹם מַתְרִיעִין עֲלֵיהֶן מִפְּנֵי שֶׁהִיא מַכַּת בַּצּוֹרֶת:

Mishnah 1: The order of these fast-days was said for the first period of rains. But about abnormal growth one sounds the alarm immediately[1]. Also if rains stopped for 40 days between rainy periods one raises the alarm about it since it is a sign of drought[2].

1 While the extended prayers and shofar blowing are instituted if there are no rains in the entire month of Marheshwan, even though the need becomes apparent in the second half of the month, a fast-day instituted because of danger to growing crops (such as widespread fungus) is proclaimed on the first Monday after the phenomenon was observed and accompanied by blowing the *shofar*.

2 Since the crop which started to grow after the first rains will wither and be lost before the second rains.

(66b line 67) סֵדֶר תַּעֲנִיּוֹת הָאֵילוּ הָאָמוּר כול'. אֵי זֶהוּ מִיָּד שֶׁלָּהֶן. רַב אָמַר. שֵׁינִי וַחֲמִישִׁי וְשֵׁינִי. שָׁנוּ בַשֵּׁינִי. מָהוּ לְהַתְרִיעַ עֲלֵיהֶן בַּחֲמִישִׁי. רִבִּי זְעוּרָה שָׁמַע לָהּ מִן הָדָא. וַיֹּאמֶר אֵלַי אַל־תִּירָא דָנִיֵּאל כִּי | מִן־הַיּוֹם הָרִאשׁוֹן אֲשֶׁר נָתַתָּה אֶת־לִבְּךָ לְהָבִין וּלְהִתְעַנּוֹת לִפְנֵי יְיָ אֱלֹהֶיךָ נִשְׁמְעוּ דְבָרֶיךָ. כְּבָר נִשְׁמְעוּ דְבָרֶיךָ. וְכָאן מִכֵּיוָן שֶׁנְּתָנוּ בֵית דִּין נַפְשָׁן לַעֲשׂוֹת כְּמִי שֶׁעָשׂוּ.

"The order of these fast-days was said," etc. What is their "immediately"? Rav said, Monday[3], Thursday, and Monday. If it became abnormal on Monday, what about sounding the alarm on Thursday[4]? Rebbi Ze`ira understood it from the following[5]: *He said to me, do not fear, Daniel, since from the first day when you intended to fast before the Eternal, your God, your words were heard.* Already your words were heard. And here, since the Court were determined to do it is as if they did[6].

3 The first Monday after the need became evident. Babli 19b.

4 But Mishnah 2:15 forbids to start a series of fast-days on Thursdays.

5 *Dan.* 10:12.

6 The fast-day is proclaimed immediately but executed only the next Monday.

(66b line 72) תַּנֵּי. כְּשֵׁם שֶׁמַּתְרִיעִין עֲלֵיהֶן בְּשְׁאָר יְמֵי שָׁבוּעַ כָּךְ מַתְרִיעִין עֲלֵיהֶן בַּשְּׁבִיעִית מִפְּנֵי פַרְנָסַת אֲחֵרִים. מַהוּ מִפְּנֵי פַרְנָסַת אֲחֵרִים. חֲבֵרַיָיא אָמְרֵי. מִפְּנֵי פַרְנָסַת גּוֹיִם. רִבִּי זְעוּרָא אָמַר מִפְּנֵי פַרְנָסַת חֲשׂוּדִים. אַתְיָיא דְּרִבִּי זְעוּרָה כְּרִבִּי. וְדַחֲבֵרַיָיא כְּרִבִּי פִּינְחָס בֶּן יָאִיר. דְּרִבִּי זְעוּרָה כְּרִבִּי. חַד סָפַר הֲוָה חָשִׁיד עַל פֵּירוֹת שְׁמִיטְתָא. אַיְיתוּנֵיהּ גַּבֵּי רִבִּי. אֲמַר לוֹן. וּמָה יַעֲבִיד עֲלִיבָא וּבְגִין חַיָּיו הוּא עֲבַד. וְדַחֲבֵרַיָּא כְּרִבִּי פִּינְחָס בֶּן יָאִיר. רִבִּי בָּעָא מִישְׁרֵי שְׁמִיטְתָא. סְלֵק רִבִּי פִּינְחָס בֶּן יָאִיר לְגַבֵּיהּ. אֲמַר לֵיהּ. מָה עִיבּוּרַיָּא עֲבִידִין. אֲמַר לֵיהּ. עוּלְשִׁין יָפוּת. וּמָה עִיבּוּרַיָּא עֲבִידִין. אֲמַר לֵיהּ. עוּלְשִׁין יָפוּת. יָדַע רִבִּי דְּלֵית הוּא מַסְכָּמָה עִמֵּיהּ. אֲמַר לֵיהּ. מִישְׁגַּח רִבִּי מֵיכוּל עִימָּן פָּטֵל צִיבְחַר יוֹמָא דֵין. אֲמַר לֵיהּ. אִין. מִי נְחִית חָמָא מוּלְוָנָתָא דְרִבִּי קַיָּימִין. אֲמַר. כָּל־אִילֵּין יְהוּדָיֵי זַיְינִין. אִיפְשָׁר דְּלָא חֲמֵי סָבַר אַפּוֹיי. מִן כְּדוֹן [שִׁמְעוֹן קָלֵיהּ.] אֲזַלוּן וְאָמְרוֹן לְרִבִּי. שָׁלַח רִבִּי בָּעֵי מְפַיְּיסָתֵיהּ. מָטוּן בֵּיהּ גַּבֵּי קַרְתֵּיהּ. אֲמַר. בְּנֵי קַרְתִּי קוֹרְבִין לִי. נַחְתוּן בְּנֵי קַרְתֵּיהּ וְאָקְפוּן עֲלוֹי. אֲמָרוּן לוֹן. רִבִּי דוּ בָעֵי מְפַיְּיסָתֵיהּ. שָׁבְקוּנֵיהּ וַאֲזָלוּן לוֹן. אֲמַר. בְּנֵי דִילִי קוֹרְבִין לִי. נַחְתָּא אִישְׁתָּא מִן שְׁמַיָּיא וְאַקְפַת עֲלוֹי. חָזְרוּן וְאָמְרוּן לְרִבִּי. אֲמַר. הוֹאִיל וְלָא זָכִינָן מִישְׁבַּע מִינֵּיהּ בְּעָלְמָא הָדֵין. נִיזְכֵּי וְנִישְׁבַּע מִינֵּיהּ לְעָלְמָא דְאָתֵי.

6 עיבוריא | ד עבוריה   7 עיבורייא | ד עבוריה ידע | ד וידע   8 פטל ציבחר | ד ציבחר פטל ליה | ד לון   9 זיינין | ד זנין   [...] | ד -   11 דו | ד -   ואזלון | ד ואזול   12 דילי | ד דידי שמייא | ד שמיא   חזרון ואמרון | אזלון אמרון   12 לעלמא | ד בעלמא

It was stated[7]: "Just as one sounds the alarm during the other years of a Sabbatical period, so one sounds the alarm during the Sabbatical because of the livelihood of others." What means "because of the livelihood of others"? The colleagues said, because of the livelihood of Gentiles. Rebbi Ze`ira said, because of the livelihood of the suspect ones[8]. That of Rebbi Ze`ira follows Rebbi, that of the colleagues follows Rebbi Phineas ben Yair. That of Rebbi Ze`ira follows Rebbi: A teacher[9] was suspected in matters of Sabbatical produce. They brought him before Rebbi who said to them, what should this wretch do, he does it for his livelihood. But that of the colleagues follows Rebbi Phineas ben Yair. [10]Rebbi wanted to permit the Sabbatical year[11]. Rebbi Phineas ben Yair went to him. He said to him: how is the grain doing? He answered him: endives[12] are doing fine. He said to him: how is the grain doing? He answered him: endives are doing fine. From this, Rebbi understood that he did not agree with him. He said to him: Would the Rabbi care to eat a bite with me today? He said to him, yes. When he came, he saw the she-mules[13] of Rebbi standing. He said, are all these fed by Jews? He will not see me again! They went and told this to Rebbi. Rebbi sent and wanted to pacify him. They found him in his city. He said, the people of my city should come close to me. The people of his city came and surrounded him. They said to them, Rebbi wants to make peace with him. They left him and went away. He said, my sons should come close to me. Fire descended from Heaven and surrounded him. They returned and told Rebbi. He said, since we did not have merit to eat our fill from him in this world, may we be worthy to eat our fill from him in the World to Come.

7 Tosephta 2:8; Babli 19b.

8 People suspected of dealing in Sabbatical produce. While the poor and everybody else are permitted to collect spontaneously growing produce on any field in the Holy Land, nobody is permitted to use any of these as an object of trade.

9 Possibly one may read סַפָּר "barber". But it is difficult to see why a barber should be disciplined by Rebbi.

10 From here on the text also is in *Demay* 1:3 (Notes 145-149,ד).

11 Since in the absence of a Temple and the distribution of land as ordered in the Torah the Sabbatical year is observed as a rabbinic ordinance, Rebbi wanted to permit cultivation of the land to help pay real estate taxes which were imposed irrespective of yield. A generation later R, Yannay did just this.

12 They are irrelevant for taxes or a payment in kind (*annona*) to the Roman army.

13 Latin *mulus*. In Yoma 8:5 it is stated that the kick of a white mule is life threatening; white mules should not be kept by Jews.

(fol. 66b) **משנה ב:** יָרְדוּ לַצְּמָחִים אֲבָל לֹא לָאִילָן לָאִילָן אֲבָל לֹא לַצְּמָחִים לָזֶה וְלָזֶה אֲבָל לֹא לַבּוֹרוֹת לַשִּׁיחִין וּמְעָרוֹת מַתְרִיעִין עֲלֵיהֶן מִיָּד:

Mishnah 2: If they descended on produce but not on trees[14], on trees but not on produce, on both but not on cisterns, ditches, or caves[15], one sounds the alarm immediately.

14 Rain beneficial to fields but not to orchards

15 The water reservoirs for the dry seasons.

(66c line 13) **הלכה ב:** יָרְדוּ לַצְּמָחִים אֲבָל לֹא לָאִילָן. צִיבְחַר צִיבְחַר. לָאִילָן אֲבָל לֹא לַצְּמָחִים. סַכִּין סַגִּין. לָזֶה וְלָזֶה אֲבָל לֹא לַבּוֹרוֹת לַשִּׁיחִין וְלַמְּעָרוֹת מַתְרִיעִין עֲלֵיהֶן מִיָּד: תַּנֵּי. מַתְרִיעִין עַל הָאִילָן בְּפֶרָס הַפֶּסַח. לַבּוֹרוֹת לַשִּׁיחִין וּמְעָרוֹת בְּפֶרָס הָעֲצֶרֶת. מֵאַתָּה אֲפִילוּ יוֹתֵר מִיכָּן. יוֹתֵר מִיכָּן מַעֲשֵׂה נִיסִּים. וְאֵין מַתְרִיעִין עַל מַעֲשֵׂה נִיסִּים.

רִבִּי בֶּרֶכְיָה רִבִּי חֶלְבּוֹ פַּפָּא בְשֵׁם רִבִּי לָעְזָר. פְּעָמִים שֶׁהַגְּשָׁמִים יוֹרְדִין בִּזְכוּת אָדָם אֶחָד בִּזְכוּת עֵשֶׂב אֶחָד בִּזְכוּת שָׂדֶה אֶחָד. וּשְׁלָשְׁתָּן בְּפָסוּק אֶחָד וּמְטַר־גֶּשֶׁם יִתֵּן לָהֶם לְאִישׁ עֵשֶׂב בַּשָּׂדֶה: לְאִישׁ אֲבָל לֹא לַאֲנָשִׁים. לְעֵשֶׂב אֲבָל לֹא לַעֲשָׂבִים. בַּשָּׂדֶה אֲבָל לֹא בַשָּׂדוֹת.

Halakhah 2: "If they descended on produce but not on trees," little by little, "on trees but not on produce," only heavy downpours, "on both but not on cisterns, ditches, or caves, one sounds the alarm immediately." It was stated[7]: "One sounds the alarm about trees half a month before Passover[16], about cisterns, ditches and caves half a month before Pentecost." Then even later[17]? Later it would be a miracle, and one does not sound the alarm expecting miracles.

Rebbi Berekhiah, Rebbi Ḥelbo Pappos in the name of Rebbi Eleazar: Sometimes rains fall because of the merit of one person, the merit of one grass blade, the merit of one field. All three are from one verse[18], *and rain showers He will give to you, to a man, grass, in the field. To a man*, but not to men. To *a grass*, but not to grasses. *In the field*, but not in fields.

16 Since Passover is the time of the barley harvest, it is too late for saving produce but still in time to save vines and olive trees.
17 Since if water reservoirs are empty at the end of the rainy season, everybody's life is in danger.
18 Sach. 10:1.

(fol. 66b) **משנה ג:** וְכֵן עִיר שֶׁלֹּא יָרְדוּ עָלֶיהָ גְשָׁמִים כַּכָּתוּב וְהִמְטַרְתִּי עַל־עִיר אַחַת וְעַל־עִיר אַחַת לֹא אַמְטִיר חֶלְקָה אַחַת תִּמָּטֵר וְחֶלְקָה אֲשֶׁר־לֹא־תַמְטִיר עָלֶיהָ תִּיבָשׁ: אוֹתָהּ הָעִיר מִתְעַנָּה וּמַתְרַעַת וְכָל־סְבִיבוֹתֶיהָ מִתְעַנּוֹת וְלֹא מַתְרִיעוֹת. רִבִּי עֲקִיבָה אוֹמֵר מַתְרִיעוֹת אֲבָל לֹא מִתְעַנּוֹת:

Mishnah 3: And also a town on which no rain fell[19], as it is written[20]: *I shall give rain on one town and on another town I shall not give rain; one parcel will receive rain but the leaves of a parcel which does not receive rain will wilt.* This town fasts and blows the *shofar* and all its surroundings[21] fast but do not blow the *shofar;* Rebbi Aqiba says they blow the *shofar* but do not fast.

19 While the rest of the country got rain.
20 *Amos* 4:7. Description of a curse.
21 While they have crops, they are at risk since the increased demand from the town without crops will drive prices higher.

(66c line 22) **הלכה ג**: אָמַר רִבִּי סִימוֹן. כָּתוּב. וְהִמְטַרְתִּי עַל־עִיר אֶחָת וְעַל־עִיר אַחַת לֹא אַמְטִיר חֶלְקָה אַחַת תִּמָּטֵר וְחֶלְקָה אֲשֶׁר־לֹא־תַמְטִיר עָלֶיהָ תִּיבָשׁ: זְכוּתָא דְחַקְלָא עָבְדָא.

מִפְּנֵי אַרְבָּעָה דְבָרִים יוֹרְדִין מִלְמַעְלָן. מִפְּנֵי בַעֲלֵי זְרוֹעַ. וּמִפְּנֵי טְלָלִים הָרָעִים. וְשֶׁיְּהֵא הָעֶלְיוֹן שׁוֹתֶה כָּנָמוּךְ. וְשֶׁיְּהוּ הַכֹּל תּוֹלִין עֵינֵיהֶם אֶל הַשָּׁמַיִם. בִּזְכוּת שְׁלֹשָׁה דְבָרִים הַגְּשָׁמִים יוֹרְדִין. בִּזְכוּת הָאָרֶץ. בִּזְכוּת הַחֶסֶד. בִּזְכוּת הַיִּיסוּרִין. וּשְׁלָשְׁתָּן בְּפָסוּק אֶחָד אִם־(לְחֶסֶד) [לְשֵׁבֶט] אִם־לְאַרְצוֹ אִם־(לְשֵׁבֶט) [לְחֶסֶד] יַמְצִאֶנּוּ:

בַּעֲוֹן אַרְבָּעָה דְבָרִים הַגְּשָׁמִים נֶעֱצָרִין. בַּעֲוֹן עוֹבְדֵי עֲבוֹדָה זָרָה וּמְגַלֵּי עֲרָיוֹת וְשׁוֹפְכֵי דָמִים וּפוֹסְקִין בָּרַבִּים וְאֵינָן נוֹתְנִין. בַּעֲוֹן עוֹבְדֵי עֲבוֹדָה זָרָה מְנַיִין. הִשָּׁמְרוּ לָכֶם פֶּן־יִפְתֶּה לְבַבְכֶם וְסַרְתֶּם וַעֲבַדְתֶּם אֱלֹהִים אֲחֵרִים וגו׳. מַה כְּתִיב בַּתְרֵיהּ. וְחָרָה אַף־י״י בָּכֶם וְעָצַר אֶת־הַשָּׁמַיִם וְלֹא־יִהְיֶה מָטָר. בַּעֲוֹן מְגַלֵּי עֲרָיוֹת מְנַיִין. וַתַּחֲנִיפִי אֶרֶץ בִּזְנוּתֵךְ וּבְרָעָתֵךְ: מַהוּ עוֹנְשׁוֹ שֶׁלַּדָּבָר. וַיִּמָּנְעוּ רְבִבִים וּמַלְקוֹשׁ לֹא הָיָה. בַּעֲוֹן שׁוֹפְכֵי דָמִים מְנַיִין. כִּי הַדָּם הוּא יַחֲנִיף אֶת־הָאָרֶץ. כִּי הַדָּם הוּא יִתֵּן אַף עַל הָאָרֶץ. בַּעֲוֹן פּוֹסְקִין בָּרַבִּים וְאֵינָן נוֹתְנִין מְנַיִין. נְשִׂיאִים וְרוּחַ וְגֶשֶׁם אָיִן אִישׁ מִתְהַלֵּל בְּמַתַּת־שָׁקֶר:

חֲמִשָּׁה שֵׁמוֹת נִקְרְאוּ לוֹ. אֵיד עָב עָנָן נָשִׂיא חֲזִיז. אֵיד מְנַיִין. וְאֵד יַעֲלֶה מִן־הָאָרֶץ. עָב [שֶׁהוּא מְעַבֶּה אֶת הָרָקִיעַ]. הִנֵּה אָנֹכִי בָּא אֵלֶיךָ בְּעַב הֶעָנָן. עָנָן. שֶׁהוּא עוֹשֶׂה אֶת הַבִּרְיוֹת עֲנָוִים אֵילּוּ לְאֵילּוּ. נָשִׂיא. שֶׁהוּא עוֹשֶׂה בַּעֲלֵי בָתִּים כִּנְשִׂיאִים. מַעֲלֶה נְשִׂאִים מִקְצֵה הָאָרֶץ. חֲזִיז. שֶׁהוּא עוֹשֶׂה אֶת הָרָקִיעַ חֶזְיוֹנוֹת חֶזְיוֹנוֹת. י״י עָשָׂה חֲזִיזִים.

Halakhah 3: Rebbi Simon said, it is written[20]: *I shall give rain on one town and on another town I shall not give rain; one parcel will receive rain but the leaves of a parcel which does not receive rain will wilt*. The merit of the field does it.

[22]For four causes the rains fall down; because of violent men[23], because of noxious dew, and that the high country drink like the low country, and that everybody direct his eyes to Heaven. [24]By the merit of three causes does rain fall. By the merit of the Land, by the merit of charity, and by the merit of sufferings; and all are in one verse[25]: *If for (charity) [the stick], if for the Land, if for (the stick) [for charity] you will find it*.

[26]Four sins cause the rains to be halted. The sins of idolatry, incestuous and adulterous behavior, spilling blood, and of those who pledge publicly for charity but do not pay up. By the sin of idolatry from where? [27]*Guard*

yourselves, that your heart not be led astray so you deviate and worship other powers, etc. What is written next? *The Eternal's rage will be inflamed against you; He will arrest the sky and there will be no rain.* By the sin of incestuous and adulterous behavior, from where? [28]*You pollute the Land by your whoring and your criminality.* What is the punishment for this? *It prevents rain showers, and there will be no late rain.* By the sin of the spillers of blood, from where? [29]*For the blood pollutes the Land.* The blood will make anger rest on the Land. By the sin of those who pledge publicly for charity but do not pay up, from where? [30]*Clouds and wind but no rain, a man who takes credit for a lying gift.*

[31]It is called by five names: fog, canopy, cloud, prince, and storm-cloud. From where "fog"? *And fog rose from the earth*[32]. "Thick cloud," [which thickens the sky][33], *behold, I shall come to you in a canopy of cloud*[34]. "Cloud", because it makes people meek with one another. "Prince" because it turns owners of houses into princes: *He raises rain-clouds from the ends of the earth*[35]. "Storm-clouds" because it turns the sky into multiple visions[36]: *The Eternal makes storm clouds*[37].

22 Gen. rabba 13(5). The problem is that in the Creation it is asserted that fog from below created the conditions for agriculture but its continued existence depends on rain from the clouds. In *Gen. rabba:* For 4 causes the Holy One, praise to Him, changed nature so that the earth should be irrigated from above.
23 Who are prevented from monopolizing water resources.
24 Babli 8b.
25 *Job.* 37:13.
26 Part of a larger story in *Qiddušin* 4:1 (Notes 54-58), copied in Babli *Yebamot* 78b;

Midrash Samuel 28[5]; *Num. rabba* 8(4).
27 *Deut.* 11:16-17.
28 *Jer.* 3:2-3.
29 *Num.* 35:33.
30 *Prov.* 25:14.
31 *Gen. rabba* 13(11).
32 *Gen.* 2:6.
33 Corrector's addition from *Gen. rabba*.
34 *Ex.* 19:9.
35 *Ps.* 135:7.
36 Deriving the unexplained word as *pilpel* form of חזה "to have a vision".
37 *Sach.* 10:1.

(66c line 42) וְכָל־סְבִיבוֹתֶיהָ מִתְעַנּוֹת וְלֹא מַתְרִיעוֹת. שֶׁכֵּן מָצָאנוּ בְיוֹם הַכִּפּוּרִים. מִתְעַנִּין אֲבָל לֹא מַתְרִיעִין. רִבִּי עֲקִיבָה אוֹמֵר מַתְרִיעוֹת וְלֹא מִתְעַנּוֹת. שֶׁכֵּן מָצָאנוּ בְרֹאשׁ הַשָּׁנָה. מַתְרִיעִין אֲבָל לֹא מִתְעַנִּין.

"All its surroundings[21] fast but do not blow the *shofar*;" since we find that on the Day of Atonement one fasts but does not blow the *shofar*. "Rebbi Aqiba says they blow the *shofar* but do not fast," since we find that on New Year's Day one blows the *shofar* but does not fast.

(fol. 66b) **משנה ד**: וְכֵן עִיר שֶׁיֵּשׁ בָּהּ דֶּבֶר אוֹ מַפּוֹלֶת אוֹתָהּ הָעִיר מִתְעַנָּה וּמַתְרַעַת וְכָל־סְבִיבוֹתֶיהָ מִתְעַנּוֹת וְלֹא מַתְרִיעוֹת. רַבִּי עֲקִיבָה אוֹמֵר מַתְרִיעוֹת וְלֹא מִתְעַנּוֹת.

Mishnah 4: Similarly, a town in which there is an epidemic or a building collapse, this town fasts and blows the *shofar*, and all its surroundings[21] fast but do not blow the *shofar*; Rebbi Aqiba says they blow the *shofar* but do not fast.

(66c line 45) **הלכה ד**: מוֹתְנָא הֲוָה בְצִיפּוֹרִין. לֹא הֲוָה עֲלִיל גּוֹ אִשְׁקָקָה דַּהֲוָה רִבִּי חֲנִינָה שָׁרֵי בְּגַוֵּיהּ. וַהֲווֹן צִיפּוֹרָאֵיי אֲמְרִין. מָה הָהֵן סָבָא בֵּינָכִי וְיָתַב שְׁלֵם וּשְׁכוּנְתֵּיהּ וּמְדִינְתָּא אֲזָלָה בְּבָאִישׁוּת. עָאל וַאֲמַר קוֹמֵיהוֹן. זִמְרִי אֶחָד הָיָה בְדוֹרוֹ וְנָפְלוּ מִיִּשְׂרָאֵל עֶשְׂרִים וְאַרְבָּעָה אֶלֶף. וְאָנוּ כַמָּה זִמְרִי יֵשׁ בְּדוֹרֵינוּ וְאַתֶּם מִתְרַעֲמִין.

Halakhah 4: There was an epidemic in Sepphoris but it did not touch the avenue where Rebbi Ḥanina was dwelling. The Sepphoreans were saying, why is this old man amongst us sitting in peace while the neighborhood and the town is ruined? He came to preach and said before them: There was one Zimry in his generation but 24'000 fell of Israel[38]. But we, how many Zimry are in our generation[39] and you are complaining?

חַד זְמַן צְרָכוּן מֵיעֲבַד תַּעֲנִי וְלֹא נְחַת מִיטְרָא. עֲבַד רִבִּי יְהוֹשֻׁעַ בְּדָרוֹמָא [תַּעֲנִיתָא] וּנְחַת מִטְרָא. וַהֲווֹן צִיפּוֹרָאֵיי אָמְרִין. רִבִּי יְהוֹשֻׁעַ בֶּן לֵוִי מָחִית מִיטְרָא לַדְּרוֹמָאֵיי. וְרִבִּי חֲנִינָה עֲצַר מִיטְרָא מִן צִיפּוֹרָאֵיי. צְרָכוּן מֵיעֲבַד זְמָן תִּינְיָינוּת. שְׁלַח וְאַיְיתֵי לְרִבִּי יְהוֹשֻׁעַ בֶּן לֵוִי. אֲמַר לֵיהּ. מִישְׁגַּח מָרִי מֵיפוּק עִימָּן לְהִתְעַנּוֹת. נַפְקוּן תְּרֵיהוֹן לְתַעֲנִיתָא וְלֹא נְחַת מִיטְרָא. עָאל וַאֲמַר קוֹמֵיהוֹן. לֹא רִבִּי יְהוֹשֻׁעַ בֶּן לֵוִי מָחִית מִיטְרָא לַדְּרוֹמָאֵיי וְלֹא רִבִּי חֲנִינָה עֲצַר מִיטְרָא מִן צִיפּוֹרָאֵיי. אֶלָּא דְרוֹמָאֵיי לִיבְּהוֹן רַכִּיךְ וּשָׁמְעִין מִילָה דְאוֹרָיָיא וּמִתְכַּנְעִין. וְצִיפְרָאֵיי לִיבְּהוֹן קַשִׁי וּשָׁמְעִין מִילָה דְאוֹרָיָיא וְלָא מִתְכַּנְעִין. מִי עֲלִיל תְּלָה עֵינוֹי וַחֲמָא אֲוִירָא שָׁיֵיף. אֲמַר. עַד כְּדוֹן הָכֵין. מִיַּד נְחַת מִיטְרָא. וּנְדַר עַל גַּרְמֵיהּ דְּלָא לְמֶעֱבַד כֵּן תּוּבָן. אֲמַר. מָה אֲנָא מֵימוֹר לְמָרֵי חוֹבָא דְּלָא יַגְבֵּי חוֹבְיֵהּ.

One time they needed to proclaim a fast but no rain fell. Rebbi Joshua ben Levi made (one) [a fast][40] in the South[41] and rain fell. The Sepphoreans were saying, Rebbi Joshua ben Levi brought rain to the Southerners, but Rebbi Hanina[42] stopped water for the Sepphoreans. They needed to make a fast a second time. He sent and brought Rebbi Joshua ben Levi. He said to him, would my Master be willing to go with us to fast. They both went to the fast but no rain fell. He came to preach and said before them, not Rebbi Joshua ben Levi brought rain to the Southerners, nor Rebbi Hanina stopped water for the Sepphoreans. Only the Southerners' hearts are soft and they hear words of instruction and submit. But the Sepphoreans' hearts are hard; they hear words of instruction and do not submit. When he came home he raised his eyes and saw the air clear. He said, is it still like this[43]? Immediately rain fell. He vowed by himself not to do this again. He said, who am I to tell to the creditor not to collect his due?

רִבִּי זְעוּרָה בְּשֵׁם רִבִּי חֲנִינָה. מַה יַּעֲשׂוּ גְדוֹלֵי הַדּוֹר וְאֵין הַצִּיבּוּר נִידּוֹן אֶלָּא אַחַר רוּבּוֹ. שֶׁכֵּן מָצָאנוּ שֶׁכָּל־שְׁלֹשִׁים וּשְׁמוֹנֶה שָׁנִים שֶׁהָיוּ יִשְׂרָאֵל כִּמְנוּדִּים לֹא הָיָה מְדַבֵּר עִם מֹשֶׁה. שֶׁנֶּאֱמַר. וַיְהִי כַאֲשֶׁר־תַּמּוּ כָּל־אַנְשֵׁי הַמִּלְחָמָה לָמוּת מִקֶּרֶב הַמַּחֲנֶה. מַה כָּתוּב בַּתְרֵיהּ. וַיְדַבֵּר יי אֵלַי לֵאמֹר׃ רִבִּי יַעֲקֹב בַּר אִידִי בְּשֵׁם רִבִּי יְהוֹשֻׁעַ בֶּן לֵוִי. מַה יַּעֲשׂוּ גְדוֹלֵי הַדּוֹר וְאֵין הַצִּיבּוּר נִידּוֹן אֶלָּא אַחַר רוּבּוֹ. שֶׁכֵּן מָצָאנוּ שֶׁאִילּוּלֵי שֶׁאָמְרוּ יִשְׂרָאֵל בְּהַר הַכַּרְמֶל יי הוּא הָאֱלֹהִים יי הוּא הָאֱלֹהִים לֹא יָרְדָה הָאֵשׁ מִן הַשָּׁמַיִם וְשָׂרְפָה אֶת הַקָּרְבָּנוֹת.

Rebbi Ze'ira in the name of Rebbi Hanina: What should the great men of a generation do since the public is judged only according to its majority? So we find that during the 38 years during which Israel were as in a ban, He did not speak with Moses, as it is said[44]: *It was when all the warriors finished dying from inside the camp.* What is written next? *The Eternal spoke to me to give orders.* Rebbi Jacob bar Idi in the name of Rebbi Joshua ben Levi: What should the great men of a generation do since the public is judged only according to its majority? So we find that if Israel had not said[45], *The Eternal is the supreme power, the Eternal is the supreme power*, no fire would have come down from heaven and burned the sacrifices[46].

רִבִּי יְהוֹשֻׁעַ בֶּן יָאִיר בְּשֵׁם רִבִּי פִּינְחָס בֶּן יָאִיר. שְׁלֹשָׁה בָּרָא הַקָּדוֹשׁ בָּרוּךְ הוּא וְתָהָא שֶׁבְּרָאָן. וְאֵילּוּ הֵן. כַּשְׂדִּים וְיִשְׁמְעֵאלִים וְיֵצֶר הָרָע. כַּשְׂדִּים הֵן | אֶרֶץ כַּשְׂדִּים זֶה הָעָם לֹא הָיָה. הַלְוַואי לֹא הָיָה. יִשְׁמְעֵאלִים. יֹשְׁבֵי אֹהָלִים | לִשְׁדֻדִים וּבְטוּחוֹת לְמַרְגִּיזֵי אֵל לַאֲשֶׁר הֵבִיא

אֱלוֹהַּ בְּיָדוֹ: יֵצֶר הָרָע. בַּיּוֹם הַהוּא נְאֻם־י"י אֹסְפָה הַצֹּלֵעָה וְהַנִּדָּחָה אֲקַבֵּצָה וַאֲשֶׁר הֲרֵעוֹתִי: רִבִּי בֵּרֶכְיָה רִבִּי אַבָּא בַּר כַּהֲנָא רִבִּי יְהוֹשֻׁעַ בֶּן יָאִיר בְּשֵׁם רִבִּי פִינְחָס בֶּן יָאִיר. הֲרֵי הוּא כְאִילוּ הֲרֵעוֹתִי.

Rebbi Joshua ben Yair in the name of Rebbi Phineas ben Yair. Three created the Holy One, praise to Him, and was wondering why He created them. These are the Chaldeans, the Arabs, and evil inclinations. Chaldeans: *this is the land of the Chaldeans, of the non-existing people*[47]. If only they did not exist. Arabs: *unkept tents of robbers, trusted by those who irritate God, those who God brought in His hand*[48]. Evil inclinations: *On this day, this is the Eternal's oracle, I shall gather the lame, and collect the disowned, and to whom I did wrong*[49]. Rebbi Berekhiah, Rebbi Abba bar Cahana, Rebbi Joshua ben Yair in the name of Rebbi Phineas ben Yair: it is as if I did wrong to them[50].

רִבִּי לִיעֶזֶר עֲבַד תַּעֲנִי וְלָא אִיתְנָחַת מִיטְרָא. עֲבַד רִבִּי עֲקִיבָא תַּעֲנִי וּנְחַת מִיטְרָא. עָאַל וְאָמַר קוֹמֵיהוֹן. אֶמְשׁוֹל לָכֶם מָשָׁל לְמָה הַדָּבָר דּוֹמֶה. לְמֶלֶךְ שֶׁהָיוּ לוֹ שְׁתֵּי בָנוֹת אַחַת חֲצוּפָה וְאַחַת כְּשֵׁירָה. אֵימַת דַּהֲוַת בְּעָיָה הַהִיא חֲצִיפְתָּא עָלַת קוֹמוֹי. הֲוָה אָמַר. יָבוּן לָהּ מַה דְּהִיא בְעָיָא וְתֵיזִיל לָהּ. וְאֵימַת דַּהֲוַת הַהִיא כְשֵׁירְתָּא עָלַת קוֹמוֹי. הֲוָה מַאֲרִיךְ רוּחֵיהּ מִתְחַמֵּד מִישְׁמוֹעַ שַׁוְעָתָהּ. וְאִית שָׁרֵי מֵימַר כֵּן? אֶלָּא שֶׁלֹּא לְחַלֵּל שֵׁם שָׁמַיִם בֵּירְבִּי אֱלִיעֶזֶר.

Rebbi Eliezer organized a fast but no rain fell. Rebbi Aqiba organized a fast and rain fell. He preached and said before them: I shall tell you a parable, to what the situation is comparable. To a king who had two daughters, one insolent and one well-behaved. When the insolent one wanted to come before him, he said, give her what she wants and let her go away. But when the well-behaved came before him, he was patient and liked to hear her request. Is it permitted to say this[50]? Only not to desecrate the Name of Heaven through Rebbi Eliezer.

רִבִּי אֲחָא עֲבַד תְּלַת עֶשְׂרֵה תַעֲנִיָּין וְלָא נְחַת מִיטְרָא. מִי עֲלִיל פְּגַע בֵּיהּ חַד כּוּתָיי. אָמַר לֵיהּ. רִבִּי. רִבִּי. עֲתוֹר גּוּלָתָךְ מִן מִיטְרָא. אָמַר לֵיהּ. חַיָּיו דְּהַהוּא גַבְרָא. שְׁמַיָּיא מֵיעֲבַד נִיסִין וְשָׁתָּא מַצְלְחָה וְהַהוּא גַבְרָא לֵית הוּא מֵיחֵי. וְעָבְדוּן שְׁמַיָּא נִיסִין וְאַצְלְחַת שַׁתָּא וּמִית הַהוּא כּוּתַיָּיא. וַחֲווֹן כָּל־עַמָּא אֳמָרִין. אַיתוּן חָמוּן פּוֹרִין דְּשֶׁמֶשׁ.

Rav Aḥa organized thirteen fast days[52] but no rain fell. When he went home he encountered a Samaritan who said to him: Rabbi, Rabbi, squeeze your garment because of the rain. He answered him, by the life of this man,

Heaven will perform wonders and the year will be successful but this man will not then live. Heaven performed wonders, the year was successful, but this Samaritan died, and people were saying, come and see the fruits of the sun[53].

38 *Num.* 25:9,14. Zimri's sin was to sleep with a non-Jewish woman who offered herself to him.

39 Visiting the bordellos in Roman Sepphoris.

40 Unnecessary corrector's addition.

41 Lydda.

42 The local Chief Rabbi.

43 That his sermon had no influence on the people and therefore, while the drought was not his fault as explained in the next paragraph, it was his failure as a preacher which was the indirect cause. For this he felt very badly; Heaven sent rain to make feel him better. All these Aramaic texts are sermon concepts.

44 *Deut.* 2:16-17. Babli 30b.

45 *1K.* 18:39.

46 However the verse makes it clear that the people answered <u>after</u> the fire had descended.

47 *Is.* 23:13.

48 *Job* 12:6 (to be combined with the statement there v. 9 that the Eternal had created all this.)

49 *Micah* 4:6.

50 Extended Babli *Sukkah* 52b; cf. Babli *Berakhot* 31b/32a and Rashi's commentary, first line of 32a; *Ta`anit* 25b in the name of Samuel Minor.

51 Is a famous rabbi permitted to call himself insolent? Cf. Babli 25b where it is explained that R. Eliezer was obstinate but R. Aqiba accommodating to other opinions.

52 As described in Chapter 2.

53 That there were abundant fruits without rains.

(66d line 11) וְכָל־סְבִיבוֹתֶיהָ מִתְעַנּוֹת וְלֹא מַתְרִיעוֹת. שֶׁכֵּן מָצָאנוּ בְיוֹם הַכִּפּוּרִים. מִתְעַנִּין אֲבָל לֹא מַתְרִיעִין. רִבִּי עֲקִיבָה אוֹמֵר מַתְרִיעוֹת אֲבָל לֹא מִתְעַנּוֹת. שֶׁכֵּן מָצָאנוּ בְרֹאשׁ הַשָּׁנָה. מַתְרִיעִין אֲבָל לֹא מִתְעַנִּין.

"All its surroundings[21] fast but do not blow the *shofar*;" since we find that on the Day of Atonement one fasts but does not blow the *shofar*. "Rebbi Aqiba says they blow the *shofar* but do not fast," since we find that on New Year's Day one blows the *shofar* but does not fast.

(fol. 66b) **משנה ה**: אֵיזֶהוּ דֶּבֶר עִיר הַמּוֹצִיאָה חֲמֵשׁ מֵאוֹת רַגְלִי יָצְאוּ מִמֶּנָּה שְׁלֹשָׁה מֵתִים בִּשְׁלֹשָׁה יָמִים זֶה אַחַר זֶה.

Mishnah 5: What is an epidemic[54]? A town which could mobilize 500 soldiers[55] and there were taken out three dead persons on three consecutive days[56].

54 That one fasts and/or blows the *shofar* to bring people to repentance.
55 Able bodied males between the ages of 20 and 50.
56 Who die because of the same disease.

(66d line 14) **הלכה ה**׃ אָמַר רִבִּי לֵוִי. כָּתוּב יַדְבֵּק יְיָ בְּךָ אֶת־הַדָּבֶר. לָאִשָּׁה הַזֹּאת שֶׁהִיא מַדְבֶּקֶת שְׁלֹשָׁה כִּכָּרִים זֶה אַחַר זֶה. הָא עֲבִידָא אֵינוֹ יוֹתֵר מִיכָּן צְרִיכָה שִׁיעוּר אַחֵר. נִשְׁמְעִינָהּ מִן הָדָא. אֲפִילוּ עִיר גְּדוֹלָה כְּאַנְטוֹכְיָא וְיָצְאוּ מִמֶּנָּה שְׁלֹשָׁה מֵתִים בִּשְׁלֹשָׁה יָמִים זֶה אַחַר זֶה. הָדָא אָמְרָה. יוֹתֵר מִיכָּן צְרִיכָה שִׁיעוּר אַחֵר. בָּתִּים שֶׁאָמְרוּ בְּרִיאִים אֲבָל לֹא מְרוֹעָעִים. וְדִכְוָתָהּ. בַּחוּרִים אֲבָל לֹא זְקֵינִים. תַּנֵּי. אַסְכָּרָה. כָּל־שֶׁהִיא שְׁנַיִם בַּדֶּבֶר וְאֶחָד בָּאַסְכָּרָה. אִיתָא חֲמֵי. אַסְכָּרָה כָּל־שֶׁהִיא. וְאַתְּ אָמַר הָכֵין. לָכֵן צְרִיכָה. כְּשֶׁהִתְרִיעוּ עַל הָאַסְכָּרָה וְהָלְכָה לָהּ. וְאַחַר כָּךְ מֵתוּ שְׁנַיִם בַּדֶּבֶר וְאֶחָד בָּאַסְכָּרָה.

Halakhah 5: Rebbi Levi said, it is written[57]: *The Eternal will stick to you the epidemic.* {A parable} of a woman who sticks three loaves together[58]. How is this acted on? Is it not that larger it needs another rate[59]? Let us hear it from the following: Even a city large as Antiochia, and there were brought out three dead persons during three consecutive days. This implies that larger it needs another rate[60]. The houses about which they spoke[61], healthy but not shaky. And similarly, young people but not old ones. It was stated: Diphtheria any; two by plague and one by diphtheria. Come and see, "diphtheria any" and you are saying so[62]? It is needed for the case that they blew the *shofar* about diphtheria and it went away and after that two died of a plague and one of diphtheria[63].

57 *Deut.* 28:21.
58 A plague for which one fasts is a infectious disease.
59 Goes a town larger than that mentioned in the Mishnah by different rules both in the number of victims and in the number of days?
60 The interpretation of this sentence depends on the interpretation of the expression "rate". If this means "percentage" then instead of "needs" one has to read "does not need". If it means "absolute numbers" then the text as it stands is correct. Since there is no corrector's addition, the second interpretation is to be accepted.
61 In Mishnah 4; one fasts only for unforeseeable building collapses.
62 If one fasts for one deadly case of diphtheria (Tosephta 2:9), why the mention

of two deaths by another communicable disease?
63 In the case of diphtheria, the requirement is waived that to declare an epidemic the causes of death must be the same infection.

(fol. 66b) **משנה ו**: עַל אֵילּוּ מַתְרִיעִין בְּכָל־מָקוֹם וְעַל הַשִּׁדָּפוֹן וְעַל הַיֵּרָקוֹן עַל הָאַרְבֶּה וְעַל הֶחָסִיל וְעַל חַיָּה רָעָה וְעַל הַחֶרֶב מַתְרִיעִין עָלֶיהָ מִפְּנֵי שֶׁהִיא מַכָּה מְהַלֶּכֶת:

Mishnah 6: About the following one blows the *shofar* everywhere: About blight and canker[64], about locusts and *hasil*[65], about dangerous beasts, and on war[66] one blows the *shofar* since it is a moving plague.

64 These destroy the harvest.
65 Kinds of locust as explained in the Halakhah.
66 Mainly civil war.

(66d line 22) **הלכה ו**: רִבִּי חָמָא בַּר עוּקְבָה בְּשֵׁם רִבִּי יוֹסֵי בֶּן חֲנִינָה. מַתְרִיעִין עַל פְּרַגְיָא שֶׁלְפִּשְׁתָּן. מַה טַעַם. שַׂמָּה וְשַׁעֲרוּרָה נִהְיְיתָה בָּאָרֶץ׃ רִבִּי שְׁמוּאֵל בַּר נַחְמָן בְּשֵׁם רִבִּי יוֹנָתָן. מַתְרִיעִין עַל הַשָּׁרָב. מַה טַעַם. קֹדֵר הִלַּכְתִּי בְּלֹא חַמָּה קַמְתִּי בַקָּהָל אֲשַׁוֵּעַ׃ אָמַר רִבִּי לְעָזָר. אוֹקִיר לְאַסְיָיךְ עַד דְּלָא תִצְטְרִיךְ לֵיהּ. מַה טַעַם. הֲיַעֲרוֹךְ שׁוּעֲךָ לֹא בְצָר וְכֹל מַאֲמַצֵּי־כֹחַ׃ רִבִּי יוֹחָנָן וְרִבִּי שִׁמְעוֹן בֶּן לָקִישׁ. רִבִּי יוֹחָנָן אָמַר. אִם סִידַּרְתָּה תְפִילָּה [לֹא יְהֵא לָךְ צָרֵי עַיִן מִלְמַעֲלָה. אֶלָּא הַכֹּל יְהוּא מְאַמְּצִין כֹּחַ]. וְכֹל מַאֲמַצֵּי־כֹחַ׃ וְרִבִּי שִׁמְעוֹן בֶּן לָקִישׁ אָמַר. אִם סִדַּרְתָּה תְפִילָּה] לֹא יְהֵא לָךְ מֵיצַר פִּיךְ. אֶלָּא הַרְחֶב־פִּיךָ וַאֲמַלְאֵהוּ׃

לֹא סוֹף דָּבָר אַרְבֶּה אֶלָּא אֲפִילּוּ כָנָף. וְלָמָּה נִקְרָא שְׁמוֹ חָסִיל. שֶׁהוּא חוֹסֵל אֶת הַכֹּל. וְלָמָּה נִקְרָא שְׁמוֹ גוּבַּאי. דּוּ גְּבֵי דִּינָא דְּמָרֵיהּ. לֹא סוֹף דָּבָר חַיָּה רָעָה אֶלָּא אֲפִילּוּ בְהֵמָה רָעָה. כְּבָר הָיוּ שָׁנִים בְּאֶרֶץ יִשְׂרָאֵל חֲמוֹר נוֹשֵׁךְ וּמֵמִית שׁוֹר נוֹשֵׁךְ וּמֵמִית. לֹא סוֹף דָּבָר חֶרֶב שֶׁלְּמִלְחָמָה אֶלָּא אֲפִילּוּ חֶרֶב שֶׁלְּשָׁלוֹם. שֶׁכְּבָר עָשָׂה רוֹשֶׁם בִּימֵי יֹאשִׁיָּהוּ.

Halakhah 6: Rebbi Ḥama bar Uqba in the name of Rebbi Yose ben Ḥanina: One blows the *shofar* for the failure of the flax crop. What is the reason? *Horrible and execrable things happened in the land*[67]. Rebbi Samuel bar Naḥman in the name of Rebbi Jonathan: One blows the *shofar* about hot East wind[68]. What is the reason? *I went black without sun*[69], *I rose in the assembly to pray*[70]. Rebbi Eleazar said, honor your healer before you need him[71]. What is the reason? *If your prayer had preceded your need, and all efforts of power*[72]. Rebbi Joḥanan and Rebbi Simeon ben Laqish. Rebbi Joḥanan said, [if you prayed, no one up high will begrudge you, but all will reinforce your power, *and all efforts of power*. Rebbi Simeon ben Laqish said, if you prayed,][73] do not keep your mouth narrow, but *open your mouth and I shall fill it*[74].

Not only a locust but even a wing[75]. And why is it called *ḥasil* because it eliminates everything[76]. And why is called *govai*? Because it forecloses the claims of its Master[77]. Not only a dangerous beast but even a dangerous domestic animal. Already there were years in the Land of Israel when a donkey's bite was deadly, a steer's bite was deadly. Not only declared war, but also war in peacetime[78], which already happened in the time of Josiah.

67 *Jer.* 5:30.
68 Which coming from the Arabian desert is very dry and threatens to dry out growing crops.
69 The sand blown by the East wind makes the sun disappear in a haze.
70 *Job* 30:28.
71 A quote from *Sirachides* 38:1.
72 *Job* 36:19. Just as one should have good relations with one's doctor before sickness strikes, so one should pray to prevent bad things to happen. The *ḥamsin* itself is not dangerous but it points to dangerous consequences.
73 Corrector's addition from the quote in *Yalqut Job* #920. A different, more explicit, version in the Babli, *Sanhedrin* 44b.
74 *Ps.* 81:11.
75 Since a wing recognizable as from a dangerous locust proves their presence. Babli 22a.
76 The words used in the Mishnah for "locusts" are biblical. In Talmudic times the name was *govai*, possibly Arabic גואב "traveller through the desert."
77 Is an instrument of Divine retribution.
78 Or the Roman army in Roman territory since its pay was mostly plunder. Babli 22a.

(fol. 66b) **משנה ז**: מַעֲשֶׂה שֶׁיָּרְדוּ זְקֵנִים מִירוּשָׁלַם לְעָרֵיהֶם וְגָזְרוּ תַעֲנִית עַל שֶׁנִּרְאָה כִמְלֹא פִי תַנּוּר שִׁדָּפוֹן בְּאַשְׁקְלוֹן. וְעוֹד גָּזְרוּ תַעֲנִית לְמָחָר עַל שֶׁאָכְלוּ זְאֵבִים שְׁנֵי תִינוֹקוֹת בְּעֵבֶר הַיַּרְדֵּן. רִבִּי יוֹסֵי אוֹמֵר לֹא עַל שֶׁאָכְלוּ אֶלָּא שֶׁנִּרְאָה:

Mishnah 7: It happened that Elders left Jerusalem for their cities to decree a fast since blight to fill an oven[79] was seen in Ascalon[80]. Also they decreed a fast the following day because wolves ate two children in Transjordan. Rebbi Yose says, not that they ate but that they were seen.

79 Enough grain which if healthy would have been enough to form a cake filling a small portable clay oven.

80 A Philistine city just outside the borders of Hasmonean Judua.

(66d line 36) **הלכה ז:** הָדָא דְאַתְּ אָמַר בִּמְכוּנָס. אֲבָל בִּמְפוּזָר אֲפִילוּ פָּרָא מִיכֵּן. אָמַר רִבִּי מָנָא. נִרְאוּ רָצִין אַחֲרֵיהֶן. אָמַר רִבִּי יוֹסֵי בֵּירִבִּי בּוּן. נִרְאוּ בְמָקוֹם שֶׁאֵין רָאוּי לָהֶם.

Halakhah 7: That is, if collected. But dispersed even less than that[81]. Rebbi Mana said, if the are seen one pursues them[82]. Rebbi Yose ben Rebbi Abun said, they were seen at a place inappropriate for them[83].

81 Since every incidence of blight is a focus of infection, dispersed incidences of blight are much more dangerous. "Less" is Latin *parum*.

82 If one has time to organize a pursuit, one chases the wild predators away until they do no longer present a danger. R. Yose's remark seems unjustified.

83 While in general wild predators are only a danger if they form a pack, if they are seen in town even a single one is an indication that he is part of a pack and therefore dangerous. R. Yose's remark is justified. The Babli 22a has a different criterion.

(fol. 66b) **משנה ח:** וְעַל אֵילוּ מַתְרִיעִין בַּשַּׁבָּת עַל עִיר שֶׁהִקִּיפוּהָ גוֹיִם אוֹ נָהָר וְעַל הַסְּפִינָה הַמּוּטְרֶפֶת בַּיָּם. רִבִּי יוֹסֵי אוֹמֵר לְעֶזְרָה אֲבָל לֹא לִצְעָקָה. שִׁמְעוֹן הַתִּימְנִי אוֹמֵר אַף עַל הַדֶּבֶר וְלֹא הוֹדוּ לוֹ חֲכָמִים:

Mishnah 8: About the following one blows the *shofar* on a Sabbath: About a town surrounded by Gentiles[84] or a river[85], and a ship in danger in the ocean. Rebbi Yose said, to help[86] but not to vociferation. Simeon from Timna says, also about an epidemic but the Sages did not agree with him[87].

84 Who come as enemies.
85 In a flood.
86 Blowing the *shofar* on a Sabbath is rabbinically forbidden; it only is permitted as a military signal to mobilize all available personnel in a situation where lives are at stake.

87 Since the only people who can help are the doctors who certainly are already on duty.

(66d line 38) **הלכה ח:** רַב אֲמַר. עֲנָנֵי יי עֲנָנִי. מַתְנִיתָה פְּלִיגָא עַל רַב. רִבִּי יוֹסֵי אוֹמֵר לְעֶזְרָה אֲבָל לֹא לִצְעָקָה. וְהָא תַנַּייָא קַדְמָייָא סָבַר מֵימַר. אֲפִילוּ לִצְעָקָה.

לֵוִי בֶּן סִיסִי בָּאוּ הַגַּיָּיסוֹת לְעִירוֹ. נָטַל סֵפֶר תּוֹרָה וְעָלָה לְרֹאשׁ הַגַּג. אָמַר. רִבּוֹן הָעוֹלָמִים.
אִין בַּטְלִית הָדָא מִילָה מֶן הָדֵין סֵפֶר אוֹרָיְתָא יַעֲלוּן לוֹן. וְאִין לָא יֵיזְלוּן לוֹן. מִיַּד אִיתְבְּעוּן וְלָא
אִשְׁתַּכְּחוּן. תַּלְמִידֵיהּ עֲבַד כֵּן. יָבְשַׁת יָדֵיהּ וְאָזְלוּן לוֹן. תַּלְמִיד תַּלְמִידֵיהּ עֲבַד כֵּן. לָא יָבְשַׁת
יָדֵיהּ וְלָא אָזְלוּן לוֹן. לוֹמַר שֶׁאֵין שׁוֹטֶה נִפְגָּע וְלֹא בְשַׂר הַמֵּת מַרְגִּישׁ בָּאוּזְמֵל.

Halakhah 8: Rav said, *answer me, Eternal, answer me*[88]. The Mishnah disagrees with Rav: "Rebbi Yose said, to help[86] but not to vociferation." Therefore the first Tanna holds even for vociferation[89].

Armies came against Levi ben Sisi's town. He took a Torah scroll and climbed onto the roof. He said: Master of the worlds. If I neglected one word of this Torah scroll they may come; if not, they shall leave. Immediately they were looked for but not found. His student did the same; his hand was paralyzed and they left[90]. His student's student did the same; his hand was not paralyzed and they did not leave. To say that the idiot is not hurt and dead flesh does not feel the knife[91].

88 *1K*. 18:37. According to the Babli 14a the reference is not to this verse but to the standard prayer on fast day, Halakhah 2:2, Notes 107-108. He holds that one never sounds the *shofar* on the Sabbath for any reason whatsoever, but he permits penitentiary prayers on a Sabbath (which other authorities permit only on a Day of Atonement which is a Sabbath.)

89 Since R. Yose must refer to *shofar* blowing, and the Mishnah brings his opinion as a modification of, not a contradiction to, the anonymous Tanna's statement, it follows that the anonymous Mishnah refers to actual *shofar* blowing.

90 Not every holy man can claim the status of Levi ben Sisi..

91 A popular adage.

(fol. 66b) **משנה ט**: עַל כָּל־צָרָה שֶׁלֹּא תָבוֹא עַל הַצִּיבּוּר מַתְרִיעִין עָלֶיהָ חוּץ מֵרוֹב גְּשָׁמִים.

Mishnah 9: One blows the *shofar* because of any danger which menaces the public except an overabundance of rain.

(66d line 46) **הלכה ט**: רִבִּי יוֹנָה שִׁמְעוֹן בַּר בָּא בְּשֵׁם רִבִּי יוֹחָנָן. דָּבָר שֶׁאִיפְשַׁר לָךְ לוֹמַר עָלָיו
דַּייִ הִיא בְרָכָה. רִבִּי בֶּרֶכְיָה רִבִּי חֶלְבּוֹ רַב אַבָּא בַּר עִילַאי בְּשֵׁם רַב. עַד שֶׁיְּבַלְלוּ שִׂפְתוֹתֵיכֶם
מְלוֹמַר. דַּייֵנוּ בְרָכָה דַּייֵנוּ בְרָכָה.

Halakhah 9: Rebbi Jonah, Simeon bar Abba in the name of Rebbi Johanan: The thing about which it is impossible to say "enough". Rebbi

Berekhiah, Rebbi Helbo, Rav Abba bar Ilay in the name of Rav: Until your lips will wear out saying, we have enough blessings, we have enough blessings[92].

92 An incomplete copy of a section in *Berakhot* 9:7 (Note 290). The beginning is missing which states that this is an explanation of *Mal.* 3:10: *I shall pour out blessing over you until 'without enough'*.

(fol. 66b) **משנה י**׃ מַעֲשֶׂה שֶׁאָמְרוּ לְחוֹנִי הַמְעַגֵּל הִתְפַּלֵּל שֶׁיֵּרְדוּ גְשָׁמִים. אָמַר לָהֶן צְאוּ וְהַכְנִיסוּ תַנּוּרֵי פְסָחִים בִּשְׁבִיל שֶׁלֹּא יִמָּקוּ. וְהִתְפַּלֵּל וְלֹא יָרְדוּ גְשָׁמִים. עָג עוּגָה וְעָמַד בְּתוֹכָהּ וְאָמַר רִבּוֹנוֹ שֶׁל עוֹלָם בָּנֶיךָ שָׂמוּ פְנֵיהֶם עָלַי שֶׁאֲנִי כְבֶן בַּיִת לְפָנֶיךָ. נִשְׁבָּע אֲנִי בְשִׁמְךָ הַגָּדוֹל שֶׁאֵינִי זָז מִכָּאן עַד שֶׁתְּתָרֵחֵם עַל בָּנֶיךָ.

Mishnah 10: It happened that they said to Onias the circle-drawer, pray for rain. He said to them, go and shelter the Passover ovens so they should not get softened. He prayed but no rain fell. What did he do? He drew a circle, stood inside it, and said: Master of the World! Your children trusted me since I am like a familiar before You. I am swearing by Your great Name that I shall not move from here until You show mercy for Your children.

(66d line 49) **הלכה י**׃ מַעֲשֶׂה שֶׁאָמְרוּ לְחוֹנִי הַמְעַגֵּל הִתְפַּלֵּל שֶׁיֵּרְדוּ גְשָׁמִים. אָמַר לָהֶן צְאוּ וְהַכְנִיסוּ תַנּוּרֵי פְסָחִים בִּשְׁבִיל שֶׁלֹּא יִמָּקוּ. הָדָא אֲמָרָה. עֶרֶב פְּסָחִים הָיָה. וְתַנֵּי כֵן. בְּעֶשְׂרִין בֵּיהּ צָמוּן כָּל־עַמָּא לְמִיטְרָא וּנְחַת לוֹן.

Halakhah 10: "It happened that they said to Onias the circle-drawer, pray for rain. He said to them, go and shelter the Passover ovens so they should not get softened." This implies that it was close to Passover[93]. It also was stated thus[94]: "On the twentieth all the people fasted for rain and it fell on them."

93 Verbally "Passover eve."
94 *Megillat Ta`anit*, Month of Adar, 25 days before Passover. The *baraita* to this statement, copied in Babli 23a, defines it as Onias's fast.

(66d line 52) וְנִתְפַּלֵּל וְלֹא יָרְדוּ גְשָׁמִים. אָמַר רִבִּי יוֹסֵי בֵּירִבִּי בּוּן. שֶׁלֹּא בָא בַעֲנָוָה. אָמַר רִבִּי יוּדָן גִּירְיָא. הָדֵין חוֹנִי הַמְעַגֵּל בַּר בְּרֵיהּ דְּחוֹנִי הַמְעַגֵּל הֲוָה סָמִיךְ לְחָרְבַּן בֵּית מוּקְדְּשָׁא. נְפַק

לְטוּרָא לְגַבֵּי פָעֲלֵיי. עַד דּוּ תַמָּן נְחַת מִיטְרָא. עָאֵל לֵיהּ לִמְעַרְתָּא. מִן יְתִיב נָם וּדְמַךְ לֵיהּ. וַעֲבַד שְׁקִיעַ בְּשִׁינְתֵּיהּ שׁוּבְעִין שְׁנִין עַד דַּחֲרַב בֵּית מוּקדְּשָׁא וְאִיתְבְּנֵי זְמַן תִּנְיָינוּת. לְסוֹף שׁוּבְעִין שְׁנִין אִיתְעַר מִן שִׁינְתֵּיהּ. נְפַק לֵיהּ מִן מְעַרְתָּא וַחֲמָא עָלְמָא מֵחֲלָף. זָוֵי דַהֲוַות כְּרָמִין עֲבִידָא זֵיתִין. זָוֵי דַהֲוָות זֵייתִין עֲבִידָא זַרְעוּ. שָׁאַל לֵיהּ לִמְדִינָתָא. אָמַר לוֹן. מָה קָלָא בָעָלְמָא. אָמְרוּן לֵיהּ. וְלֵית אַתְּ יָדַע מָה קָלָא בָעָלְמָא. אֲמַר לוֹן. לָא. אֲמָרִין לֵיהּ. מָאן אַתְּ. אֲמַר לוֹן. חוֹנִי הַמְעַגֵּל. אֲמָרוּן לֵיהּ. שְׁמַעְנָן דַּהֲוָה עָלֵיל לַעֲזָרָה וְהִיא מְנַהֲרָה. עָאֵל וְאַנְהָרַת. וְקָרָא עַל גַּרְמֵיהּ בְּשׁוּב יְיָ אֶת־שִׁיבַת צִיּוֹן הָיִינוּ כְּחוֹלְמִים:

"He prayed but no rain fell.." Rebbi Yose ben Rebbi Abun said, because he did not come in meekness. [95]Rebbi Yudan son of proselytes said, this Onias the circle drawer was the grandson of Onias the circle-drawer {who lived} close to the destruction of the Temple. He went to a mountain to his workers. While he was there, rain fell. He went to a cave; when he was sitting down he slumbered and fell asleep. He stayed in his sleep for 70 years, while the Temple was destroyed and rebuilt. At the end of 70 years he awoke from his sleep. He left the cave and found the world changed. At a place where there had been vineyards were olive trees. At a place were there had been olive trees was a field. He asked about the province, and said to them, what is news in the world? They answered him, do you not know what is news in the world? He said, no. They asked him, who are you? He answered them, Onias the circle-drawer. They told him, we heard that when he entered the Temple courtyard it lit up. He went there and it lit up. He recited about himself, *when the Eternal leads back the return of Zion we were like sleepers*[96].

95 A different version of this story which knows only of one Onias the circle-drawer is in the Babli 23a. Both versions are reported in *Midrash Psalms* 126.

96 *Ps.* 126:1.

(fol. 66b) **משנה יא**: הִתְחִילוּ הַגְּשָׁמִים מְנַטְּפִין. אָמַר לֹא כָךְ שָׁאַלְתִּי אֶלָּא גִּשְׁמֵי בוֹרוֹת שִׁיחִין וּמְעָרוֹת. יָרְדוּ בְּזַעַף. אָמַר לֹא כָךְ שָׁאַלְתִּי אֶלָּא גִּשְׁמֵי רָצוֹן בְּרָכָה וּנְדָבָה. יָרְדוּ כְתִקְנָן עַד שֶׁעָלוּ יִשְׂרָאֵל מִירוּשָׁלַיִם לְהַר הַבַּיִת מִפְּנֵי הַגְּשָׁמִים. אָמְרוּ לוֹ כְּשֵׁם שֶׁנִּתְפַּלַּלְתָּ עֲלֵיהֶם שֶׁיֵּרְדוּ כָּךְ הִתְפַּלֵּל שֶׁיֵּלְכוּ לָהֶם. אָמַר לָהֶן צְאוּ וּרְאוּ אִם נִמְחֵית אֶבֶן הַטּוֹעִים.

Mishnah 11: Rain started to drip. He said, that is not what I was asking for, but rain {to fill} cistern, ditches, and caves. It rained in a raging storm. He said, that is not what I was asking for, but rain of goodwill, blessing, and donation. It rained normally until Israel moved from Jerusalem to the Temple Mount because of the rain. They came and said to him, just as you prayed for them to come, so pray to remove them. He told them, go and check whether the losers' stone was wiped away.

(66d line64) הִתְחִילוּ גְשָׁמִים מְנַטְּפִין. אָמְרוּ. לֹא בָאוּ אֵילוּ אֶלָּא לְהַתִּיר נִדְרוֹ שֶׁלָּזֶה.

"Rain started to drip.." They said, this happened only to eliminate this one's vow[97].

אָמַר לֹא כָךְ שָׁאַלְתִּי אֶלָּא גִּשְׁמֵי בוֹרוֹת שִׁיחִין וּמְעָרוֹת. יָרְדוּ בְזַעַף. תַּנֵּי שְׁמוּאֵל. כְּמִפִּי הַנּוֹד.

"He said, that is not what I was asking for, but rain {to fill} cistern, ditches, and caves. It rained in a raging storm." Samuel stated, as pouring from a water-skin.

אָמַר לֹא כָךְ שָׁאַלְתִּי אֶלָּא גִּשְׁמֵי רָצוֹן בְּרָכָה וּנְדָבָה. יָרְדוּ כְתִיקְנָן עַד שֶׁעָלוּ יִשְׂרָאֵל מִירוּשָׁלַיִם לְהַר הַבַּיִת מִפְּנֵי הַגְּשָׁמִים. הָדָא אֲמָרָה. הַר הַבַּיִת מְקוֹרֶה הָיָה. וְתַנִּי כֵן. אִסְטָיו לִפְנִים מִסְטָיו הָיָה.

"He said, that is not what I was asking for, but rain of goodwill, blessing, and donation. It rained normally until Israel moved from Jerusalem to the Temple Mount because of the rain." This implies that the Temple Mount was covered by a roof. And it was stated so: There was a stoa inside a stoa[98].

אָמְרוּ לוֹ כְּשֵׁם שֶׁנִּתְפַּלַּלְתָּ עֲלֵיהֶם שֶׁיֵּרְדוּ כָּךְ הִתְפַּלֵּל בַּעֲלֵיהֶם שֶׁיֵּלְכוּ לָהֶם. אָמַר לָהֶן צְאוּ וּרְאוּ אִם נִמְחֵית אֶבֶן הַטּוֹעִים. מָה עִיסְקָהּ דְּהָדָא אֶבֶן הַטּוֹעִים. אֶלָּא כָּל־מַאן דְּהֲוָה מוֹבֵד מִילָה הֲוָה נָסַב לָהּ מִן תַּמָּן. וְכָל־מַאן דַּהֲוָה מַשְׁכַּח מִילָה הֲוָה מֵייבַל לָהּ לְתַמָּן. אָמַר לָהֶן. כְּשֵׁם שֶׁאִי אֶיפְשָׁר לָאֶבֶן הַזֹּאת לְהִימָּחוֹת מִן הָעוֹלָם. כָּךְ אִי אֶיפְשָׁר לְהִתְפַּלֵּל עַל הַגְּשָׁמִים שֶׁיֵּלְכוּ לָהֶם. אֶלָּא צְאוּ וְהָבִיאוּ לִי פַּר שֶׁלְּהוֹדָיוֹת. וְיָצְאוּ וְהֵבִיאוּ לוֹ פַּר שֶׁלְּהוֹדָיוֹת. וְסָמַךְ שְׁתֵּי יָדָיו וְאָמַר. רִבּוֹנִי. הֲבֵאתָהּ רָעָה עַל בָּנֶיךָ וְלֹא יָכְלוּ לַעֲמוֹד בָּהּ. הֲבֵאתָהּ טוֹבָה עַל בָּנֶיךָ וְלֹא יָכְלוּ לַעֲמוֹד בָּהּ. אֶלָּא יְהִי רָצוֹן מִלְּפָנֶיךָ שֶׁתָּבִיא רְוָחָה. מִיַּד נָשְׁבָה הָרוּחַ וְנִתְפַּזְּרוּ הֶעָבִים וְזָרְחָה הַחַמָּה וְנִתְנַגְּבָה הָאָרֶץ. וְיָצְאוּ וּמָצְאוּ מִדְבָּר מָלֵא כְּמֵהִים.

"They said to him, just as you prayed for them to come, so pray to remove them. He told them, go and check whether the losers' stone was wiped away." What was the purpose of the losers' stone. Only that anybody who lost something was taking it from there and anybody who found something was bringing it there⁹⁹. He told them that just as it is impossible for this stone to be wiped off from the world, so it is impossible to pray that the rains should stop. But go and bring me a bull as thanksgiving offering. They went and brought him a bull as thanksgiving offering. He leaned on it with both of his hands and said, my Master! You brought evil on Your children and they could not stand it; You brought benefit on Your children and they could not stand it, but may it be Your pleasure to bring relief. Immediately the wind blew, the clouds dissolved, the sun shone, and the earth dried. They went out and found the desert full of truffles¹⁰⁰.

שָׁאֲלוּ אֶת רִבִּי אֱלִיעֶזֶר. מֵאֵימָתַי מִתְפַּלְלִין עַל הַגְּשָׁמִים שֶׁיֵּלְכוּ לָהֶם. אָמַר לָהֶן. כְּדֵי שֶׁיְּהֵא אָדָם עוֹמֵד בְּקֶרֶן הָעוֹפֶל וּמְשַׁקְשֵׁק אֶת יָדָיו בְּנַחַל קִדְרוֹן. אֲבָל בְּטוּחִים אָנוּ בְּבַעַל הָרַחֲמִים שֶׁאֵינוּ מֵבִיא מַבּוּל לָעוֹלָם. מַה טַּעַם. כִּי־מֵי נֹחַ זֹאת לִי אֲשֶׁר נִשְׁבַּעְתִּי מֵעֲבֹר מֵי־נֹחַ עוֹד עַל־הָאָרֶץ.

¹⁰¹They asked Rebbi Eliezer, when may one pray for the rains to stop? He told them, if a person stands on top of the Ophel and with his hands¹⁰² makes noise in the Kidron brook. But we trust the merciful Father that He will not bring a deluge over the world. What is the reason? *This is to Me like the waters of Noe; as I swore not to bring Noe's waters another time over the earth*¹⁰³

97 Babli 23a.
98 Babli *Berakhot* 33b (referring to Herod's Temple.)
99 Babli *Bava meṣiaʿ* 28b.
100 Babli 23a.
101 Babli 22b.
102 In the Babli: his feet.
103 *Is.* 54:9.

(fol. 66b) **משנה יב**: שָׁלַח לוֹ שִׁמְעוֹן בֶּן שָׁטַח וְאָמַר לוֹ צָרִיךְ אַתָּה לְנַדּוֹת. אֲבָל מָה אֶעֱשֶׂה לָךְ וְאַתָּה מִתְחַטֵּא לִפְנֵי הַמָּקוֹם כְּבֵן שֶׁהוּא מִתְחַטֵּא לְאָבִיו וְעוֹשֶׂה לוֹ רְצוֹנוֹ. וְעָלֶיךָ הַכָּתוּב אוֹמֵר יִשְׂמַח־אָבִיךָ וְאִמֶּךָ וְתָגֵל יוֹלַדְתֶּךָ:

Mishnah 12: Simeon ben Shataḥ sent to him and told him, you should be excommunicated¹⁰⁴, but what can I do since you are misbehaving before the Omnipresent like a son who misbehaves towards his father who does his will.

About you the verse says[105], *your father and mother will enjoy and the one who bore you jubilate.*

104 According to Maimonides, the excommunication would have been because at the end Onias found a way to pray for the end of the rains. The text of the Mishnah here is that of Maimonides's autograph; different from the Babli version.

105 *Prov.* 23:28.

(67a line 9) **הלכה יב**: שָׁלַח לוֹ שִׁמְעוֹן בֶּן שָׁטָח. אָמַר לוֹ. צָרִיךְ אַתָּה לִנָּדוֹת. שֶׁאִילּוּ נִגְזְרָה גְזֵירָה כְשֵׁם שֶׁנִּגְזְרָה בִימֵי אֵלִיָּהוּ לֹא נִמְצֵאתָה מֵבִיא אֶת הָרַבִּים לִידֵי חִלּוּל הַשֵּׁם. שֶׁכָּל־הַמֵּבִיא אֶת הָרַבִּים לִידֵי חִלּוּל הַשֵּׁם צָרִיךְ נִידּוּי. [וְתַמָּן תַּנִּינָן. שָׁלַח לוֹ רַבָּן גַּמְלִיאֵל אִם מְעַכֵּב אַתָּה אֶת הָרַבִּים נִמְצֵאתָ מֵבִיא מַבּוּל לְעוֹלָם. לֹא נִמְצֵאתָ מְעַכֵּב רַבִּים מִלַּעֲשׂוֹת מִצְוָה. וְכָל־הַמְעַכֵּב רַבִּים מִלַּעֲשׂוֹת מִצְוָה צָרִיךְ נִידּוּי.] וְאָמַר לוֹ. וְאֵין הַקָּדוֹשׁ בָּרוּךְ הוּא מְבַטֵּל גְּזֵירָתוֹ מִפְּנֵי גְזֵירָתוֹ שֶׁלְּצַדִּיק. אָמַר לוֹ. [הֵן.] הַקָּדוֹשׁ בָּרוּךְ הוּא מְבַטֵּל גְּזֵירָתוֹ מִפְּנֵי גְזֵירָתוֹ שֶׁלְּצַדִּיק. וְאֵין הַקָּדוֹשׁ בָּרוּךְ הוּא מְבַטֵּל גְּזֵירָתוֹ שֶׁלְּצַדִּיק מִפְּנֵי גְזֵירָתוֹ שֶׁלְּצַדִּיק חֲבֵירוֹ.

Halakhah 12: "Simeon ben Shataḥ sent to him and told him, you should be excommunicated." For if there had been a decision made as it was decided in the days of Elijah[106], would you not have caused a desecration of the Name in public[107]? And everybody who causes a public desecration of the Name must be excommunicated. [There, we have stated: Rabban Gamliel sent to him, if you hinder the public you will cause a deluge. Would you not hinder the public from performing a meritorious act? And any who would hinder the public from performing a meritorious act must be excommunicated.][108] He answered him, but does not the Holy One, praise to Him, cancel His decision because of the decision of a just person[109]? He said to him, [yes][110]. The Holy One, praise to Him, may cancel His decision because of the decision of a just person, but He will not cancel the decision of one just person because of the decision of his just colleague[111].

106 When the decision about rainfall was delegated by God to Elijah (*1K.* 17:1; cf. *Sanhedrin* 10:2, Notes 147ff.).

107 If the decision had been given into the hands of another holy man, his prayer would have been ineffective and people would conclude that prayer is ineffective and stop praying.

108 Corrector's addition; totally garbled copy from *Roš Haššanah* 1:5, Note 279.

109 This is the standard interpretation of *Ps.* 145:19, *the pleasure of those who fear Him He will do* and similar verses as explained in the next paragraph. Babli *Mo`ed qatan* 16b.

110 Corrector's addition, unnecessary.
111 This is the essence of the reference to Elijah.

(67a line 17) אֲבָל מָה אֶעֱשֶׂה לָךְ שֶׁאַתָּה מִתְחַטֵּא לִפְנֵי הַמָּקוֹם כְּבֵן שֶׁהוּא מִתְחַטֵּא עַל אָבִיו וְהוּא עוֹשֶׂה לוֹ רְצוֹנוֹ. רִבִּי בֶּרֶכְיָה רִבִּי אַבָּא בַּר כַּהֲנָא רִבִּי זְעוּרָה בְּשֵׁם רַב יְהוּדָה. וְאִית דְּאָמְרִין לָהּ בְּשֵׁם רַב חִסְדָּא. וְאִית דְּאָמְרִין לָהּ בְּשֵׁם רַב מַתָּנָה. וְתִגְזַר אוֹמֶר וְיָקָם לָךְ. מַה תַּלְמוּד לוֹמַר לָךְ. אֶלָּא אֲפִילוּ אֲנָא אָמַר הָכֵין וְאַתְּ אָמַר הָכֵין. דִּידָךְ קַיָּימָא וְדִידִי לָא קַיָּימָא. וְעַל־דְּרָכֶיךָ נָגַהּ אוֹר: אָמַר רִבִּי חִייָה בַּר בָּא. זוֹ יְרִידַת גְּשָׁמִים. אַף־בְּרִי יַטְרִיחַ עָב יָפִיץ עֲנַן אוֹרוֹ: כִּי־הִשְׁפִּילוּ וַתֹּאמֶר גֵּוָה. אֲנִי אָמַרְתִּי לְהַשְׁפִּילָן וְאַתָּה אָמַרְתָּ לִגְאוֹתָן. דִּידָךְ קַיָּימָא וְדִידִי לָא קַיָּימָא. וְשַׁח עֵינַיִם יוֹשִׁעַ: אֲנִי אָמַרְתִּי לִשְׁחוֹת עֵינֵיהֶן בְּרָעָה. וְאַתָּה אָמַרְתָּ לְהוֹשִׁיעָן. דִּידָךְ קַיָּימָא וְדִידִי לָא קַיָּימָא. אֲנִי אָמַרְתִּי יְמַלֵּט אִי־נָקִי וְאַתָּה [אָמַרְתָּ] יִימַלֵּט אַף עַל פִּי שֶׁאֵינוּ נָקִי. דִּידָךְ קַיָּימָא וְדִידִי לָא קַיָּימָא. מָהוּ וְנִמְלַט בְּבֹר כַּפֶּיךָ: בִּבְרִירוּת כַּפֶּיךָ. בִּזְכוּת מִצְוֹת וּמַעֲשִׂים טוֹבִים שֶׁהָיוּ בְיָדְךָ מֵרֵאשִׁיתָךְ.

"But what can I do since you are misbehaving before the Omnipresent like a son who misbehaves towards his father who does his will." Rebbi Berekhia, Rebbi Abba bar Cahana, Rebbi Ze`ira in the name of Rav Jehudah. But some say it in the name of Rav Hisda, and some say it in the name of Rav Mattanah. *You decide the command and He confirms it for you*[112]. Why does the verse say, "for you"? But even if I am saying so and you are saying otherwise, yours is enduring, Mine is not enduring. *On your paths shines light*; Rebbi Hiyya bar Abba said, this is rainfall. *As heavy as He has loaded the rain-cloud, His light will disperse the cloud*[113]. *For those humbled you order elevation*[114]; if I said to humble them and you say to elevate them, yours is enduring, Mine is not enduring. *And the one of low eyes will be saved;* I said to bring their eyes down by misfortune but you are saying to save them, yours is enduring, Mine is not enduring. I said, *may the not-innocent escape*[115]? But you [said][116], he shall escape even though he is not innocent, yours is enduring, Mine is not enduring. What means, *and he will escape by the purity of your hands*, by the choice of your hands, by the merit of meritorious deeds and good works which were in your hands from before.

112 *Job* 22:28. All these verses are interpreted to show that God executes the judgment of the just.
113 *Job* 37:11; justifying Onias against Simeon ben Shatah.
114 *Job* 22:29.
115 *Job* 22:30.
116 Corrector's addition.

(67a line 30) עָלֶיךָ הַכָּתוּב אוֹמֵר יִשְׂמַח־אָבִיךָ וְאִמֶּךָ וְתָגֵל יוֹלַדְתֶּךָ׃ מַה תַּלְמוּד לוֹמַר יוֹלַדְתֶּךָ׃ רִבִּי מָנָא אָמַר. אוּמָתָךְ. רִבִּי יוֹסֵה בֵּירִבִּי בּוּן אָמַר. שַׁעֲתָךְ. וְרַבָּנִן אָמְרִי. כְּשֵׁם שֶׁהוּא מְקַלְלָה בְּכִפְלַיִים. כָּךְ הוּא מְשַׂמְּחָהּ בְּכִפְלַיִים. [שֶׁנֶּאֱמַר] כַּעַס לְאָבִיו בֵּן כְּסִיל וּמֶמֶר לְיוֹלַדְתּוֹ׃ בֵּן חָכָם יְשַׂמַּח־אָב וּבֵן כְּסִיל תּוּגַת אִמּוֹ׃ מָהוּ תּוּגַת אִמּוֹ׃ אָמַר רִבִּי לוּדָה. לִישָׁן גִּימַטְרִיּוֹן הוּא. אַפְרָא בְּעֵינֵי אִימֵּיהּ. וּמְנַיִין שֶׁהוּא מְשַׂמְּחָהּ בְּכִפְלַיִים. שְׂמַח־אָבִיךָ וְאִמֶּךָ וְתָגֵל יוֹלַדְתֶּךָ׃

"About you the verse says[105], *your father and mother will enjoy and the one who bore you jubilate.*" Why does the verse say, "the one who bore you"[117]? Rebbi Mana said, your nation. Rebbi Yose ben Rebbi Abun said, your time[118]. But the rabbis are saying, just as he brings double curse, so he brings double joy. [As it is said:] *a silly son is anger to his father and bitterness to the one who bore him. A wise son brings joy to his father but a silly son is sadness to his mother*[119]. What means *tugah* of his mother? Rebbi Ludah said, it is encrypted language, ashes in his mother's eyes[120]. And from where that he brings double joy to her? *Your father and mother will enjoy and the one who bore you jubilate.*

117 What is the difference between the mother and the one who bore him?

118 The date of his birth will be counted as lucky time.

119 *Prov.* 17:25, 10:1. The silly son brings pain once to his mother and once to the one who bore him. The wise son brings joy to both in one verse.

120 If letters are represented by numbers from 1 to 22, תוגת is represented by 22 6 3 22. If *n* is replaced by 23-*n* (the *atbash* rule) one obtains 1 17 20 1 which is אפרא. The prime example is *Jer.* 51:1, the curses against לב קמי which by the same rule are כשדים.

(fol. 66b) **משנה יג**: הָיוּ מִתְעַנִּין וְיָרְדוּ לָהֶן גְּשָׁמִים קוֹדֶם לְהָנֵץ הַחַמָּה לֹא יַשְׁלִימוּ. לְאַחַר הָנֵץ הַחַמָּה יַשְׁלִימוּ. רִבִּי אֱלִיעֶזֶר אוֹמֵר קוֹדֶם לַחֲצוֹת לֹא יַשְׁלִימוּ לְאַחַר חֲצוֹת יַשְׁלִימוּ.

Mishnah 13: If they were fasting and it rained before sunrise, they do not finish[121]; after sunrise they finish. Rebbi Eliezer says, before noon they do not finish, after noontime they finish.

121 They do not continue fasting until evening.

(67a line 37) **הלכה יג**: הָיוּ מִתְעַנִּין וְיָרְדוּ לָהֶן גְּשָׁמִים קוֹדֶם לְהָנֵץ הַחַמָּה לֹא יַשְׁלִימוּ. שֶׁנֶּאֱמַר וְהָיָה טֶרֶם־יִקְרָאוּ וַאֲנִי אֶעֱנֶה. לְאַחַר הָנֵץ הַחַמָּה יַשְׁלִימוּ. עוֹד הֵם מְדַבְּרִים וַאֲנִי אֶשְׁמָע. אוֹ חֲלַף. אָמַר רִבִּי תַנְחוּמָא. וְתַנֵּי כֵן. אֵין עֲנִייָה אֶלָּא סָמוּךְ לַקְּרִיאָה. וְאֵין קְרִיאָה אֶלָּא סָמוּךְ לַעֲנִייָה. בְּיוֹמוֹי דְּרִבִּי יוּדָן גָּזְרִין תַּעֲנִי וּנְחַת מִיטְרָא בְרוּמְשָׁא. סָלַק רִבִּי מָנָא לְגַבֵּיהּ. אֲמַר לֵיהּ. בְּגִין דַּאֲנָא צְחִי מָהוּ דְנִישְׁתֵּי. אֲמַר לֵיהּ. אוֹרִיךְ. שֶׁמָּא יִמָּלְכוּ לְהַשְׁלִים.

Halakhah 13: "If they were fasting and it rained before sunrise, they do not finish," as it is said[122], *before they will call I shall answer*. "After sunrise they finish," *still they are talking and I shall hear*. Or may be the other way around[123]? Rebbi Tanḥuma said, it was stated so: there is no answer but close to calling, and no calling but close to answering[124]. In the days of Rebbi Yudan they decided on a fast; then rain fell in the night. Rebbi Mana went up to him; he said to him: since I am thirsty, may I drink? He said to him, wait. Maybe they will take counsel to finish[125].

122 *Is.* 65:24.
123 Maybe the verse could be read differently: "Still they are talking" about convening the prayer service on the next day; "before they will call" during regular service in the morning before the prayers for rain.
124 Identifying "calling" with "public prayer" as in the second interpretation of the verse.
125 If the fast was no longer needed because of the drought, maybe they decided that a penitentiary service was needed for other reasons. The individual is not permitted to break the fast until the fast is suspended by official notice.

(67a line 43) רִבִּי אָחָא רִבִּי אַבָּהוּ בְשֵׁם רִבִּי יוֹסֵי בַּר חֲנִינָה. אָסוּר לְהִתְעַנּוֹת עַד שֵׁשׁ שָׁעוֹת בַּשַּׁבָּת. אָמַר רִבִּי יוֹסֵי בֵּירִבִּי בּוּן. מַתְנִיתָה אָמְרָה כֵן. קוֹדֶם לַחֲצוֹת לֹא יַשְׁלִימוּ. עַד כְּבוֹן צַפְרָא. לְאַחַר חֲצוֹת יַשְׁלִימוּ. כְּבָר עָבַר רוּבּוֹ שֶׁלְיוֹם בִּקְדוּשָׁה.

1 בר | נ בן   אסור | נ אסור לאדם   2 ביר' בון | נ -   3 צפרא | נ צפרא הוא כבר | נ שכבר

Rebbi Aḥa, Rebbi Abbahu, in the name of Rebbi Yose ben Ḥanina: One is forbidden to fast until the sixth hour on the Sabbath. Rebbi Yose ben Rebbi Abun said, the Mishnah states this: "before noon they should not finish," because it is morning; "after noontime they should finish," since most of the day already was spent in holiness[125].

125 The text is repeated in *Nedarim* 8:1 (Notes 17-19,**ג**). Since (*Is.* 58:13) *you shall call the Sabbath a delight*, fasting on the Sabbath is forbidden. The Mishnah implies that not eating into the afternoon is called fasting; therefore on the Sabbath one must eat before noon.

(67a line 46) רַבָּן יוֹחָנָן בֶּן זַכַּיי כַּד הֲוָה בָּעֵי יֵיחוֹת מִיטְרָא הֲוָה אָמַר לְסַפְּרֵיהּ. קוּם לָךְ קוֹמֵי הֵיכְלָא. בְּגִין דְּרַבִּי בָּעֵי מְסַפְּרָא וְלֵית בְּחֵיילֵיהּ מִצְטָעֵר. מִיָּד הֲוָה מִטְרָא נְחִית. רַב אָדָא בַּר אַחֲוָוה כַּד הֲוָה בָּעֵי יֵיחוֹת מִיטְרָא הֲוָה שָׁלַח מְסָאנֵיהּ. כַּד הֲוָה שָׁלַח תְּרֵיהוֹן הֲוָה עָלְמָא טָיֵיף. מַפַּלְתָּא הֲווָן תַּמָּן וַהֲוָה רַב מֵיתַב חַד מִן תַּלְמִידֵיהּ בְּבֵיתָא עַד דַּהֲווֹן מְפַנִּין בֵּיתָא. וְכֵן דַּהֲוָה נְפַק מִן בֵּיתָא הֲוָה בֵּייתָא רָבַע. וְאִית דְּאָמְרִין. רַב אָדָא בַּר אַחֲוָוה הֲוָה. שָׁלְחוּ חֲכָמִים וְאָמְרוּ לוֹ. מַה מַעֲשִׂים טוֹבִים יֵשׁ בְּיָדָךְ. אָמַר לָהֶן. מִיָּמַיי לֹא קִדְּמַנִי אָדָם לְבֵית הַכְּנֶסֶת. וְלֹא הִינַּחְתִּי אָדָם בְּבֵית הַכְּנֶסֶת וְיָצָאתִי לִי. וְלֹא הִילַּכְתִּי אַרְבַּע אַמּוֹת בְּלֹא תוֹרָה. וְלֹא הִזְכַּרְתִּי דִּבְרֵי תוֹרָה בְּמָקוֹם מְטוּנָּף. וְלֹא הִיצַּעְתִּי וְיָשַׁנְתִּי שֵׁינַת קֶבַע. וְלֹא צָעַדְתִּי בֵּין הַחֲבֵירִים. וְלֹא כִּינִּיתִי שֵׁם לַחֲבֵירִי. וְלֹא שָׂמַחְתִּי בְּתַקָּלַת חֲבֵירִי. וְלֹא בָּאת קִלְלַת חֲבֵירִי עַל מִיטָתִי. וְלֹא הִילַּכְתִּי בַּשּׁוּק אֵצֶל מִי שֶׁהוּא חַיָּיב לִי. מִיָּמַיי לֹא הִקְפַּדְתִּי בְּתוֹךְ בֵּיתִי. לְקַייֵם מַה שֶּׁנֶּאֱמַר אֶתְהַלֵּךְ בְּתָם־לְבָבִי בְּקֶרֶב בֵּיתִי:

When Rabban Joḥanan ben Zakkai desired that it rained, he said to his barber: stand in front of the Temple: because my rabbi needs to be groomed and is not strong enough to suffer; then immediately it started to rain. When Rav Ada bar Ahawa desired that it rained, he took off his shoe. If he took both off the world was swamped. There were building collapses; Rav let one of his students sit there until they had emptied the house. After that one left the house, the house collapsed. But some are saying, this was Rav Ada bar Ahawah[126]. The Sages sent and asked him, what good deeds did you do? He told them, never came a person earlier than me to the synagogue, and I never left a person in the synagogue before I left. I did not walk four cubits without Torah[127], but never mentioned words of the Torah at a smelly place[128]. I never prepared my bed and slept deep sleep[129], and never walked among the colleagues[130]. I never called a colleague by a nickname[131], and never enjoyed the calamity of a colleague. The curse of a colleague never came on my bed[132], and I never went in public to a person who was in debt to me[133]. I never was angry with my family, to fulfill what was said[134], *I shall walk in the simplicity of my heart in the midst of my house.*

126 In the Babli 20b told of Rav Huna. But the follow-up is there also in the name of Rav Ada bar Ahawa.

127 But mentally repeating subjects of Torah study; a necessity as long as oral law never was written down.

128 A formal prohibition (cf. *Berakhot* 2:3).

129 In order to study Torah "day and night".

130 When the students were sitting on the ground, the teacher may not pass through them since it would look as if he stepped on their heads; he has to go along the wall.

131 A grave sin; Babli *Bava meṣia`* 58b.
132 But I forgave him immediately.
133 Not to embarrass him if he could not pay.
134 *Ps.* 101:2.

(fol. 66b) **משנה יד**: מַעֲשֶׂה שֶׁגָּזְרוּ תַעֲנִית בְּלוֹד וְיָרְדוּ לָהֶן גְּשָׁמִים קוֹדֶם לַחֲצוֹת. אָמַר לָהֶן רִבִּי טַרְפוֹן צְאוּ וְאִכְלוּ וּשְׁתוּ וַעֲשׂוּ יוֹם טוֹב. וְיָצְאוּ וְאָכְלוּ וְשָׁתוּ וְעָשׂוּ יוֹם טוֹב וּבָאוּ בֵּין הָעַרְבַּיִם וְקָרְאוּ הַלֵּל הַגָּדוֹל: אֵי זֶהוּ הַלֵּל הַגָּדוֹל הוֹדוּ לֵאלֹהֵי הָאֱלֹהִים כִּי־טוֹב כִּי לְעוֹלָם חַסְדּוֹ: הוֹדוּ לַאֲדֹנֵי הָאֲדֹנִים וְגוֹמֵר.

Mishnah 14: It happened that they decided on a fast at Lydda when it rained before noon. Rebbi Tarphon said to them, go, eat, drink, and make a holiday[135]. They went, ate, drank, made a holiday, and returned in the evening and recited the Great Hallel. What is the Great Hallel? *Give thanks to the supreme Power; truly, His kindness is forever. Give thanks to the Master of masters,* [136]*etc.*

135 Deciding practice following R. Eliezer.   in the synagogue.
136 *Ps.* 136, the only Hallel recited at night

(67a line 60) **הלכה יד**: אֵיזוֹ הִיא הַלֵּל הַגָּדוֹלָה. רִבִּי פַּרְנָךְ בְּשֵׁם רִבִּי חֲנִינָה. הוֹדוּ לֵאלֹהֵי הָאֱלֹהִים כִּי לְעוֹלָם חַסְדּוֹ: הוֹדוּ לַאֲדֹנֵי הָאֲדֹנִים כִּי לְעוֹלָם חַסְדּוֹ: אָמַר רִבִּי יוֹחָנָן. וּבִלְבַד מְשַׁעְמָדִים בְּבֵית יְיָ. לָמָּה בְּאִילֵּין תַּרְתֵּין פַּרְשָׁתָא. רִבִּי זְעוּרָא רִבִּי אַבָּהוּ בְּשֵׁם רִבִּי שְׁמוּאֵל בַּר נַחְמָן. מִפְּנֵי שֶׁיְּרִידַת גְּשָׁמִים כְּלוּלָה בָּהֶן. עַל דַּעְתֵּיהּ דְּרִבִּי יוֹחָנָן נִיחָא. דִּכְתִיב מַעֲלֶה נְשִׂיאִים מִקְצֵה הָאָרֶץ. וּכְרִבִּי חֲנִינָה מַה. בְּגִין דִּכְתִיב נוֹתֵן לֶחֶם לְכָל־בָּשָׂר כִּי לְעוֹלָם חַסְדּוֹ: רִבִּי בָּא וְרִבִּי סִימוֹן תְּרֵיהוֹן אָמְרִין. הָדָא דִידָן. רִבִּי יְהוֹשֻׁעַ בֶּן לֵוִי אָמַר. הָדָא דִידָן. בַּר קַפָּרָא אָמַר. הָדָא דִידָן. בַּר קַפָּרָא כְדַעְתֵּיהּ. דְּתַנִּינָן תַּמָּן. מִיָּמֶיהָ שֶׁלַּכַּת הַשְּׁלִישִׁית לֹא הִגִּיעָה לְאָהַבְתִּי כִּי יִשְׁמַע יְיָ מִפְּנֵי שֶׁעַמָּהּ מְמוּעָטִין: תַּנֵּי בַּר קַפָּרָא. זוֹ הִיא הַלֵּל הַגָּדוֹלָה. חַד בַּר אַבַּיֵי עֲבַר קוֹמֵי תֵיבוּתָא. אָמַר לוֹן. עָנוּן בַּתְרַיי מַה דַּנָּה אָמַר. הָדָא אָמְרָה. לֵית הָדָא דִידָן. [אָמַר רִבִּי מָנָא. הָדָא דִידָן]. נְסָא הֲוָה רַב. בְּגִין כֵּן אָמַר לוֹן. עָנוּן בַּתְרַיי מַה דַּנָּא אָמַר.

Halakhah 14: [137]What is the Great *Hallel*? Rebbi Parnakh in the name of Rebbi Ḥaninah; *Give thanks to the supreme Power; truly, His kindness is forever. Give thanks to the Master of masters; truly, His kindness is forever.* Rebbi Joḥanan said, on condition of *who stand in the Eternal's house*[138]. Why these two chapters? Because rainfall is included in them. In the opinion of

Rebbi Johanan it is understandable, for it is written[139], *He brings up vapors from the ends of the earth.* How is it for Rebbi Haninah? Because it is written[136], *He gives nourishment to all flesh; truly, His kindness is forever.* Rebbi Abba, Rebbi Simon, both are saying, ours[140]. Rebbi Joshua ben Levi said, ours. Bar Qappara said, ours. Bar Qappara follows his opinion, as it was stated[141]: "during the existence of a third group they never reached *I am loving; truly the Eternal listened to my voice, my supplication,* since its people were few." Bar Qappara stated, this is the Great Hallel. A patrician stood before the Ark[122]; he said to them, repeat after me what I am saying. This implies that it is not ours[143]. [Rebbi Mana said, it is ours.][144] The miracle was great; therefore he said to them, repeat after me what I am saying[145]

137 The text is repeated from *Pesaḥim* 5:7, Notes 208-216.
138 *Ps.* 135 as introduction to *Ps.* 136.
139 *Ps.* 135:7.
140 *Ps.* 113-118, the "Egyptian Hallel".
141 Mishnah *Pesaḥim* 5:7.
142 To be the reader in a service of thanksgiving for rain relieving a drought.

143 If it were the regular *Hallel*, the congregation would not repeat the verses but answer every half-verse with "Hallelujah" (cf. *Šabbat* 16, Note 59).
144 Corrector's addition from *Pesaḥim*.
145 Because of the extraordinary nature of the event, he changed the usual response to repetition of the entire *Hallel*.

בשלשה פרקים פרק רביעי תעניות

(fol.67b) **משנה א**: בִּשְׁלֹשָׁה פְרָקִים הַכֹּהֲנִים נוֹשְׂאִין אֶת כַּפֵּיהֶן אַרְבָּעָה פְעָמִים בַּיּוֹם בְּשַׁחֲרִית וּבַמּוּסָף וּבַמִּנְחָה וּבִנְעִילַת שְׁעָרִים. בַּתַּעֲנִיּוֹת וּבַמַּעֲמָדוֹת וּבְיוֹם הַכִּפּוּרִים:

Mishnah 1: On three occasions the Cohanim lift their hands[1] four times a day, during morning prayers, *musaf*, afternoon prayers, and at the closing of the doors[2]: On fast-days[3], for the bystanders[4], and on the Day of Atonement.

1 To pronounce the priestly blessing in the synagogue.
2 *Ne`ilah*, a synagogue service close to sundown.
3 Fast days for rain.
4 As explained in Mishnah 2.

(67b line 53) בִּשְׁלֹשָׁה פְרָקִים כול'. אַתְּ שְׁמַע מִינָהּ תְּלַת. אַתְּ שְׁמַע מִינָהּ (שֶׁמִּתְפַּלְּלִין) [שֶׁמִּתְעַנִּין] בַּמַּעֲמָדוֹת. וְשֶׁמִּתְפַּלְּלִין אַרְבַּע. וְאֵין נְשִׂיאַת כַּפַּיִם בַּלַּיְלָה אֶלָּא בַיּוֹם. וְיִשָּׂא אֶת כַּפָּיו וְאַל יִתְפַּלֵּל. מָצָאנוּ תְפִילָה בְלִי נְשִׂיאַת כַּפַּיִם וְלֹא מָצָאנוּ נְשִׂיאַת כַּפַּיִם בְּלֹא תְפִילָה. תַּנֵּי. זוֹ דִבְרֵי רִבִּי מֵאִיר. רִבִּי זְעוּרָה בְּשֵׁם רִבִּי יוֹחָנָן. בָּעֵירוּבִין וּבְתַעֲנִית צִיבּוּר נָהֲגוּ הַכֹּל כְּרִבִּי מֵאִיר. רִבִּי יַעֲקֹב בַּר אָחָא בְּשֵׁם רִבִּי יוֹחָנָן. אַף בִּמְגִילַּת אֶסְתֵּר נָהֲגוּ הַכֹּל כְּרִבִּי מֵאִיר.

"On three occasions," etc. One understands from three things. One understands that the bystanders (pray) [fast][5], and that they pray[6] four times, and lifting of the hands is not during nighttime, only during daytime[7]. Could one not lift his hands without praying? We find prayer without lifting of hands; we do not find lifting of hands without prayer[8]. It was stated, these are the words of Rebbi Meïr[9]. [10]Rebbi Ze`ira in the name of Rebbi Joḥanan: In matters of *eruvin* and public fast-days everybody follows Rebbi Meïr. Rebbi Jacob bar Aḥa in the name Rebbi Joḥanan: Even about the reading of the Esther scroll everybody follows Rebbi Meïr[11].

5 Here it seems that the corrector's text [in brackets] is correct. The argument is that the recitation of the priestly blessing is a sacral act and as such forbidden to Cohanim under the influence of alcohol (*Lev.* 10:8-11). Since they have to recite the blessing late in the afternoon, they could not have drunk any alcohol during the day and therefore would not have eaten either.
6 In a technical sense, "to pray" means "to recite the *Amidah* prayer". In a synagogue setting the priests recite the blessing only during the reader's recitation of the *Amidah*.

7 Since there is no priestly blessing during evening prayers (whose status in Mishnaic times was not well defined.)
8 Outside the Temple. The priestly blessing during synagogue service is a strictly pharisaic institution; it seems from the Manual of Discipline that at least at Qumran the priests only recited poetic allusions to the biblical priestly blessing.
9 Tosephta 3:1. In this text, the opponents of R. Meïr only admit priestly blessing during the two morning services.

This is compatible with the scribe's text in this paragraph.
10 Babli 26b. Copied in *Eruvin* 6, Note 102.
11 In *Eruvin* one follows R. Meïr that *eruv* for courtyards and participation for alleys must be separate acts, Chapter 6, Note 99; in *Megillah* 2:1, Note 62, he requires that the Esther scroll has to be read from beginning to end; Babli 72a. These rules are popular usage, not rabbinic decrees.

(67b line 59) רִבִּי זְעוּרָה רִבִּי חִיָּיה רִבִּי יְהוֹשֻׁעַ בֶּן לֵוִי בְשֵׁם בַּר פְּדָיָה. מִפְּנֵי מַה סָמַךְ הַכָּתוּב פָּרָשַׁת נָזִיר לִנְשִׂיאַת כַּפַּיִם. לְלַמֶּדְךָ כְּשֵׁם שֶׁהַנָּזִיר אָסוּר בַּיַּיִן כָּךְ נְשִׂיאַת כַּפַּיִם אֲסוּרָה בַּיַּיִן. אִי מַה הַנָּזִיר אָסוּר בַּחַרְצָנִים וּבַזּוֹגִין אַף נְשִׂיאַת כַּפַּיִם אֲסוּרָה בַּחַרְצָנִים וּבַזּוֹגִין. רִבִּי יוֹנָה אָמַר. אִיתְפַּלְּגוּן יֵשׁוּעַ בַּר גְּזוֹרָה וְרִבִּי זְעוּרָה. חַד יָלִיף לָהּ מִן הַנָּזִיר. וְחַד יָלִיף לָהּ מִן הַשֵּׁירוּת. וְלָא יָדְעִין מָאן יָלִיף לָהּ מִן הַנָּזִיר. וּמָאן יָלִיף לָהּ מִן הַשֵּׁירוּת. מָאן דִּיליף לָהּ מִן הַנָּזִיר. אִי מַה הַנָּזִיר אָסוּר בַּחַרְצָנִים וּבַזּוֹגִים אַף נְשִׂיאַת כַּפַּיִם אֲסוּרָה בַּחַרְצָנִים וּבַזּוֹגִין. וּמָאן דִּיליף לָהּ מִן הַשֵּׁירוּת. אִי מַה הַשֵּׁירוּת אָסוּר בְּבַעֲלֵי מוּמִין אַף נְשִׂיאַת כַּפַּיִם אָסוּר בְּבַעֲלֵי מוּמִין.

וְהָא תַנֵּי. אִם הָיָה דָשׁ בְּעִירוֹ מוּתָּר. כְּהָדָא רִבִּי נַפְתָּלִי הֲוַת אֶצְבַּעְתֵּיהּ עֲקוּמָה. אֲתָא שְׁאַל לְרִבִּי מָנָא. אֲמַר לֵיהּ. מִכֵּיוָן שֶׁאַתָּה דָשׁ בְּעִירָךְ מוּתָּר. רַב חוּנָה מְעַבֵּר זַלְדְּקָן. וְהָא תַנֵּי. אִם הָיָה דָשׁ בְּעִירוֹ מוּתָּר. אֲמַר רִבִּי מָנָא. רִיגְלָא הֲוַת. בְּגִין שֶׁלֹּא יְהוּ אוֹמְרִין. רָאִינוּ קָטָן נוֹשֵׂא אֶת כַּפָּיו. אֲמַר רִבִּי יוֹסֵה. זֹאת אוֹמֶרֶת שֶׁאָסוּר לְהִסְתַּכֵּל בַּכֹּהֲנִים בַּשָּׁעָה שֶׁהֵן מְבָרְכִין. אֲמַר רִבִּי חַגַּיי. כְּלוּם אֲמָרוּ. אֵין מִסְתַּכְּלִין. לֹא מִפְּנֵי הֶסֵּיעַ דַּעַת. מֹשֶׁה. דַּאֲנָא מִסְתַּכְּלְנָא וְלָא מַסְעָה דַּעְתִּי.

1 כהדא | מ - עקומה | מ עקימה 2 חונה | מ חונא 3 ריגלא הוות | מ רגליה [הוי] סגין 4 מברכין | מ מברכין את ישראל 5 מסתכלנא | מ מסתכל 6 מסעה | מ מסע

Rebbi Ze`ira, Rebbi Ḥiyya, Rebbi Joshua ben Levi in the name of Bar Pedaya: Why did the verse join the chapter of the *nazir* to the chapter of lifting the hands[12]? To teach you that just as the *nazir* is forbidden wine so lifting the hands is forbidden wine. Then since the *nazir* is forbidden skins and kernels, also lifting the hands has to be forbidden skins and kernels[13]. Rebbi Jonah said, Joshua the son of the Circumciser and Rebbi Ze`ira disagreed. One infers it from the *nazir*, the other infers it from Temple service. But we do not know who inferred it from the *nazir* and who inferred it from Temple service. For him who inferred it from the *nazir,* since the *nazir* is forbidden skins and kernels, also lifting the hands has to be forbidden skins and kernels. For him who inferred it from Temple service, since the service is forbidden to bodily defective persons, so lifting the hands has to be forbidden to bodily defective persons[14].

[15]But was it not stated, if he was known in his town he is permitted[16]? As the following: The finger of Rebbi Naftali was bent[17]. He came and asked Rebbi Mana, who said to him, since you are known in your town it is permitted. Rav Huna disqualified one with sparse facial hair. But was it not stated, if he was known in his town he is permitted? Rebbi Mana said, it was a holiday[18]; so they should not say, we saw a minor lifting his hands[19]. Rebbi Yose said, this[20] implies that one is forbidden to look at the Cohanim at the moment when they are blessing. Rebbi Haggai, when they said, one does not look, was it not because of inattention[21]? By Moses, I shall look and my attention will not be diverted.

12 The rules of the *nazir* are *Num.* 6:1-21 and those of the priestly blessing 6:22-27.
13 But there is no prohibition for priests serving in the Temple to eat grapes and non-alcoholic grape products.
14 Which is shown also to be not applicable to the priestly blessing.
15 The following is copied from *Megillah,* Halakhah 4:8(**נ**).
16 Babli *Megillah* 24b.
17 In the quote of this passage by Tosaphot *Megillah* 24 b *s.v.* אם: A Cohen with deformed hands came before Rebbi Naftali.
18 In *Megillah:* he had short legs.
19 Since as explained later, reciting the priestly blessing is a biblical command, it cannot be performed by an underaged Cohen.
20 The statement on the Mishnah in *Megillah* that a Cohen with stained hands may not lift them for the priestly blessing.
21 The person blessed can benefit from the blessing only if his mind is concentrated on the Heavenly blessing.

(66b line 75) מְנַיָין לִנְשִׂיאוּת כַּפַּיִם. כֹּה תְבָרֲכוּ אֶת־בְּנֵי יִשְׂרָאֵל. עַד כָּאן בְּשַׁחֲרִית. בְּמוּסָף. וַיִּשָּׂא אַהֲרֹן אֶת־יָדָיו אֶל־הָעָם. הַמִּקְרָא הַזֶּה מְסוֹרָס הוּא. וַהֲלֹא לֹא צָרִיךְ לוֹמַר אֶלָּא וַיֵּרֶד מֵעֲשׂוֹת הַחַטָּאת וְהָעֹלָה וְהַשְּׁלָמִים וְאַחַר כָּךְ וַיִּשָּׂא אַהֲרֹן אֶת־יָדָיו וגו'. אֶלָּא מְלַמֵּד שֶׁבְּיָרִידָתוֹ לַמִּזְבֵּחַ הָיָה נוֹשֵׂא אֶת כַּפָּיו וּמְבָרֵךְ אֶת הָעָם. וַיְבָרְכֵם. בָּעֲמִידָה. יָכוֹל שֶׁלֹּא בָעֲמִידָה. תַּלְמוּד לוֹמַר בָּם בָּחַר יי אֱלֹהֶיךָ לְשָׁרְתוֹ וּלְבָרֵךְ בִּשְׁמוֹ. מַקִּישׁ בְּרָכָה לַשֵּׁירוּת. מַה שֵּׁירוּת בָּעֲמִידָה. אַף בְּרָכָה בָּעֲמִידָה. וְכֵן הוּא אוֹמֵר וַיָּקוּמוּ הַכֹּהֲנִים הַלְוִיִּם וַיְבָרְכוּ אֶת־הָעָם וגו'. בְּדוֹרוֹ שֶׁלְחִזְקִיָּהוּ שֶׁהָיוּ יְגֵיעִים בַּתּוֹרָה הַכָּתוּב מְדַבֵּר. אֲבָל בְּדוֹרוֹת אֲחֵרִים שֶׁהָיוּ עוֹבְדִים עֲבוֹדָה זָרָה מָהוּ אוֹמֵר.

וּבְפָרְשְׂכֶם כַּפֵּיכֶם אַעְלִים עֵינַיי מִכֶּם. וַיְבָרֲכֵם. בְּרָכָה סְתוּמָה. אֲבָל לֹא שָׁמַעְנוּ אֵי זוֹ הִיא עַד שֶׁבָּא הַכָּתוּב וּפֵירְשָׁהּ. יְבָרֶכְךָ יי וְיִשְׁמְרֶךָ: יָאֵר יי | פָּנָיו אֵלֶיךָ וִיחֻנֶּךָּ: יִשָּׂא יי | פָּנָיו אֵלֶיךָ וְיָשֵׂם לְךָ שָׁלוֹם:

From where the lifting of hands? So you shall bless the Children of Israel[22]. *So far during the morning prayers*[23]. At *musaf*? *Aaron lifted his hands for the people*[24]. Is not this verse distorted? Should it not read: *he descended from making the purification sacrifice, and the elevation sacrifice, and the well-being sacrifice,* and after this, *Aaron lifted his hands for the people*? But it teaches[25] that while descending from the altar he lifted his hands and blessed the people. [26]*And he blessed them,* standing. I could think, not while standing. The verse says[27], *the Eternal, your God, selected them to serve Him and to bless in His Name.* It combines blessing with service. Since service is done standing, also blessing is done standing. And so it says[28], *the Levitic Cohanim rose and blessed the people.* The verse speaks of the generation of Ezechias, when they toiled in the Torah. But in other generations, when they were serving foreign worship, what does it say? *When you spread your hands my eyes shall disregard you*[29]. [22]*And he blessed them,* any blessing. But we did not hear which it was until the verse came and explained it[30]: *The Eternal shall bless you and guard you. The Eternal shall enlighten His presence to you and show you favor. The Eternal shall turn His presence to you and give you peace.*

22 *Num.* 6:22.
23 Since in the Temple the priestly blessing was recited at the time of the morning sacrifice, the inspiration for the morning prayer service.
24 *Lev.* 9:22, description of the special inauguration service of the Tabernacle.
25 The verse mentioning blessing before descent.
26 Babli *Sotah* 38a.
27 *Deut.* 21:5.
28 *2Chr.* 30:27.
29 *Is.* 1:15.
30 *Num.* 6:24-26.

(67c line 12) וּמִנַּיִין לִנְעִילָה. אָמַר רִבִּי [לֵוִי]. גַּם כִּי־תַרְבּוּ תְפִלָּה אֵינֶנִּי שׁוֹמֵעַ. מִיכָּן שֶׁכָּל־הַמַּרְבֶּה בִּתְפִילָּה נַעֲנֶה. מַחְלָפָה שִׁיטָתֵיהּ דְּרִבִּי לֵוִי. תַּמָּן אָמַר רִבִּי אַבָּא בְּרֵיהּ דְּרִבִּי פַּפִּי רִבִּי יְהוֹשֻׁעַ דְּסִיכְנִי בְּשֵׁם רִבִּי לֵוִי. בְּכָל־עֶצֶב יִהְיֶה מוֹתֵר וּדְבַר־שְׂפָתַיִם אַךְ־לְמַחְסוֹר: חַנָּה עַל יְדֵי שֶׁרִיבַת בִּתְפִילָּתָהּ קִיצְרָה בְיָמָיו שֶׁלִּשְׁמוּאֵל. שֶׁאָמְרָה וְיָשַׁב שָׁם עַד־עוֹלָם: וַהֲלֹא אֵין עוֹלָם שֶׁל לֵוִי אֶלָּא חֲמִשִּׁים שָׁנָה. דִּכְתִיב וּמִבֶּן חֲמִשִּׁים שָׁנָה יָשׁוּב מִצְּבָא הָעֲבֹדָה. וְהַיי דִילוֹן חַמְשִׁין

וְתָרְתֵּיי. אָמַר רִבִּי יוֹסֵי בֵּירִבִּי בּוּן. וּשְׁתַּיִם שֶׁגְּמָלַתּוּ. וְכָא הוּא אָמַר הָכֵין. כָּאן בְּיָחִיד. כָּאן בְּצִיבּוּר. רִבִּי חִייָה בְשֵׁם רִבִּי יוֹחָנָן רִבִּי שִׁמְעוֹן בֶּן חַלְפוּתָה בְשֵׁם רִבִּי מֵאִיר. וְהָיָה כִּי הִרְבְּתָה לְהִתְפַּלֵל. מִיכָּן שֶׁכָּל־הַמַּרְבֶּה בִתְפִילָה נֵעֲנֶה.

1 וּמניין | ב מניין איני שומע | ב -   3 דסכני | ב דסיכנין   4 בתפילתה | ב בתפילה קצרה | ב קיצרה   5 ויהי דילון | ב והויין ליה   6 וכא | ב וכה הוא | ב -   הכין | ב הכן ביחיד | ב ליחיד בציבור | ב לציבור   7 חייא | ב חייה חלפותה | ב חלפתא | - | ב אל לי

[31]From where Neʿilah[2]? Rebbi [Levi][32] said: *Even if you prolong your prayers I shall not hear*[29]. From here that everyone who increases his prayers will be answered[33]. The argument of Rebbi Levi is inverted. There says Rebbi Abba the son of Rebbi Pappai, Rebbi Joshua of Sikhnin in the name of Rebbi Levi: *In all excitement there is something superfluous; and the word of the lips is but for deficit*[34]. Hannah, because she prayed too long, reduced the years of Samuel because she said, *he shall dwell there forever*[35] but "forever" for a Levite is only 50 years, as it is written: *at age fifty he should return from the worshipping hosts*[36]. But in fact it was 52[37]. Rebbi Yose ben Rebbi Abun said two years until she weaned him. And here you say so? One for private, the other for public prayers. Rebbi Ḥiyya in the name of Rebbi Joḥanan, Rebbi Simeon bar Ḥalaphta in the name of Rebbi Meïr: *when she prayed very long*[38]; it follows that everyone who extends his prayers will be answered[39].

31 From here to the end of the Halakhah the text is from *Berakhot* 4:1, Notes 64-124 (ב).
32 Corrector's addition from *Berakhot*.
33 Since Isaiah presents this as a particular curse, it follows that as a rule people will be heard if they increase their prayers.
34 *Prov.* 14:23.
35 *1Sam.* 1:22; not part of Hannah's prayer but a statement to her husband.
36 *Num.* 8:25.
37 Not a biblical statement but an inference of *Seder Olam* Chapter 13 (in the author's edition pp. 134-135.)
38 *1 Sam.* 1:12.
39 Denied in Babli *Berakhot* 32b.

(67c line 22) עַד אֵימָתַי הִיא נְעִילָה. רַבָּנָן דְּקַיְסָרִין אֲמְרִין. אִיתְפַּלְּגוּן רַב וְרִבִּי יוֹחָנָן. רַב אָמַר. בִּנְעִילַת שַׁעֲרֵי שָׁמַיִם. רִבִּי יוֹחָנָן. בִּנְעִילַת שַׁעֲרֵי הֵיכָל. אָמַר רִבִּי יוּדָן עַנְתּוֹנְדְּרְיָּא. מַתְנִיתָה מְסַיְיעָא לְרִבִּי יוֹחָנָן. בִּשְׁלֹשָׁה פְרָקִים הַכֹּהֲנִים נוֹשְׂאִין אֶת כַּפֵּיהֶן אַרְבַּע פְּעָמִים בַּיוֹם בַּשַּׁחֲרִית בַּמּוּסָף בַּמִּנְחָה בִּנְעִילַת שְׁעָרִים. אִית לָךְ מֵימַר. נְעִילַת שַׁעֲרֵי שָׁמַיִם בַּיּוֹם.

1 עד ב -   2 ר' יוחנן | ב ור' יוחנן אמ'. ענתונדריא | ב עמתידריא   4 בנעילת | ב ובנעילת | - | ב בתעניות ובמעמדות וביום הכיפורים

אֲתָוָה דְּאִימֵּיהּ דְּרַב אָדָא הֲוָה צַיָּיר גּוּלָתֵיהּ דְּרַב בְּצוֹמָא רַבָּא. אָמַר לֵיהּ. כַּד תֵּיחְמֵי שִׁימְשָׁא בְרֵישׁ דִּיקְלֵי יְהִיב לִי גּוּלָתִי דְּנִצְלֵי נְעִילַת שְׁעָרִים. מִחְלְפָה שִׁיטָתֵיהּ דְּרַב. תַּמָּן הוּא

אָמַר. בִּנְעִילַת שַׁעֲרֵי שָׁמַיִם. וְכָא הוּא אָמַר. בִּנְעִילַת שַׁעֲרֵי הֵיכָל. אָמַר רִבִּי מַתַּנְיָה. עַל יְדֵי דַהֲוָה מַעֲרִיךְ בִּצְלוּתֵיהּ סַגִּין הֲוָה מַגִּיעַ סָמוּךְ לִנְעִילַת שַׁעֲרֵי שָׁמַיִם.

1 אחוה | ב אחוי דאימי | ב דאימא 2 את יהיב | ב תיתב 4 מעריך | ב במעריך רב סמוך | ב -

Until when is *Ne`ilah*? The rabbis of Caesarea say: Rav and Rebbi Joḥanan disagree. Rav said, when the gates of Heaven are locked[40]. Rebbi Joḥanan: when the gates of the Temple are locked. Rebbi Yudan Antordaya said, the Mishnah supports Rebbi Joḥanan: "On three occasions do the Cohanim lift their hands four times in one day, mornings, *Musaph*, *Minḥah*, and at the locking of the gates." May you say that the gates of heaven are locked while it is still daytime[41]?

The maternal uncle of Rebbi Ada had rolled up the kaftan of Rav on the great fast. He said to him: When you see the sun on the top of the date palms, give me my kaftan so that we may pray the Locking of the Gates. The argument of Rav is inverted. There he says "the locking of the Gates of Heaven" and here he says "the locking of the gates of the Temple[42]." Rebbi Mattanah said: Since Rav needed a lot of time to pray, he reached the Locking of the Gates of Heaven.

40 It is not clear when the Gates of Heaven are locked. Maybe it is at sundown when the sun disappears, but it is more likely sometime after that when on a very clear day one may notice a sudden darkening of the sky in the middle of the gradual dusk. The gates of the Temple were locked for the public at the time of the lighting of the candelabra in the Sanctuary, which must be before sundown.

41 Since the priestly blessing may be recited only during daytime, the "locking of the gates" mentioned in the Mishnah must have been during daytime and cannot have been in the night.

42 Since the sun is on the top of the date palms quite some time before sunset, Rav cannot possibly pray at the Locking of the Gates of Heaven. Hence, his actions contradict his teachings.

(67c line 32) נְעִילָה מָהוּ שֶׁתִּפְטוֹר אֶת שֶׁלְעֶרֶב. רִבִּי בָּא רַב חוּנָה בְּשֵׁם רַב. נְעִילָה פּוֹטֶרֶת שֶׁלְעֶרֶב. אָמַר רִבִּי בָּא לְרַב חוּנָה. וְאֵיכָן הוּא מַזְכִּיר שֶׁלְאַבְדָּלָה. אָמַר רִבִּי יוֹנָה לְרִבִּי בָּא. וְהֵיאַךְ יְהוּ שֶׁבַע פּוֹטְרוֹת שְׁמוֹנֶה עֶשְׂרֵה. אָמַר לֵיהּ. וְלָא כְבָר אִיתְּתָבַת. אָמַר לֵיהּ. וּבְגִין דְּאִיתְּתָבַת תִּיבָּטֵל. אָמַר רִבִּי יוֹסֵה. מַה דְּקַשֵּׁי רִבִּי בָּא קַשֵּׁי יָאוּת. מַה דְּקַשֵּׁי רִבִּי יוֹנָה לָא קַשֵּׁי יָאוּת. קַל הֵיקִילוּ עָלָיו מִפְּנֵי תַעֲנִיתוֹ שֶׁיְּהוּ שֶׁבַע פּוֹטְרוֹת שְׁמוֹנֶה עֶשְׂרֵה. רִבִּי בָּא בַּר מָמָל אָמַר לַחֲבֵרַיָּיא. מָרַיי. מָן כּוּלְּכוֹן שְׁמָעִית שֶׁאֵין נְעִילָה פּוֹטֶרֶת שֶׁלְעֶרֶב. רִבִּי סִימוֹן בְּשֵׁם רִבִּי לֵוִי. אֵין

נְעִילָה פּוֹטֶרֶת שֶׁלְּעֶרֶב. אָמַר רִבִּי יוֹסֵי בֵּירִבִּי בּוּן. וְתַנֵּי רִבִּי חִייָה כֵן. בְּכָל־יוֹם אָדָם מִתְפַּלֵּל שְׁמוֹנֶה עֶשְׂרֵה. בְּמוֹצָאֵי שַׁבָּת וּבְמוֹצָאֵי יוֹם הַכִּיפּוּרִים וּבְמוֹצָאֵי תַעֲנִית צִיבּוּר.

1 את | ב - בא | ב אבא רב חונה | ב ורב חונא   2 אמ' | ב אמ' ליה בא | ב אבא (2) רב חונה | ב ורב הונא ואיכן | ב היאך שלאבדלה | ב של הבדלה   3 והיאך | ב היאך ובגין | ב בגין   4 תיבטל | ב תיבטיל יוסה | ב יוסי דקשי | ב דאקשי בא | ב אבא   5 היקילו | ב היקלו בא | ב אבא   6 לוי | ב יהושע בן לוי   7 חייה כן | ב חייא

May Neʻilah free one from evening prayers? Rebbi Abba, Rav Huna in the name of Rav: Neʻilah frees one from evening prayers[43]. Rebbi Abba said to Rav Huna: How may he mention *havdalah*[44]? Rebbi Jonah said to Rebbi Abba: How may seven free one from eighteen[45]? He said to him, did I not already contradict it? He said to him: Because you contradicted it, should it be abandoned? Rebbi Yose said, what Rebbi Abba asked is truly difficult. What Rebbi Jonah asked is not at all difficult; they made it easy on people because of the fast, that seven should free one from eighteen. Rebbi Abba bar Mamal said to his colleagues: From all of them I understand that Neʻilah does not free one from evening prayers. Rebbi Simon in the name of Rebbi <Joshua ben>[46] Levi: Neʻilah does not free one from evening prayers. Rebbi Yose bar Abun said: Did not Rebbi Hiyya state this? "Every day one prays eighteen benedictions, including the end of Sabbath, end of Yom Kippur, and end of public fast days.[47]"

43 According to Rav's original opinion that one prays at the Locking of the Gates of Heaven, Neʻilah may be started only when evening prayers may already be said. It does not make sense to recite two different prayers at the same time.

44 At the end of Sabbath or holiday work is permitted only if *havdalah* ("distinction") was recited, preferably in the evening Amidah. Hence, Rav's decision seems to be impossible.

45 The seven benedictions of the holiday Amidah cannot accommodate the 18 of the weekday prayers.

46 Added from the text in *Berakhot*. R. Levi was a popular preacher, neither a legal authority nor a teacher of R. Simon.

47 Fast days in a drought.

(67c line 42) רִבִּי יִצְחָק בַּר נַחְמָן בְּשֵׁם רִבִּי יְהוֹשֻׁעַ בֶּן לֵוִי. יוֹם הַכִּיפּוּרִים שֶׁחָל לִהְיוֹת בַּשַּׁבָּת אַף עַל פִּי שֶׁאֵין נְעִילָה בַשַּׁבָּת מַזְכִּיר שֶׁלְשַּׁבָּת בִּנְעִילָה. רִבִּי סִימוֹן בְּשֵׁם רִבִּי יְהוֹשֻׁעַ בֶּן לֵוִי. שַׁבָּת שֶׁחָלָה לִהְיוֹת בַּחֲנוּכָה אַף עַל פִּי שֶׁאֵין מוּסָף בַּחֲנוּכָה מַזְכִּיר שֶׁלַחֲנוּכָה בַּמּוּסָף. אוּסְפוּן עֲלָהּ רֹאשׁ חוֹדֶשׁ שֶׁחָל לִהְיוֹת בַּתַעֲנִית אַף עַל פִּי שֶׁאֵין נְעִילָה בְּרֹאשׁ חוֹדֶשׁ מַזְכִּיר שֶׁלְרֹאשׁ חוֹדֶשׁ בִּנְעִילָה. רֹאשׁ חוֹדֶשׁ וְתַעֲנִית אֵיכָן הוּא מַזְכִּיר שֶׁל רֹאשׁ חוֹדֶשׁ. רִבִּי זְעוּרָה אָמַר. בְּהוּדָיָּיה. רִבִּי בָּא בַּר מָמָל אָמַר. בָּעֲבוֹדָה. רִבִּי אֲבוּנָה אָמַר. אוֹמְרָהּ בְּרָכָה רְבִיעִית. אָמַר רִבִּי בָּא. מַה

מָצָאנוּ בְכָל־מָקוֹם אוֹמְרָהּ בְּרָכָה רְבִיעִית.   אַף כָּאן בְּרָכָה רְבִיעִית.   וּנְפַק עוֹבְדָא כְּהָדָא דְרִבִּי בָּא.

[48]Rebbi Isaac bar Naḥman in the name of Rebbi Joshua ben Levi: If the Day of Atonement happens to be on the Sabbath, one mentions Sabbath in *Ne`ilah* even though there is no *Ne`ilah* for Sabbath[49]. Rebbi Simon in the name of Rebbi Joshua ben Levi: On a Sabbath that falls on Ḥanukkah, one mentions Ḥanukkah for *Musaf* even though there is no *Musaf* for Ḥanukkah[50]. They added to it: If the New Moon happens to be on a public fast-day, one mentions the New Moon in *Ne`ilah* even though there is no *Ne`ilah* for the New Moon. When the New Moon falls on a fast-day, how does one mention the New Moon? Rebbi Ze`ira said, in "thanksgiving". Rebbi Abba bar Mamal said, in "Temple service". Rebbi Abuna said, one says it as the fourth benediction[51]. Rebbi Abba said, since we find everywhere that one says it as the fourth benediction, here also as the fourth benediction. And so it was acted upon according to Rebbi Abba[52].

48 While this paragraph also is in *Berakhot*, the text there is in very bad shape and not directly comparable to the text here.

49 Babli *Šabbat* 24b in the name of R. Joshua ben Levi.

50 Babli *Šabbat* 24a.

51 These sentences are difficult to understand and the greatest authorities of the Middle Ages, Rashba on Babli *Berakhot* 32b and Rosh to *Berakhot* Chap. 5, #10 felt compelled to emend the text. Since three of the four prayers of the New Moon are weekday prayers with an addition added in "Temple service" (the 16th benediction in the Yerushalmi version) as prescribed in *Berakhot* 5:2, the only question can be about *Musaf*. However, we never hear that the particular inserts in the morning prayers of a fast day were recited also for *Musaf*. On the other hand, as Rosh points out, the previous paragraph certainly implies that the עֲנֵנוּ prayer recited on all fast-days except Yom Kippur, not only on those for rain, must be recited also for *Musaf* since the day requires that the text be inserted in all prayers. One may at least understand the position of Rebbi Abba that on a fast day for rain which coincides with a day of the New Moon, one recites the usual *Musaf* with an additional fifth benediction which deals with the fast day, after the fourth for the New Moon. The dissenting opinions of Rebbis Ze`ira and Abba bar Mamal seem to imply that *Musaf* on a fast day consisted of the introductory and final benedictions that are common to all prayers and the additional benedictions for the fast day, whereas the section on the New Moon, for which *Musaf* is recited in the first place, is moved from its regular place to an insert in either the 16th or the 17th ("thanksgiving") benediction.

52 A reported action on an opinion is the

best proof that this is accepted practice.

(67c line 51) בַּמֶּה קוֹרִין. רִבִּי יוֹסֵי אוֹמֵר. קוֹרִין בְּרָכוֹת וּקְלָלוֹת. אֲמַר לוֹן רִבִּי מָנָא. בְּגִין מוֹדַעְתּוֹן דִּי תַעֲנִיתָא רְבִיעִין עַל מֵעֵיהוֹן. וְלָא יָדְעִין דִּי תַעֲנִיתָא. אֲמַר לֵיהּ. לְהוֹדִיעֲךָ שֶׁקּוֹרִין בְּרָכוֹת וּקְלָלוֹת. רִבִּי יוּדָן קַפּוֹדְקַיָיא אָמַר קוֹמֵי רִבִּי יוֹסֵה בְּשֵׁם רִבִּי יוּדָה בַּר פָּזִי. קוֹרִין בְּרֹאשׁ חוֹדֶשׁ. קָם רִבִּי יוֹסֵה עִם רִבִּי יוּדָה בַּר פַּפֵּי. אֲמַר לֵיהּ. אַתָּה שְׁמַעְתָּ מִן אָבוּךְ הָדָא מִילְתָא. אֲמַר לֵיהּ. אַבָּא לֹא אָמַר כֵּן. אֶלָּא בְּעֵינֵי טָב. עַל־יְדֵי דְּאִינּוּן יָדְעִין דְּהוּא רֵישׁ יַרְחָא הֵן קוֹרִין בְּרֹאשׁ חוֹדֶשׁ. וּשְׁאָר כָּל־הַמְּקוֹמוֹת קוֹרִין בְּרָכוֹת וּקְלָלוֹת.

1 או' **ב** אמ' | לון **ב** ליה בגין | **ב** כגון   2 די | **ב** בי R דהיא תעניתא | **ב** תענית   3 קפודקייא | **ב** קפודקיא יוסה **ב** יוסי בר | **ב** בן   4 יוסה **ב** יוסי בר | **ב** בן אתה | **ב** את   5 אמר | **ב** היה אמר בעייני | **ב** בעין   6 ושאר | **ב** הא שאר

[53]And what does one read? Rebbi Yose said, one reads "blessings and curses." Rebbi Mana said to him, since they know it is a fast day they are falling on their bellies, do they not know that it is a fast day? He said to him, to tell you that one reads "blessings and curses." Rebbi Yudan from Kappadokia said before Rebbi Yose in the name of Rebbi Jehudah bar Pazi, one reads about the New Moon. Rebbi Yose met Rebbi Jehudah bar Pappai; he said to him, did you hear this from your father? He said to him, my father said this only about Eintab. Since they know that it is the New Moon, they are reading about the New Moon. At all other places they are reading "blessings and curses."

53 In addition to the text in *Berakhot*, this paragraph is copied from *Ta`aniot* Halakhah 2:15, Notes 241-245.

(67c line 58) יִרְמִיָה סַפְרָא שָׁאִיל לְרַב יִרְמִיָה. רֹאשׁ חוֹדֶשׁ שֶׁחָל לִהְיוֹת בַּשַּׁבָּת בַּמֶּה קוֹרִין. אֲמַר לֵיהּ. קוֹרִין בְּרֹאשׁ חוֹדֶשׁ. אָמַר רִבִּי חֶלְבּוֹ קוֹמֵי רִבִּי אִימִּי. מַתְנִיתָא אֲמָרָה כֵן. לַכֹּל מַפְסִיקִין. לְרָאשֵׁי חֳדָשִׁים לַחֲנוּכָּה וּלְפוּרִים.

1 שאיל | **מ** שאל לרב | **ב** לר'   2 אימי | **ב** אמי מתני' | **ב** ומתניתא

יִצְחָק סְחוֹרָה שָׁאַל לְרִבִּי יִצְחָק. רֹאשׁ חוֹדֶשׁ שֶׁחָל בַּחֲנוּכָּה בַּמֶּה קוֹרִין. אֲמַר לֵיהּ. קוֹרִין שְׁלֹשָׁה בְּרֹאשׁ חוֹדֶשׁ וְאֶחָד בַּחֲנוּכָּה. רִבִּי פִּינְחָס רִבִּי סִימוֹן רִבִּי אַבָּא בַּר זְמִינָא מַטֵּי בָהּ בְּשֵׁם רִבִּי אַבְדּוּמָא דְחֵיפָה. קוֹרִין שְׁלֹשָׁה בַּחֲנוּכָּה וְאֶחָד בְּרֹאשׁ חוֹדֶשׁ. לְהוֹדִיעֲךָ שֶׁלֹּא בָא הָרְבִיעִי אֶלָּא מַחֲמַת רֹאשׁ חוֹדֶשׁ. בַּר שְׁלָמְיָה סַפְרָא שָׁאַל לְרִבִּי מָנָא. הַגַּע עַצְמָךְ שֶׁחָל רֹאשׁ חוֹדֶשׁ שֶׁלַּחֲנוּכָּה לִהְיוֹת בַּשַּׁבָּת. וְלָא שִׁבְעָה קָרוֹיִין אִינּוּן. אִית לָךְ מֵימַר שֶׁלֹּא בָא הָרְבִיעִי אֶלָּא מַחֲמַת רֹאשׁ חוֹדֶשׁ. אֲמַר לֵיהּ. וְהָדָא שְׁאִילְתֵּיהּ דְּסָפָר.

1 סחורה | **ב** סחורא שחל | **מב** שחל להיות   2 ר' סימון | **ב** ור' סימון ר' אבא | **מ** ור' אבא מטי | **ב** מטו   3 אבדומא | **ב** אבדימא דחיפה | **ב** דמן חיפה   4 שלמיה | **מ** שילמיא **ב** שלמיא   5 קרויין אינון | **ב** אינון קורין

מימר | ב למימר — 6 - | ב שאילתינהו לספרא שאילתיה | ב שאלתא

Jeremiah the Scribe asked before (Rav) <Rebbi>⁵⁴ Jeremiah: What does one read if the day of the New Moon is a Sabbath? He said to him: One reads about the New Moon. Rebbi Ḥelbo said before Rebbi Immi: The Mishnah says so: "One interrupts for everything, for New Moons, for Ḥanukkah, and for Purim."

Isaac the trader asked Rebbi Isaac: What does one read on a New Moon that falls on Ḥanukkah? He said to him: Three for the New Moon and one for Ḥanukkah. Rebbi Phineas, Rebbi Simon, Rebbi Abba bar Zamina brought it in the name of Rebbi Eudaimon of Haifa: Three read of Ḥanukka and one of the New Moon, to tell you that the fourth one comes only because of the New Moon⁵⁵. Bar Shelemiah the scribe asked Rebbi Mana: Think of it, if the New Moon of Ḥanukkah falls on a Sabbath, do not seven read? How can you say, to tell you that the fourth one comes only because of the New Moon? He said to him: That is a true question of a scribe⁵⁶.

54 The reading "Rebbi" from *Berakhot* is the only one possible. The question could have been asked only in Palestine with its 3½ year cycle, when no more than one Torah scroll was removed from the Ark at any time. In Babylonia, place of Rav Jeremiah, with its tight one-year cycle, all exceptional readings always were done with a second scroll read by the *maftir*.

55 Mishna *Megillah* 3:6.

56 Usually on Ḥanukkah only three people read from the Torah since it is a regular workday. On the day of the New Moon, four persons read since it is a day with a *Musaf* sacrifice in the Temple. On the Sabbath, seven read (and the *maftir* reads one additional portion). Hence, it seems impossible that the fourth person should read about Ḥanukkah.

57 In *Berakhot* it is stated that the scribe asked the question on behalf of others and he was rebuked by R. Mana for not thinking by himself that the natural place for reading about Ḥanukkah was the additional partion of the *maftir*.

These paragraphs also are in *Megillah* 3:6. Babli *Megillah* 29b.

(67c line 67) רִבִּי מַפְקֵד לְאַבָּא דוּ אֲמוֹרֵיהּ. אַכְרִיז קוֹמֵיהוֹן. מָאן דְּמַצְלֵי יַצְלֵי דְרַמְשָׁא עַד דְּיוֹמָא קָאִים. רִבִּי חִיָּיה בַּר בָּא מַפְקִיד לַאֲמוֹרֵיהּ. אַכְרִיז קוֹמֵיהוֹן. מָאן דְּמַצְלֵי יַצְלֵי דְרַמְשָׁא עַד דְּיוֹמָא קַיָּים. אֲמַר רִבִּי חֲנִינָה. מַשְׁכְּנֵי רִבִּי יִשְׁמָעֵאל בֵּירִבִּי יוֹסֵי אֵצֶל פּוּנְדְּקִי אֶחָד וְאָמַר לִי. כָּאן נִתְפַּלֵּל אַבָּא שְׁלָלֵילֵי שַׁבָּת בְּעֶרֶב שַׁבָּת. אָמַר רִבִּי אִימִי. רִבִּי יוֹחָנָן פָּלִיג וְלָא הֲוָה צָרִיךְ מִתְפַּלְגָה. לָמָּה. שֶׁכֵּן מוֹסִיפִין מֵחוֹל עַל קוֹדֶשׁ. וְעוֹד דְּסַלְקוֹן חַמָּרַיָּיא מִן עֶרֶב לְצִיפּוֹרִין

וְאָמְרוּן. כְּבָר שָׁבַת רִבִּי חֲנִינָה בֶּן דּוֹסָא בְּעִירוֹ. וְהַיְידָא אָמַר. דְּאָמַר רִבִּי חֲנִינָה. מָשְׁכֵנִי רִבִּי יִשְׁמָעֵאל בֵּירִבִּי יוֹסֵי אֶצֶל פּוּנְדְּקִי אֶחָד וְאָמַר לִי. כָּאן נִתְפַּלֵּל אַבָּא שֶׁלְמוֹצָאֵי שַׁבָּת בַּשַּׁבָּת. וַאֲפִילוּ עַלָה לָא הֲוָה צָרִיךְ מִתְפַּלְגָה. דְּרִבִּי מַפְקֵד לְאַבְדָּן אֲמוֹרֵיהּ. אַכְרִיז קוֹמֵיהוֹן. מָאן דְּיַצָּלֵי יַצָּלֵי דְּרַמְשָׁא עַד דְּיוֹמָא קַיָּם. רִבִּי חִייָה בַּר בָּא מַפְקֵד לַאֲמוֹרֵיהּ. אַכְרִיז קוֹמֵיהוֹן. מָאן דְּמַצָּלֵי יַצָּלֵי דְּרוּמְשָׁא עַד דְּיוֹמָא קַיָּם. דְּבֵית רִבִּי יַנַּאי אָמְרִין. עָלָה אָדָם לְמִיטָתוֹ אֵין מַטְרִיחִין עָלָיו שֶׁיֵרֵד. אָמַר רִבִּי זְעוּרָה. כָּל־זְמָן דַּהֲוִינָא עָבַד כֵּן הֲוֵינָא מִתְפַּחֵד בַּלַּיְלַיָּא. לֵית לָךְ אֶלָּא כְּהָדָא דְּרִבִּי מַפְקֵד לְאַבְדָּן אֲמוֹרֵיהּ. אַכְרִיז קוֹמֵיהוֹן. מָאן דְּמַצָּלֵי יַצָּלֵי דְּרַמְשָׁא עַד דְּיוֹמָא קַיָּם. רִבִּי חִייָה בַּר אַבָּא מַפְקֵד לַאֲמוֹרֵיהּ. אַכְרִיז קוֹמֵיהוֹן. מָאן דְּמַצָּלֵי יַצָּלֵי דְּרַמְשָׁא עַד דְּיוֹמָא קַיָּם.

1 לאבא | ב לאבדן קומיהון | ב קומי ציבורא   2 דיומא | ב יומא   חייה בר בא | ב חייא בר ווא   מפקיד | ב מפקד   3 קיים | ב קאים חנינה | ב חנינא פונדקי | ב פונדק ואמ' | ב אמ'   4 אימי | ב אמי   5 מתפלגה | ב מפלגה על הדא חמרייא | ב חומרייא   6 ואמרון | ב ואמרין חנינה | ב חנינא (2) | והיידא | ב והידא אמ' | ב אמרה דא   7 פונדקי | ב פונדוק ואמ' | ב אמ'   8 ואפילו | ב ואפי' אף מתפלגה | ב מיפלגה   קומיהון | ב קומי ציבורא קיים | ב קאים חייה בר בא | ב חייא בר ווא אכריז קומיהון | ב אכרייזו קומי ציבורא   10 יצלי | ב מצלי   דיומא קיים | ב יומא קאים   11 שירד | ב לירד   זעורה | ב זעורא מתפחד | ב מפחד בלילייא | ב בליליא   12 קומיהון | ב קומי ציבורא דיומא | ב יומא חייה בר בא | ב חייא בר ווא אכריז... קיים | ב -

[58]Rebbi commanded (Abba who was) his speaker <Abdan>[59]: Proclaim before them that he who wants to pray, should pray evening prayers as long as it is still daylight[60]. Rebbi Ḥiyya bar Abba[61] commanded his speaker: Proclaim before them that he who wants to pray should pray evening prayers as long as it is still daylight. Rebbi Ḥanina said: Rebbi Ismael ben Rebbi Yose drew me to an inn and said to me: Here my father prayed Sabbath {Friday night} prayers on Friday. Rebbi Immi said: Rebbi Joḥanan disagrees[62] but he should not have disagreed since one adds from the profane to the holy time; in addition, donkey drivers come from Arab[63] to Sepphoris and say, Rebbi Ḥanina ben Dosa already did consecrate the Sabbath in his town. But so it has been said, that Rebbi Ḥanina said: Rebbi Ismael ben Rebbi Yose drew me to an inn and said to me, here my father prayed Saturday night prayers on the Sabbath[64]. But even with that he should not have disagreed, since Rebbi commanded his speaker Abdan: Proclaim before them that he who wants to pray should pray evening prayers as long as it is still daylight. Rebbi Ḥiyya bar Abba[61] commanded his speaker: Proclaim before them that he who wants to pray should pray evening prayers as long as it is still daylight. In the house of Rebbi Yannai they said: If a man went to bed, one does not bother him to get up. Rebbi Ze`ira said, all the time that I followed this rule, I was afraid in the night. You have only what Rebbi commanded his speaker Abdan: Proclaim before them that he who wants to

pray should pray evening prayers as long as it is still daylight. Rebbi Ḥiyya bar Abba commanded his speaker: Proclaim before them that he who wants to pray should pray evening prayers as long as it is still daylight.

58 The text appears in modified form also in *Gen. rabba* 8:10, *Pesiqta rabbati* 23; the parallel in Babli *Berakhot* 27b disagrees fundamentally with the practice explained here.

59 It seems that his name was Abba Yudan; therefore both the version here and that in *Berakhot* are acceptable.

60 According to Mishnah *Berakhot* 4:1, the time of afternoon prayers is until 5/4 hours before sundown for Rebbi Jehudah and until sundown for the other Sages. As a corollary, the time of evening prayers starts at 5/4 hours before sundown for Rebbi Jehudah and at sundown for the others. Since Rebbi was a student of Rebbi Jehudah, it seems that he followed his teacher and himself was followed by his own student R. Ḥiyya. It is assumed here that we already know the result of the next paragraph, that evening prayer is not obligatory (this is also accepted in the Babli), and that because of this one permits evening prayer before sundown because it is a minor obligation and in Galilee apparently was not recited in the synagogue. [The Babli states that evening prayers should be said in the night, that this is also Rebbi's position as reported in the Babli, but that in case of error, under very dark clouds, one does not have to repeat the prayer which in Babylonia was recited in the synagogue.]

61 This R. Ḥiyya bar Abba is not the student of R. Joḥanan who usually is called by this name but Rebbi's student R. Ḥiyya (the Elder) bar Abba bar Aḥa Karsala.

62 As Levi Ginzberg explains, it seems from Mishnah *Berakhot* that originally there were 5 prayer times every day, 3 times for the Amidah prayer and twice for the recitation of the *Shema`*. R. Joḥanan is the first Amora who requires that the recitation of the *Shema`*, whose times are determined differently from those of the *Amidah*, nevertheless be combined with the *Amidah* in that the benediction following the recitation be the introduction to the *Amidah*. Since the time of the evening *Shema`* is in the night proper, he has to oppose an early recitation.

63 The village of Arrabeh, North of Kafr Kanah in lower Galilee.

64 To say weekday prayers on the Sabbath certainly is possible only if the time allotted to the prayer is dissociated from actual time.

(67d line 11) אָמַר רִבִּי יַעֲקֹב בַּר אָחָא. וְתַנֵּיי תַּמָּן. תְּפִילַת הָעֶרֶב מָהוּ. רַבָּן גַּמְלִיאֵל אוֹמֵר. חוֹבָה. רִבִּי יְהוֹשֻׁעַ אוֹמֵר. רְשׁוּת. אָמַר רִבִּי חִינְנָא. אַתְיָין אִילֵּין פְּלוּגְוָותָא כְּהֵינֵּין פְּלוּגְוָותָא. מָאן דְּאָמַר חוֹבָה. אֵין נְעִילָה פּוֹטֶרֶת שֶׁלְעָרֶב. מָאן דְּאָמַר. רְשׁוּת. נְעִילָה פּוֹטֶרֶת שֶׁלְעָרֶב.

1 ותניי | ב תניי   2 חיננא | ב חנינא   פלוגוותא | ב פלגוותא (2)   3 דאמ׳ | ב דמר (2)   מאן | ב ומאן

מַעֲשֶׂה בְּתַלְמִיד אֶחָד שֶׁבָּא וְשָׁאַל אֶת רִבִּי יְהוֹשֻׁעַ. תְּפִילַת הָעֶרֶב מָה הִיא. אָמַר לוֹ. רְשׁוּת. וּבָא וְשָׁאַל אֶת רַבָּן גַּמְלִיאֵל. תְּפִילַת הָעֶרֶב מָה הִיא. אָמַר לוֹ. חוֹבָה. אָמַר לוֹ. וַהֲלֹא רִבִּי

יְהוֹשֻׁעַ אָמַר לִי. רְשׁוּת. אָמַר לוֹ. לְמָחָר כְּשֶׁאֵיכָּנֵס לְבֵית הַוַּעַד עֲמוֹד וּשְׁאַל אֶת הַהֲלָכָה הַזֹּאת. וְעָמַד אוֹתוֹ הַתַּלְמִיד וְשָׁאַל אֶת רַבָּן גַּמְלִיאֵל. תְּפִילַת הָעֶרֶב מַה הִיא. אָמַר לוֹ. חוֹבָה. אָמַר לוֹ. וְהָא רִבִּי יְהוֹשֻׁעַ אוֹמֵר. רְשׁוּת. אָמַר לוֹ רַבָּן גַּמְלִיאֵל לְרִבִּי יְהוֹשֻׁעַ. אַתְּ הוּא שֶׁאוֹמֵר. רְשׁוּת. אָמַר לוֹ. לָאו. אָמַר לוֹ. עֲמוֹד עַל רַגְלֶיךָ וִיעִידוּךְ. וְהָיָה רַבָּן גַּמְלִיאֵל יוֹשֵׁב וְדוֹרֵשׁ וְרִבִּי יְהוֹשֻׁעַ עוֹמֵד עַל רַגְלָיו. עַד שֶׁרִינְּנוּ בוֹ כָּל־הָעָם. אָמְרוּ לְרִבִּי חוּצְפִּית הַתּוּרְגְּמָן. הַפְטֵר אֶת הָעָם. אָמְרוּ לְרִבִּי זֵינוֹן הַחַזָּן. אֱמוֹר. הִתְחִילוּ וְאָמְרוּ. הִתְחִילוּ וְעָמְדוּ כָל־הָעָם עַל רַגְלֵיהֶם. אָמְרוּ לוֹ. וְכִי עַל־מִי לֹא־עָבְרָה רָעָתְךָ תָּמִיד: מִיַּד הָלְכוּ וּמִינּוּ אֶת רִבִּי אֶלְעָזָר בֶּן עֲזַרְיָה בִּישִׁיבָה. בֶּן שֵׁשׁ עֶשְׂרֵה שָׁנָה הָיָה וְנִמְלָא כָל־רֹאשׁוֹ שֵׂיבוֹת. וְהָיָה רִבִּי עֲקִיבָה יוֹשֵׁב וּמִצְטַעֵר וְאוֹמֵר. לֹא שֶׁהוּא בֶן תּוֹרָה יוֹתֵר מִמֶּנִּי אֶלָּא שֶׁהוּא בֶן גְּדוֹלִים יוֹתֵר מִמֶּנִּי. אַשְׁרֵי אָדָם שֶׁזָּכוּ לוֹ אֲבוֹתָיו. אַשְׁרֵי אָדָם שֶׁיֵּשׁ לוֹ יָתֵד לְהִתָּלוֹת בּוֹ. וּמֶה הָיְתָה יְתֵידָתוֹ שֶׁלְּרִבִּי אֶלְעָזָר בֶּן עֲזַרְיָה. שֶׁהוּא עֲשִׂירִי לְעֶזְרָא. כַּמָּה סַפְסָלִים הָיוּ שָׁם. רִבִּי יַעֲקֹב בַּר סוֹסַיי אָמַר. שְׁמוֹנִים סַפְסָלִים שֶׁלְּתַלְמִידֵי חֲכָמִים הָיוּ שָׁם חוּץ מִן הָעוֹמְדִים מֵאַחוֹרֵי הַגָּדֵר. אָמַר רִבִּי יוֹסֵי בְּירִבִּי בּוּן. שְׁלֹשׁ מֵאוֹת סַפְסָלִין שֶׁלְּתַלְמִידֵי חֲכָמִים הָיוּ שָׁם חוּץ מִן הָעוֹמְדִים מֵאַחוֹרֵי הַגָּדֵר. כַּהֲיָא דִתְנִינַן תַּמָּן. בְּיוֹם שֶׁהוֹשִׁיבוּ אֶת רִבִּי אֶלְעָזָר בֶּן עֲזַרְיָה בַּיְשִׁיבָה. תַּמָּן תַּנִּינָן. זֶה מִדְרָשׁ דָּרַשׁ רִבִּי אֶלְעָזָר בֶּן עֲזַרְיָה לִפְנֵי חֲכָמִים בַּכֶּרֶם בְּיַבְנֶה. וְכִי כֶרֶם הָיָה שָׁם. אֶלָּא אֵילוּ תַלְמִידֵי חֲכָמִים שֶׁהָיוּ עֲשׂוּיִים שׁוּרוֹת שׁוּרוֹת כְּכֶרֶם. מִיַּד הָלַךְ לוֹ רַבָּן גַּמְלִיאֵל אֶצֶל כָּל־אֶחָד וְאֶחָד בְּתוֹךְ בֵּיתוֹ לְפַיְּיסוֹ. אֲתָא גַבֵּי רִבִּי יְהוֹשֻׁעַ וְאַשְׁכְּחֵיהּ דְּהָוָה עָבִיד מַחֲטִין. אָמַר לֵיהּ. מִן אִילֵּין אַתְּ חַיי. וְעַד כְּדוֹן אַתְּ בָּעֵי מֵידַע. אִי לוֹ לְדוֹר שֶׁאַתְּ פַּרְנָסוֹ. אָמַר לוֹ. נֶעֱנֵיתִי לָךְ. שָׁלְחוּן גַּבֵּי רִבִּי לְעָזָר בֶּן עֲזַרְיָה חַד קַצָּר. וְאִית דְּאָמְרִין רִבִּי עֲקִיבָה הֲוָה. אָמַר לֵיהּ. מִי שֶׁהוּא מַזֶּה יַזֶּה. מִי שֶׁאֵינוֹ לֹא מַזֶּה וְלֹא בֶן מַזֶּה יֹאמַר לְמַזֶּה בֶן מַזֶּה. מֵימֶיךָ מֵימֵי מְעָרָה וְאֶפְרְךָ אֶפֶר מִקְלֶה. אָמַר לָהֶן. נִתְרַצֵּיתֶם. אֲנִי וְאַתֶּם נַשְׁכִּים לְפִתְחוֹ שֶׁלְּרַבָּן גַּמְלִיאֵל. אַף עַל פִּי כֵן לֹא הוֹרִידוּ אוֹתוֹ מִגְּדוּלָּתוֹ אֶלָּא מִינּוּ אוֹתוֹ אַב בֵּית דִּין.

Rebbi Jacob bar Abba said: There, they did state, what is the status of evening prayer? Rabban Gamliel said, it is obligatory. Rebbi Joshua said, it is voluntary[65]. Rebbi Hanina said, this difference parallels the other difference: He who holds that evening prayer is obligatory, holds that *Neʿilah* does not free one from evening prayers. He who holds that it is voluntary, holds that *Neʿilah* frees one from evening prayers.

[66]It happened that one student came and asked Rebbi Joshua: What is about evening prayer? He said to him: It is voluntary. He asked Rabban Gamliel: What is about evening prayer? He said to him: It is obligatory. He said to him: But Rebbi Joshua told me that it was voluntary. He said to him: Tomorrow, when I enter the assembly hall, stand up and ask me about this practice. The next day, this student stood up and asked Rabban Gamliel: What is about evening prayer? He said to him: It is obligatory. He said to him: But Rebbi Joshua told me that it was voluntary. Rabban Gamliel said to Rebbi Joshua: Are you the one who says it is voluntary? He answered him: No. He said to him: Stand up on your feet so that they may testify against you. Then Rabban Gamliel was sitting down and lecturing while Rebbi Joshua was standing up until the people started talking and said to Rebbi Huspit the interpreter: Send the people home. They said to Rebbi Zenon the *hazan*: Start[67]! He said: Start! All the people stood up and said to him: *Certainly, on whom did your evil not pass always*[68]? They immediately appointed Rebbi Eleazar ben Azariah to the Yeshivah when he was 16 years old; his head became all white. Rebbi Aqiba sat and was sad; he said, not that he is a greater Torah scholar than I am, but he comes from a greater family than I do; hail to the man whose forefathers created merit for him, hail to the man who has a peg to hang on to. What was Rebbi Eleazar ben Azariah's peg? He was the tenth generation after Ezra[69]. How many seats were there? Rebbi Jacob ben Sisi said: Eighty seats were there of accomplished scholars, not to count those standing behind the railing. Rebbi Yose ben Rebbi Abun said 300 were there, not to count those standing behind the railing. As we have stated there[70]: "On the day Rebbi Eleazar ben Azariah was appointed to the Academy." There we have stated[71]: "This inference did Rebbi Eleazar ben Azariah present before the Sages at the vineyard of Jabneh." Was there a vineyard? It means that the scholars sat there in rows like vines in a vineyard. Rabban Gamliel went immediately to pacify each one in his house. He came to Rebbi Joshua and found him occupied with the making of needles. He asked him: This is how you earn your living? He answered him: Until now you did not know? Woe to the generation whose caretaker you are! He said to him: I humble myself before you. They sent a washerman to Rebbi

Eleazar ben Azariah, but some say that it was Rebbi Aqiba. He told him: The sprinkler, son of a sprinkler, should sprinkle. Should anyone who is neither a sprinkler nor the son of a sprinkler say to the sprinkler: your water is water from a cave and your ashes are ashes from a fireplace? He said to him: You made your peace with him! I and you shall go in the morning to Rabban Gamliel's door. Nevertheless they did not remove him from his dignity but made him head of the court.

65 In a dispute between R. Joshua and Rabban Gamliel, practice should follow R. Joshua. But there is never a doubt that the recitation of *Shema`* in the night is obligatory, and as stated before, evening prayers are still needed for mental health. In addition, following R. Johanan's later combination of *shema`* and prayer, the recitation of the *shema`* induces the obligation of the *Amidah*, which makes the dispute almost moot. Babli *Berakhot* 27b.

66 The story of this dispute should be compared with the Babli version, *Berakhot* 27b, where R. Joshua's profession is given as a charcoal burner. Since Rabban Gamliel in the aftermath of the destruction of the Temple insisted not only on uniformity of practice but also of doctrine (and in this was successful in eliminating Sadduceeism) and R. Joshua was known for his dislike of public quarrels, Rabban Gamliel thought that he was taking little risk in provoking a quarrel.

67 The hazan was not only the reader in congregational prayers, but also the general organizer of religious affairs. In outlying communities he was the ritual slaughterer and the conduit through whom questions of religious practice were addressed to the Academies. Here it seems that he had to recite the prayer at the end of a study which it was customary to start with a Bible verse and that the people spontaneously chose one which was a curse on the speaker.

68 *Nah*. 3:19.

69 Also he was very rich and could afford the expenses of representing the Jewish population before the Roman government.

70 Mishnah *Zevahim* 1:3.

71 Mishnah *Ketubot* 4:6.

(fol. 67b) משנה ב: אֵילוּ הֵן הַמַּעֲמָדוֹת צַו אֶת בְּנֵי יִשְׂרָאֵל אֶת קָרְבָּנִי לַחְמִי לְאִשַּׁי. וְכִי הֵיאַךְ קָרְבָּנוֹ שֶׁל אָדָם קָרֵב וְהוּא אֵינוֹ עוֹמֵד עַל גַּבָּיו אֶלָּא שֶׁהִתְקִינוּ הַנְּבִיאִים הָרִאשׁוֹנִים עֶשְׂרִים וְאַרְבַּע מִשְׁמָרוֹת. וְעַל כָּל מִשְׁמָר וּמִשְׁמָר הָיָה מַעֲמָד בִּירוּשָׁלַיִם שֶׁל כֹּהֲנִים וְשֶׁל לְוִיִם וְשֶׁל יִשְׂרָאֵל. הִגִּיעַ זְמַן הַמִּשְׁמָר כֹּהֲנָיו וּלְוִיָּיו עוֹלִין לִירוּשָׁלַיִם וְיִשְׂרָאֵל שֶׁבְּאוֹתוֹ הַמִּשְׁמָר מִתְכַּנְּסִין בְּעָרֵיהֶן וְקוֹרְאִין בְּמַעֲשֵׂה בְרֵאשִׁית:

Mishnah 2: These are the bystanders. *Command the Children of Israel: My sacrifice, My offering as My gift*[72]. How could a person's sacrifice be offered not in his presence[73]? But the earlier prophets[74] instituted 24 watches. For each watch there was a presence[75] in Jerusalem of priests, and of Levites, and of Israel[76]. At the time of service of each watch, its priests and Levites come to Jerusalem, and Israel belonging to this watch congregate in their towns and read about Creation[77].

72 *Num.* 28:2.
73 The daily sacrifices commanded in the verse are paid by the yearly *sheqel*, which was not paid by Cohanim (*Šeqalim* 1:6). Therefore the officiating Cohanim are not the owners of the sacrifice; a representation of the taxpayers is needed.
74 David and Samuel.
75 A scheduled presence.

76 The Land was divided into 24 districts, centered around the cities of priests.
77 In contrast to all other times when there is a Torah reading only on Mondays and Thursdays, during the week of service there is a daily reading, also some fasting, and other changes in the regular service as described in the Halakhot.

(67d line 47) **הלכה ב**: לָא צוּרְכָא דִי לָא אִילּוּ הֵן הַמַּעֲמָדוֹת מִתְכַּנְּסִיו בְּעָרֵיהֶן וְקוֹרְאִין בְּמַעֲשֵׂה בְרֵאשִׁית: בָּא לְהַתְחִיל מִתְּחִילַת הַפָּרָשָׁה.

Halakhah 2: It would only have been necessary: "These are the bystanders; they congregate in their towns and read about Creation[78]." He comes to start from the beginning of the subject.

78 The reason the bystanders are mentioned in the Mishnah is the special fasts which they organize. Since it was stated earlier that the priests on duty in the Temple do not fast on minor fastdays, the mention of Cohanim and Levites in this context seems superfluous. They are only mentioned because without sacrifices to be offered by the non-owning Cohanim there would be no need for bystanders.

(67d line 49) אָמַר רְבִּי יוֹנָה. אִילֵּין תְּמִידִין קָרְבְּנוֹתֵיהֶן שֶׁלְּכָל־יִשְׂרָאֵל אִינּוּן. אִם יִהְיוּ כָל־יִשְׂרָאֵל עוֹלִין לִירוּשָׁלַם. לֵית כְּתִיב אֶלָּא שָׁלוֹשׁ פְּעָמִים | בַּשָּׁנָה יֵרָאֶה כָל־זְכוּרְךָ. אִם יִהְיוּ כָל־יִשְׂרָאֵל יוֹשְׁבִין וּבְטֵילִין. וְהָכְתִיב וְאָסַפְתָּ דְגָנֶךָ. מִי אוֹסֵף לָהֶם אֶת הַדָּגָן. אֶלָּא שֶׁהִתְקִינוּ הַנְּבִיאִים הָרִאשׁוֹנִים עֶשְׂרִים וְאַרְבַּע מִשְׁמָרוֹת. וְעַל כָּל־מִשְׁמָר וּמִשְׁמָר הָיָה עָמוּד בִּירוּשָׁלַם שֶׁלְּכֹהֲנִים וְשֶׁלְלְוִיִּם וְשֶׁלְיִשְׂרָאֵל. תַּנֵּי. עֶשְׂרִים וְאַרְבָּעָה אֶלֶף עָמוּד מִירוּשָׁלַם וַחֲצִי עָמוּד מִירִיחוֹ. אַף יְרִיחוֹ הָיְתָה יְכוֹלָה לְהוֹצִיא עָמוּד שָׁלֵם. אֶלָּא בִשְׁבִיל לַחֲלוֹק כָּבוֹד לִירוּשָׁלַם הָיְתָה מוֹצִיאָה

חֲצִי עָמוּד. הַכֹּהֲנִים לַעֲבוֹדָה וְהַלְוִיִּם לַדּוּכָן וְיִשְׂרָאֵל מוֹכִיחִין עַל עַצְמָן שֶׁהֵן שְׁלוּחֵיהֶן שֶׁלְּכָל־יִשְׂרָאֵל.

[79]Rebbi Jonah said, these daily sacrifices are the offerings of all of Israel[80]. Could all of Israel ascend to Jerusalem? Is it not written[81], *three times a year all your males shall be seen*? If all of Israel would sit there and do nothing, is there not written[82], *you shall harvest your grain*? Who would harvest their grain? But the early prophets instituted 24 watches; from each watch there were [Cohanim, Levites, and Israel] present in Jerusalem. It was stated, *twenty-four thousand*[83]. A stand-by group[84] from Jerusalem, and half a stand-by group from Jericho. Jericho also could have produced a full stand-by group, but to give precedence to Jerusalem it only produced half a stand-by group. The Cohanim for service, the Levites for the podium[85], and the Israel as proof that they are the agents for all of Israel[86].

79 This text and the following paragraphs are copied from *Pesahim* 4:1.
80 Since it is shown in *Pesahim* that during the offering of a sacrifice the owner is forbidden work, no man in Israel would be permitted to work both in the morning and in the evening.
81 *Deut.* 16:16.
82 *Deut.* 11:14. The Babli *Berakhot* 35b infers from the verse that it is a religious obligation on a Torah scholar to earn a livelihood.
83 *1Chr.* 27:1. The verse is read as meaning that every month there were 24'000 representatives of the people at the Temple.
84 Since the Cohanim were changed every week, the people's representatives also were changed every week; only one quarter of the 24'000 on stand-by were actually needed for one week. The Babylonian term for עָמוּד is מַעֲמָד (Babli 27a). The actual numbers in Second Temple times were small.
85 For the musical accompaniment of the Temple service.
86 These are forbidden any work while the Daily Sacrifice is offered but everybody else may work.

(67d line 58) תָּנֵי רִבִּי שִׁמְעוֹן. הַכֹּהֲנִים וְהַלְוִיִּם וְיִשְׂרָאֵל וְשִׁיר מְעַכְּבִין אֶת הַקָּרְבָּן. רִבִּי אָבוּן בְּשֵׁם רִבִּי לֶעְזָר. טַעֲמֵיהּ דְּרִבִּי שִׁמְעוֹן. כָּל הַקָּהָל מִשְׁתַּחֲוִים. אֵילוּ יִשְׂרָאֵל. וְהַשִּׁיר מְשׁוֹרֵר אֵילוּ הַלְוִיִּם. וְהַחֲצֹצְרוֹת מַחְצְרִים אֵילוּ הַכֹּהֲנִים. עַד לִכְלוֹת הָעוֹלָה. הַכֹּל מְעַכְּבִין אֶת הַקָּרְבָּן. רִבִּי תַנְחוּמָא בְשֵׁם רִבִּי לֶעְזָר שָׁמַע לָהּ מִן הָדָא. וָאֶתְּנָה אֶת־הַלְוִיִּם נְתֻנִים | לְאַהֲרֹן וּלְבָנָיו מִתּוֹךְ בְּנֵי יִשְׂרָאֵל. אֵילוּ הַלְוִיִּם. לַעֲבֹד אֶת־עֲבֹדַת בְּנֵי־יִשְׂרָאֵל. אֵילוּ הַכֹּהֲנִים. וּלְכַפֵּר עַל־בְּנֵי יִשְׂרָאֵל. זֶה הַשִּׁיר. וְלֹא יִהְיֶה בִּבְנֵי יִשְׂרָאֵל נֶגֶף בְּגֶשֶׁת בְּנֵי־יִשְׂרָאֵל אֶל־הַקֹּדֶשׁ. אֵילוּ יִשְׂרָאֵל.

מִנַּיִין שֶׁהַשִּׁיר קָרוּי כַּפָּרָה. חִינְנָה אֲבוֹי דְּרַב נָטָה בְשֵׁם רִבִּי בְנָיָה. לְכַפֵּר עַל־בְּנֵי יִשְׂרָאֵל. זֶה הַשִּׁיר. מִנַּיִין שֶׁהַשִּׁיר מְעַכֵּב. רִבִּי יַעֲקֹב בַּר אָחָא רִבִּי שִׁמְעוֹן בּוּלֵיוָטָה בְשֵׁם רִבִּי חֲנִינָה. לְכַפֵּר עַל־בְּנֵי יִשְׂרָאֵל. זֶה הַשִּׁיר.

[87]It was stated: "Rebbi Simeon[88] said, Cohanim, Levites, Israel, and song invalidate the sacrifice[89]." Rebbi Abun[90] in the name of Rebbi Eleazar, the reason of Rebbi Simeon ben Eleazar: [91]*The entire congregation were bowing down*, these are Israel, *and the song was sung*, these are the Levites, *and the trumpets were trumpeting*, these are the Cohanim, *everything up to the end of the elevation offering*, all are indispensable for the sacrifice. Rebbi Tanhuma in the name of Rebbi Eleazar understood it from here[92]: *And I gave the Levites to Aaron and his sons from the midst of the Children of Israel*, these are the Levites, *to work the service of the Children of Israel in the Tent of Meeting*, these are the Cohanim, *and to atone for the Children of Israel*, that is the song[93], *so there shall be no plague when the Children of Israel approach the Sanctuary*, these are Israel.

From where that the song is called atonement? Ḥinena the father of Bar Nata in the name of Rebbi Banaia: *and to atone for the Children of Israel, that is the song*. From where that the song invalidates? Rebbi Jacob bar Aḥa, Rebbi Simeon βουλευτής[94], in the name of Rebbi Ḥanina, *and to atone for the Children of Israel*, that is the song.

87 The first sentence is also in *Eruvin* 10 (Note 141). The text there reads "musical instruments", which is required by the context there and must be understood here also since the choir is subsumed under "Levites".
88 In the other sources: R. Simeon ben Eleazar.
89 A sacrifice requiring a wine offering is invalid if not accompanied by the Levite's song.
90 In the other sources: Abbin.
91 *2Chr.* 29:28. Since this is not a pentateuchal verse it only can prove what people did or, as explained there in v. 25, what was prophetic instruction.

93 *Num.* 8:19.
93 In this version the implication is incomprehensible. It is understandable in the Babli, *Arakhin* 11a, where it is a tannaitic statement: "Song invalidates the sacrifice, the words of R. Meïr, but the Sages say, it does not invalidate. What is R. Meïr's reason? The verse says, *and I gave the Levites to Aaron and his sons from the midst of the Children of Israel, to work the service of the Children of Israel in the Tent of Meeting, and to atone for the Children of Israel*." The Levites had three biblical obligations in the Sanctuary, viz., to carry the Tent, to be its watchmen, and to sing.

Since only the third can be classified as ritual service, it must be what is referred to as atoning.

94 "The city councillor".

(67d line 69) רִבִּי יַעֲקֹב בַּר אָחָא רִבִּי חִייָה בְשֵׁם רִבִּי יוֹחָנָן. שְׁמוֹנֶה מִשְׁמָרוֹת כְּהוּנָה הֶעֱמִיד מֹשֶׁה. אַרְבַּע מִשֶּׁלְאֶלְעָזָר וְאַרְבַּע מִשֶּׁלְאִיתָמָר. עַד שֶׁעָמַד דָּוִד וּשְׁמוּאֵל הָרוֹאֶה וְהוֹסִיפוּ עֲלֵיהֶן עוֹד שְׁמוֹנֶה. אַרְבַּע מִשֶּׁלְאֶלְעָזָר וְאַרְבַּע מִשֶּׁלְאִיתָמָר. וּבִיקְּשׁוּ לְהוֹסִיף עוֹד שְׁמוֹנָה וְלַעֲשׂוֹתָן עֶשְׂרִים וְאַרְבָּעָה. וּמָצְאוּ מִשֶּׁלְאֶלְעָזָר וְלֹא מָצְאוּ מִשֶּׁלְאִיתָמָר. הָדָא הוּא דִכְתִיב וַיִּמָּצְאוּ בְנֵי־אֶלְעָזָר רַבִּים לְרָאשֵׁי הַגְּבָרִים מִן־בְּנֵי אִיתָמָר וגו'. רִבִּי יַעֲקֹב בַּר אָחָא רִבִּי חוּנָה רַבָּה דְצִיפּוֹרִין בְּשֵׁם רִבִּי יוֹחָנָן. בֵּית־אָב אֶחָד בֵּית־אָב אֶחָד לְאֶלְעָזָר. שֶׁנִּיתּוֹסַף לוֹ בָּתֵּי אָבוֹת אֲחֵרִים וְאָחֵז | אָחֵז לְאִיתָמָר. מַה שֶׁתָּפַס תָּפַס. רִבִּי זְעוּרָה בְשֵׁם רַב חוּנָה. לְחֶזִיר שִׁבְעָה עָשָׂר. שֶׁחָזַר הַמַּחְזוֹר לְאֶלְעָזָר.

לַעֲשׂוֹתָן עֶשְׂרִים וְשָׁלֹשׁ אֵין אַתְּ יָכוֹל. דִּכְתִיב הֵמָּה יִסַּד דָּוִיד וּשְׁמוּאֵל הָרוֹאֶה בֶּאֱמוּנָתָם בֶּאֱמוּנָתָם. אוֹמָנוּת גְּדוֹלָה הָיְתָה שָׁם. שֶׁאֵין מִשְׁמָר נוֹטֵל וְשׁוֹנֶה בִשְׂדֵה אֲחוּזָה עַד שִׁיטּוֹל חֲבֵירוֹ. אָמַר רִבִּי אַבָּהוּ. חִישַׁבְתִּים שֶׁאֵין מִשְׁמָר נוֹטֵל וְשׁוֹנֶה בִשְׂדֵה אֲחוּזָה עַד שֶׁיִּטּוֹל חֲבֵירוֹ.

Rebbi Jacob bar Aḥa, Rebbi Ḥiyya in the name of Rebbi Joḥanan: Moses instituted eight watches, four from Eleazar and four from Ithamar[95], until David and Samuel the Seer added another eight, four from Eleazar and four from Ithamar. They wanted to add another eight to bring them to 24, and found from Eleazar but did not find from Ithamar. This is what is written[96]: *it was found that the descendants of Eleazar were more heads than the descendants of Ithamar,* etc. Rebbi Jacob bar Aḥa, the Elder Rebbi Ḥuna from Sepphoris in the name of Rebbi Joḥanan: *One clan, one clan selected from Eleazar*[97], other clans were added for him; *and selected, selected for Ithamar,* what he had, he had. Rebbi Ze`ira in the name of Rav Ḥuna: For Ḥezir, seventeen[98]. The cycle came back to Eleazar.

[99]One could not make them 23, as it is written[100], *these are the institutions of David and Samuel the Seer in their professionalism.* It was a great feat of professionalism that no watch was taking and repeating in inheritance fields before the other could take[101]. Rebbi Abbahu said, I computed it that no watch was taking and repeating in inheritance fields before the other could take.

95 Babli 27a; Tosephta 3:2.
96 *1Chr.* 24:4.
97 *1Chr.* 24:6. The repetition is not in the MT.

98 *1Chr.* 24:15. It is claimed that ranks 1-8, 17-24 in the cycle of watches are from Eleazar.
99 This text is from *Sukkah* 5:8, explaining

the discrimination against the Bilgah watch. 100 *1Chr.* 9:22.

101 It is prescribed in *Lev.* 27:21 that real estate dedicated to the Temple by a person whose ancestor received this land in the original distribution under Joshua and which is not redeemed by the next Jubilee becomes property of the Cohanim. This is read to mean that it becomes property of the watch which regularly is on duty on the day of Atonement in the Jubilee year (*Lev.* 25:9).

(Property bought, not inherited, *must* be redeemed, *Lev.* 27:23-24.) It now is asserted that no watch repeats serving on the Day of Atonement in a Jubilee year after less than 24 Jubilee periods (or 1200 years). Since we have no details about the calendar rules of the First Temple period, at the end of which the rules of original distribution became moot, the statement can be neither verified nor falsified.

(8 line 68a) אַרְבַּע מִשְׁמָרוֹת עָלוּ מִן הַגּוֹלָה. יְדַעְיָה חָרִים פַּשְׁחוּר וְאִמֵּר. וְהִתְנוּ עִמָּהֶן הַנְּבִיאִים שֶׁבֵּינֵיהֶן שֶׁאֲפִילוּ יְהוֹיָרִיב עוֹלֶה מִן הַגּוֹלָה שֶׁלֹּא יִדְחֶה אֶת הַמִּשְׁמָר שֶׁלְּפָנָיו אֶלָּא יֵיעָשֶׂה טְפֵילָה לוֹ. וְעָמְדוּ הַנְּבִיאִים שֶׁבֵּינֵיהֶן וְעָשׂוּ עֶשְׂרִים וְאַרְבַּע גּוֹרָלוֹת וְהִטִּילוּם בְּקַלְפֵּי. וּבָא יְדַעְיָה וְנָטַל חָמֵשׁ וְהוּא הֲרֵי שֵׁשׁ. וּבָא חָרִים וְנָטַל חָמֵשׁ וְהוּא הֲרֵי שֵׁשׁ. [וּבָא פַּשְׁחוּר וְנָטַל חָמֵשׁ וְהוּא הֲרֵי שֵׁשׁ. וּבָא אִמֵּר וְנָטַל חָמֵשׁ וְהוּא הֲרֵי שֵׁשׁ.] וְהִתְנוּ עִמָּהֶן הַנְּבִיאִים שֶׁבֵּינֵיהֶן שֶׁאֲפִילוּ יְהוֹיָרִיב עוֹלֶה מִן הַגּוֹלָה שֶׁלֹּא יִדְחֶה אֶת הַמִּשְׁמָר שֶׁלְּפָנָיו אֶלָּא יֵיעָשֶׂה טְפֵילָה לוֹ. וְעָמְדוּ רָאשֵׁי מִשְׁמָרוֹת וְעָשׂוּ עַצְמָן בָּתֵּי אָבוֹת. וְיֵשׁ מִשְׁמָר שֶׁהָיָה בּוֹ חֲמִשָּׁה שִׁשָּׁה שִׁבְעָה שְׁמוֹנָה תִּשְׁעָה. מִשְׁמָר שֶׁהָיָה בּוֹ חֲמִשָּׁה שְׁלֹשָׁה מַקְרִיבִין שְׁלֹשָׁה יָמִים וּשְׁנַיִם מַקְרִיבִין אַרְבָּעָה יָמִים. מִשְׁמָר שֶׁהָיָה בּוֹ שִׁשָּׁה חֲמִשָּׁה מַקְרִיבִין חֲמִשָּׁה יָמִים וְאֶחָד מַקְרִיב שְׁנֵי יָמִים. מִשְׁמָר שֶׁהָיָה בּוֹ שִׁבְעָה כָּל־אֶחָד וְאֶחָד מַקְרִיב אֶת יוֹמוֹ. מִשְׁמָר שֶׁהָיָה בּוֹ שְׁמוֹנָה שִׁשָּׁה מַקְרִיבִין שִׁשָּׁה וּשְׁנַיִם מַקְרִיבִין יוֹם אֶחָד. מִשְׁמָר שֶׁהָיָה בּוֹ תִּשְׁעָה חֲמִשָּׁה מַקְרִיבִין חֲמִשָּׁה יָמִים וְאַרְבָּע מַקְרִיבִין שְׁנֵי יָמִים. וְיֵשׁ מֵהֶן שֶׁקָּבְעוּ עַצְמוֹן לְעוֹלָם. מִשְׁמָר שֶׁהָיָה בְשַׁבָּת הָיָה בְשַׁבָּת לְעוֹלָם. בְּמוֹצָאֵי שַׁבָּת הָיָה בְמוֹצָאֵי שַׁבָּת לְעוֹלָם. וְיֵשׁ מֵהֶן שֶׁהָיוּ מַקְרִיבִין עַל כָּל־מִשְׁמָר וּמִשְׁמָר. וְיֵשׁ מֵהֶן שֶׁהָיוּ מַגְרִילִין עַל כָּל־שָׁבוּעַ וְשָׁבוּעַ.

Four watches returned from the Diaspora: Yedaya, Harim, Pashhur, and Immer[102]. The prophets among them stipulated that even if Yehoyariv would return from the Diaspora that it would not displace the watch taking its place but would be made an appendix to it[103]. The prophets among them took the initiative and made 24 lots which they put in an urn. Yedaya came and took five; with his own this makes six[104]. Harim came and took five; with his own this makes six. [Pashhur came and took five; with his own this makes six. Immer came and took five; with his own this makes six.] The prophets among them stipulated that even if Yehoyariv[105] would return from the Diaspora that it would not displace the watch taking its place but would be made an appendix to it. The heads of the watches took the initiative and made themselves heads of clans. There were watches containing five, six, seven, eight, or nine. For a watch containing five, three were sacrificing during three days and two were sacrificing during four days[106]. For a watch containing six, five were sacrificing during five days and one was sacrificing during two days. For a watch containing seven, each single one was sacrificing on its day. For a watch containing eight, six were sacrificing during six days, and two were sacrificing on one day. For a watch containing nine, five were sacrificing during five days and four were sacrificing during two days. There were those who fixed themselves permanently. A watch[107] who served on the Sabbath always served on the Sabbath, after the end of the Sabbath always served after the Sabbath. They were those of them which were sacrificing with every watch[108]; and those who drew lots for every week[109].

102 *Ezra* 2:36-39, *Neh.* 7:39-42.
103 This sentence should be deleted; its place is at later in the text.
104 The 24 watches which served in the Second Temple were really subdivisions of the four which returned from Babylonia.
105 The leading watch in *Chr.*
106 As explained in Mishnah 2:12, each clan served one day during the week allotted to its watch. That Mishnah seemed to presume that each watch is composed of exactly 7 clans. But numbers from 5 to 9 can be accommodated.

107 One has to read "clan" instead of "watch".
108 This sentence is slightly garbled. It seems to mean: There were those which were serving at different days each time their watch was called to Jerusalem.
109 There were watches which organized a drawing of lots among their clans. Because of the different meanings of "week" this either means every time their watch was going to officiate, or once in a Sabbatical period.

(68a line 26) רִבִּי הֲוָה מַמְנֵי תְּרֵין מִינּוּיִין. אִין הֲווֹן כְּדַיי הָיוּ מִתְקַיְימִין. וְאִין לָא הֲווֹן מִסְתַּלְּקִין. מִדְדָמַךְ פָּקִיד לִבְרֵיהּ. אָמַר. לָא תַעֲבִיד כֵּן אֶלָּא מְנֵי כּוּלְהוֹן כְּחָדָא. וּמְנִי לְרִבִּי חָמָא בַּר חֲנִינָה בְּרֹאשָׁה. וְלָמָּה לָא מְנִיתֵיהּ הוּא. אָמַר רִבִּי דְרוֹסָה. בְּגִין דְּצַוְוחִין עֲלוֹי צִיפּוֹרָאֵי. וּבְגִין צְוָוחָה עֲבָדִין. אָמַר רִבִּי לְעָזֶר בֵּירִבִּי יוֹסֵה. עַל שֶׁהֵשִׁיבוֹ טַעַם בָּרַבִּים. רִבִּי הֲוָה יָתִיב מַתְנֵי. וְזָכְרוּ פְלִיטֵיהֶם אוֹתִי וְהָיוּ אֶל־הֶהָרִים כְּיוֹנֵי הַגֵּאָיוֹת כּוּלָּם הוֹמִיּוֹת. אָמַר לֵיהּ. חוֹמוֹת. אָמַר לֵיהּ. הֵן קָרִיתָהּ. אָמַר לֵיהּ. קֳדָם רַב הַמְנוּנָא דְּבָבֶל. אָמַר לֵיהּ. כַּד תֵּיחוֹת לְתַמָּן אֱמוֹר לֵיהּ דִּמְנַיְיתָךְ חַכִּים. וְיָדַע דְּלָא מִיתְמַנֵּי בְּיוֹמוֹי. מָן דִּדְמָךְ בָּעָא בְרֵיהּ מַמְנִיתֵיהּ וְלָא קָבִיל עֲלֵיהּ

מִתְמַנְיָיא. אֲמַר. לֵית אֲנָא מְקַבֵּל עֲלַי מִתְמַנְיָיא עַד זְמַן דְּיִתְמַנֵּי רִבִּי פֵּס דְּרוֹמָא קָמָיי. וַהֲוָה תַּמָּן חַד סָב. אֲמַר. אִין חֲנִינָה קֳדָמַיי אֲנָא תִּינְיָין. אִין רִבִּי פֵּס דְּרוֹמַיָּא קֳדָמַיי אֲנָא תִּינְיָין. וּקְבִיל עֲלוֹי רִבִּי חֲנִינָה מִתְמַנְיָיא תְּלִיתָאֵי.

Rebbi used to ordain double ordinations[110]. If they were worthy of it they were continuing; if not they were disappearing[111]. When he was to die, he commanded his son; he said, do not act thus but ordain all of them together, and ordain Rebbi Ḥama bar Ḥanina[112] first. Why did he not ordain him himself? Rebbi Derosa said, because the Sepphoreans complained about him[113]. And because of complaints one acts? Rebbi Eleazar ben Rebbi Yose said, because he corrected him in public. Rebbi was sitting, stating: *Their refugees will remember Me*[114], *on the mountains like valley doves, all of them cooing*[115]. He said to him, *all of them cooing*[116]. He asked him, where did you study this text? He said, before the Babylonian Rav Hamnuna. He said to him, if you will descend there, tell him that he should ordain you as *Ḥakham*. He understood that he[117] never would be ordained in his lifetime. After he died, his son wanted to ordain him, but he did not accept to be ordained unless Rebbi Ephes the Southerner was ordained before him. There was there an old man who said, if Ḥanina precedes me, I have to be the second; if Rebbi Ephes the Southerner precedes me, I have to be the second. Rebbi Ḥanina accepted to be ordained as third[118].

110 This ordination was not simply the granting of an ecclesiastical degree but carried with it the appointment as *Ḥakham* to a rabbinic post which it was the Patriarch's duty to see to it that it was filled.

111 If those appointed by Rebbi were found worthy of the posts given to them in the eyes of heaven, they lived a long life; otherwise they would die an early death.

112 One has to read either simply Ḥanina (as in the parallel *Eccl. rabba* 7(16)) or Ḥanina bar Ḥama (Babli *Ketubot* 103b). As the name Ḥama shows and the story confirms, he was a Babylonian (Babylonian Aramaic from the Accadic חמי "to protect, guard, trust".)

113 That he was too strict in his rabbinic rulings, being a recognized scholar but not appointed by the Patriarch.

114 *Ez.* 7:9.

115 *Ez.* 7:16. For "cooing", Rebbi used rabbinic Hebrew *hōmiōt*.

116 In correct biblical Hebrew (almost MT) *hōmōt*.

117 R. Ḥanina understood that he would not become *Ḥakham* in Rebbi's lifetime.

118 According to both parallel sources he agreed to be the third in rank in the Academy of Rebbi's successor.

(68a line 39) אָמַר רִבִּי חֲנִינָה. זָכִית מַאַרְכָה יוֹמִין. אִין בְּגִין הָדָא מִילְתָא לֵית אֲנָא יָדַע. אִין בְּגִין דַּהֲוֵית סָלִיק מִן טִיבֶּרְיָא לְצִיפּוֹרִין. [וַהֲוֵינָא] עָקִים אִיסְרָטִין מֵיעוֹל מִישְׁאוֹל בִּשְׁלָמֵיהּ דְּרִבִּי שִׁמְעוֹן בֶּן חַלְפוּתָא בְּעֵין תִּינֶן לֵית אֲנָא יָדַע.

Rebbi Ḥanina said, I merited to live a long life. Whether because of this matter I do not know, or whether when I was climbing from Tiberias to Sepphoris I made a detour to ask about the well-being of Rebbi Simeon ben Ḥalfuta I do not know.

שְׁמוּאֵל וְאִילֵּין דְּבֵית שִׁילָא הָווֹן שָׁאֲלִין בִּשְׁלָמֵיהּ דִּנְשִׂיָּיא בְּכָל-יוֹם. וַהֲווֹן אִילֵּין דְּבֵית שִׁילָא עָלִין קֳדָמֵיי וְיָתְבִין קֳדָמֵיי. פָּלְגוּן אִיקָר לִשְׁמוּאֵל וְאַיְיתִיבוּנֵיהּ קֳדָמֵיי. עָאַל רַב לְתַמָּן וּפָלַג לֵיהּ שְׁמוּאֵל אִיקָר [וְאוֹתְבוּנֵיהּ קֳדָמֵיי.] אָמְרִין אִילֵּין דְּבֵית שִׁילָה. אֲנָן תִּינְיָינִין אֲנָן. וְקִיבֵּל שְׁמוּאֵל מֵיתַב תְּלִיתָאֵי.

Samuel and those of the family Shilo asked about the Patriarch's well-being every day; those of the family Shilo entered first and sat down first. They honored Samuel and brought him in first. Rav immigrated from there and Samuel honored him [and brought him in first.] Those of the House of Shilo said, we are the second ones. Samuel accepted to sit as third[118].

(48a line 46) שְׁלֹשָׁה סְפָרִים מָצְאוּ בָעֲזָרָה. סֵפֶר מְעוֹנִי. וְסֵפֶר זַעֲטוּטֵי. וְסֵפֶר הִיא. בְּאֶחָד מָצְאוּ כָתוּב מְעוֹן אֱלֹהֵי קֶדֶם. וּבִשְׁנַיִם כָּתוּב מְעוֹנָה אֱלֹהֵי קֶדֶם. וְקִייְמוּ שְׁנַיִם וּבִיטְלוּ אֶחָד. בְּאֶחָד מָצְאוּ כָתוּב וַיִּשְׁלַח אֶת זַעֲטוּטֵי בְּנֵי יִשְׂרָאֵל. וּבִשְׁנַיִם כָּתוּב וַיִּשְׁלַח אֶת־נַעֲרֵי בְּנֵי יִשְׂרָאֵל. וְקִייְמוּ שְׁנַיִם וּבִיטְלוּ אֶחָד. בְּאֶחָד מָצְאוּ כָתוּב תֵּשַׁע הִיא. וּבִשְׁנַיִם כָּתוּב אַחַד עֶשְׂרֵה הִיא. וְקִייְמוּ שְׁנַיִם וּבִיטְלוּ אֶחָד.

Three scrolls were found in the Temple courtyard[119], the *Meone* scroll, the *Zaatute* scroll, the *hee* scroll. In one they found written *me`ôn is the preexisting God*, but in two was written *me`ônāh is the preexisting God*[120]. They confirmed the two and annulled the one. In one they found written *he sent the za`ᵃtûtē of the Children of Israel* but in two was written *he sent the na`ᵃrē of the Children of Israel*[121]. They confirmed the two and annulled the one. In one they found written nine היא, but in two they found eleven היא[122]. They confirmed the two and annulled the one.

אָמַר רִבִּי לֵוִי. מְגִילַּת יוֹחֲסִין מָצְאוּ בִירוּשָׁלַם וְכָתוּב בָּהּ. הִלֵּל מִן דְּדָוִד. בֶּן יָצָף מִן דְּאָסָף. בֶּן צִיצִית הַכֶּסֶת מִן דְּאַבְנֵר. בֶּן קוּבִיסִין מִן דְּאַחְאָב. בֶּן כַּלְבָּא שָׁבוּעַ מִן דְּכָלֵב. רִבִּי יַנַּאי מִן דְּעֵלִי. מִן יְהוּדָה מִן צִיפּוֹרִין. רִבִּי חִייָה רַבָּה מִבְּנֵי שְׁפַטְיָה בֶּן אֲבוּטָל. רִבִּי יוֹסֵי בֵּירִבִּי חֲלַפְתָּא מִבְּנֵי יוֹנָדָב בֶּן רֵכָב. רִבִּי נְחֶמְיָה מִן נְחֶמְיָה הַתִּרְשָׁתָא.

[123]Rebbi Levi said, they found a genealogical scroll in Jerusalem and in it was written: Hillel from David, Ben Yaṣaf[124] from Asaph, Ben Ṣiṣit Hakkeset from Abner, Ben Qubisin[125] from Ahab, Ben Kalba Savua` from Kaleb[126], Rebbi Yannai from Eli, Men Yehudah[127] from Sepphoris, the Elder Rebbi Ḥiyya from the sons of Shephatya ben Abutal[128], [129]Rebbi Yose ben Rebbi Ḥalaphta from the sons of Yonadav ben Rekhav, Rebbi Nehemiah from Nehemiah the governor.

119 It is asserted that even before the work of the Masoretes, the received text of the Pentateuch was a scholarly edition.

120 *Deut.* 33:26.

121 *Ex.* 24:5. The LXX translate *za`ᵃtûtē* (Babli *Megillah* 9a, bottom) as "young men" but *na`ar* (*Ex.* 33:11) as "boy".

122 This is the accepted *mesorah*. The irregular spelling is found in *Gen.* 14:3,20:5, 38:5; *Lev.* 11:39,13:10,13:21,16:31,20:17, 21:9; *Num.* 5:13,5:14.

123 A parallel text is in *Gen. rabba* 58(13); M. Sokoloff, *The Genizah fragmentss of Genesis rabba* (Jerusalem 1982) #110, lines 27-30.

124 In *Gen. rabba*: the family Yaṣah; in the Genizah: the House Ṣisit.

125 In the Genizah: *Kobyses*.

126 These three families are mentioned as the richest of Jerusalem before the first revolt.

127 In *Gen. rabba:* The family Yehu.

128 A son of David, *2S.* 3:4.

129 The last two late Tannaim are not mentioned in *Gen. rabba*.

(68a line 57) [תַּנֵּי.] סֵדֶר הֵסֵב. בַּזְּמַן שֶׁהֵן שְׁתֵּי מִיטוֹת הַגָּדוֹל שֶׁבָּהֶן [עוֹלֶה] מֵיסַב בְּרֹאשׁ הָעֶלְיוֹנָה. וְהַשֵּׁינִי לוֹ לְמַטָּה מִמֶּנּוּ. בַּזְּמַן שֶׁהֵן שָׁלֹשׁ מִיטוֹת הַגָּדוֹל שֶׁבָּהֶן עוֹלֶה וּמֵיסַב בְּרֹאשׁ הָאֶמְצָעִית. וְהַשֵּׁינִי לוֹ לְמַעְלָה וְהַשְּׁלִישִׁי לוֹ לְמַטָּה הֵימֶנּוּ. וְכֵן מְסֻדָּרִין וְהוֹלְכִין. אָמַר רְבִּי שְׁמוּאֵל בַּר רַב יִצְחָק. אָבוֹת דֶּרֶךְ הֵסֵב הֵן קְבוּרִין.

רִבִּי יַעֲקֹב בַּר אָחָא בְשֵׁם רִבִּי יָסָא. לְעוֹלָם אֵין הָעוֹלָם עוֹמֵד אֶלָּא עַל הַקָּרְבָּנוֹת. תַּמָּן תַּנִּינָן. שִׁמְעוֹן הַצַּדִּיק הָיָה מִשְּׁיָרֵי כְּנֶסֶת הַגְּדוֹלָה. הוּא הָיָה אוֹמֵר. עַל שְׁלֹשָׁה דְבָרִים הָעוֹלָם עוֹמֵד. עַל הַתּוֹרָה וְעַל הָעֲבוֹדָה וְעַל גְּמִילוּת חֲסָדִים: וּשְׁלָשְׁתָּן בְּפָסוּק אֶחָד. וָאֶשִׂים דְּבָרַי בְּפִיךָ. זוֹ תוֹרָה. וּבְצֵל יָדִי כִּסִּיתִיךָ. זֶה גְמִילוּת חֲסָדִים. לִלְמָדְךָ שֶׁכָּל־מִי שֶׁהוּא עָסוּק בַּתּוֹרָה וּבִגְמִילוּת חֲסָדִים זָכָה לֵישֵׁב בְּצִילוֹ שֶׁלְהַקָּדוֹשׁ בָּרוּךְ הוּא. הֲדָא הִיא דִכְתִיב מַה־יָּקָר חַסְדְּךָ אֱלֹהִים וּבְנֵי אָדָם בְּצֵל כְּנָפֶיךָ יֶחֱסָיוּן: לִנְטוֹעַ שָׁמַיִם וְלִיסוֹד אָרֶץ. אֶלָּא הַקָּרְבָּנוֹת. וְלֵאמֹר לְצִיּוֹן עַמִּי־אָתָּה: אֵילוּ יִשְׂרָאֵל. אָמַר רְבִּי חִינְנָא בַּר פָּפָּא. חִיזַּרְנוּ עַל כָּל־הַמִּקְרָא וְלֹא מָצָאנוּ שֶׁיִּקְרְאוּ יִשְׂרָאֵל צִיּוֹן אֶלָּא זֶה. וְלֵאמֹר לְצִיּוֹן עַמִּי־אָתָּה: תַּמָּן תַּנִּינָן. רַבָּן שִׁמְעוֹן בֶּן גַּמְלִיאֵל אוֹמֵר. עַל שְׁלֹשָׁה דְבָרִים הָעוֹלָם עוֹמֵד. עַל הַדִּין וְעַל הָאֱמֶת וְהַשָּׁלוֹם. וּשְׁלָשְׁתָּן דָּבָר אֶחָד הֵן. נַעֲשָׂה הַדִּין נַעֲשָׂה אֱמֶת.

נַעֲשָׂה אֱמֶת נַעֲשָׂה שָׁלוֹם. וְאָמַר רִבִּי מָנָא. שְׁלָשְׁתָּן בְּפָסוּק אֶחָד. אֱמֶת וּמִשְׁפַּט שָׁלוֹם שִׁפְטוּ בְּשַׁעֲרֵיכֶם:

[It was stated:][130] "The order of lying on couches. If there are two couches, the most important personality [goes and] lies down at the head of the upper one, and the next one next to him[131]. If they are three couches the most important personality goes and lies down at the head of the middle one; the second one before him and the third one below him. In this way one continues to organize." Rebbi Samuel bar Rav Isaac said, the Patriarchs are buried in the way of lying on couches[132].

Rebbi Jacob bar Aḥa in the name of Rebbi Yasa: The world only continues to exist by the sacrifices[133]. There, we stated[134]: "Simeon the Just was of the remainders of the Great Assembly. He used to say, the world continues to exist by three things, by the Torah, by worship, and by labors of love[135]." All three are in one verse[136]: *I shall put My word in your mouth*, that is Torah. *By the shadow of My hands I shall cover you*, these are labors of love; to teach you that he who is occupied with Torah and labors of love merits to dwell in the shadow of the Holy One, praise to Him. That is what is written[137], *how precious is Your grace, o God, and humans take shelter in Your wings' shadow*. *To plant the Heavens and give foundation to the earth*[136], these are the sacrifices, *and to say to Zion, you are My people*, these are Israel. Rebbi Ḥinena bar Pappa said, we went over all of Scripture and only found this one that Israel was called Zion, *and to say to Zion, you are My people*. There, we stated[138]: "Rabban Simeon ben Gamliel says, the world is existing on three things, on justice, on truth, and on peace. All three are one: If justice is done, truth is accomplished. If truth is accomplished, peace is established. Rebbi Mana said, and all are in one verse[139], *judge truth and law of peace in your gates*.

130 Corrector's addition; essential only in Babylonian style. Tosephta *Berakhot* 5:5, Babli *Berakhot* 46b.

131 In the dining hall (triclinium) two couches were arranged parallel to one another; three couches were arranged in the form of Π. Each couch had room for three occupants.

132 Abraham and Sarah in the middle, flanked on one side by Isaac and Rebekka and on the other by Jacob and Leah.

133 In the absence of a Temple, this means that the daily recitation of the rules of daily sacrifices are necessary for the continued

existence of the world. In Amoraic times this implied that the institution of the rules for bystanders to be explained in the following Halakhot was still followed, continuing the cycle of priestly watches uninterrupted theoretically from the time of Ezra (or practically from Hasmonean times.)
134 Mishnah *Avot* 1:2.
135 Labors for which no thanks can be given, such as burying the dead or giving charity anonymously.
136 *Is.* 51:16.
137 *Ps.* 36:8.
138 Mishnah *Avot* 1:18. The following text shows that the verse quoted at the end was not part of the Yerushalmi Mishnah (and is not part of Maimonides's autograph Mishnah.)
139 *Zach.* 8:16.

(fol. 67b) **משנה ג**: בַּיּוֹם הָרִאשׁוֹן קוֹרִין בְּרֵאשִׁית וִיהִי רָקִיעַ. בַּשֵּׁנִי יְהִי רָקִיעַ יִקָווּ הַמַּיִם. בַּשְּׁלִישִׁי יִקָווּ הַמַּיִם יְהִי מְאוֹרוֹת. בָּרְבִיעִי יְהִי מְאוֹרוֹת יִשְׁרְצוּ הַמַּיִם. בַּחֲמִישִׁי יִשְׁרְצוּ הַמַּיִם וְתוֹצֵא הָאָרֶץ. בַּשִּׁשִּׁי וְתוֹצֵא הָאָרֶץ וַיְכוּלּוּ הַשָּׁמַיִם וְהָאָרֶץ וְכָל־צְבָאָם.

Mishnah 3: On Sunday one reads, *In the Beginning, there shall be a spread.* On Monday, *there shall be a spread, the waters shall come together.* On Tuesday, *the waters shall come together, there shall be lights.* On Wednesday, *there shall be lights, the water shall swarm.* On Thursday, *the water shall swarm, the earth shall produce.* On Friday, *the earth shall produce, the heavens and earth and all their hosts were finished*[140].

140 These are the details of the Torah readings by the bystanders mentioned in Mishnah 2. The problem is that the Mishnah in *Megillah* states that three people have to be called to read the Torah, each one a minimum of three verses, and if one starts a new paragraph one must read at least two verses from it, and at the end of a paragraph one must read at least three verses. Every day one reads two paragraphs in the story of Creation (*Gen.* 1:1-2:3), but paragraph 1 only has five verses and paragraph 2 three. According to the rules, paragraph 1 should not be split. Similarly, on day 2 paragraph 2 has three verses but paragraph 3 has five, which raise the question how to accommodate second and third readers. The other days are no problem since paragraph 4 has six verses, paragraph 5 four, paragraph 6 eight, and paragraph 9 (*Gen.* 2:1-3) three.

(68a line 75) **הלכה ג**: רַב חוּנָה אָמַר. שְׁלֹשָׁה קְרִיוֹת שֶׁבַּתּוֹרָה לֹא יְפְחֲתוּ מֵעֲשָׂרָה פְּסוּקִים. חִזְקִיָּה אָמַר. כְּנֶגֶד עֲשֶׂרֶת הַדִּיבְּרוֹת. וְהָא תַנִּינָן. בַּיּוֹם הָרִאשׁוֹן בְּרֵאשִׁית וִיהִי רָקִיעַ. וְהָא לֵית בְּהוֹן אֶלָּא תְמָנִייָא. רִבִּי אִידִי אֲמַר. אִיתְפַּלְגוּן כָּהֲנָא וְאַסָּא. חַד אָמַר. חוֹזֵר. וְחוֹרָנָה אָמַר.

חוֹתֵךְ. מָאן דְּאָמַר. חוֹזֵר. חוֹזֵר שְׁנֵי פְסוּקִים. מָאן דְּאָמַר. וַיְהִי־עֶרֶב וַיְהִי־בֹקֶר פָּסוּק בִּפְנֵי עַצְמוֹ. וְהָא תַנִּינָן. בַּשֵּׁנִי יְהִי רָקִיעַ וְיִקָּווּ הַמַּיִם. חַד אָמַר. חוֹזֵר. וְחוֹרָנָה אָמַר. חוֹתֵךְ. מָאן דְּאָמַר. חוֹזֵר. חוֹזֵר שְׁנֵי פְסוּקִין. מָאן דְּאָמַר. חוֹתֵךְ. אֲפִילוּ חוֹתֵךְ לֵית בֵּיהּ. הוֹתֵיב רִבִּי פְלִיפָּה בַּר פְּרִיטָה קוֹמֵי רִבִּי זְעוּרָה. וַהֲרֵי פָּרָשַׁת עֲמָלֵק. אָמַר לֵיהּ. שַׁנְיָיה הִיא. שֶׁהוּא סִידְרוֹ שֶׁלְּיוֹם. הָתִיב רִבִּי לַעְזָר בַּר מָרוֹם קוֹמֵי רִבִּי יוֹנָה. וְהָא תַנֵּי. הַמַּפְטִיר בַּנָּבִיא לֹא יִפְחוֹת מֵעֶשְׂרִים וְאֶחָד פְּסוּקִים.

Halakhah 3: [141]Rav Huna said, three people reading in the Torah shall not do less than ten verses[142]. Hizqiah said, corresponding to the Ten Commandments[143]. But did we not state, "on Sunday, *In the Beginning* and *there shall be a spread*"? And these are only eight! Rebbi Idi said, Cahana and Assi disagreed[144]. One said, he repeats. But the other said, he splits. He who says that he repeats, he repeats two verses. He who says he splits, he splits *it was evening, it was morning*, as a separate verse[145]. But did we not state, "on Monday, *there shall be a spread* and *the waters shall come together*"? One said, he repeats. But the other said, he splits. He who says that he repeats, he repeats two verses. He who says he splits, he could not split[146]. Rebbi Philippos ben Perita objected before Rebbi Ze`ira, is there not the paragraph about Amalek? He said to him, there is a difference since this is the topic of the day[147]. Rebbi Eleazar from Merom asked before Rebbi Jonah; was it not stated, the one who reads the conclusion from Prophets should not do less than 21 verses[148]?

141 This Halakhah is repeated in *Megillah* 4:2.

142 Each one may not read less than three verses but one has to read at least 4. Babli *Megillah* 21b.

143 Babli *Megillah* 21b, as one of two explanations.

144 In Babli *Megillah* 22a, disagreement of Rav and Samuel.

145 He splits it off from v. 5 and reads it as separate sentence. In contrast to the Babli which prescribes only one sentence to be repeated, the Yerushalmi has the three readers reading a total of 10 verses as required by Rav Huna.

146 Since *"it was evening, it was morning, the third day"* already is a separate verse.

147 The reading for Purim, for which three readers are called on a weekday, is *Ex.*17:8-16. The reading is not connected to the text before or after, it cannot be augmented. Since there are 9 verses and the Mishnaic requirement can be satisfied without problems, there is no need to change anything to satisfy the additional Amoraic rule. Tosaphot *Megillah* 21b *s.v.* אין.

148 Babli *Megillah* 23a. The question would be that since we require that one

reader at least read 4 verses, should there not be at least 22 verses? The question needs no answer since there is no reading from Prophets on weekdays; the number 21 refers to the seven people called to read on a Sabbath; cf. *Megillah* 4:2 Note 74.

(fol. 67b) **משנה ד**: פָּרָשָׁה גְדוֹלָה קוֹרִין אוֹתָהּ בִּשְׁנַיִם וְהַקְּטַנָּה בְּיָחִיד. בְּשַׁחֲרִית וּבַמּוּסָף וּבַמִּנְחָה נִכְנָסִין וְקוֹרִין עַל פִּיהֶן כְּקוֹרִין אֶת שְׁמַע. עֶרֶב שַׁבָּת בַּמִּנְחָה לֹא הָיוּ נִכְנָסִין מִפְּנֵי כְּבוֹד הַשַּׁבָּת:

Mishnah 4: A large paragraph is read by two persons, and a small one by an individual[149] in the morning and for *musaf*; for afternoon prayers[150] they were assembling and read by heart as one reads the *shema`*. Friday afternoon they were not assembling[151] because of the honor of Sabbath.

149 A paragraph of 5 sentences may be split into 2 readings as explained in Halakhah 3.
150 Since there are bystanders 365 days a year, they also hold their special services on days which require a *musaf* prayer; in contrast to all other Torah readings one reads both after morning and after *musaf* prayers; Tosephta 3:4.
151 For extended services.

(68b line 10) **הלכה ד**: תַּנֵּי. אַנְשֵׁי מִשְׁמָר הָיוּ מִתְעַנִּים בְּכָל־יוֹם. בַּשֵּׁנִי הָיוּ מִתְעַנִּין עַל מַפְרְשֵׁי יַמִּים. וַיֹּאמֶר אֱלֹהִים יְהִי רָקִיעַ בְּתוֹךְ הַמָּיִם. בַּשְּׁלִישִׁי הָיוּ מִתְעַנִּין עַל יוֹצְאֵי דְרָכִים. וַיֹּאמֶר אֱלֹהִים יִקָּווּ הַמַּיִם מִתַּחַת הַשָּׁמַיִם. בָּרְבִיעִי הָיוּ מִתְעַנִּין עַל הַתִּינוֹקוֹת שֶׁלֹּא תַעֲלֶה אַסְכָּרָה לְתוֹךְ פִּיהֶם. וַיֹּאמֶר אֱלֹהִים יְהִי מְאֹרֹת. מְאֹרֹת כָּתוּב. בַּחֲמִישִׁי הָיוּ מִתְעַנִּין עַל הַמְּעוּבָּרוֹת שֶׁלֹּא יַפִּילוּ וְעַל הַמֵּינִיקוֹת שֶׁלֹּא יָמוּתוּ בְנֵיהֶן. וַיֹּאמֶר אֱלֹהִים יִשְׁרְצוּ הַמַּיִם שֶׁרֶץ נֶפֶשׁ חַיָּה. תַּנֵּי. לֹא הָיוּ מִתְעַנִּין לֹא בָעֶרֶב שַׁבָּת וְלֹא בְמוֹצָאֵי שַׁבָּת מִפְּנֵי כְבוֹד שַׁבָּת. תַּנֵּי. סַנְהֶדְרִין גְּדוֹלָה הָיְתָה מִתְעַנָּה עִמָּהֶן. וְסַנְהֶדְרִין יְכוֹלָה לְהִתְעַנּוֹת בְּכָל־יוֹם. מְחַלְּקִין הָיוּ עַצְמָן עַל בָּתֵּי אָבוֹת. וְאֵין מִתְעַנִּין עַל שְׁנֵי דְבָרִים כְּאַחַת. מִן הָדָא. וַנָּקוּמָה וּנְבַקְשָׁה מֵאֱלֹהֵינוּ עַל־זֹאת. אָמַר רִבִּי תַּנְחוּמָה. לֹא מִן הָדָא אֶלָּא מִן הָדָא. וְרַחֲמִין לְמִיבְעָא מִן־קֳדָם אֱלָהּ שְׁמַיָּא עַל־רָזָא דְנָה. רִבִּי חַגַּי בְּשֵׁם רִבִּי זְעוּרָה. שֶׁאִם הָיוּ שְׁנֵי דְבָרִים. כְּגוֹן עֲצִירַת גְּשָׁמִים וְגוֹבַי. מַתְרִיעִין עֲלֵיהֶן. רִבִּי חַגַּי כַּד דַּהֲוָה נָפֵק לְתַעֲנִיתָא הֲוָה אָמַר קוֹמֵיהוֹן. אָחֵינוּ. אַף עַל גַּב דְּאִית בְּלִיבֵּינָן עָקוֹן סַגִּין אֶלָּא לְהֵן דַּאֲתִינָן.

It was stated[152]: The people of the watch[153] are fasting every day. On Monday they were fasting for travellers at sea; *God commanded, there shall be a spread in midst of the water*[154]. On Tuesday they are fasting for road travellers; *God commanded, the waters under the sky shall congregate*[155]. On Wednesday they are fasting for children that diphteria should not develop in their mouths; *God commanded, there shall be lights*[156]. "Curses" is written[157]. On Thursday they are fasting that pregnant women should not miscarry and that the children of nursing women should not die; *God commanded, let the waters teem with living creepers*[158]. They fasted neither on Friday nor on Sunday in order to honor the Sabbath. It was stated: The Great Synhedrion was fasting with them. Can the Synhedrion fast every day? They split themselves into clans. "One does not fast for two reasons simultaneously[159], from the following: *we rose and asked of our God for this*[160]." Rebbi Tanḥuma said, not because of this but because of the following, *to ask for mercy from the God of Heaven for this secret*[161]. For if there were two reasons, such as a drought and locusts, one blows the *shofar* about them. When Rebbi Ḥaggai went for a fast, he said before them: Our brothers, even though in our hearts are many worries, this is for what we came.

152 Babli 27b.
153 Meaning the bystanders who do not work in this week.
154 *Gen.* 1:6.
155 *Gen.* 1:9.
156 *Gen.* 1:14.
157 Reading מְאֵרוֹת as מְאֹרֹת.
158 *Gen.* 1:20.

159 Babli 8b.
160 *Ezra* 8:23, misquoted. The same misquote is in the Munich ms. of the Babli (*Diqduqe Soferim Ta`anit* p. 38, Note ס). Therefore the misquote is a Midrash, not a scribal error. Editors of the printed Babli corrected the quote.
161 *Dan.* 2:18.

(fol. 67b) **משנה ה**: כָּל יוֹם שֶׁיֵּשׁ בּוֹ הַלֵּל אֵין בּוֹ מַעֲמָד שַׁחֲרִית. קָרְבַּן מוּסָף אֵין בּוֹ נְעִילָה. וְקָרְבַּן עֵצִים אֵין בּוֹ מִנְחָה דִּבְרֵי רַבִּי עֲקִיבָה. אָמַר לוֹ בֶן עַזַּאי, כָּךְ הָיָה רַבִּי יְהוֹשֻׁעַ שׁוֹנֶה קָרְבַּן מוּסָף אֵין בּוֹ מִנְחָה וְקָרְבַּן עֵצִים אֵין בּוֹ נְעִילָה. חָזַר רַבִּי עֲקִיבָה לִהְיוֹת שׁוֹנֶה כְדִבְרֵי בֶן עַזַּאי:

Mishnah 5: On any day of *hallel*[162] there is no bystanding for morning prayers[163], on a *musaf* sacrifice there is no *ne`ilah*[164]; on an offering of wood[165] there is none for the afternoon prayers, the words of Rebbi Aqiba. Ben Azzai said to him, so was Rebbi Joshua stating: on a *musaf* sacrifice[166] there is none for the afternoon prayers; on an offering of wood no *ne`ilah*[167]. Rebbi Aqiba changed to state following Ben Azzai's words.

162 The first day of Passover, Pentecost, the eight days of Tabernacles and the eight days of Hanukkah.

163 Since these are festive days and the prayers of the bystanders are penitential prayers.

164 For the same reason as before; most *musaf* sacrifices were on festive days and *ne`ilah* is characteristic of fastdays.

165 Offerings of firewood to the Temple as described in Halakhah 6.

166 When except for the Day of Atonement there can be no *ne`ilah*.

167 Since the day is a festive day.

(68b line 25) **הלכה ה:** מַתְנִיתָה דְּרִבִּי מֵאִיר. דְּרִבִּי מֵאִיר אָמַר. מִתְפַּלְלִין וְקוֹרִין מִתְפַּלְלִין וְקוֹרִין. בְּרַם כְּרַבָּנָן. מִתְפַּלְלִין וְקוֹרִין מִתְפַּלְלִין וְהוֹלְכִין לָהֶן. הָא מוּסָף יֶשׁ בּוֹ. מַתְנִיתָה דְּרִבִּי מֵאִיר. דְּרִבִּי מֵאִיר אָמַר. מִתְפַּלְלִין וְקוֹרִין. אִית תַּנָּיֵי תַּנֵּי וּמַחֲלַף. רִבִּי אֲחָא בְּשֵׁם רִבִּי יָסָא כְּמַתְנִיתָן. אָמַר רִבִּי סִימוֹן סוּבְרָא דְקִיסָא טְרַד. אָמַר רִבִּי מָנָא. מִפְּנֵי סְעוּדוֹת רֹאשׁ חוֹדֶשׁ. אָמַר רִבִּי לְעָזָר. עַל שֵׁם כָּל־הַתָּדִיר מֵחֲבֵירוֹ קוֹדֵם אֶת חֲבֵירוֹ.

קִרְיָיא מְסַיֵּיעַ לְרִבִּי יוֹחָנָן וַיְהִי מִמָּחֳרַת הַחוֹדֶשׁ הַשֵּׁנִי. אִין תֵּימַר. תְּרֵין יַרְחִין הֲווֹן. וְהָא כְתִיב מַדּוּעַ לֹא־בָא בֶן־יִשַׁי גַּם־תְּמוֹל גַּם־הַיּוֹם אֶל־הַלָּחֶם: אָמַר רִבִּי חִיָּיא בַּר בָּא. רִבִּי יוֹחָנָן מְפַקֵּד לִכְנִישְׁתָּא דְכוּפְרָא. סָבוֹן מֵעוֹל עַד דּוּ אִימָמָא וְאַתּוּן אָמְרִין זִמְנוֹ וְעִיבּוּרוֹ.

Halakhah 5: The Mishnah is Rebbi Meïr's, as Rebbi Meïr said, one prays and reads, one prays and reads. But following the Rabbis, one prays and reads, one prays and leaves[168]. Therefore on it[169] is a *musaf*. Is the Mishnah Rebbi Meïr's since Rebbi Meïr said, one prays and reads? There are Tannaim who state it inversely. Rebbi Aḥa in the name of Rebbi Yasa following our Mishnah[170]. Rebbi Simon said, is the load of firewood such an exertion[171]? Rebbi Mana said, because of the meal of the New Moon. Rebbi Eleazar said, because of "what is more frequent than something else has precedence over the other.[172]"

The verse supports Rebbi Joḥanan: *It was in the morning of the second New Month*[173]. If you would say, there were two months, is it not written: *why did Jesse's son come neither yesterday not today to the meal*[174]? Rebbi Ḥiyya bar Abba said, Rebbi Joḥanan commanded those of the Kufra synagogue[175], make sure that you come home when it is still daytime and you should mention its time and its addition[176].

168 On a festive day, the service of the bystanders ends after the Torah reading from *Gen*. The *musaf* service is the regular one, disregarding the bystanders.

169 A festive day with *musaf* prayer which falls into the week in which the community observes the rules of bystanders, such as New Year's Day of Nisan (Mishnah 6).

170 Irrespective of the attribution of names one follows the rule of the Mishnah (since, as noted earlier, the rotation of the obligation of bystanders was continued after the destruction of the Temple.)

171 Since the bystanders did not work the entire day, even in Temple times there was no reason not to follow the rules both of the New Moon and the bystanders.

172 Since the New Moon happens 12 times a year but Temple service of the clan only about twice a year.

173 *IS.* 20:27.

174 Which shows that even in the early monarchy, New Month was celebrated for two days at places (such as Saul's Gibea) far from the religious center (at Nob).

175 A synagogue in Tiberias.

176 If the New Moon was not seen on day 30 of the previous month, in the evening prayers one uses the text for New Moons and mentions that the day is New Moon's Day, and continues the same for a second day the next evening and the following day. (in a different context *Roš Haššanah* 4, Notes 42-43.)

(fol. 67b) **משנה ו**: זְמַן עֲצֵי כֹהֲנִים וְהָעָם תִּשְׁעָה. בְּאֶחָד בְּנִיסָן בְּנֵי אָרַח בֶּן יְהוּדָה. בְּעֶשְׂרִים בְּתַמּוּז בְּנֵי דָוִד בֶּן יְהוּדָה. בַּחֲמִשָּׁה בְּאָב בְּנֵי פַרְעֹשׁ בֶּן יְהוּדָה. בְּשִׁבְעָה בּוֹ בְּנֵי יוֹנָדָב בֶּן רֵכָב. בַּעֲשָׂרָה בּוֹ בְּנֵי סְנָאָה בֶּן בִּנְיָמִין. בַּחֲמִשָּׁה עָשָׂר בּוֹ בְּנֵי זַתּוּאֵל בֶּן יְהוּדָה וְעִמָּהֶם כֹּהֲנִים וּלְוִיִם וְכָל מִי שֶׁטָּעָה בְשִׁבְטוֹ. בְּנֵי גוֹנְבֵי עֱלִי בְּנֵי קוֹצְעֵי קְצִיעוֹת בְּעֶשְׂרִים בּוֹ. בְּנֵי פַחַת מוֹאָב בֶּן יְהוּדָה בְּעֶשְׂרִים בֶּאֱלוּל. בְּנֵי עָדִין בֶּן יְהוּדָה בְּאֶחָד בְּטֵבֵת. שָׁבוּ בְנֵי פַרְעֹשׁ שְׁנִיָּה בְּאֶחָד בְּטֵבֵת לֹא הָיָה בּוֹ מַעֲמָד שֶׁהָיָה בּוֹ הַלֵּל וְקָרְבַּן מוּסָף וְקָרְבַּן עֵצִים:

Mishnah 6: The times of wood offerings[177] of the priests and the people are nine. On the first of Nisan, the family Arah[178] from the tribe of Judah. On the twentieth of Tammuz, the family of David from the tribe of Judah. On the fifth of Av, the family of Par`osh[179] from the tribe of Judah. On the seventh, the family of Yonadav ben Rekhav[180]. On the tenth, the family of Senaah[181] from the tribe of Benjamin. On the fifteenth the family of Zatuel[182] from the tribe of Judah, and with them priests and Levites and everybody who is unsure of his tribe. The families of the pestle stealers and the fig hackers[183] on the twentieth. The family of Pahat Moab[184] from the tribe of Judah on the twentieth of Elul. The family of Adin[185] from the tribe of Judah on the first of

Tevet. The family of Parosh came a second time. On the first of Tevet was no bystanding since there was *hallel*, *musaf*, and wood offering[186].

177 Even though fire wood for the altar as a necessity of sacrifices could be bought with money from the Temple tax, the families mentioned in the Mishnah had the privilege of offering fire wood to the Temple as explained in Halakhah 6, and their wood had to be used before any bought by tax money could be used.
178 *Neh.* 7:10, *Ezr.* 2:9.
179 *Neh.* 7:8, *Ezr.* 2:3.
180 *Jer.* 35:16.
181 *Neh.* 7:38, *Ezr.* 2:35.

182 *Neh.* 7:13, *Ezr.* 2:8.
183 These names are explained in Halakhah 7.
184 *Neh.* 7:11, *Ezr.* 2:6.
185 *Neh.* 7:20, *Ezr.* 2:15.
186 Since the New Moon of Tevet always is a day of Hanukkah, there can be no morning bystanding because of the Hallel to be recited, and none afterwards because of *musaf* and the additional festivities of the wood offering.

(68b line 35) **הלכה ו׃** מָה רָאָה זְמַן עֲצֵי כֹהֲנִים וְהָעָם לְהִימָּנוֹת. אֶלָּא בְּשָׁעָה שֶׁעָלוּ יִשְׂרָאֵל מִן הַגּוֹלָה וְלֹא מָצְאוּ עֵצִים בַּלִּישְׁכָּה. וְעָמְדוּ אֵילּוּ וְנִתְנַדְּבוּ עֵצִים מִשֶּׁלְעַצְמָן וּמָסְרוּם לַצִּיבּוּר וְקָרְבוּ מֵהֶן קָרְבְּנוֹת צִיבּוּר. וְהִתְנוּ עִמָּהֶן הַנְּבִיאִים שֶׁבֵּינֵיהֶן שֶׁאֲפִילוּ לִשְׁכָּה מְלֵיאָה עֵצִים [שֶׁיִּהְיוּ מְבִיאִין מֵעַצְמָן.] וְעָמְדוּ אֵילּוּ וְנִתְנַדְּבוּ עֵצִים מִשֶּׁלְעַצְמָן. שֶׁלֹּא יְהֵא קָרֵב מִתְקָרֵב אֶלָּא מִשֶּׁלָּהֶן תְּחִילָּה. אָמַר רִבִּי אֲחָא. דְּרִבִּי יוֹסֵי הִיא. דְּרִבִּי יוֹסֵי אָמַר. אַף הָרוֹצֶה מִתְנַדֵּב שׁוֹמֵר חִנָּם. רִבִּי יוֹסֵי בְשֵׁם רִבִּי אִילָא. דִּבְרֵי הַכֹּל הִיא. מָה פְלִיגִין. בְּגוּפוֹ שֶׁלַּקָּרְבָּן. אֲבָל בְּמַכְשִׁירֵי קָרְבָּן כָּל־עַמָּא מוֹדֵיי שֶׁהוּא מִשֶּׁתַּנֶּה [מִן] קָרְבַּן יָחִיד (מִקָּרְבַּן) [לְקָרְבַּן] צִיבּוּר. תַּנֵּי. אִשָּׁה שֶׁעָשַׂת כֶּתוֹנֶת לִבְנָהּ צְרִיכָה לְמָסְרָה לַצִּיבּוּר. אָמַר רִבִּי אֲחָא. דְּרִבִּי יוֹסֵי הִיא. דְּרִבִּי יוֹסֵי אָמַר. אַף הָרוֹצֶה מִתְנַדֵּב שׁוֹמֵר חִנָּם. רִבִּי יָסָא בְשֵׁם רִבִּי אִילָא. דִּבְרֵי הַכֹּל הִיא. מָה פְלִיגִין. בְּגוּפוֹ שֶׁלַּקָּרְבָּן. אֲבָל בְּמַכְשִׁירֵי קָרְבָּן כָּל־עַמָּא מוֹדֵיי שֶׁהוּא מִשֶּׁתַּנֶּה [מִ]קָּרְבַּן יָחִיד (מִקָּרְבַּן) [לְקָרְבַּן] צִיבּוּר. מַתְנִיתָא פְלִיגָא עַל רִבִּי יוֹסֵי. אוֹתָן הַיָּמִים נוֹהֲגִין בָּהֶן בִּשְׁעַת קָרְבָּן וְשֶׁלֹּא בִשְׁעַת קָרְבָּן. רִבִּי יוֹסֵה אוֹמֵר. אֵינָן נוֹהֲגִין אֶלָּא בִּשְׁעַת קָרְבָּן. וְעוֹד מִן הָדָא דְּתַנֵּי. אָמַר רִבִּי אֶלְעָזָר בֵּירִבִּי יוֹסֵי. אֲנוּ הָיִינוּ מִבְּנֵי סְנָאָה בֶן בִּנְיָמִן. וְחָל תִּשְׁעָה בְאָב לִהְיוֹת בַּשַּׁבָּת. וְדָחִינוּ אוֹתוֹ לְמוֹצָאֵי שַׁבָּת וְהָיוּ מִתְעַנִּין וְלֹא מַשְׁלִימִין.

[187]For what reason were the times of wood by the priests and the people to be counted? Only that at the time when Israel returned from the Diaspora and did not find wood in the chamber, those came forward and volunteered wood from their own and donated it to the public. It was used to offer public sacrifices. The prophets among them stipulated that even if the chamber was full of wood [they would bring of their own][188]. If those came and offered and

volunteered wood from their own, that the sacrifice should only be brought first from theirs. Rebbi Aḥa said, this is Rebbi Yose's, since Rebbi Yose said, also he may volunteer as unpaid trustee. Rebbi Yose[189] in the name of Rebbi Ila, it is the opinion of everybody. Where do they disagree? About the body of the offering. But for enablers of the offering everybody agrees that a private offering can be turned into public offering. It was stated, a woman[190] who made a coat for her son has to surrender it to the public. Rebbi Aḥa said, this is Rebbi Yose's, since Rebbi Yose said, also he may volunteer as unpaid trustee. Rebbi Yasa[191] in the name of Rebbi Ila, it is the opinion of everybody. Where do they disagree? About the body of the offering. But for enablers of the offering everybody agrees that a private offering can be turned into public offering.. A *baraita* disagrees with Rebbi Yose: [192]"Those days are observed at the time of sacrifices and not at the time of sacrifices; Rebbi Yose says, they are observed only at the time of sacrifices." Also from the following: "Rebbi Eleazar ben Rebbi Yose[193] said, we were of the descendants of Senaah ben Benjamin. When the Ninth of Av fell on a Sabbath, we postponed it to the end of the Sabbath and they were fasting but not completing.[194]"

187 This paragraph was copied from here in *Šeqalim* 4:1 (Notes 10-18). It also is copied in *Megillah* 1:1. (Babli 28a).

188 Unnecessary corrector's addition, missing in all parallels.

189 This is R. Yose the late Amora, in contrast to R. Yose the Tanna quoted in the preceding sentence.

190 A priestly woman who makes a garment for her son serving in the Temple. All priestly garments for serving in the Temple must be public property.

191 This must be R. Yose (the Amora) as noted in the parallels; R. Yasa was a teacher, not a student of R. Ila.

192 Tosephta *Ta`aniot* 3:6.

193 With the parallels and the Babli 12a read : R. Ṣadoq. Since R. Yose denies that these festival days had meaning after the destruction of the Temple, his son cannot report that his family celebrated the holiday on the national day of mourning.

194 This disproves the second statement reported due to R. Yose, that the festive days were not celebrated after the destruction of the Temple, but supports R. Aḥa's statement that the Mishnah must follow R. Yose since the offering of firewood must have the status of a sacrifice if it is important enough to push aside the fast of the Ninth of Av.

(68b line 52) **הלכה ז:** מָהוּ בְּנֵי גוֹנְבֵי עֲלִי בְּנֵי קוֹצְעֵי קְצִיעוֹת. אֶלָּא בְּשָׁעָה שֶׁהוֹשִׁיב יָרָבְעָם בֶּן נְבָט פְּרָסְדָאוֹת עַל הַדְּרָכִים לֹא הָיוּ מַנִּיחִין אֶת יִשְׂרָאֵל לַעֲלוֹת לִירוּשָׁלֵָם. כָּל־מִי שֶׁהָיָה כָּשֵׁר וִירֵא חֵטְא בְּאוֹתוֹ הַדּוֹר הָיָה מֵבִיא אֶת בִּכּוּרָיו וְנוֹתְנָן בְּתוֹךְ הַסַּל וּמְחַפֶּה אוֹתָן קְצִיעוֹת וְנוֹטֵל אֶת הָעֱלִי וְנוֹתֵן אֶת הַסַּל עַל כְּתֵיפוֹ וְנוֹטֵל אֶת הָעֱלִי בְּיָדוֹ. וְכֵיוָן שֶׁהָיָה מַגִּיעַ בְּאוֹתוֹ הַמִּשְׁמָר הָיוּ אוֹמְרִים לוֹ. לְאֵיכָן אַתָּה הוֹלֵךְ. וְהוּא אוֹמֵר לוֹ. אֵינִי הוֹלֵךְ אֶלָּא לַעֲשׂוֹת קְצָת קְצִיעוֹת הַלָּלוּ כְּפוֹת אֶחָד שֶׁלִּדְבֵילָה בַּעֲלִי הַזֶּה שֶׁבְּיָדִי. וְכֵיוָן שֶׁהָיָה עוֹבֵר אֶת אוֹתוֹ הַמִּשְׁמָר הָיָה מְעַטְּרָן וּמַעֲלֶה אוֹתָן לִירוּשָׁלֵָם. מָהוּ אוֹמֵר בְּנֵי סַלְמַיי הַנְּתִיצָתִי. אֶלָּא כָּל־מִי שֶׁהָיָה מִתְנַדֵּב עֵצִים וּגְזִירִים לַמַּעֲרָכָה הָיָה מֵבִיא עֵצִים וְעוֹשֶׂה אוֹתָן כְּמִין שְׁלַבִּין וְעוֹשֶׂה אוֹתָן כְּמִין סוּלָּם וְנוֹתְנָן עַל כְּתֵיפָיו. וְכֵיוָן שֶׁהָיָה מַגִּיעַ לְאוֹתוֹ הַמִּשְׁמָר הָיָה אוֹמֵר לוֹ. לְאֵיכָן אַתָּה הוֹלֵךְ. וְהוּא אוֹמֵר לוֹ. אֵינִי הוֹלֵךְ אֶלָּא לְהָבִיא שְׁנֵי גוֹזָלוֹת הַלָּלוּ מִן הַשּׁוֹבָךְ זֶה שֶׁלְּפָנַיי בַּסּוּלָם הַזֶּה שֶׁעַל כְּתֵיפַיי. וְכֵיוָן שֶׁהָיָה עוֹבֵר אֶת אוֹתוֹ הַמִּשְׁמָר הָיָה מְפָרְקָן וּמַעֲלֶה אוֹתָן לִירוּשָׁלֵָם. עַל יְדֵי שֶׁנָּתְנוּ אֶת נַפְשָׁם לַמִּצְווֹת זָכוּ לִקְנוֹת שֵׁם טוֹב בָּעוֹלָם. וַעֲלֵיהֶם הוּא אוֹמֵר זֵכֶר צַדִּיק לִבְרָכָה.

Halakhah 7: What are "the families of the pestle stealers and the fig hackers"? [195]But when Jeroboam ben Nabat installed border guards on the roads which did not permit Israel to make a pilgrimage to Jerusalem, everybody who was qualified and sin-fearing in that generation brought his first fruits, put them in a basket, covered them with dried figs and took the pestle. He takes the basket on his shoulder and the pestle in his hand. When he reaches that guard-post they were asking him, where are you going? He answered him, I am only going to make these few dried figs into a single fig cake with this pestle in my hand. After he had passed this guard, he adorned them and brought them to Jerusalem. [196]Why does one say, the family of Salmai[197] the puller-down? But anybody who was volunteering logs and firewood for the altar brought wood and makes them into a kind of steps, assembles them into a kind of ladder, and puts them on his shoulder. When he reaches that guard he asks him, where are you going? He answers him, I am only going to bring two pigeon chicks from this dovecote over there using the ladder on my shoulder. After he had passed this guard, he disassembled {his package} and brought it to Jerusalem. Since they put themselves in danger for the meritorious deed that merited a good reputation in the world, and about them he says[198], *the remembrance of the just is a blessing.*

195 In the Babli 28a, the story is told of the Roman government "acting in the manner of Jeroboam". In the Tosephta 3:7 it is "Greek government acting in the manner of

Jeroboam." In both Babylonian sources the occurrences are dated to the Second commonwealth, which is a more reasonable scenario.

196 Babli 28a, Tosephta 3:8, as before.

197 In both Babylonian texts, *Salmay from Netofa*. The reference probably is to "the family of Salma from Bethlehem and Netofa" (*1Chr.* 2:54), Calebites. This makes sense for the Babylonian texts which date the story to the Second Commonwealth, but not for the Yerushalmi version.

198 *Prov.* 10:7.

(fol. 67b) **משנה ז**: חֲמִשָּׁה דְבָרִים אֵירְעוּ אֶת אֲבוֹתֵינוּ בְּשִׁבְעָה עָשָׂר בְּתַמּוּז וַחֲמִשָּׁה בְּתִשְׁעָה בְּאָב. בְּשִׁבְעָה עָשָׂר בְּתַמּוּז נִשְׁתַּבְּרוּ הַלּוּחוֹת וּבָטַל הַתָּמִיד וְהוּבְקְעָה הָעִיר וְשָׂרַף אֲפוֹסְטוֹמוֹס אֶת הַתּוֹרָה וְהֶעֱמִיד צֶלֶם בַּהֵיכָל. בְּתִשְׁעָה בְּאָב נִגְזַר עַל אֲבוֹתֵינוּ שֶׁלֹּא יִכָּנְסוּ לָאָרֶץ וְחָרַב הַבַּיִת בָּרִאשׁוֹנָה וּבַשְּׁנִיָּה וְנִלְכְּדָה בֵּיתָר וְנֶחְרְשָׁה הָעִיר.

Mishnah 7: Five things happened to our forefathers on the Seventeenth of Tammuz and five on the Ninth of Av[199]. On the Seventeenth of Tammuz were the tablets broken, the daily sacrifice ceased[200], the city was breached[201], Apostomos[202] burned the Torah, and put up an idol in the Temple. On the Ninth of Av was decided that our forefathers would not enter the Land[203], the Temple was destroyed the first and second times, Betar was taken, and the city ploughed over[204].

199 Or at least these two days commemorate these events even if the dates may not be correct, as explained in the Halakhah.

200 During a siege of Jerusalem.

201 Jerusalem surrendered to Nebukadnezar, and its walls were breached by Titus.

202 This personality cannot be identified since he cannot be dated.

203 After the return of the scouts, *Num.* 14:23.

204 By Hadrian, imitating the mythical foundation of Rome in the founding of pagan Aelia Capitolina. Described in a coin of Hadrian minted 130 C.E.

(68b line 69) **הלכה ח**: כָּתוּב וַיִּשְׁכֹּן כְּבוֹד־יְ"י עַל־תַּר סִינַי וַיְכַסֵּהוּ הֶעָנָן שֵׁשֶׁת יָמִים וַיִּקְרָא אֶל־מֹשֶׁה בַּיּוֹם הַשְּׁבִיעִי. שְׁבִיעִי שֶׁהוּא לְאַחַר הַדִּיבְּרוֹת וּתְחִילָה לָאַרְבָּעִים. אָמַר לָהֶן מֹשֶׁה. אַרְבָּעִין יוֹמִין אֲנָא מֵיעֲבַד בְּטוּרָא. כֵּיוָן שֶׁהִגִּיעַ יוֹם אַרְבָּעִים וְלֹא בָא. מִיַּד וַיַּרְא הָעָם כִּי־בוֹשֵׁשׁ מֹשֶׁה לָרֶדֶת מִן־הָהָר. וְכֵיוָן שֶׁהִגִּיעַ שֵׁשׁ שָׁעוֹת וְלֹא בָא. מִיַּד וַיִּקָּהֵל הָעָם עַל־אַהֲרֹן וַיֹּאמְרוּ אֵלָיו קוּם | עֲשֵׂה־לָנוּ אֱלֹהִים אֲשֶׁר יֵלְכוּ לְפָנֵינוּ וגו׳. וַיֹּאמֶר יְ"י אֶל־מֹשֶׁה לֶךְ־רֵד כִּי שִׁחֵת

עַמֶּךְ וגו'. וַיִּשְׁמַע יְהוֹשֻׁעַ אֶת־קוֹל הָעָם בְּרֵעֹה וַיֹּאמֶר אֶל־מֹשֶׁה קוֹל מִלְחָמָה בַּמַּחֲנֶה. אָמַר מֹשֶׁה. אָדָם שֶׁהוּא עָתִיד לְהַנְהִיג שְׁרָרָה עַל שִׁשִּׁים רִיבּוֹא אֵינוֹ יוֹדֵעַ לְהַבְחִין בֵּין קוֹל לְקוֹל. וַיֹּאמֶר אֵין קוֹל עֲנוֹת גְּבוּרָה וְאֵין קוֹל עֲנוֹת חֲלוּשָׁה קוֹל עַנּוֹת אָנֹכִי שׁוֹמֵעַ. אָמַר רִבִּי יָסָא. קוֹל קִילּוּס עֲבוֹדָה זָרָה אָנֹכִי שׁוֹמֵעַ. רִבִּי יוּדָן בְּשֵׁם רִבִּי יָסָא. אֵין כָּל־דּוֹר וָדוֹר שֶׁאֵין בּוֹ אוּנְקִי אַחַת מֵחֶטְיוֹ שֶׁלְעֵגֶל. וַיְהִי כַּאֲשֶׁר קָרַב אֶל־הַמַּחֲנֶה וַיַּרְא אֶת־הָעֵגֶל וּמְחֹלוֹת. רִבִּי חִלְקִיָּה בְשֵׁם רִבִּי אָחָא. מִיכָּן שֶׁלֹּא יְהֵא אָדָם דָּן (עוּמָדוֹת) [אוּמָדוֹת]. דָּרַשׁ מֹשֶׁה מִקַּל הַחוֹמֶר. מָה אִם פֶּסַח שֶׁהִיא מִצְוָה יְחִידִית נֶאֱמַר בּוֹ וְכָל־עָרֵל לֹא־יֹאכַל בּוֹ. הַתּוֹרָה שֶׁכָּל־הַמִּצְווֹת כְּלוּלוֹת בָּהּ אַל אַחַת כַּמָּה וְכַמָּה. וַיִּחַר־אַף מֹשֶׁה וַיַּשְׁלֵךְ מִיָּדָיו אֶת־הַלּוּחוֹת וַיְשַׁבֵּר אוֹתָם תַּחַת הָהָר: תַּנֵּי רִבִּי יִשְׁמָעֵאל. הַקָּדוֹשׁ בָּרוּךְ הוּא אָמַר לוֹ שֶׁשְּׁבָרָם. [שֶׁנֶּאֱמַר] וְאֶכְתּוֹב עַל־הַלֻּחֹת אֶת־הַדְּבָרִים אֲשֶׁר הָיוּ עַל־הַלֻּחֹת הָרִאשֹׁנִים אֲשֶׁר שִׁבַּרְתָּ. אָמַר לוֹ. יָפֶה עָשִׂיתָ שֶׁשִּׁיבַּרְתָּ. רִבִּי שְׁמוּאֵל בַּר נַחְמָן בְּשֵׁם רִבִּי יוֹנָתָן. הַלּוּחוֹת הָיָה אוֹרְכָּן שִׁשָּׁה טְפָחִים וְרָחְבָּן שְׁלֹשָׁה. וְהָיָה מֹשֶׁה תָּפוּשׂ בִּטְפָחַיִים וְהַקָּדוֹשׁ בָּרוּךְ הוּא בִּטְפָחַיִים וּטְפָחַיִּים רֶיוַח בָּאֶמְצַע. כֵּיוָן שֶׁעָשׂוּ יִשְׂרָאֵל אוֹתוֹ מַעֲשֶׂה בִּיקֵּשׁ הַקָּדוֹשׁ בָּרוּךְ הוּא לְחוֹטְפָן מִיָּדוֹ שֶׁלְּמֹשֶׁה. וְגָבְרָה יָדוֹ שֶׁלְּמֹשֶׁה וַחֲטָפָן מִמֶּנּוּ. הוּא שֶׁהַכָּתוּב מְשַׁבְּחוֹ בַסּוֹף וְאוֹמֵר וּלְכֹל הַיָּד הַחֲזָקָה. יֵיֵי שְׁלָמָא עַל יָדָא דְגָבְרַת עַל מִינָא. רִבִּי יוֹחָנָן בְּשֵׁם רִבִּי יוֹסֵה בַּר אַבַּיֵּי. [הַלּוּחוֹת] הָיוּ מְבַקְשִׁין לִפְרוֹחַ וְהָיָה מֹשֶׁה תוֹפְשָׂן. [דִּכְתִיב] וָאֶתְפּוֹשׂ בִּשְׁנֵי הַלֻּחוֹת. תַּנֵּי בְשֵׁם רִבִּי נְחֶמְיָה. הַכְּתָב עַצְמוֹ פָּרַח. רִבִּי עֶזְרָה בְּשֵׁם רִבִּי יְהוּדָה בֵּירִבִּי סִימוֹן. הַלּוּחוֹת הָיוּ מַשָּׂאוֹי אַרְבָּעִים סְאָה וְהַכְּתָב הָיָה סוֹבְלָן. כֵּיוָן שֶׁפָּרַח הַכְּתָב כָּבְדוּ עַל יָדָיו שֶׁלְּמֹשֶׁה וְנָפְלוּ וְנִשְׁתַּבְּרוּ.

19 ייא A | יהא A מינא A | ימינא   20 יוסה בר אביי A | יוסי בר בא   21 [דכת׳] A | ומה טעם עצמו A - | עזרה A | עזריה   22 יהודה ביר׳ סימון A | יודן משאיי A | משאון   23 שלמשה A -

It is written[205]: *The glory of the Eternal dwelt on Mount Sinai; the cloud covered it for six days; He called to Moses on the Seventh Day. Moses ascended*[206]. The Seventh after the Ten Commandments, the start of the Forty. Moses said to them, I shall be occupied on the Mountain for 40 days[207]. When the fortieth day came and he did not come, immediately *the people saw that Moses tarried in descending from the Mountain*[208]. When noontime came and he did not come, immediately *the people congregated on Aaron and said to him, rise and make us gods which shall go before us,* etc. *The Eternal said to Moses, descend, for your people corrupted*[209], etc. *And Joshua heard the sound of the people in its dealings; he said to Moses, there is sound of war in the camp*[210]. Moses said, a man who in the future will rule over 600'000 does not know to distinguish between sound and sound? *He said, there is no sound of shouts of strength nor sound of sounds of weakness, a sound of shouts I am hearing*[211]. Rebbi Yasa said, a sound of acclaim of foreign worship I am hearing. Rebbi Yudan in the name of Rebbi Yasa: There is no generation in which there is not an ounce[212] of the sin of the Calf[213]. *It was when he approached the camp that he saw the Calf and fifes*[214]. Rebbi Hilkiah in the name of Rebbi Aha: From here[215] that a person should not argue from guesses. Moses made an argument *de minore ad majus*. Since for the *pesaḥ* sacrifice, which is an isolated obligation, it is said *no uncircumcised may eat from it*[216], the Torah in which all commandments are contained not so much more? *Moses got angry and he threw the tablets from his hand and broke them below the Mountain*[214]. Rebbi Ismael stated, the Holy One, praise to Him, told him to break them, [as it is said,] *I shall write on the tablets the words which were on the first tablets luckily you broke*[217]. He said to him, you did well that you broke. Rebbi Samuel bar Naḥman in the name of Rebbi Jonathan: The tablets were six hand-breadths long and three wide. Moses held two hand-breadth, the Holy One, praise to Him two hand-breadth, and two hand-breadths of space were between them. When Israel sinned in that way, the Holy One wanted to seize them from Moses's hand, but Moses's hand had the better of it and seized them from Him. That is what the verse praises him at the end and says, *and all the strong hand*[218], [219]peace shall be on the hand which had the better on mine. Rebbi Joḥanan in the name of Rebbi Yose ben Abbai: the tablets wanted to fly off but Moses held them, [as is written,] *I grabbed the two tablets*[220]. It was stated in the name of Rebbi Nehemiah, the writing itself flew off[221]. Rebbi Ezra in the name of Rebbi Jehudah ben Rebbi Simon: The tablets were a load of forty *seah* but the writing was carrying them. When the writing flew off they were too heavy for Moses's hands, they fell, and broke[221].

205 *Ex.* 24:16.
206 *Ex.* 24:13.
207 This is the argument which shows that the tablets were broken on the 17th of Tammus (Babli 28b). In rabbinic tradition, Pentecost (Siwan 6) is the anniversary of the epiphany of Mount Sinai. If one assumes that at the Exodus this month had 30 days and counts 40 days from the following day one has 13 days in Siwan and 17 in Tammuz for a sum of 40. Therefore the date of 17 Tammuz presupposes not only the rabbinic date for the giving of the Ten Commandments but also that Moses did not eat during the six days of waiting for permission to ascend the Mountain.

The remainder of the paragraph consists of sermon concepts; presupposing like many sermons that the persons acting in biblical history had foreknowledge of what was going to happen, such as Moses knowing that he would spend 40 days on the Mountain. Similarly, the crass anthropomorphism of the sermon about the tablets would be inadmissible in a discussion with possible consequences for rules of behavior.

208 *Ex.* 32:1.
209 *Ex.* 32:7.
210 *Ex.* 32:17.
211 *Ex.* 32:18.
212 Latin *uncia*.
213 Any trouble for the Jewish people contains some punishment for the sin of the Golden Calf. Babli *Sanhedrin* 102a.
214 *Ex.* 32:19.
215 Even though Moses correctly analyzed the sound, he did not act until he had visual confirmation that his analysis was correct.
216 *Ex.* 12:48. Babli *Šabbat* 87a.
217 *Deut.* 10:2, taking אשר not as relative pronoun but as derived from the root אשר "riches, happiness".
218 *Deut.* 34:12.
219 Here starts an Ashkenazic text edited by J. Sussman (A), differing from the Leiden ms. mostly in the names of the tradents. The readings of the Leiden ms. are more reliable; they are confirmed by excerpts from this Chapter published by L. Ginzberg.
220 *Deut.* 9:17.
221 Babli *Pesahim* 87b, last line.

(68c line 24) וּבָטַל הַתָּמִיד. רַבִּי סִימוֹן בְּשֵׁם רַבִּי יְהוֹשֻׁעַ בֶּן לֵוִי. בִּימֵי מַלְכוּת יָוָן הָיוּ מְשַׁלְשְׁלִין לָהֶם שְׁתֵּי קוּפּוֹת שֶׁלְּזָהָב וְהָיוּ מַעֲלִין שְׁנֵי כְבָשִׂים. פַּעַם אַחַת שִׁילְשְׁלוּ לָהֶם שְׁתֵּי קוּפּוֹת שֶׁלְּזָהָב וְהֶעֱלוּ לָהֶן שְׁנֵי גְדָיִים. בְּאוֹתָהּ שָׁעָה הֵאִיר הַקָּדוֹשׁ בָּרוּךְ הוּא אֶת עֵינֵיהֶם וּמָצְאוּ שְׁנֵי טְלָאִים בְּלִישְׁכַּת הַטְּלָאִים. עַל אוֹתָהּ שָׁעָה הֵעִיד רַבִּי יְהוּדָה בֶּן אַבָּא עַל תָּמִיד שֶׁלְּשַׁחַר שֶׁקָּרַב בְּאַרְבַּע שָׁעוֹת. וְאָמַר רַבִּי לֵוִי. אַף בִּימֵי מַלְכוּת הָרְשָׁעָה הַזֹּאת הָיוּ מְשַׁלְשְׁלִין לָהֶם שְׁתֵּי קוּפּוֹת שֶׁלְּזָהָב וְהָיוּ מַעֲלִין לָהֶם שְׁנֵי גְדָיִים. וּבַסּוֹף שִׁילְשְׁלוּ לָהֶם שְׁתֵּי קוּפּוֹת שֶׁלְּזָהָב וְהֶעֱלוּ לָהֶם שְׁנֵי חֲזִירִים. לֹא הִסְפִּיקוּ לְהַגִּיעַ לְמַחֲצִית הַחוֹמָה עַד (שֶׁנָּתַז) [שֶׁנָּעַץ] הַחֲזִיר וְקָפַץ מֵאֶרֶץ יִשְׂרָאֵל אַרְבָּעִים פַּרְסָה. בְּאוֹתָהּ הַשָּׁעָה גָרְמוּ הָעֲוֹנוֹת וּבָטַל הַתָּמִיד וְחָרַב הַבַּיִת.

2 להם | ב להן (2) שני | ב להן שני כבשים | ב טליים 3 והעלו | ב והיו מעלין את | ב - 4 טלאים | ב טליים יהודה | ב יודה 5 ואמ' | ב אמ' הרשעה | ב רשעה להם | ב להן 6 גדיים | ב כבשים להם | ב להן 7 חזירים | ב חזיריץ למחצית החומה | ב לחצי חומה החזיר | ב החזיר בחומה ונזדעזעה החומה מארץ ישראל ארבעים פרסה | ב ארבעים פרסה מארץ ישראל

תַּנֵּי רַבִּי שִׁמְעוֹן בֶּן יוֹחַי. עֲקִיבָה רַבִּי הָיָה דּוֹרֵשׁ. כֹּה־אָמַר יי צְבָאוֹת צוֹם הָרְבִיעִי וְצוֹם הַחֲמִישִׁי וְצוֹם הַשְּׁבִיעִי וְצוֹם הָעֲשִׂירִי יִהְיֶה לְבֵית־יְהוּדָה לְשָׂשׂוֹן וּלְשִׂמְחָה. צוֹם הָרְבִיעִי זֶה שִׁבְעָה עָשָׂר בַּתַּמּוּז. יוֹם שֶׁנִּשְׁתַּבְּרוּ הַלּוּחוֹת. וּבָטַל הַתָּמִיד. וְהוּבְקְעָה הָעִיר. וְשָׂרַף אַפּוֹסְטוֹמוֹס אֶת הַתּוֹרָה. וְהֶעֱמִיד צֶלֶם בַּהֵיכָל. צוֹם הַחֲמִישִׁי. זֶה תִּשְׁעָה בְאָב. שֶׁבּוֹ חָרַב הַבַּיִת בָּרִאשׁוֹנָה וּבַשְּׁנִיָּה. צוֹם הַשְּׁבִיעִי זֶה שְׁלֹשָׁה בְּתִשְׁרֵי שֶׁנֶּהֱרַג בּוֹ גְּדַלְיָה בֶּן אֲחִיקָם. צוֹם הָעֲשִׂירִי. זֶה עֲשָׂרָה בְטֵבֶת. יוֹם שֶׁסָּמַךְ מֶלֶךְ בָּבֶל עַל יְרוּשָׁלָ͏ִם.

"The daily sacrifice ceased." [222]Rebbi Simon said in the name of Rebbi Joshua ben Levi: In the time of the hellenistic government[223] they[224] lowered them two boxes with gold and they gave them two lambs to pull up. Once they lowered them two boxes with gold and they gave them two kid goats[225] to pull up. At that moment the Holy One, praise to Him, enlightened their eyes and they found two lambs in the hall of lambs[226]. About that time did Rebbi Yehudah bar Abba testify that the perpetual morning sacrifice was brought at four hours. Rebbi Levi said: Also in the days of the present evil government[227] they lowered them two boxes with gold and they gave them two kid goats[228] to pull up. Once they lowered them two boxes with gold and they gave them two swine to pull up[229]. They did not manage to get to half the height of the wall when the swine (damaged) [clawed][230] the wall and jumped 40 parasangs from the Land of Israel. At that time the sins caused that the perpetual sacrifice was stopped and the Temple destroyed.

[231]Rebbi Simeon ben Yoḥai stated: So was my teacher Aqiba explaining. *So says the Eternal of Hosts, the fast of the fourth, the fast of the fifth, the fast of the seventh, and the fast of the tenth will be for the House of Israel enjoyment and joy*[232]. The fast of the fourth is the Seventeenth of Tammuz, the day when the tablets were broken, the daily sacrifice ceased, the city was breached, Apostomos burned the Torah, and put an idol in the Temple. The fast of the fifth is the Ninth of Av, when the Temple was destroyed the first and the second times. The fast of the seventh is the third of Tishre, when Gedalya ben Aḥiqam was murdered[233]. The fast of the tenth is the Tenth of Tevet, the day when the King of Babylonia closed in on Jerusalem[234].

222 This paragraph is copied from *Berakhot* 4:1 (Notes 22-28, ב). Babli *Roš Haššanah* 18b.

223 The Babli (*Menaḥot* 64b) telescopes this story and the next into one and dates it at the civil war of the two Hasmonean brothers Hyrkanos and Aristobulos.

224 The officials of the Temple lowered the boxes from the wall of besieged Jerusalem; in each box was payment for the lamb to be placed in it for the daily sacrifice.

225 Which cannot be used for the perpetual sacrifice.

226 Since the verse (*Num.* 28:3) requires that the perpetual sacrifice be "a yearling sheep without blemish" the sheep were usually held in a separate "hall of lambs" and were inspected three times before being used as sacrifice.

227 In both Talmudim, the "evil government" or simply "government" is the Roman government.

228 This obviously is a copyist's error (Note 225); with the text of *Berakhot* one has to read "lambs".

229 In the Babli (*Menaḥot* 64b), there was

only one swine and not only the wall but the entire Land of Israel trembled. (The civil war was at the time when Pompey conquered the East for Rome but the story here clearly speaks of the war of Titus. However, it seems that the Babli tradition in this case is more correct.)

230 The change by the corrector follows the text ב. However, there one reads "the swine clawed the wall and the wall trembled",

which is well described by the term used by the Leiden scribe.

231 This paragraph is repeated again in this Halakhah. Since the later text shows that the text here is incomplete, its correct place is there.

232 *Sach.* 8:19.

233 *Jer.* 41:2-3.

234 *Ez.* 24:2.

(68c line 41) וְהֻבְקְעָה הָעִיר. כָּתוּב בְּתִשְׁעָה לַחוֹדֶשׁ הֻבְקְעָה הָעִיר וְאַתְּ אָמַר הָכֵין. אָמַר רִבִּי תַּנְחוּם בַּר חֲנִילָאִי. קִילְקוּל חֶשְׁבּוֹנוֹת יֵשׁ כָּאן. הָדָא הִיא דִכְתִיב וַיְהִי בְּעַשְׁתֵּי־עֶשְׂרֵה שָׁנָה בְּאֶחָד לַחוֹדֶשׁ הָיָה דְבַר־יי אֵלַי לֵאמֹר׃ בֶּן־אָדָם יַעַן אֲשֶׁר אָמְרָה צֹּר עַל־יְרוּשָׁלַםִ הֶאָח. מָהוּ הֶאָח. אֵין תֵּימַר. בְּאֶחָד בָּאב. עֲדַיִין לֹא נִשְׂרָף. אֵין תֵּימַר בְּאֶחָד בְּאֱלוּל. [בַּ]יּוֹם וָלַיְלָה נָפַק בַּלְדָרָה מִן יְרוּשָׁלַם וּבָא לְצוֹר. אֶלָּא קִילְקוּל חֶשְׁבּוֹנוֹת יֵשׁ כָּאן. רִבִּי יוֹחָנָן וְרִבִּי שִׁמְעוֹן בֶּן לָקִישׁ. רִבִּי יוֹחָנָן אָמַר. לַמֶּלֶךְ שֶׁהָיָה יוֹשֵׁב וּמְחַשֵּׁב חֶשְׁבּוֹנוֹת. בָּאוּ וְאָמְרוּ לוֹ. נִשְׁבָּה בְּנָךְ. וְנִתְקַלְקְלוּ חֶשְׁבּוֹנוֹתָיו. אָמַר. יֵיעָשֶׂה זֶה רֹאשׁ לַחֶשְׁבּוֹנוֹת. רִבִּי שִׁמְעוֹן בֶּן לָקִישׁ אָמַר. לַמֶּלֶךְ שֶׁהָיָה יוֹשֵׁב וּמְחַשֵּׁב חֶשְׁבּוֹנוֹתָיו. בָּאוּ וְאָמְרוּ לוֹ. נִשְׁבָּה בְּנָךְ וְנִתְקַדֵּשׁ. אָמַר. יֵיעָשֶׂה זֶה רֹאשׁ לַחֶשְׁבּוֹנוֹת. רִבִּי מָנָא בָעֵי. נִיחָא נִתְקַלְקְלוּ לְשֶׁעָבַר. דִּילְמָא לְהַבָּא. בֵּין כְּמָאן דְּאָמַר. בְּתִשְׁעָה לַחוֹדֶשׁ. בֵּין כְּמָאן דְּאָמַר. בְּשִׁבְעָה עָשָׂר. [מָה בֵינֵיהוֹן.] עֶשְׂרִים וְאֶחָד יוֹם מִיּוֹם שֶׁהֻבְקְעָה הָעִיר וְעַד יוֹם שֶׁחָרַב בֵּית הַמִּקְדָּשׁ. אָמַר רִבִּי אֲבוּנָה. סִימָנָא מֵקֵל שָׁקֵד אֲנִי רוֹאֶה. מָה הַלּוּז הַזֶּה מִשֶּׁהוּא מוֹצִיא אֶת נִיצּוֹ וְעַד שֶׁהוּא גוֹמֵר אֶת פֵּירוֹתָיו עֶשְׂרִים וְאֶחָד יוֹם. כָּךְ מִיּוֹם שֶׁהֻבְקְעָה הָעִיר וְעַד יוֹם שֶׁחָרַב הַבַּיִת עֶשְׂרִים וְאֶחָד יוֹם. מָאן דְּאָמַר. בְּתִשְׁעָה לַחוֹדֶשׁ. [בְּאֶחָד] בְּאב חָרַב הַבַּיִת. מָאן דְּאָמַר בְּשִׁבְעָה עָשָׂר. בְּתִשְׁעָה בְּאב חָרַב הַבָּיִת.

תַּנֵּי רִבִּי שִׁמְעוֹן בֶּן יוֹחַאי. עֲקִיבָה רִבִּי הָיָה דוֹרֵשׁ. כֹּה־אָמַר יי צְבָאוֹת צוֹם הָרְבִיעִי וְצוֹם הַחֲמִישִׁי וְצוֹם הַשְּׁבִיעִי וְצוֹם הָעֲשִׂירִי וגו׳. צוֹם הָרְבִיעִי זֶה שִׁבְעָה עָשָׂר בַּתַּמּוּז. יוֹם שֶׁנִּשְׁתַּבְּרוּ הַלּוּחוֹת. וּבָטַל הַתָּמִיד. וְהֻבְקְעָה הָעִיר. וְשָׂרַף אַפּוֹסְטוֹמוֹס אֶת הַתּוֹרָה. וְהֶעֱמִיד צֶלֶם בַּהֵיכָל. צוֹם הַחֲמִישִׁי. זֶה תִּשְׁעָה בְּאב. שֶׁבּוֹ חָרַב הַבַּיִת בָּרִאשׁוֹנָה וּבַשְּׁנִיָּה. צוֹם הַשְּׁבִיעִי זֶה שְׁלֹשָׁה בְּתִשְׁרֵי. יוֹם שֶׁנֶּהֱרַג בּוֹ גְדַלְיָה בֶּן אֲחִיקָם. צוֹם הָעֲשִׂירִי. זֶה עֲשָׂרָה בְטֵבֵת. יוֹם שֶׁסָּמַךְ מֶלֶךְ בָּבֶל עַל יְרוּשָׁלַםִ. הָדָא הִיא דִכְתִיב וַיְהִי־יי אֵלַי בַּשָּׁנָה הַתְּשִׁיעִית בַּחֹדֶשׁ הָעֲשִׂירִי בֶּעָשׂוֹר לַחֹדֶשׁ לֵאמֹר׃ בֶּן־אָדָם כְּתָב־לְךָ אֶת־שֵׁם הַיּוֹם אֶת־עֶצֶם הַיּוֹם הַזֶּה סָמַךְ מֶלֶךְ־בָּבֶל עַל יְרוּשָׁלַםִ. וַאֲנִי אוֹמֵר. צוֹם הָעֲשִׂירִי זֶה חֲמִשָּׁה בְטֵבֵת. יוֹם שֶׁבָּאת שְׁמוּעָה לַגּוֹלָה. הָדָא הִיא דִכְתִיב וַיְהִי בִּשְׁתֵּי עֶשְׂרֵה שָׁנָה בַּחֲמִישִׁי בַּחֲמִשָּׁה לַחֹדֶשׁ בְּגָלוּתֵנוּ בָּא־אֵלַי הַפָּלִיט מִירוּשָׁלַםִ לֵאמֹר הֻבְּכְתָה הָעִיר׃ אֶלָּא שֶׁבִּיהוּדָה מִתְעַנִּין עַל הַמַּעֲשֶׂה. וּבַגָּלִיּוֹת עַל הַשְּׁמוּעָה. רִבִּי עֲקִיבָה דָרַשׁ

רִאשׁוֹן אַחֲרוֹן וְאַחֲרוֹן רִאשׁוֹן. וַאֲנִי דוֹרֵשׁ רִאשׁוֹן רִאשׁוֹן וְאַחֲרוֹן אַחֲרוֹן. וַאֲנִי רוֹאֶה אֶת דְּבָרַיי מִדִּבְרֵי רִבִּי עֲקִיבָה.

"And the city was breached." It is written, *on the Ninth of the month the city was breached*[235], and you are saying so? Rebbi Tanḥum bar Ḥanilai said, here is an erroneous computation[236]. That is what is written, *it was in the twelfth year, on the first of the month, was the Eternal's word to me, saying: Son of man, since Tyre said about Jerusalem hurrah*[237]. What "hurrah"? If you are saying on the first of Av, it still was not burned. If you are saying on the first of Ellul, cannot in one day and night the messenger leave Jerusalem and arrive at Tyre? But here is an erroneous computation[238]. Rebbi Joḥanan and Rebbi Simeon ben Laqish. Rebbi Joḥanan said, {a parable} of a king who was sitting and computing computations. They came and told him, your son was kidnapped; his computations became erroneous. He said, let this be the beginning of computations[239]. Rebbi Simeon ben Laqish said, {a parable} of a king who was sitting and computing computations. They came and told him, your son was kidnapped and incapacitated; his computations became erroneous. He said, let this be the beginning of computations. Rebbi Mana asked, one understands this that they were erroneous for the past; maybe for the future[240]? Whether one follows him who said on the ninth of the month, or the one who said on the seventeenth, [in what do they differ?][241] there are twenty-one days from the day the city was breached to the day the Temple was destroyed. Rebbi Abuna said, an indication[242], *I am seeing an almond stick*[243]. Since this almond tree from sprouting its flower to finishing its fruit needs twenty-one days, so from the day the city was breached to the day the Temple was destroyed twenty-one days. He who says on the Ninth of the month, the Temple was destroyed on the first of Av[244]. He who says on the Seventeenth, the Temple was destroyed on the Ninth of Av.

Rebbi Simeon ben Yoḥai stated: So was my teacher Aqiba explaining. *So says the Eternal of Hosts, the fast of the fourth, the fast of the fifth, the fast of the seventh, and the fast of the tenth will be for the House of Israel enjoyment and joy*[232]. The fast of the fourth is the Seventeenth of Tammuz, the day when the tablets were broken, the daily sacrifice ceased, the city was breached, Apostomos burned the Torah, and put an idol in the Temple. The fast of the fifth is the Ninth of Av, when the Temple was destroyed the first and the second times. The fast of the seventh is the third of Tishre, when Gedalya ben Ahiqam was murdered[233]. The fast of the tenth is the Tenth of Tevet, the day when the King of Babylonia closed in on Jerusalem[234]. That is what is written[245], *the Eternal's word came to me in the ninth year, in the tenth month, on the tenth of the month, saying: Son of man, write down the name of this day. On this very day the king of Babylonia closed in on Jerusalem.* But I am saying that the fast of the tenth is the Fifth of Tevet, the day when the news came to the diaspora. That is what is written[246], *it was in the eleventh year of our exile, in the fifth, on the fifth of the month, the fugitive came to me from Jerusalem, saying, the city was breached.* Only that in Judea one fasts on the act, and in the exile on the news. Rebbi Aqiba explains the first last and the last first; but I am explaining the first first and the last last[247]; and I hold my words more intelligible than Rebbi Aqiba's words.

235 *Jer.* 39:2. The date is confirmed *2K.* 25:3.

236 The Babli 28b disagrees and states that the city surrendered on Tammuz 9 to the Babylonians and was breached Tammuz 17 by the Romans.

237 *Ez.* 26:1-2. The verse makes it clear that the joy was about the destruction of Jerusalem, for which the prophecy gives a date *post quem*.

238 But Ezechiel implicitly states that Jerusalem was destroyed on Av 1.

239 What actually was Av 9 is now called Av 1.

240 Maybe the participants in the destruction, Jeremiah and the author of Kings, erred in the date. But Ezechiel sitting safely in Babylonia and being divinely instructed cannot be assumed to err in his date.

241 Corrector's addition from a source similar to A. There it is clear that one has to read: In what do they differ? Are there not (according to everybody) twenty-one days from the day the city was breached to the day the Temple was destroyed?

242 Greek σημεῖον.

243 *Jer.* 1:11.

244 The dating in *Ez.* is consistent with that of *Jer.* and *2K.*; there is no error in the computations.

245 *Ez.* 24:2.

246 *Ez.* 32:21.

247 I am following the order of verses in *Ez.*

(68c line 74) וְשָׂרַף אַפּוֹסְטּוֹמוֹס אֶת הַתּוֹרָה. אֵיכָן שְׂרָפָהּ. רִבִּי אָחָא אָמַר. בְּמַעֲבַרְתָּא דְלוֹד. וְרַבָּנָן אָמְרֵי. בְּמַעֲבַרְתָּא דְטַרְלוֹסָה. וְהֶעֱמִיד צֶלֶם בַּהֵיכָל. אִית תַּנָּיֵי תַנֵּי. הוּעֲמַד. מָאן דְּאָמַר הוּעֲמַד. צַלְמוֹ שֶׁלִּמְנַשֶּׁה. מָאן דְּאָמַר. הֶעֱמִיד. צַלְמוֹ שֶׁלְאַפּוֹסְטּוֹמוֹס. מִפְּנֵי מַה לֹא קָבְעוּ אוֹתוֹ תַעֲנִית. חִינָּנָא אָבוֹי דְּבַר יַנְטָה בְשֵׁם רִבִּי בְּנָיָה. שֶׁלֹּא קִיבְּלוּ רוֹב צִיבּוּר עֲלֵיהֶם. אָמַר רִבִּי

יְהוֹשֻׁעַ בֶּן לֵוִי. כָּל־מַה שֶּׁנַּעֲשָׂה בָזֶה חָזַר. וְכָל־מַה שֶּׁנַּעֲשָׂה בָזֶה לֹא חָזָר. אָמַר רבִּי לֵוִי. כָּתוּב אֲשֶׁר יַעֲשֶׂה אֹתָם הָאָדָם וָחַי בָּהֶם. וְאֵין מָאוֹר עֵינָיו שֶׁלְּאָדָם חוֹזֵר אֶלָּא לְאַחַר אַרְבָּעִים יוֹם.

1 ר' אחא | A רב במעברתא | A במערכתה 2 במעברתא | A במערכתה דטרלוסה | A דטרו לוטה 3-4 לא קבעו אותו תענית | A לא גזרו תענית יום שילוח מרגלים חיננא | A ר' חננא דבר ינטה | A דאמרנטה בנייה | A בנטה 5 יהושע | A יהושוע בזה לא | A לא

"Apostomos²⁰² burned the Torah." Where did he burn it? Rebbi Aha said, at the ford of Lydda. But the rabbis are saying, at the ford of Tarlosa²⁴⁸. "And put up an idol in the Temple." There are Tannaim who state, "was put up." He who says, "was put up," Manasse's idol. He who said, "put up", Apostomos's idol²⁴⁹. Why was it not fixed as a fast day²⁵⁰? Hinnena the father of Bar Yanta in the name of Rebbi Banaia: Because most of the community did not accept it as obligation²⁵¹. Rebbi Joshua ben Levi said, all that happened on this was repeated, all that happened on that was not repeated²⁵². Rebbi Levi said, it is written, *which a person shall do and live by them*²⁵³, and the light in a person's eyes only returns after 40 days²⁵⁴.

248 Place not identified. In A one reads "exercise field" instead of "ford".

249 A here has an insert from *Seder Olam* which identifies Apostomos with the Emperor Caligula.

250 The question here is why the Seventeenth of Tammuz is not a full 24 hr. fast day like the Ninth of Av. The question in A, why was the day when the scouts were sent not made a fast day (since they caused the people to stay in the wilderness for 40 years and fixed the day for the double destruction of the Temple) is incompatible with the statement of R. Joshua ben Levi and has to be classified as gloss.

251 And a rabbinic institution which is not accepted by a majority of the people is invalid.

252 The happenings on Tammuz 17 do not have the severity of those on Av 9.

253 *Lev.* 18:5. The verse shows that danger to life or limb supersedes religious obligations.

254 Therefore full 24 hr. fast-days must be spaced at least 40 days apart. This forbids making Tammuz 17 a full fast-day.

(68d line 7) הָדָא הִיא דִכְתִיב וַיְהִי בַּשָּׁנָה הַשֵּׁינִית בַּחוֹדֶשׁ הַשֵּׁינִי בְּעֶשְׂרִים בַּחוֹדֶשׁ וגו'. וְכָתוּב וַיִּסְעוּ מֵהַר יי דֶּרֶךְ שְׁלֹשֶׁת יָמִים. רבִּי זְכַרְיָה חַתְנֵיהּ דְּרבִּי לֵוִי. לְאִילֵּין טַלְיָיא דְמִתְפַּנֵּי מִן סִיפְרָא וְנַפְקִין לוֹן [בכ]פָרֵיי. בּוֹ בַיּוֹם נִתְאַוּוּ תַאֲוָה. עַד חוֹדֶשׁ יָמִים עַד אֲשֶׁר־יֵצֵא מֵאַפְּכֶם. וּבְשִׁבְעַת יְמֵי מִרְיָם. וַתִּסָּגֵר מִרְיָם מִחוּץ לַמַּחֲנֶה. וּבְאַרְבָּעִים יוֹם שֶׁל מְרַגְּלִים. וַיָּשׁוּבוּ מִתּוּר הָאָרֶץ מִקֵּץ אַרְבָּעִים יוֹם: וַיֵּלְכוּ וַיָּבֹאוּ אֶל־מֹשֶׁה וְאֶל־אַהֲרֹן וגו'. אֲתוֹן אַשְׁכְּחִינוֹן עֲסִיקִין בְּהִילְכוֹת חַלָּה וְעָרְלָה. אָמְרוּ לָהֶן. לָאָרֶץ אֵין אַתֶּם נִכְנָסִין וְאַתֶּם עֲסוּקִין בְּהִילְכוֹת חַלָּה וְעָרְלָה. מִיָּד וַתִּשָּׂא כָּל־הָעֵדָה וַיִּתְּנוּ אֶת־קוֹלָם וַיִּבְכּוּ הָעָם בַּלַּיְלָה הוּא. אָמַר לָהֶן. אַתֶּם בְּכִיתֶם לְפָנַי

בְּכִיָּה שֶׁלְּתִפְלוּת. חַיַּי. עֲתִידִין אַתֶּם לִבְכּוֹת בִּכְיָיה שֶׁלְמַמָּשׁ. בָּכֹה תִבְכֶּה בַּלָּיְלָה. תָּנֵי רִבִּי שִׁמְעוֹן בֶּן יוֹחַי. כָּתוּב וַיִּשְׁמַע מֹשֶׁה אֶת־הָעָם בּוֹכֶה לְמִשְׁפְּחוֹתָיו וגו'. עַל שֵׁשׁ עֲרָיוֹת שֶׁאָסַר לָהֶן מֹשֶׁה.

[255]That is what is written[256], *it was in the second year in the second month on the twentieth of the month*, etc. And it is written[257], *they travelled from the Eternal's mountain a distance of three days*. Rebbi Zacharia, the son-in-law of Rebbi Levi: {a parable} like children who are freed from <school> (books)[258] and leave to run[259]. On that very day they desired a desire[260]; *up to a month, until it will come out of your noses*. And the seven days of Miriam; *Miriam was secluded outside the camp*[261]. And the 40 days of the scouts, *they returned from scouting the Land at the end of 40 days. They walked and came to Moses and Aaron*[262] etc. They came and found them occupied with the rules for *hallah*[263] and *orlah*[264]. They said to them, you are not going to enter the Land and you are studying the rules for *hallah* and *orlah*? Immediately, *the entire congregation raised their voices; the people cried in that night*[265]. He said to them, you cried before Me a pointless crying. By My life, in the future you shall cry a substantial crying. *Crying she will cry in the night*[266]. Rebbi Simeon ben Yoḥai stated: It is written[267], *Moses heard the people crying for its families*, etc. About the six incest prohibitions which Moses forbade them[268].

255 Here the heading is missing: "On the Ninth of Av was decided that our forefathers would not enter the Land." The date of the return of the scouts is not directly spelled out in *Num*.

256 *Num*. 10:11.

257 *Num*. 10:33.

258 The text in < > is from A (and also in a clearly wrong text in a Genizah excerpt, *Yerushalmi Fragments*, p. 184.)

259 The letters [בכ] added by the corrector indicate a text like A: "leave to villages." The word is missing in the Genizah excerpt. These changes misunderstand the text. R. Zacharia notes that they did not travel for three days, but the distance of three days, implying that the actual travel time was one day.

260 *Num*. 11:20. No new date is indicated; an unqualified added month is 30 days.

261 *Num*. 12:15.

262 *Num*. 13:25.

263 The heave to be taken from bread dough "when you come into the Land" (*Num*. 15:18).

264 The fruits to be stripped from a tree during its first three years "when you come to the Land" (*Lev*. 19:23).

265 *Num*. 14:1.

266 *Thr*. 1:2, referring to the Ninth of Av.

The computation goes as follows. Starting from the 20th of the second month one counts this day for travel, 7 days for Miryam's seclusion, 30 days for the quail, and 40 days for the scouts, for a total of 97 days after the first of the 2nd month. The year is supposed to start with a full 30 day first month. Therefore the 2nd and 4th months have 29 days, the 3rd month 30 days, for a total of 88 days. The count ends on the 9th of the 5th month, Q. E. D. Differently in the Babli 29a.

267 *Num.* 11:10. This is the second unnecessary crying mentioned in the verse.

268 They cried about the paternal and maternal half-sisters, the maternal and paternal aunts, the sister-in-law, and the menstruating woman, which are permitted to Gentiles but forbidden to Israelites. Babli *Yoma* 75a.

(68d line 18) אָמַר לוֹן. אֲפִילוּ כֵן מַה חֲמִיתוֹן. אֲמָרוּן לֵיהּ. אֶרֶץ אוֹכֶלֶת יוֹשְׁבֶיהָ הִיא. כָּל־קֵירְוָא דַהֲוֵינָן עָלִין תַּמָּן הֲוֵינָן מַשְׁכְּחִין מֵתִין. אָמַר לָהֶן הַקָּדוֹשׁ בָּרוּךְ הוּא. בְּטוֹבָה שֶׁעָשִׂיתִי לָכֶם אֲמַרְתֶּם אֶרֶץ אוֹכֶלֶת יוֹשְׁבֶיהָ הִיא. כָּל־קִרְיָה דַהֲווֹן עָלִין בָּהּ הֲוָה טַב קַרְתָּא מָיֵית. עַד דַּהֲווֹן מִיטַפְּלִין בֵּיהּ הֲווֹן מְיַילְלִין קַרְתָּא וְנָפְקִין לוֹן וּבַר נַשׁ לָא יָדַע בְּהוֹן. וְלֹא עוֹד אֶלָּא דְאָמַרְתּוֹן וַנְּהִי בְעֵינֵינוּ כַּחֲגָבִים וְכֵן הָיִינוּ בְּעֵינֵיהֶם: יָדְעִין הֲוִיתוֹן מַה דַּהֲוֵינָא עֲבַד לְכוֹן בְּאַפֵּיהוֹן. אָמַר רִבִּי שִׁמְעוֹן בֶּן לָקִישׁ. דִּיבְּרוּ [דְבָרִים] כְּלַפֵּי לְמַעֲלָן. כִּי־חָזָק הוּא מִמֶּנּוּ: אֲמָרוּ. כִּבְיָכוֹל אֲפִילוּ לָא יָכִיל לְחוֹן. רִבִּי לֵוִי בְּשֵׁם רִבִּי חָמָא בַר חֲנִינָה. לְקוֹל | הֲמוּלָה גְדוֹלָה. לְקוֹל (הַתְמִילָה) [הֲמוּלָה] הַגְּדוֹלָה שֶׁאֲמַרְתֶּם. הִצִּית אֵשׁ עָלֶיהָ וְרָעוּ דָּלִיּוֹתָיו:

He said to them[269], even so, what did you see? They told him, *it is a Land devouring its inhabitants*[270]; in any town we entered there people had died. The Holy One, praise to Him, said to them: Because of the benefit which I gave you, you are saying *it is a Land devouring its inhabitants*? In any town which they entered, a head of the town died. While they were occupied with him, they passed through the town and left before anybody noticed them. Not only this, but you said, *we were in our eyes like locusts, and so we were in their eyes*[271]. You knew what I made you in their eyes. Rebbi Simeon ben Laqish said, they said things against Heaven: *for he is stronger than Him*[272]; even He can do nothing against them. Rebbi Levi in the name of Rebbi Hama bar Hanina: *with a big uproar*[273], by the noise of the big (word) [uproar][274] which you pronounced, *He started a fire which broke its branches*.

269 Moses to the scouts. One explains why the sin of the scouts, which kept the people 38 years in the desert, is the equivalent of the destruction of the Temple and merits inclusion in the fast of the Ninth of Av. Babli *Sotah* 35a.

270 *Num.* 13:32.

271 *Num.* 13:33.

272 *Num.* 13:31.
273 *Jer.* 11:16.
274 The text of the scribe (in parentheses) is preferable to that of the [corrector] since it refers to the blasphemous character of the statement in *Num.* 13:31. The public blasphemy started the fire.

(68d line 28) תַּנֵּי. רִבִּי יוֹסֵי אוֹמֵר. יוֹם שֶׁחָרַב הַבַּיִת הָיָה מוֹצָאֵי שַׁבָּת וּמוֹצָאֵי שְׁמִיטָה וּמִשְׁמַרְתּוֹ שֶׁלִּיהוֹיָרִיב בְּתִשְׁעָה בְּאָב. וְכֵן בַּשֵּׁנִי. בָּזֶה וּבָזֶה הָיוּ הַלְוִים עוֹמְדִין עַל הַדּוּכָן וְאוֹמְרִין וַיָּשֶׁב עֲלֵיהֶם | אֶת־אוֹנָם וּבְרָעָתָם יַצְמִיתֵם יַצְמִיתֵם יי אֱלֹהֵינוּ׃ רִבִּי שִׁמְעוֹן בֶּן לָקִישׁ בְּעָא קוֹמֵי רִבִּי יוֹחָנָן. מָהוּ לוֹמַר שִׁיר בְּלָא נְסָכִים. אָמַר לֵיהּ. נִשְׁמְעִינַהּ מִן הָדָא דְתַנֵּי. בָּזֶה וּבָזֶה הָיוּ הַלְוִים עוֹמְדִין עַל הַדּוּכָן וְאוֹמְרִין וַיָּשֶׁב עֲלֵיהֶם | אֶת־אוֹנָם וגו'. רִבִּי אַבָּהוּ אָמַר. אִיתְפַּלְגוֹן רִבִּי יוֹחָנָן וְרִבִּי שִׁמְעוֹן בֶּן לָקִישׁ. רִבִּי יוֹחָנָן אָמַר. אוֹמְרִין שִׁיר בְּלָא נְסָכִים. רִבִּי שִׁמְעוֹן בֶּן לָקִישׁ אָמַר. אֵין אוֹמְרִין שִׁיר בְּלָא נְסָכִים. הָתִיב רִבִּי יוֹחָנָן לְרִבִּי שִׁמְעוֹן בֶּן לָקִישׁ. וְהָתַנֵּי. בָּזֶה וּבָזֶה הָיוּ הַלְוִים עוֹמְדִים עַל הַדּוּכָן וְאוֹמְרִין וַיָּשֶׁב עֲלֵיהֶם | אֶת־אוֹנָם. אָמַר לֵיהּ רִבִּי שִׁמְעוֹן בֶּן לָקִישׁ. מָה אַתְּ שְׁמַע מִינָהּ. אָמַר לֵיהּ. מֵאַחַר שֶׁאִילּוּ נְסָכִים הָיוּ זְמַנּוֹ שֶׁלְשִׁיר הָיָה. רִבִּי יוֹחָנָן אָמַר. שִׁירוֹ שֶׁל יוֹם. רִבִּי שִׁמְעוֹן בֶּן לָקִישׁ אָמַר. שִׁירוֹ שֶׁל אֶתְמוֹל.

אָמַר רִבִּי לֵוִי. יְהוֹיָרִיב גַּבְרָה. מֵירוֹן קַרְתָּה. מְסַרְבֵּיי. מָסַר בֵּייתָהּ לִשְׂנָאַיָא. אָמַר רִבִּי בֶּרֶכְיָה. [וִיהוֹיָרִיב] י"ה הֵרִיב עִם בָּנָיו עַל שֶׁמָּרוּ וְסָרְבוּ בוֹ. יְדַעְיָה עָמוֹק צִיפּוֹרִים. יָדַע יָ"הּ עֵיצָה עֲמוּקָה שֶׁבְּלִיבָּם וְהִגְלָם לְצִיפּוֹרִין.

It was stated[275]: Rebbi Yose says, the day of the destruction of the Temple was after the end of the Sabbath, at the end of a Sabbatical year[276], during the watch of Yehoyariv, on the Ninth of Av. And so it happened the second time. Both times the Levites were standing on the platform and singing, *He turned on them their wrongs, in their malice he eradicates them, eradicates them the Eternal, our God*[277]. Rebbi Simeon ben Laqish asked before Rebbi Johanan; may one sing without libations[278]? He said to him, let us hear from what was stated: "both times the Levites were standing on the platform and singing, *He turned on them their wrongs,* etc." Rebbi Abbahu said, Rebbi Johanan and Rebbi Simeon ben Laqish disagreed. Rebbi Johanan said, one may sing without libations. Rebbi Simeon ben Laqish said, one may not sing without libations. Rebbi Johanan objected to Rebbi Simeon ben Laqish: Was it not stated, "both times the Levites were standing on the platform and singing, *He turned on them their wrongs*"? Rebbi Simeon ben Laqish said to him, what do you conclude from this? He said to him, since if there were libations it would have been time for the song. Rebbi Johanan said, the daily song. Rebbi Simeon ben Laqish said, yesterday's song[279].

Rebbi Levi said, Yehoyariv, a person. Meron, a town. Mesarbei. He delivered His House to the enemies[280]. Rebbi Berekhia said, [Yehoyariv], Yah quarrelled with His children since they rebelled and rejected Him. Yeda`ya Amoq Sipporim[281]. Yah knew the deep counsel in their hearts and exiled them to Sepphoris[283].

275 Babli 29a, *Arakhin* 11b.//
276 69 C.E.//
277 *Ps*. 94:23.//
278 If there are sacrifices, the Levites have to sing the daily song at the time the libations accompanying the daily sacrifice are poured. Since daily (and all other animal) sacrifices stopped on Tammuz 17, the question is whether the Levites may sing at all.//
279 In this version, R. Johanan disputes either whether the song was *Ps*. 94 or that the destruction was on a Sunday, since the song is the one for Wednesday. He holds that if there are no sacrifices, one performs the services which are possible under the circumstances. R. Simeon ben Laqish holds that no service can be performed if not all rules can be observed; for him the song here was not a service but a dirge.//
280 It seems that the clans of Yehoyariv serving on that day were Meron and Mesarbei.//
281 Also name of a watch and two of its clans.//
282 While we know from the poems of Yannai and Kalir that most priestly watches in their times were settled in Galilee, this may be a post-Bar Kokhba development except for Yedaya who dwelt in Sepphoris. This is called an exile since the road to Jerusalem crossed Samaritan territory (*Hagiga* 3:4). To serve in the Temple they had to come early to be purified.

(68d line 43) וְנִלְכְּדָה בֵּיתָתַר. רִבִּי הֲוָה דָרֵשׁ עֶשְׂרִין וְאַרְבָּעָה עוֹבְדִין בְּבִלַּע יי וְלֹא חָמַל. וְרִבִּי יוֹחָנָן דָּרַשׁ אֲשִׁיתִין. וְרִבִּי יוֹחָנָן יַתִּיר עַל רִבִּי. אֶלָּא עַל יְדֵי דְּרִבִּי הֲוָה סָמִיךְ לַחֻרְבַּן בֵּית מוּקְדְּשָׁא הֲוָה תַמָּן סַבִּין נְהִירִין וַהֲוָה דָרֵשׁ וְאִינּוּן בָּכֵי וּמִשְׁתַּתְּקִין וְקַיְימִין לוֹן. תַּנֵּי. אָמַר רִבִּי יְהוּדָה בֵּירִבִּי אִלְעָאִי. בָּרוּךְ רִבִּי הָיָה דּוֹרֵשׁ הַקּוֹל קוֹל יַעֲקֹב וְהַיָּדַיִם יְדֵי עֵשָׂו: קוֹלוֹ שֶׁלְיַעֲקֹב צָוַוח מִמָּה שֶׁעָשׂוּ לוֹ יָדָיו שֶׁלְעֵשָׂו בְּבֵיתָתַר.

תַּנֵּי רִבִּי שִׁמְעוֹן בֶּן יוֹחַי. עֲקִיבָה רִבִּי הָיָה דוֹרֵשׁ דָּרַךְ כּוֹכָב מִיַּעֲקֹב. דָּרַךְ כּוֹזְבָּא מִיַּעֲקֹב. רִבִּי עֲקִיבָה כַּד הֲוָה חֲמֵי בַר כּוֹזְבָה הֲוָה אָמַר. דֵּין הוּא מַלְכָּא מְשִׁיחָא. אָמַר לֵיהּ רִבִּי יוֹחָנָן בַּר תּוֹרְתָא. עֲקִיבָה. יַעֲלוּ עֲשָׂבִים בִּלְחָיֶיךָ (וְאַדַּיִין) [וַאֲדַיִין] בֶּן דָּוִד [לֹא] יָבֹא. אָמַר רִבִּי יוֹחָנָן. קוֹל אַדְרִיָּינוּס קֵיסָר הוֹרֵג בְּבֵיתָתָר שְׁמוֹנִים אֶלֶף רִיבּוֹא. אָמַר רִבִּי יוֹחָנָן. שְׁמוֹנִים [אֶלֶף] זוּג שֶׁלְתוֹקְעֵי קְרָנוֹת הָיוּ מַקִּיפִין אֶת בֵּיתָתָר. וְכָל־אֶחָד וְאֶחָד הָיָה מְמוּנֶּה עַל כַּמָּה חַיָילוֹת. וְהָיָה שָׁם בֶּן כּוֹזְבָה וְהָיָה לוֹ מָאתַיִם אֶלֶף מְטִיפֵי אֶצְבַּע. שָׁלְחוּ חֲכָמִים וְאָמְרוּ לוֹ. עַד אֵימָתַי אַתָּה

עושה את ישראל בעלי מומין. אמר להן. וכי היאך איפשר לבודקן. אמרו לו. כל־מי שאינו רוכב על סוסו ועוקר ארז מן לבנון לא יהיה נכתב באיסרטיא שלך. והיו לו מאתים אלף כך ומאתים אלף כך. וכד דהוה נפק לקרבא הוה אמר. ריבוניה דעלמא. לא תסעוד ולא תכסוף]. הלא־אתה אלהים זנחתנו ולא־תצא אלהים בצבאותינו. שלש שנים ומחצה עשה אדריינוס מקיף על ביתתר. והוה רבי אלעזר המודעי יושב על השק ועל האפר ומתפלל בכל־יום ואומר. רבון העולמים. אל תשב בדין היום. אל תשב בדין היום. בעא אדריינוס מיזל ליה. אמר ליה חד כותיי. לא תיזיל לך. דאנא חמי מה מיעבד ומשלים לך מדינתא. עאל ליה מן ביבא דמדינתא. עאל ואשכח רבי אלעזר המודעי קאים מצלי. עבד נפשיה לחיש ליה בגו אודניה. חמוניה בני מדינתא ואייתוניה גבי בן כוזבא. אמרון ליה. חמינן הדין סבא משתעי לחביבך. אמר ליה. מה אמרת ליה ומה אמר לך. אמר ליה. <אין> אנא אמר לך מלכא קטל לי. ואי לא אנא אמר לך את קטיל לי. טב לי מלכא קטל יתי ולא את. אמר ליה. אמר לי דאנא משלים מדינתא. אתא גבי רבי אלעזר המודעי. אמר ליה. מה אמר לך הדין כותייא. אמר ליה. לא כלום. מה אמרת ליה. אמר ליה. לא כלום. יהב ליה חד בעוט וקטליה. מיד יצאת בת קול ואמרה. הוי רועי האליל עזבי הצאן חרב על־זרועו ועל־עין ימינו זרועו יבש תיבש ועין ימינו כהה תכהה: הרגת את רבי אלעזר המודעי זרוען שלכל־ישראל ואין ימינם. לפיכך זרועו שלאותו האיש יבוש תיבש ועין ימינו כהה תכהה. מיד נלכדה ביתתר ונהרג בן כוזבה. אתון טעיניו רישיה גבי אדריינוס. אמר לון. מאן קטל הדין. אמר ליה חד כותייא. אנא קטלתיה. אמר ליה. חמי לי פטומיה. חמי ליה פטומיה. אשכח חכינה כריכה עלוי. אמר. אלולי אלהא דקטליה מאן הוה יכיל קטליה. וקרא עלוי. אם־לא כי־צורם מכרם וי'י הסגירם: והיו חורגין בהם והולכין עד ששקע הסוס בדם עד חוטמו. והיה הדם מגלגל סלעים משאוי ארבעים סאה עד שהלך הדם בים ארבעת מיל. אם תאמר שהיא קרובה לים. והלא רחוקה מן הים ארבעים מיל. אמרו. שלש מאות מוחי תינוקות מצאו על אבן אחת. ומצאו שלש קופות שלקצוצי תפילין שלתשע תשע סאין. ויש אומרים. תשע של שלש שלש סאין. תני רבן שמעון בן גמליאל אומר. חמש מאות בתי סופרים היו בביתתר. והקטן שבהן אין פחות מחמש מאות תינוקות. והיו אומרים. אם באו השונאים עלינו במכתובים הללו אנו יוצאין עליהן ומנקרין את עיניהם. וכיון שגרמו עונות היו כורכים כל־אחד ואחד בספרו ושורפין אותו. ומכולם לא נשתייר אלא אני. וקרא על גרמיה. עיני עוללה לנפשי מכל בנות עירי: כרם גדול היה לאדריינוס הרשע. שמונה עשר מיל על שמונה עשר מיל כמין טיברייא לציפורי. והקיפו גדר מהרוגי ביתתר מלא קומה ופישוט ידיים. ולא נזר עליהם שייקברו. עד שעמד מלך אחר וגזר עליהם שייקברו.

"Bettar was taken." [283]Rebbi used to preach 24 facts about *the Eternal swallowed and showed no mercy*[284], but Rebbi Johanan 60. So Rebbi Johanan more than Rebbi? Only since Rebbi was closer to the destruction of the Temple, there were there old men remembering, and those would cry and continuously silence him. It was stated: Rebbi Jehudah ben Rebbi Illai said, Baruch my teacher used to preach, *the voice is Jacob's voice but the hands are Esau's hands*[285]. Jacob's voice cries about what Esau's hands did at Bettar.

Rebbi Simeon ben Yohai stated: Aqiba my teacher used to preach, *there appeared a star out of Jacob*[286] there appeared Koziba out of Jacob. When Rebbi Aqiba saw Bar Koziba he said, this is King Messias. Rebbi Johanan ben Torta said to him, Aqiba! Grass will grow from your jaws and still David's son (still has to) [will not have][287] come. Rebbi Johanan said, the voice of Emperor Hadrian killing eighty thousand myriads at Bettar[288]. Rebbi Johanan said, eighty [thousand] couples of horn-blowers[289] were encircling Bettar, each of which was commanding several army units. There was Ben Koziba who had 200'000 with him missing a finger. The Sages sent, how long will you turn Israel into defective persons? He told them, how would it be possible to test them? They said to him, anyone who riding on his horse cannot uproot a cedar of Lebanon should not be enrolled in your army[290]. He had 200'000 of either kind. When he went into battle he said, Master of the World: Do not support and do not hinder, *did not you, God, neglect us, and do not go out with our armies*[291]. Three and a half years did Hadrian encircle Bettar. Rebbi Eleazar from Modiin was sitting in sackcloth and ashes, praying every day and saying, Master of the World, do not sit in judgment today, do not sit in judgment today. Hadrian wanted to go away. A Samaritan said to him, do not go away, for I am seeing what to do that the city will submit to you. He went to the city gate, entered, and found Rebbi Eleazar from Modiin standing in prayer. He showed himself as if he would whisper into his ear. The people of the city saw him and brought him to Ben Koziba. They said to him, we saw this old man turning to your uncle. He asked him, what did you say to him and what did he say to you? He answered, if I shall tell you, the king will kill me; but if I do not tell you, you will kill me. It is better that the king should kill me but not you. He told him, he said to me, I will make the town submit to the king. He came to Rebbi Eleazar from Modiin. He asked him, what did this Samaritan say to you. He answered, nothing. What did you say to him? He answered, nothing. He kicked him and killed him. Immediately there came an unembodied voice and said, *woe, criminal shepherds, who abandon the flock, a sword on his arm and on his right eye. His arm shall dry up and his right eye darken*[292]. You killed Rebbi Eleazar from Modiin, the arm of Israel, and their right eye. Therefore this man's arm shall dry up and his right eye darken. Immediately Bettar was taken and Ben Koziba killed. They came carrying his head to Hadrain. He asked them, who killed him? A Samaritan said to him, I killed him. He said to him, show me his body. He showed him his body; he found a poisonous snake wrapped around him. He said, if God had not killed him, who could kill him? He recited over him, *if not that their Rock had sold them, and the Eternal handed them over*[293]. They killed them continuously until the horse was immersed in blood up to his nose. The blood was moving rocks of 40 seah loads, until the blood colored the sea for four *mil*. If you would say that it was close to the sea, in fact it is 40 *mil* distant from the sea. They said, 300 children's brains were found on one stone, and they found three boxes of *tefillin* capsules of nine *seah* each, but some say nine of three each. It was stated, Rabban Simeon ben Gamliel says, 500 schools were in Bettar, the smallest one for not less than 500 children. They were saying, if the haters come against us we shall go out against them with these stylos and blind them. When the sins caused, they were binding each single one into his book and burning him; and of them only I remained. He recited referring to himself, *my eye hurts my soul more than all daughters of my city*[294]. The evil Hadrian had a large vineyard, eighteen *mil* by eighteen *mil*, as from Tiberias to Sepphoris. He fenced it in with the slain of Bettar standing up with outstretched arms, and did not decide that they should be buried, until another king arose[295] who decided that they should be buried.

283 A parallel text is *Thr. rabba* 3(38); cf. also Babli *Gittin* 57a-58a, *Sanhedrin* 93b.
284 *Thr.* 2:2.
285 *Gen.* 27:22.
286 *Num.* 24:17.
287 The corrector's [text] is from the Midrash. The scribe's text asserts that the Messiah always will be coming.

288 In *Cant. rabba* 2(36) the number is 90'000'000. *Thr. rabba* shows that the statement here is copied in the wrong place; it belongs to the previous paragraph, explaining the sound of Esau.
289 Roman army commanders.
290 Greek στρατιά.
291 *Ps.* 60:12.

292 *Zach.* 11:17.
293 *Deut.* 32:30.
294 *Thr.* 3:51.

295 An expression used for a new dynasty, in this case Septimius Severus.

(69a line 22) אָמַר רַב חוּנָה. מִשֶּׁנִּיתְנוּ הֲרוּגֵי בֵיתָּר לִקְבוּרָה נִקְבְּעָה הַטוֹב וְהַמֵּטִיב. הַטוֹב שֶׁלֹא נִסְרְחוּ. וְהַמֵּטִיב שֶׁנִּיתְנוּ לִקְבוּרָה. תַּנֵּי. רִבִּי יוֹסֵי אוֹמֵר. חֲמִשִּׁים וּשְׁתַּיִם שָׁנָה עָשְׂתָה בֵיתָּר לְאַחַר חֻרְבַּן בֵּית הַמִּקְדָּשׁ. וְלָמָה חָרְבָה. עַל שֶׁהִדְלִיקָה נֵירוֹת לְאַחַר חֻרְבַּן בֵּית הַמִּקְדָּשׁ. וְלָמָה הִדְלִיקָה נֵירוֹת. שֶׁהָיוּ בּוּלְוֹטֵי יְרוּשָׁלֵם יוֹשְׁבִים בְּאַמְצַע הַמְּדִינָה. וּכְדוֹ דַהֲוָון חָמֵיי בַּר נָשׁ סָלִיק לִירוּשָׁלֵם הָווֹן אָמְרִין לֵיהּ. בְּגִין דִּשְׁמָעִינָן עֲלָךְ דְּאַתְּ בָּעֵי מִתְעַבְדָה אַרְכוֹנְטָס וּבוּלְבִּיטָס. וְהוּא אֲמַר לוֹן. לֵית בְּדַעְתִּי. בְּדִיל דִּשְׁמָעִינָן עֲלָךְ דְּאַתְּ בָּעֵי מַזְבָּנָה אוֹסִיָּא דִילָךְ. וְהוּא אֲמַר לוֹן. לֵית בְּדַעְתִּי. וַהֲוָה חַבְרֵיהּ אֲמַר לֵיהּ. מַה אַתְּ בָּעֵי מִן דֵּין. כְּתוֹב וַאֲנָא חֲתַם. וַהֲוָה כָתִיב וְחַבְרֵיהּ חֲתַם. וַהֲווֹן מְשַׁלְחִין אוּנְיָיתָא לְבַר בֵּיתָהּ וְאָמְרִין לֵיהּ. אִין אֲתָא פְלָנָיָא מֵיעוֹל לְאוֹסִיָּא דִידֵיהּ לָא תִשְׁבְּקוּנֵיהּ דְּהִיא זְבִינָא גְּבוֹן. וְכֵיוָן דַּהֲוָה שָׁמַע מִינְהוֹן כָּךְ הֲוָה אֲמַר. הָלְוַוי אִיתְבַּר רִיגְלֵיהּ דַּהֲהוּא גַּבְרָא. וְלָא סְלֵיק לִירוּשָׁלֵם. הָדָא הוּא דִכְתִיב צָדוּ צְעָדֵינוּ מִלֶּכֶת בִּרְחוֹבוֹתֵינוּ. צָדוּ צְעָדֵינוּ. אַצְדֵי אוֹרְחָתַהּ דְּהַהוּא בֵּייתָא. קָרַב קֵיצֵינוּ. קָרַב קִיצֵּהּ דַּהֲהוּא בֵּיתָא. מָלְאוּ יָמֵינוּ. מָלְאוּ יוֹמוֹי דְּהַהוּא בֵּיתָא. אוֹף אִינוּן לָא נַפְקוּן טַבָאוּת. שָׂמֵחַ לְאֵיד לֹא יִנָּקֶה.

[שְׁנֵי אַחִים הָווֹן בִּכְפַר חֲרִיבָה. וַהֲוָון רוֹמִים אַזְלִין עֲלֵיהוֹן וּמְקַטְלִין לוֹן. וְאָמְרִין. כָּל סַמָּא דְּמִילְתָא נֵיתֵי כְלִילָא עַל רֵישֵׁיהוֹן. אָמְרִין. מַבְדִּיקָן אוּף חַד זְמָן. מְנַפְּקִין פְּגַע בֵּיהּ חַד סַב. אָמַר לוֹן. בָּרַיְיכוֹן סְעוֹדִינְכוֹן. אֲמַר. לָא יִסְעוֹד וְלֹא [יִסְמוֹךְ] ‹יִכְסוֹף› הֲלֹא־אַתָּה אֱלֹהִים זְנַחְתָּנוּ.]

שְׁנֵי אֲרָזִים הָיוּ סְדַר הַמִּשְׁחָה. בְּתַחַת אֶחָד מֵהֶן הָיוּ מוֹכְרִין אַרְבַּע חֲנוּיוֹת טַהֲרוֹת. וְהָאֶחָד הָיוּ מוֹצִיאִין מִמֶּנּוּ אַרְבָּעִים סְאָה גוֹזָלוֹת בְּכָל־חוֹדֶשׁ וָחוֹדֶשׁ. וּמֵהֶן הָיוּ מְסַפְּקִין קִינִּים לְכָל־יִשְׂרָאֵל. טוּר שִׁמְעוֹן הֲוָה מַפִּיק תְּלַת מְאוּן דְּגַרְבִּין דְּמַרְקוֹעַ לִקְיָיטָא כָּל־עֲרוּבַת שׁוּבָּא. וְלָמָה חָרַב. יֵשׁ אוֹמְרִים. מִפְּנֵי הַזְּנוּת. וְיֵשׁ אוֹמְרִין. שֶׁהָיוּ מְשַׂחֲקִין בַּכַּדּוּר. עֲשֶׂרֶת אֲלָפִים עֲיָירוֹת הָיוּ בְּהַר הַמֶּלֶךְ. וּלְרִבִּי אֶלְעָזָר בֶּן חַרְסוֹם אֶלֶף מְכּוּפָל. וּכְנֶגְדָּן אֶלֶף סְפִינוֹת בַּיָּם. וְכוּלְּהֶם חָרָבוּ. שָׁלֹשׁ עֲיָירוֹת הָיָה קַטְמוֹס שֶׁלָּהֶן עוֹלֶה לִירוּשָׁלֵם בַּעֲגָלָה. כָּבוּל וְשִׁיחִין וּמִגְדַּל צְבָעַיָּיא. וּשְׁלָשְׁתָּן חָרְבוּ. כָּבוּל מִפְּנֵי הַמַּחֲלוֹקֶת. שִׁיחִין מִפְּנֵי כְּשָׁפִים. וּמִגְדַּל צְבָעַיָּיא מִפְּנֵי הַזְּנוּת. שְׁלֹשָׁה כְּפָרִים כָּל־אֶחָד וְאֶחָד הָיָה מוֹצִיא כְּפָלַיִם כְּיוֹצְאֵי מִצְרַיִם. כְּפָר בִּישׁ וּכְפָר שִׁיחֲלַיָּיא וּכְפָר דִּיכְרַיָּיא. וְלָמָה הוּא קְרֵי לוֹן כְּפָר בִּישׁ. דְּלָא הֲווֹן מְקַבְּלִין לַעֲבוֹרָא. וְלָמָה הוּא קְרֵי לוֹן כְּפָר שִׁיחֲלַיָּיא. דַּהֲווֹן מְרַבְּיָין בְּנֵיהוֹן כְּאִילֵּין תַּחְלוֹסַיָּא. וְלָמָה הוּא קְרֵי לוֹן כְּפָר דִּיכְרַיָּיא. דַּהֲווֹן כָּל־נְשֵׁיהוֹן יַלְדָן דִּיכְרִין. אִי לָא הֲוַות חָדָא מִינְהוֹן נַפְקָא מִן תַּמָּן לָא הֲוַות יַלְדָא נוּקְבָה. אָמַר רִבִּי יוֹחָנָן. שְׁמוֹנִים זוּגִים אַחִים כֹּהֲנִים נִישְּׂאוּ לִשְׁמוֹנִים זוּגוֹת אֲחָיוֹת כֹּהֲנוֹת בְּלַיְלָה אֶחָד בְּהָדָא גוּפְנָא. חוּץ מֵאַחִים בְּלֹא אֲחָיוֹת. חוּץ מֵאֲחָיוֹת בְּלֹא אַחִים. חוּץ מַלְקִיִּים. חוּץ מִיִּשְׂרָאֵל. אָמַר רִבִּי יוֹחָנָן. שְׁמוֹנִים חֲנוּיוֹת שֶׁלְּאוֹרְגֵי פְלָגָס הָיוּ בְּמִגְדַּל צְבָעַיָּא. אָמַר רִבִּי חִיָּיא בַּר בָּא.

שְׁמוֹנִים חֲנוּיוֹת שֶׁלְּמוֹכְרֵי טַהֲרוֹת הָיוּ בִּכְפַר אִימְרָא. רִבִּי יִרְמְיָה בְשֵׁם רִבִּי חִייָה בַּר בָּא. שְׁמוֹנִים שִׁידוֹת שֶׁלְּמַתֶּכֶת הָיוּ בְשִׁיחִין. אָמַר רִבִּי יַנַּאי. שִׁידָה לֹא הָיְתָה בְיָמֵינוּ. רִבִּי זְעוּרָה בְשֵׁם רַב חוּנָא. אִימֵּר הִיא הָיְתָה קְטַנָּה שֶׁבַּמִּשְׁמָרוֹת. וְהִיא הָיְתָה מוֹצִיאָה שְׁמוֹנִים וַחֲמִשָּׁה אֶלֶף פִּרְחֵי כְהוּנָּה.

[296]Rav Huna said, when the slain of Bettar were permitted to be buried, "the good and the benefactor" was fixed. "The good" that they did not decompose, "the benefactor" that they were permitted for burial[297]. It was stated, Rebbi Yose said, 52 years Bettar existed after the destruction of the Temple. And why was it destroyed? For they lit lights after the destruction of the Temple. Why did they light lights? Because the council members[298] of Jerusalem were dominating the center of the city. When they were seeing a person moving to Jerusalem they said to him, since we heard about you that you are aspiring to be made judge[299] or councillor; he would say to them, that is not my intention[300]. Because we heard about you that you intend to sell your property[301]; he would say to them, that is not my intention. His colleague would say to him, what are you arguing with this one, write and I shall sign[302]. He would write and his colleague would sign. They would send the sale document[303] to his house companion and told him, if X comes to enter his property, do not let him, because it is sold to us. When he heard this from them he said, if only this man's leg had been broken before he came to Jerusalem. That is what is written[304], *they caught our steps, not to walk in our streets. They caught our steps*, destroy the way to that House, *our end is near*, the end of this House is near, *our days are fulfilled*, the days of this House are fulfilled. They also did not come out well, *he who enjoys disaster will not be acquitted*[305].

[306][Two brothers were in Kefar Ḥariba; the Romans went out against them and they would kill them. They said, the medicine for this is for us to bring a crown to their heads. They said, let us try a last time. When they went out, an old man met them and said, your Maker may support you. They said, may He neither help nor [support] <obstruct>[307], *did not you, God, neglect us*[291].]

[308]There grew two cedars on the Mount of Olives. Under one of them there were four shops selling in purity[309]; from the other they were bringing 40 *seah* of pigeon chicks every single month and from there were providing all of Israel with nests[310]. Mount Simon[311] was producing 200 barrels of fig pieces

every Friday. Why was it destroyed? Some say, because of whoring; but some say it was because they were playing ball[312]. 10'000 towns were on King's Mountain[313]; Rebbi Eleazar ben Harsom owned 1'000 of them, and correspondingly 1'000 ships on the Sea. And all of them were destroyed[314]. Of three villages was the *qtmos*[315] brought to Jerusalem in carts, Kabul, Shihin, and Magdala of the dyers[316] All three were destroyed. Kabul because of quarrel, Shihin because of sorcery, and Magdala of the dyers because of whoring. Three villages of which each one was populated by twice the number of those leaving Egypt[317], the evil village, the cress village, and the boys' village. Why was it called evil village? Because they did not receive travellers. Why was it called cress village? Because they were growing children like cress. Why was it called boys' village? Because all their women gave birth to boys. If one of them never left from there she would not give birth to a girl. Rebbi Johanan said, 80 pairs of priestly brothers married 80 pairs of priestly sisters at Gufna[318] in one night, not counting brothers but not sisters, sisters but not brothers, not counting Levites, not counting Israel. Rebbi Johanan said, in Magdala of the dyers there were 80 establishments of fustian. Rebbi Hiyya bar Abba said, 80 stores selling in purity were in Kefar Imra. Rebbi Jeremiah in the name of Rebbi Hiyya bar Abba, 80 metal *shidda*[319] were in Shihin. Rebbi Yannai said, in our time was no *shidda*. Rebbi Ze`ira in the name of Rav Huna: Immer was the smallest of the watches, and it was producing 85'000 young priests.

296 This paragraph has no parallel in *Thr. rabba*.
297 The fourth benediction of Grace. Babli 31a; *Berakhot* 1:8 (Note 278), 7:1 (Notes 35,36), Babli 48b.
298 Greek βουλευτής.
299 Greek ἄρχων, - οντος.
300 To become elected and to pay bribes for the purpose.
301 Greek ου῎σία.
302 Since a sale document is valid if it is testified to by two witnesses; it needs no signature of any of the parties to the sale.

303 A Semitic form of Greek ὠνή.
304 *Thr.* 3:18.
305 *Prov.* 17:5.
306 This again is found in *Thr. rabba*, but the corrector's insert is copied from *Yalqut Haazinu* (§946), to which tradition also belongs the text of A (which ends here). In the traditional text of *Thr. rabba* it is very clear that the story belongs to the legend of Bar Kochba since there the crown is to be offered to Simon (bar Koziba).
307 The word <added> is from A; it might be Arabic سكف "to put a step on an entrance",

as sign of an obstacle, or כסף "affairs go badly".

308 From here to the last paragraph of the Halakhah most of the text is found in *Thr. rabba* 3(38).

309 They only sold food of guaranteed purity for pilgrims to the Temple (and Pharisees eating all food in purity).

310 A "nest" is a couple of birds required for purification by many people whose impurity was caused by their own body. Cf. Babli *Berakhot* 44a.

311 Unidentified.

312 Possibly the sin was not the ball playing but the accessory wagering.

313 The hill region N of Jerusalem and W of Antipatris.

314 Babli *Yoma* 35b.

315 A word for which no reasonable source or meaning is found in the literature.

316 All places in Galilee.

317 1'200'000.

318 N of Jerusalem.

319 A person or things transported by שִׁדָּה תֵּיבָה וּמִגְדָּל made of wood do not become impure if transported through impure territory (Mishnah *Kelim* 18:3); according to Maimonides a box containing at least 40 *seah*, about half a cubic meter. R. Yannai denies knowledge of the exact dimensions required.

(69a line 65) אָמַר רִבִּי יוֹחָנָן. שְׁמוֹנִים אֶלֶף פִּירְחֵי כְהוּנָּה נֶהֶרְגוּ עַל דָּמוֹ שֶׁלִזְכַרְיָה. רִבִּי יוּדָן שָׁאַל לְרִבִּי אֲחָא. אֵיכָן הֲרָגוּ אֶת זְכַרְיָה. בְּעֶזְרַת הַנָּשִׁים אוֹ בְעֶזְרַת יִשְׂרָאֵל. אָמַר לוֹ. לֹא בְעֶזְרַת יִשְׂרָאֵל וְלֹא בְעֶזְרַת הַנָּשִׁים אֶלָּא בְעֶזְרַת הַכֹּהֲנִים. וְלֹא נָהֲגוּ בְדָמוֹ לֹא כְדָם הָאַיִל וְלֹא כְדָם הַצְּבִי. תַּמָּן כָּתוּב וְשָׁפַךְ אֶת־דָּמוֹ וְכִסָּהוּ בֶּעָפָר. בְּרַם הָכָא כִּי דָמָהּ בְּתוֹכָהּ הָיָה עַל־צְחִיחַ סֶלַע שָׂמַתְהוּ. כָּל־כָּךְ לָמָּה. לְהַעֲלוֹת חֵימָה וְלִנְקוֹם נָקָם נָתַתִּי אֶת־דָּמָהּ עַל־צְחִיחַ סֶלַע בְּלִי הִכָּסוֹת. שֶׁבַע עֲבֵירוֹת עָבְרוּ יִשְׂרָאֵל בְּאוֹתוֹ הַיּוֹם. הָרְגוּ כֹהֵן וְנָבִיא וְדַיָּין. וְשָׁפְכוּ דָם נָקִי. וְטִימְּאוּ אֶת הָעֲזָרָה. וְשַׁבָּת וְיוֹם הַכִּיפּוּרִים הָיָה. וְכֵיוָן שֶׁעָלָה נְבוּזַרְאֲדָן לְכָאן רָאָה אֶת הַדָּם תּוֹסֵס. אָמַר לָהֶן. מַה טִּיבוֹ שֶׁלָּזֶה. אָמְרוּ לוֹ. דַּם פָּרִים וּכְבָשִׂים וְאֵילִים שֶׁהָיִינוּ מַקְרִיבִין עַל גַּבֵּי הַמִּזְבֵּחַ. מִיַּד הֵבִיא פָּרִים וְאֵילִים וּכְבָשִׂים וּשְׁחָטָן עָלָיו [וַאֲדַיִין] [וַעֲדַיִין] הַדָּם תּוֹסֵס. וְכֵיוָן שֶׁלֹּא הוֹדוּ לוֹ תְּלָיָין בְּגַרְדּוֹן. אָמְרוּ. הוֹאִיל וְהַקָּדוֹשׁ בָּרוּךְ הוּא רוֹצֶה לִתְבּוֹעַ דָּמוֹ מִיָּדֵינוּ. אָמְרוּ לוֹ. דַּם כֹּהֵן וְנָבִיא וְדַיָּין הוּא שֶׁהָיָה מִתְנַבֵּא עָלֵינוּ [כָּל־]מַה שֶׁאַתָּה עוֹשֶׂה לָנוּ]. וַעֲמַדְנוּ עָלָיו וַהֲרַגְנוּהוּ. מִיַּד הֵבִיא שְׁמוֹנִים אֶלֶף פִּירְחֵי כְהוּנָּה וּשְׁחָטָן עָלָיו. וַאֲדַיִין הַדָּם תּוֹסֵס. בְּהַהִיא שַׁעְתָא נָזַף בֵּיהּ. אָמַר לֵיהּ. מַה אַתְּ בָּעֵי נוֹבַד כָּל־אוּמָּתָךְ עֲלָךְ. מִיַּד נִתְמַלֵּא הַקָּדוֹשׁ בָּרוּךְ הוּא רַחֲמִים וְאָמַר. מָה אִם זֶה שֶׁהוּא בָשָׂר וָדָם וְאַכְזָרִי נִתְמַלֵּא רַחֲמִים עַל בָּנַיי. אֲנִי שֶׁכָּתוּב בִּי כִּי אֵל רַחוּם יְיָ אֱלֹהֶיךָ לֹא יַרְפְּךָ וְלֹא יַשְׁחִיתֶךָ וְלֹא יִשְׁכַּח אֶת־בְּרִית אֲבוֹתֶיךָ. עַל אַחַת כַּמָּה וְכַמָּה. מִיַּד רָמַז לַדָּם וְנִבְלַע בִּמְקוֹמוֹ.

[320]Rebbi Joḥanan said, 80'000 young priests were slaughtered for the blood of Zachariah[321]. Rebbi Yudan asked Rebbi Aḥa, where did they kill Zachariah? In the women's courtyard or in Israel's courtyard[322]? He said to

him, neither in Israel's courtyard nor in the women's courtyard but in the priests' courtyard. They treated his blood neither as ram's blood nor as gazelle's blood[323]. There is written, *he shall pour out its blood and cover it with dust*[324]. But here[325], *for its blood was in its midst, on a bare rock he put it*. Why all this? *To arise rage, to avenge vengeance, I put its blood on a bare rock, without being covered*[326]. Seven sins did Israel commit on that day. They killed a priest, prophet, and judge, spilled innocent blood, defiled the Temple courtyard, and it was a Sabbath and Day of Atonement. When Nebuzaraddan[327] came here and saw the blood bubbling, he asked them, what is the matter with this? They told him, it is the blood of bulls, sheep, and rams, which we were sacrificing on the altar. Immediately he brought bulls, rams, and sheep and slaughtered them on it, but the blood still was bubbling. Since they did not confess, he hung them on gallows. They said, since the Holy One, praise to Him, wants to ask for his blood from us, they told him, it is the blood of a priest, prophet, and judge who was prophesying for us [all that you are doing to us.] We conspired against him and killed him. Immediately he brought 80'000 young priests and slaughtered them on it, but the blood was still bubbling. At this moment he got angry with him[328], and said to him, do you want to destroy your entire people because of you? Immediately the Holy One, praise to Him, was filled with mercy and said, if this one who is flesh and blood, and cruel, is filled with mercy for My children, I, where it is written about Me[329], *for a compassionate power is the Eternal, your God, He will not destroy you nor forget the covenant of your forefathers*, not so much more? Immediately he indicated to the blood and it was absorbed on its place.

320 A slightly shortened version of *Thr. rabba*; cf. Babli *Gittin* 57b, *Sanhedrin* 94b.
321 *2Chr.* 24:20-22. In dying he invoked God's vengeance.
322 Herod's Temple had an outer courtyard accessible to women, a middle one accessible to Israel males, and an inner one reserved uniquely for the sacrificial service by Cohanim.

323 Ram's blood has to be poured on the base of the altar; deer's blood has to be covered as indicated in the verse.
324 *Lev.* 17:13.
325 *Ez.* 24:7.
326 *Ez.* 24:8. In the verse: "impossible to cover."
327 Sent to burn down Jerusalem after its surrender and the exile of its inhabitants.

328 Zachariah.   329 *Deut.* 4:31.

(69b line 10) אָמַר רִבִּי יוֹחָנָן. שְׁמוֹנִים אֶלֶף פִּירְחֵי כְהוּנָּה בֵּרְחוּ לָהֶם לְתוֹךְ קַלְתּוּתִים שֶׁלְּבֵית הַמִּקְדָּשׁ. וְכוּלָּם נִשְׂרָפוּ. וּבְכוּלָּם לֹא נִשְׁתַּיֵּיר אֶלָּא יְהוֹשֻׁעַ בֶּן יְהוֹצָדָק הַכֹּהֵן הַגָּדוֹל. שֶׁנֶּאֱמַר הֲלוֹא זֶה אוּד מוּצָּל מֵאֵשׁ:

אָמַר רִבִּי יוֹחָנָן. שְׁמוֹנִים אֶלֶף פִּירְחֵי כְהוּנָּה (בָּקְעוּ) [בָּרְחוּ] לְתוֹךְ חַיָילוֹתָיו שֶׁלִנְבוּכַד נֶצַר. וְהָלְכוּ לָהֶן אֵצֶל יִשְׁמְעֵאלִים. אָמְרוּן לוֹן. הָבוּ חָן נִשְׁתֵּי דַּאֲנָן צָהֵיי. הֵבִיאוּ לִפְנֵיהֶן מִינֵי מְלוּחִים וְנוֹדוֹת נְפוּחוֹת. אָמְרוּן לוֹן. אָכְלוּן וְאַתּוּן שָׁתֵיי. וְכֵיוָן דַּהֲוָה חַד מִינְהוֹן שָׁרֵי זִיקָא וִיהַב לֵיהּ גּוֹ פּוּמֵיהּ. הֲוָה רוּחָא נָפַק וַהֲוָה חָנֵק לֵיהּ. הָדָא הוּא דִכְתִיב מַשָּׂא בַּעְרָב. מְטוּל רַב בַּעֲרָבִיָּיא. בַּיַּעַר בַּעְרָב תָּלִינוּ. מִי נְתוּנִים בְּיַעַר הַלְּבָנוֹן בַּעֲרָב תָּלִינוּ. אֶלָּא אוֹרְחוֹת דְּדָנִים: כֵּן אוֹרְחֲהוֹן דִּבְנֵי דוֹדַיָּיא עָבְדִין. יִשְׁמָעֵאל שֶׁצָּמֵא לֹא לִקְרַאת צָמֵא הֵתֵיוּ מָיִם. וַיִּפְקַח אֱלֹהִים אֶת־עֵינֶיהָ וַתֵּרֶא בְּאֵר מָיִם. לֹא מִן טִיבוּתְכוֹן אָתוּן לְגַבֵּיכוֹן. כִּי־מִפְּנֵי חֲרָבוֹת נָדָדוּ מִפְּנֵי | חֶרֶב נְטוּשָׁה. שֶׁלֹּא רָצוּ לְשַׁמֵּר אֶת שְׁמִיטֵיהֶם. כְּמָה דְאַתְּ אָמַר וְהַשְּׁבִיעִית תִּשְׁמְטֶנָּה וּנְטַשְׁתָּהּ. וּמִפְּנֵי קֶשֶׁת דְּרוּכָה. שֶׁלֹּא רָצוּ לְשַׁמֵּר שַׁבְּתוֹתֵיהֶם. כְּמָה דְאַתְּ אָמַר בַּיָּמִים הָהֵמָּה רָאִיתִי בִיהוּדָה | דּוֹרְכִים גִּיתּוֹת בַּשַּׁבָּת. וּמִפְּנֵי כּוֹבֶד מִלְחָמָה: שֶׁלֹּא רָצוּ לְהִלָּחֵם בְּמִלְחַמְתָּהּ שֶׁלַּתּוֹרָה. [כְּמָה דְאַתְּ אָמַר] עַל־כֵּן יֵאָמַר בְּסֵפֶר מִלְחֲמוֹת יי.

[330]Rebbi Joḥanan said, 80'000 young priests fled into the hollows[331] of the Temple, and all of them were burned. Of all of them only Joshua ben Yehoṣadaq the High Priest was left, as it is said, *is he not a wooden poker saved from fire*[332]?

[333]Rebbi Joḥanan said, 80'000 young priests (broke through) [fled to] Nebuchadnezzar's armies and went to the Ismaelites. They said to them, give us to drink for we are thirsty. They brought before them salted fish and inflated waterskins. They said to them, eat and then you can drink. When one of them opened the waterskin and put it into his mouth, the wind came out and suffocated him. That is what is written[334], *load in Arabia*, a large load on Arabia. *In a forest in Arabia they will stay*, those that should have been in the forest of Lebanon, *in Arabia they will stay*. But *the ways of Dedanians*[335], that is the way the Dedanians act. When Ismael was thirsty, did they not *bring water towards the thirsty? God opened her eyes and she saw a water cistern*[336]. Not voluntarily they came to you, *for they fled from swords. From the unfettered sword,* because they did not want to keep their Sabbaticals, as you are saying, *and the seventh unfetter and abandon*[337]. And because of

cocked bows, because they did not want to keep their Sabbaths, as you are saying, in these days I saw in Jehudah people pressing wine-presses on the Sabbath[338]. *And because of the difficulty of war*, they did not want to engage in the Torah's war, [as you are saying], *therefore it was said in the book of the wars of the Eternal*[339].

330 This paragraph is not in *Thr. rabba*.
331 The word usually is used for a hollow into which a portable stove is brought for cooking.
332 *Zach*. 3:2.
333 Similarly *Thr. rabba* 3(38), *Yalqut Prophets* 421; cf. Tanḥuma *Yitro* 5.

334 *Is*. 21:13-15.
335 A grandson of Abraham by Qetura.
336 *Gen*. 21:19.
337 *Ex*. 23:11.
338 *Neh*. 13:15.
339 *Num*. 21:14.

(69b line 27) אָמַר רִבִּי יוֹחָנָן. מִגִּבְתָּ וְעַד אַנְטִיפָּרִיס שִׁשִּׁים רִיבּוֹא עֲיָירוֹת הָיוּ. הַקְּטַנָּה שֶׁבָּהֶן הָיְתָה בֵית שֶׁמֶשׁ. דִּכְתִיב בָּהּ וַיַּךְ בְּאַנְשֵׁי בֵית־שֶׁמֶשׁ כִּי רָאוּ בַּאֲרוֹן י' וגו'. וְאֵילוּ מֵרוּחַ אַחַת הָיוּ. אֵין אַתְּ מְבַצֵּעַ לָהּ קָנַיי לָא נָסְיָיה. אָמַר רִבִּי חֲנִינָה. קָפְצָה לָהּ אֶרֶץ יִשְׂרָאֵל.
1 מגבת | מ מגבות אנטיפריס | מ אנטיפטריס הקטנה | מ [והקטנה] 2 דכת' | מ מה כת' בה 3 אין | מ וכדון אין נסייה | מ נסבה

אָמַר רִבִּי זְעִירָא. בּוֹא וּרְאֵה מַה חֲצִיפָה הִיא אֶרֶץ יִשְׂרָאֵל שֶׁהִיא עוֹשָׂה פֵירוֹת. מִפְּנֵי מָה הִיא עוֹשָׂה פֵירוֹת. תְּרֵין אֲמוֹרִין. חַד אָמַר. מִפְּנֵי שֶׁמְּזַבְּלִין אוֹתָהּ. וְחוֹרָנָה אָמַר. מִפְּנֵי שֶׁהוֹפְכִין אֶת אֲפָרָהּ. עוֹבָדָא הֲוָה בְּחַד דַּהֲוָה קָאִים זָרַע בְּחָדָא בְּקַעַת אַרְבֵּל. וְכָבַשׁ יָדֵיהּ וְנָפַק עַפְרָא יְקִידָא וְאוֹקִיד זַרְעָא.

[340]Rebbi Joḥanan said, from Gibbethon[341] to Antipatris there were 60'000 villages. The smallest among them was Bet Shemesh, about which is written[342], *He smote of the men of Bet Shemesh, for they looked at the Ark of the Eterna,* etc. These were in one direction. If you execute this with reeds it will not carry it. Rebbi Ḥanina said, the Land of Israel folded its fist.

[343]Rebbi Ze`ira said, come and see how insolent is the Land of Israel, that it yields fruit[344]. Why does it yield fruit? Two Amoraim. One said, because one fertilizes it. The other one said, because one turns its earth over. It happened that a person was sowing in the valley of Arbel when he dug down with his hand and brought up burning dust which burned the seeds.

340 *Thr. rabba* 3(38), *Megillah* 1:1 (מ).
341 The full biblical name is spelled out in *Thr. rabba*.
342 *1S*. 6:19.
343 This paragraph in *Thr. rabba, Petiḥta* 34.

344 Since it is written (*Deut.* 29:22) *sulfur and salt, burns all over its land*, describing the land after the destruction of the Temple, how can it have regained agricultural productivity?

(69b line 35) תַּנֵי. רִבִּי יוֹסֵי אוֹמֵר. חֲמִשִּׁים וּשְׁתַּיִם שָׁנָה לֹא נִרְאָה עוֹף טַס בְּאֶרֶץ יִשְׂרָאֵל. מָה טַעַם. מֵעוֹף וְעַד־בְּהֵמָה נָדְדוּ הָלָכוּ. אָמַר רִבִּי חֲנִינָה. קוֹדֶם לְאַרְבָּעִים שָׁנָה עַד שֶׁלֹּא גָלוּ יִשְׂרָאֵל לְבָבֶל נָטְעוּ תְמָרִים בְּבָבֶל. עַל יְדֵי שֶׁיִּהוּ לְהוּטִים אַחַר מְתִיקָה. שֶׁהִיא מְרַגֶּלֶת אֶת הַלָּשׁוֹן לַתּוֹרָה. אָמַר רִבִּי חֲנִינָה בְּרֵיהּ דְּרִבִּי אַבָּהוּ. שְׁבַע מֵאוֹת מִינֵי דָגִים טְהוֹרִים וּשְׁמוֹנֶה מֵאוֹת מִינֵי חֲגָבִים טְהוֹרִים וְלָעוֹף אֵין מִסְפָּר כּוּלְּהֹם גָּלוּ עִם יִשְׂרָאֵל לְבָבֶל. וּכְשֶׁחָזְרוּ כּוּלְּהֹם חָזְרוּ עִמָּהֶן חוּץ מִן הַדָּג הַנִּקְרָא שִׁיבּוּטָא. וְדָגִים הֵיאַךְ גָּלוּ. רִבִּי חוּנָה בַּר יוֹסֵף אָמַר. דֶּרֶךְ הַתְּהוֹם גָּלוּ וְדֶרֶךְ הַתְּהוֹם חָזְרוּ.

2 מעוף G | מעוף השמים   לארבעים G | ארבעים   שלא גלו | G גלו שלא   3 על ידי שיהו | G שהיו   את | G -
4 אבהו | G | אבה   ושמונה | G שמונה   5 כולהם | G כולהון   (2) | וכשחזרו | G וכיון שחזרו   6 ודגים | G ודגין
היאך | G היכן   חונה בר | G הונא אמר בשם רב

[345]It was stated: Rebbi Yose says, for 52 years no bird was flying in the Land of Israel. What is the reason? *From the bird <of the sky> to the domesticated animal, they moved, they went away*[346]. Rebbi Ḥanina said, 40 years before Israel was exiled to Babylonia they planted date palms in Babylonia, so they should be ardent after sweets since this accustoms the tongue to Torah[347]. Rebbi Ḥanina the son of Rebbi Abbahu said, 700 kinds of pure fish and 800 kinds of pure locusts and innumerable birds all were exiled with Israel to Babylonia; and when they returned, all of them returned, except the fish called turbot. How did fish migrate? Rebbi Huna (bar Joseph) <in the name of Rav Joseph>[348] said, they went into exile through the abyss end returned through the abyss.

345 From here on there exists another Genizah fragment edited by Ginzberg (G). Cf. also *Seder Olam* Chap. 27 (in the author's edition p. 234), Babli *Šabbat* 145b.

346 *Jer.* 9:9.
347 Babli *Pesaḥim* 87b/88a.
348 Since no R. Huna bar Joseph is otherwise known, prefer the reading of <G>.

(69b line 43) אָמַר רִבִּי יוֹחָנָן. אַשְׁרֵי מִי שֶׁהוּא רוֹאָה בְּמַפַּלְתָּהּ שֶׁלְּתַדְמוֹר. שֶׁהִיא הָיְתָה שׁוּתֶּפֶת בְּחֻרְבַּן הַבַּיִת הָרִאשׁוֹן וּבְחֻרְבַּן הַבַּיִת הַשֵּׁינִי. בְּחֻרְבָּן הָרִאשׁוֹן הֶעֱמִידָה שְׁמוֹנִים אֶלֶף קַשָּׁטִים. וּבְחֻרְבָּן הַשֵּׁינִי הֶעֱמִידָה שְׁמוֹנַת אֲלָפִים קַשָּׁטִים.

1 אמ' ר' יוחנן | G -   שהוא רואה | G שראה   2 בחרבן הבית הראשון ובחרבן הבית בשיני | G -   אלף | G -
קשטים | G קשטין

[340]Rebbi Joḥanan said, hail to him who sees the downfall of Palmyra, for it was partner in the destruction of the first Temple and the destruction of the second Temple. In the first destruction it put up 80'000[349] archers and in the second destruction 8'000 archers.

349 In G: 80. In *Thr. rabba* different numbers are given by different Amoraim of later generations.

(69b line 46) וְנֶחְרְשָׁה הָעִיר. חָרַשׁ רוּפוּס שְׁחִיק עֲצָמוֹת אֶת הַהֵיכָל.

"And the city was ploughed over." Rufus[350], may his bones be ground, ploughed over the Temple[204].

350 Tineius Rufus, prefect of Judea at the start of Bar Kokhba's uprising. This sentence is missing in G (and in the Midrashim.) Babli 29a.

(fol. 67b) **משנה ח**: מִשֶּׁנִּכְנַס אָב מְמַעֲטִין בְּשִׂמְחָה: שַׁבָּת שֶׁחָל תִּשְׁעָה בְּאָב לִהְיוֹת בְּתוֹכָהּ אֲסוּרִין מִלְּסַפֵּר וּמִלְּכַבֵּס וּבַחֲמִישִׁי מוּתָּרִין מִפְּנֵי כְבוֹד הַשַּׁבָּת.

Mishnah 8: From the start of Av one restricts happy occasions. The week in which the Ninth of Av falls one is forbidden to barber and to launder, but on Thursday one is permitted for the honor of the Sabbath.

(69 line 47) **הלכה ט**: אָמַר רִבִּי יְהוֹשֻׁעַ בֶּן לֵוִי. הָדָא דְאַתְּ אָמַר בְּבִנְיָן שֶׁלְּשִׂמְחָה. אֲבָל אִם הָיָה כוֹתְלוֹ גּוֹחֶה סוֹתְרוֹ וּבוֹנֵהוּ. שְׁמוּאֵל אָמַר. בְּכוֹתְלָא דְגָנֵיי בֵיהּ. רִבִּי בָּא בַר כֹּהֵן אָמַר קוֹמֵי רִבִּי יוֹסֵי. רִבִּי אֲחָא בְשֵׁם רִבִּי יַעֲקֹב בַּר אִידִי. אָסוּר לְאָרֵס אִשָּׁה בְּעֶרֶב שַׁבָּת. הָדָא דְאַתְּ אָמַר שֶׁלֹּא לַעֲשׂוֹת סְעוּדַת אֵירוּסִין. הָא לְאָרֵס יְאָרֵס. אֲפִילוּ בְתִשְׁעָה בְּאָב יְאָרֵס. שֶׁלֹּא יְקַדְּמֶנּוּ אַחֵר. מַחְלְפָה שִׁיטָתֵיהּ דִּשְׁמוּאֵל. תַּמָּן הוּא אָמַר. אֱלֹהִים | מוֹשִׁיב יְחִידִים | בַּיְתָה. בְּמֹאזְנַיִם לַעֲלוֹת הֵמָּה מֵהֶבֶל יָחַד: וְהָכָא הוּא אָמַר הָכֵין. אֶלָּא שֶׁלֹּא יְקַדְּמֶנּוּ אַחֵר בִּתְפִילָּה. אֲפִילוּ כֵן לֹא קַיְימַהּ.

1 הדא G | הדה בבניין G | בבנין 2 אמ' | G | ביה - G | בה 3 הדא G | הדה 4 אמ' | G - G | 6 הכין G | הכן

Halakhah 9: Rebbi Joshua ben Levi said, that is a building of enjoyment. But if his wall was inclined, he tears it down and rebuilds it. Samuel said, the wall where he sleeps[351]. [352]Rebbi Abba bar Cohen said before Rebbi Yose: Rebbi Aḥa in the name of Rebbi Jacob bar Idi: A man may not preliminarily marry on a Friday. That means, to make an engagement feast[353]. This implies that the preliminary marriage itself is permitted. Samuel says, even on the Ninth of Av a preliminary marriage is permitted, lest another forestall him. The argument of Samuel seems inverted. There[354], he says, *God puts singles in a house*; *To rise on scales; they all are of vapor!* And here, he says so[355]? That means, that he should not forestall him in prayer. Even so, it would not be permanent.

351 Chapter 1, Notes 247-248.
352 The following is in *Yom Tov* 5:2 (Notes 65-70), *Ketubot* 1:1 (Notes 34-42).
353 Since this would impinge on the Sabbath meal. It is in order to make the preliminary marriage on Friday and arrange the festive meal as Sabbath meal.
354 *Ps.* 68:7, 62:10. This means that marriages are pre-ordained in Heaven. (*Lev. rabba* 29(5), Babli *Mo`ed qatan* 18b.)
355 If marriages are pre-ordained, why should anybody be afraid that another man could snatch the bride preselected for him? Another man might by his prayer cause the Heavenly decree to be changed, but this would lead to the early death of one of the partners of the marriage. Babli *Sota* 2a, *Sanhedrin* 22a.

(69b line 55) אָמַר רִבִּי יוֹנָה. הָדָא דְאַתְּ אָמַר מַרְוֵחַ וּמַלְבּוּשׁ. בְּרַם מַרְוֵחַ וּמִתְקָנָה. כֵּן אֲנָן אָמְרִין. הָדֵין קַצָּרָא אָסִיר לֵיהּ מֵיעֲבַד עֲבִידְתֵּיהּ. מַתְנִיתָא פְלִיגָא עַל רִבִּי יוֹנָה. שַׁבָּת שֶׁחָל תִּשְׁעָה בְאָב לִהְיוֹת בְּתוֹכָהּ אֲסוּרִין מִלְסַפֵּר וּמִלְכַּבֵּס וּבַחֲמִישִׁי מוּתָּרִין מִפְּנֵי כְבוֹד הַשַּׁבָּת. רִבִּי יוֹנָה בְשֵׁם רַב הַמְנוּנָא. (לְתוֹסֶפֶת) [לְתִסְפּוֹרֶת] הוּשְׁבָה. רִבִּי בָּא בַר כֹּהֵן אָמַר קוֹמֵי רִבִּי יוֹסֵה רִבִּי אָחָא בְשֵׁם רִבִּי אַבָּהוּ. תִּשְׁעָה בְאָב שֶׁחָל לִהְיוֹת בַּשַּׁבָּת שְׁתֵּי שַׁבָּתוֹת מוּתָּרוֹת. לְאַחֲרָיו מָהוּ. רִבִּי יוֹחָנָן אָמַר. לְאַחֲרָיו אָסוּר. רִבִּי שִׁמְעוֹן בֶּן לָקִישׁ אָמַר. לְאַחֲרָיו מוּתָּר. דְּרָשָׁהּ רִבִּי חִייָה בַּר בָּא לְצִיפּוֹרָאֵי וְלָא קַבְּלוּן עֲלֵיהוֹן. אָמַר רִבִּי אִימִי לְרִבִּי [נָסִי]. וְאֵין בֶּן אֲחוֹי שֶׁלְרִבִּי חִייָה הַגָּדוֹל חָלוּק עָלָיו. אָמַר לֵיהּ. בְּפֵירוּשׁ פְּלִיגִין. רִבִּי יוֹחָנָן אָמַר. לְאַחֲרָיו אָסוּר. רִבִּי שִׁמְעוֹן בֶּן לָקִישׁ אָמַר. לְאַחֲרָיו מוּתָּר. מָה עֲבַד לָהּ רִבִּי שִׁמְעוֹן בֶּן לָקִישׁ. פָּתַר לָהּ תִּשְׁעָה בְאָב שֶׁחָל לִהְיוֹת בַּשַּׁבָּת. וְלֵית שְׁמַע מִינָהּ כְּלוּם. רִבִּי יִצְחָק בֶּן אֶלְעָזָר מִן דַּהֲוָה תִּשְׁעָה בְאָב נָפַק הֲוָה מַכְרִיז. יִפְתְּחוּן סַפְרַיָּא וּמָאן דְּבָעֵי יַסְפְּדָא יַסְפּוֹד. כָּתוּב וְהָשְׁבַּתִּי כָּל־מְשׂוֹשָׂהּ חַגָּהּ חָדְשָׁהּ וְשַׁבַּתָּהּ וְכָל מוֹעֲדָהּ. דְּרוֹמָאֵי נְהַגִין חַגָּהּ. צִיפּוֹרָאֵי נְהַגִין חָדְשָׁהּ. טִיבֶּרְיָאֵי נְהַגִין שַׁבַּתָּהּ. חָזְרִין רַבָּנִין דְּטִיבֶּרְיָּא לְמִינְהוֹג כְּרַבָּנִין דְּצִיפּוֹרִין.

1 הדא G | הדה   2 קצרא G | קצארא   מיעבד G | למעבד   3 השבת G | שבת   4 יוסה G | יוסי   5 אבהו |
G אבהוא   מהו G | מהוא   7 לציפוראיי G | לציפראי   קבלון G | קבלין   אימי G | אמי   [נסי] G | אמי אחוי |
G אחוי   10 בן G | ביר'   11 ספרייא G | ספרייה   ומאן G | ומן   יספדא G | יספדנה   וכל מועדה G | -
12 טיבריאי G | טיבראי

Rebbi Jonah said, what you are saying refers to washing to wear; but washing to mend? So we are saying, this washerman is forbidden to work in his trade[356]? Our Mishnah disagrees with Rebbi Jonah, "the week in which the Ninth of Av falls one is forbidden to barber and to launder, but on Thursday[357] one is permitted for the honor of the Sabbath." Rebbi Jonah in the name of Rav Hamnuna, it was repeated regarding (addition) [barbering.][358] Rebbi Abba bar Cohen said before Rebbi Yose: Rebbi Aha in the name of Rebbi Abbahu. If the Ninth of Av falls on a Sabbath, both weeks are permitted[359]. What is afterwards? Rebbi Johanan said, afterwards is forbidden; Rebbi Simeon ben Laqish said, afterwards is permitted[360]. Rebbi Hiyya bar Abba preached it to the Sepphoreans but they did not accept it. Rebbi Immi said to Rebbi [Yasa][361]. Does not the nephew of the Great Rebbi Hiyya[362] disagree with him? He answered, they disagree explicitly: Rebbi Johanan said, afterwards is forbidden; Rebbi Simeon ben Laqish said, afterwards is permitted. How does Rebbi Simeon ben Laqish explain it[363]? He explains it if the Ninth of Av falls on a Sabbath, and one cannot infer anything. Rebbi Isaac ben Eleazar announced at the end of the Ninth of Av, the barbers shall open[364], any who has to eulogize may eulogize[365]. It is written[366], *I shall eliminate all her enjoyment, her holiday, her month, her Sabbath, and all her feast.* The Southerners have the custom of *her holiday*[367], the Sepphoreans have the custom of *her month*[368], the Tiberians have the custom of *her week*[369]. The Rabbis of Tiberias changed to follow the Rabbis of Sepphoris.

356 Since the Mishnah only forbids people to wash their garments but not washermen to exercise their trade, there must be washing activities which are permitted. The Babli 29b decides otherwise.

357 If the Ninth of Av falls during the week, the following Sabbath already is after the fast and it is permitted to wash during the week in order to wear after the fast.

358 The reading of the scribe is confirmed by G; the corrector's change is indicated in *Or zarua`* §414. The corrector's text means that barbering does not follow the rules of washing and is strictly forbidden before and during the fast. The scribe's text seems to mean that there is no extension of the fast (following R. Simeon ben Laqish and R. Isaac ben Eleazar); immediately after the end of the fast all activities are permitted.

359 If the Ninth of Av falls on a Sabbath there is no week in which the Ninth of Av falls.

360 A disagreement of Babylonian authorities in Babli 29b.

361 A necessary correction of the text of G: "R. Ammi asked R. Ammi".

362 Rav.

363 The Mishnah which forbids the entire week if the fast was Sunday or Tuesday.

364 Their shops.

365 All commentators read יספר "barber" for יספד "eulogize" but this seems to be impossible in light of the evidence of G. While the rule not to eulogize on the Ninth of Av appears in the sources as Medieval Ashkenazic (*Šulḥan Arukh Oraḥ Ḥayyim* 559:10) this may be indicated here since the Ashkenazic (originally, South-Italian) order of prayers is based on the Yerushalmi.

366 *Hos.* 2:13.

367 They start the mourning rites already on the New Moon of Av.

368 They follow them the entire month and do not stop after the fast.

369 The rule presented in the Mishnah.

(69b line 72) רִבִּי יִרְמְיָה בְשֵׁם רִבִּי חִיָּיה בַּר בָּא. בַּדִּין הָיָה שֶׁיִּהוּ מִתְעַנִּין בָּעֲשִׂירִי שֶׁבּוֹ נִשְׂרַף בֵּית אֱלֹהֵינוּ. וְלָמָּה בַּתְּשִׁיעִי. שֶׁבּוֹ הִתְחִילָה הַפּוּרְעָנוּת. וְתַנֵּי כֵן. בַּשְּׁבִיעִי נִכְנְסוּ לְתוֹכוֹ. בַּשְּׁמִינִי הָיוּ מְקַרְקְרִין בּוֹ. בַּתְּשִׁיעִי הִצִּיתוּ בוֹ אֶת הָאוּר. וּבָעֲשִׂירִי נִשְׂרַף. רִבִּי יְהוֹשֻׁעַ בֶּן לֵוִי צְיַּים תְּשִׁיעִי וָעֲשִׂירִי. רִבִּי אָבוּן צְיַים תְּשִׁיעִי וָעֲשִׂירִי. רִבִּי לֵוִי צְיַּים תְּשִׁיעִי וְלֵילֵי עֲשִׂירִי. רִבִּי בָּא בַּר זַבְדָּא בְשֵׁם רִבִּי חֲנִינָה. בִּיקֵּשׁ רִבִּי לַעֲקוֹר תִּשְׁעָה בְאָב וְלֹא הִנִּיחוּ לוֹ. אָמַר לוֹ רִבִּי לָעְזָר. עִמָּךְ הָיִיתִי וְלֹא אִיתְאָמַרַת הָכִי. אֶלָּא בִּיקֵּשׁ רִבִּי לַעֲקוֹר תִּשְׁעָה בְאָב שֶׁחָל לִהְיוֹת בַּשַׁבָּת וְלֹא הִנִּיחוּ לוֹ. אָמַר. הוֹאִיל וְנִדְחָה יִדָּחֶה. אָמְרוּ [לוֹ]. יִדָּחֶה לְמָחָר. וְנַגֵי לֵיהּ הַהִיא דְּתָנִינָן תַּמָּן. רִבִּי יוֹחָנָן בֶּן בְּרוֹקָה אוֹמֵר. עַל שְׁנֵיהֶן הוּא אוֹמֵר וַיְבָרֶךְ אוֹתָם אֱלֹהִים וַיֹּאמֶר לָהֶם אֱלֹהִים פְּרוּ וּרְבוּ וגו'. רִבִּי לָעְזָר בְּשֵׁם רִבִּי חֲנִינָה. הֲלָכָה כְרִבִּי יוֹחָנָן בֶּן בְּרוֹקָה. אָמַר לֵיהּ רִבִּי בָּא בַּר זַבְדָּא. עִמָּךְ הָיִיתִי וְלֹא אִיתְאָמַרַת. אֶלָּא אִם הָיְתָה תּוֹבַעַת לְהִינָּשֵׂא הַדִּין עִמָּהּ. וְקָרָא עֲלֵיהוֹן. טוֹבִים הַשְּׁנַיִם מִן־הָאֶחָד.

1 שיהו G | שיהוא שבו G | וכשבו 2 בית אלהינו | מG - כן G כאן 3 מקרקרין | מ מקרקרים ובעשירי | מ בעשירי 4 ר' אבון צייס תשיעי ועשירי | מ - ולילי עשירי G | ליל ועשירי בא G | אבא 5 אמ' לו G | - לעזר | מ אלעזר 6 הכי | מG - 7 [לו] | מ לו G - וגוי | מ וגזה ליה G - | ההיא G | וה' מ ההוא 8 או | G אמ' שניהן G | שניהם אלהים G | אלוהים וגו' | מG - 10 אתאמרת G מ איתאמרת אם G | מ - היתה | G היתה השנים G | השניים

³⁷⁰Rebbi Jeremiah in the name of Rebbi Ḥiyya, it should have been logical that one should fast on the Tenth, since on it our God's Temple was burned. Why on the Ninth? Because the calamity started on it³⁷¹. So it was stated, on the Seventh they entered, on the Eighth they were misbehaving in it, on the Ninth they started the fire, and on the Tenth it was burned³⁷². Rebbi Joshua ben Levi fasted Ninth and Tenth. Rebbi Abun fasted Ninth and Tenth. Rebbi Levi fasted on the Ninth and the night of the Tenth. Rebbi Abba bar Zavda in the name of Rebbi Ḥanina: Rebbi wanted to uproot the Ninth of Av but they did not let him³⁷³. Rebbi Eleazar said to him, I was with you but it was not said so, but Rebbi wanted to uproot the Ninth of Av which fell on a Sabbath but they did not let him. He said, because it was pushed aside, let it be pushed

aside. They said to him, let it be pushed to the next day. In a similar case, that which we stated there[374]: "Rebbi Johanan ben Beroqa said, for both of them it says, *God blessed them and God said to them, be fruitful and multiply*[375], etc." Rebbi Eleazar in the Name of Rebbi Hanina: Practice follows Rebbi Johanan ben Beroqa. Rebbi Abba bar Zavda said to him, I was with you and it was only said, if she asks to be married the law is on her side[376]. He said about them, *two are better than one*[377].

370 This paragraph also appears in *Megillah* 1:6 (מ).
371 *2K.* 25:8.
372 Babli 29a, Tosephta 3:10.
373 Babli *Megillah* 5b.
374 Mishnah *Yebamot* 6:6.
375 *Gen.* 1:28.
376 If a woman is married childless for ten years she may ask the court to force her husband to give her a divorce with full payment of her *ketubah*. In her application to the court she must state that her request is in order to be able to marry another man (who implicitly is supposed to be more fertile than the first.) In the Babli *Yebamot* 65b she is required to state explicitly that she wants to marry another man in order to have children who will be able to care for her in her old age.
377 *Eccl.* 4:9.

(fol. 67b) **משנה ט**: עֶרֶב תִּשְׁעָה בְאָב לֹא יֹאכַל שְׁנֵי אָדָם תַּבְשִׁילִין לֹא יֹאכַל בָּשָׂר וְלֹא יִשְׁתֶּה יָיִן. רַבָּן שִׁמְעוֹן בֶּן גַּמְלִיאֵל אוֹמֵר יְשַׁנֶּה. רִבִּי יְהוּדָה מְחַיֵּיב בִּכְפִיַּית הַמִּטָּה וְלֹא הוֹדוּ לוֹ חֲכָמִים:

Mishnah 9: In the day before the Ninth of Av a person may not eat two dishes, he may not eat meat nor drink wine[378]. Rabban Simeon ben Gamliel says, he shall alterate. Rebbi Jehudah obligates him to turn up his couch[378] but the Sages did not agree with him.

378 He has to behave as if a close relative had died. R. Jehudah requires this in all respects, the anonymous majority only in matters of the meal preceding the fast.

(69c line 12) **הלכה י**: מַהוּ יְשַׁנֶּה. יַחֲלֹף. אִין הֲוָה יְלִיף אֲכִיל לִיטְרָא דְקוּפָד יֵיכוּל פַּלְגָּא. אִין הֲוָה יְלִיף שָׁתֵי קַסְט דַּחֲמַר יִשְׁתֶּה פַּלְגָא. אָמַר רִבִּי יוֹחָנָן. וּבִלְבַד עִיקַר סְעוּדַת תִּשְׁעָה בְאָב. אָמַר רַב הוֹשַׁעְיָה. וּבִלְבַד מִשֵּׁשׁ שָׁעוֹת וּלְמַעֲלָן. אָמַר רִבִּי יוֹסֵי. תַּרְתֵּיהוֹן לְקוּלָּא. אָכַל סְעוּדַת תִּשְׁעָה בְאָב מִשֵּׁשׁ שָׁעוֹת וּלְמַטָּן אֲפִילוּ עוֹלָה עַל שׁוּלְחָנוֹ כִּסְעוּדַת שְׁלֹמֹה מוּתָּר. אָכַל סְעוּדָתוֹ מִשֵּׁשׁ שָׁעוֹת וּלְמַעֲלָן אֲפִילוּ עוֹלָה עַל שׁוּלְחָנוֹ כִּסְעוּדַת שְׁלֹמֹה בְּשַׁעְתּוֹ מוּתָּר. תַּנֵּי. תִּשְׁעָה בְאָב

שֶׁחָל לִהְיוֹת עֶרֶב שַׁבָּת. וְכֵן עֶרֶב תִּשְׁעָה בְּאָב שֶׁחָל לִהְיוֹת בַּשַּׁבָּת. אֲפִילוּ עוֹלֶה עַל שׁוּלְחָנוֹ כִּסְעוּדַת שְׁלֹמֹה בְּשַׁעֲתוֹ מוּתָּר. רַב מִן דַּהֲוָה אָכַל כָּל־צוֹרְכֵיהּ הֲוָה צָבַע פִּיסְתֵּיהּ בְּקִיטְמָא וְאָמַר. זוֹ הִיא עִיקַּר סְעוּדַת תִּשְׁעָה בְּאָב. לְקַיֵּים מַה שֶׁנֶּאֱמַר וַיַּגְרֵס בֶּחָצָץ שַׁנָּי הִכְפִּישַׁנִי בָּאֵפֶר:

1 מהו G | מהוא יחלף G | יחליף ייכול G | יאכל 3 רב G | ר' יוסי G | יוסה 4 מותר G | בשעתה מותר
5 בשעתו G | בשעתה 7 בשעתו G | בשעתה מן G | מאן בקיטמא | ג גו קטמא 8 עיקר | ג עקר הכפישני באפר | ג וג'

Halakhah 10: What means "he shall alterate"? He shall change. If he is used to eat a pound[379] of meat he shall eat half; if he is used to drink a sextarius[380] of wine he shall drink half. Rebbi Johanan said, but only for the main meal of the Ninth of Av. Rav[381] Hoshaia said, and only in the afternoon. Rebbi Yose says, both statements are for leniency. If he ate the main meal of the Ninth of Av before noon, even if he brings on his table like Salomon's meal it is permitted. If he ate his meal[382] in the afternoon, even if he brings on his table like Salomon's meal in his time[383] it is permitted. It was stated: If the Ninth of Av fell on a Friday or the day before the Ninth of Av on a Sabbath, even if he brings on his table like Salomon's meal in his time it is permitted[384]. Rav after he had eaten his fill was coloring his piece of bread with ashes and said, this is the main meal of the Ninth of Av, to keep what is said[385], *He filled me with asperity, made me imbue poison.*

379 A Roman pound of 12 unciae, 345g.
380 Possibly Greek ξέστης; in both Talmudim the equivalent of a *log* (.53 l) but in the Galilean Targumim the equivalent of a *hin*, 12 *log* (6.5 l). Babli 30a.
381 In G: Rebbi. In the Babli, Rav Jehudah.

382 Intending to eat another later in the afternoon.
383 *1K.* 5:2-3.
384 Babli 29b.
385 *Thr.* 3:16. Mentioned in *Thr. rabba ad loc.*

(69c line 23) יָאוּת אָמַר רִבִּי יְהוּדָה. מַה טַעֲמוֹן דְּרַבָּנָן. עָשׂוּ אוֹתוֹ כְּמִי שֶׁמֵּתוֹ מוּטָּל לְפָנָיו. אֵינוֹ לֹא כּוֹפֶה אֶת מִיטָּתוֹ וְלֹא יָשֵׁן עַל מִיטָּה כְפוּיָה.

Rebbi Jehudah says it correctly; what is the Rabbis' reason? They made him like one whose deceased is lying before him[386]; he neither overturns his couch nor sleeps on an overturned couch.

386 As long as a person is occupied with arranging a burial, the formal rules of mourning do not apply to him. Since the mourner is not supposed to leave his house but the person who fasts on a public fast day is supposed to leave his house, no public fast can imitate the rules of formal mourning.

(fol. 67b) **משנה י**: אָמַר רַבָּן שִׁמְעוֹן בֶּן גַּמְלִיאֵל לֹא הָיוּ יָמִים טוֹבִים לְיִשְׂרָאֵל כַּחֲמִשָּׁה עָשָׂר בְּאָב וּכְיוֹם הַכִּפּוּרִים שֶׁבָּהֶן בְּנֵי יְרוּשָׁלַיִם יוֹצְאִין בִּכְלֵי לָבָן שְׁאוּלִים שֶׁלֹּא לְבַיֵּשׁ אֶת מִי שֶׁאֵין לוֹ. כָּל־הַכֵּלִים טְעוּנִין טְבִילָה. וּבְנוֹת יְרוּשָׁלַיִם יוֹצְאוֹת וְחוֹלוֹת בַּכְּרָמִים.

משנה יא: וּמֶה הָיוּ אוֹמְרִים. בָּחוּר שָׂא נָא עֵינֶיךָ וּרְאֵה מָה אַתָּה בוֹרֵר לָךְ. אַל תִּתֵּן עֵינֶיךָ בַּנּוֹי תֵּן עֵינֶיךָ בַּמִּשְׁפָּחָה. וְכֵן הוּא אוֹמֵר צְאֶינָה וּרְאֶינָה בְּנוֹת צִיּוֹן בַּמֶּלֶךְ שְׁלֹמֹה וגו׳. בְּיוֹם חֲתוּנָתוֹ זוֹ מַתַּן תּוֹרָה. וּבְיוֹם שִׂמְחַת לִבּוֹ זֶה בִּנְיַן בֵּית הַמִּקְדָּשׁ שֶׁיִּיבָּנֶה בִּמְהֵרָה בְיָמֵינוּ.

Mishnah 10: Rabban Simeon ben Gamliel said, Israel had no holidays like the Fifteenth of Av and the Day of Atonement, when the people of Jerusalem went out in borrowed white garments, not to embarrass those who had none. All garments need immersion[387]. The daughters of Jerusalem went out and played flutes[388] in the vineyards.

Mishnah 11: What were they saying? Young man, lift your eyes and see what you are choosing for yourself. Do not fix your eye on beauty, fix your eyes on the extraction[389]. And so it says[390], *Daughters of Zion go out and see king Solomon*[391], etc. *The day of His enjoyment*[391] is the giving of the Torah; *and the day of His heart's joy*[391] is the building of His Temple which may be built soon in our days.

---

387 So that all were pure. In this version, also the men who were looking for a bride had to appear in a plane white kaftan.

388 Usually one translates "dance" but it is impossible to dance in a tightly planted vineyard. On the other hand one may not play musical instruments on the Day of Atonement. Therefore it seems that the correct wording is in Maimonides's autograph Mishnah: חונות "stay".

389 The text in the Babli and the independent Mishnah mss. is much longer, confirmed by Maimonides's autograph.

390 *Cant.* 3:11. In the allegorical interpretation of the Song of Songs, any "Solomon" refers to the King of Peace.

(69c line 25) **הלכה יא**: נִיחָה בְיוֹם הַכִּיפּוּרִים שֶׁהוּא כַפָּרָה עַל יִשְׂרָאֵל. בַּחֲמִשָּׁה עָשָׂר בְּאָב לָמָּה. רִבִּי יַעֲקֹב בַּר אֲחָא בְשֵׁם רִבִּי יָסָא. שֶׁבּוֹ זְמַן קִיצָה יָפָה לָעֵצִים. שֶׁכָּל־עֵצִים שֶׁהֵן נִקְצָצִין בּוֹ אֵינָן עוֹשִׂין מַאֲכוֹלֶת. כַּהִיא דְתַנִּינָן תַּמָּן. כָּל־עֵץ שֶׁנִּמְצָא בוֹ תוֹלַעַת פָּסוּל מֵעַל גַּבֵּי הַמִּזְבֵּחַ. רַב חִייָה בַּר אַשִׁי בְשֵׁם רַב. שֶׁבּוֹ הִתִּיר הוֹשֵׁעַ בֶּן אֵלָה אֶת פְּרוֹסְדִיּוֹת שֶׁהוֹשִׁיב יָרָבְעָם בֶּן נְבָט עַל

הַדְּרָכִים. כַּהֲנָא שָׁאַל [לְרַב]. כָּל־הֲדָא טִיבוּתָא רַבְּתָא עֲבַד וּכְתִיב בֵּיהּ עָלָיו עָלָה שַׁלְמַנְאֶסֶר מֶלֶךְ אַשּׁוּר. אָמַר לֵיהּ. עַל יְדֵי שֶׁשָּׁמַט אֶת הַקּוֹלָר מִצַּוָּארוֹ וּתְלָיוֹ בְּצַוְּאר הָרַבִּים. לָא אָמַר. כָּל־עַמָּא יִסְקוּן. אֶלָּא מָאן דְּבָעֵי מִיסּוּק יִסּוּק. רִבִּי שְׁמוּאֵל בַּר רַב יִצְחָק. וְאָמְרִין לָהּ בְּשֵׁם רִבִּי שְׁמוּאֵל בַּר נַחְמָן. שֶׁבּוֹ הוּתְּרוּ שְׁבָטִים לָבוֹא זֶה בָזֶה. דִּכְתִיב לֹא־תִסֹּב נַחֲלָה מִבְּנֵי יִשְׂרָאֵל מִמַּטֶּה אֶל־מַטֶּה אַחֵר כִּי אִישׁ בְּנַחֲלַת אֲבֹתָיו יִדְבְּקוּ בְּנֵי יִשְׂרָאֵל: וּכְתִיב וְכָל־בַּת יֹרֶשֶׁת נַחֲלָה מִמַּטּוֹת בְּנֵי יִשְׂרָאֵל וגו'. וְכִי אֶיפְשַׁר לְבַת לִירַשׁ שְׁנֵי מַטּוֹת. תִּיפְטָר שֶׁהָיָה אָבִיהָ מִשֵּׁבֶט אֶחָד וְאִמָּהּ מִשֵּׁבֶט אֶחָד. וְרַבָּנָן אָמְרֵי. שֶׁבּוֹ הוּתַּר שִׁבְטוֹ שֶׁלְבִּנְיָמִין לָבוֹא בַקָּהָל. דִּכְתִיב אָרוּר נוֹתֵן אִשָּׁה לְבִנְיָמִן: מִקְרָא קָרְאוּ וְקֵירְבוּהוּ. מִקְרָא קָרְאוּ וְרִיחֲקוּהוּ. מִקְרָא קָרְאוּ וְקֵירְבוּהוּ. אֶפְרַיִם וּמְנַשֶּׁה כִּרְאוּבֵן וְשִׁמְעוֹן יִהְיוּ־לִי: מִקְרָא קָרְאוּ וְרִיחֲקוּהוּ. גּוֹי וּקְהַל גּוֹיִם יִהְיֶה מִמֶּךָּ וּמְלָכִים מֵחֲלָצֶיךָ יֵצֵאוּ: וַעֲדַיִין לֹא נוֹלַד בִּנְיָמִן. רִבִּי אָבוּן אָמַר. שֶׁבּוֹ בָטַל הַחֲפָר. וְאָמַר רִבִּי לֵוִי. בְּכָל־עֶרֶב תִּשְׁעָה בְאָב הָיָה מֹשֶׁה מוֹצִיא כָּרוֹז בְּכָל־הַמַּחֲנֶה וְאוֹמֵר. צְאוּ לַחֲפָר צְאוּ לַחֲפָר. וְהָיוּ יוֹצְאִין וְחוֹפְרִין לָהֶן קְבָרִים וִישֵׁינִים. וּבַשַּׁחַר הָיוּ עוֹמְדִין וּמוֹצְאִין עַצְמָן חֲסֵרִים חֲמִשָּׁה עָשָׂר אֶלֶף וּפְרוֹטְרוֹט. וּבַשָּׁנָה הָאַחֲרוֹנָה עָשׂוּ כֵן וְעָמְדוּ וּמָצְאוּ עַצְמָן שְׁלֵמִים. אָמְרוּ. דִּילְמָא דְטָעִינַן בְּחוּשְׁבָּנָא. וְכֵן בַּעֲשָׂרָה וְכֵן בְּאַחַד עָשָׂר וּבִשְׁנַיִם עָשָׂר וּבִשְׁלֹשָׁה עָשָׂר וּבְאַרְבַּע עָשָׂר וּבַחֲמִשָּׁה עָשָׂר. כֵּיוָן דְּאַשְׁלַם זִיתְרָא אָמְרוּ. דּוּמֶה שֶׁבִּיטֵּל הַקָּדוֹשׁ בָּרוּךְ הוּא אוֹתָהּ הַגְּזֵירָה קָשָׁה מֵעָלֵינוּ. וְעָמְדוּ וְעָשׂוּ יוֹם טוֹב.

Halakhah 11: [391]One understands the Day of Atonement which is atonement for all of Israel. [392]Why on the Fifteenth of Av? Rebbi Jacob bar Aha in the name of Rebbi Yasa: For this is the good time to cut wood, because any wood cut on this day does not develop worms; as we have stated there, "any wood containing a worm is disqualified from the altar.[393]" Rav Hiyya bar Ashi in the name of Rav, because on it Hoshea ben Ela abolished the guards which Jeroboam ben Nabath posted on the roads[394]. Cahana asked [Rav]. He did all this good deed and it is written about him[395], *against him came Salmanessar the king of Assyria*? He answered him, because he removed the collar from his neck and hung it on the community's neck. He did not say, all the people should go on pilgrimage, but, any one who wants to go may go. Rebbi Samuel bar Rav Isaac, but some say in the name of Rebbi Samuel bar Nahman: On it the tribes were permitted to intermarry. As it is written[396], *family heritage should not be transferred from tribe to tribe; but the Children of Israel shall stick everyone to the family heritage of his forefathers*, etc. And it is written[397], *any daughter inheriting family heritage in the tribes of the Children of Israel*, etc. How is it possible for a daughter to inherit from two tribes? Explain it if her father was from one tribe and her mother from another tribe[398]. But the Rabbis say, on it the tribe of Benjamin was permitted to intermarry, as it is written[399], *cursed be he who gives a wife to Benjamin.* They read a verse and included him; they read a verse and excluded him. They read a verse and included him[400], *Ephraim and Manasse shall be to me like Reuben and Simeon.* They read a verse and excluded him, *a people and community of peoples shall be from you and kings will come from your loins*[401], and Benjamin was not yet born. [402]Rebbi Abun said, digging stopped on it, as Rebbi Levi said, on every eve of the Ninth of Av, Moses had a declaration published in all the encampment and said, go out for digging, go out for digging. They went out, dug graves for themselves, and slept. In the morning they were getting up and found themselves missing 15'000 and detail[403]. In the last year they did that, got up, and found themselves whole. They said, maybe we erred in the computation. The same on the Tenth, the Eleventh, the Twelfth, the Thirteenth, and the Fifteenth. Since the moon was full they said, it seems that The Holy One, praise to Him, vacated this hard judgment against us. They got up and made a holiday.

391 Babli 30b.
392 Babli 30b,31a; *Bava batra* 121a.
393 Mishnah *Middot* 2:5. In the Babli the reason is given that this is the last day on which wood for the altar may be cut before the rainy season.
394 To prohibit pilgrimages to Jerusalem.
395 *2K.* 17:3.
396 *Num.* 36:7.
397 *Num.* 36:8.
398 According to the Babli, a later generation read *Num.* 36 to apply only to the daughters of Salpaad and their contemporaries.
399 *Jud.* 21:18.
400 *Gen.* 48:5.

401 *Gen.* 35:11.
In the explanations, the terms "included" and "excluded" have to be switched. The text follows the usual pattern, that if possibilities A and B are raised, B is explained before A. Since the number 12 of tribe cannot be changed, either Joseph is counted as one tribe and Benjamin is included (35:11), or Ephraim and Manasse are counted as full tribes, there seems to be no place for Benjamin. This logic is not followed by the Babli.
402 *Thr. rabba, Introduction* (33).
403 If always the same number died on the Ninth of Av and nobody during the year, the number would be $600'000:38 = 15'789.47$.

(69c line 51) כָּל־הַכֵּלִים טְעוּנִין טְבִילָה. וּבְנוֹת יְרוּשָׁלַיִם יוֹצְאוֹת וְחוֹלוֹת בַּכְּרָמִים. רִבִּי יַנַּאי בֵּירִבִּי יִשְׁמָעֵאל אָמַר. וַאֲפִילוּ נְתוּנִים בַּתֵּיבָה. נְתוּנִים בַּתֵּיבָה וְאַתְּ אָמַר הָכֵן. מִתּוֹךְ שֶׁאַתְּ עוֹשֶׂה כֵן הוּא מַשְׁאִילָן.

1 ינאי ביר' | G ינייִ בר   2 מתוך | G מיתוך

"All garments need immersion. The daughters of Jerusalem went out and played flutes in the vineyards." Rebbi Yannai ben Rebbi Ismael said, even if put in a box[404]. Put in a box and you are saying so? Because you are doing that, he will lend them.

404 He required that all plain white garments had to be immersed in a *miqweh* even if it was obvious that they were pure and there was no intention to use them.

(59c line 54) וּמֶה הָיוּ אוֹמְרוֹת. בָּחוּר שָׂא נָא עֵינֶיךָ וּרְאֵה מָה אַתָּה בּוֹרֵר לָךְ. אַל תִּתֵּן עֵינֶיךָ בַּנּוֹאי תֵּן עֵינֶיךָ בַּמִּשְׁפָּחָה כול'. הָיְתָה בִּתּוֹ שֶׁלַּמֶּלֶךְ שׁוֹאֶלֶת מִבִּתּוֹ שֶׁלַּכֹּהֵן גָּדוֹל. בִּתּוֹ שֶׁלַּכֹּהֵן גָּדוֹל שׁוֹאֶלֶת מִבִּתּוֹ שֶׁלַּמֶּלֶךְ. הַכָּאוּרוֹת הָיוּ אוֹמְרוֹת. אַל תִּתֵּן עֵינֶיךָ(בַּנּוֹאי) [בַּנּוֹי]. וְהַנָּאוֹת הָיוּ אוֹמְרוֹת. תֵּן עֵינֶיךָ בַּמִּשְׁפָּחָה. וְכֵן הוּא אוֹמֵר צְאֶינָה וּרְאֶינָה בְּנוֹת צִיּוֹן בַּמֶּלֶךְ שְׁלֹמֹה בָּעֲטָרָה שֶׁעִיטְּרָה לּוֹ אִמּוֹ בְּיוֹם חֲתוּנָּתוֹ וּבְיוֹם שִׂמְחַת לִבּוֹ. בְּיוֹם חֲתוּנָּתוֹ זוֹ מַתַּן תּוֹרָה. וּבְיוֹם שִׂמְחַת לִבּוֹ זֶה בִּנְיַן בֵּית הַמִּקְדָּשׁ שֶׁיִּיבָּנֶה בִּמְהֵרָה בְיָמֵינוּ.

2 בתו | G ביתו   מבתו | G מביתו   2-3 בתו ... שלמלך | - G   5 לבו G ליבו   6 שייבנה | G יהי רצון שיבנה במהרה | G בימהרה

"What were they saying? Young man, lift your eyes and see what you are choosing for yourself. Do not fix your eye on beauty, fix you eyes on the extraction, etc." If she was the king's daughter she was borrowing from the High Priest's daughter; the High Priest's daughter was borrowing from the king's daughter[405]. The ugly ones did say, "do not fix your eye on beauty[406]," and the beautiful ones did say, "fix you eyes on the extraction." "And so it says[390], *Daughters of Zion go out and see king Solomon*[391], *with the crown with which his mother crowned him on the day of his marriage and the day of his heart's joy*. *The day of His enjoyment* is the giving of the Torah; *and the day of His heart's joy* is the building of His Temple which may be built soon in our days."

405 Babli 31a.
406 The corrector's spelling follows the (Babylonian) consensus, the spelling in both Yerushalmi texts is the etymologically correct one.

Introduction to Tractate Megillah

The name of the Tractate refers to the Esther scroll which is read connected to the festivities of Purim, but not necessarily on Purim. As a popular festivity, rejected by Sadducees, the celebration is justified in Pharisaic tradition by equating the Esther scroll with the Torah. This is aided by the fact that the Esther scroll is totally profane and therefore the general rule does not apply that Hagiographa and Prophets cannot serve as sources of religious rules, only as evidence of religious practices. The ninth Chapter of *Esther* therefore is analyzed as if it were a pentateuchal text. This can be qualified as anti-Sadducee demonstration.

The first part of the first Chapter discusses the dates of the reading under different circumstances; the festivities themselves are fixed on the 15th of Adar for fortified ancient places and the 14th for every other place. Since "Adar" in an intercalary year is repeated, this section is concluded with an enumeration of the differences regarding Purim between first and second Adar in such a year. The second part of the Chapter then is devoted to enumerations of differences in and extended discussion of the rules for related subjects, such as Sabbath and Holidays, different categories of vows, etc. Halakhot 1:2-5 contain some discussion of the computed calendar; Halakhah 1:11 mentions the Torah written in paleo-Hebrew script.

The second Chapter concentrates on the rules of the actual reading of the scroll and the weekly portions from the Pentateuch. The third Chapter brings the rules of synagogue buildings, synagogue services, and synagogue readings. The last Chapter then continues the rules of Torah and ancillary synagogue readings, with an appendix detailing the rules for *tefillin* and *mezuzzot*. The editor of the Venice *editio princeps* here invented a rule, proclaimed to originate in Moses's teachings on Mount Sinai, that the boxes of *tefillin* have to be black, while in both Talmudim the only rules are that the boxes be "square", i. e. cubes, and the straps black.

מגילה נקראת פרק ראשון מגילה

(fol.69d) **משנה א**: מְגִילָּה נִקְרֵאת בְּאַחַד עָשָׂר בִּשְׁנֵים עָשָׂר בִּשְׁלֹשָׁה עָשָׂר בְּאַרְבָּעָה עָשָׂר בַּחֲמִשָּׁה עָשָׂר לֹא פָחוֹת וְלֹא יָתֵר. כְּרַכִּים הַמּוּקָּפִין חוֹמָה מִימוֹת יְהוֹשֻׁעַ בֶּן נוּן קוֹרִין בַּחֲמִשָּׁה עָשָׂר. כְּפָרִים וַעֲיָירוֹת גְּדוֹלוֹת קוֹרִין בְּאַרְבָּעָה עָשָׂר אֶלָּא שֶׁהַכְּפָרִים מַקְדִּימִין לְיוֹם הַכְּנִיסָה:

Mishnah 1: The scroll[1] is read on the Eleventh, the Twelfth, the Thirteenth, the Fourteenth, the Fifteenth[2], no less and no more. Places walled[3] from the days of Joshua bin Nun[4] read on the Fifteenth. Hamlets[5] and large villages read on the Fourteenth, except that hamlets precede to the market day[6].

1 The Esther scroll read on Purim.
2 Of Adar; in an intercalary year the Adar preceding Nisan.
3 Greek χάραξ "palisade".
4 The reason is explained in the third paragraph of the Halakhah.
5 Who either have no organized prayer service since they count less than ten adult males or they have nobody competent to read the scroll.
6 Monday or Thursday preceding Purim.

On these days one reads the scroll in the local synagogue for the benefit of the peasants who come to town to sell their produce on the market. If the 14th, Purim, is on Sunday, one reads for the peasants on the 11th. If it falls on Wednesday or Sabbath, one reads on the 12th; on Tuesday or Friday one reads on the 13th. (In the computed calendar, the 14th never falls on Monday, Wednesday, or Sabbath; Note 89.)

(69d line 60) מְגִילָּה נִקְרֵאת כול'. רִבִּי אִילָא שִׁמְעוֹן בַּר בָּא בְּשֵׁם רִבִּי יוֹחָנָן. כָּתוּב לְקַיֵּים אֶת־יְמֵי הַפּוּרִים הָאֵלֶּה בִּזְמַנֵּיהֶם. מַה תַּלְמוּד לוֹמַר בִּזְמַנֵּיהֶם. רִבִּי יוֹנָה וְרִבִּי יוֹסֵה. רִבִּי יוֹנָה אָמַר. לִיתֵּן לָהֶן זְמַנִּים אֲחֵרִים. רִבִּי יוֹסֵה אוֹמֵר. זְמַנִּים שֶׁקָּבְעוּ לָהֶם חֲכָמִים. וַאֲפִילוּ הֵן. אַחַד עָשָׂר וּשְׁנֵים עָשָׂר וּשְׁלֹשָׁה עָשָׂר וְאַרְבָּעָה עָשָׂר וַחֲמִשָּׁה עָשָׂר. אוֹ אֵינוֹ אֶלָּא שִׁשָּׁה עָשָׂר וְשִׁבְעָה עָשָׂר. רִבִּי אַבָּהוּ בְשֵׁם רִבִּי לָעְזָר. לֹא יַעֲבֹר. וְלֹא יַעֲבֹר. רִבִּי יִצְחָק בַּר נַחְמָן בְּשֵׁם שְׁמוּאֵל. לֹא יַעֲבֹר. וְלֹא יַעֲבֹר. אוֹ אֵינוֹ אֶלָּא תְּשִׁיעִי וַעֲשִׂירִי. שְׁמוּאֵל בַּר נַחְמָן בְּשֵׁם רִבִּי יוֹנָתָן. יָמִים אֵין כָּתוּב כָּאן אֶלָּא כַּיָּמִים. תֵּן יָמִים כְּנֶגֶד יָמִים. אַחַד עָשָׂר וּשְׁנֵים עָשָׂר כְּנֶגֶד אַרְבָּעָה עָשָׂר וַחֲמִשָּׁה עָשָׂר. אוֹ שְׁנֵים עָשָׂר וּשְׁלֹשָׁה עָשָׂר כְּנֶגֶד אַרְבָּעָה עָשָׂר וַחֲמִשָּׁה עָשָׂר. אָמַר רִבִּי חֶלְבּוֹ. יוֹם שְׁלֹשָׁה עָשָׂר יוֹם מִלְחָמָה הָיָה. הוּא מוֹכִיחַ עַל עַצְמוֹ שֶׁאֵין בּוֹ נִיחָה. מֵעַתָּה אַל יִקְרָאוּ בוֹ. לְפָנָיו וּלְאַחֲרָיו קוֹרִין וּבוֹ אֵינָן קוֹרִין. אוֹ אֵינוֹ אֶלָּא תְּשִׁיעִי וַעֲשִׂירִי. כַּיָּמִים. יָמִים שֶׁהֵן סְמוּכִין לַיָּמִים.

וְאִם יָמִים שֶׁהֵן סְמוּכִין לַיָּמִים. אֵינָן אֶלָּא שִׁשָּׁה עָשָׂר וְשִׁבְעָה עָשָׂר. לֵית יְכִיל. דְּאָמַר רִבִּי אַבָּהוּ בְּשֵׁם רִבִּי אֶלְעָזָר. וְלֹא יַעֲבֹר. וְלֹא יְעַבֵּר. [רִבִּי יִצְחָק בַּר נַחְמָן בְּשֵׁם שְׁמוּאֵל. לֹא יַעֲבֹר. וְלֹא יַעֲבֹר.]

"The scroll is read," etc. Rebbi Ila, Simeon bar Abba in the name of Rebbi Johanan: *To confirm these Purim days in their times*[7]. Why does the verse say, *in their times*? Rebbi Jonah and Rebbi Yose. Rebbi Jonah says, to give them other times[8]. Rebbi Yose says, times which the Sages fixed for them. And those are these: the Eleventh, the Twelfth, the Thirteenth, the Fourteenth, the Fifteenth[9]. Or maybe only the Sixteenth and the Seventeenth? Rebbi Abbahu in the name of Rebbi Eleazar: *and it shall not pass by*[10], one shall not impregnate[11]. Rebbi Isaac bar Nahman in the name of Samuel: *and it shall not pass by*, and one shall not let it pass[12]. Maybe it is only the Ninth and the Tenth? Samuel bar Nahman in the name of Rebbi Jonathan: It is not written "days" but *like the days*[13], pair days with days, the Eleventh and Twelfth corresponding to Fourteenth and Fifteenth. Or the Twelfth and Thirteenth corresponding to Fourteenth and Fifteenth? Rebbi Helbo said, the Thirteenth was a day of war[14]. It proves for itself that it was not a day of comfort. Then one should not read on this day. One reads before and after, on the day one should not read[15]? Or only the Ninth and the Tenth? *Like the days*, days close to the days. But if days close to the days, {maybe} only Sixteenth and Seventeenth? You cannot, for Rebbi Abbahu said in the name of Rebbi Eleazar: *and it shall not pass by*, one shall not impregnate[11]. [Rebbi Isaac bar Nahman in the name of Samuel: *and it shall not pass by*, and one shall not let it pass.[16]]

7 *Esth.* 9:31.

8 He would allow other days than those enumerated in the Mishnah if circumstances demand it.

9 Since the days enumerated in the Mishnah are supposed to have been decreed by the Great Assembly, they could be modified only by an assembly of greater authority. It is unlikely that such an assembly ever could be convened. Differently in the Babli, 2a.

10 *Esth.* 9:27.

11 The language is taken from calendar computation where "intercalation" is called "impregnation". Here it means "changing the usual calendar data."

12 Reading the root עבר not as rabbinic Hebrew "to be pregnant" but as biblical Hebrew "to pass by". One may not celebrate Purim later than the last date mentioned in the Scroll, the 15th of Adar.

13 *Esth.* 9:22.
14 *Esth.* 9:1.
15 Excluding the 13th would be technically impossible. Cf. Meïri *Megillah,* ed. M. Herschler, pp. 14/15.
16 Corrector's addition from the earlier text, totally out of place since one speaks of predating, not postdating.

(70a line 2) תַּנֵּי בְשֵׁם רִבִּי נָתָן. כָּל־הַחוֹדֶשׁ כָּשֵׁר לִקְרִיאַת הַמְּגִילָה. מַה טַעַם. וְהַחוֹדֶשׁ אֲשֶׁר נֶהְפַּךְ לָהֶם מִיָּגוֹן לְשִׂמְחָה וגו׳. אָמַר רִבִּי חֶלְבּוֹ. וּבִלְבַד עַד חֲמִשָּׁה עָשָׂר. דְּאָמַר רִבִּי אַבָּהוּ בְשֵׁם רִבִּי לְעָזָר. לֹא יַעֲבוֹר. וְלֹא יַעֲבוֹר. רִבִּי יִצְחָק בַּר נַחְמָן בְּשֵׁם שְׁמוּאֵל. לֹא יַעֲבוֹר. וְלֹא יַעֲבוֹר. הָדָא דְאַתְּ אָמַר. לִקְרִיַּת הַמְּגִילָה. אֲבָל לַעֲשׂוֹת סְעוּדָה אֵינָן עוֹשִׁין אֶלָּא בְאַרְבָּעָה עָשָׂר וּבַחֲמִשָּׁה עָשָׂר. וְאֵין מְחַלְּקִין [לָעֲנִיִּים] אֶלָּא בְאַרְבָּעָה עָשָׂר וּבַחֲמִשָּׁה עָשָׂר. אֵין עֵינֵיהֶם שֶׁלְּעֲנִיִּים תְּלוּיוֹת אֶלָּא בְאַרְבָּעָה עָשָׂר וּבַחֲמִשָּׁה עָשָׂר. וְיִהְיוּ אֵילּוּ לִקְרִיאָה וְאֵילּוּ לִסְעוּדָה. רִבִּי חֶלְבּוֹ רִבִּי חוּנָה בְשֵׁם רַב. וְהַיָּמִים הָאֵלֶּה נִזְכָּרִים וְנַעֲשִׂים. נִזְכָּרִים בִּקְרִיאָה. וְנַעֲשִׂים בִּסְעוּדָה. זֹאת אוֹמֶרֶת שֶׁמְּגִלַּת אֶסְתֵּר נִיתְּנָה לְהִידָּרֵשׁ. רִבִּי חֶלְבּוֹ רִבִּי יָסָא בְשֵׁם רִבִּי לְעָזָר. נֶאֱמַר כָּאן דִּבְרֵי שָׁלוֹם וֶאֱמֶת׃ וְנֶאֱמַר לְהַקֵּל אֱמֶת קְנֵה וְאַל־תִּמְכּוֹר. הֲרֵי הִיא כַּאֲמִיתָּהּ שֶׁלַּתּוֹרָה. מָה זוֹ צְרִיכָה סִירְטוּט אַף זוֹ צְרִיכָה סִירְטוּט. מַה זוֹ נִיתְּנָה לְהִידָּרֵשׁ אַף זוֹ נִיתְּנָה לְהִידָּרֵשׁ. רִבִּי יִרְמְיָה בְשֵׁם רִבִּי שְׁמוּאֵל בַּר רַב יִצְחָק. מְגִילָּה שֶׁמָּסַר שְׁמוּאֵל לְדָוִד נִיתְּנָה לְהִידָּרֵשׁ. מַה טַעַם. הַכֹּל בִּכְתָב. זוֹ הַמְּסוֹרֶת. מִיַּד יְיָ׳. זוֹ רוּחַ הַקּוֹדֶשׁ. עָלַי הִשְׂכִּיל. מִיכָּן שֶׁנִּיתְּנָה לְהִידָּרֵשׁ. רִבִּי יִרְמְיָה בָעֵי. וְלָמָּה לֵינָן אֳמְרִין. וְתַבְנִית כֹּ"ל אֲשֶׁר הָיָה בָרוּחַ עִמּוֹ. אָמַר רִבִּי מָנָא. בְּרוּחַ פִּיו.

It was stated in the name of Rebbi Nathan: The entire month is qualified for reading the scroll[17]. What is the reason? *The month which for them was turned from sorrow to joy*[18]. Rebbi Ḥelbo said, but only up to the Fifteenth. As Rebbi Abbahu said in the name of Rebbi Eleazar: *and it shall not pass by*, one shall not impregnate[11]. Rebbi Isaac bar Naḥman in the name of Samuel: *and it shall not pass by*, and one shall not let it pass. That is what you are saying to read the scroll. But making a dinner[19] one makes only on the Fourteenth and the Fifteenth; and one distributes [to the poor][20] only on the Fourteenth and the Fifteenth. The eyes of the poor are only directed to the Fourteenth and the Fifteenth[21]. Then these should be for reading and those for the dinner? Rebbi Ḥelbo, Rebbi Huna in the name of Rav: *These days are remembered and executed*[22]. *Remembered* by reading. *And executed* by dinner. This implies that the Scroll is given to be analyzed[23] Rebbi Ḥelbo, Rebbi Yasa in the name of Rebbi Eleazar: It is said here[24], *words of peace and truth.* And it is said there,[25] *truth buy but do not sell*[26]. It is like the truth of the Torah. This one needs ruling, that one needs ruling[27]. This one is given to be analyzed, that one is given to be analyzed. Rebbi Jeremiah in the name of Rebbi Samuel bar Rav Isaac: The scroll which Samuel handed to David[28] is given to be analyzed. What is the reason? [29]*Everything in writing*, that is the Masora. *For the hand of the Eternal,* that is the Holy Spirit. *To me for understanding*, from here that it is given to be analyzed. Rebbi Jeremiah asked, and why do we not say, *the plan of everything was in spirit with him*[30]? Rebbi Mana said, the wind of his mouth[31].

17 For example a person going on a trip who probably will not have a scroll available to him on the days enumerated in the Mishnah can discharge his obligation by reading the scroll before his departure.

18 *Esth.* 9:22.

19 The obligatory dinner to celebrate Purim.

20 A separate obligation to give to the poor, *Esth.* 9:22.

21 Babli 4b.

22 *Esth.* 9:28.

23 While in principle a text posterior to the Pentateuch cannot prescribe any new obligation, only testify to the practice of earlier generations in the interpretation of the law, an exception is made for the Esther scroll, whose prescriptions are considered divine and in which the story is repeated in Chapter 9 for legal interpretation only. Since Sadducees did not recognize Esther as a canonical book, this elevation of the scroll to Pentateuchal status must be considered an anti-Sadducee demonstration.

24 *Esth.* 9:30.

25 *Prov.* 23:23.

26 It is permitted to pay for instruction in the Torah but forbidden to take money for teaching others. "Truth" in *Proverbs* always refers to the Torah.

27 Torah verses, as well as a Torah scroll, may only be written on lines, if parchment or leather impressed into the material with a metal ruler, if on paper the latter must be lined. (Babli 16b.)

28 With the plan for the building of the Temple.

29 *1Chr.* 28:19.

30 *1Chr.* 28:12.

31 רוח may be interpreted as Divine inspiration only if indicated as such in the verse.

(7a line 21) כְּרַכִּים הַמּוּקָפִין חוֹמָה מִימוֹת יְהוֹשֻׁעַ בֶּן נוּן קוֹרִין בַּחֲמִשָּׁה עָשָׂר. רִבִּי סִימוֹן בְּשֵׁם רִבִּי יְהוֹשֻׁעַ בֶּן לֵוִי. חִלְקוּ כָבוֹד לָאָרֶץ יִשְׂרָאֵל שֶׁהָיְתָה חֲרֵיבָה בְאוֹתָן הַיָּמִים וְתָלוּ אוֹתָהּ מִימוֹת יְהוֹשֻׁעַ בֶּן נוּן. וְיִקְרְאוּ הַכֹּל בַּחֲמִשָּׁה עָשָׂר. רִבִּי אַבָּהוּ דָּרַשׁ יְשִׁיבָה יְשִׁיבָה. מַה יְשִׁיבָה שֶׁנֶּאֱמַר לְהַלָּן מִימוֹת יְהוֹשֻׁעַ בֶּן נוּן אַף יְשִׁיבָה שֶׁנֶּאֱמַר כָּאן מִימוֹת יְהוֹשֻׁעַ בֶּן נוּן. וְיִקְרְאוּ הַכֹּל בְּאַרְבָּעָה עָשָׂר. רִבִּי יוּדָה בַּר פָּזִי דָּרַשׁ פְּרָזִי פְּרָזוֹת. נֶאֱמַר כָּאן פְּרָזוֹת וְנֶאֱמַר לְהַלָּן לְבַד מֵעָרֵי הַפְּרָזִי הַרְבֵּה מְאֹד: מַה פְּרָזִי שֶׁנֶּאֱמַר לְהַלָּן מִימוֹת יְהוֹשֻׁעַ בֶּן נוּן אַף פְּרָזִי שֶׁנֶּאֱמַר כָּאן מִימוֹת יְהוֹשֻׁעַ בֶּן נוּן. תַּנֵּי. רִבִּי יְהוֹשֻׁעַ בֶּן קָרְחָה אוֹמֵר. מִימוֹת אֲחַשְׁוֵרוֹשׁ. אָמַר לֵיהּ רִבִּי יוֹסֵי בֵּירִבִּי יְהוּדָה. וְכִי

מָה עִנְיָין שׁוּשַׁן הַבִּירָה לָבוֹא לְכָאן. אִם מִשּׁוּשַׁן הַבִּירָה אַתְּ לָמֵד מֵעַתָּה בְשׁוּשַׁן הַבִּירָה אֲל יִקְרְאוּ וּשְׁאָר כָּל־הַמְּקוֹמוֹת יִקְרָאוּ. הָא תְלָתָא תַנָּיִין. תַּנָּיָיא קַדְמָייָא סָבַר מֵימַר. מִימוֹת יְהוֹשֻׁעַ בֶּן נוּן. תַּנָּיָיא אַחֲרָייָא סָבַר מֵימַר. מִימוֹת אֲחַשְׁוֵרוֹשׁ. תַּנָּיָיא אַחֲרָייָא סָבַר מֵימַר. עִיר מִכָּל־מָקוֹם. נִמְצֵאתָה אוֹמֵר. רִבִּי יְהוֹשֻׁעַ בֶּן קָרְחָה וְרִבִּי יוֹסֵי בֵּירְבִּי יְהוּדָה שְׁנֵיהֶם אֲמָרוּ דָבָר אֶחָד. אֶלָּא שֶׁזֶּה לָמַד מִטַּעַם אֶחָד וְזֶה לָמַד מִטַּעַם אֶחָד. וְתַנֵּי כֵן. הַסָּמוּךְ לַכְּרַךְ וְהַנִּרְאֶה עִמּוֹ הֲרֵי הוּא כְיוֹצֵא בוֹ. רִבִּי אַייְבוֹ בַר נַגָּרֵי בְשֵׁם רִבִּי חִייָה בַר בָּא. כְּגוֹן הָדָא חֲמָתָה. לֹא אָמַר אֶלָּא כְּגוֹן. הָא חֲמַתָּה עַצְמָהּ מוּקֶּפֶת חוֹמָה מִימוֹת יְהוֹשֻׁעַ בֶּן נוּן. מִן הָדָא. וְעָרֵי מִבְצָר הַצִּדִּים צֵר וְחַמַּת רַקַּת וְכִינָרֶת: הַצִּידִים כְּפַר חִטַיָּיא. צֵר דִּסְמִיכָה לָהּ. חַמַּת חֲמָתָה. רַקַּת טִיבֶּרְיָא. כִּינֶּרֶת גִּינִיסַר. תָּתִיב רִבִּי לֵוִי. וְהֶכְתִיב וְהָעֲרָבָה וְהַיָּם כִּנְר֑וֹת. מֵעַתָּה שְׁנֵי גִּינִיסַרְיוֹת הָיוּ. אוֹ לֹא הָיוּ אֶלָּא שְׁנֵי אַבְטוֹנִיּוֹת. כְּגוֹן בֵּית יֶרַח וְצִינְבָרֵי. שֶׁהֵן מִגְדָּלוֹת כִּינָרִים. וְחָרַב הַכְּרַךְ וְנַעֲשָׂה שְׁלְגוֹיִם. אִיתָא חֲמֵי. בּוֹ אֵינָן קוֹרִין וּבְחוּצָה לָהּ קוֹרִין.

"Places walled from the days of Joshua bin Nun read on the Fifteenth." Rebbi Simon in the name of Rebbi Joshua ben Levi: They honored the Land of Israel which was desolate in those days and attached it to the days of Joshua bin Nun. Then should not everybody read on the Fifteenth? Rebbi Abbahu analyzed "dwelling, dwelling". Since "dwelling" mentioned there refers to the days of Joshua bin Nun, so also "dwelling" mentioned here refers to the days of Joshua bin Nun[32]. Then should not everybody read on the Fourteenth? Rebbi Jehudah bar Pazy analyzed "open, openness." It is said here "openness" and it said there[33] *except for very many open towns*. Since "open" mentioned there refers to the days of Joshua bin Nun, so also "openness" mentioned here refers to the days of Joshua bin Nun[34]. It was stated[35]: "Rebbi Joshua ben Qorḥa says, from the days of Ahasuerus. Rebbi Yose ben Rebbi Jehudah said to him, what has the reference to Susa the Fortress to do here? If you are inferring from Susa the Fortress then one should read in Susa the Fortress, but not read at any other place[36]." It seems that there are three Tannaim. The first Tanna intends to say, from the days of Joshua bin Nun. Another Tanna intends to say, from the days of Ahasuerus. Another Tanna intends to say, "town" in any case[37]. It turns out that you may say that Rebbi Joshua ben Qorḥa and Rebbi Yose ben Rebbi Jehudah say the same[38], only that each one of them infers from a separate argument; and it was stated so[35]: "what is close to a walled place and what is seen with it has the same standing as it[39]." Rebbi Ayvo bar Naggari in the name of Rebbi Ḥiyya bar Abba: For example like Ḥamata. Since he only said "like", therefore Ḥamata itself was walled in the days of Joshua bin Nun. From the following[40]: *Fortified towns, Haṣṣiddim, Ṣer, and Ḥamat, Raqqat, and Kinneret.* Haṣṣiddim is Wheat village[41], Ṣer is next to it, Ḥamat Ḥamata[42], Raqqat Tiberias[43], Kinneret, Genezareth. Rebbi Levi objected, is it not written[44], *the prairie to the Kinneret lake?* Were there two Genesareths[45]? Or were there only two autonomous districts[46], like Bet Yeraḥ and Zinbarai, which are towers on Lake Kinneret, where the fortification was abandoned and taken over by Gentiles. Come and see, there one does not read, outside one reads[47]?

32 The basis for this argument and the next one is *Esth.* 9:19: *Therefore the dispersed Jews who dwell in open towns celebrate the Fourteenth of the Month of Adar.* While this does not prove that the inhabitants of walled cities read on the Fifteenth, it makes clear that those in open towns do not read on the Fifteenth. The only question is whether the town has to be open at the time of reading or had to be open at the time of the conquest. Now "dwelling" is mentioned in the verse, and it is mentioned as a duty to dwell in the Land after the conquest in *Deut.* 12:10.

33 *Deut.* 3:5.

34 This argument to exclude dwellers in towns that are not open from reading on the 14th is quoted in the Babli 2b.

35 Tosephta 1:1.

36 Not even in the city of Susa which in the Scroll is clearly distinguished from the government complex, the Fortress.

37 In any town not walled at the time of reading one reads on the 14th.

38 It is not proven that R. Yose ben R. Jehudah disagrees with R. Joshua ben Qorḥa in practice since he does not proffer an alternative.

39 As Amoraic statement Babli 2b. These places read on the 15th.

40 *Jos.* 19:35, in the description of the territory of Naftali. Cf. Babli *Makkot* 10a.

41 Possibly Hattim on the plain above Tiberias.

42 In the Babli 6a this is identified as the hot springs of Tiberias (which, however, has no archeological remains of the time of Joshua.)

43 Tell Raqqat is slightly to the North of Herodian Tiberias.

44 *Jos.* 12:3, as Northern border of the kingdom of Sihon, given to the tribe of Gad.

45 Since the Jordan plain of Gad ended at the Southern end of the Sea of Galilee whereas Genezareth is close to its Northern end.

46 Greek ’αυτονομία.

47 Since this is unreasonable, one may only read in the suburbs on the 15th if there is organized communal reading in the city on the 15th.

(70a line 46) חִזְקִיָּה קָרֵי לָהּ בְּאַרְבָּעָה עָשָׂר וּבַחֲמִשָּׁה עָשָׂר. דּוּ חֲשַׁשׁ לָהִיא דְּתַנֵּי רִבִּי שִׁמְעוֹן בֶּן יוֹחַי. וְאִישׁ כִּי־יִמְכֹּר בֵּית־מוֹשַׁב עִיר חוֹמָה. פְּרָט לִטִיבֶּרְיָא שֶׁהַיָּם חוֹמָה לָהּ. רִבִּי יוֹחָנָן קָרֵי לָהּ בִּכְנִישְׁתָּא דְּכִיפְרָא. וְאָמַר. הָדָא הִיא עִיקַר טִיבֶּרְיָא קַדְמִייָתָא. וְלָא חֲשַׁשׁ לְהָדָא דְּתַנֵּי רִבִּי שִׁמְעוֹן בֶּן יוֹחַי. קַל הֵיקִילוּ בִקְרִייָאתָהּ. דְּתַנִּינָן תַּמָּן. כֹּל שֶׁהוּא לִפְנִים מִן הַחוֹמָה הֲרֵי הוּא כְּבָתֵּי עָרֵי חוֹמָה חוּץ מִן הַשָּׂדוֹת. רִבִּי מֵאִיר אוֹמֵר. אַף הַשָּׂדוֹת. וְתַנֵּי כֵן. הַסָּמוּךְ לַכַּרָךְ וְהַנִּרְאֶה עִמּוֹ הֲרֵי הוּא כְיוֹצֵא בּוֹ.

Hizqiah read it[48] on the Fourteenth and the Fifteenth, since he was apprehensive about what Rebbi Simeon ben Yoḥay had stated, *a person who would sell a dwelling-house in a walled city*[49], that excludes Tiberias whose wall is the lake[50]. Rebbi Johanan read it in the Kifra synagogue and said, this is the main ancient Tiberias[51]; he was not apprehensive about what Rebbi Simeon ben Yoḥay had stated. They were lenient in matters of reading it, as we have stated there[52]: "Anything inside the walls is treated as a house of a walled city except fields. Rebbi Meïr says, even fields." And it was stated so[35]: "what is close to a walled place and what is seen with it has the same standing as it.[53]"

48 The Esther scroll in Tiberias. Babli 5b.
49 *Lev.* 25:29.
50 While Herodian Tiberias had a wall on the land side since there was none on the lake side it was of little military value. The question is whether such military value is required for the definition of "walled city" both for the laws of the Jubilee and for reading the Scroll.
51 It seems that this synagogue (at other places called Kufra) was outside the wall. In his opinion this was the original Raqqat which was encroached upon by Herod building Tiberias.
52 Mishnah *Arakhin* 9:5, about the rules of houses in walled cities for which there exists a right of buying back only during one year.
53 While R. Simeon ben Yoḥay may be correct for the laws of the Jubilee, his argument is irrelevant for reading the Scroll.

(70a line 53) אָמַר רִבִּי יוֹחָנָן. מִגִּבְּתוֹן וְעַד אַנְטִיפַּרִיס שִׁשִּׁים רִיבּוֹא עֲיָירוֹת הָיוּ. [וְהַקְּטַנָּה] שֶׁבָּהֶן הָיְתָה בֵית שֶׁמֶשׁ. מַה כְּתִיב בָּהּ וַיַּךְ בְּאַנְשֵׁי בֵית־שֶׁמֶשׁ כִּי רָאוּ בָּאֲרוֹן י"י וגו'. וְאִילּוּ מֵרוּחַ אַחַת הָיוּ. וּכְדוֹן אִין אַתְּ מְבַצֵּעַ לָהּ קָנַיי לָא נְסַבָה. אָמַר רִבִּי חֲנִינָה. קָפְצָה לָהּ אֶרֶץ יִשְׂרָאֵל.

[54]Rebbi Johanan said, from Gibbethon to Antipatris there were 60'000 villages. The smallest among them was Bet Shemesh, about which it is written[55], *He smote of the men of Bet Shemesh, for they looked at the Ark of*

the Eternal, etc. These were in one direction. If you execute this with reeds it will not carry it. Rebbi Ḥanina said, the Land of Israel folded its fist.

54 *Taʿaniot* 4:8, Notes 340-342.   55 *1S.* 6:19.

(70a line 57) כָּל־הָעֲיָירוֹת שֶׁמָּנָה יְהוֹשֻׁעַ אֲפִילוּ מֵאָה אֵינוּן. רִבִּי שִׁמְעוֹן בֶּן לָקִישׁ אָמַר. מוּקָפוֹת חוֹמָה מָנָה. רִבִּי יוֹסֵי בַּר חֲנִינָה אָמַר. הַסְּמוּכוֹת לִסְפַר מָנָה. קִרְיָיא מְסַייֵעַ לְרִבִּי יוֹסֵי בַּר חֲנִינָה. וַיְהִי גְבוּלָם מֵחֶלֶף (מֵאֵילוֹן בְּצַעֲנַנִּים) [וגו׳. וְקַטָּת וְנַהֲלָל וְשִׁמְרוֹן וְיִדְאֲלָה וּבֵית לֶחֶם]. מֵחֶלֶף חֶלֶף. מֵאֵילוֹן אַיְילִין. בְּצַעֲנַנִּים אֲגַנַּיָּיא דְקֶדֶשׁ. הַנֶּקֶב צַיְידָתָה. וְיַבְנְאֵל כְּפַר יַמָּא. עַד־לַקּוּם לוֹקִים. וְקַטָּת קְטוּנִית. וְנַהֲלָל מַהֲלוּל. וְשִׁמְרוֹן סִימוֹנִיָּיה. וְיִדְאֲלָה חִירִיָּה. בֵּית לֶחֶם בֵּית לֶחֶם צָרִיָּיה.

רִבִּי אֲחָא רִבִּי יוּדָה בֶן לֵוִי רִבִּי יְהוֹשֻׁעַ בֶּן לֵוִי בְּשֵׁם רִבִּי. לוֹד וְגֵיא הַחֲרָשִׁים מוּקָפוֹת חוֹמָה מִימוֹת יְהוֹשֻׁעַ בֶּן נוּן. וְלָמָּה לֹא אָמַר וְאוֹנוֹ. בְּגִין דִּכְתִיב. וְהָא כְתִיב לוֹד וְאִיתְאֲמָרַת. אֶלָּא בְגִין דִּתְנִינָן. וְגִמְלָא וְגָדוּר וְחָדִיד וְאוֹנוֹ וִירוּשָׁלַיִם וְכֵן כַּיּוֹצֵא בָהֶן. וְהָכְתִיב וּבְנֵי אֶלְפַּעַל עֵבֶר וּמִשְׁעָם וָשֶׁמֶר הוּא בָּנָה אֶת־אוֹנוֹ וְאֶת־לוֹד וּבְנוֹתֶיהָ. אָמַר רִבִּי לָעָזָר בֵּירִבִּי יוֹסֵה. בִּימֵי פִילֶגֶשׁ בַּגִּבְעָה חָרְבָה וְעָמַד אֶלְפַּעַל וּבְנָיָּיהּ. הָדָא הִיא דִכְתִיב גַּם כָּל־הֶעָרִים הַנִּמְצָאוֹת שִׁלְּחוּ בָאֵשׁ. רִבִּי חֲנַנְיָה בְּשֵׁם רִבִּי פִינְחָס. לוֹד וְאוֹנוֹ הֵן הֵן גֵּיא הַחֲרָשִׁים.

All the towns which Joshua enumerated are at least one hundred. Rebbi Simeon ben Laqish said, he enumerated those walled. Rebbi Yose bar Ḥanina said, he enumerated those close to the border. The verse supports Rebbi Yose bar Ḥanina: *their border was Meḥelef*[56] [etc. *And Qaṭṭat, and Nahallal, and Shimron, and Yedeala, and Bet Leḥem*[57].] *Meḥelef,* Ḥelef. *Me'elon,* Aylin. *Basaʿananim,* Basin of Qedesh. *And Adami,* Damin. *Ḥanneqeb,* Saidata. *And Yabneel,* Kefar Yama. *Up to Laqqum,* Loqim[58]. *And Qaṭṭat,* Qetonit. *And Nahallal,* Mahlul. *And Shimron,* Simonieh. *And Yedeala,* Ḥirieh. *And Bet Leḥem,* Bet Leḥem Ṣarieh[59].

Rebbi Aḥa, Rebbi Jehudah ben Levi, Rebbi Joshua ben Levi in the name of Rebbi: Lod and *Ge-Haharašim*[60] were walled from the times of Joshua bin Nun. Why did he not say, "and Ono"? Because it is written[61]. But so is Lod and it was mentioned. But because it was stated[62], "Gamla, Gedor, Ḥadid, and Ono, and Jerusalem, and those similar to them." But is it not written[63], *The sons of Elpaʿal: Ever, and Misham, and Shemer; he built Ono and Lod and its dependencies?* Rebbi Eleazar ben Rebbi Yose said, it was destroyed in the times of the Concubine at Gibea[64]; Elpaʿal rebuilt it. That is what is written[65], *also all existing towns they put to the fire.* Rebbi Ḥanania in the name of Rebbi Phineas: Lod and Ono are *Ge-Haharašim*⁶⁶.

56 *Jos.* 19:33. The verse establishes that the localities mentioned in *Jos.* are boundary markers, in this case of Naftali. All localities mentioned in the verse will be identified later in the paragraph.

57 *Jos.* 19:15, description of the border between Zevulun and Naftali. Addition by the corrector since the localities will later be discussed in the text. But since of the first verse only one locality was named, the addition seems to be unwarranted. Clearly, the interest is on Tiberias and its wider neighborhood.

58 Most of the places are not identified. If the root of בצעננים is בצעה "swamp", the translation would have to be "swamp near Qedesh Naftali." *Damin* seems to be the village of *Dameh* near Tiberias. *Ḥanneqeb* seems to be Arabic נקב "hole, breach", a good description for the mountain pass controlling the road from Tiberias to the Mediterranean. *Kefar Yama* may be the place Yamnia mentioned by Josephus (*Bell.* II.xx.6) in Galilee.

59 The places mentioned in *Jos.* 19:15, in the center of Lower Galilee; in Talmudic times the region of Sepphoris. Except for the Galilean Bet Leḥem the places are unidentified.

60 Mentioned first in *Neh.* 11:35 as settlements in the region of Benjamin. Babli 4a.

61 *Neh.* 11:35.

62 Mishnah *Arakhin* 9:6, describing walled cities.

63 *1Chr.* 8:12, descendants of Benjamin.

64 Babli 4a.

65 *Jud.* 20:48.

66 It is possible to read *Neh.* 11:35 as: *Lod and Ono are Ge-Harašim* (valley of the artisans.) He therefore disagrees with Rebbi's statement.

(70a line 73) רִבִּי חֶלְבּוֹ רִבִּי חוּנָה בְּשֵׁם רִבִּי חִייָה רַבָּה. הַכֹּל יוֹצְאִין בְּאַרְבָּעָה עָשָׂר שֶׁהִיא זְמַן קְרִיאָתָהּ. לֹא בָא אֶלָּא לְלַמְּדָךְ שֶׁהַמִּצְווֹת נוֹהֲגוֹת בָּאֲדָר שֵׁינִי. רִבִּי יוֹסֵי וְרִבִּי אָחָא הָוון יְתִיבִין. אָמַר רִבִּי יוֹסֵי לְרִבִּי אָחָא. לֹא מִסְתַּבְּרָא לְשֶׁעָבַר אֲבָל לַבָּא. וְהָא תַנֵּי. מְקוֹם שֶׁנָּהֲגוּ לִקְרוֹתָהּ שְׁנֵי יָמִים קוֹרִין אוֹתָהּ שְׁנֵי יָמִים. אָמַר לֵיהּ. אוֹף אֲנָא סָבַר כֵּן. אָמַר רִבִּי מָנָא. וְיָאוּת. אִילוּ מִי שֶׁקְּרָייָהּ בְּאַרְבָּעָה עָשָׂר וְחָזַר וּקְרָייָהּ בַּחֲמִשָּׁה עָשָׂר שֶׁמָּא אֵין שׁוֹמְעִין לוֹ. אִם אוֹמֵר אַתְּ כֵּן שֶׁמָּא נִמְצֵאתָהּ עוֹקֵר זְמַן כָּרְכִים בְּיָדָיו.

Rebbi Ḥelbo, Rebbi Huna in the name of the Great Rebbi Ḥiyya. Everybody may fulfill his obligation on the Fourteenth, which is the time of its reading⁶⁷. It only comes to teach you that the obligations apply to the Second Adar⁶⁸. Rebbi Yose and Rebbi Aḥa were sitting together. Rebbi Yose said to Rebbi Aḥa, it is only reasonable for the past; but for the future⁶⁹? And did we not state, at a place where one is used to read it on two days, one reads it on two days? He said to him, I also am of this opinion. Rebbi Mana said, this is correct. If somebody read it on the Fourteenth and read it again on the Fifteenth, would one not listen to him? If you are saying so[70], with your hand you uproot the time of walled places.

67 *Šeqalim* 1:1, Note 24; also quoted twice in the sequel. He asserts that even though villagers may read early and inhabitants of walled cities have to read on the Fifteenth, reading on the Fourteenth satisfies the basic requirement. Those who are reading on both days, as mentioned later, because the tradition about the existence of a walled settlement in the days of Joshua bin Nun is not reliable, do not recite a benediction on the second day.

68 As explained in *Šeqalim*, if the Scroll was read on the 15th of Adar and then an intercalary month was declared, the reading has to be repeated but even in a walled town may be read on the 14th.

69 If the scroll was read by error on the 14th it does not have to be repeated since the basic obligation was fulfilled, but a place which by tradition is obligated to read on the 15th cannot be permitted in the future to read on the 14th.

70 That a place reading and celebrating on the 15th may be permitted to change to the 14th.

(4 line 70b) נַחְמָן בְּרֵיהּ דְּרִבִּי שְׁמוּאֵל בַּר נַחְמָן. שִׂמְחָה וְשָׂשׂוֹן מִיכָּן שֶׁהֵן אֲסוּרִין בְּהֶסְפֵּד. וּמִשְׁתֶּה מִיכָּן שֶׁאֲסוּרִין בְּתַעֲנִית. וְיוֹם טוֹב מִיכָּן שֶׁאֲסוּרִין בַּעֲשִׂיַּית מְלָאכָה. אָמַר רִבִּי חֶלְבּוֹ. זִימְנִין סַגִּין יָתְבִית קוֹמֵי רִבִּי שְׁמוּאֵל בַּר נַחְמָן וְלָא שְׁמָעִית מִינֵיהּ הָדָא מִילְתָא. אֲמַר לֵיהּ. כָּל־מַה דַּהֲוָה אַבָּא שְׁמִיעַ אַתְּ שְׁמִיעַ. מִילְתֵיהּ דְּרִבִּי פְּלִיגָא. דְּרִבִּי הָיָה מְפַרְסֵם עַצְמוֹ שְׁנֵי יָמִים בַּשָּׁנָה. רוֹחֵץ בְּשִׁבְעָה עָשָׂר בְּתַמּוּז וְנוֹטֵעַ נְטִיעוֹת בְּפוּרִים. רִבִּי חֲבִיבָה בְּשֵׁם רַבָּנָן דְּתַמָּן. בְּכָל־מָקוֹם [שֶׁכָּתוּב] יוֹם טוֹב אֵין כָּתוּב וְקִיבֵּל. בְּכָל־מָקוֹם שֶׁכָּתוּב וְקִיבֵּל אֵין כָּתוּב יוֹם טוֹב. וְכָאן כָּתוּב יוֹם טוֹב וְכָתוּב וְקִיבֵּל. רִבִּי סִימוֹן בְּשֵׁם רִבִּי שְׁמוּאֵל בַּר נַחְמָן. מִשְׁפָּחָה וּמִשְׁפָּחָה אֵילוּ הַכְּפָרִים. מְדִינָה וּמְדִינָה אֵילוּ הַכְּרָכִים. וְעִיר וָעִיר אֵילוּ הָעֲיָירוֹת.

Nahman the son of Rebbi Samuel bar Nahman: *Joy and enjoyment*[71], this implies that eulogies are forbidden. *And festive dinner*, this implies that fasting is forbidden. *And holiday,* this implies that work is forbidden[72]. Rebbi Helbo said, many times I sat before Rebbi Samuel bar Nahman but did not hear these things from him. He said to him, did you hear all the traditions which my father had? The action of Rebbi disagrees, for Rebbi acted demonstratively on two days in the year. He took a bath on the Seventeenth of Tammuz[73] and planted saplings on Purim[74]. Rebbi Habiba in the names of the Rabbis of there: Any place where it is written *holiday* it is not written *they accepted*, and any place where it is written *they accepted* it is not written *holiday*⁷⁵. And here it is written *holiday* and it is written *they accepted*⁷⁶? Rebbi Simon in the name of Rebbi Samuel bar Naḥman: *Family and family*, these are the hamlets. *City and city*, these are the fortified places. *Town and town*, these are the small towns⁷⁷.

71 The entire statement is an explanation of *Esth.* 9:10, but the expression "joy and enjoyment" is from 8:17 instead of the correct "joy" (as in the Babli, 5b.)

72 The Babli notes that it is not clear from the statement whether this refers to both days of Purim or only to the day celebrated in the community.

73 To emphasize that the restrictions of the 9ᵗʰ of Av do not apply to the 17ᵗʰ of Tammuz.

74 To make it clear that work is not forbidden on Purim; Babli 5b.

75 In the list of *Esth.* 9:19 "holiday" is mentioned, but in the note 9:22 that the Jews accepted the rules of Purim, only joy and dinner are mentioned (in addition to obligations to send food to one another and gifts to the poor.)

76 This can be read either as proof of R. Helbo's position (as a question), or (as a statement) by Nahman that 9:23 asserts that the Jews accepted all that Mordocai had written to them, implicitly endorsing the holiday status.

77 *Esth.* 9:28; Babli 2b.

(70b line 15) תַּנֵּי שְׁמוּאֵל. מִפְּנֵי מַה מַקְדִּימִין לְיוֹם הַכְּנִיסָה. כְּדֵי שֶׁיְּסַפְּקוּ [מַיִם וּ]מָזוֹן לַאֲחֵיהֶם שֶׁבַּכְּרָכִים. רִבִּי פִילִיפָּא בַּר פְּרוֹטָא אָמַר קוֹמֵי רִבִּי יוֹנָה. לֵית הָדָא אֲמָרָה שֶׁאָסוּר בַּעֲשִׂיַּת מְלָאכָה. אָמַר לֵיהּ. אִין מִן הָדָא לֵית שְׁמַע מִינָהּ כְּלוּם. הֲרֵי חוֹלוֹ שֶׁלְּמוֹעֵד הֲרֵי הוּא אָסוּר בַּעֲשִׂיַּת מְלָאכָה וְהֵן מְסַפְּקִין מָזוֹן לַאֲחֵיהֶם שֶׁבַּכְּרָכִים. לֵית לָךְ אֶלָּא כְהָדָא דְרִבִּי. דְּרִבִּי הָיָה מְפָרְסֵם עַצְמוֹ שְׁנֵי יָמִים בַּשָּׁנָה. רוֹחֵץ בְּשִׁבְעָה עָשָׂר בְּתַמּוּז וְנוֹטֵעַ נְטִיעוֹת בְּפוּרִים.

Samuel stated: Why do they⁷⁸ precede to the market day? So they may provide [water and]⁷⁹ food to their brothers in the fortified places⁷⁹. Rebbi Philippos ben Protos said before Rebbi Jonah: Could this mean that it is forbidden for {agricultural} work⁸⁰? He said to him, if from this you can conclude nothing. Are there not the intermediate days of holidays which are forbidden for {agricultural} work⁸¹ but they provide food to their brothers in the fortified places. You only have this from Rebbi, for Rebbi acted demonstratively on two days in the year. He took a bath on the Seventeenth of Tammuz⁷³ and planted saplings on Purim⁸².

78 The inhabitants of isolated hamlets.

79 Corrector's addition from the Babli 4a, to be deleted. Water is drawn from local wells.

80 If you invite the farmers to listen to the reading of the scroll in the city synagogue because you want them to bring their produce to the local market, do you not tell them to harvest their produce early in the morning and this certainly is agricultural work.

81 As explained in *Mo`ed qaṭan*, work forbidden on the intermediate days of holidays essentially is agricultural work.

82 Therefore Rebbi choose agricultural work to perform in public on Purim.

(70b line 21) רִבִּי יוּסְטָא בֵּירְבִּי שׁוּנֶם בְּעָא קוֹמֵי רִבִּי מָנָא. וְלֹא עֶזְרָה תִּיקֵן שֶׁיְּהוּ קוֹרִין בַּתּוֹרָה בַּשֵּׁינִי וּבַחֲמִישִׁי וּבַשַּׁבָּת בַּמִּנְחָה. וּמָרְדְּכַי וְאֶסְתֵּר מְתַקְּנִים אַל מַה שֶׁעֶזְרָה עָתִיד לְהַתְקִין. אָמַר לֵיהּ. מִי שֶׁסִּידֵּר אֶת הַמִּשְׁנָה סָמְכָהּ לַמִּקְרָא. מִשְׁפָּחָה וּמִשְׁפָּחָה מְדִינָה וּמְדִינָה וְעִיר וָעִיר.

Rebbi Justus ben Rebbi Shunem asked before Rebbi Mana: Did not Ezra institute that one reads in the Torah Mondays, Thursdays, and Sabbath afternoon[83]? And Mordocai and Esther institute on basis of what Ezra will institute in the future[84]? He said to him, he who ordered the Mishnah based it on Scripture: *Family and family, city and city, town and town*[85].

83 Babli *Bava qamma* 82a (and below Halakhah 4:1, 75a l. 21). The Torah reading on Sabbath morning is attributed to Moses.

84 Since the text dates Purim to Xerxes but Ezra to Artaxerxes, basing a date for the reading of the Scroll on an institution of Ezra clearly is anachronistic.

85 *Esth.* 9:28. No fixed dates are indicated, only that there are variable times according to circumstances. The fixation of market days to Monday and Thursday is a later development in the many centuries between Persian rule and Mishna composition.

(fol. 69d) **משנה ב:** כֵּיצַד חָל לִהְיוֹת בַּשֵּׁנִי כְּפָרִים וַעֲיָירוֹת גְּדוֹלוֹת קוֹרִין בּוֹ בַּיּוֹם וּמוּקָּפוֹת חוֹמָה לְמָחָר. חָל לִהְיוֹת בַּשְּׁלִישִׁי אוֹ בָּרְבִיעִי כְּפָרִים מַקְדִּימִין לְיוֹם הַכְּנִיסָה וַעֲיָירוֹת גְּדוֹלוֹת קוֹרִין בּוֹ בַּיּוֹם וּמוּקָּפוֹת חוֹמָה לְמָחָר.

Mishnah 2: How is this? If it falls on Monday, hamlets and large villages read on this day, but walled cities the next day. If it falls on Tuesday or Wednesday, hamlets precede to the market day, large villages read on this day, but walled cities the next day.

(70b line 25) **הלכה ב:** כָּל־הֵן דְּתַנִּינָן חָל לִהְיוֹת בְּאַרְבָּעָה עָשָׂר אֲנָן קַיָּימִין. אָמַר רִבִּי יוֹסֵה. מַתְנִיתָא אֲמָרָהּ כֵּן. מוּקָּפוֹת חוֹמָה לְמָחָר. אָמַר רִבִּי יוֹסֵה. לֵית כָּאן חָל לִהְיוֹת בַּשֵּׁינִי נוֹלֵית

כָּאן] חָל לִהְיוֹת בַּשַׁבָּת. חָל לִהְיוֹת בַּשֵּׁינִי צוֹמָא רַבָּא בְּחַד בְּשׁוּבָא. חָל לִהְיוֹת בַּשַׁבָּת צוֹמָא רַבָּא בַּעֲרוּבְתָא.

Halakhah 2: In all cases where we are stating "if it falls" it refers to the Fourteenth[86]. Rebbi Yose said, the Mishnah implies this, "walled cities the next day." Rebbi Yose[87] said, there is no "if it falls on Monday", [there is no] "if it falls on the Sabbath.[88]" If it falls on Monday, the Great Fast Day is on Sunday; if it falls on the Sabbath, the Great Fast Day falls on Friday[89].

---

86 Of Adar (II).

87 Who published the calendar rules which insure that the Day of Atonement never falls on Friday or Sunday (*Eruvin* Chapter 3, Note 199.)

88 Mishnah 4.

89 In the computed calendar only the lengths of the Months Marḥeshwan and Kislew are variable. Therefore if the day of the week of any date after 1 Tevet is known, the day of week of any later date in the year may easily be computed. In addition, the Adar preceding Nisan always has 29 days. After the 14th, there are 15 days left in Adar. From Nisan 1 to Tishre 1 are three months of 30 days and three of 29 days. Together with the 10 days of Tishre to the Day of Atonement this makes

15+90+87+10 = 202 = 29×7 - 1.

Therefore the day of the week of the Day of Atonement is the day of the week of the 13th of Adar.

The calendar rules give an easy mnemonic rule for the determination of the days of the week for the holidays (the first days of the holidays in the Diaspora): One writes the 6 first letters of the alphabet (representing numbers), and under them the 6 last in inverse order (representing holidays):

א ב ג ד ה ו
ת ש ר ק צ פ

which is read as: The first day of Passover is the same weekday as the Ninth of Av (תשעה באב); the second day the same weekday as Pentecost (שבועות), the third day the same weekday as New Year's day (ראש השנה); the fourth day used not to have a counterpart; today it is Israel Independence Day (קוממיות); the fifth day is the same weekday as the Day of Atonement (צום כיפור), the sixth day the same as the preceding Purim (פורים). This shows that the following Day of Atonement always is on the weekday preceding that of the 14th of Adar. Since the calendar rules (explained in the author's edition of *Seder Olam*) are made to exclude New Year's Day from Sunday, Wednesday, and Friday, or the Day of Atonement from Tuesday, Friday, Sunday, they automatically exclude Monday, Thursday, and Sabbath from being the 14th of Adar. The question remains why the exclusion of Thursday is not mentioned by R. Yose. While the exclusion of Friday and Sunday from being the Day of Atonement is a necessity because of the Fast, the exclusion of Tuesday is only a desideratum (cf. *Sukkah* 4:2, Note 20.)

(fol. 69d) **משנה ג**: חָל לִהְיוֹת בַּחֲמִישִׁי כְּפָרִים וַעֲיָירוֹת גְּדוֹלוֹת קוֹרִין בּוֹ בַּיּוֹם וּמֻקָּפוֹת חוֹמָה לְמָחָר.

משנה ד: חָל לִהְיוֹת עֶרֶב שַׁבָּת כְּפָרִים מַקְדִּימִין לְיוֹם הַכְּנִיסָה וַעֲיָירוֹת גְּדוֹלוֹת וּמֻקָּפוֹת חוֹמָה קוֹרִין בּוֹ בַּיּוֹם.

Mishnah 3: If it falls on Thursday, hamlets and large villages read on this day, but walled cities on the next day.

Mishnah 4: If it falls on Friday, hamlets precede to the market day[90], large villages and walled cities read on this day[91].

90 Thursday.
91 One forbids reading the scroll on a Sabbath, to avoid having a person carrying the scroll in the public domain in a place having no *eruv*.

(70b line 30) **הלכה ג**: בָּעוּן קוֹמֵי רִבִּי זְעִירָא. אִיתָא חֲמֵי. חָל לִהְיוֹת לַכְּרַכִּים בַּשַּׁבָּת קוֹרִין בְּעֶרֶב שַׁבָּת. חָל לִהְיוֹת לַעֲיָירוֹת בַּשַּׁבָּת יִדָּחוּ לְיוֹם הַכְּנִיסָה. אָמַר רִבִּי לָא. מִפְּנֵי כְבוֹד הַכְּרַכִּים. שֶׁלֹּא יְהוּ אוֹמְרִין. רָאִינוּ כַרְכִּים וַעֲיָירוֹת קוֹרִין כְּאַחַת. מֵעַתָּה לֹא יִדָּחוּ לְיוֹם הַכְּנִיסָה. שֶׁלֹּא יְהוּ אוֹמְרִין. רָאִינוּ כְּפָרִים וַעֲיָירוֹת קוֹרִין כְּאַחַת. מֵעַתָּה חָל לִהְיוֹת בַּשֵּׁינִי. חָל לִהְיוֹת בַּחֲמִישִׁי. חָל לִהְיוֹת בַּשַּׁבָּת. אַשְׁכַּח תַּנֵּי. כְּפָרִים [וַעֲיָירוֹת] וַכְרַכִּים קוֹרִין כְּאַחַת. וְהָהֵן תַּנָּיָיה לָא נָסַב (אֲפִילוּ) [אַפָּה] לַבִּירְיָיה. דְּאִית לֵיהּ שֶׁלֹּא יְקַדְּמוּ כְרַכִּים לַעֲיָירוֹת. דְּאִית לֵיהּ כָּל־שֶׁהוּא נִדְחֶה מִמְּקוֹמוֹ יִדָּחֶה לְיוֹם הַכְּנִיסָה. רִבִּי אוֹמֵר. כּוֹלְהוֹן יִדָּחוּ לְיוֹם הַכְּנִיסָה. דְּאִית לֵיהּ שֶׁלֹּא יְקַדְּמוּ כְרַכִּים לַעֲיָירוֹת. דְּאִית לֵיהּ. כָּל־שֶׁהוּא נִדְחֶה מִמְּקוֹמוֹ יִדָּחֶה לְיוֹם הַכְּנִיסָה. הֵיךְ עֲבָדִין עוֹבְדָא. אָמַר רִבִּי יוֹסֵה. כְּמַתְנִיתָהּ.

Halakhah 3: They asked before Rebbi Ze`ira[92]: Come and see, if it falls so that in walled cities one should read on the Sabbath, one reads on Friday[93]. If it falls so that in villages one should read on the Sabbath, it is being pushed to the market day[94]! Rebbi La said, because of the honor of walled cities, that one should not say, we saw walled cities and villages read at the same day. Then it should not be pushed to the market day, that one should not say, we saw hamlets and villages read on the same day. Then if it falls on Monday, falls on [Thursday, falls on][95] the Sabbath? It was found stated, Hamlets [and villages][96] and walled cities may read together; and this Tanna does not show (respect) [even][97] for any creature. He holds that walled cities cannot precede villages; he holds that any which is pushed away is pushed to the market day. "Rebbi says, all shall be pushed to the market day.[98]" For he holds that walled cities cannot precede villages; for he holds that any which is pushed away is pushed to the market day. How does one act? Rebbi Yose said, following the Mishnah[99].

92 Two generations before R. Yose, when the 14th on Monday and Sabbath was not impossible.
93 Mishnah 4.
94 Mishnah 5.
95 Corrector's addition, probably against the intent of the original compiler, cf. Note 87.
96 Corrector's addition. Since villages always read between hamlets and walled cities, the note is correct but logically unnecessary.
97 The [corrector's] note is incomprehensible; follow the (scribe's) text.
98 Tosephta 1:2; Babli 4b.
99 In all actual cases one follows the applicable one of Mishnaiot 2-5

(fol. 69d) **משנה ה**: חָל לִהְיוֹת בַּשַּׁבָּת כְּפָרִים וַעֲיָירוֹת גְּדוֹלוֹת מַקְדִּימִין וְקוֹרִין לְיוֹם הַכְּנִיסָה וּמוּקָּפוֹת חוֹמָה לְמָחָר.

Mishnah 5: If it falls on the Sabbath, hamlets and large villages precede and read on the market day, but walled cities on the next day.

(70b line 41) **הלכה ד**: בָּעוּן קוֹמֵי רִבִּי זְעוּרָה. כְּמָה דְּאַתְּ אָמַר תַּמָּן. חָל לִהְיוֹת לַכְּרַכִּים בַּשַּׁבָּת קוֹרִין בְּעֶרֶב שַׁבָּת. חָל לִהְיוֹת לַעֲיָירוֹת בַּשַּׁבָּת יִקְרְאוּ בְּעֶרֶב שַׁבָּת. אֶלָּא מַתְנִיתָה בִּתְרֵין תַּנָּיִיא. תַּנָּיָיא קַדְמָייָא סְבַר מֵימָר. כָּל־שֶׁהוּא נִדְחֶה מִמְּקוֹמוֹ יִדָּחֶה לְיוֹם הַכְּנִיסָה. [וְתַנָּיָיא חוֹרָנָא סְבַר מֵימָר. כָּל־שֶׁהוּא נִדְחֶה מִמְּקוֹמוֹ לֹא יִדָּחֶה לְיוֹם הַכְּנִיסָה.] אָמַר לוֹן. כֵּן אָמַר רַב. חַד תַּנָּיָיא הוּא. מִפְּנֵי מָה אָמְרוּ. חָל לִהְיוֹת לַכְּרַכִּים בַּשַּׁבָּת קוֹרִין בְּעֶרֶב שַׁבָּת. דְּאָמַר רִבִּי חֶלְבּוֹ רַב חוּנָה רַב בְּשֵׁם רִבִּי חִייָה רַבָּה. הַכֹּל יוֹצְאִין בְּאַרְבָּעָה עָשָׂר שֶׁהוּא זְמַן קְרִיאָתָהּ. וְדִכְוָותָהּ. חָל לִהְיוֹת לַעֲיָירוֹת בַּשַּׁבָּת. דְּאָמַר רִבִּי חֶלְבּוֹ. יוֹם שְׁלֹשָׁה עָשָׂר יוֹם מִלְחָמָה הָיָה. וְהוּא מוֹכִיחַ עַל עַצְמוֹ שֶׁאֵין בּוֹ נִיחָה. אַשְׁכַּח תַּנֵּי. כְּפָרִים קוֹרִין בְּעֶרֶב שַׁבָּת. וַעֲיָירוֹת גְּדוֹלוֹת יִידָּחוּ לְיוֹם הַכְּנִיסָה. וּמוּקָּפוֹת חוֹמָה לְאַחַר הַשַּׁבָּת. הֵיךְ עַבְדִּין עוֹבְדָא. אָמַר רִבִּי יוֹסֵה. לֵית אִיפְשָׁר. וְאִין אִיפְשָׁר כְּמַתְנִיתָה.

Halakhah 4: They asked before Rebbi Ze`ira[92]: As you are saying there, if it falls so that in walled cities one should read on the Sabbath, one reads on Friday[93]. If it falls so that in villages one should read on the Sabbath, should one not read it on Friday[100]? But the Mishnah must be by two Tannaim. The first Tanna is of the opinion that any which is pushed away is pushed to the market day[101]. [The other Tanna is of the opinion that not everything which is pushed away is pushed to the market day.][102] He said to them, so says Rav: it is one Tanna. Why did they say, if for walled cities it falls on a Sabbath, one reads it on Friday? Because Rebbi Helbo, Rebbi Huna in the name of the Great Rebbi Hiyya: Everybody may fulfill his obligation on the Fourteenth, which is the time of its reading[67,103]. And similarly, if for villages it would fall on the Sabbath[104]; as Rebbi Helbo said, the Thirteenth was a day of war[14]. It proves for itself that it was not a day of comfort. It is found stated, hamlets read on Friday[105]; large villages are pushed to the market day, and walled cities after the Sabbath. How does one act? Rebbi Yose said, it is impossible[87], but if one would be possible, following the Mishnah[99].

100 Since if the 15th is on a Sabbath one reads on the 14th, on Friday, there seems to be no reason why one should not read on Friday if the 14th is on the Sabbath, against the Mishnah.
101 This is the Mishnah.
102 Corrector's addition. Probably not part of the original text, in which Rebbi Ze`ira immediately states that one follows Rav who explains that all Mishnaiot are consistent.
103 If for walled cities it is a Sabbath, then Friday is the 14th and is valid reading for everybody (after the fact).
104 But if Sabbath is the 14th, Friday is not acceptable following R. Helbo, and there are two reasons why one should read on Thursday.
105 Following R. La in the preceding Halakhah. Babli 5a.

(70b line 55) **הלכה ה**: רִבִּי בָּא בְשֵׁם רַב יְהוּדָה. כָּל־שֶׁאָמְרוּ. יִדָּחֶה מִמְּקוֹמוֹ. וּבִלְבַד בַּעֲשָׂרָה. וַאֲנָן חַמְיָין רַבָּנָן. אֲפִילוּ בַיָּחִיד. רִבִּי אֲבוּנָה בְשֵׁם רִבִּי אַסִּי. כָּל־שֶׁאָמְרוּ. יִדָּחֶה לְיוֹם הַכְּנִיסָה. וּבִלְבַד בַּעֲשָׂרָה. רִבִּי חֲנַנְיָה אָמַר. אִיתְפַּלְגוּן רַב חוּנָה וְרַב יְהוּדָה. חַד אָמַר. וּבִלְבַד בַּעֲשָׂרָה. וְחוֹרָנָה אָמַר. אֲפִילוּ בְיָחִידִי. מָתִיב מָאן דְּאָמַר. וּבִלְבַד בַּעֲשָׂרָה. לְמָאן דְּאָמַר. אֲפִילוּ בְיָחִידִי. עַד שֶׁהוּא בִמְקוֹמוֹ יִקְרָא.

אָמַר רִבִּי. סֵלְקַת מַתְנִיתָהּ אֶחָד עָשָׂר וּשְׁנַיִם עָשָׂר וּשְׁלֹשָׁה עָשָׂר וְאַרְבָּעָה עָשָׂר וַחֲמִשָּׁה עָשָׂר.

Halakhah 5: Rebbi Abba in the name of Rav Jehudah: In any case they said, it should be pushed away from its place, only with ten[106]. But we see Rabbis even single? Rebbi Abuna in the name of Rebbi[107] Assi: In any case they said, any that is pushed to the market day, only with ten. Rebbi Hanania said, Rav Huna and Rav Jehudah disagree. One says, only with ten; the other one says, even singly. The one who said only for ten objected to the one who said even singly: then why does he not read at his place[108]?

Rebbi said, the Mishnah comes out on the Eleventh, the Twelfth, the Thirteenth, the Fourteenth, the Fifteenth[109].

106 For the Yerushalmi it is clear that on the 14th (or for walled cities the 15th), reading the Scroll is not a sacral act and public worship; therefore it does not have to be performed in public by 10 adult males. The only problem is if the scroll has to be read on another day; where in one opinion it remains a private act but in the other it needs publicity, a public reading in the presence of at least ten adult males. Babli 5a.

107 Read: Rav.

108 Why should not everybody read privately on the 14th?

109 The 11th appears as a day of reading the scroll only if the 14th is a Sunday, and this case is missing in the Mishnah in the Yerushalmi; it is in the Mishnah in the Babli (and in Maimonides's autograph Mishnah). Rebbi declares the Mishnah in the Babli and independent Mishnah mss. as the correct last edition of the text.

(fol. 69d) **משנה ו**: אֵיזוֹ הִיא עִיר גְּדוֹלָה כָּל־שֶׁיֵּשׁ בָּהּ עֲשָׂרָה בַטְלָנִין. פָּחוֹת מִיכֵּן הֲרֵי זֶה כְפָר. בְּאֵילוּ אָמְרוּ מַקְדִּימִין וְלֹא מְאַחֲרִין. אֲבָל זְמַן עֲצֵי כֹהֲנִים וְהָעָם וְתִשְׁעָה בְאָב וַחֲגִיגָה וְהַקְהֵל מְאַחֲרִין וְלֹא מַקְדִּימִין. אַף עַל פִּי שֶׁאָמְרוּ מַקְדִּימִין וְלֹא מְאַחֲרִין מוּתָּרִין בְּהֶסְפֵּד וּבְתַעֲנִית וּמַתָּנוֹת לָאֶבְיוֹנִים. אָמַר רִבִּי יְהוּדָה אֵימָתַי מָקוֹם שֶׁנִּכְנָסִין בַּשֵּׁנִי וּבַחֲמִישִׁי. אֲבָל מָקוֹם שֶׁאֵין נִכְנָסִין לֹא בַשֵּׁנִי וְלֹא חֲמִישִׁי קוֹרִין אוֹתָהּ בִּזְמַנָּהּ:

Mishnah 6: What is a large village? Any in which there are ten unoccupied people[110]. Less than that is a hamlet. About these[111] it was said that one precedes and does not trail. But for the times of offering of wood by the priests and the people[112], and the Ninth of Av[113], and the festive offering[114], and the public assembly[115], one trails but does not precede[116]. Even though they said, one precedes but does not trail, one is permitted to eulogize, and to fast[117], and gifts to the poor[118]. Rebbi Jehudah said, when has this been said? At places where one assembles Monday and Thursday. But at a place where one assembles neither Monday nor Thursday one reads on its time[110].

110 Since a day laborer is supposed to work from sunrise to sunset, and the farmer or householder who hires him must supervise and work with him during that time, regular

synagogue service during the week is possible only if there are at least 10 adult males available after sunrise and before sunset for public morning and afternoon services. Since the inhabitants of hamlets are supposed to come to the synagogue to hear the reading of the scroll, if the synagogue is not open they cannot come. If the community has people able to read the scroll but cannot support a daily synagogue service, they are reading on the 14th.

111 The days preceding Purim.

112 As described in Mishnah *Ta`anit* 4:6.

113 Which is pushed to the 10th if the 9th is a Sabbath.

114 The festival offering required from every pilgrim at one of the three yearly festivals of pilgrimage cannot be offered prior to the start of the festival, but may be offered anytime in the holiday week (which in case of Pentecost is after the end of the holiday).

115 The public Torah reading on Tabernacles of the Sabbatical year; *Deut.* 31:10-13.

116 If any of these dates falls on a Sabbath, the obligation is transferred to the following Sunday.

117 The prohibition of mourning and fasting refers only to Purim itself, not to the dates of reading the scroll if these precede the 14th of Adar.

118 As stated before (Note 21), these obligations also are independent of the date of reading the scroll.

(70b line 63) **הלכה ו**: תַּנֵּי. עֲשָׂרָה בְטֵילִים מִמְּלַאכְתָּן לְבֵית הַכְּנֶסֶת. רַב יְהוּדָה אָמַר. כְּגוֹן אָנוּ שֶׁאֵין אָנוּ צְרִיכִין לְתַלְמוּדֵינוּ. תַּנֵּי. כְּפָר שֶׁאֵין בּוֹ עֲשָׂרָה. תְּקָנָתוֹ קַלְקָלָתוֹ וְנַעֲשָׂה כְעִיר.

Halakhah 6: It was stated: Ten who are free from work for the synagogue[119]. Rav Jehudah said, like us who do not need time to study[120]. It was stated, a place with less than ten inhabitants, its improvement is by its deficiency and is treated like a village[121].

119 It is not implied that these people do not work at all; only that they are free to go to the synagogue mornings and evenings. Babli 5a.

120 He already has passed all his exams and obtained a job as communal rabbi; therefore he is free (probably better: obligated) to come to the synagogue every morning and evening.

121 If there are less than 10 inhabitants it is not worth while for the nearby village to organize a reading for them; since the market day is irrelevant for them automatically they have to read on the 14th.

(70b line 65) בְּאֵילּוּ אָמְרוּ מַקְדִּימִין וְלֹא מְאַחֲרִין. קְרִיאַת מְגִילָה וּתְרוּמַת שְׁקָלִים מַקְדִּימִין וְלֹא מְאַחֲרִין. סְעוּדַת רֹאשׁ חוֹדֶשׁ וּסְעוּדַת פּוּרִים מְאַחֲרִין וְלֹא מַקְדִּימִין. רִבִּי זְעוּרָה בָּעָא קוֹמֵי רִבִּי אַבָהוּ. וְיַעֲשׂוּ אוֹתָן בַּשַּׁבָּת. אָמַר לֵיהּ. לַעֲשׂוֹת אוֹתָם יְמֵי מִשְׁתֶּה וְשִׂמְחָה. אֶת שֶׁשִּׂמְחָתוֹ תְּלוּיָה בְּבֵית דִּין. יָצָא זֶה שֶׁשִּׂמְחָתוֹ תְּלוּיָה בִּידֵי שָׁמַיִם.

מַגְבַּת פּוּרִים לְפוּרִים. אָמַר רִבִּי לָעֲזָר. וּבִלְבַד שֶׁלֹּא יְשַׁנֶּה מִמֶּנָּה הֶעָנִי רְצוּעָה לְמִנְעָלוֹ. אֵין מְדַקְדְּקִין בְּמִצְוַת פּוּרִים אֶלָּא כָּל־מִי שֶׁהוּא פּוֹשֵׁט אֶת יָדוֹ לִיטוֹל נוֹתְנִין לוֹ. אֵין מְשַׁנִּין בְּמָעוֹת פּוּרִים. הָא שְׁאָר כָּל־הַמָּעוֹת מְשַׁנִּין. אֶלָּא כָּל־הַמָּעוֹת עַד שֶׁלֹּא יִינָתְנוּ לַגִּיזְבָּרִין אַתְּ רַשַּׁאי לְשַׁנּוֹתָן. מִשֶּׁנִּיתְּנוּ לַגִּיזְבָּרִין אֵין אַתְּ רַשַּׁאי לְשַׁנּוֹתָן.

"About these[111] it was said that one precedes and does not trail." Reading the Scroll and paying the *Sheqel* tax one precedes and does not trail; the Meal of the New Moon and the Purim Meal one trails[122] but does not precede. Rebbi Ze`ira said before Rebbi Abbahu: then could one make it on the Sabbath[123]? He answered him, *to make them days of drinking and joy*[124]; those whose joy depends on the court[125]; this excludes those whose joy depends on Heaven.

"[126]The Purim collection is for Purim[127]. Rebbi Eleazar[128] said, only that the poor should not change it from its destination to {buy from it} laces for his shoes. One does not check eligibility for the money given as Purim charity; one gives to anybody who extends his hand to take." One may not change Purim monies; does this imply that other {charity} monies one may change[129]? But the intended use of any monies may be changed[130] before they are given into the hands of the administrators; after they are given into the hands of the administrators they may not be changed.

122 The meal at which the New Moon is declared by the calendar court by its nature cannot be celebrated before the New Moon has been declared; the Purim meal is scheduled for the afternoon of the 14th (or 15th), probably extending into the next night.
123 For which one has to go to the expenses of a festive meal anyhow.
124 *Esth.* 9:22.
125 The calendar court, before the publication of the computed calendar. After the publication, every date is permanently depending on R. Yose's court.
126 Tosephta 1:5; Babli *Bava mesia`* 78b.
127 The gifts to the poor demanded by *Esth.* 9:22 must be used by the poor to buy food for the Purim meal.
128 The ms. sources (Note 126) are about evenly split between Eleazar and Eliezer.
129 Mishnah *Qiddušin* 1:6 states that a promise to Heaven has the legal consequences of delivery to persons. If monies promised to charity must be delivered, what else may be changed?
130 While the fact that the monies must be given to charity cannot be changed, the name and nature of the charity may be changed before the monies are delivered to the administrators of the charity. Tosephta 2:15, Babli *Arakhin* 6a.

1) אֲבָל זְמַן עֲצֵי כֹּהֲנִים. מָה רָאָה זְמַן עֲצֵי כֹהֲנִים וְהָעָם לְהִימָּנוֹת. אֶלָּא בְשָׁעָה שֶׁעָלוּ (70c line
יִשְׂרָאֵל מִן הַגּוֹלָה וְלֹא מָצְאוּ עֵצִים בַּלִּישְׁכָּה וְעָמְדוּ אֵילּוּ וְנִתְנַדְּבוּ עֵצִים מִשֶּׁלְעַצְמָן וּמְסָרוּם
לַצִּיבּוּר וְנִקְרְבוּ מֵהֶן קָרְבְּנוֹת צִיבּוּר. וְהִיתְנוּ עִמָּהֶן הַנְּבִיאִים שֶׁבֵּינֵיהֶן שֶׁאֲפִילוּ לִשְׁכָּה מְלֵיאָה
עֵצִים וְעָמְדוּ אֵילּוּ וְנִתְנַדְּבוּ עֵצִים מִשֶּׁלְעַצְמָן שֶׁלֹּא יְהֵא קָרְבָּן מִתְקָרֵב אֶלָּא מִשֶּׁלָּהֶן תְּחִילָּה.
אָמַר רִבִּי אֲחָא. דְּרִבִּי יוֹסֵי הִיא. דְּרִבִּי יוֹסֵי אָמַר. אַף הָרוֹצֶה מִתְנַדֵּב שׁוֹמֵר חִנָּם. רִבִּי יוֹסֵה
בְשֵׁם רִבִּי אִילָא. דִּבְרֵי הַכֹּל הִיא. מַה פְלִיגִין. בְּגוּפוֹ שֶׁלְּקָרְבָּן. אֲבָל בְּמַכְשִׁירֵי קָרְבָּן כָּל־עַמָּא
מוֹדֵיי שֶׁהוּא מִשְׁתַּנֶּה קָרְבָּן יָחִיד מִקָּרְבָּן צִיבּוּר. תַּנֵּי. אִשָּׁה שֶׁעָשְׂת כֻּתּוֹנֶת לִבְנָהּ צְרִיכָה לִמְסוֹר
לַצִּיבּוּר. אָמַר רִבִּי אֲחָא. דְּרִבִּי יוֹסֵי הִיא. דְּרִבִּי יוֹסֵי אָמַר. אַף הָרוֹצֶה מִתְנַדֵּב שׁוֹמֵר חִנָּם. רִבִּי
יוֹסֵה בְשֵׁם רִבִּי אִילָא. דִּבְרֵי הַכֹּל הִיא. מַה פְלִיגִין. בְּגוּפוֹ שֶׁלְּקָרְבָּן. אֲבָל בְּמַכְשִׁירֵי קָרְבָּן
כָּל־עַמָּא מוֹדֵיי שֶׁהוּא מִשְׁתַּנֶּה קָרְבָּן יָחִיד מִקָּרְבָּן צִיבּוּר. מַתְנִיתָא פְלִיגָא עַל רִבִּי יוֹסֵה. אוֹתָן
הַיָּמִים נוֹהֲגִין בִּשְׁעַת קָרְבָּן וְשֶׁלֹּא בִּשְׁעַת קָרְבָּן. רִבִּי יוֹסֵי אוֹמֵר. אֵינָן נוֹהֲגִין אֶלָּא בִּשְׁעַת קָרְבָּן.
וְעוֹד מִן הָדָא דְתַנֵּי. אָמַר רִבִּי לַעֲזָר בֵּירִבִּי צָדוֹק. אֲנִי הָיִינוּ מִבְּנֵי סְנָאָה בֶן בִּנְיָמִן וְחָל תִּשְׁעָה
בְאָב לִהְיוֹת בַּשַּׁבָּת וְדָחִינוּ אוֹתוֹ לְמוֹצָאֵי שַׁבָּת וְהָיִינוּ מִתְעַנִּין וְלֹא מַשְׁלִימִין.

[131]"But for the times of offering of wood by the priests." For what reason were the times of wood by the priests and the people to be counted? Only that at the time when Israel returned from the Diaspora and did not find wood in the chamber, those came forward and volunteered wood from their own and donated it to the public. It was used to offer public sacrifices. The prophets among them stipulated for them that even if the chamber was full of wood, if those came and offered and volunteered wood from their own, that the sacrifice should only be brought first from theirs. Rebbi Aḥa said, this is Rebbi Yose's, since Rebbi Yose said, also he may volunteer as unpaid trustee. Rebbi Yose in the name of Rebbi Ila, it is the opinion of everybody. Where do they disagree? About the body of the offering. But for enablers of the offering everybody agrees that a private offering can be turned into public offering. It was stated, a woman who made a coat for her son has to surrender it to the public. Rebbi Aḥa said, this is Rebbi Yose's, since Rebbi Yose said, also he may volunteer as unpaid trustee. Rebbi Yose in the name of Rebbi Ila, it is the opinion of everybody. Where do they disagree? About the body of the offering. But for enablers of the offering everybody agrees that a private offering can be turned into public offering.. A *baraita* disagrees with Rebbi Yose: "Those days are observed at the time of sacrifices and not at the time of sacrifices; Rebbi Yose says, they are observed only at the time of sacrifices."

Also from the following: "Rebbi Eleazar ben Rebbi Sadoq said, we were of the descendants of Senaah ben Benjamin. When the Ninth of Av fell on a Sabbath, we postponed it to the end of the Sabbath and we were fasting but not completing."

131 This paragraph also is *Ta`aniot* 4:6 (Notes 187-194), *Šeqalim* 4:1 (Notes 10-18); Babli *Ta`anit* 12a.

(70c line 17) וּבְתִשְׁעָה בְּאָב. רִבִּי יִרְמְיָה בְּשֵׁם רִבִּי חִייָה בַּר בָּא. בַּדִּין הָיָה שֶׁיְהוּ מִתְעַנִּין בָּעֲשִׂירִי. שֶׁבּוֹ נִשְׂרַף. וְלָמָּה בַּתְּשִׁיעִי. שֶׁבּוֹ הִתְחִילָה הַפּוּרְעָנוּת. וְתַנֵּי כֵן. בַּשְּׁבִיעִי נִכְנְסוּ לְתוֹכוֹ. בַּשְּׁמִינִי הָיוּ מְקַרְקְרִים בּוֹ. בַּתְּשִׁיעִי הִצִּיתוּ בוֹ אֶת הָאוּר. בָּעֲשִׂירִי נִשְׂרַף. רִבִּי יְהוֹשֻׁעַ בֶּן לֵוִי צַייָם תְּשִׁיעִי וַעֲשִׂירִי. רִבִּי לֵוִי צַייָם תְּשִׁיעִי וְלֵילֵי עֲשִׂירִי. רִבִּי בָּא בַּר זַבְדָּא בְּשֵׁם רִבִּי חֲנִינָה. בִּיקֵּשׁ רִבִּי לַעֲקוֹר תִּשְׁעָה בְּאָב וְלֹא הִנִּיחוּ לוֹ. אָמַר לוֹ רִבִּי אֶלְעָזָר. עִמָּךְ הָיִיתִי וְלֹא אִיתְאֲמָרַת אֶלָּא בִּיקֵּשׁ רִבִּי לַעֲקוֹר תִּשְׁעָה בְּאָב שֶׁחָל לִהְיוֹת בַּשַּׁבָּת וְלֹא הִנִּיחוּ לוֹ. אָמַר. הוֹאִיל וְנִדְחָה יִדָּחֶה. אָמְרוּ לוֹ. יִדָּחֶה לְמָחָר. וְנָגַה לֵיהּ הַהִיא דְּתַנִּינָן תַּמָּן. רִבִּי יוֹחָנָן בֶּן בְּרוֹקָה אוֹמֵר. עַל שְׁנֵיהֶם הוּא אוֹמֵר. וַיְבָרֶךְ אוֹתָם אֱלֹהִים וַיֹּאמֶר לָהֶם אֱלֹהִים פְּרוּ וּרְבוּ. רִבִּי לְעָזָר בְּשֵׁם רִבִּי חֲנִינָה. הֲלָכָה כְּרִבִּי יוֹחָנָן בֶּן בְּרוֹקָה. אָמַר לֵיהּ רִבִּי בָּא בַּר זַבְדָּא. עִמָּךְ הָיִיתִי וְלֹא אִיתְאֲמָרַת אֶלָּא הָיְתָה תּוֹבַעַת לְהִינָּשֵׂא חַדְיִן עִמָּהּ. וְקָרָא עֲלֵיהוֹן. טוֹבִים הַשְּׁנַיִם מִן־הָאֶחָד.

"And the Ninth of Av." [132]Rebbi Jeremiah in the name of Rebbi Hiyya, it should have been logical that one should fast on the Tenth, since on it it was burned. Why on the Ninth? Because the calamity started on it. So it was stated, on the Seventh they entered, on the Eighth they were misbehaving in it, on the Ninth they started the fire, and on the Tenth it was burned. Rebbi Joshua ben Levi fasted Ninth and Tenth. Rebbi Levi fasted on the Ninth and the night of the Tenth. Rebbi Abba bar Zavda in the name of Rebbi Hanina: Rebbi wanted to uproot the Ninth of Av but they did not let him. Rebbi Eleazar said to him, I was with you but it was not said so, but Rebbi wanted to uproot the Ninth of Av which fell on a Sabbath but they did not let him. He said, because it was pushed aside, let it be pushed aside. They said to him, let it be pushed to the next day. In a similar case, that which we stated there: "Rebbi Johanan ben Beroqa said, for both of them it says, *God blessed them and God said to them, be fruitful and multiply*[133], etc." Rebbi Eleazar in the Name of Rebbi Hanina: Practice follows Rebbi Johanan ben Beroqa. Rebbi Abba bar Zavda said to him, I was with you and it was only said, if she asks to be married the law is on her side. He said about them, *two are better than one*[134].

132 This paragraph also is in *Ta'aniot* 4:9, Notes 370-377.
133 *Gen.* 1:28.
134 *Eccl.* 4:9.

(70c line 31) וּבַחֲגִיגָה. כָּתוּב אֶחָד אוֹמֵר. וְחַג הַקָּצִיר בִּכּוּרֵי מַעֲשֶׂיךָ. וְכָתוּב אֶחָד אוֹמֵר. כָּל־מְלֶאכֶת עֲבוֹדָה לֹא תַעֲשׂוּ. אָמַר רִבִּי חֲנַנְיָה. הָא כֵיצַד יִתְקַיְּימוּ שְׁנֵי כְתוּבִים. בְּשָׁעָה שֶׁהוּא חָל בַּחוֹל אֵת חוֹגֵג וְשׁוֹבֵת. בְּשָׁעָה שֶׁהוּא חָל בַּשַּׁבָּת לְמָחָר אֵת חוֹגֵג וְקוֹצֵר. אָמַר רִבִּי יוֹסֵה בֵּירִבִּי בּוּן. וּבִלְבַד שִׁיבָּלִים לְעִיסָּתָהּ. כְּהָדָא דְתַנֵּי. לָהֵן אִינָשׁ דִּיהֵוֵי עֲלוֹי אָעִין וְבִכּוּרִין. הָאוֹמֵר. הֲרֵי עָלַי עֵצִים לַמִּזְבֵּחַ וְגִיזִּירִים לַמַּעֲרָכָה. אָסוּר בְּהֶסְפֵּד וּבְתַעֲנִית וּמִלְעֲשׂוֹת מְלָאכָה בּוֹ בַיּוֹם.

"And the festive offering." One verse says, *the harvest festival, the first fruits of your work*[134*]. Another verse says, *any productive work you shall not do*[135]. Rebbi Hanania said, how could both verses be sustained? If it falls on a weekday you bring the festival offering and refrain from work. If it falls on the Sabbath, the following day you bring the festival offering and harvest[136]. Rebbi Yose ben Rebbi Abun said, only ears for her dough[137]. As what was stated[138], "therefore anybody who has an obligation for wood and first fruits. He who says, I am taking upon me {to bring} wood for the altar and logs for the arrangement[139] on that day are forbidden funeral orations, and fasting, and working[140]."

134* *Ex.* 23:16.
135 *Lev.* 23:21. The first verse seems to require harvesting on Pentecost, the second verse forbids it. Babli *Hagigah* 17b.
136 Since Pentecost is only one day, the next day is a regular work day.
137 On a day of sacrificing one is forbidden gainful work, as on a holiday. Therefore on the Sunday after Pentecost on Sabbath the only harvesting permitted is collecting for immediate consumption.
138 *Pesaḥim* 4:1, Notes 6-7; *Megillat Ta'anit* Chapter 5.
139 The arrangement of firewood on the altar.
140 Work is not forbidden in a formal sense as on the Sabbath or holiday, only any gainful employment, including harvest for later sale.

(70c line 37) וּבְהַקְהֵל. רִבִּי בָּא בְּרֵיהּ דְּרִבִּי חִייָה בַּר בָּא אָמַר. מִפְּנֵי הַתְּקִיעָה. רִבִּי יִצְחָק בֵּירִבִּי חִייָה אָמַר. מִפְּנֵי הַבִּימָה. וְיַעֲשׂוּ אוֹתָם מֵאֶתְמוֹל. שֶׁלֹּא לִדְחוֹק אֶת הָעֲזָרָה. אָמַר רִבִּי מַתַּנְיָה. עַל שֵׁם לֹא־תִטַּע לְךָ אֲשֵׁרָה כָּל־עֵץ.

"And the public assembly." Rebbi Abba, son of Rebbi Hiyya bar Abba, said, because of horn blowing[141]. Rebbi Isaac ben Rebbi Ḥiyya said, because of the platform[142]. Could they not make it the day before? Not to compress the courtyard[143]. Rebbi Mattaniah said, because of *you shall not plant any wooden Ashera*[144].

141 Tosephta *Sotah* 7:15 states that Cohanim blow golden trumpets at the public assembly. There is no horn blowing on the Sabbath.

142 On which the king sits to read from the Torah, Tosephta *Sotah* 7:13. This argument follows the opinion that the Torah was read inside the Temple enclosure, not on the Temple Mount outside the enclosure following R. Eliezer ben Jacob.

143 The Torah is read on the first of the intermediate days of Tabernacles. The courtyard is rather small and could not accommodate the worshippers on the first day of the holiday if it already had been constructed there. Quoted by Rashi 5a.

144 *Deut*. 16:21. In his opinion, any permanent wooden construction is forbidden in the Temple precinct. R. Eliezer ben Jacob reads the verse as forbidding any wooden structure in the Temple precinct (*Sifry Deut*. 145); therefore he must hold that the reading was outside on the Mount. This raises the question whether R. Mattaniah quotes the verse in support of R. Isaac ben R. Hiyya or in opposition since for R. Eliezer ben Jacob only R. Abba ben R. Ḥiyya's reason would be valid (Maimonides *Hagigah* 3:7).

(70c line 40) מַתְנִיתָה דְרִבִּי מֵאִיר. [דְּאָמַר רִבִּי מֵאִיר.] דִּילָא לְמִיסְפַּד. אָסוּר לְהִתְעַנּוֹת. וְדִילָא לְהִתְעַנּוֹת. מוּתָּר בְּהֶסְפֵּד. וְדִי לָא סְתָם כְּדִילָא לְהִתְעַנְיָיה. אָמַר רִבִּי יוֹנָה. אִילֵּין יוֹמַיָּא דִילָא לְהִתְעַנָאָה בְהוֹן וּמִקְצָתָן דִּילָא לְמִיסְפַּד בְּהוֹן. אָמַר רַבָּן שִׁמְעוֹן בֶּן גַּמְלִיאֵל. מַה תַּלְמוּד לוֹמַר בְּהוֹן בְּהוֹן שְׁנֵי פְעָמִים. אֶלָּא מְלַמֵּד שֶׁהַלַּיְלָה מוּתָּר וְהַיּוֹם אָסוּר. כְּהָדָא דְתַנֵּי. לָהֵן אִינָשׁ דִּיהֲוֵי עֲלוֹהִי אֲסָר בִּצְלוֹ. אָמַר רִבִּי יוֹסֵי בֵּירִבִּי בּוּן. שֶׁהוּא צָרִיךְ לְהַזְכִּיר מִבְּעָרֶב. וְאַתְיָא כַהִיא דְאָמַר רִבִּי זְעוּרָה בְשֵׁם רַב חוּנָה. אוֹמְרוֹ כְלֵילֵי שַׁבָּת וְכְיוֹמוֹ.

The Mishnah is Rebbi Meïr's, since Rebbi Meïr said, "not to eulogize" one is forbidden to fast, "not to fast" one is permitted to eulogize. "Not to" unspecified is as "not to fast." Rebbi Jonah said, "these are the days not to fast on them, and partially not to eulogize on them." Rabban Simeon ben Gamliel said, why does it say "on them" twice? To teach that the night is permitted but the day forbidden. As it was stated, "therefore a person who takes it on himself has to forbid himself in prayer." Rebbi Yose ben Rebbi Abun said, that he must mention it on the preceding evening. This comes following what Rebbi Ze`ira said in the name of Rav Huna: Similar to Friday night and Sabbath day.

145 This and the following texts to almost the end of the Halakhah are repeated from *Ta`aniot* 2:13-14, Notes 194-230.

(70c line 48) מַתְנִיתָה אוֹ בְּאֶחָד עָשָׂר כְּרִבִּי יוֹסֵי. אוֹ בִשְׁנֵים עָשָׂר כְּרִבִּי מֵאִיר. וְקַשְׁיָא עַל דְּרִבִּי מֵאִיר. לָא כֵן תַּנֵּי. בִּתְרֵין עָשָׂר בֵּיהּ יוֹם טִירְיוֹן. וְאָמַר רִבִּי יַעֲקֹב בַּר אָחָא. בָּטֵל יוֹם טִירְיוֹן. יוֹם שֶׁנֶּהֱרַג לוּלִיָּנוֹס וּפַפּוֹס. בִּתְלַת־עֲשַׂר בֵּיהּ יוֹם נִיקָנוֹר. מָהוּ יוֹם נִיקָנוֹר. שִׁלְטוֹן מִשִּׁלְמַלְכוּת יָוָן הָיָה עוֹבֵר לְאָלֶכְּסַנְדְּרִיאָה וְרָאָה אֶת יְרוּשָׁלֵם וְחֵירֵף וְנִיאֵץ וְגִידֵּף וְאָמַר. בְּשׁוּבִי בְשָׁלוֹם אֶתּוֹץ אֶת־הַמִּגְדָּל הַזֶּה. וְיָצָא אֶחָד מִשֶּׁלְחַשְׁמוֹנַיי וְהָיָה הוֹרֵג בְּחֵיָילוֹתָיו עַד שֶׁהִגִּיעַ לְקָרוּכִין שֶׁלּוֹ. וְכֵיוָן שֶׁהִגִּיעַ לְקָרוּכִין שֶׁלּוֹ קָטַע אֶת יָדָיו וְחָתַךְ אֶת רֹאשׁוֹ וְתַחְבָּן בָּעֵץ. וְכָתַב מִלְּמַטָּן. הַפֶּה שֶׁדִּיבֵּר בְּאַשְׁמָה וְהַיָּד שֶׁפָּשְׁטָה בְגַאֲוָה. וְתָלְיָין בְּקוֹנְטָס נֶגֶד יְרוּשָׁלַם. עַל דַּעְתֵּיהּ דְּרִבִּי מֵאִיר נִיחָא. בָּא לוֹסַר לְפָנָיו. עַל דַּעְתֵּיהּ דְּרִבִּי יוֹסֵה מַה בָּא לוֹסַר. לְפָנָיו לֵית לֵיהּ. עַצְמוֹ אָסוּר מִפְּנֵי אַרְבָּעָה עָשָׂר. בָּא לְהוֹדִיעֲךָ שֶׁהוּא אָסוּר בְּהֶסְפֵּד. וַאֲפִילוּ עַל דְּרִבִּי מֵאִיר לֵית הִיא מַקְשְׁיָיא. לָא כֵן תַּנֵּי. בִּתְרֵין עָשָׂר בֵּיהּ יוֹם טִירְיוֹן. וְאָמַר רִבִּי יַעֲקֹב בַּר אָחָא. בָּטֵל יוֹם טִירְיוֹן. יוֹם שֶׁנֶּהֱרַג לוּלִיָּנוֹס וּפַפּוֹס. בְּאַרְבַּעַת־עָשָׂר וּבַחֲמֵשֶׁת־עָשָׂר פּוּרַיָיא דִּילָּא לְמִיסְפַּד. בְּשִׁית־עֲשַׂר שָׁרוּן לְמִיבְנָא שׁוּר יְרוּשָׁלֵם דִּילָּא לְמִיסְפַּד. עַל דַּעְתֵּיהּ דְּרִבִּי מֵאִיר נִיחָא. בָּא לוֹסַר לְפָנָיו. עַל דַּעְתֵּיהּ דְּרִבִּי יוֹסֵה מַה בָּא לֶאֱסַר. לֶאֱסוֹר לְפָנָיו לֵית לֵיהּ. עַצְמוֹ אָסוּר מִפְּנֵי חֲמִשָּׁה עָשָׂר. בָּא לְהוֹדִיעֲךָ שֶׁהוּא אָסוּר בְּהֶסְפֵּד.

The Mishnah either follows Rebbi Yose on the eleventh or Rebbi Meïr on the twelfth. But it is difficult for Rebbi Meïr. Was it not stated, "on the twelfth of it is Tirion Day?" But Rebbi Jacob bar Aḥa said, Tirion Day was disestablished; the day when Julianus and Pappos were killed. "On the thirteenth of it is Nikanor Day." What is Nikanor Day? "A commander of the Greek government was passing by on his way to Alexandria when he saw Jerusalem, and insulted, blasphemed, and vituperated and said, *when I shall return in peace I shall destroy this tower* One of the Hasmoneans went out against him, killed his soldiers until he came to his car When he came to his car he hacked off his hand and cut off his head, stuck them on a piece of wood and wrote under it, the mouth which spoke in guilt and the hand stretched out in haughtiness, and hang it on a pole outside Jerusalem." In Rebbi Meïr's opinion it is understandable, it comes to forbid the previous day. What does it come to forbid for Rebbi Yose? To forbid the day before he does not need since itself it forbidden because of the fourteenth. It comes to inform you that eulogies are forbidden. And also for Rebbi Meïr it is not difficult; was it not stated, "on the twelfth of it is Tirion Day?" But Rebbi Jacob bar Aḥa said, Tirion Day was disestablished; the day when Julianus and Pappos were killed. "On the fourteenth and the fifteenth is Purim, not to eulogize. On the sixteenth they started to build the wall of Jerusalem, not to eulogize." In Rebbi Meïr's opinion it is understandable, it comes to forbid the previous day. What does it come to forbid for Rebbi Yose? To forbid the day before he does not need since itself is forbidden because of the fifteenth. It comes to inform you that eulogies are forbidden.

(70c line 66) בְּשׁוּבְעַת עָשָׂר בֵּיהּ קָמוּן עַמְמַיָּא עַל פְּלֵיטַת סָפְרַיָּא בִּמְדִינַת כַלְקִיס וּבֵית זְבָדִין וַהֲוָה פֶרְקָן. עַל דַּעְתֵּיהּ דְּרִבִּי מֵאִיר נִיחָא. בָּא לֶאֱסוֹר עַצְמוֹ. עַל דַּעְתֵּיהּ דְּרִבִּי יוֹסֵה מָה בָא לֶאֱסוֹר. אָמַר רִבִּי יוֹסֵי. כָּל־אִילֵּין מִילַּיָּא לָא מְסַייְעָן וְלָא תָבְרִן. לָא עַל דְּרִבִּי מֵאִיר וְלָא עַל דְּרִבִּי יוֹסֵי. לֹא בָא אֶלָּא לִמְנוֹת יָמִים שֶׁנַּעֲשׂוּ בָהֶן נִסִּים לְיִשְׂרָאֵל. תֵּדַע לָךְ שֶׁהוּא כֵן. דְּתַנִּינָן. בְּרֵישׁ יַרְחָא דְנִיסָן דִּיתְקַם תְּמִידָא דִּי לָא לְמִיסְפַּד. בְּלֹא כֵן אֵינוֹ אָסוּר מִשּׁוּם רֹאשׁ חוֹדֶשׁ. אֲבָל בַּשַּׁבָּתוֹת וּבְיָמִים טוֹבִים מִתְעַנִּין לִפְנֵיהֶן וּלְאַחֲרֵיהֶן. מָה רָאִיתָה לְהָקֵל בְּאִילּוּ וּלְהַחֲמִיר בְּאִילּוּ. שֶׁאִילּוּ דִּבְרֵי תוֹרָה וְאֵין דִּבְרֵי תוֹרָה צְרִיכִין חִיזּוּק. וְאֵילּוּ דִּבְרֵי סוֹפְרִים וְדִבְרֵי סוֹפְרִין צְרִיכִין חִיזּוּק. הָדָא דְּאַתְּ אָמַר. עַד שֶׁלֹּא בֶטְלָה בְטֵילַת מְגִילַת תַּעֲנִית. אֲבָל מִשֶּׁבֶּטְלָה מְגִילַת תַּעֲנִית בָּטְלוּ כָּל־אֵילוּ. רִבִּי חֲנִינָה וְרִבִּי יְהוֹשֻׁעַ בֶּן לֵוִי תְּרֵיהוֹן אָמְרִין. בֶּטְלָה מְגִילַת תַּעֲנִית. רִבִּי בָּא וְרִבִּי סִימוֹן אָמְרֵי. בֶּטְלָה מְגִילַת תַּעֲנִית. רִבִּי יוֹנָתָן אָמַר. בֶּטְלָה מְגִילַת תַּעֲנִית. אָמַר רִבִּי יוֹחָנָן. אֶמֶשׁ הָיִיתִי יוֹשֵׁב וְשׁוֹנֶה מַעֲשֶׂה שֶׁגָּזְרוּ תַּעֲנִית בַּחֲנוּכָּה בְּלוֹד. וְאָמְרוּ עָלָיו עַל רִבִּי אֱלִיעֶזֶר שֶׁסִּיפֵּר וְעַל רִבִּי יְהוֹשֻׁעַ שֶׁרָחַץ. אָמַר לָהֶן רִבִּי יְהוֹשֻׁעַ. צְאוּ וְהִתְעַנּוּ עַל מַה שֶּׁהִתְעַנִּיתֶם. וְאַתְּ אָמַר. בֶּטְלָה מְגִילַת תַּעֲנִית. אָמַר רִבִּי בָּא. אַף עַל גַּב דְּאַתְּ אָמַר. בֶּטְלָה מְגִילַת תַּעֲנִית. חֲנוּכָּה וּפוּרִים לָא בֶטְלוּ.

"On the seventeenth of it Gentiles attacked the remainder of the Sopherim at the city of Khalkis and Bet-Zabdin and there was relief." In Rebbi Meïr's opinion it is understandable, it comes to forbid the {day} itself. What does it come to forbid for Rebbi Yose? Rebbi Yose said, all these matters neither support nor contradict either Rebbi Meïr or Rebbi Yose; they only come to report the days on which miracles were done for Israel. You have to understand that this is so since we have stated: "On the New Moon of Nisan the Daily Offering was settled, one may not eulogize." Without this is it not already forbidden to him because of the New Moon? "But on Sabbath and holidays one fasts before and after them. What do you understand to be lenient with these and restrictive with those? For these are words of the Torah, and words of the Torah do not need reinforcement. But those are words of the Sopherim, and words of the Sopherim need reinforcement." That is what you were saying, as long as *Megillat Ta`anit* was not abolished. But since *Megillat Ta`anit* was abolished, all these were abolished. Rebbi Ḥanina and Rebbi Joshua ben Levi both said, *Megillat Ta`anit* was abolished. Rebbi Abba and Rebbi Simon both said, *Megillat Ta`anit* was abolished. Rebbi Jonathan said, *Megillat Ta`anit* was abolished. Rebbi Joḥanan said, yesterday I was repeating, "it happened that in Lydda they decided on a fast-day on Hanukkah. They said about Rebbi Eliezer that he got a haircut, and about Rebbi Joshua that he took a {thermal} bath. Rebbi Joshua said to them, go and fast because you fasted." And you are saying, *Megillat Ta`anit* was abolished? Rebbi Abba said, even if you are saying that *Megillat Ta`anit* was abolished, Hanukkah and Purim were not abolished.

(70d line 8) מֵילֵיהוֹן דְּרַבָּנָן אָמְרִין. בֶּטְלָה מְגִילַת תַּעֲנִית. רִבִּי אָבוּן צַיֵּים כָּל־עֲרוּבַת שׁוּבָּא. רִבִּי יוֹנָתָן צַיֵּים כָּל־עֲרוּבַת רֵישׁ שַׁתָּא. רִבִּי זְעוּרָה צָם תְּלַת מָאוָון דְּצוֹמִין. וְאִית דְּאָמְרִין. תְּשַׁע מָאוָון. וְלֹא חָשׁ עַל מְגִילַת תַּעֲנִית. רִבִּי יַעֲקֹב בַּר אָחָא מְפַקֵּד לְסָפְרַיָּה. אִין אֲתַת אִיתָּא מִשְׁאֲלָנְכוֹן. אִימְרִין לָהּ. בַּכֹּל מִתְעַנִּין חוּץ מִשַּׁבָּתוֹת וְיָמִים טוֹבִים וְרָאשֵׁי חֳדָשִׁים וְחוּלוֹ שֶׁלְּמוֹעֵד וַחֲנוּכָּה וּפוּרִים.

The actions of the rabbis imply that *Megillat Ta`anit* was abolished. Rebbi Jonathan fasted every New Year's Day's eve. Rebbi Abun fasted every Sabbath eve. Rebbi Ze`ira fasted 300 fasts, and some say 900, and disregarded *Megillat Ta`anit*. Rebbi Jacob bar Aḥa commanded the schoolteachers, if a woman comes to ask you, tell her that one may fast any time except Sabbaths, holidays, New Moons, intermediate days of holidays, Hanukkah and Purim.

(70d line 14) שִׁמְעוֹן בַּר בָּא אָמַר. אֲתַא עוֹבְדָא קוֹמֵי רִבִּי יוֹחָנָן וְהוֹרֵי כְרִבִּי יוֹסֵי וַהֲוָה רִבִּי לֶעְזֶר מִצְטָעֵר וְאָמַר. שֶׁבְקִין סְתָמָא וְעָבְדִין כְּיִחִידָיָא. אַשְׁכַּח תַּנֵּי לָהּ רִבִּי חִייָה בְּשֵׁם רִבִּי מֵאִיר. כַּד שְׁמַע דְּתַנֵּי לָהּ רִבִּי חִייָה בְּשֵׁם רִבִּי מֵאִיר אָמַר. יָאוּת סַבָּא יָדַע פִּרְקֵי גַרְמֵיהּ. רִבִּי מָנָא בָעָא קוֹמֵי רִבִּי יוּדָן. לֹא כֵן אָמַר רִבִּי חִזְקִיָּה רִבִּי אַבָּהוּ בְּשֵׁם רִבִּי לֶעְזֶר. כָּל־מָקוֹם שֶׁשָּׁנָה רִבִּי

מַחֲלוֹקֶת וְאַחַר כָּךְ שָׁנָה סְתָם הֲלָכָה כִּסְתָם. אָמַר לֵיהּ. לָא רִבִּי. דִּילְמָא חוֹרָן. מָה הֵן. אוּ דְאַשְׁכַּח רִבִּי מַחֲלוֹקֶת וְחָזַר וְשָׁנָה סְתָם הֲלָכָה כִּסְתָם. אָתַר דְּלָא אַשְׁכַּח רִבִּי מַתְנֵי מַחֲלוֹקֶת אֶלָּא אֲחֵרִים שָׁנוּ מַחֲלוֹקֶת וְרִבִּי שָׁנָה סְתָם. לֹא כָל־שֶׁכֵּן שֶׁתְּהֵא הֲלָכָה כִּסְתָם. אָתָא רִבִּי חִזְקִיָּה רִבִּי יַעֲקֹב בַּר אָחָא רִבִּי שִׁמְעוֹן בַּר אַבָּא בְשֵׁם רִבִּי לְעָזָר. וַאֲפִילוּ אֲחֵרִים שָׁנוּ מַחֲלוֹקֶת וְרִבִּי שָׁנָה סְתָם הֲלָכָה כִּסְתָם. וְלָמָּה הוּא מוֹרֶה לֵיהּ כְּיִחִידָיָיא. רִבִּי שְׁמוּאֵל בַּר יַנַּאי בְשֵׁם רִבִּי אָחָא. הָדָא דְאַתְּ אָמַר בִּשְׁאֵין מַחֲלוֹקֶת אֵצֶל סְתָם. אֲבָל אִם יֵשׁ מַחֲלוֹקֶת אֵצֶל סְתָם לָא בְדָא הֲלָכָה כִּסְתָם.

Simeon bar Abba said, there came a case before Rebbi Johanan and he instructed following Rebbi Yose. Rebbi Eleazar was sorry about this; he said, does one disregard the anonymous {Mishnah} and follow an isolated opinion? He found that Rebbi Ḥiyya stated this in the name of Rebbi Meïr. When he understood that Rebbi Ḥiyya stated this in the name of Rebbi Meïr, he said, the old man understands his chapters well. Rebbi Mana asked before Rebbi Yudan: Did not Rebbi Ḥizqiah, Rebbi Abbahu say in the name of Rebbi Eleazar, every place where Rebbi taught a disagreement and afterwards taught it anonymously, practice follows the anonymous statement. He said to him, and if not Rebbi, maybe somebody else. How is this? If it is found that Rebbi taught a disagreement and afterwards taught it anonymously, then practice follows the anonymous statement. In a case where Rebbi did not teach a disagreement but others taught it in disagreement and Rebbi taught it anonymously, certainly practice has to follow the anonymous text. There come Rebbi Ḥizqiah, Rebbi Jacob bar Aḥa, Rebbi Simeon bar Abba in the name of Rebbi Eleazar, every place where Rebbi taught a disagreement and afterwards taught it anonymously, practice follows the anonymous statement. Why does he instruct here following the isolated opinion? Rebbi Samuel bar Ina in the name of Rebbi Aḥa: That is, if no disagreement is stated together with the anonymous opinion. But if a disagreement is stated together with the anonymous opinion, practice does not follow the anonymous opinion.

(70d line 28) רִבִּי יוּדָן נְשִׂיָּיא שָׁלַח לְרִבִּי הוֹשַׁעְיָה רַבָּה חֲדָא עֲטָם וְחַד לָגִין דַּחֲמַר. שָׁלַח וְאָמַר לֵיהּ. קִיַּימְתְּ בָּנוּ וּמַתָּנוֹת לָאֶבְיוֹנִים. חָזַר וְשָׁלַח לֵיהּ חַד עֵגֶל וְחַד גְּרָב דַּחֲמַר. שָׁלַח וְאָמַר לֵיהּ. קִיַּימְתָּ בָּנוּ וּמִשְׁלוֹחַ מָנוֹת אִישׁ לְרֵעֵהוּ.

[146]Rebbi Yudan the Patriarch sent the Great Rebbi Hoshaia a roast and a pitcher[147] of wine. He sent and told him, you fulfilled with us *gifts to the needy*. Then he sent him a calf and a barrel of wine. He sent and told him, you fulfilled with us, *sending meals one person to the other*.

146 Babli 7a/b, where however the text in the printed editions is unreliable and originally was a metathesis of the Yerushalmi text; cf. *Dikduke Soferim Megillah* pp. 24-25, Notes ב-ג. Since this story illustrates the meaning of *sending meals one person to the other and gifts to the poor* which is mentioned in Mishnah 7, it seems that this paragraph, which has no connection with the subjects of Mishnah 6, really belongs to the next Halakhah.

147 Greek λάγηνος, Latin *lagena*.

(fol. 69d) **משנה ז**: קָרְאוּ אֶת הַמְּגִילָּה בַּאֲדָר הָרִאשׁוֹן וְנִתְעַבְּרָה הַשָּׁנָה קוֹרִין אוֹתָהּ בַּאֲדָר הַשֵּׁנִי. אֵין בֵּין אֲדָר הָרִאשׁוֹן לַאֲדָר שֵׁנִי אֶלָּא מִקְרָא מְגִילָּה וּמַתָּנוֹת לָאֶבְיוֹנִים:

Mishnah 7: If the Scroll was read during the first Adar and then the year was intercalated[148] one has to read it during the second Adar. There is no difference between first and second Adar except reading the Scroll and gifts to the needy[149].

148 While the Scroll was read correctly, since now actually the Adar preceding Nisan is the next month the reading has to be repeated.

149 In this form it is not quite correct since the intercalation also makes the first Adar 30 days but the second is 29 days. One has to explain that on the 14th (or 15th) of the second one reads the scroll, gives gifts to the needy and sends food to friends, but the prohibition of fasting and mourning extends to the same days in the first Adar.

(70d line 31) **הלכה ז**: תַּנֵּי. בְּמָקוֹם (שֶׁמְסַכְּנִין) [שֶׁנִּכְנָסִין] קוֹרִין אוֹתוֹ בְּאַרְבָּעָה עָשָׂר. רִבִּי יוֹסֵה בָעֵי. אִם בְּמָקוֹם (שֶׁמְסַכְּנִין) [שֶׁנִּכְנָסִין] אַל יִקְרְאוּ אוֹתָהּ כָּל־עִיקָּר.

Halakhah 7: It was stated: In a place (where they are in danger) [where they assemble][150] one reads it on the Fourteenth. Rebbi Yose asked: If it is a place (where they are in danger) [where they assemble] they should not read it at all[151].

150 Obviously the text of the (scribe) is the correct one; the [corrector's] has to be deleted. The scribe's text is quoted by R. S. Nathanson in *Ziun Yerushalaim* in the name

of Nahmanides in the Wilna edition of the Yerushalmi; the quote is not found in Nahmanides"s *Novellae* to *Megillah* edited by M. Goldstein, Jerusalem 1973.

151 A customary obligation is not to be executed if it leads to danger of life.

(70d line 33) מַתְנִיתָה בְּשֶׁעִיבְּרוּ וְאַחַר כָּךְ קָרְאוּ אוֹתָהּ. אֲבָל אִם קָרְאוּ אוֹתָהּ וְאַחַר כָּךְ עִיבְּרוּ לֹא בְדָא. מַתְנִיתָה לֹא אָמְרָה כֵן אֶלָּא קָרְאוּ אֶת הַמְּגִילָּה בַּאֲדָר הָרִאשׁוֹן וְנִתְעַבְּרָה הַשָּׁנָה קוֹרִין אוֹתָהּ בַּאֲדָר הַשֵּׁינִי. רִבִּי סִימוֹן בְּשֵׁם רִבִּי יְהוֹשֻׁעַ בֶּן לֵוִי. כָּתוּב לְקַייֵם אֶת אִגֶּרֶת הַפּוּרִים הַזֹּאת. מַה תַּלְמוּד לוֹמַר הַשֵּׁינִית: אֶלָּא מִיכָּן שֶׁאִם קָרְאוּ אוֹתָהּ בַּאֲדָר הָרִאשׁוֹן וְנִתְעַבְּרָה הַשָּׁנָה קוֹרִין אוֹתָהּ בַּאֲדָר הַשֵּׁינִי.

The Mishnah if it was intercalated and afterwards they read it; but if they read it and after that it was intercalated it does not apply[152]. The Mishnah does not say so, but "if the Scroll was read during the first Adar and then the year was intercalated one has to read it during the second Adar." Rebbi Simon in the name of Rebbi Joshua ben Levi: it is written[153], *to validate this Purim letter*; why does the verse say, *the second*? But from here that If the Scroll was read during the first Adar and then the year was intercalated one has to read it during the second Adar.

152 In this rejected opinion, if the reading the first time was legitimate, it does not have to be repeated. The accepted opinion leaves open the question whether also the benedictions recited for the reading have to be repeated. Differently Babli 6b-7a.
153 *Esth.* 9:29.

(70d line 39) רִבִּי יִרְמְיָה בְּשֵׁם רִבִּי שְׁמוּאֵל בַּר רַב יִצְחָק. מֶה עָשׂוּ מָרְדֳּכַי וְאֶסְתֵּר. כָּתְבוּ אִגֶּרֶת וְשָׁלְחוּ לְרַבּוֹתֵינוּ. שֶׁכֵּן אָמְרוּ לָהֶם. מְקַבְּלִין אַתֶּם עֲלֵיכֶם שְׁנֵי יָמִים הַלָּלוּ בְּכָל־שָׁנָה. אָמְרוּ לָהֶן. לֹא דַּייָן הַצָּרוֹת הַבָּאוֹת עָלֵינוּ אֶלָּא שֶׁאַתֶּם רוֹצִין לְהוֹסִיף עָלֵינוּ עוֹד צָרָתוֹ שֶׁלְהָמָן. חָזְרוּ וְכָתְבוּ לָהֶן אִגֶּרֶת שְׁנִייָה. הָדָא הִיא דִכְתִיב לְקַייֵם אֶת אִגֶּרֶת [הַפּוּרִים] הַזֹּאת הַשֵּׁנִית: מֶה הָיָה כָּתוּב בָּהּ. אָמְרוּ לָהֶן. אִם מִדָּבָר זֶה אַתֶּם מִתְיָירְאִים הֲרֵי הִיא כְתוּבָה וּמַעֲלָה בָּאַרְכַיִּים. הֲלוֹא־הֵם כְּתוּבִים עַל־סֵפֶר דִּבְרֵי הַיָּמִים לְמַלְכֵי מָדַי וּפָרֶס: רִבִּי שְׁמוּאֵל בַּר נַחְמָן בְּשֵׁם רִבִּי יוֹנָתָן. שְׁמוֹנִים וַחֲמִשָּׁה זְקֵינִים וּמֵהֶם שְׁלֹשִׁים וְכַמָּה נְבִיאִים הָיוּ מִצְטַעֲרִין עַל הַדָּבָר הַזֶּה. אָמְרוּ. כָּתוּב אֵלֶּה הַמִּצְוֹת אֲשֶׁר צִוָּה יי אֶת־מֹשֶׁה. אִילּוּ הַמִּצְווֹת שֶׁנִּצְטַוִּוינוּ מִפִּי מֹשֶׁה. כָּךְ אָמַר לָנוּ מֹשֶׁה. אֵין נָבִיא אַחֵר עָתִיד לְחַדֵּשׁ לָכֶם דָּבָר מֵעַתָּה. וּמָרְדֳּכַי וְאֶסְתֵּר מְבַקְשִׁים לְחַדֵּשׁ לָנוּ דָּבָר. לֹא זָזוּ מִשָּׁם נוֹשְׂאִים וְנוֹתְנִין [בַּדָּבָר] עַד שֶׁהֵאִיר הַקָּדוֹשׁ בָּרוּךְ הוּא אֶת עֵינֵיהֶם וּמָצְאוּ אוֹתָהּ כְּתוּבָה בַּתּוֹרָה וּבַנְּבִיאִים וּבַכְּתוּבִים. הָדָא הִיא דִכְתִיב וַיֹּאמֶר יי אֶל־מֹשֶׁה כְּתוֹב זֹאת זִכָּרוֹן בַּסֵּפֶר. זֹאת תּוֹרָה. כְּמָה דְתֵימַר וְזֹאת הַתּוֹרָה אֲשֶׁר־שָׂם מֹשֶׁה לִפְנֵי בְּנֵי יִשְׂרָאֵל: זִכָּרוֹן

אֵילוּ הַנְּבִיאִים. וַיִּכְתֹּב סֵפֶר זִכָּרוֹן לְפָנָיו לְיִרְאֵי י'י וגו'׃ בַּסֵּפֶר אֵילוּ הַכְּתוּבִים. וּמַאֲמַר אֶסְתֵּר קִיַּם דִּבְרֵי הַפּוּרִים הָאֵלֶּה וְנִכְתָּב בַּסֵּפֶר׃

רַב וְרִבִּי חֲנִינָה וְרִבִּי יוֹנָתָן וּבַר קַפָּרָא וְרִבִּי יְהוֹשֻׁעַ בֶּן לֵוִי אָמְרוּ. הַמְגִילָּה הַזֹּאת נֶאֶמְרָה לְמֹשֶׁה בְּסִינַי. אֶלָּא שֶׁאֵין מוּקְדָּם וּמְאוּחָר בַּתּוֹרָה. רִבִּי יוֹחָנָן וְרִבִּי שִׁמְעוֹן בֶּן לָקִישׁ. רִבִּי יוֹחָנָן אָמַר. הַנְּבִיאִים וְהַכְּתוּבִים עֲתִידִין לִיבָּטֵל. וַחֲמֵשֶׁת סִפְרֵי תוֹרָה אֵינָן עֲתִידִין לִיבָּטֵל. מַה טַעְמָא. קוֹל גָּדוֹל וְלֹא יָסָף. רִבִּי שִׁמְעוֹן בֶּן לָקִישׁ אָמַר. אַף מְגִילַּת אֶסְתֵּר וַהֲלָכוֹת אֵינָן עֲתִידִין לִיבָּטֵל. נֶאֱמַר כָּאן קוֹל גָּדוֹל וְלֹא יָסָף. וְנֶאֱמַר לְהַלָּן וְזִכְרָם לֹא־יָסוּף מִזַּרְעָם׃ הֲלָכוֹת. הֲלִיכוֹת עוֹלָם לוֹ׃

[154]Rebbi Jeremiah in the name of Rebbi Samuel bar Rav Isaac: What did Mordocai and Esther do? They wrote a letter and sent to our rabbis[155]. So they said to them, do you accept upon yourselves these two days every year? They answered them, are not the troubles which come upon us enough, that you want to add to ours the trouble of Haman? They insisted and wrote them a second letter; that is what is written[156], *to confirm to them this second [Purim]letter*. What was written in it? They told them, if this is your fear, already it is written and deposited in Archives[157]: *are these not written in the annals of the kings of Media and Persia*[158]. Rebbi Samuel bar Naḥman in the name of Rebbi Jonathan: 85 Elders and among them more than 30 prophets[159] were sorry about this matter. They said, it is written[160]: *These are the commandments which the Eternal commanded to Moses*. These are the commandments which we were commanded by Moses's saying. So did Moses say to us: No other prophet will reveal to you anything afterwards. And Mordocai and Esther want to introduce something new[161]? They did not move from there but discussed [the matter][162] until the Holy One, praise to Him, illuminated their eyes and they found it written in the Torah, in Prophets, and in Hagiographs. This is what is written[163], *the Eternal said to Moses, write this in a book for remembrance*. *This* is the Torah, as you are saying, *this is the Torah which Moses put before the Children of Israel*[164]. *Remembrance* are the Prophets, *a book of remembrance is being written before Him for those who fear the Eternal,*[165] etc. *In a book* are the Hagiographs, *Esther's word confirmed the matter of these Purim days and it was written in a book*[166].

Rav, and Rebbi Ḥanina, and Rebbi Jonathan, and Bar Qappara, and Rebbi Joshua ben Levi said, this scroll had be said to Moses on Sinai; only there is no earlier and later in the Torah[167]. Rebbi Joḥanan and Rebbi Simeon ben Laqish. Rebbi Joḥanan said, Prophets and Hagiographs will in the future be nullified, but the five books of the Torah will never be nullified. What is the reason? *A strong voice, never ending*[168]. Rebbi Simeon ben Laqish said, also the Esther scroll and practices will never be nullified. It is said here, *a strong voice, never ending*, and it is said there, *their remembrance will not end from their descendants*[169]. Practices? *His practices are eternal*[170].

154 Babli 7a.
155 The established rabbinate in the Holy Land, the only one authorized to decree practices valid everywhere.
156 *Esth.* 9:29.
157 Greek 'αρχεῖον.
158 *Esth.* 10:2.
159 In Babli sources: 120 Elders.
160 *Lev.* 27:34. Quoted in the same sense in the Babli *Šabbat* 104a, *Yoma* 80b, *Temurah* 16b.
161 Since from the middle of Chapter 9 to the end of the Scroll the rules of Purim are written to be interpreted as biblical laws. This cannot be compared to Ḥanukkah which is a purely rabbinical time of remembrance. Writing new rules of biblical status is a clear violation of the prohibition *neither to add nor to subtract* (*Deut.* 4:2). This is a sufficient reason for Sadducees to reject the scroll and the attendant questionable activities.
162 Corrector's addition in Babylonian style.
163 *Ex.* 17:14.
164 *Deut.* 4:44.
165 *Mal.* 3:16.
166 *Esth.* 9:32.
167 Babli *Pesahim* 6a. Since the Torah is a timeless document, the historical succession must be irrelevant. In philosophical terms, they support Mendelssohn and possibly Maimonides, proponents of an abstract Judaism, against Jehudah Hallevi's Judaism as historical religion. The argument, *mutatis mutandis*, is found again in the attempts at justification of the medieval pseudepigraph *Zohar* as Tannaitic document.
168 *Deut.* 5:19.
169 *Esth.* 9:28.
170 *Hab.* 3:6. R. Joḥanan follows the first generation Amoraim in accepting Judaism as an abstract religion, which therefore is open to total re-interpretation [which even envisages disappearance of biblical holidays (*Midrash Mishle* 9[2]; Responsa Rashba #93.] R. Simeon ben Laqish accepts Judaism as historical religion whose rules do evolve but cannot be revolutionized.

(70d line 64) רִבִּי לֵוִי בְשֵׁם רִבִּי שִׁמְעוֹן בֶּן לָקִישׁ. צָפָה הַקָּדוֹשׁ בָּרוּךְ הוּא שֶׁהָמָן הָרָשָׁע עָתִיד לִשְׁקוֹל כַּסְפּוֹ עַל יִשְׂרָאֵל. אָמַר. מוּטָב שֶׁיַּקְדִּים כַּסְפָּן שֶׁלְבָנַיי לְכַסְפֵּי שֶׁלְאוֹתוֹ הָרָשָׁע. לְפִיכָךְ מַקְדִּימִין וְקוֹרִין בְּפָרָשַׁת שְׁקָלִים.

Rebbi Levi in the name of Rebbi Simeon ben Laqish. The Holy One, praiuse to Him, saw that the evil Haman in the future would weigh his money against Israel. He said, it is better that my children's money should precede this evil one's money. Therefore one precedes and reads the paragraph about *Šeqalim*[171].

171 A fundraising sermon concept to accompany the reading of *Ex.* 30:11-16 on the Sabbath preceding or falling on the New Moon of Adar (2). Originally this was introduced as a proclamation that the Temple tax was due. After the destruction of the Temple this reason disappeared and the Temple tax was turned into charity money and merged with the gifts due to the poor on Purim. Babli 13b.

(70d line 67) רִבִּי אַבָּהוּ בְשֵׁם רִבִּי לְעָזָר. בְּכָל־שָׁנָה וְשָׁנָה: הִקִּישׁ שָׁנָה שֶׁהִיא מְעוּבֶּרֶת לְשָׁנָה שֶׁאֵינָה מְעוּבֶּרֶת. מַה שָׁנָה שֶׁאֵינָה מְעוּבֶּרֶת אֲדָר סָמוּךְ לְנִיסָן אַף שָׁנָה שֶׁהִיא מְעוּבֶּרֶת אֲדָר סָמוּךְ לְנִיסָן. אָמַר רִבִּי חֶלְבּוֹ. כְּדֵי לִסְמוֹךְ גְּאוּלָּה לִגְאוּלָּה.

רִבִּי לֵוִי בְשֵׁם רִבִּי חָמָא בַּר חֲנִינָא. אוֹתָהּ הַשָּׁנָה הָיְתָה מְעוּבֶּרֶת. מַה טַעַם. מִיּוֹם | לְיוֹם וּמֵחוֹדֶשׁ לְחוֹדֶשׁ שְׁנֵים־עָשָׂר הוּא־חוֹדֶשׁ אֲדָר: אֲדָר הָרִאשׁוֹן תּוֹסֶפֶת. אֲדָר הַשֵּׁינִי תּוֹסֶפֶת. מַה בֵּינֵיהוֹן. רִבִּי שְׁמוּאֵל בַּר רַב יִצְחָק אָמַר. שְׁנֵי כִבְשֵׂי עֲצֶרֶת בֵּינֵיהוֹן. נוֹלַד בַּחֲמִשָּׁה עָשָׂר בָּאֲדָר בְּשָׁנָה שֶׁאֵינָה מְעוּבֶּרֶת וְנִכְנַס לְשָׁנָה שֶׁהִיא מְעוּבֶּרֶת. אִין תֵּימַר. אֲדָר הָרִאשׁוֹן תּוֹסֶפֶת. שָׁנָה אֲרוּכָה הִיא. אִין תֵּימַר. אֲדָר הַשֵּׁינִי תּוֹסֶפֶת. אֵין לוֹ אֶלָּא עַד חֲמִשָּׁה עָשָׂר בָּאֲדָר הָרִאשׁוֹן. אָמַר רִבִּי אַייבוּ בַּר נַגְרִי. מַתְנִיתָהּ אֶמְרָה כֵן. אֲדָר הָרִאשׁוֹן תּוֹסֶפֶת. דְּתַנִינָן תַּמָּן. הֵן הֵעִידוּ שֶׁמְּעַבְּרִין אֶת הַשָּׁנָה כָל־אֲדָר. שֶׁהָיוּ אוֹמְרִים. עַד הַפּוּרִים. הֵן הֵעִידוּ שֶׁמְּעַבְּרִין אֶת הַשָּׁנָה עַל תְּנַאי. הָדָא אֶמְרָה. אֲדָר הָרִאשׁוֹן תּוֹסֶפֶת. אִין תֵּימַר. אֲדָר הַשֵּׁינִי תּוֹסֶפֶת. לֹא קַיָּים עַל שַׁתָּא וּמְעַבֵּר לָהּ. מַר עוּקְבָא אַשְׁכַּח תְּרֵין אִיגְּרִין. בַּחֲדָא כְתִיב. וּשְׁפַר בְּאַפַּיי וּבְאַפֵּי חֲבֵרַיי מוֹסְפָה עַל שַׁתָּא תַּלְתִּין יוֹמִין. וּבַחֲדָא כְתִיב. וּשְׁפַר בְּאַפַּיי וּבְאַפֵּי חֲבֵרַיי מוֹסָפָה עַל שַׁתָּא יְרַח יוֹמִין. מָאן דְּאָמַר תַּלְתִּין יוֹמִין. אֲדָר הָרִאשׁוֹן תּוֹסֶפֶת. וּמָאן דְּאָמַר. יְרַח יוֹמִין. אֲדָר הַשֵּׁינִי תּוֹסֶפֶת. אֵין מִן הָדָא לֵית שְׁמַע מִינָהּ כְּלוּם. דְּאָמַר רִבִּי יַעֲקֹב בַּר אָחָא וְרִבִּי יוּדָן גְּזוֹרֵי רִבִּי סִימוֹן בְּשֵׁם רִבִּי יְהוֹשֻׁעַ בֶּן לֵוִי. לְעוֹלָם שְׁנֵי חֳדָשִׁים מְעוּבָּרִין. עִיבֵּר אֶת הָרִאשׁוֹן וְלֹא עִיבֵּר אֶת הַשֵּׁינִי מַה שֶּׁעָשָׂה עָשׂוּי. לְעוֹלָם אֲדָר סָמוּךְ לְנִיסָן חָסֵר.

Rebbi Abbahu in the name of Rebbi Eleazar: *Every year by year*[172]. It bundled an intercalary year with one which is not intercalary. Since in a year which is not intercalary Adar is next to Nisan, also in an intercalary year Adar is next to Nisan. Rebbi Helbo said, in order to make one liberation close to the other liberation[173].

Rebbi Levi in the name of Rebbi Hama bar Hanina: That year[174] was intercalary. What is the reason? *From day to day, and from month to month, to the twelfth month which is the month of Adar*[175]. Is the first Adar additional? Is the second Adar additional? What is the difference between them? Rebbi Samuel ben Rav Isaac said, the two lambs of Pentecost are between them[176]. If it was born on the fifteenth of Adar in a non-intercalary year and it enters an intercalary year; if you are saying that the first Adar is additional, it is a long year. If you are saying that the second Adar is additional, it[176*] has only up to the fifteenth of the first Adar. Rebbi Ayvo bar Naggari said, a Mishnah states that the first Adar is additional, as we have stated there[177]: "They testified that one may intercalate the year during all of Adar; for there were those who said, until Purim. They testified that one may intercalate the year conditionally[178]." This implies that the first Adar is additional. If you would say that the second Adar is the addition[179], it no longer is the year and he intercalates it? Mar Uqba found two letters[180]. In one was written, "it is good in my eyes and the eyes of my colleagues to add thirty days to the year." And in one it was written, "it is good in my eyes and the eyes of my colleagues to add a month to the year." He who says "thirty days" implies that the first Adar is additional[181]; he who says "a month" implies that the second Adar is additional. If from there, you cannot infer anything, as Rebbi Jacob bar Aha and Rebbi Yudan from Gezur, Rebbi Simon in the name of Rebbi Joshua ben Levi said, forever both months may be augmented[182]. If he augmented the first and did not augment the second, what he did is well done. Always the Adar close to Nisan is defective[183].

172 *Esth.* 9:21. The implication is that Purim should be celebrated in an intercalary year the way it is celebrated in a regular year.

173 In the Babli 6b both reasons are attributed to Rabban Simeon ben Gamliel. The opposing opinion of R. Eleazar ben R. Yose is not mentioned in the Yerushalmi.

174 The year described in the Esther Scroll.

175 *Esth.* 3:7, describing Haman's casting of lots (following the Babylonian calendar in which the intercalary month also was Adar.)

176 They are prescribed to be yearlings. On the face of it, they have nothing to do with the rules of Adar since they are due in

Siwan. The meaning of the statement is that if the first Adar is the addition, the second Adar is the last in the year and the year is stretched to 13 months. But if the second Adar is the addition then a month-year by definition has 12 months; the thirteenth month is neither of the preceding nor of the following year. (This argument is not found otherwise in the Talmudim.) In the first case, a lamb is a yearling up to the date of its birth in the following year; in the second case it is a yearling for 12 months from the date of its birth.

176* The lamb as a yearling.

177 Mishnah *Idiut* 7:7.

178 The calendar court has the entire month of Adar (necessarily the first) to decree the year as intercalary (and thereby changing the current Adar from 29 to 30 days) In the absence of the Patriarch the court may decree an intercalation subject to later approval by the Patriarch.

179 See Note 176.

180 This is the traditional style in which the Patriarch's court announces intercalation; cf. *Sanhedrin*: Yerushalmi 1:1 Notes 179ff., Tosephta 2:2-11, Babli 11b. In this case these were letters addressed to the Head of the Diaspora in Babylonia.

181 Since as noted at the end, the regular Adar preceding Nisan has 29 days.

182 The rule that the Adar preceding Nisan has 29 days is a desideratum; its violation does not invalidate any religious act.

183 Without explicit change from a competent authority.

(71a line 14) תַּנֵּי. רַבָּן שִׁמְעוֹן בֶּן גַּמְלִיאֵל אוֹמֵר. מִצְוֹת הַנּוֹהֲגוֹת בָּאֲדָר הַשֵּׁינִי אֵינָן נוֹהֲגוֹת בָּאֲדָר הָרִאשׁוֹן חוּץ מִן הֶסְפֵּד וּמִן הַתַּעֲנִית שֶׁהֵן שָׁוִין בָּזֶה וּבָזֶה. רִבִּי בָּא רַב יִרְמְיָה בְּשֵׁם רַב רִבִּי סִימוֹן בְּשֵׁם רִבִּי יְהוֹשֻׁעַ בֶּן לֵוִי. הֲלָכָה כְּרַבָּן שִׁמְעוֹן בֶּן גַּמְלִיאֵל. רִבִּי חוּנָה רַבָּהּ דְּצִיפּוֹרִין אָמַר. הִנְהִיג רִבִּי חֲנִינָה דְצִיפּוֹרִין כְּהָדָא דְרַבָּן שִׁמְעוֹן בֶּן גַּמְלִיאֵל. לֹא אָמַר אֶלָּא הִנְהִיג. הָא לַהֲלָכָה לֹא. אֲבָל לְעִנְיָין שְׁטָרוֹת כּוֹתְבִין. אֲדָר הָרִאשׁוֹן וַאֲדָר הַשֵּׁינִי. אֶלָּא שֶׁכּוֹתְבִין אֲדָר הַשֵּׁינִי תִּינְיָין. רִבִּי יְהוּדָה אוֹמֵר. אֲדָר הַשֵּׁינִי כּוֹתֵב תי"ן וְדַיּוֹ.

[184]It was stated: Rabban Simeon ben Gamliel says, Obligations which apply to the Second Adar do not apply to the First Adar except for eulogy and for fasting which are equal for both[185]. Rebbi Abba, Rebbi Jeremiah in the name of Rav, Rebbi Simeon in the name of Rebbi Joshua ben Levi: Practice follows Rabban Simeon ben Gamliel. Rebbi Huna, the rabbi of Sepphoris said, Rebbi Ḥanina made it a custom in Sepphoris following Rabban Simeon ben Gamliel. He only said custom, therefore not as practice[186]. But in matters of documents one writes the First Adar, the Second Adar, only that for the Second Adar one writes תִּינְיָין. Rebbi Jehudah says, the Second Adar one writes ת, and it is enough[187].

184 A parallel text for this and the following paragraph is in *Šeqalim* 1:1, Notes 51 ff.

185 Tosephta 1:6, Babli 6b.

186 It is obligatory only in places which adopted the ruling.

187 In the anonymous opinion for both months one writes Adar, but the second one is qualified by "second" (in Aramaic, the language of contracts in both Talmudim.) R. Jehudah agrees that "Adar" alone means the First Adar in an intercalary year, but the Second may be indicated by a single letter ת, first letter of the Aramaic word "second". Babli *Nedarim* 63a.

(71a line 21) תַּמָּן תַּנִּינָן. אֵין בֵּין אֲדָר הָרִאשׁוֹן לַאֲדָר הַשֵּׁינִי אֶלָּא קְרִיאַת הַמְּגִילָה וּמַתָּנוֹת לָאֶבְיוֹנִים: רִבִּי סִימוֹן בְּשֵׁם רִבִּי יְהוֹשֻׁעַ בֶּן לֵוִי. אַף שִׁימוּעַ שְׁקָלִים וְכִלְאַיִם יֵשׁ בֵּינֵיהֶן. רִבִּי חֶלְבּוֹ וְרַב חוּנָה רַב בְּשֵׁם רִבִּי חִייָה רַבָּה. הַכֹּל יוֹצְאִין בְּאַרְבָּעָה עָשָׂר שֶׁהוּא זְמָן קְרִיאָתָהּ. אָמַר רִבִּי יוֹסֵה. וְיֵאוּת. כְּלוּם אֲמְרוּ. מַשְׁמִיעִין עַל הַשְּׁקָלִים. לֹא כְּדֵי שֶׁיָּבִיאוּ יִשְׂרָאֵל שִׁקְלֵיהֶן בְּעוֹנָתָן. אִם אוֹמֵר אַתְּ. בַּאֲדָר הָרִאשׁוֹן. עַד כְּדוֹן אִית בַּשַּׁתָּא שִׁיתִּין יוֹמִין. כְּלוּם אֲמְרוּ יוֹצְאִין אַף עַל הַכִּלְאַיִם לֹא כְּדֵי שֶׁיִּהוּ הַצְּמָחִין נִיכָּרִין. אִם אוֹמֵר אַתְּ בַּאֲדָר הָרִאשׁוֹן. עַד כְּדוֹן אִינּוּן דַּקִּיקִין.

[188]There, we have stated: "The only difference between a First Adar and a Second Adar is the reading of the Esther scroll and gifts to the poor". Rebbi Simon in the name of Rebbi Joshua ben Levi, also proclamations regarding *sheqalim* and *kilaim* are between them[189]. Rebbi Helbo and Rav Huna, Rav in the name of the Great Rabbi Hiyya: Everybody may fulfill his obligation on the Fourteenth, which is the time of its reading[67]. Rebbi Yose said, this[190] is correct. Did they not say,. one proclaims about *sheqalim*, so that Israel should bring their *sheqalim* in time? If you would say on the First Adar, there still would be sixty days {left} in the year. Did they not say, also one goes to inspect for *kilaim*, not that the plants should be recognizable? If you would say in the First Adar, they still would be small.

188 The origin of this paragraph is *Šeqalim* 1:1 (Notes 19 ff.); therefore the Mishnah here is quoted as "there".

189 Mishnah *Sheqalim* 1:1 in an intercalary year refers to the first day of Second Adar.

190 This refers to the statement of R. Simon.

(fol. 69d) **משנה ח**: אֵין בֵּין יוֹם טוֹב לַשַׁבָּת אֶלָּא אוֹכֶל נֶפֶשׁ בִּלְבָד. אֵין בֵּין שַׁבָּת לְיוֹם הַכִּיפּוּרִים אֶלָּא שֶׁזֶּה זְדוֹנוֹ בִּידֵי אָדָם וְזֶה זְדוֹנוֹ בְּהִיכָּרֵת:

Mishnah 8: The only difference between holiday and Sabbath refers to preparation of food[191]. The only difference between Sabbath and the Day of Atonement is that in the first case its intentional desecration is punished by man and in the second case by extirpation[192].

191 There are many differences in the rules which are different for holidays and for the Sabbath. What is stated here is that what is biblically forbidden on the Sabbath (enumerated in *Sabbath* 7:2) is biblically forbidden on a holiday except anything used for the preparation of food which is explicitly exempted from prohibition (*Ex.* 12:16.

192 Anything biblically forbidden on a Sabbath is forbidden on the Day of Atonement without exception (but eating is forbidden on the Day of Atonement and required on the Sabbath.)

(71a line 29) **הלכה ח**: [תַּנֵּי בְשֵׁם רִבִּי יְהוּדָה. אַף מַכְשִׁירֵי אוֹכֶל נֶפֶשׁ הִתִּירוּ. מַה בֵּינֵיהוֹן. רַב חִסְדָּי אוֹמֵר. לְחַדֵּד רֹאשׁוֹ שֶׁל שַׁפּוּד בֵּינֵיהוֹן. רִבִּי חֲנִינָא בְּרֵיהּ דְּרִבִּי אַבָּהוּ. הוֹצִיא אֵשׁ מֵהָאֲבָנִים בֵּינֵיהוֹן. תַּנָּא רִבִּי יְהוּדָה בַּר פָּזִי דְּבַרְזִילָה. הוּא הַדָּבָר. מָהוּ הוּא הַדָּבָר. לְחַדֵּד רֹאשׁוֹ שֶׁלְשַׁפּוּד הוּא הַדָּבָר אוֹ לְהוֹצִיא אֵשׁ מֵהָאֲבָנִים הוּא הַדָּבָר. לֵית לָךְ אֶלָּא כְהָדָא. אֵין מַשְׁחִיזִין אֶת הַסַּכִּין אֲבָל מַשִּׁיאָהּ עַל גַּבֵּי חֲבֶירְתָּהּ. אָמַר רַב חִסְדָּי. דְּרִבִּי יוּדָא הִיא. דָּמַר רִבִּי יוּדָא בְשֵׁם שְׁמוּאֵל. דִּבְרֵי הַכֹּל הִיא. כְּדֵי לְהַעֲבִיר שַׁמְנוּנִית שֶׁעָלֶיהָ.

Halakhah 8: [193][It was stated in the name of Rebbi Jehudah, they also permitted actions preparatory to the preparation of food[194]. What is between them? Rav Ḥisday said, to sharpen the tip of the spit is between them. Rebbi Hanania the son of Rebbi Abbahu said, to produce fire from stones is between them. Rebbi Jehudah bar Pazi stated from Barzilah: what is the matter? Is the matter to sharpen the tip of the spit, or to produce fire from stones? You only have the following[195]: "One does not sharpen the knife but he cleanses it on another." Rav Ḥisday said, this is Rebbi Jehudah's, for Rebbi Jehudah in the name of Samuel said, it is everybody's opinion, to remove the fat on it.]

193 Corrector's addition. Except for the introductory sentence this is copied from *Yom Ṭov* 5:2 (Notes 82-88).
194 Tosephta 1:7. Since the preparation of food is permitted on a holiday but prohibited on a Sabbath, there necessarily is a gray area where the decision between permitted and prohibited actions must be rabbinical by biblical standards.
195 *Yom Ṭov* 3:8.

(71a line 36) כָּל־אֵילוּ בְּיוֹם טוֹב אֵין צוֹרֶךְ לוֹמַר בַּשַּׁבָּת. אֵילֵין אִינּוּן. וְהָא אִית לָךְ חוֹרָנִין. סְקִילָה בַּשַּׁבָּת. אֵין סְקִילָה בַּיּוֹם טוֹב. כָּרֵת בַּשַּׁבָּת. אֵין כָּרֵת בַּיּוֹם טוֹב. מַכּוֹת בַּיּוֹם טוֹב. אֵין מַכּוֹת בַּשַּׁבָּת. אֵין תֵּימַר. בִּדְבָרִים שֶׁיֵּשׁ בָּהֶן אוֹכֶל נֶפֶשׁ אֲתֵינָן מִיתְנֵי. וְהָא תַנִּינָן. מַשְׁחִילִין פֵּירוֹת דֶּרֶךְ אֲרוּבָּה בְּיוֹם טוֹב אֲבָל לֹא בַשַּׁבָּת. וְעוֹד מִן הָדָא. שׁוֹחֲקִין עֲצֵי בְשָׂמִים לַמִּילָה בְּיוֹם טוֹב אֲבָל לֹא בַשַּׁבָּת. אָמַר רִבִּי יוֹסֵה. וְהוּא שֶׁמָּל. וְעוֹד מִן הָדָא דְתַנֵּי. מוֹדִין חֲכָמִים לְרִבִּי מֵאִיר בְּחוֹתָמוֹת שֶׁבַּקַּרְקַע שֶׁמְּפַקְפְּקִין וּמַפְקִיעִין וּמַתִּירִין וְחוֹתְכִין. בַּשַּׁבָּת מְפַקְפְּקִין אֲבָל לֹא מַפְקִיעִין וְלֹא מַתִּירִין וְלֹא חוֹתְכִין. וּבַכֵּלִים בַּשַּׁבָּת מוּתָּר. אֵין צוֹרֶךְ לוֹמַר בְּיוֹם טוֹב.

[196]"All these were said on a holiday, so much more on the Sabbath.." Are these it? Are there no others[197]? There is stoning on the Sabbath, there is no stoning on a holiday. There is extirpation on the Sabbath, there is no extirpation on a holiday. There is flogging on a holiday, there is no flogging on the Sabbath[198]. If you would say, we are coming to state cases connected with food, did we not state: "one lowers produce through a skylight on the holiday but not on the Sabbath[199]"? In addition from the following, one grinds aromatic wood for a circumcision on a holiday but not on the Sabbath[200]. Rebbi Yose said, only if he circumcised[201]. In addition from what was stated[202], "The Sages agree with Rebbi Meïr about seals in the ground that one pushes aside, and removes, and unties, and cuts. On the Sabbath one pushes aside but one does not remove nor untie nor cut. For implements on the Sabbath it is permitted; it is not necessary to mention on a holiday."

196 The paragraph is from *Yom Tov* 5:2, Notes 77 ff., based on the quote from Mishnah 5:2.
197 One proves that the list is incomplete.
198 Desecrating the Sabbath is a capital crime, intentional desecration being punishable by stoning if there are witnesses, by divine extirpation otherwise. Desecration of a holiday is a simple transgression, intentional desecration before witnesses is punishable by flogging.
199 Mishnah *Yom Tov* 5:1.
200 Babli *Šabbat* 134a.
201 Since grinding aromatic wood is not preparation of food it may be done if the necessity is clearly established, not in advance of an expected event.
202 The following is copied from *Yom Tov* 4:2, Notes 60-61.

(71a line 45) אֵין בֵּין שַׁבָּת לְיוֹם הַכִּיפּוּרִים אֶלָּא שֶׁזֶּה זְדוֹנוֹ בִּידֵי אָדָם וְזֶה זְדוֹנוֹ בְּהִיכָּרֵת: הָא בְּתַשְׁלוּמִין שְׁנֵיהֶן שָׁוִין. מַתְנִיתָהּ דְּרִבִּי נְחוּנְיָה בֶּן הַקָּנָה. דְּתַנֵּי. רִבִּי נְחוּנְיָה בֶּן הַקָּנָה אוֹמֵר. יוֹם הַכִּיפּוּרִים כַּשַּׁבָּת בַּתַּשְׁלוּמִין. רִבִּי שִׁמְעוֹן בֶּן מְנַסְיָא אוֹמֵר. מְחוּיָּבֵי כָרֵתוֹת כִּמְחוּיָּבֵי מִיתוֹת בֵּית דִּין. מַה נָּפַק מִבֵּינֵיהוֹן. רִבִּי אָחָא בְשֵׁם רִבִּי אֲבוּנָא. נַעֲרָה נִדָּה בֵּינֵיהוֹן. רִבִּי מָנָא

אָמַר. אַף אֲחוֹת אִשְׁתּוֹ בֵּינֵיהוֹן. עַל דַּעְתֵּיהּ דְּרִבִּי נְחוּנְיָיה בֶּן הַקָּנָה. מַה שַּׁבָּת אֵין לָהּ הֵיתֵּר אַחַר אִיסוּרָהּ אַף יוֹם הַכִּיפּוּרִים אֵין לוֹ הֵיתֵּר אַחַר אִיסוּרוֹ. וְאִילּוּ הוֹאִיל וְיֵשׁ לָהֶן הֵיתֵּר אַחַר אִיסוּרָן מְשַׁלֵּם. עַל דַּעְתֵּיהּ דְּרִבִּי שִׁמְעוֹן בֶּן מְנַסְיָא. מַה שַּׁבָּת יֵשׁ בָּהּ כָּרֵת אַף יוֹם הַכִּיפּוּרִים יֵשׁ בּוֹ כָּרֵת. וְאִילּוּ הוֹאִיל וְיֵשׁ בָּהֶן כָּרֵת אֵינוֹ מְשַׁלֵּם. רִבִּי יוּדָה בַּר פָּזִי אָמַר. מַכּוֹת וְכָרֵת מַה אֲמָרִין בָּהּ אִילֵּין תַּנָּיָיא. אָמַר רִבִּי יוֹסֵה. צְרִיכָה לְרַבָּנָן. רִבִּי יוֹנָה בָעֵי. וְלָמָּה לֹא שָׁמַע לָהּ מִן הָדָא דְּתַנֵּי רִבִּי שִׁמְעוֹן בֶּן יוֹחַי. דְּתַנֵּי רִבִּי שִׁמְעוֹן בֶּן יוֹחַי. רִבִּי טַרְפוֹן אוֹמֵר. נֶאֱמַר כָּרֵת בַּשַּׁבָּת וְנֶאֱמַר כָּרֵת בְּיוֹם הַכִּיפּוּרִים. מַה כָּרֵת שֶׁנֶּאֱמַר בַּשַּׁבָּת אֵין מַכּוֹת אֵצֶל כָּרֵת. אַף כָּרֵת שֶׁנֶּאֱמַר בְּיוֹם הַכִּיפּוּרִים אֵין מַכּוֹת אֵצֶל כָּרֵת. אָמַר רִבִּי מָנָא קוֹמֵי רִבִּי יוֹסֵי. מַה צְרִיכָה לֵיהּ. כְּרִבִּי שִׁמְעוֹן בֶּן לָקִישׁ. בְּרַם כְּרִבִּי יוֹחָנָן. אִם מַכּוֹת אֵצֶל מִיתָה יֵשׁ לוֹ לֹא כָּל־שֶׁכֵּן מַכּוֹת אֵצֶל כָּרֵת. דְּאִיתַּפַּלְגוֹן. הַשּׁוֹחֵט אוֹתוֹ וְאֶת בְּנוֹ לְשֵׁם עֲבוֹדָה זָרָה. רִבִּי יוֹחָנָן אָמַר. אִם הִתְרוּ בוֹ לְשֵׁם אוֹתוֹ וְאֶת בְּנוֹ לוֹקֶה. לְשֵׁם עֲבוֹדָה זָרָה נִסְקָל. רִבִּי שִׁמְעוֹן בֶּן לָקִישׁ אָמַר. אֲפִילוּ הִתְרוּ בוֹ לְשֵׁם אוֹתוֹ וְאֶת בְּנוֹ אֵינוֹ לוֹקֶה. מֵאַחַר שֶׁהִתְרוּ בוֹ לְשֵׁם עֲבוֹדָה זָרָה נִסְקָל. אָמַר לֵיהּ. אֲפִילוּ כְּרִבִּי יוֹחָנָן צְרִיכָה לֵיהּ. תַּמָּן לִשְׁנֵי דְבָרִים וְהָכָא לְדָבָר אֶחָד.

2 נחונייה (2) | כ נחונייא 3 בתשלומין | כ לתשלומין 4 נפק מביניהון | כ ביניהון אבונא | כ אבינא נדה | כ נידה 5 אף | ת אוף נחונייה | כ נחונייא לה | כ לו 8 ויש | כ אין אמ' | כ בעא 9 תנייא | כ תני יוסה | כ יוסי לרבנן | כ לרבניין בעי | כ בעא ולמה | כ למה 12 ליה | כ - 13 אם | כ מה לא | כ - 14 אם | כ - לשם | כ משם 15 נסקל | כ היה נסקל לשם | כ משם 16 שהתרו | כ שאילו התרו נסקל | כ היה נסקל 17 ליה | כ לו לשני | כ שני והכא | כ וכא לדבר | כ דבר

[203]"The only difference between Sabbath and the Day of Atonement is that in the first case its intentional desecration is punished by man and in the second case by extirpation." Therefore, for payment both follow the same rules[204]. This is by Rebbi Nehoniah ben Haqanah since Rebbi Nehoniah ben Haqanah says, the Day of Atonement follows the rules of Sabbath for payment. But Rebbi Simeon ben Menassiah says those subject to extirpation equal those subject to capital punishment. What is between them? Rebbi Aha in the name of Rebbi Abuna said, a menstruating adolescent girl is between them[205]. Rebbi Mana said, also his wife's sister is between them[206]. In the opinion of Rebbi Nehoniah ben Haqanah, just as the Sabbath does not become permitted after its prohibition started; so the Day of Atonement does not become permitted after its prohibition started. However, these may become permitted after their prohibition started, he has to pay. But Rebbi Simeon ben Menassiah said, extirpation applies to the Sabbath and the day of Atonement; extirpation does not apply to these, he has to pay. Rebbi Judah bar Pazi asked: What say these Tannaim about whipping and extirpation[207]? Rebbi Yose said, that is a problem for the rabbis. Rebbi Jonah said, why can we not understand

it from what Rebbi Simeon ben Yoḥai stated? As Rebbi Simeon ben Yoḥai stated: Rebbi Tarphon says, extirpation was mentioned for the Sabbath[208] and the Day of Atonement. Since for extirpation mentioned for the Sabbath there can be no whipping connected to extirpation[209], so for extirpation mentioned for the Day of Atonement there is no whipping in a case involving extirpation. Rebbi Mana said before Rebbi Yose: When do we need this? Not for Rebbi Simeon ben Laqish? But for Rebbi Joḥanan, if he admits flogging in death penalty cases, certainly flogging in extirpation cases, since they disagreed: If somebody slaughters an animal and its young for idolatrous purposes[210]. Rebbi Joḥanan says, if he was cautioned about an animal and its young, he is flogged, about idolatry, he is stoned to death[211]. Rebbi Simeon ben Laqish said, even if he was cautioned about an animal and its young, he is not flogged since he would be stoned to death had he been cautioned about idolatry[212]. He said to him, we need it even for Rebbi Joḥanan! Here are two cases, there it is one case[213].

203 This paragraph appears also in *Ketubot* 3:1 (כ), and in slightly different form in *Terumot* 7:1, in both cases in a much longer discussion about payment for torts inflicted during the commission of a crime. It is commonly held that civil claims cannot be enforced if the perpetrator is subject to criminal prosecution in a capital case; there is dispute whether this extends to cases punishable by whipping and/or extirpation by judgment of Heaven.

204 Payments for torts committed while desecrating the Day of Atonement are treated as if they were committed on the Sabbath.

205 If a single girl close to adulthood is raped, the rapist is subject to a fine and he has to marry her (*Deut.* 22:28-29). If he has sexual relations with her, he is subject to extirpation (*Lev.* 20:18).

206 The wife's sister is forbidden during the wife's lifetime (*Lev.* 18:18). No punishment is indicated in that verse, but in v. 26 all incest prohibitions are treated as equal; therefore it is implied that the wife's sister is prohibited under penalty of extirpation by Heaven.

207 Since the prior discussion (not repeated here) was between R. Joḥanan and R. Simeon ben Laqish, it is of interest to know what are the positions of the Tannaim R. Nehoniah ben Haqanah and R. Simeon ben Menassiah.

208 While desecrating the Sabbath is a capital crime, a desecration can be prosecuted in a human court only if the act was witnessed and criminal intent was proven by testimony that the perpetrator was duly warned before the act not to commit a capital crime. A Sabbath desecration not prosecutable in court is punishable by Heaven by extirpation (*Ex.* 31:14).

209 In the Babli, *Ketubot* 34b/35a, this is deduced from *Ex.* 21:22-23, where payment is due if a pregnant woman is injured and an abortion caused, but no payment is due if the woman is murdered.

210 Slaughtering an animal and its young on the same day is a simple prohibition (*Lev.* 22:28), punishable by whipping. Slaughter as idolatrous sacrifice is a capital crime.

211 Since no conviction is possible without proof of criminal intent, actual prosecution is possible only if the nature of the crime to be committed was known to the perpetrator. For R. Johanan the rules apply only to cases that actually come before the court.

212 For R. Simeon ben Laqish the rules of capital cases apply if capital punishment is a legal possibility even if the circumstances of the actual case prohibit its imposition.

213 The prohibiton of slaughtering an animal and its young also applies to profane slaughter; it is unrelated to the prohibition of idolatry. The parallel discussion in the Babli is *Hulin* 81b, where it is pointed out that one has to presume that the first animal was slaughtered for food but the second for idolatry; only in that case does one act result in two transgressions. But in the question asked here one deals with one transgression which, however, cannot be prosecuted for lack of witnesses.

(71a line 65) עַל דַּעְתֵּיהּ דְּרִבִּי שִׁמְעוֹן בֶּן לָקִישׁ. מַה בֵּין אִילֵּין תַּנָּיָיא לְאִילֵּין רַבָּנָן. לָאוִים. לֹא כְרִיתוֹת. רִבִּי יוּדָן אָמַר. הַבָּא עַל הַמַּמְזֶרֶת אִית בֵּינֵיהוֹן. רִבִּי חֲנַנְיָה אָמַר. אַף הַמַּצִּית גְּדִישׁוֹ שֶׁלַחֲבֵירוֹ בְּיוֹם טוֹב בֵּינֵיהוֹן. עַל דַּעְתּוֹן דְּאִילֵּין תַּנָּיָיא. הוֹאִיל וְאֵין בָּהֶן כָּרֵת מְשַׁלֵּם. עַל דַּעְתּוֹן דְּאִילֵּין רַבָּנָן. הוֹאִיל וְיֵשׁ בָּהֶן מַכּוּת אֵינוֹ מְשַׁלֵּם. מֵעַתָּה אֵילּוּ נְעָרוֹת שֶׁיֵּשׁ לָהֶן [קְנָס] לֹא כְרַבָּנָן. אָמַר רִבִּי מַתַּנְיָה. תִּיפְתָּר. דִּבְרֵי הַכֹּל בְּמַמְזֵר שֶׁבָּא עַל הַמַּמְזֶרֶת. וְאֵשֶׁת אָחִיו לֹא יְבִמְתּוֹ הִיא. אָמַר רִבִּי מַתַּנְיָה. תִּיפְתָּר. שֶׁהָיוּ לְאָחִיו בָּנִים וְאֵירֵס אִשָּׁה וָמֵת וּבָא אָחִיו וְאָנְסָהּ.

1 מה | כ מה איכא תנייא | כ תנאי רבנן | כ רבנין לאוים | כ לאוין   2 אית | כ -   אף | כ - גדישו | כ גדיש
3 שלחבירו | כ חבירו טוב | כ הכיפורים תנייא | כ תנאי   4 דאילין רבנן | כ דרבנין - | כ דאילו לא | כ דלא

[214]According to Rebbi Simeon ben Laqish, what is between these Tannaim and those rabbis[215]? Prohibitions without extirpation. Rebbi Judan said, he who sleeps with a bastard girl is between them[216]. Rebbi Hananiah said, he who puts fire to the grain stack of his neighbor on a holiday[217] is between them. These Tannaim think, since there is no extirpation, he pays. Those rabbis think, since there is flogging he does not pay. But then "these are the adolescent girls who can claim a fine" cannot follow the rabbis[218]! Rebbi Mattaniah said, explain it according to everybody if it refers to a bastard male who sleeps with a bastard girl[216] But is his brother's wife[219] not his sister-in-law? Explain it that the man's brother had children and had

performed the preliminary wedding with a woman when he died and his brother came and raped her[220].

214 This paragraph is the end of the long discussion about the possibility of fines if a crime was committed and has absolutely no connection with the topic discussed here. It is copied from *Ketubot* together with the preceding paragraph.

215 The Tannaim quoted in the preceding paragraph and the rabbis (presumed to be R. Meïr and his students) who formulated Mishnah *Ketubot* 3:1 which states that fines are due in all cases except capital crimes.

216 The bastard is a child born from adulterous or incestuous sexual relations. It is stated in *Deut.* 23:2: *No bastard may come into the Eternal's congregation.* This may be read (with Maimonides, *Issure Biah* 15:2) that marriage with a (male or female) bastard is punishable; then the rape of an unmarried bastard girl unquestionably requires a fine. Or it may be read (with RAVaD) that "come to" in rabbinic interpretation everywhere means sexual relations; then the rape of a bastard girl also incurs the penalty of flogging. Only relations and marriage between a male and a female certain bastards are permitted according to everybody.

217 Whose violation is punished by flogging; there is no extirpation.

218 Since it clearly states that crimes punishable by Heaven incur fines in human courts.

219 This is a separate Note, not connected to the preceding. According to the Mishnah the brother's virgin wife is entitled to the fine if she is raped by the brother in law. If the brother is alive, it is adultery, a capital crime. If the brother is dead, since she still is a virgin she has no children. If the brother has no children from another woman, any sex act between her and her brother in law, even rape, makes her the brother in law's wedded wife, with a claim to *ketubah* but no fine.

220 She is forbidden to him (*Lev.* 18:16) and by the argument of Note 206 there is extirpation.

(fol. 69d) **משנה ט**: אֵין בֵּין הַמּוּדָּר הֲנָאָה מֵחֲבֵירוֹ לַמּוּדָּר מִמֶּנּוּ מַאֲכָל אֶלָּא דְּרִיסַת הָרֶגֶל וְכֵלִים שֶׁאֵין עוֹשִׂין בָּהֶן אֹכֶל נָפֶשׁ. אֵין בֵּין נְדָרִים לִנְדָבוֹת אֶלָּא שֶׁהַנְּדָרִים מֵתוּ אוֹ נִגְנְבוּ חַיָּבִין בְּאַחֲרָיוּתָן וּנְדָבוֹת מֵתוּ אוֹ נִגְנְבוּ אֵין חַיָּבִין בְּאַחֲרָיוּתָן:

Mishnah 9: The only difference between one who is under a vow {not to have} usufruct from another[221] and one who is under a vow about use of food is passing through his real estate[222] and vessels that cannot be used to prepare food. The only difference between vows and voluntary gifts[223] is that for vows one is responsible if they died or were lost, and for voluntary gifts one is not responsible if they died or were lost.

221 Mishnah *Nedarim* 4:1. A is restricted in that B made a vow that A may have no usufruct from him. (If A makes a vow that B may have no usufruct of him, the active mode is used.)
222 Setting his foot on the other's property.
223 Dedications of animals as Temple sacrifices.

(71a line 73) **הלכה ט**: הָא דָבָר שֶׁעוֹשִׂין בּוֹ אוֹכֶל נֶפֶשׁ אָסוּר. לֹא מִמַּאֲכָל נָדַר. רִבִּי שִׁמְעוֹן בֶּן לָקִישׁ אָמַר. כֵּינִי מַתְנִיתָא. אֵין בֵּין הַמּוּדָּר הֲנָייָה מֵחֲבֵירוֹ לַמּוּדָּר הֲנָיַית מַאֲכָל מֵחֲבֵירוֹ. וְתַנֵּי דְּבֵית רִבִּי כֵּן. הַמּוּדָּר הֲנָיַית מַאֲכָל מֵחֲבֵירוֹ לֹא יַשְׁאִילֶנּוּ נָפָה וּכְבָרָה רֵיחַיִם וְתַנּוּר. תַּנֵּי. אֲבָל מַשְׁאִיל הוּא לוֹ כּוֹסוֹת וּקְעָרוֹת וְתַמְחוּיִין. שֶׁאֵינָן מְהַנִּין אֶת הָאוֹכֶל אֲבָל מַכְנִיסִין אֶת הָאוֹכֵל. לַפָּסִין וּקְדֵירוֹת אָסוּר. לִטְחוֹן וְלִדְרוֹךְ אָסוּר. לִקְצוֹר צְרִיכָה. לִבְצוֹר צְרִיכָה. הֲנָיַית מַאֲכָל מָהוּ. תַּנֵּי. אֲבָל מַשְׁאִילוֹ הוּא קוּרְדּוֹם. הַוֵּינָן סָבְרִין מֵימַר. בְּקַרְדֹּם שֶׁלְבִּיקוֹעַ. תִּיפְתָּר בְּקוּרְדּוֹם שֶׁלְנִיכּוּשׁ. וְלֵית שְׁמַע מִינָהּ כְּלוּם. רִבִּי אָבוּנָא אָמַר. רִבִּי יִרְמְיָה בָּעֵי. הָהֵן זוסטא מִכֵּיוָן שֶׁהוּא מַרְחִיק וְאִתְּ חֲשַׁר בֵּיהּ קִימְחָא. כְּמִי שֶׁהוּא נָפָח.

1 לא | נ ולא ר' שמעון בן לקיש אמ' | נ אמ' ר' שמעון בן לקיש   2 המודר | נ מודר   ותניי | נ תניי   4 משאיל הוא | נ משאילו   5 לפסין | נ לפסים   לבצור צריכה | נ ולבצור צריכא מאכל | נ -   6 הוא | נ -   בקרדום | נ בקורדום שלביקוע | נ שלבקעי   7 שלניכוש | נ שלמכוש זוסטא | נ יוסטה שהוא | נ -   8 מרחיק | נ די מרחק   ואת חשר | נ וחשר   כמי שהוא נפח | נ אסיר מישאל ליה

Halakhah 9: [224]Therefore vessels used to prepare food are forbidden. But did he not make the vow about food? Rebbi Simeon ben Laqish: so is the Mishnah: The only difference between one who is under a vow {not to have} usufruct from another and one who is under a vow about use for food. In the House of Rebbi it was stated thus: "One who is under a vow about use[225] of food should not borrow from him a fine or coarse sieve, a grindstone, or an oven." It was stated: But he may borrow from him cups and bowls and fruit bowls, since these are not used to prepare food, only to serve food. Pans[226] and pots are forbidden. To mill grain and to press grapes is forbidden. Harvesting grain is a problem, harvesting grapes is a problem. What kind of usufruct of food? It was stated: But he may borrow an axe from him. We wanted to say, an axe to split. Explain it by a hatchet for weeding, and you cannot infer anything. Rebbi Abuna said, that *zwsta*[227] since one removes and separates the bran from flour with it, it is like a sieve.

224 This is copied from *Nedarim* 4:1 (Notes 5-12,נ) since it refers to parts of Mishnah
Nedarim 4:1 not repeated in *Megillah* 1:9. Cf. Babli *Nedarim* 33a.

225 This is the text of Mishnah *Nedarim* 4:1 in the Yerushalmi; in the Babli "use for" is missing. It indicates that the original Yerushalmi Mishnah was the same as the Babli.
226 Greek λοπάς.
227 Neither the form given in *Megillah* nor that in *Nedarim* are satisfactorily explained.

(71b line 8) אֵי זֶהוּ נֶדֶר שֶׁאֲמָרוּ. בָּאוֹמֵר. הֲרֵי עָלַי עוֹלָה. וְאֵי זֶהוּ נְדָבָה שֶׁאֲמָרוּ. בָּאוֹמֵר. הֲרֵי זוֹ עוֹלָה. רִבִּי חָמָא חַבְרִין דְּרַבָּנָן בָּעֵי. אָמַר. הֲרֵי עָלַי. וְחָזַר וְאָמַר. הֲרֵי זֶה. רִבִּי חִינְנָה בָּעֵי. לֹא מִסְתַּבְּרָא [דִּידָהּ] אָמַר. הֲרֵי זֶה. וְחָזַר וְאָמַר. הֲרֵי עָלַי. אִיסּוּר חָמוּר חָל עַל אִיסּוּר קַל. אֵין אִיסּוּר קַל חָל עַל אִיסּוּר חָמוּר.

[228]"What is the vow about which they spoke? He who says, on me is the obligation for an elevation offering[229]. What is the voluntary gift about which they spoke? He who says, this one is for an elevation offering."[230] Rebbi Ḥama the colleague of the rabbis asked, if he said, "on me is the obligation", and came back and said, "this one is"[231]? Rebbi Ḥinena asked, would it not be reasonable if he said, "this one is", and came back and said, "on me is the obligation"? A severe prohibition falls one a simple prohibition but a simple prohibition does not fall on a severe prohibition[232].

227 Copied from *Roš Haššanah* 1:1 (Notes 136-141).
228 His obligation is extinguished only by the offering of a qualified animal as sacrifice, irrespective of other circumstances.
229 His obligation is limited to this particular animal. If it dies or develops a disqualifying blemish, his obligation is terminated.
230 Mishnah *Qinnim* 1:1. Babli 8a, *Roš Haššanah* 6a, *Ḥulin* 139a.
231 Is this a new obligation or is it a dedication of a specific animal intended to fulfill its prior general obligation? It is presumed that the second statement immediately follows the first.
232 In the second case, the voluntary gift is transformed into a vow. In the first case, the vow is not transformed into a voluntary gift.

(fol. 69d) **משנה י**: אֵין בֵּין זָב הָרוֹאֶה שְׁתֵּי רְאִיּוֹת לְרוֹאֶה שָׁלֹשׁ אֶלָּא קָרְבָּן. אֵין בֵּין מְצוֹרָע מוּסְגָּר לִמְצוֹרָע מוּחְלָט אֶלָּא פְּרִיעָה וּפְרִימָה תִּגְלַחַת וְצִפֳּרִים:

Mishnah 10: The only difference between a sufferer from flux who experienced two episodes and one who experienced three is the sacrifice[233]. The only difference between a sufferer from skin disease who is quarantined and one declared absolute is torn clothing, untended hair, shaving, and birds[234].

233 The impurity of the sufferer, a male from gonorrhea or a female from any genital emission, is the topic of *Lev.* 15:1-30 and Tractate *Zavim*. After one emission of fluid the sufferer becomes impure; he needs immersion in a *miqweh* and becomes pure at sundown. If he has two emissions in one day or in two successive days, he is a source of severe impurity and cannot become pure unless he was seven consecutive days without symptoms. If he has three emissions in at most three consecutive days, he cannot participate in any kind of sacred offerings unless after his purification he brings a sacrifice of two birds (*Lev.* 15:14,29).

234 In a number of cases of skin disease when the diagnosis is not clear cut, the sufferer is quarantined 7 or 14 days (*Lev.* 13:4,5,21,26,31. Even if after the quarantine the priest declares him not impure, he has to immerse himself and the clothing he wore during his quarantine in a *miqweh*, but during the quarantine he does not have to wear torn clothing and dishevelled hair like the person declared as certain sufferer (*Lev.* 13:45). After he is healed he still has to immerse himself and the clothing he wore during his impurity, but he does not have to undergo the purification ceremony described in *Lev.* 14:1-32. (Tractate *Nega`im*).

(71b line 12) **הלכה י**׃ אָמַר רִבִּי יוּדָה בַּר פָּזִי. דְּרִבִּי לְעָזֶר הִיא. דְּרִבִּי לְעָזֶר אָמַר. [אַף] בַּשְּׁלִישִׁית בּוֹדְקִין אוֹתוֹ מִפְּנֵי הַקָּרְבָּן׃ בְּרַם כְּרַבָּנָן. הַשְּׁנִיָּיה מְאוֹנָס טָהוֹר. וְהַשְּׁלִישִׁית מְאוֹנָס טָמֵא. אָמַר רִבִּי יוֹסֵה. אִין לֵית הִיא דְּרַבָּנָן וְלָא אוּף דְּרִבִּי לְעָזֶר לֵית הִיא. דְּתַנֵּי. אָמַר רִבִּי לְעָזָר. לֹא לְסוֹתְרוֹ אָמַרְתִּי אֶלָּא שֶׁלֹּא יָבִיא קָרְבָּן. לֹא אָמַרְתִּי שֶׁאֵינוֹ זָב לִסְתּוֹר זָב. הוּא לִסְתּוֹר לֹא אָמַרְתִּי אֶלָּא שֶׁלֹּא יָבִיא קָרְבָּן. הָדָא אֲמָרָה. דִּבְרֵי הַכֹּל הִיא. אִין תֵּימַר. דְּרִבִּי לְעָזֶר הִיא. נִיתְנֵי. הַשְּׁנִיָּיה בִסְתִירָה וְלֹא בְקָרְבָּן וְהַשְּׁלִישִׁית בִּסְתִירָה וּבְקָרְבָּן. עַל דַּעְתֵּיהּ דְּרִבִּי לְעָזֶר. רָאָה שְׁתַּיִם בְּשׁוּפִי וְאַחַת בְּקוֹשִׁי סוֹתֶרֶת וְאֵינָהּ מְבִיאָה קָרְבָּן.

Halakhah 10: Rebbi Jehudah bar Pazi said, this is Rebbi Eleazar's, for "Rebbi Eleazar said, [also] the third time one checks him out because of the sacrifice.[235]" But for the rabbis, the second time if forced he is pure, but the third time if forced is impure[236]. Rebbi Yose said, if it is not the rabbis', it also is not Rebbi Eleazar's, as it was stated: Rebbi Eleazar said, I did not say to undo his count[237], only that he may not bring a sacrifice. I did not say that he is not a sufferer from flux to undo the count of episodes; not to upset his status did I say but that he may not bring a sacrifice. This implies that it[238] is everybody's opinion. If you would say it is Rebbi Eleazar's it should state:

the second time is subject to undoing but not a sacrifice, the third time to undoing and sacrifice[239]. In Rebbi Eleazar's opinion, if she experienced two episodes of easy flux[240] and one in difficulty she undoes[241] and does not bring a sacrifice.

235 Mishnah *Zavim* 2:2. The Mishnah states that the male sufferer from flux is impure only if he has a discharge for a medical condition. If it is possible that the discharge is an ejaculation of semen because of some exterior influence, he still is impure and needs immersion but this is not cumulative and does not start a count. Then the Mishnah restricts this investigation to the first two times. A third episode within 3 days establishes a pattern; the cause must be medical.

The majority of sources including Maimonides's autograph Mishnah (and the organization of the Mishnah) indicate that the name is correctly "Eleazar" and not "Eliezer".

236 According to the anonymous majority, the Mishnah should mention that there is another difference between two and three times flux, that the second may be checked and eliminated whereas the third may not.

237 He agrees that two consecutive counts establish a pattern which creates severe impurity but he holds that an obligatory sacrifice may be brought only if the obligation is clearly established, whereas impurity in most cases has to be observed on a suspicion.

238 Mishnah 10.

239 Similar to what was noted for the majority in Note 236, but with a different background.

240 Which establishes severe impurity.

241 If the third time would not be counted had it been the second, it cannot be counted for a sacrifice. If therefore an unquestionable third episode happens on a later date, the count for sacrifice has to start anew.

(71b line 21) אָמַר רִבִּי יוּדָן. מַתְנִיתָה בִּשְׁנֵי בְנֵי אָדָם. אָמַר רִבִּי חֲנִינָה. מַתְנִיתָה אָמְרָה כֵן. אֵין בֵּין מְצוֹרָע מוּסְגָּר לִמְצוֹרָע מוּחְלַט אֶלָא פְרִיעָה וּפְרִימָה וְתִגְלַחַת וְצִיפֳּרִים: הֲדָא אָמְרָה. בִּשְׁנֵי בְנֵי אָדָם אֲנָן קַייָמִין. אִין תֵּימַר. בְּאָדָם אֶחָד. נִיתְנֵי. אֵין בֵּין בַּהֶרֶת גְּדוֹלָה לַבַּהֶרֶת קְטַנָה. הֵיךְ מַה דְאַתְּ אֲמַר תַּמָּן בִּשְׁנֵי בְנֵי אָדָם אֲנָן קַייָמִין. וְהָכָא בִּשְׁנֵי בְנֵי אָדָם אֲנָן קַייָמִין.

פֵּרְחָה בוֹ מִתּוֹךְ הֶסְגֵּר. רִבִּי יוֹחָנָן אָמַר. טָעוּן צִפֳּרִים. רִבִּי לָעֶזֶר אָמַר. אֵין טָעוּן צִפֳּרִים. אֵין אָמַר רִבִּי בָּא בַּר מָמָל. מַתְנִיתָה מְסַייְעָא לְרִבִּי יוֹחָנָן. מִן־הַצָּרוּעַ: לְהָבִיא אֶת שֶׁפֵּרְחָה בְכוּלוֹ שֶׁיְּהֵא טָעוּן צִפֳּרִים. [וַ]הֲלֹא דִין הוּא. מַה אִם מִי שֶׁטָּהַר וְאֵין סִימָנֵי מְטַמְאָיו עִמּוֹ יְהֵא טָעוּן צִפֳּרִים. מִי שֶׁטָּהַר וְסִימָנֵי מְטַמְאָיו עִמּוֹ (לֹא) [אֵינוֹ דִין שֶׁ]יְהֵא טָעוּן צִפֳּרִים. [וַהֲלֹא] שֶׁעָמַד בּוֹ שְׁנֵי שָׁבוּעוֹת יוֹכִיחַ. שֶׁטָּהַר וְסִימָנֵי מְטַמְאָיו עִמּוֹ וְאֵין טָעוּן צִיפֳּרִים. אַף אַתָּה אַל תִּתְמַהּ עַל מִי שֶׁפֵּרְחָה בְכוּלוֹ. שֶׁאַף עַל פִּי שֶׁטָּהַר וְסִימָנֵי מְטַמְאָיו עִמּוֹ וְאֵין טָעוּן צִפֳּרִים. תַּלְמוּד לוֹמַר מִן־הַצָּרוּעַ: לְהָבִיא אֶת שֶׁפֵּרְחָה בְכוּלוֹ שֶׁיְּהֵא טָעוּן צִפֳּרִים. אִם אוֹמֵר [אַתְּ]

[ל]טַהַר מִתּוֹךְ הֶסְגֵּר לֹא יְהֵא טָעוּן צִפֳּרִים. וִיתִיבִינֵיהּ. לֹא מוּטָב לְהָשִׁיב פְּרִיחָה עַל פְּרִיחוֹת וְלֹא עֲמִידָה עַל פְּרִיחוֹת. אָמַר רִבִּי חֲנַנְיָה חֲבֵרוֹן דְּרַבָּנָן. מַתְנִיתָהּ מְסַייְעָה לְרִבִּי יוֹחָנָן. דְּכֵן תַּנְיָיא מָתִיב לַחֲבֵרֵיהּ. לֹא. אִם אָמַרְתְּ בָּזֶה שֶׁאֵינוֹ נִזְקָק לַחֲלִיטָה תֹּאמַר בָּזֶה שֶׁהוּא נִזְקָק לַחֲלִיט. הוֹאִיל וְהוּא נִזְקָק לְהַחֲלִיט יְהֵא טָעוּן צִיפֳּרִים. אָמַר רִבִּי יַעֲקֹב בַּר אָחָא. סוֹפָה מְסַייְעָה לְרִבִּי לְעָזָר. הַטָּהַר מִתּוֹךְ הֶסְגֵּר פָּטוּר מִפְּרִימָה וּמִפְּרִיעָה וּמִתִּגְלַחַת וּמִצֳּפֳּרִים: כָּל־מַה דַּאֲנָן קַייָמִין הָכָא. בַּפְּרִיחוֹת. אָמַר רִבִּי שְׁמוּאֵל בַּר אַבְדוּמָא. מַה פְּלִיגִין. לְהָבִיא צִפֳּרִים. אֲבָל לְהָבִיא קָרְבָּן כָּל־עַמָּא מוֹדֵיי שֶׁאֵינוֹ מֵבִיא קָרְבָּן. וְתַנֵּי כֵין. בַּשְּׁבִיעִי יְגַלַּח וּבַשְּׁמִינִי יָבִיא. אֶת שֶׁהוּא טָעוּן תִּגְלַחַת מֵבִיא קָרְבָּן. אֶת שֶׁאֵינוֹ טָעוּן תִּגְלַחַת אֵינוֹ מֵבִיא קָרְבָּן. רִבִּי חָמָא בַּר עוּקְבָה בְּשֵׁם רִבִּי יוֹסֵי בֵּרִבִּי חֲנִינָה. כָּל־יְמֵי אֲשֶׁר הַנֶּגַע בּוֹ יִטְמָא. אֶת שֶׁטּוּמְאָתוֹ תְלוּיָה בְנִגְעוֹ. יָצָא זֶה (שֶׁטָּהֲרָתוֹ) [שֶׁטּוּמְאָתוֹ] תְלוּיָה בִסְפִירוֹת יָמָיו. עַד כְּדוֹן פְּרִיעָה וּפְרִימָה. תִּגְלַחַת וְצִפֳּרִים מְנַיִין. רִבִּי לְעָזָר דְּרוֹמָייָא בְשֵׁם רִבִּי שַׁמַּי. זֹאת תִּהְיֶה תוֹרַת הַמְצוֹרָע בְּיוֹם. אֶת שֶׁהוּא מִיטַּמֵּא וּמִיטַּהֵר בְּיוֹם אֶחָד. יָצָא זֶה שֶׁאֵינוֹ מִיטַּמֵּא וּמִיטַּהֵר בְּיוֹם אֶחָד.

[242]Rebbi Yudan said: The Mishnah is about two persons[243]. Rebbi Ḥanina said, the Mishnah says so, "the only difference between a sufferer from skin disease who is quarantined and one declared absolute is torn clothing, untended hair, shaving, and birds." This implies that we are dealing with two persons. If you would say about one person, one should state: "the only difference between a large white spot and a small white spot.[244]" Just as you are saying there, we are dealing with two persons, so also here we are dealing with two persons[245].

If it spread while in quarantine[246], Rebbi Joḥanan said, he needs birds. Rebbi Eleazar said, he does not need birds. Rebbi Abba bar Mamal said, a *baraita* supports Rebbi Joḥanan: [247]*"From the sufferer from skin disease*[248]; to include one on whom it spread on his entire person that he needs birds. Is that not a logical argument? If a person became pure and the signs of what made him impure are not on him shall need birds[249], (should not) [is it not logical that][250] one who became pure and the signs of what made him impure are on him [shall] need birds? [But] the one on whom it was stable for two weeks[251] shall disprove it, since he became pure and the signs of what made him impure are on him, but he does not need birds. So do not wonder if one on whom it spread while in quarantine and the signs of what made him impure are on him does not need birds. The verse says, *from the sufferer of skin disease* to include one on whom it spread on his entire person that he needs birds." If you would say that one becoming pure in quarantine does not need birds, should he not have objected that it would have been better to argue spreading against spreadings and not staying stable against spreadings[252]? Rebbi Hananiah the colleague of the rabbis: the *baraita* supports Rebbi Johanan since the Tanna answers his colleague, no. If you are saying about this one who never was up to be declared absolute, what can you say about the one who was to be declared absolute[253]? Because he was to be declared absolute, he needs birds. Rebbi Jacob bar Aha said, the closing statement[254] supports Rebbi Eleazar. The one becoming pure in quarantine is not liable for torn clothing, and untended hair, and shaving, and birds. All of this is what we are considering here, about spreadings[255]. Rebbi Samuel bar Eudaimon said, all they are disagreeing is about bringing birds. But in the matter of bringing a sacrifice everybody agrees that he does not bring a sacrifice. It was stated thus: On the seventh he has to shave, on the eighth he shall bring[256]; one who needs shaving brings a sacrifice, one who does not need shaving does not bring a sacrifice. Rebbi Hama bar Uqba in the name of Rebbi Yose ben Rebbi Hanina: *All days on which the skin disease is on him he will be impure*[257], one whose impurity is caused by his skin disease. This excludes him whose (purity) [impurity][258] depends on the count of his days[259]. So far torn clothing and unkempt hair. From where shaving and birds[260]? Rebbi Eleazar the Southerner in the name of Rebbi Shammai: *This shall be the doctrine of the sufferer from skin disease on the day*[261]. One who may become impure and pure on one day; this excludes one who cannot become impure and pure on one day[262].

242 Here starts the discussion of the second part of the Mishnah, the sufferer from skin disease.

243 Not the rare case of a person about to be declared pure after quarantine when suddenly in the presence of the Cohen signs of impurity appear; Mishnah *Nega`im* 7:3.

244 A large white spot is one looking depressed and containing a white hair which is impure (*Lev.* 13:3). A small one is one not looking depressed and without a white hair (*Lev.* 13:4) which requires quarantine.

245 Also the first sentence of the Mishnah refers to two different people.

246 *Lev.* 13:13. If the entire skin of the patient is diseased, he is pure. Naturally while the disease is spreading he satisfies all conditions of severe purity, but since this requires a pronouncement by the Cohen, if there were no clear signs of impurity when

he was put in quarantine and at the end of the quarantine the entire skin already was diseased, the Cohen who sees him only at the start and the end of his 7 days of quarantine has to declare him pure out of quarantine without ever pronouncing him absolutely impure.

247 *Sifra Meṣora`* Introduction 6-8.

248 *Lev.* 14:3. As introduction to the bird ceremony the Cohen has "to see that the skin disease was healed from the sufferer from skin disease." Skin disease can be healed only from a sufferer from the disease; the final remark seems to be redundant. It is added to include also a sufferer who never was declared as such.

249 The disappearance of his symptoms is the sign that he is healed, in contrast to the person who is pure but far from healed in that all his skin is infected.

250 The corrector's changes are from the (Babylonian style) *Sifra*.

251 *Lev.* 13:6. If the white spot does not grow within 14 days nor develop a white hair, the person has to be declared pure (after immersion) even though his problem skin is still visible.

252 This is the proof that the *Sifra* supports the opinion of R. Johanan since following R. Eleazar instead of appealing to purity after a lengthy quarantine the Tanna should have mentioned the case of fast spreading skin disease which at the next inspection by the Cohen already has changed from a sign of impurity to one of purity and does not need birds.

253 The case of dispute between R. Johanan and R. Eleazar is not comparable to other cases of skin disease since the Cohen is not empowered to inspect during the quarantine; the patient never was in a state to be declared absolutely impure.

254 The second sentence of the Mishnah.

255 This seems to refer to a statement similar to the wording of the Mishnah in the Babli: The only difference between one declared pure after quarantine and one declared pure after being absolutely impure is shaving and birds. Since this envisages a situation like the one discussed here, it explicitly supports the Babylonian R. Eleazar.

256 *Lev.* 14:9,10.

257 *Lev.* 13:46.

258 Both the scribe's and the corrector's texts give the same meaning; the correction is unnecessary.

259 Since the Cohen cannot judge him during the intermediate days of his quarantine.

260 What is the biblical source of the statement of the Mishnah regarding these items?

261 *Lev.* 14:2.

262 Since quarantine makes impure for a minimum of 7 days.

(fol. 69d) **משנה יא**: אֵין בֵּין סְפָרִים לִתְפִילִּין וּמְזוּזוֹת אֶלָּא שֶׁהַסְּפָרִים נִכְתָּבִין בְּכָל־לָשׁוֹן וּתְפִילִּין וּמְזוּזוֹת אֵינָן נִכְתָּבוֹת אֶלָּא אַשּׁוּרִית. רַבָּן שִׁמְעוֹן בֶּן גַּמְלִיאֵל אוֹמֵר אַף בַּסְּפָרִים לֹא הִתִּירוּ שֶׁיִּכָּתְבוּ אֶלָּא יְוָנִית:

Mishnah 11: The only difference between Torah scrolls and Tefillin[263] and Mezuzot[264] is that Torah scrolls may be written in any language[265] but Tefillin and Mezuzot may be written only in Hebrew square script. Rabban Simeon ben Gamliel says, also Torah scrolls they only permitted to be written in Greek[266].

263 Boxes containing parchment with the verses *Ex.* 13:2-12,11-16, *Deut.* 6:4-9,11:13-21, "to be tied to the arms and be a sign between the eyes."

264 A single sheet with the same verses, "to be affixed to the doorposts of your house and your gates."

265 In translation for the purpose of study.

266 In translation, not in phonetic transcription into Greek letters as in Origenes's Hexapla.

(71b line 51) **הלכה יא**: כָּתוּב וַיְהִי כָל־הָאָרֶץ שָׂפָה אֶחָת וּדְבָרִים אֲחָדִים. רִבִּי לְעָזָר וְרִבִּי יוֹחָנָן. חַד אָמַר. שֶׁהָיוּ מְדַבְּרִים בְּשִׁבְעִים לָשׁוֹן. וְחוֹרָנָה אָמַר. שֶׁהָיוּ מְדַבְּרִין בִּלְשׁוֹן יְחִידוֹ שֶׁלְעוֹלָם בִּלְשׁוֹן הַקּוֹדֶשׁ. תַּנֵּי בַּר קַפָּרָא. יַפְתְּ אֱלֹהִים לְיֶפֶת וְיִשְׁכֹּן בְּאָהֳלֵי־שֵׁם. שֶׂיִּהוּ מְדַבְּרִין בִּלְשׁוֹנוֹ שֶׁלְיֶפֶת בָּאוֹהֲלוֹ שֶׁלְשֵׁם. בְּנֵי יֶפֶת גּוֹמֶר וּמָגוֹג וְיָוָן וְתוּבָל וּמֶשֶׁךְ וְתִירָס. גּוֹמֶר גֶּרְמַמְיָה. מָגוֹג גּוֹתִיָיא. מָדַי כִּשְׁמוּעָהּ. יָוָן אֶוָוסוּס. תּוּבָל וּתְנִיָּיה. מֶשֶׁךְ מוּסְיָיא. תִּירָס. רִבִּי סִימוֹן אָמַר. פָּרָס. וְרַבָּנָן אָמְרֵי. תְּרָקָא. בְּנֵי גוֹמֶר אַשְׁכְּנַז וְרִיפַת וְתוֹגַרְמָה. אַסְיָיא וְהַדְיַת וְגֶרְמָנִיקְיָה. בְּנֵי יָוָן אֱלִישָׁה וְתַרְשִׁישׁ כִּתִּים וְדוֹדָנִים. אֶלְסְטַרְסֶם אָבֵיָּה וְדַרְדְּנִיָּה. אֶת הָאַרְוָדִי רוֹדוֹס. אֶת־הַצְּמָרִי חָמָץ. אֶת־הַחֲמָתִי חֲמַת. עַד־לֶשַׁע. רִבִּי לְעָזָר אָמַר. עַד קַלְרָה. רִבִּי יוּדָן בַּר שָׁלוֹם אָמַר. מִיכָּן לַתַּרְגּוּם.

Halakhah 11: It is written[267] *all Earth was one tongue and unified words*. Rebbi Eleazar and Rebbi Johanan. One said, they were speaking seventy languages[268]. But the other said, they were speaking in the language of the Unique of the World, the holy language. Bar Qappara stated, *may God embellish Japhet and dwell in the tents of Shem*[269], that one should speak Japhet's language in Shem's tents[270]. *The sons of Japhet: Gomer and Magog, and Yawan, and Tubal, and Meshekh, and Tiras*[271]. Gomer, Germamia[272]. Magog, Gothica. Madai, as it is understood[273]. Yawan, Ephesus[274]. Tuval, Bythinia. Meshekh, Moesia. Tiras, Rebbi Simon said Persia, but the rabbis said Thrace. *The sons of Gomer: Ashkenaz, and Riphat, and Togarma*[275]. Asia[276], and Adiabene, and Germanicia[277]. *The sons of Yawan: Elisha, and Tarshish, Kittim and Dodanim*[278]. Elis[279], Tarsos, Euboea, and Dardania[280]. *The Arwadite*[281], Rhodos. *The Ṣamarite*, Homs. *The Hamatite*, Hama. *Up to*

Lasha`. Rebbi Eleazar said, to Kallirrhoe. Rebbi Yudan bar Shalom said, from here about the Targum[282].

267 *Gen.* 11:1.

268 Everybody understood all languages of the 70 peoples mentioned as descendants of Noah.

269 *Gen.* 9:27.

270 Greek was the common language of all Jews in the Roman Empire.

271 *Gen.* 10:2.

272 The district Jerma in N. Assyria. It is to be noted that Saadia Gaon in his Arabic Pentateuch translation disregards the determinations both of the Yerushalmi and the Babli (*Yoma* 10a) for the descendants of Sem and Japhet but follows the determinations given here for the descendants of Ham (*Gen.* 10:18-19).

273 Media.

274 Representing all of Ionia.

275 *Gen.* 10:3.

276 Not the continent, nor Asia Minor, but probably the city of Sardis.

277 A city in the province of Comagene, near the border of Cappadocia.

278 *Gen.* 10:4.

279 Possibly Aeolis. Note that in the text two names are written as one.

280 Dardanos in the Troas.

281 *Gen.* 10:18.

282 Since the names in the Hebrew text are unintelligible, the text itself authorizes translations which make it intelligible.

(71b line 63) אָמַר רִבִּי יוֹנָתָן דְּבֵית גּוּבְרִין. אַרְבָּעָה לְשׁוֹנוֹת נָאִים שֶׁיִּשְׁתַּמֵּשׁ בָּהֶן הָעוֹלָם. וְאֵילוּ הֵן. לַעַז לַזֶּמֶר. רוֹמִי לַקְּרָב. סוּרְסִי לְאִילְיָיא. עִבְרִי לַדִּיבּוּר. וְיֵשׁ אוֹמְרִים. אַף אֲשׁוּרִי לִכְתָב. אֲשׁוּרִי יֵשׁ לוֹ כְתָב וְאֵין לוֹ לָשׁוֹן. עִבְרִי יֵשׁ לוֹ לָשׁוֹן וְאֵין לוֹ כְתָב. בָּחֲרוּ לָהֶם כְּתָב אֲשׁוּרִי וְלָשׁוֹן עִבְרִי. וְלָמָּה נִקְרָא שְׁמוֹ אֲשׁוּרִי. שֶׁהוּא מְאוּשָּׁר בִּכְתָבוֹ. אָמַר רִבִּי לֵוִי. עַל שֵׁם שֶׁעָלָה בְיָדָם מֵאַשּׁוּר. תַּנֵּי. רִבִּי יוֹסֵי אוֹמֵר. רָאוּי הָיָה עֶזְרָא שֶׁתִּינָּתֵן תּוֹרָה עַל יָדוֹ אֶלָּא שֶׁקְּדָמוֹ דוֹר מֹשֶׁה. אַף עַל פִּי שֶׁלֹּא נִיתְּנָה הַתּוֹרָה עַל יָדָיו אַף הוּא נִיתַּן כְּתָב וְלָשׁוֹן עַל יָדוֹ. וּכְתָב הַנִּשְׁתְּוָון כָּתוּב אֲרָמִית וּמְתוּרְגָּם אֲרָמִית: וְלֹא־כָהֲלִין כְּתָבָא לְמִיקְרֵי. מְלַמֵּד שֶׁבּוֹ בַיּוֹם נִיתָּן. רִבִּי נָתָן אוֹמֵר. בְּדַעַץ נִיתְּנָה הַתּוֹרָה. וְאָתְיָיא כְרִבִּי יוֹסֵה. רִבִּי אוֹמֵר. אֲשׁוּרִית נִיתְּנָה הַתּוֹרָה. וּכְשֶׁחָטְאוּ נֶהְפַּךְ לָהֶן לְרַעַץ. וּכְשֶׁזָּכוּ בִּימֵי עֶזְרָא נֶהְפַּךְ לָהֶן אֲשׁוּרִית. גַּם־הַיּוֹם מַגִּיד מִשְׁנֶה אָשִׁיב לָךְ׃ וְכָתַב לוֹ אֶת־מִשְׁנֵה הַתּוֹרָה הַזֹּאת עַל־סֵפֶר. כְּתָב שֶׁהוּא עָשׂוּי לְהִשְׁתַּנּוֹת. תַּנֵּי. רִבִּי שִׁמְעוֹן בֶּן אֶלְעָזָר אָמַר מִשּׁוּם רִבִּי אֶלְעָזָר בֶּן פְּרָטָא שֶׁאָמַר מִשּׁוּם רִבִּי לְעָזָר הַמּוֹדָעִי. כְּתָב אֲשׁוּרִי נִיתְּנָה הַתּוֹרָה. מַה טַעַם. וָוֵי הָעַמּוּדִים. שֶׁיְּהוּ וָוִים שֶׁלַּתּוֹרָה דוֹמִים לָעַמּוּדִים. אָמַר רִבִּי לֵוִי. מָאן דְּאָמַר. בְּדַעַץ נִיתְּנָה הַתּוֹרָה. עַיִ"ן מַעֲשֵׂה נִסִּים. מָאן דְּאָמַר. אֲשׁוּרִי נִיתְּנָה הַתּוֹרָה. סַמֶּ"ךְ מַעֲשֵׂה נִסִּים. רִבִּי יִרְמְיָה בְּשֵׁם רִבִּי חִיָּיה בַּר בָּא וְרִבִּי סִימוֹן תְּרֵיהוֹן אָמְרִין. תּוֹרַת הָרִאשׁוֹנִים לֹא הָיָה לֹא הֵ"א שְׁלָהֶם וְלֹא מֵ"ם שֶׁלָּהֶן סָתוּם. הָא סַמֶּ"ךְ סָתוּם.

Rebbi Jonathan from Bet Guvrrin said, four languages are appropriate that the world should use them, and they are these: The Foreign Language[283] for song, Latin for war, Syriac for elegies, Hebrew for speech. Some are saying, also Assyrian[284] for writing.

Assyrian has a script but no language; Hebrew has a language but no script. They choose for themselves Assyrian script and Hebrew language[285]. Why is it called Assyrian? Because it is beautiful script; Rebbi Levi said, because they brought it with them from Assyria[286]. It was stated: Rebbi Yose said, Ezra was worthy that the Torah could have been given through him, only Moses's generation preceded him. Even though the Torah was not given through him, but he gave writing and language[285]; *and the script of the letter written in Aramaic and explained in Aramaic*[287]. *And they could not read this script*[288]; this teaches that it was given on that day[289]. Rebbi Nathan says, the Torah was given in paleo-Hebrew; this follows Rebbi Yose[290]. Rebbi said, the Torah was given in Assyrian, but when they sinned it was changed into paleo-Hebrew. When they merited it in the days of Ezra it was changed into Assyrian: *Also today I shall return to you what was told to change*[291]; *he shall write for himself this changing Torah in a scroll*[292], a script which in the future is apt to change. It was stated: Rebbi Simeon ben Eleazar says in the name of Rebbi Eleazar ben Protos who said it in the name of Rebbi Eleazar from Modiin, the Torah was given in Assyrian script. What is the reason? *The hooks of the pillars*[293], that the letters *vav* of the Torah look like pillars[294]. Rebbi Levi said, for him who said, the Torah was given in paleo-Hebrew, the letter *ayin* was a miracle[295]. He who said, the Torah was given Assyrian, the letter *samekh* was a miracle. Rebbi Jeremiah in the name of Rebbi Hiyya bar Abba and Rebbi Simon both were saying, in earlier copies of the Torah neither *he* nor final *mem* were closed[296]. Therefore *samekh* was closed[297].

283 Greek, the non-Hebrew language common to the Jews in the Roman Empire.

284 Hebrew square script, adopted from the Aramaic script of Northern Iraq, used by the Persian administration of the territories West of the Euphrates for their Reichsaramaic.

285 This refers to the tradition quoted in the Babli, *Sanhedrin* 21a: "Originally the Torah was given to Israel in Hebrew script and the Holy Language. It was given to them a second time in the days of Ezra in Assyrian script and Aramaic language. Israel chose for themselves Assyrian script and the Holy language." For this entire passage the Babli reference is *Sanhedrin* 21b-22a.

286 In the first version the name of the script has nothing to do with Assyria. In the second it is asserted that it is the Aramaic

script of what earlier was Assyria.

287 *Ezra* 4:7.

288 *Dan.* 5:8.

289 The Babylonian sages could not read the script on the wall because it was new. This claims divine origin for the square script.

290 The Babylonian R. Nathan follows the Babylonian tradition that traces Targum Onkelos to Ezra and asserts that he transcribed the Torah into Aramaic script.

291 *Zach.* 9:12. The translation here tries to express the homily implied by the quotes.

292 *Deut.* 17:18.

293 *Ex.* 27:10.

294 In paleo-Hebrew the letter *vav*, meaning "hook", really looks like a hook on a stick. In square script the hook is lost, only the stick is left.

295 This does not refer to the Torah but to the stone tablets. From the description that the tablets were written on both sides it is inferred that the letters pierced the stone; the same letters were visible on both sides. This creates a problem for circular shaped letters, *ayin* in paleo-Hebrew and *samekh* in square script.

296 The open final *mem* is exemplified in the Aramaic inscription of King Uziahu's ossuary. In early Medieval mss. the *he* looks like a ה, only that the left leg is not at the left end but touching the vertical bar somewhat to the right. The open *he* is recommended in the Babli, *Menahot* 29b. For a thorough discussion, cf. S. Liebermann, *Tarbiz* 4 (1933) pp. 292-293.

297 This justifies R. Levi's remark that only *samekh* but not final *mem* represented a problem.

(71c line 7) תַּנֵּי. רַבָּן שִׁמְעוֹן בֶּן גַּמְלִיאֵל אוֹמֵר. אַף בִּסְפָרִים לֹא הִתִּירוּ שֶׁיִּכָּתְבוּ אֶלָּא יְוָנִית. בָּדְקוּ וּמָצְאוּ שֶׁאֵין הַתּוֹרָה יְכוֹלָה לְהִיתַּרְגֵּם כָּל־צוֹרְכָהּ אֶלָּא יְוָנִית. בּוּרְגָּנִי אֶחָד בְּיָדָהּ לָהֶם אֲרָמִית מִתּוֹךְ יְוָנִית. רִבִּי יִרְמְיָה בְּשֵׁם רִבִּי חִייָה בַּר בָּא. תִּירְגֵּם עֲקִילַס הַגֵּר הַתּוֹרָה לִפְנֵי רִבִּי אֱלִיעֶזֶר וְלִפְנֵי רִבִּי יְהוֹשֻׁעַ וְקִילְסוּ אוֹתוֹ [וְאָמְרוּ לוֹ]. יָפְיָפִיתָ מִבְּנֵי אָדָם. רִבִּי יוּדָה בַּר פָּזִי אָמַר. רִבִּי יְהוֹשֻׁעַ בֶּן לֵוִי שָׁאַל. וְלָמָּה לִי נָן אָמְרִין. יֵשׁ בִּסְפָרִים מַה שֶׁאֵין בַּתְּפִילִין וּמְזוּזוֹת. שֶׁהַסְפָרִים נִכְתָּבִין בִּשְׁנֵי דַפִּים וּתְפִילִין וּמְזוּזוֹת אֵינָן נִכְתָּבִים אֶלָּא בְדַף אֶחָד. הָתִיב רִבִּי יִצְחָק בְּרֵיהּ דְּרִבִּי חִייָה כְּתוּבָה. דְּרַבָּה. שֶׁהַסְפָרִים נִכְתָּבִין בִּשְׁתֵּי עוֹרוֹת וּתְפִילִין וּמְזוּזוֹת אֵינָן נִכְתָּבוֹת אֶלָּא בְעוֹר אֶחָד. אֲמָרוּן חֲבֵרַיָיא קוֹמֵי רִבִּי מָנָא. אוֹ נֹאמַר. דַּף אֶחָד בִּשְׁנֵי עוֹרוֹת. לֵית הִיא דְּרַבָּה. אָמַר לוֹן. שֶׁכֵּן אֲפִילוּ סְפָרִים אֵינָן נִכְתָּבִים כֵּן. תּוֹלִין בִּסְפָרִים. אֵין תּוֹלִין לֹא בַתְּפִילִין וְלֹא בִמְזוּזוֹת. סְפָרִים שֶׁכְּתָבָן כִּתְפִילִין וְכִמְזוּזוֹת אֵין תּוֹלִין בָּהֶן. תְּפִילִין וּמְזוּזוֹת שֶׁכְּתָבָן כִּסְפָרִים תּוֹלִין בָּהֶן. רִבִּי זְעוּרָה בְּשֵׁם רִבִּי אִימִּי. הָיָה כּוֹתֵב. אלה עם. אִם הָיְתָה הַפָּרָשָׁה עֲשׂוּיָה כֵּן כָּשֵׁר. וְאִם לָאו פָּסוּל. רִבִּי זְעוּרָה בְּשֵׁם רִבִּי אִימִּי בַּר חִינָּנָא. כְּכְתָב סְפָרִים כֵּן כְּתָב תְּפִילִין וּמְזוּזוֹת.

It was stated: Rabban Simeon ben Gamliel says, even Torah scrolls they only permitted to be written in Greek. They investigated and found that the Torah may be correctly translated only into Greek. A villager invented for them Aramaic from the Greek[298]. Rebbi Jeremiah in the name of Rebbi Hiyya bar Abba: Akylas the proselyte translated the Torah[299] before Rebbi Eliezer and Rebbi Joshua; they praised him [and said to him], *you are a superhuman beauty*[300]. Rebbi Jehudah bar Pazy said, Rebbi Joshua ben Levi asked, why do we not say there is a rule valid for Torah scrolls which does not apply to Tefillin and Mezuzot, in that Torah scrolls may be written on two sheets[301], but Tefillin and Mezuzot may only be written on single sheets. Rebbi Isaac the son of Rebbi Hiyya the scribe asked, a stronger question, in that Torah scrolls may be written on two hides[302], but Tefillin and Mezuzot may only be written on single hides. The colleagues said before Rebbi Mana, or should we say, one column of two different hides? Is that not stronger? He said to them, because even scrolls are not written in this way[303]. One suspends in scrolls[304]; one suspends neither in Tefillin nor in Mezuzot. One does not suspend in scrolls which were written as Tefillin and Mezuzot; one suspends in Tefillin and Mezuzot written as scrolls[305]. Rebbi Ze`ira in the name of Rebbi Immi: If he was writing אלא עם, if the paragraph was made in this way it is qualified, otherwise disqualified[306]. Rebbi Ze`ira in the name of Rebbi Immi bar Hinena: The script of scrolls is used as script of Tefillin and Mezuzot[307].

298 This disqualifies all Aramaic translations, even Targum Onkelos canonized in Babylonia.

299 Into Greek. In the Babli 3a he is credited with the Aramaic translation as restoration of Ezra's Aramaic translation.

300 *Ps.* 45:3.

301 Even a single book of the Torah is written on many sheets which then are sewn together. The short texts of Tefillin and Mezuzot must be written on single sheets. Babli *Menahot* 33a.

302 The leather on which the scroll is written does not have to be prepared from a single hide.

303 Rectangular sheets of leather may be sewn together to form a scroll; the stiches must be between the columns and may not intrude into the writing.

304 If a letter or a word in the text was forgotten it may be added between the lines over of the place to which it belongs.

305 If in writing the paragraphs required for Tefillin or Mezuzot one has the choice to use the written text either as part of a scroll or as Tefillin or Mezuzah, one must follow the more stringent rules. But if these paragraphs are written as part of columns of a scroll, they cannot be used in Tefillin or Mezuzot and errors may be corrected by suspending the missing letters or words.

306 If a line is short, in this example 6 spaces (the Babli requires a minimum of 9) it is acceptable if and only if the entire column is equally slim.

307 Babli *Menahot* 29b.

(71c line 24) רִבִּי זְעוּרָה בְשֵׁם רַב. נִיקַב נֶקֶב בְּיְרִיכוֹ שֶׁלְהֵ"א. אִם גּוֹרְדוֹ וְנִשְׁתַּיֵּיר שָׁם יֶרֶךְ קְטַנָּה כָּשֵׁר. וְאִם לָאו פָּסוּל. רִבִּי זְעוּרָה בְשֵׁם רַב חִסְדָּא. הָיָה הַגִּימֶ"ל מְכַלֶּה אֶת (הַגְּבוּל) [הַגְּוִיל]. אִם גּוֹרְדוֹ וְנִשְׁתַּיֵּיר שָׁם יֶרֶךְ קְטַנָּה כָּשֵׁר. וְאִם לָאו פָּסוּל. רִבִּי זְעוּרָה בְשֵׁם אֲשִׁיָּיאן בַּר נִדְבָּה. נִיקַב נֶקֶב בְּאֶמְצַע בֵּי"ת. אִם הָיָה (הַגְּבוּל) [הַגְּוִיל] מַקִּיפוֹ מִכָּל־צַד כָּשֵׁר. וְאִם לָאו פָּסוּל. אָמַר רִבִּי זְעוּרָה. אַתְיָא דְרַב חִסְדָּא כְרַב וּתְרֵיהוֹן פְּלִיגִין עַל שִׁיטָתֵיהּ דַּאֲשִׁיָּיאן בַּר נִדְבָּה. חַבְרַיָּיא אָמְרֵי. אַתְיָא דַּאֲשִׁיָּיאן בַּר נִדְבָּה כְּרִבִּי יוֹחָנָן.

דְּתַנֵּי. עִירַב אֶת הָאוֹתִיּוֹת. אִית תַּנֵּיי תַנֵּי. כָּשֵׁר. אִית תַּנֵּיי תַנֵּי. פָּסוּל. רִבִּי אָדָא בַּר שִׁמְעוֹן בְּשֵׁם רִבִּי יוֹחָנָן. מָאן דְּאָמַר כָּשֵׁר. מִלְמַטְּן. מָאן דְּאָמַר פָּסוּל. מִלְמַעְלָן. מִלְמַעְלָן. כְּגוֹן אַרְצֵינוּ תִפְאַרְתֵּינוּ. אַרְצְךָ צְרִיכָה. תִּפְאַרְתָּךְ צְרִיכָה.

1 אית | ב ואית אדא | ב אידי בר | ב בשם ר'   2 מאן דאמ' | ב מן דמר (2)

Rebbi Ze`ira in the name of Rav: If there is a hole in the hip of a *he*, if one shaves it off and there remains a small hip it is qualified, otherwise it is disqualified[308]. Rebbi Ze`ira in the name of Rav Ḥisda: If a *gimel* was at the end (of the border) [of the leather][309]. If one shaves it off and there remains a small hip it is qualified, otherwise it is disqualified. Rebbi Ze`ira in the name of Ashian bar Nidba[310]. If there was a hole in the middle of a *bet*. If the (border) [leather] surrounds it on every side it is qualified, otherwise it is disqualified[311]. Rebbi Ze`ira said, it turns out that Rav Ḥisda follows Rav and both disagree with the system of Ashian bar Nidba. The colleagues are saying, Ashian bar Nidba parallels Rebbi Joḥanan.

[312]As it was stated. If he mixed the letters. There are Tannaim who state, it is qualified. There are Tannaim who state, it is disqualified. Rebbi Ada bar Simeon[313] in the name of Rebbi Joḥanan: He who says qualified, at the top. He who says disqualified, at the bottom; for example ארצינו, תפארתינו. ארצך is questionable, תפארתך is questionable[314].

308 If there is a hole in the leather where the right hand side vertical stroke of ה is written, the letter is not complete and therefore unacceptable. Rav permits to shave off the ink around the hole and below. If a small vertical stroke is left, the letter now is legible and entire; the text may be used for public reading from the scroll or as Tefillin or Mezuzah.

309 It seems that the corrector's change is the result of his misunderstanding the text. It is required that each letter in the text be surrounded by blank space. If a letter reaches the border of the sheet, Rav Ḥisda permits shaving off a little bit to create the blank space if the remaining writing still is legible.

310 In the Babli *Menaḥot* 29a his name is Ashian bar Nidbakh.

311 He denies that the space around the

letter can be created by shaving off some ink from the letter in question. He then requires that the entire letter be removed and rewritten.

312 The following two paragraphs are also in *Berakhot* 2:3 (Notes 145-152), as part of a series of statements of R. Idi in the name of R. Simon. Factually the first paragraph has no relevance in *Berakhot* and the second does not fit here.

313 As noted, read: R. Idi in the name of R. Simon (ben Laqish).

314 (Rashba Responsa 1:711.) If a letter is completely written and its foot accidentally touches the following letter, as with a slightly too long foot of נ in גנ, one may scratch off the superfluous length and has a complete acceptable letter. But when a letter has its head elongated, so that from the start the letter was not standing free, then the entire letter has to be scratched out and the writing has to start anew. The questionable case is a situation with a letter that is hanging down below the line, as in the combination תך when the small foot of ת meets the downward stroke of ך. In that case, the ת was complete but the ך was not; this case remains unsettled (i. e., for practical rulings both letters have to be erased and rewritten.)

(71b line 34) רִבִּי אָחָא בִּירִבִּי שִׁמְעוֹן בְּשֵׁם רִבִּי יוֹחָנָן. לֹא יַעֲמוֹד אָדָם וְיִתְפַּלֵּל בְּמָקוֹם גָּבוֹהַּ. מַה טַעַם. אָמַר רִבִּי בָּא בְשֵׁם רִבִּי פַּפָּא. מִמַּעֲמַקִּים קְרָאתִיךָ יְיָ. רִבִּי אָדָא בַּר שִׁמְעוֹן בְּשֵׁם רִבִּי יוֹחָנָן. לֹא יַעֲמוֹד אָדָם וְיִתְפַּלֵּל וְצָרִיךְ לִנְקוּבָיו. מַה טַעַם. הִכּוֹן לִקְרַאת־אֱלֹהֶיךָ יִשְׂרָאֵל׃ אָמַר רִבִּי סִימוֹן. הִתְכַּווֵן לִקְרַאת אֱלֹהֶיךָ יִשְׂרָאֵל׃ אָמַר רִבִּי אַלְכְּסַנְדְרִי. שְׁמוֹר רַגְלְךָ כַּאֲשֶׁר תֵּלֵךְ אֶל־בֵּית הָאֱלֹהִים. שְׁמוֹר עַצְמְךָ מִן הַטִּיפִים הַיּוֹצְאִין מִבֵּין רַגְלֶיךָ. הָדָא דְאַתְּ אָמַר. בַּדַּקִּים. אֲבָל בַּגַּסִּים אִם יָכוֹל לִסְבּוֹל יִסְבּוֹל. רִבִּי יַעֲקֹב בַּר אֲבַיָּה בְּשֵׁם רִבִּי אָחָא. שְׁמוֹר רַגְלְךָ כַּאֲשֶׁר תֵּלֵךְ אֶל־בֵּית הָאֱלֹהִים. שְׁמוֹר עַצְמְךָ כְּשֶׁתְּהֵא נִקְרָא אֶל־בֵּית הָאֱלֹהִים שֶׁתְּהֵא טָהוֹר וְנָקִי. אָמַר רִבִּי בָּא. יְהִי־מְקוֹרְךָ בָרוּךְ. יְהִי מִקְרָאֲךָ לַקֶּבֶר בָּרוּךְ. אָמַר רִבִּי בְּרֶכְיָה. עֵת לָלֶדֶת וְעֵת לָמוּת. אַשְׁרֵי אָדָם שֶׁשְּׁעַת מִיתָתוֹ כִּשְׁעַת לֵידָתוֹ. מַה שְׁעַת לֵידָתוֹ נָקִי אַף בִּשְׁעַת מִיתָתוֹ יְהֵא נָקִי.

1 אחא | ב אידי יוחנן | ב יוסי   2 בא | ב אבא בשם ר' | ב בריה דר' ר' אדא | ב אמ' ר' אידי בר | ב בר'   3 לנקוביו | ב לנקביו   5 היוצאין | ב היוצאות דאת אמ' | ב דתימ'   6 אביה | ב אביי   8 בא | ב אבא   9 כשעת ... יהא | ב [כשעת ... יהא]

Rebbi Aḥa the son of Rebbi Simeon[313] in the name of Rebbi Johanan: No man should stand at an elevated place and pray. What is the reason? Rebbi Abba the son of R. Pappai said: *From the depth I call on You, Eternal!*[315] Rebbi Ada bar Simeon in the name of Rebbi Johanan said: No man should pray when he has an urge to go to the bathroom. What is the reason? *Israel, prepare yourself before Your God.*[316] Rebbi Alexandri said: *Watch your feet when you go to God's house*[317]; watch yourself from the drops that drip from between your feet. That means, for urine. But for defecation, if he can bear it, let him bear it. Rebbi Jacob bar Abiah in the name of Rebbi Aha: *Watch your feet when you go to God's house*; watch yourself when you are called to God's house that you should be pure and innocent. Rebbi Abba said: *Your fountain shall be blessed*[318], your being called to the grave shall be blessed. Rebbi Berekhiah said: *A time to be born and a time to die*[319], hail to the man whose hour of death is like the hour of his birth; just as at the hour of his birth he was innocent so at the hour of his death may he be innocent.

315 *Ps.* 130:1.
316 *Am.* 4:12.
317 *Eccl.* 4:17.
318 *Prov.* 5:18.
319 *Eccl.* 3:2.

(71c line 46) רִבִּי בָּא בְשֵׁם רַב יְהוּדָה. הָיָה עָשׂוּי כַּחֲצִי חֲלִיטָה. שׁוּרָה הָעֶלְיוֹנָה שֶׁיֵּשׁ לְמַטָּה הֵימֶנָּה שְׁתַּיִם צָרִיךְ שֶׁיְּהֵא בָהּ שָׁלֹשׁ תֵּיבוֹת. הָאֶמְצָעִית שְׁתַּיִם. הַתַּחְתּוֹנָה אֲפִילוּ [עַל] הָאָרֶץ. רִבִּי זְעוּרָה בְשֵׁם רַב חִסְדָּא. הָיָה עָשׂוּי בְּמִין סִימְפּוֹן. שׁוּרָה הָעֶלְיוֹנָה שֶׁיֵּשׁ לְמַטָּה שְׁתֵּי תֵיבוֹת. הַתַּחְתּוֹנָה שְׁתַּיִם. וְהָאֶמְצָעִית אֵינִי יוֹדֵעַ. רִבִּי יִרְמְיָה אָמַר לָהּ רִבִּי זְעוּרָה בְּשֵׁם רַב חִסְדָּא. רִבִּי יוֹנָה וְרִבִּי יוֹסֵה תְּרֵיהוֹן אֲמְרִין. רִבִּי זְעוּרָה בְּשֵׁם אַשְׁיָין בַּר נִדְבָּה. חַבְרַיָּא אֲמְרִין. רִבִּי זְעוּרָה בְּשֵׁם רַב חֲנַנְאֵל. אִם הָיָה הַדְּיוֹ יוֹצְאָה מִבֵּין הַנְּקָבִים פָּסוּל. כֵּיצַד הוּא עוֹשֶׂה. לוֹחֲכָהּ בִּלְשׁוֹנוֹ וְהִיא עוֹמֶדֶת. טָעָה וְהִשְׁמִיט אֶת הַשֵּׁם. אִית תַּנָּיֵי תַנֵּי. תּוֹלֶה אֶת הַשֵּׁם. אִית תַּנָּיֵי תַנֵּי. מוֹחֵק אֶת הַחוֹל וְכוֹתֵב אֶת הַשֵּׁם וְתוֹלֶה אֶת הַחוֹל. רִבִּי זְעוּרָה רַב חֲנַנְאֵל בְּשֵׁם רַב. הֲלָכָה כְמִי שֶׁאוֹמֵר. מוֹחֵק אֶת הַחוֹל וְכוֹתֵב אֶת הַשֵּׁם וְתוֹלֶה אֶת הַחוֹל. רִבִּי זְעוּרָה רַב חֲנַנְאֵל בְּשֵׁם רַב. וְאִם הָיָה כְגוֹן אֲנִי יְהוָֹה אֱלֹהֵיכֶם מוּתָּר. לָמָּה. מִפְּנֵי שֶׁהֵן שָׁלֹשׁ תֵּיבוֹת אוֹ מִפְּנֵי שֶׁיֵּשׁ בּוֹ חוֹל. מַה נָּפַק מִן בֵּינֵיהוֹן. אֵל | אֱלֹהִים | יי. אִין תֵּימַר. מִפְּנֵי שֶׁהֵן שָׁלֹשׁ תֵּיבוֹת. הֲרֵי הֵן שָׁלֹשׁ תֵּיבוֹת. אִין תֵּימַר. מִפְּנֵי שֶׁיֵּשׁ בּוֹ חוֹל. הֲרֵי אֵין בּוֹ חוֹל. לֵית צְרִיכָה. בַּיי צְרִיכָה.

Rebbi Abba in the name of Rav Jehudah: if it was made like half a bagel[320]. The uppermost line under which are two others must contain at least three words, the middle one two, the lowest one even [*on the*] *earth*[321]. Rebbi Ze`ira in the name of Rav Hisda: if it was made like a double flute[322], the uppermost line under which are two others must contain at least three words, the lowest two. The middle one I do not know[323]. Rebbi Jeremiah said it: Rebbi Ze`ira in the name of Rav Hisda; Rebbi Jonah and Rebbi Yose both say, Rebbi Ze`ura in the name of Ashian bar Nidba; the colleagues say, Rebbi Ze`ira in the name of Rav Hananel. If the ink comes out of the holes it is disqualified. What does he do? He licks it off with his tongue and it jells[323].

If he made an error and omitted the Name. There are Tannaim who state, he suspends the Name. There are Tannaim who state, he erases the profane, writes the Name, and suspends the profane[324]. Rebbi Ze`ira, Rav Ḥananel in the name of Rav: practice follows him who says, he erases the profane, writes the Name, and suspends the profane. Rebbi Ze`ira, Rav Ḥananel in the name of Rav: but if it was like *I am the Eternal your God*[325] it is permitted. Why? Because these are three words or because part of it is profane? What is the difference between them? *God, Highest Power, Eternal*[326]. If you are saying because they are three words, they are three words. If you are saying, because part of it is profane, nothing there is profane. *For the Eternal* is questionable, *by the Eternal* is questionable[327].

320 If a Mezuzah is written in calligraphy in the shape of half-circles one inside the other then the inner arcs are shorter than the outer ones and contain fewer words.

321 *Deut.* 11:21. The addition by the corrector clearly has to be deleted.

322 Greek συμφωνία. It is _/-shaped, having the two mouth pieces close together but the bodies of the flutes diverging.

323 Whether it need 2 or 3 words. Therefore 3 certainly are sufficient. The Babli *Menaḥot* 30b quotes the first Tanna as R. Yose (whom Babylonian practice follows), the second one as R. Jehudah's.

324 If there is a hole in the leather or parchment which is visible once the ink has dried, the letter is incomplete and disqualified. But if the ink when dry covers the hole completely so that the reader will not notice the hole, it is qualified. Babli *Šabbat* 108a.

325 *Num.* 15:41.

326 *Jos.* 22:22. The situation does not occur in the Pentateuch.

327 Since it will be stated later that prefixes of the Name may be erased while suffixes may not, the question is whether an erasable prefix has the same status as a profane word preceding the Name.

(71c line 62) רַב שֶׁשָּׁעָה בְרֵיהּ דְּרַב חֲנַנְאֵל אָמַר. צָרִיךְ לִכְתּוֹב הֵ"א לְמַטָּה מֵאַרְכּוּבָתוֹ שֶׁלְּלָמֶ"ד. הֲלִי'י תִּגְמְלוּ־זֹאת. הָא לִי'י תִּגְמְלוּ־זֹאת. מְזוּזָה. אִית תַּנָּיֵי תַנֵּי. פְּתוּחָה. אִית תַּנָּיֵי תַנֵּי. סְתוּמָה. שְׁמוּאֵל בַּר שִׁילַת מִשְּׁמֵיהּ דְּרַב. הֲלָכָה כְּמִי שֶׁאוֹמֵר פְּתוּחָה. שֶׁאֵין זֶה מְקוֹמָהּ. פְּתוּחָה מֵרֹאשָׁהּ סְתוּמָה. פְּתוּחָה מְסוֹפָהּ פְּתוּחָה. פְּתוּחָה מִיכָּן וּמִיכָּן סְתוּמָה. טָעָה וְהִשְׁמִיט פָּסוּק אֶחָד. אִם יֵשׁ בּוֹ שְׁתַּיִם שָׁלֹשׁ שִׁיטִּין מְתַקְּנוֹ וְקוֹרֵא בוֹ. אַרְבַּע אֵינוֹ קוֹרֵא בוֹ. רִבִּי זְעוּרָה בְשֵׁם רַב חֲנַנְאֵל. אַף בְּקֶרַע כֵּן. תַּנֵּי. סֵפֶר שֶׁיֶּשׁ בּוֹ [שְׁתַּיִם וְשָׁלֹשׁ טָעִיּוֹת בְּכָל־דַּף וְדַף מְתַקְּנוֹ וְקוֹרֵא בוֹ. אַרְבַּע אֵינוֹ קוֹרֵא בוֹ. וְהָא תַנֵּי סֵפֶר שֶׁיֶּשׁ בּוֹ] שְׁמוֹנִים וְחָמֵשׁ טָעִיּוֹת כְּפָרָשַׁת וַיְהִי בִּנְסֹעַ הָאָרֹן מְתַקְּנוֹ וְקוֹרֵא בוֹ. אָמַר רִבִּי שַׁמִּי. כָּאן בְּסֵפֶר גָּדוֹל וְכָאן בְּסֵפֶר קָטוֹן. רִבִּי זְעוּרָה בְשֵׁם רַב חֲנַנְאֵל.

HALAKHAH 11

מָצָא בּוֹ דַף אֶחָד שָׁלֵם מַצִּיל אֶת כּוּלּוֹ. מַה. שָׁלֵם שֶׁאֵין בּוֹ [שָׁלֹשׁ] טָעִיּוֹת. אוֹ שָׁלֵם שֶׁאֵין בּוֹ אַרְבַּע. חֲגְרָא אֲחוֹי דְּרִבִּי בָּא בַּר בִּינָה יְהַב אוֹרַייְתָא לְרַב חֲנַנְאֵל וְקָרָא בָהּ. אָמַר לֵיהּ. הָדָא אוֹרַייְתָךְ צְרִיכָה צְלוֹ. וּבַסּוֹף מָצָא בָהּ דַף אֶחָד שָׁלֵם וְהִצִּיל אֶת כּוּלּוֹ. מַה. שָׁלֵם שֶׁאֵין בּוֹ טָעִיּוֹת. אוֹ שָׁלֵם שֶׁאֵין בּוֹ אַרְבַּע.

Rav Shesha the son of Rav Hananel said, one has to write ה below the knee joint of the ל, *so you want to repay to the Eternal*? In this way you want to repay to the Eternal[328]? The Mezuzah. There are Tannaim who state, open; there are Tannaim who state, closed[329]. Samuel bar Shilat in the name of Rav: Practice follows him who said open, since that is not its place[330]. Open at the start is closed. Open at the bottom is open. Open on both sides is closed[331]. If in error he omitted one verse, if it is two or three lines one repairs and reads from it; four one does not read from it[332]. Rebbi Ze`ira in the name of Rav Hananel, the same holds for a tear[333]. It was stated, a scroll in which there are [two or three errors on every page one fixes and reads from it. Four one does not read from it. But was it not stated, a scroll in which there are][334] 85 errors, as the paragraph *it was when the Ark travelled*[335], one repairs and reads from it? Rebbi Shammai said, here in a large scroll, there in a small scroll[336]. Rebbi Ze`ira in the name of Rav Hananel, if he found in it one page which is whole, it saves everything. How? Whole in that there are (no) [not three][337] errors? Or whole that there are no four? Hagra the brother of Rebbi Abba bar Bina gave a Torah scroll to Rav Hananel who checked it. He said to him, this your Torah scroll needs prayer[338]. At the end he found in it a page which was whole, which saved everything. How? Whole in that there are no errors? Or whole that there are no four[339]?

328 In *Deut.* 32:6 one has to write ה לי, an enlarged *he* of which, however, the horizontal bar has to be aligned with the horizontal bar of the following *lamed*. The larger size will appear at the bottom where the vertical bars of this *he* are longer than those of the following Name.

329 Paragraphs in the Hebrew Bible are either ending in a blank space of a third of a line, with the next paragraph starting on the same line on which the previous paragraph ended, this is called a closed paragraph. The other possibility is that the remainder of the last line remains empty; this is called open paragraph. Both paragraphs written in a Mezuzah, *Deut.* 6:4-9, 11:13-21, are closed in a Torah scroll; the first one follows an open paragraph, the second a closed one.

330 The Babli disagrees (*Menahot* 32a).

331 "Open at the start" means that the

writing of the first paragraph starts only in the middle of the line. This is normal for paragraphs following a closed paragraph. Open at the bottom means that the remainder of the last line of the paragraph remains empty; this is the definition of an open paragraph. Open on both sides implies open at the start.

332 The scroll may not be used for public readings.

333 A tear in the parchment damaging up to three lines may be fixed by sewing the tear. If it is greater the page has to be removed and buried.

334 It seems that the corrector's addition is necessary from the statements following.

335 *Num.* 10:35-36 is a separate text and contains exactly 85 letters.

336 A small scroll is one of 28 colums, which may exhibit 3 errors on each column and not reach 85. A large scroll has more columns; one has to check each column for the number of errors.

337 The later text shows clearly that the corrector's text has to be deleted.

338 There are so many errors that the scribe clearly sinned when writing the scroll.

339 Since no answer is given, in praxi one requires a column totally without error. Babli *Mehahot* 29b.

(71d line 1) רִבִּי זְעוּרָה רַב חֲנַנְאֵל בְּשֵׁם רַב. תִּיפוּרָהּ הֲלָכָה לְמשֶׁה מִסִּינַי. רִבִּי יִרְמְיָה בְּשֵׁם רִבִּי שְׁמוּאֵל בַּר רַב יִצְחָק. קִשְׁרֵי תְפִילִּין הֲלָכָה לְמשֶׁה מִסִּינַי. רִבִּי יִרְמְיָה אַפְסְקַת רְצוּעָתָהּ דִתְפִילָּתָהּ. שָׁאַל לְרִבִּי בָּא בַר מָמָל. אָמַר לֵיהּ. וּקְשָׁרְתֶּם. אֲפִילוּ קְשִׁירָה תַּמָּה. רִבִּי זְעוּרָה אַפְסִיק גוּדָא דְרצוּעָתָא. שָׁאַל לְרַב חוּנָה וּלְרַב קַטִינָא וְשָׁרוֹן לֵיהּ. אַפְסִיק זְמַן תִּנְיָינוּת וְשָׁרוֹן לֵיהּ דְּלָא מִן אוּלְפָן. רִבִּי בָּא בְּרֵיהּ דְּרִבִּי חִייָה בַּר בָּא. רִבִּי חִייָה בְּשֵׁם רִבִּי יוֹחָנָן. הֲלָכָה. זֶה שֶׁהוּא תוֹפֵר צָרִיךְ שֶׁיְהֵא מְשַׁיֵּיר מִלְמַעֲלָן וּמִלְמַטָּן כְּדֵי שֶׁלֹּא יְקָרַע. וּמַחֲוִי לֵיהּ עַל מוֹחָא. אִם הֲלָכָה לָמָּה לֹא יְקָרַע. וְאִם לֹא יְקָרַע לָמָּה הֲלָכָה. הֲלָכָה לְמשֶׁה מִסִּינַי שֶׁיְהוּ כוֹתְבִין בְּעוֹרוֹת וְכוֹתְבִין בִּדְיוֹ וּמְסַרְגְּלִין בְּקָנֶה וְכוֹרְכִין בְּשֵׂיעָר וְטוֹלִין בְּמַטְלִית וְדוֹבְקִין בַּדֶּבֶק וְתוֹפְרִין בְּגִידִין. וּכְשֶׁהוּא תוֹפֵר יְהֵא תוֹפֵר כְּתֶפֶר הַזֶּה. וְצָרִיךְ שֶׁיְהֵא מְשַׁיֵּיר בֵּין שִׁיטָה לְשִׁיטָה [כ]מְלוֹא שִׁיטָה. בֵּין תֵּיבָה לְתֵיבָה כִּמְלוֹא אוֹת. בֵּין אוֹת לְאוֹת כָּל־שֶׁהוּא. בֵּין דַּף לְדַף מְלֹא גוֹדָל. עָשָׂה סוֹף הַדַּף שָׁוֶה לִתְחִילָּתוֹ פָּסַל. צָרִיךְ לִיתֵּן רֶיוַח בַּסֵּפֶר מִלְמַעֲלָן שְׁתֵּי אֶצְבָּעוֹת וּמִלְמַטָּן שָׁלֹשׁ. רִבִּי אוֹמֵר. בַּתּוֹרָה מִלְמַעֲלָן שָׁלֹשׁ וּמִלְמַטָּן טֶפַח. וְצָרִיךְ שֶׁיְהֵא מְשַׁיֵּיר בֵּין סֵפֶר לְסֵפֶר כִּמְלוֹא אַרְבַּע שִׁיטִין. וּבַנְּבִיאִים שְׁלֹשָׁה עָשָׂר שָׁלֹשׁ. וְצָרִיךְ שֶׁיְהֵא גוֹמֵר בְּאֶמְצַע הַדַּף וּמַתְחִיל בְּאֶמְצָעִיתוֹ. וּבַנְּבִיאִים גּוֹמֵר בְּסוֹפוֹ וּמַתְחִיל בְּרֹאשׁוֹ. וּבַנְּבִיאִים שְׁלֹשָׁה עָשָׂר אָסוּר. אֵין עוֹשִׂין יְרִיעָה פְחוּתָה מִשְּׁלֹשָׁה דַפִּין וְלֹא יוֹתֵר עַל שְׁמוֹנָה. הָדָא דְאַתְּ אֲמַר. בַּתְּחִילָה. אֲבָל בַּסּוֹף אֲפִילוּ כָּל־שֶׁהוּא. וּבַקְּלָפִים לֹא נָתְנוּ חֲכָמִים שִׁיעוּר.

Rebbi Ze`ira, Rav Hananel in the name of Rav: Its sewing[340] is practice of Moses from Sinai. Rebbi Jeremiah in the name of Rebbi Samuel bar Rav Isaac: the knots of Tefillin[341] are practice of Moses from Sinai. A Tefillin strip of Rebbi Jeremiah broke; he asked Rebbi Abba bar Mamal who said to him, *and you stall tie them*³⁴², even simple tying³⁴³. Rebbi Ze`ira's wall of the strip broke³⁴⁴. He asked Rav Huna and Rav Qatina, and they permitted him. It broke a second time and they permitted him, not from what they had learned³⁴⁵. Rebbi Abba the son of Rebbi Hiyya bar Abba, Rebbi Hiyya in the name of Rebbi Johanan: The practice is that he who sews must leave space on top and bottom³⁴⁶ so it should not tear. They hit him on the skull, if it is practice why "should not tear"? And if "should not tear" why practice³⁴⁷? It is practice of Moses from Sinai that one write on leather, and write with ink, and rule with a ruler³⁴⁸, and ties with hair³⁴⁹, and patches with a patch³⁵⁰, and glues with glue³⁵¹, and sews³⁵² with sinews. As he sews, he has to sew this stitch³⁵³. One needs to leave between line and line the width of a line, between word and word the width of a letter, between letter and letter something, between column and column a thumb-width³⁵⁴. If he made the end of the column equal to its beginning he disqualified it³⁵⁵. One must leave on the top of the scroll {a margin of} two finger-breadths and at the bottom three. Rebbi says, in the Torah at the top three and at the bottom a hand-breadth. Between book and book one has to leave four lines empty³⁵⁶, in the Twelve Prophets three. One has to end in the middle of a column and start in its middle³⁵⁷; but for a Prophet he ends at the bottom and starts at the top³⁵⁸; but for the Twelve Prophets it is forbidden³⁵⁹. One makes no sheet less than three columns and none more than eight³⁶⁰. That you are saying, at the start. But at the end even a little³⁶¹; and for parchment³⁶² the Sages did not give any size.

340 That the leaves of a Torah scroll and the Tefillin cases must be sewn together with sinews. Babli *Makkot* 11a.
341 The straps of the Tefillin on the arm must be tied together with a small knot imitating the shape of י; the straps of the head Tefillin must be tied behind the head in a ד. Babli *Menahot* 35b.
342 *Deut.* 6:8.
343 The suffix תם is read as a separate word, "unblemished, straight-forward." The knots *must* be at the prescribed places; the shapes are desideratum (since the shapes would not fit if Moses wrote paleo-Hebrew.)
344 The Tefillin are small cubes sitting on a square leather base. To this base is added a rectangular tube through which the strap is drawn (in Babylonian sources called תִּיתוֹרָא "augmentation".) The wall became defective. Since it is augmentation, not the essence of Tefillin, it may be patched up.
345 To permit patch of a patch was their decision, not traditional practice.
346 If one sews leather sheets together, the top and bottom stitches should not be too close to the rim. Babli 19b.

347 Since "practice" here means "practice from Moses on Sinai", it needs no justification.

348 The lines on which the horizontal bars of the letters are written must be impressed with a wooden or metal tool, not drawn by pencil.

349 The sheets used for Tefillin are made into scrolls which then are tied with animal hair before being out into Tefillin boxes. Babli *Sabbat* 108a.

350 If the leather on which the Torah scroll is written has a tear, it can be patched up at the back with a leather patch.

351 If the text of the arm-Tefillin were written on separate sheets, they may be glued together to form one page.

352 The Torah scroll and the cases for Tefillin.

353 The stitches must be evenly spaced.

354 Babli *Menahot* 30a; *Soferim* 2:2.

355 One may not start writing on a page below the top, that it may not look deficient.

356 Between the books of the Pentateuch. Babli *Bava batra* 13b; *Soferim* 2:3.

357 In writing a Torah scroll containing all five books.

358 Since the books of Prophets are independent of one another.

359 A sheet of a single column is possible at the end of Deuteronomy.

360 *Menahot* 30a; *Soferim* 2:6.

361 Since the Twelve Prophets form a single book.

362 Or rather split leather. Babli *Bava batra* 14a.

(71d line 21) וְצָרִיךְ שֶׁיְּהֵא כוֹתֵב עַל הַגְּוִיל בְּמָקוֹם הַשֵּׂיעָר וְעַל הַקְּלָף בִּמְקוֹם נְחוּשָׁתוֹ. אִם שִׁינָּה פָּסַל. לֹא יְהֵא כוֹתֵב חֶצְיוֹ עַל הָעוֹר וְחֶצְיוֹ עַל הַקְּלָף. אֲבָל כּוֹתֵב הוּא חֶצְיוֹ עַל עוֹר בְּהֵמָה טְהוֹרָה וְחֶצְיוֹ עַל עוֹר חַיָּה טְהוֹרָה. אֵין כּוֹתְבִין אֶלָּא עַל עוֹר בְּהֵמָה טְהוֹרָה. מַה טַעַם. תְּהְיֶה תּוֹרַת יְיָ בְּפִיךָ. מִמַּה שֶׁאַתָּה נוֹתֵן בְּפִיךָ. וְהָא תַנֵּי. כּוֹתְבִין עַל עוֹר נְבֵילוֹת וּטְרֵיפוֹת. מִינָא דְאַתְּ נוֹתֵן בְּפִיךָ. וְעוֹשִׂין עַמּוּד לְסֵפֶר בְּסוֹפוֹ לַתּוֹרָה מִיכָּן וּמִיכָּן. לְפִיכָךְ גּוֹלְלִין הַסֵּפֶר לִתְחִילָּתוֹ. וְהַתּוֹרָה לְאֶמְצָעִיתָהּ. רִבִּי שְׁמוּאֵל רִבִּי זְעוּרָה בְשֵׁם רַב חִייָה בַּר יוֹסֵף. אֲפִילוּ שְׁתֵּי יְרִיעוֹת. רִבִּי זְעוּרָה שְׁמוּאֵל בַּר שִׁילַת בְּשֵׁם כַּהֲנָא. וּבִלְבַד מְקוֹם הַתֵּפֶר. רִבִּי אָחָא בְשֵׁם רִבִּי שְׁמוּאֵל בַּר נַחְמָן. סֵפֶר שֶׁאֵין עָלָיו מַפָּה הוֹפְכוֹ עַל הַכְּתָב כְּדֵי שֶׁלֹּא יִתְבַּזֶּה הַכְּתָב.

It is required that he write on leather on the place of the hair and on parchment on the place of its split[363]. If he changed this, he disqualified it. One should not write half of it on leather and half of it on parchment, but he may write on leather from a pure domestic animal and half on leather from a pure wild animal. One only writes on leather from a pure animal[364]. What is the reason? *That the Eternal's teaching be in your mouth*[365], from what you are putting into your mouth. But was it not stated, one writes on leather from carcasses and torn animals[364]? The kind which you are putting into your mouth[366]. One makes a staff at the end of a book, but for the Torah one on both sides. Therefore one rolls a book up to its beginning but the Torah to its middle[367]. Rebbi Samuel, Rebbi Ze`ira in the name of Rav Ḥiyya bar Joseph: Even two sheets[368]. Rebbi Ze`ira, Samuel bar Shilat in the name of Kahana: but only at the place of the suture[369]. Rebbi Aḥa in the name of Rebbi Samuel bar Naḥman: A scroll which has no cover one turns on the writing so the writing should not be degraded[370].

363 Where the script is more readable. Babli *Menaḥot* 32a.
364 Babli *Šabbat* 108a.
365 *Ex.* 13:9.
366 Since hide and leather are inedible anyhow.

367 The Torah scroll can be stored to open at the place where one stopped reading.
368 The scroll shows two sheets when it is opened.
369 Babli 32a.
370 *Eruvin* 10 (Note 79); *Soferim* 3:16.

(71d line 32) כָּל־הָאוֹתִיּוֹת הַכְּפוּלִים בָּאָלֶף־בֵּית כּוֹתֵב אֶת הָרִאשׁוֹנִים בִּתְחִלַּת הַתֵּיבָה וּבְאֶמְצַע הַתֵּיבָה. וְאֶת הָאַחֲרוֹנִים בְּסוֹפָהּ. וְאִם שִׁינָּה פָּסַל. מִשֵּׁם רִבִּי מַתְיָה בֶּן חָרָשׁ אָמְרוּ. מנצפ"ך הֲלָכָה לְמֹשֶׁה מִסִּינַי. מָהוּ מנצפ"ך. רִבִּי יִרְמְיָה בְּשֵׁם רִבִּי שְׁמוּאֵל בַּר רַב יִצְחָק. מַה שֶׁהִתְקִינוּ לָךְ הַצּוֹפִים. מָאן אִינּוּן אִילֵּין צוֹפִין. מַעֲשֶׂה בְּיוֹם סַגְרִיר שֶׁלֹּא נִכְנְסוּ חֲכָמִים לְבֵית הַוַּעַד וְנִכְנְסוּ הַתִּינוֹקוֹת. אָמְרִין. אִיתוֹן נֲעֲבִיד בֵּית וַעֲדָא דְלָא יִבָּטֵל. אָמְרִין. מָהוּ דֵין תִּכְתִּיב מֵ"ם מֵ"ם נוּ"ן נוּ"ן צַדֵּ"י צַדֵּ"י פֵּ"ה פֵּ"ה כַּ"ף כַּ"ף. מִמַּאֲמַר לְמַאֲמַר. מִנֶּאֱמָן לְנֶאֱמָן. מִצַּדִּיק לְצַדִּיק. מִפֶּה לְפֶה. מִכַּף יָדוֹ שֶׁלְהַקָּדוֹשׁ בָּרוּךְ הוּא לְכַף יָדוֹ שֶׁלְשְׁלֹמֹה. וְסִיְּימוּ אוֹתָן חֲכָמִים וְעָמְדוּ כּוּלָּן בְּנֵי אָדָם גְּדוֹלִים. אָמְרוּן. רִבִּי לִיעֶזֶר וְרִבִּי יְהוֹשֻׁעַ הֲוֹון מִינְּהוֹן. רִבִּי יִרְמְיָה בְּשֵׁם רִבִּי חִייָה בַּר בָּא וְרִבִּי סִימוֹן תְּרֵיהוֹן אָמְרִין. תּוֹרַת הָרִאשׁוֹנִים לֹא הָיָה לֹא הֵ"א שְׁלָהֶם וְלֹא מֵ"ם שְׁלָהֶן סָתוּם. הָא סַמֶּ"ךְ סָתוּם.

רִבִּי סִימוֹן וְרִבִּי שְׁמוּאֵל בַּר נַחְמָן תְּרֵיהוֹן אָמְרִין. אַנְשֵׁי יְרוּשָׁלַם הָיוּ כוֹתְבִין. יְרוּשָׁלַיִם יְרוּשָׁלַיְמָה. וְלֹא הָיוּ מַקְפִּידִין. וְדִכְוָתָהּ צָפוֹן צְפוֹנָה. תֵּימָן תֵּימָנָה.

Of all double letters[371] in the alphabet one writes the first form at the start of a word and in the middle of a word, but the last form at the end, and if one changed this he disqualified it. In the name of Rebbi Matthew ben Ḥarash they said, מנצפ"ך is a practice of Moses from Sinai. What is מנצפ"ך? Rebbi Jeremiah in the name of Rebbi Samuel bar Rav Isaac: what the seers instituted for you[372]. Who are those seers? [373]It happened on a day of rainstorm that the Sages did not come to the assembly hall, but the children entered. They said, come and let us form an assembly that it should not be cancelled. They said, what is that that it is written *mem mem, nun nun, ṣade ṣade, peh feh, kaf khaf.*

From utterance to utterance, from trustworthy to trustworthy, from just to just, from mouth to mouth, from the hand of the Holy One, praise to Him, to the hand of Moses[374]. The Sages identified them and they all grew to become important personalities. They said, Rebbi Eliezer and Rebbi Joshua were from these. Rebbi Jeremiah in the name of Rebbi Ḥiyya bar Abba and Rebbi Simon both were saying, in earlier copies of the Torah neither *he* nor final *mem* were closed[296]. Therefore *samekh* was closed[297].

Rebbi Simon and Rebbi Samuel bar Naḥman both were saying, the people of Jerusalem were writing Jerusalem, to Jerusalem, and were not differentiating. And similarly North, to North; South, to South[375].

371 The letters which in square script have two forms, as indicated in the next sentences.

372 While R. Matthew ben Ḥarash holds that the Torah was given in square script, R. Jeremiah dates square script to the time of the (later) prophets; he holds that the Torah was given in Paleo-Hebrew. Babli 2b.

373 Babli *Šabbat* 104a.

374 The entire homily refers to the giving of the Torah, from utterance of God to utterance of Moses, etc.

375 In the Hebrew of late Second Temple times, as exemplified in the Qumran texts, locative is freely used as nominative (already noted by Geiger, Urschrift p. 233; cf. S. Liebermann *Tarbiz* 4(1933) p.293, E. Kutscher, Isaiah Scroll, p. 67).

(71d line 46) שְׁלשָׁה עָשָׂר דָּבָר שִׁינוּ חֲכָמִים לְתַלְמַי הַמֶּלֶךְ. כָּתְבוּ לוֹ. אֱלֹהִים בָּרָא בְרֵאשִׁית. אֶעֱשֶׂה אָדָם בְּצֶלֶם וּבִדְמוּת. זָכָר וּנְקוּבָיו בְּרָאָם. וַיְכַל בַּשִּׁשִּׁי וַיִּשְׁבּוֹת בַּשְּׁבִיעִי. הָבָא אֵרְדָה. וַתִּצְחַק שָׂרָה בִּקְרוֹבֶיהָ לֵאמוֹר. כִּי בְאַפָּם הָרְגוּ שׁוֹר וּבִרְצוֹנָם עִקְּרוּ אֵבוּס. וַיִּקַּח מֹשֶׁה אֶת אִשְׁתּוֹ וְאֶת בָּנָיו וַיַּרְכִּיבֵם עַל נוֹשְׂאֵי בְנֵי אָדָם. וּמוֹשַׁב בְּנֵי יִשְׂרָאֵל אֲשֶׁר יָשְׁבוּ בְמִצְרַיִם וּבְכָל־הָאֲרָצוֹת שְׁלשִׁים שָׁנָה וְאַרְבַּע מֵאוֹת שָׁנָה. וְאֶת־הָאַרְנֶבֶת אֶת צְעִירַת הָרַגְלַיִם. אָמוּ שֶׁלְּתַלְמַי הַמֶּלֶךְ אַרְנַבְתָּא הֲוָת שְׁמָהּ. לֹא חֶמֶד אֶחָד מֵהֶם נָשָׂאתִי. אֲשֶׁר חָלַק יי אֱלֹהֶיךָ אוֹתָם לְהָאִיר לְכֹל הָעַמִּים תַּחַת כָּל־הַשָּׁמָיִם: אֲשֶׁר לֹא צִוִּיתִי לְאוּמוֹת לְעָבְדָם.

Thirteen things they changed for King Ptolemy. They wrote for him, "God created the beginning[376]." "I shall make man in stature and form[377]." "Male and his openings He created them[378]." "He finished on the Sixth and rested on the Seventh[379]" "Now I shall descend[380]." "Sarah laughed in her surroundings, saying.[381]" "For in their rage they slew a bull and in their will uprooted a trough[382]." "Moses took his wife and his sons and let them ride on people-carriers[383]." "The dwelling of the Children of Israel, which they dwelled in Egypt and other lands, was 430 years.³⁸⁴" *And the hare*³⁸⁵, "and the young of foot." King Ptolemy's mother was called "hare³⁸⁶". "Not one precious thing I took from them³⁸⁷" "Which the Eternal, your God, distributed them to give light to all peoples under all the heavens.³⁸⁸" "Which I did not command peoples to worship them.³⁸⁹"

376 *Gen*. 1:1; change not found in LXX.
377 *Gen*. 1:26; change not found in LXX.
378 *Gen*. 1:27; change not found in LXX.
379 *Gen*. 2:2; change found in LXX.
380 *Gen*. 11:7; change found in LXX.
381 *Gen*. 18:12; LXX: "in herself".
382 *Gen*. 49:6; change not found in LXX.
383 *Ex*. 4:20. LXX: "beast of burden".
384 *Ex*. 12:40. LXX: "In the land of Egypt and the land of Canaan."
385 *Lev*. 11:6 (in LXX 11:5). LXX: "rough-foot", a designation of the hare.

386 The dynasty of the Ptolemies was called the Lagides, after an ancestor Lagos "hare".
387 *Num*. 16:15; change found in LXX.
388 *Deut*. 4:19; change not found in LXX.
389 *Deut*. 17:3; change not found in LXX.

The comparisons with the LXX text was done on the basis of Rahlfs's edition; the history of the text between the time of the Jewish translation in Alexandria and its adaptation by Christian editors in the Roman Empire is unknown. The same list is in the Babli 9a.

(71d line 55) כָּל־הָאוֹתִיּוֹת הַכְּתוּבִים עִם הַשֵּׁם מִלְּפָנָיו הֲרֵי אֵילוּ חוֹל וְנִמְחָקִין. כְּכוֹן לַיִ"י בַּיִ"י כַּיִ"י שֶׁיִ"י. שֶׁכֵּן מָצָאנוּ בַּצִּיץ שֶׁהוּא מוּבְדָּל מִמֶּנּוּ. קוֹדֶשׁ לַמַ"ד מִלְּמַטָּן וְהַשֵּׁם מִלְמַעְלָן. כָּל־הָאוֹתִיּוֹת הַכְּתוּבִים עִם הַשֵּׁם מֵאַחוֹרָיו הֲרֵי אֵילוּ קוֹדֶשׁ וְאֵינָן נִמְחָקִין. כְּגוֹן אֱלֹהֵינוּ אֱלֹהֵיכֶם. אֵילוּ שֵׁמוֹת שֶׁאֵינָן נִמְחָקִין. הַכּוֹתֵב אֶת הַשֵּׁם בְּאַרְבַּע אוֹתִיּוֹת. בְּיוּ"ד וּבְהֵ"א. בָּאָלֶ"ף וּבָדָלֶ"ת. אֵל אֱלֹהִים אֱלֹהֶיךָ אֱלֹהֵי אֱלֹהֵינוּ אֱלֹהֵיכֶם שַׁדַּי צְבָאוֹת אֶהְיֶה אֲשֶׁר אֶהְיֶה. כָּתַב אָלֶ"ף דָּלֶ"ת מֵיְ"י. אָלֶ"ף הֵ"א מֵאֶהְיֶה. שִׁי"ן דָּלֶ"ת מִשַּׁדַּי. צָדֵ"י בֵּי"ת מִצְּבָאוֹת. הֲרֵי אֵילוּ נִמְחָקִין וּמוֹחֵק אֶת טְפִילוּתֵיהֶם. לֵאלוֹהִים מוֹחֵק אֶת לַמַ"ד. לַיִ"י מוֹחֵק אֶת לָמֵד. כָּתַב יוּד הֵ"א מֵאַרְבַּע אוֹתִיּוֹת. אָלֶ"ף לָמֵד מֵאֱלֹהִים אֵינוֹ נִמְחָק. כְּלָלוֹ שֶׁלַדָּבָר. כָּל־שֶׁכְּיוֹצֵא בוֹ שֵׁם מִתְקַיֵּים בְּמָקוֹם אַחֵר אֵינוֹ נִמְחָק.

All letters written with the Name as prefix are profane and may be erased, e. g., to the Eternal, by the Eternal, as the Eternal, that the Eternal, since we find that on the diadem it was separate from it, "holy to" at the bottom, "the Eternal" at the top³⁹⁰. All letters written with the Name as suffix are holy and may not be erased, e. g., our God, your God. These are the Names which may not be erased: one who writes the Name of four letters, whether YH or AD³⁹¹. "El, Elohim, Elohei, Elohenu, Elohekhem, Shadday, Sabaoth, Ehye-Ašer-Ehye." If one writes AD from Adonai, EH from Ehye, ŠD from

Shadday, ṢB from Sabaoth, these may be erased and one erases their additions³⁹². "To Elohim" one erases "to"; "to the Eternal" one erases "to"³⁹³. If he wrote YH³⁹⁴ of the four-letter Name, EL from Elohim, it may not be erased. This is the rule: Any which at another place is a permanent Name may not be erased.

390 *Yoma* 4:1 Note 27; Babli *Šabbat* 63b, *Sukkah* 5a. For the following, *Ševuot* 35b.
391 The Name אֲדֹנָי used as pronunciation of the Tetragrammaton. If the intention is to אֲדֹנָי "my masters", the word is profane and may be erased.

392 אֵד "vapor", אָה has no sense, שַׁד "female breast" שַׁד "spirit", צָב "turtle" are profane words.
393 As noted at the start of the paragraph.
394 Which is a divine Name in its own right and should have been mentioned in the list.

(71d line 66) תַּנֵּי. רִבִּי יוֹסֵי אוֹמֵר. שֶׁלְבֵית חֲגִירָה כּוֹתְבָנִים אוּמָנִים הָיוּ בִירוּשָׁלַם. הָיוּ מוֹחֲקִין צְבָאוֹת. שֶׁכֵּן הוּא שֵׁם חוֹל בְּמָקוֹם אַחֵר. וּפְקֻדֵי שָׂרֵי צְבָאוֹת בְּרֹאשׁ הָעָם׃ כָּל־הַשֵּׁמוֹת הַכְּתוּבִים בְּאַבְרָהָם אָבִינוּ קוֹדֶשׁ חוּץ מֵאֶחָד שֶׁהוּא חוֹל. וַיְהִי כַּאֲשֶׁר הִתְעוּ אֹתִי אֱלֹהִים מִבֵּית אָבִי. וְיֵשׁ אוֹמְרִים. אַף הוּא קוֹדֶשׁ. שֶׁאִילּוּלֵי אֱלֹהִים כְּבָר הִתְעוּ אוֹתִי. כָּל־הַשֵּׁמוֹת הַכְּתוּבִים בְּמִיכָה אַף עַל פִּי שֶׁהֵן כְּתוּבִין בְּיו"ד וּבְהֵ"א הֲרֵי אֵילוּ חוֹל חוּץ מֵאֶחָד שֶׁהוּא קוֹדֶשׁ. כָּל־יְמֵי הֱיוֹת בֵּית־הָאֱלֹהִים בְּשִׁלֹה׃ כָּל־הַשֵּׁמוֹת הַכְּתוּבִים בְּנָבוֹת אַף עַל פִּי שֶׁהֵן כְּתוּבִין בְּאֵלֶ"ף לָמֶד הֲרֵי אֵילוּ קוֹדֶשׁ. בֵּרֵךְ נָבוֹת אֱלֹהִים וָמֶלֶךְ. אֲבָל חַנּוּן וְרַחוּם אֶרֶךְ אַפַּיִם וְרַב חֶסֶד מֶלֶךְ מְלָכִים מְרוֹמָם וְנָדוֹל וְנוֹרָא וְעֶלְיוֹן אַדִּיר צַדִּיק יָשָׁר חָסִיד תָּמִים גִּיבּוֹר הֲרֵי אֵילוּ חוֹל. אֵילוּ שֵׁמוֹת שֶׁאֵינָן נֶחְלָקִין. עַמִּיאֵל עַמִּישַׁי צוּרְאֵל צוּרִישַׁדָּי גַּמְלִיאֵל פְּדָהצוּר פְּדָהאֵל אֵינָן נֶחְלָקִין. אֵילוּ שֵׁמוֹת שֶׁהֵן נֶחְלָקִין. בֵּית־אֵל בֵּית־ אָוֶן וְתָרָה אַף וְתָרָה אַפִּי פוּטִי־פֶרַע צָפְנַת־פַּעְנֵחַ.

It was stated: Rebbi Yose says, the family Hagira were professional scribes in Jerusalem, who were erasing Sabaoth since it is a profane substantive at another place, *the military commanders take position at the head of the people*³⁹⁵. All Names written regarding our father Abraham are holy except one which is profane, *it was when the gods made me err from my father's house*³⁹⁶. But some are saying, this one also is holy, "for unless God, they already would have made me err." All Names written regarding Micha³⁹⁷ are profane, even though they are written with YH, except one which is holy, *all time that the House of God was at Siloh*³⁹⁸. All Names written regarding Naboth, even though they are written with EL are holy, *Naboth cursed God and King*³⁹⁹. But "merciful and compassionate, patient and full of grace, King of kings, elevated, and great, and awesome, and supreme, powerful, just, straight, saintly, flawless, strong," these are profane[400]. The following are the names which cannot be split: Amiel, Amishadday, Suriel, Surishaddai, Gamliel, Pedahzur, Pedahel, may not be split[401] These are names that may be split, Beth-El[402], Beth-Awen, getting angry, I shall get angry, Poti-phera, Safenath-Paneaḥ.

395 *Deut.* 20:9.
396 *Gen.* 20:13. Babli *Ševuot* 35b.
397 *Jud.* 17-18.
398 *Jud.* 18:31.
399 *1K.* 21:13. *Ševuot* 35b.
400 These are attributes, not Names.
401 While theophoric names are profane, isolating the divine name by splitting the word would create a word which may not be erased since the syllable was intended as a Name.
402 A geographic name, written without any intent of endowing it with holiness.

(72a line 4) הַלְלוּ יָ'הּ. רַב וּשְׁמוּאֵל. חַד אָמַר הַלְלוּ יָ'הּ. וְחוֹרָנָה אָמַר הַלְלוּיָהּ. מָאן דְּאָמַר הַלְלוּ יָ'הּ. נֶחֱלַק וְאֵינוֹ נִמְחָק. מָאן דְּאָמַר הַלְלוּיָהּ. נִמְחָק וְאֵינוֹ נֶחֱלַק. וְלָא יָדְעִין מָאן אָמַר דָּא וּמָאן אָמַר דָּא. מִן מַה דַּאֲמַר רַב. שְׁמָעִית מִן חָבִיבִי. אִם יִתֵּן לִי אָדָם סֵפֶר תִּילִים שֶׁלְּרַבִּי מֵאִיר מוֹחֵק אֲנִי אֶת כָּל־הַלְלוּ יָהּ שֶׁבּוֹ. שֶׁלֹּא נִתְכַּוֵּון לְקַדְּשׁוֹ. הֲוֵי דוּ אָמַר הַלְלוּיָהּ. מִילֵּיהוֹן דְּרַבָּנָן פְּלִיגִין. דְּאָמַר רִבִּי סִימוֹן בְּשֵׁם רִבִּי יְהוֹשֻׁעַ בֶּן לֵוִי. בַּעֲשָׂרָה לְשׁוֹנוֹת שֶׁלְּשֶׁבַח נֶאֱמַר סֵפֶר תִּילִים. בְּאִישׁוּר בְּנִיצוּחַ בְּנִיגּוּן בְּשִׁיר בְּמִזְמוֹר בְּהַשְׂכֵּל בְּרִינָּה [בְּתוֹדָה] בִּתְפִילָּה בִּבְרָכָה. הַמְאוּשָּׁר שֶׁבְּכוּלָּן הַלְלוּ יָהּ. שֶׁהַשֵּׁם וְהַשֶּׁבַח כְּלוּלִין בּוֹ.

[403]Rav and Samuel. One said *hallelu yah,* and the other one said *hallēluja.* For him who said *hallelu yah* it is split but cannot be erased. For him who said *hallelujah* it may be erased but cannot be split. We do not know who said what. Since Rav said, I heard from my uncle, if somebody would give me a book of Psalms written by Rebbi Meïr I could erase all *hallelujah* in it since he did not intend to sanctify them. This implies that he said *hallelujah.* The words of the rabbis disagree, as Rebbi Simon said in the name of Rebbi Joshua ben Levi, the book of Psalms was said with ten expressions of praise, with "hail", with "excellence", with melody, with song, with chant, with instruction, with shout, [with thanksgiving,] with prayer, with blessing. The most beatific of all of them is *hallelujah* since both the Name and praise are contained in it.

רִבִּי זְעוּרָה בָּעָא קוֹמֵי רִבִּי אַבָּהוּ. מַה נַעֲנֵי. אֲמַר לֵיהּ הָכָא (כִּיפָה) [בָּפֶּה] קוֹמָךְ. רִבִּי יוֹנָה עָנֵי הָכֵן וְהָכֵן. רִבִּי לְעָזָר עָנֵי הָכֵין וְהָכֵין. דְּתַנֵּי. שָׁמַע וְלֹא עָנָה יָצָא. עָנָה וְלֹא שָׁמַע לֹא יָצָא. רַב

בְּשֵׁם רִבִּי אַבָּא בַּר חָנָה. וְאִית דְּאָמְרִין. רִבִּי אַבָּא בַּר חָנָה בְּשֵׁם רַב. וְהוּא שֶׁעָנָה רָאשֵׁי פְרָקִים. רִבִּי זְעוּרָה בָּעֵי. הַיי לֵין אִינּוּן רָאשֵׁי פְרָקִים. הַלְלוּיָהּ | הַלְלוּ עַבְדֵי יי הַלְלוּ אֶת־שֵׁם יי. בְּעוֹן קוֹמֵי רִבִּי חִייָה בַּר בָּא. מְנַיִין אִם שָׁמַע וְלֹא עָנָה יָצָא. אֲמַר לוֹן. מִן מַה דַּאֲנַן חֲמֵיי רַבָּנִין רַבְרְבַיָּא קַייָמִין בְּצִיבּוּרָא וְאִילֵּין אָמְרִין בָּרוּךְ הַבָּא. וְאִילֵּין אָמְרִין. בְּשֵׁם יי. וְאִילּוּ וְאִילּוּ יוֹצְאִין יְדֵי חוֹבָתָן.

Rebbi Ze`ira asked before Rebbi Abbahu: He told him, (on top) [in the mouth] before you. Rebbi Jonah answered both ways. Rebbi Eleazar answered both ways. As it was stated, if he heard but did not answer, he fulfilled his obligation; if he answered but did not hear he did not fulfill his obligation[404]. Rav in the name of Rebbi Abba bar Ḥana; but some say Rebbi Abba bar Ḥana in the name of Rav: Only if he answered at the start of the Chapters. Rebbi Ze`ira asked, what are the starts of Chapters? *Hallelujah, praise, servants of the Eternal, praise the Name of the Eternal*[405]. They asked before Rebbi Ḥiyya bar Abba: From where that he who heard but did not answer has fulfilled his obligation? He told them, since we are seeing great rabbis standing among the public when these say *praised be he who comes* and the others say *in the name of the Eternal*[406], and both have fulfilled their obligation.

תַּנֵּי רִבִּי הוֹשַׁעְיָה. עוֹנֶה הוּא אָדָם אָמֵן אַף עַל פִּי שֶׁלֹּא אָכַל. אֵינוֹ אוֹמֵר. בָּרוּךְ שֶׁאָכַלְנוּ. אֶלָּא אִם כֵּן אָכַל. תַּנֵּי. אֵין עוֹנִין אָמֵן יְתוֹמָה וְלֹא אָמֵן קְטוּפָה. בֶּן עַזַּאי אוֹמֵר. הָעוֹנֶה אָמֵן יְתוֹמָה יְהִיוּ בָנָיו יְתוֹמִין. קְטוּפָה. תִּיקָּטֵף נִשְׁמָתוֹ. אֲרוּכָה. יַאֲרִיךְ יָמִים בְּטוֹבָה. אֵי זוֹ הִיא אָמֵן יְתוֹמָה. אָמַר רַב חוּנָה. הָהֵן דְּחָב לִמְבָרְכָה וְהוּא עָנֵי וְלֹא יְדַע מַה הוּא עָנֵי. תַּנֵּי. גּוֹי שֶׁבֵּירַךְ אֶת הַשֵּׁם עוֹנִין אַחֲרָיו אָמֵן. בַּשֵּׁם. אֵין עוֹנִין אַחֲרָיו אָמֵן. אָמַר רִבִּי תַנְחוּמָה. אִם בֵּירַכְךָ גּוֹי עֲנֵה אַחֲרָיו אָמֵן. דִּכְתִיב בָּרוּךְ תִּהְיֶה מִכָּל־הָעַמִּים. גּוֹי אֶחָד פָּגַע בְּרִבִּי יִשְׁמָעֵאל וּבֵירְכוֹ. אֲמַר לֵיהּ. כְּבָר מִילְּתָךְ אֲמִירָא. אַחֵר פָּגַע בּוֹ וְקִילְּלוֹ. אֲמַר לֵיהּ. כְּבָר מִילְּתָךְ אֲמִירָה. אָמְרוּ לֵיהּ תַּלְמִידוֹי. רִבִּי. הֵיךְ מַה דְּאָמְרַתְּ לְהֵן אֲמַרְתְּ לָהֵן. אֲמַר לוֹן. וְלֹא כֵן כְּתִיב. אוֹרְרֶיךָ אָרוּר וּמְבָרֲכֶיךָ בָּרוּךְ:

Rebbi Hoshaya stated: One answers Amen even if he did not eat, but he may not say: "Let us praise Him, of Whose bounty we ate," except if he did eat. It is stated: "One answers neither an orphan Amen, nor a plucked Amen. Ben Azai said, if one answered an orphan Amen, may his children be orphans; hurried, may the end of his days be hurried; plucked, may his soul be plucked off. For a long Amen, they lengthen his days and years in a good way. What is an orphan Amen? Rebbi Huna said, that is one who is obligated to recite a blessing, he answers Amen, and is not conscious for what he answered Amen.

It is stated: One answers Amen after a Gentile who recited a benediction for the Eternal. By the Name, one does not answer Amen after him. Rebbi Tanḥuma said, if a Gentile blesses you, answer after him Amen since it is written[407] *You shall be blessed by all peoples.* A Gentile met Rebbi Ismael and blessed him. He answered: The word about you has already been said. He met a second one who cursed him; he answered: The word about you has already been said. His students said to him: Rebbi, did you say to the one what you said to the other? He said to them, so it is written[408] *Those who curse you are cursed, but those who bless you are blessed.*

403 The text from here to the end of the Halakhah is copied in *Sukkah* 3:12 (Notes 117-136).
404 The recitation of the holiday *Hallel* (*Ps.* 13-18).
405 *Ps.* 113:1.
406 *Ps.* 118:26.
407 *Deut.* 7:14.
408 *Gen.* 27:29.

(fol. 69d) **משנה יב**: אֵין בֵּין כֹּהֵן מָשׁוּחַ בְּשֶׁמֶן הַמִּשְׁחָה לִמְרוּבֶּה בְּגָדִים אֶלָּא פַּר הַבָּא עַל כָּל־הַמִּצְוֹת. אֵין בֵּין כֹּהֵן שֶׁשִּׁמֵּשׁ לְכֹהֵן שֶׁעָבַר אֶלָּא פַּר יוֹם הַכִּפּוּרִים וַעֲשִׂירִית הָאֵיפָה׃

Mishnah 12: The only difference between a High Priest anointed with the anointing oil and one invested[409] is the bull which comes for all commandments. The only difference between an acting High Priest and a deactivated High Priest[410] is the bull of the Day of Atonement and the Tenth of an Epha[416].

409 The making of the anointing oil is described in *Ex.* 30:22-33 as a personal obligation of Moses. It cannot be duplicated by any other person. Therefore only the High Priests of the Tabernacle, of Siloh, and the First Temple could be anointed for their duties. The High Priests of the Second Temple were invested with the vestments of their office but could not be anointed. The special purification offering of the High Priest of a bull described in *Lev.* 4:3-12 is restricted to the "anointed priest". The purification offering of a High Priest of the Second Temple period was that of common people, a female goat or sheep; *Lev.* 4:27-35.
410 Removed by a king of the Herodian dynasty or a Roman procurator.

(72a line 31) **הלכה יב:** תַּנֵּי. כֹּהֵן מָשִׁיחַ מֵבִיא פָר. אֵין הַמְרוּבֶּה בְגָדִים מֵבִיא פָר. וּדְלֹא כְרִבִּי מֵאִיר. דְּרִבִּי מֵאִיר אָמַר. הַמְרוּבֶּה בְגָדִים מֵבִיא פָר. מַה טַעֲמֵיהּ דְּרִבִּי מֵאִיר. מָשִׁיחַ. מַה תַלְמוּד לוֹמַר כֹּהֵן. לְרַבּוֹת אֶת הַמְרוּבֶּה [בְגָדִים]. מַה טַעֲמוֹן דְּרַבָּנָן. מָשִׁיחַ. יָכוֹל זֶה הַמֶּלֶךְ. תַלְמוּד לוֹמַר כֹּהֵן. אִי כֹהֵן יָכוֹל אַף מְרוּבֶּה בְגָדִים. תַלְמוּד לוֹמַר מָשִׁיחַ. אוֹ יָכוֹל שֶׁאֲנִי מַרְבֶּה אַף מְשׁוּחַ מִלְחָמָה. תַלְמוּד לוֹמַר מָשִׁיחַ. שֶׁאֵין עַל גַּבָּיו מָשִׁיחַ. מְחִלְפָה שִׁיטָתוֹן דְּרַבָּנָן. הָכָא כְּתִיב מָשִׁיחַ וְהָכָא כְּתִיב מָשִׁיחַ. הָכָא אִינּוּן אָמְרִין. לְרַבּוֹת מְרוּבֶּה בְגָדִים. וְהָכָא אִינּוּן אָמְרִין. לְהוֹצִיא אֶת הַמְרוּבֶּה בְגָדִים. אָמַר רִבִּי אִילָא. כָּל־מִדְרָשׁ וּמִדְרָשׁ בְּעִנְיָינוֹ. תַּמָּן כָּל־הַפָּרָשָׁה אֲמוּרָה בְאַהֲרֹן. לְאִי־זֶה דָבָר נֶאֱמַר כֹּהֵן. לְרַבּוֹת אֶת הַמְרוּבֶּה בְגָדִים. בְּרַם הָכָא אֵין הַפָּרָשָׁה אֲמוּרָה בְאַהֲרֹן. אִילּוּ נֶאֱמַר מָשִׁיחַ וְלֹא נֶאֱמַר כֹּהֵן. הָיִיתִי אוֹמֵר. [לְעוֹלָם עַל הֶעְלֵם דָּבָר מֵבִיא פָר וְעַל שִׁגְגַת מַעֲשֶׂה מֵבִיא שָׂעִיר. הֱוֵי צוֹרֶךְ הוּא שֶׁיֹּאמַר כֹּהֵן. אוֹ אִילּוּ נֶאֱמַר כֹּהֵן וְלֹא נֶאֱמַר מָשִׁיחַ. הָיִיתִי אוֹמֵר.] זֶה הַמֶּלֶךְ. אִין תֹּאמַר. כְּבָר קָדְמָה פָרָשַׁת הַמֶּלֶךְ. הָיִיתִי אוֹמֵר. עַל הֶעְלֵם דָּבָר מֵבִיא פָר וְעַל שִׁגְגַת מַעֲשֶׂה מֵבִיא שָׂעִיר. הֱוֵי צוֹרֶךְ הוּא שֶׁיֹּאמַר מָשִׁיחַ וְצוֹרֶךְ הוּא שֶׁיֹּאמַר כֹּהֵן.

[411]**Halakhah 12:** It was stated: The Anointed Priest brings a bull, the one clothed in multiple garb does not bring a bull. This disagrees with Rebbi Meïr, for Rebbi Meïr said, the one clothed in multiple garb brings a bull[412]. What is Rebbi Meïr's reason? *The Anointed.* Why does the verse say *priest*? To add the one clothed in multiple garb[413]. What is the rabbis' reason? *The anointed.* I could think that this is the king. The verse says, *priest.* If priest, I could think the one clothed in multiple garb. The verse says, *anointed*[414]. Then I could think that I am adding also the one anointed for war[415]. The verse says, *Anointed*; one who has no anointed person over him. The argument of the rabbis seems inverted. Here[416] is written *anointed* and there is written *anointed.* Here they say, to include the one clothed in multiple garb[417]. But here[418] they say, to exclude the one clothed in multiple garb. Rebbi Hila said, each inference refers to its meaning. There the entire paragraph is said for Aaron. Why is said *priest*? To include the one clothed in multiple garb[419]. But here the paragraph does not mention Aaron. If it had said *the Anointed* but not *priest*, I would have said, [he brings a bull for forgetting a topic, but for acting in error he brings a goat. Therefore it is necessary that it would mention *priest*. But if it had mentioned *priest* but not *the Anointed*, I would have said,][420] this refers to the king[421]. If you would say already this precedes the paragraph about the king[422], I would have said that for forgetting a topic he

brings a bull but for acting in error he brings a goat[423]. Therefore it is necessary that it mention *the Anointed* and that it mention *priest*.

411 The entire Halakhah is also in *Horaiot* 3:3 (Notes 132-188). The copy of the first paragraph in *Horaiot* is incomplete; the later paragraphs are also in *Yoma* 1:1 (Notes 123-149).

412 The definite article used in *Lev.* 4:3, *the priest*, would alone have sufficed to characterize the High Priest, biblically distinguished from all others.

413 Tosephta *Horaiot* 2:3.

414 The double restriction, *the* priest (the High Priest), *anointed,* makes it clear that only an anointed high priest is meant. The rabbinic disagreement implies that no High Priest of Second Temple times ever brought a purification sacrifice for himself.

415 The one mentioned in *Deut.* 20:3 charged with addressing the army. He also is called *the* priest (*Sotah* Chapter 8) and bound by all restrictions imposed on the High Priest in *Lev.* 21:10-15 (Tosephta 2:1).

416 *Lev.* 6:15, on the daily flour sacrifice of the High Priest.

417 Mishnah *Horaiot* 3:4 mentions the daily offering of a tenth of an *ephah* as duty of the High Priest clothed in multiple garb [*Sifra Saw Pereq* 5(1)].

418 In the Chapter on purification sacrifices.

419 Aaron and his successors are mentioned in v. 13. In v. 15, the mention of "the priest, anointed from his descendants in his stead" does not seem to require a mention of anointing as a definition.

420 Unnecessary corrector's addition.

421 Since *Cohen* may simply mean "public servant" (*2S.* 8:18).

422 Which is only the third in the Chapter.

423 As explained in *Horaiot* 2:3, The High Priest may offer a bull only for his forgetting a topic in religious law. One could argue that for simple acting in error, he should bring a commoner's sacrifice (or, since a male animal is mentioned, the goat characterized earlier as sacrifice for inadvertent idolatry). The specific mention of *priest* bars him from a commoner's sacrifice.

(72a line 47) אָמַר רִבִּי יוֹחָנָן עָבַר וְהֵבִיא עֲשִׂירִת הָאֵיפָה שֶׁלּוֹ כָּשֵׁר.

Rebbi Johanan said, if he transgressed and offered his tenth of an *ephah* it is valid[424].

424 This refers to the statement in the Mishnah that the only difference between acting and emeritus High Priests are the High Priest's bull on the Day of Atonement and the daily flour offering of a tenth of an *ephah*. It is now stated that if the ex-High Priest, who, as will be explained later in the Halakhah, should be unfit to serve as High Priest and is barred from serving as common priest, nevertheless acts as High Priest, the offering is legitimate.

(47c line 3) מַתְקִינִין לוֹ כֹהֵן אַחֵר תַּחְתָּיו שֶׁמָּא יֶאֱרַע בּוֹ פְסוּל. מַה. מְיַיחֲדִין לֵיהּ עִימֵּיהּ. אָמַר רִבִּי חַגַּי. מֹשֶׁה. דִּינּוּן מְיַיחֲדִין לֵיהּ עִימֵּיהּ דּוּ קָטִיל לֵיהּ. אוֹתוֹ. אֶחָד מוֹשְׁחִין וְאֵין מוֹשְׁחִין שְׁנַיִם. אָמַר רִבִּי יוֹחָנָן. מִפְּנֵי אֵיבָה.

[425]"One arranges for another Cohen as his replacement, maybe a disqualification of his will happen.[426]" How? Does one leave them alone together? Rebbi Ḥaggai said, by Moses! If one would leave them alone together, he would kill him! Him[427]. One anoints one, one does not anoint two. Rebbi Joḥanan said, because of rivalry[428].

425 Here starts the parallel in *Yoma* 1:1.

426 Mishnah *Yoma* 1:1. Since the entire service of the Day of Atonement is valid only if conducted by the High Priest, a replacement must be available in case the High Priest becomes impure or otherwise incapacitated. The High Priest undergoes a week of preparation for the service, to train for a very crowded program. The question then arises whether the designated backup also has to undergo the same training, possibly at the same place.

427 *Lev.* 6:12; the offering of the High Priest starting with the day he is anointed for his office. *Sifra Ṣaw Parašah* 3(3). The singular indicates that only one High Priest can be appointed at one time. This implies that the reserve appointee for the day of Atonement cannot have the status of High Priest unless he actually is needed.

428 He disagrees and holds that while the two could not have been anointed on the same day, they could have been anointed on different days. The rule that the back-up Cohen has lower status is practical, not biblical, as is the entire institution of the back-up.

(72a line 50) עָבַר זֶה וְשִׁימֵּשׁ זֶה. הָרִאשׁוֹן כָּל־מִצְוֹת כְּהוּנָּה עָלָיו. הַשֵּׁינִי אֵינוֹ כָשֵׁר לֹא לְכֹהֵן גָּדוֹל וְלֹא לְכֹהֵן הֶדְיוֹט. אָמַר רִבִּי יוֹחָנָן. עָבַר וְעָבַד עֲבוֹדָתוֹ כְשֵׁירָה. עֲבוֹדָתוֹ מִשֶּׁל מִי. נִשְׁמְעִינָהּ מִן הָדָא. מַעֲשֶׂה בְבֶן אִילֵם מִצִּיפּוֹרִין שֶׁאֵירַע קָרִי לְכֹהֵן גָּדוֹל בְּיוֹם הַכִּיפּוּרִים וְנִכְנַס בֶּן אִילֵם וְשִׁימֵּשׁ תַּחְתָּיו בִּכְהוּנָּה גְדוֹלָה. וְאָמַר לַמֶּלֶךְ כְּשֶׁיָּצָא. אֲדוֹנִי הַמֶּלֶךְ. פַּר וְשָׂעִיר שֶׁל יוֹם מִשֶּׁלִּי הֵן קְרֵיבִים אוֹ מִשֶּׁלְּכֹהֵן גָּדוֹל. וְיָדַע הַמֶּלֶךְ מַה שׁוֹאֲלוֹ. אָמַר לוֹ. בֶּן אִילֵם. לֹא דַייָךְ אֶלָּא שֶׁשִּׁימַּשְׁתָּה שָׁעָה אַחַת לִפְנֵי מִי שֶׁאָמַר וְהָיָה הָעוֹלָם דַּייָךְ. וְיָדַע בֶּן אִילֵם שֶׁהוּסַע מִכְּהוּנָּה גְדוֹלָה.

If one was incapacitated and the other officiated. The first has all the sanctity of the High Priesthood on him; the second one is qualified neither as High Priest nor as common priest[429]. Rebbi Joḥanan said, if he transgressed and officiated, his officiating is valid[430]. Whose officiating? [431]Let us hear from the following: It happened to Ben Illem from Sepphoris that the High

Priest experienced an emission of semen on the Day of Atonement[432]; Ben Illem entered and officiated in his stead. He asked the king when he went out: "The bull and the goat which are brought today, from whose property are they offered? From mine or from the High Priest's?" The king understood what he was asking and answered him, "Ben Illem, is it not enough for you that you served once before Him Who spoke and the world was created? It is enough for you." Ben Illem understood that he was removed from the High Priesthood.

429 As the Babli explains (*Yoma* 12b), "one increases in sanctity but never decreases" (cf. *Bikkurim* 3:3, Note 57; *Yoma* 3:8 Note 201, *Ševuot* 1:8 Note 169). Since the service of the Day of Atonement is valid only if performed by the High Priest, the substitute becomes a temporary High Priest. He cannot act as a High Priest if the actual High Priest's temporary disability is removed and he is permanently barred from acting as a common priest. As the Babli points out, if the High Priest dies, the substitute automatically becomes his successor.

430 A doubt about the legitimacy of officiating in the Temple does not invalidate the offering (*Terumot* 8:1, Note 26).

431 The case is told not only in the two parallels in *Horaiot* and *Yoma*, but also in abbreviated form in the Babli, *Yoma* 12b where, however, the ruling is not the king's (necessarily of the Herodian dynasty) but "the rabbis'." There is no reason to doubt the historicity of the Yerushalmi version.

432 The High Priest is taken to live in the Temple, and therefore deprived of sexual activity, for seven days preceding the Day of Atonement. In the night of the Day of Atonement he is deprived of sleep (*Yoma* Mishnah 1:7) to avoid the danger of him having an involuntary emission. If he has one anyhow, he is disqualified for the entire day even if he immediately purifies himself in a *miqweh* since the disqualification by temporary impurity is not removed by the removal of the impurity until the following sundown (*Lev.* 22:7; cf. *Ma`aser Šeni* 3:2, Notes 21-22.)

(72 line 58) מַעֲשֶׂה בְשִׁמְעוֹן בֶּן קַמְחִית שֶׁיָּצָא לְדַבֵּר עִם מֶלֶךְ עֲרָבִי [עֶרֶב יוֹם הַכִּיפּוּרִים עִם חֲשֵׁיכָה] וְנִתְזָה צִינּוֹרָה שֶׁלְרוֹק מִפִּיו עַל בְּגָדָיו וְטִימְאַתּוּ וְנִכְנַס יְהוּדָה אָחִיו וְשִׁימֵּשׁ תַּחְתָּיו בִּכְהוּנָה. וְרָאֲתָה אִימָּן שְׁנֵי בָנֶיהָ כֹּהֲנִים גְּדוֹלִים בְּיוֹם אֶחָד. שִׁבְעָה בָנִים הָיוּ לְקַמְחִית וְכוּלְּהֹם שִׁימְּשׁוּ בִּכְהוּנָּה גְדוֹלָה. שָׁלְחוּ חֲכָמִים וְאָמְרוּ לָהּ. מַה מַעֲשִׂים טוֹבִים יֵשׁ בְּיָדֵךְ. אָמְרָה לָהֶן. יָבוֹא עָלַי אִם רָאוּ קוֹרוֹת בֵּיתִי שְׂעָרוֹת רֹאשִׁי וְאִימְרַת חָלוּקִי מִיָּמַיי. אָמְרִין. כָּל־קִמְחַיָּא קֶמַח וְקִמְחָא דְקֵימְחִית סוֹלֶת. וְקָרְוּן עָלָהּ כָּל־כְּבוּדָּה בַת־מֶלֶךְ פְּנִימָה מִמִּשְׁבְּצוֹת זָהָב לְבוּשָׁהּ:

[433]It happened that Simeon ben Qimḥit went out for a walk with an Arab king [on the evening before the Day of Atonement at sundown][434] and a drop

of spittle squirted on his garment and defiled him. His brother Jehudah entered and officiated in his stead. Their mother saw two of her sons as High Priests on the same day. Qimḥit had seven sons; all of them served as High Priests[435]. The Sages sent and asked Qimḥit, what good deeds are in your hand? She told them, there should come over me if the beams of the roof of my house ever saw the hair on my head or the seam of my undershirt[436]. They said, all flours are flour but Qimḥit's flour is fine flour[437]. They recited about her[438]: *All the honor of the king's daughter is inside; gold settings her garments*[439].

433 In addition to the two parallels there is a short version in the Babli, *Yoma* 47a. There, the names are Ismael and Joseph. The passages are discussed in detail by Grätz, *Geschichte der Juden* vol. 3/2⁴ Note 19/II. Josephus transcribes בֶּן קִמְחִית as τοῦ Καμύδου.

434 The different versions of this text are discussed in *Horaiot*, Note 157. Probably it should read "with the king at sundown before the Day of Atonement." If the Arab was not converted to Judaism, the High Priest would have had to leave the holy precinct on the Day of Atonement, a most unlikely happening before he had finished all his duties.

The version of the text presupposes that the king had immersed himself in a *miqweh* so he could enter the restricted area on the Temple Mount. Nevertheless, (Mishnah *Hagigah* 2:7) "The garments of the vulgar are severely impure for Pharisees; the garments of Pharisees are severely impure for those eating heave; the garments of those eating heave are severely impure for those sacrificing." The severe impurity of מִדְרָס referred to here is the impurity of seats or beds used by a sufferer from gonorrhea or a menstruating woman, which makes anyone touching it impure and requires immersion in water and waiting until sundown. Since the king could not sacrifice on the Day of Atonement, he could not have immersed himself with an intention which would make him co-pure with the High Priest. Since the incident happened at sundown, the High Priest was automatically disqualified for the next 24 hours.

While a living Gentile is not under the rules of biblical impurity, rabbinically every Gentile is impure and this impurity cannot be removed by immersion in water (Babli *Avodah zarah* 36b).

435 Under the Herodian kings, when the High Priesthood was conferred and removed at the whim of the king.

436 It is indecent for a married woman to be seen in public with uncovered hair. She was clothed at home as she was for the street and never undressed except in the dark. The Babli notes that many women follow this custom.

437 A pun on the name of *Qimḥit* "flour lady".

438 *Ps.* 45:14.

439 According to Rashi's commentary in

Yoma, the argument means that the reward of a woman who behaves with dignity in her home is that her son will be High Priest whose garment is adorned with golden settings for precious stones. (Cf. *Tanhuma Wayyišlaḥ* 6, *Bemidbar* 3.)

(72a line 66) יָכוֹל לֹא יְהֵא מְשׁוּחַ מִלְחָמָה מֵבִיא עֲשִׂירִית הָאֵיפָה [שֶׁלּוֹ. תַּלְמוּד לוֹמַר תַּחְתָּיו מִבָּנָיו. אֶת שֶׁבְּנוֹ עוֹבֵד תַּחְתָּיו מֵבִיא עֲשִׂירִית הָאֵיפָה] שֶׁלּוֹ. יָצָא מְשׁוּחַ מִלְחָמָה שֶׁאֵין בְּנוֹ עוֹבֵד תַּחְתָּיו. וּמְנַיִין לִמְשׁוּחַ מִלְחָמָה שֶׁאֵין בְּנוֹ עוֹבֵד תַּחְתָּיו. תַּלְמוּד לוֹמַר יִלְבָּשָׁם הַכֹּהֵן תַּחְתָּיו מִבָּנָיו. אֶת שֶׁהוּא בָא אֶל אוֹהֶל מוֹעֵד לְשָׁרֵת בַּקּוֹדֶשׁ בְּנוֹ עוֹבֵד תַּחְתָּיו. יָצָא מְשׁוּחַ מִלְחָמָה שֶׁאֵינוֹ בָא אֶל אוֹהֶל מוֹעֵד לְשָׁרֵת בַּקּוֹדֶשׁ [אֵין בְּנוֹ עוֹבֵד תַּחְתָּיו]. מְנַיִין שֶׁהוּא מִתְמַנֶּה כֹהֵן גָּדוֹל. [שֶׁנֶּאֱמַר] פִּינְחָס בֶּן־אֶלְעָזָר נָגִיד הָיָה עֲלֵיהֶם לְפָנִים יְיָ עִמּוֹ. רִבִּי יוֹסֵה כַּד דַּהֲוָה בָעֵי לְמִקַנְתְּרָה לְרִבִּי לְעָזָר בֵּירִבִּי יוֹסֵי הֲוָה אָמַר לֵיהּ. לְפָנִים עִמּוֹ: לְפָנִים עִמּוֹ: בִּימֵי זִמְרִי מִיחָה וּבִימֵי פִילֶגֶשׁ בְּגִבְעָה לֹא מִיחָה.

I could think that the one anointed for war[415] should bring his tenth of an *ephah*[416]. [The verse says[440], *in his stead, of his sons*. One whose son will serve in his stead brings his tenth of an *ephah*.] This excludes the one anointed for war whose sons will not serve in his stead does not bring a tenth of an *ephah*. From where that the son of the anointed for war will not serve in his stead? The verse says[440], *seven days shall the priest wear them*, etc. If one officiates in the Tent of Meeting, his son will stand in his stead. This excludes the one anointed for war who does not officiate in the Tent of Meeting, [his son will not stand in his stead.] From where that he can be appointed as High Priest[441]? [As is written,] [442]*Phineas the son of Eleazar was leader over them; in earlier times the Eternal was with him*. When Rebbi Yose wanted to needle[443] Rebbi Eleazar ben Rebbi Yose[444], he said to him, "before, he was with him." *Before, he was with him*. In the days of Zimri[445], he protested. In the days of the concubine at Gibea[446], he did not protest.

440 *Ex.* 29:30. As often, the proof is from the part of the verse not quoted: *Seven days the priest shall wear them, who of his sons will stand in his stead to officiate in the Sanctuary*. The only hereditary office in Divine Service is that of the High Priest. Babli *Yoma* 72b/73a.

441 Since the Anointed for War is under the restrictions valid for the High Priest, one has to ascertain that his office be subordinate, not coordinate, to the High Priesthood and that an appointment to High Priesthood does not violate the rule that one may not reduce the holiness of one's position (Note 151).

442 *1Chr.* 9:20. The leader of the priests is the High Priest. Phineas was appointed Anointed for War by Moses, *Num.* 31:6.

443 Hebrew verb built on a Greek root; cf.

Berakhot 3, Note 96.
444 R. Yose seems to have complained about a lack of leadership on the part of his son.
445 *Num.* 27:1-15.
446 *Jud.* 19-21. In the opinion of *Seder Olam,* based on the teachings of R. Yose the Tanna (who is meant here), the affair at Gibea happened at the start of the period of the Judges, when Phineas was High Priest. Cf. the author's edition of *Seder Olam* (Northvale NJ 1998), pp. 122-123.

(72a line 75) מְנַיָין שֶׁהוּא נִשְׁאַל בִּשְׁמוֹנָה. ר' בָּא רִבִּי חִייָה בְשֵׁם רִבִּי חִייָה רִבִּי חִייָה בְשֵׁם רִבִּי יוֹחָנָן. וּבִגְדֵי הַקוֹדֶשׁ אֲשֶׁר לְאַהֲרֹן יִהְיוּ לְבָנָיו. מַה תַּלְמוּד לוֹמַר אַחֲרָיו. אֶלָּא לִגְדוּלָה שֶׁלְאַחֲרָיו. מְנַיָין שֶׁהוּא עוֹבֵד בִּשְׁמוֹנָה. רִבִּי אִימִּי בְשֵׁם רִבִּי יוֹחָנָן. וּבִגְדֵי הַקוֹדֶשׁ אֲשֶׁר לְאַהֲרֹן יִהְיוּ לְבָנָיו. מַה תַּלְמוּד לוֹמַר אַחֲרָיו. אֶלָּא לִגְדוּלָה שֶׁלְאַחֲרָיו. אָמַר לֵיהּ רִבִּי יוֹנָה. עִמָּךְ הָיִיתִי. לֹא אָמַר עוֹבֵד אֶלָּא נִשְׁאַל. בַּמֶּה הוּא נִשְׁאַל. אַייתֵי רַב הוֹשַׁעְיָה מַתְנִיתָא דְּבַר קַפָּרָא מִן דְּרוֹמָא וְתַנָּא. וַחֲכָמִים אוֹמְרִים. אֵינוֹ כָשֵׁר לֹא בִשְׁמוֹנָה שֶׁל כֹּהֵן גָּדוֹל וְלֹא בְאַרְבָּעָה שֶׁל כֹּהֵן הֶדְיוֹט. אָמַר רִבִּי בָּא. בְּדִין הָיָה שֶׁיְּהֵא עוֹבֵד בְּאַרְבָּעָה. וְלָמָּה אֵינוֹ עוֹבֵד. שֶׁלֹּא יְהוּ אוֹמְרִין. רָאִינוּ כֹהֵן גָּדוֹל פְּעָמִים עוֹבֵד בְּאַרְבָּעָה פְּעָמִים שֶׁהוּא עוֹבֵד בִּשְׁמוֹנָה. אָמַר רִבִּי יוֹנָה. וְלֹא מִבִּפְנִים הוּא עוֹבֵד וְלֹא מִבַּחוּץ הוּא נִשְׁאָל. וְטוֹעִים בֵּין דָּבָר מִבִּפְנִים לַבַּחוּץ. וְכִי רִבִּי טַרְפוֹן אֲבִיהֶן שֶׁלְּכָל־יִשְׂרָאֵל לֹא טָעָה בֵין תְּקִיעַת הַקָּהֵל לִתְקִיעַת קָרְבָּן. דִּכְתִיב וּבְנֵי אַהֲרֹן הַכֹּהֲנִים יִתְקְעוּ בַּחֲצוֹצְרוֹת. תְּמִימִים לֹא בַעֲלֵי מוּמִין. דִּבְרֵי רִבִּי עֲקִיבָה. אָמַר לוֹ רִבִּי טַרְפוֹן. אֲקַפַּח אֶת בָּנַיי אִם לֹא רָאִיתִי אֶת שִׁמְעוֹן אֲחִי אִימָּא חִיגֵּר מֵרַגְלָיו עוֹמֵד בָּעֲזָרָה וַחֲצוֹצַרְתּוֹ בְיָדוֹ וְתוֹקֵעַ. אָמַר לוֹ רִבִּי עֲקִיבָה. שֶׁמָּא לֹא רְאִיתוֹ אֶלָּא בִשְׁעַת הַקְהֵל. וַאֲנִי אוֹמֵר. בִּשְׁעַת הַקָּרְבָּן. אָמַר לוֹ רִבִּי טַרְפוֹן. אֲקַפַּח אֶת בָּנַיי שֶׁלֹּא הִיטִּיתָה יָמִין וּשְׂמֹאל. אֲנִי הוּא שֶׁרָאִיתִי אֶת הַמַּעֲשֶׂה וְשָׁכַחְתִּי. וְאַתָּה דוֹרֵשׁ וּמַסְכִּים עַל הַשְּׁמוּעָה. הָא כָל־הַפּוֹרֵשׁ מִמָּךְ כְּפוֹרֵשׁ מֵחַיָּיו.

And from where that he was asked in eight[447]? Rebbi Abba, Rebbi Ḥiyya, Rebbi Ḥiyya in the name of Rebbi Joḥanan: *And Aaron's holy garments shall be for his descendants in his stead*[440]. Why does the verse say, *in his stead*? For greatness after him[448]. And from where that he officiated in eight[449]? Rebbi Immi in the name of Rebbi Joḥanan: *And Aaron's holy garments shall be for his descendants.* Why does the verse say, *in his stead*? For greatness after him. Rebbi Jonah said to him[450], I was with you; he did not say "officiated" but "was asked". Rav Hoshaia brought a Mishnah of Bar Qappara from the South which stated: But the Sages are saying that he is qualified neither in the four of a common priest nor in the eight of a High Priest[449]. Rebbi Abba said, it would be logical that he officiate in four[451]. Why did they say that he does not officiate? Lest people say, we saw a High

Priest, sometimes he officiates in four, sometimes he officiates in eight[452]. Rebbi Jonah said, would he not officiate inside and would he not be asked outside? Does one err between inside and outside? But did Rebbi Tarphon, the father of all of Israel, not err between blowing for assembly and the blowing for a sacrifice? As it is stated: *The descendants of Aaron, the priests, shall blow the trumpets*[453], blameless ones, not with bodily defects, the words of Rebbi Aqiba. Rebbi Tarphon said to him, I would hit my sons[454] if I did not see Simeon, my mother's brother, lame in one of his legs, standing in the Temple court with his trumpet in his hand and blowing! Rebbi Aqiba answered him, maybe you saw him only at the time of assembly[455]; but I was saying, at the time of sacrifices[456]. Rebbi Tarphon said to him, I would hit my sons but you did not deviate right or left. I am the one who saw the act and forgot. You derive it and agree with tradition. Therefore, anybody who separates from you is as if he separated himself from his life[457].

447 The Anointed for War has two jobs. One is to address the army as described in *Deut.* 20:1-9, the other to ask the Urim and Tummim oracle on behalf of the army commander. Since this oracle is mentioned only in connection with the High Priest's garments (*Ex.* 28:30) it is obvious that the Anointed for War must wear one of these garments for the oracle. But since all eight garments of the High Priest form an indivisible unit, he must wear all of them.

448 Also for a secondary greatness.

449 This seems logical. Since the Anointed for War is required to wear the High Priest's garb, "one increases in sanctity but does not decrease" (cf. Note 429). The opposing opinion disqualifies the Anointed for War from all office in the Sanctuary.

450 The name of R. Jonah's interlocutor is not given; it is presumed to be his colleague R. Yose. He notes that R. Immi's statement was identical to that of of R. Hiyya. In the Babli, *Yoma* 73a, the students of R. Johanan already point out that R. Johanan only gave his opinion on interrogation of the oracle, not of officiating.

452 He holds that as a matter of principle, the Anointed for War could use the eight garments of the High Priest strictly for his duties outside the sanctuary and still be a common priest inside without violating the principle of Note 429. The Babli disagrees (*Yoma* 73a) and bases the rule strictly on that principle. In contrast to the Babli, this would be strictly a rabbinic rule, not based on biblical principles, and therefore not a historical reconstruction by a new rule for the days of the Messiah.

453 *Num.* 10:8.

454 His oath formula, cursing himself if his statement should be found false. Babli

Šabbat 17a.
455 The command to call all the community in the desert by the sound of trumpets (*Num.* 10:3) is extended to use trumpets to introduce the public Torah reading in the Temple at Tabernacles in the Sabbatical Year (*Deut.* 31:10-13).
456 *Num.* 10:10; cf. *Sanhedrin* 3:3 Note 155.
457 A similar text in *Sifry Num.* 75 (a better text *Yalqut* #725).

(72b line 19) וְכִפֶּר הַכֹּהֵן אֲשֶׁר־יִמְשַׁח אֹתוֹ. מַה תַּלְמוּד לוֹמַר. לְפִי שֶׁכָּל־הַפָּרָשָׁה אֲמוּרָה בְאַהֲרֹן. אֵין לִי אֶלָּא אַהֲרֹן עַצְמוֹ. מִנַּיִין לִרְבוֹת כֹּהֵן אַחֵר. תַּלְמוּד לוֹמַר. אֲשֶׁר־יִמְשַׁח אֹתוֹ. אֵין לִי אֶלָּא מָשׁוּחַ בְּשֶׁמֶן הַמִּשְׁחָה. הַמְרוּבֶּה בְגָדִים מְנַיִין. תַּלְמוּד לוֹמַר וַאֲשֶׁר יְמַלֵּא אֶת־יָדוֹ. מְנַיִין לִרְבוֹת כֹּהֵן הַמִּתְמַנֶּה. תַּלְמוּד לוֹמַר וְכִפֶּר הַכֹּהֵן. בַּמֶּה הוּא מִתְמַנֶּה. רַבָּנָן דְּקַיְסָרִין בְּשֵׁם רִבִּי חִייָה בַּר יוֹסֵף. בְּפֶה. אָמַר רִבִּי זְעוּרָה. הָדָא אָמְרָה שֶׁמְּמַנִּין זְקֵינִים בַּפֶּה. אָמַר רִבִּי חִייָה בַּר אָדָא. מַתְנִיתָא אָמְרָה כֵן. חֲזוֹר בָּךְ בְּאַרְבָּעָה דְבָרִים שֶׁהָיִיתָ אוֹמֵר וְנַעַשְׂךָ אַב בֵּית דִּין.

The priest shall atone who was anointed[458]. Since the entire chapter is said about Aaron, from where to include another priest[459]? The verse says, *who was anointed*; not only the anointed with the anointing oil; from where the one clothed in multiple garb? The verse says, *who was inducted into office.* And from where another who was appointed[460]? The verse says, *the priest shall atone*[461]. How is he being appointed? The rabbis of Caesarea in the name of Rebbi Ḥiyya bar Joseph, by mouth[462]. Rebbi Ze`ira said, this implies that one may ordain Elders by word of mouth. Rebbi Ḥiyya bar Ada said, a Mishnah says so: "Recant the four things that you are used to say and we shall make you president of the Court.[463]"

458 *Lev.* 16:32. The problem is the legitimacy of a priest appointed *ad hoc* as High Priest to conduct the service of the Day of Atonement for which common priests are disqualified.
459 The first 30 verses of the Chapter mention Aaron exclusively.
460 In an emergency of the Day of Atonement where no formal session of a court can be held. Even when anointing oil was available, simple investiture was enough.
461 Since it does not stress "the High Priest", it follows that any priest can be appointed to fill the office.
462 It does not need the laying on of hands nor a document of appointment. (Tosaphot *Yoma* 12b s, v. כהן).
463 Mishnah *Idiut* 5:6. The oral promise was irrevocable.

(fol. 69d) **משנה יג**: אֵין בֵּין בָּמָה גְדוֹלָה לְבָמָה קְטַנָּה אֶלָּא פְּסָחִים. זֶה הַכְּלָל כָּל שֶׁהוּא נִידָּר וְנִידָּב קָרֵב בַּבָּמָה. וְכָל־שֶׁאֵינוֹ לֹא נִידָּר וְלֹא נִידָּב אֵינוֹ קָרֵב בַּבָּמָה:

משנה יד: אֵין בֵּין שִׁילֹה לִירוּשָׁלַיִם אֶלָּא שֶׁבְּשִׁילֹה אוֹכְלִין קָדָשִׁים קַלִּין וּמַעֲשֵׂר שֵׁנִי בְּכָל־הָרוֹאֶה וּבִירוּשָׁלַיִם לִפְנִים מִן הַחוֹמָה. כָּאן וְכָאן קָדְשֵׁי קָדָשִׁים נֶאֱכָלִין לִפְנִים מִן הַקְּלָעִים. קְדוּשַׁת שִׁילֹה יֵשׁ אַחֲרֶיהָ הֶיתֵּר וּקְדוּשַׁת יְרוּשָׁלַיִם אֵין אַחֲרֶיהָ הֶיתֵּר:

Mishnah 13: The only difference between a public altar and a private altar was the Pesaḥ sacrifice[464]. This is the principle: Anything which can be vowed or donated[223] is sacrificed on a private altar; but nothing which cannot be vowed or donated is sacrificed on a private altar.

Mishnah 14: The only difference between Shilo and Jerusalem was that at Shilo one ate simple sacrifices[465] and Second Tithe at sight[466] and in Jerusalem inside the wall. In both cases most holy sacrifices[467] are eaten inside the curtains[468]. After the holiness of Shilo {temporary altars} were permitted but after Jerusalem {temporary altars} are not permitted[469].

464 The public altar is the one constructed for the Tabernacle at Sinai, which was the common altar for all tribes. The rules given in *Deut.* are interpreted to mean that if the altar and the Tabernacle were at one place, Shilo in the time of the Judges, and Jerusalem, private altars were forbidden, but when altar and Tabernacle were at different places, in the time between the destruction of Shilo and the building of the Temple when the Tent was in Nob, the Ark at Bet Shemesh, Qiryat Yearim, or Jerusalem and the altar at Gibeon, private altars were permitted since a place can be considered to be "selected by the Eternal" only if it is the place both of the altar and the complete Tent. Mishnah *Zevahim* 14:4-10.

465 Sacrifices parts of which were eaten by laity.

466 Any place at which the Tabernacle could be seen.

467 Sacrifices either burned as holocaust or eaten in part by priests only.

468 The enclosure of the sacred domain which for the Tabernacle was formed by curtains.

469 When Shilo was destroyed the historical record shows that Samuel and Saul sacrificed at several places, none of which could claim to be "chosen by the Eternal." But Solomon declared the Temple to be God's place *forever* (*1K.* 8:13; *2Chr.* 6:2).

(72b line 27) **הלכה יג**: [אֵין בֵּין בָּמָה גְדוֹלָה לְבָמָה קְטַנָּה כו']. רִבִּי יוֹחָנָן עָבַד תְּלַת שְׁנִין וּפְלַג דְּלָא נְחַת לְבֵית וַעֲדָא מִן צַעֲרָא. בְּסוֹפָא חֲמָא רִבִּי אֶלְעָזָר בַּחֵילְמֵיהּ. לְמָחָר סִינַי נָחַת וּמְחַדֵּת לְכוֹן מִילָה. עָאַל וְאָמַר קוֹמֵיהוֹן. מֵאֵיכָן קָשַׁט הַקּוֹשֵׁט הַזֶּה שֶׁפִּתְּחָא עֲבוֹדָה בִּבְכוֹרוֹת. מִן הֲדֵין קִרְיָיה. כִּי לִי כָּל־בְּכוֹר בְּיוֹם הַכּוֹתִי כָל־בְּכוֹר בְּאֶרֶץ מִצְרַיִם וגו'. וְכָתוּב וּבְכָל־אֱלֹהֵי מִצְרַיִם

אֲעֶשֶׂה שְׁפָטִים וגו'. קוֹדֶם לָכֵן מַה הָיוּ עוֹשִׂין. וַתִּקַּח רִבְקָה אֶת־בִּגְדֵי עֵשָׂו בְּנָהּ הַגָּדֹל הַחֲמוּדֹת אֲשֶׁר אִתָּהּ בַּבָּיִת. מָהוּ הַחֲמוּדוֹת. שֶׁהָיָה מְשַׁמֵּשׁ בִּכְהוּנָּה גְדוֹלָה. אָמַר רִבִּי לֵוִי. שָׁבַר יי׳ מַטֵּה רְשָׁעִים. אֵילוּ הַבְּכוֹרוֹת שֶׁהִקְרִיבוּ לַעֵגֶל תְּחִילָה.

Halakhah 13: ["The only difference between a public altar and a private altar, etc."] Rebbi Joḥanan spent three years that he did not visit the house of assembly because of pain. At the end Rebbi Eleazar saw in his dream: Tomorrow Sinai will come down and bring a new insight. He came and said before them, from where is this truth verified that divine service is by firstborns?[470] From this verse[471], *for Mine is every firstborn; on the day when I smote every firstborn in the Land of Egypt*, etc. And it is written[472], *and on all gods of Egypt I shall pass judgment*, etc. Before that what were they doing? *Rebecca took the desirable garments of her older son Esaw, which were with her in the house*[473]. What are "the desirable"? That he was acting as High Priest. Rebbi Levi said, *the Eternal broke the staff of the evildoers*[474], these are the firstborn who were the first to sacrifice to the Calf[475].

470 Mishnah *Zevaḥim* 14:4: Before the Tabernacle was erected private altars were permitted and the service was in the hands of the firstborn.

471 *Num.* 3:13. The reference is to the later part of the verse, *I sanctified for Me every firstborn in Israel.*

472 *Ex.* 12:12. The firstborn were sanctified to God because the gods of Egypt were destroyed.

473 *Gen.* 27:15.

474 *Is.* 14:5.

475 *Num. rabba* 4(5).

(72b line 35) הַכֹּל קָרֵב בַּבָּמָה. בְּהֵמָה וְחַיָּה וְעוֹפוֹת גְּדוֹלִים וּקְטַנִּים זְכָרִים וּנְקֵיבוֹת תְּמִימִין [אֲבָל לֹא] (וּ)בַעֲלֵי מוּמִין. טְהוֹרִים אֲבָל לֹא טְמֵאִים. הַכֹּל קָרֵב עוֹלָה וְאֵינָן טְעוּנִין הַפְשֵׁט וְנִיתּוּחַ. וְגוֹיִם בַּזְּמַן הַזֶּה רְשָׁאִין לַעֲשׂוֹת כֵּן. זְכָרִים וּנְקֵיבוֹת מְנַיִין. רִבִּי אַבָּהוּ בְּשֵׁם רִבִּי יוֹסֵי בַּר חֲנִינָה. וְאֶת־הַפָּרוֹת הֶעֱלוּ עֹלָה לַיי׳׃ תְּמִימִים [אֲבָל לֹא] (וּ)בַעֲלֵי מוּמִין מְנַיִין. אָמַר רִבִּי יָסָא. פָּשַׁט רִבִּי לָעֵזֶר לַחֲבֵרַייָא. מִכָּל־הַחַי מִכָּל־בָּשָׂר. שֶׁיְּהוּ שְׁלֵמִים בְּאֵיבְרֵיהֶן. מֵירְטִים. פָּשַׁט רִבִּי לָעֵזֶר. כָּל צִפּוֹר כָּל־כָּנָף. פְּרָט לַמֵּירְטִים. טְהוֹרִים אֲבָל לֹא טְמֵאִים מְנַיִין. רִבִּי אַבָּא בְּרֵיהּ דְּרִבִּי פַּפִּי רִבִּי יְהוֹשֻׁעַ דְּסִיכְנִין בְּשֵׁם רִבִּי לֵוִי. הִנֵּה נֹחַ תּוֹרָה מִתּוֹךְ תּוֹרָה. אָמַר. כְּבָר נֶאֱמַר לִי כְּיֶרֶק עֵשֶׂב נָתַתִּי לָכֶם אֶת־כֹּל׃ לְאֵיזֶה דָבָר רִיבָה הַכָּתוּב בַּטְּהוֹרִין. לְקָרְבָּנוֹת. וְגוֹיִם בַּזְּמַן הַזֶּה רְשָׁאִין לַעֲשׂוֹת כֵּן. רִבִּי בָּא בְשֵׁם רַב יְהוּדָה. אָסוּר לְיִשְׂרָאֵל לְסַיְּיעוֹ וְאָסוּר לְהֵיעָשׂוֹת לוֹ שָׁלִיחַ.

[476]"Everything is brought on an altar[477], domestic and wild animals[478], large and small birds[479], male and female[480], whole [but not] (and)[481] defective,

pure[482] but not impure. All are brought as elevation sacrifice and do not need stripping and partitioning[483]. Gentiles today are permitted to do this." From where male and female? Rebbi Abbahu in the name of Rebbi Yose bar Hanina: *and the cows they offered as elevation offering to the Eternal.*[484] From where whole [but not] (and)[481] defective? Rebbi Yasa said, Rebbi Eleazar made it clear to the colleagues, *from all living, from integer flesh*[485], that they should be complete in their limbs. Plucked? Rebbi Eleazar made it clear, *any bird, any wing*[486], to exclude plucked ones. From where pure but not impure? Rebbi Abba the son of Rebbi Pappai, Rebbi Joshua from Sikhnin in the name of Rebbi Levi: Noah pondered a lesson from the Torah. He said, it already was said to me, *like vegetables from the field I gave you everything*[487]. Why did Scripture increase the pure ones? For sacrifices. And Gentiles today are permitted to do this. Rebbi Abba in the name of Rav Jehudah, it is forbidden to a Jew to help him and it is forbidden to become his agent[488].

476 Babli *Zevahim* 115b, Tosefta *Zevahim* 13:1.
477 A private altar when it is legitimate. The detailed rules of sacrifices spelled out in *Lev.* are valid only for places of public worship.
478 On a public altar only cattle, sheep and goats are permitted.
479 On a public altar only pigeons and turtle doves are permitted.
480 By the rules of *Lev.* 1:3,10, an elevation sacrifice can only be a male animal.
481 Clearly the text of the [corrector] is the only acceptable one.
482 Kosher animals and birds, *Lev.* 11.
483 In the Babylonian sources (Note 476): they need stripping (remove the hide) and partitioning.
484 *1S.* 6:14, referring to the cows which drew the cart on which the Philistines returned the Ark to Bet Shemesh. Since the place at Shilo was inactive without the Ark in the Tabernacle, it was a time when private altars were permitted.
485 *Gen.* 6:19. The animal must be complete from the outside. It does not need inspection of its internal organs as required for kosher consumption of the meat or as sacrifice on a public altar. Babli *Zevahim* 116a.
486 *Gen.* 7:14. If the feathers are removed, the bird has no more wings.
487 *Gen.* 9:3. While Adam was created as a vegetarian (*Gen.* 1:29), Noah was told to be an omnivore.
488 Since private altars were forbidden after the building of the Temple, Jews cannot be involved in any way in building or serving such an altar. Babli *Zevahim* 116b.

(72b line 46) אַנְטוֹנִינוֹס שָׁאַל לְרַבִּי. מָהוּ לִבְנוֹת מִזְבֵּחַ. אֲמַר לֵיהּ. בְּנֵיהוּ וּגְנוֹז אֲבָנָיו. מַהוּ לַעֲשׂוֹת לוֹ קְטוֹרֶת. אֲמַר לֵיהּ. חַסֵּר בָּהּ אַחַת מִסַּמְמָנֶיהָ. לֹא כֵן תַּנֵּי. לֹא תַעֲשׂוּ לָכֶם. לָכֶם אֵין אַתֶּם עוֹשִׂין [אֲבָל] עוֹשִׂין הֵם אֲחֵרִים לָכֶם. אֲמַר רִבִּי חֲנַנְיָה. בְּגִין רִבִּי רוֹמָנוֹס דְּשַׁלְּחֵיהּ רִבִּי יַעֲבְּדִינֵיהּ לֵיהּ. אִית מִילִּין אֲמָרִין דְּאִתְגַּיַּיר (אַנְטוֹלִינוֹס) [אַנְטוֹנִינוֹס]. אִית מִילִּין אֲמָרִין דְּלָא אִתְגַּיַּיר (אַנְטוֹלִינוֹס) [אַנְטוֹנִינוֹס]. רָאוּ אוֹתוֹ יוֹצֵא בְמִנְעָל פָּחוּת בְּיוֹם הַכִּיפּוּרִים. מַה אַתְּ שָׁמַע מִינָהּ. שֶׁכֵּן אֲפִילוּ יְרֵיאֵי שָׁמַיִם יוֹצְאִין בְּכָךְ. (אַנְטוֹלִינוֹס) [אַנְטוֹנִינוֹס] אֲמַר לְרַבִּי.. מֵייכְלָתִי אַתְּ מִן לִוְיָתָן לְעָלְמָא דַאֲתֵי. אֲמַר לֵיהּ. אִין. אֲמַר לֵיהּ. מִן אִימֵּר פִּיסְחָא לָא אַייכְלְתָּנִי וּמִן לִוְיָתָן אַתְּ מֵיכַל לִי. אֲמַר לֵיהּ. מַה נַעֲבִיד לָךְ וּבְאִימֵּר פִּיסְחָא כְּתִיב וְכָל־עָרֵל לֹא־יֹאכַל בּוֹ. כֵּיוָן דְּשָׁמַע כֵּן אֲזַל וְגָזַר. אֲתָא לְגַבֵּיהּ. אֲמַר לֵיהּ. רִבִּי. חֲמֵי גְזוּרָתִי. אֲמַר לֵיהּ. בְּדִידִי לָא אִיסְתַּכְּלִית מִן יוֹמוֹי אֶלָּא בְדִידָךְ. וְלָמָּה נִקְרָא שְׁמוֹ רַבֵּינוּ הַקָּדוֹשׁ. שֶׁלֹּא הִבִּיט בְּמִילָתוֹ מִיָּמָיו. וְלָמָּה נִקְרָא שְׁמוֹ נַחוּם אִישׁ קוֹדֶשׁ הַקֳּדָשִׁים. שֶׁלֹּא הִבִּיט בְּצוּרַת מַטְבֵּעַ מִיָּמָיו.. הֲדָא אָמְרָה דְּאִתְגַּיַּיר (אַנְטוֹלִינוֹס) [אַנְטוֹנִינוֹס]. מֵילֵיהוֹן דְּרַבָּנָן אֲמָרִין. (לֹא) נִיתְגַּיֵּיר (אַנְטוֹלִינוֹס) [אַנְטוֹנִינוֹס]. דְּאָמַר רִבִּי חִזְקִיָּה רִבִּי אַבָּהוּ בְּשֵׁם רִבִּי לָעָזָר. אִם בָּאִין הֵן גִּירֵי הַצֶּדֶק לֶעָתִיד לָבוֹא (אַנְטוֹלִינוֹס) [אַנְטוֹנִינוֹס] בָּא בְרֹאשָׁם.

Antoninus[489] asked Rebbi, may I build an altar? He said to him, build it and hide its stones. May one make incense for him? He said to him, make it without one of its ingredients. Was it not stated, *you may not make for yourselves*[490]? You may not make for yourselves [but] others may make for you[491]. Rebbi Ḥanania said, this was for Rebbi Romanos[492] whom Rebbi sent to make it for him. [493]There are indications implying that (Antolinus) [Antoninus] converted; there are indications implying that (Antolinus) [Antoninus] did not convert. One saw him walking with a slight shoe on the Day of Atonement[332]. What do you infer since even God-fearing people go outside thus? (Antolinus) [Antoninus] said to Rebbi, can I eat from the Leviathan[495] in the World to Come? He said to him, yes. He told him, from the Passover lamb you would not let me eat, but from Leviathan you make me eat? He answered, what can we do for you since about the Passover lamb it is written that *no uncircumcised man may eat from it*[496]. When he heard this, he went and circumcized. He came to Rebbi and said to him, look at my circumcision. He answered him, at mine I never looked[497], and at yours I should look? Why is he called our holy teacher? Because he never in his life looked at his circumcision. And why is his name Nahum the holiest of holies[498]? Because he never in his life looked at the figure on a coin. This implies that (Antolinus) [Antoninus] converted. The statement of the rabbis implies that (Antolinus) [Antoninus] did (not) convert, as [331]Rebbi Ḥizqiah, Rebbi Abbahu in the name of Rebbi Eleazar said: When in the Future World the proselytes come, (Antolinus) [Antoninus] comes at the head of all of them.

489 A crypto-Jewish Roman Emperor, probably of the Severan dynasty. It is futile to try to determine to whom one refers; cf. *Kilaim* 9:4, Note 79. It was implied already in Halakhah 1 that Gentiles may have part in the World to Come.

490 *Ex.* 30:37.

491 Gentiles may make the incense for non-sacral use.

492 Rebbi's agent for matters to be done outside the seat of the Patriarchate.

493 A parallel, in slightly different order, is in Sanhedrin 10:6 (Notes 331-338). There, in Halakhah 3:12, and in Midrashic sources, the Emperor is called Antolinus.

494 The wearing of leather shoes is forbidden on the Day of Atonement (except where it is necessary, as when walking on muddy streets.) That Antoninus did not wear leather shoes on the Day of Atonement is no proof that he became a proselyte since many "God-fearing people", Gentiles known as "Friends of the Synagogue", do the same.

495 The just feasting on Leviathan meat in the World to Come are also mentioned in *Lev. rabba* 22(7), Babli *Bava batra* 74b-75a.

496 *Ex.* 12:48.

497 It is indecent to look at sexual organs. Other references to this insert are *Megillah* 3:3 (74a 1.39); *Avodah zarah* 3:1 (42c 1.5); Babli *Šabbat* 118b, *Pesahim* 104a.

498 An otherwise unknown personality.

(72b line 61) רִבִּי לֶעְזָר וְרִבִּי יוֹסֵי בֶּן חֲנִינָה. רִבִּי לֶעְזָר אָמַר. שְׁלָמִים הִקְרִיבוּ בְּנֵי נֹחַ. רִבִּי יוֹסֵי בֶּן חֲנִינָה אָמַר. עוֹלוֹת הִקְרִיבוּ בְּנֵי נֹחַ. הָתִיב רִבִּי לֶעְזָר לְרִבִּי יוֹסֵי בֶּן חֲנִינָה. וְהָכְתִיב וְהֶבֶל הֵבִיא גַם־הוּא מִבְּכוֹרוֹת צֹאנוֹ וּמֵחֶלְבֵהֶן. מַה עֲבַד לָהּ רִבִּי יוֹסֵי בֶּן חֲנִינָה. מִן שְׁמֵנַּיְיהוֹן. הָתִיב רִבִּי לֶעְזָר לְרִבִּי יוֹסֵי בֶּן חֲנִינָה. וְהָא כְתִיב וַיִּשְׁלַח אֶת־נַעֲרֵי בְּנֵי יִשְׂרָאֵל וַיַּעֲלוּ עוֹלוֹת וגו'. מַה עֲבַד לָהּ רִבִּי יוֹסֵי בֶּן חֲנִינָה. שְׁלֵימִין בְּגוּפָן בְּלֹא הַפְשֵׁט וּבְלֹא נִיתּוּחַ. הָתִיב רִבִּי לֶעְזָר לְרִבִּי יוֹסֵי בֶּן חֲנִינָה. [וְהָכְתִיב וַיִּקַּח יִתְרוֹ חוֹתֵן מֹשֶׁה עוֹלָה וּזְבָחִים לֵאלֹהִים. מַה עֲבַד לָהּ רִבִּי יוֹסֵי בַּר חֲנִינָא.] כְּמָאן דְּאָמַר. לְאַחַר מַתַּן תּוֹרָה בָא יִתְרוֹ. רִבִּי חוּנָה אָמַר. אִיתְפַּלְגוּן יְהוּדָה בִּיְרִבִּי וְרִבִּי יַנַּאי. חַד אָמַר. קוֹדֶם מַתַּן תּוֹרָה בָא יִתְרוֹ. וְחוֹרָנָה אָמַר. לְאַחַר מַתַּן תּוֹרָה בָא יִתְרוֹ. וְהָא יָדְעִין מָאן אָמַר דָּא וּמָאן אָמַר דָּא. נִישְׁמְעִינָהּ מִן הָדָא. וַיִּשְׁמַע יִתְרוֹ כֹהֵן מִדְיָן חוֹתֵן מֹשֶׁה. מַה שָׁמַע. חִזְקִיָּה אָמַר. קְרִיעַת יַם סוּף שָׁמַע. רִבִּי יְהוֹשֻׁעַ אָמַר. קְרִיעַת יַם סוּף שָׁמַע. [וְרִבִּי לֵוִי אָמַר. מִלְחֶמֶת עֲמָלֵק שָׁמַע.] יְהוּדָה בִּיְרִבִּי אָמַר. מַתַּן תּוֹרָה שָׁמַע. הֲוֵי דוּ אָמַר. לְאַחַר מַתַּן תּוֹרָה בָא יִתְרוֹ. רִבִּי בָּא וְרִבִּי חִיָּיה בְּשֵׁם רִבִּי יוֹחָנָן. וְדָא מְסַיְיעָה לְרִבִּי יוֹסֵי בֶּן חֲנִינָה. עוּרִי צָפוֹן וּבוֹאִי תֵימָן. עוּרִי צָפוֹן זֶה הָעוֹלָה שֶׁנִּשְׁחֶטֶת בַּצָּפוֹן. מַהוּ עוּרִי. דָּבָר שֶׁהָיָה יָשֵׁן וְנִתְעוֹרֵר. וּבוֹאִי תֵימָן. אֵילוּ שְׁלָמִים שֶׁהֵן נִשְׁחָטִין בַּדָּרוֹם. מָהוּ בוֹאִי. דָּבָר שֶׁהָיָה שֶׁלְּחִידּוּשׁ. מַה עֲבַד לָהּ רִבִּי יוֹסֵי בַּר

חֲנִינָה. לִכְשֶׁיִּתְעוֹרְרוּ הַגָּלִיּוֹת שֶׁהֵן נְתוּנוֹת בַּצָּפוֹן וְיָבוֹאוּ וְיִבְנוּ בֵּית הַמִּקְדָּשׁ שֶׁהוּא נָתוּן בַּדָּרוֹם. רִבִּי אַבָּא בְּרֵיהּ דְּרִבִּי פַּפֵּי רִבִּי יְהוֹשֻׁעַ דְּסִיכְנִין בְּשֵׁם רִבִּי לֵוִי. אוּף דֵּין קִרְיָיה מְסַיֵּיעַ לְרִבִּי יוֹסֵי בֶּן חֲנִינָה. זֹאת תּוֹרַת הָעוֹלָה הִיא הָעוֹלָה. שֶׁהָיוּ בְּנֵי נֹחַ מַקְרִיבִין. כַּד הוּא אֲתֵי גַּבֵּי שְׁלָמִים אֲמַר. זֹאת תּוֹרַת זֶבַח הַשְּׁלָמִים. אֲשֶׁר הִקְרִיב אֵין כָּתוּב כָּאן אֶלָּא אֲשֶׁר יַקְרִיב. מִיכָּן וּלְהַבָּא.

Rebbi Eleazar and Rebbi Yose ben Ḥanina. Rebbi Eleazar said, the Sons of Noah brought well-being offerings. Rebbi Yose ben Ḥanina said, the Sons of Noah brought elevation offerings[499]. Rebbi Eleazar objected to Rebbi Yose ben Ḥanina: Is it not written, *and Abel also brought from the firstlings of his sheep and of their excellence*[500]. What does Rebbi Yose ben Ḥanina do with this? From their luxurious ones. Rebbi Eleazar objected to Rebbi Yose ben Ḥanina: Is it not written, *he sent the young men of Israel and they offered elevation offerings*[501], etc.? What does Rebbi Yose ben Ḥanina do with this? Entire in their bodies, without stripping and partitioning[502]. Rebbi Eleazar objected to Rebbi Yose ben Ḥanina: [Is it not written, *Jethro, Moses's in-law, took elevation and well-being offerings for God*[503]?] What does Rebbi Yose ben Ḥanina do with this? Following him who said that Jethro came after the giving of the Torah[504]. Rebbi Huna said, Jehudah the great one and Rebbi Yannai disagreed. One said, Jethro came before the giving of the Torah; but the other one said, Jethro came after the giving of the Torah. We did not know who said what. Let us hear from the following: *Jethro, the priest of Midyan, Moses's in-law, heard*[505]. What did he hear? Hizqiah said, he heard the parting of the Reed Sea. Rebbi Joshua said, he heard the parting of the Reed Sea. [Rebbi Levi said, he heard the war of Amaleq.] The Great Jehudah said, he heard the giving of the Torah. Therefore he must be the one who said, Jethro came after the giving of the Torah. Rebbi Abba and Rebbi Ḥiyya in the name of Rebbi Johanan, the following supports Rebbi Yose ben Ḥanina: *Awake North, and come South*[506]. *Awake North* refers to the elevation sacrifice which is slaughtered in the North. What means "awake"? What was sleeping[507] and awoke. *And come South* refers to well-being sacrifices which are slaughtered in the South. What means "come"? Something new[508]. What does Rebbi Yose ben Ḥanina do with this? When the diasporas in the North awake and build the Temple in the South. Rebbi Abba the son of Rebbi Pappai, Rebbi Joshua from Sikhnin in the name of Rebbi Levi: also the following verse supports Rebbi Yose ben Hanina: *This is the teaching about the elevation sacrifice*[509]. *This is the elevation sacrifice* which the Sons of Noah were sacrificing. When he comes to well-being sacrifice he says, *this is the teaching about the well-being sacrifice*[510]. It is not written "which one brought" but *shall bring* from now on..

499 Noah certainly sacrificed elevation sacrifices (*Gen.* 8:20); therefore these are certainly permitted on any private altar. Well-being sacrifices can be permitted on a private altar only if they are permitted to Gentiles, the children of Noah. In order to permit well-being sacrifices on private altars one must find examples of such sacrifices from the time preceding the epiphany on Sinai. Babli *Zevahim* 116a.

500 *Gen.* 4:4. In Torah law, firstlings are sacrificed as special well-being offerings.

In *Lev.* it is quite clear that "fat" in general is חֵלֶב; פֶּדֶר is used only for fat destined to the altar and forbidden to humans. The suffixed form is חֶלְבְּהֶן. In *Gen.* the suffixed form is וּמֵחֶלְבְהֶן; one has to explain חֵלֶב in 4:4 and 45:18 from Accadic *ḫilibū* "magnificence, splendor, excellence." This interpretation is accepted here.

501 *Ex.* 24:5. The argument is the part of the verse which is not quoted: *they sacrificed oxen as well-being sacrifices to the Eternal.*

502 Instead of שְׁלָמִים he reads שְׁלָמִים. Cf. Babli *Hagigah* 6b.

503 *Ex.* 18:12. While the corrector's addition seems to be a logical necessity, it probably is taken from Babli *Zevahim* 116a.

504 His sacrifices followed all rules of *Lev.*

505 *Ex.* 18:1.

506 *Cant.* 4:16.

507 Old practices resurrected.

508 This is R. Yose ben Hanina's argument that well-being sacrifices were introduced only by the Torah.

509 *Lev.* 6:2.

510 *Lev.* 7:11. Again the argument is from the continuation of the verse, not quoted.

(72c line 11) פָּרִים הַנִּשְׂרָפִים וּשְׂעִירִים הַנִּשְׂרָפִין אֵיכָן הֵן נִשְׂרָפִין. עַל גַּבֵּי הַקֶּבֶר. מִן מַה דְתַנִּינָן אֵין בֵּין בָּמָה גְדוֹלָה לְבָמָה קְטַנָּה אֶלָּא פְסָחִים. כֵּינֵי מַתְנִיתָא. אֵין בֵּין בָּמָה גְדוֹלָה לְבָמָה קְטַנָה אֶלָּא פְסָחִים בִּלְבַד. וּדְלָא כְרַבִּי יוּדָה. דְּרַבִּי יוּדָה אָמַר. חַטָּאת פֶּסַח לְיָחִיד בְּבָמָה גְדוֹלָה. אֵין חַטָּאת פֶּסַח לְיָחִיד בְּבָמָה קְטַנָּה. תַּנֵּי. אָמַר רַבִּי יְהוּדָה. כָּל־מַה שֶׁהַצִּיבּוּר מַקְרִיב בְּאוֹהֶל מוֹעֵד שֶׁבַּמִּדְבָּר הוּא מַקְרִיב בְּאוֹהֶל מוֹעֵד שֶׁבַּגִּלְגָּל. מַה בֵּין אוֹהֶל מוֹעֵד שֶׁבַּמִּדְבָּר לְאוֹהֶל מוֹעֵד שֶׁבַּגִּלְגָּל. אוֹהֶל מוֹעֵד שֶׁבַּמִּדְבָּר לֹא הָיָה לוֹ הֵיתֵּר בָּמָה. אוֹהֶל מוֹעֵד שֶׁבַּגִּלְגָּל הָיָה לוֹ הֵיתֵּר בָּמָה. וּבָמָתוֹ בָרֹאשׁ גַּגּוֹ וְאֵין מַקְרִיב עָלֶיהָ אֶלָּא עוֹלָה וּשְׁלָמִים בִּלְבַד. וַחֲכָמִים אוֹמְרִים. כָּל־מַה שֶׁהַצִּיבּוּר מַקְרִיבִין וְהַיָּחִיד מַקְרִיבִין בְּאוֹהֶל מוֹעֵד שֶׁבַּמִּדְבָּר מַקְרִיבִין בְּאוֹהֶל מוֹעֵד שֶׁבַּגִּלְגָּל. מַה טַעֲמָא דְּרַבִּי יוּדָה. לֹא תַעֲשׂוּ בַּגִּלְגָּל כְּכֹל אֲשֶׁר אֲנַחְנוּ עוֹשִׂים פֹּה הַיּוֹם. מַה תַּעֲשׂוּ שָׁם. דָּבָר שֶׁהוּא בָא לִידֵי יַשְׁרוּת. וְאֵי זוֹ זוֹ. זוֹ עוֹלָה וּשְׁלָמִים. מַה טַעֲמוֹן דְּרַבָּנָן. בִּמְקוֹם

אִישׁ כָּל־הַיָּשָׁר בְּעֵינָיו יַעֲשֶׂה. לֹא תַעֲשׂוּן כְּכֹל אֲשֶׁר אֲנַחְנוּ עוֹשִׂים פֹּה הַיּוֹם. וּמַה תַּעֲשׂוּ שָׁם. דָּבָר שֶׁהוּא בָא לִידֵי יַשְׁרוּת. וְאֵי זוּ זוּ. זוּ עוֹלָה וּשְׁלָמִים. רִבִּי יְהוּדָה אוֹמֵר. הַיָּחִיד הוּזְהָר וְהַיָּחִיד הוּתָּר. הוּזְהָר וּבָמָתוֹ בְרֹאשׁ גַּגּוֹ וְהוּתַּר לְעוֹלָה וּשְׁלָמִים. רַבָּנָן אָמְרֵי. אַף הַצִּיבּוּר וְהַיָּחִיד הוּזְהָרוּ. צִיבּוּר תּוּתַּר מִכְּלָלוֹ. יָחִיד לָן בְּאִיסוּרוֹ.

Where are burned oxen and burned goats burned[511]? On a grave[512]. Since we have stated, the only difference between a public altar and a private altar was the *Pesaḥ* sacrifice[513]? So in the Mishnah: The only difference between a public altar and a private altar was the *Pesaḥ* sacrifice exclusively[514]; not following Rebbi Jehudah, since Rebbi Jehudah said, purification sacrifice and *Pesaḥ* for the individual on the public altar, no purification sacrifice and *Pesaḥ* for the individual on a private altar. It was stated[515]: "Rebbi Jehudah said, anything the community sacrifices at the Tent of Meeting in the desert it sacrifices at the Tent of Meeting at Gilgal[516]. What is the difference between the Tent of Meeting in the desert and the Tent of Meeting at Gilgal? At the Tent of Meeting in the desert was no permission of a private altar; at the Tent of Meeting at Gilgal was permission of a private altar. His altar may be on his roof, but he may sacrifice there only elevation and well-being sacrifices. But the Sages are saying, everything which community or private person sacrifice at the Tent of Meeting in the desert they sacrifice at the Tent of Meeting at Gilgal[517]." What is Rebbi Jehudah's reason? *Do not do* at Gilgal *everything which we are doing here today*[518]. What may you do there? Anything straight-forward[519]. What is that? That are elevation and well-being sacrifices. What is the rabbis' reason? At a place where any man may do what is right in his eyes. *Do not do everything which we are doing here today.* What may you do there? Anything straight-forward. What is that? That are elevation and well-being sacrifices. Rebbi Jehudah says, the individual was warned and the individual was permitted. He was warned, and his private altar is on his roof, and he is permitted elevation and well-being sacrifices. The rabbis are saying, also community and individuals were warned. The community was comprehensively permitted. The individual stays in his prohibition[520].

511 *Lev.* 6:23. Any purification offering whose blood was brought inside the Sanctuary has to be burned (the purification sacrifices of the anointed High Priest, the

community, and those of the Day of Atonement.)

512 The paradigm of a place of impurity. In *Lev.* 4:12 it is ordered that the High Priest's bull be burned on a place of purity. It is stated here that this applies only to the functioning Sanctuary in the desert, at Shilo, and in the Temple, but not at any other public altar.

513 Since purification sacrifices to be burned are public offerings they seem to be improper on private altars. Does the Mishnah authorize them on private altars?

514 This means either that all purification sacrifices are permitted on private altars when such altars are permitted, or that no purification sacrifices are permitted on any altar when private altars are permitted.

515 Babli *Zevahim* 117a, Tosephta *Zevahim* 13:15.

516 The temporary place of the Tabernacle during the conquest of Canaan under Joshua.

517 Everybody agrees that on a private altar one could bring only voluntary offerings.

On the public altar according to R. Jehudah only public sacrifices are possible; according to the rabbis also obligatory sacrifices of individuals.

518 *Deut.* 12:8.

519 A reformulation of the end of *Deut.* 12:8.

520 A commandment in the plural is directed to individuals, in the singular it is interpreted as a collective and addressed to the community as a whole. In *Deut.* 12:8 the first part is in the plural, the second in the singular. R. Jehudah reads the entire verse as addressed to the individual; therefore on a public altar one may not sacrifice what one cannot do on a private altar (except the case of the *Pesaḥ* treated in the next paragraph which is a private well-being sacrifice required to be brought on the public altar), whereas the majority splits the verse to permit all kinds of public sacrifices on the public altar. In the tradition of the Babli *Zevahim* 117a the roles are switched.

(72c line 29) תַּנֵּי בְשֵׁם רִבִּי שִׁמְעוֹן. הַצִּיבּוּר אֵינוֹ מֵבִיא אֶלָּא מַה שֶׁקָּבַע עָלָיו הַכָּתוּב. סָבַר רִבִּי שִׁמְעוֹן. מִשֶּׁנִּקְבַּע מַעֲשֵׂר שֵׁינִי עוֹד לֹא פָסָק. רִבִּי בָּא בַר מָמָל אָמַר. פַּר הֶעֱלָם דָּבָר בֵּינֵיהוֹן. רִבִּי יוֹסֵה אוֹמֵר. נִדְבַת הַצִּיבּוּר בֵּינֵיהוֹן. תַּנֵּי. אֶחָד הָאִישׁ וְאֶחָד הָאִשָּׁה. אָמַר רִבִּי יוֹחָנָן. לֵית כָּאן אִשָּׁה. אִישׁ כָּתוּב בַּפָּרָשָׁה. תַּנֵּי. אַף הַנְּזִירוּת. אָמַר רִבִּי יוֹחָנָן. לֵית כָּאן נְזִירוּת. נְזִירוּת חוֹבָה הִיא. תַּנֵּי. אַף הַנְּסָכִים. אָמַר רִבִּי יוֹסֵה בֵּירִבִּי בּוּן. מָאן תַּנָא נְסָכִים דְּלָא כְרִבִּי. דְּתַנֵּי. רִבִּי אוֹמֵר. אוֹמֵר אֲנִי. אַף מִשֶּׁנִּכְנְסוּ יִשְׂרָאֵל לָאָרֶץ אֵין נִיסְכִים קְרֵיבִין אֶלָּא מִבִּפְנִים. מַה טַעַם. בַּקּוֹדֶשׁ הַסֵּךְ נֶסֶךְ שֵׁכָר לַיי' אֵין כָּתוּב בְּלֹא תַעֲשֶׂה אֶלָּא מִבִּפְנִים. מְנַיִין מִבַּחוּץ. נִישְׁמְעִינָהּ מִן הָדָא. מְנַיִין לַשּׁוֹחֵט לַפֶּסַח וּלְיָחִיד וּלְבָמַת יָחִיד וּלְבָמַת צִיבּוּר בִּשְׁעַת אִיסּוּר בָּמָה שֶׁהוּא עוֹבֵר בְּלֹא תַעֲשֶׂה. תַּלְמוּד לוֹמַר לֹא תוּכַל לִזְבּוֹחַ אֶת־הַפֶּסַח בְּאַחַת. עָנוּשׁ כָּרֵת וְאַתְּ אָמַר הָכֵין. רִבִּי שִׁמְעוֹן בֶּן לָקִישׁ אָמַר. בְּשׁוֹחֵט מֵשֵׁשׁ שָׁעוֹת וּלְמַעְלָן שֶׁלֹּא לִשְׁמוֹ בִּשְׁעַת הֶיתֵּר בָּמָה. וְלָמָּה הוּא אוֹמֵר בִּשְׁעַת אִיסּוּר בָּמָה. בִּשְׁעַת אִיסּוּר בָּמָתוֹ. וְלָמָּה לִי שֶׁלֹּא לִשְׁמוֹ. שֶׁלֹּא תֹאמַר. שְׁלָמִים הֵן וְהֵן כְּשֵׁירִין. וְעוֹד מִן הָדָא. יָכוֹל אִם שְׁחָטוֹ מֵשֵׁשׁ שָׁעוֹת וּלְמַעְלָן יְהֵא כָשֵׁר.

מָה אִית לָךְ מְשֵׁשׁ שָׁעוֹת (וּלְמַעְלָן יְהֵא כָשֵׁר) [וּלְמַטָּן יְהֵא פָּסוּל]. לֹא. שֶׁלֹּא לִשְׁמוֹ. אָמַר רִבִּי יוֹסֵה. חָדָא אֱמָרָח. שְׁלָמִים הַבָּאִין מַחֲמַת פֶּסַח כְּשֵׁירִים בַּבָּמָה. עוֹלָה הַבָּאָה מַחֲמַת אָשָׁם. עַל דַּעְתֵּיהּ דְּרִבִּי לְעֶזֶר מַהוּ שֶׁתְּהֵא כְשֵׁירָה בַּבָּמָה. נִשְׁמְעִינָהּ מִן הָדָא. זֶה הַכְּלָל כָּל־שֶׁהוּא נִידָּר וְנִידָב קָרֵב בַּבָּמָה. וְכָל־שֶׁאֵינוֹ לֹא נִידָּר וְלֹא נִידָּב אֵינוֹ קָרֵב בַּבָּמָה:

אָמַר רִבִּי יוֹסֵי בֶּן חֲנִינָה. אֵין הַבָּמָה נִיתֶּרֶת אֶלָּא בְּנָבִיא. מַה טַעַם. הִשָּׁמֶר לְךָ פֶּן־תַּעֲלֶה עוֹלוֹתֶיךָ בְּכָל־מָקוֹם אֲשֶׁר תִּרְאֶה׃ כִּי אִם־בַּמָּקוֹם וגו'. וְאֵלִיָּהוּ מַקְרִיב בִּשְׁעַת אִיסּוּר הַבָּמוֹת. אָמַר רִבִּי שְׂמְלָאִי. דְּבִירָא אָמַר לֵיהּ. וּבִדְבָרֶךָ עָשִׂיתִי. וּבְדִיבּוּרְךָ עָשִׂיתִי.

It was stated in the name of Rebbi Simeon[521]: "The community only brings what Scripture fixed for it." Rebbi Simeon is of the opinion that since when Second Tithe was introduced it was not interrupted[522]. What is between them[523]? Rebbi Abba bar Mamal said, the bull of hidden things[524] is between them. Rebbi Yose says, voluntary offerings of the community are between them. It was stated, both men and women[525]. Rebbi Joḥanan said, there is no woman here, "man" is written in the paragraph[526]. It was stated, also a nazir's sacrifices[527]. Rebbi Joḥanan said, there are no nazir's sacrifices here; nazir's sacrifices are an obligation. It was stated, also libations[528]. Rebbi Yose ben Rebbi Abun said, he who states "libations" does not hold with Rebbi, as it was stated, Rebbi says, I am saying that also after Israel entered the Land, libations only are brought inside[529]. What is the reason? *In the Sanctuary pour alcoholic libations to the Eternal*[530]. A prohibition is written only for inside; from where for the outside? Let us hear from the following. From where that one who slaughters as *Pesah* for an individual on a private altar or the public altar in a time where altars are forbidden, that he transgresses a prohibition? The verse says, *you may not slaughter the Pesah at one*[531]. He is punished with extirpation and you are saying so[532]? Rebbi Simeon ben Laqish said, this is about one who slaughters in the afternoon not for its name[533] in a time when altars are permitted. Then why does he say, in a time when altars are forbidden? In a time when his altar is forbidden[534]. Why not for its name? That you should not say, it is well-being offering[535] and qualified. In addition, from the following: I could think that if he slaughtered it in the afternoon it should be qualified. Why do you have (in the afternoon it should be qualified) [in the morning it should be disqualified][536]? No. It is not for its name[533]. Rebbi Yose said, this implies that well-being sacrifices brought because of *Pesaḥ*[536] are qualified on an altar. Would an elevation offering be brought because of a reparation sacrifice be qualified on an altar according to Rebbi Eleazar? Let us hear from the following: "This is the principle: Anything which can be vowed or donated[223] is sacrificed on a private altar; but nothing which cannot be vowed or donated is sacrificed on a private altar."

Rebbi Yose ben Hanina said, the altar is permitted only by a prophet. What is the reason? *Guard yourself lest you bring your elevation offerings at any place you are seeing, except at a place* [537]etc. [538]And Elijah sacrifices when local altars are forbidden? Rebbi Simlai said, the Word He said to him[539]: *I acted on Your saying.* I acted following Your Word.

---

521 Tosephta *Zevaḥim* 13:15. The only sacrifices authorized on a public altar are those fixed beforehand, not depending on circumstances. In the Tosephta, the statement is attributed to R. Jehudah. But since the following text starts with "in addition, R. Simeon says . . .", the prior text must be R. Simeon's (Note of *Pene Moshe*.)

522 This statement does not belong here, it was copied from Halakhah 14. Second Tithe is the farmer's property to be consumed in purity "before the Eternal" (*Deut.* 14:23). When the Tent was at Nob, the altar at Gibeon, and the Ark at Qiryat Yearim, it is difficult to see where "before the Eternal" was. He posits that the duty of Second Tithe was in force in the interval between Siloh and Solomon's Temple.

523 R. Simeon and the majority who permit on the public altar anything sacrificed in the desert.

524 *Lev.* 4:13-21, the purification offering for erroneous acts of the community.

525 May sacrifice on a private altar.

526 *Deut.* 12:8.

527 May be brought on a private altar. Babli *Temurah* 14b.

528 As detailed in *Num.* 15:1-16, required for the sacrifices authorized on private altars. Babli *Zevaḥim* 111a.

529 At the altar standing in a sanctified enclosure of the Tabernacle.

530 *Num.* 28:7.

531 *Deut.* 16:6, read as: only at one place for all of Israel.

532 Since the sacrifice as described is one at an unauthorized place and this is punished by extirpation (*Lev.* 17:4), whereas the verse quoted treats this as a simple misdemeanor.

533 Which disqualifies the sacrifice from fulfilling any obligation; Mishnah *Zevaḥim* 1:1.

534 Since *Pesaḥ* may not be brought on a private altar and is a modified well-being offering, a private altar on the afternoon of the 14th of Nisan is disqualified for any kind of well-being offering.

535 An animal vowed for *Pesaḥ* but not used for this purpose automatically is dedicated as well-being offering.

536 The corrector's text is to be deleted.

537 *Deut.* 12:13-14. The argument is from the part not quoted, *except at a place which the Eternal will chose*, by informing a

prophet of His choice.
538 *Ta`aniot* 2:8, Notes 164-165.
539 *1K.* 18:36.

(line 53 72c) [**הלכה יד**:] רִבִּי יוֹחָנָן בַּר מַרְיָיה שָׁמַע לָהּ מִן הָדָא. אָז יִבְנֶה יְהוֹשֻׁעַ מִזְבֵּחַ לַי"י אֱלֹהֵי יִשְׂרָאֵל בְּהַר עֵיבָל: אֵין לִי אֶלָא הַר עֵיבָל. שִׁילוֹ מְנַיִין. וַיִּקַּח שְׁמוּאֵל טְלֵה חָלָב אֶחָד וַיַּעֲלֵהוּ עוֹלָה כָּלִיל לַי"י. אָמַר רִבִּי אַבָּא בַּר כַּהֲנָא. שָׁלֹשׁ עֲבֵירוֹת הוּתְּרוּ בְשֵׂייוֹ שֶׁלִּשְׁמוּאֵל. הוּא (וּעִירוּ) [וְעוּרוּ] וּמְחוּסַּר זְמַן וְלֵוִי הָיָה. אָמַר רִבִּי יוֹסֵה. אִין מִן הָדָא לֵית שְׁמַע מִינָהּ כְּלוּם. דְּאָמַר רִבִּי אַבָּא בַּר כַּהֲנָא. שֶׁבַע עֲבֵירוֹת הוּתְּרוּ בְּפָרוֹ שֶׁלְגִּדְעוֹן. אֲבָנִים פְּסוּלוֹת וַעֲצֵי אֲשֵׁירָה וּמוּקְצָה וְנֶעֱבַד וְלַיְלָה וְזָר וְאִיסוּר בָּמָה. מָאן דְּבָעֵי יִשְׁמָעִינָהּ טַבָאוּת מִן הַהִיא דְרַבִּי שְׁמוּאֵל בַּר נַחְמָן. וּתְשׁוּבָתוֹ הָרָמָתָה כִּי־שָׁם בֵּיתוֹ וְשָׁם שָׁפַט אֶת־יִשְׂרָאֵל וַיִּבֶן־שָׁם מִזְבֵּחַ לַי"י. כָּתוּב וַיָּרֶם הַטַּבָּח אֶת־הַשּׁוֹק וְהֶעָלֶיהָ וַיָּשֶׂם | לִפְנֵי שָׁאוּל וגו'. רִבִּי שְׁמוּאֵל בַּר נַחְמָן אָמַר. שָׁקָא וְשׁוּפָה. רִבִּי יוֹחָנָן אָמַר. שָׁקָא וְאַלְיָה. רִבִּי לְעָזָר אָמַר. חָזֶה וָשׁוֹק. דְּאָמַר רִבִּי לְעָזָר. חָזֶה וָשׁוֹק לַכֹּהֲנִים בְּבָמָה גְדוֹלָה וְלַבְּעָלִים בְּבָמָה קְטַנָּה. רִבִּי זְעוּרָה בְשֵׁם רִבִּי לְעָזָר. עוֹר הָעוֹלָה לַכֹּהֲנִים בְּבָמָה גְדוֹלָה וְלַבְּעָלִים בְּבָמָה קְטַנָּה. רִבִּי זְעוּרָה בְשֵׁם רַב יִרְמְיָה. תְּרוּמַת תּוֹדָה לַכֹּהֲנִים בְּבָמָה גְדוֹלָה וְלַבְּעָלִים בְּבָמָה קְטַנָּה. רִבִּי יוֹחָנָן בָּעֵי. הַלַּיְלָה מָהוּ שֶׁיְּהֵא כָשֵׁר בַּבָּמָה. הֵתִיב רִבִּי לְעָזָר. וְהָכְתִיב וַיֹּאמֶר שָׁאוּל פֻּצוּ בָעָם וַאֲמַרְתֶּם לָהֶם הַגִּישׁוּ אֵלַי אִישׁ שׁוֹרוֹ וגו'. וּכְתִיב וַיַּגִּידוּ לְשָׁאוּל לֵאמֹר הִנֵּה הָעָם חוֹטִאים לַיהוָֹה לֶאֱכֹל עַל־הַדָּם וגו'. הָא כֵיצַד. הַלַּיְלָה לַחוּלִין וְהַיּוֹם לַמּוּקְדָּשִׁין. כַּד שְׁמַע רִבִּי יוֹחָנָן אָמַר. יָפָה לִימְּדָנוּ רִבִּי לְעָזָר.

[540][**Halakhah 14**:] Rebbi Johanan bar Marius understood it from the following[541]: *Then Joshua would build an altar for the Eternal, the God of Israel, on Mount Ebal.* Not only Mount Ebal, from where Shilo[542]? *Samuel took a milk lamb and brought it up totally as elevation offering for the Eternal*[543]. Rebbi Abba bar Cahana said, three sins were permitted for Samuel's sheep: It and its hide[544], and deficient in time[545], and he was a Levite[546]. Rebbi Yose said, if about this it implies nothing, since Rebbi Abba bar Cahana said, seven sins were permitted for Gideon's bull[547]: Disqualified stones, and Asherah wood, and separated, and worshipped, and night, and outsider, and altar prohibition. He who wants may understand it well from that by Rebbi Samuel bar Nahman: *When he returned to Rama, for there was his house, and there he judged Israel, and there he built an altar for the Eternal*[548]. It is written[549], *the cook lifted the thigh and what was on it and put before Saul*, etc. Rebbi Samuel bar Nahman said, the thigh and meat[550]. Rebbi Johanan said, the thigh and the fat tail[551]. Rebbi Eleazar said, the thigh and the breast[550], as Rebbi Eleazar said, the thigh and the breast belong to the

Cohanim at a public altar but to the owner at a private altar. Rebbi Ze`ira in the name of Rebbi Eleazar: The hide of the elevation sacrifice belongs to the Cohanim at a public altar[552] but to the owner at a private altar. Rebbi Ze`ira in the name of Rav Jeremiah: The contribution of a thanksgiving sacrifice[553] belongs to the Cohanim at a public altar but to the owner at a private altar. Rebbi Johanan asked, is the night qualified at a private altar[554]? Rebbi Eleazar answered, is it not written,[555] *Saul said, disperse under the people and tell them, every man shall bring to me his ox*, etc. And it is written[556], *they told Saul saying, behold the people are sinning against the Eternal by eating on the blood*, etc. How is this? The night for profane {slaughter}, and the day for sacrificial. When Rebbi Johanan heard this, he said, well did Rebbi Eleazar teach us[557].

540 Corrector's addition, inserted at the wrong place since this paragraph is a direct continuation of the preceding one, showing that at all times a prophet may legally build an altar separate from the official sanctuary. As noted in N. 537, Deuteronomy nowhere declares that only one sanctuary is tolerated, but only that the place of sacrifices must have been chosen by the Eternal. The high cost of official worship as demanded in *Num*. 28-29 automatically restricts permanent worship to one place, making any additional place used on the authority of a recognized prophet a temporary matter.

541 *Jos*. 8:30. Since the altar on Mount Ebal was built at the time when the Tent and Moses's altar were at Gilgal, this proves that at this time secondary public altars were not forbidden.

542 That several official and private altars were permitted after the destruction of Shilo.

543 *1S*. 7:9.

544 In *Lev*. 1:6 it is decreed that an elevation offering is burned without its hide. Babli *Zevahim* 120a.

545 This is not spelled out in the verse. No lamb may be sacrificed on an official altar if it is not at least 8 days old; *Lev*. 23:27.

546 He was a descendant of Qorah, and only descendants of Aaron may officiate at a public altar.

547 *Jud*. 6:25-27. The stones had been used for an altar of Baal, therefore they were forbidden for all usufruct together with the wood of the Asherah tree. They could have been used only by direct commandment from God. That the bull had been worshipped as a deity is deduced from the involved language in the verse, where a single bull is called "second" to show that two sins were committed with it. (Babli *Temurah* 28b.) That sacrifices are permitted only during daytime is deduced from *Lev*. 7:38 (Halakhah 2:5). In Gideon's time the sanctuary of Shilo was in existence.

548 *1S*. 8:17, after the destruction of Shilo.

549 *1S*. 9:24.

550 The thigh belongs to the officiating Cohen (*Ex*. 29:27-28); Saul could have received it only if no Cohen was officiating

at the altar. Babli *Avodah zarah* 25a, *Zevahim* 119b.
551 The fat tail is to be burned on the altar, *Lev.* 3:9.
552 In *Lev.* 7:8 it is decreed that the hide belongs to the officiating Cohen. Since a non-Cohen was shown to be able to officiate at a private altar, the hide belongs to the owner. Babli *Zevahim* 119b.
553 The officiating Cohen's part of the breads accompanying the sacrifice, *Lev.* 7:14.
554 Since on an official altar sacrifices are possible only during daytime, Halakhah 2:5.
555 *1S.* 14:34. It is stated in the verse that the slaughter was in the night; in v. 35 it is stated that Saul built an altar.
556 *1S.* 14:33, they engaged in pagan slaughter.
557 That the verse emphasizes profane slaughter during nighttime. Babli *Zevahim* 120a.

(73c line 72) רִבִּי פִּינְחָס בְּשֵׁם רִבִּי יוֹסֵה בֵּירִבִּי אִילְעַאי. כָּתוּב אֶחָד אוֹמֵר. וַיִּטּשׁ מִשְׁכַּן שִׁילֹה. וְכָתוּב אַחֵר אוֹמֵר וַתְּבִאֵהוּ בֵית־י'י שִׁלֹה. הָא כֵיצַד. בַּיִת שֶׁלַאֲבָנִים מִלְּמַטָּן וִירֵעוֹת מִלְמַעֲלָן. וְהִיא הָיְתָה מְנוּחָה. אָמַר רִבִּי זְעוּרָה. וּבִלְבַד עֲשָׂרָה טְפָחִים כְּבִנְיַין הַבַּיִת. וְהָא תַנֵּי. כְּשֵׁם שֶׁהָיָה אוֹהֶל מוֹעֵד נָטוּי כָּךְ אוֹהֶל שֶׁבְּשִׁילֹה נָטוּי. אָמַר רִבִּי יוֹסֵי בֵּירִבִּי בּוּן. קְרָסָיו קְרָשָׁיו בְּרִיחָיו וַאֲדָנָיו וְעַמּוּדָיו: וְהָיוּ הַקְּרָסִים נִרְאִין מִתּוֹכוֹ כְּכוֹבָבִים בָּרָקִיעַ.

Rebbi Phineas in the name of Rebbi Yose ben Rebbi Ila`y. One verse says, *he abandoned the dwelling at Shilo*[558], but an other verse says, *she brought him to the Eternal's House at Shilo*[559]. How is this? A stone house below and the gobelins on top[560], and this was "rest."[561] Rebbi Ze`ira said, a minimum of ten hand-breadths, as in building a house. But was it not stated, just as the Tent of Meeting was erected so was the Tent at Shilo erected? Rebbi Yose ben Rebbi Abun said, *its poles, its planks, its latches, its bases, and its columns*[562]. Its poles were visible inside like stars in the sky.

558 *Ps.* 78:60. The argument is based on the second part of the verse, *a Tent He made dwell among mankind.*
559 *1Sam.* 1:25.
560 The three layers of covers of the Tent of Meeting were drawn over a stone wall. Babli *Zevahim* 118a.
561 Private altars are prohibited in *Deut.* 12:9 when Israel comes *to the rest and the inheritance.* "Rest" is defined as Shilo, "inheritance" as Jerusalem. Babli 10a.
562 *Ex.* 39:33.

(72d line 1) רִבִּי חִייָה רַבָּה אָמַר לְרִבִּי שִׁמְעוֹן בְּרִבִּי. אֲנִי שְׁמַעְתִּי מֵאָבִיךְ שֶׁכָּל־חוּפוֹת [שֶׁהָיוּ] לֹא הָיוּ אֶלָּא בְחֶלְקוֹ שֶׁלְבִנְיָמִין. מַה טַעֲמָא. וּבֵין כְּתֵפָיו שָׁכֵן: וְהָא כְתִיב וַיִּמְאַס בְּאֹהֶל יוֹסֵף וּבְשֵׁבֶט אֶפְרַיִם לֹא בָחָר. וַיִּבְחַר בְּשֵׁבֶט יְהוּדָה. וְכִי בִיהוּדָה בָחָר. אֶלָּא בְחִירָה וּבְחִירָה. מַה בְחִירָה שֶׁנֶּאֶמְרָה לְהַלָן בְּנִיָמִן בִּכְלָל. אַף בְּחִירָה שֶׁנֶּאֶמְרָה כָאן בִּנְיָמִן בִּכְלָל. רִבִּי יוֹנָה רִבִּי אַבָּהוּ

בְּשֵׁם רִבִּי יוֹסֵי בֶּן חֲנִינָה. וּרְצוֹן שֹׁכְנִי סְנֶה. קֳדָשִׁים הַמֻּרְצִין נֶאֱכָלִין בְּחֶלְקוֹ שֶׁלְיוֹסֵף. אָמַר רִבִּי אֶבְדּוּמָא דְּצִיפּוֹרִין. כְּרֹאשׁ תּוֹר הָיָה נִכְנַס מִתּוֹךְ חֶלְקוֹ שֶׁלְיוֹסֵף לְתוֹךְ חֶלְקוֹ שֶׁלְבִּנְיָמִן וְהָיָה הַמִּזְבֵּחַ נָתוּן עָלָיו. מַה טַעַם. וְנָסַב הַגְּבוּל מִזְרָחָה תַּאֲנַת שִׁלֹה. עַד אִיסְכּוּפְיָה דְשִׁילה. רִבִּי יוֹנָה רִבִּי אַבָּהוּ בְּשֵׁם רִבִּי יוֹסֵי בֶּן חֲנִינָה. וּרְצוֹן שֹׁכְנִי סְנֶה. שֶׁשָּׁרֵת שְׁכִינָה בְּסַנְאָיו שֶׁלְיוֹסֵף.

The Great Rebbi Ḥiyya said to Rebbi Simeon ben Rebbi: I heard from your fathers that all covers[563] [which existed] only were in Benjamin's part. What is the reason? *He rests between his shoulders*[564]. But is it not written, *He despised the Tent of Joseph and did not choose the tribe of Ephraim, but chose the tribe of Judah*[565]. Did he choose Judah[566]? But choosing, choosing. Since choosing there includes Benjamin, so choosing here includes Benjamin[567]. Rebbi Jonah, Rebbi Abbahu in the name of Rebbi Yose ben Ḥanina: *and the pleasure of the Dweller in the senna*[568]. Sacral meat given to atonement is consumed in the part of Joseph[569]. Rebbi Eudaimon of Sepphoris said, like vertex of a trapezoid[570] entered from Joseph's part into Benjamin's part; on it the altar was situated. What is the reason? *The border turned eastward to Taanat-Shilo*[571], up to the door-sill[572] of Shilo. Rebbi Jonah, Rebbi Abbahu in the name of Rebbi Yose ben Ḥanina: *and the pleasure of the Dweller in the senna*. That the Divine Presence dwelt in the greatness[573] of Joseph.

563 The Tabernacles and the Temple erected in the Land, including Nob and Gibeon; Babli *Zevaḥim* 118b..
564 *Deut.* 33:12, in the blessing of Benjamin.
565 *Ps.* 78:67-68. This locates the Temple in the territory of Judah even though *Jos.* 15:8 puts the Northern border of Judah in the Hinnom valley (and probably Jaffa Street.)
566 Since it was stated earlier that the Temple building was in Benjamin.
567 If the place at Shiloh was chosen in Benjamin, the one in Jerusalem also was in Benjamin (while occupied by Jebusites.)
568 *Deut.* 33:15, in the blessing of Joseph.
569 Even if the Tent at Shiloh was on Benjamin territory, the place outside the Tent reserved for the priests' eating of sacral meat was in Joseph.
570 A technical term otherwise used in the laws of *Kilaim* 1:9, Note 202.

It would make more sense to read "from Benjamin's part into Joseph's part."
571 *Jos.* 16:6. Since this identifies *Taanat Shilo* ("the fig tree of Shilo") as a suburb of Shilo, they must read the description of the Ephraimite border in the verse as description of the Southern border. Babli *Zevaḥim* 118b.
572 An Accadic word, *askuppu*.
573 Reading the otherwise undocumented סנא as Arabic "elevation, greatness".

(72d line 12) רִבִּי לְעָזָר בְּשֵׁם רִבִּי הוֹשַׁעְיָה. מִמָּה שֶׁנֶּאֶכְלוּ קָדָשִׁים קַלִּים וּמַעֲשֵׂר שֵׁינִי בְּכָל־הָרוֹאֶה לֹא צָרַךְ הַשּׁוֹנֶה לְהַזְהִיר עַל אֲכִילָתָן אֶלָּא עַל עֲלִיָּיתָן. מַה טַּעַם. הִשָּׁמֶר לְךָ פֶּן־תַּעֲלֶה עוֹלוֹתֶיךָ. פֶּן תַּעֲלֶה עֲלִיָּיתֶיךָ. רִבִּי שִׁמְעוֹן בַּר מְיָישָׁא בְּעָא קוֹמֵי רִבִּי לְעָזָר. מַהוּא הָרוֹאֶה. שִׁילֹה אוֹ שִׁילֹה וּמִשְׁכַּן שִׁילֹה. אָמַר לֵיהּ. שִׁילֹה וּמִשְׁכַּן שִׁילֹה. כְּגוֹן הָדָא בֵית מָעוֹן. אֶלָּא שֶׁזֶּה מַפְסִיק וְזֶה אֵינוּ מַפְסִיק.

Rebbi Eleazar in the name of Rebbi Hoshaia: Since simple sacrifices and Second Tithe were eaten at sight[466] the person who stated the Mishnah did not need to warn about the consumption but about its bringing[574]. What is the reason? *Guard yourself, lest you bring your elevation sacrifices*[575], lest you bring what you are obliged to offer[576]. Rebbi Simeon bar Miasha asked before Rebbi Eleazar: What means "at sight"? Shilo or Shiloh and the Sanctuary at Shilo? He told him, Shiloh and the Sanctuary at Shilo, as for example Bet-Maon, only that there is an interruption and here is no interruption[577].

574 The main point in Mishnah 14 is not that these have to be eaten there but, by implication, that they are forbidden except at the official Sanctuary. Babli *Zevahim* 118a.
575 *Deut.* 12:13, the verse forbidding altars which are not legitimized by a prophet.

576 To an illegitimate place.
577 It is necessary not only that the Sanctuary be seen but also that it be possible to reach the Sanctuary from the place of consumption without leaving the area from which it is seen. Babli *Zevahim* 118b.

(72d line 17) רִבִּי יָסָא בְּשֵׁם רִבִּי יוֹחָנָן. זֶה סִימָן. כָּל־זְמַן שֶׁהָאָרוֹן מִבִּפְנִים הַבָּמוֹת אֲסוּרוֹת. יָצָא הַבָּמוֹת מוּתָּרוֹת. רִבִּי זְעוּרָא בְּעָא קוֹמֵי רִבִּי יָסָא. אֲפִילוּ לְשָׁעָה. כְּגוֹן הַהוּא דְּעֵילִי. רִבִּי אַבָּהוּ בְּשֵׁם רִבִּי יוֹחָנָן. שָׁם שָׁם. מַה שָּׁם שֶׁנֶּאֱמַר לְהַלָּן הַבָּמוֹת אֲסוּרוֹת. אַף שָׁם שֶׁנֶּאֱמַר כָּאן הַבָּמוֹת אֲסוּרוֹת. רִבִּי שִׁמְעוֹן בֶּן לָקִישׁ בְּעָא קוֹמֵי רִבִּי יוֹחָנָן. מֵעַתָּה אִם אֵין אָרוֹן אֵין פֶּסַח. אָמַר רִבִּי יוֹסֵי בֵּירִבִּי בּוּן. אַזְכָּרָה אַזְכָּרָה. מַה אַזְכָּרָה שֶׁנֶּאֱמַר לְהַלָּן הַבָּמוֹת אֲסוּרוֹת. אַף אַזְכָּרָה שֶׁנֶּאֱמַר כָּאן הַבָּמוֹת אֲסוּרוֹת. וְכֵן הָיָה רִבִּי יוּדָה וְרִבִּי שִׁמְעוֹן אוֹמְרִים. מַעֲשֵׂר שֵׁינִי בְּנוֹב וּבְגִבְעוֹן. נִיחָא כְּרִבִּי יוּדָה. דְּרִבִּי יוּדָה אָמַר. חַטָּאת פֶּסַח לְיָחִיד בְּבָמָה גְדוֹלָה. אֵין חַטָּאת פֶּסַח לְיָחִיד בְּבָמָה קְטַנָּה. כְּרִבִּי שִׁמְעוֹן. דְּרִבִּי שִׁמְעוֹן אָמַר. אַף הַצִּיבּוּר אֵינוּ מֵבִיא אֶלָּא מַה שֶׁקָּבַע עָלָיו הַכָּתוּב. סָבַר רִבִּי שִׁמְעוֹן. מִשֶּׁנִּקְבַּע מַעֲשֵׂר שֵׁינִי עוֹד לֹא פָסַק.

Rebbi Yasa in the name of Rebbi Johanan: This is the indication: Any time the Ark is inside[578], private altars are forbidden; once it left, private altars are permitted. Rebbi Ze`ura asked before Rebbi Yasa: even temporarily, as in the case of Eli[579]? Rebbi Abbahu in the name of Rebbi Johanan, "there", "there". Just as in the case of "there" mentioned there private altars are forbidden, so in the case of "there" mentioned here private altars are forbidden[580]. Rebbi Simeon ben Laqish asked before Rebbi Joḥanan, in that case if there is no Ark is there no *Pesaḥ*[581]? Rebbi Yose ben Rebbi Abun said, "appellation", "appellation". Just as in the case of "appellation" mentioned there private altars are forbidden, so in the case of "appellation" mentioned here private altars are forbidden[582]. And so Rebbi Jehudah and Rebbi Simeon were saying, Second Tithe in Nob and Gibeon. One understands Rebbi Jehudah, since Rebbi Jehudah said, purification sacrifice and *Pesaḥ* for the individual on the public altar, no purification sacrifice and *Pesaḥ* for the individual on a private altar[583]. Following Rebbi Simeon? Since Rebbi Simeon said, "The community only brings what Scripture fixed for it.[584]" Rebbi Simeon is of the opinion that since when Second Tithe was introduced it was not interrupted[522].

578 The Tabernacle or the Temple.

579 *1S.* 4:4. While it turned out that the absence of the Ark was permanent, it was intended to be temporary. What was the status of private altars between the removal of the Ark from Shilo and its installation in Qiryat Yearim?

580 It is not quite clear to which verses this refers. In *Zevaḥim* 119a Rashi refers to the prohibition of private altars, where "there" is used both in *Deut.* 12:7 and 14:23 regarding the obligation to sacrifice at the public shrine, and *Ex.* 40:3 regarding the place of the Ark in the Tabernacle.

581 In that case there could not have been any *Pesaḥ* sacrifice in the Second Temple, whose basic institutions were approved by Zachariah, Haggai, and Malachia. Since we know that the *Pesaḥ* was sacrificed there, the argument presented must be invalid.

582 It is not clear what this means. It cannot refer to the biblical meaning of the word אַזְכָּרָה, the declaration by the priest that the part taken is God's part to be burned on the altar, since this does not apply to the items in question. Therefore it must refer to the rabbinic meaning of אַזְכָּרָה, the Name YHWH, which appears many times both in reference to permitted and prohibited altars.

583 He expressly endorses *Pesaḥ* on any public altar, without reference to the Ark.

584 But *Pesaḥ* depends on the calendar, it is not fixed beforehand and therefore should be forbidden on a public altar. The same holds a fortiori for Second Tithe which depends on the crop; Note 521.

(72d line 28) מִנַּיִין שֶׁהַכֹּהֲנִים יוֹצְאִין יְדֵי חוֹבָתָן בַּחַלָּה וּבַתְּרוּמָה וְיִשְׂרָאֵל בְּמַעֲשֵׂר שֵׁינִי בַּפֶּסַח. תַּלְמוּד לוֹמַר תֹּאכְלוּ מַצּוֹת. רִיבָה. יָכוֹל יֵצְאוּ יְדֵי חוֹבָתָן בַּבִּיכּוּרִים. תַּלְמוּד לוֹמַר בְּכֹל מוֹשְׁבוֹתֵיכֶם תֹּאכְלוּ מַצּוֹת: מַצָּה הַנֶּאֱכֶלֶת בְּכָל־מוֹשָׁב. יָצְאוּ בִיכּוּרִים שֶׁאֵינָן נֶאֱכָלִין בְּכָל־מוֹשָׁב.

הָתִיבוּן. הֲרֵי מַעֲשֵׂר שֵׁינִי הֲרֵי הוּא נֶאֱכָל בְּכָל־מוֹשָׁב. רָאוּי הוּא לְהִיפָּדוֹת וּלְהֵיאָכֵל בְּכָל־מוֹשָׁב. רִבִּי בּוּן בַּר חִייָה בָעֵי. מֵעַתָּה הַלָּקוּחַ בְּכֶסֶף מַעֲשֵׂר שֵׁינִי טָמֵא כְרִבִּי יְהוּדָה. הוֹאִיל וְאֵינוֹ רָאוּי לְהִיפָּדוֹת וּלְהֵיאָכֵל בְּכָל־מוֹשָׁב אֵין יוֹצְאִין בּוֹ. רִבִּי שִׁמְעוֹן בֶּן לָקִישׁ בָּעֵי. [מֵעַתָּה] חַלַּת עִיסַת מַעֲשֵׂר שֵׁינִי בִּירוּשָׁלַם. הוֹאִיל וְאֵינָהּ רְאוּיָה לְהִיפָּדוֹת וּלְהֵיאָכֵל בְּכָל־מוֹשָׁב אֵין יוֹצְאִין בָּהּ.

יָכוֹל יֵצֵא יְדֵי חוֹבָתָן בַּחֲלוֹת תּוֹדָה וּבְרְקִיקֵי נָזִיר. תַּלְמוּד לוֹמַר שִׁבְעַת יָמִים מַצּוֹת תֹּאכֵלוּ. מַצָּה הַנֶּאֱכֶלֶת כָּל־שִׁבְעָה. יָצְאוּ חַלּוֹת תּוֹדָה וּרְקִיקֵי נָזִיר שֶׁאֵינָן נֶאֱכָלִין כָּל־שִׁבְעָה. רִבִּי יוֹנָה בְשֵׁם רִבִּי שִׁמְעוֹן בֶּן לָקִישׁ. מִמָּה שֶׁנֶּאֱכְלוּ חַלּוֹת תּוֹדָה (וּשְׂעִירֵי) [וּרְקִיקֵי] נָזִיר בְּכָל־עָרֵי יִשְׂרָאֵל לֹא צָרַךְ הַשּׁוּנֶה לְהוֹצִיאָן מִמּוֹשָׁב. רִבִּי יוֹסֵה בְשֵׁם רִבִּי שִׁמְעוֹן בֶּן לָקִישׁ. זֹאת אוֹמֶרֶת שֶׁנֶּאֶכְלוּ חַלּוֹת תּוֹדָה וּרְקִיקֵי נָזִיר בְּכָל־עָרֵי יִשְׂרָאֵל לֹא צָרַךְ הַשּׁוּנֶה לְהוֹצִיאָן מִמּוֹשָׁב. נִיחָא חַלּוֹת תּוֹדָה. רְקִיקֵי נָזִיר. לֹא כֵן אָמַר רִבִּי יוֹחָנָן. לֵית כָּאן נְזִירוּת. נְזִירוּת חוֹבָה הִיא. אָמַר רִבִּי בּוּן בַּר כַּהֲנָא. תִּיפְתָּר שֶׁקְּרָבָה חַטָּאתוֹ בְשִׁילֹה. עוֹלָתוֹ וּשְׁלָמָיו בְּנוֹב וּבְגִבְעוֹן. רִבִּי חֲנַנְיָה רִבִּי עֶזְרָה בְעוֹן קוֹמֵי רִבִּי מָנָא. לֹא כֵן אָמַר רִבִּי בְשֵׁם רִבִּי יוֹסֵה. שַׁלְמֵי חֲגִיגָה הַבָּאִים בְּבָמָה כְשֵׁירִים אֶלָּא שֶׁלֹּא עָלוּ לַבְּעָלִים לְשֵׁם חוֹבָה. אֶלָּא כְרִבִּי יוּדָה. דְּרִבִּי יוּדָה אָמַר. חַטָּאת פֶּסַח לַיָּחִיד בְּבָמָה גְדוֹלָה. אֵין חַטָּאת פֶּסַח לַיָּחִיד בְּבָמָה קְטַנָּה. לֹא אַתְיָא אֶלָּא כְרִבִּי שִׁמְעוֹן. דְּרִבִּי שִׁמְעוֹן אָמַר. מִכֵּיוָן שֶׁנִּזְרַק עָלָיו אֶחָד מִן הַדָּמִים הוּתַּר הַנָּזִיר בַּיַּיִן וְלִיטַּמֵּא לַמֵּתִים:

[585]From where that the Cohanim may fulfill their obligation with *hallah* or heave, and Israel with Second Tithe on Passover? The verse says, *you shall eat mazzot*[586]; this adds. Could I think that they may fulfill their obligation with First Fruits? The verse says, *in all your dwelling places you shall eat mazzot*[587], *mazzah* which may be eaten at any dwelling place; this excludes First Fruits which are not eaten at any dwelling place. They objected, but may Second Tithe be eaten at any dwelling place? It may be redeemed and be eaten at any dwelling place. Rebbi Abun bar Hiyya asked: What was bought with tithe money and became impure, following Rebbi Jehudah, since it is not subject to being redeemed and eaten at any dwelling place, one may not fulfill one's obligation with it. Rebbi Simeon ben Laqish asked: *Hallah* from dough made from Second Tithe in Jerusalem, since it is not subject to being redeemed and eaten at any dwelling place, one may not fulfill one's obligation with it.

I could think that they may fulfill their obligation with flat cakes for a thanksgiving offering and wafers of a *nazir*. The verse says, *seven days you shall eat mazzot*[588]; *mazzah* which may be eaten all seven days. This excludes thanksgiving offering and wafers of a *nazir* which may not be eaten all seven days. Rebbi Jonah in the name of Rebbi Simeon ben Laqish: since flat cakes for a thanksgiving offering and (goats) [wafers][589] of a *nazir* may be eaten in the entire domain of the Land of Israel, the presenter could not exclude because of "dwelling place". Rebbi Yose in the name of Rebbi Simeon ben Laqish: this implies that wafers of a *nazir* may be eaten in the entire domain of the Land of Israel, the presenter could not exclude because of "dwelling place". One understands about flat cakes for a thanksgiving offering. But it is not so for wafers of a *nazir*. Rebbi Johanan said, there is no *nazir* here; *nezirut* is an obligation[527]. Rebbi Abun bar Cahana said, explain it if his purification offering was presented in Shiloh but his elevation and well-being offerings in Nob or Gibeon. Rebbi Hananiah, Rebbi Ezrah asked before Rebbi Mana: Did not the teacher say in the name of Rebbi Yose: Holiday well-being offerings brought at an elevated place are qualified but they are not counted against an obligation of the owner? But it must be for Rebbi Jehudah, as Rebbi Jehudah said, purification and Passover offerings of individuals at a principal elevated place, but no purification and Passover offerings of individuals at a private altar. It only follows Rebbi Simeon, since "Rebbi Simeon said, when one of the bloods was sprinkled, the *nazir* is permitted to drink wine and to defile himself for the dead.[590]"

585 This text is from *Pesahim* 2:4 (Notes 210-227) except for an unwarranted addition by the corrector in the *Pesahim* text.
586 *Ex.* 12:18,20. *Mekhilta dR. Simeon ben Yohay* 12:20 (p. 24).
587 *Ex.* 12:20.
588 *Ex.* 12:15.
589 The scribe's text clearly is in error.
590 Mishnah *Nazir* 6:11. Therefore only the first sacrifice of the *nazir* is obligatory, the others together with the bread may be offered locally.

(72d line 53) אִית תַּנָּיֵי תַנֵּי. מְנוּחָה זוֹ שִׁילֹה. נַחֲלָה זוֹ יְרוּשָׁלֵַם. אִית תַּנָּיֵי תַנֵּי. מְנוּחָה זוֹ יְרוּשָׁלֵַם. נַחֲלָה זוֹ שִׁילֹה. מָאן דְּאָמַר. מְנוּחָה זוֹ שִׁילֹה. כִּי לֹא־בָאתֶם עַד־עָתָּה אֶל־הַמְּנוּחָה. נַחֲלָה זוֹ יְרוּשָׁלֵַם. הָעַיִט צָבוּעַ נַחֲלָתִי לִי. מָאן דְּאָמַר. נַחֲלָה זוֹ שִׁילֹה. הָיְתָה־לִּי נַחֲלָתִי כְּאַרְיֵה בַיָּעַר. מְנוּחָה זוֹ יְרוּשָׁלֵַם. זֹאת־מְנוּחָתִי עֲדֵי־עַד וגו'. לְאֶחָד שֶׁעָשָׂה לוֹ חֲבִילָה וְהָיָה נִיְנַח בָּהּ. כָּךְ בְּאֹהֶל מוֹעֵד נֶאֶסְרוּ הַבָּמוֹת. בַּגִּלְגָּל הוּתְּרוּ הַבָּמוֹת. בְּשִׁילֹה נֶאֶסְרוּ הַבָּמוֹת. בְּנוֹב וּבְגִבְעוֹן הוּתְּרוּ הַבָּמוֹת. בִּירוּשָׁלֵַם נֶאֶסְרוּ הַבָּמוֹת. לַמֶּלֶךְ שֶׁאָמַר לְעַבְדּוֹ. אַל תִּשְׁתֶּה יַיִן לֹא מִטִּיבֶּרְיָא וְלֹא מִקֵּיסָרִין וְלֹא מִצִּיפּוֹרִין. הָא בֵּינְתַיִים מוּתָּר. כָּךְ בְּאֹהֶל מוֹעֵד עָשׂוּ אַרְבָּעִים חָסֵר אַחַת.

בְּגִלְגָּל עָשׂוּ אַרְבַּע עֶשְׂרֵה. שֶׁבַע שֶׁכִּיבְּשׁוּ וְשֶׁבַע שֶׁחָלְקוּ. בְּשִׁילֹה עָשׂוּ שְׁלֹשׁ מֵאוֹת וְשִׁשִּׁים וְתֵשַׁע. בְּנוֹב וּבְגִבְעוֹן עָשׂוּ חֲמִשִּׁים וְשֶׁבַע. שְׁלֹשׁ עֶשְׂרֵה בְנוֹב וְאַרְבָּעִים וְאַרְבַּע בְּגִבְעוֹן. וּבִירוּשָׁלַם עָשׂוּ בְּבִנְיָן הָרִאשׁוֹן אַרְבַּע מֵאוֹת וָעֶשֶׂר וּבְבִנְיָן הָאַחֲרוֹן אַרְבַּע מֵאוֹת וְעֶשְׂרִים. לְקַיֵּים מַה שֶׁנֶּאֱמַר גָּדוֹל יִהְיֶה כְּבוֹד הַבַּיִת הַזֶּה הָאַחֲרוֹן מִן־הָרִאשׁוֹן.

There are Tannaim who state, *rest* is Shilo, *inheritance* is Jerusalem. There are Tannaim who state, *rest* is Jerusalem, *inheritance* is Shilo[591]. He who says that *rest* is Shilo, *because up to now you did not come to the rest*[592]. *Inheritance* is Jerusalem, *My inheritance is a vulture, a hyena for Me*[593]. He who said, *inheritance* is Shilo, *My inheritance like a lion in the forest*[594]; *rest* is Jerusalem, *this is My rest forever*[595], etc.; like one who made a bundle and rested with it[596]. At the Tent of Meeting private altars were forbidden. At Gilgal private altars were permitted. At Shilo private altars were forbidden. At Nob and Gibeon private altars were permitted. At Jerusalem private altars were forbidden. {A parable of} a king who said to his slave, drink wine neither from Tiberias, nor from Caesarea[597], nor from Sepphoris. Therefore from in-between is permitted. So at the Tent of Meeting they spent 39 years. At Gilgal they spent fourteen years, seven when they conquered and seven when they distributed[598]. At Shilo they spent 369 years[599], at Nob and Gibeon they spent 57, thirteen at Nob[600] and 44 at Gibeon[601]. But in Jerusalem they spent 410 years at the first Temple and 420 at the last Temple[602], to confirm what has been said, *the glory of this last Temple will be greater than that of the first*[603].

591 Since in the verse quoted next the times when private altars are forbidden is called *rest* and *inheritance*. Babli 10a, *Zevahim* 119a.

592 *Deut.* 12:9.

593 *Jer.* 12:9.

594 *Jer.* 12:8.

595 *Ps.* 132:14.

596 Even if he has to work on the bundle, once he has assembled it he feels like being able to rest. So it is with Jerusalem, even though it was repeatedly destroyed, it is not to be replaced.

597 Caesarea Philippi, as always.

598 As inferred from verses in *Seder Olam* 11 (in the author's edition, pp. 116-119); Babli *Zevahim* 118b.

599 *Seder Olam* 11 (p. 117).

600 *Seder Olam* 13 (p. 131).

601 Since Solomon started building the Temple in year 480 after the Exodus (*1K.* 6:1), the time at Gibeon was 480 - (40+14+369+13). This is not quite correct since the altar at Gibeon was closed only at the inauguration of the Temple, after a building period of 7 years.

602 Babli *Yoma* 9a. The computation which gives too few years for the Second Temple is analyzed by the author in *Seder Olam*, pp. 248-250.

603 *Hag.* 2:9.

הקורא את המגילה פרק שני מגילה

(fol.72d) **משנה א**: הַקּוֹרֵא אֶת הַמְּגִילָה לְמַפְרֵעַ לֹא יָצָא. קְרָאָהּ עַל פֶּה קְרָאָהּ תַּרְגּוּם בְּכָל־לָשׁוֹן לֹא יָצָא. אֲבָל קוֹרִין אוֹתָהּ לַלּוֹעֲזוֹת בְּלַעַז. וְהַלּוֹעֵז שֶׁשָּׁמַע אַשּׁוּרִית יָצָא:

Mishnah 1: He who reads the Scroll out of order[1] did not fulfill his obligation. If he read it by heart, read it in Aramaic or any language[2], he did not fulfill his obligation except that one may read to Greek speakers in Greek. The Greek speaker who heard it from Hebrew square script did fulfill his obligation.

1   Not in the order the verses are written in the text.

2   Except Greek as stated in the Mishnah.

(73a line 18) הַקּוֹרֵא אֶת הַמְּגִילָה לְמַפְרֵעַ לֹא יָצָא. דִּכְתִיב כִּכְתָבָם. קְרָאָהּ עַל פֶּה לֹא יָצָא. דִּכְתִיב כִּכְתָבָם. קְרָאָהּ תַּרְגּוּם לֹא יָצָא. דִּכְתִיב כִּכְתָבָם. בְּכָל־לָשׁוֹן לֹא יָצָא. דִּכְתִיב כִּכְתָבָם וְכִלְשׁוֹנָם.

רִבִּי יוֹנָה אָמַר. תַּנֵּי נַחְמָן בַּר אָדָא. רִבִּי יוֹסֵה אָמַר. תַּנֵּי נַחְמָן סַבָּא. וְהָיוּ. כְּדֶרֶךְ הֲוָיָיתָן יְהוּ. תַּנֵּי. אַף בְּהַלֵּל וּבִקְרִיַת שְׁמַע הַמְּגִילָה כֵּן. נִיחָא בִקְרִיאַת הַמְּגִילָה דִּכְתִיב כִּכְתָבָם. בְּרַם בַּהֲלֵילָא. בְּגִין דִּכְתִיב מִמִּזְרַח־שֶׁמֶשׁ עַד־מְבוֹאוֹ מְהוּלָל שֵׁם יי· מְהוּלָל שֵׁם יי מְמִזְרָח שֶׁמֶשׁ וְעַד מְבוֹאוֹ. מָה אַתְּ שְׁמַע מִינָהּ. אָמַר רִבִּי אָבוּן. עוֹד הִיא אֲמוּרָה עַל הַסֵּדֶר. בְּצֵאת יִשְׂרָאֵל מִמִּצְרַיִם לְשֶׁעָבַר. לֹא לָנוּ יי לֹא לָנוּ לַדּוֹרוֹת הַלָּלוּ. אָהַבְתִּי כִּי־יִשְׁמַע | יי לִימוֹת הַמָּשִׁיחַ. אֲסָרוּ־חַג בַּעֲבֹתִים לִימוֹת גּוֹג וּמָגוֹג. אֵלִי אַתָּה וְאוֹדֶךָּ לֶעָתִיד לָבוֹא.

"He who reads the Scroll out of order did not fulfill his obligation." For it is written, *as in their writing*[3]. If he read it by heart he did not fulfill his obligation for it is written, *as in their writing*. If he read it in Aramaic he did not fulfill his obligation for it is written, *as in their writing*. In any language he did not fulfill his obligation for it is written, *in their writing and in their language*[4].

[5]Rebbi Jonah said that Naḥman bar Ada stated; Rebbi Yose said that Naḥman the Old stated: *They shall be*[6], they shall be unaltered[7]. We have stated: "The same holds for Hallel and reading of *Shema*[8] the Scroll." One understands this for the Scroll since it is written, *as in their writing*. But for

Hallel, since it is written, *from sunrise to sunset may the Name of the Eternal be praised*[9]? The Name of the Eternal is praised from sunrise to sunset. What can you understand from that[10]? Rebbi Abun said, still it is said in order. *When Israel left Egypt*[11], in the past, *not for us, Eternal, not for us*[12], in current generations, *I loved, truly the Eternal listened to my voice*[13] in the days of the Messiah, *bind the holiday sacrifice with ropes*[14] in the days of Gog and Magog, *You are my God and I shall thank You*[15], in the future world.

3 *Esth,* 9:27.
4 *Esth,* 8:9. Different in Babli 17a,18a.
5 This text is a slightly enlarged copy of a text in *Berakhot* 2:4 (Notes 183-185) referring to the Mishnah which states that reading the *Shema* not in the sequence of its verses is not fulfilling one's obligation.
6 *Deut.* 6:6.
7 Understanding the verb "to be" as "to stay, to exist".
8 Word to be deleted in this context; it belongs to the text of Tosephta 2:1.

9 *Ps.* 113:1.
10 If there is no difference between East and West, earlier and later, as declared at the start of *Hallel*, why should it be important that the Psalms be recited in order? Differently in the Babli 17a, *Pesahim* 118a.
11 *Ps.* 114:1.
12 *Ps.* 115:1.
13 *Ps.* 116:1.
14 *Ps.* 118:27.
15 *Ps.* 118:28.

(73a line 29) רִבִּי יוֹסֵה בְשֵׁם רִבִּי אֲחָא רִבִּי זְעוּרָה בְשֵׁם רִבִּי לְעָזָר. וְהִיא שֶׁתְּהֵא כְתוּבָה בְלַעַז. מָה אֲנָן קַייָמִין. אִם בְּשֶׁהָיְתָה כְתוּבָה אֲשׁוּרִית וְתִירְגְּמָהּ בְּלַעַז. הָדָא דְתַנִּינָן בְּכָל־לָשׁוֹן. אִם בְּשֶׁהָיְתָה כְתוּבָה בְלַעַז וְתִירְגְּמָהּ אֲשׁוּרִית. הָדָא הִיא דְתַנֵּי. מַה בֵּין סְפָרִים לִמְגִילַת אֶסְתֵּר. אֶלָּא שֶׁהַסְּפָרִים נִכְתָּבִין בְּכָל־לָשׁוֹן וּמְגִילַת אֶסְתֵּר אֵינָהּ נִכְתֶּבֶת אֶלָּא אֲשׁוּרִית. אָמַר רִבִּי שְׁמוּאֵל בַּר סוּסַרְטַי. תִּיפְתָּר שֶׁהָיְתָה כְתוּבָה גִינַנְטוֹן. תַּנֵּי שְׁמוּאֵל. טָעָה וְהִשְׁמִיט פָּסוּק אֶחָד וְתִרְגְּמוֹ הַמְתַרְגֵּם יָצָא. בְּכָל־לָשׁוֹן לֹא יָצָא. וְאִתְּ אָמַר הָכֵין. שְׁמוּאֵל כְּדַעְתֵּיהּ. [דִ]שְׁמוּאֵל אָמַר. הָיְתָה כְתוּבָה כְהִילְכָתָהּ הַלּוֹעֵז יוֹצֵא בָהּ בְּלַעַז. רִבִּי אַבָּהוּ בְשֵׁם רִבִּי לְעָזָר יוֹדֵעַ אֲשׁוּרִית וְיוֹדֵעַ לַעַז יוֹצֵא בָהּ [בְּלַעַז וַ]אֲשׁוּרִית. בְּלַעַז וּצָא בָהּ בְּלַעַז. יוֹדֵעַ אֲשׁוּרִית וְיוֹדֵעַ לַעַז מָהוּ שְׁיוֹצִיא אֲחֵרִים בְּלַעַז. יָבֹא כְהָדָא. כָּל־שֶׁאֵינוֹ חַיָּב בַּדָּבָר אֵינוֹ מוֹצִיא אֶת הָרַבִּים יְדֵי חוֹבָתָן.

Rebbi Yose in the name of Rebbi Aḥa, Rebbi Ze`ira in the name of Rebbi Eleazar: Only if it was written in Greek[16]. Where do we hold? If it was written in square script and he translated it into Greek, that is what we have stated "in any language." If it was written in Greek and he translated it into {the language of}square script, that is what was stated, which is the difference between Torah scrolls and the Esther scroll? Only that Torah scrolls may be written in any language but the Esther scroll may only be written in square script. Rebbi Samuel bar Sosartai said, explain it if it was written *gignton*[17]. Samuel stated: If in error he omitted one verse but the translator translated it, he fulfilled his obligation. We are saying "in any language," and you are saying so[18]? Samuel follows his opinion [since] Samuel said, if it was written according to its rules the Greek speaker fulfills his obligation in Greek. Rebbi Abbahu in the name of Rebbi Eleazar: If he knows the language of square script and he knows Greek, he fulfills his obligation [in Greek or][19] in the language of square script. Greek, he fulfills his obligation in Greek. If he knows the language of square script and he knows Greek, may he absolve the public from their obligation in Greek? This shall come following: anybody who is not obligated in a matter cannot not absolve the public of their obligation[20].

16 This refers to the statement in the Mishnah that Greek speakers satisfy their obligation by hearing the Megillah read in Greek translation. This implies that it must be read from a Greek text, not being freely translated from a Hebrew text; but writing a Greek text is not permitted as explained in this paragraph. Babli *Šabbat* 115b.

17 No reasonable explanation of this word is known. As far as the meaning is concerned, the most acceptable conjecture is that of Pene Moshe, that the scroll was written in two columns, one in Hebrew square script and the other in Greek; but the word in the text cannot be read δίγλωττον (Brüll). The suggestion by S. Fränkel, to read και 'εγένετο, the start of the LXX translation of the masoretic text of Esther, to the exclusion of the apocryphal additions, does not fit the context.

18 If it is a translation on the spot, Greek is forbidden like any other translation.

19 Corrector's addition which totally misunderstands the text; to be deleted. A person understanding Hebrew must hear the text in Hebrew. As noted in the text, if he speaks both Hebrew and Greek, he must hear the text in Hebrew and cannot read the scroll for Greek speakers ignorant of Hebrew. Only a person ignorant of Hebrew may in public read the Greek text from a bilingual scroll.

20 Mishnah *Roš Haššanah* 3:9.

(fol. 72d) **משנה ב**: קְרָאָהּ סֵירוּגִין נִתְנַמְנֵם יָצָא. הָיָה כּוֹתְבָהּ דּוֹרְשָׁהּ וּמַגִּיהָהּ אִם כִּיוֵּן לִבּוֹ יָצָא. וְאִם לָאו לֹא יָצָא. הָיְתָה כְּתוּבָה בַּסַּם וּבַסִּיקְרָא וּבַקּוֹמוֹס וּבַקַּנְקַנְתּוֹם עַל הַנְּיָיר וְעַל הַדִּיפְתְרָא לֹא יָצָא עַד שֶׁתְּהֵא כְּתוּבָה אַשּׁוּרִית עַל הַסֵּפֶר בַּדְּיוֹ:

Mishnah 2: If he read it piecewise while dozing[20] he fulfilled his obligation. If he wrote it, studied it, corrected it, if he had the intention[21] he fulfilled his obligation. If it was written with a chemical, or vermillion, or gum, or vitriol[22], on papyrus, or on vellum[23], he did not fulfill his obligation unless it is written in square letters on a scroll in ink.

20 He was awake and had the intention of reading the Scroll as an obligation on Purim, only he fell asleep between passages. He does not not have to repeat on condition that he did not skip anything nor change the order of the verses.

21 He intended to read the entire scroll while reading, or studying, or correcting a correctly written scroll.
22 Greek χάλκανθος.
23 Greek διφθέρα.

(73a line 41) **הלכה ב**: תַּנֵּי. סֵירוּגִים יָצָא. סֵירוּסִים לֹא יָצָא. סֵירוּגִין קִיטּוּעִין. סֵירוּסִין חַד פָּרָה חַד.

אָמַר רִבִּי חַגַּי. סֵירוּגִים וַחֲלוֹגְלוֹגוֹת וּמִי גָדוֹל בְּחָכְמָה אוֹ בַשָּׁנִים אִיצְרָכַת לַחֲבֵרַיָּיא. אָמְרוּן. נִיסּוֹק נִישְׁאוֹל לְבֵית רִבִּי. סַלְקוֹן מִישְׁאוֹל וְאָמְרוּן. יָצָאת שִׁפְחָה מִשֶּׁלְבֵית רִבִּי. אָמְרַת לְהֶם. הִיכָּנְסוּ לִשְׁנַיִם. אָמְרוּן. יֵיעוֹל פְּלָן קָמַי. יֵיעוֹל פְּלָן קָמַי. שָׁרוֹן עָלוֹן קִטְעִין קִטְעִין. אָמְרָה לְהֵן. לָמָּה אַתֶּם נִכְנָסִין סֵירוּגִין. חַד רִבִּי הֲוָה טָעִין פַּרְחִינִין וְנָפְלוּ מִינֵּיהּ. אָמְרָה לֵיהּ. רִבִּי. נִתְפַּזְּרוּ חֲלָגְלוּגָיךְ. אָמְרָה לָהּ. אַיְיתָא מְטַאְטָא. וְאַיְיתַת אַלְבִּינָה.

It was stated: Piecewise, he fulfilled his obligation. Transposed[24], he did not fulfill his obligation. Piecewise means in pieces. Transposed, one minus one[25].

[26]Rebbi Ḥaggai said, the colleagues did know neither what סֵירוּגִין, חֲלוֹגְלוּגוֹת, means nor "who is superior, in wisdom or in years?[27]" They said, let us go and ask in the house of Rebbi. They went to ask; a slave girl from the house of Rebbi came out and told them, enter in pairs. Each one said, that one should enter before me. They started to enter one by one. She said to them, why do you enter in סֵירוּגִין? One rabbi was carrying purslain; it fell from him. She said to him, Rabbi, your חֲלוֹגְלוּגוֹת are dispersed. She said to her[28], bring a broom[29]; she brought a willow-broom[30].

24 The order of verses switched.
25 Greek παρά, cf. E. and H. Guggenheimer, Lešonenu 39 (1975) pp. 60-61.
26 A very similar paragraph is in *Ševi`it* 9:1 (Notes 11-12).
27 *Serugin* is from the Mishnah here, *Halaglugot* from Mishnah *Ševi`it* 9:1, and the problem whether wisdom or age gives preference arises in connection with Mishnah *Sanhedrin* 4:2 that in criminal cases the senior judge has to give his opinion last.
28 This sentence is missing in *Ševi`it* 9:1. It seems that the pure Hebrew speaking head-slave ordered one of her underlings to bring a broom.
29 The problem is the *hapax* in *Is*. 12:23.
30 The Aramaic equivalent of the Hebrew expression for "broom". Babli 18a.

(49 line 73a) רִבִּי מָנָא אָמַר בְּשֵׁם רִבִּי יוּדָה שֶׁאָמַר מִשֵּׁם רִבִּי יוֹסֵה הַגְּלִילִי. הִפְסִיק בָּהּ כְּדֵי לִקְרוֹת אֶת כּוּלָּהּ לֹא יָצָא יְדֵי חוֹבָתוֹ. רִבִּי בָּא רַב יִרְמְיָה בְשֵׁם רַב. הֲלָכָה כְרִבִּי מָנָא שֶׁאָמַר מִשֵּׁם רִבִּי יְהוּדָה שֶׁאָמַר מִשֵּׁם רִבִּי יוֹסֵי הַגְּלִילִי. הִפְסִיק בָּהּ. רִבִּי יוֹחָנָן בְּשֵׁם רִבִּי שִׁמְעוֹן בֶּן יוֹצָדָק. אַף בַּהַלֵּל וּבַמְּגִילָּה כֵּן. אַבָּא בַּר חוּנָא וְרַב חִסְדָּא הֲווֹן יָתְבִין אָמְרִין. אַף בִּתְקִיעוֹת כֵּן. סַלְקוֹן לְבֵית רִבִּי וּשְׁמָעוּן רַב חוּנָא בְשֵׁם רַב. אֲפִילוּ שְׁמָעָן עַד תֵּשַׁע שָׁעוֹת יָצָא. אָמַר רִבִּי זְעוּרָה. עַד דַּאֲנָא תַמָּן אִיצְרְכַת לִי. סָלְקִית לְהָכָא שְׁמָעִית דְּאָמַר רִבִּי יָסָא בְשֵׁם רִבִּי יוֹחָנָן. אֲפִילוּ שְׁמָעָן כָּל־הַיּוֹם יָצָא וְהוּא שֶׁשְּׁמָעָן עַל סֵדֶר. רִבִּי יוֹסֵה בָעֵי. הָיָה זֶה צָרִיךְ לִפְשׁוּטָה רִאשׁוֹנָה וְזֶה צָרִיךְ לִפְשׁוּטָה אַחֲרוֹנָה. תְּקִיעָה אַחַת מוֹצִיאָה יְדֵי שְׁנֵיהֶן. רִבִּי בּוּן בַּר חִיָּיה בָעֵי. כְּגוֹן קְרִיַת שְׁמַע וּבִרְכוֹתֶיהָ. הִיא וְלֹא בְרְכוֹתֶיהָ. בְּרְכוֹתֶיהָ וְלֹא הִיא. הִפְסִיק שְׁלִישָׁהּ וְחָזַר וְהִפְסִיק שְׁלִישָׁהּ. וּבְקוֹרֵא מְשָׁעָרִים וּבְכָל־אָדָם מְשָׁעָרִים. אָמַר רִבִּי מַתַּנְיָה. לֹא מִסְתַּבְּרָא בְּקוֹרֵא.

1 מנא | ב מני בשם | ב משום משם | ב משום הפסיק | ב אם הפסיק   2 מנא | ב מינא   3 משם | ב משום (2) הפסיק בה | ב -   4 ובמגילה | ב ובקריאת המגילה חונא | ב רב הונא הוון | ב הוו   5 ר' | ב רב   6 זעורה | ב זעירא איצרכת | ב צריכת סלקית | ב וכד סלקת דאמר | ב -   7 היה | ב הוה לפשוטה | ב פשוטה 8 לפשוטה | ב פשוטה שניהן | ב שתיהון בון בר חייה | ב אבין בר חייא   9 כגון | ב -   10 ובקורא | ב בקורא ובכל | ב או בכל מתניה | ב מתניא לא | ב -

[31]Rebbi Mana said in the name of Rebbi Jehudah who said in the name of Rebbi Yose the Galilean: If one interrupted so that he would have been able to read all of it, he did not fulfill his duty[32]. Rebbi Abba, Rav Jeremiah in the name of Rav: The practice follows Rebbi Mana who said in the name of Rebbi Jehudah who said in the name of Rebbi Yose the Galilean, "if one interrupted.". Rebbi Johanan in the name of Rebbi Simeon ben Josadaq: The same applies to Hallel and the Esther Scroll. Abba bar Rav Huna and Rav Hisda sat together and said, the same rule applies to blowing the Shofar[33]. They went up to (Rebbi's) <Rav's>[34] Yeshivah and heard Rav Huna in the name of Rav: Even if one heard it in up to nine hours he fulfilled his

obligation. Rebbi Ze`ira said: When I was there, this was a problem for me. When I came here, I heard Rebbi Yasa in the name of Rebbi Johanan: Even if one heard it during an entire day, one has fulfilled one's obligation. But only if one heard it in the correct order[35]. Rebbi Yose investigated: If one needed to hear the initial simple tone and another one the final simple tone, one blow of the Shofar serves the requirements of both of them[36]. Rebbi Abun bar Hiyya investigated: The recitation of Shema` with its benedictions, the recitation of Shema` without its benedictions, its benedictions without it[37]? If he interrupted after a third, interrupted after a second third[38]? Does one estimate by the reader's speed or by the average speed of all men? Rebbi Mattaniah said, is it not reasonable by the reader's?

31 This paragraph is copied from *Berakhot* 2:1, Notes 24-39 (ב).
32 This does not refer to reading the scroll, which is mentioned later, but to reading the *Shema`* as part of the morning and evening services, the topic of *Berakhot* 1-3. For the Megillah, Babli 18b.
33 When one is required to hear 9 sounds in prescribed order.
34 The *Berakhot* <text> is the correct one.
35 While there are no time limits, the prescribed order cannot be changed.
36 The obligation is to hear, not to blow the *shofar*. While the person who blows must have intent to let the listeners fulfill their religious duty, the listener must have intent to listen to the prescribed sound, which may vary from person to person.
37 This again refers to reading the *Shema`* which is preceded and followed by prescribed benedictions. In computing the maximal time limit allowed for interruption, are these three different occasions or only one? No answer is given.
38 This also applies to reading the *Megillah*. If there are several interruptions, does the time limit apply to each one separately or to the total time of interruptions? No answer is given.

(73a line 62) מְנַשֶׁה הֲוָה יָתִיב קוֹמֵי רִבִּי זְעוּרָה וְאִינַמְנַם. אָמַר לֵיהּ. חֲזוֹר לָךְ דְּלָא כַוְונִית.

Menasheh was sitting before Rebbi Ze`ira and was dozing. He said to him, repeat because I did not concentrate[39].

39 While the Mishnah permits the reader to be dozing occasionally because when he is reading he cannot do this without intent, the listener cannot be dozing and fulfill the obligation to hear the Scroll from beginning to end.

(73a line 63) הָיָה כּוֹתְבָהּ. הָדָא אָמְרָה שֶׁהוּא מוּתָּר בַּעֲשִׂיַּת מְלָאכָה. נֹאמַר. בְּאַרְבָּעָה עָשָׂר בַּכְּרַכִּים. וְדוֹרְשָׁהּ. וּבִלְבַד שֶׁלּוֹא יַפְלִיג עַצְמוֹ וְעִינְיָנוֹת אֲחֵרִים. וּמַגִּיהָהּ. תַּנֵּי. אֵין מְדַקְדְּקִין בְּטָעִיוֹתֶיהָ. רִבִּי יִצְחָק בַּר אַבָּא בַּר מְחַסְיָה וְרַב חֲנַנְאֵל הֲווֹן יְתִיבִין קוֹמֵי רַב. חַד אָמַר יְהוּדִים. וְחַד אָמַר יְהוּדִיִּים. וְלֹא חָזַר חַד מִינְּהוֹן. רִבִּי יוֹחָנָן הֲוֵי קָרֵי כּוּלָּהּ יְהוּדִים. רִבִּי חֶלְבּוֹ רַב יִרְמְיָה בְּשֵׁם רַב. כָּתוּב אֶחָד אוֹמֵר סֵפֶר. וְכָתוּב אַחֵר אוֹמֵר אִיגֶּרֶת. הָא כֵיצַד. קַל קִקִילוּ בִּתְפִירָתָהּ. שֶׁאִם תָּפַר בָּהּ שְׁנַיִם אוֹ שְׁלשָׁה תַפִּים שֶׁהִיא כְשֵׁירָה.

"If he wrote it," this implies that work is permitted. Should we say on the Fourteenth, in walled cities[39]? "Studied it," only he should not let his mind wander to other topics. "He corrected it." It was stated: one is not explicit about its mistakes. Rebbi Isaac bar Abba from Meḥasia and Rebbi Ḥananel were sitting before Rav. One said, *Yehudim*. And the other one said, *Yehudiim*, and neither of them changed his opinion. Rebbi Joḥanan was reading always "Yehudim[40]". Rebbi Ḥelbo, Rav Jeremiah in the name of Rav: One verse says "book[41]", another verse says "letter.[42]" How is this? They made it light for sewing. They were lenient regarding its sewing, that if he stitched two or three stitches it is qualified[43].

39 Since the 14th Adar is not Purim in a fortified city but reading the Scroll on the 14th always is valid (Chapter 1 Note 67).
40 Irrespective of how it was written.
41 *Esth.* 9:32.
42 *Esth.* 9:26.
43 Babli 19a.

(fol. 72d) **משנה ג:** בֶּן עִיר שֶׁהָלַךְ לִכְרַךְ וּבֶן כְּרַךְ שֶׁהָלַךְ לְעִיר אִם עָתִיד לַחֲזוֹר לִמְקוֹמוֹ קוֹרֵא בִּמְקוֹמוֹ. וְאִם לָאו קוֹרֵא עִמָּהֶם. מֵאֵיכָן קוֹרֵא אָדָם אֶת הַמְּגִילָּה וְיוֹצֵא בָּהּ יְדֵי חוֹבָתוֹ רִבִּי מֵאִיר אוֹמֵר כּוּלָּהּ. רִבִּי יְהוּדָה אוֹמֵר מֵאִישׁ יְהוּדִי. וְרִבִּי יוֹסֵי אוֹמֵר, מֵאַחַר הַדְּבָרִים הָאֵלֶּה:

Mishnah 3: A villager who went to a walled city, or a dweller in a walled city who went to a village, if he intends to return to his place[44] he reads as at his place; otherwise he reads with them. From where does a person start to read and fulfills his duty? Rebbi Meïr says, all of it. Rebbi Jehudah says, from *a Jewish man*[45]. Rebbi Yose says, from *after these matters*[46].

44 In time for the reading of the Scroll.
45 *Esth.* 2:5.
46 *Esth.* 3:1.

(73a line 71) **הלכה ג**: נִיחָא בֶּן כַּרַךְ שֶׁהָלַךְ לָעִיר שֶׁזְּמַנּוֹ מוּאַחַר. בֶּן עִיר שֶׁהָלַךְ לַכְּרַךְ וְאֵין זְמַנּוֹ מוּקְדָּם. אָמַר רִבִּי יוּדָן. לֵית כָּאן בֶּן עִיר שֶׁהָלַךְ לַכְּרַךְ. וְתַנֵּיי דְּבֵית רִבִּי כֵן. בֶּן כַּרַךְ שֶׁהָלַךְ לָעִיר. אָמַר רִבִּי יוֹסֵה. אוֹף כָּאן בְּעָתִיד לְהִשְׁתַּקֵּעַ עִמָּהֶן. אָמַר רִבִּי יוֹסֵה. וְהוּא שֶׁיֵּצֵא קוֹדָם לְשֶׁהֵאִיר מִזְרָח. אֲבָל אִם יָצָא לְאַחַר שֶׁהֵאִיר הַמִּזְרָח כְּבָר נִפְטָר. רַב נַחְמָן בַּר יַעֲקֹב בָּעֵי. מֵעַתָּה גֵּר שֶׁמָּל לְאַחַר שֶׁהֵאִיר הַמִּזְרָח כְּבָר נִפְטָר. רִבִּי בּוּן בַּר חִייָה בָּעֵי. בֶּן עִיר שֶׁעָקַר דִּירָתוֹ לֵילֵי חֲמִשָּׁה עָשָׂר [נִתְחַיֵּיב כָּאן. וּבֶּן כַּרַךְ שֶׁעָקַר דִּירָתוֹ בְּלֵיל אַרְבַּע עָשָׂר] נִפְטָר מִכָּאן וּמִכָּאן.

Halakhah 3: One understands the dweller in a walled city whose time is later. Is the time of a village dweller who went to a walled city not earlier? Rebbi Yudan said, there is here no village dweller who went to a walled city[47]. And it was stated in the House of Rebbi so: the dweller in a walled city who went to a village[48]. Rebbi Yose said, also here if he will stay with them[49]. Rebbi Yose said, only if he left before dawn, but if he left after dawn he already is not liable[50]. Rav Naḥman bar Jacob asked, then a proselyte who circumcised after dawn already is not liable[51]? Rebbi Abun bar Ḥiyya asked, the village dweller who changed his abode in the night of the Fifteenth [is obligated here; and a dweller in a walled city who changed his abode in the night of the Fourteenth] is not liable at either place[52]?

47 If the Mishnah refers only to the situation on the day of Purim, then for the villager it should make no difference whether he wants to return to his place or not since he will be unable to read at his place.

48 There are versions of the Mishnah which do not include the statement objected to by R. Yudan.

49 The Mishnah in its entire formulation can be retained if one adds people intending to move from one place to the other, even if for the purpose of moving they have to return to their earlier place of residence.

50 If the dweller in a walled town left the village during the night, the rules for villages have no relevance for him (the Mishnah does not mention reading the Scroll in the night, only that the entire day is qualified for the reading, Mishnah 5.) But immediately at dawn he becomes obligated.

51 If the proselyte was not obligated at dawn because he was not yet Jewish, he cannot become obligated in the middle of the day.

52 The text as it stands makes no sense. The corrector's addition has to be deleted; both R. Isaya II of Trani and Rashba quote the text without his addition. The text is quoted by Rashba, Responsa 3:414, as: "the village dweller who changed his abode in the night of the Fourteenth is not liable at either place" if he arrived at the walled city after dawn of the 15th since then on Purim he is neither a village dweller nor a city dweller. This text is confirmed by Meïri (ed. M. Herschler, Jerusalem 1962, p. 55), who questions Rashba's interpretation.

(73b line 4) בֶּן עִיר מָהוּ שֶׁיּוֹצִיא בֶּן כַּרָךְ יְדֵי חוֹבָתוֹ. יָבֹא כְהָדָא. כֹּל שֶׁאֵינוֹ חַיָּיב בַּדָּבָר אֵינוֹ מוֹצִיא אֶת הָרַבִּים יְדֵי חוֹבָתָן׃ בֶּן כַּרָךְ מָהוּ שֶׁיּוֹצִיא בֶּן עִיר יְדֵי חוֹבָתוֹ. כֹּל שֶׁאֵינוֹ חַיָּיב בַּדָּבָר אֵינוֹ מוֹצִיא אֶת הָרַבִּים יְדֵי חוֹבָתָן׃ אוֹ יָבֹא כָהִיא דְּאָמַר רִבִּי חֶלְבּוֹ רַב חוּנָה בְשֵׁם רִבִּי חִייָה רַבָּה. הַכֹּל יוֹצְאִין בְּאַרְבָּעָה עָשָׂר שֶׁהִיא זְמַן קְרִיאָתָהּ. רִבִּי יוּדָן בָּעֵי. [בֶּן עִיר שֶׁ]נָּתַן דַּעְתּוֹ לַעֲקוֹר דִּירָתוֹ לֵילֵי חֲמִשָּׁה עָשָׂר. לֹא מַתְנִיתָהּ הִיא. בֶּן עִיר שֶׁהָלַךְ לַכְּרָךְ. מַתְנִיתָה בְּשֶׁהָיָה בַּכְּרָךְ. מַה צְּרִיכָה לֵיהּ. בְּשֶׁהָיָה בָעִיר. אֲבָל מַפְרְשֵׁי יָמִים וְהוֹלְכֵי מִדְבָּרוֹת קוֹרְאִין כְּדַרְכָּן בְּאַרְבָּעָה עָשָׂר. אָמַר רִבִּי מָנָא. בְּעָתִיד לַחֲזוֹר לִמְקוֹמוֹ. אָמַר רִבִּי פִינְחָס. עַל־כֵּן הַיְּהוּדִים הַפְּרָזִים. פָּרוּז הָיָה בְאוֹתָהּ שָׁעָה.

May a village dweller free a city dweller of his obligation? Should it follow "anybody not obligated for something may not free the public from their obligation"[53]? May a city dweller free a village dweller of his obligation? Should it follow "anybody not obligated for something may not free the public from their obligation"? Or should it follow what "Rebbi Ḥelbo said, Rebbi Huna in the name of the Great Rebbi Ḥiyya: Everybody may fulfill his obligation on the Fourteenth, which is the time of its reading[54]"? Rebbi Yudan asked. [A village dweller who] decided to move in the night of the Fifteenth? Is that not the Mishnah, "a villager who went to a walled city"? The Mishnah if he was in the walled city. What is problematic for him, if he was in a village. But those on an ocean trip or passing through deserts read normally on the Fourteenth. Rebbi Mana said, if he intended to return to his place. Rebbi Phineas said, *therefore the dispersed Jews*[55], in that hour he was dispersed[56].

53 Mishnah *Roš Haššanah* 3:8. By this argument, neither the village dweller on the 15th nor the city dweller on the 14th may read for another person's benefit.
54 Chapter 1, Note 67. By this argument, everybody may read for other persons on the 14th. The question is not resolved (but Tosaphot *Yebamot* 14a, s.v. כי read the text as following the first opinion.)
55 *Esth.* 9:19.
56 Since he could not possibly reach his home on Purim. Babli 19a.

(73b line 14) מֵאֵיכָן קוֹרֵא אָדָם אֶת הַמְּגִילָה וְיוֹצֵא בָהּ יְדֵי חוֹבָתוֹ. רִבִּי מֵאִיר אוֹמֵר. אֶת כּוּלָּהּ. רִבִּי יְהוּדָה אוֹמֵר. מֵאִישׁ יְהוּדִי. רִבִּי יוֹסֵי אוֹמֵר. מֵאַחַר הַדְּבָרִים הָאֵלֶּה׃ רִבִּי אַבָּהוּ בְּשֵׁם רִבִּי לְעָזָר. מָאן דְּאָמַר כּוּלָּהּ. עַל־כֵּן עַל־כָּל־דִּבְרֵי הָאִיגֶּרֶת הַזֹּאת. מָאן דְּאָמַר. מֵאִישׁ יְהוּדִי. וּמַה־רָאוּ עַל־כָּכָה. מָאן דְּאָמַר. מֵאַחַר הַדְּבָרִים הָאֵלֶּה. וּמָה הִגִּיעַ אֲלֵיהֶם׃ רִבִּי סִימוֹן בְּשֵׁם רִבִּי יְהוֹשֻׁעַ בֶּן לֵוִי. מָאן דְּאָמַר כּוּלָּהּ. וְכָל־מַעֲשֵׂה תּוֹקְפוֹ וּגְבוּרָתוֹ. מָאן דְּאָמַר מֵאִישׁ יְהוּדִי.

וּפָרָשַׁת גְדוּלַת מָרְדֳּכַי. וּמָאן דְּאָמַר מֵאַחַר הַדְּבָרִים הָאֵלֶּה. אֲשֶׁר גִּדְּלוֹ הַמֶּלֶךְ. רִבִּי יוֹסֵי בֵּירִבִּי בּוּן בְּשֵׁם רִבִּי יְהוֹשֻׁעַ בֶּן לֵוִי. תּוֹקֶף. כָּל־תּוֹקֶף. אֶת־כָּל־תּוֹקֶף. תּוֹקֶף זֶה תוֹקְפּוֹ שֶׁלְהָמָן. כָּל־תּוֹקֶף זֶה תוֹקְפּוֹ שֶׁלְמָרְדֳּכַי. אֶת־כָּל־תּוֹקֶף זֶה תוֹקְפּוֹ שֶׁלְאַחַשְׁוֵרוֹשׁ. תַּנֵּי. רִבִּי שִׁמְעוֹן בֶּן יוֹחַי אוֹמֵר. מִבַּלַּיְלָה הַהוּא. מִמְּקוֹם שֶׁהָיְתָה מַפַּלְתּוֹ שֶׁלְהָמָן מִשָּׁם הָיְתָה גְדוּלָתוֹ שֶׁלְמָרְדֳּכַי.

"From where does a person start to read and fulfills his duty? Rebbi Meïr says, all of it. Rebbi Jehudah says, from *a Jewish man*[45]. Rebbi Yose says, from *after these matters*[46]." Rebbi Abbahu in the name of Rebbi Eleazar: He who says all of it, *about all words of this letter*[57]. He who says from *a Jewish man, what they understood about it*[57]. He who says from *after these matters, and what happened to them*[57]. Rebbi Simon in the name of Rebbi Joshua ben Levi. He who says all of it, *all the facts of his strength and mightiness*[58]. He who says from *a Jewish man, the Chapter of the greatness of Mordocai*[58]. He who says from *after these matters, how the King aggrandized him*[58]. Rebbi Yose ben Rebbi Abun in the name of Rebbi Joshua ben Levi: *strength, all strength, with all strength*[59]. *Strength*, is Haman's strength. *All strength*, is Mordocai's strength. *With all strength*, is Ahasuerus's strength. It was stated[60]: Rebbi Simeon ben Yoḥay says, from *in that night*[61]. From the place where there was Haman's downfall came Mordocai's rise.

57 *Esth.* 9:26.
58 *Esth.* 10:2.
59 *Esth.* 9:29.
60 Babli 19a. In Tosephta 2:9 in the name of R. Simeon ben Eleazar.
61 *Esth.* 6:1.

(73b line 25) רִבִּי בָּא רַב יִרְמְיָה בְּשֵׁם רַב. הֲלָכָה כְּרִבִּי מֵאִיר דְּהוּא אָמַר. כּוּלָּהּ. רִבִּי זְעוּרָה בְּשֵׁם רִבִּי יוֹחָנָן. בָּעֵירוּבִין וּבְתַעֲנִית צִיבּוּר נָהֲגוּ הַכֹּל כְּרִבִּי מֵאִיר. רִבִּי יַעֲקֹב בַּר אָחָא בְּשֵׁם רִבִּי יוֹחָנָן. אַף בִּמְגִילַת אֶסְתֵּר נָהֲגוּ הַכֹּל כְּרִבִּי מֵאִיר

רִבִּי חֶלְבּוֹ רַב מַתָּנָה רַב יוֹסֵי בַּר מָנַיְישָׁא בְּשֵׁם רַב. בֵּין כְּמָאן דְּאָמַר. כּוּלָּהּ. בֵּין כְּמָאן דְּאָמַר. מֵאִישׁ יְהוּדִי. בֵּין כְּמָאן דְּאָמַר. מֵאַחַר הַדְּבָרִים הָאֵלֶּה. וּבִלְבַד מִסְפָּר שָׁלֵם. רִבִּי חֶלְבּוֹ רַב מַתָּנָה יוֹסֵי בַּר מָנַיְישָׁא בְּשֵׁם רַב. אִם הָיְתָה כְּתוּבָה חוּמָשִׁין אֵין קוֹרְאִין בָּהּ בָּרַבִּים. אָמַר רִבִּי תַּנְחוּמָא. מִפְּנֵי הַהֶדְיוֹטוֹת. עוּלָּא בֵּירִיָּה רִבִּי לֶעְזָר בְּשֵׁם רִבִּי חֲנִינָא. רָגִיל צָרִיךְ לִקְרוֹתָהּ בַּלַּיְלָה וּלְשָׁנוֹתָהּ בַּיּוֹם. הֲוֵינָן סָבְרִין מֵימַר. לִשְׁנוֹת מִשְׁנָתָהּ. אָמַר רִבִּי אַבָּא מָרִי בַּבְלָיָיה. לִשְׁנוֹת קְרִיָּיתָהּ.

Rebbi Abba, Rav Jeremiah in the name of Rav: practice follows Rebbi Meïr who says, all of it[62]. Rebbi Ze`ira in the name of Rebbi Joḥanan: In matters of *eruvin* and public fast-days everybody follows Rebbi Meïr. Rebbi Jacob bar Aḥa in the name Rebbi Johanan: Even about the reading of the Esther scroll everybody follows Rebbi Meïr[63].

Rebbi Ḥelbo, Rav Mattanah, Yose bar Menashia in the name of Rav: Following whom who says, all of it, or who says from *a Jewish man,* or whom who said from *after these matters,* but only from a complete scroll[63]. Rebbi Ḥelbo, Rav Mattanah, Yose bar Menashia in the name of Rav: If it was written like fifths[64] one does not read from it in public. Rebbi Tanḥuma said, because of the uneducated. Ulla from Bireh, Rebbi Eleazar in the name of Rebbi Ḥanina: The learned fundraiser[65] has to read it in the night and to repeat during the day. We were of the opinion to say, to teach its Mishnah[66]. Rebbi Abba Mari the Babylonian said, to repeat its reading[67].

62 Babli 18b,19a.

63 *Eruvin* Chapter 6, Note 102. In *eruvin* one follows R. Meïr that *eruv* for courtyards and participation for alleys must be separate acts; in *Ta`aniot* that on a public fast day the priestly blessing is given three times. Babli *Eruvin* 72a. These rules are popular usage, not rabbinic decrees.

64 A *Ḥumash* is a single book of the Pentateuch. One may not read from an Esther text written together with other Hagiographs since the Esther scroll is not holy and Hagiographs are no source of Halakhah.

65 For the title *"ragil"* for the outstanding scholar who acts as fundraiser, cf. S. Liebermann *Tarbiz* 4 (1933) pp. 378-9; *Eruvin* Chapter 3, Note 150. The Babli (4a, 20a) has the same statement formulated as obligation for everybody.

66 Since the technical term for teaching Mishnah is "to repeat".

67 Even the fundraiser who wants to visit as many places as possible has to read the Scroll during the day; his reading in the night following Babylonian practice does not excuse him from the obligation to read it during daytime.

(73b line 35) רִבִּי בֶּרֶכְיָה רִבִּי חֶלְבּוֹ עוּלָּא בִירִיָּיה רִבִּי לְעָזָר בְּשֵׁם רִבִּי חֲנִינָה. עָתִיד הַקָּדוֹשׁ בָּרוּךְ הוּא לְהֵיעָשׂוֹת רֹאשׁ חוּלָה לַצַּדִּיקִים לְעָתִיד לָבוֹא. מַה טַעַם. שִׁיתוּ לִבְּכֶם | לְחֵילָה. לְחוֹלָה כְּתִיב. וְהַצַּדִּיקִים מַרְאִין אוֹתוֹ בְּאֶצְבַּע וְאוֹמְרִים. כִּי זֶה | אֱלֹהִים אֱלֹהֵינוּ עוֹלָם וָעֶד הוּא יְנַהֲגֵנוּ עַלְמוּת: עַלְמוּת בַּעֲלִימוּת. [בְּזָרִיזוּת]. עַלְמוּת. כְּאִילֵין עֲלָמוֹת. תִּירְגְּמָהּ עֲקִילַס. אֲתָא־נַסְיָיא. עוֹלָם שֶׁאֵין בּוֹ מָוֶת. וְהַצַּדִּיקִים מַרְאִין אוֹתוֹ בְּאֶצְבַּע וְאוֹמְרִים. כִּי זֶה | אֱלֹהִים אֱלֹהֵינוּ עוֹלָם וָעֶד הוּא יְנַהֲגֵנוּ עַלְמוּת: הוּא יְנַהֲגֵנוּ בָּעוֹלָם הַזֶּה. הוּא יְנַהֲגֵנוּ לְעָתִיד לָבוֹא.

1 בירייה | ק בירייא ר ביריא   2 להיעשות | קר ליעשות   4 [...] | קר - עלמות | קר עולימותא אתא נסייא | קר אתנא סירא   6 ינהגנו | ק ניהגנו   לעתיד לבוא | ר לעולם הבא

רִבִּי חֶלְבּוֹ רַב חָמָא בַּר גּוּרְיָא בְשֵׁם רַב חָמָא בַּר עוּקְבָא בְשֵׁם רִבִּי יוֹסֵי בֶּן חֲנִינָה. מִשְׁפָּחָה וּמִשְׁפָּחָה. מִיכָּן לְמִשְׁמָרוֹת כְּהוּנָּה וּלְוָיָה שֶׁיִּהוּ בְטֵילִין. אָמַר רִבִּי חֶלְבּוֹ. מִיכָּן לְבֵית הַוַועַד שֶׁיְּהֵא בָטֵל. שִׁמְעוֹן בַּר בָּא בְשֵׁם רִבִּי יוֹחָנָן. וְזִכְרָם לֹא־יָסוּף מִזַּרְעָם: מִיכָּן שֶׁקָּבְעוּ לָהּ חֲכָמִים מַסֶּכֶת.

Rebbi Berekhia, Rebbi Ḥelbo, Ulla from Bireh, Rebbi Eleazar in the name of Rebbi Ḥanina[68]: In the future the Holy One, praise to Him, will lead a circular dance for the Just ones. What is the reason? *Put your hearts to its walls*[69], it is written "to its circular dance.[70]" And the Just one will point with their finger and say, *Truly, He is GOD, our Power, Forever; He will lead us beyond death*[71]! *Almut*, in strength, [in agility.][72] *Almut*, like these girls. Akilas translated 'αθανασία, a world without death. And the Just one will point with their finger and say, *Truly, He is GOD, our Power, Forever; He will lead us beyond death!* He will lead us in this world, He well lead us in the future[73].

Rebbi Ḥelbo, Rav Ḥama bar Guria in the name of Rav Ḥama bar Uqba in the name of Rebbi Yose ben Ḥanina: *Family and family*[74], from here that the watches of priests and Levites will be unoccupied[75]; Rebbi Ḥelbo said, from here that the house of assembly will be empty[76]. Simeon bar Abba in the name of Rebbi Joḥanan, *and their remembrance will not disappear from their descendants*[74], from here that the Sages dedicated a Tractate to it.

---

68 This has no material connection with the preceding text; it is added because it is a tradition of Ulla from Bireh as is the preceding one. A parallel text is in *Moed qatan* 3:7 (in two texts, קר), shortened in the Babli, *Ta`anit* 31a, Midrash *Ps.*, *Ps.* 48[5].
69 *Ps.* 48:14.
70 This reading is not found in masoretic texts.
71 *Ps.* 48:15.
72 Corrector's addition from *Megillah*.
73 "Lead us in worlds" is the translation of LXX.

74 *Esth.* 9:28.
75 Since sexual activity pollutes and purity is regained only at sundown following immersion in water, priests and Levites officiating in the Temple have to serve far from their families. If they have to join their families for the celebration of Purim, the Temple service has to stop. Babli 3a.
76 While the previous remark was theoretical, this one is practical and forbids sessions of the Academy in the afternoon of Adar 14.

(fol. 72d) **משנה ד**: הַכֹּל כְּשֵׁרִין לִקְרוֹת אֶת הַמְּגִילָּה חוּץ מֵחֵרֵשׁ שׁוֹטֶה וְקָטָן. רִבִּי יְהוּדָה מַכְשִׁיר בְּקָטָן. אֵין קוֹרִין אֶת הַמְּגִילָּה וְלֹא מוֹלִין וְלֹא טוֹבְלִין וְלֹא מַזִּין. וְכֵן שׁוֹמֶרֶת יוֹם כְּנֶגֶד יוֹם לֹא תִטְבּוֹל עַד שֶׁתָּנֵץ הַחַמָּה. וְכוּלָּן שֶׁעֲשׂוּ מִשֶּׁעָלָה עַמּוּד הַשַּׁחַר כָּשֵׁר:

Mishnah 4: Everybody is qualified to read the Scroll[77] except the deaf-and-dumb[78], the insane, and the underage. Rebbi Jehudah qualifies the underage[79]. One does nor read the scroll, nor circumcises, nor immerses[80], nor sprinkles[81], nor may the woman observing a day for a day immerse herself[82], before sunrise. But all who did it after dawn are qualified.

77 In order to absolve others of their obligation.

78 He would have to use sign language. But the deaf-and-dumb is not obligated for any religious observance. He does not have to read and therefore cannot do it for others (Note 20).

79 The other Sages hold that the parent of a minor has the obligation to teach his son to read the scroll and to make him read it. This is not a personal obligation of the minor and therefore he is unable to absolve the public of their obligation.

80 In a *miqweh*.

81 With ashes of the Red Cow.

82 A woman has a discharge during the 11 days following the week of her menstruation. The discharge cannot be menstrual; therefore she has to observe one day without discharge, immerse herself in a *miqweh* in order to be pure at sundown.

(73b line 47) **הלכה ד**: הַכֹּל כְּשֵׁרִין לִקְרוֹת אֶת הַמְּגִילָּה חוּץ מֵחֵרֵשׁ שׁוֹטֶה וְקָטָן. אָמַר רַב מַתָּנָה. דְּרִבִּי יוֹסֵי הִיא. אָמַר רִבִּי יוֹסֵה. הֲוֵינָן סָבְרִין מֵימַר. מַה פְּלִיגִין רִבִּי יוֹסֵה וְרַבָּנָן. בִּשְׁמַע. דִּכְתִיב בָּהּ שְׁמַע. הָא שְׁאָר כָּל־הַמִּצְוֹת לֹא. מִן מַה דְּרַב מַתָּנָה אָמַר. דְּרִבִּי יוֹסֵי הִיא. הֲדָא אֲמָרָה. הִיא שְׁמַע הִיא שְׁאָר כָּל־הַמִּצְוֹת. וּמַה טַעֲמָא דְרִבִּי יוֹסֵה. וְהַאֲזַנְתָּ לְמִצְוֹתָיו. שְׁמַע אָזְנֶיךָ מַה שֶׁפִּיךָ מְדַבֵּר. רַב חִסְדָּא אָמַר. לֵית כָּאן חֵרֵשׁ. בְּאַשְׁגָּרַת לָשׁוֹן הִיא מַתְנִיתָא. אָמַר רִבִּי יוֹסֵה. מִסְתַּבְּרָא יוֹדֶה רַב חִסְדָּא בִּתְרוּמוֹת דְּהִיא דְרִבִּי יוֹסֵי. אָתָא רִבִּי חֲנַנְיָה בְּשֵׁם רַב חִסְדָּא. דְּרִבִּי יוֹסֵה הִיא. אָמַר רִבִּי יוֹסֵה בֵּירִבִּי בּוּן. עַל כּוֹרְחַךְ אַתְּ אָמַר דְּהִיא דְרִבִּי יוֹסֵה. דְּתַנִּינָן חֲמִשְׁתֵּי קַדְמַייָתָא וְלֹא תַגֵּינָתָהּ עִמְּהוֹן. אִם מִשֵּׁם שֶׁאֵין תְּרוּמָתוֹ תְּרוּמָה. דְּתַנִּינָן חֲמִשְׁתֵּי אַחֲרִייָתָא וְלֹא תַגֵּינָתָהּ עִמְּהוֹן. הֲוֵי סוֹפָךְ מֵימַר. דְּרִבִּי יוֹסֵה הִיא.

2 יוסה | **בת** יוסי ר' יוסה ורבנן | **ב** רבנן ור' יוסי **ת** ר' יוסי ורבנין   3 מה דרב מתנה אמ' | **ב** דמר רב מתנה **ת** דאמר רב מתנה הדא אמרה | **ב** הוי   4 המצות | **ת** המצוות שבתורה יוסה | **בת** יוסי שמע | **ב** ישמעו   5 אזניך | **ת** לאוזניך באשרת | **ב** השגרת **ת** אשגרת היא | **ת** הי - | **ב** לר' יודה   6 יוסה | **בת** יוסי יודה | **ב** דידה **ת** יודי חנניה | **ב** חנינא   7 יוסה | **בת** יוסי (3) | כורחיך | **ב** כורחיך את אמר | **בת** איתמר   8 חמשתי | **ת** חמישתי (2) קדמייתא | **ת** קדמיתא תנינתא | **ב** תנינתה אם | **ת** ואין משם | **בת** משום תרומתו | **ב** תרומתן דתנינן | **ב** והא תנינן **ת** והתנינן   9 אחרייתא | **ת** אחריתא | **ב** אחרנייתא

Halakhah 4: "Everybody is qualified to read the Scroll except the deaf-and-dumb, the insane, and the underage." [83]Rav Mattanah said: That formulation is Rebbi Yose's. Rebbi Yose said: We could be of the opinion that the rabbis and Rebbi Yose disagree only about *Shemaʿ* since there it is written: *hear*!, but not about any other obligations. Since Rav Mattanah said "that formulation is Rebbi Yose's", it is the same for all obligations. What is the reason of Rebbi Yose? *Bend your ear to His commandments*[84], your ears should hear what your mouth says. Rav Hisda said: The deaf and dumb person is not mentioned, it is a formula[85]. Rebbi Yose said: It is reasonable to think that Rav Hisda concedes that the statement from *Terumot* is from Rebbi Yose. Rabbi Hanania came in the name of Rav Hisda, this one is by Rebbi Yose. Rebbi Yose bar Rebbi Abun said: It must be said that that one is Rebbi Yose's since we have stated the first five cases[86] and did not include it, because their heave is no heave. Then we have stated the five later ones and did not include it. So in the end you must say, that one is by Rebbi Yose[87].

83 This paragraph appears also in *Berakhot* 2:4 (Notes 160-166,ב) and *Terumot* 1:2 (Notes 90-93,ת). The Mishnah in *Berakhot* states that in reading the *Shemaʿ* one must hear what one says. The majority holds that this is a desideratum but not an absolute necessity. R. Yose the Tanna disagrees and therefore a person who is deaf but able to speak still cannot read the *Shemaʿ*. Heave is the part of the harvest which is given to the Cohen as sanctum to be eaten in purity. The dedication must be a conscious act; therefore in Mishnah *Terumot* 1:1 the deaf-and-dumb person is excluded from those who may dedicate heave.

84 *Ex.* 15:26.

85 In all legal matters depending on a conscious act, "insane, deaf-and-dumb, and underage" are excluded. The formula should have been modified here but, since the Mishnah was transmitted orally and could not be written down, was not modified, to ease memorization.

86 Mishnah *Terumot* 1:1: Five categories of people cannot consecrate heave and if they did it anyhow, their actions are null and void: the deaf-and-dumb, the insane, minors, one who is not the owner, and a non-Jew." The sixth Mishnah then reads: Five categories of people should not consecrate heave (since a priori it requires the recitation of a benediction) but if they did it anyhow their actions are valid: the speechless, the drunk, the naked, the blind, those impure by emission of semen." In between it is explained that חֵרֵשׁ means a deaf-and-dumb person who is not legally capable of acting but that the deaf who can talk belongs to the same category as the second group of five.

87 Therefore, Mishnah *Terumot* 1:2, explaining that the deaf person who is able to speak can give heave, has to be formulated separately and could not be included in *Terumot* 1:6 since the first and sixths Mishnayot are Rebbi Yose's who will

object to the inclusion of the deaf person in the second group but not to that of the speechless.

(73b line 58) רַבִּי יְהוּדָה מַכְשִׁיר בְּקָטָן. אָמַר רִבִּי יְהוּדָה. קָטָן הָיִיתִי וּקְרִיתִיהָ לִפְנֵי רִבִּי טַרְפוֹן בְּלוֹד. אָמְרוּ לוֹ. קָטָן הָיִיתָ וְאֵין עֵידוּת לְקָטָן. אָמַר רִבִּי. מַעֲשֶׂה שֶׁקְּרִיתִיהָ לִפְנֵי רִבִּי יוּדָה בְאוּשָׁה. אָמְרוּ לוֹ. אֵין זוּ רְאָיָיה. הוּא שֶׁהוּא מַתִּיר. מִיכָּן וְהֵילַךְ נָהֲגוּ הָרַבִּים לִקְרוֹתָהּ בְּבֵית הַכְּנֶסֶת. בַּר קַפָּרָא אָמַר. צָרִיךְ לִקְרוֹתָהּ לִפְנֵי נָשִׁים וְלִפְנֵי קְטַנִּים שֶׁאַף אוֹתָם הָיוּ (בַּמִּסְפֵּק) [בַּסָּפֵק]. רִבִּי יְהוֹשֻׁעַ בֶּן לֵוִי עָבַד כֵּן. מְכַנֵּשׁ בָּנוֹי וּבְנֵי בֵייתֵיהּ וְקָרֵי לָהּ קוֹמֵיהוֹן.

"Rebbi Jehudah qualifies the underage." "Rebbi Jehudah said, I was a minor and read it in front of Rebbi Tarphon at Lydda. They said to him, you were a minor and there is no testimony from minors. Rebbi said, it happened and I read it in the presence of Rebbi Jehudah at Usha. They said to him, that is no proof since he is the one who permits it." From then on the public used to read it in the synagogue[88]. Bar Qappara said, one has to read it in front of women and children because they also were in the doubt[89]. Rebbi Joshua ben Levi acted thus; he assembled his sons and the people of his house[90] and read it in front of them.

88 If one reads הָרַבִּים then it means that one chooses to make a synagogal act out of reading the Esther scroll (replacing the earlier private ceremonies), since then the Scroll would be read by the communal חַזָּן who certainly is an adult. But if one reads הָרַבִּים then the translation is "from then on the youths would read it in the synagogue", permitting minors to read in public, Tosephta 2:8.
89 The doubt whether they all would be killed. The corrector replaced the Yerushalmi word, which he did not understand, by the equivalent Babli word.
90 The women of his household. Babli 4a.

(73b line 64) אֵין קוֹרִין אֶת הַמְּגִילָּה עַד שֶׁתָּנֵץ הַחַמָּה. דִּכְתִיב בַּיּוֹם אֲשֶׁר סִבְּרוּ אוֹיְבֵי הַיְּהוּדִים לִשְׁלוֹט בָּהֶם.
וְלֹא מוֹלִים. דִּכְתִיב וּבַיּוֹם הַשְּׁמִינִי יִמּוֹל בְּשַׂר עָרְלָתוֹ.
וְלֹא טוֹבְלִין. דִּכְתִיב וְהִזָּה וְטָבַל. מַה הַזָּיָיה בַּיּוֹם. אַף טְבִילָה בַּיּוֹם. מְנַיִין שֶׁהַהַזָּיָיה בַּיּוֹם. דִּכְתִיב וְהִזָּה הַטָּהוֹר עַל־הַטָּמֵא בַּיּוֹם הַשְּׁלִישִׁי. כָּל־מְחוּיְּבֵי טְבִילוֹת טוֹבְלִין כְּדַרְכָּן בַּיּוֹם חוּץ מִן הַנִּידָה וְיוֹלֶדֶת שֶׁאֵינָהּ טוֹבֶלֶת אֶלָּא בַלַּיְלָה. נִידָה שֶׁעִיבֵּר זְמַנָּהּ טוֹבֶלֶת בֵּין בַּיּוֹם וּבֵין בַּלַּיְלָה. דְּרָשָׁהּ רִבִּי חִייָה בַּר בָּא לְצוּרָאֵי. נִידָה שֶׁעִיבֵּר זְמַנָּהּ טוֹבֶלֶת בֵּין בַּיּוֹם בֵּין בַּלַּיְלָה. תַּמָּן אָמְרִין.

אֲפִילוּ עִיבֵּר זְמַנָּהּ לֹא. מִפְּנֵי חֲמוֹתָהּ וּמִפְּנֵי כַלָּתָהּ. אִשָׁה אַחַת מִשֶּׁלְבֵּית רַבּוֹתֵינוּ רָאוּ אוֹתָהּ טוֹבֶלֶת כְּדַרְכָּהּ בַּיּוֹם. נֹאמַר. מְעוֹבֶרֶת זְמַן הֲוָת.

"One does nor read the scroll before sunrise." For it is written[91], *on the day the enemies of the Jews thought they would rule over them.*

"Nor circumcises," for it is written[92], *on the eighth day one circumcises the prepuce of his flesh.*

"Nor immerses," for it is written, *he sprinkles, he immerses*[93]. Since sprinkling is during daytime, also immersion is during daytime. From where that sprinkling is during daytime? For it is written[94], *the pure one sprinkles on the impure one on the third day.* [95]All who require immersion immerse themselves normally during daytime except for the woman after her period and one who gave birth who only immerses herself during the night[96]. A woman after her period whose time has passed[97] immerses herself either during the day or during the night. Rebbi Hiyya bar Abba preached this to the people of Tyre[98], a woman after her period whose time has passed immerses herself either during the day or during the night. There[99] they say, even one whose time has passed not, because of her mother-in-law and her daughter-in-law. They saw a woman of the family of our rabbis[100] immersing herself normally during daytime. We shall say that her time had passed.

91   *Esth.* 9:1.
92   *Lev.* 12:3.
93   *Num.* 19:18.
94   *Num.* 19:19.
95   From here on this paragraph and the next are from *Šabbat* 2, Notes 63-71. This paragraph is connected with the Mishnah here since it states only that immersion of males has to be during daytime. The next paragraph has no connection, it simply is copied from *Šabbat*.
96   Babli *Šabbat* 121a, *Pesahim* 90b, *Yoma* 6a, 87a.
97   After the first evening she could have immersed herself after her period; cf. *Niddah* 4:1 Note 3. Babli *Niddah* 67b.
98   As practice to be followed.
99   In Babylonia, where the statement was attributed to R. Joḥanan; *Niddah* 67b. There, the reason is given "because of the discipline of her daughter", that she should learn the rules clearly.
100 The household of R. Jehudah Nesia. The deviation of Galilean from Babylonian practice is confirmed.

(73b line 73) נִדָּה שֶׁנֶּאֶנְסָה וְטָבְלָה. רִבִּי שַׁמַּי בְּשֵׁם רַב. טְהוֹרָה לְבֵיתָהּ וּטְמֵיאָה לְטַהֲרוֹת. רִבִּי לְעָזָר בְּשֵׁם רִבִּי חֲנִינָה. טְמֵיאָה בֵין לְבֵיתָהּ בֵּין לְטַהֲרוֹת. מַה טַעַם. וְכוּבַּס שֵׁנִית וְטָהֵר. מַה הָרִאשׁוֹנָה לְדַעַת אַף הַשְּׁנִייָה לְדַעַת. מְנַיִּין שֶׁהָרִאשׁוֹנָה לְדַעַת. וְצִוָּה הַכֹּהֵן וְכִבְּסוּ. לְדַעַת. וַאֲנָן חֲמִיָין רַבָּנָן מְקַדְּמִין לְעִיבּוּרָה. רִבִּי נַחְמָן בְּשֵׁם רִבִּי מָנָא. מִצְוָה לְהַקְדִּים כְּדֵי לָרוּץ בַּמִּצְוֹת.

A woman after her period who was immersed by accident, Rebbi Shammai in the name of Rav: she is pure for her house but impure for purities[101]. Rebbi Eleazar in the name of Rebbi Ḥanina, she is impure both for her house and purities. What is the reason? *It should be washed a second time and will be pure*[102]. Since the first time it was intentionally, also the second time it must be intentionally. And from where that the first time it was intentionally? *The Cohen has to order that they should wash*[103]. Intentionally. And we see that rabbis are early for intercalations. Rav Naḥman in the name of Rebbi Mana: It is an obligation to be early, to hasten in commandments[104].

101 She unintentionally fell into water which qualifies as a *miqweh*. In this opinion, an intent to become pure by immersion is needed only to be able to prepare pure food ("purities") whereas to be permitted to her husband ("pure for her house") she only has to be immersed since in the relevant biblical paragraph (*Lev.* 15:19-24) immersion is explicitly required only of people coming in contact with movables on which she sat during her period of impurity. The opposing opinion requires intent for any purification. Babli *Ḥulin* 31a.

102 *Lev.* 15:59, about impurity of textiles. The remark "a second time" is taken as indication that the second washing has to follow the rules of the first; Babli *Ḥulin* 31b. A different interpretation in *Sifra Tazria`*

Pereq 16(11)

103 *Lev.* 13:54.

104 This refers to something completely different in the rules of Sabbath observation. Rebbi Naḥman requires the husband to direct his household to light Sabbath lights, and therefore begin the observance of the Sabbath, somewhat before the time of sundown since in the fulfilling of divine commandments one has to show eagerness. As an example it is noted that the rabbis who form the court which decrees intercalations always arrive early for the deliberations. This is a commentary on the last statement of the last Mishnah in Chapter *Šabbat* 2.

(fol. 73a) **משנה ה**: כָּל־הַיּוֹם כָּשֵׁר לִקְרִיאַת הַמְּגִילָּה וְלִקְרִיאַת הַהַלֵּל וְלִתְקִיעַת שׁוֹפָר וְלִנְטִילַת לוּלָב וְלִתְפִילַּת הַמּוּסָפִין וְלָמוּסָפִין לְוִידּוּי פָּרִים וּלְוִידּוּי מַעֲשֵׂר וּלְוִידּוּי יוֹם הַכִּפּוּרִים.

Mishnah 5: The entire day is qualified for reading the Scroll, and to read the *Hallel*[105], and to blow the *shofar*[106], and to take the *lulav*[107], and for the *musaf* prayer[108], and for *musaf* sacrifices, for confessions with bulls[109], and for the declaration of tithes[110] and for the confessions of the Day of Atonement[111].

105 *Ps*. 113-118, to be recited on holidays. The recitation of *Hallel* after morning prayers is customary, not obligatory.
106 On New Year's Day. If a person is unable to go to the synagogue, he may hear the required sounds during the entire day.
107 The recitation of *musaf* after the Torah reading is customary, not obligatory.
108 The confessions of the anointed priest (*Lev*. 4:3) and the representatives of the people (*Lev*. 4:14), as well as the *musaf* sacrifices, may be performed at any time after the daily morning and before the evening sacrifices.
110 The farmer's declaration, *Deut*. 26:13-15, as well as the declaration on the occasion of presentation of first fruits, *Deut*. 26:3-10.
111 The confession of the High Priest (*Lev*. 16:21).

(73c line 4) **הלכה ה**: כָּל־הַיּוֹם כָּשֵׁר לִקְרִיאַת הַמְּגִילָּה. דִּכְתִיב בַּיּוֹם אֲשֶׁר שִׂבְּרוּ אֹיְבֵי הַיְּהוּדִים לִשְׁלוֹט בָּהֶם. לִקְרִיאַת הַהַלֵּל. דִּכְתִיב זֶה־הַיּוֹם עָשָׂה יי נָגִילָה וְנִשְׂמְחָה בוֹ: לִתְקִיעַת שׁוֹפָר. דִּכְתִיב יוֹם תְּרוּעָה יִהְיֶה לָכֶם: לִנְטִילַת לוּלָב דִּכְתִיב וּלְקַחְתֶּם לָכֶם בַּיּוֹם הָרִאשׁוֹן. לִתְפִילַת הַמּוּסָפִין וְלַמוּסָפִין. דִּכְתִיב בְּיוֹם צַוֹּתוֹ אֶת־בְּנֵי יִשְׂרָאֵל וגו'.

Halakhah 5: "The entire day is qualified to read the Scroll," as it is written[91], *on the day the enemies of the Jews thought they would rule over them*. To read the *Hallel*, as it is written[112], *this is the day the Eternal made, let us enjoy and be happy on it*. To blow the *shofar*, as it is written[113], *a day to shofar blowing it shall be for you*. To take the *lulav*, as it is written[114], *you shall take for yourselves on the first day*. For the *musaf* prayer, and for *musaf* sacrifices, as it is written[115], *on the day on which He commanded the Children of Israel*, etc.

112 *Ps*, 118:24.
113 *Num*. 29:1.
114 *Lev*. 23:40
115 *Lev*. 7:38. The verse continues: *to bring their sacrifices to the Eternal*.

(fol. 73a) **משנה ו**: לִסְמִיכָה לִשְׁחִיטָה לִתְנוּפָה וּלְהַגָּשָׁה לִקְמִיצָה לְהַקְטָרָה לִמְלִיקָה לְקַבָּלָה לְהַזָּיָיה וּלְהַשְׁקָיַית סוֹטָה וְלַעֲרִיפַת הָעֶגְלָה וּלְטַהֲרַת הַמְצוֹרָע:

Mishnah 6: [116]For leaning on[117], slaughter, weaving[118] and presenting[119], taking a handful[120], burning on the altar, breaking the neck[121], receiving[122], sprinkling[123], and to let the suspected adulteress drink[124], and to break the neck of the calf[125], and to purify the sufferer from skin disease[126].

116 A continuation of the sentence starting with: "the entire day is qualified."

117 Confession of the votary when bringing his sacrifice, while leaning on the head of the sacrificial animal; *Lev.* 1:4, 3:2,8,13, 4:24,29,33.

118 An act required for certain sacrifices, mostly well-being sacrifices, *Lev.* 7:30.

119 Presenting flour sacrifices and first fruits to the altar.

120 Of the flour offering to be burned on the altar.

121 Of a bird offered as elevation or purification sacrifice (*Lev.* 1:15,5:8).

122 The sacrificial blood to be brought to the altar.

123 The blood on the horns of the altar.

124 *Num.* 5:11-31.

125 In case of an unsolved murder, *Deut.* 21:1-9.

126 *Lev.* 14:1-32.

(73c line 9) **הלכה ו**: לִסְמִיכָה לִשְׁחִיטָה לִתְנוּפָה לְהַגָּשָׁה לִקְמִיצָה לְהַקְטָרָה לִמְלִיקָה לְקַבָּלָה לְהַזָּיָיה. דִּכְתִיב בְּיוֹם צַוּוֹתוֹ אֶת־בְּנֵי יִשְׂרָאֵל.

Halakhah 6: "For leaning on, slaughter, weaving, presenting, taking a handful, burning on altar, breaking the neck, receiving, sprinkling." As it is written[115], *on the day on which He commanded the Children of Israel.*

(fol. 73a) **משנה ז**: כָּל־הַלַּיְלָה כָּשֵׁר לִקְצִירַת הָעוֹמֶר לְהֶקְטֵר חֲלָבִים וְאֵיבָרִים. זֶה הַכְּלָל דָּבָר שֶׁמִּצְוָתוֹ בַיּוֹם כָּשֵׁר כָּל־הַיּוֹם. וּשֶׁמִּצְוָתוֹ בַלַּיְלָה כָּשֵׁר כָּל־הַלַּיְלָה:

Mishnah 7: The entire night is qualified for the cutting of the *omer*[127], and to burning fat and parts[128]. This is the principle: Anything commanded to be done by day is qualified the entire day, anything commanded to be done by night is qualified the entire night.

126 The first cut of the new barley harvest to be brought to the Temple, *Lev.* 23:9-14.

127 Burning on the altar of the leftovers of the sacrifices of the previous day; *Lev.* 6:5.

(73c line 11) **הלכה ז**: כָּל־הַלַּיְלָה כָּשֵׁר לִסְפִירַת הָעוֹמֶר. אָמַר רִבִּי יוֹחָנָן. דְּרִבִּי אֶלְעָזָר בֶּרִבִּי שִׁמְעוֹן הִיא. דְּרִבִּי אֶלְעָזָר בֶּרִבִּי שִׁמְעוֹן אָמַר. מֵהָחֵל לִקְצוֹר תָּחֵל לִסְפּוֹר. מֵעַתָּה יֵצֵא לוֹ חוּץ לִתְחוּם כֵּיוָן שֶׁחֲשֵׁיכָה יַתְחִיל לִקְצוֹר. אֵיפְשָׁר לוֹ לְכַוֵּין. לְפִיכָךְ כָּל־הַלַּיְלָה כָּשֵׁר. הָיָה מַקְרִיב מִנְחַת הָעוֹמֶר וְנִטְמֵאת בְּיָדוֹ. אוֹמֵר וּמְבִיאִין לוֹ אַחֶרֶת. וְאִם לָאו אוֹמְרִים לוֹ. הֱוֵי פִיקֵּחַ וּשְׁתוֹק. הֱוֵי פִיקֵּחַ וּשְׁתוֹק. דִּבְרֵי רִבִּי. רִבִּי אֶלְעָזָר בֶּרִבִּי שִׁמְעוֹן אוֹמֵר. לְעוֹלָם אוֹמְרִים לוֹ. הֱוֵי פִיקֵּחַ וּשְׁתוֹק. שֶׁאֵין עוֹמֶר שֶׁנִּקְצַר שֶׁלֹּא לִמְצְוָתוֹ כָּשֵׁר. סָבַר רִבִּי אֶלְעָזָר בֶּרִבִּי שִׁמְעוֹן. שֶׁאֵין הָעוֹמֶר בָּא מִן הָעֲלִייָה. אָמַר רִבִּי יוֹחָנָן. אַתְיָא דְּרִבִּי לְעָזָר בֶּרִבִּי שִׁמְעוֹן כְּשִׁיטַת רִבִּי עֲקִיבָה רַבּוֹ שֶׁלְּאָבִיב. דְּתַנִּינָן תַּמָּן. כְּלָל אָמַר רִבִּי עֲקִיבָה. כָּל־מְלָאכָה שֶׁאֵיפְשָׁר לָהּ לֵעָשׂוֹת מֵעֶרֶב שַׁבָּת אֵינָהּ דּוֹחָה אֶת הַשַּׁבָּת. וְכָל־מְלָאכָה שֶׁאֵי אֵיפְשָׁר לָהּ לְהֵיעָשׂוֹת מֵעֶרֶב שַׁבָּת דּוֹחָה אֶת הַשַּׁבָּת. וְהָא תַנִּינָן. מַעֲשֶׂה שֶׁעָבְרוּ יוֹתֵר מֵאַרְבָּעִים זוּג וְעִיכְּבָן רִבִּי עֲקִיבָה בְּלוֹד. מִפְּנֵי שֶׁהָיוּ אַרְבָּעִים זוּג. אֲבָל אִם הָיָה זוּג אֶחָד לֹא הָיָה מְעַכְּבוֹ.

Halakhah 7: "The entire night is qualified for the counting[128] of the *omer*." Rebbi Johanan said, this is Rebbi Eleazar ben Rebbi Simeon's, since Rebbi Eleazar ben Rebbi Simeon said, from the start of cutting you shall start to count[129]. Then he should leave the Sabbath domain at nightfall and start to cut. It is impossible to be exact[130]; therefore the entire night is qualified.

If he was sacrificing the flour offering of the *omer* and it became impure in his hand, he says it[131] and one brings him another one; otherwise[132] one tells him, be intelligent and shut up, be intelligent and shut up, the words of Rebbi. Rebbi Eleazar ben Rebbi Simeon says, always one tells him, be intelligent and shut up, since no *omer* which was not cut for its purpose is qualified. Rebbi Eleazar ben Rebbi Simon is of the opinion that the *omer* cannot come from storage[133]. Rebbi Johanan said, that of Rebbi Eleazar ben Rebbi Simon parallels the system of Rebbi Aqiba, his father's teacher, as we have stated there[134]: "Any work which is possible to be performed on Friday does not push the Sabbath away; but any which is impossible to be performed on Friday pushes the Sabbath away." But did we not state[135], "It happened that more than 40 couples passed by and Rebbi Aqiba held them back in Lydda." Because they are 40 couples. But if it had been a single couple he would not have held them back[138].

128 Counting the 50 days between the bringing of the *omer* and Pentecost (*Lev.* 23:15-16). The verse puts the start of the count at the bringing of the *omer* which must be during daytime, but rabbinically it is connected to the cutting of the *omer* in the night preceding to offering. Since the statement is given as a quote, one has to

assume that a Yerushalmi Mishnah mentioned "counting", a continuing obligation also without a Temple, instead of "cutting", which became obsolete with the destruction of the Temple. Both "cutting" and "counting" are mentioned in the Mishnah in Alfasi, confirmed there by the commentary "Rashi", cf. *Dikduke Soferim Megillah* 56a Note (כ).

129 And since the verse requires the cutting at the end of the holiday, counting has to occur immediately after the end of the holiday. But then one should not have the entire night for both cutting and counting.

130 Since "immediately after" is a vague notion, in particular involving a complicated matter, moving vessels and sickle to a field, etc., by necessity the entire night has to be qualified.

131 That the grain became impure and he needs new one.

132 If no grain is left from the cutting done in the preceding night.

133 A minority opinion in both Talmudim, explicitly contradicted in Tosephta *Menaḥot* 10:33. Babli *Menaḥot* 72a.

134 Mishnah *Šabbat* 19:1, about preparations for a circumcision required to be performed on the Sabbath. R. Aqiba then must hold that if the 16th of Nisan is a Sabbath, the *omer* must be cut on the Sabbath.

135 *Roš Haššanah* 1:6, Note 278.

136 While testimony for a New Moon cannot be given before the New Moon is seen, if that day be a Sabbath it may not be used for massive disregard of Sabbath prohibitions.

(73c line 23) קְצִירַת הַיּוֹם מָה אַתְּ עָבַד לָהּ. כִּקְצִירַת הַלַּיְלָה אוֹ כְּבָא מִן הָעֲלִיָּיה. אִין תֵּימַר. כִּקְצִירַת הַלַּיְלָה. אַשְׁכַּחַת אֲמַר. הָדָא פַלְגוּ בֵּין רִבִּי לְעָזָר בֵּירִבִּי שִׁמְעוֹן וּבֵין רַבָּנָן. דְּרַבָּנָן אָמְרִין. קְצִירַת הַיּוֹם כִּקְצִירַת הַלַּיְלָה. וְרִבִּי אֶלְעָזָר בְּרִבִּי שִׁמְעוֹן אוֹמֵר. אֵין קְצִירַת הַיּוֹם כִּקְצִירַת הַלַּיְלָה. אִין תֵּימַר. כְּבָא מִן הָעֲלִייָה. תַּרְתֵּין פְּלֻגְוָון בֵּין רִבִּי אֶלְעָזָר בֵּירִבִּי שִׁמְעוֹן וּבֵין רַבָּנָן. דְּרַבָּנָן אָמְרֵי. קְצִירַת הַיּוֹם כִּקְצִירַת הַלַּיְלָה. וְרִבִּי לְעָזָר בְּרִבִּי שִׁמְעוֹן אוֹמֵר. אֵין קְצִירַת הַיּוֹם כִּקְצִירַת הַלַּיְלָה. וְרַבָּנָן אָמְרֵי. הַבָּא מִן הָעֲלִיָּיה כָּשֵׁר. וְרִבִּי לְעָזָר בְּרִבִּי שִׁמְעוֹן אוֹמֵר. הַבָּא מִן הָעֲלִייָה פָּסוּל.

What are you doing with cutting during daytime[137]? Like cutting during nighttime or coming from storage? If you would say, like cutting during nighttime, you would find to say that the disagreement between Rebbi Eleazar ben Rebbi Simeon and the Rabbis is that the Rabbis are saying, cutting during daytime is like cutting during nighttime, while Rebbi Eleazar ben Rebbi Simeon is saying, cutting during daytime is not like cutting during nighttime. If you would say, like coming from storage, you would find to say that there are two disagreements between Rebbi Eleazar ben Rebbi Simeon and the Rabbis. For the Rabbis are saying, cutting during daytime is like cutting during nighttime, while Rebbi Eleazar ben Rebbi Simeon is saying, cutting during daytime is not like cutting during nighttime. And the Rabbis are saying, what is coming from storage is qualified, while Rebbi Eleazar ben Rebbi Simeon is saying, what is coming from storage is disqualified.

137 If we state as certain that the Mishnah is R. Eleazar ben R. Simeon's it follows that the Rabbis hold that the *omer* also may be cut during the day when its offering is due in the Temple, and by implication also that the *omer* count may be done during daytime.

To allow the grain for *omer* to be taken from storage is a much greater leniency since the *omer* is clearly labelled as offering from the new harvest (*Lev.* 23:10). The two questions are not logically connected.

(73c line 31) רִבִּי שִׁמְעוֹן בֶּן לָקִישׁ בָּעֵי. קְצִירַת הָעוֹמֶר מָהוּ שֶׁיִּדְחֶה אֶת הַשַּׁבָּת בַּיּוֹם. הָתִיב רִבִּי אַבַּיי. וְהָא תַּנִּינָן. מִצְוָתוֹ לִקְצוֹר בַּלַּיְלָה. נִקְצַר בַּיּוֹם כָּשֵׁר וְדוֹחֶה אֶת הַשַּׁבָּת: וְלֹא קַבְּלֵיהּ. אָמַר רִבִּי אָחָא. חָזַר רִבִּי שִׁמְעוֹן בֶּן לָקִישׁ מִן הָדָא. כֵּיוָן שֶׁחֲשֵׁיכָה אָמַר לָהֶן. בָּא הַשֶּׁמֶשׁ. אוֹמְרִים הֵין. בָּא הַשֶּׁמֶשׁ. אוֹמְרִים הֵין. מַה אֲנַן קַיָּימִין. אִם לַלַּיְלָה. כְּבָר הוּא אָמוּר. אֶלָּא אִם אֵינוֹ עִנְיָין לַלַּיְלָה תְּנֵיהוּ לַיּוֹם. דָּבָר שֶׁהוּא דוֹחֶה אֶת הַשַּׁבָּת בַּיּוֹם מַכְשִׁירָיו מָהוּ שֶׁיִּדְחוּ אֶת הַשַּׁבָּת בַּלַּיְלָה. וְהָא תַּנִּינָן. הֶעֱמִידוּ עוֹשֵׂי חֲבִיתִּיי לַעֲשׂוֹת חֲבִיתִּין: תִּיפְתָּר בַּחוֹל. תַּנָּה רִבִּי חִייָה בַּר אַדָא. זֶהוּ סֶדֶר תָּמִיד לַעֲבוֹדַת בֵּית אֱלֹהֵינוּ. בֵּין בַּחוֹל וּבֵין בַּשַּׁבָּת. וְהָא תַּנִּינָן. קְצָרוּהוּ וּנְתָנוּהוּ בְקוּפוֹת וְהֶבִיאוּהוּ בָעֲזָרָה וְהָיוּ מְהַבְהֲבִין אוֹתוֹ בָאוּר [כְּדֵי לְקַיֵּים בּוֹ מִצְוַת קָלִי.] אָמַר רִבִּי יוֹסֵה. מִכֵּיוָן שֶׁהִתְחִיל בַּמִּצְוָה אוֹמְרִים לוֹ. מָרוֹק. הָתִיב רִבִּי יוּדָן קַפּוֹדְקָייָא קוֹמֵי רִבִּי יוֹסֵי. הַגַּע עַצְמוֹךְ שֶׁבָּא מִן הָעֲלִייָה. מִכֵּיוָן שֶׁלֹּא הִתְחִיל בַּמִּצְוָה אֵין אוֹמְרִים לוֹ. מָרֵק. הָתִיב רִבִּי יַעֲקֹב בַּר סוֹסִי קוֹמֵי רִבִּי יוֹסֵה. וְהָא תַּנִּינָן. שֶׁעַל מַהֲלַךְ לַיְלָה וְהַלַּיְלָה יוֹם מְחַלְּלִין אֶת הַשַּׁבָּת וְיוֹצְאִין לְעֵדוּת הַחוֹדֶשׁ. אָמַר לֵיהּ. מִכֵּיוָן שֶׁהַיּוֹם צָרִיךְ לַלַּיְלָה וְהַלַּיְלָה צָרִיךְ לַיּוֹם כְּמִי שֶׁכּוּלּוֹ יוֹם. אָמַר רִבִּי יוֹסֵה בֵּירִבִּי בּוּן. וְלֹא לְמַפְרִיעוֹ הוּא קָדֵשׁ. מִכֵּיוָן שֶׁהוּא קָדֵשׁ לְמַפְרִיעוֹ הוּא יוֹם הוּא לַיְלָה.

1 שידחה | ה שתדחה   2 קבליה   ה קיבלה   3 חזר | ה חזר ביה   4 אמור | ה או'   5 ליום | ה ענינין ליום מכשיריו | ה מכשירין   6 והא תנינן | ה והתנינן עושי | ה עושה תנה | ה תנא   7 זהו | ה זה והא תנינן | ה והתנינן   8 והביאוהו | ה הביאוהו בעזרה | ה לעזרה - | ה דברי ר' מאיר אמ' ר' יוסה | ה [ר' יוסי אומר]   9 מרוק | ה מרק יוסי | ה יוסה   10 שלא התחיל | ה שהתחיל   11 סוסי קומי ר' יוסה | ה סוסיי והא תנינן | ה והתנינן   12 ליה | ה להן יוסה | ה יוסי   13 קדש | ה קדוש (2)

Rebbi Simeon ben Laqish asked, does cutting the `*omer* during daytime push aside the Sabbath[138]? Rebbi Abbai objected, did we not state[139], "its obligation is to harvest during nighttime. If it was cut during daytime it is qualified and pushes the Sabbath aside." But he did not accept it[140]. Rebbi Aha said, Rebbi Simeon ben Laqish changed his opinion because of this[141]: "After nightfall he says to them, did the sun set? They say, yes. Did the sun set? They say, yes.[142]" Where do we hold? If about nighttime, that already was said[143]. But if it does not refer to nighttime, let it refer to daytime; it is a matter that pushes aside the Sabbath during daytime. Do the preparations[144] push aside the Sabbath during nighttime? Did we not state[145], "they made the maker of pan-baked breads make pan-baked breads." Explain it, on a weekday. Rebbi Hiyya bar Ada stated[146], "this is the daily order of service of our God's Temple," whether on a weekday or a Sabbath. But did we not state[147], "they harvested it and put it in boxes, brought it to the Temple courtyard, and were parching it in fire to fulfill the commandment of roasting. Rebbi Yose[148] said, since he started the meritorious work, one tells him to complete it." Rebbi Judah from Kappadokia objected before Rebbi Yose: Think of it, if it came from storage. Since he did not start the meritorious work, there is no reason to tell him to complete it[149]. Rebbi Jacob bar Sosai objected before Rebbi Yose, did we not state, "for on a distance of walking a night and a day one desecrates the Sabbath and goes for testimony of the new moon"[150]? He said to them, since the daytime needs the nighttime[151] and the nighttime needs the daytime, it is as if it were all daytime. Rebbi Yose ben Rebbi Abun said, is it not sanctified retroactively[152]? Since it is sanctified retroactively there is no difference between day and night.

138 This paragraph is copied in *Roš Haššanah* 1:10 (ה).

Since the `omer must be brought at a fixed time, in pharisaic-rabbinic tradition on the 16th of Nisan (in the standard Sadducee tradition of the Book of Jubilees on Nisan 22, in Boethusian tradition on the Sunday of the Passover week), the fixed date overrules any Sabbath prohibition. Since the grain has to be parched (*Lev.* 2:14), the offering involves a Sabbath violation. It is prescribed that the grain be newly cut (*Lev.* 23:10). By tradition this has to be done in the night of Nisan 16. The question is whether it may be done the next morning if the 16th of Nisan is a Sabbath, since in this case the commandment would not be executed in the best manner.

139 Mishnah *Menahot* 10:9. The Mishnah seems to exclude any doubt about R. Simeon ben Laqish's question.

140 He interprets the clause "and pushes the Sabbath aside" only as referring to cutting during nighttime.

141 The clause must refer to the entire statement of the Mishnah.

142 Mishnah *Menahot* 10:3, describing the cutting of the barley for the `omer on a Sabbath.

143 Why does the priest charged with the cutting have to ask the attending crowd twice whether this is the right time to do the cutting? (The Babli takes it as an anti-Sadducee-Boethusian demonstration.)

144 Transporting the scythe and the storage boxes to the place of harvesting.

145 Mishnah *Tamid* 1:3. The pan-baked breads are for the daily offering by the High Priest (cf. *Yoma* 1:1, Note 26.) Baking the breads only is a preparation for the offering.

146 Mishnah *Tamid* 7:3, covering all the preceding rules, without distinction between Sabbath and weekday.

147 Mishnah *Menaḥot* 10:4, again about the `omer. Parching the grain usually is done during nighttime but there are no rules prohibiting doing it early in the morning.

148 The Amora. He notes that the Mishnah has no relevance for the question about preparations. Since cutting the grain in the night was a Sabbath violation, it is clear that there is authorization to finish the entire ceremony on the Sabbath. This implies nothing if there was no action during the night.

149 If no new grain was growing by Passover and grain from storage was used, there seems to be no authorization to parch it on the Sabbath.

150 As a matter of principle testimony may be received only during daytime. If people leave their Sabbath domain during nighttime in order to testify during daytime, the action in the night has the status of preparation for the main event during daytime.

151 Otherwise they could not appear in Court during daytime.

152 If the day is determined to be one of the New Moon (or in Tishre New Year's day) it receives this status from the preceding evening. Therefore every year one has to observe the restrictions of the holiday starting with the evening of the 30th of Elul even if no witnesses of the New Moon are yet known.

בני העיר פרק שלישי מגילה

(fol.72d) **משנה א**: בְּנֵי הָעִיר שֶׁמָּכְרוּ רְחוֹבָהּ שֶׁל עִיר לוֹקְחִין בְּדָמָיו בֵּית הַכְּנֶסֶת. בֵּית הַכְּנֶסֶת לוֹקְחִין תֵּיבָה. תֵּיבָה לוֹקְחִין מִטְפָּחוֹת. מִטְפָּחוֹת לוֹקְחִין סְפָרִים. סְפָרִים לוֹקְחִין תּוֹרָה. אֲבָל אִם מָכְרוּ תּוֹרָה לֹא יִקְחוּ סְפָרִים. סְפָרִים לֹא יִקְחוּ מִטְפָּחוֹת. מִטְפָּחוֹת לֹא יִקְחוּ תֵּיבָה. תֵּיבָה לֹא יִקְחוּ בֵּית הַכְּנֶסֶת. בֵּית הַכְּנֶסֶת לֹא יִקְחוּ אֶת הָרְחוֹב. וְכֵן בְּמוֹתְרֵיהֶן.

Mishnah 1: The people of a town who sold the town plaza[1] buy with the proceeds a synagogue[2], a synagogue they buy an Ark[3], an Ark they buy ribands[4], ribands they buy books[5], books the buy a Torah[6]. But if they sold a Torah they may not buy books, books they may not buy ribands, ribands they may not buy an Ark, an Ark they may not buy a synagogue, a synagogue they may not buy a town plaza. The same holds for their excess[7].

1 The town plaza has some holiness since it is the place of public prayer in times of draught (Ta`aniot 2:1).

2 The sanctity of the synagogue as permanent place of prayer is greater than that of the town plaza. The general principle is that if an object of holiness was sold, the proceeds have to be used to buy an object of greater holiness.

3 The (movable) chest in which the Torah scrolls are kept.

4 The bands, in Germany called wimpels and elaborately decorated, which are used to tie the Torah scrolls.

5 Texts of Prophets and Hagiographs.

6 Torah scrolls qualified to be read in public.

7 Excess money after the replacement has been bought does not lose its sanctity and may not be used for profane purposes.

(73d line 11) בְּנֵי הָעִיר שֶׁמָּכְרוּ רְחוֹבָהּ שֶׁל עִיר כול'. אָמַר רִבִּי יוֹחָנָן. דְּרִבִּי מְנַחֵם בֵּירִבִּי יוֹסֵה הִיא. דְּרִבִּי מְנַחֵם בֵּירִבִּי יוֹסֵה אָמַר. רְחוֹבָהּ שֶׁלָּעִיר יֵשׁ לָהּ קְדוּשָּׁה. שֶׁכֵּן מוֹצִיאִין סֵפֶר תּוֹרָה וְקוֹרִין בּוֹ בָרַבִּים. בְּרַם כְּרַבָּנָן. עָשׂוּ אוֹתוֹ כְּחַרְחֵק אַרְבַּע אַמּוֹת.

"The people of a town who sold the town plaza," etc. Rebbi Johanan said, this is Rebbi Menahem ben Rebbi Yose's, for Rebbi Menahem ben Rebbi Yose said, the town plaza has holiness since one brings a Torah scroll and reads from it in public[1]. But following the Rabbis one treats it like a distance of four cubits[8].

8 As explained in the next paragraph, one may pray everywhere if one is at a distance of 4 cubits from bad smells, excrement, etc. Since the public square is used for prayer on very rare occasions, it is treated as a place of occasional prayer which has no intrinsic sanctity. Babli 26a.

(73d line 15) רִבִּי יִרְמְיָה רִבִּי שְׁמוּאֵל בַּר חָלָף בְּשֵׁם רַב אָדָא בַּר אֲחֲוָה. הַמִּתְפַּלֵּל לֹא יָרוֹק עַד שֶׁיְּהַלֵּךְ אַרְבַּע אַמּוֹת. אָמַר רִבִּי יוֹסֵה בֵּירִבִּי בּוּן. וְכֵן הָרוֹקִין אַל יִתְפַּלֵּל עַד שֶׁיְּהַלֵּךְ אַרְבַּע אַמּוֹת. תַּנֵּי. הַמִּתְפַּלֵּל לֹא יַטִּיל מַיִם עַד שֶׁיְּהַלֵּךְ אַרְבַּע אַמּוֹת. וְכֵן הַמֵּטִיל מַיִם אַל יִתְפַּלֵּל עַד שֶׁיְּהַלֵּךְ אַרְבַּע אַמּוֹת. אָמַר רִבִּי יַעֲקֹב בַּר אֲחָא. לֹא סוֹף דָּבָר עַד שֶׁיְּהַלֵּךְ אַרְבַּע אַמּוֹת אֶלָּא אֲפִילוּ שָׁהָא כְּדֵי הִילּוּךְ אַרְבַּע אַמּוֹת. אִם אוֹמֵר אַתְּ. עַד שֶׁיְּהַלֵּךְ אַרְבַּע אַמּוֹת יְהֵא אָסוּר. אַף אֲנִי אוֹמֵר. אַחֵר בָּא וְהִיטִּיל שָׁם.

1 חלף | ב חלפתא לא | ב אל   2 יוסה | ב יוסי בון | ב אבון הרוקין | ב הרוקק   3 לא | ב אל   5 - | ב אמ' ר' אמי את | ב אתה אף | ב -

⁹Rebbi Jeremiah, Rebbi Samuel bar Ḥalaph in the name of Rav Ada bar Ahava: He who prayed should not spit until he walked four cubits. Rebbi Yose bar Rebbi Abun said, similarly (spittle) <he who spat>¹⁰ should not pray until he walked four cubits. He who urinates should not pray until he walks four cubits¹¹. Rebbi Jacob bar Aḥa said: not only that he walks four cubits but even if he waits corresponding to a walk of four cubits. If you say that he is forbidden until he removes himself four cubits, I say that somebody else came and urinated there¹².

9 This is copied from a longer discussion in *Berakhot* 3:5 (6d line 60, Notes 251-252,ב).
10 The text <from *Berakhot*> is the correct one.
11 In the Tosephta (*Berakhot* 2:19), the language is more restrictive: "A person should not urinate at the place where he prays unless he removes himself four cubits. Once he urinated he should not pray unless he removed himself four cubits. If it is dry or absorbed (in the earth) it is permitted." This text is the basis of the discussion of the Babli 27b but not of the Yerushalmi.
12 And there is no place in the world where he could pray. The Babli (*Berakhot* 25a) explicitly rules out this argument and states that one is forbidden only at a place where certainly somebody urinated and the moisture is still recognizable.

(73d line 22) בַּיְישָׁנָאֵי שְׁאָלוֹן לְרִבִּי אִימִּי. מַהוּ לִיקַּח אֲבָנִים מִבֵּית הַכְּנֶסֶת זוֹ וְלִבְנוֹת בְּבֵית הַכְּנֶסֶת אַחֶרֶת. אָמַר לוֹן. אָסוּר. אָמַר רִבִּי חֶלְבּוֹ. לֹא אָסַר רִבִּי אִימִּי אֶלָּא מִפְּנֵי עֲגְמַת נֶפֶשׁ. רִבִּי גּוּרְיוֹן אָמַר. מוּגְדְּלָאֵי שְׁאָלוֹן לְרִבִּי שִׁמְעוֹן בֶּן לָקִישׁ. מַהוּ לִיקַּח אֲבָנִים מֵעִיר זוֹ וְלִבְנוֹת בְּעִיר אַחֶרֶת. אָמַר לוֹן. אָסִיר. הוֹרֵי רִבִּי אִימִּי. אֲפִילּוּ מִמִּזְרָחָהּ לְמַעֲרָבָהּ אָסוּר מִפְּנֵי חוּרְבָּן

אוֹתוֹ מָקוֹם. מַהוּ לִמְכּוֹר בֵּית הַכְּנֶסֶת וְלִיקַּח בֵּית הַמִּדְרָשׁ. מִילְתֵיהּ דְּרִבִּי יְהוֹשֻׁעַ בֶּן לֵוִי אָמְרָה. שָׁרֵי. דְּאָמַר רִבִּי יְהוֹשֻׁעַ בֶּן לֵוִי. וַיִּשְׂרֹף אֶת־בֵּית־י'י. זֶה בֵּית הַמִּקְדָּשׁ. וְאֶת־בֵּית הַמֶּלֶךְ. זֶה פָּלָטִין שֶׁלְצִדְקִיָּהוּ. וְאֵת כָּל־בָּתֵּי יְרוּשָׁלָם. אִילוּ אַרְבַּע מֵאוֹת וּשְׁמוֹנִים בַּתֵּי כְנֵסִיּוֹת שֶׁהָיוּ בִירוּשָׁלָם. דְּאָמַר רִבִּי פִּינְחָס בְּשֵׁם רִבִּי הוֹשַׁעְיָה. אַרְבַּע מֵאוֹת וּשְׁמוֹנִים בַּתֵּי כְנֵסִיּוֹת הָיוּ בִירוּשָׁלָם וְכָל־אַחַת וְאַחַת הָיָה לָהּ בֵּית סֵפֶר וּבֵית תַּלְמוּד. [בֵּית סֵפֶר] לְמִקְרָא וּבֵית תַּלְמוּד לְמִשְׁנָה. וְכוּלְּהוֹן עָלָה אֶסְפַּסְיָינוּס. וְאֶת־כָּל־בֵּית הַגָּדוֹל שָׂרַף בָּאֵשׁ. זֶה מִדְרָשׁוֹ שֶׁלְּרַבָּן יוֹחָנָן בֶּן זַכַּי. שֵׁשָׁה הָיוּ מַתְנִין גְּדוּלוֹתָיו שֶׁלְהַקָּדוֹשׁ בָּרוּךְ הוּא. כְּגוֹן סַפְּרָה־נָא לִי אֵת כָּל־הַגְּדוֹלוֹת אֲשֶׁר־עָשָׂה אֱלִישָׁע: רִבִּי שְׁמוּאֵל בַּר נַחְמָן בְּשֵׁם רִבִּי יוֹנָתָן. הָדָא דְּאַתְּ אָמַר. בְּבֵית הַכְּנֶסֶת שֶׁלְיָחִיד. אֲבָל בְּבֵית הַכְּנֶסֶת שֶׁלְרַבִּים אָסוּר. אֲנִי אוֹמֵר. אֶחָד מִסּוֹף הָעוֹלָם קָנוּי בּוֹ. וְהָא תַנֵּי. מַעֲשֶׂה בְרִבִּי אֶלְעָזָר בֵּירִבִּי צָדוֹק שֶׁלָּקַח בֵּית הַכְּנֶסֶת שֶׁלְאֲלֶכְּסַנְדְּרִיִּים וְעָשָׂה בָהּ צְרָכָיו. אֲלֶכְּסַנְדְּרִיִּים עָשׂוּ אוֹתָהּ מִשֶּׁלְעַצְמָן. עַד כְּדוֹן בִּשְׁבָּנְיָיהּ לְשֵׁם בֵּית הַכְּנֶסֶת. בְּנָיָיהּ לְשֵׁם חָצֵר וְהִקְדִּישָׁהּ מָהוּ. נִישְׁמְעִינָהּ מִן הָדָא. קוֹנָם לַבַּיִת זֶה שֶׁאֵינִי נִכְנָס. וְנַעֲשָׂה בֵית הַכְּנֶסֶת. הָדָא אָמְרָה. בְּנָיָיהּ לְשֵׁם חָצֵר וְהִקְדִּישָׁהּ קָדְשָׁה. אֵימָתַי קָדְשָׁה. מִיַּד [אוֹ] בִּשְׁעַת הַתַּשְׁמִישׁ. נִישְׁמְעִינָהּ מִן הָדָא. הָעוֹשֶׂה תֵיבָה לְשֵׁם סֵפֶר וּמִטְפָּחוֹת לְשֵׁם סֵפֶר. עַד שֶׁלֹּא נִשְׁתַּמֵּשׁ בָּהֶן הַסֵּפֶר מוּתָּר לְהִשְׁתַּמֵּשׁ בָּהֶן הֶדְיוֹט. מִשֶּׁנִשְׁתַּמֵּשׁ בָּהֶן הַסֵּפֶר אָסוּר לְהִשְׁתַּמֵּשׁ בָּהֶן הֶדְיוֹט. [וּמַה] אִם אֵילּוּ שֶׁנַּעֲשׂוּ לְשֵׁם סֵפֶר אֵינָן קְדִישׁוֹת אֶלָּא בִּשְׁעַת הַתַּשְׁמִישׁ. זוֹ שֶׁבְּנָיָיהּ לְשֵׁם חָצֵר לֹא כָל־שֶׁכֵּן. אֵילוּ שֶׁעֲשָׂאָן לְשֵׁם חוּלִין וְהִקְדִּישָׁן מָה הֵן. כְּמָה דְּאַתְּ אָמַר תַּמָּן. בְּנָיָיהּ לְשֵׁם חָצֵר וְהִקְדִּישָׁהּ קָדְשָׁה. וְהָכָא עֲשָׂאָם לְשֵׁם חוּלִין וְהִקְדִּישָׁן קָדַשׁ.

The people of Bet Shean asked Rebbi Immi, may one take stones from one synagogue to build another synagogue[13]? He said to them, it is forbidden. Rebbi Ḥelbo said, Rebbi Immi forbade it only to make them feel bad[14]. Rebbi Gorion said, the people from Magdala asked Rebbi Simeon ben Laqish: May one take stones from one village to build in another village? He said to them, it is forbidden[14]. Rebbi Immi instructed, even from East to West is forbidden because of the destruction of that place. May one sell a synagogue to buy a school? Rebbi Joshua ben Levi's word implies that it is permitted. For Rebbi Joshua ben Levi said, *he burned the Eternal's House*[15], that is the Temple, *and the king's house,* that is Sedecias's palace, *and all the houses of Jerusalem*, these are the 480 synagogues which were in Jerusalem[16]. As Rebbi Phineas said in the name of Rebbi Hoshaia: There were 480 synagogues in Jerusalem, each of which had a school and a Talmud study; [the school] for Bible and the Talmud study for Mishnah. Against all of them came Vespasian. *And every large house he burned in fire,* that is the study of Rabban Joḥanan ben Zakkai where one was telling the great deeds of the Holy One, praise to Him, in the sense of *tell please of the great deeds which Elisha accomplished*[17]. Rebbi Samuel bar Naḥman in the name of Rebbi Jonathan: That you are saying about a private synagogue. But with a public synagogue it is forbidden; I am saying that one at the end of the world has part in it[18]. But did we not state, "it happened that Rebbi Eleazar ben Rebbi Ṣadoq bought the synagogue of the Alexandrians and used it for all his needs"? The Alexandrians made it from their own[19]. So far if it was built as a synagogue. If it was built as a court and he dedicated it, what is the rule? Let us hear from the following: "A *qônam*[20] that I shall not enter this house and it was turned into a synagogue.[21]" This implies that if it was built as a court and he dedicated it, it became sanctified. When is it sanctified, immediately [or] at the moment of use? Let us hear from the following: If one builds a chest for a scroll[22] or makes ribands for a scroll. As long as it was not used for a scroll profane use is permitted; after it was used for the scroll private use is prohibited. Therefore, if these who were made for a scroll are not sanctified until used, this which was built as court not so much more? What is the rule for these if they were made for profane use? Since you are saying there, if it was built as a court and he dedicated it, it is sanctified, so here if they were made for profane use and he dedicated them they are sanctified[23].

13 In a different place or neighborhood. If the synagogue was destroyed and has to be rebuilt on its plot or nearby, the old stones have to be re-used if at all possible.

14 The ruling is not invariable religious law, but an *ad hoc* ruling at a time when the Christian government of the Roman Empire tried to eliminate Jewish settlement in the Holy Land.

15 *2K*. 25:9.

16 While this refers to Jerusalem in post-Herodian times (Babli *Ketubot* 105a) and the verse describes the destruction of the first Temple, this should not be considered an anachronism. Since the verse is formulated as part of Scripture, it is meaningful outside of time and space.

17 *2K*. 8:4.

18 He would have to be asked to vote on the sale of the property. Babli 26a/b,27a.

19 Tosephta 2:17. In the Babli 26a it is the synagogue of the metal smelters, a local guild, so no far-away person may have a say in it. Therefore their vote is undisputed.

20 A formula to confirm an oath, Phoenician for *qorbān*; cf. Introduction to Tractate *Nedarim*.

21 Mishnah *Nedarim* 9:2. Since the Mishnah states that this vow may be dissolved, it confirms that the dedication of

profane building turns it into a synagogue.
22 A Torah scroll.

23 The rules for dedication of real estate and of movables are identical.

(73d line 51) כְּלֵי שָׁרֵת מֵאֵימָתַי הֵן קְדֵישִׁין. מִיַּד אוֹ בִשְׁעַת הַתַּשְׁמִישׁ. אִין תֵּימַר. מִיַּד. נִיחָא. אִין תֵּימַר. בִּשְׁעַת הַתַּשְׁמִישׁ. כְּאַחַת הֵן קְדֵישִׁים וּמִתְקַדְּשִׁין. נִיחָא שֶׁל מֹשֶׁה שֶׁנִּתְקַדְּשׁוּ בְשֶׁמֶן הַמִּשְׁחָה וּבְדָם. וְשֶׁל שְׁלֹמֹה כְּאַחַת הֵן קְדֵישִׁים וּמִתְקַדְּשִׁין. בִּכְנִיסָתָן לָאָרֶץ הָיוּ מְפַנִּין מִתּוֹךְ שֶׁלְּמֹשֶׁה לְתוֹךְ שֶׁלִּשְׁלֹמֹה. לֹא הָיָה שָׁם שֶׁלְּמֹשֶׁה כְּאַחַת הֵם קְדֵישִׁים וּמִתְקַדְּשִׁים. בַּעֲלִיָּיתָן מִן הַגּוֹלָה הָיוּ מְפַנִּין מִתּוֹךְ שֶׁלִּשְׁלֹמֹה לְתוֹךְ שֶׁלָּהֶן. לֹא הָיָה שָׁם שֶׁלִּשְׁלֹמֹה כְּאַחַת הֵן קְדֵישִׁים וּמִתְקַדְּשִׁים.

אֲבָנִים שֶׁחֲצָבָן לְשֵׁם מֵת אֲסוּרוֹת בַּהֲנָיָיה. לְשֵׁם חַי וּלְשֵׁם מֵת מוּתָּרִין בַּהֲנָיָיה. הַזּוֹרֵק כְּלִי לִפְנֵי מִיטָתוֹ שֶׁל מֵת לְתוֹךְ אַרְבַּע אַמּוֹת [שֶׁלּוֹ] אָסוּר בַּהֲנָיָיה. חוּץ לְאַרְבַּע אַמּוֹת מוּתָּר בַּהֲנָיָיה.

[24] From which moment on are vessels of Temple service holy? Immediately[25] or at the moment of use? If you are saying immediately, it is understandable. If you are saying at the moment of use, simultaneously they become holy and make holy. One can understand for those of Moses which became holy by the anointing oil and the blood[26]. But those of Solomon simultaneously became holy and made holy. When they entered the Land they transferred from Moses's to Solomon's[27]. If none of Moses's was available, they simultaneously became holy and made holy. When they returned from the Diaspora, they transferred from Solomon's[28] to theirs. If none of Solomon was available, they simultaneously became holy and made holy.

[29] Stones quarried for a corpse are forbidden for usufruct[30]. For a corpse or a living person[31] they are permitted for usufruct. If somebody throws an implement near the bier of a corpse, within four cubits [of him][32] it is forbidden for usufruct; anything outside four cubits is permitted for usufruct.

24 Copied from *Yoma* 3:6, Notes 120-126.
25 Is a declaration of intent to use the vessel in the Temple the equivalent of a formal dedication and donation to the Temple, or not? Since the contents of a sacred vessel automatically become holy, in the second case the holiness of the vessel and its power to convert profane to sacral start at the same moment.

26 Before they were actually used. This is an action, not a declaration of intent.
27 But first to the Tabernacle at Shiloh.
28 The vessels given by Cyrus from the treasury of Babylon.
29 Copied from *Yoma*, not approppriate here.
30 Since a grave and its appurtenances are forbidden for usufruct.
31 Babli *Sanhedrin* 48a: A mausoleum

(73d line 60) כָּל־כְּלֵי בֵית הַכְּנֶסֶת כְּבֵית הַכְּנֶסֶת. סַפְסְלָה וּקְלֵטִירָה כְּבֵית הַכְּנֶסֶת. כִּילָה דְעַל אָרוֹנָא כְּאָרוֹנָא. רִבִּי אַבָּהוּ יְהַב גּוּלְתָּה תַּחְתּוֹי הָהֵן בִּילָן. רַב יְהוּדָה בְשֵׁם שְׁמוּאֵל. בִּימָה וּלוּחוֹתָיו אֵין בָּהֶן קְדוּשַׁת אָרוֹן [וְ]יֵשׁ בָּהֶן מִשּׁוּם קְדוּשַׁת בֵּית הַכְּנֶסֶת. אינגלין אֵין בּוֹ מִשּׁוּם קְדוּשַׁת אָרוֹן. יֵשׁ בּוֹ מִשּׁוּם קְדוּשַׁת בֵּית הַכְּנֶסֶת. רִבִּי יִרְמְיָה אֲזַל לְגוֹלְנָה. חֲמִיתוֹן יְהָבִין מַכּוּשָׁא בְּגוֹ אָרוֹנָא. אֲתָא שְׁאַל לְרִבִּי אִימִּי. אֲמַר לֵיהּ. אֲנִי אוֹמֵר. לְכָךְ הִתְנוּ עָלָיו מִבַּתְּחִילָה. רִבִּי יוֹנָה עֲבַד לֵיהּ מִגְדָּל וְאַתְנֵי עֲלוֹי. עִילִיחָא דְסִיפְרִין וְאַרְעֲיָיא דְמָאנִין.

All appurtenances of the synagogue are like the synagogue[33]. The bench[34] and the arm-chair[35] are like the synagogue. The cover over the Ark is like the Ark. Rebbi Abbahu gave a jacket under the curtain[36]. Rav Jehudah in the name of Samuel: The podium[37] and its plates do not have the sanctity of the Ark but the sanctity of the synagogue. The lectern[38] does not have the sanctity of the Ark; it has the sanctity of the synagogue. Rebbi Jeremiah went to the Gaulanitis. He saw them putting a hammer into the Ark. He went and asked Rebbi Immi, who told him, I am saying that they stipulated this from the start. Rebbi Jonah made for himself a chest and stipulated about it, the upper part for scrolls, the lower part for implements[39].

32 Corrector's addition, not in *Yoma*, To be deleted as unjustified. built for a person still living is permitted for usufruct.

33 In that they become dedicated to sacral use by being used the first time. Tosephta 2:13.
34 Latin *subsellium*.
35 Greek κλιντήρ.
36 Latin *vellum*.
37 Where the public Torah reading is performed. Babli 32a; cf. Meïri and Rosh *ad loc.*
38 It is difficult to know how this was pronounced. In Mishnah *Kelim* 16:7 אנלגין, Greek 'αναλογεῖον.
39 To confirm that it is possible to stipulate before an implement is given to the synagogue that it may be used for specified profane purposes as long as these do not interfere with the intended sacral use. Nevertheless if the implement is sold, the rules of tHe Mishnah do apply.

(73d line 67) מִטְפָּחוֹת לוֹקְחִין סְפָרִים. אֲפִילוּ מִטְפְּחוֹת תּוֹרָה וְחוּמָשִׁין לוֹקֵחַ בָּהֶן נְבִיאִים וּכְתוּבִים.

"Ribands they buy books[5]." Even for ribands of Torah and *Ḥumash*[40] one buys Prophets and Hagiographs.

40 Scrolls containing a single book of the Pentateuch which cannot be used for public readings.

(73d line 68) סְפָרִים לֹא יְקְחוּ מִטְפָּחוֹת. אֲפִילוּ נְבִיאִים וּכְתוּבִים [אֵינוֹ] לוֹקֵחַ בָּהֶן מִטְפָּחוֹת תּוֹרָה וְחוּמָשִׁים. כּוֹרְכִים תּוֹרָה בְמִטְפָּחוֹת תּוֹרָה. חוּמָשִׁים בְּמִטְפָּחוֹת חוּמָשִׁים. [נְבִיאִים בְּמִטְפָּחוֹת נְבִיאִים.] תּוֹרָה וְחוּמָשִׁים בְּמִטְפָּחוֹת נְבִיאִים וּכְתוּבִים. אֲבָל לֹא נְבִיאִים וּכְתוּבִים בְּמִטְפָּחוֹת תּוֹרָה וְחוּמָשִׁים. נוֹתְנִין תּוֹרָה עַל גַּבֵּי תוֹרָה. וְחוּמָשִׁים עַל גַּבֵּי חוּמָשִׁים. תּוֹרָה וְחוּמָשִׁים עַל גַּבֵּי נְבִיאִים וּכְתוּבִים. אֲבָל לֹא נְבִיאִים וּכְתוּבִים עַל גַּבֵּי תּוֹרָה וְחוּמָשִׁין. רִבִּי יִרְמְיָה בְשֵׁם רִבִּי זְעוּרָה. תּוֹרָה וְחוּמָשִׁין עָרֵק תַּנָּיָה מִינָהּ.

כּוֹתְבִין תּוֹרָה נְבִיאִים כְּאַחַת. דִּבְרֵי רִבִּי מֵאִיר. וַחֲכָמִים אוֹמְרִים. אֵין כּוֹתְבִין תּוֹרָה וּנְבִיאִים כְּאַחַת אֲבָל כּוֹתְבִין תּוֹרָה נְבִיאִים וּכְתוּבִים כְּאַחַת. רִבִּי יִרְמְיָה בְשֵׁם רִבִּי שְׁמוּאֵל בַּר רַב יִצְחָק. תּוֹרָה וְחוּמָשִׁין קְדוּשָׁה אַחַת הֵן. אֵין עוֹשִׂין תּוֹרָה חוּמָשִׁין אֲבָל עוֹשִׁין חוּמָשִׁין תּוֹרָה. אָמַר רִבִּי יוֹסֵה. הָדָא אֲמָרָה. תּוֹרָה שֶׁעֲשָׂאָהּ חוּמָשִׁין בִּקְדוּשָׁתָהּ הִיא. רִבִּי שְׁמוּאֵל בַּר נַחְמָן בְּשֵׁם רִבִּי יוֹנָתָן. תּוֹרָה חֲסֵירָה אֵין קוֹרְאִין בָּהּ בָּרַבִּים. וְהָא תַנֵּי. בְּבְרֵאשִׁית עַד הַמַּבּוּל. בְּוַיִּקְרָא עַד וַיְהִי בַּיּוֹם הַשְּׁמִינִי. בְּוַיְדַבֵּר עַד וַיְהִי בִּנְסוֹעַ הָאָרוֹן. מוּתָּר לִקְרוֹת בּוֹ בָּרַבִּים. חָדָא אֲרַסְקִינָס אוֹקִיד אוֹרַיְיתָא דְּצִנְבְּרַאֵי. אִלּוּ שָׁאֲלוּן לְרִבִּי יוֹנָה וּלְרִבִּי יוֹסֵה. מַהוּ לִקְרוֹת בַּסֵּפֶר בָּרַבִּים. אָמְרוֹן לוֹן. אָסִיר. לָא דְאָסִיר אֶלָּא מִן גּוֹ דְּנַפְשְׁהוֹן עֲגִימָה אִינּוּן זָבְנִין לְהוֹן אָחוֹרִי.

"Books, they may not buy ribands." Even from Prophets and Hagiographs one may [not] buy ribands for Torah or *Humashim*. One ties a Torah with ribands of Torah, *Humashim* with ribands of *Humashim*, [Prophets with ribands of Prophets]; Torah and *Humashim* with ribands of Prophets and Hagiographs, but not Prophets and Hagiographs with ribands of Torah and *Humashim*. One may put a Torah on top of a Torah, *Humashim* on top of *Humashim*, Torah and *Humashim* on top of Prophets and Hagiographs but not Prophets and Hagiographs on top of Torah and *Humashim*. Rebbi Jeremiah in the name of Rebbi Ze`ira: The Tanna fled from Torah and *Humashim*[41].

One writes Torah and Prophets together, the words of Rebbi Meïr. But the Sages are saying, one does not write Torah and Prophets together, but one may write Torah, Prophets, and Hagiographs together[42]. Rebbi Jeremiah in the name of Rebbi Samuel bar Rav Isaac: Torah and *Humashim* have the same sanctity. One does not split a Torah into *Humashim*, but one turns *Humashim* into a Torah. Rebbi Yose said, this implies that a Torah which was split into *Humashim* remains in its sanctity[43]. Rebbi Samuel bar Nahman in the name of Rebbi Jonathan: One does not read in public from an incomplete Torah[44]. But was it not stated: [45]It is permitted to read in public in

Genesis up to the deluge, in *Leviticus* up to *it was on the eighth day*[46], in *Numbers* up to *it was when the Ark travelled*[47]? This Ursicinus[48] set fire to the Torah of the Sennabarites[49]. They came and asked Rebbi Jonah and Rebbi Yose, whether one may read from the scroll in public. They told them, it is forbidden. Not that it is forbidden but since they will feel so badly they will buy another one.

41 He does not address the problem whether a wimpel used for a single *Humash* may be used for a complete Torah scroll and vice versa. A partial answer is given in the Babli 27a.

42 While the sanctity of Torah is greater than that of the other parts of the Bible, one may write an entire Bible together, but not a Torah together with the portions of the prophets read as weekly *Haftarah*. Babli *Bava Batra* 13b.

43 Since the *Humashim* may be put together to form a complete Torah, they could not have lost their sanctity by being split.

44 Babli *Gittin* 60a.

45 This indicates how deficient a book may be and still be used in public.

46 *Lev.* 9:1.

47 *Num.* 10:35.

48 Legate of the Emperor Gallus.

49 From a place near Tiberias.

(74a line 10) וְכֵן בְּמוֹתְרֵיהֶן. מִמַּה שֶׁגָּבוּ גַּבָּאֵי צְדָקָה וְהוֹתִירוּ. כְּהָדָא רִבִּי חִיָּיה בַּר בָּא אֲזַל לְחָמָץ וִיהָבוּ לֵיהּ פְּרִיטִין [לְ]מִפְלְגָא לְיַתְמַיָּא וּלְאַרְמְלָאתָא. נְפַק וּפִלְגוֹן לְרַבָּנָן. מַהוּ שֶׁצָּרִיךְ לְהַפְרִישׁ תַּחְתֵּיהֶן. רִבִּי בָּא בַּר מָמָל אָמַר. צָרִיךְ לְהַפְרִישׁ תַּחְתֵּיהֶן. רִבִּי זְעוּרָה אָמַר. צָרִיךְ לְהַפְרִישׁ תַּחְתֵּיהֶן. רִבִּי אִילָא אָמַר. אֵינוֹ צָרִיךְ לְהַפְרִישׁ תַּחְתֵּיהֶן. רִבִּי יָסָא בְשֵׁם רִבִּי לְעָזָר אוֹמֵר. אֵינוֹ צָרִיךְ לְהַפְרִישׁ תַּחְתֵּיהֶן. רִבִּי יַעֲקֹב בַּר אָחָא רִבִּי יָסָא רִבִּי לְעָזָר בְּשֵׁם רִבִּי חֲנִינָה. כָּל־הַמִּצְוֹת עַד שֶׁלֹּא יִינָּתְנוּ לַגִּיזְבָּרִין אַתְּ רַשַּׁאי לְשַׁנּוֹתָם. מִשֶּׁנִּיתְּנוּ לַגִּיזְבָּרִין אֵין אַתְּ רַשַּׁאי לְשַׁנּוֹתָם.

"The same holds for the excess." From what the administrators of charity collected[50]. As the following: Rebbi Hiyya bar Abba went to Homs where they gave him monies to distribute to orphans and widows. He went and distributed it to the rabbis. Does he have to replace them? Rebbi Abba bar Mamal said, he has to replace them. Rebbi Ze'ira[51] said, he has to replace them. Rebbi Ila said, he does not have to replace them. Rebbi Yasa in the name of Rebbi Johanan says, he does not have to replace them. Rebbi Jacob bar Aha, Rebbi Yasa, Rebbi Eleazar in the name of Rebbi Hanina, the intended use of any charity monies may be changed before they are given into the hands of the administrators; after they are given into the hands of the administrators they may not be changed[52].

50 Since charity money is given as a religious obligation, it acquires sanctity which makes illegitimate use sinful until the money is delivered to an entitled recipient. Cf. Babli 27a.

51 Since he was a direct student of R. Ḥiyya bar Abba, his opinion probably is that of his teacher.

52 Halakhah 1:6, Note 130. Babli *Arakhin* 6a.

(fol. 73c) **משנה ב**: אֵין מוֹכְרִין אֶת שֶׁל רַבִּים לַיָחִיד מִפְּנֵי שֶׁמּוֹרִידִין אוֹתוֹ מִקְּדוּשָּׁתוֹ דִּבְרֵי רִבִּי מֵאִיר. אָמְרוּ לוֹ אִם כֵּן אַף לֹא מֵעִיר גְּדוֹלָה לְעִיר קְטַנָּה:

Mishnah 2: One does not sell public property to a private person because one diminishes its sanctity[53], the words of Rebbi Meïr. They said to him, if this be so, then not even from a large town to a small town.

53 Since *the King's splendor is the multitude of people* (*Prov.* 14:28).

(74a line 18) **הלכה ב**: שְׁלֹשָׁה מִבֵּית הַכְּנֶסֶת כְּבֵית הַכְּנֶסֶת וְשִׁבְעָה מִבְּנֵי הָעִיר כָּעִיר. מָה אֲנָן קַיָּימִין. אִם בְּשֶׁקִּיבְּלוּ עֲלֵיהֶן. אֲפִילוּ אֶחָד. אִם בְּשֶׁלֹּא קִיבְּלוּ עֲלֵיהֶן. אֲפִילוּ כַּמָּה. אֶלָּא כֵן אֲנָן קַיָּימִין. בִּסְתָם.

Halakhah 2: Three from a synagogue act for the synagogue, seven from a town act for the town. Where do we hold? If they accepted it, even one; if they did not accept, even many. But we hold in the normal case[54].

54 In order to legally act for a synagogue or a town, the heads have to be duly elected by the membership of the synagogue or the inhabitants of the town. The normal case is to elect a board of 3 members to run the affairs of a synagogue and a board of 7 as town council.

(74a line 20) בֶּן עִיר שֶׁפָּסַק בְּעִיר אַחֶרֶת נוֹתֵן עִמָּהֶן. בְּנֵי הָעִיר שֶׁפָּסְקוּ בְּעִיר אַחֶרֶת נוֹתְנִין בִּמְקוֹמָן. רִבִּי חִייָה בְשֵׁם רִבִּי יוֹחָנָן. כְּגוֹן הָהֵן סִיפְסְלָא דִמְעוֹנְיָא. כְּהָדָא. רִבִּי חֶלְבּוֹ הֲוָה דָרֵשׁ בְּצִיפּוֹרִין. פָּסַק תַּמָּן. אֲתָא בָעֵי לְמֵיתַּן הָכָא. אָמַר לֵיהּ רִבִּי אִימִּי. יְחִידְיי אַתְּ. הָעוֹשֶׂה נֵר וּמְנוֹרָה לְבֵית הַכְּנֶסֶת עַד שֶׁלֹּא נִשְׁתַּכַּח שֵׁם הַבְּעָלִים מֵהֶן אֵין אַתְּ רַשַּׁאי לְשַׁנּוֹתָן לְמָקוֹם אַחֵר. אִם מִשֶּׁנִּשְׁתַּכַּח שֵׁם הַבְּעָלִים מֵהֶן אַתְּ רַשַּׁאי לְשַׁנּוֹתָן לְמָקוֹם אַחֵר. רִבִּי חִייָה בְשֵׁם רִבִּי יוֹחָנָן. אִם הָיָה שֵׁם הַבְּעָלִים חָקוּק עֲלֵיהֶן כְּמִי שֶׁלֹּא נִשְׁתַּכַּח שֵׁם הַבְּעָלִים מֵהֶן.

HALAKHAH 2

כְּחָדָא. אַנטוֹלִינוּס עָשָׂה מְנוֹרָה לְבֵית הַכְּנֶסֶת. שָׁמַע רִבִּי וְאָמַר. בָּרוּךְ אֱלֹהִים אֲשֶׁר נָתַן בְּלִיבּוֹ לַעֲשׂוֹת מְנוֹרָה לְבֵית הַכְּנֶסֶת. רִבִּי שְׁמוּאֵל בַּר רַב יִצְחָק בָּעֵי. מַה אָמַר רִבִּי. בָּרוּךְ אֱלֹהִים. בָּרוּךְ אֱלֹהֵינוּ. אִין אָמַר. בָּרוּךְ אֱלֹהִים. הָדָא אֲמָרָה [דְלָא] אִיתְגַּיַּיר אַנטוֹלִינוּס. אִין אָמַר. בָּרוּךְ אֱלֹהֵינוּ. הָדָא אֲמָרָה [דְ]אִיתְגַּיַּיר אַנטוֹלִינוּס.

A person from one town who pledged[55] in an other town gives with them. The people of one town[56] who pledged in an other town give at their place. Rebbi Ḥiyya in the name of Rebbi Joḥanan, like these benches[57] of Maon. As the following: Rebbi Ḥelbo was preaching in Sepphoris. He pledged there. He came and wanted to give here[58]. Rebbi Immi said to him, you are a single person[59].

If somebody[60] makes a light or a candelabrum for the synagogue, as long as the name of their owner is not forgotten, one is not empowered to change them to another place; if the the name of their owner is forgotten, one is empowered to change them to another place. Rebbi Ḥiyya in the name of Rebbi Joḥanan: if the owner's name was engraved on it, it is as if the name of their owner is not forgotten. Antoninus[61] made a candelabrum for the synagogue. Rebbi heard and said, praise to God Who inspired him to make a candelabrum for the synagogue. Rebbi Samuel ben Rav Isaac asked, what did Rebbi say? Praise to God or praise to our God? If he said praise to God, this implies that Antoninus did not convert; if he said praise to our God this implies that Antoninus did convert.

55 For charity.
56 As an organized group with a known administrator of charity who can be trusted to collect all pledges.
57 This most probably either is misspelling for סיפסרא "broker", or it stands for this word by a dialectal change of liquids. The brokers from Maon formed a distinguished group in Tiberias and therefore pay their pledges in Maon.
58 In Tiberias.
59 And you have to pay in Sepphoris.
60 Either a Jew or a Gentile "friend of the synagogue".
61 For this and the following cf. Halakhah 1:13 Notes 489 ff.

(74a line 41) [אִית מִילִין דְּאִתְגַּיַּיר אַנטוֹנִינוּס וְאִית מִילִין אָמְרִין דְּלָא אִתְגַּיַּיר אַנטוֹנִינוּס]. רָאוּ אוֹתוֹ יוֹצֵא בְּמִנְעָל פָּחוּת בְּיוֹם הַכִּיפּוּרִים. מַה אַתְּ שָׁמַע מִינָהּ. שֶׁכֵּן אֲפִילוּ יְרֵאֵי שָׁמַיִם יוֹצְאִין בְּכָךְ. אַנטוֹלִינוּס אָמַר לְרִבִּי. מֵייכַלְתֵּי אַתְּ מִן לִוְיָתָן לְעָלְמָא דְאָתֵי. אֲמַר לֵיהּ. אִין. אֲמַר לֵיהּ. מִן אִימַּר פִּיסְחָא לָא אוֹכַלְתַּנִי וּמִן לִוְיָתָן אַתְּ מֵייכִיל לִי. אֲמַר לֵיהּ. וּמַה נַּעֲבִיד לָךְ וּכְתִיב בֵּיהּ

וְכָל עָרֵל לֹא־יֹאכַל בּוֹ: כֵּיוָן דְּשָׁמַע מִינֵיהּ כֵּן אֲזַל וּגְזַר. אֲתָא לְגַבֵּיהּ. אֲמַר לֵיהּ. רִבִּי. חֲמִי
גְזוּרְתִי. אֲמַר לֵיהּ. בְּדִידִי לָא אִיסְתַּכְּלִית מִיָּמַי אֶלָּא בְדִידָךְ. וְלָמָּה נִקְרָא שְׁמוֹ רַבֵּינוּ הַקָּדוֹשׁ.
שֶׁלֹּא הִבִּיט בְּמִילָתוֹ מִיָּמָיו. [וְלָמָּה נִקְרָא שְׁמוֹ נָחוּם אִישׁ קוֹדֶשׁ הַקֳּדָשִׁים. שֶׁלֹּא הִבִּיט בְּצוּרַת
מַטְבֵּעַ מִיָּמָיו.] הָדָא אָמְרָה דְאִתְגַּיֵּיר אַנְטוֹלִינוּס. מִילֵּיהוֹן דְּרַבָּנָן אָמְרִין. (דְּלֹא) אִיתְגַּיֵּיר
אַנְטוֹלִינוּס. דְּאָמַר רִבִּי חִזְקִיָּה רִבִּי אַבָּהוּ בְשֵׁם רִבִּי לָעְזָר. אִם בָּאִין הֵן גֵּירֵי צֶדֶק לֶעָתִיד לָבוֹא
אַנְטוֹלִינוּס בָּא בְרֹאשָׁם.

[62][There are indications implying that Antoninus converted; there are indications implying that Antoninus did not convert.] One saw him walking with a house shoe on the Day of Atonement, what do you infer since even God-fearing people go outside thus. Antolinus said to Rebbi, can I eat from the Leviathan[5] in the World to Come? He said to him, yes. He told him, from the Passover lamb you would not let me eat, but from Leviathan you make me eat? He answered, what can we do for you since about the Passover lamb it is written that *no uncircumcised man may eat from it*. When he heard this, he went and circumcised. He came to Rebbi and said to him, look at my circumcision. He answered him, at mine I never looked[497], and at yours I should look? Why is he called our holy teacher? Because he never in his life looked at his circumcision. [And why is his name Nahum the holiest of holies? Because he never in his life looked at the figure on a coin.] This implies that Antolinus converted. The statement of the rabbis implies that Antolinus did (not) convert., as Rebbi Ḥizqiah, Rebbi Abbahu in the name of Rebbi Eleazar said: When in the Future World the proselytes come, Antolinus comes at the head of all of them.

62 This is copied from Halakhah 1:13. The corrector's additions only make it a copy; this shows that from the start it was intended as a reference and not a stand-alone text.

(74a line 43) מַהוּ מִיכְתּוֹב תְּרֵיי תָלַת מִילִין מִן פְּסוּקָא. מַר עוּקְבָּא מִישְׁלַח כְּתַב לְרֵישׁ גָּלוּתָא
דַּהֲוָה דְּמִיךְ וְקָאִים בְּזִימְרִין. אַל־תִּשְׂמַח יִשְׂרָאֵל | אֶל־גִּיל. רִבִּי אָחָא כָּתַב זֵיכֶר צַדִּיק לִבְרָכָה.
רִבִּי זְעוּרָה כָּתַב וְלֹא־זָבָר יוֹאָשׁ הַמֶּלֶךְ. רִבִּי יִרְמְיָה מִישְׁלַח כְּתַב לְרַבִּי יוּדָן נְשִׂיָּיא. לְשָׂנוֹא
אֶת־אֹהֲבֶיךָ לְאַהֲבָה אֶת־שׂוֹנְאֶיךָ. רִבִּי חִייָה רִבִּי יָסִי רִבִּי אִימִּי דָּנוּן לְתָמָר. אֲזַלַת וּקְרָבַת עֲלֵיהוֹן
לְאַנְטִיפּוֹטָא דְקַיְסָרִין. שְׁלָחוּן וְכָתְבוּן לְרִבִּי אַבָּהוּ. שָׁלַח רִבִּי אַבָּהוּ וְכָתַב לְחוֹן. (תְּרֵי) [כְּבָר]
פִּייַּסְנוּ לִשְׁלֹשָׁה לִיטוּרִין. לְטוּב יֶלֶד לְטוּב לָמַד וְתִרְשִׁישׁ. אֲבְדוּקִיס אָבְמַסִיס תַּלְתַּסְס. אֲבָל

תָּמָר תַּמְרוּרִים בְּתַמְרוּרֶיהָ הִיא עוֹמֶדֶת וּבִיקַּשְׁנוּ לְמָתְקָהּ וְלַשָּׁוְא צָרַף צָרוֹף. רִבִּי מָנָא מִשְׁלַח כְּתַב לְרִבִּי הוֹשַׁעְיָה בֵּירִבִּי שַׁמַּי. רֵאשִׁיתְךָ מִצְעָר מְאֹד תִּשְׂגֶּא אַחֲרִיתֶךָ:

May one write two or three words from a verse[63]? Mar Uqba sent a letter to the Head of the Diaspora who went to sleep and got up with song: *Israel, do not enjoy like the Gentiles*[64]. Rebbi Aha wrote, *the remembrance of the just is a blessing*[65]. Rebbi Ze`ura wrote, *Joash the King did not remember*[66]. Rebbi Jeremiah sent a letter to Rebbi Jehudah Nesia, *to hate your lovers, to love your hater*[67]. Rebbi Ḥiyya, Rebbi Yasa, and Rebbi Immi judged Tamar. She went and complained about them to the prefect[68] of Sepphoris. They sent and wrote to Rebbi Abbahu[69], who wrote back to them, (twice) [already][70] we pacified the three informers[71], the well born, the well learned, and Tarshish, Eutokos, Eumathes, Thalassios[72]; but the rebellious Tamar remains in her rebellious state; we tried to soften her but *in vain did one smelt to refine*[73]. Rebbi Mana sent a letter to Rebbi Hoshaia ben Rebbi Shammai, *your beginnings were small,* your future may be much expanding[74].

63 Is it permitted to use parts of verses to make a point in a letter, implying that the words were written without the required ruled lines and not in square script. Instead of a reasoned answer it is pointed out that not only did Amoraim of all generations use biblical quotes in their letters but also that they did not adhere closely to the text.

64 *Hos.* 9:1.

65 *Prov.* 10:7.

66 *2Chr.* 24:22.

67 *2S.* 19:10. The order of the quotes is inverted.

68 Greek 'ανθύπατος.

69 Who was Rabbi of Caesarea Philippi, residence of the prefect's superior. The judgment rendered by the three rabbis could be interpreted by the Roman authorities as an act of rebellion, usurping the role of Roman criminal courts. Since the Talmudim do not indicate that the rabbis were killed or jailed, R. Abbahu must have been more successful than he indicates in his letter.

70 The reading of the (scribe) has to be preferred over that of the [corrector].

71 Reading *delatores* with Graetz.

72 Conjectured name.

73 *Jer.* 6:29.

74 *Job* 8:7. In the second half of the verse, the word order and spelling are changed.

(fol. 73c) **משנה ג**: אֵין מוֹכְרִין בֵּית הַכְּנֶסֶת אֶלָּא עַל תְּנַאי אֵימָתַי שֶׁיִּרְצוּ יַחֲזִירוּהוּ דִּבְרֵי רִבִּי מֵאִיר. וַחֲכָמִים אוֹמְרִים מוֹכְרִים אוֹתוֹ מִמְכַּר עוֹלָם מֵאַרְבָּעָה דְבָרִים חוּץ מֵאַרְבָּעָה דְבָרִים לַמֶּרְחָץ וְלַבּוּרְסְקִי וְלַטְּבִילָה וּלְבֵית הַמַּיִם. רִבִּי יְהוּדָה אוֹמֵר מוֹכְרִין אוֹתוֹ לְשֵׁם חָצֵר וְהַלּוֹקֵחַ מַה שֶּׁיִּרְצֶה יַעֲשֶׂה:

Mishnah 3: One may sell a synagogue only on the condition that they could take it back any time they so desire, the words of Rebbi Meïr. But the Sages are saying that one may sell it permanently except for four things[75], a bath house, a tannery, a ritual bath, and a urinal. Rebbi Jehudah says, one sells it as a courtyard[76] and the buyer may use it as he pleases.

75 They exclude the (thermal) bath house and the (cold) ritual bath because people stand there naked, and tannery and urinal because of the bad smell. Both are considered inappropriate for what had been a place of worship.

76 It can be sold unconditionally as building plot.

(74a line 54) **הלכה ג**: אָמַר רִבִּי יוֹחָנָן. לֵית כָּאן. מָה אֲנָן קַיָּימִין. אִם כְּרִבִּי מֵאִיר אֵין מוֹכְרִין בֵּית הַכְּנֶסֶת אֶלָּא עַל תְּנַאי. אִם כְּרַבָּנָן. מוֹכְרִין אוֹתוֹ מִמְכַּר עוֹלָם חוּץ מֵאַרְבָּעָה דְבָרִים. רִבִּי חִייָה בְשֵׁם רִבִּי יוֹחָנָן. תִּיפְתָּר בְּסֵפֶר תּוֹרָה.

Halakhah 3: Rebbi Johanan, it does not apply[77]. Where do we hold? If following Rebbi Meïr, one may sell a synagogue only conditionally. If following the rabbis, one may sell it permanently except for four things! Rebbi Hiyya in the name of Rebbi Johanan, explain it for a Torah scroll.

77 Mishnah 3 and Mishnah 2 contradict one another; if Mishnah 2 is confirmed then Mishnah 3 cannot apply. Mishnah 2 prohibits selling public property in a way which reduces its sanctity; the Mishnah 3 cannot permit selling it when its sanctity is certainly diminished, even if the buyers are not individuals. Not even R. Meïr's prescription conforms with Mishnah 2. The answer must be that Mishnah 2 does not apply to real estate, only to the contents of public buildings, including the Torah scrolls.

(fol. 73c) **משנה ד**: וְעוֹד אָמַר רִבִּי יְהוּדָה בֵּית הַכְּנֶסֶת שֶׁחָרַב אֵין מַסְפִּידִין לְתוֹכוֹ וְאֵין מַפְשִׁילִין בְּתוֹכוֹ חֲבָלִים וְאֵין פּוֹרְשִׂין לְתוֹכוֹ מְצוּדוֹת וְאֵין שׁוֹטְחִין עַל גַּגּוֹ פֵּרוֹת וְאֵין עוֹשִׂין אוֹתוֹ קַפֶּנְדַּרְיָא שֶׁנֶּאֱמַר וַהֲשִׁמּוֹתִי אֶת מִקְדְּשֵׁיכֶם. קְדוּשָּׁתָן אַף כְּשֶׁהֵן שׁוֹמֵמִין. עָלוּ בוֹ עֲשָׂבִים לֹא יִתְלוֹשׁ מִפְּנֵי עָגְמַת נֶפֶשׁ:

Mishnah 4: In addition, Rebbi Jehudah said, in a destroyed synagogue[78] one does not eulogize, nor twine ropes, nor set in it traps, nor on its roof lay out produce[79], nor use it as a short-cut[80], for it is said[81], *I shall lay waste your holy places*, they are in their holiness even if laid waste. If grasses are growing there one shall not tear them out because of the bad feeling[82].

78 Collapsed, destroyed by fire, or otherwise unusable.
79 For example to make raisins or fig cakes.
80 Latin *compendiarium* (*iter*).
81 *Lev.* 26:31.
82 People should feel badly enough in seeing weeds grow that they raise the money to rebuild the synagogue.

(74a line 57) הלכה ד: הָדָא דְאַתְּ אָמַר בְּבֵית הַכְּנֶסֶת שֶׁלְיָחִיד. אֲבָל בְּבֵית הַכְּנֶסֶת שֶׁלְרַבִּים אֲפִילוּ בָּנוּי אָסוּר. אָמַר רִבִּי חִייָה בַּר בָּא. רִבִּי יוֹחָנָן מֵיקַל לַנַּשְׁיָיא דְשָׁטְחָן בִּגְדֵיהוֹן עַל אֲוִירָא דְּבֵי מִדְרָשָׁא.

Halakhah 4: This you are saying for a private synagogue. But for a public synagogue it is forbidden even if it is built up[83]. Rebbi Hiyya bar Abba said, Rebbi Johanan was cursing women who hung their clothing in the air of the study hall.

83 For an existing private synagogue the owner can give permission for use. For a public one there is nobody who would have the authority to give permission.

(74a line 59) שְׁמוּאֵל אָמַר. נִכְנַס שֶׁלֹּא לַעֲשׂוֹתוֹ קַפַּנְדַּרְיָא מוּתָּר לַעֲשׂוֹתוֹ קַפַּנְדַּרְיָא. תַּנֵּי. בָּתֵּי כְנֵסִיּוֹת וּבָתֵּי מִדְרָשׁוֹת אֵין נוֹהֲגִין בָּהֶן קַלּוּת רֹאשׁ. לָא אוֹכְלִין וְלֹא שׁוֹתִין בָּהֶן וְלֹא מְטַיְילִין בָּהֶן וְלֹא יְשֵׁנִים בָּהֶן וְלֹא נִכְנָסִין בָּהֶן לֹא בַחַמָּה בִּימוֹת הַחַמָּה וְלֹא בַגְשָׁמִים בִּמוֹת הַגְּשָׁמִים. אֲבָל שׁוֹנִין וְדוֹרְשִׁין בָּהֶן. רִבִּי יְהוֹשֻׁעַ בֶּן לֵוִי אָמַר. בָּתֵּי כְנֵסִיּוֹת וּבָתֵּי מִדְרָשׁוֹת לַחֲכָמִים וּלְתַלְמִידֵיהֶם. רִבִּי חִייָה רִבִּי יָסָא מִיקַבְּלִין בְּגוֹ כְנִישְׁתָּא. רִבִּי אִימִּי מְפַקַּד לְסַפְרַיָּא. אִין אֲתָא בַּר נַשׁ מְלַכְלַךְ בְּאוֹרַיְיתָא [וְלַגַבְּכוֹן] תְּהַוֹון מְקַבְּלִין לֵיהּ וּלְחַמְרֵיהּ וּלְמָנוֹי. רִבִּי בֶּרֶכְיָה אֲזַל לִכְנִישְׁתָּא דְבֵית שְׁאָן. חֲמָא בַּר נַשׁ מַשְׁזִיג יָדוֹי וְרַגְלוֹי מִן גּוֹרְנָה. אֲמַר לֵיהּ. אָסִיר לָךְ. לְמָחָר חַמְתֵּא הַהוּא גַבְרָא מַשְׁזִיג יָדוֹי וְרַגְלוֹי מִן גּוֹרְנָה. אֲמַר לֵיהּ. רִבִּי. לָךְ שָׁרֵי וְלִי אֲסִיר. אֲמַר לֵיהּ. אִין. אֲמַר לֵיהּ. לָמָּה. אֲמַר לֵיהּ. כֵּן אָמַר רִבִּי יְהוֹשֻׁעַ בֶּן לֵוִי. בָּתֵּי כְנֵסִיּוֹת וּבָתֵּי מִדְרָשׁוֹת לַחֲכָמִים וּלְתַלְמִידֵיהֶם. הָהֵן פְּרָוְורָה מָהוּ מִיעֲבוֹר בְּגַוֵּיהּ. רִבִּי אַבָּהוּ עָבַר בִּפְרָוְורָה. מַה דְשָׁרֵי. אָמַר רִבִּי זְכַרְיָה חַתְנֵיהּ דְּרִבִּי לֵוִי. סַפְרָא הֲוָה אֵימָתָן וְאִין לָא הֲוָה רִבִּי אַבָּהוּ עָבַר לָא הֲוָה מִפְּנֵי טַלְיָיא.

Samuel said, if he entered without intending to use it as a short-cut he may use it as short-cut[84]. It was stated[85]: "One may not behave unbecomingly in synagogues and houses of study. One neither eats nor drinks in them, nor takes walks in them, nor sleeps in them, nor enters into them because of the sun in summer or because of the rain in winter, but one studies and preaches in them." Rebbi Joshua ben Levi said, synagogues and houses of study are for the sages and their students[86]. Rebbi Hiyya, Rebbi Yasa were received in the synagogue.[87] Rebbi Immi commanded to the teachers, if a person comes to you who is dirtied by study[88], accept him and his donkey and his implements. Rebbi Berekhiah went to the synagogue of Bet-Shean. He saw a man washing his hands and feet from its pail. He told him, it is forbidden to you. On the next day this man saw him washing his hands and feet from its pail. He said to him, Rabbi, to you it is permitted and to me it is forbidden? He answered him, yes. He asked, why? He said to him, so says Rebbi Joshua ben Levi: synagogues and houses of study are for the sages and their students. These fore-courts, may one pass through them[89]? Rebbi Abbahu passed through its fore-court. Is it permitted[90]? Rebbi Zachariah the son-in-law of Rebbi Levi said, the teacher was intimidating and if Rebbi Abbahu had not passed through he would not have let go the children[91].

84 If somebody enters for a legitimate reason, if then he leaves he may use the exit closest to his destination even if his total path then shows that he shortened his route by passing through the house of study. Babli 29a.

85 Tosephta 2:18, Babli 28a.

86 He disagrees with the Tosephta and permits Sages and students to use synagogues and houses of study as dormitories. Babli 28b.

87 They are reported to have taught at many different places. When they were traveling they stayed at synagogues.

88 If it is clear that he studied, even if not at the level of any degree.

89 Even though one may not take a short-cut through a synagogue or a house of study, what is the rule about the surrounding real estate?

90 Does the act of R. Abbahu show that fore-courts may be used as short-cuts?

91 In this version, the fore-courts have the same status as the houses of study themselves and may be used as short-cuts only if one enters for a legitimate reason.

(fol. 73c) **משנה ה:** רֹאשׁ חֹדֶשׁ אֲדָר שֶׁחָל לִהְיוֹת בְּשַׁבָּת קוֹרִין בְּפָרָשַׁת שְׁקָלִים. חָל לִהְיוֹת בְּתוֹךְ הַשַּׁבָּת מַקְדִּימִין לְשֶׁעָבַר וּמַפְסִיקִין לְשַׁבָּת אַחֶרֶת.

Mishnah 5: If the New Moon of Adar falls on a Sabbath, one reads the paragraph of *Šeqalim*[92]. If it falls on a weekday one precedes it and interrupts the next Sabbath[93].

92 The Mishnah follows the Palestinian rule that one never reads from more than one Torah scroll in the morning service of Sabbaths and holidays. The rule is that one interrupts the regular sequence of Torah readings (in the 3½ year cycle) and reads the paragraph about *Šeqalim* (*Ex.* 30:11-16) on or just preceding the start of Adar (in an intercalary year, Adar II), then about Amaleq (*Deut.* 25:17-19) on the Sabbath preceding Purim, about purification through the ashes of the Red Cow (*Num.* 19:1-22) on the Sabbath after Purim and about the coming Passover (*Ex.* 12:1-20) on the Sabbath preceding or on the New Moon of Nisan. Since 7 readers have to be called and each of them has to read at least three verses, in most cases this means that the paragraph has to be read several times.

93 One interrupts with the special readings and returns to the regular reading cycle. Between *Šeqalim* and Purim there always is one regular reading; between Purim and Nisan there may or may not be a regular reading.

(74a line 74) **הלכה ה:** רִבִּי לֵוִי בְשֵׁם רִבִּי שִׁמְעוֹן בֶּן לָקִישׁ. צָפָה הַקָּדוֹשׁ בָּרוּךְ הוּא שֶׁהָמָן הָרָשָׁע עָתִיד לִשְׁקוֹל כַּסְפּוֹ עַל יִשְׂרָאֵל. אָמַר. מוּטָב שֶׁיַּקְדִּים כַּסְפָּן שֶׁלְּבָנַיי לְכַסְפּוֹ שֶׁלְּאוֹתוֹ הָרָשָׁע. לְפִיכָךְ מַקְדִּימִין וְקוֹרִין בְּפָרָשַׁת שְׁקָלִים.

Rebbi Levi in the name of Rebbi Simeon ben Laqish. The Holy One, praiuse to Him, saw that the evil Haman in the future would weigh his money against Israel. He said, it is better that my children's money should precede this evil one's money. Therefore one precedes and reads the paragraph about *Šeqalim*[94].

94 From Chapter 1:7, Note 121.

(74a line 76) חָל לִהְיוֹת בְּעֶרֶב שַׁבָּת בְּמַה קוֹרִין. רִבִּי זְעוּרָה אָמַר. קוֹרִין לְשֶׁעָבַר. רִבִּי אִילָא רִבִּי אַבָּהוּ בְשֵׁם רִבִּי יוֹחָנָן. קוֹרִין לָבָא. וַהֲוָה רִבִּי זְעוּרָה מִסְתַּכֵּל בֵּיהּ. אֲמַר לֵיהּ. מָה אַתְּ מִסְתַּכֵּל בִּי. אֲנָא אֲמַר לָךְ מִן שְׁמוּעָה וְאַתְּ אֲמַר מִן דִּיעָה וְאַתְּ מִסְתַּכֵּל בִּי. מַתְנִיתָהּ מְסַייְעָא לְדֵין וּמַתְנִיתָהּ מְסַייְעָא לְדֵין. מַתְנִיתָהּ מְסַייְעָא לְרִבִּי זְעוּרָה. אֵי זוֹ הִיא שַׁבָּת הָרִאשׁוֹנָה. כָּל-שֶׁחָל רֹאשׁ חוֹדֶשׁ שֶׁלַּאֲדָר לִהְיוֹת בְּתוֹכָהּ. אֲפִילוּ בְּעֶרֶב שַׁבָּת. תַּנֵּי שְׁמוּאֵל מְסַייְעָא לְרִבִּי אִילָא. אֵי זוֹ הִיא שַׁבָּת הַשְּׁנִייָה. כָּל-שֶׁחָל הַפּוּרִים לִהְיוֹת בְּתוֹכָהּ. וַאֲפִילוּ עֶרֶב שַׁבָּת. רַב נַחְמָן

בַּר יַעֲקֹב בָּעֵי. הַגַּע עַצְמָךְ שֶׁחָל חֲמִשָּׁה עָשָׂר לִהְיוֹת בַּשַּׁבָּת. לִקְרוֹת בִּמְגִילַת אֶסְתֵּר אֵין אַתְּ יָכוֹל. שֶׁאֵין קוֹרִין בְּכִתְבֵי הַקּוֹדֶשׁ אֶלָּא מִן הַמִּנְחָה וּלְמַעֲלָן. וְיִקְרְאוּ זָכוֹר. אָמַר לֵיהּ. כֵּן אָמַר רַב. וְהַיָּמִים הָאֵלֶּה נִזְכָּרִים וְנַעֲשִׂים. שֶׁתְּהֵא אַזְכָּרָתָן קוֹדֶם לַעֲשִׂיָּיתָן. רִבִּי אַבָּא בְּרֵיהּ דְּרִבִּי פַּפֵּי בָּעֵי. הַגַּע עַצְמָךְ שֶׁחָל אַרְבָּעָה עָשָׂר לִהְיוֹת בַּשַּׁבָּת. הֲרֵי שֶׁקְּדָמָה אַזְכָּרָתָן לַעֲשִׂיָּיתָן. אָמַר לֵיהּ. וְלֹא כְבַר אִיתוֹתָבַת דְּלֵית אֵיפְשָׁר. וְאִם אֵיפְשָׁר אִיחוּר הוּא לַעֲיָירוֹת.

What does one read if it[95] falls on a Friday? Rebbi Ze`ira says, one reads earlier[96]. Rebbi Ila, Rebbi Abbahu in the name of Rebbi Joḥanan: one reads later[97]. Rebbi Ze`ira was looking at him. He said to him, why are you looking at me? I said to you from tradition, and you are saying an opinion[98]; why are you looking at me? A *baraita* supports one and a *baraita* supports the other. A *baraita* supports Rebbi Ze`ira: What is the first week? Any in which the New Month of Adar falls, even on Friday. What Samuel stated supports Rebbi Ila: What is the second week[99]? Any in which Purim falls, even on Friday. Rav Naḥman bar Jacob asked, think of it if the Fifteenth fell on a Sabbath? You may not read in the Esther scroll since one reads in Hagiographs only after afternoon prayers[100]. Could they not read *remember*[101]? He said to him, so says Rav, *these days are remembered and executed*[102], that the remembrance precedes the execution. Rebbi Abba the son of Rebbi Pappai asked, think of it if the Fourteenth fell on a Sabbath? Does not the remembrance precede the execution[103]? He said to him, was this not already contradicted, it cannot happen[104]. And if it could happen it would be belated for towns[105].

95 The New Moon of Adar.
96 The Sabbath preceding. Babli 30a.
97 The Sabbath following. Babli 30a.
98 R. Ila quotes R. Joḥanan while R. Ze`ira holds his opinion as a logical inference from Mishnah 5.
99 The problem is that as they are formulated Mishnaiot 5 and 6 contradict one another. Mishnah 5 states that if *Šeqalim* is read before the day of New Moon then on the next Sabbath one reads a section in the regular sequence of Torah reading while Mishnah 6 supposes that one reads the 4 extra paragraphs (Note 92) one after the other without interruption and only afterwards returns to the regular readings. This is possible only if *Šeqalim* is read later and justifies R. Joḥanan. Babli 30a.
100 It seems from the old Midrash collections that after the Torah reading in the afternoon of the Sabbath one read a *Haftara* from Hagiographs, while in the morning the public reading after the Torah reading had to be from Prophets.
101 The reading *Deut.* 25:17-19.
102 *Esth.* 9:28.

| 103 If one reads about Amaleq on the 14th and then, because the Scroll cannot be read on the Sabbath one reads it on the 15th, Rav's condition is satisfied.
104 In the computed calendar; Chapter 1 | Note 89.
105 Since it was determined that the Scroll may not be read after the appointed time (Chapter 1 Note 12), one would have to read the Scroll in towns on the 12th or the 13th. |
|---|---|

(fol. 73c) **משנה ו**: בַּשְּׁנִיָּה זָכוֹר. בַּשְּׁלִישִׁית פָּרָה אֲדוּמָּה. בָּרְבִיעִית הַחֹדֶשׁ הַזֶּה לָכֶם. בַּחֲמִישִׁית חוֹזְרִין לְכִסְדְּרָן. לַכֹּל מַפְסִיקִין לְרָאשֵׁי חֳדָשִׁים לַחֲנוּכָּה וּלְפוּרִים בַּתַעֲנִיּוֹת וּבַמַּעֲמָדוֹת וּבְיוֹם הַכִּפּוּרִים.

Mishnah 6: On the second, *red cow*[92]. On the third, *this month is for you*[92]. On the fifth one returns to the regular sequence. One interrupts[106] for everything, for New Months, for Ḥanukkah, and for Purim, on fast days, and for bystanders[107] and on the Day of Atonement.

106 The regular sequence of readings is interrupted for any special occasions (when in the Babylonian rite usually a second Torah scroll is used).	107 To support the local priests who went serving in the Temple; *Ta`aniot* 4:1 Note 4, 4:2, Note 77.

(74b line 14) **הלכה ו**: רִבִּי בָּא בְשֵׁם רִבִּי חִייָה בַּר אַשִׁי. אֵין מַפְסִיקִין בֵּין פּוּרִים לְפָרָה. רִבִּי לֵוִי בְשֵׁם רִבִּי חָמָא בַּר חֲנִינָה. אֵין מַפְסִיקִין בֵּין פָּרָה לְהַחוֹדֶשׁ. אָמַר רִבִּי לֵוִי. סִימָנֵיהוֹן דְּאִילֵּין פֵּרָשָׁתָא. בֵּין הַכּוֹסוֹת הַלָּלוּ אִם רוֹצֶה לִשְׁתּוֹת יִשְׁתֶּה. בֵּין שְׁלִישִׁי לִרְבִיעִי לֹא יִשְׁתֶּה. רִבִּי לֵוִי בְשֵׁם רִבִּי חָמָא בַּר חֲנִינָה. בְּדִין הוּא שֶׁתִּקְדּוֹם הַחוֹדֶשׁ לְפָרָה. שֶׁבְּאֶחָד לַנִּיסָן הוּקַם הַמִּשְׁכָּן וּבַשֵּׁינִי נִשְׂרְפָה הַפָּרָה. וְלָמָּה פָרָה קוֹדֶמֶת. שֶׁהִיא טָהֳרָתָן שֶׁלְכָּל־יִשְׂרָאֵל.

Halakhah 6: Rebbi Abba in the name of Rebbi Ḥiyya bar Ashi: One does not interrupt between Purim and *cow*. Rebbi Levi in the name of Rebbi Ḥama bar Ḥanina: One does not interrupt between *cow* and *this month*[108]. Rebbi Levi said, a sign for these paragraphs, "between these cups, he may drink if he wants to drink; between the third and the fourth he may not drink.[109]" Rebbi Levi in the name of Rebbi Ḥama bar Ḥanina, it would have been logical that *this month* should precede *cow* since the Tabernacle was erected on the First of Nisan and the cow was burned on the Second[110]. Why does *cow* precede? Because it is the purification of all of Israel.

108 Babli 30a.

109 Babli 30a. The Babli points out that the tradition of R. Ḥama bar Ḥanina contradicts that of R. Ḥiyya bar Ashi if Purim falls on Thursday and therefore the first of Nisan falls on the Sabbath.

109 Mishnah *Pesahim* 10:8. This permits interruptions between first, second, and third special Torah readings.

110 *Seder Olam* Chapter 7.

(74b line 20) יִרְמְיָה סָפְרָא שָׁאַל לְרַב יִרְמְיָה. רֹאשׁ חוֹדֶשׁ שֶׁחָל לִהְיוֹת בַּשַּׁבָּת בַּמֶּה קוֹרִין. אָמַר לֵיהּ. קוֹרִין בְּרֹאשׁ חוֹדֶשׁ. אָמַר רִבִּי חֶלְבּוֹ קוֹמֵי רִבִּי אִימִּי. מַתְנִיתָא אָמְרָה כֵן. לַכֹּל מַפְסִיקִין. לְרָאשֵׁי חֳדָשִׁים לַחֲנוּכָּה וּלְפוּרִים.

יִצְחָק סְחוֹרָה שָׁאַל לְרִבִּי יִצְחָק. רֹאשׁ חוֹדֶשׁ שֶׁחָל לִהְיוֹת בַּחֲנוּכָּה בַּמֶּה קוֹרִין. אָמַר לֵיהּ. קוֹרִין שְׁלֹשָׁה בְּרֹאשׁ חוֹדֶשׁ וְאֶחָד בַּחֲנוּכָּה. רִבִּי פִּינְחָס רִבִּי סִימוֹן וְרִבִּי אַבָּא בַּר זְמִינָא מַטֵּי בָהּ בְּשֵׁם רִבִּי אֶבְדּוּמָא דְחֵיפָה. קוֹרִין שְׁלֹשָׁה בַּחֲנוּכָּה וְאֶחָד בְּרֹאשׁ חוֹדֶשׁ. לְהוֹדִיעֲךָ שֶׁלֹּא בָא הָרְבִיעִי אֶלָּא מַחֲמַת רֹאשׁ חוֹדֶשׁ. בַּר שִׁילְמִיָה סָפְרָא שָׁאַל לְרִבִּי מָנָא. הַגַּע עַצְמְךָ שֶׁחָל רֹאשׁ חוֹדֶשׁ שֶׁלַּחֲנוּכָּה לִהְיוֹת בַּשַּׁבָּת. וְלֹא שִׁבְעָה קְרוּיִין אִינּוּן. אִית לָךְ מֵימַר שֶׁלֹּא בָא הָרְבִיעִי אֶלָּא מַחֲמַת רֹאשׁ חוֹדֶשׁ. אָמַר לֵיהּ. וְהָדָא שְׁאִילְתֵּיהּ דְּסַפָּר.

[111]Jeremiah the Scribe asked before Rav Jeremiah: What does one read if the day of the New Moon is a Sabbath? He said to him: One reads about the New Moon. Rebbi Ḥelbo said before Rebbi Immi: The Mishnah says so: "One interrupts for everything, for New Moons, for Ḥanukkah, and for Purim."

Isaac the trader asked Rebbi Isaac: What does one read on a New Moon that falls on Ḥanukkah? He said to him: Three for the New Moon and one for Ḥanukkah. Rebbi Phineas, Rebbi Simon, Rebbi Abba bar Zamina brought it in the name of Rebbi Eudaimon of Haifa: Three read of Ḥanukka and one of the New Moon, to tell you that the fourth one comes only because of the New Moon. Bar Shelemiah the scribe asked Rebbi Mana: Think of it, if the New Moon of Ḥanukkah falls on a Sabbath, do not seven read? How can you say, to tell you that the fourth one comes only because of the New Moon? He said to him: That is a true question of a scribe.

111 This is from *Ta`aniot* 4:1, Notes 54-56.

(fol. 73c) **משנה ז**: בַּפֶּסַח קוֹרִין בְּפָרָשַׁת מוֹעֲדוֹת שֶׁבְּתוֹרַת כֹּהֲנִים. בָּעֲצֶרֶת שִׁבְעָה שָׁבוּעוֹת. בְּרֹאשׁ הַשָּׁנָה בַּחֹדֶשׁ הַשְּׁבִיעִי. בְּיוֹם הַכִּפּוּרִים אַחֲרֵי מוֹת. בְּיוֹם טוֹב הָרִאשׁוֹן שֶׁל חָג קוֹרִין בְּפָרָשַׁת מוֹעֲדוֹת שֶׁבְּתוֹרַת כֹּהֲנִים וּשְׁאָר כָּל־יְמוֹת הֶחָג קוֹרִין בְּקָרְבְּנוֹת הֶחָג:

Mishnah 7: On Passover one reads the section about holidays in *Leviticus*[112]. On Pentecost, *seven weeks*[113]. On New Year's Day, *in the Seventh month on the First of the month*[114] On the Day of Atonement, *after the death*[115] On the first day of Tabernacles one reads the section about holidays in *Leviticus*; on the remaining days about the sacrifices of the holiday[116].

112 *Lev*. 23:1-44.
113 *Deut*. 16:9-12 to be repeated five times.
114 *Lev*. 23:23-25 to be repeated five times.
115 *Lev*. 17:1-34.
116 The appropriate verses from *Num*. 29:17-39.

(74b line 31) **הלכה ז**: וּבָעֲצֶרֶת שִׁבְעָה שָׁבוּעוֹת. אִית תַּנָּיֵי תַנֵּי. בַּחוֹדֶשׁ הַשְּׁלִישִׁי. וּבְרֹאשׁ הַשָּׁנָה וּבַחוֹדֶשׁ הַשְּׁבִיעִי. אִית תַּנָּיֵי תַנֵּי. וַיְיָ פָּקַד אֶת־שָׂרָה. בְּיוֹם הַכִּפּוּרִים אַחֲרֵי מוֹת. וּבְיוֹם טוֹב הָרִאשׁוֹן שֶׁל חָג קוֹרִין בְּפָרָשַׁת מוֹעֲדוֹת שֶׁבְּתוֹרַת כֹּהֲנִים וּשְׁאָר כָּל־יְמוֹת הֶחָג קוֹרִין בְּקָרְבְּנוֹת הֶחָג: רִבִּי יַעֲקֹב בַּר אֲחָא בְּשֵׁם רִבִּי יָסָא. לְלַמְּדָךְ שֶׁאֵין הָעוֹלָם עוֹמֵד אֶלָּא עַל הַקָּרְבָּנוֹת.

Halakhah 7: "On Pentecost, *seven weeks*." There are Tannaim who state, *in the third month*[117] "And on New Year's Day, *and in the Seventh month*[118]." There are Tannaim who state, *and the Eternal counted Sarah*[119]. "On the Day of Atonement, *after the death*. On the first day of Tabernacles one reads the section about holidays in *Leviticus*; on the remaining days about the sacrifices of the holiday." Rebbi Jacob bar Aḥa in the name of Rebbi Yasa, to teach you that the world only exists by the sacrifices.

117 *Ex*. Chapters 19-20. While Pharisaic and Sadducee traditions differ about the date of Pentecost, both are in agreement that the holiday celebrates the anniversary of the theophany of Sinai and the giving of the Ten Commandments, the theme of these Chapters. Tosephta 3:5.
118 In this version the reading is *Num*. 29:1-5.
119 *Gen*. Chapter 21. The reading is appropriate because v. 21:17 states that a person is judged only by his state at the moment of judgment; if he is repentant then his prior misdeeds are disregarded; a proper reading for the Day of Judgment. Tosephta 3:6 For the Babylonian rite, Babli 31a.

(74b line 36) תַּמָּן תַּנִּינָן. שִׁמְעוֹן הַצַּדִּיק הָיָה מִשְּׁיָרֵי כְּנֶסֶת הַגְּדוֹלָה. הוּא הָיָה אוֹמֵר. עַל שְׁלֹשָׁה דְבָרִים הָעוֹלָם עוֹמֵד. עַל הַתּוֹרָה וְעַל הָעֲבוֹדָה וְעַל גְּמִילוּת חֲסָדִים: וּשְׁלָשְׁתָּן בְּפָסוּק אֶחָד. וָאָשִׂים דְּבָרַי בְּפִיךָ. זֶה תַלְמוּד תּוֹרָה. וּבְצֵל יָדִי כִּסִּיתִיךָ. זוֹ גְמִילוּת חֲסָדִים. לְלַמְּדָךְ שֶׁכָּל־מִי שֶׁהוּא עוֹסֵק בַּתּוֹרָה וּבִגְמִילוּת חֲסָדִים זוֹכֶה לֵישֵׁב בְּצִילּוֹ שֶׁלְהַקָּדוֹשׁ בָּרוּךְ הוּא. הֲדָא הִיא דִכְתִיב מַה־יָּקָר חַסְדְּךָ אֱלֹהִים וּבְנֵי אָדָם בְּצֵל כְּנָפֶיךָ יֶחֱסָיוּן: לִנְטוֹעַ שָׁמַיִם וְלִיסוֹד אָרֶץ. אִילּוּ הַקָּרְבָּנוֹת. וְלֵאמֹר לְצִיּוֹן עַמִּי־אָתָּה: אָמַר רִבִּי חִינָנָא בַּר פָּפָּא. חִיזַּרְנוּ עַל כָּל־הַמִּקְרָא וְלֹא מָצֵאנוּ שֶׁנִּקְרְאוּ יִשְׂרָאֵל צִיּוֹן אֶלָּא זֶה. וְלֵאמֹר לְצִיּוֹן עַמִּי־אָתָּה: תַּמָּן תַּנִּינָן. רַבָּן שִׁמְעוֹן בֶּן גַּמְלִיאֵל אוֹמֵר. עַל שְׁלֹשָׁה דְבָרִים הָעוֹלָם עוֹמֵד. עַל הַדִּין וְעַל הָאֱמֶת וְעַל הַשָּׁלוֹם. וּשְׁלָשְׁתָּן דָּבָר אֶחָד הֵן. נַעֲשָׂה הַדִּין נַעֲשָׂה אֱמֶת. נַעֲשָׂה אֱמֶת נַעֲשָׂה הַשָּׁלוֹם. אָמַר רִבִּי מָנָא. וּשְׁלָשְׁתָּן בְּפָסוּק אֶחָד. אֱמֶת וּמִשְׁפַּט שָׁלוֹם שִׁפְטוּ בְּשַׁעֲרֵיכֶם:

[120]There, we stated: "Simeon the Just was of the remainders of the Great Assembly. He used to say, the world continues to exist by three things, by the Torah, by worship, and by labors of love" All three are in one verse: *I shall put My word in your mouth*, that is Torah. *By the shadow of My hands I shall cover you*, these are labors of love; to teach you that he who is occupied with Torah and labors of love merits to dwell in the shadow of the Holy One, praise to Him. That is what is written, *how precious is Your grace, o God, and humans take shelter in Your wings' shadow. To plant the Heavens and give foundation to the earth*, these are the sacrifices, *and to say to Zion, you are My people*. Rebbi Ḥinena bar Pappa said, we went over all of Scripture and only found this one that Israel was called Zion, *and to say to Zion, you are My people*. There, we stated: "Rabban Simeon ben Gamliel says, the world is existing on three things, on justice, on truth, and on peace. All three are one: If justice is done, truth is accomplished. If truth is accomplished, peace is established. Rebbi Mana said, and all are in one verse, *judge truth and law of peace in your gates*.

120 From Ta`aniot 4:2, Notes 134-139.

(fol. 73d) **משנה ח**: בַּחֲנוּכָּה בַּנְּשִׂיאִים. בַּפּוּרִים וַיָּבֹא עֲמָלֵק. בְּרָאשֵׁי חֳדָשִׁים וּבְרָאשֵׁי חָדְשֵׁיכֶם. בַּמַּעֲמָדוֹת בְּמַעֲשֵׂה בְרֵאשִׁית. בַּתַּעֲנִיּוֹת בְּרָכוֹת וּקְלָלוֹת. אֵין מַפְסִיקִין בַּקְּלָלוֹת אֶלָּא אֶחָד קוֹרֵא אֶת כּוּלָּן. בַּשֵּׁנִי וּבַחֲמִישִׁי וּבְשַׁבָּת בַּמִּנְחָה קוֹרִין כְּסִדְרָן וְאֵינוּ עוֹלֶה לָהֶן מִן הַחֶשְׁבּוֹן שֶׁנֶּאֱמַר וַיְדַבֵּר מֹשֶׁה אֶת מֹעֲדֵי ה' אֶל בְּנֵי יִשְׂרָאֵל מִצְוָתָן שֶׁיְּהוּ קוֹרִין כָּל־אֶחָד וְאֶחָד בִּזְמַנּוֹ:

Mishnah 8: On Hanukkah, about the princes[121]. On Purim, *Amaleq came*[122]. On New Moons, *on the start of your months*[123]. For the bystanders, the Creation[124]. On fast days, blessings and curses[125]. One does not interrupt curses, but one person reads them entirely. On Monday, Thursday, and Sabbath afternoon one reads regularly but they may not count it in the series[126], as it is said[127], *Moses spoke to the Children of Israel about the holidays of the Eternal*; the obligation is that each one be read in its time.

121 *Num.* 7:12-59 (-89), on each day of Hanukkah one reads the princes' offerings for that day of the dedication of the Tabernacle.
122 *Ex.* 17:8-16.
123 *Num.* 28:11-15.
124 On each day of the week one reads the corresponding day of Creation; *Gen.* 1:1-2:3.
125 Either *Lev.* 26:3-46 or *Deut.* Chapter 28.
126 One reads the start of the portion to be read on the next Sabbath; this has no influence on the text to be read on the Sabbath.
127 *Lev.* 23:44.

(74b line 49) **הלכה ח**: אֵין מַפְסִיקִין בַּקְּלָלוֹת. אָמַר רִבִּי חִייָה בַּר גַּמְדָּא. אַל תָּקוּץ בְּתוֹכַחְתּוֹ. אַל תַּעֲשֵׂם קוֹצִים קוֹצִים. אָמַר רִבִּי לֵוִי. אָמַר הַקָּדוֹשׁ בָּרוּךְ הוּא. אֵינוֹ בְדִין שֶׁיְּהוּ בָנַיי מִתְקַלְלִים וַאֲנִי מִתְבָּרֵךְ. אָמַר רִבִּי יוֹסֵה בֵּירִבִּי בּוּן. לֹא מִטַּעַם הַזֶּה. אֶלָּא זֶה שֶׁהוּא עוֹמֵד לִקְרוֹת בַּתּוֹרָה צָרִיךְ שֶׁיְּהֵא פוֹתֵחַ בְּדָבָר טוֹב וְחוֹתֵם בְּדָבָר טוֹב. לֵוִי בַּר פָּאטִי שָׁאַל לְרַב חוּנָה. אִילֵּין אָרוּרַיָּיא מָהוּ דִיקְרִינוֹן חַד וִיבָרֵךְ לִפְנֵיהֶן וּלְאַחֲרֵיהֶן. אָמַר לֵיהּ. אֵין לָךְ טָעוּן בְּרָכָה לְפָנָיו וּלְאַחֲרָיו אֶלָּא קַלָּלוֹת שֶׁבְּתוֹרַת כֹּהֲנִים וּקְלָלוֹת שֶׁבְּמִשְׁנֵה תוֹרָה. רִבִּי יוֹנָתָן סַפְרָא דְגוּפְתָא נְחַת לְהָכָא. חֲמָא לְבַר אָבוּנָא סַפְרָא קָרֵי שִׁירַת הַבְּאֵר וּמְבָרֵךְ לְפָנֶיהָ וּלְאַחֲרֶיהָ. אֲמַר לֵיהּ. וְעָבְדִין כֵּן. אֲמַר לֵיהּ. וַאֲדַיִין אַתְּ לְזוֹ. כָּל־הַשִּׁירוֹת טְעוּנוֹת בְּרָכָה לִפְנֵיהֶן וּלְאַחֲרֵיהֶן. אִישְׁתְּאָלַת לְרִבִּי סִימוֹן. אָמַר לוֹן רִבִּי סִימוֹן בְּשֵׁם רִבִּי יְהוֹשֻׁעַ בֶּן לֵוִי. אֵין לָךְ טָעוּן בְּרָכָה לְפָנָיו וּלְאַחֲרָיו אֶלָּא שִׁירַת הַיָּם וַעֲשֶׂרֶת הַדִּבְּרוֹת וּקְלָלוֹת [שֶׁבְּתוֹרַת כֹּהֲנִים וּקְלָלוֹת] שֶׁבְּמִשְׁנֵה תוֹרָה. אָמַר רִבִּי אַבָּהוּ. אֲנִי לֹא שְׁמַעְתִּי. נִרְאִין דְּבָרִים בַּעֲשֶׂרֶת הַדִּבְּרוֹת. רִבִּי יוֹסֵה בֵּירִבִּי בּוּן. תּוּמָנְתֵּי פְּסוּקַיָּיא אַחֲרַיָּיא דְּמִשְׁנֵה תוֹרָה טְעוּנִין בְּרָכָה לִפְנֵיהֶן וּלְאַחֲרֵיהֶן. בְּלֹא כָךְ אֵין הַפּוֹתֵחַ וְהַחוֹתֵם מְבָרֵךְ לְפָנֶיהָ וּלְאַחֲרֶיהָ. לָכֵן צְרִיכָה. רֹאשׁ חוֹדֶשׁ שֶׁחָל לִהְיוֹת בַּשַּׁבָּת.

Halakhah 8: "One does not interrupt curses." Rebbi Hiyya bar Gamda said, *do not be repelled by his reproach*[128], do not split it into many thorns[129]. Rebbi Levi said, the Holy One, praise to Him, said that it is not logical that My children be cursed and I praised. Rebbi Yose ben Rebbi Abun said, not because of that reason[130] but because one who stands up to read in the Torah needs to start with something good and conclude with something good. Levi bar Paṭi asked Rav Huna: these curses[131] which we read as one, should one recite a benediction before and after? He said to him, nothing needs a benediction before and after except the curses in *Leviticus* and the curses in *Deuteronomy*[125]. Rebbi Jonathan the scribe of Gufta came down here[132]; he saw Bar Abuna reading the Song of the Well[133] and recite a benediction before and after. He said to him, does one do this? He answered him, you still are about this? All songs need a benediction before and after. Rebbi Simon was asked. Rebbi Simon told them in the name of Rebbi Joshua ben Levi, only the Song on the Sea[134], and the Ten Commandments, and the curses [in *Leviticus* and the curses][135] in *Deuteronomy* need a benediction before and after. Rebbi Abbahu said, I did not hear[136]. It seems reasonable for the Ten Commandments[137]. Rebbi Yose ben Rebbi Abun: the eight verses in *Deuteronomy*[138] need a benediction before and after. Without this do not the one who starts and the one who finishes recite the benediction before and after[139]? But it is needed for a New Moon which falls on a Sabbath[140].

128 *Prov.* 3:11. Babli 31b. The entire paragraph is more or less reproduced in *Soferim* 12:1-6.

129 An untranslatable pun, identifying the roots קוץ "to be repelled" (Accadic קצץ "to be enraged") and קוץ "thorn" (without obvious cognate).

130 He rejects the homiletic reason given by preachers (accepted in the Babli 31b) and points to a simple technicality which makes stopping during the reading of the curses impossible.

131 The curse formulas *Deut.* 27:15-26.

132 To Tiberias.

133 *Num.* 21:17-20.

134 *Ex.* 15:1-19.

135 The addition by the corrector is questionable since the Babli requires benedictions only for the text of *Lev.* and excludes that of *Deut.*

136 The topic never came up in his studies.

137 The special treatment accorded here to the Song on the Sea and the Ten Commandments may be the reason for the Ashkenazic custom to stand during the recitation of these texts; a custom otherwise unexplained.

138 The last 8 verses, *Deut.* 34:5-12, about Moses's death and its aftermath, which are ascribed either to Joshua or to Moses who wrote them by Divine command without separation of words. Babli *Bava batra* 15a.

139 The original Palestinian usage was that a benediction was recited before the start of the Torah reading ("Who choose us from all peoples and gave us His Torah") and after the end ("Who gave us His Torah") recited, respectively, by the first reader before and the last reader after his reading. Separate benedictions for every reader, which make

all the preceding discussion unnecessary, are Babylonian usage. It follows that the benedictions mentioned here for the Song on the Sea, the Ten Commandments, and Blessings and Curses, must be different from the beginning and ending benedictions.

140 Since the reading has only 5 verses (Note 123) it cannot be split; the text has to be recited seven times. Since starting and finishing readers read the same text, it remains questionable why they should differ in their benedictions.

(74b line 65) אָמַר רִבִּי יוֹסֵה בֵּירִבִּי בּוּן. שִׁירַת הַלְוִיִּם לֹא יִפְחֲתוּ לָהּ מִשִּׁשָּׁה קְרִיאִיּוֹת. סִימָנֵיהּ הזי"ו ל"ך. רִבִּי זְעוּרָה רִבִּי יִרְמְיָה בְשֵׁם רַב. [שִׁירַת הַיָּם] וְשִׁירַת דְּבוֹרָה נְכְתָּבִים אֲרִיחַ עַל גַּבֵּי לְבֵינָה וּלְבֵינָה עַל גַּבֵּי אָרִיחַ. עֲשֶׂרֶת בְּנֵי הָמָן וּמַלְכֵי כְנַעַן נְכְתָּבִין אָרִיחַ עַל גַּבֵּי אָרִיחַ וּלְבֵינָה עַל גַּבֵּי לְבֵינָה. דְּכָל־בִּנְיָין דְּכֵן לָא קָאִים. מַאי כְדוֹן. לְמִצְוָה [אוֹ] לְעִיכּוּב. אָמַר רִבִּי לְרִבִּי חֲנַנְיָה בַּר אֲחוֹי דְּרַב הוֹשַׁעְיָה. נָהִיר אַתְּ דַּהֲוִינַן קַיָּימִים קֳדָם חָנוּתָהּ דְּרַב הוֹשַׁעְיָה חָבִיבָךְ. עָבַר רִבִּי בָא בַּר זַבְדָּא וּשְׁאִלְינַן לֵיהּ וַאֲמַר בְּשֵׁם רַב. לְעִיכּוּב.

[141]Rebbi Yose ben Rebbi Abun said, in the Levites' song they should not have less than six readings[142]; its mnemonic is *hazayu lak*[143]. Rebbi Ze'ira, Rebbi[144] Jeremiah in the name of Rav: [the Song on the Sea] and Deborah's song are written space on brick and brick on space[145]. The ten sons of Haman[146] and the kings of Canaan[147] are written space on space and brick on brick[148], since any such building will not stand. How is that, as meritorious act or as impediment[149]? Rebbi[150] said to Rebbi Ḥanania the son of Rav Hoshaia's brother, do you remember when we were standing in front of your uncle's store that Rebbi Abba bar Zavda passed by and we asked him when he said in the name of Rav: an impediment?

141 *Soferim* 12:8-12.
142 The song Mosis (*Deut.* 32:1-43), parts of which are sung during the presentation of the *musaf* sacrifice of Sabbath has to be split into six parts, to be sung during six consecutive Sabbaths.
143 The starting letters of verses 1,7,13,19,29,40 which determine the text to be sung. Babli *Roš Haššanah* 31a.
144 Read "Rav".
145 These songs have to be written

etc. Babli 16b.
146 *Esth.* 9:7-10.
147 *Jos.* 12:9-24.
148 These songs have to be written

etc.
149 If they are written differently, may the scroll be used in public service or not?
150 In *Soferim* 13:4: R. Yose bar Ḥanina the brother of Rebbi Hoshaia said . . .

(74b line 71) רִבִּי חִייָה בְּרֵיהּ דְּרִבִּי אָדָא דְיָפּוֹ בְשֵׁם רִבִּי זְעוּרָה. צָרִיךְ לְאוֹמְרָן בִּנְפִיחָה אַחַת וַעֲשֶׂרֶת בְּנֵי הָמָן עִמָּהֶן. אָמַר רִבִּי יוֹסֵי בֵּירִבִּי בּוּן. צָרִיךְ שֶׁיְּהֵא אִישׁ בְּרֹאשׁ דַּפָּא וְאֶת בְּסוֹפָהּ. שֶׁכֵּן הוּא (סְלִיק) [שְׁנִיץ] וּנְחַת כְּהָדֵין קֵונְטְרָה. רַב אָמַר. צָרִיךְ לֵאמַר. אָרוּר הָמָן אֲרוּרִים בָּנָיו. אָמַר רִבִּי פִּינְחָס. צָרִיךְ לוֹמַר. חַרְבּוֹנָה זָכוּר לַטּוֹב. רִבִּי בֶּרֶכְיָה רִבִּי יִרְמְיָה רִבִּי חִייָה בְשֵׁם רִבִּי יוֹחָנָן. רִבִּי יוֹנָתָן כַּד דַּהֲוָה מַטֵי לְהַהוּא פְסוּקָא אֲשֶׁר הֶגְלָה נְבוּכַדְנֶצַּר הֲוָה אֲמַר נְבוּכַדְנֶצַּר שְׁחִיק עֲצָמוֹת. שֶׁכָּל־ נְבוּכַדְנֶצַּר דִּכְתִיב בְּיִרְמְיָה חַי הָיָה. בְּרַם הָכָא מֵת הָיָה.

Rebbi Ḥiyya the son of Rebbi Ada from Jaffa in the name of Rebbi Ze`ira: One has to recite them in one breath together with "the ten sons of Haman.[151]" Rebbi Yose ben Rebbi Abun said, one has to write *ish* at the top of the column and *the* at the end[152] since so it (rises) [is compressed][153] and sinks like a plumb-line[154]. Rav said, one has to say[155], Haman be cursed, his sons be cursed. Rebbi Phineas said, one has to say, Harbona be remembered for good. Rebbi Berekhiah, Rebbi Jeremiah, Rebbi Ḥiyya in the name of Rebbi Joḥanan: When Rebbi Jonathan came to this verse, *whom Nebuchadnezzar exiled*[156], he used to say, Nebuchadnezzar, may his bones be pulverized; for all "Nebuchadnezzar" written in Jeremiah refer to the living, but here he was dead[157].

151 Verses 9:6-9 together with the first three words of v. 10 have to be recited in one breath. *Soferim* 13:5, Babli 16b.
152 The last word of *Esth.* 9:6 has to be on top of a column of 11 lines, under it the names of the ten sons of Haman. Otherwise the lines are empty except for the word ואת at the right end of the line for the first 10 lines. In contrast to what is prescribed here on the 11th line one currently writes עשרת at the end and then starts the next full column with בני המן. *Soferim* 13:6.
153 The corrector's change is from *Soferim*, to be deleted.
154 Greek κέντρον.
155 After the reading of the scroll. *Gen. rabba* 49(1).
156 *Esth.* 2:6.
157 *Gen. rabba* 49(1); *Soferim* 14:7.

(74c line 3) וְאֵין עוֹלֶה לָהֶם מִן הַחֶשְׁבּוֹן. אִית תַּנָּיֵי תַנֵּי. עוֹלֶה לָהֶם מִן הַחֶשְׁבּוֹן. רִבִּי זְעוּרָה אַבָּא בַּר יִרְמְיָה רַב מַתָּנָה בְשֵׁם שְׁמוּאֵל. הֲלָכָה כְּמִי שֶׁהוּא אוֹמֵר. אֵינוֹ עוֹלֶה לָהֶם מִן הַחֶשְׁבּוֹן. כְּמַתְנִיתִין.

"But they may not count it in the series." There are Tannaim who state, "they may count it in the series[158]." Rebbi Ze`ira, Abba bar Jeremiah, Rav

Mattanah in the name of Samuel: Practice follows him whom said, they may not count it in the series; as the Mishnah.

158 In Babli 31b and Tosephta 3:10, the Mishnah is attributed to R. Jehudah, who holds that at the place where one stops the reading on Sabbath morning there one starts the reading on the next Sabbath. Rebbi Meïr holds that where one stops Sabbath morning there one reads Sabbath afternoon; where one stops Sabbath afternoon there one reads on Monday, where one stops on Monday there one reads on Thursday; where one stops on Thursday there one reads on the next Sabbath morning.

(74c line 6) אִית תַּנָּיֵי תַנֵי. פּוֹתֵחַ וְרוֹאֶה גּוֹלֵל וּמְבָרֵךְ. אִית תַּנָּיֵי תַנֵי. פּוֹתֵחַ וְרוֹאֶה וּמְבָרֵךְ. רִבִּי זְעוּרָה אַבָּא בַּר יִרְמְיָה רַב מַתָּנָה בְשֵׁם שְׁמוּאֵל. הֲלָכָה כְמִי שֶׁהוּא אוֹמֵר. פּוֹתֵחַ וְרוֹאֶה וּמְבָרֵךְ. וּמָה טַעַם. וּכְפִתְחוֹ עָמְדוּ כָל־הָעָם. וּמָה כְתִיב בַּתְרֵיהּ. וַיְבָרֶךְ עֶזְרָא אֶת־יְיָ הָאֱלֹהִים הַגָּדוֹל. בַּמֶּה גִידְלוֹ. רִבִּי גִידּוּל אָמַר. בְּשֵׁם הַמְפוֹרָשׁ. רַב מַתָּנָה אָמַר. בִּבְרָכָה גִידְלוֹ. רִבִּי סִימוֹן בְּשֵׁם רִבִּי יְהוֹשֻׁעַ בֶּן לֵוִי. לָמָּה נִקְרְאוּ אַנְשֵׁי כְנֶסֶת הַגְּדוֹלָה. שֶׁהֶחֱזִירוּ אֶת הַגְּדוּלָּה לְיוֹשְׁנָהּ. אָמַר רִבִּי פִינְחָס. מֹשֶׁה הִתְקִין מַטְבִּיעָהּ שֶׁלְּתְּפִילָה. הָאֵל הַגָּדוֹל הַגִּבּוֹר וְהַנּוֹרָא. יִרְמְיָה אָמַר. הָאֵל הַגָּדוֹל הַגִּבּוֹר. וְלֹא אָמַר נוֹרָא. וְלָמָּה הוּא גִיבּוֹר. לָזֶה נָאֶה לְהִיקָּרוֹת גִּיבּוֹר. שֶׁהוּא רוֹאֶה חוּרְבַּן בֵּיתוֹ וְשׁוֹתֵק. וְלָמָּה לֹא אָמַר נוֹרָא. אֵין נוֹרָא אֶלָּא בֵּית הַמִּקְדָּשׁ. דִּכְתִיב נוֹרָא אֱלֹהִים מִמִּקְדָּשֶׁיךָ. דָּנִיאֵל אָמַר. הָאֵל הַגָּדוֹל וְהַנּוֹרָא. וְלָמָּה לֹא אָמַר גִּיבּוֹר. בָּנָיו מְסוּרִין בְּקוֹלָרִין. אֵיכָן הִיא גְבוּרָתוֹ. וְלָמָּה הוּא אָמַר נוֹרָא. לָזֶה נָאֶה לְהִיקָּרוֹת נוֹרָא. בְּנוֹרָאוֹת שֶׁעָשָׂה עִמָּנוּ בְּכִבְשָׁן הָאֵשׁ. וְכֵיוָן שֶׁעָמְדוּ אַנְשֵׁי כְנֶסֶת הַגְּדוֹלָה הֶחֱזִירוּ אֶת הַגְּדוּלָּה לְיוֹשְׁנָהּ. וְעַתָּה אֱלֹהֵינוּ הָאֵל הַגָּדוֹל הַגִּבּוֹר וְהַנּוֹרָא שׁוֹמֵר הַבְּרִית וְהַחֶסֶד אַל־יִמְעַט לְפָנֶיךָ וגו'. וּבָשָׂר וָדָם יֵשׁ בּוֹ כֹחַ לִיתֵּן קִצְבָה בִדְבָרִים הַלָּלוּ. אָמַר רִבִּי יִצְחָק בַּר לְעָזָר. יוֹדְעִין הֵן הַנְּבִיאִים שֶׁאֱלוֹהָן אֲמִיתִּי וְאֵינָן מַחֲנִיפִין לוֹ.

3 האלהים | ב אלהי   4 גידלו | ב גודלו ר' גידלו | ב גדול ברכה גידל | ב גודלו בברכה   5 נקראו | ב נקרו
7 הוא | ב אמ' גיבור | ב הגיבור להיקרות | ב לקרות   8 אין | ב אלא שאין דכת' | ב שני   9 גיבור | ב הגבור
10 איכן | ב היכן הוא | ב - להיקרות | ב לקרות   11 את | ב -   12 שומר...וגו' | ב -   13 לעזר | ב אלעזר

There are Tannaim who state, he opens, looks, rolls up, and recites the benediction. There are Tannaim who state, he opens, looks, and recites the benediction. Rebbi Ze`ira, Abba bar Jeremiah, Rav Mattanah in the name of Samuel, Practice follows him who said, he opens, looks, and recites the benediction[159]. And what is the reason? *When he opened it, the entire people stood up*[160]. What is written afterwards? [161]*Ezra praised the Eternal, the Great God*[162]. In what did he declare Him great? Rebbi Giddul said, by the explicit Name. Rav Mattanah said, he declared Him great by the benediction. Rebbi Simon in the name of Rebbi Joshua ben Levi: Why are they called the men of the Great Assembly? Because they re-instituted the grandeur to its old glory[163]. Rebbi Phineas said, Moses instituted the prayer formula, *the God, the Great, the Strong, and the Awesome*[164]. Jeremiah said, *the Great and Strong God*[165]; he did not mention "the Awesome". Why is He strong? He is appropriately called strong since He sees the destruction of His Temple and is silent. Why did he not mention "Awesome"? Awesome is only the Temple, as it is written, *God Awesome in Your Sanctuary*[166]. Daniel said *the Great and Awesome God*[167]. Why did he not mention "the Strong"? His sons are delivered to iron collars[168]; where is His strength? But why does he say, *Awesome*? He is appropriately called awesome by the awesome deeds he made for us in the fiery oven. But when the men of the Great Assembly arose they re-instituted the grandeur to its old glory: *But now, our God, the Power, the Great, the Strong, and the Awesome, keeper of Covenant and grace, may it not be little in Your eyes*[169], etc. But does flesh and blood have the power to state limits in these matters[170]? Rebbi Isaac bar Eleazar said, the prophets know that their God is truthful and they do not flatter him.

---

159 A person who comes to read from the Torah must first recognize the place from which he is going to read and then pronounce the benediction. The Babli 32a explains that the first opinion (attributed to R. Meïr) requires him to close the scroll so people should not think that the benediction is written in the text. The second opinion (attributed to R. Jehudah) notes that everybody knows the benediction by heart and therefore will know that the benediction is not written in the scroll.

160 *Neh.* 8:5.

161 From here on there is a parallel in *Berakhot* 7:4, 11c line 29 ff.

162 *Neh.* 8:8.

163 Babli *Yoma* 69b.

164 *Deut.* 10:17, incorporated into the first benediction of the Amidah.

165 *Jer.* 32:18.

166 *Ps.* 68:36.

167 *Dan.* 9:4.

168 Latin *collare*.

169 *Neh.* 9:32.

170 Is it possible to ascribe criticism of God to Prophets and Sages?

הקורא עומד פרק רביעי מגילה

(fol.74c) **משנה א**: הַקּוֹרֵא אֶת הַמְּגִילָּה עוֹמֵד וְיוֹשֵׁב. קְרָאָהּ אֶחָד קְרָאוּהָ שְׁנַיִם יָצָא. מָקוֹם שֶׁנָּהֲגוּ לְבָרֵךְ יְבָרֵךְ. שֶׁלֹּא לְבָרֵךְ לֹא יְבָרֵךְ. בַּשֵּׁנִי וּבַחֲמִישִׁי וּבַשַּׁבָּת בַּמִּנְחָה קוֹרִין שְׁלֹשָׁה. אֵין פּוֹחֲתִין מֵהֶן וְאֵין מוֹסִיפִין עֲלֵיהֶן. וְאֵין מַפְטִירִין בַּנָּבִיא. הַפּוֹתֵחַ וְהַחוֹתֵם בַּתּוֹרָה מְבָרֵךְ לְפָנֶיהָ וּלְאַחֲרֶיהָ:

Mishnah 1: One who reads the scroll either stands or sits. If one read it or two read it[1], one[2] has fulfilled his obligation. On a place where one is used to recite a benediction, he has to recite the benediction[3]; where one is used not to recite a benediction, he does not recite the benediction. On Monday, Thursday and Sabbath afternoon three are reading[4], no less and no more, and one does not conclude with a Prophet[5]. The one who starts and the one who ends in the Torah recites the benediction, before or after[5].

1 Simultaneously.
2 The hearer.
3 At the conclusion of the reading.
4 Three different readers read from the Torah scroll one after the other.
5 In contrast to Sabbath and holiday mornings when a reading from the prophets is obligatory.

(74c line 71) הַקּוֹרֵא אֶת הַמְּגִילָּה עוֹמֵד וְיוֹשֵׁב כול׳. מָה. לְשֶׁעָבַר. הָא כַתְּחִילָּה לֹא. וְהָא תַנֵּי. מַעֲשֶׂה בְּרִבִּי מֵאִיר שֶׁקְּרָיָיהּ מְיוּשָׁב בְּבֵית הַכְּנֶסֶת שֶׁלְטִיבְעִין וּנְתָנָהּ לְאַחֵר וּבֵירַךְ עָלֶיהָ. כֵּינִי מַתְנִיתָא. מוּתָּר לְקָרוֹתָהּ עוֹמֵד וּמוּתָּר לְקָרוֹתָהּ יוֹשֵׁב. מַה נוֹתְנָהּ לְאַחֵר וּמְבָרֵךְ עָלֶיהָ. זֶה קוֹרֵא וְזֶה מְבָרֵךְ. רִבִּי הוּנָא בְשֵׁם רַב יִרְמְיָה. מִיכָּאן שֶׁהַשּׁוֹמֵעַ כְּקוֹרֵא. כָּתוּב אֲשֶׁר קָרְאוּ לִפְנֵי מֶלֶךְ יְהוּדָה. וְלֹא שֶׁפָּן קְרָיָיהּ. אֶלָּא מִיכָּן שֶׁהַשּׁוֹמֵעַ כְּקוֹרֵא.

"One who reads the scroll either stands or sits," etc. How? In the past? Therefore not a priori? But was it not stated[6], "it happened that Rebbi Meïr read it in the synagogue of Tiveon while sitting; he gave it to another who recited the benediction." So is the Mishnah: one is permitted to read it standing; one is permitted to read it sitting. How may he give it to another who recited the benediction? One reads and another recites the benediction? Rebbi[7] Huna in the same of Rav Jeremiah: from here that the hearer is like the reader. It is written[8], *which the King of Judea read.* But did not Shafan read it? But from here that the hearer is like the reader.

6   Tosephta 2:5.
7   Read: Rav.

8   2K. 22:16. The Torah scroll found by the High Priest.

(74d line 1) מָהוּ לַעֲמוֹד מִפְּנֵי סֵפֶר תּוֹרָה. רִבִּי חִלְקִיָּה רִבִּי סִימוֹן בְּשֵׁם רִבִּי לֶעְזָר. מִפְּנֵי בְּנָהּ הוּא עוֹמֵד. לֹא כָל־שֶׁכֵּן מִפְּנֵי תוֹרָה עַצְמָהּ. זֶה שֶׁהוּא עוֹמֵד לִקְרוֹת בַּתּוֹרָה מִפְּנֵי מַה הוּא עוֹמֵד. מִפְּנֵי כְבוֹדָהּ אוֹ מִפְּנֵי כְבוֹד הָרַבִּים. אִין תֵּימַר. מִפְּנֵי כְבוֹדָהּ. אֲפִילוּ בֵינוֹ לְבֵינָהּ. אִין תֵּימַר. מִפְּנֵי כְבוֹד הָרַבִּים. אֲפִילוּ בֵינוֹ לְבֵין עַצְמוֹ. אִם אוֹמֵר אַתְּ כֵּן אַף הוּא מִתְעַצֵּל וְאֵינוֹ קוֹרֵא.

Does one stand before a Torah scroll? Rebbi Hilkiah, Rebbi Simon in the name of Rebbi Eleazar: One stands before her son[9], not so much more before the Torah itself? The one who stands to read in the Torah, why does he stand? Because of its honor or the honor of the public? If you say, because of its honor, even in private. If you say, because of the honor of the public, even alone[10]? If you would say so, he will be lazy and not read.

9   One has to stand in front of a Sage, *Lev.* 19:32. Babli *Qiddušin* 33b.
10 If one stands only because of the public, it is obvious that for private Torah reading one does not have to stand. If standing in front of the public is an additional obligation over that to stand for any Torah reading, it leads to undesirable consequences.

(747 line 7) רִבִּי שְׁמוּאֵל בַּר רַב יִצְחָק עָאַל לַכְּנִישְׁתָּא. חַד בַּר נָשׁ קָאִים מְתַרְגֵּם סָמִיךְ לַעֲמוּדָא. אֲמַר לֵיהּ. אָסוּר לָךְ. כְּשֵׁם שֶׁנִּיתְּנָה בְּאֵימָה וְיִרְאָה כָּךְ אָנוּ צְרִיכִין לִנְהוֹג בָּהּ בְּאֵימָה וְיִרְאָה. רִבִּי חַגַּיי אָמַר. רִבִּי שְׁמוּאֵל בַּר רַב יִצְחָק עָאַל לַכְּנִישְׁתָּא. חֲמָא חוּנָה קָאִים מְתַרְגֵּם וְלָא מֵקִים בַּר נָשׁ תַּחְתּוֹי. אֲמַר לֵיהּ. אָסִיר לָךְ. כְּשֵׁם שֶׁנִּתְּנָה עַל יְדֵי סִרְסוּר כָּךְ אָנוּ צְרִיכִין לִנְהוֹג בָּהּ עַל יְדֵי סִרְסוּר. עָאַל רִבִּי יוּדָה בַּר פָּזִי וְעָבְדָהּ שְׁאֵילָה. אָנֹכִי עוֹמֵד בֵּין־יי ובֵינֵיכֶם בָּעֵת הַהִיא לְהַגִּיד לָכֶם אֶת־דְּבַר יי. רִבִּי חַגַּיי אָמַר. רִבִּי שְׁמוּאֵל בַּר רַב יִצְחָק עָאַל לַכְּנִישְׁתָּא. חֲמָא חַד סְפַר מוֹשֵׁט תַּרְגּוּמָא מִן גּוֹ סִיפְרָא. אֲמַר לֵיהּ. אָסִיר לָךְ. דְּבָרִים שֶׁנֶּאֶמְרוּ בַּפֶּה בַּפֶּה וּדְבָרִים שֶׁנֶּאֶמְרוּ בִכְתָב בִּכְתָב.

Rebbi Samuel bar Rav Isaac went to a synagogue. A man stood up to translate while leaning on a pillar. He said to him, this is forbidden to you; just as it was given in trembling and fear so we have to treat it in trembling and fear. Rebbi Haggai said, Rebbi Samuel bar Rav Isaac went to a synagogue. He saw Huna[11] standing up translating without putting up another person in his stead. He said to him, this is forbidden to you; just as it was given by an agent, so we have to treat it by an agent. Rebbi Jehudah bar Pazi went and turned it into a question[12], *I was standing between the Eternal and you at that time to tell you the Eternal's word*[13]. Rebbi Ḥaggai said, Rebbi Samuel bar Rav Isaac went to a synagogue. He saw a teacher delivering the translation from a book. He said to him, this is forbidden to you; matters which were said orally orally[14], matters which were said in writing in writing[15].

11 With Rif (§1133) where the entire paragraph is copied, for חונה read: חזנה "the rabbi", the organizer of the religious services, who in an unlearned congregation both read the Torah and delivered the Aramaic translation. However, the Ashkenazic *Qonteros Aḥaron* (ed. L. Ginzberg) also reads הונא.

12 He turned the statement that the Torah was given by Moses as God's agent into a question-and-answer matter of study.

13 *Deut.* 5:5.

14 This declares the accepted *Targum*, Onkelos in the East and an unknown Targum in the West, as part of the oral tradition made by Ezra into an organic part of Judaism.

15 Babli *Gittin* 60b.

(74d line 17) רִבִּי חַגַּיי בְּשֵׁם רִבִּי שְׁמוּאֵל בַּר נַחְמָן. נֶאֶמְרוּ דְבָרִים בַּפֶּה וְנֶאֶמְרוּ דְבָרִים בִּכְתָב וְאֵין אָנוּ יוֹדְעִין (אֵילוּ) [אֵיזֶה מֵהֶן] חָבִיבִים. אֶלָא מִן מָה דִכְתִיב כִּי עַל־פִּי ׀ הַדְּבָרִים הָאֵלֶּה כָּרַתִּי אִתְּךָ בְּרִית וְאֶת־יִשְׂרָאֵל: אוֹתָן שֶׁבַּפֶּה אֲמָרָה. הָדָא אֲמָרָה. רִבִּי יוֹחָנָן וְרִבִּי יוּדָן בֵּירִבִּי שִׁמְעוֹן. חַד אָמַר. אִם שִׁימַרְתָּ מַה שֶׁבַּפֶּה וְשִׁימַרְתָּ מַה שֶׁבִּכְתָב אֲנִי כוֹרֵת אִתְּךָ בְּרִית. וְאִם לָאו אֵינִי כוֹרֵת אִתְּךָ בְּרִית. וְחוֹרָנָה אָמַר. אִם שִׁימַרְתָּ מַה שֶׁבַּפֶּה וְשִׁימַרְתָּ מַה שֶׁבִּכְתָב אַתְּ נוֹטֵל שָׂכָר. וְאִם לָאו אֵין אַתְּ נוֹטֵל שָׂכָר. אָמַר רִבִּי יְהוֹשֻׁעַ בֶּן לֵוִי. עֲלֵיהֶם וַעֲלֵיהֶם דְּבָרִים הַדְּבָרִים כָּל כָּכָל. מִקְרָא מִשְׁנָה וְתַלְמוּד וְאַגָּדָה. וַאֲפִילוּ מַה שֶׁתַּלְמִיד וָתִיק עָתִיד לְהוֹרוֹת לִפְנֵי רַבּוֹ כְּבָר נֶאֱמַר לְמֹשֶׁה מִסִּינַי. הָדָא הוּא דִכְתִיב יֵשׁ דָּבָר שֶׁיֹּאמַר רְאֵה־זֶה חָדָשׁ הוּא. וַחֲבֵירוֹ מֵשִׁיבוֹ. כְּבָר הָיָה לְעוֹלָמִים אֲשֶׁר הָיָה מִלְּפָנֵינוּ:

2 (אילו) | פ - [איזה מהן] | ח [איזו] חביבים | ח חביבין פ חביב 4 שימרת | פ שימרתה 5 וחורנה | פ וחרנה ושימרת | פ וקיימת נוטל | חפ מקבל 6 נטל | חפ מקבל דברים הדברים כל ככל | חפ כל ככל דברים הדברים 7 ואגדה | ח הלכות ואגדות 8 וחבירו | חפ חבירו - | חפ ואו' לו

[16]Rebbi Ḥaggai in the name of Rebbi Samuel bar Naḥman: Things have been said orally and things have been said in writing, and we do not know which ones are preferred. From what is written[17]: *by the mouth of these words I concluded a covenant with you and Israel,* it follows that the oral traditions are preferred[18]. Rebbi Joḥanan and Rebbi Yudan bar Rebbi Simeon. One said that if you kept what is oral tradition and kept what is written I will conclude a

covenant with you, otherwise I shall not conclude a covenant with you. The other one said, if you watched all that is oral tradition and kept all that is written you will receive your reward, otherwise you will not receive any reward. Rebbi Joshua ben Levi said[19]: *On them, and on them*; *words, the words all, like all;*; Bible, Mishnah, Talmud, and Aggadah. Even what a competent student[20] will discover[21] before his teacher was said to Moses on Sinai. What is the reason? *There is something about which one would say, look, this is new!* His colleague will answer, *it already has been forever*[22].

16 The same text appears in *Peah* 1:6 (Notes 104-109,פ) and *Ḥagigah* 1:8 (Note 189,ח).

17 *Ex.* 34:27.

18 This argument is somewhat specious since the full verse reads: *The Eternal said to Moses, write down these words for yourself, because by the mouth of these words I concluded a covenant with you and Israel.* In Babli *Gittin* 60b, R. Simeon ben Laqish explains the verse as part of the covenant and states that written verses may not be recited by heart and oral traditions not written down as declared here at the end of the previous paragraph.

19 The reference is to Deut. 9:10: *The Eternal gave to me the two stone tablets, written by the Divine Finger, and on them like all the words that the Eternal spoke to you on the mountain on the day of assembly.* The three underlined expressions are all unnecessary for the understanding of the sentence; these are interpreted as referring to the three divisions of oral law contained in the complete Torah. Babli 19b.

20 Arabic وثيق "strong, safe, secure, dependable, reliable". The interpretations of the untrained and incompetent are worthless.

21 Since a student may not rule, or teach, before his teacher, the root of the word להורות must be "to become pregnant," in this case, with an idea.

22 *Eccl.* 1:10.

(74d line 29) תַּנֵי. לֹא יְהוּ שְׁנַיִם קוֹרִין בַּתּוֹרָה וְאֶחָד מְתַרְגֵּם. אָמַר רִבִּי זְעוּרָה. מִפְּנֵי הַבְּרָכָה. וְהָא תַּנֵי. לֹא יְהוּ שְׁנַיִם מְתַרְגְּמִין וְאֶחָד קוֹרֵא. אִית לָךְ מֵימַר. מִפְּנֵי הַבְּרָכָה. אֶלָּא מִשֵּׁם [שֶׁאֵין] שְׁנֵי קוֹלוֹת נִכְנָסִין בְּאוֹזֶן אַחַת. תַּנֵי. שְׁנַיִם קוֹרְאִין בַּתּוֹרָה. אֵין שְׁנַיִם קוֹרְאִין בַּנָּבִיא. אָמַר רִבִּי עוּלָּא. קְרָאוֹת בַּתּוֹרָה. אֵין קְרָאוֹת בַּנָּבִיא.

1 זעורה | ב זעורא   2 והא תני | ב והתני   3 באוזן | ב לתוך אוזן   קוראין | ב קורין   קוראין | ב מפטירין   4 קראות | ב קריוות (2)

תַּנֵי. אֶחָד קוֹרֵא בַתּוֹרָה וְאֶחָד מְתַרְגֵּם. לֹא אֶחָד קוֹרֵא וּשְׁנַיִם מְתַרְגְּמִין. לֹא שְׁנַיִם מְתַרְגְּמִין וְאֶחָד קוֹרֵא. לֹא שְׁנַיִם קוֹרְאִין וּשְׁנַיִם מְתַרְגְּמִין. וּבְנָבִיא אֶחָד קוֹרֵא וְאֶחָד מְתַרְגֵּם [וְאֶחָד קוֹרֵא] וּשְׁנַיִם מְתַרְגְּמִין. לֹא שְׁנַיִם קוֹרִין וְאֶחָד מְתַרְגֵּם וְלֹא שְׁנַיִם קוֹרִין וּשְׁנַיִם מְתַרְגְּמִין. וּבַמְּגִילָּה אֶחָד קוֹרֵא וְאֶחָד מְתַרְגֵּם. אֶחָד קוֹרֵא וּשְׁנַיִם מְתַרְגְּמִין. שְׁנַיִם קוֹרִין וְאֶחָד מְתַרְגֵּם.

שְׁנַיִם קוֹרִין וּשְׁנַיִם מְתַרְגְּמִין. וְהַתַּרְגּוּם מְעַכֵּב. אָמַר רִבִּי יוֹסֵה. מִן מַה דַּאֲנַן חַמְיָין רַבָּנִן נָפְקִין לְתַעֲנִיתָא וּקְרָאֵיי וְלָא מְתַרְגְּמִין הָדָא אֲמָרָה שֶׁאֵין הַתַּרְגּוּם מְעַכֵּב. אָמַר רִבִּי יוֹנָה. אַף עַל גַּב דְּאַתְּ אָמַר. אֵין הַתַּרְגּוּם מְעַכֵּב. טָעָה מַחֲזִירִין אוֹתוֹ.

רִבִּי יוֹנָה רִבִּי יִרְמְיָה. חַד מְחַזֵּר. וְחוֹרָנָה מְחַזֵּר. פְּטִירִין עִם יַרְקוֹנִין. נֹאמַר פְּטִירִין עִם מְרוֹרִין. וְלָא יַדְעִין מָאן אָמַר דָּא וּמָאן אָמַר דָּא. מִן מַה דָּאָמַר רִבִּי [יוֹנָה]. מָהוּ לַהֲבִיאָן בְּתַמְחוּיִין שֶׁלְכֶסֶף. הֲוִי דְּהוּא מְחַזֵּר. מָנָא. וְיֹאמַר. סַלָּא. רִבִּי פִּינְחָס מְחַזֵּר. פְּטִימִין בְּנֵי תוֹרִין. וְיֹאמַר תּוֹרִין בְּנֵי תוֹרִין.

1 ר' | א ור'   חד' | א חד אמ'   וחורנה | א וחרנה אמ'   ירקונין | א (יסקונין)   נאמר | א דאת אמר   2 מרורין | א מרורין יגעין | א ידעינן   3 דהוא | א הוא דאמ'   ויאמר | א די אמ'   סלא | א כלה   ר' | א דר'   - | א אמ'   4 ויאמר | א די אמ'

[23]It was stated: Two should not read in the Torah[24] and one translate. Rebbi Ze`ira said, because of the benediction. But was it not stated, not two shall translate and one read. Could you say, because of the benediction? But because [not] two voices enter one ear. It was stated: Two read in the Torah, but not two read in Prophets. Rebbi Ulla said, there are readers for the Torah, there are no readers in Prophets[25].

It was stated: One reads in the Torah and one translates. Not one reads and two translate nor two read and one translates, nor two read and two translate. But in a Prophet, one reads and one translates, [or one reads] and two translate; not two read and two translate nor two read[26] and two translate. In the Esther scroll, one reads and one translates, one reads and two translate; two read and one translates, or two read and two translate[27]. Does translation obstruct[28]? Rebbi Yose said, since we are seeing that rabbis come on fast-days and read but do not translate, this implies that the translation is not obstructing. Rebbi Jonah said, even though you are saying that the translation is not obstructing, if he makes an error one corrects him.

[29]Rebbi Jonah and Rebbi Jeremiah. One says, one repeats "vessels"[30]. The other one says, one repeats "unleavened with vegetables" because you have to say "unleavened with bitter herbs". We do not know who said what. Since Rebbi [Jonah] said[31], may one bring in large silver baskets, it shows that he must have said that one repeats "vessels". One has to say "basket". Rebbi Phineas said, one must repeat "fattened ones and young bulls" because one must say "bulls and young bulls."[32]

23 *Berakhot* 5:4 (Notes 143-148,ב); Tosephta 3:20 (Babli *Roš Haššanah* 27a).
24 Simultaneously.
25 The second *baraita* does not contradict the first; it refers to consecutive readers, not simultaneous ones. Readings from Prophets never are split among different readers.
26 Only one person may read, but two may translate for different sections of the public since Prophets are not a source of law.
27 Since the reading of the Esther scroll always is a noisy affair.
28 Is reading without translation legitimate?

29 *Bikkurim* 3:5 (Notes 85-87,א).
30 While in principle the translator may choose his own words (since he is forbidden to read from a prepared text), in a few places rabbinic authorities insist that certain expressions are too imprecise. The first one is the translation of טנא (*Deut.* 26:2) by "vessel" instead of "basket", the second one that of מצות ומרורים (*Num.* 9:11) by "unleavened bread and vegetables."
31 *Bikkurim* 3:5, Note 84, referring to the presentation of First Fruits in the Temple.
32 *Lev.* 4:3, in both Onkelos and Pseudo-Jonathan.

(74d line 47) מְנַיִין לְתַרְגּוּם. רִבִּי זְעוּרָא בְשֵׁם רַב חֲנַנְאֵל. וַיִּקְרְאוּ בַסֵּפֶר תּוֹרַת. זֶה הַמִּקְרָא. מְפָרֵשׁ זֶה תַרְגּוּם. וְשׂוֹם שֶׂכֶל אֵילּוּ הַטְּעָמִים. וַיָּבִינוּ בַּמִּקְרָא זֶה הַמְּסוֹרֶת. וְיֵשׁ אוֹמְרִים. אֵילוּ הַהַכְרָעִים. וְיֵשׁ אוֹמְרִים. אֵילוּ רָאשֵׁי פְסוּקִים. רִבִּי זְעוּרָה בְשֵׁם רַב חֲנַנְאֵל. אֲפִילוּ רָגִיל בַּתּוֹרָה כְעֶזְרָא לֹא יְהֵא הוֹגֶה מִפִּיו וְקוֹרֵא (כְּמוֹת) [כְּמוֹ] שֶׁנֶּאֱמַר בְּבָרוּךְ. וַמְפִּיו יִקְרָא אֵלַי כָּל־הַדְּבָרִים הָאֵלֶּה וַאֲנִי כּוֹתֵב עַל־הַסֵּפֶר בַּדְּיוֹ: וְהָא תַנֵּי. מַעֲשֶׂה בְרִבִּי מֵאִיר שֶׁהָיָה בְאַסְיָיא וְלֹא הָיָה שָׁם מְגִילָּה כְתוּבָה עִבְרִית וּכְתָבָהּ מִפִּיו וּקְרָיָיהּ. אֵין לְמֵידִין מִשְׁעַת הַדְּחָק. וְיֵשׁ אוֹמְרִים. שְׁתַּיִם כָּתַב. כָּתַב אֶת הָרִאשׁוֹנָה מִתּוֹךְ פִּיו וְכָתַב אֶת הַשְּׁנִייָה מִתּוֹךְ הָרִאשׁוֹנָה וְגָנַז הָרִאשׁוֹנָה וְקָרָא בַשְּׁנִייָה. רִבִּי יִשְׁמָעֵאל בֵּירִבִּי יוֹסֵי אוֹמֵר. יָכִיל אֲנָא כְתַב כָּל־קִרְיָיא מִן פִּימִי. רִבִּי חִייָה רַבָּה אָמַר. יָכִיל אֲנָא כְתַב כָּל־קִרְיָיא בִּתְרֵין מָנָיי. הֵיךְ עֲבִידָא. זְבַן בִּתְרֵין מָנָיי זֶרַע דְּכִיתָּן וּזְרַע לֵיהּ וַחֲצַד לֵיהּ וַעֲבַד חַבְלִין וְתָפַשׂ טָבֵיי וְכָתַב כָּל־קִרְיָיא עַל מַשְׁכֵּיהוֹן. שָׁמַע רִבִּי וְאָמַר. אַשְׁרֵי (הגוי) [הַדּוֹר] שֶׁאַתֶּם בְּתוֹכוֹ.

From where the translation? Rebbi Ze`ira in the name of Rav Ḥananel: *They read in the Scroll of the Torah*[33], that is the reading. *Explained*, that is the translation[34]. *Making sense*, these are the accents[35]. *And understood the reading*, this is the Masora, and some say, these are the decisions[36], and some say, these are the starts of verses[37]. Rebbi Ze`ira in the name of Rav Ḥananel: Even an expert in the Torah like Ezra should not pronounce with his mouth[38] and read as it is said about Baruch: *And from his mouth he would read all these words to me and I was writing on a scroll with ink*[39]. But was it not stated[40], "it happened that Rebbi Meïr was in Essia where there was no Esther scroll written in Hebrew, when he wrote it by heart and read it. One does not infer from emergency situations. But there are those who say that he wrote two. He wrote the first by heart, and copied the second one from the first one, put away the first and read from the second." Rebbi Ismael ben Rebbi Yose says, I can write the entire Torah from memory. The Elder Rebbi Ḥiyya said, I can write the entire Torah for two minas[41]. How would he do it? He buys flax seed for two minas, sowed and harvested it, made ropes to catch deer and wrote the entire Torah on their hides. Rebbi heard it and said, happy is (the people) [the generation][42] to which you belong.

33 *Neh.* 8:8.
34 Since this is proved from a text in Hagiographs, the Targum has the status of an institution of the Men of the Great Assembly.
35 Which indicate the divisions of sentences into logical units.
36 The sentences where the caesura and therefore the meaning is not obvious. *Avodah zarah* 2:8, Notes 325 ff.
37 The division of the text into verses is oral tradition since no punctuation is permitted in the text. The last three options are variants of the theme that the text is intelligible only on the basis of traditional pronunciation. Babli 3a, *Nedarim* 37b.
38 One may not recite a Torah text by heart (nor, as pointed out in the sequel, write the text by heart.) Babli 18b.
39 *Jer.* 36:18.
40 Babli 18b, Tosephta 2:5.
41 Babli *Bava meṣia`* 85b.
42 The corrector's change is unnecessary since Rebbi is known as proponent of correct use of Hebrew; for him גוי means "people", not "Gentile".

(74c line 61) כֵּיצַד הוּא מְבָרֵךְ עָלֶיהָ. זַכַּיי טַבָּחָא בְשֵׁם רִבִּי יוֹחָנָן. הָרָב אֶת רִיבָךְ וְהַנּוֹקֵם אֶת נִקְמָתָךְ הַגּוֹאֲלָךְ וְהַמּוֹשִׁיעֲךָ מִכַּף עָרֶצֶיךָ. עַד כְּדוֹן בַּסּוֹף. בַּתְּחִילָּה. הֲרֵי הִיא כְּכָל־שְׁאָר מִצְוֹתֶיהָ שֶׁלַּתּוֹרָה. מַה שְׁאָר כָּל־מִצְוֹתֶיהָ שֶׁלַּתּוֹרָה טְעוּנוֹת בְּרָכָה אַף זוֹ טְעוּנָה בְרָכָה.

How does one make the benediction for it[43]? Zakkai the butcher in the name of Rebbi Johanan: "He Who fights your fight, and Who avenges your vengeance, your Savior, and your Redeemer from all your oppressors." So far at the end; at the start? It is like all other commandments of the Torah. Just as all other commandments of the Torah require a benediction at the start, so this one also requires a benediction at the start[44].

43 The reading of the Esther scroll. The Babylonian version of the text given here is in the Babli 21b.
44 While this text only prescribes a single benediction, "Who sanctified us by His commandments and commanded us about

reading the Scroll", the Babli (also on testimony of a person not otherwise mentioned in the Talmudim) adds another two, "Who performed wonders for our fathers in those days at this time" and "Who let us live, supported us, and let us reach this time."

(74d line 65) כָּתוּב בַּתּוֹרָה בְּרָכָה לְפָנֶיהָ וְאֵין כָּתוּב בָּהּ בְּרָכָה לְאַחֲרֶיהָ. מַה כָּתוּב בָּהּ לְפָנֶיהָ. כִּי שֵׁם יְ'י אֶקְרָא הָבוּ גוֹדֶל לֵאלֹהֵינוּ. וְכָתוּב בַּמָּזוֹן בְּרָכָה לְאַחֲרָיו וְאֵין כָּתוּב בָּהּ בְּרָכָה לְפָנָיו. מַה כָּתוּב בּוֹ לְאַחֲרָיו. וְאָכַלְתָּ וְשָׂבָעְתָּ וּבֵרַכְתָּ וגו'. מְנַיִין לִיתֵּן אֶת הָאָמוּר בָּזֶה בָזֶה וְאֶת הָאָמוּר בָּזֶה בָזֶה. רִבִּי שְׁמוּאֵל בַּר נַחְמָן בְּשֵׁם רִבִּי יוֹנָתָן. שֵׁם שֵׁם לִגְזֵירָה שָׁוָה. מַה שֵׁם שֶׁנֶּאֱמַר בַּתּוֹרָה [בְּרָכָה] לְפָנֶיהָ אַף שֵׁם שֶׁנֶּאֱמַר בַּמָּזוֹן בְּרָכָה לְפָנָיו. וּמַה שֵּׁם שֶׁנֶּאֱמַר בַּמָּזוֹן בְּרָכָה לְאַחֲרָיו אַף שֵׁם שֶׁנֶּאֱמַר בַּתּוֹרָה בְּרָכָה לְאַחֲרֶיהָ. עַד כְּדוֹן כְּרִבִּי עֲקִיבָה. כְּרִבִּי יִשְׁמָעֵאל. רִבִּי יוֹחָנָן בְּשֵׁם רִבִּי יִשְׁמָעֵאל קַל וָחוֹמֶר. מָה אִם מָזוֹן שֶׁאֵין טָעוּן בְּרָכָה לְפָנָיו טָעוּן לְאַחֲרָיו. תּוֹרָה שֶׁהִיא טְעוּנָה בְרָכָה לְפָנֶיהָ אֵין דִּין שֶׁתְּהֵא טְעוּנָה בְרָכָה לְאַחֲרֶיהָ. עַד כְּדוֹן תּוֹרָה. מָזוֹן. מָה אִם תּוֹרָה שֶׁאֵינָהּ טְעוּנָה בְרָכָה לְאַחֲרֶיהָ טְעוּנָה לְפָנֶיהָ. מָזוֹן שֶׁהוּא טָעוּן לְאַחֲרָיו אֵינוֹ דִין שֶׁיְּהֵא טָעוּן לְפָנָיו. רִבִּי יִצְחָק וְרִבִּי נָתָן. רִבִּי יִצְחָק אָמַר. כִּי־הוּא יְבָרֵךְ הַזֶּבַח וְאַחֲרֵיכֶן יֹאכְלוּ הַקְּרוּאִים. רִבִּי נָתָן אוֹמֵר. וַעֲבַדְתֶּם אֵת יְ'י אֱלֹהֵיכֶם וּבֵרַךְ אֶת־לַחְמְךָ וְאֶת־מֵימֶיךָ. אֵימָתַי הוּא קָרוּי לַחְמְךָ. עַד שֶׁלֹּא אֲכַלְתּוֹ. רִבִּי אוֹמֵר. מָה אִם בְּשָׁעָה שֶׁאָכַל וְשָׂבַע אַתְּ אָמַר. צָרִיךְ לְבָרֵךְ. בְּשָׁעָה שֶׁהוּא תָאֵב לֹא כָל־שֶׁכֵּן. עַד כְּדוֹן מָזוֹן. תּוֹרָה. מָה אִם מָזוֹן שֶׁאֵינוֹ אֶלָּא חַיֵּי שָׁעָה טָעוּן בְּרָכָה לְפָנָיו וּלְאַחֲרָיו. תּוֹרָה שֶׁהִיא חַיֵּי עֲדֵי עַד לֹא כָל־שֶׁכֵּן.

1 בה | ב בתורה   2 וכתוב | ב כתיב לאחריו | ב לאחריה בה | ב -   3 בו | ב -   וגו' | ב -   מניין | ב ומניין   4 נחמן | ב נחמני   - | ב [אתיא]   5 לפניה | ב לפניו   7 לאחריו | ב ברכה לאחריו   8 אין | ב אינו   9 שהוא טעון | ב שטעון   שיהא טעון | ב שטעון   10 ואחריכן | ב ואחר כך   11 לחמך ואת מימיך | ב לחמך   12 אכלתו | ב אכלת את אמר | ב -   13 תאב | ב תאב לאכול

רִבִּי זְעוּרָה בָעֵי. אִילֵּין שְׁלֹשָׁה קְרִיוֹת מָה אַתְּ עָבֵד לוֹן. כִּשְׁלֹשָׁה שֶׁאֲכָלוּ כְאַחַת אוֹ כִשְׁלֹשָׁה שֶׁאֲכָלוּ זֶה בִּפְנֵי עַצְמוֹ וְזֶה בִּפְנֵי עַצְמוֹ. אִין תַּעֲבָדִינוֹן כִּשְׁלֹשָׁה שֶׁאֲכָלוּ כְאַחַת. הָרִאשׁוֹן מְבָרֵךְ בְּרָכָה רִאשׁוֹנָה וְהָאַחֲרוֹן מְבָרֵךְ בְּרָכָה הָאַחֲרוֹנָה וְהָאֶמְצָעִי אֵינוֹ מְבָרֵךְ כָּל־עִיקָּר. אִין תַּעֲבָדִינוֹן כִּשְׁלֹשָׁה שֶׁאֲכָלוּ זֶה בִּפְנֵי עַצְמוֹ וְזֶה בִּפְנֵי עַצְמוֹ. אֲפִילוּ הָאֶמְצָעִי מְבָרֵךְ לְפָנֶיהָ וּלְאַחֲרֶיהָ. אָמַר רִבִּי שְׁמוּאֵל בַּר אַבְדּוּמָא. לָמְדוּ בִּרְכַּת הַתּוֹרָה מִבִּרְכַּת הַמָּזוֹן אֶלָּא לָרַבִּים. אִם לָרַבִּים אֲפִילוּ בֵינוֹ לְבֵין עַצְמוֹ אֵינוֹ מְבָרֵךְ. אָמַר רִבִּי אַבָּא מָרִי אֲחוֹי דְּרִבִּי יוֹסֵף. עֲשָׂאוּהָ כִּשְׁאָר כָּל־הַמִּצְוֹת שֶׁבַּתּוֹרָה. מַה שְׁאָר כָּל־הַמִּצְוֹת טְעוּנוֹת בְּרָכָה אַף זוֹ טְעוּנָה בְרָכָה.

1 זעורה | ב זעורא   עבד | ב עביד   2 - | ב וזה בפני עצמו   3 מברך | ב - האחרונה | ב אחרונה   4 לפניה ולאחריה | ב לפניו ולאחריו   5 אבדומא | ב אבדימא   למדו | ב לא למדו   המזון R הזימון | ב המזון   אם | ב ואם   6 אינו | ב לא   אבא | ב אב   יוסה | ב יוסי   7 שבתורה | ב שלתורה

[45]For Torah[46] there is written a benediction before, but no benediction is written after. What is written before it? *For I am invoking the name of the Eternal, attribute greatness to our God*[47]. For food there is written a benediction after, but no benediction is written before. What is written after

it? *You will eat and be satiated, then you must praise*[48]. From where that which is said about one on the other and vice-versa? Rebbi Samuel bar Naḥman in the name of Rebbi Jonathan: The Name is mentioned in both verses as parallel expressions[49]. Just as the Name that is mentioned concerning Torah implies a benediction before, so the Name that is mentioned concerning food implies a benediction before. And just as the Name that is mentioned concerning food implies a benediction after, so the Name that is mentioned concerning Torah implies a benediction after. That follows Rebbi Aqiba. How following Rebbi Ismael[50]? Rebbi Joḥanan in the name of Rebbi Ismael, an inference *de minore ad majus*[51]. If food that needs no explicit benediction before, needs a benediction afterwards, regarding Torah which needs a benediction before, it is only logical that it should need a benediction afterwards. That works for Torah; what about food? If Torah which needs no benediction afterwards, needs a benediction before, regarding food which needs a benediction afterwards, it is only logical that it should need a benediction before. Rebbi Isaac and Rebbi Nathan say, *For he will recite the benediction over the sacrifice and after that the invited guests will eat*[52]. Rebbi Nathan said, *you shall serve the Eternal, your God, and give praise for your bread and your water*[53]; when is it called your bread and your water, before you eat[54]. Rebbi said, if he has to give praise when he ate and is satiated, so much more at a time when he is hungry for food. That is for food, what about Torah? If food, which sustains only temporary life, needs a benediction before and after, Torah, which sustains eternal life, so much more[55].

Rebbi Ze`ira asked: These three that are called[56], how are you treating them? As three who ate together or as three who ate each one for himself? If you treat them as three who ate together then the first one recites the benediction before, the last one recites the benediction after, and the middle one does not recite any benediction at all. If you treat them as three who ate each one for himself then even the middle one recites benedictions before and after. Rebbi Samuel ben Eudaimon said, they did learn the benedictions for the Torah from Grace only in public[57]. If in public, then in private one should not recite any benediction! Rebbi Abba Mari, the brother of Rebbi Yose, said: They made it equal to other commandments of the Torah. Just as other commandments of the Torah need benedictions, this also needs a benediction[58].

45 The following is quoted from *Berakhot* 7:1, Notes 40-52 (ב).
46 Torah study, including Torah reading.
47 *Deut.* 32:3.
48 *Deut.* 8:10.
49 In general, it is assumed in the system of Rebbi Aqiba that a word can have only one meaning in the Pentateuch. A stronger implication, agreed to by all tannaitic authorities, is a "parallel expression". The technical term is *equal cut*. The formal definition of the school of R. Ismael is that if one has a tradition that two equal or synonymous expressions are written in the Torah for purposes of comparison and if these two words are not used for any other inference, then all laws connected with one word apply to the other and vice-versa. The derivation here does not fulfill these conditions; hence, it is labelled to follow the rules of R. Aqiba who is not known to require too much formality in case the verse is used to give a biblical base to an old tradition.
50 The rules of R. Ismael are systematized in his 13 hermeneutical rules given in the introduction to *Sifra* on Leviticus.
51 The first rule of R .Ismael. If there are two commandments, A and B, and if every rule for A is no more stringent than the corresponding rule for B, then a rule expressed for A that has no equivalent for B is valid also for B. The Babli (*Berakhot* 21a) quotes the following in the name of R. Johanan only and points out that the application here is not justified since it is self-contradictory. The Yerushalmi seems to be of the opinion that in the formulation given here, with "not more stringent" instead of "less stringent", the argument is logically admissible.
52 *1S.* 9:13. In the Babli (*Berakhot* 48b) and in the Mekhilta dR. Ismael (Ba 16, ed. Horovitz-Rabin p. 61) this is given in the name of R. Nathan only. A verse from *Samuel* (Biblical but not Pentateuchal) cannot prove a commandment but can prove a practice.
53 *Ex.* 23:25. In the Babli and the Mekhilta, this appears in the name of Rebbi Isaac.
54 The full verse seems to read: *You shall serve the Eternal, your God, then He will bless your bread and your water and I will remove sickness from your midst.* The switch from third to first person is awkward in any case. In the Babli (in particular, in the Sephardic incunabula print) it is spelled out: Do not read וּבֵרַךְ *He will bless* but וּבָרֵךְ "and praise". The Bible Concordance of G. Lisowsky (Stuttgart 1958) takes the verse, as it stands, to mean *You shall serve the Eternal, your God, and praise for your bread and your water, then I will remove sickness from your midst.* One may recite a benediction on one's bread and one's water only before it is consumed; afterwards one may speak only of nourishment and sustenance.
55 In the Babli and the Mekhilta this is an argument of Rebbi Ismael.

56 The minimum number of people called to read the Torah in public. Since the preceding arguments tied benedictions over Torah reading to Grace, one has to ask in which way they are comparable. In the Babli 21b there is a baraita: "(In reading the Torah) he who starts recites the benediction before and he who finishes recites the benediction after." On that, the Gemara notes: But today, all recite benedictions before and after. Tthe baraita seems to represent early Babylonian practice; we do not know of any direct Yerushalmi source that let people read the Torah without benediction. Rebbi Ze`ira, the Galilean head of academy who had come from Babylonia, is the right person to ask for the reasons and the correct practice. Since his questions remain without answers, both practices might be acceptable.

57 R. Samuel ben Eudaimon seems to object to reciting a benediction after Torah study. Also, since Torah study is a permanent obligation (*Jos.* 1:8) one benediction in the morning is enough to cover all Torah study during the day and evening; one does not have to recite a new benediction for study after an interruption.

58 Most commandments need only a benediction before, not after their execution. Thus, the benediction for the Torah in private study follows the general rule of benedictions over commandments. The quote for benediction for the Torah before the reading, *Deut.* 32:3, is clearly addressed to the public and, therefore, not applicable to private study.

(75a line 17) אָמַר רִבִּי שְׁמוּאֵל בַּר נַחְמָן. רִבִּי יוֹנָתָן עֲבַר קוֹמֵי סִידְרָא. שְׁמַע קָלוֹן קְרוּיֵי וְלֹא הֲוָה מְבָרְכִין. אָמַר לוֹן. עַד מָתַי אַתֶּם עוֹשִׂין אֶת הַתּוֹרָה קְרָחוֹת קְרָחוֹת. מֹשֶׁה הִתְקִין אֶת יִשְׂרָאֵל שֶׁיְּהוּ קוֹרִין בַּתּוֹרָה בַּשַּׁבָּתוֹת וּבַיָּמִים טוֹבִים וּבְרָאשֵׁי חֳדָשִׁים וּבְחוּלוֹ שֶׁלְּמוֹעֵד. שֶׁנֶּאֱמַר וַיְדַבֵּר מֹשֶׁה אֶת־מוֹעֲדֵי יי אֶל־בְּנֵי יִשְׂרָאֵל׃ עֶזְרָא הִתְקִין לְיִשְׂרָאֵל שֶׁיְּהוּ קוֹרִין בַּתּוֹרָה בַּשֵּׁינִי וּבַחֲמִישִׁי וּבַשַּׁבָּת בַּמִּנְחָה. הוּא הִתְקִין טְבִילָה לְבַעֲלֵי קְרָיִין. הוּא הִתְקִין בָּתֵּי דִינִין יוֹשְׁבִין בַּעֲיָירוֹת בַּשֵּׁינִי וּבַחֲמִישִׁי. הוּא הִתְקִין שֶׁיְּהוּ הָרוֹכְלִין מְחַזְּרִין בַּעֲיָירוֹת מִפְּנֵי כְבוֹדָן שֶׁלְּבָנוֹת יִשְׂרָאֵל. הוּא הִתְקִין שֶׁיְּהוּ מְכַבְּסִין בַּחֲמִישִׁי מִפְּנֵי כְבוֹד הַשַּׁבָּת. הוּא הִתְקִין שֶׁיְּהוּ אוֹפִין פַּת בְּעַרְבֵי שַׁבָּתוֹת. שֶׁתְּהֵא פְרוּסָה מְצוּיָה לֶעָנִי. הוּא הִתְקִין שֶׁיְּהוּ אוֹכְלִין שׁוּם בְּלֵילֵי שַׁבָּתוֹת. שֶׁהוּא מַכְנִיס אַהֲבָה וּמוֹצִיא תַאֲוָה. הוּא הִתְקִין שֶׁיְּהוּ הַנָּשִׁים מְדַבְּרוֹת זוֹ עִם זוֹ בְּבֵית הַכִּסֵּא. הוּא הִתְקִין שֶׁתְּהֵא אִשָּׁה חוֹגֶרֶת בַּסִּינָר בֵּין מִלְּפָנֶיהָ בֵּין מִלְאַחֲרֶיהָ. אָמַר רִבִּי תַנְחוּם בַּר חִייָה. מִפְּנֵי מַעֲשֶׂה שֶׁאֵירַע. מַעֲשֶׂה בְאִשָּׁה שֶׁבָּעֲלָהּ קוֹף מִכְּדַרְכָּהּ וּשְׁלֹא כְדַרְכָּהּ. הוּא הִתְקִין שֶׁתְּהֵא אִשָּׁה חוֹפֶפֶת וְסוֹרֶקֶת קוֹדֶם לִטְהֳרָתָהּ שְׁלֹשָׁה יָמִים. רִבִּי יוֹסֵה בְשֵׁם דְּבֵית רִבִּי יַנַּאי רִבִּי בָּא בַּר כֹּהֵן בְּשֵׁם רַב חוּנָה. כְּדֵי לַשַּׁבָּת וְלִשְׁנֵי יָמִים טוֹבִים שֶׁלְּגָלִיּוֹת. רִבִּי זְעוּרָה בְשֵׁם רַב יְהוּדָה. וְהוּא שֶׁהִגִּיעַ זְמַנָּהּ לִטְבוֹל בְּנָתַיִים. רִבִּי בָּא בְשֵׁם רַב יְהוּדָה. וַאֲפִילוּ הִגִּיעַ זְמַנָּהּ לִטְבוֹל בַּסּוֹף. וַהֲוָה רִבִּי זְעוּרָה מִסְתַּכֵּל בֵּיהּ. אָמַר לֵיהּ. מָה אַתְּ מִסְתַּכֵּל בִּי. מַה־יְּדַעְתְּ וְלֹא נֵדָע תָּבִין וְלֹא־עִמָּנוּ הוּא׃ אֲתָא רִבִּי אָחָא בְשֵׁם רִבִּי תַנְחוּם בֵּירִבִּי חִייָה וְאָמַר טַעֲמָא. וַאֲפִילוּ הִגִּיעַ זְמַנָּהּ לִטְבוֹל בַּסּוֹף. שֶׁמָּא מַעֲיָינָהּ רָחוֹק וְהִיא מִתְעַצֶּלֶת וְאֵינָהּ טְהוֹרָה.

Rebbi Samuel bar Naḥman said, Rebbi Jonathan passed by the synagogue. He heard their voices reading without benedictions. He said to them, how long are you making the Torah out of bald spots[59]! Moses instituted that the Torah should be read on Sabbath, holidays, New Moons, and on the intermediate days of holidays. Ezra instituted that the Torah should be read on Mondays and Thursdays, and on Sabbath afternoon[60]. He instituted immersion for people with emissions of semen[61]. He instituted that law courts should sit in large villages on Mondays and Thursdays[62]. He instituted that peddlars make the circuit of villages because of the honor of the daughters of Israel[63]. He instituted that one should wash on Thursdays for the honor of the Sabbath. He instituted that one should bake bread on Fridays so that a piece be available for the poor. He instituted that one eat garlic on Friday Night, because it brings love and removes desire[64]. He instituted that women should talk with one another in the toilet[65]. He instituted that a woman wear an apron[66] front and back. Rebbi Tanḥum bar Hiyya said, because of what had happened. It happened that a woman was raped by an ape, both regular and irregular intercourse[67]. He instituted that a woman may wash and comb her hair up to three days before her purity[68]. Rebbi Yose in the name of the House of Rebbi Yannai, Rebbi Abba bar Cohen in the name of Rav Huna: Corresponding to the Sabbath and the two days of holiday in the Diaspora. Rebbi Ze`ira in the name of Rav Jehudah: only if the time of her immersion is in the meantime. Rebbi Abba in the name of Rav Jehudah: even if the time of her immersion is at the end[69]. Then Rebbi Ze`ira was looking at him. He said to him, what are you looking at me? *What do you know that we do not know, you understand what is not with us*[70]? There came Rebbi Aḥa in the name of Rebbi Tanḥum ben Rebbi Ḥiyya and reported the reason: even if the time of her immersion is at the end; I am saying that maybe her spring is far away and she is lazy and not pure.

---

59 He required that every one reading in the Torah pronounce the benedictions before and after. This implies that in practical terms the question was resolved already in the first generation of Amoraim and benedictions required from everybody.

60 Differently in the Babli, *Bava qamma* 82a.

61 He forbade Torah study and prayer before immersion in a *miqweh*, *Berakhot* 3:4.

62 It is presumed that in walled cities one

has access to courts every day.

63 That every woman have access to cosmetics and perfumes.

64 Since marital relations are a religious duty for the husband on Friday nights, it seems that garlic increases virility but is not an aphrodisiac and therefore improves the moral qualities of the children to be conceived.

65 To warn away men. In the Babli, *Sanhedrin* 19a, this is a late institution of R. Yose (the Tanna) in Sepphoris.

66 This is Maimonides's explanation. Rashi (*Šabbat* 92a) explains as underpants.

67 The technical term irregular intercourse is used for absence of penetration.

68 If she immerses herself after her period, the water has to touch "all of her body"; this is interpreted to mean that no dirt may be either on her body or her hair. Since the combing is forbidden on Sabbath and holiday, if she has to immerse herself on one of these days she is told to cleanse her hair before the Sabbath or holiday.

69 The dispute between R. Ze`ira and R. Abba is if the holiday in the Diaspora is Thursday-Friday and she has to immerse herself after the end of the Sabbath. R. Ze`ira holds that since she may both cleanse and immerse herself after the end of the Sabbath, there is no reason to permit the cleansing on Wednesday. R. Abba disagrees for the reason given in the text.

70 *Job* 15:9.

(fol. 74c) **משנה ב**: וּבְרָאשֵׁי חֳדָשִׁים וּבְחוּלוֹ שֶׁל מוֹעֵד קוֹרִין אַרְבָּעָה. אֵין פּוֹחֲתִין מֵהֶן וְאֵין מוֹסִיפִין עֲלֵיהֶן וְאֵין מַפְטִירִין בַּנָּבִיא. הַפּוֹתֵחַ וְהַחוֹתֵם בַּתּוֹרָה מְבָרֵךְ לְפָנֶיהָ וּלְאַחֲרֶיהָ. זֶה הַכְּלָל כָּל־שֶׁיֵּשׁ בּוֹ מוּסָף וְאֵינוֹ יוֹם טוֹב קוֹרִין אַרְבָּעָה.

Mishnah 2: On New Moon's Days and on the intermediate days of holidays four are reading, no less and no more, and one does not close with a reading from Prophets. The ones who start and finish the Torah reading recite the benediction before and after the reading[71]. This is the principle: four are reading on any {day} when there is *musaf*[72] and it is not a holiday.

71 The one who starts recites the benediction before and the one who ends recites the benediction after, according to the old standard abolished in Amoraic times.

72 Either referring to Temple times, a *musaf* sacrifice as prescribed in *Num.* 28-29, or in Mishnaic times a *musaf* prayer after the reading from the Torah.

(75a line 39) **הלכה ב**: רַב חוּנָה אָמַר. שְׁלֹשָׁה קְרִיוֹת שֶׁבַּתּוֹרָה לֹא יִפְחֲתוּ מֵעֲשָׂרָה פְּסוּקִים. חִזְקִיָּה אָמַר. כְּנֶגֶד עֲשֶׂרֶת הַדִּיבְּרוֹת. [וְהָא תַנִּינָן. בַּיּוֹם הָרִאשׁוֹן בְּרֵאשִׁית וִיהִי רָקִיעַ. וְהָא לֵית בְּהוֹן אֶלָּא תְמַנְיָא. רִבִּי אִידִי אוֹמֵר. אִיתְפַּלְגוּן כָּהֲנָא וְאָסִי. חַד אָמַר. חוֹזֵר. וְחוֹרָנָא אָמַר.

חוֹתֵךְ. מָאן דְּאָמַר. חוֹזֵר. חוֹזֵר שְׁנֵי פְסוּקִים. וּמָאן דָּמַר. חוֹתֵךְ. וַיְהִי־עֶרֶב וַיְהִי־בֹקֶר פָּסוּק בִּפְנֵי עַצְמוֹ. וְהָא תַנִּינָן. בַּשֵּׁנִי יְהִי רָקִיעַ וְיִקָווּ הַמַּיִם. מָאן דְּאָמַר. חוֹזֵר. חוֹזֵר שְׁנֵי פְסוּקִין. וּמָאן דָּמַר. חוֹתֵךְ. אֲפִילוּ חוֹתֵךְ אֵין בּוֹ. הוֹתִיב רִבִּי פְלִיפִּי בַּר פְּרוֹטָה קוֹמֵי רִבִּי יוֹנָה. וַהֲרֵי פָּרָשַׁת עֲמָלֵק. אָמַר לֵיהּ. שַׁנְיָיא הִיא. שֶׁהִיא סִידּוּרָהּ שֶׁלְּיוֹם.] הָתִיב רִבִּי לְעָזָר בַּר מָרוֹם. וְהָא תַאנֵי. הַמַּפְטִיר בַּנָּבִיא לֹא יִפְחוֹת מֵעֶשְׂרִים וְאֶחָד פְּסוּקִים. וְיִהְיוּ עֶשְׂרִים וּשְׁלֹשָׁה. תְּלָתָא עֲשָׂרָה וּתְלָתָא עֲשָׂרָה וְחַד שְׁלֹשָׁה.

Halakhah 2: [73]Rav Huna said, three people reading in the Torah shall not do less than ten verses. Hizqiah said, corresponding to the Ten Commandments [But did we not state, "on Sunday, *In the Beginning* and *there shall be a spread*"? And these are only eight! Rebbi Idi said, Cahana and Assi disagreed. One said, he repeats. But the other said, he splits. He who says that he repeats, he repeats two verses. He who says he splits, he splits *it was evening, it was morning,* as a separate verse. But did we not state, "on Monday, *there shall be a spread* and *the waters shall come together*"? He who says that he repeats, he repeats two verses. He who says he splits, he could not split. Rebbi Philippos ben Protos objected before Rebbi Jonah, is there not the paragraph about Amalek? He said to him, there is a difference since this is the topic of the day.] Rebbi Eleazar from Merom asked, was it not stated, the one who reads the conclusion from Prophets should not do less than 21 verses. Should there not be 23? Three for ten, three for ten, and one three[74].

73 This is repeated (mostly by the corrector) from *Ta`aniot* 4:3, Notes 141-148.

74 He reads the statement of Rav Huna to mean that any time three people read in the Torah they together must read 10 verses. Then on a Sabbath, when 3+3+1 readers are called, they must read a minimum of 23 verses. Corresponding to this the reader from Prophets should have to read 23 verses. The fact that he has to read only 21 shows that we have to read Rav Huna's remark as referring only to the weekday and Sabbath afternoon readings.

(fol 74c) **משנה ג:** בְּיוֹם טוֹב חֲמִשָּׁה. בְּיוֹם הַכִּיפּוּרִים שִׁשָּׁה. בְּשַׁבָּת שִׁבְעָה. אֵין פּוֹחֲתִין מֵהֶן אֲבָל מוֹסִיפִין עֲלֵיהֶן וּמַפְטִירִין בַּנָּבִיא. הַפּוֹתֵחַ וְהַחוֹתֵם בַּתּוֹרָה מְבָרֵךְ לְפָנֶיהָ וּלְאַחֲרֶיהָ:

Mishnah 3: On a holiday five, on the Day of Atonement six, on the Sabbath seven, no less but one may add to them, and one closes with a reading from Prophets. The ones who start and finish the Torah reading recite the benediction before and after the reading[71].

(75a line 50) **הלכה ג**: וּבְיוֹם הַכִּיפּוּרִים שִׁשָּׁה. אִית תַּנֵּיֵי תַנֵּי. שִׁבְעָה. מָאן דְּאָמַר. שִׁשָּׁה. מִפְּנֵי הַתְּפִילָה. מָאן דְּאָמַר. שִׁבְעָה. כְּהָדָא דְתַנֵּי. בַּשַּׁבָּת מְמַהֲרִים לָבוֹא וּמְמַהֲרִין לָצֵאת. בְּיוֹם טוֹב מְאַחֲרִין לָבוֹא וּמְמַהֲרִין לָצֵאת. בְּיוֹם הַכִּיפּוּרִים מְמַהֲרִין לָבוֹא וּמְאַחֲרִין לָצֵאת.

Halakhah 3: "And on the Day of Atonement six." There are Tannaim who state, seven. He who says six, because of the prayer[75]. He who says seven, following what was stated, on a Sabbath one comes early and leaves early[76]; on a holiday one comes late and leaves early[77], on the Day of Atonement one comes early and leaves late[78].

75 To have time for the prayers which are extra long.

76 Since one may not cook on the Sabbath, all food is prepared and one may come early; one leaves early to enjoy the Sabbath. Babli 23a.

77 One comes late since one may prepare the holiday food early in the morning.

78 One comes early since nothing is there to prepare and one leaves late since on this day there is nothing to do but pray.

(75a line 532) הַלּוֹעֲזוֹת לָא נָהֲגוּ כֵן. אֶלָּא אֶחָד קוֹרֵא כָּל־הַפָּרָשָׁה כּוּלָּהּ. הָיָה יוֹדֵעַ אֶחָד אֶת הַפָּרָשָׁה קוֹרֵא אֶת כּוּלָּהּ. שִׁבְעָה יוֹדְעִין שְׁלֹשָׁה פְסוּקִין כּוּלְּהוֹן קָרְאֵיי. אֶחָד יוֹדֵעַ שְׁלֹשָׁה פְסוּקִים קָרֵי וַחֲזַר קָרֵי. רִבִּי זְעוּרָה בְשֵׁם רַב יִרְמְיָה. הָעֶבֶד עוֹלֶה לְמִנְיָין שִׁבְעָה. וַיְדַבֵּר עוֹלֶה מִשְׁלֹשָׁה פְסוּקִים. לֹא כֵן אָמַר רִבִּי חָמָא בַּר עוּקְבָּה בְשֵׁם רִבִּי יוֹסֵי בֵּירִבִּי חֲנִינָה. אָסוּר לְלַמֵּד אֶת עַבְדּוֹ תוֹרָה. תִּיפְתָּר. שֶׁלָּמַד מֵאֵילָיו אוֹ שֶׁלִּימְּדוֹ רַבּוֹ כְּטָבִי.

The Greek speakers did not use to do this, but a single person reads the entire portion[79]. If one knew the portion he reads it completely. If of seven persons each one knows three verses, they all read[80]. If one knows three verses he reads them repeatedly[81]. Rebbi Ze`ira in the name of Rav Jeremiah, a slave is counted for the count of seven[82]; "and spoke" is counted as one of three verses[83]. But did not Rebbi Ḥama bar Uqba say in the name of Rebbi Yose ben Rebbi Ḥanina, it is forbidden to teach Torah to one's slave[84]? Explain it if he learned it by himself or that his master taught him like Tabi[85].

79 If the congregation knows no Hebrew, a professional reader will read it for them. Tosephta 3:13.
80 Even though the customary reading is longer, if the congregation manages to find among their members three who together can read 21 verses, they can conduct regular services.
81 If no professional is available, one person may read 3 verses 7 times.
82 Even though he is not counted in a quorum of ten adult males.
83 The short verse, *the Eternal spoke to Moses as follows*, is counted as a full verse of the required three. Babli 21b.
84 Babli *Ketubot* 28a.
85 The slave in Rabban Gamliel's house for whom the master warranted that he was a moral person.

(75a line 59) רִבִּי חֶלְבּוֹ רִבִּי מַתָּנָה רְבִּי שְׁמוּאֵל בַּר שִׁילַת בְּשֵׁם רַב. שִׁבְעָה חוּץ מִן הַמַּפְטִיר. הָתִיב רִבִּי חֲנַנְיָה בֶּן פָּזִי. וְהָתַנִּינֻן. הַמַּפְטִיר בַּנָּבִיא לֹא יִפְחוֹת מֵעֶשְׂרִים וְאֶחָד פְּסוּקִין. הוּא אָמְרָהּ וְאָמַר טַעַם. בְּשֶׁאֵין שָׁם תּוּרְגְּמָן. אֲבָל אִם יֵשׁ שָׁם תּוּרְגְּמָן קוֹרְאִים שְׁלֹשָׁה. אָמַר רִבִּי חֶלְבּוֹ קוֹמֵי רִבִּי אַבָּהוּ קוֹמֵי רִבִּי יוֹחָנָן. קָרַאי תְּלָתָה. אָמַר לֵיהּ. [וְ]לֹא (הוּא) [יְהֵא] רִבִּי יוֹחָנָן כְּתוּרְגְּמָן.

Rebbi Ḥelbo, Rebbi Mattanah, Samuel bar Shilat in the name of Rav: Seven not counting the closer[86]. Rebbi Ḥananiah ben Pazi objected, did we not state, the one who reads the conclusion from Prophets should not do less than 21 verses[87]? He said it and he gave the reason, if there is no translator. But if there is a translator, one has to read three[88]. Rebbi Ḥelbo said before Rebbi Abbahu, before Rebbi Joḥanan they are reading three. He said to him, (is not) [should not be] Rebbi Joḥanan like a translator[89]?

86 The one who reads from Prophets has first to read three verses in the Torah, but (on Sabbath and holidays) cannot be counted among the seven who deliver the required reading.
87 Then a minimum of 24 verses will have been read; why do we not require that 24 verses be read from Prophets? Babli 24a.
88 If the text has been explained to the congregation there is no requirement to read 21 verses, and certainly not 24.
89 Since R. Joḥanan will have explained or preached about the topics read, in his synagogue the required reading is 3 verses.

(fol. 74c) **משנה ד:** אֵין פּוֹרְסִין עַל שְׁמַע וְאֵין עוֹבְרִין לִפְנֵי הַתֵּבָה וְאֵין נוֹשְׂאִין כַּפֵּיהֶם וְאֵין קוֹרִין בַּתּוֹרָה וְאֵין מַפְטִירִין בַּנָּבִיא וְאֵין עוֹשִׂין מַעֲמָד וּמוֹשָׁב וְאֵין אוֹמְרִים בִּרְכַּת אֲבֵלִים וַחֲתָנִים וְאֵין מְזַמְּנִין עַל הַמָּזוֹן בַּשֵּׁם פָּחוֹת מֵעֲשָׂרָה. וּבַקַּרְקָעוֹת תִּשְׁעָה וְכֹהֵן. וְאָדָם כַּיּוֹצֵא בָּהֶן:

Mishnah 4: One does not split the *Shema*`[90], nor stand in front of the Ark[91], nor lift his hands[92] nor read in the Torah[93], nor close with Prophets[93], nor proceed standing and sitting[94], nor recite benedictions for mourners[95] or bridegrooms[96], nor say Grace invoking the Name, with less than ten attendants; in matters of real estate[97] nine and a Cohen, and similarly about humans[98].

90 פּוֹרֵס "to split" is Rashi's reading in the Babli, which he explains that if a group of at least ten adult males come late to the synagogue, they can have their own reader who leads them in an abbreviated service. The text of Maimonides is פּוֹרֵשׂ "to spread out"; he interprets "spreading out the *Shema*`" as the regular synagogue service leading to the public recitation of the *Shema*` and the following *Amidah*. The Yerushalmi Halakhah clearly supports Maimonides.

91 As a reader for the *Amidah*.

92 The priestly blessing as part of the *Amidah*.

93 Public reading.

94 Returning from a funeral to town they had seven places where they sat down for additional eulogies.

95 Addition to Grace in a house of mourning.

96 The seven benedictions required at a definitive wedding and following Grace in the wedding week.

97 To determine the value of real estate dedicated to the Temple. *Lev.* 27:14-25; Tractate *Arakhin*.

98 To determine the amount of money dedicated to the Temple for the "value of somebody" (*Lev.* 27:1-8), 9 lay people and 1 Cohen also are required.

(75a line 64) **הלכה ד**: מִכֵּיוָן דְּתַנִּינָן. אֵין פּוֹרְסִין אֶת שְׁמַע פָּחוֹת מֵעֲשָׂרָה. וְלֵיי דָא מִילָּה תַנִּינָן. אֵין עוֹבְרִין לִפְנֵי הַתֵּבָה פָּחוֹת מֵעֲשָׂרָה. לָכֵן צְרִיכָה. כְּהָדָא דְתַנֵּי. אֵין פּוֹרְסִין אֶת שְׁמַע פָּחוֹת מֵעֲשָׂרָה. הִתְחִילוּ בַּעֲשָׂרָה וְהָלְכוּ לָהֶן מִקְצָתָן גּוֹמֵר. אֵין עוֹבְרִין לִפְנֵי הַתֵּבָה פָּחוֹת מֵעֲשָׂרָה. הִתְחִילוּ בַּעֲשָׂרָה וְהָלְכוּ לָהֶן מִקְצָתָן גּוֹמֵר. אֵין נוֹשְׂאִין אֶת כַּפֵּיהֶן פָּחוֹת מֵעֲשָׂרָה. הִתְחִילוּ בַּעֲשָׂרָה וְהָלְכוּ לָהֶן מִקְצָתָן גּוֹמֵר. אֵין קוֹרְאִין בַּתּוֹרָה פָּחוֹת מֵעֲשָׂרָה. הִתְחִילוּ בַּעֲשָׂרָה וְהָלְכוּ לָהֶן מִקְצָתָן גּוֹמֵר. אֵין מַפְטִירִין בַּנָּבִיא פָּחוֹת מֵעֲשָׂרָה. הִתְחִילוּ בַּעֲשָׂרָה וְהָלְכוּ לָהֶן מִקְצָתָן גּוֹמֵר. וְעַל כּוּלָּם הוּא אוֹמֵר. וְעוֹזְבֵי יְיָ יִכְלוּ׃

Halakhah 4: Since we had stated, "one does not spread out the *Shema*` with less than ten attendants", for which purpose did we state, "one does not stand before the Ark with less than ten attendants"? It is necessary for what was stated, "one does not spread out the *Shema*` with less than ten attendants; if they started with ten and some left, he finishes. One does not stand before the Ark with less than ten attendants; if they started with ten and some left, he finishes. One does not lift his hands with less than ten attendants; if they started with ten and some left, he finishes. One does not read in the Torah with less than ten attendants; if they started with ten and some left, he finishes. One does not close with Prophets with less than ten attendants; if they started with ten and some left, he finishes. About all these He says, *those who abandon the Eternal will disappear.*[99]"

99 *Is.* 1:28. Cf. Babli *Berakhot* 8a, bottom.

(75a line 72) אֵין עוֹשִׂין מַעֲמָד וּמוֹשָׁב. עָמְדוּ יְקָרִים. שְׁבוּ יְקָרִים. שִׁבְעָה פְעָמִים.

"One does not proceed standing and sitting.[94]" Stand, dears; sit down, dears, seven times[94].

(75a line 73) אֵין אוֹמְרִים בְּרְכַּת אֲבֵלִים וַחֲתָנִים. תַּנֵּי. אוֹמְרִים בְּרְכַּת חֲתָנִים כָּל־שִׁבְעָה. רִבִּי יִרְמְיָה סְבַר מֵימַר. מַפְקִין כַּלָּתָה כָּל־שִׁבְעָה. אָמַר לֵיהּ רִבִּי יוֹסֵה. וְהָא תַנֵּי רִבִּי חִייָה. אוֹמֵר בְּרְכַּת אֲבֵלִים כָּל־שִׁבְעָה. אִית לָךְ מֵימַר. מַפְקִין מֵיתָא כָּל־שִׁבְעָה. מַאי כְדוֹן. מַה כָּאן מְשַׂמֵּחַ עִמּוֹ אַף כָּאן מְנַחֵם עִמּוֹ. מַה כָּאן מַזְכִּירִין אַף כָּאן מַזְכִּירִין.

אִית תַּנֵּי תַנֵּי. אֵין אֲבֵלִים עוֹלִין מִן הַמִּנְיָין. [וְאִית תַּנּוּיֵי תַנֵּי. אֲבֵלִים עוֹלִים מִן הַמִּנְיָין.] אָמַר רִבִּי אֲבוּנָה. מָאן דְּאָמַר. אֵין אֲבֵלִים עוֹלִים מִן הַמִּנְיָין. בַּאֲבֵילֵי אוֹתוֹ הַמֵּת. מָאן דְּאָמַר. אֲבֵלִים עוֹלִים מִן הַמִּנְיָין. בַּאֲבֵילֵי מֵת אַחֵר. וְהָא תַנֵּי. יוֹצֵא לְהִתְנַחֵם אֲבָל לֹא לְנַחֵם.

"One does not recite benedictions for mourners or bridegrooms." [100]It was stated, the marriage benedictions are said all seven days[96]. Rebbi Jeremiah wanted to say that one re-enacts the marriage all seven days. Rebbi Yose said to him, did not Rebbi Ḥiyya state, the benedictions for mourners are said all seven days? Can you say that one buries the dead all seven days? How is that? Since here he enjoys with him, so there he consoles with him. As here one remembers, so there one remembers[101].

There are Tannaim who state, the mourners are not counted in the quorum. [There are Tannaim who state, the mourners are counted in the quorum.] Rebbi Abuna said, he who said, the mourners are not counted in the quorum, the mourners of this deceased. He who said, the mourners are counted in the quorum, the mourners of another deceased. But was it not stated, he leaves to be comforted but not to comfort[102]?

100 An incomplete copy of this text is in *Ketubot* 1:1, Notes 78-83.
101 The topic of conversation in a house of mourning is the deceased; the topic of conversation with the newlyweds is the marriage ceremony.

102 Therefore there can be no other mourners in the first week of mourning present at the meal in the house of mourning. R. Abuna's explanation is rejected, there is genuine disagreement how the numbers have to be counted. Babli 23b.

(75b line 6) תָּנֵי שְׁמוּאֵל. אֵין קִידּוּשׁ הַחוֹדֶשׁ אֶלָּא בַעֲשָׂרָה. רִבִּי בָּא רִבִּי יָסָא בְשֵׁם רִבִּי יוֹחָנָן. נֶאֱמַר כָּאן עֵדָה וְנֶאֱמַר לְהַלָּן עַד־מָתַי לָעֵדָה הָרָעָה הַזֹּאת. מָה עֵדָה הָאֲמוּרָה לְהַלָּן עֲשָׂרָה אַף כָּאן עֲשָׂרָה. אָמַר רִבִּי סִימוֹן. נֶאֱמַר כָּאן תּוֹךְ וְנֶאֱמַר לְהַלָּן וַיַּבֹאוּ בְּנֵי יִשְׂרָאֵל לִשְׁבּוֹר בְּתוֹךְ הַבָּאִים. מַה תּוֹךְ שֶׁנֶּאֱמַר לְהַלָּן עֲשָׂרָה אַף כָּאן עֲשָׂרָה. אָמַר לֵיהּ רִבִּי יוֹסֵה בֵּירִבִּי בּוּן. אִם מִתּוֹךְ אַתְּ לָמֵד. סַגִּין אִינּוּן. [אֶלָּא נֶאֱמַר כָּאן בְּנֵי יִשְׂרָאֵל וְנֶאֱמַר לְהַלָּן בְּנֵי יִשְׂרָאֵל. מַה לְהַלָּן עֲשָׂרָה אַף כָּאן עֲשָׂרָה.]

Samuel stated, the sanctification of the New Moon is only by ten {attendants}[103]. [104]Rebbi Abba, Rebbi Yasa in the name of Rebbi Johanan: It is said here community, and it is said there, *how long this bad community*. Since "community" mentioned there are ten, so also "community" mentioned here are ten[105]. Rebbi Simon said, it is said here, in midst, and it is said there[106], *the sons of Israel came to buy in midst of the comers*. Since "in midst" mentioned there are ten, so also "in midst" mentioned here are ten[107]. Rebbi Yose ben Rebbi Abun said to him, if you infer from "in midst", there are many[108]. [But it is said here "the sons of Israel", and it is said there "the sons of Israel". Since there are ten, also here are ten.[109]]

103 In *Sanhedrin* 1:2 (Note 120) this is quoted as Amoraic statement of Samuel. It is not the determination of the day of the New Moon, which can be made by a competent court of three, but the solemn declaration of the start of a new month.
104 *Gen. rabba* 91(1).
105 *Lev.* 19:2 reads, *speak to the community of Israel, you shall be holy*. From this one wants to prove that all matters called "holy" need a community of at least ten adult males. Since the ten bad scouts are called a "bad community" in *Num.* 14:17, it follows that in Pentateuchal usage a group is called "community" if it has 10 members. Since we do not find the expression used for a smaller number, 10 is the required minimum. Babli 23b.
106 *Gen.* 42:5.
107 Here the reference is to *Lev* 22:32: *I shall be sanctified in the midst of the Children of Israel*. One intends to prove that God may be sanctified by any group of at least 10 of the Children of Israel.
108 There are two possible interpretations of this statement. Since *Lev* 22:32 is the

conclusion of statements about the Temple service, it may refer to all the people and therefore require a minimum of 600'000 people, or it may refer to the large number of times the lexeme "in the midst" is used in the Pentateuch, from which nothing can be inferred.

108 Added from *Gen. rabba*. Since it implies the identity of "Children of Israel" with "sons of Israel, Jacob", one may doubt whether it is intended here.

(75b line 13) וּבְקַרְקָעוֹת תִּשְׁעָה וְכֹהֵן. כְּנֶגֶד עֲשָׂרָה כֹּהֲנִים הָאֲמוּרִין בַּפָּרָשָׁה. וְיִהְיוּ כוּלָם כֹּהֲנִים. רִיבּוּי אַחַר רִיבּוּי לְמָעֵט. וְיִהְיוּ כוּלָן יִשְׂרָאֵל. אֵין הַפָּרָשָׁה יוֹצְאָה בְלֹא כֹהֵן. עַד כְּדוֹן בְּמַקְדִּישׁ גּוּפָהּ שֶׁלְשָׂדֶה. אָמַר. דְּמֵי שָׂדִי עָלַי. נִישְׁמְעִינָהּ מִן הָדָא. עֲרָכִים הַמִּיטַּלְטְלִיו בִּשְׁלשָׁה. וְיֵשׁ עֲרָכִים שֶׁאֵינָן מִיטַּלְטְלִיו. רִבִּי יַעֲקֹב בַּר אָחָא רִבִּי שִׁמְעוֹן בַּר אַבָּא בְשֵׁם רִבִּי חֲנִינָה. בָּאוֹמֵר. הֲרֵי עֶרְכִּי עָלַי. וּבָא לְסַדֵּר מִן הַקַּרְקַע. שָׁמִין לוֹ בָעֲשָׂרָה. מִן הַמִּיטַּלְטְלִיו. שָׁמִין לוֹ בִּשְׁלשָׁה. הָאוֹמֵר. הֲרֵי עֶרְכִּי עָלַי. אֵינוֹ כָאוֹמֵר. דְּמֵי שָׂדִי עָלַי. אֲבָל אִם אָמַר. הֲרֵי עָלַי מֵאָה מָנֶה לַהֶקְדֵּשׁ. שָׁמִין לוֹ בִּשְׁלשָׁה. לִכְשֶׁיַּעֲשִׁיר. נִידּוֹן בְּהֶשֵּׂג יָד.

"In matters of real estate[97] nine and a Cohen." Corresponding to the ten times "Cohen" is mentioned in the paragraph[109]. Then should they not all be Cohanim? An inclusion after an inclusion is an exclusion[110]. Then could they all be Israel? The paragraph has no result without a Cohen. That is, if one dedicated the body of a field. But if he said, I am vowing the value of my field for the Temple, [111]let us hear from the following: "Appraisal of movables by three {appraisers}." Do there exist appraisals not of movables[112]? Rebbi Jacob bar Aha, Rebbi Simeon bar Abba in the name of Rebbi Ḥanina: If somebody says, I am vowing my appraisal, and comes to settle his debt by real estate, one appraises it by ten {persons}, by movables by three[113]. Is one who says, I am vowing my appraisal not like one who says, I am vowing my field's value[114]? But if he said, I am vowing a hundred mina for the Temple, one appraises him by three. Should he become rich, he will be judged by what he can afford[115].

109 The word "Cohen" is mentioned 3 times in *Lev.* 27:8, 2 times each in vv. 14,14, and once in vv. 11,21,23, for a total of 10.

110 Therefore *n* consecutive inclusions are an inclusion for *n* odd, an exclusion for *n* even. Babli 23b, *Yoma* 43a.

111 This text is from *Sanhedrin* 1:4, discussing Mishnah 1:4 quoted in this sentence.

112 By definition, "appraisals" refers to the sums of money detailed in *Lev.* 27:1-8. Money always is movable.

113 Real estate by the rules of Mishnah *Megillah* 4:4, movables by *Sanhedrin* 1:4.
114 Since the rules of appraisal are the same in both categories.
115 This is difficult to understand; since the text is confirmed by two copies, it cannot be emended. By biblical law, a reduction of payments for the poor is mandated only for appraisals (*Lev.* 27:8), not for dedications of specified sums. The reduction, based on what he can afford, is determined by a committee of three which must include a Cohen. If the poor person paid only part of the reduced sum and then becomes rich, the original sum is reinstated as soon as he can afford it. If the poor person made his vow (in the *Megillah* version for 100 minas) in order to induce God to make him rich so he may fulfill his vow, it might be in the interest of the Temple to wait with the collection of the debt until the person became affluent.

(75b line 22) תַּנֵּי. עֲבָדִים וּשְׁפָחוֹת וּמִיטַּלְטְלִין אֵין לָהֶם אִיגֶּרֶת בִּיקּוֹרֶת. מָהוּ אִיגֶּרֶת בִּיקּוֹרֶת. רִבִּי יוּדָה בַּר פָּזִי אָמַר. אַכְרָזָה. עוּלָּה בַר יִשְׁמָעֵאל אָמַר. עֲבָדִים שֶׁלֹּא יִבְרְחוּ. שְׁטָרוֹת וּמִיטַּלְטְלִין שֶׁלֹּא יִיגָּנְבוּ. רִבִּי בָּא בַר כֹּהֵן בְּעָא קוֹמֵי רִבִּי יוֹסֵה. לֵית הָדָא אָמְרָה שֶׁעֲבָדִים נִפְדִּין בִּשְׁלֹשָׁה. אָמַר לֵיהּ. אִין. וְהָתַנֵּינָן וּבַקַּרְקָעוֹת תִּשְׁעָה וְכֹהֵן וְאָדָם כַּיּוֹצֵא בָהֶן. אָמַר לֵיהּ. אָדָם דְּהָכָא בֶּן חוֹרִין הוּא. חִינָנָה בַר שְׁלֶמְיָה בְּשֵׁם רַב. אֲתָא עוֹבָדָא קוֹמֵי רִבִּי וּבְעָא מֵיעֲבַד כְּרַבָּנָן. אֲמַר לֵיהּ רִבִּי לַעֲזָר בֶּן בְּנוֹ שֶׁלְרִבִּי לַעֲזָר בֶּן פְּרָטָא. רִבִּי. לֹא כֵן לִימַּדְתָּנוּ בְשֵׁם זְקֵינָיךְ. אֶלָּא אִם כֵּן עָשׂוּ כֵן אִיגֶּרֶת בִּיקּוֹרֶת. וַחֲזַר בֵּיהּ וַעֲבַד כְּרַבָּן שִׁמְעוֹן בֶּן גַּמְלִיאֵל.

[116]It was stated: One does not make public tender for slaves, and girl slaves[117], and movables. What is public tender? Rebbi Jehudah ben Pazi said, announcement. Ulla bar Ismael said, slaves lest they flee, securities and movables lest they be stolen. Rebbi Abba bar Cohen asked before Rebbi Yose: Does this not imply that a slave be redeemed in front of three people? He answered him, yes. But did we not state: "Real estate nine and a Cohen. The same holds for humans"? He answered him, but the human here is a free person.

Ḥanania bar Šelemiah in the name of Rav: A case came before Rebbi who wanted to act following the rabbis. Rebbi Eleazar ben Proteus, the grandson of Rebbi Eleazar ben Proteus, said to him: Rebbi, did you not teach us in your grandfather's name, "except if he offered public tender"? He answered, yes, changed his mind, and acted following Rabban Simeon ben[118] Gamliel.

116 *Sanhedrin* 1:4, Note 258. The origin of these paragraphs is in *Ketubot* 11:6, explained there in Notes 116-128. The final

paragraph, while also found in *Sanhedrin*, makes sense only in *Ketubot*.

117 Copyist's error from שְׁטָרוֹת "documents (of indebtedness)".

118 The last two words have to be deleted with the two other sources. Rebbi was the son of Rabban Simeon ben Gamliel.

(fol. 74c) **משנה ה**: הַקּוֹרֵא בַּתּוֹרָה לֹא יִפְחוֹת מִשְּׁלֹשָׁה פְּסוּקִים. וְלֹא יִקְרָא לַמְתוּרְגְּמָן יוֹתֵר מִפָּסוּק אֶחָד וּבַנָּבִיא שְׁלֹשָׁה. אִם הָיוּ שְׁלָשְׁתָּן שָׁלֹשׁ פָּרָשִׁיּוֹת קוֹרִין אֶחָד אֶחָד. מְדַלְּגִין בַּנָּבִיא וְאֵין מְדַלְּגִין בַּתּוֹרָה. וְעַד כַּמָּה הוּא מְדַלֵּג עַד כְּדֵי שֶׁלֹּא יַפְסִיק הַתּוּרְגְּמָן:

Mishnah 5: One who reads in the Torah may not read less than three verses. He should not read for the translator more than one verse, but in Prophets three. If all three were three paragraphs he reads them singly[119]. One skips in Prophets but one does not skip in the Torah. How far may he skip[120]? As long as the translator did not stop.

119 For example *Is.* 45:8-10 can be read only in single sentences. While in the translation of Torah one requires exactitude, in Prophets one requires clarification of the meaning; but different paragraphs usually have different emphasis.

120 How much time does he have to scroll? It is obvious that in Prophets one cannot switch scrolls; this means that one may switch subjects only within one prophet except for the 12 minor prophets written on one scroll.

(75b line 31) **הלכה ה**: רִבִּי בָּא בְּרֵיהּ דְּרִבִּי חִייָה בַּר בָּא רִבִּי חִייָה בְּשֵׁם רִבִּי יוֹחָנָן. הָיָה קוֹרֵא בַּתּוֹרָה וְנִשְׁתַּתֵּק. זֶה שֶׁהוּא עוֹמֵד תַּחְתָּיו יַתְחִיל מִמָּקוֹם שֶׁהִתְחִיל הָרִאשׁוֹן. אִין תֵּימַר. מִמָּקוֹם שֶׁהִפְסִיק. הָרִאשׁוֹנִים נִתְבָּרְכוּ לִפְנֵיהֶן וְלֹא נִתְבָּרְכוּ לְאַחֲרֵיהֶן. הָאַחֲרוֹנִים נִתְבָּרְכוּ לְאַחֲרֵיהֶן וְלֹא נִתְבָּרְכוּ לִפְנֵיהֶן. וְכָתוּב תּוֹרַת יְיָ תְּמִימָה. שֶׁתְּהֵא כּוּלָּהּ תְּמִימָה.

1 בא | ב אבא   2 אין תימר | ב אם אומ' את   3 שהפסיק | ב שפסק   האחרונים | ב והאחרונים   4 | - ב משיבת נפש

Halakhah 5: [121]Rebbi Abba, the son of Rebbi Hiyya bar Abba in the name of Rebbi Johanan: If one became paralyzed while reading in the Torah[122], the one who steps in for him should start from the place the first one started. For if you would say from the place he stopped, the first verses would have been blessed before them but not after them, the last ones after them but not before them, but it is written[123] *The Torah of the Eternal is perfect,* that it should be totally perfect.

121 The text also appears in *Berakhot* 5:4 (Notes 141,142,**ב**).
122 In public.
123 *Ps.* 19:8.

(75b line 36) הָיְתָה הַפָּרָשָׁה שֶׁלְחֲמִשָּׁה פְּסוּקִים קוֹרֵא אֶת כּוּלָּהּ. לֹא עָשָׂה כֵן אֶלָּא קָרָא שְׁלֹשָׁה. זֶה שֶׁהוּא עוֹמֵד [תַּחְתָּיו] צָרִיךְ לִקְרוֹת שְׁנֵי פְסוּקִים הָאַחֲרוֹנִים וּשְׁלֹשָׁה מִפָּרָשָׁה הָאַחֶרֶת לֹא עָשָׂה כֵן מָהוּ שֶׁיְּעַכֵּב. רִבִּי יוֹנָה וְרִבִּי יוֹסֵה סָלְקוּן מֵיחֲמֵייהּ אַפִּין לְאָחוֹי דִיהוּדָה בַּר תַּמּוּזָה קְרִיבֵיהּ דְּרִבִּי יוֹסֵה בֶּן חֲנִינָה בִּכְנִישְׁתָּא דְּסוֹבָנַייָא וַהֲוָה שָׁם רִבִּי יִרְמְיָה וְעִכֵּב. אָמַר רִבִּי יוֹנָה לְרִבִּי יוֹסֵה. וְכוֹפִין. אָמַר לֵיהּ. וְהָא רַבָּךְ מְעַכֵּב. רִבִּי יִרְמְיָה רִבִּי שִׁמְעוֹן שָׂרָה רִבִּי חִינְנָא בַּר אַנְדְּרֵיי בְּשֵׁם רִבִּי זַכַּיי דְּכָבוּל. טָעָה בֵּין תֵּיבָה לְתֵיבָה מַחֲזִירִין אוֹתוֹ. אָמַר רִבִּי יִרְמְיָה לְרִבִּי זְעוּרָה. וְעָבְדִין כֵּן. אָמַר לֵיהּ. וְאַדַּיִין אַתְּ לָזוֹ. אֲפִילוּ טָעָה בֵּין אִם לְוְאִם מַחֲזִירִין אוֹתוֹ. רִבִּי שִׁמְעוֹן סַפְרָא דְטַרְבֶּנֶת אָמְרוּן לֵיהּ בְּנֵי קַרְתֵּיהּ. קְטַע בְּדִיבָּרַייָּא דְּקְרוֹנוּן בְּנַינָן. אֲתָא שְׁאַל לְרִבִּי חֲנִינָה. אָמַר לֵיהּ. אִין קְטָעִין רֵישָׁךְ לָא תִשְׁמַע לוֹן. וְלָא שָׁמַע לוֹן וְשָׁרוֹן לֵיהּ מִן סַפְרוּתֵיהּ. בָּתַר יוֹמִין נְחַת לְהָכָא. קָם עִימֵּיהּ רִבִּי שִׁמְעוֹן בֶּן יוֹסִינָה. אָמַר לֵיהּ. מַה אַתְּ עָבִיד בְּהַהוּא קַרְתָּךְ. וְתַנֵּי לֵיהּ עוֹבְדָא. אָמַר לֵיהּ. וְלָמָה לֹא שְׁמַעַתְּ לוֹן. אָמַר לֵיהּ. וְעָבְדִין כֵּן. אָמַר לֵיהּ. וְלִינַן מְקַטְעִין לוֹן בְּסִידְרָא. אָמַר לֵיהּ. וְלִינַן חֲזָרִין וְכֵלְלִין לוֹן. אָמַר רִבִּי זְעוּרָה. אִילּוּ הֲוָה הַהוּא סַפְרָא בְּיוֹמוֹי מַנִּיתִי חֲכִים.

If the paragraph was of five verses, he reads all of them. If he did not do so, the following one has to read the two last verses and three from the next paragraph[124]. If he did not do this, does it obstruct? Rebbi Jonah and Rebbi Yose went to visit the brother of Jehudah bar Tammuza the relative of Rebbi Yose ben Ḥanina in the synagogue of the neck-cloth makers[125]. Rebbi Jeremiah was there and he stopped them[126]. Rebbi Jonah said to Rebbi Yose, does one force? He answered him, here your teacher is stopping them. Rebbi Jeremiah, Rebbi Simeon Shara, Rebbi Ḥinena bar Andreas in the name of Rebbi Zakkai from Kabul: If he erred between one word and another one lets him repeat. Rebbi Jeremiah said to Rebbi Ze`ira, does one act like this? He told him, is that still a problem for you? Even if he erred between *if* and *and if* one makes him repeat. The people of his town told Rebbi Simeon, the teacher of Terbenth, cut the sentences which our sons are reading[127]. He went and asked Rebbi Ḥanina, who told him, do not listen to them even if they cut off your head. He did not listen to them and they freed him from his teaching position. After some time he came down here. Rebbi Simeon ben Yosina associated with him. He asked him, what goes on in your town? He told him the affair. He asked him, why did you not listen to them? He answered, does one do this? He answered, do we not cut them in the study? He answered, but we repeat and take them together[128]. Rebbi Ze`ira said, if this teacher had been in my time, I would have appointed him Rabbi.

124 Babli 22a.
125 Greek σάβανον "fine cloth". It appears that this was a synagogue in Tiberias.
126 He forced the second reader to read five verses before they could continue with the public Torah reading.

127 In teaching them to read Torah, they wanted him to split the verses into small parts which are easier to memorize.
128 If a verse is analyzed in its parts in advanced study it is always summarized as a complete sentence.

(75b line 52) רַב אָמַר. כְּגוֹן הוֹי רָב אֶת־יוֹצְרוֹ.

Rav said, for example *Woe him who fights his creator*[119].

מְדַלְגִין בַּנְּבִיא וְאֵין מְדַלְגִין בַּתּוֹרָה. מְדַלְגִין בַּנָּבִיא. אֵין מְדַלְגִין מִנָּבִיא לְנָבִיא. וּבִנְבִיא שֶׁלִּשְׁנַיִם עָשָׂר מוּתָּר.

[129]"One skips in Prophets but one does not skip in the Torah." One skips in prophets; one does not skip from one prophet to another prophet, but with the twelve prophets it is permitted[120].

אֵין מְדַלְגִין בַּתּוֹרָה. רִבִּי יִרְמְיָה בְשֵׁם רִבִּי שִׁמְעוֹן בֶּן לָקִישׁ. שֶׁאֵין גּוֹלִים סֵפֶר תּוֹרָה בָּרַבִּים. רִבִּי יוֹסֵה בָעֵי. הַגַע עַצְמָךְ שֶׁהָיְתָה פָרָשָׁה קְטַנָּה. אָמַר לֵיהּ. כְּדֵי שֶׁיַּשְׁמְעוּ אֶת יִשְׂרָאֵל הַתּוֹרָה עַל סֵדֶר. וְהָא תַנִּינָן. קוֹרֵא אַחֲרֵי מוֹת וְאַךְ בֶּעָשׂוֹר. שַׁנְיָיא הִיא. שֶׁהִיא סִדְרוֹ שֶׁל יוֹם. תֵּדַע לָךְ. דְּאָמַר רִבִּי שִׁמְעוֹן בֶּן לָקִישׁ. בְּכָל־מָקוֹם אֵינוֹ קוֹרֵא עַל פֶּה. וְהָכָא קוֹרֵא עַל פֶּה. רִבִּי יוֹסֵה מְפַקֵּד לְבַר עוּלָא חַזָּנָא דִכְנִישְׁתָּא דְּבַבְלָיָיא. כַּד דְּהִיא חָדָא אוֹרְיָיא תְּהֵוֵי גְוִילָא אֲחוֹרֵי פָרוֹכְתָא. כַּד דְּאִינּוּן תַּרְתֵּיי תֵּי מְיַיבֵּל חָדָא [וּמַיְיתֵי חָדָא].

"One does not skip in the Torah." Rebbi Jeremiah in the name of Rebbi Simeon ben Laqish: Because one does not scroll the book of the Torah in public. Rebbi Yose asked, think of it, if it was a small paragraph[130]? But so that Israel should hear the Torah in due order. But did we not state[131]: "he reads *after the death*[132] and *but on the tenth day*"[133]? There is a difference since this is the order of the day. You should know this, as Rebbi Simeon ben Laqish said, one never recites from memory but here he recites. Rebbi Yose ordered Bar Ulla, the beadle of the synagogue of the Babylonians: If there is one Torah[134], scroll it behind a curtain. If there are two, take away one and bring the other[28].

129 This and the next paragraph are in *Sotah* 7:6 and *Yoma* 7:1 (Notes 25-28).
130 If one continues on the same page after an interruption, nothing has to be scrolled.
131 Mishnah *Yoma* 7:1.
132 *Lev.* 16.
133 *Num.* 29:7-11. The sacrifices detailed in *Num.* 29:7-11 (offered by the High Priest in his year-round "golden" garments) are completely different from those required by *Lev.* 16, for whose service white linen garments are prescribed. Therefore mention of the text in *Num.* 19 is essential, but scrolling such a large distance would be an interruption of the public service.
134 On a day which in the Babylonian rite requires reading two different sections, such as a New Moon celebrated on a Sabbath, or a holiday. Then the Torah has to be scrolled, but this should not be done in public.

(75b line 61) עַד אֵיכָן. אָמַר רִבִּי אָחָא. כְּגוֹן פָּרָשַׁת יְהוֹיָדָע כֹּהֵן גָּדוֹל.

How far? Rebbi Aḥa said, as the paragraph of Joyada the High Priest[135].

135 This refers to the time one has to skip from one place in the scroll to another. It is the time the translator needs to translate or explain the paragraph of 4 verses, *2K.* 11:17-20.

(fol. 74c) **משנה ו**: הַמַּפְטִיר בַּנָּבִיא הוּא פּוֹרֵס אֶת שְׁמַע וְהוּא עוֹבֵר לִפְנֵי הַתֵּבָה וְהוּא נוֹשֵׂא אֶת כַּפָּיו. וְאִם הָיָה קָטָן אָבִיו אוֹ רַבּוֹ עוֹבְרִין עַל יָדוֹ:

Mishnah 6: He who closes with Prophets spreads out the *Shema*ʿ[90], or stands before the Ark[91] or lifts his hands[92,136]. If he was under age, his father or teacher stand in his stead.

136 Since reading from Prophets is less prestigious than reading from the Torah, the person who agrees to study Prophets to be able to read in public is induced to accept by being offered the honor to lead the congregation in reciting the *Shema*ʿ and its attendant benedictions, or the *Amidah*, or if he be a Cohen to pronounce the priestly blessings.

(75b line 62) **הלכה ו**: לָא צוֹרְכָה דִּילָא הַפּוֹרֵשׁ אֶת שְׁמַע הוּא עוֹבֵר לִפְנֵי הַתֵּבָה וְהוּא נוֹשֵׂא אֶת כַּפָּיו. רִבִּי יוֹסֵי בֶּן חֲנִינָה אָמַר. כְּדֵי לְזָרְזוֹ.

וְאִם הָיָה קָטָן אָבִיו אוֹ רַבּוֹ עוֹבְרִין עַל יָדוֹ: וְהָא תַנִּינָן. קָטָן לֹא יִפְרוֹשׁ אֶת שְׁמַע. אָמַר רִבִּי יוּדָן. כָּאן בְּשֶׁהֵבִיא שְׁתֵּי שְׂעָרוֹת וְכָאן בְּשֶׁלֹּא הֵבִיא שְׁתֵּי שְׂעָרוֹת.

Halakhah 6: Is not necessarily the one who spreads out the *Shemaʿ* the one who stands before the Ark and who lifts his hands[137]? Rebbi Yose ben Ḥanina said, in order to hasten him[138].

"If he was under age, his father or teacher do it in his stead." But was it not stated, a minor may not spread out the *Shemaʿ*? Rebbi Judan said, here if he grew two pubic hairs, there if he did not grow two pubic hairs[139].

137 Since at least in Amoraic times the *Amidah* immediately follows the recitation of the benediction concluding the *Shemaʿ*, by necessity the one who spreads out the *Shemaʿ* continues as the one who stands before the Ark, and if he is a Cohen is obligated to bless the congregation in his repetition of the *Amidah*.

138 While it is true that once he is chosen to spread out the *Shemaʿ* the other offices follow automatically, to increase the attraction of the job one gives it three titles.

139 Since a person may not absolve the public from its duty unless he himself is equally obligated and a minor cannot be obligated, the minor cannot do any of the three jobs with which he should be honored. Then why does the Mishnah formulate the replacement in terms of "standing", which only refers to the *Amidah*? The answer is that for purely religious obligation a person is an adult as soon as he grows two pubic hairs, but for public standing it also is required that he be 13 years and one day. If he grows 2 pubic hairs while only 12 years old, he might be able to spread out the *Shemaʿ* but he cannot stand before the Ark.

משנה ז: קָטָן קוֹרֵא בַּתּוֹרָה וּמְתַרְגֵּם אֲבָל אֵינוֹ פּוֹרֵס אֶת שְׁמַע וְאֵינוֹ עוֹבֵר לִפְנֵי (fol. 74c) הַתֵּיבָה וְאֵינוֹ נוֹשֵׂא אֶת כַּפָּיו. פּוֹחֵחַ פּוֹרֵס אֶת שְׁמַע וּמְתַרְגֵּם אֲבָל אֵינוֹ קוֹרֵא בַּתּוֹרָה וְאֵינוֹ עוֹבֵר לִפְנֵי הַתֵּבָה וְאֵינוֹ נוֹשֵׂא אֶת כַּפָּיו. סוּמָא פּוֹרֵס אֶת שְׁמַע וּמְתַרְגֵּם. רִבִּי יְהוּדָה אוֹמֵר כֹּל שֶׁלֹּא רָאָה מְאוֹרוֹת מִיָּמָיו לֹא פּוֹרֵס אֶת שְׁמַע:

Mishnah 7: A minor reads in the Torah and translates[140] but he does not spread out the *Shemaʿ*, nor stands before the Ark, nor lifts his hands. The uncovered[141] spreads out the *Shemaʿ* and translates, but he may not read in the Torah nor stand before the Ark, nor lift his hands. A blind man spreads out the *Shemaʿ*[142] and translates. Rebbi Jehudah says, a person who never saw light does not spread out the *Shemaʿ*[143].

140 Since these activities depend only on ability, not personal obligation.

141 In *Is.* 20, Jonathan translates עָרוֹם by

פֻּחֵחַ (while at all other occurrences the translation is ערטילאי). Rif explains: פוּחֵחַ means one whose clothing is torn and his shoulder and arms are naked. Rashi quotes *Soferim* 14:15: פוּחֵחַ is one whose feet are naked, or whose clothing is torn, or whose head is uncovered. He may do anything which is not visible in public.

142 This Tanna holds that blindness is not a disability freeing from religious observances.

143 Since the first benediction preceding the *Shema`* is a praise of God for the creation of light.

(75b line 67) **הלכה ז**: תַּמָּן תַּנֵּינָן. סוּמָא אֵינוֹ גוֹלֶה דִּבְרֵי רִבִּי יְהוּדָה. רִבִּי מֵאִיר אוֹמֵר גּוֹלֶה. וּשְׁנֵיהֶן מִקְרָא אֶחָד הֵן דּוֹרְשִׁין. בְּלֹא רְאוֹת. רִבִּי יְהוּדָה אוֹמֵר. לְרַבּוֹת אֶת הַסּוּמָא. רִבִּי מֵאִיר אוֹמֵר. פְּרָט לַסּוּמָא. וְכָא תַנֵּינָן. כֹּל שֶׁלֹּא רָאָה מְאוֹרוֹת מִיָּמָיו לֹא יִפְרוֹשׂ אֶת שְׁמַע: הָא אִם רָאָה פּוֹרֵשׂ. רִבִּי חַגַּיי בָּעָא קוֹמֵי רִבִּי יוֹסֵה. מִחְלְפָה שִׁיטָתֵיהּ דְּרִבִּי יְהוּדָה. תַּמָּן הוּא אָמַר. פְּרָט. וְהָכָא הוּא אָמַר. לְרַבּוֹת. אָמַר רִבִּי חֲנַנְיָה בְּרֵיהּ דְּרִבִּי הִלֵּל. בְּיוֹשֵׁב בְּבַיִת אָפֵל הִיא מַתְנִיתָא. כָּךְ אָנוּ אוֹמְרִים. הַיּוֹשֵׁב בְּבַיִת אָפֵל לֹא יִפְרוֹשׂ אֶת שְׁמַע: בְּרַם הָכָא בְּלֹא רְאוֹת לְרַבּוֹת אֶת הַסּוּמָא.

Halakhah 7: [144]There, we have stated, "A blind person is not exiled, the words of Rebbi Jehudah; Rebbi Meïr says, he is exiled." And both of them explained the same verse, *without seeing*[145]. Rebbi Jehudah says, to include the blind person. Rebbi Meïr says, excluding the blind person. And here we have stated, "a person who never saw light does not spread out the *Shema`*[143]." Therefore if he saw he spreads. Rebbi Haggai asked before Rebbi Yose, is the argument of Rebbi Jehudah inverted? There he says, excluding, but here he says, to include. Rebbi Hanania the son of Rebbi Hillel said, the Mishnah is about one sitting in a dark house. So we are saying, "one sitting in a dark house may not spread the *Shema`*." But here, *without seeing*, to include the blind person.

144 This paragraph is a reformulation of a paragraph in *Makkot* 2:7 Notes 41-44.

145 *Num.* 35:23.

(fol. 74c) **משנה ח**: כֹּהֵן שֶׁיֵּשׁ בְּיָדָיו מוּמִין לֹא יִשָּׂא אֶת כַּפָּיו. רִבִּי יְהוּדָה אוֹמֵר אַף מִי שֶׁהָיוּ יָדָיו צְבוּעוֹת אִסַטִּיס לֹא יִשָּׂא אֶת כַּפָּיו מִפְּנֵי שֶׁהָעָם מִסְתַּכְּלִין בּוֹ:

Mishnah 8: A Cohen whose hands are defective shall not lift his hands[146]. Rebbi Jehudah says, also a person whose hands are colored by woad[147] hall not lift his hands since people look at him.

146 Since the Cohen has to stand in front of the Ark and lift his hands over his head when reciting the priestly blessing.

147 Greek ἰσάτις.

(75b line 75) **הלכה ח**: תַּנֵּי. וּבְפָנָיו. וְהָא תַנֵּי. אִם הָיָה דָשׁ בְּעִירוֹ מוּתָּר. רִבִּי נַפְתָּלִי הֲוָות אֶצְבָּעָתֵיהּ עֲקִימָה. אֲתָא שְׁאִיל לְרִבִּי מָנָא. אָמַר לֵיהּ. מִכֵּיוָן שֶׁאַתָּה דָשׁ בְּעִירָךְ מוּתָּר. רַב חוּנָה מְעַבֵּר זַלְדְּקָן. וְהָא תַנֵּי. אִם הָיָה דָשׁ בְּעִירוֹ מוּתָּר. אָמַר רִבִּי מָנָא. רַגְלֵיהּ [הֲוֵי] סַגִּין. בְּגִין שֶׁלֹּא יְהוּ אוֹמְרִין. רָאִינוּ קָטָן נוֹשֵׂא אֶת כַּפָּיו. אָמַר רִבִּי יוֹסֵה. זֹאת אוֹמֶרֶת שֶׁאָסוּר לְהִסְתַּכֵּל בַּכֹּהֲנִים בְּשָׁעָה שֶׁהֵן מְבָרְכִין אֶת יִשְׂרָאֵל. אָמַר רִבִּי חַגַּיי. כְּלוּם אָמְרוּ. אֵין מִסְתַּכְּלִין. לֹא מִפְּנֵי הֶסֵּיעַ דַּעַת. מֹשֶׁה. דַּאֲנָא מִסְתַּכְּלָנָא וְלָא מְסַעָה דַעְתִּי.

Halakhah 8: [148]It was stated, in his face. But was it not stated, if he was known in his town he is permitted? As the following: The finger of Rebbi Naftali was bent. He came and asked Rebbi Mana, who said to him, since you are known in your town it is permitted. Rav Huna disqualified one with sparse facial hair. But was it not stated, if he was known in his town he is permitted? Rebbi Mana said, it was a crowded holiday; so they should not say, we saw a minor lifting his hands. Rebbi Yose said, this implies that one is forbidden to look at the Cohanim at the moment when they are blessing Israel. Rebbi Haggai, when they said, one does not look, was it not because of inattention? By Moses, I shall look and my attention will not be diverted.

148 This is Ta`aniot 4:1, Notes 15-21.

(fol. 74c) **משנה ט**: הָאוֹמֵר אֵינִי עוֹבֵר לִפְנֵי הַתֵּבָה בִּצְבוּעִין אַף בִּלְבָנִים לֹא יַעֲבוֹר. בְּסַנְדָּל אֵינִי עוֹבֵר אַף יָחֵף לֹא יַעֲבוֹר. הָעוֹשֶׂה תְפִילָּתוֹ עֲגוּלָּה סַכָּנָה וְאֵין בָּהּ מִצְוָה. נְתָנָהּ עַל מִצְחוֹ אוֹ עַל פַּס יָדוֹ הֲרֵי זוֹ דֶּרֶךְ הַמִּינוּת. צִפָּהּ זָהָב וּנְתָנָהּ עַל בֵּית אוּנְקְלִי שֶׁלּוֹ הֲרֵי זוֹ דֶּרֶךְ הַחִיצוֹנִין:

Mishnah 9: If somebody said, I shall not stand before the Ark in coloreds, also in whites he shall not stand. With sandals I shall not stand, also barefoot he shall not stand[149]. He who makes his *tefillah* round puts himself in danger and it is no meritorious deed[150]. If he places it on his forehead or on his hand, it is the way of heretics[151]. If he covered it with gold and put it on his sleeve, it is the way of outsiders[152].

149 We suspect him of belonging to a heretical sect which does not follow pharisaic/rabbinic instructions, such as the Jewish sect in Arabia from whom Mohammed received the ways of divine worship, who did not follow the rabbinic reduction of 5 daily prayers (2 times *Shema`* and 3 times *Amidah*) to 3.

150 When Jewish worship was forbidden during the Hadrianic persecutions, changing the traditional forms of *tefillin* is not acceptable.

151 Since the verse (*Ex.* 13:9) requires *a sign on your hand and remembrance* (or *declaration*) *between your eyes*, Sadducee *Tefillin* were put on the hand and on the forehead between the eyes, in contrast to rabbinic practice which puts them above the elbow and on the hair.

152 Non-Jewish gnostic sects.

(75c line 6) **הלכה ט**׃ תָּנָה רִבִּי יוֹסֵי בֶּן בְּבַי. תַּפִילִין מְרוּבָּעוֹת [שְׁחוֹרוֹת] הֲלָכָה לְמֹשֶׁה מִסִּינַי.

Halakhah 9: Rebbi Yose ben Bevai stated: Square [black][153] *tefillin* are practice from Moses on Sinai[154].

153 Corrector's addition, of unknown source. The Babli only declares black strips as practice from Moses on Sinai.

154 Babli 24b, *Šabbat* 28b, *Menaḥot* 35a.

(fol. 74c) **משנה י**׃ הָאוֹמֵר יְבָרְכוּךָ טוֹבִים הֲרֵי זוֹ דֶּרֶךְ הַמִּינוּת. עַל קַן צִפּוֹר יַגִּיעוּ רַחֲמֶיךָ וְעַל טוֹב יִזָּכֵר שְׁמֶךָ מוֹדִים מוֹדִים מְשַׁתְּקִין אוֹתוֹ. הַמְכַנֶּה בָּעֲרָיוֹת מְשַׁתְּקִין אוֹתוֹ. הָאוֹמֵר וּמִזַּרְעֲךָ לֹא תִתֵּן לְהַעֲבִיר לַמּוֹלֶךְ וּמִזַּרְעָךְ לָא תִתֵּן לְאַעְבָּרָא בְּאַרְמָיּוּתָא מְשַׁתְּקִין אוֹתוֹ בִּנְזִיפָה׃

Mishnah 10: He who says, may the good ones bless You, is the way of heretics[155]. To the bird's nest reaches your mercy[156], Your name may be mentioned on good things[157] we thank we thank[158]: one silences him. One who circumscribes in incest prohibitions[159], one silences him. He who translates *and do not give of your offspring to be burned for Moloch*[160] as "do not allow your semen to impregnate a Gentile woman"[161]: one silences him with rebuke.

155 It is heretic to permit only the predestined few to Divine worship and to designate everybody else as belonging to Satan since every human has the capacity to repent and become good.

156 Referring to *Deut.* 22:6. To give sermons about presumed reasons for biblical commandments is sinful.

157 But not on bad ones; this contradicts the obligation to praise God for the Bad as one

does for the Good, Mishnah *Berakhot* 9:5.
158 If the beginning of the penultimate benediction of the Amidah is repeated without stop in between it looks like an affirmation of the existence of dual powers.

159 *Lev.* Chap. 18. For example, changing *your father* into "his father", or, as in Pseudo-Jonathan, "debase" for *uncover*.
160 *Lev.* 18:21.
161 Pseudo-Jonathan's translation.

(75c line 7) **הלכה י**: הָאוֹמֵר יְבָרְכֶיךָ טוֹבִים. שְׁתֵּי רְשׁוּיוֹת.

Halakhah 10: "He who says, may the good ones bless You." Two powers[155].

רִבִּי פִּינְחָס בְּשֵׁם רִבִּי סִימוֹן. כְּקוֹרֵא תִיגֶּר עַל מִדּוֹתָיו שֶׁלְהַקָּדוֹשׁ בָּרוּךְ הוּא. עַל קַן צִפּוֹר הִגִּיעוּ רַחֲמֶיךָ וְעַל אוֹתוֹ הָאִישׁ לֹא הִגִּיעוּ רַחֲמֶיךָ. רִבִּי יוֹסֵי בְּשֵׁם רִבִּי סִימוֹן. בְּנוֹתֵן קִיצְבָה עַל מִדּוֹתָיו שֶׁלְהַקָּדוֹשׁ בָּרוּךְ הוּא. עַד קַן צִיפּוֹר הִגִּיעוּ רַחֲמֶיךָ. אִית תַּנָּיֵי תַנֵּי. עַד. אִית תַּנָּיֵי תַנֵּי. עַל. מָאן דְּאָמַר. עַל. מְסַיֵּיעַ לְרִבִּי פִּינְחָס. מָאן דְּאָמַר. עַד. מְסַיֵּיעַ לְרִבִּי יוֹסֵה. אָמַר רִבִּי יוֹסֵה בֵּירִבִּי בּוּן. לֹא עָבְדִין טַבָאוּת. שֶׁהֵן עוֹשִׂין [מִדּוֹתָיו שֶׁלְהַקָּדוֹשׁ בָּרוּךְ הוּא רַחֲמִים. אִילֵּין דִּמְתַרְגְּמִין. עַמִּי בְּנֵי יִשְׂרָאֵל. כְּמָה דַּאֲנָן רַחֲמִין בַּשְׁמַיָּא כֵּן תְּהַוֹון רַחֲמָנִין בְּאַרְעָא. תּוֹרְתָא אוֹ רְחִילָה יָתָהּ וְיַת בְּרָהּ לָא תְכָסִין תְּרוֹוַיְהוֹן בְּיוֹמָא חַד. לֹא עָבְדִין טַבָאוּת. שֶׁהֵן עוֹשִׂין] גְּזֵירוֹתָיו שֶׁלְהַקָּדוֹשׁ בָּרוּךְ הוּא רַחֲמִים.

1 פינחס | ב S יצחק R פינחס 3 עד | ב על 4 על | ב עד דאמ' | ב דמר מאן | ב ומן דאמ' | ב דמר יוסה | ב יוסי (2) 5 טבאות | ב טבות שהן עושין | ב שעושין [מדותיו | ב למידותיי אילין | ב ואילין 6 רחמין בשמייא | ב רחמן בשמיא כן | ב כך

[162]Rebbi Phineas in the name of Rebbi Simeon: He is like one who quarrels with the measures of the Holy One, praise to Him: Your mercies reached[163] over a bird's nest but did not reach this man[164]! Rebbi Yose in the name of Rebbi Simeon: He is like one who makes finite the measures of the Holy One, praise to Him: Your mercies reach down to the bird's nest[165]. Some Tannaim formulate "over", some Tannaim formulate "to". He who says "over" supports Rebbi Phineas, he who says "to" supports Rebbi Yose. Rebbi Yose bar Abun said[166]: They do not act well who declare [the measures of the Holy One, praise to Him, to be mercy. And those[167] who translate "My people Israel, just as I am merciful in Heaven so you should be merciful on earth. A cow or a mother sheep, it and its young you should not slaughter together on one day," they do not act well because they declare] the measures of the Holy One, praise to Him, to be mercy.

162 Originally a shortened reference to a text in *Berakhot* 5:3 (Notes 122-126), extended to a full copy by the corrector.
163 All Mishnah manuscripts, all

Yerushalmi sources of the Mishnah, and all Babli sources (25a, *Berakhot* 33b) have יגיע but all texts in the discussion have הגיע.
164 "This man" in Talmudic speech means "me".
165 His mercies reach down to a bird's nest but not to insects and worms.
166 In Babli sources (25a, *Berakhot* 33b), the statement is attributed either to R. Yose bar Abun or to R. Yose bar Zabida.
167 Targum Pseudo-Jonathan to Lev. 22:28, with minor changes.

(75c line 19) וְדִכְוָותָהּ. אָמֵן אָמֵן. שְׁמַע שְׁמַע. תּוּרְגְּמָן שֶׁהוּא עוֹמֵד לִפְנֵי חָכָם אֵינוֹ רַשַּׁאי לֹא לִשְׁנוֹת וְלֹא לְכַנּוֹת וְלֹא לְהוֹסִיף אֶלָּא אִם כֵּן הָיָה אָבִיו אוֹ רַבּוֹ. רִבִּי פְּדָת הֲוָה אָמוֹרָא דְרִבִּי יָסָא. מִילִין דִּשְׁמַע מִן אָבוֹי הֲוָה אָמַר. כָּךְ אָמַר רִבִּי בְּשֵׁם אַבָּא. מִילִין דְּלָא שְׁמַע מִן אָבוֹי הֲוָה אָמַר. כָּךְ אָמַר רִבִּי בְּשֵׁם רִבִּי לְעָזָר. בַּר יָשִׁיטָא הֲוָה אָמוֹרָא דְרִבִּי אָחָא. מִילִין דִּשְׁמַע מִן אָבוֹי הֲוָה אָמַר. כָּךְ אָמַר רִבִּי בְּשֵׁם אַבָּא. מִילִין דְּלָא שְׁמַע מִן אָבוֹי הֲוָה אָמַר. כָּךְ אָמַר רִבִּי בְּשֵׁם רִבִּי חִינְנָה. רִבִּי מָנָא כַּד דַּהֲוָה מוֹרֵי בַּחֲבוּרָתָה. מִילִין דִּשְׁמַע מִן אָבוֹי בְּבֵיתָא הֲוָה אָמַר. כֵּן אָמַר רִבִּי בְּשֵׁם רִבִּי יוֹנָה. מִילִין דִּשְׁמַע מִן אָבוֹי בְּבֵית וַעֲדָא הֲוָה אָמַר. כֵּן אָמַר רִבִּי יוֹנָה.

And similarly, Amen Amen[168], hear hear[169]. An interpreter who stands in front of a Sage is permitted neither to change, nor to circumlocute, nor to add unless he was his father or his teacher. Rebbi Pedat[170] was the speaker of Rebbi Yasa. Things which he had heard from his father he referred to: so says my teacher in my father's name. Things which he had not heard from his father he referred to: so says my teacher in Rebbi Eleazar's name. Bar Yashita was the speaker of Rebbi Aha. Things which he had heard from his father he referred to: so says my teacher in my father's name. Things which he had not heard from his father he referred to: so says my teacher in Rebbi Ḥinena's name. When Rebbi Mana was instructing in a group, things which he had heard from his father in his house he referred to: so says my teacher in Rebbi Jonah's name[171]. Things which he had heard from his father in the Academy he referred to: so says Rebbi Jonah.

168 The expression Amen Amen appears as very positive expression twice in the Bible (*Num.* 5:22, *Neh.* 8:6); both times the two words are separated by *pasek*. In addition, 3 times one finds Amen, we-Amen. One has to conclude that the only act which is rejected here is if the word is repeated immediately, without hiatus. The same argument has to be applied to *Modim Modim* in the Mishnah.
169 Not to give the impression that one has to hear instructions from two different deities.
170 The son of R. Eleazar ben Pedat.
171 This text is problematic. R. Mana II was R. Jonah's son and R. Yose's student.

(75c line 28) הַמְכַנֶּה בָּעֲרָיוֹת. בְּעַרְיָיתָא דְּאָבוֹי וּבְעַרְיָיתָא דְּאִימֵּיהּ. מִזַּרְעָךְ לֹא תִתֵּן לְהַעֲבִיר לַמּוֹלֶךְ. מִן זַרְעָךְ לָא תִתֵּן לְאַעְבָּרָא בְּאַרְמָיְיתָא. תַּנֵּי רִבִּי יִשְׁמָעֵאל. זֶה שֶׁהוּא נוֹשֵׂא אֲרָמִית וּמַעֲמִיד מִמֶּנּוּ בָנִים מַעֲמִיד אוֹיְבִים לַמָּקוֹם.

"One who circumscribes in incest prohibitions[159]," incest prohibitions regarding his father and his mother.

Do not give of your offspring to be burned for Moloch[160], "do not allow your semen to impregnate a Gentile woman". Rebbi Ismael stated, he who marries a Gentile woman and has children from her raises enemies of the Omnipresent[172].

172 The Babli 25a explicitly characterizes this as R. Ismael's interpretation of *Lev.* 18:21.

(fol. 74c) **משנה יא**: מַעֲשֶׂה רְאוּבֵן נִקְרָא וְלֹא מִיתַּרְגֵּם. מַעֲשֶׂה תָמָר נִקְרָא וּמִיתַּרְגֵּם. מַעֲשֶׂה עֵגֶל הָרִאשׁוֹן נִקְרָא וּמִיתַּרְגֵּם. וְהַשֵּׁנִי נִקְרָא וְלֹא מִיתַּרְגֵּם.

Mishnah 11: The story of Reuben[173] is read but not translated. The story of Tamar[174] is read and translated. The first story of the Calf[175] is read and translated, but the second[176] is read and not translated.

173 His rape of Bilha, *Gen.* 35:22.
174 The incest story of Jehudah and Tamar, *Gen.* 38:1-30. The story is made acceptable by Jehudah's confession.
175 The Golden Calf, *Ex.* 32:1-6.
176 Aaron's version and its aftermath, *Ex.* 32:20-35.

(75c line 31) **הלכה יא**: אֲשֶׁר־חֲכָמִים יַגִּידוּ וְלֹא כִחֲדוּ מֵאֲבוֹתָם: מַה שָּׂכָר נָטְלוּ עַל כָּךְ. לָהֶם לְבַדָּם נִתְּנָה הָאָרֶץ וְלֹא־עָבַר זָר בְּתוֹכָם:

Halakhah 11: *What Sages tell, they did not hold back anything from their ancestors*[177]. What reward did they take for this[178]? *To them alone the Land was given, no stranger passed in their midst*[179].

177 *Job* 15:18.
178 Not to hide the disreputable actions of Reuben and Jehudah.
179 *Job* 15:19.

(75c line 33) אֵי זֶהוּ מַעֲשֵׂה עֵגֶל הַשֵּׁינִי. רִבִּי סִימוֹן בְּשֵׁם רִבִּי יְהוֹשֻׁעַ בֶּן לֵוִי. מִתְּשׁוּבָה שֶׁהֱשִׁיב מֹשֶׁה אֶת אַהֲרֹן עַד כִּי־פְרָעֹה אַהֲרֹן לְשִׁמְצָה בְּקָמֵיהֶם. חֲנַנְיָה בַּר שְׁלֶמְיָה בְּשֵׁם רַב. מִתְּשׁוּבָה שֶׁהֱשִׁיב אַהֲרֹן אֶת מֹשֶׁה עַד כִּי־פְרָעֹה אַהֲרֹן לְשִׁמְצָה בְּקָמֵיהֶם. רִבִּי אָחָא בְשֵׁם רִבִּי בָא. וּמִחָא יי' יַת עַמָּא עַל אֲשֶׁר עָשׂוּ אֶת־הָעֵגֶל אֲשֶׁר עָשָׂה אַהֲרֹן׃ רִבִּי מַר עוּקְבָּן בְּשֵׁם רַבָּנַן דְּתַמָּן. לֹא דּוֹמָה גְנַאי יָחִיד בְּצִיבּוּר לִגְנָיֵי צִיבּוּר בְּצִיבּוּר.

וְאַתְיָיא כַּהִיא דְאָמַר רִבִּי חֶלְבּוֹ בְּשֵׁם רַב חוּנָה. בִּרְכוֹת כֹּהֲנִים נִקְרָאוֹת וְלֹא מִיתַּרְגְּמוֹת. רִבִּי בָּא בַּר כֹּהֵן בְּעָא קוֹמֵי רִבִּי יוֹסֵה. מַה טַּעַם. אָמַר לֵיהּ. כֹּה תְבֶרֲכָֽוּ. לִבְרָכָה נִיתְּנָה. לֹא נִיתְּנָה לִקְרָאָה.

What is the second story of the Calf? Rebbi Simon in the name of Rebbi Joshua ben Levi: From the answer Moses gave to Aaron up to *for Aaron had let it become dissolute, a disgrace before their opponents*[180]. Hanania bar Shelemia in the name of Rav: From the answer Aaron gave Moses to up to *for Aaron had let it become dissolute, a disgrace before their opponents*. Rebbi Aha in the name of Rebbi Abba: "And the Eternal smote the people *because they made the Calf which Aaron made.*[181]" Rebbi Mar Uqban in the name of the rabbis there: the shame of a single person in the public is not comparable to the shame of the public in matters of the public[182].

It follows what Rebbi Helbo said in the name of Rav Huna: The priestly blessings are read but not translated[183]. Rebbi Abba bar Cohen asked before Rebbi Yose, what is the reason? He told him, *so you shall bless*[184], it was given as blessing, it was not given to be read.

180 *Ex.* 32:25.
181 *Ex.* 32:35. Tosephta 3:36, Babli 25b.
182 The first story of the Calf centers on the people whose guilt is diluted by their numbers. The second story centers on Aaron and declares his incompetence as leader.
183 This refers to the first sentence in Mishnah 12. The first sentence presupposes a reading "is read but not translated" as in the Babli whereas the question of R. Abba bar Cohen is based on the reading here which declares that the priestly blessing is not read from the Torah. There is no indication in the Palestinian Midrashim that this was actual practice.
184 *Num.* 6:22.

(fol. 24c) **משנה יב**: בִּרְכַּת כֹּהֲנִים וּמַעֲשֵׂה דָוִד וְאַמְנוֹן לֹא נִיקְרִין וְלֹא מִיתַּרְגְּמִין. וְאֵין מַפְטִירִין בַּמֶּרְכָּבָה רִבִּי יְהוּדָה מַתִּיר. וְרִבִּי אֱלִיעֶזֶר אוֹמֵר אֵין מַפְטִירִין בְּהוֹדַע אֶת יְרוּשָׁלַיִם אֶת תּוֹעֲבוֹתֶיהָ:

Mishnah 12: The priestly blessing[185], the stories of David[186] and Amnon[187] are neither read nor translated. One does not close with the Chariot[188], but Rebbi Jehudah permits. And Rebbi Eliezer says, one does not close with *tell Jerusalem its abominations*[189].

185 *Num.* 6:24-27.
186 The story of David and Batsheva, *2S.* 11.
187 The rape of Tamar, *2S.* 13:1-22.
188 *Ez.* Chapter 1, the traditional reading from Prophets on Pentecost.
189 *Ez.* Chap. 16.

(75c line 42) **הלכה יב**: אֵין מַפְטִירִין בַּמֶּרְכָּבָה וְרִבִּי יְהוּדָה מַתִּיר. רִבִּי אֱלִיעֶזֶר אוֹמֵר. אֵין מַפְטִירִין בְּהוֹדַע אֶת יְרוּשָׁלַיִם אֶת תּוֹעֲבוֹתֶיהָ: מַעֲשֶׂה בְּאֶחָד שֶׁהִפְטִיר בְּהוֹדַע אֶת יְרוּשָׁלַיִם אֶת תּוֹעֲבוֹתֶיהָ: אָמַר לוֹ רִבִּי אֱלִיעֶזֶר. יֵלֵךְ אוֹתוֹ הָאִישׁ וְיֵדַע בְּתוֹעֲבוֹתֶיהָ שֶׁלְּאִמּוֹ. וּבָדְקוּ אַחֲרָיו וְנִמְצָא מַמְזֵר.

Halakhah 12: "One does not close with the Chariot[188], but Rebbi Jehudah permits. And Rebbi Eliezer says, one does not close with *tell Jerusalem its abominations*[189]. It happened that somebody closed with *tell Jerusalem its abominations*. Rebbi Eliezer said to him, may this man go and be informed of the abominations of his mother. They checked him out and he was found to be a bastard.[190]"

190 Babli 25b, Tosephta 3:34.

(75c line 45) וְדָא מְזוּזָה יְהָבִין לָהּ הֵיכָא. רִבִּי זְעוּרָה רַב יְהוּדָה בְּשֵׁם שְׁמוּאֵל. מְשַׁלְּשׁוֹ וְנוֹתְנוֹ בִּתְחִילַּת שְׁלִישׁ הָעֶלְיוֹן. רִבִּי חֶלְבּוֹ בְּשֵׁם רַב חוּנָה. חוֹצֶה אֶת הַפֶּתַח וּמְשַׁלְּשׁוֹ וְנוֹתְנָה בְּסוֹף הַשְּׁלִישׁ הַתַּחְתּוֹן. מַה בֵּינֵיהוֹן. מְקוֹם מְזוּזָה בֵּינֵיהוֹן. בַּר טַבְרִי שָׁאַל לְרִבִּי יִצְחָק. הַגַּע עַצְמָךְ שֶׁהָיָה שַׁעַר גָּבוֹהַּ. אָמַר לֵיהּ. נוֹתְנָהּ כְּנֶגֶד כְּתֵיפָיו. בֵּית מִדְרָשֵׁיהּ דְּרִבִּי חֲנִינָה עֲבִיד כֵּן. רִבִּי יִרְמְיָה בְּשֵׁם רִבִּי שְׁמוּאֵל בַּר רַב יִצְחָק. בֵּית מְזוּזָתוֹ שֶׁלְרִבִּי הָיָה עָשׂוּי כְּמִין נַגָּר. תְּלוּיָה בַּדֶּלֶת. סַכָּנָה שֶׁאֵין בָּהּ מִצְוָה. חָקַק בְּרֹאשׁ הַמַּקֵּל וְהִנִּיחוֹ בְּמָקוֹם שֶׁאֵינוֹ רָאוּי לוֹ. סַכָּנָה שֶׁאֵין בָּהּ מִצְוָה. רִבִּי בָּא בְּשֵׁם רַב יְהוּדָה. וַאֲפִילוּ [לֹא] סְמָרוֹ. וְהָא תַּנֵּי. וְהוּא שֶׁסְּמָרוֹ. אָמַר רִבִּי יוֹסָה. וְהוּא שֶׁיִּיחֲדוֹ לְכֵן. שֶׁלְּבֵית מַלוֹנוֹ הָיוּ עוֹשִׂין כֵּן בְּפוּלְמָסִיּוֹת. שְׁמוּאֵל אָמַר. נְתָנָהּ לִפְנִים מִטֶּפַח פְּסוּלָה. רִבִּי זְעוּרָה בְּשֵׁם שְׁמוּאֵל. צָרִיךְ שֶׁיְּהֵא שֹׁמֵעַ שֶׁלֹּה רוֹאֶה אֶת הַפֶּתַח. רִבִּי יִרְמְיָה בְּשֵׁם

רִבִּי זְעוּרָה. כֵּינֵי מַתְנִיתָהּ. צִיר שֶׁיֵּשׁ לוֹ שְׁנֵי פְתָחִים נוֹתֵן עַל אֵיזֶה מֵהֶן שֶׁיִּרְצֶה. הֵיאַךְ שְׁמַע שֶׁלָּהּ רוֹאֶה אֶת הַפֶּתַח. בַּיִת שֶׁיֵּשׁ לוֹ שְׁנֵי פְתָחִים נוֹתֵן בָּרָגִיל. הָיוּ שְׁנֵיהֶן רְגִילִין נוֹתֵן בַּחֲזִית. הָיוּ שְׁנֵיהֶן חֲזִית נוֹתֵן עַל אֵיזֶה מֵהֶן שֶׁיִּרְצֶה. פֶּתַח שֶׁהוּא פָתוּחַ לַגַּג וּלְגִינָּה הֲרֵי הוּא כְּפָתוּחַ לֶחָיִל. דִּבְרֵי רִבִּי יוֹסֵי בֵּירִבִּי יְהוּדָה. וַחֲכָמִים אוֹמְרִים. הֲרֵי הוּא כְּפָתוּחַ לַשּׁוּק.

[191]Where does one put this *mezuzah*? Rebbi Ze'ira in the name of Samuel: one divides it into three parts and puts it at the start of the uppermost third. Rebbi Ḥelbo in the name of Rav Huna: One divides the door into half, then into thirds, and puts it at the top of the lowest third. What is between them? The place of the *mezuzzah* is between them[192]. Bar Tabari asked Rebbi Isaac, think of it, if it was a high gate? He said to him, he puts it at his shoulder's height. The house of study of Rebbi Ḥanina was made so. Rebbi Jeremiah in the name of Rebbi Samuel bar Rav Isaac: the container of Rebbi's *mezuzzah* was made like a bolt[193]. If it was hung on the door, a danger and it is no meritorious deed[150,202]. If he excavated the top of a stick and put it at an unbecoming place, a danger and it is no meritorious deed[150]. Rebbi Abba in the name of Rav Jehudah: even if he (nailed) [did not nail] it[194]. But did we not state, on condition that he nailed it? Rebbi Yose said, on condition that he dedicated {the place} for it[195]. Those of the family Malwan did so in the wars.[196] Samuel said, if it was put inside[197] more than a hand-breadth it is disqualified. Rebbi Ze'ira in the name of Samuel: It is necessary that its *shemaʿ* see the door[198]. Rebbi Jeremiah in the name of Rebbi Ze'ira: So is the *baraita*, a doorpost serving two doors he puts it on the one he chooses. How can its *shemaʿ* see the door[199]? If a house[200] has two doors, he puts it on the one usually used. If both were usually used he puts it in front. If both were in front he puts it on the one he chooses. A door which opens to the roof or to a garden is as if open to a wall, the words of Rebbi Yose ben Rebbi Jehudah. But the Sages are saying, it is as open to the market[201,202].

191 This has no connection with the preceding. Since *mezuzzah* was mentioned in an earlier Mishnah and since there is no Yerushalmi Tractate *Menahot*, the rules of *mezuzzah* are collected here.

192 According to Samuel, the box containing the *mezuzzah* has to be fixed so that its lower end be at $^2/_3$ of the height of the door-post. Rav Huna divides the height of the door-post into sixths (first halves and then each half into thirds). For him the upper rim of the *mezuzzah* case has to be at the upper end of the fourth sixth, which is two thirds. Therefore the place of the lower end

for Samuel is the place of the upper end for Rav Huna. Babli *Menahot* 33a.

193 It was attached horizontally, satisfying both Samuel and Rav Huna. Babli *Menahot* 33a.

194 The corrector's addition should be deleted. Rav Jehudah disqualifies a long stick with a *mezuzzah* placed inside even if it is nailed to a door-post.

195 Rebbi Yose accepts the stick if it truly is permanently affixed.

196 One of the uprisings against the Romans, cf. *Yoma* 5:7, Note 172. They affixed their *mezuzzah* that it was securely attached but still easily removed in times of danger.

197 Away from the outer rim of the door-post. Babli *Menahot* 33b.

198 He requires that the paragraph starting with *shema*` be written last on the sheet. The sheet then has to be rolled so that the last paragraph is on the outside.

199 If there are two doors, and the *shema*` is on the side of one door, it is pointing away from the other door.

200 Usually a "house" is a one-room piece. It is then stated that a one-room house needs only one *mezuzzah*; the *mezuzzah* is an obligation attached to the house, not the door.

201 And therefore acceptable as unique *mezuzzah*. Babli *Menahot* 33b.

202 Babli *Menahot* 32b; Tosephta 3:30.

(75c line 62) הַדָּר בְּחוּצָה לָאָרֶץ וְהַדָּר בְּפוּנְדְּקֵי אֶרֶץ יִשְׂרָאֵל שְׁלֹשִׁים יוֹם אֵינוֹ צָרִיךְ לִיתֵּן מְזוּזָה. יוֹתֵר מִיכֵּן צָרִיךְ לִיתֵּן מְזוּזָה. הַדָּר בְּבוּרְגָּנִין שְׁלֹשִׁים יוֹם צָרִיךְ לִיתֵּן מְזוּזָה. הַשּׂוֹכֵר בַּיִת מִיִּשְׂרָאֵל צָרִיךְ לִיתֵּן מְזוּזָה. הַשּׂוֹכֵר בַּיִת מִגּוֹי צָרִיךְ לִיתֵּן מְזוּזָה. וּכְשֶׁהוּא יוֹצֵא נוֹטֵל. וּבְשֶׁלְיִשְׂרָאֵל אָסוּר לַעֲשׂוֹת כֵּן. רִבִּי יַעֲקֹב בַּר אֲחָא בְשֵׁם רִבִּי יֹאשִׁיָּה. מִפְּנֵי מַעֲשֶׂה שֶׁאִירַע. מַעֲשֶׂה בְּאֶחָד שֶׁנָּטַל וְהָיָה קוֹבֵר אֶת בָּנָיו. הַדָּר בְּפוּנְדְּקֵי חוּצָה לָאָרֶץ שְׁלֹשִׁים יוֹם אֵינוֹ צָרִיךְ לִיתֵּן מְזוּזָה. אִם נָתַן לֹא יִטּוֹל. רִבִּי יַעֲקֹב בַּר אֲחָא בְשֵׁם רִבִּי יֹאשִׁיָּה. מִפְּנֵי מַעֲשֶׂה שֶׁאִירַע. מַעֲשֶׂה בְּאֶחָד שֶׁנָּטַל וְהָיָה קוֹבֵר אֶת בָּנָיו.

He who dwells outside the Land or dwells in a hostelry in the Land of Israel for thirty days need not put up a *mezuzzah*[203]. Longer than that he has to put up a *mezuzzah*. He who dwells in a rural tower for thirty days has to put up a *mezuzzah*. He who rents a house from a Jew has to put up a *mezuzzah*[204]. He who rents a house from a Gentile has to put up a *mezuzzah*, and when he leaves he removes it, but from a Jew it is forbidden to act in this way. Rebbi Jacob bar Aha in the name of Rebbi Josias, because of what happened. It happened that a person removed and was burying his children. He who dwells dwells in a hostelry outside the Land of Israel for thirty days need not put up a *mezuzzah*. If he put up, he may not remove it. Jacob bar Aha in the name of

Rebbi Josias, because of what happened. It happened that a person removed and was burying his children.

203 Babli *Menahot* 44a.
204 The renter is responsible to supply the *mezuzzah*. Babli *Pesahim* 4a, *Bava mesia`* 102a.

(75c line 70) חוּלְדַּת הַמּוּלִים חַיָּיבֶת בִּמְזוּזָה. חַלּוֹן שֶׁהוּא אַרְבַּע עַל אַרְבַּע שֶׁעֲבָדִים יוֹשְׁבִין שָׁם וּמְנִיפִין לְרַבּוֹנֵיהֶם חַיָּיבִין בִּמְזוּזָה. לוּלִים אֵילּוּ עַל גַּב אֵילּוּ חַיָּיבִין בִּמְזוּזָה. הֵן דּוּ דָרַס אַסְכּוּפְתָּא אֲרַעִייָתָא. רִבִּי יוֹסֵי הֲוָה מִצְטָעֵר דְּלָא חֲמָא לוּלָא דְרִבִּי אִילְעָא דַהֲוָה עָבִיד מִן דַּעְתְּהוֹן דְּכָל־רַבָּנָן.

[205]*Huldat hammulim*[206] is liable for *mezuzah*. A window, four by four {cubits} wide, in which slaves sit and make wind for their masters are liable for *mezuzah*. Coops one on top of the other are liable for *mezuzah*; one steps on the doorstep below[207]. Rebbi Yose was sorry not to have seen the coop of Rebbi Ilai which he had made according to all rabbis[208].

205 These lines are copied in *Yoma* 1:1, Notes 108-111.
206 A direct translation would be "mole of circumcised", which makes no sense. The explanation of *Qorban haEdah*, "entrances of cave dwellings" has no linguistic basis and would be superfluous. A possibility is Jastrow's explanation, "loading and unloading dock for mules", from מולא, Latin *mulus, mula*, the mule.
207 If the chicken coops are part of the house and are directly accessible from the doorstep, and the areas of the openings add up to four-by-four cubits.
208 That it was required to have a *mezuzzah* according to everybody.

(75c line 74) תְּפִילָּה וּמְזוּזָה מִי קוֹדֵם. שְׁמוּאֵל אָמַר. מְזוּזָה קוֹדֶמֶת. רַב חוּנָה אָמַר. תְּפִילָּה קוֹדֶמֶת. מַה טַעֲמֵיהּ דִּשְׁמוּאֵל. שֶׁכֵּן הִיא נוֹהֶגֶת בַּיָּמִים טוֹבִים וּבַשַּׁבָּתוֹת. מַה טַעֲמֵיהּ דְּרַב חוּנָה. שֶׁכֵּן הִיא נוֹהֶגֶת בְּפַמְפַּרְשֵׁי יַמִּים וְהוֹלְכֵי מִדְבָּרוֹת. מַתְנִיתָהּ מְסַייְעָה לִשְׁמוּאֵל. תְּפִילָּה שֶׁבָּלַת עוֹשִׂין אוֹתָהּ מְזוּזָה. מְזוּזָה שֶׁבָּלַת אֵין עוֹשִׂין אוֹתָהּ תְּפִילָּה. לָמָּה. שֶׁמַּעֲלִין בַּקּוֹדֶשׁ וְלֹא מוֹרִידִין.

Tefillin and *mezuzzah,* which one has precedence? Samuel said, *mezuzzah* has precedence. Rav Huna said, *tefillin* have precedence. What is Samuel's reason? Since it applies on holidays and Sabbath[209]. What is Rav Huna's reason? Since it applies to travellers on the Seas and those who cross deserts. A *baraita*[210] supports Samuel: "A worn-out *tefillah* one may make into *mezuzzah*, a worn out *mezuzzah* one may not make into a *tefillah*. Why? Because one increases in holiness but may not decrease."

209 Whereas *tefillin* are strictly only worn on working days.

210 *Soferim* 14:20.

Introduction to Tractate Ḥagigah

As their name indicates, the holidays of pilgrimage trigger two obligations: to appear in the Temple as pilgrims, and to observe the holiday as time of happiness. Since also one may not appear in the Temple empty-handed (*Ex.* 23:14) the pilgrim has to bring two sacrifices: an elevation sacrifice to celebrate his entry to the Temple with a gift, and a well-being sacrifice to provide the meal for the family celebration of the holiday. The Tractate contains the rules of both sacrifices together with many connected subjects. The First Chapter details the rules of the pilgrimage and its sacrifices. Since the holiday obligations may be satisfied only on a holiday, this leads to examples of what in Proverbs is described as *what is crooked cannot be made straight.* This again leads to a list of traditional rules with little, or no biblical background. The Second Chapter starts with a list of topics unfit for public treatment, followed by a discussion of the disagreement between Pharisaic schools about the handling of the required sacrifices on the holiday proper, including the special rules for the one-day holiday of Pentecost. The end of the Chapter, and the entirety of Chapter Three, are devoted to the levels of purity required for profane food, non-Temple *sancta*, and Temple *sancta*, together with the special holiday rules enacted to include all of Israel in the celebrations with no regard to the level of observation of the rules of purity particular to the individual celebrant.

הכל חייבין פרק ראשון חגיגה

(fol.75d) **משנה א**: הַכֹּל חַיָּיבִין בָּרְאִיָּה חוּץ מֵחֵרֵשׁ שׁוֹטֶה וְקָטָן וְטוּמְטוּם וְאַנְדְּרוֹגִינוֹס נָשִׁים וַעֲבָדִים שֶׁאֵינָן מְשׁוּחְרָרִים הַחִיגֵּר וְהַסּוּמָא וְהַחוֹלֶה וְהַקָּטָן וְכָל־מִי שֶׁאֵינוֹ יָכוֹל לַעֲלוֹת בְּרַגְלָיו. אֵיזֶהוּ קָטָן כֹּל שֶׁאֵינוֹ יָכוֹל לִרְכּוֹב עַל כְּתֵפוֹ שֶׁל אָבִיו וְלַעֲלוֹת מִירוּשָׁלַיִם לְהַר הַבַּיִת דִּבְרֵי בֵית שַׁמַּאי. וּבֵית הִלֵּל אוֹמֵר כֹּל שֶׁאֵינוֹ יָכוֹל לֶאֱחוֹז בְּיָדוֹ שֶׁל אָבִיו וְלַעֲלוֹת מִירוּשָׁלַיִם לְהַר הַבַּיִת שֶׁנֶּאֱמַר שָׁלֹשׁ רְגָלִים:

Mishnah 1: All are obligated to appear[1] except the deaf-mute, the insane, and the child, and the sexless, and the hermaphrodite, women, and unemancipated slaves, the lame, and the blind, and the sick, and the child, and anybody who cannot ascend on his feet. Who is a child? Any who cannot ride on his father's shoulder from Jerusalem to the Temple Mount, the words of the House of Shammai. But the House of Hillel say, any who cannot hold on to his father's hand and climb from Jerusalem to the Temple Mount, as it is said, *three walking occasions*[2].

1 To fulfill the biblical commandment to "be seen" before God on the occasion of the three festivals of pilgrimage which are called either *steps* (Ex. 23:17, Deut. 16:16) or *walking occasions* (Ex. 23:14, 34:23). The cases exempted from this biblical duty are defined in the Halakhah.

2 Ex. 23:14.

(75d line 51) הַכֹּל חַיָּיבִין בָּרְאִיָּיה כוּל׳. מַתְנִיתָהּ בִּרְאִיַּית קָרְבָּן. אֲבָל בִּרְאִיַּית פָּנִים אֲפִילוּ קָטָן חַיָּיב. מִן הָדָא הַקְהֵל אֶת־הָעָם הָאֲנָשִׁים וְהַנָּשִׁים וְהַטָּף. וְאֵין קָטָן גָּדוֹל מִטָּף.

דְּתַנֵּי. מַעֲשֶׂה בְּרַבִּי יוֹחָנָן בֶּן בְּרוֹקָה וְרַבִּי אֶלְעָזָר חִסְמָא שֶׁהָיוּ מְהַלְּכִין מִיַּבְנֶה לְלוֹד וְהִקְבִּילוּ רַבִּי יְהוֹשֻׁעַ בִּבְקִיעִין. אָמַר לָהֶן. מַה חִידּוּשׁ הָיָה לָכֶם בְּבֵית הַמִּדְרָשׁ הַיּוֹם. אָמְרוּ לוֹ. הַכֹּל תַּלְמִידֶיךָ וּמֵימֶיךָ אָנוּ שׁוֹתִין. אָמַר לָהֶן. אַף עַל פִּי כֵן אֵי אֶיפְשָׁר לְבֵית הַמִּדְרָשׁ שֶׁלֹּא יְהֵא בּוֹ דָּבָר חָדָשׁ בְּכָל־יוֹם. מִי שָׁבַת שָׁם. אָמְרוּ לוֹ. רִבִּי לָעְזָר בֶּן עֲזַרְיָה. מֶה הָיְתָה פָרָשָׁתוֹ. הַקְהֵל אֶת־הָעָם הָאֲנָשִׁים וְהַנָּשִׁים וְהַטָּף. פָּתַח בָּהּ אָמַר. הוֹאִיל וְהָאֲנָשִׁים בָּאִים לִלְמוֹד וְהַנָּשִׁים לִשְׁמוֹעַ. הַטָּף לָמָּה בָא. אֶלָּא כְּדֵי לִיתֵּן שָׂכָר לִמְבִיאֵיהֶן. אָמַר לָהֶן. אֵין הַדּוֹר יָתוֹם שֶׁרַבִּי לָעְזָר בֶּן עֲזַרְיָה בְּתוֹכוֹ.

2 ר׳ | ס את ר׳ אמרו | ס ואמרו 3 אע״פ | ס אפי׳ 4 מה | ס ומה 5 פתח בה אמר | ב ומה אמ׳ בה ללמד | ס ללמוד 6 לשמוע | ס באות לשמוע כדי | ס - לעזר | ס אלעזר

אָתְיָא דְרִבִּי לָעְזָר בֶּן עֲזַרְיָה דְלָא כְּבֶן עֲזָאי. דְּתַנִּינָן תַּמָּן. מִכָּאן אוֹמֵר בֶּן עַזַּאי. חַיָּיב אָדָם לְלַמֵּד אֶת בִּתּוֹ תוֹרָה שֶׁאִם תִּשְׁתֶּה תֵּדַע שֶׁהַזְּכוּת תּוֹלָה לָהּ.

"All are obligated to appear," etc. The Mishnah is about the sacrifice of appearance[3], but the child is obligated in the personal appearance[4]. From the following, *assemble the people, men, women, and toddlers*[5]. And are not children[6] older than toddlers?

[7]As it was stated: It happened that Rebbi Joḥanan ben Beroqa and Rebbi Eleazar Ḥasma were walking from Jabneh to Lydda when they were visiting Rebbi Joshua in Beqi`in[8]. He asked them, what was new today in the House of Study? They said to him, we all are your students and drink from your waters. He said to them, even so, it is impossible that there not be a new idea every day in the House of Study. Who stayed there over the Sabbath? They said to him, Rebbi Eleazar ben Azariah. And what was his text? *Assemble the people, men, women, and toddlers*. He started by saying, since men come to learn and women to listen, why do the toddlers come? It must be to give a reward to those who bring them. He said to them, a generation is not orphaned which counts Rebbi Eleazar ben Azariah among them.

It follows that Rebbi Eleazar ben Azariah disagrees with Ben Azzai, as we have stated there[9]: "From here Ben Azzai said, a person is obligated to teach Torah to his daughter, that in case she would drink she knows that merit suspends."

---

3   While it is an obligation to appear in the Temple on one of the holidays of pilgrimage, it is sinful to enter there without bringing a personal sacrifice during the holiday (as specified in Mishnah 2), *Ex.* 34:20.

4   The obligation of *Ex.* 34:20 cannot apply to children, who are not subject to monetary obligations. They also cannot be obligated in any other way, but their parents are obligated to instruct them to do the right things. Quoted by Rashi *ad* 2a.

5   *Deut.* 31:12.

6   The expression קטן in the Mishnah is used to designate children with a measure of understanding, in contrast to תינוק.

7   The same text is in *Soṭah* 3:4 (Notes 107-109,ס); *Avot dR. Nathan A* Chap. 18.

8   An unidentified place. It cannot be the place of the same name in Galilee.

9   Mishnah *Soṭah* 3:4. R. Eleazar ben Azariah does not agree that women come to study Torah equally with the men.

(75d line 64) חֵרֵשׁ. חַבְרַיָּיא בְשֵׁם רִבִּי לָעֶזֶר. לָמַּעֲן יִשְׁמְעוּן וּלְמַעַן יִלְמָדוּן. עַד כָּדוֹן בִּמְדַבֵּר וְאֵינוֹ שׁוֹמֵעַ. חֵרֵשׁ שׁוֹמֵעַ וְאֵינוֹ מְדַבֵּר. רִבִּי אִילָא בְשֵׁם רִבִּי לָעֶזֶר. לְמַעַן יִלְמָדוּן. וּלְמַעַן יְלַמְּדוּן. אָמַר רִבִּי יוֹנָה. הָדָא אָמְרָה דְלֵית כְּלָלֵי דְרַבִּי כְּלָלִין. דְּתַנִּינָן תַּמָּן. חֵרֵשׁ הַמְדַבֵּר וְאֵינוֹ שׁוֹמֵעַ לֹא יִתְרוֹם. וְסָבְרִינָן מֵימַר. מְדַבֵּר וְאֵינוֹ שׁוֹמֵעַ חֵרֵשׁ. שׁוֹמֵעַ וְאֵינוֹ מְדַבֵּר [אֵינוֹ] חֵרֵשׁ. וְתַנִּינָן. הַחֵרֵשׁ שֶׁנֶּחֱלַץ וְהַחֵרֶשֶׁת שֶׁחָלְצָה וְהַחוֹלֶצֶת לַקָּטָן חֲלִיצָתָהּ פְּסוּלָה. אָמַר רִבִּי יוֹחָנָן. בְּשֶׁאֵין יְכוֹלִין לוֹמַר. וְאָמַר וְאָמְרָה. וְתַנִּינָן. חֵרֵשׁ שֶׁדִּיבְּרוּ חֲכָמִים בְּכָל מָקוֹם שֶׁאֵינוֹ לֹא שׁוֹמֵעַ וְלֹא מְדַבֵּר. וְדָא מְסַייְעָה לְרִבִּי יוֹנָה. דְּרִבִּי יוֹנָה אָמַר. הָדָא אָמְרָה דְלֵית כְּלָלֵי דְרַבִּי כְּלָלִין.

1 חברייא | ת חבריא במדבר | ת מדבר   2 חרש | תי -   אילא | תי הילא | תי -   ילמדון | י ילמדון   3 כללי | ת כללוי י כללין תמן | ת -   4 [אינו] | תי -   ותנינן | ת והתנינן   5 אמ' | תי ואמ' בשאין | ת בשאינו י שאין   6 - | י בו
7 ודא | תי הדא מסייעה | ית מסייעא דלית | י לית כללי | ת כללוי י כללין

The deaf-mute. [10]The colleagues in the name of Rebbi Eleazar: *So they should hear and learn*[11]. So far one who speaks but cannot hear; what about one who hears but cannot speak? Rebbi Ila in the name of Rebbi Eleazar: *So they should learn,* so they should teach[12]. Rebbi Jonah said, this means that the principles of Rebbi are no principles, since we have stated[13]: "A *hereš* who speaks and does not hear should not give heave" and we thought that one who speaks but does not hear is *hereš*, one who hears but does not speak is [not][14] *hereš*. But we have stated:[15] "*Ḥaliṣah* is invalid if performed for a *hereš* man, or by a *hereš* woman, or by a woman for an underage male." And Rebbi Joḥanan said, because they cannot say *he shall say*[16], *she shall say*[17]. We also have stated[13]: "A *hereš* mentioned anywhere by the Sages is a deaf-mute." This supports Rebbi Jonah, for Rebbi Jonah said that the principles of Rebbi are no principles[18].

10 This text also appears in *Terumot* 1:2, Notes 94-102 (**ת**), *Yebamot* 12:5, Note 104 (**י**).
11 *Deut.* 31:12.
12 Excluding the mute who cannot teach. Babli 3a.
13 Mishnah *Terumot* 1:2.
14 To be deleted as shown by the parallel texts.

15 Mishnah *Yebamot* 12:5.
16 *Deut.* 25:8.
17 *Deut.* 25:9. Without these declarations the procedure is invalid. Therefore the deaf but not mute may participate in valid *ḥaliṣah*. Babli *Yebamot* 104b.
18 Since the use of *hereš* as a technical term is inconsistent in the Mishnah.

(75d line 73) רִבִּי יוֹחָנָן בָּעֵי. חֵרֵשׁ בְּאָזְנוֹ אַחַת מָהוּ. אָמַר רִבִּי יוֹסֵי בֵּירִבִּי בּוּן. מַחֲלוֹקֶת רִבִּי יוֹסֵי וְרַבָּנָן. דְּתַנֵּי וְלִבְנֵי אַהֲרֹן תַּעֲשֶׂה כּוּתָּנוֹת. רַבָּנָן אָמְרֵי. שְׁתֵּי כוּתָּנוֹת לְכָל־אֶחָד וְאֶחָד. רִבִּי

יוֹסֵי אָמַר. אֲפִילוּ כּוּתֶּנֶת אַחַת לְכָל־אֶחָד וְאֶחָד. מַה טַּעֲמוֹן דְּרַבָּנָן. וְלִבְנֵי אַהֲרֹן תַּעֲשֶׂה כֻתֳּנֹת. מַה טַּעֲמֵיהּ דְּרִבִּי יוֹסֵי. לְמֵאָה בְנֵי אַהֲרֹן תַּעֲשֶׂה כֻתֳּנֹת. וְהָכָא תִּקְרָא אֶת־הַתּוֹרָה הַזֹּאת נֶגֶד כָּל־יִשְׂרָאֵל בְּאָזְנֵיהֶם: רַבָּנָן אָמְרֵי. שְׁתֵּי אָזְנַיִים לְכָל־אֶחָד וְאֶחָד. רִבִּי יוֹסֵה אוֹמֵר. אֲפִילוּ אוֹזֶן אַחַת לְכָל־אֶחָד וְאֶחָד.

Rebbi Johanan asked, what about a person deaf in one ear[19]? Rebbi Yose ben Rebbi Abun said, the disagreement between the Rabbis and Rebbi Yose. As it was stated, *and for Aaron's sons make coats*[20]. The Rabbis said, two coats for each one[21]. Rebbi Yose said, even one coat for each one. What is the Rabbis' reason? *And for Aaron's sons make coats.* What is Rebbi Yose's reason? For a hundred sons of Aaron make coats[22]. And here, *read this Torah in front of all of Israel into their ears*[23]. The Rabbis are saying, two ears for each of them. Rebbi Yose is saying, even a single ear for each of them.

19 Is he required to appear in the Temple at Tabernacles in the Sabbatical year? Babli *Ḥagigah* 3a.
20 *Ex.* 28:40.
21 Since "coats" is a plural and an otherwise undetermined plural always means 2. Cf. H. Guggenheimer, *Logical Problems in Jewish Tradition*, in: Confrontations with Judaism, ed. Ph. Longworth; London 1967.
22 The plural may be explained without reference to the persons involved since the coats are public property.
23 *Deut.* 31:11.

(76a line 5) שׁוֹטֶה. אָמַר רִבִּי לְעָזָר. אַתָּה הָרְאֵתָ לָדַעַת.

קָטָן. רִבִּי יִרְמְיָה וְרִבִּי אַיְיבוּ בַּר נַגְרֵי הֲווֹן יְתִיבִין. אָמְרִין. אֵיזֶהוּ קָטָן כֹּל שֶׁאֵינוֹ יָכוֹל לִרְכּוֹב עַל כְּתֵפוֹ שֶׁלְּאָבִיו. וְקָטָן שׁוֹמֵעַ וְקָטָן מְדַבֵּר. חֲזֵרוּן וְאָמְרוּן. כָּל־זְכוּרְךָ. לְרַבּוֹת אֶת הַקָּטָן. וַיֵּימַר. כָּל־זְכוּרְךָ. לְרַבּוֹת אֶת הַחֵרֵשׁ. לְמַעַן יִשְׁמְעוּן וּלְמַעַן יִלְמְדוּן. פְּרָט (לְקָטָן) [לְחֵרֵשׁ]. [וְיֵימַר לְמַעַן יִשְׁמְעוּן וּלְמַעַן יִלְמְדוּן. פְּרָט לְקָטָן]. אָמַר רִבִּי יוֹסֵה. מֵאַחַר שֶׁכָּתוּב אֶחָד מַרְבֶּה וְכָתוּב אֶחָד מְמַעֵט. מַרְבֶּה אֲנִי אֶת הַקָּטָן שֶׁהוּא רָאוּי לָבוֹא לְאַחַר זְמָן. וּמוֹצִיא אֶת הַחֵרֵשׁ שֶׁאֵינוֹ רָאוּי לָבוֹא לְאַחַר זְמָן. שְׁמוּאֵל בַּר אַבָּא בְּעָא קוֹמֵי רִבִּי זְעוּרָה. קָטָן חֵרֵשׁ מַהוּ שֶׁיְּהֵא חַיָּיב. אָמַר לֵיהּ. אִיתָא חֲמֵי. יָצִיבָא (בַּשָּׁמַיָּא) [בָּאַרְעָא] וְגִיּוֹרָא בִּשְׁמֵי שְׁמַיָּא. אִילּוּ גָדוֹל חֵרֵשׁ פָּטוּר. קָטָן חֵרֵשׁ לֹא כָּל־שֶׁכֵּן. אָמַר רִבִּי יִרְמְיָה. בְּדִין הָיָה קָטָן וְלֹא חֵרֵשׁ יְהֵא פָטוּר. גְּזֵירַת הַכָּתוּב הוּא. כָּל־זְכוּרְךָ. לְרַבּוֹת אֶת הַקָּטָן. הָיִיתִי אוֹמֵר. אִילּוּ (קָטָן) [גָּדוֹל] חֵרֵשׁ יְהֵא חַיָּיב. שֶׁלֹּא לַחֲלוֹק בְּהִילְכוֹת זְכוּרְךָ. הֲוֵי צוֹרְכָה לְהַהִיא דְאָמַר רִבִּי יוֹסֵה. מֵאַחַר שֶׁכָּתוּב אֶחָד מַרְבֶּה וְכָתוּב אֶחָד מְמַעֵט. מַרְבֶּה אֲנִי אֶת הַקָּטָן שֶׁהוּא רָאוּי לָבוֹא לְאַחַר זְמָן. וּמוֹצִיא אֶת הַחֵרֵשׁ שֶׁאֵינוֹ רָאוּי לָבוֹא לְאַחַר זְמָן.

"The insane." Rebbi Eleazar said, *you were shown to know*[24].

"The child." Rebbi Jeremiah and Rebbi Ayvo bar Naggari were sitting. They said, we have stated: Who is a child? Any who cannot ride on his father's shoulder." And can a child hear and can a child speak[25]? They turned around and said, *all your males*[26], to include the child. Or should we say, to include the deaf-mute? *So they should hear and learn*[1], to exclude (the child) [the deaf-mute. Or should we say, *so they should hear and learn,* to exclude the child?][27] Rebbi Yose said, since one verse excludes and one verse includes, I am including the child who will be able to come in the future, and excluding the deaf-mute who will not be able to come in the future. Samuel bar Abba asked before Rebbi Ze`ira: May a deaf-mute child be liable[28]? He said to him, come and see; the permanent dweller (in Heaven) [on earth][29] and the traveller in the highest Heaven? Since an adult deaf-mute is not liable, a child deaf-mute not *a fortiori*? Rebbi Jeremiah said, it would have been logical that a child who is no deaf-mute should be not liable[30]. It is the decision of the verse, *all your males*, to include the child. I would say, but a (child) [adult][31] deaf-mute should be liable, not to split the practice of *males*. Therefore what Rebbi Yose said is necessary: since one verse excludes and one verse includes, I am including the child who will be able to come in the future, and excluding the deaf-mute who will not be able to come in the future.

24 *Deut.* 4:35.

25 While a child can hear and speak, it usually will not understand (meant here by "hear") and it cannot teach (understood by "speak").

26 *Ex.* 23:17, *Deut.* 16:16, description of who is required to appear in the Temple on a festival of pilgrimage. Babli 4a; *Mekhilta dR. Ismael Mišpatim* Chap. 20 (ed. Horovitz-Rabin p. 333).

27 Corrector's addition, unnecessary.

28 According to the Babli, 6a, this question refers to a deaf-mute child whom the experts give a chance of recovering hearing and/or speech.

29 The corrector's change introduces the Babli's idiom; it should be deleted. The expression means that one was seeking proof in extraneous sources when the answer is readily available intrinsically.

30 In this discussion, it should be pointed out that the child is never liable, and cannot be liable before becoming an adult. The question is whether the parent is liable to bring the child to the Temple.

31 Corrector's change, misunderstanding the text, to be deleted. The scribe's text also implies that there should be no distinction

(76a line 21) טוּמְטוּם. הַכֹּל מוֹדִין בְּטוּמְטוּם שֶׁנִּקְרַע וְנִמְצָא זָכָר בְּיוֹם טוֹב הָרִאשׁוֹן שֶׁהוּא חַיָּב. מַה פְּלִיגִין. בִּשְׁאָר הַיָּמִים. חִזְקִיָּה אָמַר. יֵרָאֶה יֵרָאֶה אֶת שֶׁהוּא חַיָּב בָּרִאשׁוֹן חַיָּב בַּשֵּׁנִי. אֶת שֶׁאֵינוֹ חַיָּב בָּרִאשׁוֹן אֵינוֹ חַיָּב בַּשֵּׁנִי. אָמַר רִבִּי יוֹחָנָן. כָּל־שִׁבְעָה תַּשְׁלוּמִין לָרִאשׁוֹן. אָמַר רִבִּי אִילָא. מִפֶּסַח הַשֵּׁנִי לָמַד רִבִּי יוֹחָנָן. כְּמָה דְרִבִּי יוֹחָנָן אָמַר תַּמָּן. פֶּסַח שֵׁינִי תַּשְׁלוּמִין לָרִאשׁוֹן. כֵּן הוּא אָמַר הָכָא. כָּל־שִׁבְעָה תַּשְׁלוּמִין לָרִאשׁוֹן. רִבִּי הוֹשַׁעְיָה אָמַר. כָּל־ שִׁבְעָה חוֹבָה. מַה נָּפַק מִן בֵּינֵיהוֹן. גֵּר שֶׁנִּתְגַּייֵר בִּשְׁאָר הַיָּמִים. עַל דַּעְתֵּיהּ דְּחִזְקִיָּה פָּטוּר. עַל דַּעְתֵּיהּ דְּרִבִּי יוֹחָנָן וּדְרִבִּי הוֹשַׁעְיָה חַיָּב. אַף בְּטָמֵא כֵן. נִיטְמָא בִּשְׁאָר הַיָּמִים. עַל דַּעְתֵּיהּ דְּחִזְקִיָּה פָּטוּר. עַל דַּעְתֵּיהּ דְּרִבִּי יוֹחָנָן וּדְרִבִּי הוֹשַׁעְיָה חַיָּב. אָמַר רִבִּי יוֹסֵה. תַּמָּן רָאוּי הוּא. קְרִיעָה הִיא שֶׁגְּרָמָה. בְּרַם הָכָא הַטָּמֵא עַצְמוֹ אֵינוֹ רָאוּי.

"The sexless." Everybody agrees that a sexless who was torn open and turned out to be a male[32] on the first day of a holiday is liable. Where do they disagree? On the remaining days. Ḥizqiah said, *he shall be seen, he shall be seen*[33], he who is liable on the first {day} is liable on the second; he who is not liable on the first {day} is not liable on the second. Rebbi Joḥanan said, all seven {days} are make-up for the first. Rebbi Ila said, Rebbi Joḥanan inferred this from the Second *Pesaḥ*. As Rebbi Joḥanan said there[34], the Second *Pesaḥ* is make-up for the first, so he says here, all seven {days} are make-up for the first. Rebbi Hoshaia said, all seven {days} are obligatory[35]. What results between them? A proselyte who converted on one of the other days. In Ḥizqiah's opinion he is not liable; in Rebbi Joḥanan's and Rebbi Hoshaia's opinions he is liable. Is it the same for the impure one[36]? In Ḥizqiah's opinion is he not liable; in Rebbi Joḥanan's and Rebbi Hoshaia's opinions is he liable? Rebbi Yose said, there he is suitable[37]; the tearing caused it. But here the impure person himself is not suitable[38].

32 By an accident or an operation his skin was torn and it turned out that he had penis and testicles. Then he is a male and liable for all obligations of a male. Since a male is required to appear in the Temple on a holiday, but not before, now that he knows that he is a male he is liable like everybody else.

33 *Ex.* 23:17,34:23. In both places only Passover is mentioned as going on for 7 days; Pentecost and Tabernacles appear as single holidays. Since the obligation to appear is repeated, it follows that the seven day holiday has to be treated like a one-day holiday. A person not obligated on the one day cannot become obligated later.

34 Babli 2a, 9a, *Pesaḥim* 93a. Since the Second *Pesaḥ* is biblical institution for people not liable to bring the first of the 14th of Nisan, it proves that make-up days

are also for people not liable for appearance on the first day of a holiday.

35 They are independent possibilities for fulfilling the obligation of appearance, including the six days following the one-day holiday of Pentecost.

36 A person impure on the first day, to become pure on a later day.

37 Therefore he certainly is not liable for Ḥisqia and R. Joḥanan; the question remains open for R. Hoshaia.

(76a line 30) אַנְדְּרוֹגִינוֹס. כָּל־זְכוּרְךָ. פְּרָט לְאַנְדְּרוֹגִינוֹס. תַּמָּן תַּנִּינָן. סָפֵק אַנְדְּרוֹגִינוֹס אֵין מְחַלְּלִין עָלָיו אֶת הַשַּׁבָּת. רִבִּי יְהוּדָה מַתִּיר בָּאַנְדְּרוֹגִינוֹס: מַה אָמַר כָּא רִבִּי יְהוּדָה. נִישְׁמְעִינָהּ מִן הָדָא. יוֹחָנָן בֶּן דַּהֲבַאי מִשֵּׁם רִבִּי יְהוּדָה. אַף הַסּוּמָא. וְלֵית בַּר־נַשׁ אָמַר אַף אֶלָּא דְּהוּא מוֹדֵי עַל קַדְמִייָתָא. מִחְלְפָא שִׁיטָתֵיהּ דְּרִבִּי יְהוּדָה. תַּמָּן הוּא אָמַר. פְּרָט. וְהָכָא הוּא אָמַר. לְרַבּוֹת. רִבִּי יְהוּדָה וְרַבָּנָן מִקְרָא אֶחָד הֵן דּוֹרְשִׁין. רַבָּנָן דּוֹרְשִׁין עָרֵל. מַה תַּלְמוּד לוֹמַר עָרֵל זָכָר. עַד שֶׁיְּהֵא כוּלוֹ זָכָר. רִבִּי יוּדָה דָּרַשׁ זָכָר. מַה תַּלְמוּד לוֹמַר עָרֵל. וַאֲפִילוּ מְקָצָתוֹ עָרֵל. בְּרַם הָכָא. כָּל־זְכוּרְךָ. פְּרָט לְאַנְדְּרוֹגִינוֹס.

"The hermaphrodite." *All your males*[26], to exclude the hermaphrodite. There[38], we have stated: "One does not desecrate the Sabbath for a case of doubt[39] {or} for a hermaphrodite; Rebbi Jehudah permits for the hermaphrodite." What does Rebbi Jehudah say in this case[40]? Let us hear from the following: Joḥanan ben Dahavai said in the name of Rebbi Jehudah, neither does the blind one[41]. Nobody says "neither" unless he agrees with the preceding statement[42]. The argument of Rebbi Jehudah seems inverted. There he says except, but here he says including. Rebbi Jehudah and the rabbis explain the same verse[43]. The rabbis explain *uncircumcised*. Why does the verse say, *an uncircumcised male*? Only if he be totally male[44]. Rebbi Jehudah explains *male*[45]. Why does the verse say, *uncircumcised*? Even if he is only partially uncircumcised. But here, a*ll your males*, to exclude the hermaphrodite.

38 Mishnah *Shabbat* 19:3. The entire paragraph essentially is found in *Šabbat* 19, Notes 99-109, *Yebamot* 8:1.

39 Whether the baby was actually born on a Sabbath or maybe on Friday or Sunday. In the latter case he may not be circumcised on the Sabbath.

40 Does R. Jehudah agree with the Mishnah which excludes the hermaphrodite from the duty of pilgrimage?

41 Who is excluded from the duty of pilgrimage. Tosephta 1:1, Babli 2a, *Sanhedrin* 4b, *Arakhin* 2b.

42 That the hermaphrodite is excluded.

43 *Gen.* 17:14, establishing the duty of circumcision. The verse emphasizing *male*

is not needed to exclude female circumcision since the limb to be circumcised always is referred to as *flesh*, and therefore designates the only boneless limb, the penis, which characterizes males.

44 While the hermaphrodite can be circumcised, having a penis, and has to be circumcised since his maleness may be the dominant trait, he cannot be classified as male.

45 Babli *Šabbat* 137a. Instead of *all your males*, he reads *your total maleness*.

(76a line 38) נָשִׁים. כָּל־זְכוּרְךָ. פְּרָט לְנָשִׁים.

עֲבָדִים. נִשְׁמְעִינָהּ מִן הָדָא. שָׁלֹשׁ פְּעָמִים בַּשָּׁנָה יֵרָאֶה כָל־זְכוּרְךָ. אֶת שֶׁאֵין לוֹ אָדוֹן אֶלָּא הַקָּדוֹשׁ בָּרוּךְ הוּא. יָצָא הָעֶבֶד שֶׁיֵּשׁ לוֹ אָדוֹן אַחֵר. אָמַר רִבִּי יְהוֹשֻׁעַ בֶּן לֵוִי. מִנַּיִין שֶׁכָּל־הַמְקַיֵּים מִצְוַת רְאִיָּה כְּאִילּוּ מְקַבֵּיל פְּנֵי שְׁכִינָה . מִן הָדָא שָׁלֹשׁ פְּעָמִים בַּשָּׁנָה יֵרָאֶה כָל־זְכוּרְךָ אֶל־פְּנֵי הָאָדֹן | יי' וגו'.

חִיגֵּר. דִּכְתִיב רְגָלִים.

חוֹלֶה. דִּכְתִיב וְשָׂמַחְתָּ.

זָקֵן. דִּכְתִיב רְגָלִים. אָמַר רִבִּי יוֹסֵה. תַּרְתֵּיהוֹן לְקוּלָּא. יָכוֹל לִשְׂמוֹחַ וְאֵינוּ יָכוֹל לְהַלֵּךְ. קוֹרֵא אֲנִי עָלָיו רְגָלִים. יָכוֹל לְהַלֵּךְ וְאֵינוּ יָכוֹל לִשְׂמוֹחַ. קוֹרֵא אֲנִי עָלָיו וְשָׂמַחְתָּ.

"Women". *All your males*[26], excluding women[46].

"Slaves". Let us hear from the following: *Three times a year shall all your males be seen*[47], anybody who has no master but the Holy One, praise to Him. This excludes the slave who has another master. Rebbi Joshua ben Levi said, from where that anybody who keeps the commandment of appearance is like one who greets the Divine Presence? From this, *Three times a year shall all your males be seen before the face of the Master, the Eternal*, etc[47].

"The lame", for it is written, *walking occasions*[1].

"The sick", for it is written, *you shall enjoy*[48]. "The old", for it is written, *walking occasions*. Rebbi Yose said, both are for leniency. If he can enjoy but not walk, I am reading for him *walking occasions*. If he can walk but not enjoy, I am reading for him *you shall enjoy*.

46 *Sifry Deut.* 143; *Mekhilta dR. Ismael Mišpatim* Chap. 20 (ed. Horovitz-Rabin p. 333).

47 *Ex.* 23:17. Babli 4a.

48 *Deut.* 16:14. *Mekhilta dR. Ismael Mišpatim* Chap. 20 (ed. Horovitz-Rabin p. 333).

(76a line 45) רִבִּי יוֹחָנָן בְּשֵׁם רִבִּי יַנַּאי. בֵּית שַׁמַּי וּבֵית הִלֵּל מִקְרָא אֶחָד הֵן דּוֹרְשִׁין. בֵּית שַׁמַּי אוֹמְרִים. כָּתוּב אֶחָד אוֹמֵר זְכוּרְךָ. וְכָתוּב אֶחָד אוֹמֵר רְגָלִים. טוּל בֵּנְתַיִם אֶת שֶׁהוּא יָכוֹל לִרְכּוֹב

עַל כְּתֵיפוֹ שֶׁלְאָבִיו. וַאֲפִילוּ קָטָן יָכוֹל הוּא לִרְכּוֹב יָצָא. אֶלָּא אֶת שֶׁהוּא רוֹאֶה כְּתֵיפוֹ שֶׁלְאָבִיו וּמַפְסֵעַ. בֵּית הִלֵּל דּוֹרְשִׁין. כָּתוּב אֶחָד אוֹמֵר זְכוּרְךָ. וְכָתוּב אֶחָד אוֹמֵר רְגָלִים. טוּל בֵּנְתַיִם אֶת שֶׁהוּא יָכוֹל לֶאֱחוֹז בְּיָדוֹ שֶׁלְאָבִיו. וּלְעִנְיָין טַהֲרוֹת אַתְּ אָמַר. אֶת שֶׁהוּא תָפוּס בְּיַד אָבִיו סְפֵיקוֹ כְּפִיקֵחַ. אָבִיו תּוֹפֵשׂ בְּיָדוֹ [סְפֵיקוֹ] כְּחֵרֵשׁ. בְּרַם הָכָא בֵין כָּךְ וּבֵין כָּךְ חַיָּב.

Rebbi Johanan in the name of Rebbi Yannai: The House of Shammai and the House of Hillel explain the same verse. The House of Shammai are saying, one verse says *your males*[26], and another verse says, *walking occasions*[1]. Take in between them the one able to ride on his father's shoulder. But even a {very} small one can ride on his father's shoulder; must he fulfill his obligation? But one who sees his father's shoulder and runs to him[49]. The House of Hillel explain: one verse says *your males*, and another verse says, *walking occasions*. Take in between them the one able to grab his father's hand. But in matters of purity you are saying, if he grabs his father's hand, in matters of doubt he is treated as intelligent being[50]. If his father grabs his hand, [in case of doubt][51] he is treated as deaf-and-dumb. But here in both cases he is liable[52].

49 For the House of Shammai the obligation of appearance extends to all boys able to ride on their father's shoulders without being held by their father.

50 By Pentateuchal standards, only intelligent Jews can become impure (Mishnah *Taharot* 3:6). (The impurity of Gentiles is rabbinic, i. e., popular usage traceable to First Temple times.) Therefore a baby cannot be impure (but he cannot be pure either and as such is prevented from entering the Temple). It is now stated that as long as a parent has to grab his hand to make him walk with the parent he is considered unable to be asked in matters of purity and therefore impervious to purity. If such a child touches food prepared in purity, it remains pure. But if the child by himself takes his parent's hand, he is treated as intelligent being and since he may be asked whether he touched certain things he is subject to impurity and if he touched pure food and does not remember what he did before this the food has to be treated as impure.

51 Corrector's addition; correct but unnecessary in Yerushalmi style.

52 The rules of appearance (which refer to the parent's obligation to bring his child) and those of impurity (which refer to the status of the child) are not comparable.

(76a line 53) רִבִּי בּוּן בַּר חִייָה בְּעָא קוֹמֵי רִבִּי זְעוּרָה. אֵיכָן הָיוּ מַרְאִים פָּנִים. בְּהַר הַבַּיִת אוֹ בָעֲזָרוֹת. אָמַר לֵיהּ. נִשְׁמְעִינָהּ מִן הָדָא. הַטָּמֵא פָּטוּר מִן הָרְאִיָּיה. דִּכְתִיב וּבָאתָ שָׁמָּה וַהֲבֵאתֶם שָׁמָּה. וְאֵין טָמֵא מֵת נִכְנָס לְהַר הַבַּיִת. הָדָא אָמְרָה. בָּעֲזָרָה הָיוּ מַרְאִים פָּנִים. מֵאֵיכָן אַתְּ מוֹדֵד. מִן הַחוֹמָה אוֹ מִן הַבָּתִּים. תַּנֵּי שְׁמוּאֵל. מִן הַשִּׁילוֹחַ. וְשִׁילוֹחַ הָיָה בְּאֶמְצַע הַמְּדִינָה.

רִבִּי בּוּן בַּר חִייָה בְּעָא קוֹמֵי רִבִּי זְעוּרָה. מָהוּ לְשַׁלֵּחַ חֲגִיגָתוֹ בְּיַד אַחֵר. אָמַר לֵיהּ. נִשְׁמְעִינָהּ מִן הָדָא. מוּכֵּי שְׁחִין וּפוֹלִפְסִין פְּטוּרִין מִן הָרְאִיָּיה. דִּכְתִיב וּבָאתָ שָׁמָּה וַהֲבֵאתֶם שָׁמָּה. הַטָּמֵא פָּטוּר מִן הָרְאִיָּיה. דִּכְתִיב בְּבוֹא כָל־יִשְׂרָאֵל לֵרָאוֹת וגו'. הָרָאוּי לָבוֹא עִם כָּל־יִשְׂרָאֵל מֵבִיא. וְשֶׁאֵינוֹ רָאוּי לָבוֹא עִם כָּל־יִשְׂרָאֵל אֵינוֹ מֵבִיא. וְיִשְׁלַח חֲגִיגָתוֹ בְּיַד אַחֵר. אָמַר רִבִּי יוֹסֵי. זֹאת אוֹמֶרֶת שֶׁאֵינוֹ מְשַׁלֵּחַ חֲגִיגָתוֹ בְּיַד אַחֵר. רִבִּי שַׁמַּי בָּעֵי. אוֹ חִילּוּף. מוּכֵּי שְׁחִין וּפוֹלִפְסִין (פְּטוּרִין מִן הָרְאִיָּיה. דִּכְתִיב בְּבוֹא כָל־יִשְׂרָאֵל. חָזַר רִבִּי שַׁמַּי וְאָמַר. מוּכֵּי שְׁחִין וּפוֹלִפְסִין אַף עַל פִּי שֶׁאֵינָן רְאוּיִין) לָבוֹא עִם כָּל־יִשְׂרָאֵל רְאוּיִין הֵן לָבוֹא בִּפְנֵי עַצְמָן. הַטָּמֵא אֵינוֹ רָאוּי לֹא בִּפְנֵי עַצְמוֹ וְלֹא עִם כָּל־יִשְׂרָאֵל.

Corrector's text

רִבִּי שַׁמַּי בָּעֵי. אוֹ חִילּוּף. מוּכֵּי שְׁחִין וּפוֹלִפְסִין [פְּטוּרִין מִן הָרְאִיָּיה. דִּכְתִיב בְּבוֹא כָל־יִשְׂרָאֵל לֵרָאוֹת]. הַטָּמֵא פָּטוּר מִן הָרְאִיָּיה. דִּכְתִיב וּבָאתָ שָׁמָּה וַהֲבֵאתֶם שָׁמָּה. חָזַר רִבִּי שַׁמַּי וָאַמַר. מוּכֵּי שְׁחִין וּפוֹלִפְסִין אַף עַל פִּי שֶׁאֵינָן רְאוּיִין] לָבוֹא עִם כָּל־יִשְׂרָאֵל רְאוּיִין הֵן לָבוֹא בִּפְנֵי עַצְמָן. הַטָּמֵא אֵינוֹ רָאוּי ...

Rebbi Abun bar Ḥiyya asked before Rebbi Ze`ira: Where does one appear[53]? On the Temple Mount or in the Temple courtyards? He told him, let us hear from the following[54]: "The impure is exempt from appearance, for it is written, *you shall come there and bring there*." And one impure in the impurity of the dead may not enter the Temple Mount[55]. This implies that appearance is in the Temple courtyards.

From where does one measure[56]? from the wall or from the houses? Samuel stated, from the Siloam. And the Siloam was in the middle of the capital[57].

Rebbi Abun bar Ḥiyya asked before Rebbi Ze`ira: May one send one's appearance sacrifice[58] by another person? He said to him, let us hear from the following: "Those afflicted by scabies or polyps[59] are exempt from appearance, since it is written *you shall come there and bring there*[60]. The impure is exempt from appearance since it is written, *when all of Israel comes*[61], etc. The one able to come with all of Israel brings; the one unable to come with all of Israel does not bring." Could he not send his appearance sacrifice by another person? Rebbi Yose said, this implies that he may not send his appearance sacrifice by another person. Rebbi Shammai asked, or maybe the other way. Those afflicted by scabies or polyps (are exempt from appearance, since it is written *when all of Israel comes*. Rebbi Shammai turned around and said, Those afflicted by scabies or polyps) even though they cannot come with all of Israel, they can come by themselves[62]. The impure one is unable to come by himself and with all of Israel[63].

Corrector's text[64]

Rebbi Shammai asked, or maybe the other way. Those afflicted by scabies or polyps [are exempt from appearance, since it is written *when all of Israel comes to appear*. The impure is exempt from appearance since it is written, *you shall come there and bring there*. Rebbi Shammai turned around and said, Those afflicted by scabies or polyps] even though they cannot come with all of Israel, they can come by themselves. The impure one is unable . . .

53 While the lay person is forbidden to appear in the Temple without a sacrifice (*Ex.* 23:15, 34:20), this is an obligation separate from that of appearance. The question is if the latter is satisfied only in the Temple district or already in the enlarged sacred district, representing the camp of the Levites in the desert (*Num.* 1:50).

54 Tosephta 1:1. Babli 4b, *Yebamot* 72b, from another verse *Mekhilta dR. Ismael Mišpatim* Chap. 20 (ed. Horovitz-Rabin p. 333). Since a sacrifice may be brought only in the Temple and the impure person may not enter, he may not bring; one concludes that he need not come.

55 This is not quite exact, Mishnah *Kelim* 1:8. The person whose impurity originates in his body may not enter the Temple Mount; the one impure by the impurity of the dead may not enter the immediate surroundings of the Temple domain; the person not impure but not pure may not enter the Temple courtyards.

56 This refers to the statement of the Mishnah that the minor must be brought to the Temple if he is able to walk from Jerusalem to the Temple.

57 The pond is rather close to the Temple but at the foot of a steep hill. No indications are given how differences in level are to be commuted into distances.

58 Which is required (Note 53) and its minimal value determined in Mishnah 2. May one satisfy the obligation of appearance by paying another person to present the sacrifice in the payor's name?

59 Greek πολύπους "multipede", according to the commentators of the Babli a putrid growth on the nose which is extremely bad smelling.

60 *Deut.* 12:5-6. *You shall come* is in singular form, to be interpreted as collective. *You shall bring* is in the plural, addressed to every pilgrim separately. This version exempts everybody unable to join a group, in this case because of his unbearable body smell (Babli 4b).

61 *Deut.* 31:12.

62 Since *coming* and *bringing* are

| mentioned in separate verses, they are separate obligations. The person who smells bad is exempt from joining a group but still obligated to appear in the Temple. | 63 He is prohibited from bringing a sacrifice and exempt from joining a group which he would contaminate by his touch.
64 An unnecessary rearrangement. |

(76a line 68) הִפְרִישׁ חֲגִיגָתוֹ וָמֵת. הַיּוֹרְשִׁים מָהוּ שֶׁיָּבִיאוּ אוֹתָהּ. רִבִּי אִילָא אָמַר. יֵרָאֶה יֵרָאֶה. הָרָאוּי לָבֹא מֵבִיא. וְשֶׁאֵינוֹ רָאוּי לָבֹא אֵינוֹ מֵבִיא. אָמַר רִבִּי זְעוּרָה כַּהִיא דְרִבִּי יוֹחָנָן וְרִבִּי יוֹנָתָן תְּרֵיהוֹן אָמְרִין. כָּל בְּכוֹר בָּנֶיךָ תִּפְדֶּה. אֲפִילוּ לְאַחַר מִיתָה. וְהָכָא וְלֹא־יֵרָאוּ פָנַי רֵיקָם: אֲפִילוּ לְאַחַר מִיתָה. אָמַר רִבִּי בָּא בַּר מָמָל. מַחֲלוֹקֶת שְׁמוּאֵל וְרִבִּי יוֹחָנָן. דְּתַנִּינָן תַּמָּן. הָאִשָּׁה שֶׁהֵבִיאָה חַטָּאתָהּ וָמֵתָה יָבִיאוּ הַיּוֹרְשִׁין עוֹלָתָהּ. עוֹלָתָהּ וָמֵתָה. לֹא יָבִיאוּ הַיּוֹרְשִׁין חַטָּאתָהּ: שְׁמוּאֵל אָמַר. בְּמוּפְרֶשֶׁת. רִבִּי יוֹחָנָן אָמַר. אֲפִילוּ אֵינָהּ מוּפְרֶשֶׁת. מָה אֲנָן קַיָּימִין. אִם בְּשֶׁיֵּרְשׁוּ קַרְקַע. בְּהָדָא אָמַר שְׁמוּאֵל. בְּמוּפְרֶשֶׁת. אִם בְּשֶׁיֵּרְשׁוּ מִיטַּלְטְלִין. בְּהָדָא רִבִּי יוֹחָנָן אָמַר. אֲפִילוּ אֵינָהּ מוּפְרֶשֶׁת. מַה נָּפַק מִן בֵּינֵיהוֹן. יֵרְשׁוּ קַרְקַע. עַל דַּעְתֵּיהּ דִּשְׁמוּאֵל לִתְבֹּעַ אֵין תּוֹבְעִין וּלְמַשְׁכֵּן אֵין מְמַשְׁכְּנִין. עַל דַּעְתֵּיהּ דְּרִבִּי יוֹחָנָן אוֹף לְמַשְׁכֵּן מְמַשְׁכְּנִין. יֵרְשׁוּ מִטַּלְטְלִין. עַל דַּעְתֵּיהּ דְּרִבִּי יוֹחָנָן לִתְבֹּעַ תּוֹבְעִין וּלְמַשְׁכֵּן [אֵין] מְמַשְׁכְּנִין. עַל דַּעְתֵּיהּ דִּשְׁמוּאֵל אַף לִתְבֹּעַ אֵין תּוֹבְעִין.

If he separated[65] his festival offering and died, do the heirs have to bring it? Rebbi Ila said, *shall be seen*, has to be seen[66]. He who can come brings, he who cannot come does not bring. Rebbi Ze`ira said, following Rebbi Johanan and Rebbi Jonathan who both said, *you have to redeem any first born of your sons*, even after death, and here, *they shall not appear before My Presence empty-handed*, even after death[67]. Rebbi Abba bar Mamal said, there is a disagreement between Samuel and Rebbi Johanan, regarding what we have stated there[68], "A woman[69] who brought her purification sacrifice and died, the heirs have to bring her elevation sacrifice. Her elevation sacrifice and she died, the heirs shall not bring her purification sacrifice[69]." Samuel said, if it was separated[70]. Rebbi Johanan said, even if it was not separated. Where do we hold? If they inherited real estate[71], does Samuel say if it was separated? If they inherited movables[72], does Rebbi Johanan say, even if it was not separated? What is the difference between them? If they inherited real estate, in Samuel's opinion one does neither claim it nor taking pledges for it[73]; in Rebbi Johanan's opinion one even takes pledges. If they inherited movables, in Rebbi Johanan's opinion one claims it (and is) [but is not][74] taking pledges for it. In Samuel's opinion one does not claim it.

65 He designated an animal from his herd as his sacrifice for the coming pilgrimage. Since it does not say "he dedicated", the designation is not a formal dedication. Nevertheless, Mishnah *Qiddušin* 1:7 states that a promise to Heaven is to be enforced like delivery to a person.

66 Since the deceased is buried, the designation becomes void.

67 *Ex.* 34:20. There seems to be no reason why the redemption of the first-born is mentioned in the same verse as the prohibition to appear in the Temple empty-handed. It is explained that just as the redemption of the first born is an obligation not eliminated by the absence of a father, so the obligation of the sacrifice of appearance is not eliminated by the death of the votary.

68 Mishnah *Qinnim* 2:5.

69 After childbirth, which obligates here for a purification and an elevation sacrifice (*Lev.* 12:1-8.)

70 Since a purification sacrifice in all cases is a personal obligation, at the death of the person any purification sacrifice already dedicated as such can neither be sacrificed nor redeemed. If it is not yet dedicated it cannot be dedicated. Therefore it is technically impossible for the heirs to bring her purification sacrifice.

71 By strict talmudic rules only real estate is subject to claims by creditors. The extension of liens to movables is Gaonic, not relevant here. The rule of Mishnah *Qiddušin* 1:7 creates a lien on the estate only if it contains real estate. Since the woman's obligation was created at the moment of childbirth, there seems to be no reason why Samuel could limit the obligation.

72 In the absence of real estate, according to the rule explained in the preceding Note the obligation should be unenforceable even for R. Johanan.

73 The Temple authorities are required to insist on prompt liquidation of all dues to the Temple. The verse (*Deut.* 23:22) require prompt payment of all vows. By rabbinic interpretation this means before the passing of the next three festivals of pilgrimage. Since there is a time limit, the officers of the Temple are required to ask for the prompt fulfillment of the vow and are entitled to take pledges from the votary to enforce their demand. But since the heirs did not make any vow, the time limit cannot be applied to them and the powers of the Temple officials are limited; for Samuel they are eliminated but not for R. Johanan.

74 There seems to be no justification for the corrector's addition. According to Samuel, *Qiddušin* 1:7 declares that a promise to Heaven is the equivalent of a civil contract; if the contract would become unenforceable, so is the obligation to Heaven. According to R. Johanan the obligation can be enforced since the equivalent of the sacrifice was Heaven's property and as such could not be part of the estate.

(fol. 75d) **משנה ב**: בֵּית שַׁמַּאי אוֹמְרִים הָרְאִיָּה שְׁתֵּי כֶסֶף וְהַחֲגִיגָה מָעָה כָּסֶף. וּבֵית הִלֵּל אוֹמְרִים הָרְאִיָּה מָעָה כֶסֶף וַחֲגִיגָה שְׁתֵּי כָסֶף:

Mishnah 2: The House of Shammai say, the sacrifice of appearance is two silver coins, and the festival sacrifice one obolus[75]. But the House of Hillel say, the sacrifice of appearance is one silver obolus, and the festival sacrifice two silver coins.

75 The sacrifice of appearance is an elevation sacrifice, not for human consumption. The festival sacrifice is a family well-being sacrifice providing the meat to the festival meal to be consumed in purity as part of the commandment to enjoy the holiday. The obolus in the Augustean system is the smallest silver coin, $1/6$ of a silver denar, about 0.6g of silver.

(76b line 5) **הלכה ב**: רְאִיָּה עוֹלוֹת וַחֲגִיגָה שְׁלָמִים. בֵּית שַׁמַּי אוֹמְרִים. מַרְבִּין בָּעוֹלוֹת וּמְמָעֲטִים בַּשְּׁלָמִים. בֵּית הִלֵּל אוֹמְרִים. מְמָעֲטִין בָּעוֹלוֹת וּמַרְבִּין בַּשְּׁלָמִים. רִבִּי תַּנְחוּם בַּר עִילָאי בְּשֵׁם רִבִּי יוֹסֵי בֶּן חֲנִינָה. בֵּית שַׁמַּי יָלְפִין לָהּ מִקָּרְבָּנוֹת [הָעֲצֶרֶת. בֵּית הִלֵּל יָלְפִין לָהּ מִקָּרְבָּנוֹת] הַנְּשִׂיאִים. אָמְרוּ בֵית הִלֵּל לְבֵית שַׁמַּי. לֹא מוּטָב לִלְמוֹד קָרְבַּן יָחִיד מִקָּרְבָּן יָחִיד. אָמְרוּ לָהֶם בֵּית שַׁמַּי. מוּטָב לִלְמוֹד דָּבָר שֶׁהוּא נוֹהֵג לַדּוֹרוֹת מִדָּבָר שֶׁהוּא נוֹהֵג לַדּוֹרוֹת. וְאַל תָּבֵא לִי קָרְבַּן נְשִׂיאִים שֶׁאֵינוֹ נוֹהֵג לַדּוֹרוֹת.

Halakhah 2: The sacrifice of appearance is elevation offerings, but the festival sacrifice is well-being offerings. The House of Shammai are saying, one increases elevation offerings and diminishes well-being offerings. The House of Hillel are saying, one diminishes elevation offerings and increases well-being offerings. Rebbi Tanḥum bar Ilai in the name of Rebbi Yose ben Ḥanina: The House of Shammai infer from the sacrifices [of Pentecost[76]; the House of Hillel infer from the sacrifices] of the princes[77]. The House of Hillel said to the House of Shammai, is it not better to be instructed from a private offering about private offerings? The House of Shammai said to them, it is better to be instructed by something applicable to the future; do not refer to the sacrifice of the princes which is not applicable to the future.

76 The only holiday offering by the public including well-being sacrifices. The presentation of bread from the new wheat harvest is accompanied by elevation sacrifices of one bull, 2 rams, and 7 sheep, as well as a well-being sacrifice of 2 sheep (*Lev.* 23:18-19).

77 All of the tribal leaders brought the

same sacrifice for the inauguration of the Tent of Meeting, 1 bull, 1 ram, 1 sheep as elevation offering but 2 bulls, 5 rams, 5 goats, 5 sheep as well-being sacrifice (*Num.* 7). Babli 6a.

(76b line 12) תַּנֵּי. יֵשׁ בָּרְאִיָּיה מַה שֶׁאֵין בַּחֲגִיגָה. וּבַחֲגִיגָה מַה שֶׁאֵין בָּרְאִיָּיה. שֶׁהָרְאִיָּיה כוּלָהּ לַגְּבוֹהַּ. מַה שֶּׁאֵין כֵּן בַּחֲגִיגָה. חֲגִיגָה נוֹהֶגֶת לִפְנֵי הַדִּיבֵּר וּלְאַחַר הַדִּיבֵּר. מַה שֶׁאֵין כֵּן בָּרְאִיָּיה. חֲגִיגָה נוֹהֶגֶת לִפְנֵי הַדִּיבֵּר. לְשׁוֹן חֲגִיגָה נוֹהֶגֶת לִפְנֵי הַדִּיבֵּר. שַׁלַּח אֶת־עַמִּי וְיָחוֹגּוּ לִי בַּמִּדְבָּר: וּבַשִּׂמְחָה מַה שֶׁאֵין כֵּן בִּשְׁנֵיהֶן. שֶׁהַשִּׂמְחָה נוֹהֶגֶת בֵּין בְּדָבָר שֶׁהוּא מִשֶּׁלּוֹ בֵּין בְּדָבָר שֶׁהוּא מִשֶּׁלַּאֲחֵרִים. בֵּין בְּדָבָר שֶׁדַּרְכּוֹ לָכֵן בֵּין בְּדָבָר שֶׁאֵין דַּרְכּוֹ לָכֵן. וְאֵילּוּ אֵינָן נוֹהַגִין אֶלָּא מִשֶּׁלּוֹ. וּבִלְבַד מִדָּבָר שֶׁדַּרְכּוֹ לָכֵן. רִבִּי יוֹסֵי בָעֵי. וְלָמָּה לִי נָן אֲמָרִין. כָּל־שֶׁהוּא חַיָּיב בָּרְאִייָה חַיָּיב בַּשִּׂמְחָה. וְיֵשׁ שֶׁהוּא חַיָּיב בַּשִּׂמְחָה וְאֵינוֹ חַיָּיב בָּרְאִייָה. נָשִׁים חַיָּיבוֹת בַּשִּׂמְחָה וְאֵינָן חַיָּיבוֹת בָּרְאִייָה. רִבִּי יְהוֹשֻׁעַ בֶּן לֵוִי אָמַר. וְשָׂמַחְתָּ֒. אֲפִילּוּ מִמַּקִילוֹן. אָמַר רִבִּי לָעֲזָר. נֶאֱמַר כָּאן שִׂמְחָה וְנֶאֱמַר לְהַלָּן שִׂמְחָה. מַה שִׂמְחָה הָאֲמוּרָה לְהַלָּן שְׁלָמִים אַף כָּאן שְׁלָמִים. רַב חוּנָה אָכַל (פשוש) [פשוט] כָּל־שִׁבְעָה.

It was stated[78]: "There is about the sacrifice of appearance what does not apply to the festival sacrifice, and about the festival sacrifice what does not apply to the sacrifice of appearance. For the sacrifice of appearance is totally for the High[79]; this does not apply to the festival sacrifice. The festival sacrifice was in use before the Word[80] and after the Word; this does not apply to the sacrifice of appearance." Was the festival sacrifice in use before the Word[81]? The language of festival sacrifice was in use before the Word[82]: *send My people that they present Me with festival sacrifices in the desert.* "[78]And joy applies to matters which are his property and matters which are others' property; whether matters usually used for the purpose or matters not usually used for the purpose[83]. But those apply only to his own property and matters usually used for the purpose." Rebbi Yose said, and why do we not say, anybody liable for a sacrifice of appearance is liable for joy but there are those liable for joy but not liable for a sacrifice of appearance: "Women are liable for joy but not liable for a sacrifice of appearance[84]"? Rebbi Joshua ben Levi said, *and you shall enjoy*[85], even from a butcher shop[86]. Rebbi Eleazar said, *joy* is mentioned here and *joy* in mentioned there. Since the joy mentioned there refers to well-being sacrifices so also *joy* mentioned here refers to well-being sacrifices[87]. Rav Huna ate (deflated things) [simply][88] all seven days[89].

78 Tosephta 1:4; cf. Babli 6a/b.
79 Everything is burned on the altar; there is no part even for the Cohanim.
80 The theophany of Sinai.
81 Before the Giving of the Torah there could be no commandments and no commanded sacrifices.
82 *Ex.* 5:1.
83 One may enjoy the holiday being invited to somebody else's well-being sacrifice, and even with meat from an animal not admissible as sacrifice.
84 Tosephta 1:4; obviously not part of R. Yose's *baraita* text.
85 "Enjoyment" of the meat of well-being sacrifices is mentioned without any reference to holidays in *Deut.* 12:12, and as a requirement of the holidays in *Deut.* 16:11,14,15.

86 Latin *macellum*. According to his argument, the duty to eat meat on holidays is biblical also after the destruction of the Temple when sacrificial meat is not available.
87 The comparison of the verses quoted in Note 85 shows that the biblical requirement is intrinsically connected with well-being sacrifices and therefore became moot with the destruction of the Temple.
88 The corrector considered the scribe's otherwise unknown פשש as scribal error and replaced it with a known word with similar letters. The scribe may have intended a word like Arabic פס "to deflate".
89 Following R. Eleazar he did not accept the duty to eat meat on a holiday as scriptural and ate simple fare during the holiday week.

(76b line 24) אָמַר רִבִּי יוֹחָנָן. מָעָה כֶסֶף וּשְׁתֵּי כֶסֶף דְּבַר תּוֹרָה. תַּנָּא רִבִּי יָסָא קוֹמֵי רִבִּי יוֹחָנָן. רְאִיָּיה כָּל־שֶׁהִיא. חֲכָמִים הֵם שֶׁאֲמָרוּ. מָעָה כֶסֶף וּשְׁתֵּי כֶסֶף. אָמַר לֵיהּ. וְיֵשׁ כָּן זוֹ. אָמַר רִבִּי יוֹנָה. וְכָל־הַשִּׁיעוּרִין לֹא חֲכָמִים הֵם שֶׁנְּתָנוּם. כְּזַיִת מִן הַמֵּת. כְּזַיִת מִן הַנְּבֵילָה. וְכָעֲדָשָׁה מִן הַשֶּׁרֶץ. לֹא אֲתָא מִישְׁאוֹל אֶלָּא כַּיֵּי דְּתַנֵּי רִבִּי הוֹשַׁעְיָה. דְּתַנֵּי רִבִּי הוֹשַׁעְיָה. וְלֹא־יֵרָאוּ פָנַי רֵיקָם: אֲפִילוּ כָּל־שֶׁהוּא. חֲכָמִים הֵם שֶׁאֲמָרוּ. מָעָה כֶסֶף וּשְׁתֵּי כֶסֶף. וְקַשְׁיָא. מִן דּוּ סָמַךְ לָהּ לִדְבַר תּוֹרָה הוּא אָמַר. חֲכָמִים הֵם שֶׁאֲמָרוּ. מָעָה כֶסֶף וּשְׁתֵּי כֶסֶף. אָמַר רִבִּי יוֹסֵי בֵּירִבִּי בּוּן. רִבִּי יוֹחָנָן כְּדַעְתֵּיהּ וְרִבִּי הוֹשַׁעְיָה כְּדַעְתֵּיהּ. רִבִּי יוֹחָנָן כְּדַעְתֵּיהּ. דְּרִבִּי יוֹחָנָן דּוּ אָמַר. כָּל־הַשִּׁיעוּרִין הֲלָכָה לְמֹשֶׁה מִסִּינַי. חֲוֵי דּוּ אָמַר. מָעָה כֶסֶף וּשְׁתֵּי כֶסֶף דְּבַר תּוֹרָה. רִבִּי הוֹשַׁעְיָה כְּדַעְתֵּיהּ. רִבִּי הוֹשַׁעְיָה דּוּ אָמַר. הָאוֹכֵל אִיסּוּר בַּזְּמַן הַזֶּה צָרִיךְ לִשְׁנוֹת לְפָנָיו אֶת הַשִּׁיעוּרִין. שֶׁמָּא יַעֲמוֹד בֵּית דִּין אַחֵר וִישַׁנֶּה עָלָיו אֶת הַשִּׁיעוּרִין. וִיהֵא יוֹדֵעַ מֵאֵי זֶה שִׁיעוּר אָכַל. חֲוֵי דּוּ אָמַר רְאִיָּיה כָּל־שֶׁהִיא. חֲכָמִים הֵם שֶׁאֲמָרוּ. מָעָה כֶסֶף וּשְׁתֵּי כֶסֶף. אָמְרִין. חָזַר בֵּיהּ רִבִּי יוֹחָנָן מִן הָדָא. רִבִּי יוֹנָה וְרִבִּי יוֹנָתָן תְּרֵיהוֹן אָמְרִין. לֹא חָזַר בֵּיהּ. וְעוֹד מִן הָדָא דְּאָמַר רִבִּי לֹא בְשֵׁם רִבִּי אִימִּי. אִיתְפַּלְגוֹן חִזְקִיָּה וְרִבִּי יוֹחָנָן. חִזְקִיָּה אָמַר. אָדָם חוֹלֵק חוֹבָתוֹ לִשְׁתֵּי בְהֵמוֹת. רִבִּי יוֹחָנָן אָמַר. אֵין אָדָם חוֹלֵק חוֹבָתוֹ לִשְׁתֵּי בְהֵמוֹת. אֶלָּא צָרִיךְ שֶׁיְּהֵא בְיָדוֹ שְׁתֵּי כֶסֶף לְכָל־אַחַת וְאַחַת. רִבִּי

שִׁמְעוֹן בֶּן לָקִישׁ בְּשֵׁם חִזְקִיָּה. אָדָם טוֹפֵל בְּהֵמוֹת לִבְהֵמָה וְאֵין אָדָם טוֹפֵל מָעוֹת לְמָעָה. רִבִּי יוֹחָנָן אָמַר. אָדָם טוֹפֵל מָעוֹת לְמָעָה וְאֵין אָדָם טוֹפֵל בְּהֵמוֹת לִבְהֵמָה. הֵיךְ עֲבִידָה. הָיוּ לְפָנָיו עֶשֶׂר בְּהֵמוֹת. הִקְרִיב חָמֵשׁ בְּיוֹם טוֹב הָרִאשׁוֹן. וְהַמּוֹתָר מָהוּ שֶׁיִּדְּחוּ אֶת יוֹם טוֹב הָאַחֲרוֹן. רִבִּי קְרִיסְפִּי אָמַר. אִיתְפַּלְגוּן רִבִּי יוֹחָנָן וְרִבִּי שִׁמְעוֹן בֶּן לָקִישׁ. חַד אָמַר. דּוֹחֶה. וְחוֹרָנָה אָמַר. אֵינוֹ דּוֹחֶה. וְלָא יָדְעִין מָאן אָמַר דָּא וּמָאן אָמַר דָּא. אָמַר רִבִּי זְעוּרָה. נָפְרֵשׁ מִילֵּיהוֹן דְּרַבָּנִין מִן מִילֵּיהוֹן. דְּרִבִּי יוֹחָנָן דּוּ אָמַר. אָדָם טוֹפֵל מָעוֹת לְמָעָה. אֵין אָדָם טוֹפֵל בְּהֵמוֹת לִבְהֵמָה. הוּא דוּ אָמַר דּוֹחֶה. רִבִּי שִׁמְעוֹן בֶּן לָקִישׁ דּוּ אָמַר. אָדָם טוֹפֵל בְּהֵמוֹת לִבְהֵמָה. אֵין אָדָם טוֹפֵל מָעוֹת לְמָעָה. הוּא דוּ אָמַר. אֵינוֹ דוֹחֶה. שִׁמְעוֹן בַּר בָּא בְשֵׁם רִבִּי יוֹחָנָן. לְעוֹלָם הוּא מוֹסִיף וְהוֹלֵךְ וְדוֹחֶה אֶת יוֹם טוֹב עַד שֶׁיֹּאמַר. עוֹד אֵין בְּדַעְתִּי לְהוֹסִיף.

[90]Rebbi Johanan said: "One silver obolus and two silver coins[91] are words of the Torah." Rebbi Yasa stated before Rebbi Johanan: The appearance is with anything[92]; the Sages only said: "One silver obolus, two silver coins." He said to him: Is there anything like that? Rebbi Jonah said, are not all measures determined by the Sages[93]? They said: The volume of an olive from a corpse[94], the volume of an olive from a cadaver[95], the volume of a lentil from a dead reptile[96]. The question here is only what Rebbi Hoshaia stated: *They should not be seen before Me empty-handed*[97], with anything; the Sages only said: "A silver obolus, two silver coins." The difficulty is that this[98] is support for the opinion that it is based on words of the Torah. He said that only the Sages instituted: "one silver obolus, two silver coins." Rebbi Yose ben Rebbi Abun said: Rebbi Johanan follows his own opinion and Rebbi Hoshaia follows his own opinion. Rebbi Johanan follows his own opinion since Rebbi Johanan said that all measures are practice taught by Moses at Sinai; he says that "one obolus and two silver coins are the word of the Torah." Rebbi Hoshaia follows his own opinion; Rebbi Hoshaia is the one who said: he who eats forbidden food in the present time has to study the quantities[99]; maybe a new court will arise and change the measures for him; then he will know what measure he ate. Therefore he is the one who said, the appearance is with anything; the Sages only said: "one silver obolus, two silver coins." They said, Rebbi Johanan changed his mind about this. Rebbis Jonah and Jonathan[100] said, he did not change his mind; additionally, Rebbi La said in the name of Rebbi Ammi: Hizqiah and Rebbi Johanan disagreed. Hizqiah said, a man may split his obligation for two animals[101]. Rebbi Johanan said, nobody

may split his obligation for two animals, but for each one he has to have two silver coins in his hand. Rebbi Simeon ben Laqish in the name of Hizqiah: A person adjoins an animal to an animal but no person may adjoin money to money[102]. Rebbi Johanan said, a person may adjoin money to money but no person may adjoin animals to an animal. What may be done? There were before him ten animals, he sacrificed five of them on the first holiday. May the remainder push aside the last holiday[103]? Rebbi Crispus said, Rebbi Johanan and Rebbi Simeon ben Laqish disagree. One said, they push; the other one said, they do not push. We do not know who said what. Rebbi Ze`ira said, we may explain the words of the rabbis by their own words. Rebbi Johanan said: a person may adjoin coins to coins but not animals to an animal; he must say, they push[104]. But Rebbi Simeon ben Laqish said, a person adjoins an animal to an animal but no person may adjoin money to money; he must say, they do not push[105]. Simeon bar Abba came in the name of Rebbi Johanan: He adds[106] and pushes the holiday further until he says: I do not intend to add further.

90 This text is parallel to a somewhat defective text in *Peah* 1:1 (Notes 37-57); in places the Rome ms. of *Zeraim* has a more complete text.

91 The amounts stated in Mishnah 2 have biblical status.

92 One may appear in the Temple with one sacrifice for the appearance and one for the family holiday; no minimal expenditure is required. The monetary minimum is purely a rabbinic one. Babli 7a.

93 There are many biblical precepts that are applied only to some minimal amount and volume. None of these are spelled out in the Torah; they are all customary or rabbinic formulations.

94 All rules of defilement by parts of a corpse apply only if a minimum size of the volume of one olive is present. Hence, somebody in a house in which less than that volume of a corpse is present may go to the Temple without the purification procedure of the ashes of the Red Cow even though going there in impurity is a strict biblical prohibition.

95 To bring a sin offering for having eaten meat from a cadaver needs this minimum amount; the same minimum applies to the impurity caused by touching or carrying pieces of the cadaver of an otherwise kosher animal.

96 The minimum volume from a carcass that causes the severe impurity incurred by touching dead reptiles.

97 *Ex.* 23:15, 34:20.

98 These verses (and an additional one in *Deut.*) insist that one may not appear empty-handed; this must mean that a negligible amount is counted as nothing and, therefore, is forbidden by the Torah.

99 Since one is required and permitted to bring a sin-offering only if he ate more than the volume of an olive, he is forbidden to bring one if he ate less than that volume. Hence, the determination of that volume is essential. In the Babli *Yoma* 80a the interpretation is that not the rule of "volume of an olive" might change but rather its interpretation. Not only are antique measures never defined to exact standards, also modern interpretations of "volume of an olive" vary on a scale of 1 to 30. Hence, once the Temple is rebuilt an authoritative re-interpretation is needed even according to R. Johanan.

100 Instead of this totally impossible reading (R. Jonathan precedes R. Johanan) read with the *Peah* text: R. Yose.

101 In the Babli 8a it is explained that the obligation to spend an obolus and two silver coins must be satisfied by unencumbered money. Now four years out of seven there is a second tithe on agricultural produce of the Land of Israel. That second tithe is the property of the farmer but it must be consumed in Jerusalem; it also may be redeemed by money and the money taken to Jerusalem and there spent on food to be consumed in Jerusalem. So one may assume that many people on their pilgrimage for the holiday have money and, in case they are priests, animals of the tithe that they want to eat in Jerusalem to absolve themselves at the same time of the obligations of pilgrimage and Second Tithe. According to Hizqiah, on the first day of the holiday one may bring small and cheap animals as obligatory sacrifices and then use the money of tithes for additional *Hagigah* offerings but one may not add the money of Second Tithes to profane money to buy one large animal for any of the two obligations.

102 R. Johanan holds that one may add money (if only the basic amount is profane) but not animals (since no animal worth less than two pieces of silver is acceptable as *Hagigah*.)

103 If these animals retain the status of *Hagigah*, they may be sacrificed on the last day of Pesah or Sukkot which are also full holidays. If, however, they have only the status of sacrifices in fulfillment of a vow (since any dedication as sacrifice is a vow to bring the animal to the Temple), then they may be slaughtered only during the intermediate days of the holiday or after its conclusion, and they do not push aside holiday prohibitions. (Babli 8b.)

104 Since each animal was bought with money dedicated for *Hagigah*, they all have the status of *Hagigah*.

105 Since one may not adjoin money, only the first animal was *Hagigah*, the rest are not and cannot be used on a full holiday.

106 Even during the intermediate days of the holiday, when one's biblical obligation of appearing in the Temple with a sacrifice has already been satisfied, he can add money to the original money and still the animals bought will fall under the category of Hagigah. But when he declares that it is enough, the next money spent will no longer buy Hagigah sacrifices. This extension of R. Johanan's statement is not a logical consequence of his earlier one.

(fol. 75d) **משנה ג**: עוֹלוֹת בַּמּוֹעֵד בָּאוֹת מִן הַחוּלִין וּשְׁלָמִים מִן הַמַּעֲשֵׂר. בְּיוֹם טוֹב הָרִאשׁוֹן שֶׁל חַג, בֵּית שַׁמַּאי אוֹמְרִים מִן הַחוּלִין. וּבֵית הִלֵּל אוֹמְרִים מִן הַמַּעֲשֵׂר:

Mishnah 3: Elevation sacrifices on a holiday come from profane money[107] and well-being offerings from tithe money[108]. On the first day of any holiday[109], the House of Shammai are saying from profane money[110] but the House of Hillel are saying from tithe money.

107 Since nothing of the sacrifice is permitted to humans, and Second Tithe money must be spent on food for the farmer's family, tithe money may never be used for elevation sacrifices, holiday or no holiday.

108 Even though a small part of any well-being sacrifice is burned on the altar, it is explicitly permitted by a verse to use tithe money; *Deut.* 12:6.

109 This is the meaning of the word here, not "Tabernacles."

110 The House of Shammai permit slaughter of sacrifices on a full holiday only if they are an obligation of the holiday. Therefore they permit on the full holiday only the holiday sacrifice which for them must have the value of one (profane) obolus, and forbid to add money of Second Tithe to this profane amount. But the House of Hillel, for whom the basic obligation is 2 profane oboloi, permit to add tithe money to buy a large animal for the family celebration.

(76b line 53) **הלכה ג**: רִבִּי תַּנְחוּם בַּר עִילַאי בְּשֵׁם רִבִּי יוֹסֵי בֵּירְבִּי חֲנִינָה. כָּךְ מְשִׁיבִין בֵּית שַׁמַּי לְבֵית הִלֵּל. דָּבָר שֶׁהוּא בָא חוֹבָה בָּא מִן הַמַּעֲשֵׂר. אָמְרוּ לָהֶן. אִילוּ בָחוֹל שֶׁמָּא אֵינוֹ מֵבִיא אַחַת מִן הַחוּלִין וְטוֹפֵל לַמַּעֲשֵׂר. וָכָא מֵבִיא אַחַת מִן הַחוּלִין וְטוֹפֵל לַמַּעֲשֵׂר. וּמְנַיְין שֶׁהוּא טוֹפֵל [לַמַּעֲשֵׂר]. אָמַר רִבִּי יוֹסֵי בֶּן חֲנִינָה. נֶאֱמַר כָּאן מִשָּׁת וְנֶאֱמַר לְהַלָּן כִּי לֹא תוּכַל שְׂאֵתוֹ. מַה שְּׂאֵת הָאֲמוּר לְהַלָּן מַעֲשֵׂר אַף כָּאן מַעֲשֵׂר. אָמַר רִבִּי לַעֲזָר. נֶאֱמַר כָּאן שִׂמְחָה וְנֶאֱמַר לְהַלָּן שִׂמְחָה. מַה שִּׂמְחָה הָאֲמוּרָה לְהַלָּן מַעֲשֵׂר אַף כָּאן מַעֲשֵׂר. וְיָבִיא כוּלָּם מִן הַמַּעֲשֵׂר. עוּלָּא בַּר יִשְׁמָעֵאל אָמַר. נֶאֱמַר כָּאן מִשָּׁת וְנֶאֱמַר לְהַלָּן וַתֵּרֶב מַשְׂאַת בִּנְיָמִן. מַה מַשְׂאַת שֶׁנֶּאֱמַר לְהַלָּן שֶׁנֶּאֱמַר אַחַת עִיקָר וְהַשְּׁאָר טְפֵילָה. אַף מִשָּׁת שֶׁנֶּאֱמַר כָּאן אַחַת עִיקָר וְהַשְּׁאָר טְפֵילָה. אָמַר רִבִּי יוֹסֵי בֵּירְבִּי בּוּן. וַהֲלֹא שַׁלְמֵי נְדָבָה כְשַׁלְמֵי חֲגִיגָה הֵן. וְלָמָּה הוּא טָפַל לוֹן לְאִילֵין קְרָאהַיָּיא. לְלַמְּדָךְ שֶׁדּוֹחִין עֲלֵיהֶן יוֹם טוֹב.

Halakhah 3: Rebbi Tanḥum bar Ilai in the name of Rebbi Yose ben Ḥanina: So answer the House of Shammai to the House of Hillel: May any obligatory sacrifice come from tithe[111]? They said to them, if it were a weekday, could he not bring one from profane money and add the tithe money? And here he brings one from profane money and adds tithe money[112]. From where that one may add [tithe money]? Rebbi Yose ben Hanina said, it is said here *measure*[113], and it is said there, *for you cannot carry it*[114]. Since *carrying* mentioned there refers to tithe, so also here tithe. Rebbi Eleazar said, it mentions joy here and it mentions joy there[115]. Since joy mentioned there refers to tithe, so also joy mentioned here refers to tithe. Could not all of them be brought from tithe money? Ulla bar Ismael said, it is said here *measure* and it is said there, *the gift for Benjamin exceeded*[116]. Since *gift* which is mentioned there refers to one as principal[117] and the remainder addition, so also here one is principal and the remainder addition. Rebbi Yose ben Rebbi Abun said, are not the voluntary well-being offerings like the well-being offerings of the holiday? Why does he add those verses?[118] To tell you that for them one pushes aside the holiday[119].

111 It is implied in Halakhah 2 that the 1 and 2 oboloi required in Mishnah 2 must be profane money.
112 Also on the holiday.
113 *Deut.* 16:10, referring to the holiday of Pentecost which has no intermediary days. The root of the word is taken (with many moderns) to be נשא.
114 *Deut.* 14:24, referring to Second Tithe; same root.
115 "Joy" as commandment to enjoy meat is repeatedly mentioned for holidays in *Deut.* 16, and referring to Second Tithe in *Deut.* 14:26.
116 *Gen.* 43:34, same root.
117 The gift to every brother.
118 Why are those somewhat shaky derivations needed at all?
119 To justify the House of Hillel who in matters of well-being sacrifices treat full holidays on the same level as the intermediate days.

(fol. 75d) **משנה ד**: יִשְׂרָאֵל יוֹצְאִין יְדֵי חוֹבָתָן בִּנְדָרִים וּבִנְדָבוֹת וּבְמַעֲשֵׂר בְּהֵמָה. וְהַכֹּהֲנִים בַּחַטָּאת וּבָאָשָׁם וּבֶחָזֶה וּבַשּׁוֹק וּבִבְכוֹר. אֲבָל לֹא בָעוֹפוֹת וְלֹא בַמְּנָחוֹת:

Mishnah 4: Israel fulfill their obligation with vows[120], and voluntary gifts[121] and animal tithe[122], and the Cohanim with purification sacrifices, and reparation sacrifices[123], and breast and thigh[125], and firstlings[124], but not with birds[126] or cereal sacrifices.

120 An animal brought to fulfill a vow that the votary takes upon himself the obligation

HALAKHAH 4

to bring a certain kind of sacrifice.

121 A voluntary gift is a vow to bring a designated animal as sacrifice. If this animal dies or becomes disqualified for the altar the votary has no obligation to offer a replacement.

122 From the rancher's herd every tenth calf has to be brought to the Temple as sacrifice and is to be consumed by the rancher's family in purity; no part is given to the Cohanim. All these sacrifices have no connection with the holiday but since the pilgrimage is the natural occasion to liquidate all obligations towards the Temple, they are recommended as means to fulfill the obligation to celebrate the joy of holiday by the consumption of meat.

123 These are most holy sacrifices and the parts not burned on the altar have to be consumed by the adult male Cohanim in the Temple domain.

124 They are brought as sacrifice and consumed by the Cohen's family in purity within the walls of the city.

125 The parts given to the Cohen from well-being sacrifices, to be consumed by the Cohen's family in purity within the walls of the city.

126 Which according to biblical standards do not qualify as "meat".

(76b line 65) **הלכה ד**: רִבִּי זְעוּרָה עוּלָא בַּר יִשְׁמָעֵאל בְּשֵׁם רִבִּי לְעָזָר. שַׁלְמֵי חֲגִיגָה שֶׁשְּׁחָטָן מֵעֶרֶב הָרֶגֶל אֵינוֹ יוֹצֵא בָהֶן יְדֵי חוֹבָתוֹ בָּרֶגֶל. הָתִיב רִבִּי בָא. וְהָא תַּנֵּי. חֲגִיגַת אַרְבָּעָה עָשָׂר יוֹצְאִין בָּהּ מִשֵּׁם שִׂמְחָה. וְאֵין יוֹצְאִין בָּהּ מִשֵּׁם שְׁלָמִים. [אָמַר רִבִּי זְעִירָא. תִּיפְתָּר בְּשֶׁשְּׁחָטוֹ בָּרֶגֶל. אָמַר לֵיהּ רִבִּי בָא. אִם בְּשֶׁשְּׁחָטוֹ בָּרֶגֶל אֵין זוֹ חֲגִיגַת אַרְבָּעָה עָשָׂר. מַאי כְדוֹן.] אָמַר רִבִּי זְעוּרָה. עַד דַּאֲנָא תַּמָּן שְׁמַע תַּנָּא עוּלָא בַּר יִשְׁמָעֵאל בְּשֵׁם רִבִּי לְעָזָר. כַּד סַלְקִית לְהָכָא שְׁמַע תַּנָּא רִבִּי חִייָה בְּשֵׁם רִבִּי לְעָזָר. וְהַיְיתָ אַךְ שָׂמֵחַ· לְרַבּוֹת לֵילֵי יוֹם טוֹב הָאַחֲרוֹן לְשִׂמְחָה. אוֹ יָכוֹל אַף לֵילֵי יוֹם טוֹב הָרִאשׁוֹן. תַּלְמוּד לוֹמַר אַךְ. אוֹ חִלּף. רִבִּי חִייָה בְּשֵׁם רִבִּי לְעָזָר. וְשָׂמַחְתָּ בְּחַגֶּךָ. מִשֶּׁאַתְּ מִתְחַייֵב בַּחֲגִיגָה אַתְּ מִתְחַייֵב בַּשִּׂמְחָה. הָתִיבוּן. וְהָא תַּנִּינָן. הַהַלֵּל וְהַשִּׂמְחָה שְׁמוֹנָה. הַגַּע עַצְמָךְ שֶׁחָל יוֹם טוֹב הָרִאשׁוֹן לִהְיוֹת בְּשַׁבָּת. לְשׁוּחֲטָן מֵעֶרֶב הָרֶגֶל אֵין אַתְּ יָכוֹל. דְּאָמַר רִבִּי זְעוּרָה עוּלָא בַּר יִשְׁמָעֵאל בְּשֵׁם רִבִּי לְעָזָר. שַׁלְמֵי חֲגִיגָה שֶׁשְּׁחָטָן מֵעֶרֶב הָרֶגֶל אֵינוֹ יוֹצֵא בָהֶן יְדֵי חוֹבָתוֹ בָּרֶגֶל. לְשׁוּחֲטָן בָּרֶגֶל אֵין אַתְּ יָכוֹל. שֶׁכְּבָר לָמַדְנוּ שֶׁאֵין חֲגִיגָה דּוֹחָה שַׁבָּת. אֵימָתַי אָמְרוּ. הַהַלֵּל וְהַשִּׂמְחָה שְׁמוֹנָה. אָמַר רִבִּי יוֹסֵי. קִיְימָהּ רַב אָבְדּוּמֵי נְחוּתָא בְּכֹהֲנִים וּבִשְׂעִיר.

Halakhah 4: [127]Rebbi Ze`ira, Ulla bar Ismael in the name of Rebbi Eleazar: With pilgrimage well-being offerings which were slaughtered on the eve of a festival one does not satisfy his obligation for the pilgrimage[128]. Rebbi Abba objected, was it not stated: With the pilgrimage offering of the Fourteenth one fulfills the obligation of joy but one does not fulfill the one of well-being offerings? Rebbi Ze`ira said, explain it that he slaughtered it on the holiday. Rebbi Abba said, if he slaughtered it on the holiday it is not a festival offering of the Fourteenth. What about it? Rebbi Ze`ira said, when we still were there, we heard stated Ulla bar Ismael in the name of Rebbi Eleazar. When we came up to here we heard stated, Rebbi Ḥiyya in the name of Rebbi Eleazar: *only be joyful*[129], to add the night of the las festival day for joy. Or maybe also the nights of the firs day of the festival? Or inverse? Rebbi Ḥiyya in the name of Rebbi Eleazar: *and you shall be joyous on your festival of pilgrimage*[130]. When you are obligated for a sacrifice of pilgrimage you are obligated for joy. They objected, did we not state, "*hallel* and joy eight"[131]? Think of it, if the first day of the holiday falls on a Sabbath! He cannot slaughter on the eve of the holiday since Rebbi Ze`ira, Ulla bar Ismael in the name of Rebbi Eleazar said, with pilgrimage well-being offerings which were slaughtered on the eve of a festival one does not satisfy his obligation for the pilgrimage. He cannot slaughter on the holiday since we already have learned that the pilgrimage offering does not push aside the Sabbath. When did they say, *Hallel* and joy eight? Rebbi Yose said, Rav Eudaimon the emigrant explained it for Cohanim and the goat[132].

127 This paragraph also is *Sukkah* 5:4, explained there in Notes 73-82.
128 As regards the obligation to bring well-being sacrifices for the consumption of meat.
129 *Deut.* 16:15.
130 *Deut.* 16:14.
131 Mishnah *Sukkah* 4:1.
132 If the first day is a Sabbath, all required holiday sacrifices are brought on the altar. They all are holocausts except for the goat as purification offering whose meat is eaten by the Cohanim. But since it is a Sabbath, it may not be cooked or roasted for private use and the meat must be eaten raw. The Babli *Pesahim* 71a holds that eating raw meat is no joy.

(76c line 4) אֲבָל לֹא בָעוֹפוֹת וְלֹא בַמְּנָחוֹת: דִּכְתִיב זֶבַח.

"But not with birds or cereal sacrifices." For it is written *slaughter*[133].

133 "Joy" is connected with bloody sacrifice in *Deut.* 27:7. Different verses are quoted to the same effect in *Sifry Deut.* 141,142.

(fol. 75d) **משנה ה**: מִי שֶׁיֵּשׁ לוֹ אוֹכְלִין מְרוּבִּין וּנְכָסִים מְמוּעָטִים מֵבִיא שְׁלָמִים מְרוּבִּין וְעוֹלוֹת מְמוּעָטוֹת. אוֹכְלִין מְעוּטִין וּנְכָסִים מְרוּבִּין מֵבִיא עוֹלוֹת מְרוּבּוֹת וּשְׁלָמִים מְמוּעָטִין. זֶה וָזֶה

מְמוּעָטִין עַל זֶה נֶאֱמַר מָעָה כֶסֶף וּשְׁתֵּי כָסֶף. זֶה וְזֶה מְרוּבִּין עַל זֶה נֶאֱמַר אִישׁ כְּמַתְּנַת יָדוֹ
כְּבִרְכַּת יְיָ אֱלֹהֶיךָ אֲשֶׁר נָתַן לָךְ:

Mishnah 5: He who has many eaters and a small budget brings many well-being offerings and few elevation offerings. Few eaters and a large budget, he brings many elevation offerings and few well-being offerings[134]. Both few, for this one it was said "one obolus, two silver coins." Both ample, for this one it was said[135], *each man according to his means, corresponding to the blessing by the Eternal, your God, which He gave you.*

134 The meat of a well-being offering has to be consumed by the end of the following	day. One has to avoid letting sacral meat become disqualified. 135 *Deut.* 16:17.

(76c line 4) **הלכה ה**: עָנִי וְיָדוֹ רְחָבָה. קוֹרֵא אֲנִי עָלָיו. אִישׁ כְּמַתְּנַת יָדוֹ. עָשִׁיר וְיָדוֹ מְעוּטָה. קוֹרֵא אֲנִי עָלָיו. אִישׁ כְּמַתְּנַת יָדוֹ. עָשִׁיר וְיָדוֹ מְעוּטָה. קוֹרֵא אֲנִי עָלָיו. כְּבִרְכַּת יְיָ אֱלֹהֶיךָ אֲשֶׁר נָתַן־לָךְ: עָנִי וְיָדוֹ מְעוּטָה. עַל זֶה נֶאֱמַר. אֵין פָּחוּת מִשְּׁתֵּי כָסֶף.
אִישׁ. פְּרָט לְקָטָן. רִבִּי יִרְמְיָה בָּעֵי. אָמַר. הֲרֵי עָלַי חֲגִיגָה בְּחָמֵשׁ סְלָעִים. וְהֵבִיא בִשְׁתַּיִם. יָצָא אוֹ כְבָר נִקְבַּע. אָמַר לֵיהּ רִבִּי יוֹסֵי. וְלָמָּה לֹא. אִילּוּ מִי שֶׁאָמַר הֲרֵי עָלַי אָשָׁם בְּחָמֵשׁ סְלָעִים. שֶׁמָּא לֹא נִקְבַּע. וְכָא נִקְבַּע.

Halakhah 5: If he is poor but generous, I am reading for him, *each man according to his means*, rich but stingy, I am reading for him, *corresponding to the blessing by the Eternal, your God, which He gave you.* If he is poor and stingy, on this one it was said, not less than two silver coins[136].

"Each man", to exclude the minor[137]. Rebbi Jeremiah asked, if he said, it is on me to bring a festival offering worth five tetradrachmas, but he brought for two; did he fulfill his obligation or is he already fixed[138]? Rebbi Yose said to him, why not? If somebody said, it is on me to bring a reparation sacrifice for five tetradrachmas[139], is he not fixed? And here he is fixed.

136 In this interpretation, the Mishnah is read to explain moral, not prescribed, behavior. However it also is possible to read the text differently: "If he is poor with a large family, I am reading for him, *each man according to his means*, rich but with a small family, I am reading for him, *corresponding to the blessing by the Eternal, your God, which He gave you.* If he is poor with a small family, on this one it was said, no less than two silver coins." In this version the Mishnah is prescriptive. The poor person has to provide meat for his entire family but it may be done as cheaply

as possible, subject to the lower limit of 2 oboloi. The rich man who has no use for many well-being offerings has to bring many elevation offerings.

137 Even though the minor is obligated to appear in the Temple, *Deut.* 16:17 does not apply to him.

138 The festival offering is an obligation whose minimal value is set at $^1/_3$ of a denar, $^1/_{12}$ of a tetradrachma. If he made a vow for a voluntary offering, it would be clear that the vow is fulfilled only if all its terms are fulfilled. The question is whether the private stipulation overrides the general rule.

139 Nobody can make a vow for a reparation offering if he is not obligated to bring one. By biblical decree the value of the offering is 2 tetradrachmas (*Lev.* 5:15). Nevertheless, if he vows to increase the value, his sacrifice is accepted by the Temple only if he spends at least 5 tetradrachmas. This shows that even for obligatory sacrifices a prior vow raises the biblical or rabbinic minimum to the level of the vow.

(fol. 75d) **משנה ו**: מִי שֶׁלֹּא חָג בְּיוֹם טוֹב הָרִאשׁוֹן שֶׁל חָג חוֹגֵג אֶת כָּל־הָרֶגֶל וְיוֹם טוֹב הָאַחֲרוֹן. עָבַר הָרֶגֶל וְלֹא חָג אֵינוֹ חַיָּב בְּאַחֲרָיוּתוֹ. עַל זֶה נֶאֱמַר מְעֻוָּת לֹא יוּכַל לִתְקוֹן וְחֶסְרוֹן לֹא יוּכַל לְהִמָּנוֹת:

Mishnah 6: Someone who did not bring his holiday sacrifice on the first day of the holiday may bring it during the entire festival including the last day of the festival[140]. Once the festival has passed he is not liable for its warranty[141]. On that it was said[142], *the distorted cannot be repaired and the deficient cannot be made whole.*

140 Even though the last day is a full holiday with all the restrictions imposed on such a day; the only day not suitable for the holiday sacrifice is the Sabbath.

141 While in general the Temple has the power to force people to perform the sacrifices due, this does not extend to the holiday sacrifice even though it becomes a fixed obligation with the votary's entry into the Temple domain. The neglect of the duty cannot be made up by a later sacrifice. On Pentecost which is one day only the festival sacrifice may also be brought during the six days following.

142 *Eccl.* 1:15.

(76c line 10) **הלכה ו**: רִבִּי יוֹחָנָן בְּשֵׁם רִבִּי יִשְׁמָעֵאל. נֶאֱמַר חֲמִשָּׁה עָשָׂר בַּפֶּסַח וְנֶאֱמַר חֲמִשָּׁה עָשָׂר בֶּחָג. מַה חֲמִשָּׁה עָשָׂר שֶׁנֶּאֱמַר בַּפֶּסַח יוֹם טוֹב הָאַחֲרוֹן תַּשְׁלוּמִין לָרִאשׁוֹן. אַף חֲמִשָּׁה עָשָׂר שֶׁנֶּאֱמַר בַּחַג יוֹם טוֹב הָאַחֲרוֹן תַּשְׁלוּמִין לָרִאשׁוֹן. יְהוּדָה בַּר סַפְרָא בְּשֵׁם רִבִּי הוֹשַׁעְיָה.

וְחַגֹּתֶם אֹתוֹ חַג לַיהֹוָה שִׁבְעַת יָמִים. וְכִי שִׁבְעָה הֵם. וַהֲלֹא שְׁמוֹנָה הֵם. אֶלָּא צֵא שַׁבָּת מֵהֶם הֲרֵי שִׁבְעָה. אָמַר רִבִּי יוֹסֵי. וְכִי מִיכָּן לְמֵדְנוּ שֶׁאֵין חֲגִיגָה דוֹחָה אֶת הַשַּׁבָּת. לֹא מִמָּקוֹם אַחֵר. הָתִיב רִבִּי יוֹחָנָן אָחוֹי דְרַב סַפְרָא. וְהָא תַנֵּי. אַף בַּפֶּסַח כֵּן. מֵעַתָּה צֵא שַׁבָּת מֵהֶם הֲרֵי שִׁשָּׁה. הַגַּע עַצְמָךְ שֶׁחָל יוֹם טוֹב הָרִאשׁוֹן וְיוֹם טוֹב הָאַחֲרוֹן לִהְיוֹת בַּשַּׁבָּת. מֵעַתָּה צֵא מֵהֶם שְׁנֵי יָמִים הֲרֵי שִׁשָּׁה. אָתָא רִבִּי חֲנַנְיָה יְהוּדָה בַּר סַפְרָא בְּשֵׁם רִבִּי הוֹשַׁעְיָה. וְחַגֹּתֶם אֹתוֹ חַג לַיהֹוָה שִׁבְעַת יָמִים. וְכִי שִׁבְעָה הֵם. וַהֲלֹא שְׁמוֹנָה הֵם. אֶלָּא צֵא שַׁבָּת מֵהֶם. שֶׁכְּבָר לָמַדְנוּ שֶׁאֵין חֲגִיגָה דוֹחָה שַׁבָּת. מַה תַּלְמוּד לוֹמַר תְּחָגּוּהוּ. אֶלָּא מְלַמֵּד שֶׁיּוֹם טוֹב הָאַחֲרוֹן תַּשְׁלוּמִין לָרִאשׁוֹן.

אָמַר רִבִּי יוֹחָנָן. וְתַנֵּי כֵן. שְׁמִינִי כֶן. שְׁמִינִי רֶגֶל בִּפְנֵי עַצְמוֹ. פַּיִיס בִּפְנֵי עַצְמוֹ. בְּרָכָה בִּפְנֵי עַצְמָהּ. קָרְבָּן בִּפְנֵי עַצְמוֹ. רֶגֶל. דְּאָמַר רִבִּי אַבּוּן בְּשֵׁם רִבִּי אַחָא. בְּכוּלְּהוֹן כְּתִיב וּבַיּוֹם וְכָאן כְּתִיב בַּיּוֹם. לְלַמְּדָךְ שֶׁהוּא רֶגֶל בִּפְנֵי עַצְמוֹ. פַּיִיס. אָמַר רִבִּי יוֹסֵי. מַתְנִיתָא אֲמָרָה כֵן. בַּשְּׁמִינִי חָזְרוּ לַפַּיִיס כְּרְגָלִים. בְּרָכָה. אָמַר רִבִּי לָא. זְמָן. קָרְבָּן. פַּר אֶחָד אַיִל אֶחָד.

Halakhah 6: Rebbi Johanan in the name of Rebbi Ismael: It is said *fifteenth* regarding Passover and it is said *fifteenth* regarding Tabernacles[143]. Since for the *fifteenth* which was said regarding Passover the last day is a make-up for the first[144], also for the *fifteenth* which was said regarding Tabernacles the last day is a make-up for the first. Jehudah bar Safra in the name of Rebbi Hoshaia: *You shall bring a holiday sacrifice for the Eternal seven days*[145]. Are they seven? Are they not eight[146]? But remove Sabbath from them, there remain seven. Rebbi Yose said, do we infer from here that the holiday sacrifice does not push the Sabbath aside? Was it not from another place[147]? Rebbi Johanan the brother of Rav Safra objected, was it not stated, the same holds for Passover? Then remove Sabbath from them, there remain six[148]. Think of it, if the first and the last holiday fall on the Sabbath, then remove two days from them and there remain six! There came Rebbi Hanania[149], Jehudah bar Safra in the name of Rebbi Hoshaia: *You shall bring a holiday sacrifice for the Eternal seven days*. Are they seven? Are they not eight? But remove Sabbath from them, since we already infer that the holiday sacrifice does not push the Sabbath aside; why does the verse say, *bring on it a holiday sacrifice*[150]? But it teaches that the last day of the festival is make-up for the first.

[151]Rebbi Johanan said, it was stated so that the eighth day was a separate holiday, a separate lottery, a separate benediction, a separate sacrifice[152]. Holiday, as Rebbi Abun said in the name of Rebbi Aha, for all of them is

written *and on day*, but here is written *on day*, to teach you that it is a separate holiday[153]. Lottery, Rebbi Yose said, the Mishnah says this, "on the eighth day they returned to the lottery as on holidays." Benediction, Rebbi La said, time[154]. Sacrifice, *one bull and one ram*[155].

143 It is mentioned several times in the Pentateuch that the first day of the festival of unleavened bread, rabbinically called *Pesaḥ*, and the festival of booths both start on the 15th of their respective months. Since the particular source is not identified, the argument is informal and not binding as "equal cut".

144 Since the Seventh Day of Passover has the same public sacrifices as the first.

145 *Lev.* 23:41.

146 While it is noted in *Lev.* 23:36 that the seven days of Tabernacles are immediately followed by a separate holiday on the eighth day, in *Num.* 29:35 the holiday appears as the Eighth Day of Tabernacles. This Eighth Day therefore has a double role, as last day of Tabernacles and as separate festival.

147 Since the holiday offerings are private sacrifices they automatically are excluded on the Sabbath.

148 The argument of R. Hoshaia cannot be correct.

149 He shows that the previous discussion was based on a faulty version of R. Hoshaia's argument.

150 This is a misquote of *Ex.* 12:14 for the last word in *Lev.* 23:41, תָּחֹגּוּ אֹתוֹ *bring it as holiday sacrifice*. Since the sacrifice is mentioned in the singular it is shown that there is a single required sacrifice for the eight-day festival of which up to seven are days of sacrifice. *Sifra Emor Pereq* 17.

151 This is copied from *Sukkah* 5:7, Notes 131-135*.

152 Tosephta *Sukkah* 4:17.

153 In the list of sacrifices for days 2-7 of Tabernacles the first words always are *and on day*, *Num.* 29:17,20,23,26,29,32, but the listing for the eighth day starts *on the eighth day* without connective (*Num.* 29:35).

154 "Who let us live, and supported us, and let us reach this time."

135 *Num.* 29:36. These numbers are characteristic of the High Holidays.

(fol. 75d) **משנה ז**: רבי שמעון בן מנסיא אומר איזהו מעוות שאינו יכול לתקון זה הבא על הערוה והוליד ממזר. אם תאמר בגנב וגזלן יכול הוא לחזור ולתקן. רבי שמעון בן מנסיא אומר אין קורין מעוות אלא למי שהיה מתוקן מתחילה ונתעוות. ואיזה זה תלמיד חכם שפירש מן התורה:

Mishnah 7: Rebbi Simeon ben Menassiah says, who is *distorted cannot be repaired*? This is one committing incest or adultery and producing a bastard. If you would say a thief or robber, that one may repent and repair. Rebbi Simeon ben Menassia[136] says, one calls *distorted* only what was correct before and became distorted. Who is that? This is a scholar who separated from the Torah.

136 In all other sources: R. Simeon ben Yoḥai.

(76c line 28) **הלכה ז**: תָּנֵי רִבִּי שִׁמְעוֹן בֶּן יוֹחַי. אִם רָאִיתָ עֲיָירוֹת שֶׁנִּתְלְשׁוּ מִמְּקוֹמָן בְּאֶרֶץ יִשְׂרָאֵל דַּע שֶׁלֹּא הֶחֱזִיקוּ בִּשְׂכַר סוֹפְרִים וּמַשְׁנִים. מַה טַעַם. עַל־מָה אָבְדָה הָאָרֶץ נִצְּתָה כַמִּדְבָּר מִבְּלִי יוֹשֵׁב: וַיֹּאמֶר יי עַל־עָזְבָם אֶת־תּוֹרָתִי.

רִבִּי יוּדָן נְשִׂיָּיא שְׁלַח לְרִבִּי חִייָה וּלְרִבִּי אַסִּי וּלְרִבִּי אַמִּי לְמֵיעֲבוֹר בְּקִרְיָיתָא דְּאַרְעָא דְיִשְׂרָאֵל לִמְתַקְּנָא לוֹן סָפְרִין וּמַתְנִייָנִין. עֲלוֹן לְחַד אֲתַר וְלָא אַשְׁכְּחוֹן לָא סְפַר וְלָא מַתְנִייָן. אֲמָרִין לוֹן. אַייתוֹן לָן נְטוּרֵי קַרְתָּא. אַייתוֹן לוֹן סַנְטוּרֵי קַרְתָּא. אֲמָרוֹן לוֹן. אִילֵּין אִינּוּן נְטוּרֵי קַרְתָּא. לֵית אִילֵּין אֶלָּא חָרוֹבֵי קַרְתָּא. אֲמָרוֹן לוֹן. וּמָאן אִינּוּן נְטוּרֵי קַרְתָּא. אֲמָרוֹן לוֹן. סַפְרַיָּיא וּמַתְנִייָנַיָּא. הָדָא הִיא דִּכְתִיב אִם יי לֹא־יִבְנֶה בַיִת וגו׳.

רִבִּי חוּנָה רִבִּי יִרְמְיָה בְּשֵׁם רִבִּי שְׁמוּאֵל בַּר רַב יִצְחָק. מָצָאנוּ שֶׁוִיתֵּר הַקָּדוֹשׁ בָּרוּךְ הוּא לְיִשְׂרָאֵל עַל עֲבוֹדָה זָרָה וְעַל גִּילּוּי עֲרָיוֹת וְעַל שְׁפִיכוּת דָּמִים. וְעַל מְאָסָם בַּתּוֹרָה לֹא וִיתֵּר. מַה טַעַם. וַיֹּאמֶר יי עַל אֲשֶׁר עָשׂוּ עֲבוֹדָה זָרָה וְגִילּוּי עֲרָיוֹת וּשְׁפִיכוּת דָּמִים אֵין כָּתוּב כָּאן. אֶלָּא וַיֹּאמֶר יי עַל־עָזְבָם אֶת־תּוֹרָתִי. אָמַר רִבִּי חִייָה בַּר בָּא. אוֹתִי עָזְבוּ אַוְותְרָה. שֶׁמָּא אֶת תּוֹרָתִי שָׁמָרוּ. שֶׁאִילּוּ אוֹתִי עָזְבוּ וְתוֹרָתִי שָׁמָרוּ הַשְּׂאוֹר שֶׁבָּהּ הָיָה מְקָרְבָן אֶצְלִי. רַב הוּנָה אָמַר. לָמַד תּוֹרָה שֶׁלֹּא לִשְׁמָהּ. שֶׁמִּתּוֹךְ שֶׁלֹּא לִשְׁמָהּ אַף בָּא לִשְׁמָהּ.

רִבִּי יְהוּדָה כְּשֶׁהָיָה רוֹאֶה אֶת הַמֵּת וְאֶת הַכַּלָּה מִתְקַלְּסִין הָיָה נוֹתֵן עֵינָיו בַּתַּלְמִידִים וְאוֹמֵר. הַמַּעֲשֶׂה קוֹדֶם לַתַּלְמוּד.

Halakhah 7: Rebbi Simeon ben Yoḥai stated: When you see towns in the Land of Israel uprooted from their place, know that they did not contribute to the wages of Bible and Mishnah teachers[137]. What is the reason? *Why is the land ruined, torn down like an uninhabited wilderness? The Eternal said, because they abandoned My Torah*[138].

Rebbi Judah the Prince[139] sent Rebbi Ḥiyya[140], Rebbi Assi[141], and Rebbi Immi to tour the towns of the Land of Israel in order to give them Bible and Mishnah teachers. They came to one place where they found neither Bible nor Mishnah teacher. They said to them, bring us the watchmen of the town. They brought them the stewards[142] of the town. They told them, these are not the watchmen of the town, they are the destroyers of the town[143]. They asked them, and who would be the watchmen of the town? They told them, the Bible and Mishnah teachers. That is what is written, *if the Eternal would not build the house*[144], etc.

Rebbi Huna, Rebbi Jeremiah in the name of Rebbi Samuel bar Rav Isaac: We find that the Holy One, praise to Him, did forego[145] for Israel about idol worship, incest and adultery, and bloodshed[146]. But for their rejection of the Torah he did not forego. What is the reason? It is not written here "The Eternal said, because they committed idol worship, incest and adultery, and bloodshed," but *the Eternal said, because they abandoned My Torah*. Rebbi Hiyya bar Abba said, that they abandoned Me I could forego, maybe they would keep My Torah[147], since if they abandoned Me but kept My Torah, the leavening in it would bring them close to Me. Rav Huna said, study Torah even not for its own merit, since through {studying} not for its own merit you come to {study} for its own[148].

[149]When Rebbi Jehudah saw a funeral procession or the acclamation of a bride he looked at the students and said, deed precedes study.

137 Since at least since the time of the High Priest Joshua ben Gamla providing for elementary schooling is a communal responsibility. *Petihta Thr. rabbati* (2).
138 *Jer.* 9:11-12.
139 R. Judah II, the grandson of Rebbi.
140 R. Hiyya bar Abba.
141 His Babylonian name. In the Yerushalmi he usually appears as R. Yasa.
142 Identified by S. Liebermann as Latin *saltuarius*, administrator of an agricultural domain.
143 Since they did not include the wages of elementary school teachers in the communal budget.
144 *Ps.* 127:1.
145 He did forego meting out punishment.
146 The three cardinal sins.
147 A sermon on *Jer.* 32:23.
148 Babli *Pesahim* 50b, *Sotah* 22b,47a, *Nazir* 23b, *Sanhedrin* 105a, *Horaiot* 10b,. *Arakhin* 16b.
149 This is the introduction to the next paragraph, about the relative merits of Torah study and good deeds. Babli *Megillah* 29a.

(76c line 46) נִמְנוּ בַּעֲלִיַּית בֵּית אָרִיס. הַתַּלְמוּד קוֹדֵם לַמַּעֲשֶׂה. רִבִּי אַבָּהוּ הֲוָה בְקֵיסָרִין. שָׁלַח לְרִבִּי חֲנִינָה בְּרֵיהּ מַזְכֵּי בְּטִיבֶּרְיָה. שָׁלְחוּן וְאָמְרוּן לֵיהּ. גָּמָל הוּא חֶסֶד. שָׁלַח כָּתַב לֵיהּ. הֲמִבְּלִי אֵין קְבָרִים בְּקֵיסָרִין שְׁלַחְתִּיךָ לְטִיבֶּרְיָא. כְּבָר נִמְנוּ בַּעֲלִיַּית בֵּית אָרִיס בְּלוֹד הַתַּלְמוּד קוֹדֵם לַמַּעֲשֶׂה. רַבָּנִין דְּקֵיסָרִין אָמְרִין. הָדָא דְאַתְּ אָמַר. בְּשֶׁיֵּשׁ שָׁם מִי שֶׁיַּעֲשֶׂה. אֲבָל אִם אֵין שָׁם מִי שֶׁיַּעֲשֶׂה הַמַּעֲשֶׂה קוֹדֵם לַתַּלְמוּד. דִּלְמָא. רִבִּי חִייָה רִבִּי יָסָא רִבִּי אִמִּי עֲנָן מֵיתֵי גַּבֵּי רִבִּי

לְעֶזֶר. אֲמַר לוֹן. אִן הֲוֵיתוֹן יוֹמָא דֵין. אֲמְרוֹן לֵיהּ. גְּמַל חֶסֶד. אֲמַר לוֹן. וְלָא הֲוָה תַּמָּן חוֹרָנִין. אֲמְרִין לֵיהּ. מָגִיר הֲוָה.

[150]They voted in the upper floor of the house of Arius that study precedes action[151]. Rebbi Abbahu dwelt in Caesarea. He sent his son Rebbi Ḥanina to acquire merit in Tiberias. They sent and said to him, he does works of charity[152]. He wrote to him, are there no graves in Caesarea[153] that I sent you to Tiberias? For they already voted in the upper floor of the house of Arius in Lydda that study precedes action[154]. The rabbis of Caesaria say, that is, if there is somebody there who will do it. But if nobody is there who will do it, the action has precedence[155]. Example. Rebbi Ḥiyya, Rebbi Yasa, Rebbi Immi, were late in coming to Rebbi Eleazar. He asked them, where have you been? They told him, performing an act of charity. He asked them, where there no others? They answered him, it was a neighbor[156].

150 This text essentially is from *Pesaḥim* 3:7, Notes 142-148.
151 According to the Babli, *Qidduśin* 40b, this was an early Tannaitic decision following R. Aqiba against R. Tarphon. *Ḥagigah* 1:7.
152 Burying the dead.
153 A reference to *Ex.* 14:11.

154 Therefore he has to spend his time studying in the Academy there.
155 In particular, religious obligations of a personal nature, which cannot be delegated, have precedence over study. Babli *Moed Qatan* 9b.
156 It was an obligation irrespective of the number of attendees at the funeral.

(fol. 75d) **משנה ח**: הֶיתֵּר נְדָרִים פּוֹרְחִים בָּאֲוִיר וְאֵין לָהֶן עַל מַה שֶּׁיִּסְמֹכוּ. הִילְכוֹת שַׁבָּת חֲגִיגוֹת וּמְעִילוֹת כַּהֲרָרִים תְּלוּיִים בְּסַעֲרָה. מִקְרָא מְמוּעָט וַהֲלָכוֹת מְרוּבּוֹת. הַדִּינִים וְהָעֲבוֹדוֹת הַטַּהֲרוֹת וְהַטּוּמְאוֹת וְהָעֲרָיוֹת יֵשׁ לָהֶן עַל מַה שֶּׁיִּסְמֹכוּ. וְהֵן הֵן גּוּפֵי תּוֹרָה.

Mishnah 8: The dissolution of vows[157] flies in the air and has no support. The rules of the Sabbath, holiday sacrifices, and larceny on sancta[158] are like mountains hanging on a hair, few verses and many rules. Civil law, Temple service, purity and impurity, and forbidden sexual relations have support. All of them[159] are the body of the Torah.

157 The power of a rabbi to annul the vow of a person is based on the questionable interpretation, rejected by Sadducees and Karaites, of a single verse.

158 As mentioned in *Lev.* 5:14-15. The exact definition of what constitutes larceny on sancta is not found in the Biblical text.

(76c line 54) **הלכה ח:** תַּנֵּי. רִבִּי לִיעֶזֶר אוֹמֵר. יֵשׁ לָהֶן עַל מַה שֶׁיִּיסָמְכוּ. נִשְׁבַּעְתִּי וַאֲקַיֵּמֶה. פְּעָמִים שֶׁאֵינוֹ מְקַיֵּים. רִבִּי יְהוֹשֻׁעַ אוֹמֵר. יֵשׁ לָהֶן עַל מַה שֶׁיִּיסָמְכוּ. אֲשֶׁר־נִשְׁבַּעְתִּי בְאַפִּי. בְּאַפִּי נִשְׁבַּעְתִּ. חוֹזֵר אֲנִי בִי.

תַּמָּן תַּנִּינָן. אַרְבָּעָה נְדָרִים הִתִּירוּ חֲכָמִים. וְכָל־הַנְּדָרִים לֹא חֲכָמִים הֵם שֶׁהֵן מַתִּירִין. כָּתוּב וַיְדַבֵּר מֹשֶׁה אֶל־רָאשֵׁי הַמַּטּוֹת לִבְנֵי יִשְׂרָאֵל. תָּלָה הַפָּרָשָׁה בְּרָאשֵׁי הַמַּטּוֹת שֶׁיִּהוּ מַתִּירִין לָהֶן אֶת נִדְרֵיהֶן. רַב יְהוּדָה בְּשֵׁם שְׁמוּאֵל. כָּתוּב לֹא יַחֵל דְּבָרוֹ. הוּא אֵינוֹ מוֹחֵל דְּבָרוֹ. אַחֵר הוּא שֶׁעוֹשֶׂה דְבָרוֹ חוּלִּין. וְאֵי זֶה זֶה. זֶה חָכָם שֶׁהוּא מַתִּיר לוֹ אֶת נִדְרוֹ.

1 לא | נ לאו   2-3 להן את נדריהן | נ נדרי העם   3 כת' לא יחל דברו | נ -   הוא | נ -   4 שעושה | נ עושה לו את | נ -

Halakhah 8: [159]It was stated: Rebbi Eliezer says, they have support. *I swore and shall keep it*[160]. Sometimes I do not keep it. Rebbi Joshua says, they have support. *Which I swore in My anger*[161]. I swore in My anger, I am changing My opinion.

[162]There, we have stated[163]: "Four kinds of vows did the Sages dissolve." Do not the Sages permit all kinds of vows? It is written[164]: *Moses spoke to the heads of the tribes of the Children of Israel.* He referred the paragraph to the heads of the tribes that they should dissolve their vows. Rav Jehudah in the name of Samuel: *He shall not profane his word*[165]. He cannot profane his word; this implies that others can profane his words. Who is that? That is the Sage who dissolves the vow.

159 This text essentially appears in the Venice edition of the Yerushalmi in *Nedarim* 3:1 as an unjustified corrector's addition taken from here. Also the attribution there of R. Eliezer's statement to Hananiah the nephew of R. Joshua is unjustified; Hananiah refers to the next paragraph. The authorship of R. Eliezer of a similar statement is confirmed in the Babli 10a.

160 *Ps.* 119:106.
161 *Ps.* 95:11.
162 Text copied from *Nedarim* 3:1, Notes 6-7.
163 Mishnah *Nedarim* 3:1.
164 *Num.* 30:2.
165 *Num.* 30:3.

(76 line 62) רִבִּי זְעוּרָה רַב יְהוּדָה רַב יִרְמְיָה בַּר אַבָּא בְּשֵׁם שְׁמוּאֵל. שְׁלֹשָׁה שֶׁהֵן יוֹדְעִין לִפְתּוֹחַ מַתִּירִין כְּזָקֵן. סָבְרִין מֵימַר. בְּמָקוֹם שֶׁאֵין זָקֵן. רַבָּנָן דְּקַיְסָרִין אָמְרִין. אֲפִילוּ בְּמָקוֹם שֶׁיֵּשׁ זָקֵן.

אָמְרוּן קוֹמֵי רִבִּי יָסָא. רַב חוּנָה רֹאשֵׁי מַטּוֹת. אָמַר לֵיהּ. אִין לֵית רַב חוּנָה רָאשֵׁי מַטּוֹת מָאן אִינּוּן רָאשֵׁי מַטּוֹת. רַב חוּנָה רֹאשׁ לְרָאשֵׁי מַטּוֹת.

מָהוּ לִמְנוֹת זְקֵינִים לִדְבָרִים יְחִידִים. נִישְׁמְעִינָהּ מִן הָדָא. רַב מְנִיתֵיהּ רִבִּי לְהַתִּיר נְדָרִים וְלִרְאוֹת כְּתָמִים. מִן דִּדְמַךְ בְּעָא גַּבֵּי בְּרֵיהּ מוּמֵי בְּכוֹרוֹת. אָמַר לוֹ. אֵינִי מוֹסִיף לָךְ עַל מַה שֶׁנָּתַן לָךְ אַבָּא. אָמַר רִבִּי יוֹסֵי בֵּירִבִּי בּוּן. כּוֹלָּא יְהַב לֵיהּ. לָדִין יְחִידִי וּלְהַתִּיר נְדָרִים וְלִרְאוֹת כְּתָמִים וְלִרְאוֹת מוּמִין שֶׁבְּגָלוּי. מִן דִּדְמַךְ בְּעָא גַּבֵּי בְּרֵיהּ מוּמִין שֶׁבַּסֵּתֶר. אָמַר לֵיהּ. אֵינִי מוֹסִיף לָךְ עַל מַה שֶׁנָּתַן לָךְ אַבָּא. אַף עַל גַּב דַּתְּ אָמַר. מְמַנִּין זְקֵינִים לִדְבָרִים יְחִידִים. וְהוּא שֶׁיְּהֵא רָאוּי לְכָל־הַדְּבָרִים. כְּהָדָא רִבִּי יְהוֹשֻׁעַ בֶּן לֵוִי מַנִּי לְכָל־תַּלְמִידָיו. וַהֲוָה מִצְטַעֵר עַל חַד דַּהֲוָה (נְכִי) [בְּכִי] בְּעֵינוֹי וְלָא הֲוָה יָכִיל מַמְנִיָתֵיהּ. וִימַנְיֵיהּ לִדְבָרִים יְחִידִים. הָדָא אָמְרָה. הָרָאוּי [לְכָל־הַדְּבָרִים רָאוּי] לְדָבָר אֶחָד. [וְשֶׁאֵינוֹ] לְכָל־ הַדְּבָרִים אֲפִילוּ לְדָבָר אֶחָד אֵינוֹ רָאוּי.

מָהוּ לִמְנוֹת זְקֵינִים לְיָמִים. נִישְׁמְעִינָהּ מִן הָדָא. רִבִּי חִייָה בַּר אַבָּא אֲתָא לְגַבֵּי רִבִּי לְעָזָר. אֲמַר לֵיהּ. פַּייֵּס לִי לְרַבִּי יוּדָן נְשִׂייָא דִּי כְתוֹב לִי חֲדָא אִיגְּרָא דִיקָר. נִיפּוּק לְפַרְנָסָתִי לְאַרְעָא בְּרִייָתָא. פַּייְסֵיהּ וְכָתַב לֵיהּ. הֲרֵי שִׁילַּחְנוּ אֲלֵיכֶם אָדָם גָּדוֹל. שְׁלוּחֵינוּ וְכַיּוֹצֵא בָנוּ עַד שֶׁהוּא מַגִּיעַ אֶצְלֵינוּ. רִבִּי חִזְקִיָה רִבִּי דּוֹסְתַּי רִבִּי אַבָּא בַּר זְמִינָא. וּמְטוּ בָהּ מִשְּׁמֵיהּ דְּרִבִּי דּוֹסְתַּי סַבָּא. הָכֵין כָּתַב לֵיהּ. הֲרֵי שִׁילַּחְנוּ אֲלֵיכֶם אָדָם גָּדוֹל. וּמַה הוּא גְדוּלָּתוֹ. שֶׁאֵינוֹ בּוֹשׁ לוֹמַר. לֹא שָׁמַעְתִּי.

מָהוּ לְהַתִּיר בְּפֵילָנִיס. רִבִּי אַבָּהוּ בְשֵׁם רִבִּי יוֹחָנָן. רִבִּי הִתִּיר בְּפֵילָנִיס. רִבִּי יְהוֹשֻׁעַ בֶּן לֵוִי מַתִּיר בְּפֵילָנִיס. רִבִּי חוּנָה בְשֵׁם רִבִּי יִרְמִיָה. בְּמָקוֹם שֶׁאֵין טַלִּית. אָמַר רִבִּי יוֹסֵי בֵּירִבִּי בּוּן. לִנְדָרִים קַלִּין.

[166]Rebbi Ze`ira, Rav Jehudah, Jeremiah bar Abba in the name of Samuel: Three who know how to find an opening[167] may permit like an Elder. They thought, at a place where no Elder was available. The rabbis of Caesarea are saying: Even at a place where there is an Elder[168]. They said before Rebbi Yasa: Is Rav Huna "head of tribes"[169]? He answered them, if Rav Huna is not head of tribes, who are the heads of tribes? Rav Huna is head of the heads of tribes[170].

May one appoint Elders for selected topics[171]? Let us hear from the following: Rebbi appointed Rav to invalidate vows and to see stains[172]. After his death, he[173] asked his[174] son for {permission to judge} defects of firstlings. He said to him, I shall not add to what my father gave you. Rebbi Yose ben Rebbi Abun said, he gave him everything: To sit in judgment alone, to invalidate vows, to see stains, and to see outside blemishes[175]. After his death, he asked his son for {permission to judge} hidden defects. He said to him, I shall not add to what my father gave you. Even though you say, one appoints Elders for selected topics, only if he is competent for everything. As the following: Rebbi Joshua ben Levi ordained all his students, but he was sorry about one who (had a defect in his) [had a running] eye[176] and he could not ordain him; could he not have ordained him for selected topics? That implies (that one who is competent in one thing has to be competent in everything, even for one thing he is not competent) [one who is competent in everything is competent in one thing but one who is not competent in everything cannot be declared competent in one thing.][177]

May one appoint Elders for a fixed time? Let us hear from the following: Rebbi Hiyya bar Abba went to Rebbi Eleazar and asked him to intervene with the Patriarch Rebbi Jehudah, that the latter should write him a letter of recommendation for seeking a livelihood in a foreign country. He intervened, and {the Patriarch} wrote for him: Here we are sending you as our representative a great personality with all our powers until he shall return to us. Rebbi Hizqiah, Rebbi Dositheus, Rebbi Abba bar Zamina, and they report in the name of the old Rebbi Dositheus: He wrote him the following. Here we are sending you a great personality. What is his greatness? He will not be ashamed to say "I did not learn this"[178].

May one permit wearing a coat[179]? Rebbi Abbahu in the name of Rebbi Johanan: One permits wearing a coat. Rebbi Joshua ben Levi permitted wearing a coat. Rebbi Huna in the name of Rebbi Jeremiah: At a place where one does not wear a toga. Rebbi Yose ben Abun said, for easy vows[180].

166 This and the following paragraphs are copied from *Nedarim* 10:10 (Notes 112-128). The first paragraph is complete here and slightly defective there; the end of the second paragraph here is lacunary in the ms. and badly augmented by the corrector. The last paragraph is added from there without any reasonable connection to the topics of *Hagigah*.

167 They know the rules of invalidating vows In the Babli, *Nedarim* 78a, *Bekhorot* 36b, any three lay persons are empowered to form a court to invalidate vows.

168 Invalidation of a vow by three laymen is not infringing on the privileges of the rabbinate. The ordained rabbi has the privilege to invalidate a vow alone (Babli, *Nedarim* 78a).

169 He was the undisputed head of the Babylonian rabbinate and was of the family of the davidic Head of the Diaspora. He certainly had the right to invalidate vows, being of the "heads of the tribes" [164].

170 He is the head of all ordained rabbis, even though his Babylonian ordination is not complete as explained in the next paragraph.

171 Is it possible to give ordination without conferring all rabbinical powers on the candidate?

172 To decide whether a female genital discharge was menstrual blood or not; i. e., whether the woman would be permitted to her husband or not. This is taken as example of his power to decide in matters of ritual prohibitions and includes permission to judge in all matters of such prohibitions.

173 Rav.

174 Rebbi's.

175 Blemishes of firstlings. In the tradition of the Babli, *Sanhedrin* 5a, Rav received full rabbinic powers except the right to decide anything in matters of firstlings. (A firstling of cattle, sheep, or goats must be sacrificed unless it has a blemish which disqualifies it as a sacrifice. In the absence of a Temple, the firstling must graze until it develops a blemish; *Deut.* 15:19-23.) The full ordination was refused to him since his intent was to return to Babylonia and Rebbi disapproved of that. After him, all rabbis with the limited diaspora ordination received the title of Rav.

176 Since skin lesions (wrongly translated as "leprosy", *Lev.* 13-14) must be seen with both eyes, a one-eyed or blind person could not be ordained to decide on their ritual purity. {The meaning of the corrector's change is questionable.}

177 The scribe's text is lacunary, the corrector's wrong. One has to adopt the text from *Nedarim*: In order to be competent in one thing he has to be competent in everything; one who is not competent in everything cannot be declared competent in one thing.

178 In the first version the ordination was valid only as long as R. Hiyya served outside the Land of Israel. In the second, it was unconditional. The question is not resolved.

179 May a vow be removed informally or only in a court proceeding with the rabbi sitting as judge? "Robe" is Latin *paenula*, Greek φαινόλης, παινόλης.

180 Those which can be permitted unquestionably, for which no argument is needed.

(76d line 10) הִילְכוֹת שַׁבָּת. רִבִּי יוֹנָה אָמַר רִבִּי חָמָא בַּר עוּקְבָה מַקְשֵׁי. וַהֲלֹא אֵין כָּתוּב אֶלָּא אַךְ מַעְיָן וּבוֹר מִקְוֵה־מַיִם יִהְיֶה טָהוֹר. וְאַתְּ לָמֵד מִמֶּנּוּ כַּמָּה הֲלָכוֹת.

"The rules of the Sabbath." Rebbi Jonah said that Rebbi Ḥama bar Uqba asked, is it not written only *but a spring, or a cystern, a water pool shall be pure*[181], and you infer from this many rules[182].

181 *Lev.* 11:36.

182 He objects to the distinction made between the rules of the Sabbath and those of purity. While there are many more verses dealing with purity than those dealing with the Sabbath, there are many rules of purity derived from as slim a scriptural basis than those of the Sabbath. Cf. *Sifra Shemini Parashah* 9.

(76d line 13) רְבִּי זְעוּרָה בְשֵׁם רְבִּי יוֹחָנָן. אִם בָּאת הֲלָכָה תַּחַת יָדֶיךָ וְאֵין אַתְּ יוֹדֵעַ מַה טִיבָהּ אַל תַּפְלִיגִינָּהּ לְדָבָר אַחֵר. שֶׁהֲרֵי כַּמָּה הֲלָכוֹת נֶאֶמְרוּ לְמֹשֶׁה מִסִּינַי וְכוּלְהֹן מְשׁוּקָּעוֹת בַּמִּשְׁנָה. אָמַר רְבִּי אָבוּן. וְיָאוּת. הֲרֵי שְׁנֵי מִינֵי חִיטִּים. אִילּוּלֵי שֶׁבָּא נָחוּם וּפֵירְשָׁהּ לָנוּ יוֹדְעִין הָיִינוּ.

1 זעורה | פ זעירא   2 תפליגינה | פ תפליגנה מסיני | פ בסיני   3 אבון | פ אבין חרי | פ היא   3 ופירשה | פ ופירש לנו

[183]Rebbi Ze`ira said in the name of Rebbi Joḥanan: If you come to notice a practice of which you do not know the reason, do not push it aside as something alien since many practices were said as from Moses on Sinai[184] and all of them were absorbed into the Mishnah. Rebbi Abun said, that is correct! If Naḥum had not come and explained it to us about the two kinds of wheat, could we have known[185]?

183 From here to the last paragraph of the Chapter the text is Halakhah *Peah* 2:6, Notes 98-120 (פ). This first paragraph is intelligible only in the framework of Tractate *Peah*.

184 In the *Peah* text, including Mishnah 2:6: to Moses on Sinai. The formulation here only asserts that these practices were accepted as traditional and valid interpretations of the Law by the time of Ezra's organization of Judaism.

185 Referring to Mishnah *Peah* 2:6 where Nahum the Scribe asserts a tradition from Moses on Sinai that a farmer harvesting two different strains of wheat has to give only one *peah*.

(76d line 17) רְבִּי זְעוּרָה בְשֵׁם רְבִּי לָעֲזָר. אֶכְתָּוב־לוֹ רוּבֵּי תּוֹרָתִי. וְכִי רוּבָּהּ שֶׁלַּתּוֹרָה נִכְתְּבָה. אֶלָּא מְרוּבִּין הַדְּבָרִים הַנִּדְרָשִׁין מִן הַכָּתָב מִן הַדְּבָרִים הַנִּדְרָשִׁין מִן הַפֶּה. וְכַיְנִי. אֶלָּא חָבִיבִין הַדְּבָרִים הַסְּמוּכִין לִכְתָב מִן הַדְּבָרִים הַסְסְמוּכִין לַפֶּה. אָמַר רְבִּי יוּדָה פַּר פָּזִי. אֶכְתָּוב־לוֹ רוּבֵּי תּוֹרָתֵי. אֵילּוּ הַתּוֹכָחוֹת. אֲפִילוּ כֵן לֹא כְּמוֹ־זָר נֶחְשָׁבוּ. אָמַר רְבִּי אָבוּן. אִילּוּ כָתַבְתִּי לָךְ רוּבֵּי תּוֹרָתִי לֹא כְּמוֹ־זָר נֶחְשָׁבוּ. מָה בֵינָן לָאוּמּוֹת. אֵילוּ מוֹצִיאִין סִפְרֵיהֶן וְאֵילוּ מוֹצִיאִין סִפְרֵיהֶן. אֵילוּ מוֹצִיאִין דִּפְתְּרֵיהֶן וְאֵילוּ מוֹצִיאִין דִּפְתְּרֵיהֶן.

Rebbi Ze`ira in the name of Rebbi Eleazar: *I wrote down for him most of My teaching*[186]. But was most of the Torah written down? Rather, more things are derived from what is written than what is derived from oral tradition. Is that so? But things derived from what is supported by a verse are preferred over those supported by oral tradition. Rebbi Judah ben Pazi said: *I wrote down for him most of My teaching,* these are the admonitions. Nevertheless, is it not that *they were considered foreign*? Rebbi Abun said: If I had written down for you most of my teaching, would it not be considered Gentile[187]? What would be the difference between us and the Gentiles? These produce their books and those produce their books. These produce their parchments[188] and those produce their parchments.

186 *Hos.* 8:12.
187 Since only Jews have oral tradition as main source of a codified system of laws.
188 Greek διφθέρα.

(76d line 25) רִבִּי חַגַּיי בְּשֵׁם רִבִּי שְׁמוּאֵל בַּר נַחְמָן. נֶאֶמְרוּ דְבָרִים בְּפֶה וְנֶאֶמְרוּ דְבָרִים בִּכְתָב וְאֵין אָנוּ יוֹדְעִין (אִילוּ) [אֵיזוֹ] מֵהֶן חֲבִיבִין. אֶלָּא מִן מָה דִכְתִיב כִּי עַל־פִּי | הַדְּבָרִים הָאֵלֶּה כָּרַתִּי אִתְּךָ בְּרִית וְאֶת־יִשְׂרָאֵל: הָדָא אָמְרָה. אוֹתָן שֶׁבַּפֶּה חֲבִיבִין. רִבִּי יוֹחָנָן וְרִבִּי יוּדָן בִּירִבִּי שִׁמְעוֹן. חַד אָמַר. אִם שִׁימַּרְתָּ מַה שֶׁבַּפֶּה וְשִׁימַּרְתָּ מַה שֶׁבִּכְתָב אֲנִי כוֹרֵת אִתְּךָ בְּרִית. וְאִם לָאו אֵינִי כוֹרֵת אִתְּךָ בְּרִית. וְחוֹרָנָה אָמַר. אִם שִׁימַּרְתָּ מַה שֶׁבַּפֶּה וְשִׁימַּרְתָּ מַה שֶׁבִּכְתָב אַתְּ מְקַבֵּל שָׂכָר. וְאִם לָאו אֵין אַתְּ מְקַבֵּל שָׂכָר. אָמַר רִבִּי יְהוֹשֻׁעַ בֶּן לֵוִי. עֲלֵיהֶם וַעֲלֵיהֶם כָּל כְּכָל דְּבָרִים הַדְּבָרִים. מִקְרָא וּמִשְׁנָה תַלְמוּד הֲלָכוֹת וָאַגָּדָה. אֲפִילוּ מַה שֶׁתַּלְמִיד וָתִיק עָתִיד לְהוֹרוֹת לִפְנֵי רַבּוֹ כְּבָר נֶאֱמַר לְמֹשֶׁה בְּסִינַי. מַה טַעַם. יֵשׁ דָּבָר שֶׁיּאֹמַר רְאֵה־זֶה חָדָשׁ הוּא. חֲבֵירוֹ מְשִׁיבוֹ וְאוֹמֵר לוֹ. כְּבָר הָיָה לְעוֹלָמִים אֲשֶׁר הָיָה מִלְּפָנֵנוּ׃

[189]Rebbi Haggai in the name of Rebbi Samuel bar Naḥman: *Things have been said orally and things have been said in writing, and we do not know which ones are preferred. From what is written*[190]: *by the mouth of these words I concluded a covenant with you and Israel,* it follows that the oral traditions are preferred. Rebbi Joḥanan and Rebbi Yudan ben Rebbi Simeon. One said that if you kept what is oral tradition and kept what is written I will conclude a covenant with you, otherwise I shall not conclude a covenant with you. The other one said, if you watched all that is oral tradition and kept all that is written you will receive your reward, otherwise you will not receive any reward. Rebbi Joshua ben Levi said: *On them, and on them; all, like all; words, the words*; Bible, Mishnah, Talmud, practices and Aggadah. Even what a competent student will discover before his teacher was said to Moses on Sinai. What is the reason? *There is something about which one would say, look, this is new!* His colleague will answer, *it already has been forever*[191].

189 This paragraph also is from *Megillah* 4:1, Notes 16 ff.
190 *Ex.* 34:27.
191 *Eccl.* 1:10.

(76d line 37) רִבִּי זְעוּרָה בְּשֵׁם שְׁמוּאֵל. אֵין מוֹרִין לֹא מִן הַהֲלָכוֹת וְלֹא מִן הָאַגָּדוֹת וְלֹא מִן הַתּוֹסָפוֹת אֶלָּא מִן הַתַּלְמוּד. וְהָא תַנָא רִבִּי חֲלַפְתָּא בֶּן שָׁאוּל. הִיא שְׁנֵי מֵינֵי חִיטִּין הִיא שְׁנֵי

מִינֵי שְׂעוֹרִין. אָמַר רִבִּי זְעוּרָה. כָּךְ הָיְתָה הֲלָכָה בְיָדָם וּשְׁכָחוּהָ. הִיא שְׁנֵי מִינֵי חִיטִּין הִיא שְׁנֵי מִינֵי שְׂעוֹרִין. וְהָא תַנִּינָן. הַמַּחֲלִיק בְּצָלִים לַחִים לַשּׁוּק וּמְקַיֵּים יְבֵישִׁין לַגּוֹרֶן. אִית לָךְ מֵימַר. שׁוּק וְגוֹרֶן. כָּךְ הָיְתָה הֲלָכָה בְיָדָם וּשְׁכָחוּהָ.

Rebbi Ze'ira in the name of Samuel: One makes inferences neither from practices[192], nor from homiletics[193], nor from extraneous sources[194], but only from study[195]. Did not Rebbi Ḥalaphta ben Shaul state: The case of two kinds of wheat is the same as the case of two kinds of barley[196]? Rebbi Ze'ira said, that was part of the original practice and it was forgotten: The case of two kinds of wheat is the same as the case of two kinds of barley. But did we not state[197] "He who strips moist onions for the market and stores dry ones[198];" can you say about market and storage that this was of the original practice and was forgotten?

192 Rules of practice declared in the Mishnah; these may be overridden by arguments in the Talmud. The interpretation of this paragraph follows R. Samuel ben Meïr (Rashbam) to Babli *Bava batra* 130b.

193 Homiletics, whether incorporated in the Talmud or given in separate Midrashim. Since the sixteenth century this principle has been violated in favor of practices mentioned in the pseudepigraphic Midrash Zohar.

194 The "additional sources" are tannaitic materials not given in the Mishnah, either as single traditions or as part of a collection.

195 From study which finds the reasons for each ruling.

196 If R. Ḥalaphta ben Shaul makes the inference that the rules for barley are identical with those for wheat, does he not violate Samuel's statement that one does not draw inferences from stated practices but only from an argument about the underlying principles?

197 Mishnah *Peah* 3:3.

198 He has to give *peah* two times; this rule cannot be deduced from the stated practice regarding two kinds of wheat since one deals here with only one kind of onion. Since this Mishnah cannot be a consequence of the original Halakhah, neither may one assert that the ruling of R. Ḥalaphta ben Shaul was part of the original Halakhah. Hence, neither the statement of R. Ḥalaphta nor the Mishnah are exempt from logical scrutiny on the basis of accepted general principles.

(76d line 43) רִבִּי חֲנַנְיָה בְשֵׁם שְׁמוּאֵל. אֵין לְמֵידִין מִן הַהוֹרָיָיה. הַכֹּל מוֹדִין שֶׁאֵין לְמֵידִין מִן הַמַּעֲשֶׂה. אָמַר לֵיהּ רִבִּי מָנָא. הָדָא דַתְּ אָמַר בָּהוּא דְלָא סָבַר. בְּרַם בָּהוּא דְסָבַר עֲבִיד. אָמַר לֵיהּ. בֵּין דְּסָבַר בֵּין דְּלָא סָבַר בָּהוּא דְפָלִיג. בְּרַם בָּהוּא דְלָא פָלִיג בֵּין סָבַר בֵּין לָא סָבַר עֲבָד.

Rebbi Hananiah in the name of Samuel: One makes no inferences from a ruling[199]. Everybody agrees that one makes no inferences from an action[200].

Rebbi Mana said to him, that means somebody who does not understand[201], but he who understands may act. He said to him, whether one understands or one does not understand, if there is a disagreement[202]. But if there is no disagreement, whether one understands or one does not understand one acts[203].

199 If a rabbi was asked about a practical problem and he gave a certain decision, a third party may make no practical applications of that decision unless he understands the reasoning behind the decision and agrees with it.

200 If one saw a rabbinic authority act in a certain way, one may not act in the same way or make inferences from this action unless one knows both the background of and the reasoning for the particular action.

201 The reasoning of the rabbinic authority.

202 If in the Mishnah or another source there is mention of a disagreement between rabbis about the correct course, action is permitted only if there is an explicit understanding of and agreement with the reasoning behind the ruling.

203 In this case, one may act on the decision or imitate the action of a competent rabbinic authority even without a detailed inquiry into the arguments leading to decision or action.

Here ends the text from *Peah*.

(76d line 47) רִבִּי אַבָּהוּ בְשֵׁם רִבִּי יוֹחָנָן. כָּל־הָאֲסוּרִין שְׁרִיבָה עֲלֵיהֶן. שׁוֹגֵג מוּתָּר מֵזִיד אָסוּר. וְלֹא מַתְנִיתָה הִיא. אִם שׁוֹגֵג מוּתָּר. אִם מֵזִיד אָסוּר׃ מַתְנִיתָה בִתְרוּמָה דְרוּבָהּ. אָתָא מֵימַר לָךְ. וַאֲפִילוּ בִּשְׁאָר כָּל־הַדְּבָרִים. רִבִּי אָחָא בְשֵׁם רִבִּי יוֹנָתָן. כְּשֵׁם שֶׁמִּצְוָה לוֹמַר עַל דָּבָר שֶׁהוּא נַעֲשֶׂה כָּךְ מִצְוָה שֶׁלֹּא לוֹמַר עַל דָּבָר שֶׁאֵינוֹ נַעֲשֶׂה. אָמַר רִבִּי לְעָזָר. כְּשֵׁם שֶׁאָסוּר לְטַהֵר אֶת הַטָּמֵא כָּךְ אָסוּר לְטַמֵּא אֶת הַטָּהוֹר. רִבִּי אַבָּא בַר יַעֲקֹב בְּשֵׁם רִבִּי יוֹחָנָן. אִם בָּאת הֲלָכָה תַּחַת יָדֶיךָ וְאֵין אַתְּ יוֹדֵעַ אִם לִתְלוֹת אִם לִשְׂרוֹף. לְעוֹלָם הֱוֵי רָץ אַחַר הַשְּׂרֵיפָה יוֹתֵר מִן הַתְּלִייָה. שֶׁאֵין לָךְ חָבִיב בַּתּוֹרָה מִפָּרִים הַנִּשְׂרָפִין וּשְׂעִירִים הַנִּשְׂרָפִין וְהֵן בַּשְּׂרֵיפָה. רִבִּי יוֹסֵי בָּעֵי. וּלְמֵידִין דָּבָר שֶׁאֵין מִצְוָתוֹ לְכָאן מִדָּבָר שֶׁמִּצְוָתוֹ לְכָאן.

[204]Rebbi Abbahu in the name of Rebbi Johanan: All forbidden things[205], if one added to them in error it is permitted, intentionally it is forbidden. Is that not the Mishnah[206], "if it was in error it is permitted, if intentional it is forbidden"? The Mishnah is about addition to heave, he comes to tell you about other things. Rebbi Aha in the name of Rebbi Jonathan: Just as one has a duty to instruct about actions that should be done so one has a duty to instruct negatively about actions that should not be done. Rebbi Eleazar said, just as it is forbidden to declare the impure as pure, so it is forbidden to declare the pure as impure. Rebbi Abba bar Jacob in the name of Rebbi Johanan: If a practical case comes before you and you do not know whether

to suspend or to burn[207], always try to burn rather than to suspend since there is nothing in the Torah more distinguished than burned bulls and burned rams[208], and they are burned. Rebbi Yose asked, is it possible to infer from something whose commandment is thus for something whose commandment is not so[209]?

204 This paragraph is copied (somewhat lacunary, completed by the corrector) in *Terumot* 5:9 (Notes 112-115).

205 Which can become insignificant in an appropriate plurality of permitted food (60, 100, 200 times, as the case may be).

206 Mishnah *Terumot* 5:9.

207 The rule is that heave impure by biblical standards must be burned but heave impure only by rabbinic standards must be "suspended", *viz.*, one must leave it to rot until it is no longer food and, therefore, pure according to all standards.

208 The expiatory sacrifices whose blood was brought into the Sanctuary.

209 The argument of R. Abba bar Jacob contradicts our principle that homiletics cannot be the base of practical decisions.

אין דורשין פרק שני חגיגה

(fol.76d) **משנה א**: אֵין דּוֹרְשִׁין בָּעֲרָיוֹת בִּשְׁלֹשָׁה. וְלֹא בְּמַעֲשֵׂה בְרֵאשִׁית בִּשְׁנָיִם. וְלֹא בַּמֶּרְכָּבָה בְּיָחִיד אֶלָּא אִם כֵּן הָיָה חָכָם מֵבִין מִדַּעְתּוֹ. כָּל־הַמִּסְתַּכֵּל בְּאַרְבָּעָה דְּבָרִים רָתוּי לוֹ כְּאִילּוּ לֹא בָא לָעוֹלָם מַה לְמַעְלָן וּמַה לְמַטָּן מַה לְפָנִים וּמַה לְאָחוֹר. כָּל־שֶׁלֹּא חָס עַל כְּבוֹד קוֹנוֹ רָאוּי לוֹ כְּאִילּוּ שֶׁלֹּא בָא לָעוֹלָם:

Mishnah 1: One does not explain sexual aberrations to three {persons}, nor the Creation[1] to two, nor the Chariot[2] to one unless he was wise and understood by himself. Anybody trying to investigate four things it would have been better for him not to have come into the world: what is above and what is below, what is before and what is after[3]. And anybody not caring for the glory of his Creator[4] would have been better off not to come into the world[5].

1 To study the esoteric doctrines inspired by the biblical account of Creation which obviously is not a scientific text.
2 The details of the Divine Throne as described in the first Chapter of Ezechiel.
3 Since space and time are created, there cannot be any meaningful answer to the question what was before time and what is outside space.
4 The hypocrite who sins in secret is blaspheming every time he sins since he shows that he denies that God is all-knowing.
5 Not being born he could not be punished.

(77a line 12) אֵין דּוֹרְשִׁין בָּעֲרָיוֹת בִּשְׁלֹשָׁה כול׳. רִבִּי בָּא בְשֵׁם רַב יְהוּדָה. דְּרִבִּי עֲקִיבָה הִיא. בְּרַם כְּרִבִּי יִשְׁמָעֵאל. דְּרִבִּי יִשְׁמָעֵאל תַּנֵּי אַזְהָרוֹת לְעוֹבְדָה. מִן דְּרִבִּי אִמִּי יָתִיב מַתְנֵי. אַזְהָרָה לַשּׁוֹכֵב אַזְהָרָה לַנִּשְׁכָּב. הָדָא אֲמָרָה. הֲלָכָה כְּרִבִּי יִשְׁמָעֵאל.

"One does not explain sexual aberrations to three {persons}," etc. Rebbi Abba in the name of Rav Jehudah: This is Rebbi Aqiba's, but following Rebbi Ismael[6]? Since Rebbi Ismael states warnings to the actors[7]. Since Rebbi Immi was sitting and stating a warning for active homosexual and a warning for the passive homosexual, this implies that practice follows Rebbi Ismael[8].

6 If there can be no public discussion about the rules concerning sexual aberrations, there can be no disagreement about these rules. This is acceptable following R. Aqiba who derives prohibition for both the active and the passive homosexual from *Lev.* 18:22, noting that the unvocalized verb can be read both in active and in passive voices (cf *Sanhedrin* 7:9, Note 176.) But R. Ismael who denies that *Lev.* 18:22 contains a prohibition of passive homosexuality does derive the prohibition from an intricate derivation involving verses which on the face of it do not describe deadly sins. Therefore he must invite public discussion of his position. The Babli 11b considers the Mishnah as a moral precept, not an enforceable ruling.

7 *Sanhedrin* 7:9, Notes 177-181; Babli *Sanhedrin* 54b.

8 The Amora was openly teaching R. Ismael's opinion as authoritative; the first clause in Mishnah 1 is not accepted.

(77a line 18) וְלֹא בְמַעֲשֵׂה בְרֵאשִׁית בִּשְׁנָיִם. רִבִּי בָּא בְשֵׁם רַב יְהוּדָה. דְּרִבִּי עֲקִיבָה הִיא. בְּרַם כְּרִבִּי יִשְׁמָעֵאל דּוֹרְשִׁין לְעוֹבְדָה. מִן מַה דְּרִבִּי יוּדָה בַּר פָּזִי יְתִיב דָּרַשׁ. בַּתְּחִילָּה הָיָה הָעוֹלָם מַיִם בְּמַיִם. הָדָא אֲמָרָה. הֲלָכָה כְרִבִּי יִשְׁמָעֵאל. דָּרַשׁ רִבִּי יוּדָה בַּר פָּזִי. בַּתְּחִילָּה הָיָה הָעוֹלָם מַיִם בְּמַיִם. מַה טַעַם. וְרוּחַ אֱלֹהִים מְרַחֶפֶת עַל־פְּנֵי הַמַּיִם: חָזַר וַעֲשָׂאוּ שֶׁלֶג. מַשְׁלִיךְ קַרְחוֹ כְפִתִּים. חָזַר וַעֲשָׂאוּ אֶרֶץ. כִּי לַשֶּׁלֶג | יֹאמַר הֱוֵא אָרֶץ. וְהָאָרֶץ עוֹמֶדֶת עַל מַיִם. לְרוֹקַע הָאָרֶץ עַל־הַמָּיִם. וְהַמַּיִם עוֹמְדִים עַל הָרִים. עַל־הָרִים יַעַמְדוּ־מָיִם: וְהֶהָרִים עוֹמְדִין עַל רוּחַ. כִּי הִנֵּה יוֹצֵר הָרִים וּבוֹרֵא רוּחַ. וְהָרוּחַ תְּלוּיָה בִסְעָרָה. רוּחַ סְעָרָה עֹשָׂה דְבָרוֹ: וּסְעָרָה עֲשָׂאָהּ הַקָּדוֹשׁ בָּרוּךְ הוּא כְּמִין קָמִיעַ וּתְלָיָיהּ בִּזְרוֹעוֹ שֶׁנֶּאֱמַר וּמִתַּחַת זְרוֹעוֹת עוֹלָם.

"Nor the Creation to two." Rebbi Abba in the name of Rav Jehudah: This is Rebbi Aqiba's, but following Rebbi Ismael one investigates what happened. Since Rebbi Jehudah bar Pazi was sitting and explaining that originally the world was water in water; this implies that practice follows Rebbi Ismael. Rebbi Jehudah bar Pazi was preaching[9]: Originally the world was water in water. What is the reason? *God's wind was hovering over the water*[10]. Then He turned it into snow, *He throws his ice like small breads*[11]. Then He turned it into land, *for He will tell the snow, be land*[12]. And the land stands on water, *to Him Who spreads the earth over the water*[13]. And the water stands on mountains, *on mountains shall the water stand*[14]. And the mountains stand on wind, *behold the Maker of mountains and Creator of wind*[15]. And the wind depends on storm, *the wind storm executes His word*[16]. And the Holy One, praise to Him, turned storm into a kind of amulet and hung it on His arm, as it is said, *and below eternal arms*[17].

9 The original meaning of דרש "to investigate" has been changed into the later Amoraic-Medieval "to preach" and the interpretation of the Mishnah changed accordingly.	12 *Job* 37:6.
	13 *Ps.* 136:6. Babli 12b.
	14 *Ps.* 104:6.
	15 *Am.* 4:13.
10 *Gen.* 1:2.	16 *Ps.* 148:3
11 *Ps.* 147:17.	17 *Deut.* 33:27.

(77a line 27) כִּי הִנֵּה יוֹצֵר הָרִים וגו'. זֶה אֶחָד מִשִּׁשָּׁה מִקְרָיוֹת שֶׁהָיָה רִבִּי קוֹרֵא אוֹתָן וּבוֹכֶה. בַּקְּשׁוּ אֶת־יְ'י' כָּל־עַנְוֵי הָאָרֶץ וגו'. שִׂנְאוּ־רָע וְאֶהֱבוּ טוֹב וגו'. יִתֵּן בֶּעָפָר פִּיהוּ וגו'. כִּי אֶת כָּל הַמַּעֲשֶׂה וגו'. וַיֹּאמֶר שְׁמוּאֵל אֶל־שָׁאוּל לָמָּה הִרְגַּזְתַּנִי וגו'. אָמַר לוֹ. לֹא הָיָה לָךְ לְהַרְגִּיז אֶת בּוֹרְאֲךָ אֶלָּא בִי. עֲשִׂיתַנִי עֲבוֹדָה זָרָה שֶׁלָךְ. אֵין אַתְּ יוֹדֵעַ. כְּשֵׁם שֶׁנִּפְרָעִין מִן הָעוֹבֵד כָּךְ נִפְרָעִין מִן הַעֲבֵד. וְלֹא עוֹד אֶלָּא שֶׁהָיִיתִי סָבוּר שֶׁהוּא יוֹם הַדִּין וְנִתְיָרֵאתִי. וַהֲרֵי דְּבָרִים קַל וָחוֹמֶר. מָה אִם שְׁמוּאֵל רַבָּן שֶׁלַּנְּבִיאִים. שֶׁכָּתוּב בֵּיהּ וַיֵּדַע כָּל־יִשְׂרָאֵל מִדָּן וְעַד־בְּאֵר שֶׁבַע וגו'. נִתְיָרֵא מִיּוֹם הַדִּין. אָנוּ עַל אַחַת כַּמָּה וְכַמָּה. וְהָדֵין כִּי הִנֵּה יוֹצֵר הָרִים וּבוֹרֵא רוּחַ וגו'. אֲפִילוּ דְּבָרִים שֶׁאֵין בָּהֶן חֵטְ נִכְתָּבִין לְאָדָם עַל פִּינְקְסוֹ. וּמִי מַגִּיד לָאָדָם. הֶבֶל הַיּוֹצֵא מִפִּיו. רִבִּי חַגַּי בְשֵׁם רִבִּי יַעֲבֵץ. יוֹצֵר הָרִים וּבוֹרֵא רוּחַ. רִבִּי חַגַּי בְשֵׁם רִבִּי יַעֲבֵץ. אִילֵּין צִיפָּארֵיי. תוֹהוּ חוֹשֶׁךְ וַאֲפֵילָה.

Behold the Maker of mountains and Creator of wind, etc. This is one of six verses which Rebbi was reading and crying[18]. *Implore the Eternal, all the meek of the Land*[19], etc. *Hate evil and love goodness*,[20] etc. *He shall put dust in his mouth*[21], etc. *For all deeds*[22], etc. *Samuel said to Saul, why did you irritate me*[23], etc. He said to him, you should not have angered your Creator by me. You made me your idol. Do you not know that just as the worshipper is punished, the worshipped is punished? Not only this but I was thinking that this was the Day of Judgment and I was afraid. And is that not an inference *de minore ad majus*, if Samuel, the teacher of the Prophets, about whom it is written, *all of Israel knew, from Dan to Beer Sheva*[24], etc., was afraid of the Day of Judgment, so we so much more? And this *behold the Maker of mountains and Creator of wind*, even matters which are not sinful are written for everybody[25] on his writing tablet[26]. And who tells to a person? The breath of his mouth. Rebbi Ḥaggai in the name of Rebbi Jabeṣ. *The Maker of mountains and Creator of wind*. Rebbi Ḥaggai in the name of Rebbi Jabeṣ, those Sepphoreans, "chaos" is darkness and murkiness[27].

18 Attributed to other authors in the Babli, 4b. For the next three verses, the problem is that by their text reward for exemplary behavior is not guaranteed.
19 *Soph.* 2:3.
20 *Am.* 5:15.
21 *Thr.* 3:29.
22 *Eccl.* 12:14.
23 *1Sam.* 28:15.
24 *1Sam.* 3:20.
25 Babli 5b.
26 Greek πίναξ.
27 The last two sentences which probably are corrupt seem to explain the word "chaos" in *Gen.* 1:2.

(77a line 39) רִבִּי יוּדָה בַּר פָּזִי בְשֵׁם רִבִּי יוֹסֵי בֵּירִבִּי יוּדָה. אַדְרִיָינוּס שָׁאַל לַעֲקִילַס הַגֵּר. קוּשְׁטִין אַתּוּן אָמְרִין דְּהֵן עַלְמָא קַיָּים עַל רוּחָא. אָמַר לֵיהּ. אִין. מִן הֵן אַתְּ מוֹדַע לִי. אָמַר לֵיהּ. אַיְיתִי לִי הוֹגָנִין. אַיְיתֵי לֵיהּ הוֹגָנִין. אַטְעוּנוּנָן טַעוּנֵיהוֹן. אֲקִימוֹן וְאַרְבָּעוֹן. נַסְתּוּן וְחָנְקוֹן. אָמַר לֵיהּ. הֵא לָךְ. אֲקִימוֹן. אָמַר לֵיהּ. מִן דְּחָנָקָתוֹן. אָמַר לֵיהּ. כְּלוּם חֲסַרְתִּינוֹן. לֹא רוּחָא הִיא דְנָפְקַת מִינְּהוֹן.

Rebbi Jehudah bar Pazi in the name of Rebbi Yose ben Rebbi Jehudah: Hadrian asked Akylas the proselyte[28], is it true that you are saying that this world rest on the spirit? He told him, yes. He said to him, how can you show this to me? He told him, bring me noble camels. He brought him noble camels. He loaded them with their loads, let them stand up and lie down, lifted them and strangulated them. He told him, here they are, raise them. He said to him, after you strangulated them? He told him, I did not remove anything from them, is it not the spirit which left them?

28 Who according to tradition was a relative of the later Emperor Hadrian. As translator he is dated almost a generation earlier (*Megillah* 1:11, Note 299).

(77a line 44) וְלֹא בַּמֶּרְכָּבָה בְּיָחִיד. עוֹד הִיא כְרִבִּי עֲקִיבָה. דִּבְרֵי הַכֹּל הִיא. כְּדֵי שֶׁיְּהֵא אָדָם יוֹדֵעַ לָחוּס עַל כְּבוֹד קוֹנוֹ. לֹא כֵן אָמַר רַב. אֵין אָדָם רַשַּׁאי לוֹמַר דָּבָר (בְּנֶגַע צָרַעַת) [כְּנֶגֶד רַבּוֹ] אֶלָּא אִם כֵּן רָאָה אוֹ שִׁימֵּשׁ. כֵּיצַד הוּא עוֹשֶׂה. כַּתְּחִילָּה רַבּוֹ פוֹתֵחַ לוֹ רָאשֵׁי פְסוּקִים וּמְסַכֵּם. רִבִּי חִייָה בְשֵׁם רִבִּי יוֹחָנָן. תַּלְמִיד וָתִיק הָיָה לוֹ לְרִבִּי וְדָרַשׁ פֶּרֶק אֶחָד בְּמַעֲשֵׂה הַמֶּרְכָּבָה. וְלֹא הִסְכִּימָה דַעְתּוֹ שֶׁלְרִבִּי. וְלָקָה בְשְׁחִין. הַתּוֹרָה הַזּוֹ דוֹמָה לִשְׁנֵי שְׁבִילִין. אֶחָד שֶׁלְאוֹר וְאֶחָד שֶׁלְשֶׁלֶג. הִיטָּה בָזֶה מֵת בָּאוּר. הִיטָּה בָזוֹ מֵת בַּשֶּׁלֶג. מַה יַּעֲשֶׂה. יְהַלֵּךְ בָּאֶמְצַע.

"Nor the Chariot[2] to one." Is this still Rebbi Aqiba's? It is the opinion of everybody, so that a person know how to take care of the glory of his Maker. Did not Rav say, nobody is permitted to pronounce anything (about skin disease) [against his teacher][29] unless either he saw or he served. How does one proceed? At the start his teacher indicates the topics of the verses and summarizes[30]. Rebbi Ḥiyya in the name of Rebbi Joḥanan: Rebbi had a competent student who explained one Chapter in the Work of the Chariot to which Rebbi did not concur; he was stricken with scabies. This teaching may be compared to two roads, one of fire and the other of snow. If he takes one he dies in fire, if he takes the other he dies in snow. What should he do? Walk in the middle[31].

29 The corrector's [text] arose from a misunderstanding of the argument and has to be deleted. The scribe's (text) is based on the observation that the rules of impurity of skin disease are given an important place in *Lev*. 13-14, but already at the time of the Mishnah were not identifiable as specific illnesses. While it is important to be acquainted with the interpretation of two full Chapters in the Torah, this must be restricted to memorizing the traditional interpretations. A person is empowered to add his own statement only if he was confronted with an actual case. The same holds with the Heavenly Chariot. Unless he had his own vision, the reality behind Ezechiel's verses remains closed to him, and any statement which adds to study material is presumptuous assertion of false, since unknowable, statements.

30 The traditional interpretation of the verses.

31 Learn the traditional interpretation and refrain from adding to it.

(77a line 51) מַעֲשֶׂה בְרַבָּן יוֹחָנָן בֶּן זַכַּאי שֶׁהָיָה מְהַלֵּךְ עַל הַדֶּרֶךְ רוֹכֵב עַל הַחֲמוֹר. וְרִבִּי אֶלְעָזָר בֶּן עֲרָךְ מְהַלֵּךְ אַחֲרָיו. אָמַר לוֹ. רִבִּי. הַשְׁנִינִי פֶּרֶק אֶחָד בְּמַעֲשֵׂה הַמֶּרְכָּבָה. אָמַר לוֹ. וְלֹא כָךְ שָׁנוּ חֲכָמִים. וְלֹא בַּמֶּרְכָּבָה. אֶלָּא אִם כֵּן הָיָה חָכָם וּמֵבִין מִדַּעְתּוֹ. אָמַר לוֹ. רִבִּי. תַּרְשֵׁינִי לוֹמַר לְפָנֶיךָ אֲנִי. אָמַר לוֹ. אֱמוֹר. כֵּיוָן שֶׁפָּתַח רִבִּי לְעָזָר בֶּן עֲרָךְ בְּמַעֲשֵׂה הַמֶּרְכָּבָה יָרַד לוֹ רַבָּן יוֹחָנָן בֶּן זַכַּי מִן הַחֲמוֹר. אָמַר. אֵינוֹ בַדִּין שֶׁאֱהֵא שׁוֹמֵעַ כְּבוֹד קוֹנִי וַאֲנִי רָכוּב עַל הַחֲמוֹר. הָלְכוּ וְיָשְׁבוּ לָהֶן תַּחַת אִילָן אֶחָד. וְיָרְדָה אֵשׁ מִן הַשָּׁמַיִם וְהִקִּיפָה אוֹתָם. וְהָיוּ מַלְאֲכֵי הַשָּׁרֵת מְקַפְּצִין לִפְנֵיהֶן כִּבְנֵי חוּפָּה שְׂמֵיחִין לִפְנֵי חָתָן. נַעֲנָה מַלְאָךְ אֶחָד מִתּוֹךְ הָאֵשׁ וְאָמַר. כִּדְבָרֶיךָ אֶלְעָזָר בֶּן עֲרָךְ כֵּן הוּא מַעֲשֵׂה הַמֶּרְכָּבָה. מִיַּד פֶּתְחוּ כָּל־הָאִילוֹנוֹת (מֵהֶן) [פִּיהֶן] וְאָמְרוּ שִׁירָה. אָז יְרַנְּנוּ עֲצֵי הַיַּעַר: כֵּיוָן שֶׁגָּמַר רִבִּי לְעָזָר בֶּן עֲרָךְ בְּמַעֲשֵׂה הַמֶּרְכָּבָה עָמַד רַבָּן יוֹחָנָן בֶּן זַכַּי וּנְשָׁקוֹ עַל רֹאשׁוֹ וְאָמַר. בָּרוּךְ יְי׳ אֱלֹהֵי אַבְרָהָם יִצְחָק וְיַעֲקֹב שֶׁנָּתַן לְאַבְרָהָם אָבִינוּ בֵּן חָכָם יוֹדֵעַ לִדְרוֹשׁ בִּכְבוֹד אָבִינוּ שֶׁבַּשָּׁמַיִם. יֵשׁ לָךְ נָאֶה לִדְרוֹשׁ וְאֵינוֹ נָאֶה מְקַיֵּים. נָאֶה מְקַיֵּים וְאֵינוֹ נָאֶה דוֹרֵשׁ. אֶלְעָזָר בֶּן עֲרָךְ נָאֶה דוֹרֵשׁ וְנָאֶה מְקַיֵּים. אַשְׁרֶיךָ אַבְרָהָם אָבִינוּ. שֶׁיָּצָא מֵחֲלָצֶיךָ אֶלְעָזָר בֶּן עֲרָךְ. וְכֵיוָן שֶׁשָּׁמְעוּ רִבִּי יוֹסֵף הַכֹּהֵן וְרִבִּי שִׁמְעוֹן בֶּן נְתַנְאֵל אַף הֵם פָּתְחוּ בְּמַעֲשֵׂה הַמֶּרְכָּבָה. אָמְרוּ. יוֹם אֶחָד בִּתְקוּפַת תַּמּוּז הָיָה. וְרָעֲשָׁה הָאָרֶץ וְנִרְאֲתָה הַקֶּשֶׁת בֶּעָנָן. וְיָצְאָה בַת קוֹל וְאָמְרָה לָהֶן.

הֲרֵי הַמָּקוֹם פָּנוּי לָכֶם וְהַטְּרְקְלִין מוּצָע לָכֶם. אַתֶּם וְתַלְמִידֵיכֶם מְזוּמָּנִין לַכַּת שְׁלִישִׁית. וְאַתְיָא כְּמַאן דְּאָמַר שׂוֹבַע שְׂמָחוֹת אֶת־פָּנֶיךָ. שֶׁבַע כִּיתּוֹת שֶׁלַּצַדִּיקִים לֶעָתִיד לבוא.

[32]It happened that Rabban Johanan ben Zakkai was on the road, riding on a donkey, and Rebbi Eleazar ben Arakh was walking behind him. He said to him, my teacher, instruct me in a Chapter about the Work of the Chariot. He told him, did the Sagen not state, "nor the Chariot[2] unless he was wise and understood by himself." He said to him, my teacher, permit me to say it before you. He told him, say. When Rebbi Eleazar ben Arakh started about the Work of the Chariot, Rabban Johanan ben Zakkai descended from the donkey. He said, it is not appropriate that I should hear about the glory of my Creator riding on a donkey. They went and sat under a tree, when fire descended from Heaven and surrounded them, and the angels of Service were dancing before them like wedding guests happy with the bridegroom. An angel addressed from inside the fire and said, the Work of the Chariot is as you said, Eleazar ben Arakh. Then all trees (around them) [opened their mouths] and sang; *then all trees of the forest will sing*[33]. When Rebbi Eleazar ben Arakh finished with the Work of the Chariot, Rabban Johanan ben Zakkai rose, kissed him on his head, and said: Praised be the Eternal, the God of Abraham, Isaac, and Jacob, who gave a wise son to our father Abraham who knows to speak of the Glory of our Father in Heaven. They are good speakers who do not act well, those who act well but are no good speakers. Eleazar ben Arakh speaks well and acts well. Hail to you, our father Abraham, that Eleazar ben Arakh came from your loins. When Rebbi Yosef Hakohen and Rebbi Simeon ben Nethanael[34] heard, they also started with the Work of the Chariot. They said, it was one day after the summer solstice; the earth trembled and the Arc appeared in the cloud. An unembodied voice came and said to them, the place is free and the *triclinium* prepared for you. You and your students are invited to the third group. This parallels him who said, *seven enjoyments are before Your presence*[35], there are seven groups of just people in the Future World[36].

32 Babli 14b; Tosephta 2:1.
33 *Ps.* 96:12.
34 Cf. Mishnah *Avot* 2:8.
35 *Ps.* 16:11.
36 Who are worthy to see God's glory, *Lev. rabba* 30(2).

74 line 77a) שׁוּב מַעֲשֶׂה בְּיִרְבִּי יְהוֹשֻׁעַ שֶׁהָיָה מְהַלֵּךְ בַּדֶּרֶךְ. וּבֶן זוֹמָא בָּא כְנֶגְדּוֹ. שָׁאַל בִּשְׁלוֹמוֹ וְלֹא הֱשִׁיבוֹ. אָמַר לוֹ. מֵאַיִן וּלְאַיִן בֶּן זוֹמָא. אָמַר לוֹ. מִסְתַּכֵּל הָיִיתִי בְּמַעֲשֵׂה בְרֵאשִׁית. וְאֵין בֵּין מַיִם הָעֶלְיוֹנִים לַמַּיִם הַתַּחְתּוֹנִים אֶלָּא (אֶחָד) [כִּמְלֹא] פּוֹתֵחַ טֶפַח. נֶאֱמַר כָּאן רִיחוּף. וְנֶאֱמַר לְהַלֹּן כְּנֶשֶׁר יָעִיר קִנּוֹ עַל־גּוֹזָלָיו יְרַחֵף. מַה רִיחוּף שֶׁנֶּאֱמַר לְהַלָּן נוֹגֵעַ וְאֵינוֹ נוֹגֵעַ. אַף רִיחוּף שֶׁנֶּאֱמַר כָּאן נוֹגֵעַ וְאֵינוֹ נוֹגֵעַ. אָמַר רִבִּי יְהוֹשֻׁעַ לְתַלְמִידָיו. הֲרֵי בֶן זוֹמָא בַחוּץ. וְלֹא הָיוּ יָמִים קַלִּים עַד שֶׁנִּפְטַר בֶּן זוֹמָא.

[37]It also happened that Rebbi Joshua was on the road when Ben Zoma came towards him. He greeted him but he did not answer. He asked him, from where and whence, Ben Zoma? He told him, I was observing the Creation, and the distance between the upper waters and the lower waters is (one) [a full][38] opening of a hand-breadth. It says here "hovering", and it says there, *as an eagle watches his nest, over his chicks he hovers*[39]. Since in case of the hovering mentioned there it means barely touching, so the hovering mentioned here means barely touching. Rebbi Joshua said to his students, Ben Zoma is out. It was only a few days that Ben Zoma passed away.

37 Babli 15a.
38 The corrector's text certainly is erroneous. It uses Babli general language but contradicts the Babli here. While the Talmudim recognize units of measurement smaller than the hand-breadth, e. g., finger-widths, unless numbers are given "a hand-breadth" means a small distance of indeterminate size.
39 *Deut.* 32:11.

5.line 77b) רִבִּי יוּדָה בַּר פָּזִּי בְּשֵׁם רִבִּי יוֹסִי בְּיִרְבִּי יוּדָה. שְׁלֹשָׁה הִרְצוּ תוֹרָתָן לִפְנֵי רַבָּן. רִבִּי יְהוֹשֻׁעַ לִפְנֵי רַבָּן יוֹחָנָן בֶּן זַכַּיי. רִבִּי עֲקִיבָה לִפְנֵי רִבִּי יְהוֹשֻׁעַ. חֲנַנְיָה בֶן חֲכִינַיי לִפְנֵי רִבִּי עֲקִיבָה. מִיכָן וָהֵילָךְ אֵין דַּעְתָּן נְקִיָּה. אַרְבָּעָה נִכְנְסוּ לַפַּרְדֵּס. אֶחָד הֵצִיץ וָמֵת. אֶחָד הֵצִיץ וְנִפְגַּע. אֶחָד הֵצִיץ וְקִיצֵּץ בַּנְּטִיעוֹת. אֶחָד נִכְנַס בְּשָׁלוֹם וְיָצָא בְשָׁלוֹם. בֶּן עַזַּאי הֵצִיץ וְנִפְגַּע. עָלָיו הַכָּתוּב אוֹמֵר דְּבַשׁ מָצָאתָ אֱכוֹל דַּיֶּיךָ. בֶּן זוֹמָא הֵצִיץ וָמֵת. עָלָיו הַכָּתוּב אוֹמֵר יָקָר בְּעֵינֵי י'י הַמָּוְתָה לַחֲסִידָיו. אַחֵר הֵצִיץ וְקִיצֵּץ בַּנְּטִיעוֹת. מַנּוּ אַחֵר. אֱלִישָׁע בֶּן אֲבוּיָה. שֶׁהָיָה הוֹרֵג רָבֵי תוֹרָה. אָמְרִין. כָּל־תַּלְמִיד דַּהֲוָה חֲמֵי לֵיהּ מְשַׁבַּח בְּאוֹרַיְתָא הֲוָה קָטִיל לֵיהּ. וְלֹא עוֹד אֶלָּא דַּהֲוָה עָלִיל לְבֵית וַעֲדָא וַהֲוָה חֲמֵי טַלְיָיא קוֹמֵי סָפְרָא. וַהֲוָה אֲמַר. מָה אִילֵּין יָתְבִין עָבְדִין הָכָא. אוּמָנְתֵיהּ דְּהֵן בַּנַּאי. אוּמָנְתֵיהּ דְּהֵן נַגָּר. אוּמָנְתֵיהּ דְּהֵן צַיָּיד. וְכֵיוָן דַּהֲווֹן שָׁמְעִין כֵּן הֲווֹן שָׁבְקִין לֵיהּ וְאָזְלִין לוֹן. עָלָיו הַכָּתוּב אוֹמֵר אַל־תִּתֵּן אֶת־פִּיךָ לַחֲטִיא אֶת־בְּשָׂרֶךָ וְגוֹ'. שֶׁחִיבֵּל מַעֲשֵׂה יָדָיו שֶׁלְאוֹתוֹ הָאִישׁ. אוּף בְּשָׁעַת שׁוּמְדָא הֲווֹן מַטְעֲנִין לוֹן מְטוֹלִין. וַהֲווֹן מִתְכַּוְּונִין מִיטְעוֹן תְּרֵי חַד מְטוֹל. מִשּׁוּם שְׁנַיִם שֶׁעָשׂוּ מְלָאכָה אַחַת. אֲמַר. אַטְעוֹנִינּוּן יְחִידָאִין. אֲזַלּוֹן וְאַטְעוֹנִינּוּן יְחִידָיִין. וַהֲווֹן מִתְכַּוְּונִין מִפְרוֹק בְּכַרְמְלִית. שֶׁלֹּא לְהוֹצִיא מֵרְשׁוּת הַיָּחִיד

לִרְשׁוּת הָרַבִּים. אָמַר. אַטְעוּנִינּוּן צְלוֹחִיִין. אַזְלוּן וְאַטְעוּנִינּוּן צְלוֹחִיִין. רִבִּי עֲקִיבָה נִכְנַס בְּשָׁלוֹם וְיָצָא בְשָׁלוֹם⁴⁰. עָלָיו הַכָּתוּב אוֹמֵר מָשְׁכֵנִי אַחֲרֶיךָ נָּרוּצָה וגו'.

Rebbi Jehudah bar Pazi in the name of Rebbi Yose ben Rebbi Jehudah: Three lectured their teachings[41] in front of their teachers: Rebbi Joshua in front of Rabban Joḥana ben Zakkai, Rebbi Aqiba in front of Rebbi Joshua, Ḥananiah ben Ḥakhinai in front of Rebbi Aqiba. From there on their mind was not pure[42]. Four entered the Garden[43], One peeked and was hurt; one peeked and died; one peeked and cut saplings, one entered in peace and left in peace. Ben Azzai peeked and was hurt; about him the verse says[44], *if you found honey, eat your fill*. Ben Zoma peeked and died, about him the verse says[45], *dear in the Eternal's eyes is the death of his pious*. Aḥer peeked and cut saplings. Who is Aḥer? Elisha ben Abuya, who killed the children of Torah. They said, if he saw a student excelling in Torah he killed him. Not only this, but he went to the school house and saw children in front of their Bible teacher. He said, what are these sitting doing here? The profession of this one is builder, the profession of this one is carpenter, the profession of this one is hunter, the profession of this one is tailor. When they heard this, they left him[46] and went away. About him the verse says[47], *do not let your mouth make your flesh sin*[48], etc.; for he destroyed the deeds of himself. Also in the time of religious persecution they[49] made them[50] carry loads. They[50] intended that two together should carry one load, because of two persons who performed one work[51]. He[52] said, make them carry singly. They[49] went and made them carry singly. They[50] intended to unload in *karmelit*, in order not to carry from a private to a public domain[53]. He[52] said to them[49], let them carry flasks; they made them carry flasks[54]. Rebbi Aqiba entered in peace and left in peace; about him the verse says[55], *draw me, I shall run after you*, etc.

40 Babli 14b-15a. Tosephta 2:2-3.
41 About the Work of the Chariot.
42 Studies of *Ez.* 1 were no longer tolerated.
43 Gnostic interpretations.
44 *Prov.* 25:16. The implication is that eating more than his fill is dangerous.
45 *Ps.* 116:15.

46 The teacher.
47 *Eccl.* 5:5.
48 This quote seems to support Y. Kutscher's suggestion that "Aher" does not mean "the other" but "the one in heat", since "flesh" describes the male organ.
49 The Romans, during the Hadrianic persecutions.

50 The Jews.
51 It is implied that the Jews were forced to carry on the Sabbath. Two people carrying one load do not break a biblical prohibition. Cf. *Šabbat* Chapter 1, Note 105.
52 Elisha ben Abuya.

53 To avoid breaking a biblical prohibition, *Šabbat* Chapter 1, Note 73.
54 To be transported from one private domain to another through public domain, a biblical infraction.
55 *Cant.* 1:4. Babli 15b.

(77b line 24) רִבִּי מֵאִיר הֲוָה יָתִיב דְּרָשׁ בְּבֵית מִדְרָשָׁא דְטִיבֶּרְיָה. עָבַר אֱלִישָׁע רַבֵּיהּ רְכִיב עַל סוּסְיָא בְּיוֹם שׁוּבְתָּא. אָתוֹן וְאָמְרוֹן לֵיהּ. הָא רַבָּךְ לְבַר. פְּסַק לֵיהּ מִן דְּרָשָׁה וּנְפַק לְגַבֵּיהּ. אֲמַר לֵיהּ. מָה הֲוִיתָה דְּרָשׁ יוֹמָא דֵין. אֲמַר לֵיהּ. וַיי׳ בֵּרַךְ אֶת־אַחֲרִית וגו׳. אֲמַר לֵיהּ. וּמָה פָּתַחְתְּ בֵּיהּ. אֲמַר לֵיהּ. וַיּוֹסֶף יי׳ אֶת־כָּל־אֲשֶׁר לְאִיּוֹב לְמִשְׁנֶה: שֶׁכָּפַל לוֹ אֶת כָּל־מָמוֹנוֹ. אֲמַר. וַוי דְּמוֹבְדִין וְלָא מַשְׁכָּחִין. עֲקִיבָה רַבָּךְ לָא הֲוָה דָרֵשׁ כֵּן. אֶלָא וַיי׳ בֵּרַךְ אֶת־אַחֲרִית אִיּוֹב מֵרֵאשִׁיתוֹ. בִּזְכוּת מִצְוֹת וּמַעֲשִׂים טוֹבִים שֶׁהָיָה בְיָדוֹ מֵרֵאשִׁיתוֹ. אֲמַר לֵיהּ. וּמָה הֲוִיתָה דְרִישׁ תּוּבָן. אֲמַר לֵיהּ. טוֹב אַחֲרִית דָּבָר מֵרֵאשִׁיתוֹ. אֲמַר לֵיהּ. וּמָה פָּתַחְתְּ בֵּיהּ. אֲמַר לֵיהּ. לְאָדָם שֶׁהוֹלִיד בָּנִים בְּנַעֲרוּתוֹ וָמֵתוּ. וּבְזִקְנוּתוֹ וְנִתְקַיְּימוּ. הֱוֵי טוֹב אַחֲרִית דָּבָר מֵרֵאשִׁיתוֹ. לְאָדָם שֶׁעָשָׂה סְחוֹרָה בְּיַלְדּוּתוֹ וְהִפְסִיד. וּבְזִקְנָתוֹ וְנִשְׂתַּכֵּר. הֱוֵי טוֹב אַחֲרִית דָּבָר מֵרֵאשִׁיתוֹ. לְאָדָם שֶׁלָּמַד תּוֹרָה בְנַעֲרוּתוֹ וּשְׁכָחָהּ. וּבְזִקְנָתוֹ וְקִייְּמָהּ. הֱוֵי טוֹב אַחֲרִית דָּבָר מֵרֵאשִׁיתוֹ. אֲמַר. וַוי דְּמוֹבְדִין וְלָא מַשְׁכָּחִין. עֲקִיבָה רַבָּךְ לָא הֲוָה דָרֵשׁ כֵּן. אֶלָא טוֹב אַחֲרִית דָּבָר מֵרֵאשִׁיתוֹ. בִּזְמַן שֶׁהוּא טוֹב מֵרֵאשִׁיתוֹ. וּבִי הָיָה הַמַּעֲשֶׂה. אֲבוּיָה אַבָּא מִגְּדוֹלֵי יְרוּשָׁלֵם הָיָה. בְּיוֹם שֶׁבָּא לְמוֹהֳלֵינִי קָרָא לְכָל־גְּדוֹלֵי יְרוּשָׁלֵם וְהוֹשִׁיבָן בְּבַיִת אֶחָד. וּלְרִבִּי אֱלִיעֶזֶר וּלְרִבִּי יְהוֹשֻׁעַ בְּבַיִת אֶחָד. מִן דְּאָכְלוֹן וְשָׁתוֹן שָׁרוֹן מְחַפְּחִין וּמְרַקְּדִין. אֲמַר רִבִּי לִיעֶזֶר לְרִבִּי יְהוֹשֻׁעַ. עַד דְּאִינּוּן עֲסִיקִין בְּדִידוֹן נַעֲסוֹק אֲנָן בְּדִידָן. וְיָשְׁבוּ וְנִתְעַסְּקוּ בְּדִבְרֵי תוֹרָה. מִן הַתּוֹרָה לַנְּבִיאִים וּמִן הַנְּבִיאִים לַכְּתוּבִים. וְיָרְדָה אֵשׁ מִן הַשָּׁמַיִם וְהִקִּיפָה אוֹתָם. אָמַר לָהֶן אֲבוּיָה. רַבּוֹתַיי. מָה בָּאתֶם לִשְׂרוֹף אֶת בֵּיתִי עָלַי. אָמְרוּ לוֹ. חַס וְשָׁלוֹם. אֶלָּא יוֹשְׁבִין הָיִינוּ וְחוֹזְרִין בְּדִבְרֵי תוֹרָה. מִן הַתּוֹרָה לַנְּבִיאִים וּמִן הַנְּבִיאִים לַכְּתוּבִים. וְהָיוּ הַדְּבָרִים שְׂמֵחִים כִּנְתִינָתָן מִסִּינַי. וַהֲוָיתָה הָאֵשׁ מְלַחֶכֶת אוֹתָן כִּלְחִיכָתָן מִסִּינַי. וְעִיקַּר נְתִינָתָן מִסִּינַי לֹא נִתְּנוּ בָאֵשׁ. וְהָהָר בּוֹעֵר בָּאֵשׁ עַד־לֵב הַשָּׁמַיִם. אָמַר לָהֶן אֲבוּיָה אַבָּא. רַבּוֹתַיי. אִם כָּךְ הִיא כּוֹחָהּ שֶׁלַּתּוֹרָה. אִם נִתְקַיֵּים לִי הַבֵּן הַזֶּה לַתּוֹרָה אֲנִי מַפְרִישׁוֹ. לְפִי שֶׁלֹּא הָיְתָה כַּוָּנָתוֹ לְשֵׁם שָׁמַיִם לְפִיכָךְ לֹא נִתְקַיְּימוּ בְאוֹתוֹ הָאִישׁ. אֲמַר לֵיהּ. וּמָה הֲוִיתָה דְּרִישׁ תּוּבָן. אֲמַר לֵיהּ. לֹא־יַעַרְכֶנָּה זָהָב וּזְכוּכִית. אֲמַר לֵיהּ. וּמָה פָּתַחְתְּ בֵּיהּ. אֲמַר לֵיהּ. דִּבְרֵי תוֹרָה קָשִׁין לִקְנוֹת כִּכְלֵי זָהָב וְנוֹחִין לְאַבֵּד כִּכְלֵי זְכוּכִית. וּמָה כְלִי זָהָב וּכְלִי זְכוּכִית אִם נִשְׁתַּבְּרוּ יָכוֹל הוּא לַחֲזוֹר וְלַעֲשׂוֹתָם כֵּלִים כְּמוֹ שֶׁהָיוּ. אַף תַּלְמִיד חָכָם שֶׁשָּׁכַח תַּלְמוּדוֹ יָכוֹל הוּא לַחֲזוֹר וּלְלָמְדוֹ כַּתְּחִילָּה. אֲמַר לֵיהּ. דַּייֶךָ מֵאִיר. עַד כָּאן תְּחוּם שַׁבָּת. אֲמַר לֵיהּ. מִן הֵן אַתְּ יָדַע. אֲמַר לֵיהּ. מִן טַלְפֵי דְסוּסְיי דַּהֲוֵינָא מַנִּי וְהוֹלֵךְ אַלְפַּיִים אַמָּה. אֲמַר לֵיהּ. וְכָל־הָדָא חָכְמְתָא אִית בָּךְ וְלֵית אַתְּ חֲזַר בָּךְ. אֲמַר לֵיהּ. לֵית אֲנָא יָכִיל. אֲמַר לֵיהּ. לָמָּה. אֲמַר לֵיהּ. שֶׁפַּעַם אַחַת הָיִיתִי עוֹבֵר לִפְנֵי בֵית קוֹדֶשׁ הַקֳּדָשִׁים רָכוֹב עַל סוּסִי בְּיוֹם הַכִּפּוּרִים שֶׁחָל לִהְיוֹת

בְּשַׁבָּת וְשָׁמַעְתִּי בַּת קוֹל יוֹצֵאת מִבֵּית קוֹדֶשׁ הַקֳדָשִׁים וְאוֹמֶרֶת. שׁוּבוּ בָנִים שׁוֹבָבִים. חוּץ מִן אֱלִישָׁע בֶּן אֲבוּיָה. שֶׁיָדַע כּוֹחִי וּמָרַד בִּי. וְכָל־דָּא מִן הֵן אָתַת לֵיהּ. אֶלָּא פַּעַם אַחַת הָיָה יוֹשֵׁב וְשׁוֹנֶה בְּבִקְעַת גִּינֵּיסָר. וְרָאָה אָדָם אֶחָד עָלָה לְרֹאשׁ הַדֶּקֶל וְנָטַל אֵם עַל הַבָּנִים. וְיָרַד מִשָּׁם בְּשָׁלוֹם. לְמָחָר רָאָה אָדָם אַחֵר שֶׁעָלָה לְרֹאשׁ הַדֶּקֶל. וְנָטַל אֶת הַבָּנִים וְשִׁילַּח אֶת הָאֵם. וְיָרַד מִשָּׁם וְהִכִּישׁוֹ נָחָשׁ וָמֵת. אָמַר. כָּתוּב שַׁלֵּחַ תְּשַׁלַּח אֶת־הָאֵם וְאֶת־הַבָּנִים תִּקַּח־לָךְ לְמַעַן יִיטַב לָךְ וְהַאֲרַכְתָּ יָמִים: אֵיכָן הִיא טוֹבָתוֹ שֶׁלָּזֶה. אֵיכָן הִיא אֲרִיכוּת יָמִים שֶׁלָּזֶה. וְלֹא הֲוָה יְדַע שֶׁדְּרָשָׁהּ רִבִּי יַעֲקֹב לְפָנִים מִמֶּנּוּ. לְמַעַן יִיטַב לָךְ. לָעוֹלָם הַבָּא שֶׁכּוּלוֹ טוֹב. וְהַאֲרַכְתָּ יָמִים. לֶעָתִיד שֶׁכּוּלוֹ אָרוֹךְ. וְיֵשׁ אוֹמְרִים. עַל יְדֵי שֶׁרָאָה לְשׁוֹנוֹ שֶׁלְרִבִּי יְהוּדָה הַנַּחְתּוֹם נָתוּן בְּפִי הַכֶּלֶב שׁוֹתֵת דָּם. אָמַר. זוֹ תוֹרָה וְזוֹ שְׂכָרָהּ. זֶהוּ הַלָּשׁוֹן שֶׁהָיָה מוֹצִיא דִבְרֵי תוֹרָה כְּתִיקְנָן. זֶהוּ הַלָּשׁוֹן שֶׁהָיָה יָגִיעַ בַּתּוֹרָה כָּל־יָמָיו. [זוֹ תוֹרָה וְזוֹ שְׂכָרָהּ.] דּוֹמֶה שֶׁאֵין מַתַּן שָׂכָר וְאֵין תְּחִיַּת הַמֵּתִים. וְיֵשׁ אוֹמְרִים. אִמּוֹ כְּשֶׁהָיְתָה מְעוּבֶּרֶת בּוֹ הָיְתָה עוֹבֶרֶת עַל בָּתֵּי עֲבוֹדָה זָרָה וְהֵרִיחָה מֵאוֹתוֹ הַמִּין. וְהָיָה אוֹתוֹ הָרֵיחַ מְפַעְפֵּעַ בְּגוּפָהּ כְּאִרְסָהּ שֶׁלַּחֲכִינָה. לְאַחַר יָמִים חָלָה אֱלִישָׁע. אָתוּן וְאָמְרוּן לְרִבִּי מֵאִיר. הָא רַבָּךְ בְּאִישׁ. אֲזַל בָּעֵי מְבַקַּרְתֵּיהּ. וְאַשְׁכְּחֵיהּ בְּאִישׁ. אֲמַר לֵיהּ. לֵית אַתְּ חָזַר בָּךְ. אֲמַר לֵיהּ. וְאִין חָזְרִין מִתְקַבְּלִין. אֲמַר לֵיהּ. וְלֹא כֵן כְּתִיב. תָּשֵׁב אֱנוֹשׁ עַד־דַּכָּא. עַד דִּיכְדּוּכָהּ שֶׁלַּנֶּפֶשׁ מְקַבְּלִין. בְּאוֹתָהּ שָׁעָה בָּכָה אֱלִישָׁע וְנִפְטַר וָמֵת. וְהָיָה רִבִּי מֵאִיר שָׂמֵחַ בְּלִיבּוֹ וְאוֹמֵר. דּוֹמֶה שֶׁמִּתּוֹךְ תְּשׁוּבָה נִפְטַר רַבִּי. מִן דְּקָבְרוּנֵיהּ יָרְדָה אֵשׁ מִן הַשָּׁמַיִם וְשָׂרְפָה אֶת קִבְרוֹ. אָתוּן וְאָמְרוּן לְרִבִּי מֵאִיר. הָא קִיבְרֵיהּ דְּרַבָּךְ אַייְקַד. נְפַק בָּעֵי מְבַקַּרְתֵּיהּ. וְאַשְׁכְּחֵיהּ אַייְקַד. מָה עֲבַד. נְסַב גּוֹלְתֵיהּ וּפְרָסֵיהּ עֲלֵיהּ. אָמַר. לִינִי | הַלַּיְלָה וגו׳. לִינִי בָעוֹלָם הַזֶּה שֶׁדּוֹמֶה לַלַּיְלָה וְהָיָה בַבֹּקֶר. זֶה הָעוֹלָם הַבָּא שֶׁכֻּלּוֹ בּוֹקֶר. אִם־יִגְאָלֵךְ טוֹב יִגְאָל. זֶה הַקָּדוֹשׁ בָּרוּךְ הוּא שֶׁהוּא טוֹב. דִּכְתִיב בֵּיהּ טוֹב־י״י לַכֹּל וְרַחֲמָיו עַל־כָּל־מַעֲשָׂיו: וְאִם־לֹא יַחְפֹּץ לְגָאֳלֵךְ וּגְאַלְתִּיךְ אָנֹכִי חַי־י״י. וְאִיטְפֵיַית. אָמְרוּן לְרִבִּי מֵאִיר. אִין אָמְרוּן לָךְ בְּהַהוּא עָלְמָא. לְמַאן אַתְּ בָּעֵי מְבַקְּרָה. לְאָבוּךְ אוֹ לְרַבָּךְ. אֲמַר לוֹן. אֲנָא מְקָרֵב לְרִבִּי קַדְמַיי וּבָתַר כֵּן לְאַבָּא. אָמְרִין לֵיהּ. וּשְׁמָעִין לָךְ. אֲמַר לוֹן. וְלֹא כֵן תְּנֵינָן. מַצִּילִין תִּיק הַסֵּפֶר עִם הַסֵּפֶר, תִּיק תְּפִלִּין עִם הַתְּפִלִּין, מַצִּילִין לֶאֱלִישָׁע אַחֵר בִּזְכוּת תּוֹרָתוֹ. לְאַחַר יָמִים הָלְכוּ בְנוֹתָיו לִיטּוֹל צְדָקָה מֵרַבִּי. גָּזַר רַבִּי וְאָמַר. אַל־יְהִי־לוֹ מֹשֵׁךְ חָסֶד וְאַל־יְהִי חוֹנֵן לִיתוֹמָיו: אָמְרוּ לוֹ. רַבִּי. אַל תַּבֵּט בְּמַעֲשָׂיו. הַבֵּט בְּתוֹרָתוֹ. בְּאוֹתָהּ שָׁעָה בָּכָה רִבִּי וְכָזַר עֲלֵיהֶן שֶׁיִּתְפַּרְנְסוּ. אָמַר. מַה זֶּה שֶׁיָּגַע בַּתּוֹרָה שֶׁלֹּא לְשֵׁם שָׁמַיִם רְאוּ מַה הֶעֱמִיד. מִי שֶׁהוּא יָגֵעַ בַּתּוֹרָה לִשְׁמָהּ עַל אַחַת כַּמָּה וְכַמָּה.

[56]Rebbi Meïr was sitting and preaching in the House of Study of Tiberias when his teacher Elisha passed by riding on a horse on the Sabbath. They came and told him, your teacher is outside. He stopped his sermon and went out to him. He asked him, what did you preach today? He told him, *and the Eternal blessed the end*[57] etc. He asked him, what did you explain about this? He answered him, *and the Eternal added double all that Job had owned*[58]; that he doubled his money. He said, woe for those who are lost and not found,

your teacher Aqiba did not preach this but, *the Eternal blessed the end of Job from his beginning*, by the merit of commandments and good works which were in his hand from his beginning. He asked him, and what did you preach further? He told him, *the end of a matter is better than the beginning*[59]. He asked him, what did you explain about this? For example, a man who had children in his youth but they died, and in his old age they lived; that is *the end of a matter is better than the beginning*. For example, a man who traded in his youth and lost, and in his old age and gained; that is *the end of a matter is better than the beginning*. For example, a man who studied Torah in his youth and forgot, in his old age he remembered; that is *the end of a matter is better than the beginning*. He said, woe for those who are lost and not found, your teacher Aqiba did not preach this but, *the end of a matter is good from the beginning,* in case it is good from the start, and this applies to me. My father Abuya was one of the leading Jerusalemites. On the day he came to circumcise me he invited all the leading Jerusalemites and sat them in one room, and Rebbi Eliezer and Rebbi Joshua in another room[60]. After they ate and drank they started to clap with their hands and dance. Rebbi Eliezer and Rebbi Joshua said, while they are occupied in theirs let us be occupied with ours. They sat occupied with words of the Torah, from the Torah to Prophets, from Prophets to Hagiographs. Fire descended from Heaven and surrounded them. Abuya told them, my teachers! Why do you come to burn down my house? They told him, Heaven forbid! But we were sitting reviewing the words of the Torah, from the Torah to Prophets, from Prophets to Hagiographs, and the words were joyful as at their giving on Sinai. And was the main giving on Sinai not in fire? *And the Mountain burns in the fire up to the heart of Heaven*[61]. My father Abuya told them, my teachers! If that is the power of Torah, if this son of mine survives I dedicate him to Torah. Because his intent was not for Heaven, it did not succeed with this man. He asked him, and what did you preach further? He told him, *it cannot be valued by gold or glass*[62]. He asked him, what did you explain about this? He told him, the words of the Torah are as difficult to acquire as golden vessels, and as easy to lose as glass vessels. And like golden and glass vessels when they are broken he can make them vessels as before, also the student of the Sages who forgot his learning can learn it anew. He said to him, this is enough, Meïr, up to here is the Sabbath domain. He asked him, how do you know? He told him, from the horse's hooves which I continuously counted for 2'000 cubits. He said to him, all that wisdom is in you and you do not repent? He told him, I cannot. He asked him, why? He told him, once I was passing by the Holiest of Holies riding on a horse on the Day of Atonement which fell on a Sabbath and I heard an unembodied voice coming from the Holiest of Holies, saying, *return, erring children*[63], except for Elisha ben Abuya who knew My power and rebelled against Me. And all that came to him because he was sitting memorizing in the valley of Genezareth and saw a man climbing to the top of a date palm taking the mother with the chicks and descending safely. The next day he saw another man climbing to the top of a date palm, taking the chicks and sending away the mother. When climbing down he was bitten by a snake, and he died. He said, it is written[64], *sending away you shall send the mother, but the chicks you may take for yourself, so it will be good for you and prolong your days.* Where is the good for this one? Where is the prolongation of days of this one? He did not know that Rebbi Jacob had explained it preceding him[65], *so it will be good for you* in the future world which is all good, *and prolong your days*, in the future which is all long. But some are saying, because he saw the tongue of Rebbi Jehudah the baker in the mouth of a dog, oozing blood. He said, is this the Torah and this is its reward? This is the tongue which was delivering the words of the Torah correctly; this is the tongue which occupied itself with Torah all its days; [is this the Torah and this is its reward?] It appears that there is no reward and no resurrection of the dead. But some are saying, when his mother was pregnant with him she passed by pagan temples and smelled of this kind. And this smell was bubbling in her body like the poison of a viper. Later Elisha fell sick. They came and informed Rebbi Meïr, your teacher is sick. He went to visit him and found him sick. He asked him, are you not repenting? He asked, and if one repents, is one accepted? He told him, is it not written, *man shall repent up to extinction*[66], one receives up to the extinction of the breath. At that moment Elisha cried, passed away, and died. Rebbi Meïr was happy internally and said, it seems that my teacher passed away repentant. After they buried him, fire descended from Heaven and burned his grave. They came and informed Rebbi Meïr, your teacher's grave is on fire. He went to visit it and found it burning. What did he do? He took his kaftan and spread it over it. He said, *stay for the night*[67], etc. Stay for this world which compares to the night, *and it will be in the morning,* this is the Future World which is all morning, *if the Good One will redeem,* this is the Holy One, praise to Him, who is Good, as it is written[68], *the Eternal is good to all, and His mercies are on all His creatures. And if He does not want to redeem you I shall redeem you, living is the Eternal*[67], and it was extinguished. They asked Rebbi Meïr, if they ask you in that World, whom do you want to visit, your father or your teacher? He told them, I shall visit my teacher first and afterwards my father. They said, will they listen to you? He told them, did we not state[69], "one saves the case of a scroll with the scroll, and the case of phylacteries with the phylacteries"? One saves Elisha Aḥer by the merit of his Torah. Later his daughters went to take charity from Rebbi. Rebbi decided and said, *nobody shall show him grace nor be friendly to his orphans*[70]. They told him, Rebbi. Do not look at his deeds, do look at his Torah. At this moment Rebbi cried and decided for them that they be provided for[71]. He said, if this one who toiled in Torah not for Heaven's sake, see what he produced[72]; one who toils in the Torah for itself not so much more?

56 The legend of Aḥer is also found in *Ruth rabba* 6(6), *Eccl. rabba* 7(18); partially Babli 15a/b. Note that Aḥer's birth is dated both to Jerusalem before the first war against the Roman as also to the ascendancy of RR. Eliezer and Joshua after the death of Rabban Joḥanan ben Zakkai about 80CE. His apostasy is dated to the Hadrianic persecutions after 130, and his unmarried daughters appear before Rebbi not before 180.

57 *Job* 42:12.

58 *Job* 42:10.

59 *Eccl.* 7:8.

60 Cf. Note 56.

61 *Deut.* 4:11.

62 *Job* 28:17.

63 *Jer.* 3:14,22.

64 *Deut.* 22:7.

65 Tosephta *Hulin* 10:16.

66 *Ps.* 90:3.

67 *Ruth* 3:13.

68 *Ps.* 145:9.

69 Mishnah *Šabbat* 16:2.

70 *Ps.* 109:12.

71 This usually means to be given a dowry for a decent marriage.

72 He raised a good Jewish family.

(77c line 18) רִבִּי לְעָזָר בְּשֵׁם בַּר סִירָא. פְּלִיאָה מִמְּךָ מַה תֵּדַע. עֲמוּקָה מִשְּׁאוֹל מַה תַחְקוֹר. בְּמַה שֶׁהוּרְשֵׁיתָה הִתְבּוֹנֵן. אֵין לְךָ עֵסֶק בַּנִּסְתָּרוֹת. רַב אָמַר תֵּאָלַמְנָה שִׂפְתֵי שָׁקֶר. יִתְחָרְשׁוּ יִתְפָּרְכָוּ יִשְׁתַּתְּקוּן. יִתְחָרְשׁוּ. כְּמָה דַתְּ אָמַר וַיֹּאמֶר י'י אֵלָיו מִי שָׂם פֶּה וגו'. יִתְפָּרְכָו. כְּמָה דַתְּ אָמַר וְהִנֵּה אֲנַחְנוּ מְאַלְּמִים אֲלֻמִּים. יִשְׁתַּתְּקוּן. כִּשְׁמוּעוֹ. הַדּוֹבְרוֹת עַל־צַדִּיק עָתָק. הַדּוֹבְרוֹת עַל צַדִּיקוֹ שֶׁלְעוֹלָם דְּבָרִים שֶׁהֶעֱתִיק מִבְּרִיוֹתָיו. בְּגַאֲוָה וָבוּז. זֶה שֶׁהוּא מִתְגָּאֶה לוֹמַר. אֲנִי דוֹרֵשׁ בְּמַעֲשֵׂה בְרֵאשִׁית. סָבוּר שֶׁהוּא כִמְגָאֶה. וְאֵינוֹ אֶלָּא כִמְבַזֶּה.

Rebbi Eleazar in the name of Siracides: *What is beyond you do not have to know, what is deeper than the abyss do not investigate. Ponder what is permitted to you; you have no concern with hidden things*[73]. [74]Rav said, *may lying lips be* אלם[75]: may they become dumb, be rubbed out, silenced. May they become dumb, as you are saying, *the Eternal said to him, Who formed a mouth*[76] etc. May they be rubbed out, as you are saying, *here we were tying sheaves*[77]. May they be silenced, as it is understood. *Which talk boasting about a just one*[74], who talk about the Universal Just One in matters which He hid from His creatures. *With haughtiness and contempt*[75], that is he who is haughty to say, I am investigating the Creation. He feels like haughty but only is insulting.

73 *Siracides* 3:21-22. Babli 13a.
74 For the following, including the next paragraph, cf. *Gen. rabba* 1(7).
75 *Ps.* 31:19.

76 *Ex.* 4:11, mentioning deafness and dumbness.
77 *Gen.* 37:7. Reading the word for "sheaf" as "assembly of single stalks".

(77c line 26) אָמַר רִבִּי יוֹסֵי בֶּן חֲנִינָה. הַמִּתְכַּבֵּד בְּקָלוֹן חֲבֵירוֹ אֵין לוֹ חֵלֶק לָעוֹלָם הַבָּא. הַמִּתְכַּבֵּד בִּכְבוֹד חַי הָעוֹלָמִים לֹא כָל־שֶׁכֵּן. מַה כְתִיב בַּתְרֵיהּ. מָה רַב טוּבְךָ אֲשֶׁר־צָפַנְתָּ לִּירֵאֶיךָ. אַל יְהִי לוֹ בְּמָה רַב טוּבְךָ. אָמַר רִבִּי לֵוִי. כָּתוּב כְּבוֹד אֱלֹהִים הַסְתֵּר דָּבָר וגו'. כְּבֹד אֱלֹהִים הַסְתֵּר דָּבָר עַד שֶׁלֹּא נִבְרָא הָעוֹלָם. כְּבוֹד מְלָכִים חֲקוֹר דָּבָר. מִשֶּׁנִּבְרָא הָעוֹלָם. אָמַר רִבִּי לֵוִי. הֲנֹאת יְדַעְתָּ מִנִּי־עַד. אֲבָל אַתְּ מִנִּי שִׂים אָדָם עֲלֵי־אָרֶץ.

Rebbi Yose ben Ḥanina said, one who aggrandizes himself by the disgrace of another person has no part in the Future World. He who aggrandizes himself by the glory of the Universal Living not so much more? What is written afterwards[78]? *How great is the good which You hid for those who fear You.* He may not have part in the great good. Rebbi Levi said, it is written[79], *the glory of God is hiding things,* etc. *The glory of God is hiding things*, before the world was created; *the glory of kings is investigating things,* after the world was created. Rebbi Levi said, *do you know what happened earlier*, but you *since human was put on the earth*[80].

78 *Ps.* 31:21.
79 *Prov.* 25:2.
80 *Job* 20:4.

(77c line 32) רִבִּי יוֹנָה [בְשֵׁם] רִבִּי בָא. כָּתוּב כִּי שְׁאַל־נָא לְיָמִים רִאשׁוֹנִים אֲשֶׁר־הָיוּ לְפָנֶיךָ. יָכוֹל קוֹדֶם לְמַעֲשֵׂה בְרֵאשִׁית. תַּלְמוּד לוֹמַר לְמִן־הַיּוֹם אֲשֶׁר בָּרָא אֱלֹהִים | אָדָם עַל־הָאָרֶץ. יָכוֹל מִשִּׁישִׁי וָאֵילֵךְ. תַּלְמוּד לוֹמַר רִאשׁוֹנִים. אַחַר שֶׁרִיבָּה הַכָּתוּב מִיעֵט. הֲרֵי אָנוּ לְמֵידִין מִשִּׁישִׁי. מַה שִּׁישִׁי מְיוּחָד שֶׁהוּא מִשֵּׁשֶׁת יְמֵי בְרֵאשִׁית. אַף אַתְּ לֹא תְהֵא מֵבִיא לִי אֶלָּא אֶת שֶׁהוּא כַיּוֹצֵא בַשִּׁישִׁי. יָכוֹל לֵידַע מַה לְמַעֲלָה מִן הַשָּׁמַיִם וּמַה לְמַטָּה מִן הַתְּהוֹם. תַּלְמוּד לוֹמַר וּלְמִקְצֵה הַשָּׁמַיִם וְעַד־קְצֵה הַשָּׁמָיִם. אֶלָּא עַד שֶׁלֹּא נִבְרָא הָעוֹלָם אַתְּ דּוֹרֵשׁ וְלִיבָּךְ מַסְכִּים. מִשֶּׁנִּבְרָא הָעוֹלָם אַתְּ הוֹלֵךְ וְקוֹלָךְ הוֹלֵךְ מִסּוֹף הָעוֹלָם וְעַד סוֹפוֹ. תַּנֵּי בַּר קַפָּרָא. וּלְמִן הַיּוֹם. אַתְיָא דְּרִבִּי יוּדָה בַּר פָּזִי כְהָדָא דְבַר קַפָּרָא. וּמַה דְּתַנֵּי רִבִּי חִיָּיה כְּהָדָא דְרִבִּי בָא.

Rebbi Jonah [in the name of] Rebbi Abba: It is written[81], *but ask the first days which were before you*, I could think before the Creation. The verse says, *from the day that God created Man on the Earth*. I could think starting with the Sixth Day, the verse says, the first. After the verse added, it subtracted. Therefore we infer from the Sixth. Since the Sixth is particular that it is one of the Six Days of Creation, also you may not bring to me only ones similar to the Sixth. I could think, to know what is higher than heaven and lower than the abyss, the verse says, *from end of heaven to end of heaven*. But before the world was created you may investigate privately; after the world was created your voice may go from one end of the world to the other end[82]. Bar Qappara stated, "and from the day." It comes that Rebbi Jehudah bar Pazi[9] parallels Bar Qappara, and what Rebbi Ḥiyya stated[83] parallels Rebbi Abba.

81 *Deut.* 4:32.
82 Meaning that one is permitted to publicly preach about this subject anywhere.
83 Tosephta 2:7, Babli 11b; *Gen. rabba* 1(13).

(77c line 41) רִבִּי יוֹנָה בְּשֵׁם רִבִּי לֵוִי. בְּבֵי"ת נִבְרָא הָעוֹלָם. מַה בֵּי"ת סָתוּם מִכָּל־צְדָדָיו וּפָתוּחַ מִצַּד אֶחָד. כָּךְ אֵין לָךְ רְשׁוּת לִדְרוֹשׁ מַה לְמַעֲלָן וּמַה לְמַטָּן מַה לְפָנִים וּמַה לְאָחוֹר. אֶלָּא מִיּוֹם שֶׁנִּבְרָא הָעוֹלָם וָלָבָא. אוֹמְרִים לְבֵי"ת. מִי בְרָאָךְ. וְהוּא מַרְאֶה לָהֶן בִּנְקוּדָה וְאוֹמֵר. זֶה שֶׁלְּמַעְלָן. וּמַה שְׁמוֹ. וְהוּא מַרְאֶה לָהֶן בִּנְקוּדָה וְאוֹמֵר יי שְׁמוֹ. אָדוֹן שְׁמוֹ. דָּבָר אַחֵר. וְלָמָּה

בְּבֵי"ת. שֶׁהוּא בְּלָשׁוֹן בְּרָכָה. וְלֹא בְאָלֶף. שֶׁהוּא לָשׁוֹן אֲרִירָה. אָמַר הַקָּדוֹשׁ בָּרוּךְ הוּא. אֵינִי בוֹרֵא אֶת עוֹלָמִי אֶלָּא בְבֵי"ת. שֶׁלֹּא יְהוּא כָל־בָּאֵי עוֹלָם אוֹמְרִין. הֵיאַךְ הָעוֹלָם יָכוֹל לַעֲמוֹד. וְנִבְרָא בְלָשׁוֹן אֲרִירָה. אֶלָּא הֲרֵינִי בוֹרֵא אֶת עוֹלָמִי בְּבֵי"ת בְּלָשׁוֹן בְּרָכָה. וְאוּלַי יַעֲמוֹד.

רִבִּי אַבָּהוּ בְשֵׁם רִבִּי יוֹחָנָן. בִּשְׁתֵּי אוֹתִיּוֹת נִבְרְאוּ שְׁתֵּי עוֹלָמוֹת. הָעוֹלָם הַזֶּה וְהָעוֹלָם הַבָּא [אֶחָד בְּהֵ"א וְאֶחָד בְּיוּ"ד.] מַה טַּעַם. כִּי בְּיָהּ יי צוּר עוֹלָמִים׃ וְאֵין אָנוּ יוֹדְעִין אִי זֶה נִבְרָא בְהֵ"א וְאִי זֶה מֵהֶם נִבְרָא בְיוּ"ד. אֶלָּא מִן מַה דִכְתִיב אֵלֶּה תוֹלְדוֹת הַשָּׁמַיִם וְהָאָרֶץ בְּהִבָּרְאָם. בְּהֵ"א בְרָאָם. הֱוֵי הָעוֹלָם הַזֶּה נִבְרָא בְהֵ"א. וְהָעוֹלָם הַבָּא נִבְרָא בְיוּ"ד. מָה הֵ"ה (חָסֵר) [פָּתוּחַ] מִלְּמַטָּן. רֶמֶז לְכָל־בָּאֵי עוֹלָם שֶׁהֵן יוֹרְדִין לִשְׁאוֹל. מַה הֵ"א יֵשׁ לוֹ נְקוּדָה מִלְמַעְלָן. מְשָׁעָה שֶׁהֵן יוֹרְדִין הֵן עוֹלִין. מַה הֵ"א פָּתוּחַ מִכָּל־צַד. כָּךְ פּוֹתֵחַ פֶּתַח לְכָל־בַּעֲלֵי תְשׁוּבָה. מַה יוּ"ד כָּפוּף כָּךְ יִהְיוּ כָל־בָּאֵי עוֹלָם כְּפוּפִין. וְנֶהֶפְכוּ כָל־פָּנִים לְיֵרָקוֹן׃ כֵּיוָן שֶׁרָאָה דָוִד כָּךְ הִתְחִיל לְקַלֵּס בִּשְׁתֵּי אוֹתִיּוֹת. הַלְלוּ יָהּ | הַלְלוּ עַבְדֵי יי הַלְלוּ אֶת־שֵׁם יי׃

[84]Rebbi Jonah in the name of Rebbi Levi: The world was created with Bet. Since Bet is closed from all sides but open from one side, you have no right to investigate what is above, what is below, what is before, and what is after, except starting with the day the world was created and onwards. One asks the Bet, who created you? It points out to them its point and says, this One above. And what is His Name? It points out to them its back point and says, *the Eternal is His Name*[85], "Master" is His Name. Another explanation. Why by Bet? Because it is an expression of blessing, but not by Alef, which is an expression of accursed. The Holy One, praise to Him, said, I shall only build My world with Bet, so that the creatures should not say, how could the world remain standing if it was created in an expression of accursed. Therefore I shall create it with Bet, and expression of blessing, so it shall have a chance to endure.

[86]Rebbi Abbahu in the name of Rebbi Joḥanan: With two letters two worlds were created, this world and the Future World. [One by He and one by Yud.] What is the reason? *For in Yah, the Eternal is the Rock of Worlds*[87]. However, we did not know which one was created by He and which one by Yud. But from what is written, *these are the outcomes of Heaven and Earth in their being created*[88], He created them by He. This implies that this world was created by He, and the Future World was created by Yud. [89]Since He is (missing) [open] below, it is a hint for all creatures that they will descend to the pit. Since He has a point on top, from the moment they descend they

ascend. Since He is open from all sides, so He opens a door to all who repent. Since Yud is curved, so all creatures should be bent. *All faces turned yellow*[90]. When David saw this, he started to acclaim by two letters, *praise Yah, praise, the servants of the Eternal, praise the Name of the Eternal*[91].

84 *Gen. rabba* 1(14).	88 *Gen.* 2:4.
85 *Ex.* 15:32.	89 Babli *Menahot* 29b.
86 *Gen. rabba* 12(9).	90 *Jer.* 30:6.
87 *Is.* 26:4.	91 *Ps.* 113:1.

(77c line 60) רִבִּי יוּדָן נְשִׂייָא שָׁאַל לְרִבִּי שְׁמוּאֵל בַּר נַחְמָן. מָהוּ דֵין דִּכְתִיב סוֹלוּ לָרוֹכֵב בָּעֲרָבוֹת בְּיָהּ שְׁמוֹ וְעִלְזוּ לְפָנָיו: אָמַר לֵיהּ. אֵין לָךְ כָּל־מָקוֹם וּמָקוֹם שֶׁאֵינוֹ מְמוּנֶּה עַל בָּיהּ שֶׁלּוֹ. וּמִי מְמוּנֶּה עַל בִּיאָה שֶׁבְּכוּלָּם. הַקָּדוֹשׁ בָּרוּךְ הוּא. בְּיָהּ שְׁמוֹ. בִּי־יָהּ שְׁמוֹ. אָמַר לֵיהּ רִבִּי לְעָזָר. רַבָּךְ לָא הֲוָה דָרַשׁ כֵּן. אֶלָּא לְמֶלֶךְ שֶׁבָּנָה פַּלְטִין בְּמָקוֹם בִּיבִים בְּמָקוֹם אַשְׁפּוֹת בְּמָקוֹם סָרִיּוֹת. מִי שֶׁהוּא בָא וְאוֹמֵר. הַפַּלְטִין הַזוֹ בְּמָקוֹם בִּיבִים הוּא. בְּמָקוֹם אַשְׁפּוֹת הוּא. בְּמָקוֹם סָרִיּוֹת הוּא. אֵינוּ פוֹגֵם. בָּךְ מִי שֶׁהוּא אוֹמֵר. כַּתְּחִילָּה הָיָה הָעוֹלָם מַיִם בְּמַיִם. הֲרֵי זֶה פוֹגֵם. לְפַרְדֵּיסוֹ שֶׁלְּמֶלֶךְ וַעֲלִייָה בְנוּיָה עַל גַּבָּיו. עָלָיו לְהָצִיץ. אֲבָל לֹא לִיגַּע.

[92]Rebbi Yudan the Patriarch asked Rebbi Samuel bar Nahman: What means that which is written, *Prepare a way for the rider on clouds, His name YH, and jubilate before Him*[93]. He told him, there is no place which does not have one appointed over its life[94]. And who is appointed over the lives of all? The Holy One, praise to Him. *His name YH*, His name: Βια. Rebbi Eleazar told him, your teacher[95] was not explaining in this way, but {a parable} of a king who built a palace on a place of sewers, a place of dung heaps, a place which stinks. One who comes and says, this palace is at a place of sewers, a place of dung heaps, a place which stinks, does he not detract? So he detracts who says, originally the world was water in water[9]. {A parable} of a king's orchard and an observation deck built on it, to look at it but not to touch[96].

92 *Gen. rabba* 12(9), 1(7). Babli 16a.	96 The orchard is the world, the observation deck is Scripture, which may be enjoyed but may not be used to gain knowledge of the working of the Creation; forbidding Gnosticism.
93 *Ps.* 68:5.	
94 An otherwise undocumented feminine of Greek *m.* βίος "life".	
95 R. Jonathan.	

(77c line 68) בֵּית שַׁמַּי אוֹמְרִים. שָׁמַיִם נִבְרְאוּ תְחִילָּה וְאַחַרְכָּךְ הָאָרֶץ. וּבֵית הִלֵּל אוֹמְרִים. הָאָרֶץ נִבְרֵאת תְּחִילָה וְאַחַרְכָּךְ הַשָּׁמַיִם. אֵילּוּ מְבִיאִין טַעַם לְדִבְרֵיהֶן וְאֵילּוּ מְבִיאִין טַעַם

לְדִבְרֵיהֶן. מַה טַעֲמוֹן דְּבֵית שַׁמַּי. בְּרֵאשִׁית בָּרָא אֱלֹהִים אֵת הַשָּׁמַיִם וְאֵת הָאָרֶץ. לַמֶּלֶךְ שֶׁעָשָׂה כִסֵּא. מִשֶּׁעֲשָׂאוֹ עָשָׂה אֵפִּיפוֹדִין שֶׁלּוֹ. הַשָּׁמַיִם כִּסְאִי וְהָאָרֶץ הֲדוֹם רַגְלָי. מַה טַעֲמוֹן דְּבֵית הִלֵּל. בְּיוֹם עֲשׂוֹת יְיָ אֱלֹהִים אֶרֶץ וְשָׁמָיִם: לַמֶּלֶךְ שֶׁעָשָׂה פָלָטִין. מִשֶּׁבָּנָה אֶת הַתַּחְתּוֹנִים עָשָׂה אֶת הָעֶלְיוֹנִים. אַף־יָדִי יָסְדָה אֶרֶץ וִימִינִי טִפְּחָה שָׁמָיִם. אָמַר רִבִּי יוּדָה בַר פָּזִי. וְדָא מְסַייְעָה לבֵית הִלֵּל. לְפָנִים הָאָרֶץ יָסַדְתָּ וּמַעֲשֵׂה יָדֶיךָ שָׁמָיִם: אָמַר רִבִּי חֲנִינָה. מִמָּקוֹם שֶׁבֵּית שַׁמַּי מְבִיאִין טַעַם לְדִבְרֵיהֶן מִשָּׁם בֵּית הִלֵּל מְסַלְּקִין לוֹן. מַה טַעֲמוֹן דְּבֵית שַׁמַּי. בְּרֵאשִׁית בָּרָא אֱלֹהִים אֵת הַשָּׁמַיִם וְאֵת הָאָרֶץ. מִשָּׁם בֵּית הִלֵּל מְסַלְּקִין לוֹן. וְהָאָרֶץ הָיְתָה. כְּבָר הָיְתָה. רִבִּי יוֹחָנָן בְּשֵׁם חֲכָמִים. אִם לִבְרִיָּיה שָׁמַיִם קָדְמוּ. וְאִם לְשִׁכְלוּל הָאָרֶץ קָדְמָה. אִם לִבְרִיָּיה שָׁמַיִם קָדְמוּ. בְּרֵאשִׁית בָּרָא אֱלֹהִים וגו'. אִם לְשִׁכְלוּל הָאָרֶץ קָדְמָה. בְּיוֹם עֲשׂוֹת יְיָ אֱלֹהִים אֶרֶץ וְשָׁמָיִם: שָׁמַיִם בָּרִאשׁוֹן כְּבֵית שַׁמַּי עָשָׂה שְׁלֹשָׁה יָמִים. וְעָשׂוּ תוֹלְדוֹת רִאשׁוֹן וְשֵׁנִי וּשְׁלִישִׁי. בָּרְבִיעִי יְהִי מְאוֹרוֹת. יָם בַּשֵּׁנִי כְּבֵית שַׁמַּי עָשָׂה שְׁלֹשָׁה יָמִים. וְעָשָׂה תוֹלְדוֹת שֵׁנִי וּשְׁלִישִׁי וּרְבִיעִי. בַּחֲמִישִׁי יִשְׁרְצוּ הַמַּיִם. אֶרֶץ בַּשְּׁלִישִׁי כְּבֵית שַׁמַּי עָשָׂה שְׁלֹשָׁה יָמִים. וְעָשָׂה תוֹלְדוֹת שְׁלִישִׁי וּרְבִיעִי וַחֲמִישִׁי. בַּשִּׁשִּׁי וְתוֹצֵא הָאָרֶץ. אֶרֶץ בָּרִאשׁוֹן כְּבֵית הִלֵּל עָשַׂת שְׁנֵי יָמִים. וְעָשׂוּ תוֹלְדוֹת רִאשׁוֹן וְשֵׁנִי. בַּשְּׁלִישִׁי תַּדְשֵׁא הָאָרֶץ. שָׁמַיִם בַּשֵּׁנִי כְּבֵית הִלֵּל עָשׂוּ שְׁנֵי יָמִים. וְעָשׂוּ תוֹלְדוֹת שֵׁנִי וּשְׁלִישִׁי. בָּרְבִיעִי יְהִי מְאוֹרוֹת. יָם בַּשְּׁלִישִׁי כְּבֵית הִלֵּל עָשָׂה שְׁנֵי יָמִים. וְעָשָׂה תוֹלְדוֹת שְׁלִישִׁי וּרְבִיעִי. בַּחֲמִישִׁי יִשְׁרְצוּ הַמַּיִם. אָמַר רִבִּי שִׁמְעוֹן בֶּן יוֹחַי. תְּמֵיהַּ אֲנִי הֵיאַךְ נֶחְלְקוּ אֲבוֹת הָעוֹלָם עַל בְּרִיַּית הָעוֹלָם. שֶׁאֲנִי אוֹמֵר. שָׁמַיִם וָאָרֶץ לֹא נִבְרְאוּ אֶלָּא כְּלַפָּס הַזֶּה וּכְכִיסּוּיֵהּ. מַה טַעַם. אַף־יָדִי יָסְדָה אֶרֶץ וִימִינִי טִפְּחָה שָׁמָיִם. אָמַר רִבִּי לָעֲזָר בֵּירִבִּי שִׁמְעוֹן. אִם כְּדַעַת הַזוּ שֶׁאָמַר אַבָּא פְּעָמִים שֶׁהוּא מַקְדִּים שָׁמַיִם לָאָרֶץ. פְּעָמִים שֶׁהוּא מַקְדִּים אֶרֶץ לַשָּׁמַיִם. אֶלָּא מְלַמֵּד שֶׁשְּׁנֵיהֶן שְׁקוּלִים זֶה בָּזֶה.

[97]The House of Shammai are saying, heaven was created first and afterwards earth. But the House of Hillel are saying, earth was created first and afterwards heaven. These are bringing proof for their assertion, and those are bringing proof for their assertion. What is the reason of the House of Shammai? *In the Beginning God created heaven and earth*[98]. {A parable} of a king who made a chair. After he had made it he made its footstool[99]: *the Heavens are My throne and the Earth My footstool*[100]. What is the reason of the House of Hillel? *On the day of the Eternal's, God's, making of earth and heaven*[101] {A parable} of a king who made a palace. After he built the foundations he built the upper structure: *also My left hand founded the Earth and My right hand tended the Heavens*[102]. Rebbi Jehudah bar Pazi said, also the following supports the House of Hillel: *in earlier times You founded the Earth, and the Heavens are the work of Your hands*[103]. Rebbi Hanina said,

from the place from where the House of Shammai prove their assertion, from there the House of Hillel remove them. What is the reason of the House of Shammai? *In the Beginning God created heaven and earth.* From there the House of Hillel remove them: *and the earth was*[104], it already was. Rebbi Johanan in the name of the Sages: As for creation, the heaven preceded. As for perfecting, the earth preceded. As for creation, the heaven preceded, *in the Beginning God created.* As for perfecting, the earth preceded, *on the day of the Eternal's, God's, making of earth and heaven.* According to the House of Shammai, the heaven after the First waited three days, First, Second, Third, to have offspring. On the Fourth, *there shall be lights*[105]. According to the House of Shammai, the sea after the Second waited three days, Second, Third, Fourth, to have offspring. On the Fifth, *the waters shall teem*[106]. According to the House of Shammai, the earth after the Third waited three days, Third, Fourth, Fifth, to have offspring. On the Sixth, *the earth shall produce*[107]. According to the House of Hillel, the earth after the First waited two days, First and Second, to have offspring. On the Third, *the earth shall be covered with grass.* According to the House of Hillel, the sea after the Third waited two days, Third and Fourth, to have offspring. On the Fifth, *the waters shall teem.* Rebbi Simeon ben Yoḥai said, I am wondering how the fathers of the world could disagree about the creation of the world. Heaven and earth were only created like a pan[108] and its cover. What is the reason? *Also My left hand founded the Earth and My right hand tended the Heavens*[109]. Rebbi Eleazar ben Rebbi Simeon said, following this, my father's opinion, sometimes heaven precedes earth, sometimes earth precedes heaven, which teaches that they are equivalent one to another.

97 *Gen. rabba* 1(21), *Lev. rabba* 36(1), *Midrash Samuel* 5[1]. The Midrashim seem to be the original source since they apply R. Eleazar ben R. Simeon's final statement to other pairs of notions.
98 *Gen.* 1:1.
99 Greek 'ὑποπόδιον.
100 *Is.* 66:1.
101 *Gen.* 2:4.
102 *Is.* 48:13.
103 *Ps.* 102:26.
104 *Gen.* 1:2.
105 *Gen.* 1:14.
106 *Gen.* 1:20.
107 *Gen.* 1:24.
108 Greek λοπάς.
109 The argument is from the end of the verse, not quoted: *I am calling to them, they*

shall stand together.

(fol. 76d) **משנה ב**: יוֹסֵי בֶּן יוֹעֶזֶר אוֹמֵר שֶׁלֹּא לִסְמוֹךְ יוֹסֵי בֶּן יוֹחָנָן אוֹמֵר לִסְמוֹךְ. יְהוֹשֻׁעַ בֶּן פְּרַחְיָה אוֹמֵר שֶׁלֹּא לִסְמוֹךְ מַתַּי הָאַרְבֵּלִי אוֹמֵר לִסְמוֹךְ. יְהוּדָה בֶּן טַבַּאי אוֹמֵר שֶׁלֹּא לִסְמוֹךְ שִׁמְעוֹן בֶּן שָׁטָח אוֹמֵר לִסְמוֹךְ. שְׁמַעְיָה אוֹמֵר לִסְמוֹךְ אַבְטַלְיוֹן אוֹמֵר שֶׁלֹּא לִסְמוֹךְ. הִלֵּל וּמְנַחֵם לֹא נֶחֱלָקוּ. יָצָא מְנַחֵם נִכְנַס שַׁמַּאי. הִלֵּל אוֹמֵר לִסְמוֹךְ וְשַׁמַּאי אוֹמֵר שֶׁלֹּא לִסְמוֹךְ. הָרִאשׁוֹנִים הָיוּ נְשִׂיאִים וְהַשְּׁנִיִּים אֲבוֹת בֵּית דִּין:

Mishnah 2: Yose ben Yoezer[110] says not to lean on[111], Yose ben Johanan says to lean on. Joshua ben Peraḥia says not to lean on, Matthew from Arbel says to lean on. Jehudah ben Tabbai says not to lean on, Simeon ben Shetaḥ says to lean on. Shemaiah says to lean on, Avtalion says not to lean on. Hillel and Menaḥem did not disagree. Menaḥem left and Shammai entered; Hillel says to lean on, Shammai says not to lean on. The first ones were Patriarchs, the second Presidents of the Court.

110 The pairs enumerated here were the joint heads of the Pharisaic leadership from Hasmonean to Herodian times, as enumerated in *Avot*, Chapter 1.

111 The verse requires that the owner of a well-being sacrifice lean with his hands on the animal before it is slaughtered (*Lev.* 3:2,7,13), but there is no indication that omission of the ceremony would in any way disqualify the sacrifice. By tradition, the owner has to push down on the animal with all his force. Doing this on a holiday is at least rabbinically forbidden as illegitimate use of an animal. Now it is explained in *Eruvin* Chapter 10 that most, but not all, rabbinic restrictions on Sabbath and holidays were disregarded in the Temple. The disagreement is whether the prohibition to push down on an animal is observed in the Temple for holiday sacrifices offered on a holiday or not.

(77d line 21) **הלכה ב**: בָּרִאשׁוֹנָה לֹא הָיְתָה מַחֲלוֹקֶת בְּיִשְׂרָאֵל אֶלָּא עַל הַסְּמִיכָה בִּלְבַד. וְעָמְדוּ שַׁמַּאי וְהִלֵּל וְעָשׂוּ אוֹתָן אַרְבַּע. מִשֶּׁרַבּוּ תַּלְמִידֵי בֵית שַׁמַּי וְתַלְמִידֵי בֵית הִלֵּל וְלֹא שִׁימְּשׁוּ אֶת רַבֵּיהֶן כָּל־צָרְכָּן. וְרַבּוּ הַמַּחֲלוֹקוֹת בְּיִשְׂרָאֵל וְנֶחְלְקוּ לִשְׁתֵּי כִיתּוֹת. אֵילּוּ מְטַמְּאִין וְאֵילּוּ מְטַהֲרִין. וְעוֹד אֵינָהּ עֲתִידָה לַחֲזוֹר לִמְקוֹמָהּ עַד שֶׁיָּבוֹא בֶן דָּוִד.

רִבִּי חִייָה בְשֵׁם רִבִּי יוֹחָנָן. לֹא תְהֵא שְׁבוּת קַלָּה בְעֵינֶיךָ. שֶׁהֲרֵי סְמִיכָה אֵינָהּ אֶלָּא רְשׁוּת וְנֶחְלְקוּ עָלֶיהָ אֲבוֹת הָעוֹלָם. אָמַר רִבִּי יוֹסֵה. זֹאת אוֹמֶרֶת שֶׁאָדָם צָרִיךְ לִכְבּוֹשׁ אֶת כּוּבְדוֹ. דְּלָא כֵן מַה אֲנַן אֲמְרִין. אָסוּר לִיגַּע בַּבְּהֵמָה בְיוֹם טוֹב.

Halakhah 2: Originally the only disagreement in Israel was about leaning on. Then rose Hillel and Shammai and made it four[112]. After the students of the House of Shammai and students of the House of Hillel increased who did not sufficiently serve their teachers, disagreements increased in Israel and they were split into two sects; these declare impure and those declare pure, and the prior state will not be reconstituted until the arrival of David's son[113].

[114]Rebbi Ḥiyya in the name of Rebbi Joḥanan: Rabbinic Sabbath prohibitions shall not be unimportant in your eyes, since leaning on is only a meritorious act and the fathers of the world disagreed about it. Rebbi Yose said, this implies that one has to press down with all his weight. If it were not so we would have to say that it is forbidden to touch an animal on the Sabbath.

112 The disagreement noted here and those reported in Mishnaiot *Idiut* 1-3.

113 The Messiah.

114 Babli 16b.

(77d line 29) הִלֵּל וּמְנַחֵם לֹא נֶחֱלָקוּ. יָצָא מְנַחֵם נִכְנַס שַׁמַּי. לְאֵיכָן יָצָא. יֵשׁ אוֹמְרִים. מִמִּידָּה לְמִידָּה יָצָא. וְיֵשׁ אוֹמְרִים. כְּנֶגֶד פָּנָיו יָצָא. הוּא וּשְׁמוֹנִים זוּג שֶׁלְּתַלְמִידֵי חֲכָמִים מְלוּבָּשִׁין תִּירְקֵי זָהָב. שֶׁהִשְׁחִירוּ פְנֵיהֶן כְּשׁוּלֵי קְדֵירָה. שֶׁאָמְרוּ לָהֶן. כִּתְבוּ עַל קֶרֶן הַשּׁוֹר שֶׁאֵין לָכֶם חֵלֶק בֵּאלֹהֵי יִשְׂרָאֵל.

"Hillel and Menaḥem did not disagree. Menaḥem left and Shammai entered." Where did he leave to? Some are saying, from behavior he left to behavior[115]. But some are saying, he left against his face[116], he and eighty pairs of students of the Sages, wearing golden *tirqe*[117], whose faces became black like the rim of a pot[118] when they were told, write on a bull's horn that you have no part in the God of Israel.

115 In the Babli 16b: He left to bad behavior, which certainly means that he rejected Pharisaic Judaism but leaves unanswered the question whether he became an apostate or an adherent of a competing sect.

116 In the Babli: He left to work for the king (Herod.)

117 A word of unknown meaning and etymology. In the Babli: silk garments, not appropriate for Pharisaic Sages.

118 A clay pot.

(77d line 33) אֲנָן תַּנִּינָן. יְהוּדָה בֶּן טַבַּאי נָשִׂיא. וְשִׁמְעוֹן בֶּן שָׁטַח אַב בֵּית דִּין. אִית תַּנָּיֵי תַנֵּי וּמַחְלְףּ. מָאן דְּאָמַר. יְהוּדָה בֶּן טַבַּאי נָשִׂיא. עוֹבְדָא דַאֲלֶכְּסַנְדְּרִיאָה מְסַיֵּיעַ לֵיהּ. יְהוּדָה בֶּן טַבַּאי [הֲוָון בְּנֵי יְרוּשְׁלַם] בָּעוּן מַמְנִיתֵיהּ נָשִׂיא בִּירוּשָׁלַם. עָרַק וַאֲזַל לֵיהּ לַאֲלֶכְּסַנְדְּרִיאָה. וְהָיוּ

בְּנֵי יְרוּשָׁלַם כּוֹתְבִין. מִירוּשָׁלַם הַגְּדוֹלָה לְאָלֶכְּסַנְדְּרִיאָה הַקְּטַנָּה. עַד מָתַי אָרוּסִי יוֹשֵׁב אֶצְלְכֶם וַאֲנִי יוֹשֶׁבֶת עֲגוּמָה עָלָיו. פְּרֵישׁ מַיְתֵי גּוֹ אִילְפָא. אָמַר. דְּכוּרָה מָרְתָא דְּבַיְתָא דְּקִבַּלְתּוּן מַה הֲוַוָת חֲסֵירָה. אָמַר לֵיהּ חַד מִן תַּלְמִידוֹי. רַבִּי. עֵינָהּ הֲוַות שְׁבָרָה. אָמַר לֵיהּ. הָא תַּרְתֵּי גַּבָּךְ. חֲדָא דַּחֲשַׁדְתָּנִי. וַחֲדָא דְּאִיסְתַּכַּלְתְּ בָּהּ. מָה אֲמָרִית. יָאיָיא בְּרֵיוָא. לָא אֲמָרִית וְאֶלָּא בְּעוֹבְדָהּ. וְכָעַס עֲלוֹי וְאָזַל.

[119]We have stated: Jehudah ben Ṭabbai was Patriarch, and Simeon ben Shetaḥ President of the Court; there are Tannaim who switch. What happened in Alexandria supports him who said, Jehudah ben Ṭabbai was Patriarch. [The people of Jerusalem] wanted to appoint him Patriarch in Jerusalem. The people from Jerusalem did write: From the great Jerusalem to the small Alexandria: How long still will my betrothed live in your midst and I am sitting sorrowful about him? He took leave and started on a ship. He said, I remember the lady of the house who received us; what is she missing? One of his students told him, her eye is damaged. He told him, you have sinned twice; first that you suspected me, and second that you looked at her. Did I say that she was beautiful in looks? I only said that about her deeds. He was taking offense and he left[120].

119 This is a version of the text in *Sanhedrin* 6:5 (Notes 77 - 82), mainly following the Genizah text there.

120 He died.

(77d line 42) מָאן דְּאָמַר. שִׁמְעוֹן בֶּן שֶׁטַח נָשִׂיא. עוֹבְדָא דְּאַשְׁקְלוֹן מְסַיֵּיעַ לֵיהּ. תְּרֵין חֲסִידִין הֲווֹן בְּאַשְׁקְלוֹן אָכְלִין כְּחֲדָא וְשָׁתֵי כְּחֲדָא וְלָעֵי בְּאוֹרָיְיתָא כְּחֲדָא. דְּמִךְ חַד מִינְהוֹן וְלָא אִיתְגְּמַל לֵיהּ חֶסֶד. מִית בְּרֵיהּ דִּמְעָיְנוּ מוּכָס וּבְטֵלַת כָּל־מְדִינָתָא מִגְמוֹל לֵיהּ חֶסֶד. שׁוֹרֵי הַהוּא חֲסִידָא מִצְטַעֵר. אָמַר. וַוי דְּלֵית לְשׂוֹנְאֵיהוֹן דְּיִשְׂרָאֵל כְּלוּם. אִיתְחֲמֵי לֵיהּ בְּחֶלְמָא וַאֲמַר לֵיהּ. לָא תִּיבְזֵי בְּנֵי מָרִיךְ. דֵּין עֲבַד חֲדָא חוֹבָא וַאֲזַל בֵּיהּ. וְדֵין עֲבַד חֲדָא טִיבוּ וַאֲזַל בָּהּ. וּמָה חוֹבָא עֲבַד הַהוּא חֲסִידָא. [חַס] לֵיהּ לָא עֲבַד חוֹבָה מִן יוֹמוֹי. אֶלָּא פַּעַם אַחַת הִקְדִּים תְּפִילִּין שֶׁל רֹאשׁ לִתְפִילִּין שֶׁל יַד. וּמָה טִיבוּ עֲבַד בְּרֵיהּ דִּמְעָיְנוּ מוּכָס. חַס לֵיהּ לָא עֲבַד טִיבוּ מִן יוֹמוֹי. אֶלָּא חַד זְמַן עֲבַד אֲרִסְטוֹן לְבוּלְבָטַיָּיא וְלָא אָתוֹן אָכְלוּנֵיהּ. אָמַר. יֵיכְלוּנֵיהּ מִיסְכֵּינַיָּיא דְּלָא יְטַ[לוּן]. וְאִית דְּאָמְרִין. בְּשׁוּקָא הֲוָה עֲבַר וּנְפַל מִינֵּיהּ חַד עִיגּוּל. וַחֲמָא חַד מִסְכֵּן וּנְסַב לֵיהּ וְלָא אָמַר לֵיהּ כְּלוּם [בְּגִין דְּלָא מְסַמְקֵי אַפּוֹיי]. בָּתַר יוֹמִין חֲמָא הַהוּא חֲסִידָא לְחַסִּידָא חַבְרֵיהּ מְטַיֵּיל גּוֹ גַּנִּין גּוֹ פַּרְדֵּיסִין גּוֹ מַבּוּעִין גּוֹ דְּמַיי. וַחֲמָא לִבְרֵיהּ דִּמְעָיְנוּ מוּכָס לְשׁוֹנוֹ שׁוֹתֵת עַל פִּי הַנָּהָר. בְּעֵי מַמְטֵי מַיָּיא וְלָא מָטֵי. וַחֲמָא לְמִרְיָם בְּרַת עֲלִי בְּצָלִים. רַבִּי לְעָזָר בַּר יוֹסֵה אָמַר. תַּלְיָיא בְּחִיטֵּי בִּיזָיַיא. רַבִּי יוֹסֵי בֶּן חֲנִינָא אָמַר. צִירָא דְּתַרְעָא דְּגִהִנָּם קְבִיעָא בְּאוּדְנָהּ. אָמַר לוֹן. לָמָּה דָא כֵן.

HALAKHAH 2

437

אָמְרִין לֵיהּ. דַּהֲוַת צַיְימָא וּמְפַרְסְמָה. וְאִית דְּאָמְרֵי. דַּהֲוַת צַיְימָא חַד יוֹם וּמְקַזָּה לֵיהּ תְּרֵי. אָמַר לוֹן. עַד אֵימַת הִיא כֵן. אָמְרִי לֵיהּ. עַד דְּיֵיתֵי שִׁמְעוֹן בֶּן שָׁטַח וַאֲנָן מְרִימִין לָהּ מִן גּוֹ אוּדְנָהּ וְקָבְעִין לֵיהּ גּוֹ אוּדְנֵיהּ. [אָמַר לוֹן. וְלָמָּה. אָמְרִי לֵיהּ.] דַּאֲמַר. אֵין אֲנָא מִתְעֲבִיד נָשִׂיָּא אֲנָא מְקַטֵּל חָרָשַׁיָּא. וְהָא אִיתְעֲבִיד נָשִׂיָּא וְלָא קְטַל חָרָשַׁיָּא. וְהָא אִית תְּמָנִין נָשִׁין חָרָשִׁין יְהִיבִין גּוֹ מְעָרָתָא דְּאַשְׁקְלוֹן מְחַבְּלָן עָלְמָא. אֶלָּא אֵיזִיל אֱמוֹר לֵיהּ. אָמַר לוֹן. אֲנָא דָּחִיל דְּהוּא כְּבָר נָשִׂיָּא וְלֵית הוּא מְהֵימְנַתִי. אָמְרִי לֵיהּ. אִי הֵימְנָהּ הָא טַבָאוּת. וְאִין לָא [עֲבִיד הָדֵין סִימָנָהּ קוּמוֹי.] הַב יָדָךְ עַל עֵינָךְ וְאַפְקָהּ וְחַזְרָהּ וְהִיא חֲזָרָה. אֲזַל וְתַנֵּי לֵיהּ עוּבְדָּה. בָּעָא מֵיעֲבַד [סִימָנָא] קוּמוֹי וְלָא שָׁבְקֵיהּ. אֲמַר לֵיהּ. יָדַע אֲנָא דְּאַתְּ גְּבַר חָסִיד. יְתִיר מִן כֵּן אַתְּ יָכִיל עֲבַד. וְלֹא עוֹד אֶלָּא בְּפוּמִי לָא אַמְרִית. בְּלֵיבִּי חֲשָׁבִית. מִיָּד עָמַד שִׁמְעוֹן בֶּן שָׁטַח בְּיוֹם סַגְרִיר וּנְסַב עִמֵּיהּ תּוּמְנִין גּוּבְרִין בְּחִירִין. וִיהַב בִּידֵיהוֹן תּוּמְנֵי לְבוּשִׁין נְקִיִּים וִיבוֹנֵי גּוֹ קִידְרִין חַדְתִּין וְכָפוּנוֹן עַל רֵישֵׁיהוֹן. אָמַר לוֹן. אֵין צְפָרֵית חַד זְמַן לַבְּשׁוּן לְבוּשֵׁיכוֹן. וְאִין צְפָרֵית זְמַן תִּנְיָין עוּלוּן כּוּלְכוֹן כְּחָדָא. וְכֵיוָן דְּאָתוּן עֲלָלִין כָּל־חַד וְחַד מִינְכוֹן יְגוּף חָדָא וִיטַלְטְלִינֵּהּ מִן אַרְעָא. דְּעִיסְקֵיהּ דְּהָדֵין חָרָשָׁא טַלְטְלוּתֵיהּ מִן אַרְעָא לָא יָכִיל עֲבַד כְּלוּם. אֲזַל וְקָם לֵיהּ עַל תַּרְעָא דִּמְעָרַתָא. אֲמַר לֵיהּ. אוּים אוּים. פִּתְחוּן לִי. מִן דִּידְכָן אֲנָא. אָמְרוֹן לֵיהּ. הֵיאַךְ אֲתִית לְהָכָא בַּהֲדֵין יוֹמָא. אֲמַר לוֹן. בֵּינֵי טִיפַּיָּיא הֲוֵינָא מְהַלֵּךְ. אָמְרוֹן לֵיהּ. וּמָה אֲתִיתָא הָכָא מֵיעֲבַד. אֲמַר. מֵילַף וּמֵילְפָא. כָּל־מַטֵּי יַעֲבִיד מַה דְּהוּא חָכָם. וַהֲוַת כָּל־חָדָא מִינְּהוֹן אָמְרָה מַה דְּהִיא אָמְרָה וּמַיְיתְיָא פִּיתָּה. וְחָדָא אָמְרָה מַה דְּהִיא אָמְרָה וּמַיְיתֵי קוּפָד. אָמְרָה מַה דְּהִיא אָמְרָה וּמַיְיתֵי תַבְשִׁילִין. אָמְרָה מַה דְּהִיא אָמְרָה וּמַיְיתֵי חֲמָר. אָמְרוֹן לֵיהּ. אַתְּ מָה אִית בָּךְ עָבַד. אָמַר לוֹן. אִית בִּי צְפַר תְּרֵין צַפְרִין וּמַיְיתֵי לְכוֹן תּוּמָנִין גּוּבְרִין בְּחִירִין. הֲוֵי עִמְּכוֹן חַדֵּי וּמַחְדֵּי לְכוֹן. אָמְרִין לֵיהּ. כֵּן אֲנַן בָּעַי. צְפַר חָדָא זְמַן וְלָבְשׁוּ מָנֵיהוֹן. דִּצְפַר זְמַן תִּנְיָין וְעָלוּן כּוּלְּהוֹן כְּחָדָא. אֲמַר. כָּל־דְּמַטֵּי יַחְכּוֹם זוּגֵיהּ. וְחָעֲנוּנוֹן וְאָזְלוּן וְצָלְבוּנוֹן. הָדָא הִיא דִּתְנֵינָן. מַעֲשֶׂה בְשִׁמְעוֹן בֶּן שָׁטַח שֶׁתָּלָה נָשִׁים בְּאַשְׁקְלוֹן. [אָמְרוּ. שְׁמוֹנִים נָשִׁים תָּלָה. וְאֵין דָּנִין שְׁנַיִם בְּיוֹם אֶחָד. אֶלָּא שֶׁהָיְתָה הַשָּׁעָה צְרִיכָה לְכָךְ.]

[121]What happened in Ascalon supports him who said, Simeon ben Shetaḥ was president. Two pious men were in Ascalon. They ate together, drank together, and studied Torah together. One of them died, and nobody attended his funeral. The son of Ma`yan the publican died; the entire city stopped working to attend his funeral. The other pious man started crying and said woe, do the haters of Israel have no hope? He was shown in a dream that it was said to him, do not denigrate your Master's children. This one committed one sin and died with it, the other one did one good deed and died with it[122]. What sin did this pious man commit? Far be it that he committed a sin, but once he put on his head phylacteries before his arm phylacteries[123]. What good deed did the son of publican Ma`yan do? Far be it that he ever

committed a good deed, but once he prepared a breakfast for the city council but they did not come to eat it. He said, let the poor eat it, so it should not go to waste. Some say, he was walking in the street when a loaf fell down from him[124] and a poor person picked it up. He did not say anything [in order not to embarrass him]. After days this pious man saw his comrade the pious walking in gardens, in orchards, at water sources, and he saw the son of Ma`yan the publican with his tongue out on the river bank trying in vain to reach the water. He also saw Miriam, Onion-leaf's daughter. Rebbi Eleazar bar Yose said, she was hanging on her breast nipples. Rebbi Yose ben Ḥanina said, the hinge of Hell's door was fixed in her ear. He asked them, why? They told him, because she fasted and made herself famous[125]. Some say, she fasted one day and was dissolute two. He asked them for how long is she in this state? They told him, until Simeon ben Shetaḥ comes, when we shall remove it from her ear and put it in his ear. [He asked them, and why?] They told him, because he said, that if I would be elected Patriarch, I would kill sorcerers. But now he was made Patriarch and he did not kill them. In fact, there are eighty women sorcerers in the cave of Ascalon who hurt the world. You shall go and tell him! He told them, I am afraid that since he is Patriarch he will not believe me. They told him, if he will believe you it will be good. In case that he will not believe you, perform a sign in front of him: put your hand on an eye and take it out, put it back and it will be back. He went and told him. He wanted to perform [the miracle] before him, but he told him, I know that you are a pious person; more than that you could do. In fact, I never spoke it with my mouth[91] even though I intended so in my thoughts. Immediately Simeon ben Shetaḥ went on a stormy day and took with him eighty select men. He gave them eighty clean garments, put them in eighty new amphoras, and put them on them upside down. He told them, when I whistle once, put on your garments. When I whistle for the second time, come in all of you together. When you enter, each of you shall choose one and lift her from the ground, since the nature of this sorcery is that separated from the earth it cannot do anything. He went and stood at the entrance to the cave. He said אוים, אוים[126], open for me, I am one of yours. They asked, how did you come here on such a day? He said, I was walking between the raindrops. They asked him, what do you want to do here? He said, to learn and to teach. Every one should make what he is able to. One of them said what she said and produced bread. One of them said what she said and produced meat. One of them said what she said and produced dishes. One said what she said and produced wine. They asked him, what can you do? He told them, when I whistle twice, I shall bring here eighty select men for your pleasure and entertainment. They told him, that is what we desire. When he whistled the first time, they put on their garments; when he whistled for the second time, they all entered together. He said, every one who comes shall select his mate. They lifted them, took them away, and crucified them[127]. That is what we have stated: "It happened that Simeon ben Shetaḥ hanged women in Ascalon. [They said, he hanged eighty women but one does not try two on the same day." But the hour needed it[128].]

121 Another version of the Simeon ben Shetaḥ legend. Corrector's additions are from the version in *Sanhedrin* 6:5, Notes 83-96, *q. v.*
122 It is a general answer to the question צדיק ורע לו רשע וטוב לו "why do the just suffer and the wicked enjoy their lives?" that the wicked enjoy the rewards for their few good deeds and the just are punished for their few sins in this world, to create a clean slate for reward and punishment in the World to Come.
123 *Ex.* 13:9,16 require that the sign (*tefillin*, phylacteries) carried by the faithful be on the arm before being put on the head. The repetition emphasizes the importance of this feature.
124 And he would not have eaten it afterwards.
125 Fasting without repentance is sinful (*Nedarim* 9:1 Note 25.)
126 The meaning of these words is unknown. Cf. *Sanhedrin* 6:5, Note 93.
127 A certain anachronism.
128 He acted under the king's police powers, disregarding all judicial rules.

(78a line 14) תַּנֵּי. אָמַר רִבִּי אֶלְעָזָר בֶּן יַעֲקֹב. שָׁמַעְתִּי שֶׁעוֹנָשִׁין שֶׁלֹּא כַּהֲלָכָה וְעוֹנְשִׁין שֶׁלֹּא כַּתּוֹרָה. עַד אֵיכָן. רִבִּי לָעְזָר בֵּירִבִּי יוֹסֵי אָמַר. עַד כְּדֵי זִימְזוּם. רִבִּי יֹסֵה אוֹמֵר. בָּעֵדִים. אֲבָל לֹא בְהַתְרָיָיה. מַעֲשֶׂה בְּאֶחָד שֶׁיָּצָא לַדֶּרֶךְ רָכוּב עַל סוּסוֹ בַּשַּׁבָּת. וְהֵבִיאוּהוּ לְבֵית דִּין וּסְקָלוּהוּ. וַהֲלֹא שְׁבוּת הָיָת. אֶלָּא שֶׁהָיְתָה הַשָּׁעָה צְרִיכָה לְכֵן. שׁוּב מַעֲשֶׂה בְּאֶחָד שֶׁיָּצָא לַדֶּרֶךְ וְאִשְׁתּוֹ עִמּוֹ. וּפָנָה לַאֲחוֹרֵי הַגָּדֵר וְעָשָׂה צְרָכָיו עִמָּהּ. וְהֵבִיאוּהוּ לְבֵית דִּין וְהִלְקוּהוּ. וַהֲלֹא אִשְׁתּוֹ הָיָת. אֶלָּא שֶׁנָּהַג עַצְמוֹ בְּבִיזָּיוֹן.

It was stated[129]: "Rebbi Eliezer ben Jacob said, I heard that one punishes not according to practice and punishes not according to Torah." How far?

Rebbi Eleazar ben Rebbi Yose said, up to a murmur[130]. Rebbi Yose said, by witnesses, but without warning[131]. It happened that one went on the road riding in his horse on the Sabbath. They brought him to court and stoned him. But was it not a rabbinic violation[132]? But at the time[133] it was needed. Also it happened that one went on the road together with his wife. He turned to behind a wall and satisfied his needs with her. They brought him to court and whipped him. But was it not his wife[134]? But he behaved in a degrading way.

129 Babli *Sanhedrin* 46a, *Yebamot* 90b. In the Babylonian version is added: "not to transgress the Torah, but to make a fence around the Torah." This means that the court must act under emergency rules covered by the police powers of the king (or assumed by the court in the absence of a legitimate government.)

130 The court may act on hearsay.

131 He disputes that hearsay is ever accepted (except when expressly permitted as in the case of a husband who has disappeared) and always requires valid testimony. In emergency situations he permits rendering judgment if the criminal act was proven but not the criminal intent in that there is no proof that the perpetrator was warned by valid witnesses not commit the criminal act.

132 While the rider broke the positive biblical commandment to let his animal rest on the Sabbath, this is not a prosecutable offense. Riding on the Sabbath or holiday is a rabbinic prohibition (Mishnah *Yom Tov* 5:2), not prosecutable by biblical standards and certainly not a capital crime.

133 In the Babylonian texts: "in the times of the Greeks". He was executed not for riding on his horse on the Sabbath but for showing support for the Seleucide party during the Maccabean wars.

134 No criminal act was committed.

(fol. 76d) **משנה ג**: בֵּית שַׁמַּאי אוֹמְרִים מְבִיאִים שְׁלָמִים וְאֵין סוֹמְכִין עֲלֵיהֶן אֲבָל לֹא עוֹלוֹת. וּבֵית הִלֵּל אוֹמְרִים מְבִיאִין שְׁלָמִים וְעוֹלוֹת וְסוֹמְכִין עֲלֵיהֶן:

Mishnah 3: The House of Shammai are saying, one brings well-being offerings and does not lean on them, but no elevation offerings[135]. But the House of Hillel are saying one brings well-being and elevation offerings and leans on them[136].

135 Since most of well-being offerings is consumed and the preparation of food is permitted on a holiday, there is no question that these may be brought on a holiday. As explained in Mishnah 2, the House of Shammai follow a long tradition which holds that biblically required but rabbinically prohibited leaning on the

sacrificial animal may not be done in the Temple on a full holiday. Since nothing of elevation offerings is human food, on a full holiday they prohibit bringing private elevation offerings, even those biblically required as appearance offering.

136 Both the appearance offering as elevation offering and the holiday well-being offerings are biblically required on the holiday, which means the full holiday, as exemplified by Pentecost which is only one day. Therefore the House of Hillel admit both kinds of offerings on the full holiday and disregard the rabbinic prohibition of leaning on since most rabbinic prohibitions are disregarded in the Temple.

(78a line 21) **הלכה ג:** בֵּית שַׁמַּי אוֹמְרִים. הוּתְּרָה סְמִיכָה שֶׁלֹּא כְדַרְכָּהּ. וּבֵית הִלֵּל אוֹמְרִים. לֹא הוּתְּרָה סְמִיכָה שֶׁלֹּא כְדַרְכָּהּ. אֵי זוֹ הִיא סְמִיכָה שֶׁלֹּא כְדַרְכָּהּ. מֵאֶתְמוֹל. אָמַר רִבִּי זְעוּרָה. כָּל־עַמָּא מוֹדֵיי בְּאָשָׁם מְצוֹרָע שֶׁסָּמַךְ עָלָיו מֵאֶתְמוֹל לֹא יָצָא. שַׁלְמֵי נְדָבָה שֶׁסָּמַךְ עֲלֵיהֶן מֵאֶתְמוֹל יָצָא. מַה פְלִיגִין. בְּשַׁלְמֵי חֲגִיגָה. בֵּית שַׁמַּי עָבְדִין לוֹן כְּשַׁלְמֵי נְדָבָה. בֵּית הִלֵּל עָבְדִין לוֹן כְּאָשָׁם מְצוֹרָע. אָמַר רִבִּי יָסָא הֵן דַּתְּ אָמַר. אָשָׁם מְצוֹרָע שֶׁסָּמַךְ עָלָיו מֵאֶתְמוֹל לֹא יָצָא. בִּזְמַנּוֹ. עִיבֵּר זְמַנּוֹ נַעֲשֶׂה כְּשַׁלְמֵי חֲגִיגָה.

Halakhah 3: [137]The House of Shammai say, irregular leaning-on was permitted. But the House of Hillel say, irregular leaning-on was not permitted. What is irregular leaning-on? From the day before. Rebbi Ze'ira said, everybody agrees that he did not fulfill his obligation regarding the reparation offering of a sufferer from skin disease if he leaned on the day before; he fulfilled his obligation with voluntary well-being offerings for which he leaned on the day before. Where do they disagree? The festival well-being offerings. The House of Shammai treat them like voluntary well-being offerings; the House of Hillel treat them like the reparation offering of a sufferer from skin disease. Rebbi Yasa said, that what you are saying, he did not fulfill his obligation regarding the reparation offering of a sufferer from skin disease if he leaned on the day before, {only} on time. If its time has passed it becomes like holiday well-being offerings.

137 This Halakhah is *Yom Tov* 2:4, explained there in Notes 56-84.

(78a line 28) אָמְרוּ בֵית הִלֵּל לְבֵית שַׁמַּי. מָה אִם בְּשָׁעָה שֶׁאֲנִי אוֹסֵר לַהֶדְיוֹט הֲרֵי אֲנִי מַתִּיר לַגָּבוֹהַּ. בְּשָׁעָה שֶׁאֲנִי מַתִּיר לַהֶדְיוֹט אֵינוֹ דִין שֶׁנַּתִּיר לַגָּבוֹהַּ. אָמְרוּ לָהֶן בֵּית שַׁמַּי. וַהֲרֵי נְדָרִים וּנְדָבוֹת יוֹכִיחוּ. שֶׁהֵן מוּתָּרִין לַהֶדְיוֹט וַאֲסוּרִין לַגָּבוֹהַּ. אָמְרוּ לָהֶן בֵּית הִלֵּל. לֹא. אִם אֲמַרְתֶּם בִּנְדָרִים וּנְדָבוֹת שֶׁאֵין זְמַנָּן קָבוּעַ. תֹּאמְרוּ בַחֲגִיגָה שֶׁזְּמַנָּהּ קָבוּעַ. אָמְרוּ לָהֶן בֵּית שַׁמַּי. חֲגִיגָה אֵין זְמַנָּהּ קָבוּעַ. שֶׁאִם לֹא חָג בָּרִאשׁוֹן חוֹגֵג בַּשֵּׁנִי. שֶׁאִם לֹא חָג בַּשֵּׁנִי חוֹגֵג בַּשְּׁלִישִׁי. . אָמְרוּ

לָהֶן בֵּית הִלֵּל. חֲגִיגָה זְמַנָּהּ קָבוּעַ. שֶׁאִם לֹא חָג בָּרֶגֶל. אֵינוֹ יָכוֹל לָחוּג אַחַר הָרֶגֶל. אָמְרוּ לָהֶן בֵּית שַׁמַּי. וַהֲלֹא כְּבָר נֶאֱמַר אַךְ אֲשֶׁר יֵאָכֵל לְכָל־נֶפֶשׁ הוּא לְבַדּוֹ יֵעָשֶׂה לָכֶם׃ אָמְרוּ לָהֶם בֵּית הִלֵּל. מִשָּׁם רְאָיָיה. לָכֶם אֵינוֹ נַעֲשֶׂה. [אֲבָל] נַעֲשֶׂה הוּא לַגָּבוֹהַּ. אַבָּא שָׁאוּל אוֹמֵר טַעַם אַחֵר. מָה אִם בְּשָׁעָה שֶׁכִּירָתָךְ סְתוּמָה כִּירַת רַבָּךְ פְּתוּחָה. בְּשָׁעָה שֶׁכִּירָתָךְ פְּתוּחָה אֵינוֹ דִין שֶׁתְּהֵא כִּירַת רַבָּךְ פְּתוּחָה. דָּבָר אַחֵר. אֵינוֹ דִין שֶׁיְּהֵא שׁוּלְחָנָךְ מָלֵא וְשׁוּלְחַן (רַבָּךְ) [קוֹנָךְ] רֵיקָם.

"The House of Hillel said to the House of Shammai: Since at a time when I forbid to the private person I am permitting it for Heaven, when it is permitted for the private person is it not logical that it be permitted for Heaven? The House of Shammai said to them, vows and voluntary gifts are proof, since they are permitted to the private person but forbidden to Heaven. The House of Hillel said to them, no. If you are speaking about vows and voluntary gifts which have no fixed time, what does this imply for the festival offering which has a fixed time? The House of Shammai answered them, the festival offering has no fixed time since if he did not offer it on the first day, he may offer it on the second day, if he did not offer it on the second day, he may offer it on the third day. The House of Hillel told them, the festival offering has a fixed time, for if he did not offer it on the holiday of pilgrimage he may not offer it after the holiday. The House of Shammai said to them, is it not already said: *only what can be eaten by any person this alone may be made for you*[138]? The House of Hillel answered them, is that a proof? *For you* it may not be made, [but] it is made for Heaven. Abba Shaul says it was based on another reason: Since when your stove is closed down, your Master's stove is open, when your stove is open it only is logical that your Master's stove should be open. Another explanation: It is not in order that your table should be full but the table of your (Master) [Creator] be empty."

(78a line 42) אָמַר רִבִּי יוֹסֵי בֵּירִבִּי בּוּן. רִבִּי שִׁמְעוֹן בֶּן לָקִישׁ הֲוָה עָבַר קוֹמֵי סִדְרָא וּשְׁמַע קָלְהוֹן קָרְיֵי הָהֵן פְּסוּקָא. וַיִּזְבְּחוּ לַיי זְבָחִים וַיַּעֲלוּ עוֹלוֹת לַיי לְמָחֳרַת הַיּוֹם הַהוּא. אָמַר. מָאן דְּמִפְסַק לֵהּ כְּבֵית שַׁמַּי. מָאן דְּקָרֵי כּוּלֵּהּ כְּבֵית הִלֵּל. נִיחָא עוֹלוֹת לְמָחֳרַת הַיּוֹם הַהוּא. שְׁלָמִים לְמָחֳרַת הַיּוֹם. וְאֵין שְׁלָמִים בָּאִין כְּבֵית שַׁמַּי. אָמַר רִבִּי יוֹסֵי בֵּירִבִּי בּוּן. דָּוִד מֵת בָּעֲצֶרֶת. וְהָיוּ כָל־יִשְׂרָאֵל אוֹנְנִין וְהִקְרִיבוּ לְמָחָר.

Rebbi Yose ben Rebbi Abun said, Rebbi Simeon ben Laqish was passing by the school when he heard them reciting the verse[139], *they sacrificed animal sacrifices and brought elevation sacrifices the next day.* He said, he who interrupts follows the House of Shammai; he who reads it as one sentence follows the House of Hillel. One understands elevation sacrifices the next day; but well-being sacrifices the next day? Are not well-being sacrifices brought following the House of Shammai? Rebbi Yose ben Rebbi Abun said, David died on Pentecost; all of Israel were deep mourners and they brought the next day.

(61c line 12) מַעֲשֶׂה בְהִלֵּל הַזָּקֵן שֶׁהֵבִיא עוֹלָתוֹ לָעֲזָרָה וְסָמַךְ עָלֶיהָ. חִבְּרוּ עָלָיו תַּלְמִידֵי בֵית שַׁמַּי. הִתְחִיל מְכַשְׁכֵּשׁ בִּזְנָבָהּ. אָמַר לָהֶן. רְאוּ נְקֵיבָה הִיא וּשְׁלָמִים הֲבֵאתִיהָ. וְהִפְלִיגָן בִּדְבָרִים וְהָלְכוּ לָהֶן. לְאַחַר יָמִים גָּבְרָה יָדָן שֶׁלְּבֵית שַׁמַּי וּבִקְשׁוּ לִקְבּוֹעַ הֲלָכָה כְדִבְרֵיהֶם. וְהָיָה שָׁם בָּבָא בֶן בּוּטָא מִתַּלְמִידֵי בֵית שַׁמַּי וְיוֹדֵעַ שֶׁהֲלָכָה כְּבֵית הִלֵּל. פַּעַם אַחַת נִכְנַס לָעֲזָרָה וּמְצָאָהּ שׁוֹמֵמֶת. אָמַר. יְשַׁמּוּ בָּתֵּיהֶן שֶׁל אֵילוּ שֶׁהֵישִׁימוּ אֶת בֵּית אֱלֹהֵינוּ. מֶה עָשָׂה. שָׁלַח וְהֵבִיא שְׁלֹשֶׁת אֲלָפִים טָלִים מִצֹּאן קֵדָר וּבִיקְּרָן מִמּוּמִין. וְהֶעֱמִידָן בְּהַר הַבַּיִת וְאָמַר לָהֶן. שִׁמְעוּנִי אֲחַיי בֵּית יִשְׂרָאֵל. כָּל־מִי שֶׁהוּא רוֹצֶה יָבִיא עוֹלוֹת יָבִיא וְיִסְמוֹךְ. יָבִיא שְׁלָמִים וְיִסְמוֹךְ. בְּאוֹתָהּ שָׁעָה נִקְבְּעָה הֲלָכָה כְּבֵית הִלֵּל. וְלֹא אָמַר אָדָם דָּבָר. אָמַר רְבִּי יִצְחָק בִּירְבִּי לָעָזָר. הָדָא כַּסָּא בְּשִׁירוּתָא בָּעְיָא מוּלַיי. סָסָא דְּקִיסָא מִינֵּיהּ וּבֵיהּ. כָּל־גּוּמְרָא דְלָא כְוָויָה בְשַׁעְתָּהּ לָא כְוָיָה. מַעֲשֶׂה בְאֶחָד מִתַּלְמִידֵי בֵית הִלֵּל שֶׁהֵבִיא עוֹלָתוֹ לָעֲזָרָה וְסָמַךְ עָלֶיהָ. וְרָאהוּ אֶחָד מִתַּלְמִידֵי בֵית שַׁמַּי. אָמַר לָהֶן. מַה זוֹ סְמִיכָה. אָמַר לוֹ. מַה זוֹ שְׁתִיקָה. וְשִׁיתְּקוֹ בִנְזִיפָה וְהָלַךְ לוֹ.

"It happened that Hillel the Elder brought his elevation offering to the Temple courtyard and leaned on it. The students of the House of Shammai ganged up on him. He started to wag its tail, said to them, look, it is a female and I brought it as well-being sacrifice, and kept them talking about other matters until they left. After some time the House of Shammai became strong and they wanted to fix practice following their words. There was there Bava ben Buta from the students of the House of Shammai who realized that practice followed the House of Hillel. Once he entered the Temple courtyard and found it desolate. He said, the house of those who make our God's House desolate shall be desolate. What did he do? He sent and brought 3'000 young lambs from Qedar sheep, checked them for defects, and displayed them on the Temple Mount. He said to them, listen to me my brothers, the House of Israel. Anybody who wants to bring an elevation sacrifice may bring it and lean on it, to bring a well-being sacrifice may bring it and lean on it. At that moment, practice was fixed following the House of Hillel; and nobody said anything." Rebbi Isaac ben Rebbi Eleazar said, this cup for breakfast has to be full[81]; the worm in the wood comes from itself; any coal which does not cause a burn at the start will not cause one. "Again it happened that a student of Hillel brought his elevation offering to the Temple courtyard and leaned on it. A student of Shammai saw him and said to him, what is this leaning-on? He said to him, what about being silent? He silenced him by a reprimand and he left."

138 *Ex.* 12:16.   139 *1Chr.* 29:21.

(fol. 76d) **משנה ד**: עֲצֶרֶת שֶׁחָלָה לִהְיוֹת עֶרֶב שַׁבָּת בֵּית שַׁמַּאי אוֹמְרִים יוֹם טְבוֹחַ לְאַחַר שַׁבָּת. וּבֵית הִלֵּל אוֹמְרִים אֵין לָהֶן יוֹם טְבוֹחַ וּמוֹדִין שֶׁאִם חָלָה לִהְיוֹת בַּשַּׁבָּת שֶׁיּוֹם טְבוֹחַ לְאַחַר שַׁבָּת וְאֵין כֹּהֵן גָּדוֹל מִתְלַבֵּשׁ בְּכֵלָיו וּמוּתָרִין בְּסְפֵּד וּבְתַעֲנִית שֶׁלֹּא לְקַיֵּים דִּבְרֵי הָאוֹמְרִין עֲצֶרֶת לְאַחַר שַׁבָּת:

Mishnah 4: If Pentecost falls on a Friday, the House of Shammai are saying that its slaughter-day is after the Sabbath[140], but the House of Hillel are saying that it has no slaughter-day.[141] They agree that if it falls on the Sabbath that its slaughter-day is after the Sabbath; the High Priest does not wear his garments, and one is permitted eulogies and fasting, in order not to support the words of those who are saying that Pentecost is on Sunday[142].

140 Since the House of Shammai do not permit the elevation offerings to be brought on Friday, which is the holiday, nor on the Sabbath when they are biblically prohibited, they must declare Sunday as a minor holiday similar to the intermediate days of Passover and Tabernacles.

141 Since the holiday is only one day, every pilgrim is asked to bring all his offerings on the holiday itself.

142 In this case (which is excluded in the computed calendar), no private slaughter is possible on the holiday itself. It may not be done in advance of the holiday (Halakhah 1:4, after Note 131). Therefore the first day available for the pilgrimage offerings is Sunday. While in the biblical text Pentecost is a purely agricultural holiday, the start of the wheat harvest, both in Pharisaic as in standard Sadducee (as given in the Book of Jubilees) interpretation it is the anniversary of the theophany on Sinai and therefore the anniversary of the creation of the organized Synagogue. Only the otherwise unremarkable sect of the Boethusians insist on counting the fifty days starting from a Sunday, therefore having Pentecost on a Sunday but its calendar date variable and not available as the anniversary of anything. Since by the time of the formulation of the Mishnah Boethusians long had disappeared, one may consider these rules as intended

against Christian practice which manages to combine the Boethusian variable date with the interpretation as anniversary of the founding of the Chuch. The High Priest is prevented from serving on that day, to avoid that the day be considered festive in any way. Similarly, even though the day is an extension of the holiday, one is invited to treat it as a regular weekday on which eulogies and fasts are permitted.

(78a line 62) **הלכה ד**: עֲצֶרֶת שֶׁחָלָה לִהְיוֹת עֶרֶב שַׁבָּת. בֵּית שַׁמַּאי אוֹמְרִים. יוֹם טְבוֹחַ שֶׁלָּהּ לְאַחַר שַׁבָּת. בֵּית הִלֵּל אוֹמְרִים. אֵין לָהּ יוֹם טְבוֹחַ. אֶלָּא יוֹמָהּ הוּא טְבוּחָהּ. הָא בֵית שַׁמַּי אוֹמְרִים. יוֹם טְבוֹחַ שֶׁלָּהּ אַחַר שַׁבָּת. [וְאֵין] כֹּהֵן גָּדוֹל מִתְלַבֵּשׁ בְּכֵלָיו. (קוֹל) [מִקַּל] וָחוֹמֶר. מָה אִם בְּשָׁעָה שֶׁיֵּשׁ שָׁם שְׁלָמִים וְעוֹלוֹת כְּדִבְרֵי בֵית הִלֵּל אֵין כֹּהֵן גָּדוֹל מִתְלַבֵּשׁ בְּכֵלָיו. בְּשָׁעָה שֶׁאֵין שְׁלָמִים וְעוֹלוֹת כְּדִבְרֵי בֵית שַׁמַּי לֹא כָל־שֶׁכֵּן.

כָּתוּב אֶחָד אוֹמֵר וְחַג הַקָּצִיר בִּכּוּרֵי מַעֲשֶׂיךָ. וְכָתוּב אֶחָד אוֹמֵר כָּל־מְלֶאכֶת עֲבֹדָה לֹא תַעֲשׂוּ. אָמַר רִבִּי חֲנַנְיָה. כֵּיצַד יִתְקַיְּימוּ שְׁנֵי מִקְרָאוֹת הַלָּלוּ. בְּשָׁעָה שֶׁהוּא חָל בַּחוֹל אַתְּ חוֹגֵג וְשׁוֹבֵת. וּבְשָׁעָה שֶׁהוּא חָל בַּשַּׁבָּת לְמָחָר אַתְּ חוֹגֵג וְקוֹצֵר. אָמַר רִבִּי יוֹסֵי בֵּירִבִּי בּוּן. וּבִלְבַד שִׁיבָּלִים לְעִיסָתוֹ. כְּהָדָא דְתַנֵּי. לְהֵן אֵינָשׁ דִּיחֱוֵי עֲלוֹהִי אָעִין וּבִכּוּרִין. הָאוֹמֵר. הֲרֵי עָלַי עֲצִים לַמִּזְבֵּחַ וְגִיזִירִין לַמַּעֲרָכָה. אָסוּר (בְּסָפָד) [בַּהֶסְפֵּד] וְתַעֲנִית וּמִלַּעֲשׂוֹת מְלָאכָה בּוֹ בַּיּוֹם.

Halakhah 4: "If Pentecost falls on a Friday, the House of Shammai are saying that its slaughter-day is after the Sabbath, but the House of Hillel are saying that it has no slaughter-day." But its day is its slaughter-day. Here the House of Shammai are saying, its slaughter-day is after the Sabbath, and the High Priest (wears) [does not wear] his garments (?)[143][.] It is an argument *de minore ad majus*. Since in a time where there are well-being and elevation offerings following the House of Hillel the High Priest does not wear his garments, in a time when there are no well-being and elevation offerings following the House of Shammai, not so much more?

[144]One verse says, *the harvest festival, the first fruits of your work*[145]. Another verse says, *any productive work you shall not do*[146]. Rebbi Ḥanania said, how could both verses be sustained? If it falls on a weekday you bring the festival offering and refrain from work. If it falls on the Sabbath, the following day you bring the festival offering and harvest. Rebbi Yose ben Rebbi Bun said, only ears for her dough. As what was stated, "therefore anybody who has an obligation for wood and first fruits. He who says, I am taking upon me {to bring} wood for the altar and logs for the arrangement on that day is forbidden funeral orations, and fasts, and working."

143 The scribe's text (in parentheses) has to be accepted. The [corrector's] seems to be based on a misunderstanding of the text. The statement about the High Priest is formulated in the name of the House of Hillel. Is it rejected by the House of Shammai? The House of Shammai would have had to object to the rule formulated by the House of Hillel if they still had existed at a time when Christianity had become an factor.

144 This paragraph is copied from *Megillah* 1:3, Notes 134-140.

145 *Ex.* 23:16.

146 *Lev.* 23:21.

(78a line 75) מוֹדִים שֶׁאִם חָלָה לִהְיוֹת בַּשַׁבָּת שֶׁיּוֹם טְבוֹחַ שֶׁלָּהּ לְאַחַר שַׁבָּת. הָא בֵית הִלֵּל אוֹמְרִים. יוֹם טְבוֹחַ שֶׁלָּהּ לְאַחַר שַׁבָּת. עוֹרוֹת שֶׁל מִי. רִבִּי טָבִי בְּשֵׁם רִבִּי יֹאשִׁיָּה. אִיתְפַּלְגוּן רִבִּי יוֹחָנָן וְרִבִּי שִׁמְעוֹן בֶּן לָקִישׁ. רִבִּי יוֹחָנָן אָמַר. שֶׁלְּכָל־הַמִּשְׁמָרוֹת. רִבִּי שִׁמְעוֹן בֶּן לָקִישׁ אָמַר. שֶׁלְאוֹתוֹ הַמִּשְׁמָר. וַתְּ אָמַר. יוֹם טְבוֹחַ שֶׁלָּהּ לְאַחַר שַׁבָּת. עוֹרוֹת שֶׁלְמִי. תַּפְלוּגְתָּא דְּרִבִּי יוֹחָנָן וְרִבִּי שִׁמְעוֹן בֶּן לָקִישׁ. אָמַר רִבִּי יוֹחָנָן. עֲצֶרֶת יֵשׁ לָהּ תַּשְׁלוּמִין כָּל־שִׁבְעָה. הָתִיב רַב הוֹשַׁעְיָה. וְהָא תַנֵּי. מַה הֶחָדָשׁ לִמְנוּיָיו יוֹם אֶחָד אַף הָעֲצֶרֶת לִמְנוּיֶיהָ יוֹם אֶחָד. אָמַר רִבִּי לָא. שֶׁאִם לֹא חָג בָּרִאשׁוֹן יָחוּג כָּל־שִׁבְעָה.

"They agree that if it falls on the Sabbath that its slaughter-day is after the Sabbath." So the House of Hillel are saying, its slaughter-day is after the Sabbath. Whose are the hides[147]? Rebbi Tabi in the name of Rebbi Joshia: Rebbi Joḥanan and Rebbi Simeon ben Laqish disagree. Rebbi Joḥanan said, of all watches. Rebbi Simeon ben Laqish said, of this watch. And you are saying, its slaughter-day is after the Sabbath; whose are the hides? The disagreement between Rebbi Joḥanan and Rebbi Simeon ben Laqish[148]? Rebbi Joḥanan said, Pentecost has all of seven days as make-up[149]. Rav Hoshaia objected: was it not stated, just as the New Moon is one day after its count, to Pentecost is one day after its count? Rebbi La said, if he did not bring his holiday sacrifice on the first day, he may bring it all seven days[150].

147 By biblical decree, the hides belong to the Cohanim serving at the moment of sacrifice, *Lev.* 7:8. Now on a holiday where all of Israel is commanded to appear in the Temple, all Cohanim also are asked to appear and therefore have equal claim to all hides of holiday sacrifices. But on all other days, only the watch of service of this week has a claim; in fact, only the clan serving on that very day. Therefore if the slaughter-day is treated as an extension of the holiday, all Cohanim must be admitted to service and the hides belong to all watches. But if it is a regular weekday, only the serving clan or, if its personnel is not sufficient, the serving watch are admitted to service and to receive the prebends.

148 Is it really a problem on Pentecost

which falls on a Sabbath and the Cohanim on pilgrimage cannot leave the place of the Temple on the Sabbath and therefore are all available for service on the next day?
149 Cf. Halakhah 1:1, Note 33. Babli 17a,b.

150 It is obvious that the pilgrimage offerings are holiday offerings, to be serviced by all Cohanim who therefore are entitled to their share of the hides.

(78b line 7) רִבִּי יוֹסֵי בֵּירִבִּי בּוּן בְּשֵׁם רִבִּי יְהוֹשֻׁעַ בֶּן לֵוִי. בְּכָל־יוֹם כֹּהֵן גָּדוֹל מִתְלַבֵּשׁ בְּכֵלָיו וּבָא וּמַקְרִיב תָּמִיד שֶׁלְּשַׁחַר. אִם יֵשׁ נְדָרִים וּנְדָבוֹת הוּא מַקְרִיבָן. וְהוֹלֵךְ וְאוֹכֵל בְּתוֹךְ בֵּיתוֹ. וּבָא וּמַקְרִיב תָּמִיד שֶׁלְּבֵין הָעַרְבַּיִם. וּבָא וְלָן בְּלִשְׁכַּת פַּלְהֶדְרִין. רִבִּי עוּקְבָה בְּשֵׁם רִבִּי יְהוֹשֻׁעַ בֶּן לֵוִי. לֹא הָיָה עוֹשֶׂה כֵן אֶלָּא בַשַּׁבָּתוֹת וּבְיָמִים טוֹבִים. אִת תַּנֵּיֵי תַנֵּי. הַצִּיץ מְרַצֶּה עַל מִצְחוֹ. אִת תַּנֵּיֵי תַנֵּי. אֲפִילוּ בְזָוִית. מָאן דְּאָמַר. הַצִּיץ מְרַצֶּה עַל מִצְחוֹ. וְהָיָה עַל־מִצְחוֹ תָּמִיד. וּמָאן דְּאָמַר. אֲפִילוּ בְזָוִית. מֵהָדָא דְיוֹם הַכִּיפּוּרִים. מָאן דְּאָמַר. הַצִּיץ מְרַצֶּה עַל מִצְחוֹ. מְסַיֵּיעַ לְרִבִּי יוֹסֵי בֵּירִבִּי בּוּן. מָאן דְּאָמַר. אֲפִילוּ בְזָוִית. מְסַיֵּיעַ לְרִבִּי עוּקְבָה.

[151]Rebbi Yose ben Rebbi Abun in the name of Rebbi Joshua ben Levi: Every day[152] the High Priest dresses in his robes[153], comes, and sacrifices the daily morning sacrifice. If there are vows or voluntary sacrifices[154], he offers them. Then he goes to his house, and returns to bring the daily evening sacrifice, and comes to stay overnight in the Palhedrin lodge. Rebbi Uqba in the name of Rebbi Joshua ben Levi: He did this only on Sabbath and holidays[155]. There are Tannaim who state: the diadem[156] propitiates on his forehead. There are Tannaim who state: even in a corner. He who says, the diadem propitiates on his forehead, *it always shall be on his forehead*[157]. But he who says, even in a corner, from the Day of Atonement[158]. He who says, the diadem propitiates on his forehead, supports Rebbi Yose ben Rebbi Abun; he who says, even in a corner, supports Rebbi Uqba.

151 This text is from *Yoma* 1:1, Notes 184-190.
152 Of the seven days of preparation.
153 The eight garments prescribed for the High Priest.
154 The legal difference between a vow and a voluntary offering, which also needs dedication, is that a vow is formulated as a personal obligation, "I am taking upon me the obligation to offer such and such a sacrifice." In that case, if the animal selected for the sacrifice becomes disqualified for any reason, the maker of the vow has to bring a replacement. A voluntary offering is a dedication, "this animal shall be such-and-such a sacrifice." If the animal becomes disqualified, no replacement is due.

155 He seems to imply every Sabbath and holiday during the year, including New Year's Day and the Sabbath preceding the day of Atonement.

156 The diadem (*Ex.* 28:36-38) which is worn *to eliminate iniquities of sancta*, to legitimate sacrifices even if they do not completely satisfy the prescribed rules.

157 *Ex.* 29:38.

158 When the High Priest officiates in white robes without the diadem.

(fol.76a) **משנה ה**: נוֹטְלִין לַיָּדַיִם לַחוּלִין וְלַמַּעֲשֵׂר וְלַתְּרוּמָה. וְלַקּוֹדֶשׁ מַטְבִּילִין. וְלַחַטָּאת אִם נִטְמְאוּ יָדָיו נִטְמָא גוּפוֹ:

Mishnah 5: One washes hands[159] for profane food, tithe, and heave, but for *sancta* one immerses[160]. And for the Red Cow if his hands became impure so became his body[161].

159 The impurity of hands is rabbinic. Unless hands are consciously guarded from touching anything impure they are presumed to be impure in second degree and can be purified by having a *quartarius* (about 133 ml) of water poured over them.

160 The consumption of *sancta* requires not only a pure body, but if the eater's hands were not consciously guarded from touching anything impure after he immersed his whole body in a *miqweh*, at the time of the meal his hands have to be immersed again in a minimum if 40 *seah* (about 510 l) of water.

161 Even if according to rabbinic rules the rabbinic impurity of his hands does not imply impurity of the body, for handling the ashes of the Red Cow or water containing such ashes he must be considered impure and therefore disqualified.

(78b line 16) **הלכה ה**: וְיֵשׁ יָדַיִם לַחוּלִין. אֶלָּא כְרַבִּי שִׁמְעוֹן בֶּן אֶלְעָזָר. דְּרַבִּי שִׁמְעוֹן בֶּן אֶלְעָזָר אוֹמֵר. יֵשׁ יָדַיִם לַחוּלִין. דִּבְרֵי הַכֹּל הִיא. כְּדֵי שֶׁיְּהֵא בָדֵל מִן הַתְּרוּמָה. תַּנֵּי רִבִּי שִׁמְעוֹן בֶּן אֶלְעָזָר מִשּׁוּם רִבִּי מֵאִיר. הַיָּדַיִם תְּחִילָּה לַחוּלִין וּשְׁנִיּוֹת לַתְּרוּמָה. מַה. רִבִּי שִׁמְעוֹן בֶּן אֶלְעָזָר כְּרִבִּי עֲקִיבָה. דְּתַנִּינָן תַּמָּן. הַמַּכְנִיס יָדָיו לְבֵית הַמְּנוּגָּע יָדָיו תְּחִילָּה דִּבְרֵי רִבִּי עֲקִיבָה. וַחֲכָמִים אוֹמְרִים. יָדָיו שְׁנִיּוֹת. כְּרַבָּנָן הִיא תַמָּן. מַה טַעֲמוֹן הָכָא. מִתּוֹךְ שֶׁאַתְּ אוֹמֵר לוֹ. יָדָיו שְׁנִיּוֹת. אַף הוּא בָדֵל מִן הַתְּרוּמָה. וְלֹא מַחֲמַת מַשְׁקֶה גְזֵרוּ עֲלֵיהֶן. וְיִהְיוּ תְחִילָּה. (קוֹל) [קַל] וָחוֹמֶר. מָה אִם טְבוּל יוֹם שֶׁהוּא דְבָר תּוֹרָה אֵינוֹ אֶלָּא פוֹסֵל. יָדַיִם שֶׁהֵן מִדִּבְרֵיהֶן לֹא כָל־שֶׁכֵּן. דָּבָר אַחֵר. כְּלוּם גָּזְרוּ עַל הַיָּדַיִם לֹא כְּדֵי שֶׁיְּהֵא בָדֵל מִן הַתְּרוּמָה. מִתּוֹךְ שֶׁאַתְּ אוֹמֵר לוֹ. יָדָיו שְׁנִיּוֹת. אַף הוּא בָדֵל מִן הַתְּרוּמָה.

Halakhah 5: Is hand-washing required for profane food[162]? But it must follow Rebbi Simeon ben Eleazar, since Rebbi Simeon ben Eleazar says, hand-washing is required for profane food. It is everybody's opinion, so he should separate from heave[163]. Rebbi Simeon ben Eleazar stated in the name of Rebbi Meïr, hands are first degree impure for profane food and second degree impure for heave[164]. Does Rebbi Simeon ben Eleazar follow Rebbi Aqiba, as we have stated there[165], "if somebody puts his hands into a leprous house[166], his hands are impure in the first degree, the words of Rebbi Aqiba, but the Sages are saying, his hands are impure in the second degree"? There, it follows the rabbis; what is their reason here? Since you tell him that his hands are impure in the second degree, he will separate from heave. But did they not decide about them because of fluids; then they should be impure in the first degree[167]? It is an argument *de minore ad majus*. Since the *Tevul Yom*, which is a word from the Torah, only disqualifies[168], impure hands, which are from their words, not so much more? Another explanation: Did they not decide about hands only that he should separate from heave? Since you tell him that his hands are impure in the second degree, he will separate from heave.

162 This is a discussion of impurity imparted by unwashed hands. The basic observation is that an impure person or object which touches anything susceptible to impurity imparts impurity of one degree lower. (However, the majority opinion is that fluids do not touch but merge, and therefore transmit impurity of the same degree as the acting material.) There are three stages of biblical impurity, "grandfather of impurity", a corpse or a house in which there is a corpse, "original impurity", anything touched by a corpse or (with a few exceptions) found in a house containing a corpse, and any other impurity described in the Torah, and "impurity in the first degree", biblically imparted by contact with original impurity or rabbinically by contact with any impure fluid. The other stages are rabbinical; persons or food impure in stage n by touch impart impurity of stage $n+1$. The technical term is "impure" for anything able to impart impurity and "disqualified" for matters unusable because of impurity but not imparting impurity to others. Profane food may be impure in stage 1, it becomes disqualified (cannot be dedicated for any sacred use) in stage 2. Heave and Second Tithe (*sacra* not connected with the Temple) are impure in stages 1,2 and disqualified in stage 3. Temple *sacra* are impure in stages 1,2,3 and disqualified in stage 4.

163 Since unwashed hands rabbinically are considered impure in stage two, handling heave with unwashed hands disqualifies it.

164 Touching with unwashed hands always disqualifies. Babli *Hulin* 33b; differently Tosephta *Taharot* 1:6.

165 Mishnah *Yadaim* 3:1.

166 As described in *Lev.* 14:33-54. Bodily entrance into the house causes biblical impurity (vv. 46,47), standing outside and reaching into the house only causes rabbinic impurity.

167 Since unwashed hands touching any fluid make the fluid rabbinically impure in the first degree, it would be reasonable to consider unwashed hands as impure in the first degree.

168 An impure person can qualify to eat sancta by first immersing himself in a *miqweh*, to remove his impurity, and then waiting until sundown, when he becomes pure (*Lev.* 22:6-7). The intermediate stage, no longer impure but not yet pure, is called *Tevul Yom*, "immersed during daytime". Since the verse prohibits him to consume sacred food it is inferred that he also may not handle it. Since he is no longer impure, his touch cannot make impure. It is inferred that his touch disqualifies.

(78b line 27) תַּמָּן תַּנִּינָן. [הַתְּרוּמָה וְהַבִּכּוּרִים חַיָּבִים עֲלֵיהֶן מִיתָה וָחוֹמֶשׁ. וַאֲסוּרִים לַזָּרִים. וְהֵן נִכְסֵי כֹהֵן. וְעוֹלִין בְּאֶחָד וּמֵאָה. וּטְעוּנִין רְחִיצַת יָדַיִם וְהַעֲרֵב שֶׁמֶשׁ.] הֲרֵי אֵלּוּ בִתְרוּמָה וּבְבִכּוּרִים מַה שֶּׁאֵין כֵּן בַּמַּעֲשֵׂר: תַּמָּן אַתְּ אָמַר. אֵין הַמַּעֲשֵׂר טָעוּן רְחִיצָה. וְהָכָא אַתְּ אָמַר. הַמַּעֲשֵׂר טָעוּן רְחִיצָה. הֵן דַּתְּ אָמַר. הַמַּעֲשֵׂר טָעוּן רְחִיצָה. רַבָּנָן. הֵן דַּתְּ אָמַר. אֵין הַמַּעֲשֵׂר טָעוּן רְחִיצָה. רִבִּי מֵאִיר. דִּתְנִינָן תַּמָּן. כָּל־הַטָּעוּן בִּיאַת מַיִם מִדִּבְרֵי סוֹפְרִים מְטַמֵּא אֶת הַקּוֹדֶשׁ וּפוֹסֵל אֶת הַתְּרוּמָה וּמוּתָּר בְּחוּלִּין וּבַמַּעֲשֵׂר. דִּבְרֵי רִבִּי מֵאִיר. וַחֲכָמִים אוֹסְרִין בַּמַּעֲשֵׂר. וְלָא שְׁמִיעַ דְּאָמַר רִבִּי שְׁמוּאֵל בְּשֵׁם רִבִּי זְעוּרָה. מָהוּ וַחֲכָמִים אוֹסְרִין בַּמַּעֲשֵׂר. נִפְסַל גּוּפוֹ מִלּוֹכַל בַּמַּעֲשֵׂר. מַאי כְדוֹן. הֵן דַּתְּ אָמַר. הַמַּעֲשֵׂר טָעוּן רְחִיצָה. [בִּרְוֹצֶה לוֹכַל. וְהֵן דַּתְּאָמַר. אֵין הַמַּעֲשֵׂר טָעוּן רְחִיצָה.] בִּרְוֹצֶה לִיגַּע. וְלֹא הוּא רוֹצֶה לוֹכַל הוּא רוֹצֶה לִיגַּע. אֶלָּא מִשּׁוּם [נְטִילַת סֶרֶךְ. וְהָתַנִּינָן. תְּרוּמָה. וְכִי יֵשׁ בִּתְרוּמָה מִשּׁוּם] נְטִילַת סֶרֶךְ. אֶלָּא בְחוּלִין שֶׁנַּעֲשׂוּ עַל [גַּב] טַהֲרַת הַקּוֹדֶשׁ. וְחוּלִין שֶׁנַּעֲשׂוּ עַל גַּב הַקּוֹדֶשׁ לֹא כְחוּלִּין הֵם. תִּיפְתָּר אוֹ כְרִבִּי שִׁמְעוֹן בֶּן אֶלְעָזָר אוֹ כְרִבִּי אֶלְעָזָר בֵּירִבִּי צָדוֹק. אוֹ כְרִבִּי שִׁמְעוֹן בֶּן אֶלְעָזָר. דְּתַנֵּי רִבִּי שִׁמְעוֹן בֶּן אֶלְעָזָר אוֹמֵר מִשּׁוּם רִבִּי מֵאִיר. הַיָּדַיִם תְּחִילָה לַחוּלִּין וּשְׁנִיּוֹת לַתְּרוּמָה. אוֹ כְרִבִּי אֶלְעָזָר בֵּירִבִּי צָדוֹק. דִּתְנִינָן תַּמָּן. חוּלִין שֶׁנַּעֲשׂוּ עַל גַּב הַקּוֹדֶשׁ הֲרֵי אֵילּוּ כְחוּלִּין . רִבִּי לָעֲזָר בַּר רִבִּי צָדוֹק אוֹמֵר הֲרֵי אֵילּוּ כִּתְרוּמָה לְטַמֵּא שְׁנַיִם וְלִפְסוֹל אֶחָד:

There, we have stated[169]: ["For heave and First Fruits one incurs the penalty of death[170] or a fine of a fifth[171]; they are forbidden to lay persons, are property of the Cohen[172], may be lifted by one in 100[173], need washing of the hands and sundown.] This applies to heave and First Fruits but not to tithe." There, you are saying tithe does not need washing, but here, you are saying that tithe needs washing. When you are saying that tithe needs washing, following the rabbis; but when you are saying that tithe does not need washing, following Rebbi Meïr. As we have stated there[174], "anything which requires immersion by the words of the Sopherim[175] makes *sancta* impure and disqualifies heave but is permitted for profane food and tithe, the words of Rebbi Meïr. But the Sages forbid for tithe[176]." He did not understand that Rebbi Samuel said in the name of Rebbi Ze`ira: What means, "but the Sages forbid for tithe"? His body became disqualified from consuming tithe[177]. How it that? If you are saying, tithe needs washing, [for one who intends to eat. If you are saying, tithe does not need washing,] if he intends to touch[178]. But does not one who wants to eat also want to touch? Only because of [handwashing as discipline. But did we not state "heave"? For heave is there] handwashing as discipline[179]? Therefore about profane food prepared in the purity of *sancta*. But is profane food prepared in the purity of *sancta* not profane food[180]? Explain either following Rebbi Simeon ben Eleazar or Rebbi Eleazar ben Rebbi Ṣadoq. Either following Rebbi Simeon ben Eleazar, as it was stated, Rebbi Simeon ben Eleazar says in the name of Rebbi Meïr, hands are first degree impure for profane food and second degree impure for heave[164]. Or Rebbi Eleazar ben Rebbi Ṣadoq, as we have stated there[181]: "profane food prepared in the purity of *sancta* is profane food. Rebbi Eleazar ben Rebbi Ṣadoq says, it is like heave, to be impure in two stages and disqualified in the third[162]."

169 Mishnah *Bikkurim* 2:1. The corrector added the text presupposed by the scribe.
170 Eating them in impurity is a deadly sin.
171 If misappropriated, the restitution must be at least 125%.
172 They might be traded from one Cohen to another and a Cohen may use them as gifts to marry a wife since, even if she was a lay person before, she becomes a member of the Cohen's family by marriage and may eat heave and First Fruits.
173 If heave or First Fruits were mixed with profane food and are now no longer recognizable, if they constitute less than 1% of the mixture, 1% may be lifted and designated heave or First Fruits and the remainder freed for lay use.
174 Mishnah *Parah* 11:5. Babli 18b.
175 Part of the original institutions of Judaism formulated by Ezra and his successors.
176 Since tithe becomes impure by touch of hands or things impure in the second degree and unwashed hands always are impure in the second degree.
177 But not touching.
178 The better text probably is obtained by deleting the corrector's addition: "If you are saying, tithe needs washing, if he intends to touch? But does not one who wants to eat also want to touch?"
179 Again it is better to delete the

corrector's addition. The washing of hands is "discipline of heave".

180 Food prepared to the standards of *sancta* is not a *sanctum* unless dedicated, which in the absence of a Temple is impossible. Therefore it remains profane and its status cannot be changed by touching with hands which are impure in the second degree.

181 Mishnah *Taharot* 2:8.

(78b line 46) וְלַקּוֹדֶשׁ מַטְבִּילִין. כָּל־הֵן דְּתַנֵּינָן מַטְבִּילִין. בְּאַרְבָּעִים סְאָה אֲנָן קַיָּימִין. וְהָא תַּנִּינָן. הַנּוֹטֵל יָדָיו לַמִּקְדָּשׁ צָרִיךְ רְבִיעִית. אָמַר רִבִּי לְעָזָר. כָּאן בְּיָדַיִם טְמֵאוֹת וְכָאן בְּיָדַיִם טְהוֹרוֹת. [אָמַר רִבִּי חֲנִינָא בְּרֵיהּ דְּרִבִּי הִלֵּל. אֲפִילוּ תֵימַר. כָּאן וְכָאן בְּיָדַיִם טְהוֹרוֹת. כָּאן וְכָאן בְּיָדַיִם טְמֵאוֹת.] כָּאן בְּקוֹדְשֵׁי מִקְדָּשׁ הַמּוּקְדָּשִׁין. וְכָאן בְּחוּלִּין שֶׁנַּעֲשׂוּ עַל גַּב הַקּוֹדֶשׁ.

"But for *sancta* one immerses[160]." Anywhere we state "immerses" it means in 40 *seah*. But did we not state[182], "he who washes his hands in the Temple needs a *quartarius*"? Rebbi Eleazar said, here for impure hands, there fore pure hands. [Rebbi Ḥanina ben Rebbi Hillel said, even if you are saying here and there for pure hands, here and there for impure hands.][183] Here for dedicated Temple *sancta*, there for profane food prepared in the purity of *sancta*.

182 Cf. Tosephta *Yadaim* 1:5.

183 The provenience of the corrector's addition is unknown. The spelling חנינא is Babylonian.

(78b line 51) וְלַחַטָּאת אִם נִטְמְאוּ יָדָיו נִטְמָא גוּפוֹ׃ אָמַר רִבִּי חֲנַנְיָה. לֹא שֶׁחִידְּשׁוּ טוּמְאָה לַחַטָּאת. אֶלָּא אָמְרוּ. הַמִּיטַּמֵּא טוּמְאָה קַלָּה כְּמִיטַּמֵּא טוּמְאָה חֲמוּרָה. רִבִּי יַעֲקֹב בַּר אָחָא בְּשֵׁם רִבִּי לְעָזָר. וְאָסַף אִישׁ. מַה תַּלְמוּד לוֹמַר טָהוֹר. הַגַּע עַצְמָךְ. אֲפִילוּ אַתְּ אוֹסְפוֹ בְּמַגְרֵיפָה אָמְרָה תוֹרָה טָהוֹר. מָה אֲנָן קַיָּימִין. אִם בְּמַגְרֵיפָה שֶׁלְּמַתֶּכֶת. וַהֲלֹא פְשׁוּטֵי כְלֵי מַתָּכוֹת טְמֵאִין. אִם בְּמַגְרֵיפָה שֶׁלְּעֵץ. לֹא כְעוֹמֵד מֵחֲמַת דָּבָר טָמֵא הוּא. אָמַר רַב הוֹשַׁעְיָה. תִּיפְתָּר בְּאוֹסְפוֹ בְּנֶסֶר. וְאֵיפְשָׁר שֶׁלֹּא יַנֵּשָׂא עָלָיו. אָמַר רִבִּי דְּרִבִּי אָבוֹי יוּדָן דְּרִבִּי מַתַּנְיָה. תִּיפְתָּר בְּאוֹסְפוֹ בְּמַלְתְּרָא עָבָה. רִבִּי בָּא בַּר מָמָל בְּעָא קוֹמֵי רִבִּי אִמִּי. מַה בֵּין אָדָם טָהוֹר לַחַטָּאת לִכְלִי רֵיקָן טָהוֹר לַחַטָּאת. אָמַר לֵיהּ. וְאָסַף טָהוֹר. מַה תַּלְמוּד לוֹמַר אִישׁ. אֶלָּא לִיתֵּן טַהֲרָה מְעוּלָּה לְאִישׁ לַעֲשׂוֹתוֹ כְּמֵי חַטָּאת וּכְאֵפֶר חַטָּאת. רִבִּי יָסָא בְּשֵׁם רִבִּי שִׁמְעוֹן בֶּן לָקִישׁ. הֵיסֵט שֶׁטִּיהַרְתִּי לָךְ בַּשֶּׁרֶץ טִימֵּאתִי לָךְ כָּאן.

"And for the Red Cow if his hands became impure so became his body[161]." Rebbi Ḥanina said, not that they introduced new impurities for the Red Cow but they said, he who becomes impure in an easy impurity is like one who became impure in severe impurity[184]. Rebbi Jacob bar Aha in the name of

Rebbi Eleazar: *And it shall be collected by a man*, why does the verse say, *pure*[185]? Think of it. Even if you collect it by a shovel, the Torah requires *pure*. Where do we hold? If a metal shovel, but also flat metal implements are subject to impurity. If a wooden shovel, is it not held together because of something subject to impurity[186]? Rav Hoshaia said, explain it if he collects it with a plank[187]. Then it is impossible that he should not carry it[188]. Rebbi Yudan, the father of Rebbi Mattaniah, said, explain it if he collects it with a coarse cross-beam[189]. Rebbi Abba bar Mamal asked before Rebbi Immi: what is the difference between a person pure for the Red Cow and an empty vessel pure for the Red Cow[190]? He answered him, *And it shall be collected by a pure*, why does the the verse say, *man*? Only to prescribe extraordinary purity to the man to handle the water for ashes of the Red Cow and the ashes of the Red Cow. Rebbi Yasa in the name of Rebbi Simeon ben Laqish: The moving which I declared pure for you for crawling animals[191] I declared impure for you here[192].

184 An easy impurity is one which is removed by immersion in a *miqweh*. A severe impurity needs some additional action, either a waiting period or a sacrifice to regain access to Temple and *sancta*.

185 *Num.* 19:9.

186 Any metal object is subject to impurity. A wooden object is subject to impurity if it encloses a volume; it becomes impure by being used as a container. Therefore it seems that the collection of the ashes, required by the verse, is an impossible task.

187 A flat piece of wood is impervious to impurity.

188 In most cases of severe impurity, such as carcasses of non-kosher four-legged animals, and impurity caused by human bodies, carrying the impure object without touching it, causes the carrier to be impure (*Lev.* 11:28, 15:10). Since in relation to the ashes of the Cow any impurity is severe, there is transfer of impurity even if the ashes are carried on a wooden plank which itself cannot become impure.

189 Greek μέλαθρον. This not only is a flat piece of wood, it is so heavy that the load of ashes is not noticeable; it causes no impurity by carrying.

190 The Mishnah (Note 174) extends impurity automatically only for humans, not to vessels.

191 In the special section about impurity of dead crawling animals (*Lev.* 11:29-38), impurity by carrying is not mentioned.

192 The rabbinic restrictions in the case of the ashes of the Cow are justified biblically.

(fol. 77a) **משנה ו**: הַטּוֹבֵל לַחוּלִין וְהוּחְזַק לַחוּלִין אָסוּר בַּמַּעֲשֵׂר. הַטּוֹבֵל לַמַּעֲשֵׂר וְהוּחְזַק לַמַּעֲשֵׂר אָסוּר לַתְּרוּמָה. הַטּוֹבֵל לַתְּרוּמָה וְהוּחְזַק לַתְּרוּמָה אָסוּר לַקּוֹדֶשׁ. הַטּוֹבֵל לַקּוֹדֶשׁ וְהוּחְזַק לַקּוֹדֶשׁ אָסוּר לַחַטָּאת. הַטּוֹבֵל לֶחָמוּר הוּתַּר לַקַּל. טָבַל וְלֹא הוּחְזַק כְּאִילוּ לֹא טָבַל:

Mishnah 6: He who immersed himself for profane food and considers himself pure for profane food is prohibited tithe[193]. He who immersed himself for tithe and considers himself pure for tithe is prohibited heave. He who immersed himself heave and considers himself pure for heave is prohibited *sancta*. He who immersed himself for *sancta* and considers himself pure for *sancta* is prohibited handling ashes of the Red Cow. He who immersed himself for the more stringent is permitted the lesser one. He who immersed himself and does not consider himself pure is as if he did not immerse[194].

193 One who immersed himself to eat his profane food in ritual purity may not eat Second Tithe without immersing himself a second time with the correct intention. The other cases are to be interpreted similarly.

194 He immersed himself for cleanliness, not for purity. His immersion does not remove impurity.

(78d line 62) **הלכה ו**: וְחוּלִין צְרִיכִין כַּוָּנָה. דְּרוּבָּא אָתָא מֵימוֹר לָךְ. אֲפִילוּ טוֹבֵל לַחוּלִין וְהֻחְזַק לַחוּלִין אָסוּר בְּמַעֲשֵׂר. לֹא כֵן אָמַר רִבִּי אֶלְעָזָר. כְּמִינְיָין הַחוּלִין כֵּן מִינְיָין הַמַּעֲשֵׂר. כָּאן לַאֲכִילָה וְכָאן לַמַּגָּע. הַטּוֹבֵל סְתָם מוּתָּר בְּכוּלָם. אָמַר רִבִּי יוֹחָנָן. בִּמְזוּקָק לְכוּלָן. עוֹדֵיהוּ רַגְלָיו מְשׁוּקָּעוֹת בַּמַּיִם מַחֲזִיק עַצְמוֹ לְכָל־טַהֲרָה שֶׁיִּרְצֶה.

תַּמָּן תַּנִּינָן. מַקֵּל שֶׁהִיא מְלִיאָה מַשְׁקִין טְמֵאִים. כֵּיוָן שֶׁהִשִּׁיקָהּ לַמִּקְוֶה. טָהֲרָה. דִּבְרֵי רִבִּי יְהוֹשֻׁעַ. וַחֲכָמִים אוֹמְרִים. עַד שֶׁיִּטְבּוֹל אֶת כּוּלָּהּ. רִבִּי שִׁמְעוֹן בֶּן לָקִישׁ אָמַר. מַה פְּלִיגִין. בְּטוּמְאָה קַלָּה. אֲבָל בְּטוּמְאָה חֲמוּרָה אַף רִבִּי יְהוֹשֻׁעַ מוֹדֶה. רִבִּי יוֹחָנָן אָמַר. אַף בְּטוּמְאָה חֲמוּרָה פְּלִיגִין. מַתְנִיתָה פְּלִינָא עַל רִבִּי שִׁמְעוֹן בֶּן לָקִישׁ. עוֹדֵיהוּ רַגְלָיו מְשׁוּקָּעוֹת בַּמַּיִם מַחֲזִיק עַצְמוֹ לְכָל־טַהֲרָה שֶׁיִּרְצֶה. פָּתַר לָהּ בָּאוֹכֶל אוֹכְלִין טְמֵאִין וְשׁוֹתֶה מַשְׁקִין טְמֵאִין. לֹא כֵן אָמַר רִבִּי יַעֲקֹב בַּר זַבְדִּי רִבִּי אַבָּהוּ בְּשֵׁם רִבִּי שִׁמְעוֹן בֶּן לָקִישׁ. הָאוֹכֵל אוֹכָלִין טְמֵאִין וְשׁוֹתֶה מַשְׁקִין טְמֵאִין גּוּפוֹ טָהוֹר בְּלֹא כַוָּונָה. מִכֵּיוָן שֶׁנָּתַן דַּעְתּוֹ לַטַּהֲרָה מְעוּלָּה מִמֶּנּוּ [אֵינוֹ] צָרִיךְ כַּוָּונָה. מַתְנִיתָה פְּלִינָא עַל רִבִּי שִׁמְעוֹן בֶּן לָקִישׁ. מִקְוֶה שֶׁיֵּשׁ בּוֹ אַרְבָּעִים סְאָה מְכוּוָּנוֹת וְיָרְדוּ שְׁנַיִם וְטָבְלוּ [שְׁנֵיהֶן טְהוֹרִין.] זֶה אַחַר זֶה הָרִאשׁוֹן טָהוֹר וְהַשֵּׁינִי טָמֵא. רִבִּי יְהוּדָה אוֹמֵר. אִם הָיוּ רַגְלָיו שֶׁל רִאשׁוֹן נוֹגְעוֹת בַּמַּיִם אַף הַשֵּׁינִי טָהוֹר. וְעוֹד הִיא בָּאוֹכֵל אוֹכָלִין טְמֵאִין וְשׁוֹתֶה מַשְׁקִין טְמֵאִין. מַתְנִיתָה פְּלִינָא עַל רִבִּי שִׁמְעוֹן בֶּן לָקִישׁ. צָנוּן שֶׁבַּמְּעָרָה אִשָּׁה נִדָּה מַדִּיחָתוֹ וְהוּא טָהוֹר. הֶעֱלָתוֹ כָּל־שֶׁהוּא מִן הַמַּיִם טָמֵא. וְתַנֵּי עָלָהּ. רִבִּי יְהוּדָה מְטַהֵר מִשֵּׁם רִבִּי יְהוֹשֻׁעַ. וְנִדָּה לֹא טוּמְאָה חֲמוּרָה הִיא. הָדָא פְּלִינָא עַל רִבִּי שִׁמְעוֹן בֶּן לָקִישׁ וְלֵית לָהּ קַיָּים.

Halakhah 6: But needs profane food intention[195]? He is informing you of more: even if he immersed himself for profane food and considers himself pure for profane food he is prohibited tithe. Did not Rebbi Eleazar say, the count for profane food is the count for tithe[196]? Here it is for eating, there for touching[197]. He who immerses himself without specification is pure for all of them[198]. Rebbi Johanan said, if he had relationship with all of them. As long as his feet are in the water, he may consider himself pure for any stage he chooses[199].

There, we have stated[200]: "A staff which is full of impure fluids[201], when it touched the *miqweh* it is pure, the words of Rebbi Joshua. But the Sages are saying, only if he immerses it completely." Rebbi Simeon ben Laqish said, where do they disagree? For easy impurity; but for severe impurity[184] even Rebbi Joshua agrees. Rebbi Johanan said, they even disagree for severe impurity. A *baraita* disagrees with Rebbi Simeon ben Laqish: "As long as his feet are in the water, he may consider himself pure for any stage he chooses." Explain it about one who ate impure food and drank impure drinks[202]. Did not Rebbi Jacob bar Zavdi, Rebbi Abbahu say in the name of Rebbi Simeon ben Laqish, the body of one who ate impure food and drank impure drinks is pure without special intention[203]? From the moment he intended elevated purity he (needs) [does not need] intention[204]. A Mishnah disagrees with Rebbi Simeon ben Laqish[205]: "A *miqweh* containing exactly 40 *seah* into two persons descended, [both are pure]. One after the other, the first one is pure, the second impure[206]. Rebbi Jehudah says, if the feet of the first touched the water, the second one also is pure[207]." Still this is about one who ate impure food and drank impure drinks[202]. A *baraita* disagrees with Rebbi Simeon ben Laqish: A woman in her period may rinse a radish in a cave[208] and it is pure. If she lifted it in any way out of the water it is impure. And we have stated thereto: Rebbi Jehudah declares it pure in the name of Rebbi Joshua[209]. And represents a menstruating woman not a severe impurity? This disagrees with Rebbi Simeon ben Laqish and it has no standing[210].

195 Since profane food does not require pure bodies there should be no requirement for immersion and therefore no possibility of intention. Babli 19a.

196 Profane food only can become impure in the first degree and disqualify in the

second. The same holds for Second Tithe.

197 Eating Second Tithe needs a body pure by intention but not handling it.

198 Tosephta 3:2; Babli 19a. For R. Johanan if at the moment of immersion it was impossible for the person to eat tithe, heave, or *sancta*, the immersion cannot be valid for one of these.

199 Since water is considered one body, the person standing in the water in this respect is like one immersed and still has the choice of the degree of impurity imparted by the immersion.

200 Mishnah *Taharot* 8:9.

201 Not that the staff contains fluid but that it is covered by fluid from top to bottom. If the staff touches the water, for R. Joshua all the fluid is connected to and becomes part of the 40 *seah* which purify.

202 Whose impurity is rabbinic. Babli 18b.

203 Unless the person has the intention of being pure for heave etc., he is biblically pure and, since in this instance his rabbinic disqualification is inactive, also rabbinically.

204 The correction is unnecessary; once a higher level of purity is desired, no specific intention is needed to invalidate the prior immersion.

205 Mishnah *Miqwaot* 7:6. Babli 19a.

206 If the first one left the *miqweh* before the second entered, the water clinging to his body is missing in the *miqweh* which therefore cannot contain the full 40 *seah* needed to purify.

207 Following R. Joshua (Note 201).

208 Containing 40 *seah* of water and therefore being a natural *miqweh*.

209 But for the Sages the radish remains pure only if at all times it is fully immersed.

210 There is no explaining away and R. Johanan's opinion on the point of view of R. Joshua is proven.

(fol. 77b) **משנה ז:** בִּגְדֵי עַם הָאָרֶץ מִדְרָס לַפְּרוּשִׁים. בִּגְדֵי פְרוּשִׁים מִדְרָס לְאוֹכְלֵי תְרוּמָה. בִּגְדֵי אוֹכְלֵי תְרוּמָה מִדְרָס לַקּוֹדֶשׁ. יוֹסֵי בֶּן יוֹעֶזֶר הָיָה חָסִיד שֶׁבַּכְּהוּנָּה וְהָיְתָה מִטְפַּחְתּוֹ מִדְרָס לַקּוֹדֶשׁ. יוֹחָנָן בֶּן גּוּדְגְּדָא הָיָה אוֹכֵל עַל טָהֳרַת הַקּוֹדֶשׁ כָּל־יָמָיו וְהָיְתָה מִטְפַּחְתּוֹ מִדְרָס לַחַטָּאת:

Mishnah 7: The garments of the vulgar[211] are "support"[212] for Pharisees[213]; the garments of Pharisees are "support" for the eaters of heave; the garments of eaters of heave are "support" for the eaters of *sancta*. Yose ben Yoezer[214] was the most pious of the priests but his handkerchief[217] was "support" for *sancta*. Johanan ben Gudgada all his life ate in the purity of *sancta* but his handkerchief was "support" for the ashes of the Red Cow[215].

211 A person who disregards the rules of impurity (unless on a pilgrimage to the Temple); cf. *Introduction to Tractate Demay*.

212 Rabbinically it is considered a source of original impurity. The expression "support"

comes from the severe impurity of a menstruating woman where *Lev.* 15:21 implies that any implement which had supported her body (chair or bed) imparts impurity to anybody touching it and his garments.

213 People observing the laws on impurity in their daily lives.

214 Cf. Mishnah 2:2.

215 But not for the eaters of *sancta*. This Mishnah contradicts the practice established after the destruction of the Temple which considers profane food eaten in the purity of *sancta* not different from other profane food (Note 180).

(78 line 9) **הלכה ז**: רִבִּי יָסָא בְּשֵׁם רִבִּי יוֹחָנָן. בְּמַגָּעוֹת שָׁנוּ. רִבִּי זְעוּרָה בָּעָא קוֹמֵי רִבִּי יָסָא. מֵאֵיכָן נִיטְמָא הַבֶּגֶד הַזֶּה מִדְרָס. אָמַר לֵיהּ. תֵּיפְתָּר שֶׁהָיְתָה אִשְׁתּוֹ שֶׁלְּעַם הָאָרֶץ יוֹשֶׁבֶת עָלָיו עֲרוּמָה. שְׁמוּאֵל בַּר אַבָּא בָּעָא קוֹמֵי רִבִּי זְעוּרָה. כַּמָּה דַתְּ אָמַר תַּמָּן. אֵין הֵיסֵט בַּחוּלִין. וְיֵשׁ הֵיסֵט בַּחוּלִין עַל יְדֵי מַגָּע. וְדִכְוָותָהּ אֵין מַשָּׂא בַּחוּלִין. וְיֵשׁ מַשָּׂא בַּחוּלִין עַל יְדֵי מַגָּע. רִבִּי שְׁמוּאֵל אָחוֹי דְּרִבִּי הוֹשַׁעְיָה אָמַר. רִבִּי יִרְמְיָה בָּעֵי. יָשְׁבָה עַל הַכִּסֵּא וְנָגְעָה בּוֹ. מַה נַּפְשָׁךְ. אִם מַשָּׂא הֲרֵי מַשָּׂא. אִם מַגָּע הֲרֵי מַגָּע. כְּמָה דַתְּ אָמַר בְּמַשָּׂא. עַד שֶׁיִּנָּשֵׂא רוּבּוֹ. וְדִכְוָותָהּ בְּמַגָּע. עַד שֶׁיִּגַּע בְּרוּבּוֹ.

גּוּפוֹ שֶׁלְּפָרוּשׁ מָהוּ שֶׁיֵּיעָשֶׂה כְזָב אֵצֶל הַתְּרוּמָה. הָתֵיב רִבִּי יוֹחָנָן. וְהָא תַּנִּינָן. הַמַּנִּיחַ עִם הָאָרֶץ בְּתוֹךְ בֵּיתוֹ לְשׁוֹמְרוֹ. בִּזְמַן שֶׁהוּא רוֹאֶה אֶת הַנִּכְנָסִין וְאֶת הַיּוֹצְאִין. הָאוֹכָלִין וְהַמַּשְׁקִין וּכְלֵי חֶרֶשׂ פְּתוּחִין טְמֵאִין. אֲבָל הַמִּשְׁכָּבוֹת וְהַמּוֹשָׁבוֹת וּכְלֵי חֶרֶשׂ מוּקָּפִין צָמִיד פָּתִיל טָהוֹר. אֵין לֵימַר. עָשׂוּ גוּפוֹ כְּזָב אֵצֶל הַתְּרוּמָה. אֲפִילוּ מוּקָּפִין צָמִיד [פָּתִיל] יְהוּ טְמֵאִין. אָמַר רִבִּי יוּדָה בַּר פָּזִי. תֵּיפְתָּר בְּעַם הָאָרֶץ אֵצֶל הַפָּרוּשׁ. וְלֵית שְׁמַע מִינָהּ כְּלוּם. אָמַר רִבִּי מָנָא. כֵּן אָמַר רִבִּי יוֹסֵף רִבִּי. כָּל־מַה דַּאֲנָן קַיָּימִין הָכָא בִּתְרוּמָה אֲנַן קַיָּימִין. תֵּדַע לָךְ שֶׁהוּא כֵּן. דְּתַנִּינָן תַּמָּן. אַפִּיל מוּבָל אֲפִילוּ כָפוּת הַכֹּל טָמֵא: כְּלוּם אָמְרוּ טְמֵאִים לֹא מִשּׁוּם הֵיסֵט. לֹא כֵן אָמַר רִבִּי יוֹחָנָן. לֹא חֲצָצוֹת וְלֹא הֶסֵּיטוֹת וְלֹא [רְשׁוּת הַיָּחִיד וְלֹא] עִם הָאָרֶץ אֵצֶל תְּרוּמָה. גּוּפָהּ שֶׁלַּתְּרוּמָה מָהוּ שֶׁיֵּיעָשֶׂה כְזָב אֵצֶל הַקּוֹדֶשׁ. נִשְׁמְעִינָהּ מִן הָדָא. הַחוֹתֵךְ שֶׁפּוֹפֶרֶת שֶׁלַּקּוֹדֶשׁ. הַחוֹתָכָהּ וְהַמַּטְבִּילָהּ טָעוּן טְבִילָה. מַטְבִּילָהּ. נִיחָא חוֹתְכָהּ. וְיַכְרְכֶינָּה (בְּסִיט) [בְּסִיב] וְיַטְבִּילָהּ. אֶלָּא תִּיפְתָּר בְּשֶׁחֲתָכָהּ עַל מְנַת לְהַטְבִּילָהּ. גּוּפָהּ שֶׁלַּקּוֹדֶשׁ מָהוּ שֶׁיֵּיעָשֶׂה כְזָב אֵצֶל הַחַטָּאת. נִשְׁמְעִינָהּ מִן הָדָא. שְׁנֵי לְגִינִין. אֶחָד טָהוֹר לַקּוֹדֶשׁ וְאֶחָד טָהוֹר לַתְּרוּמָה. שֶׁנְּגָעוֹ זֶה בָזֶה. שְׁנֵיהֶן טְהוֹרִין. וְהָא מַתְנִיתָא פְלִיגָא. עָשָׂה אֶת הַטָּהוֹר לַחַטָּאת שֶׁהֵיסִיטוֹ בְּרוֹקוֹ וּבְשִׁכְבַת זַרְעוֹ שֶׁלַּטָּהוֹר לַתְּרוּמָה וְנִיטְמָא. הִיא טָהוֹר לַתְּרוּמָה הִיא טָהוֹר לַקּוֹדֶשׁ.

Halakhah 7: Rebbi Yasa in the name of Rebbi Johanan: They stated it for touchings[216]. Rebbi Ze`ira asked before Rebbi Yasa, from where did this garment become impure by support? He told him, explain it that the vulgar's wife sat on it naked[217]. Samuel bar Abba asked before Rebbi Ze`ira: As you are saying there, there is no "support" for profane food but there is "support" for profane food by touching[218], similarly there is no load for profane food but there is load for profane food by touching. Rebbi Samuel the brother of Rebbi Hoshaia said, Rebbi Jeremiah asked, if she sat on a chair and touched it[219]? As you look at it, if load, there is load; it touching there is touching[220]. As you are saying about load, on condition that most of it be carried, similarly if most of it be touched[221]?

May the body of a Pharisee be considered like that of a sufferer from gonorrhea for heave[222]? Rebbi Joḥanan asked, but did we not state[223], "somebody who let a vulgar watch his house, at times when he sees those who enter and those who leave, food, and drinks, and open clay vessels are impure. But couches and seats and clay vessels tightly wound closed are pure[224]"? If you are saying, they considered the body of a Pharisee like that of a sufferer from gonorrhea for heave then even those tightly [wound] closed should be impure[225]. Rebbi Jehudah bar Pazi said, explain it concerning a vulgar at a Pharisee's, and you cannot infer anything[226]. Rebbi Mana said, so said my teacher Rebbi Yose, all that we are considering here[227] refers to heave. You may know that this is so, since we have stated there, "even moved, even tied, everything is impure." Did they not say they are impure, not because moving[228]? Did not Rebbi Joḥanan say, concerning heave there is neither separations, nor movings, nor [private domain, nor] vulgar[229]. May heave itself be considered like a sufferer from gonorrhea in relation to *sancta*[230]? Let us hear from the following. If one cuts a tube for *sancta*, he who cuts it and he who immerses it need immersion. One understands he who cuts. He who immerses[231]? Could he not bind it with a (*sit*)[232] [fiber] and immerse it? But explain it that he cut it in order to immerse it[231]. May a *sanctum* itself be considered like a sufferer from gonorrhea in relation to the ashes of the Red Cow? Let us hear from the following. Two pitchers, one pure for *sancta* and one pure for heave, who touched one another are both pure[233]. But does not a *baraita* disagree? They made that the person pure for the ashes of the Cow who moved spittle or semen of one pure for heave that it became impure[234]. The same is pure for heave and pure for *sancta*.

216 The garments of a vulgar make a Pharisee impure by touch but not by load nor by "support".

217 If the wife of the vulgar, still a source of

original impurity from her period, sat on the garment, the latter became an original source of impurity. Therefore there is a (slim) possibility that the Pharisaic restriction correspond to a case of actual biblical impurity. Babli *Hulin* 35b.

218 Only humans and implements can become impure by load or "support" but foodstuffs become impure only by touch.

219 What is the status of the chair?

220 In both cases the status of the impurity is the same.

221 R. Jeremiah has a point; the two sources of impurity are not equivalent. For impurity by load or "support", most of the weight of the cause of impurity must be carried or must be loaded on, but the smallest amount of touching has the same consequence as touching most of the impure surface area.

222 If the garments of a Pharisee are impure like those of a sufferer from gonorrhea, is it not reasonable to expect the same from the Pharisee's body?

223 Mishnah *Taharot* 7:5.

224 As long as the Pharisee has control over the stream of visitors, only things impure by touch are considered impure; the vulgar is not supposed to cause impurity by sitting on something even though this would be the cause of biblical original impurity (not only derivative impurity as in the case of touch) if the vulgar actually were a sufferer from gonorrhea.

225 Since the exception for tightly closed vessels applies only to tent impurity.

226 The entire Mishnah refers to ordinary impurity on the level of profane food and is irrelevant for the question raised here.

227 The Mishnah in *Taharot*.

228 The part of the Mishnah quoted here refers to the situation that the Pharisee has no control over the stream of visitors which therefore may include menstruating women which may make seats and couches impure by biblical standards. This proves that these arguments do not apply to the vulgar himself and that therefore also the Mishnah here has to be read to apply to garments only and to nothing else.

229 Rabbinic extensions of impurity do not apply except in cases where they are mentioned explicitly. The corrector's addition has to be deleted since it refers to a rule, that questionable cases in private domains have to be judged restrictively, which by general consensus is of biblical status.

230 Same question as that referred to in Note 222.

231 If he prepares vessels for use with *sancta* but he himself is not pure for the consumption of *sancta,* it is clear that the vessels must be immersed since by necessity he touched them. But immersion may be done indirectly as described.

232 Here the corrector's text has to be accepted since the scribe's *sit* is a measure, half a hand-breadth.

233 Mishnah 7 applies only to humans, not to vessels.

234 Spittle is biblically original impurity for the sufferer from gonorrhea; it is pure for the person pure for heave. But semen is biblically impure from everybody. Therefore for the rabbinic extensions described in Mishnah 7 there is no difference in the rules according to levels of impurity.

חומר בקודש פרק שלישי חגיגה

(fol.78b) **משנה א**: חֹמֶר בַּקּוֹדֶשׁ מִבַּתְּרוּמָה שֶׁמַּטְבִּילִין כֵּלִים בְּתוֹךְ כֵּלִים בַּתְּרוּמָה אֲבָל לֹא בַקּוֹדֶשׁ. אֲחוֹרַיִים וְתוֹךְ וּבֵית צְבִיעָה בַּתְּרוּמָה אֲבָל לֹא בַקּוֹדֶשׁ. הַנּוֹשֵׂא אֶת הַמִּדְרָס נוֹשֵׂא אֶת הַתְּרוּמָה אֲבָל לֹא אֶת הַקּוֹדֶשׁ. בִּגְדֵי אוֹכְלֵי תְרוּמָה מִדְרָס לַקּוֹדֶשׁ. לֹא כְמִדַּת הַקּוֹדֶשׁ מִדַּת הַתְּרוּמָה שֶׁבַּקּוֹדֶשׁ מַתִּיר וּמַטְבִּיל וְאַחַר כָּךְ קוֹשֵׁר וּבַתְּרוּמָה קוֹשֵׁר וְאַחַר כָּךְ מַטְבִּיל:

Mishnah 1: Sancta are more stringent than heave in that one may immerse vessels inside vessels[1] for heave but not for *sancta*. One considers back[2], inside, and finger-holes[3] for heave but not for *sancta*. He who carries "support" may carry heave but not *sancta*[4]. The garments of eaters of heave are "support" for *sancta*[5]. The action for *sancta* is different from that for heave in that for *sancta* one unties before immersing whereas for heave one may tie and then immerse[6].

1 Vessels immersed in a *miqweh* to be pure for use with *sancta* must be immersed singly. For heave one may immerse vessels inside vessels if only it is possible for the water to touch each vessel fully inside and out.

2 Clay vessels by biblical standards become impure only from inside a cavity. Any impurity on the concave parts of the outside is rabbinical.

3 Holes on the outside of a pot or cup into which one puts his fingers to hold the cup are independent cavities. For heave, all these rules of rabbinic impurity are observed. For *sancta* any impurity of any source disqualifies the vessel.

4 A person may carry both the shoe of a sufferer from gonorrhea and heave if both of them are placed on wooden planks (impervious to impurity) and the carrier never touches shoe and heave.

5 Mishnah 2:7.

6 For heave one may assume that the water penetrates any rope with which immersed vessels are tied. For *sancta* this assumption may not be made.

(78d line 2) חֹמֶר בַּקּוֹדֶשׁ מִבַּתְּרוּמָה כול׳. רִבִּי חִייָה בְשֵׁם רִבִּי יוֹחָנָן. מִפְּנֵי שֶׁאוֹכְלֵי תְרוּמָה זְרִיזִין. וְאוֹכְלֵי קוֹדֶשׁ אֵינָן זְרִיזִין. אָמַר רִבִּי חֲנַנְיָה קוֹמֵי רִבִּי מָנָא. וְהָדָא הִיא מַעֲלָה. אִילּוּ דָבָר שֶׁהוּא שָׁוֶה בָזֶה וּבָזֶה. טָמֵא בָזֶה וְטָהוֹר בָּזֶה. וְדָא הִיא מַעֲלָה. אָמַר לֵיהּ. תִּיפְּתַר בְּמֵזִיקָק לַקּוֹדֶשׁ. רִבִּי לָא בְשֵׁם רִבִּי יוֹחָנָן. אִם הָיָה דָבָר טָמֵא [כָּבֵד] כְּלִיטְרָא אֵין מַטְבִּילִין אוֹתוֹ. אַבָּא שָׁאוּל אוֹמֵר. אַף בִּתְרוּמָה אֵין מַטְבִּילִין אוֹתוֹ אֶלָּא סַל וְנַרְגּוּתְנִי בִּלְבַד. אָמַר רִבִּי יוֹחָנָן. אַבָּא שָׁאוּל וְרִבִּי שִׁמְעוֹן שְׁנֵיהֶם אָמְרוּ דָבָר אֶחָד. דְּתַנִּינָן תַּמָּן. הָאוֹחֵז בָּאָדָם וּבַכֵּלִים וּמַטְבִּילָן

טְמֵאִים. וּכְשֶׁהוּא מַדִּיחַ אֶת יָדָיו טְהוֹרִין. רִבִּי שִׁמְעוֹן אוֹמֵר יְרַפֵּם [עַד] שֶׁיָּבוֹא בָהֶן הַמַּיִם. אָמַר רִבִּי יוֹחָנָן. מִסְתַּבְּרָא רִבִּי שִׁמְעוֹן יוֹדֵי לְאַבָּא שָׁאוּל. אַבָּא שָׁאוּל לֹא יוֹדֵי לְרִבִּי שִׁמְעוֹן. רַבָּנִן דְּקַיְסָרִין בְּשֵׁם רִבִּי יוֹחָנָן. הֲלָכָה כְאַבָּא שָׁאוּל. וְתַנֵּי כֵן. הֲלָכָה כִדְבָרָיו. אָמַר רִבִּי יוֹנָה. מַתְנִיתָהּ דְּרִבִּי מֵאִיר. אֲבָל דִּבְרֵי חֲכָמִים עוֹשִׂין כֵּן אֲפִילוּ בַקּוֹדֶשׁ. שֶׁאֵין בֵּית צְבִיעָה תּוֹךְ. כְּלִי קוֹדֶשׁ כּוּלָּן תּוֹךְ.

"*Sancta* are more stringent than heave," etc. Rebbi Ḥiyya in the name of Rebbi Joḥanan, because eaters of heave are vigilant but eaters of *sancta* are not vigilant[7]. Rebbi Ḥanania said before Rebbi Mana, is that eminence? If it were a thing equal for both but impure for one and pure for the other, that would be eminence. He said to him, explain it if it is connected to *sancta*[8]. Rebbi La in the name of Rebbi Joḥanan, if the impure was [heavy] a lb. one does not immerse it[9]. Abba Shaul said, also for heave one immerses only a basked or a willow-basket[10]. Rebbi Joḥanan said, Abba Shaul and Rebbi Simeon said the same, as we have stated there[11], "if one holds a human or vessels and immerses them, they are impure, but if he had rinsed his hands in water they are pure[12]. Rebbi Simeon said, he should hold them loosely so the water may come into them." Rebbi Joḥanan said, it is reasonable that Rebbi Joḥanan would agree with Abba Shaul but Abba Shaul not with Rebbi Simeon[13]. The rabbis of Caesarea in the name of Rebbi Joḥanan: Practice follows Abba Shaul. It was stated thus: Practice follows his words. Rebbi Jonah said, the Mishnah is Rebbi Meïr's, but the words of the Sages are that one acts thus even for *sancta*, since finger-holes are no interior; for vessels of *sancta* all is interior[14].

7   Heave as a countryside food is eaten daily by Cohanim but *sancta* only at the time of their service in the Temple, usually two weeks in a year, or by laity on pilgrimage. The eaters of heave may be expected to follow an exact procedure at all times.

8   If a Cohen happens to eat heave in the week in which he is eating *sancta*, he may not immerse vessels for heave together with those for *sancta* since they follow different rules and in this case it it obvious that for one and the same person the rules for *sancta* are more stringent.

9   The permission for eaters of heave to immerse a smaller vessel inside a larger one holds only if the smaller vessel weighs less than one Roman pound. Cf. Babli 21a.

10   Greek γύργαθος.

11   Mishnah *Miqwaot* 8:5.

12   If his hands block the access of the water in the *miqweh* to even the smallest part of the surface area, the immersion is ineffective. According to R. Simeon it is possible to hold something in the *miqweh*

without obstructing the access of the water.
13 Abba Shaul holds that joint immersion is possible only if the outer vessel is permeable; hands are not permeable.
14 Finger-holes while cavities cannot be used to store anything since they have no bottom; they are irrelevant by biblical standards. But it is agreed in the Mishnah that for vessels used for *sancta*, rabbinic impurity is treated as biblical.

(78d line 15) רִבִּי יוֹנָה בְשֵׁם רִבִּי חִיָּיה בַּר בָּא. מַעֲשֶׂה שֶׁנִּכְנְסוּ שִׁבְעָה זְקֵינִים לְעַבֵּר אֶת הַשָּׁנָה בְּבִקְעַת רִימּוֹן. וּמִי הָיוּ. רִבִּי מֵאִיר וְרִבִּי יְהוּדָה וְרִבִּי יוֹסֵי וְרִבִּי שִׁמְעוֹן וְרִבִּי נְחֶמְיָה וְרִבִּי לִיעֶזֶר בֶּן יַעֲקֹב וְרִבִּי יוֹחָנָן הַסַּנְדְּלָר. אָמְרוּ. כַּמָּה מַעֲלוֹת בַּקּוֹדֶשׁ וּבַתְּרוּמָה. רִבִּי מֵאִיר אוֹמֵר. שָׁלֹשׁ עֶשְׂרֵה. רִבִּי יוֹסֵי אוֹמֵר. שְׁתֵּים עֶשְׂרֵה. אָמַר רִבִּי מֵאִיר. כָּךְ שָׁמַעְתִּי מֵרִבִּי עֲקִיבָה. שָׁלֹשׁ עֶשְׂרֵה. אָמַר לוֹ רִבִּי יוֹחָנָן הַסַּנְדְּלָר. שִׁימַּשְׁתִּי אֶת רִבִּי עֲקִיבָה עוֹמָדוֹת מַה שֶּׁלֹּא שִׁימַּשְׁתּוֹ יְשִׁיבוֹת. אָמְרוּ. רִבִּי יוֹחָנָן הַסַּנְדְּלָר אֲלֶכְסַנְדְּרִי לַאֲמִיתּוֹ הוּא. וְעָמְדוּ מִשָּׁם בִּנְשִׁיקָה. וְכָל־מָאן דְּלָא הֲוָה לֵיהּ גּוּלָה הֲוָה חַבְרֵיהּ קָטַע פַּלְגָּא דְגוּלָתֵיהּ וְיָהַב לֵיהּ. וְלָמָּה הֲווֹן עָבְדִין כֵּן. דַּהֲווֹן כּוּלְּהוֹן דָּרְשִׁין הָדֵין פְּסוּקָא מִן שֶׁבַע שֶׁבַע אַפִּין. אָשִׁירָה נָא לִידִידִי שִׁירַת דּוֹדִי לְכַרְמוֹ. וְקַלְסוּן לַאֲחוֹרָיָא מַה אַשְׁכַּח אַפּוֹי בְּגַוָּהּ. אָמְרִין. רִבִּי שִׁמְעוֹן בֶּן יוֹחַי הֲוָה. וְלָמָּה הֲווֹן דָּחֲקִין מֵעַתָּה הָדָא מִילְּתָא. דַּהֲווֹן דָּרְשִׁין מֵימַר אֱלֹהֵי מַסֵּכָה לֹא תַעֲשֶׂה־לָּךְ: מַה כְּתִיב בַּתְרֵיהּ. אֶת־חַג הַמַּצּוֹת תִּשְׁמֹר. אָמְרִין. כָּל־מִי שֶׁסְּפִיקָה בְיָדוֹ לְעַבֵּר אֶת הַשָּׁנָה וְאֵינוֹ מְעַבְּרָהּ כְּאִילּוּ עוֹבֵד עֲבוֹדָה זָרָה. מִי אֲתֵי מֵיזַל לוֹן אָמְרִין. אַתּוּן נַחֲוֵי עוֹבְדֵינָן. וַהֲוָה תַמָּן חַד כֵּיף דַּשִּׁיִישׁ וַהֲוָה כָּל־חַד וְחַד נָסִיב חַד מַסְמֵר וְקָבַע לֵיהּ בְּגַוֵּיהּ וְהוּא נָחַת וּשְׁקַע כָּהֲדֵין לַיִישָׁא. עַד כְּדוֹן מִיתְקְרֵי כֵּיפָא מַסְמְרָא.

Rebbi Jonah in the name of Rebbi Hiyya bar Abba: It happened that seven Elders assembled in the valley of Rimmon[15]. Who were they? Rebbi Meïr, and Rebbi Jehudah, and Rebbi Yose, and Rebbi Simeon, and Rebbi Nehemiah, and Rebbi Eliezer ben Jacob, and Rebbi Johanan the Alexandrian. They said, how many distinctions have *sancta* compared to heave[16]? Rebbi Meïr says, thirteen. Rebbi Yose says, twelve. Rebbi Meïr said, so I heard from Rebbi Aqiba, thirteen. Rebbi Johanan the Alexandrian said, I served Rebbi Aqiba standing more than you served sitting[17]. They said, Rebbi Johanan the Alexandrian is a true Alexandrian. They rose kissing, and if any of them had no kaftan, his colleague cut half of his kaftan and gave it to him. And why did they do this? Because all of them were explaining the following verse, each one in seven ways: *I shall sing to my beloved, my beloved's song for his vineyard*[18]. They acclaimed the last one for the versions he found in it. They said, this was Rebbi Simeon ben Yohai. Why were they exerting themselves in this matter[19]? They were explaining, saying, *molten gods you shall not make for yourself.* What is written next? *The holiday of unleavened bread you shall observe*[20]. They said, anybody able to intercalate a year and he does not intercalate is as if he worshipped strange gods. When they were leaving they said, come and let us record our act. A rock of marble was there. Each of them took a nail and fixed it in it; it descended and sank in as in dough. Until now it is called the rock of nails.

15 In the South of Judea at a time when the main Jewish settlement was in the Galilee.
16 In all Mishnaiot together. The main difference seems to be whether back and finger-holes are one or two subjects.
17 He served standing as a member of his household whereas R. Meïr was a student in R. Aqiba's classes. Therefore his contact was more intensive and extensive.
18 *Is.* 5:1.
19 Convening a meeting at a far-out place in order to proclaim an intercalary month.
20 *Ex.* 34:17-18.

(78d line 32) אָמַר רִבִּי יוֹחָנָן. בֵּית צְבִיעָה שֶׁאָמְרוּ בֵּין בִּפְנִים בֵּין בַּחוּץ כְּדֶרֶךְ שֶׁהַנְּקִיִּים תּוֹפְסִין בּוֹ. אָמַר רִבִּי זְעוּרָה. אִיפְשַׁר לוֹמַר בְּנָגוּב. שֶׁאֵין הַיָּדַיִם מִיטַּמּוֹת בְּנָגוּב. אֲבָל אִיפְשַׁר לוֹמַר כִּמְלוֹא מַשְׁקֶה. שֶׁמִּכֵּיוָן שֶׁנָּגַע בּוֹ טִימֵּהוּ. אֶלָּא כִי נָן קַיָּימִין [בִּמְלוּכְלָךְ] בְּמַשְׁקֶה. רִבִּי יוֹחָנָן בְּשֵׁם רִבִּי בְּנָיָיה. עָשׂוּ מַשְׁקֵה בֵּית צְבִיעָה כְּמַשְׁקֶה בֵּית מִטְבַּחַיָּיא. כָּמָה דַתְּ אָמַר תַּמָּן. מַשְׁקֵה בֵּית מִטְבַּחַיָּא טְהוֹרִין בִּמְקוֹמָן וּטְמֵאִין בְּמָקוֹם אַחֵר. [וְכָה מַשְׁקֵה בֵּית צְבִיעָה טְהוֹרִין בִּמְקוֹמָן וּטְמֵאִין בְּמָקוֹם אַחֵר.] רִבִּי סִימוֹן בְּשֵׁם רִבִּי יְהוֹשֻׁעַ בֶּן לֵוִי. מַשְׁקֵה בֵּית מִטְבַּחַיָּא שֶׁיָּצָא לַחוּץ נִיטְמָא. וְהָא תַנִּינָן . מַשְׁקֵה בֵּית מִטְבַּחַיָּא שֶׁיָּצָאוּ לַחוּץ בִּקְדוּשָּׁתָן הֵן. אָמַר רִבִּי יוֹסֵה. קָיְימָה רִבִּי סִימוֹן. רִבִּי חִינָּנָא רִבִּי סִימוֹן בְּשֵׁם רִבִּי יְהוֹשֻׁעַ בֶּן לֵוִי. בְּשֶׁיָּצְאוּ וְחָזְרוּ. נִיטְמָא מַשְׁקֶה הָעֶלְיוֹן וְהָיָה שׁוֹתֵת וְיוֹרֵד. רִבִּי בָּא וְרִבִּי בּוּן בַּר חִייָה. חַד אָמַר. בִּמְקוֹמוֹ טָהוֹר. יָרַד לְמַטָּן טָמֵא. וְחוֹרָנָה אָמַר. הוֹאִיל וְהוּא בָא מִכֹּחַ טַהֲרָה טָהוֹר.

רִבִּי אָחָא בְּשֵׁם רִבִּי זְעוּרָה. הָדָא דַתְּ אָמַר. כְּמַשְׁקִין שֶׁנִּיטְמוּ בְאוֹכְלִין. אֲבָל בְּמַשְׁקִין שֶׁנִּיטְמוּ בְשֶׁרֶץ טְמֵאִים הֵן.

Rebbi Johanan said, the finger-holes which they mentioned, whether inside or outside, in the manner in which cleanly people hold it[21]. Rebbi Ze`ira said, "it is impossible to say, about one which is wiped dry, for hands are not made impure by anything wiped dry[22]. In truth it is impossible to say, if it is full of fluid, for in the moment he touched it he made it impure[23]. But we must hold that [it was dirtied] by fluid[24]." Rebbi Johanan in the name of Rebbi Banaiah: They treated fluid in a finger-hole like fluid at the slaughtering place^{25}. As you are saying there that fluids of the slaughtering place are pure at their proper place but impure at any other place^{26}, [so here, fluids in a finger-hole are pure at their proper place but impure at any other place.] Rebbi Simon in the name of Rebbi Joshua ben Levi: fluids of the slaughtering place which came outside {the Temple courtyards} become impure. But did we not state, fluids of the slaughtering place which came outside continue in their sanctity? Rebbi Yose said, Rebbi Simon explained it. Rebbi Hinena, Rebbi Simon in the name of Rebbi Joshua ben Levi. If they came out and returned^{27}. If the upper fluid became impure and flowed down, Rebbi Abba and Rebbi Abun bar Hiyya. One said, at its place it is pure, if it flows down it is impure. The other one said, since it comes from purity it is pure^{28}.

Rebbi Aha in the name of Rebbi Ze`ira: About fluids which became impure from solid food. But fluids impure from crawling things are impure^{29}.

21 Cleanly people hold the cup on the outside, so that their fingers do not touch the drink. The problem with finger-holes is that they are cavities, and as such potential subjects of biblical impurity, but since the cavities are horizontal, not vertical, they are not containers and therefore impervious to biblical impurity. Babli 22b.

22 Tosephta *Kelim Baba Batra* 3:9. Since unwashed hands rabbinically are impure in the second degree, when dry they have no influence on the status of vessels. (By touching they still disqualify heave and make sacrificial food impure.)

23 In this case it is certain that the fluid touched the hand. By rabbinic tradition any such fluid is impure in the first degree and so is the vessel containing it.

24 In the case of isolated spots of fluids one cannot say that the fluids merge; the rules of the Mishnah are reasonable if applied to this situation.

25 Mishnah *Idiut* 8:4; *Kelim* 15:6. Even though water and blood are the essential agents of biblical impurity, water used at the slaughtering place in the Temple and blood spilled there are pure, i. e., impervious to impurity and do not act to prepare food to possible impurity.

26 Outside of the Temple they just are regular fluids subject to all their rules. Babli *Pesahim* 17a.

27 If they somehow re-entered the Temple domain while pure by outside standards, they regain their immunity from the rules of impurity.

28 The slaughtering place is in the place of the Cohanim, the highest in the Temple domain. The question is the definition of the domain in which the fluids are exempt from the rules of impurity. In one opinion it only is the Cohanim's courtyard, in the other it is the entire space inside the enclosure of the Temple, including the courtyards accessible to Israel men and women.

29 This is a new remark, about the Mishnah. The impurity discussed is of rabbinic nature, such as derivative impurity

of foodstuffs; but biblical impurity, such as caused by the carcasses of crawling animals, is transmitted to vessels by biblical rules. Babli *Pesaḥim* 17b.

(78d line 46) תַּמָּן תַּנִּינָן. כָּל־הַכֵּלִים יֵשׁ לָהֶן אֲחוֹרַיִים וְתוֹךְ וְיֵשׁ לָהֶם בֵּית צְבִיעָה. רִבִּי טַרְפוֹן אוֹמֵר. לַעֲרִיבָה גְדוֹלָה שֶׁלְּעֵץ. רִבִּי עֲקִיבָה אוֹמֵר. לְכוֹסוֹת. רִבִּי מֵאִיר אוֹמֵר. לְיָדַיִם טְמֵאוֹת וּטְהוֹרוֹת. אָמַר רִבִּי יוֹסֵי. לֹא אֲמְרוּ אֶלָּא לְיָדַיִם טְהוֹרוֹת בִּלְבָד: וּכְרִבִּי מֵאִיר. הָיוּ יָדָיו טְמֵאוֹת וַאֲחוֹרֵי הַכּוֹס טְהוֹרִין מַשְׁקֶה לַחוּץ עַל גַּבֵּי הַכּוֹס וְאָחֲזוֹ בְּבֵית צְבִיעָתוֹ. פְּשִׁיטָא שֶׁאֵין מַשְׁקֶה מִיטַּמֵּא מִן הַיָּד לְטַמֵּא אֶת הַכּוֹס. כְּשֵׁם שֶׁאֵין מַשְׁקֶה מִיטַּמֵּא מִן הַיָּד לְטַמֵּא אֶת הַכּוֹס כָּךְ אֵין מַשְׁקֶה מִיטַּמֵּא מִן הַיָּד לְטַמֵּא כִכָּר בְּמָקוֹם אַחֵר. נִישְׁמְעִינָהּ מִן הָדָא. מַשְׁקִין טְהוֹרִים נְתוּנִין בַּקַּרְקַע. נָגַע בָּהֶן כִּכָּר טָמֵא טִימְּאָן. לְאֵי זֶה דָבָר טִימְּאָן. לֹא לְטַמֵּא כִכָּר בְּמָקוֹם אַחֵר. מִפְּנֵי שֶׁהֵן עַל גַּבֵּי קַרְקַע. הָא עַל גַּבֵּי הַכּוֹס לֹא. אֶלָּא מַשְׁקֶה [נָתוּן] עַל גַּבֵּי הַיָּד וְאָחֲזוֹ בְּבֵית צְבִיעָתוֹ אֲפִילוּ כֵן אֵין מַשְׁקֶה מִיטַּמֵּא מִן הַכּוֹס לְטַמֵּא אֶת הַיָּד. נִישְׁמְעִינָהּ מִן הָדָא. מַשְׁקִין טְמֵאִין נְתוּנִין בַּקַּרְקַע. נָגַע בָּהֶן כִּכָּר טָהוֹר נִיטְמָא. לָא אָמַר אֶלָּא כִכָּר. הָא יָד לֹא. וּכְרִבִּי יוֹסֵה. הָיוּ יָדָיו טְהוֹרוֹת וַאֲחוֹרֵי הַכּוֹס טְמֵאִים. מַשְׁקֶה נָתוּן עַל גַּבֵּי הַיָּד וְאָחֲזוֹ בְּבֵית צְבִיעָתוֹ. פְּשִׁיטָא שֶׁאֵין מַשְׁקֶה מִיטַּמֵּא מִן הַכּוֹס לְטַמֵּא אֶת הַיָּד. וּכְשֵׁם שֶׁאֵין מַשְׁקֶה מִיטַּמֵּא מִן הַכּוֹס לְטַמֵּא אֶת הַיָּד כָּךְ אֵין מַשְׁקֶה מִיטַּמֵּא מִן הַיָּד לְטַמֵּא כִכָּר בְּמָקוֹם אַחֵר. נִישְׁמְעִינָהּ מִן הָדָא. מַשְׁקִין טְמֵאִין נְתוּנִין בַּקַּרְקַע. נָגַע בָּהֶן כִּכָּר טָהוֹר נִיטְמָא. לְאֵי זֶה דָבָר נִיטְמָא. לֹא לְטַמֵּא כִכָּר בְּמָקוֹם אַחֵר. מִפְּנֵי שֶׁהֵן עַל גַּבֵּי קַרְקַע. הָא עַל גַּבֵּי הַיָּד לֹא. אֶלָּא מַשְׁקֶה נָתוּן עַל גַּבֵּי הַכּוֹס וְאָחֲזוֹ בְּבֵית צְבִיעָתוֹ. אֲפִילוּ כֵן אֵין מַשְׁקֶה מִיטַּמֵּא מִן הַיָּד לְטַמֵּא אֶת הַכּוֹס. נִישְׁמְעִינָהּ מִן הָדָא. מַשְׁקִין טְמֵאִים נְתוּנִין בְּבֵית צְבִיעָתוֹ שֶׁלְּכוֹס. נָגַע בָּהֶן כּוֹס שֶׁאֲחוֹרָיו טְהוֹרִים בְּבֵית צְבִיעָתוֹ נִיטְמָא.

There, we have stated[30]: "All vessels have back and interior, and they have finger-holes. Rebbi Tarphon says, concerning a large wooden trough[31]. Rebbi Aqiba says, concerning cups[32]. Rebbi Meïr says, concerning impure and pure hands. Rebbi Yose says, they referred only to pure hands[33]." Following Rebbi Meïr, if his hands were impure and the back of the cup pure, fluid outside on the cup and he touches it in his finger-hole, it is obvious that the fluid does not become impure from his hands to make the cup impure[34]. Just as the fluid does not become impure from his hands to make the cup impure, will the fluid not become impure from his hands to make a loaf impure at another place[35]? Let us hear from the following. Pure fluids are on the ground. If an impure loaf touched them, it made them impure[36]. In which respect did it make impure? Not to make a loaf impure at another place? Because they are on the ground; therefore not on a cup[37]. But maybe fluid is on the hand and he holds at finger-holes, even so does the fluid become impure from the cup to make the hand impure[38]? Let us hear from the following. Impure fluids are on the ground. If a pure loaf touched them, it became impure. It only says, a loaf; therefore not a hand[39]. And following Rebbi Yose, if his hands were pure but the back of the cup impure, there is fluid on his hand, and he holds in the finger-holes, it is obvious that the fluid does not become impure from the cup to make the hand impure[40]. Just as the fluid does not become impure from the cup to make the hand impure, will the fluid not become impure from his hands to make a loaf impure at another place[41]? Let us hear from the following. Impure fluids are on the ground. If pure loaf touched them, it became impure. In which respect did it become impure? Not to make a loaf impure at another place? Because they are on the ground; therefore not on a hand[42]. But maybe fluid is on the cup and he holds at finger-holes, even so does the fluid become impure from the hand to make the cup impure? Let us hear from the following. Impure fluids are in the finger-holes. If a cup whose back is pure touched its finger-holes it became impure[43].

30 Mishnah *Kelim* 25:7.

31 All vessels become impure, possibly by different rules, inside and out. But finger-holes apply only to heavy wooden troughs used to prepare dough.

32 The rules of finger-holes also apply to earthenware cups. The rules essentially state that finger-holes, being horizontal cavities, are rabbinic transmitters of impurity and therefore subject to rabbinic disregards of rabbinic rules.

33 Following R. Meïr, if his hands were impure and the back of the cup pure, handling the cup by finger-holes keeps the back of the cup pure. If his hands were pure and the back of the cup impure, handling the cup by finger-holes keeps the hands pure. Following R. Yose only the second case holds.

34 Since the finger-hole is a separate entity, for R. Meïr impurity of the back of the vessel is a separate affair not influenced by anything in the finger-hole, even if some of the fluid is in the finger-hole.

35 Since it was stated that the fluid does not become impure in the finger-hole, is this a statement about the fluid or about the finger-hole? In the second case the fluid will be impure in the moment it flows out of the finger-hole.

36 Since any impure fluid is impure in the first degree, even if made impure by secondary impurity.

37 The formulation excludes finger-holes; the statement was about the fluid.

38 If the fluid is on the hand outside the finger-hole, if the back of the cup is impure and it touches at the outside of the finger-hole, will the hand become impure?

39 According to R. Meïr there cannot be

connection for impurity between fingers in finger-holes and any other part of the cup.
40 For R. Yose, the exemption of finger-holes only works to protect the fingers from impurity on the back of the cup.
41 Same question as Note 35.

42 Same answer, in cases relevant for R. Yose, as Note 39.
43 Contrary to the opinion of R. Meïr, R. Yose holds that impurity can be transmitted through finger-holes.

(78d line 69) הַנּוֹשֵׂא אֶת הַמִּדְרָס נוֹשֵׂא אֶת הַתְּרוּמָה אֲבָל לֹא אֶת הַקּוֹדֶשׁ. רִבִּי בָּא בְשֵׁם רַב יְהוּדָה. מִפְּנֵי מַעֲשֶׂה שֶׁאֵירַע. מַעֲשֶׂה בְּאֶחָד שֶׁנִּיקְּבָה חָבִיתוֹ וּפְקָקָהּ בְּסַנְדָּלוֹ. רִבִּי זְעוּרָה רִבִּי יָסָא בְשֵׁם רִבִּי לְעָזָר. עָבַר וְנָשָׂא טָהוֹר. וְאִתְיָא כַהִיא דְּאָמַר רִבִּי לְעָזָר. יֵשׁ [מֵהֶן] שֶׁאָמְרוּ לֹא יִשָּׂא. עָבַר וְנָשָׂא טָמֵא. [וְיֵשׁ מֵהֶן שֶׁאָמְרוּ.] לֹא יִשָּׂא. אִם עָבַר וְנָשָׂא טָהוֹר. אָמַר רִבִּי זְעוּרָה קוֹמֵי רִבִּי מָנָא. לֵית הָדָא אָמְרָה שֶׁלֹּא עָשׂוּ גוּפוֹ כְזָב אֵצֶל הַקּוֹדֶשׁ. [אִין תֵּימַר. עָשׂוּ גוּפוֹ כְזָב אֵצֶל הַקּוֹדֶשׁ.] אֲפִילוּ עָבַר וְנָשָׂא יִהְיֶה טָמֵא. אָמַר לֵיהּ. תִּיפְתָּר בִּמְזוּקָּק לַקּוֹדֶשׁ. שֶׁלֹּא כְמִדַּת הַקּוֹדֶשׁ מִדַּת הַתְּרוּמָה. שֶׁבַּקּוֹדֶשׁ מַתִּיר אֶת הַחוּטִים וּמְנַגֵּב אֶת הַנְּקָבִים וְאַחַר כָּךְ קוֹשֵׁר וּבַתְּרוּמָה קוֹשֵׁר. וְאַחַר כָּךְ מַטְבִּיל. אוֹכְלֵי תְרוּמָה זְרִיזִין הֵן. וְהֵן חָצִין אוֹתָהּ. אוֹכְלֵי הַקּוֹדֶשׁ אֵינָן זְרִיזִין וְאֵינָן חָצִים אוֹתָהּ.

"He who carries "support" may carry heave but not *sancta*[4]. Rebbi Abba in the name of Rav Jehudah, because of a happening. It happened to a person that his amphora sprung a leak and he plugged it with his sandal[44]. Rebbi Ze`ira, Rebbi Yasa in the name of Rebbi Eleazar: If he transgressed and carried it, it is pure. This follows what Rebbi Eleazar said: some say, he shall not carry; if he transgressed and carried it is impure. [But some say,] he shall not carry; if he transgressed and carried it is pure[45]. Rebbi Ze`ira said in front of Rebbi Mana[46] does this not imply that they made his body not like a sufferer from gonorrhea[47]? [If you would say, they made his body not like a sufferer from gonorrhea,] then if he transgressed and carried he would be impure. He answered him, explain it if it is connected to *sancta*[8,48].

"The action for *sancta* is different from that for heave in that for *sancta* one unties the strings and wipes the holes and then ties whereas for heave one may tie and then immerse.[49]" Eaters of heave are vigilant and they hollow[50] it but eaters of *sancta* are not vigilant[7] and do not hollow.

44 Which was impure by "load" and made the contents of the amphora biblically impure. Babli 22b (end).
45 Since these statements refer to Temple practice, not to biblical laws, they are not subject to discussion. Babli 23a.
46 R. Mana I.
47 Therefore one may answer a question

raised earlier.
48 This implies nothing in the general case.
49 Tosephta 3:6.
50 Before any use they meticulously clean the interior of any vessel used for heave.

(fol. 78c) **משנה ב**: כֵּלִים הַנִּגְמָרִים בְּטָהֳרָה צְרִיכִין טְבִילָה לַקּוֹדֶשׁ אֲבָל לֹא לַתְּרוּמָה. הַכְּלִי מְצָרֵף מַה שֶּׁבְּתוֹכוֹ לַקּוֹדֶשׁ אֲבָל לֹא לַתְּרוּמָה. הָרְבִיעִי בַּקּוֹדֶשׁ פָּסוּל וְהַשְּׁלִישִׁי בַּתְּרוּמָה. וּבַתְּרוּמָה נִטְמֵאת אַחַת מִיָּדָיו חֲבֶרְתָּהּ טְהוֹרָה. וּבַקּוֹדֶשׁ מַטְבִּיל שְׁתֵּיהֶן. וְהַיָּד מְטַמָּא אֶת חֲבֶרְתָּהּ בַּקּוֹדֶשׁ אֲבָל לֹא בַּתְּרוּמָה:

Mishnah 2: Implements manufactured in purity need immersion for *sancta* but not for heave. A vessel combines its contents for *sancta* but not for heave[51]. For *sancta* the fourth degree is disqualified and the third for heave[52]. For heave, if one of his hands became impure the other remains pure, but for *sancta* he immerses both. One hand makes the other impure for *sancta* but not for heave[53].

51 A vessel contains disjoint morsels of food. If one piece becomes impure, this in general has no influence of the other pieces since derivative impurity of food cannot make the vessel impure and even rabbinically the other pieces are two touchings distant from the impure piece. The only exception are *sancta* for which there exists a fourth degree of impurity. Therefore morsels of *sancta* in the same vessel as a second degree impure piece of food are disqualified even if they are all physically separated.
52 Chapter 2, Note 162.
53 Since the impurity of hands is rabbinic of the second degree, the prior argument applies.

(79a line 4) **הלכה ב**: תַּנֵּי. מַעֲשֶׂה בְּאִשָּׁה אַחַת שֶׁהָיְתָה אוֹרֶגֶת בֶּגֶד אֶחָד בְּטָהֳרָה וּבָאת אֵצֶל רִבִּי יִשְׁמָעֵאל לְהִישָּׁאֵל לוֹ. אָמְרָה לוֹ. יוֹדַעַת אֲנִי שֶׁלֹּא נִיטְמָא. אֶלָּא שֶׁלֹּא נָתַתִּי דַעְתִּי לְשׁוֹמְרוֹ. מִתּוֹךְ שֶׁהוּא בּוֹדְקָהּ אָמְרָה לוֹ. נִידָּה בָּאָה וּמֵתְחָה עִמִּי בַּחֶבֶל. בְּאוֹתָהּ שָׁעָה אָמַר רִבִּי יִשְׁמָעֵאל. גְּדוֹלִים הֵם דִּבְרֵי חֲכָמִים שֶׁאָמְרוּ. כֵּלִים הַנִּגְמָרִים בְּטָהֳרָה צְרִיכִין טְבִילָה לַקּוֹדֶשׁ אֲבָל לֹא לַתְּרוּמָה. שׁוּב מַעֲשֶׂה בְּאִשָּׁה אַחַת שֶׁהָיְתָה אוֹרֶגֶת מִטְפַּחַת אַחַת בְּטָהֳרָה וּבָאת אֵצֶל רִבִּי יִשְׁמָעֵאל לְהִישָּׁאֵל לוֹ. אָמְרָה לוֹ. יוֹדַעַת אֲנִי שֶׁלֹּא נִיטְמָא. אֶלָּא שֶׁלֹּא נָתַתִּי דַעְתִּי לְשׁוֹמְרוֹ. מִתּוֹךְ שֶׁהוּא בּוֹדְקָהּ אָמְרָה לוֹ. נִפְסְקָה גֵּימָא אַחַת וּקְשַׁרְתִּיהָ בְּפִי. בְּאוֹתָהּ שָׁעָה אָמַר רִבִּי יִשְׁמָעֵאל. גְּדוֹלִים הֵן דִּבְרֵי חֲכָמִים שֶׁאָמְרוּ. כֵּלִים הַנִּגְמָרִין בְּטָהֳרָה צְרִיכִין טְבִילָה בַּקּוֹדֶשׁ אֲבָל לֹא לַתְּרוּמָה.

Halakhah 2: It was stated[54]: "It happened that a woman was weaving cloth in purity and came to Rebbi Ismael to ask him about it. She told him, I am sure that it did not become impure, only I did not concentrate to watch it. While he was interrogating her, she said to him, a menstruating woman came and helped me stretching the rope[55]. At that moment Rebbi Ismael said, great are the words of the Sages who said, 'implements manufactured in purity need immersion for *sancta* but not for heave.' Another happening: a woman was weaving a shawl in purity and came to Rebbi Ismael to ask him about it. She told him, I am sure that it did not become impure, only I did not concentrate to watch it. While he was interrogating him, she said to him, a thread broke and I tied it with my mouth[56]. At that moment Rebbi Ismael said, great are the words of the Sages who said, 'implements manufactured in purity need immersion for *sancta* but not for heave.'"

54 Tosephta *Kelim Bava Batra* 1:2-3; Babli 20a.

55 If the menstruating woman alone had stretched the warp, it would certainly be impure because moved by a person whose impurity is from her own body. Since it was a joint effort, it is possible that the warp, and therefore the cloth, was impure, but it cannot be determined whether it is. In order to be sure it is pure it has to be immersed.

55 Spittle is one of the body fluids which transmit severe impurity. Weaves are susceptible to impurity only if the surface area is at least 3 finger-widths by 3 finger-width. If the woman started the weave when she was impure from her period and the spittle was not totally dry when the weave reached the threshold of impurity, the shawl would be biblically impure. Since the fact can no longer be ascertained, the weave has to be immersed because of the doubt.

(79a line 15) הַחוֹתֵךְ מִשְׁפּוֹפֶרֶת הַקּוֹדֶשׁ. חוֹתְכָהּ וּמַטְבִּילָהּ טָעוּן טְבִילָה. נִיחָה חוֹתְכָהּ. מַטְבִּילָהּ. וְיַכְרִיכָנָּה (בְּשִׁיט) [בְּסִיב] וְיַטְבִּילָהּ. אָמַר רִבִּי אִילָא. תִּפְתָּר שֶׁחֲתָכָהּ עַל מְנָת לְהַטְבִּילָהּ. אָמַר רִבִּי יְהוֹשֻׁעַ בֶּן לֵוִי. עַד כָּאן בְּקוֹדְשֵׁי מִקְדָּשׁ הַמְקוּדָּשִׁים. מִיכָּן הָאֵילַךְ בְּחוּלִין שֶׁנַּעֲשׂוּ עַל טַהֲרַת הַקּוֹדֶשׁ.

[56]If one cuts a tube for *sancta*, he who cuts it and he who immerses it need immersion. One understands he who cuts. He who immerses? Could he not bind it with a (*sit*) [fiber] and immerse it? But explain it that he cut it in order to immerse it.

Rebbi Joshua ben Levi said, up to here about sanctified Temple *sancta*. From here on, about profane food prepared in the purity of sacrifices[57].

56 Chapter 2, Notes 231-232.
57 Mishnah 1 and the first statement of Mishnah 2 apply only to actual Temple *sancta* and therefore are inoperative after the destruction of the Temple. The later distinctions between *sancta* and heave also apply to profane food prepared in the purity of *sancta*.

(79a line 19) אָמַר רִבִּי יוֹחָנָן. מֵעֵידוּתוֹ שֶׁלְרִבִּי עֲקִיבָה הִיא. דְּתַנִּינָן תַּמָּן. הוֹסִיף רִבִּי עֲקִיבָה הַסּוֹלֶת וְהַקְּטוֹרֶת הַלְּבוֹנָה וְהַגֶּחָלִים שֶׁנָּגַע טְבוּל יוֹם בְּמִקְצָתָן. שֶׁפָּסַל אֶת כּוּלּוֹ: רִבִּי שִׁמְעוֹן בֶּן לָקִישׁ אָמַר. יוֹדְעִין הָיוּ שֶׁכְּלֵי שָׁרֵת מְחַבְּרִים. וּמַה בָא לְהָעִיד. עַל שְׁיָרֵי מְנָחוֹת שֶׁיְּהוּ מְחַבְּרִין אֶת עַצְמָן. רִבִּי יוֹסֵי בֵּירִבִּי זְמִינָה בְשֵׁם רִבִּי יוֹחָנָן. מִפְּנֵי מַה אָמְרוּ. שְׁיָרֵי מְנָחוֹת מְחַבְּרִין אֶת עַצְמָן. מִפְּנֵי שֶׁנִּזְקְקוּ לְכֵילָיו. רִבִּי אָחָא רִבִּי אִילָא בְשֵׁם רִבִּי יָסָא. יוֹדְעִין הָיוּ שֶׁכְּלֵי שָׁרֵת מְחַבְּרִין. מַה בָא לְהָעִיד. עַל הַסּוֹלֶת וְעַל הַקְּטוֹרֶת וְעַל הַלְּבוֹנָה וְעַל הַגֶּחָלִים. נִיחָא סוֹלֶת וּקְטוֹרֶת וּלְבוֹנָה. גֶּחָלִים. אָמַר רִבִּי בּוּן בַּר כָּהֲנָא. תִּיפְּתָר בִּגְחָלִים שֶׁלְיוֹם הַכִּיפּוּרִים שֶׁבַּמָּה שֶׁהוּא חוֹתֶה הוּא מַכְנִיס. אֲבָל בִּגְחָלִים שֶׁל כָּל־יוֹם [לֹא]. כַּהִיא דְתַנִּינָן תַּמָּן. נִתְפַּזֵּר מִמֶּנּוּ בְקַב גֶּחָלִים הָיָה מְכַבְּדָן לָאַמָּה. וּבַשַּׁבָּת כּוֹפִין עָלָיו פְּסַכְתֵּר. אָמַר רִבִּי מַתַּנְיָה. וְכִי סוֹלֶת וּקְטוֹרֶת וּלְבוֹנָה וּגְחָלִים יֵשׁ לָהֶן שִׁיעוּר אֵצֶל זֶה. לֹא מִפְּנֵי שֶׁנִּזְקְקוּ לְכֵילָיו. וְהָכָא מִפְּנֵי שֶׁנִּזְקְקוּ לְכֵילָיו.

Rebbi Johanan said, it is from Rebbi Aqiba's testimony[57]. As we have stated there[57], "Rebbi Aqiba added that fine flour, and incense, frankincense, and coals, part of which were touched by a *Tevul Yom* are all disqualified[58]." Rebbi Simeon ben Laqish said, they knew that vessels of Servive do combine. About what comes he to testify? About the leftovers of flour-offerings that they do combine together. Rebbi Yose ben Rebbi Zamina in the name of Rebbi Johanan: Why did they say, leftovers of flour-offerings do combine together? Because they need their vessel[59]. Rebbi Aha, Rebbi Ila in the name of Rebbi Yasa: they knew that vessels of Service do combine. About what comes he to testify? About fine flour, and incense, and frankincense, and coals[60]. One understands fine flour, and incense, and frankincense. Coals[61]? Rebbi Abun bar Cahana said, explain it about coals on the Day of Atonement which he has to carry inside in the vessel which he used to scoop up[62]. But [not][63] about every day's coals. As we have stated there[64], "If a *qab* of coals were dispersed, one sweeps them into the water canal, but on the Sabbath one covers it with a wine-cooler[65]. Rebbi Mattania said, do fine flour, and incense, frankincense, and coals, need a minimum volume in this respect?

Not because they have to be in their vessel? Here also because they have to be in their vessel[66].

57 In Mishnah *Idiut* 8:1.

58 This statement is implied by the statement of our Mishnah that vessels do combine for *sancta*. Therefore Mishnah 2 must have been formulated posterior to R. Aqiba.

59 Since the leftovers of flour offerings have to be eaten by priests, they have to be taken from the vessel in which they were presented to the altar. Since the vessel is not needed after presentation and burning of a fistful on the altar, one might think that then the vessel acts like a profane vessel and does not imply disqualification of the entire content composed of disjoint pieces if one piece became disqualified. As long as the vessel is actually used it transmits disqualification. Babli 23b.

60 These are not foods and not subject to the rules of impurity of foodstuffs up to the fourth degree.

61 They should be impervious to impurity.

62 The coals which the High Priest on the Day of Atonement has to scoop up with a fire-pan and carry into the holiest of holies with the incense (*Lev.* 16:12). These are the only coals which become disqualified if outside a dedicated Vessel of Service.

63 Corrector's addition, making explicit the text's meaning.

64 Mishnah *Tamid* 5:5.

65 Greek ψυκτήρ, a big metal vessel.

66 He holds that the Mishnah in *Idiut* applies to all coals removed from the altar. The rule is that the burned-out charcoal remainders have to be removed in dedicated fire-pans. Even if the later are spilled and swiped into the water canal crossing the inner courtyard, they were removed in a dedicated vessel, and in this case the vessel combines all its contents. The same holds for a large private flour offering, not subject to the amounts prescribed for public offerings, and which might be presented in two or more vessels. In that case, each vessel separately transmits disqualification from a part of its contents to all of it.

(79a line 31) רִבִּי בּוּן בַּר חִייָה בָעֵי. קוֹמֶץ מָהוּ שֶׁיְּיקָרֵב בִּשְׁנֵי כֵלִים. הָתִיב רִבִּי חָנִין. וְהָא תַּנִּינָן. הַכְּלִי מְצָרֵף. אִין תֵּימַר שֶׁקּוֹמֶץ קָרֵב בִּשְׁנֵי כֵלִים. וְלֵיי דָא מִילָּה תַּנִּינָן. הַכְּלִי מְצָרֵף. אָמַר רִבִּי לָעְזָר דְּרוֹמְיָיא. לֹא כֵן אָמַר רִבִּי יוֹסֵי בֵּירִבִּי זְמִינָא בְּשֵׁם רִבִּי יוֹחָנָן. מִפְּנֵי מַה אָמְרוּ. שְׁיָרֵי מְנָחוֹת מְחַבְּרִין אֶת עַצְמָן. לֹא מִפְּנֵי שֶׁנִּזְקְקוּ לְכֵילָיִין. וְהָכָא שֶׁנִּזְקְקוּ לְכֵילָיִין. אָמַר רִבִּי מַתַּנְיָה. וְכִי סוֹלֶת וּקְטוֹרֶת וּלְבוֹנָה וּגְחָלִים לֹא בְכַמָּה כֵלִים הֵן קְרֵיבִין. וְאַתְּ אָמַר. הַכְּלִי מְצָרֵף. וְהָכָא הַכְּלִי מְצָרֵף. כַּהֲנָא שָׁאַל לְרַבָּנִין דְּתַמָּן. מִנְחָה חֲלוּקָה (בְּבָסָּה) [בְּגָסָּה]. נִיטְמֵאת זוֹ נִיטְמֵאת זוֹ. אָמְרוּן לֵיהּ. נִיטְמֵאת זוֹ נִיטְמֵאת זוֹ. וְקֶפְצָה טוּמְאָה. אָמְרוּן לֵיהּ. וְקֶפְצָה טוּמְאָה. אֲפִילוּ אַחֶרֶת בֵּינְתַּיִים. אָמְרוּן לֵיהּ. אֲפִילוּ אַחֶרֶת בֵּינְתַּיִים. קוֹמֶץ מְזוֹ לָזוֹ. אָמְרוּן לֵיהּ. שְׁמוּעָה לֹא שְׁמַעְנוּ. מִשְׁנָה שָׁנִינוּ. כַּהֲיא דְתַנִּינָן לְתַמָּן. שְׁתֵּי מְנָחוֹת שֶׁלֹּא נִקְמְצוּ וְנִתְעָרְבוּ זוֹ בָזוֹ. אִם יָכוֹל לִקְמוֹץ מְזוֹ בִּפְנֵי עַצְמָהּ וּמְזוֹ בִּפְנֵי עַצְמָהּ כְּשֵׁירוֹת. וְאִם לָאו פְּסוּלוֹת. [וְ]אֵין שְׁיָרֶיהָ שֶׁל זוֹ

מַפְסִיקִין לָזוֹ. אָתָא רִבִּי יַעֲקֹב בַּר אָחָא רִבִּי יָסָא בְּשֵׁם רִבִּי יוֹחָנָן. קוֹמֶץ מִזוֹ עַל זוֹ. נִיטְמֵאת זוֹ נִיטְמֵאת זוֹ. הָאֶמְצָעִית לֹא נִיטְמֵאת. לֹא כֵן תַּנֵּי. כַּף אֶחָת. שֶׁהִיא עוֹשָׂה מַה שֶׁבְּתוֹכָהּ אֶחָת. אָמַר רִבִּי חִינְנָה. אֵין הַכֵּלִי מְצָרֵף אֶלָּא דָּבָר שֶׁהוּא אָסוּר לוֹ.

Rebbi Abun bar Ḥiyya asked: may a fistful be offered from two vessels[67]? Rebbi Ḥanin objected, did we not state, "the vessel combines"? If you would say that a fistful can be offered from two vessels, for which purpose did we state "the vessel combines"? Rebbi Eleazar the Southerner said, did not Rebbi Yose bar Zamina say in the name of Rebbi Joḥanan, why did they say, leftovers of flour-offerings do combine together? Because they need their vessel[59]. Here also because they have to be in their vessel[68]. Rebbi Mattaniah said, are not fine flour, and incense, and frankincense, and coals offered in many vessels? Nevertheless you are saying, "the vessel combines"; and here "the vessel combines"[69]. Cahana asked the rabbis there, a flour-offering split in the mixing bowl[70], if one became impure did the other become impure[71]? They said to him, if one became impure the other became impure. Did impurity jump[72]? They said to him, impurity did jump. Even if another {vessel} was in between? They said to him, even if another {vessel} was in between. Taking a fistful from one on the other[73]? They said to him, we did not hear any tradition, we studied a Mishnah, as what we did state there[74], "if two flour offerings from which no fistfuls were taken were combined together, if he is able to take a fistful from one separately and from the other separately[75] they are qualified, otherwise disqualified." Do not the remainders of one interrupt between one and the other[76]? There came Rebbi Jacob bar Aḥa, Rebbi Yasa in the name of Rebbi Joḥanan: If a fistful was taken from one for the other[77], if one became impure he other became impure. Anything in-between did not become impure. Was it not stated, "*one cup*[77]? Which makes its contents one.[78]" Rebbi Ḥinena said, a vessel combines only what is tied to it[79].

67 The regular discipline of flour offerings is that flour and oil are mixed in one sanctified vessel, then the priest takes a fistful, deposits it into a second vessel which he carries to the altar and empties into the flames. Since in any case a second vessel is involved, may the offering be brought from the start in two vessels, and the fistful taken from one and deposited into a third permits the contents of both original vessels to be consumed by the priests?

68 If the offering from the start is in two

separate vessels, where is the one vessel which combines the contents such that if part becomes disqualified everything is disqualified? As before the answer is that since no offering may be presented without being in a vessel, that vessel is a necessity of the service and the multitude of original vessels is irrelevant.

69 The previous argument is extended from flour offering to incense, which at least for the shewbreads always is in multiple containers, and the other offerings.

70 The scribe's text is the correct one, confirmed by the Babli (*Menahot* 7a,24a/b). The corrector's change is erroneous.

71 While an argument may be made that if part of a flour-offering becomes disqualified the whole becomes disqualified, does the argument extend to actual impurity (or order <4), so that the contents of a vessel can cause impurity or disqualification to anything it comes in contact with, without ever having been touched by anything impure?

72 From one vessel to another with which it is not in contact.

73 Rebbi Abun bar Hiyya's question.

74 Mishnah *Menahot* 3:3.

75 If the materials of the two offerings are recognizable as distinct.

76 One has to say that the statement that the vessel combines is a biblical one; therefore on the one hand the vessel transmits disqualification from one piece to a disjoint one, and on the other hand permits to take a fistful from the offering although certainly parts of the offering are mixed with another, which without the combining action of the vessel would disqualify.

77 Of a flour-offering presented in two or more vessels.

78 *Sifry Num.* 49, Babli 23b. The reference is to the offerings of the heads of tribes for the inauguration of the Tabernacle (*Num.*7:14, 20, 26, 32, 38, 44, 50, 56, 62, 68, 74, 80). It would have been sufficient to state that each of them brought "*a* cup full of incense". The emphasis 12 times on "*one* cup full of incense" is explained by that the cup makes the offering an indivisible entity.

79 He denies that impurity may be transferred by action at a distance.

(79a line 48) רִבִּי שִׁמְעוֹן בֶּן לָקִישׁ בָּעֵי. צָרִיד שֶׁלְמְנָחוֹת מָהוּ שֶׁיַּעֲשֶׂה מִינְיָין. הָתִיב רִבִּי לְעָזָר. וְהָכְתִיב מִכָּל־הָאוֹכֶל אֲשֶׁר יֵאָכֵל אֲשֶׁר יָבֹא עָלָיו מַיִם יִטְמָא. אֶת שֶׁטּוּמְאָתוֹ עַל יְדֵי מַיִם עוֹשֶׂה מִינְיָין. אֶת שֶׁאֵין טוּמְאָתוֹ עַל יְדֵי מַיִם אֵינוֹ עוֹשֶׂה מִינְיָין. הָתִיב רִבִּי יוֹסֵי. הֲרֵי נִבְלַת עוֹף הַטָּהוֹר הֲרֵי הִיא מְטַמָּא טוּמְאַת אוֹכָלִים בְּלֹא הֶכְשֵׁר וּבְלֹא טוּמְאָה. מִפְּנֵי שֶׁסּוֹפָהּ לְטַמְּאוֹת טוּמְאָה חֲמוּרָה. מַאי כְדוֹן. מִכָּל־הָאוֹכֶל אֲשֶׁר יֵאָכֵל. אֶת שֶׁטּוּמְאָתוֹ מִשָּׁם אוֹכֶל עוֹשֶׂה מִינְיָין. וְאֶת שֶׁאֵין טוּמְאָתוֹ מִשָּׁם אוֹכֶל אֵינוֹ עוֹשֶׂה מִינְיָין.

Rebbi Simeon ben Laqish asked: Does a dry piece of flour-offering start a count[80]? Rebbi Eleazar objected: Is it not written[81], *of all foodstuff which is edible on which comes water is susceptible to impurity*. Any whose impurity is caused by water starts a count, nothing whose impurity is not caused by water starts a count. Rebbi Yose objected: Is there not a carcass of a kosher bird which causes impurity of foodstuff without preparation and without impurity, because it ends up causing severe impurity[82]? What about this? *Of all foodstuff which is edible,* any whose impurity is caused by the category of edibles[83] starts a count, nothing whose impurity is not caused by edibles the category of starts a count.

80 A flour offering in general needs to be mixed with oil. As noted later, food becomes susceptible to impurity only by contact with water or one of the fluids compared to water in a biblical verse, including olive oil. This contact is called "preparation for impurity", cf. *Demay* 2:3, Note 141. The question now is whether flour never in contact with a fluid, which becomes disqualified by being in a combining vessel, also becomes impure to count derivative impurity of degrees 1,2,3,4 or not. Babli *Hulin* 36a.

81 *Lev.* 11:34.

82 The meat of a kosher bird which was not slaughtered once it is in the mouth makes not only the eater but also his garments causes of original biblical impurity. The garments cause impurity to anything potentially susceptible to impurity, without "preparation."

83 Even if the particular item is not kosher to eat.

(79a line 55) רִבִּי יוֹנָתָן בְּשֵׁם רִבִּי. הָאוֹכֵל אוֹכֵל שְׁלִישִׁי בַּתְּרוּמָה נִפְסַל גּוּפוֹ מְלוֹכַל בַּתְּרוּמָה. רִבִּי שְׁמוּאֵל בַּר רַב יִצְחָק בָּעֵי. מַה. רִבִּי כְרִבִּי אֱלִיעֶזֶר. דְּתַנִּינָן תַּמָּן. הָאוֹכֵל אוֹכֵל רִאשׁוֹן רִאשׁוֹן. הָאוֹכֵל אוֹכֵל שֵׁינִי שֵׁינִי. הָאוֹכֵל אוֹכֵל שְׁלִישִׁי שְׁלִישִׁי. דִּבְרֵי הַכֹּל הִיא. כְּדֵי שֶׁיְּהֵא בָדֵל מִן הַתְּרוּמָה. וְדִכְוָותָהּ. הָאוֹכֵל אוֹכֵל שֵׁינִי בְּמַעֲשֵׂר נִפְסַל גּוּפוֹ מְלוֹכַל בְּמַעֲשֵׂר. נִשְׁמְעִינָהּ מִן הָדָא. וַחֲכָמִים אוֹסְרִין בְּמַעֲשֵׂר. וְלָא שְׁמִיעַ [לָהּוּ] דְּאָמַר רִבִּי שְׁמוּאֵל בְּשֵׁם רִבִּי זְעוּרָה. מָהוּ וַחֲכָמִים אוֹסְרִין בְּמַעֲשֵׂר. נִפְסַל גּוּפוֹ מְלוֹכַל בְּמַעֲשֵׂר. וְדִכְוָותָהּ. הָאוֹכֵל אוֹכֵל רְבִיעִי בַּקּוֹדֶשׁ נִפְסַל גּוּפוֹ מְלוֹכַל בַּקּוֹדֶשׁ. נִשְׁמְעִינָהּ מִן הָדָא. דְּאָמַר רִבִּי יִרְמְיָה בְּשֵׁם רִבִּי בָּא בַר מָמָל. עָשׂוּ אוֹתוֹ כְּאוֹכֵל אוֹכֵל רְבִיעִי בַּקּוֹדֶשׁ. הָאוֹכֵל אוֹכֵל רְבִיעִי בַּקּוֹדֶשׁ נִפְסַל גּוּפוֹ מְלוֹכַל בַּקּוֹדֶשׁ. עַד כְּדוֹן בְּקָדְשֵׁי מִזְבֵּחַ הַמְּקוּדָּשִׁין. וַאֲפִילוּ בְחוּלִּין שֶׁנַּעֲשׂוּ עַל טַהֲרַת הַקּוֹדֶשׁ. נִשְׁמְעִינָהּ מִן הָדָא. [דְּתַנִּינָן תַּמָּן.] הַשּׁוֹחֵט בְּהֵמָה חַיָּה וְעוֹף וְלֹא יָצָא מֵהֶן דָּם. כְּשֵׁירִין וְנֶאֱכָלִים בְּיָדַיִם מְסוֹאָבוֹת. אַף עַל פִּי שֶׁלֹּא הוּכְשְׁרוּ בְדָם. רִבִּי שִׁמְעוֹן אוֹמֵר הוּכְשְׁרוּ בַשְּׁחִיטָה: רִבִּי לְעָזָר בְּשֵׁם רִבִּי הוֹשַׁעְיָה. מַתְנִיתָהּ בְּחוּלִּין שֶׁנַּעֲשׂוּ עַל גַּב הַקּוֹדֶשׁ כְּרִבִּי יְהוֹשֻׁעַ. רִבִּי זְעוּרָה רִבִּי יָסָא רִבִּי יוֹחָנָן רִבִּי יַנַּאי בְּשֵׁם רִבִּי. הָאוֹכֵל אוֹכֵל שְׁלִישִׁי בַּתְּרוּמָה נִפְסַל גּוּפוֹ מְלוֹכַל בַּתְּרוּמָה. וְלָא מַתְנִיתָהּ הִיא שֶׁהַשְּׁלִישִׁי שֵׁינִי לַקּוֹדֶשׁ. מַתְנִיתָהּ בְּקָדְשֵׁי מִזְבֵּחַ הַמְּקוּדָּשִׁין. דְּרַבָּא אֲתָא מֵימַר לָךְ. וַאֲפִילוּ בְחוּלִּין שֶׁנַּעֲשׂוּ עַל גַּב הַקּוֹדֶשׁ. אָמַר רִבִּי בּוּן בַּר חִיָּיה קוֹמֵי רִבִּי זְעוּרָה. מַתְנִיתָהּ אָמְרָה כֵן. כִּכְּרוֹת הַקּוֹדֶשׁ בְּתוֹךְ גּוּמוֹתֵיהֶם הַמַּיִם מְקוּדָּשִׁין. בָּאשׁ לָךְ דַּאֲתָא מֵימוֹר

לָךְ. עָשָׂה מַשְׁקֵה פִיו כְּמַשְׁקֵה קוֹדֶשׁ. אָמַר רִבִּי זְעוּרָה. בְּמַה דַּתְּ אָמַר תַּמָּן. עָשָׂה אֶת הַטָּהוֹר לַחֲטָאת כְּמִי חַטָאת וּכְאֵפֶר חַטָּאת. וְהָכָא עָשָׂה מַשְׁקֵה פִיו כְּמַשְׁקֵה קוֹדֶשׁ. רִבִּי זְעוּרָה רִבִּי יָסָא רִבִּי יוֹחָנָן רִבִּי יַנַּיי. וְלֹא יְדַעִין אֵין מַטִּי בָהּ בְּשֵׁם רִבִּי. מַתְנִיתָהּ מִינָהּ קְיוֹמָה וּמִינָהּ תְּבָרָהּ. מִינָהּ קְיוֹמָהּ. שֶׁהַשְּׁלִישִׁי שֵׁינִי לַקּוֹדֶשׁ וְאֵין שֵׁינִי לַתְּרוּמָה. שֶׁנַּעֲשָׂה לְטַהֲרַת הַתְּרוּמָה. אֲבָל אִם נַעֲשָׂה לְטַהֲרַת הַקּוֹדֶשׁ נַעֲשָׂה גוּפוֹ שֵׁינִי אֵצֶל קוֹדֶשׁ. מִינָהּ תְּבָרָהּ. שֶׁהַשְּׁלִישִׁי שֵׁינִי לַקּוֹדֶשׁ וְלֹא שֵׁינִי לַתְּרוּמָה. שֶׁנַּעֲשֵׂית לְטַהֲרַת הַקּוֹדֶשׁ. אֲבָל אִם נַעֲשָׂה לְטַהֲרַת הַתְּרוּמָה נַעֲשָׂה גוּפוֹ שֵׁינִי אֵצֶל הַתְּרוּמָה וְכָל־שֶׁכֵּן אֵצֶל הַקּוֹדֶשׁ.

Rebbi Jonathan in the name of Rebbi: If somebody eats food which is third degree impure for heave, his body is disqualified from eating heave[84]. Rebbi Samuel bar Rav Isaac asked, how? Rebbi follows Rebbi Eliezer? As we have stated there[85], "He who eats food impure in the first degree is impure in the first degree. He who eats food impure in the second degree is impure in the second degree. He who eats food impure in the third degree is impure in the third degree.[86]" It is everybody's opinion, so he should stay away from heave[87]. And similarly, if somebody eats food which is second degree impure for tithe, is his body disqualified from eating tithe? Let us hear from the following[88]: "But the Sages forbid for tithe.[89]" They had not heard that Rebbi Samuel said in the name of Rebbi Ze`ira, what means "but the Sages forbid for tithe"? His body is disqualified from eating tithe[90]. And similarly, if somebody eats food which is fourth degree impure for *sancta*, is his body disqualified from eating *sancta*? Let us hear from the following, as Rebbi Jeremiah said in the name of Rebbi Abba bar Mamal, they made him like one eating fourth degree impure food for *sancta*[91]. This implies, if somebody eats food which is fourth degree impure for *sancta*, his body is disqualified from eating *sancta*. So far in Temple *sancta* which were sanctified. Or also for profane food prepared in the standards of *sancta*? Let us hear from the following, [as we stated there][92]: "If somebody slaughters domestic animals, wild animals, or birds, and no blood came out from them, they are qualified and may be eaten with unclean hands, since they were not prepared by blood. Rebbi Simeon says, they were prepared by slaughter[93]." Rebbi Eleazar in the name of Rebbi Hoshaia: The Mishnah is about profane food prepared in the standards of *sancta* following Rebbi Joshua[86]. Rebbi Ze`ira, Rebbi Yasa, Rebbi Joḥanan, Rebbi Yannai in the name of Rebbi: If somebody eats food which is third degree impure for heave, his body is disqualified from eating heave. Is that not a Mishnah that third degree impurity is second degree impurity for *sancta*[86]? The Mishnah is about Temple *sancta* which were sanctified. He[94] tells you in addition, even for profane food prepared in the standards of *sancta*. Rebbi Abun bar Hiyya said before Rebbi Ze`ira: The Mishnah says so, "loaves of *sancta* bread; the water in their cavities is sanctified.[95]" Does it displease you that it comes to tell you that he makes fluid by your pronouncement like sanctified fluid[96]? Rebbi Ze`ira said, as you are saying there[97], one made one pure for the ashes of the Red Cow equal to the water for the ashes of the Red Cow and to the ashes of the Red Cow, and here one made fluid by your pronouncement like sanctified fluid. Rebbi Ze`ira, Rebbi Yasa, Rebbi Johanan, Rebbi Yannai, and it is unknown whether this is in the name of Rebbi: There is a Mishnah[85] which is both confirmation and disproof. From it confirmation: "For third degree impurity is second degree impurity for *sancta*, but not second degree impurity for heave, if it was prepared by the standards of heave." But if it was prepared in the standards of *sancta*, his body is second degree impure for *sancta*[98]. From it disproof: For third degree impurity is second degree impurity for *sancta*, but not second degree impurity for heave, if it was prepared by the standards of *sancta*[99]. But if it was prepared in the standards of heave, his body is second degree impure for heave and *a fortiori* for *sancta*[100].

84 Babli *Hulin* 35a. Since the third degree of impurity disqualifies but does not induce impurity for heave, the person is permitted in principle to touch heave but not to eat it.
85 Mishnah *Taharot* 2:2.
86 R. Eliezer holds that a person eating impure food subject to higher orders of derivative impurity becomes impure in the same degree as his food, whereas R. Joshua holds that impure food of the first two degrees make the body impure in the second degree, and that third degree impurity (disqualification) for heave equals second degree (impurity) for *sancta*. Since in general we are following R. Joshua against R. Eliezer, it would be astonishing to find an anonymous Mishnah following R. Eliezer against R. Joshua. Cf. Babli *Hulin* 33b.
87 While in theory he could touch heave without bad effects, since touching could lead to eating we tell him to stay away from heave in all respects. This is not a biblical rule.
88 Mishnah *Parah* 11:5.
89 The Mishnah states that anybody needing immersion in water for rabbinic impurity may without immersion eat profane food and Second Tithe according to R. Meïr,

but the majority forbids him Second Tithe.

90 There should not have been any question since the problem already was solved in a Mishnah known to all.

91 A quote from Halakhah 3, Note 136. The reference is to a deep mourner who is obligated to see to the burial of a close relative and is forbidden any sacral act. As stated here, it implies that the person eating disqualified *sancta* is forbidden any sacral act.

92 Mishnah *Hulin* 2:5.

93 For the majority, slaughtered meat is prepared for impurity (Note 80) either by the blood spilled in the act of slaughter or by cutting the animal into pieces, or by later contact with water. Since meat eaten otherwise than raw must be kashered in water, the Mishnah implies that meat not prepared by blood may be eaten raw with unwashed hands and remain untouched by impurity.

94 Rebbi in the *baraita*.

95 Mishnah *Taharot* 1:9. Bread baked to accompany *sancta* is prepared for impurity both by the water used in making the dough and by the fact that it is used in the Temple. If the bread is leavened, as required for thanksgiving offerings (*Lev.* 7:13), and some moisture remains in bubbles inside the loaves, it is considered as if outside. If the loaf is touched by disqualified (4th order impure) food, the moisture becomes impure in the first degree and the loaf actually impure; while totally dry food is not impacted by the touch of disqualified food.

96 "Fluid by his pronouncement" is profane food intentionally prepared by the standards of *sancta*. "Sanctified fluid" is fluid actually used in the Temple.

97 In Mishnah *Parah* Chapter 10.

98 The Mishnah text is R. Joshua's. Since he formulates it for profane food prepared in the standards of heave, it is clear that he excludes profane food prepared in the standards of *sancta*; his statement requires equal treatment for actual *sancta*, possible only in the Temple, and food prepared in the standards of *sancta*, possible everywhere in the Holy Land at all times (subject to the availability of ashes of the Red Cow.)

99 As stated in the Mishnah there.

100 But nothing implies that this also is valid for profane food prepared in the standards of *sancta*.

(79b line 8) תָּנֵי רִבִּי יוֹסֵי. מְנַיִין לָרְבִיעִי בַּקּוֹדֶשׁ שֶׁהוּא פָסוּל. וְדִין הוּא. מַה אִם מְחוּסַּר כִּיפּוּרִים שֶׁאֵינוֹ פוֹסֵל בִּתְרוּמָה הֲרֵי פוֹסֵל בַּקּוֹדֶשׁ. רְבִיעִי שֶׁהוּא פוֹסֵל בִּתְרוּמָה אֵינוֹ דִין שֶׁיִּפָּסוֹל בַּקּוֹדֶשׁ. הֲרֵי לָמַדְנוּ לַשְּׁלִישִׁי מִן הַכָּתוּב. וְלָרְבִיעִי (מִקּוֹל) [מִקַּל] וָחוֹמֶר. הֵתִיב רִבִּי יוֹחָנָן. הֲרֵי הָאוֹכֵל הַבָּא מַחֲמַת טְבוּל יוֹם יוֹכִיחַ. הֲרֵי הוּא פוֹסֵל בִּתְרוּמָה וְאֵינוֹ פוֹסֵל בַּקּוֹדֶשׁ. רִבִּי חֲנַנְיָה בְשֵׁם רִבִּי יוֹחָנָן. אַתְיָא דְּרִבִּי יוֹסֵה כְּשִׁיטַת רִבִּי עֲקִיבָה רַבּוֹ. כְּמָה דְּרִבִּי עֲקִיבָה אָמַר תַּמָּן. יִטְמָא יִטְמָא דְּבַר תּוֹרָה. כֵּן רִבִּי יוֹסֵה אָמַר הָכָא. יִטְמָא יִטְמָא דְּבַר תּוֹרָה. רִבִּי אַבָּהוּ בְשֵׁם רִבִּי יוֹסֵה בֶּן חֲנִינָה. לֵית רִבִּי יוֹסֵי צָרִיךְ לְהָדֵין (קוֹל) [קַל] וָחוֹמֶר. קָרְיֵי דָרַשׁ רִבִּי יוֹסֵי. וְהַבָּשָׂר אֲשֶׁר־יִגַּע. זֶה שֵׁינִי שֶׁנָּגַע בָּרִאשׁוֹן. בְּכָל־טָמֵא. זֶה שְׁלִישִׁי שֶׁנָּגַע בַּשֵּׁינִי. לֹא יֵאָכֵל. סוֹף טָמֵא לֹא יֵאָכֵל. עַד כְּדוֹן בְּאוֹכְלִין שֶׁנִּיטְמוּ מֵאֲוִיר כְּלִי חֶרֶס שֶׁנִּיטְמָא בְּשָׁרֶץ. אוֹכְלִין עַצְמָן שֶׁנִּיטְמוּ בְשֶׁרֶץ מְנַיִין. וְדִין הוּא. וּמַה אִם הַכֵּלִים שֶׁאֵינָן מִיטַּמְּאִין מֵאֲוִיר כְּלִי חֶרֶס שֶׁנִּיטְמָא

בְּשֶׁרֶץ הֲרֵי הֵן מִיטַּמִּין כְּשֶׁרֶץ לְטַמֵּא אוֹכְלִין. אוֹכְלִין עַצְמָן שֶׁנִּיטְמוּ בְשֶׁרֶץ אֵינוּ דִין שֶׁיִּיטַּמּוּ כְּשֶׁרֶץ לְטַמֵּא אוֹכְלִין. עַד כְּדוֹן כְּרבִּי עֲקִיבָה. כְּרִבִּי יִשְׁמָעֵאל. תַּנֵּי רִבִּי יִשְׁמָעֵאל. וְהַבָּשָׂר אֲשֶׁר־יִגַּע בְּכָל־טָמֵא. זֶה רִאשׁוֹן שֶׁנָּגַע בְּטָמֵא. לֹא יֵאָכֵל. לְרַבּוֹת אֶת הַשֵּׁנִי. שְׁלִישִׁי בַּתְּרוּמָה מְנַיִין. וְדִין הוּא. מָה אִם טְבוּל יוֹם שֶׁאֵינוּ פוֹסֵל בְּחוּלִין הֲרֵי הוּא פוֹסֵל בַּתְּרוּמָה. שֵׁינִי שֶׁהוּא פוֹסֵל בְּחוּלִין אֵינוּ דִין שֶׁיִּפְסוֹל בַּתְּרוּמָה. רְבִיעִי בַּקּוֹדֶשׁ מְנַיִין. וְדִין הוּא. מָה אִם מְחוּסַּר כִּיפּוּרִים שֶׁאֵינוּ פוֹסֵל בִּתְרוּמָה הֲרֵי הוּא פוֹסֵל בַּקּוֹדֶשׁ. (רְבִיעִי) [שְׁלִישִׁי] שֶׁהוּא פוֹסֵל בִּתְרוּמָה אֵינוּ דִין שֶׁיִּפְסוֹל בַּקּוֹדֶשׁ. הֲרֵי לָמַדְנוּ לָרִאשׁוֹן וּלְשֵׁינִי מִן הַכָּתוּב וְלִשְׁלִישִׁי מִן הַדִּין וְלָרְבִיעִי (מִקָּל) [וָחוֹמֶר]. דָּנִין לוֹ דִין מִן הַדִּין. שֶׁיְּהֵא הַכֹּל מְשׁוּעֲבָּד לַהֲלָכָה שֶׁיְּהֵא הַשְּׁלִישִׁי פוֹסֵל בַּתְּרוּמָה וְהָרְבִיעִי בַּקּוֹדֶשׁ.

1 ר' | ס אמ' ר'   2 פוסל | ס אוכל R פסל פוסל | ס הוא פסול רביעי | ס שלישי פוסל | ס פסול   4 הרי | ס - הרי הוא | ס שהוא   5 חנניה | ס חייה אתיא | ס אתייה יוסה | ס יוסי   6 תמן | ס -   7 בן | ס בר   9 חרס | ס חרש שניטמו | ס שניטמאו   10 ומה | ס מה מיטמין | ס מיטמין | ס מטמאין | ס מטמאין חרס | ס חרש   11 מיטמין | ס מטמאין   12-11 אוכלין עצמן שניטמו בשרץ אינו דין שייטמו כשרץ לטמא אוכלין | R - | ס אכלין שהן מטמאין מאויר כלי חרש שמיטמא בשרץ אינו דין שניטמאן בשרץ לטמא אכלין   13 בטמא \ ס בכל טמא בתרומה | ס - מה | ס ומה   14 פוסל | ס פסול   16 הרי | ס הא

[101]"Rebbi Yose stated, from where that the fourth degree is disqualified in sanctified food? It is an argument. Since one who lacks expiation[102] is not disqualified for heave[103] but disqualified for sanctified food, it is only logical that third degree[104] [impurity] which is disabled for heave should disqualify for sanctified food. That means, we learned third degree from a verse[105] and fourth degree from an argument *de minore ad majus*." Rebbi Joḥanan objected: Food that was touched by a *Tevul Yom*[106] is a counter-example, because he disqualifies in the case of heave but does not disqualify in the case of sanctified food[107]. Rebbi Ḥananiah[108] in the name of Rebbi Joḥanan: Rebbi Yose argues the method of his teacher Rebbi Aqiba. Just as Rebbi Aqiba says *impure*, impure by the words of the Torah, so Rebbi Yose says *it will be impure*, it makes impure by the words of the Torah. Rebbi Abbahu in the name of Rebbi Yose ben Ḥanina: Rebbi Yose does not need that argument *de minore ad majus*. Rebbi Yose explains the verse[109]: *Any meat which would touch*, that is second degree food because it touched primary impurity; *anything impure*, that is third degree food because it touched second degree impurity; *shall not be eaten*, the endstage of impurity may not be eaten. So far about solid food that became impure in the air space of a clay vessel which had become impure by a reptile[110]. What about solid food that became impure directly from a reptile? Is that not an argument? Since vessels, which cannot

become impure in the air space of a clay vessel that became impure by a reptile, become impure by contact with a reptile[111] to defile solid food, is it not logical that solid food itself which became impure by a reptile should become impure by contact with a reptile to defile solid food. So far, following Rebbi Aqiba. Following Rebbi Ismael? Rebbi Ismael stated: [112]*Any meat which would touch anything impure*, that is first degree food which touched any impurity, *shall not be eaten*, to add a second degree of impurity. The third degree from where? It is an argument. Since a *tevul yom* who is not disqualified for profane food disqualifies heave, it is only logical that a person secondarily impure, who disables profane food should disable heave. The fourth degree for sacrifices from where? It is an argument. Since one who lacks expiation who does not disable heave disables sanctified food, it is only logical that third degree [impurity] which disqualifies heave should disable sanctified food. That means, we learned first and second degrees from a verse, the third from an argument and the fourth from an argument *de minore ad majus*. Can one pile argument on argument[113]? Everything is subject to practice, i. e., that third degree disables heave and fourth degree disables sacrifices[114].

101 This is copied from *Soṭah* 5:2 (Notes 93-106, ט). In this paragraph, the corrector's changes are copied from *Soṭah* and have to be accepted.

102 If a person is healed whose body was an original source of impurity, he needs immersion in water to be pure and also a ceremony of expiation to be admitted to the Sanctuary and sacrifices (for the person afflicted with skin disease, *Lev*, 14:32; for the persons healed from genital discharges 15:14-15, 29-30 for the woman after childbirth 12:6-8). After immersion in water, the person is totally pure (after the following sundown) at any place other than the Sanctuary.

103 Tosephta 3:17.

104 In the text here "fourth order," not corrected by the corrector. The translated text here is from *Soṭah*.

105 Mishnah *Soṭah* 5:3 following R. Aqiba.

106 Cf. Chapter 1, Note 168.

107 Tosephta 3:16; *Sifra Emor Pereq* 4(8). It is proved that *sacra* are not in all respects more restrictive than heave. It is remarkable that the Babli does not argue against the thesis of R. Yose since it clearly violates the rule "it is enough if inference drawn from an argument be equal to the premise " (Babli *Bava qamma* 25a). According to this rule, a passive impurity in the minor cannot become an active one in the major. The Yerushalmi knows no such rule; it needs the counter-example of R. Johanan. The difference between the Talmudim is that for the Yerushalmi, *de minore ad majus* is a

rhetorical device but for the Babli it is part of a meta-logical system (cf. the author's *Logical Problems in Jewish Tradition*, in: Confrontations with Judaism, Ph. Longworth, ed., London 1966 pp. 171-196.)
108 In *Sotah*: R. Hiyya, the only possible reading since R. Hananiah was a teacher, not a student, of R. Johanan.
109 *Lev.* 7:19; *Sifra Saw Parasha* 9. A similar interpretation is given as an additional *baraita* in the Babli 24a, *Pesahim* 18b/19a, *Sotah* 29b.
110 A dead reptile from the kinds enumerated in *Lev.* 11:29-30.
111 Vessels can become impure only from original impurity (a "father" or "grandfather" of impurity, never from derivative impurity.) There is no verse which would indicate otherwise (but in *Pesahim* 1:7, R. Ismael is quoted to the effect that *Lev.* 11:33 also applies to vessels. It may be a veiled reference to the argument presented here.)
112 *Lev.* 7:19.
113 It is a principle accepted in both Talmudim that at least for any rules of sacrifices and connected matters, most hermeneutical rules cannot be used one after the other; cf. *Yebamot* 8:1, Note 19. A detailed table of legal and illegal combinations, derived from Babli *Zevahim* Chapter 5, appears in the author's paper *Über ein bemerkenswertes logisches System aus der Antike*, Methodos 1951, pp. 150-164.
114 Tosephta 3:8. "Practice" here corresponds to "Practice of Moses from Mount Sinai" in the Babli, generally accepted practice whose roots can no longer be ascertained. The status of such practice is more than rabbinic and less than biblical.

(line 32 79b) וּבַתְּרוּמָה נִטְמֵאת אַחַת מִיָּדָיו חֲבֶירְתָהּ טְהוֹרָה. לְטַמֵּא אֶת הַקּוֹדֶשׁ. דִּבְרֵי רִבִּי. רִבִּי יוֹסֵי בֵּירִבִּי יוּדָה אוֹמֵר. לִפְסוֹל בַּקּוֹדֶשׁ. מַה. רִבִּי כְרִבִּי יְהוֹשֻׁעַ. דְּתַנִּינָן תַּמָּן. כֹּל הַפּוֹסֵל אֶת הַתְּרוּמָה מְטַמֵּא אֶת הַיָּדַיִם לִהְיוֹת שְׁנִיּוֹת. וְהַיָּד מְטַמָּא אֶת חֲבֶירְתָהּ. דִּבְרֵי רִבִּי יְהוֹשֻׁעַ. וּדְרִבִּי יְהוֹשֻׁעַ רָבָא מִן דְּרִבִּי. מַה דְּאָמַר רִבִּי בַּקּוֹדֶשׁ. וּמַה דְּאָמַר רִבִּי יְהוֹשֻׁעַ בַּתְּרוּמָה.

"For heave, if one of his hands became impure the other remains pure." "To make *sancta* impure, the words of Rebbi. Rebbi Yose ben Rebbi Jehudah says, to disqualify *sancta*.[115]" How? Following Rebbi Joshua? As we have stated there[116], "anything which disqualifies heave makes hands impure in the second degree, and one hand makes the other one impure, the words of Rebbi Joshua." And Rebbi Joshua says more than Rebbi, since what Rebbi said refers to *sancta*, but Rebbi Joshua refers to heave[117].

115 Tosephta 3:10; Babli 24a. The text of the Tosephta is: A person who immerses one hand and prepares food in purity, any food prepared until he immerses the other hand is impure since one hand makes the other impure to make *sancta* impure . . ." The Tosephta implies that if one hand is impure, in preparation of *sancta* the other is impure in the second degree for Rebbi, in the third for R. Yose ben R. Jehudah.

116 Mishnah *Yadaim* 3:2.

117 Therefore the Mishnah here which treats heave (disqualified by second degree impurity) more leniently than *sancta* (disqualified by third degree impurity) cannot be R. Joshua's.

(79b line 37) רִבִּי שִׁמְעוֹן בֶּן לָקִישׁ אָמַר. לֹא שָׁנוּ אֶלָּא חֲבֵירָתָהּ. הָא אַחֶרֶת לֹא. רִבִּי יוֹחָנָן אָמַר. אֲפִילוּ אַחֶרֶת. רִבִּי יִרְמְיָה רִבִּי אִמִּי בְשֵׁם רִבִּי יוֹחָנָן. אֲפִילוּ כִכָּר. אָמְרִין. חָזַר רִבִּי יוֹחָנָן מִן הָדָא. מָה אָמַר כֹּה עַד לֹא יַחֲזוֹר בֵּיהּ. לֹא אָמַר אֶלָּא לְטַמֵּא כִכָּר. עַל שֵׁם כָּל הַפּוֹסֵל אֶת הַתְּרוּמָה מְטַמֵּא אֶת הַיָּדַיִם לִהְיוֹת שְׁנִיּוֹת. הָא לְטַמֵּא כִכָּר כָּל־עַמָּא מוֹדֵי שֶׁאֵינוֹ מְטַמֵּא. עַל שֵׁם שֶׁאֵין שֵׁינִי עוֹשֶׂה שֵׁינִי.

Rebbi Simeon ben Laqish said, they only stated "the other", not a stranger's[118]. Rebbi Johanan said, even a stranger's. Rebbi Jeremiah, Rebbi Immi in the name of Rebbi Johanan, even a loaf. They said, Rebbi Johanan retracted this; when he said so it was before he changed his mind. He only said to make a loaf impure, because of "anything which disqualifies heave makes hands impure in the second degree." Therefore to make a loaf impure everybody agrees that it does not make impure[119], since "no second degree creates second degree.[116]"

118 This refers to the statement that for *sancta* both hands have to be washed since otherwise one impure hand causes the other hand also to be impure. The problem is whether the other hand, which was not exposed to impurity, is impure in the second degree as impure hand, or of the third as derivative of second degree impurity. R. Simeon ben Laqish holds that it is impure in the third degree, R. Johanan that it is second.

119 For anything but the other hand of the person one follows the rule that induced impurity is one degree more than the inducing one. Therefore the second hand may disqualify a loaf of *sancta* but cannot possibly make it impure.

(fol. 78c) **משנה ג**: אוֹכְלִין אוֹכָלִים נְגוּבִים בְּיָדַיִם מְסוֹאָבוֹת בַּתְּרוּמָה אֲבָל לֹא בַקּוֹדֶשׁ. הָאוֹנֵן וְהַמְחוּסָּר כִּפּוּרִים צְרִיכִין טְבִילָה לַקּוֹדֶשׁ אֲבָל לֹא לַתְּרוּמָה:

Mishnah 3: One eats dry food[120] with dirty hands[121] with heave but not with *sancta*. The deep mourner[122] and one who lacks expiation need immersion for *sancta* but not for heave[123].

120 Which somehow never was wetted and therefore is impervious to impurity. But all

food eaten with sacrifices is subject to the rules of impurity.
121 Which are second degree impure and therefore have no influence on profane food, only on heave and *sancta*.
122 Who somehow is not impure in the impurity of the dead.
123 They are forbidden *sancta* but permitted heave. The immersion before their disability was removed is not counted.

(79b line 43) **הלכה ג**: אָמַר רִבִּי חֲנַנְיָה בֶּן אַנְטִיגְנֹס. וְכִי יֵשׁ אוֹכְלִין נְגוּבִין אֵצֶל הַקּוֹדֶשׁ. תּוֹחֵף אֶת הֲחַרָרָה בְּשִׁפּוּד וְאוֹכֵל עִמָּהּ כְּזַיִת בָּשָׂר בִּתְרוּמָה אֲבָל לֹא בַקּוֹדֶשׁ.

תַּמָּן תַּנִּינָן. הָיָה אוֹכֵל דְּבֵילָה בְּיָדַיִם מְסוֹאָבוֹת. הִכְנִיס יָדוֹ לְתוֹךְ פִּיו לִיטּוֹל אֶת הַצְּרוֹר. חִזְקִיָּה אָמַר. לֹא שָׁנוּ אֶלָּא דְּבֵילָה שֶׁהוּא רוֹצֶה בַּמַּשְׁקִין שֶׁעַל אֶצְבָּעוֹ. הָא שְׁאָר כָּל־הַדְּבָרִים לֹא. רִבִּי יוֹחָנָן אָמַר. לֹא שַׁנְיָא. הִיא דְּבֵילָה הִיא שְׁאָר כָּל־הַדְּבָרִים. מַתְנִיתָהּ פְּלִיגָא עַל חִזְקִיָּה מַגַּע טְמֵא מֵת שֶׁהָיוּ אוֹכְלִין וּמַשְׁקִין לְתוֹךְ פִּיו. הִכְנִיס רֹאשׁוֹ לַאֲוִיר הַתַּנּוּר טָהוֹר וְטִימְּאֵהוּ. וְטָהוֹר שֶׁהָיוּ אוֹכְלִין וּמַשְׁקִין לְתוֹךְ פִּיו. הִכְנִיס רֹאשׁוֹ לַאֲוִיר הַתַּנּוּר טָמֵא וְנִיטְמָא. נִיחָא מַשְׁקִין טְמֵאִין. אוֹכְלִין מֵאֵיכָן הוּכְשְׁרוּ. לֹא מִמַּשְׁקֵה פִיו. תִּיפְתָּר אוֹ בִדְבֵילָה שְׁמֵינָה אוֹ בְאוֹכְלִין שֶׁהוּכְשְׁרוּ עַד שֶׁהֵן מִבַּחוּץ. מַתְנִיתָהּ פְּלִיגָא עַל רִבִּי יוֹחָנָן. אוֹכְלִין אוֹכְלִין נְגוּבִין בְּיָדַיִם מְסוֹאָבוֹת בַּתְּרוּמָה אֲבָל לֹא בַקּוֹדֶשׁ. פָּתַר לָהּ בָּאוֹרֵק. אִם בָּאוֹרֵק אֲפִילוּ בַקּוֹדֶשׁ. שֶׁמָּא יִשְׁכַּח וְיִגַּע. אִם שֶׁמָּא יִשְׁכַּח וְיִגַּע אֲפִילוּ בַתְּרוּמָה יְהֵא אָסוּר. מַאי כְדוֹן. אוֹכְלֵי תְרוּמָה זְרִיזִין הֵן וְאֵינוֹ שׁוֹכֵחַ. אוֹכְלֵי הַקּוֹדֶשׁ אֵינָן זְרִיזִין וְהוּא שׁוֹכֵחַ.

Halakhah 3: "Rebbi Ḥananiah ben Antigonos said, do dry foods exist for *sancta*[124]? He impales the flat piece[125] on the spit[126] and eats with it an olive-sized bit of meat of heave but not of *sancta*.[127]"

There we have stated[128]: "If he ate a fig cake with dirty hands, put his hand into his mouth to remove a pebble, . . .[129]" Hizqiah said, one stated this only for a fig cake where he desires the fluid remaining on his finger, therefore not for anything else. Rebbi Joḥanan said, there is no difference, equally a fig cake where he desires the fluid remaining on his finger or anything other. The Mishnah[128] disagrees with Hizqiah: "Touching by a person impure in the impurity of the dead who had food or drink in his mouth: if he put his head inside a pure stove he made it impure. If a pure person with food or drink in his mouth put his head inside the impure stove he became impure.[130]" One understands drinks. From where was the food susceptible to impurity? Not from his saliva[131]! Explain it either from a moist fig cake or as food which already outside were susceptible to impurity. The Mishnah disagrees with Rebbi Joḥanan: "One eats dry food[120] with dirty hands[121] with heave but not with *sancta*." Explain it if he throws[132]. If he throws then even for *sancta*. Maybe he will forget and touch. If maybe he will forget and touch then it should be forbidden also for heave. Eaters of heave are vigilant and he will not forget but eaters of *sancta* are not vigilant[7] and he forgets.

124 Anything used with sacrificial food is susceptible to impurity; its use makes it susceptible.

125 Usually this word denotes a flat pitta bread. But here this cannot be the intended meaning since any kind of bread is made from dough containing water and therefore automatically susceptible to impurity. The reference is to a piece of food which never was in contact with any external fluid.

126 Which as a flat wooden implement is impervious to impurity.

127 Tosephta 3:12; Babli 24b.

128 Mishnah *Kelim* 8:10.

129 R. Meïr declares the fig cake impure but R. Jehudah pure. They disagree about the status of the saliva of a pure person. As noted later, saliva in the mouth does not prepare for impurity; otherwise a person never could eat in purity. R. Jehudah holds that saliva in the mouth is immune from impurity; for him the problem does not exist. R. Meïr holds that saliva is a fluid subject to the rules of impurity since the spittle of a person sick with gonorrhea is a source of biblical impurity. Since unwashed hands are impure of second degree, the saliva in his mouth makes them impure in the first degree. If then he again touches the fig cake it will be impure in the second degree.

130 The stove is made of clay. Biblically clay vessels become impure if and only if impurity is placed into its concavity with or without touching. The person himself would make the stove impure only if most of his body were inside but since the food in his head is moist and impure, putting his head inside makes the stove biblically impure. If therefore a pure person with food in his mouth puts his head inside the stove, the food becomes impure and makes the person impure.

131 Since as explained in Note 129, saliva in a pure person's body is pure and does not prepare for impurity.

132 He throws the food into his mouth so it is swallowed immediately without being wetted.

(79b line 58) תַּמָּן תַּנִּינָן. אוֹנֵן נוֹגֵעַ וְאֵינוֹ מַקְרִיב וְאֵינוֹ חוֹלֵק לֶאֱכוֹל בָּעֶרֶב. תַּמָּן אַתְּ אָמַר. מוּתָּר לִיגַּע. וְכָא אַתְּ אָמַר. אָסוּר לִיגַּע. אָמַר רִבִּי יַנַּיי. כָּאן בְּשֶׁהִסִּיעַ דַּעְתּוֹ וְכָאן בְּשֶׁלֹּא הִסִּיעַ דַּעְתּוֹ. רִבִּי יוֹסֵי בָּעֵי. אִם בְּשֶׁהִסִּיעַ דַּעְתּוֹ אֲפִילוּ בִתְרוּמָה יְהֵא אָסוּר. מַאי כְדוֹן. כַּהֲיָא דְּאָמַר רִבִּי יִרְמְיָה בְשֵׁם רִבִּי בָּא בַּר מָמָל. עָשׂוּ אוֹתוֹ כְאוֹכֵל אוֹכֵל רְבִיעִי בַּקּוֹדֶשׁ. הָדָא אָמְרָה הָאוֹכֵל אוֹכֵל רְבִיעִי בַּקּוֹדֶשׁ אָסוּר וּמוּתָּר לִיגַּע. וְכָא אָסוּר לוֹכַל וּמוּתָּר לִיגַּע. תַּמָּן תַּנִּינָן. שֶׁבֵּית שַׁמַּי אוֹמְרִים. צְרִיכָה טְבִילָה בָּאַחֲרוֹנָה. וּבֵית הִלֵּל אוֹמְרִים. אֵינָהּ צְרִיכָה טְבִילָה בָּאַחֲרוֹנָה׃ מָה אֲנָן קַייָמִין. אִם לַאֲכִילַת תְּרוּמָה קַשְׁיָא עַל דְּבֵית שַׁמַּי. וְלֹא טְבוּלַת יוֹם הִיא. וְאֵין טְבוּל יוֹם

מַעֲרִיב שִׁמְשׁוֹ וְאוֹכֵל. אִם לַאֲכִילַת קֳדָשִׁים קַשְׁיָא עַל דְּבֵית הִלֵּל. וְלָא מְחוּסָּר כַּפָּרָה הִיא. וְאֵין מְחוּסָּר כַּפָּרָה טָעוּן טְבִילָה אֵצֶל הַקּוֹדֶשׁ. אִין תֵּימַר. בַּתְּרוּמָה אֲנָן קַיָּימִין תַּמָּן. וְהָדָא דְתַנִּינָן הָכָא רֵישָׁא דְבְרֵי הַכֹּל וְסֵיפָא בְּמַחְלוֹקֶת. אִין תֵּימַר. בַּתְּרוּמָה אֲנָן קַיָּימִין הָכָא. וְהָדָא הִיא דְתַנִּינָן תַּמָּן רֵישָׁא דְבְרֵי הַכֹּל וְסֵיפָא בְּמַחְלוֹקֶת. אָמַר רִבִּי שְׁמוּאֵל בַּר אֲבָדוּמִי קוֹמֵי רִבִּי מָנָא. בַּתְּרוּמָה אֲנָן קַיָּימִין. תַּמָּן טַעֲמוֹן דְּבֵית שַׁמַּי מִפְּנֵי הַהֶדְיוֹטוֹת. שֶׁלֹּא יְהוּ אוֹמְרִים. רָאִינוּ אִשָּׁה שׁוֹפַעַת דָּם וְאוֹכֶלֶת בַּתְּרוּמָה.

There we have stated[133]: "The deep mourner touches but may not sacrifice nor take his part of meat in the evening.[134]" There you are saying, he may touch. But here you are saying, he is forbidden to touch. Rebbi Yannai said, here when he put his mind to other things, but there if he did not put his mind to other things[135]. Rebbi Yose asked, if he put his mind to other things should he not also be forbidden heave? How is this? As Rebbi Jeremiah said in the name of Rebbi Abba bar Mamal: They treated him like one who ate food which was of fourth degree for *sancta*[136]. This implies that one who ate food which was of fourth degree for *sancta* is forbidden to eat but permitted to touch. And here he is forbidden to eat but permitted to touch. There we have stated[137]: "For the House of Shammai are saying, she needs immersion at the end, but the House of Hillel are saying, she does not need immersion at the end.[138]" Where do we hold? If about eating heave it is difficult for the House of Shammai; if about eating *sancta* it is difficult for the House of Hillel[139]. Does she not lack expiation? Do people lacking expiation not need immersion for *sancta*[140]? If you are saying that there one holds about heave, regarding what we have stated here the first part is everybody's opinion and the second part in dispute. If you are saying that here one holds about heave, regarding what we have stated there the first part is everybody's opinion and the second part in dispute[141]. Rebbi Samuel bar Eudaimon said before Rebbi Mana, we are dealing with heave. There the reason of the House of Shammai is because of the unlearned[142], that they should not say, we saw a woman losing blood and eating heave[143].

133 Mishnah *Zevahim* 12:1.
134 Usually the deep mourner Cohen, the mourner before the burial, will be impure in the impurity of the dead since it is obligatory for a Cohen to defile himself for the burial of a close relative (*Lev.*. 21:1-4). In case he is prevented from participating in the burial (usually by being far from the place of burial) and is pure, he still is forbidden before the burial to participate in

any religious rite. If he is in Jerusalem and pure, at the time of distribution of the sacrificial meat he is barred from participating even if a short time later he will be able to resume all his functions.

135 The Mishnah in *Zevahim* permits the deep mourner to touch *sancta*, but the Mishnah here requires him to immerse himself, which implies that after immersion he still is prohibited touching *sancta* until sundown. This glaring contradiction can be explained in that the Mishnah here prescribes immersion for a person not directly involved in the Temple service. Babli *Zevahim* 99a.

136 Which is disqualified for *sancta* but not for heave. "He" is the deep mourner not impure in the impurity of the dead.

137 Mishnah *Niddah* 10:7.

138 The Mishnah explains the rules of the purity of women after childbirth. The verse (*Lev.* 12:2-6) declares her impure in the impurity of menstruation for 7 days after the birth of a son and 14 days after the birth of a daughter. At the end of this period she has to immerse herself. For the following 33 days after the birth of a son and 66 after that of a girl she is impervious to impurity from genital bleeding. She still is barred from the Temple and *sancta* until she has brought her sacrifice of expiation. The Houses of Shammai and Hillel disagree on whether after the expiration of her days of purity (i. e., when she again becomes susceptible to impurity) she needs another immersion.

139 In the Mishnah it is stated as unanimous opinion that the deep mourner needs immersion for *sancta* but not for heave.

140 Since the verse requires a sacrifice of expiation at the end of her period of purity it should be clear that she is lacking expiation and following the Mishnah here needs immersion for *sancta* but not for heave.

141 In the first case, the statement here about immersion is the House of Hillel's. In the second case, the reference to the first part is Mishnah *Niddah* 10:6.

142 Greek 'ἰδιώτης.

143 There is no reason in the rules of impurity preventing a woman with genital bleeding to eat heave in the days of her purity. They forbid it only so people should not draw the wrong inferences, not knowing that she is impervious to this kind of impurity.

(fol. 78c) **משנה ד**: חוֹמֶר בַּתְּרוּמָה שֶׁבִּיהוּדָה נֶאֱמָנִים עַל טַהֲרַת יַיִן וְשֶׁמֶן כָּל־יְמוֹת הַשָּׁנָה וּבִשְׁעַת הַגִּתּוֹת וְהַבַּדִּים אַף עַל הַתְּרוּמָה. עָבְרוּ הַגִּתּוֹת וְהַבַּדִּים וְהֵבִיאוּ לוֹ חָבִית שֶׁל יַיִן שֶׁל תְּרוּמָה לֹא יְקַבְּלֶנָּה מִמֶּנּוּ אֲבָל מַנִּיחָהּ לָגַת הַבָּאָה. אִם אָמַר לוֹ הִפְרַשְׁתִּי לְתוֹכָהּ רְבִיעִית קוֹדֶשׁ נֶאֱמָן. כַּדֵּי יַיִן וְכַדֵּי שֶׁמֶן הַמְדוּמָּעוֹת, נֶאֱמָנִין עֲלֵיהֶן בִּשְׁעַת הַגִּתּוֹת וְהַבַּדִּים קוֹדֶם לָגַת שִׁבְעִים יוֹם:

Mishnah 4: One is more restrictive for heave in that in Judea one is trustworthy about purity of wine and oil the entire year[144] but about heave {only} at the time of grape and olive harvest[145]. If the time of grape and olive harvest is passed and he[146] brought him[147] a barrel of heave wine he should not accept it but let it stay until the next grape harvest. Only if he said, I put into it a *quartarius* of *sanctum* he is trustworthy[148]. One is trustworthy about wine and oil barrels used for heave[149] at the time of grape and olive harvest and sixty days preceding the grape harvest.

144 This is a rule for Temple times since, as explained in the Halakhah, wine and oil for use in the Temple had to be brought from Judea. Therefore all farmers in Judea were careful in preserving the purity of oil and wine.

145 Since every farmer wanted to produce his heave in purity.

146 The vulgar, negligent in matters of purity.

147 The Cohen, observing the rules of purity.

148 Since the Temple wine makes him observant of the rules of purity.

149 Which in *Ex.* 22:28 is called דמע.

(79b line 75) **הלכה ד**: חוֹמֶר בַּתְּרוּמָה שֶׁבִּיהוּדָה נֶאֱמָנִין. הָא בַגָּלִיל לֹא. רִבִּי סִימוֹן רִבִּי יְהוֹשֻׁעַ בֶּן לֵוִי בְשֵׁם רִבִּי פְּדָיָיה. מִפְּנֵי שֶׁפְּסִיקְיָיא שֶׁלְכּוּתִיִּים מַפְסָקֶת. וְהָא תַנִּינָן. שְׁנִייָה לָהּ רֶגֶב בְּעֵבֶר הַיַּרְדֵּן. בְּלֹא כָךְ אֵין פְּסִיקְיָיא שֶׁלְכּוּתִים מַפְסָקֶת. אָמַר רִבִּי שַׁמַּי. תִּיפְתָּר בְּמֵבִיא גַּרְגְּרִים וְכוֹתְשָׁן שָׁם. וּבִיהוּדָה נֶאֱמָנִין עַל הַיַּיִן אֲבָל לֹא עַל הַקַּנְקִינִים. וּבַגָּלִיל אֵינָן נֶאֱמָנִין לֹא עַל הַיַּיִן וְלֹא עַל הַקַּנְקִינִים. רִבִּי סִימוֹן בְּשֵׁם רִבִּי יְהוֹשֻׁעַ בֶּן לֵוִי. בֶּן דָּרוֹם שֶׁאָמַר. בַּגָּלִיל הֲבֵאתִיהָ. נֶאֱמָן. וּבֶן גָּלִיל שֶׁאָמַר. מִדָּרוֹם הֲבֵאתִיהָ. אֵינוֹ נֶאֱמָן.

Halakhah 4: "One is more restrictive for heave in that in Judea one is trustworthy." Rebbi Simon, Rebbi Joshua ben Levi in the name of Rebbi Pedaiah: Because a strip of Samaritans interrupts[150]. But did we not state[151], "the second best is Regev in Transjordan"? Without this would not a strip of Samaritans interrupt[150]? Rebbi Shammai said, explain it if he brings whole olives[152] and pounds them there. And in Judea one is trustworthy about the wine but not about the flasks. Rebbi Simon in the name of Rebbi Joshua ben Levi: A Southerner who said, I brought this from Galilee is trustworthy; a Galilean who said, I brought this from Judea is not trustworthy[153].

150 This statement must be late Amoraic, after the exclusion of Samaritans from Judaism according to its rabbinic interpretation (cf. *Avodah zarah* 3:1 Note 27). The correct version is Rashi's reading in the Babli: "A strip of Gentile territory", which is impure in the general impurity of lands outside Jewish Palestine; cf. *Dikduke Sopherim Ḥagigah* 25a Note 8.

151 Mishnah *Menahot* 8:3.

152 Which never were wetted and therefore are impervious to impurity.

153 In both cases the heave is impure unless under control of a trustworthy person.

(7) ‏רִבִּי יִרְמְיָה סָבַר מֵימַר בִּתְרוּמָה שֶׁנַּעֲשִׂית עַל גַּב הַקּוֹדֶשׁ. הָא עַל גַּב עַצְמָהּ לֹא‎ (79c line ‏אָמַר רִבִּי יוֹסֵה. וַאֲפִילוּ נַעֲשִׂית עַל גַּב עַצְמָהּ. מַתְנִיתָהּ פְּלִינָא עַל רִבִּי יוֹסֵה. צָרִיךְ לַעֲמוֹד עֲלֵיהֶן‎ ‏עַד שֶׁיִּטְבּוֹלוּ. פָּתַר לָהּ שֶׁלֹּא בִשְׁעַת הַבַּד. אִית לָךְ מֵימַר שֶׁלֹּא בִשְׁעַת הַגַּת. אָמַר רִבִּי יִצְחָק‎ ‏בֵּירִבִּי לָעְזָר. אוֹ קוֹדֶם שֶׁלֹּא בָצְרוּ בָהּ שְׁלֹשָׁה בְנֵי אָדָם נָגְעוּ בּוֹ טַהֲרוֹת. בִּשְׁעַת הַגִּיתוֹת וְהַבַּדִּים‎ ‏הַטַּהֲרוֹת טְהוֹרוֹת. עָבְרוּ הַגִּיתוֹת וְהַבַּדִּים הַטַּהֲרוֹת טְמֵאוֹת. וְיֵשׁ כְּלִי חֶרֶשׂ מַשֶּׁהוּ מִטָּהֵר חוֹזֵר‎ ‏וּמִיטַּמֵּא. וְלֵית כָּל־אִילֵּין מִילַּיָּא כֵן. אֶלָּא כֵינִי. נָגְעוּ בּוֹ טַהֲרוֹת קוֹדֶם לַגִּיתוֹת וְלַבַּדִּים‎ ‏הַטַּהֲרוֹת טְהוֹרוֹת. וְיֵשׁ כְּלִי חֶרֶשׂ מַשֶּׁהוּ מִיטַּמֵּא חוֹזֵר וּמִיטָּהֵר. וְלֵית כָּל־אִילֵּין מִילַּיָּא כֵן.‎ ‏אֶלָּא כֵינִי. נָגְעוּ בּוֹ טַהֲרוֹת בְּשָׁעָה שֶׁהוּא מָלֵא הַטַּהֲרוֹת טְהוֹרוֹת. פִּינָּהוּ הַטַּהֲרוֹת טְמֵאוֹת. וְיֵשׁ‎ ‏כְּלִי חֶרֶשׂ מַשֶּׁהוּ מִיטָּהֵר חוֹזֵר וּמִיטַּמֵּא. וְלֵית כָּל־אִילֵּין מִילַּיָּא כֵן. אֶלָּא כֵינִי. נָגְעוּ בּוֹ טַהֲרוֹת‎ ‏בְּשָׁעָה שֶׁהוּא רֵיקָן הַטַּהֲרוֹת טְמֵאוֹת. מִילְּהוּ הַטַּהֲרוֹת טְהוֹרוֹת. וְיֵשׁ כְּלִי חֶרֶשׂ מַשֶּׁהוּ מִיטַּמֵּא‎ ‏חוֹזֵר וּמִיטָּהֵר. וְלֵית כָּל־אִילֵּין מִילַּיָּא כֵן.‎

Rebbi Jeremiah was of the opinion, only heave prepared in the purity of *sancta*[154]. Therefore not in its own. Rebbi Yose said, even if prepared in its own[155]. A Mishnah disagrees with Rebbi Yose[156]: "He has to watch them until they immersed themselves." Explain it: not in the time of the olive harvest. Could you say not in the time of the grape harvest[157]? Rebbi Isaac ben Rebbi Eleazar said, if food prepared in purity touched it before three people used it, at the time of olive and grape harvests the food prepared in purity remains pure, not at the time of olive and grape harvests the food prepared in purity becomes impure. Does there exist any clay vessel which is pure and then makes impure[158]? Are not all these of the same kind? But it must be the following: if food prepared in purity touched it before the time of olive and grape harvests the food prepared in purity remains pure. Does there exist any clay vessel which is impure and then pure? Are not all these of the same kind? But it must be the following: if food prepared in purity touched it when it was full the food prepared in purity remains pure. If he cleared it, the food prepared in purity becomes impure. Does there exist any clay vessel which is pure and then makes impure? Are not all these of the same kind? But it must be the following: if food prepared in purity touched it when it was empty the food prepared in purity becomes impure. If he filled it, the food prepared in purity remains pure. Does there exist any clay vessel which is pure and then makes impure? Are not all these of the same kind[159]?

154 Since the Mishnah connects purity of food prepared by the non-observant to the preparation of oil and wine for the Temple, it seems rational to restrict the entire Mishnah to food prepared to Temple standards.

155 If R. Jeremiah were correct, one could not say that the standards of heave are more strict than those of *sancta*.

156 Mishnah *Taharot* 10:3. The Mishnah prescribes that in preparation of the olive and grape harvests one requests the workers, presumed to be vulgars who do not observe the rules of purity in their daily lives, to immerse themselves in a *miqweh*. For R. Meïr it is enough if the employer leads them to the *miqweh*, but R. Yose the Tanna requires that he observe their immersion. This clearly means that the workers in olive or wine presses are not presumed to follow strictly the rules of purity.

157 Olives which remain intact being harvested may be stored and later be pressed but grapes must be pressed immediately after being harvested. Therefore the Mishnah in *Taharot* which mentions wine-press workers must refer to the time of the grape harvest.

158 Since clay utensils cannot be purified other than being broken, it does not make any sense to consider clay olive and grape presses pure one day and impure the next. Mishnaiot *Hagigah* 3:4 and *Taharot* 10:3 are incompatible.

159 There is no formulation able to bridge the conceptual contradictions between the two Mishnaiot.

(79c line 22) אָמַר רִבִּי יוֹחָנָן. כּוּשְׁתְּ וְקֵירוּיָה וּמָבוֹי וְגֵר וְעַם הָאָרֶץ. חוּמְרִין.

כּוּשְׁתְּ. כַּיי דְּתַנִּינָן תַּמָּן. הַכּוּשְׁט וְהַחֶמֶס וְרָאשֵׁי בְשָׂמִים הַתִּיָּיה וְהַחִלְתִּית וְהַפִּילְפְּלִין וְחַלּוֹת חָרִיעַ נִלְקָחִים בְּכֶסֶף מַעֲשֵׂר. וְאֵינָן מְטַמְּאִין טוּמְאַת אוֹכְלִין דִּבְרֵי רִבִּי עֲקִיבָה. אָמַר רִבִּי יוֹחָנָן בֶּן נוּרִי. אִם נִלְקָחִין בְּכֶסֶף מַעֲשֵׂר מִפְּנֵי מָה אֵינָן מְטַמּוֹת טוּמְאַת אוֹכְלִין. אִם אֵינָן מְטַמּוֹת טוּמְאַת אוֹכְלִין אַף הֵן לֹא יִלָּקְחוּ בְּכֶסֶף מַעֲשֵׂר: רִבִּי יוֹחָנָן אָמַר. חוּמְרִין. מְטַמְּאִין טוּמְאַת אוֹכְלִים וְאֵינָן נִלְקָחִין בְּכֶסֶף מַעֲשֵׂר.

קֵירוּיָיה. כַּיי דְּתַנִּינָן תַּמָּן. קֵירוּיָיה שֶׁהִטְבִּילוּהָ בְּמַיִם שֶׁהֵן רְאוּיִין לְקַדֵּשׁ מְקַדְּשִׁין בָּהּ עַד שֶׁתִּיטָּמָא. נִיטְמָא אֵין מְקַדְּשִׁין בָּהּ. רִבִּי יְהוֹשֻׁעַ אוֹמֵר אִם מְקַדְּשִׁין בָּהּ בַּתְּחִילָּה אַף בַּסּוֹף. אִם אֵינָן מְקַדְּשִׁין בָּהּ בַּסּוֹף אַף לֹא בַתְּחִילָּה. בֵּין כָּךְ וּבֵין כָּךְ לֹא יֶאֱסוֹף בְּתוֹכָהּ מַיִם מְקוּדָּשִׁין: רִבִּי יוֹחָנָן אָמַר. חוּמְרִין. אֵין מְקַדְּשִׁין בָּהּ לֹא בַתְּחִילָּה וְלֹא בַסּוֹף.

מָבוֹי. כַּיי דְּתַנִּינָן תַּמָּן. וְכֵן מָבוֹי שֶׁנִּיטְּלָה קוֹרָתוֹ אוֹ לְהָיָיו כּוּל. רִבִּי יוֹחָנָן אָמַר. חוּמְרִין. אֲסוּרִין בֵּין בְּשַׁבָּת זוֹ בֵּין בְּשַׁבָּת הַבָּאָה.

גֵּר. דְּתַנֵּי. גֵּר שֶׁנִּתְגַּיֵּיר וְהָיוּ לוֹ יֵינוֹת. אָמַר. בְּבָרִי לִי שֶׁלֹּא נִתְנַסֵּךְ מֵהֶן. בִּזְמַן שֶׁנַּעֲשׂוּ עַל גַּב עֲצָמָן. טְהוֹרִין לוֹ וּטְמֵאִין לַאֲחֵרִים. עַל גַּב אֲחֵרִים טְמֵאִין בֵּין לוֹ וּבֵין לַאֲחֵרִים. רִבִּי עֲקִיבָה

אוֹמֵר. אִם טְהוֹרִין לוֹ יְהוּ טְהוֹרִין לָאֲחֵרִים. אִם טְמֵאִין לָאֲחֵרִים יְהוּ טְמֵאִין לוֹ. רִבִּי יוֹחָנָן אָמַר. חוֹמָרִין. טְמֵאִין בֵּין לוֹ בֵּין לָאֲחֵרִים.

עַם הָאָרֶץ. דְּתַנֵּי. עַם הָאָרֶץ שֶׁנִּתְמַנָּה לִהְיוֹת חָבֵר. וְהָיוּ לוֹ טהורות וְאָמַר. בְּבָרִיא לִי שֶׁנַּעֲשׂוּ בְטַהֲרָה. בַּזְּמַן שֶׁנַּעֲשׂוּ עַל גַּב עַצְמוֹ טְהוֹרוֹת לוֹ וּטְמֵאוֹת לָאֲחֵרִים. עַל גַּב אֲחֵרִים טְמֵאוֹת בֵּין לוֹ בֵּין לָאֲחֵרִים. רִבִּי עֲקִיבָה אוֹמֵר. אִם טְהוֹרוֹת לוֹ יְהִיוּ טְהוֹרוֹת לָאֲחֵרִים. אִם טְמֵאוֹת לָאֲחֵרִים יְהִיוּ טְמֵאוֹת לוֹ. רִבִּי יוֹחָנָן אָמַר. חוֹמָרִין. טְמֵאוֹת בֵּין לוֹ וּבֵין לָאֲחֵרִים.

[160] Rebbi Joḥanan said, *costos*, and hollowed squash, and alley, and convert, and vulgar, are restrictive.

Costos as we have stated[161], "*costos*, and cardamon, and important spices,[162] and benjamin, and asa foetida, and peppers, and safflower cakes, may be bought with tithe money[163] but do not become impure by impurity of foodstuff, the words of Rebbi Aqiba. Rebbi Joḥanan ben Nuri said, if they may be bought with tithe money they become impure by impurity of foodstuff, and if they do not become impure by impurity of foodstuff they may not be bought with tithe money." Rebbi Joḥanan said, restrictive[164]: they become impure by impurity of foodstuff and may not be bought with tithe money.

Hollowed squash as we have stated[165]: "A hollowed squash which one immersed in water is suitable for sanctification, and one uses it to sanctify until it becomes impure. Once it is impure one may not use it to sanctify. Rebbi Joshua says, if one uses it to sanctify at the start then also at the end. If one does not use at the end then also not at the start." Rebbi Joḥanan said, restrictive, one may not sanctify either at the beginning or at the end.

Alley, as we have stated there[166], "or an alley whose beam was removed, etc." Rebbi Joḥanan said, restrictive, it is forbidden both on this Sabbath and the coming Sabbath.

Proselyte, as it was stated: If a proselyte converted while he had wines, and said, it is clear to me that no libations were made from it, if he made it by himself it is pure for him but impure for others[167], by others it is impure both for him and for others. Rebbi Aqiba said, if they are pure for him they should be pure for others; if impure for others they should be impure for him. Rebbi Joḥanan said, restrictive, impure for him and for others.

Vulgar, as it was stated: If a vulgar person who was inducted as a fellow[168] has food made in purity and he said, it is clear to me that it was prepared in purity, if he made it by himself it is pure for him but impure for others, by others it is impure both for him and for others. Rebbi Aqiba said, if they are pure for him they should be pure for others; if impure for others they should be impure for him. Rebbi Joḥanan said, restrictive, impure for him and for others.

160 A somewhat fuller version of a text from *Eruvin* 9:4 (Notes 60-69). The implication here is that the Mishnah in *Taharot* presents a rabbinic restriction. Since this is not a matter of logic, there is no contradiction in the basic legal foundations of both Mishnaiot.

161 Mishnah *Uqeṣin* 3:5. *Costos,-i, f.*, Greek κόστος, an Oriental aromatic plant.

162 The spices mentioned are not food but may be used as additives in the preparation of food.

163 Money dedicated as Second Tithe which may be spent only on pure food or drink in Jerusalem.

164 The Mishnah is stated as an argument, not as a statement, to permit in practice to accept each argument even though this results in two mutually contradictory restrictions.

165 Mishnah *Parah* 5:3. "Sanctify" means to put some of the ashes of the Red Cow into the water to use it to purify from the im-

purity of the dead. This water has to be taken from flowing water (*Num.* 19:17). Since the squash, used as a pot, will absorb of this water, immediately after it has been immersed in flowing water it might be used in the ceremony, but later the water retained in its walls will invalidate new water drawn by the hollowed squash. In the Mishnah, R. Joshua argues that if at the start the squash was acceptable it always should be acceptable, if later it is not acceptable neither should it be at the start (since the point in time when it becomes unacceptable is not well defined.)

166 *Eruvin* Mishnah 9:4. If the beam was in place at the start of the Sabbath, an argument is made that in the alley it closes one may continue to carry on this Sabbath.

167 As wine prepared by a Non-Jew, cf. *Avodah zarah,* Chapters 2-5.

168 A fellow is a person observing all rules of purity in the absence of a Temple, cf. Introduction to Tractate *Demay.*

(79c line 46) אָמַר רִבִּי יַנַּיי. הָרוּבִּין הָיוּ אוֹמְרִים. בִּתְרוּמָה שֶׁנַּעֲשִׂית עַל גַּב הַקּוֹדֶשׁ. הָא עַל גַּב עַצְמָהּ לֹא. וַאֲנִי אוֹמֵר. אֲפִילוּ נַעֲשִׂית עַל גַּב עַצְמָהּ. אַתְיָא דְרִבִּי יוֹסֵה כְּרִבִּי יַנַּאי וּדְרִבִּי יִרְמְיָה כְרוּבִּים.

Rebbi Yannai said, the youngsters[169] said, only heave prepared in the purity of *sancta*[154]. Therefore not in its own. But I am saying, even if prepared in its own[155]. Rebbi Yose follows Rebbi Yannai and Rebbi Jeremiah the youngsters.

169 The sons of R. Hiyya the Elder, Hizqiah and Jehudah. Since in the absence of a Temple no ruling is required about the meaning of the Mishnah, none is given.

(79c line 50) אִם אָמַר לוֹ הִפְרַשְׁתִּי לְתוֹכָהּ רְבִיעִית קוֹדֶשׁ נֶאֱמָן. מֵאַחַר שֶׁהוּא נֶאֱמָן עַל הַקּוֹדֶשׁ נֶאֱמָן עַל הַתְּרוּמָה.

כַּדֵּי יַיִן וְכַדֵּי שֶׁמֶן הַמַּדְמִיעוֹת. אָמַר רִבִּי יוֹסֵי בֵּירִבִּי בּוּן. אִילּוּ שֶׁקּוֹדְחִין בָּהֶן אֶת הַדֶּמַע.

"Only if he said, I put into it a *quartarius* of *sanctum* he is trustworthy[148]." Since he is trustworthy for the *sanctum* he is trustworthy for heave[170].

"One is trustworthy about wine and oil barrels used for heave." Rebbi Yose ben Rebbi Abun said, those in which one heats heave.

170 Babli 25b.

(fol. 78c) **משנה ה**: מִן הַמּוֹדִיעִית וְלִפְנִים נֶאֱמָנִין עַל כְּלֵי חֶרֶשׂ. וּמִן הַמּוֹדִיעִית וְלַחוּץ אֵין נֶאֱמָנִין. כֵּיצַד הַקַּדָּר שֶׁהוּא מוֹכֵר אֶת הַקְּדֵירוֹת נִכְנַס לִפְנִים מִן הַמּוֹדִיעִית הוּא הַקַּדָּר וְהֵן הַקְּדֵירוֹת וְהֵן הַלּוֹקְחִין נֶאֱמָן. יָצָא אֵינוֹ נֶאֱמָן:

Mishnah 5: From Modiin and closer one is trustworthy about clay vessels, but from Modiin and outside one is not trustworthy. How is this? The potter[171] who sells pots[172], if he is inside from Modiin then the potter, the pots, and the buyers[173], are trustworthy. If he left he is not trustworthy[174].

171 Who usually is a vulgar, not trustworthy in matters of purity.

172 The kinds used to cook *sancta* in. The problem with clay vessels is that they cannot be made pure once they are impure. Now the remainders of meat absorbed in the porous walls of clay vessels become forbidden and impure leftover meat after the time allotted to its consumption and therefore must be broken (*Lev.* 6:21). If only fellows could supply clay vessels for *sancta*, everybody would have to use expensive metal vessels.

173 The buyer who affirms that he bought the pot at a place closer to Jerusalem than Modiin.

174 Even about pots he sold at a place closer to Jerusalem than Modiin.

(79c line 52) **הלכה ה:** מַתְנִיתָא בִּכְלֵי חֶרֶשׂ הַדַּקִּים. מַתְנִיתָא אָמְרָה כֵן. הוּא הַקַּדָּר וְהֵן הַקְּדֵירוֹת וְהֵן הַלּוֹקְחִין. וּקְדֵירוֹת לֹא כְלֵי חֶרֶשׂ דַּקִּין הֵן.

נָגְעוּ בּוֹ טַהֲרוֹת. מִן הַמּוֹדִיעִית וְלִפְנִים טִימֵּא מַשְׁקֶה אֶת הַכְּלִי. הָיָה מָלֵא מַיִם. רִבִּי שִׁמְעוֹן בֶּן לָקִישׁ אָמַר. נֶאֱמָן עַל הַכְּלִי וְאֵינוּ נֶאֱמָן עַל הַמַּשְׁקֶה. רִבִּי יוֹחָנָן אָמַר. נֶאֱמָן עַל זֶה וְעַל זֶה. מַתְנִיתָא פְלִיגָא עַל רִבִּי שִׁמְעוֹן בֶּן לָקִישׁ. אִם אָמַר לוֹ הִפְרַשְׁתִּי לְתוֹכָהּ רְבִיעִית קוֹדֶשׁ נֶאֱמָן. אָמַר רִבִּי זְעוּרָה. תִּיפְתָּר בָּאוֹמֵר. עַד שֶׁאֲנִי חָבֵר הִפְרַשְׁתִּיהָ. רַבָּנִן דְּקַיְסָרִין בְּשֵׁם רִבִּי בּוּן בַּר חִיָּיה. טַעֲמָא דְּרִבִּי שִׁמְעוֹן בֶּן לָקִישׁ אֵין חֲבֵירוּת לַמַּיִם.

Halakhah 5: The Mishnah is about small clay vessels. The Mishnah implies this: "the potter, the pots, and the buyers." And are pots not small clay vessels[175]?

If food prepared in purity touched it, from Modiin and closer the fluid made the vessel impure[176]. If it was filled with water, Rebbi Simeon ben Laqish said, he is trustworthy about the vessel but not trustworthy about the fluid. Rebbi Johanan said, he is trustworthy about both. A Mishnah disagrees with Rebbi Simeon ben Laqish: "Only if he said, I put into it a *quartarius* of *sanctum* he is trustworthy[148]." Rebbi Ze'ira said, explain it about one who said, I separated it when I was fellow[177]. The rabbis of Caesarea in the name of Rebbi Abun bar Hiyya: The reason of Rebbi Simeon ben Laqish, there is no fellowship for water[178].

175 Vessels of daily use, not large vats. Babli 26a.

176 While the vulgar is to be believed if near Jerusalem he stated that a clay vessel was pure, this refers only to empty vessels. If the vessel contains food, according to R. Johanan one says that since he is trustworthy about the vessel he also is trustworthy for its contents. This is denied by R. Simeon ben Laqish; therefore the statement under consideration is R. Simeon ben Laqish's, not accepted by R. Johanan.

The text mentions fluid because impure fluids always are impure in the first degree and make clay vessels impure in their interior.

177 The vulgar is not trusted if he affirms that the food was prepared under the supervision of a fellow.

178 He holds that even on a holiday, on which all of Israel are considered fellows, no vulgar is trustworthy to testify about water.

(fol. 78c) **משנה ו:** הַגַּבָּאִים שֶׁנִּכְנְסוּ לְתוֹךְ הַבַּיִת וְכֵן הַגַּנָּבִים שֶׁהֶחֱזִירוּ אֶת הַכֵּלִים נֶאֱמָנִין לוֹמַר לֹא נָגַעְנוּ. וּבִירוּשָׁלַם נֶאֱמָנִין עַל הַקּוֹדֶשׁ וּבִשְׁעַת הָרֶגֶל אַף עַל הַתְּרוּמָה:

Mishnah 6: Tax collectors[179] who entered a house, and also tax collectors who returned implements[180], are trustworthy if they say "we did not touch".

And in Jerusalem they[181] are trustworthy about *sancta*, and on holidays also about heave.

179 Vulgar Jews entering the house of a fellow.
18 They brought back the vessels (now impure) which they took as pledge. They are to be believed if they state that they did not touch anything else in the house. The Babli has a different text.
181 Every Jew.

(79c line 61) **הלכה ו**: הַגַּבָּאִים שֶׁנִּכְנְסוּ לְתוֹךְ הַבַּיִת הַבַּיִת טָמֵא. אִם יֵשׁ עִמָּהֶן גּוֹי נֶאֱמָנִין לוֹמַר נִכְנַסְנוּ אֲבָל לֹא נָגַעְנוּ. פָּתַר לָהּ תְּרֵין פִּתָרִין. נֶאֱמָנִין לוֹמַר נִכְנַסְנוּ אֲבָל לֹא נָגַעְנוּ. בְּשֶׁיֵּשׁ עֵדִים יוֹדְעִין. וּבִירוּשָׁלַיִם נֶאֱמָנִין עַל הַקּוֹדֶשׁ אֲפִילוּ יֵשׁ עֵדִים יוֹדְעִין. פָּתַר לָהּ פֶּתֶר חוֹרָן. נֶאֱמָנִין לוֹמַר נִכְנַסְנוּ אֲבָל לֹא נָגַעְנוּ. לָכֵן צְרִיכָה בְּשֶׁיֵּשׁ עֵדִים יוֹדְעִין. וּבִירוּשָׁלַיִם נֶאֱמָנִין עַל הַקּוֹדֶשׁ אַף עַל פִּי שֶׁיֵּשׁ עֵדִים יוֹדְעִין.

אָמַר רִבִּי יְהוֹשֻׁעַ בֶּן לֵוִי. יְרוּשָׁלַם הַבְּנוּיָה כְּעִיר שֶׁחוּבְּרָה לָהּ יַחְדָּו. עִיר שֶׁהִיא עוֹשָׂה כָל־יִשְׂרָאֵל חֲבֵרִים. מֵעַתָּה אֲפִילוּ בִּשְׁאַר יְמוֹת הַשָּׁנָה. אָמַר רִבִּי זְעוּרָה. וּבִלְבַד בְּשָׁעָה שֶׁשָּׁם עָלוּ שְׁבָטִים.

Halakhah 6: "If tax collectors entered a house, the house is impure. If they are accompanied by a Gentile they are trustworthy to say, we entered but we did not touch.[182]" One may explain this by two explanations. They are trustworthy to say, we entered but we did not touch if witnesses know of it[183]. And in Jerusalem they are trustworthy about *sancta* even if witnesses know of it. One may explain by another explanation: They are trustworthy to say, we entered but we did not touch. This is necessary {to be stated} even if witnesses know of it. And in Jerusalem they are trustworthy about *sancta* even if witnesses know of it.

Rebbi Joshua ben Levi said, *Jerusalem, built like a city which combines in fellowship*[184], the city which confers fellowship on all of Israel[185]. Then even on all other days of the year? Rebbi Ze`ira said, in the time *when the tribes ascended*[186].

182 Mishnah *Taharot* 7:6. Tosephta *Taharot* 8:5 explains that even though the Gentile is no formal witness, the tax collectors fear to lie in the presence of people who know better.

183 Probably this should be read as "no witnesses know of it." In this case it would be an application of the principle, "the mouth which forbade is the mouth which permits." If no witness knows that he

entered, the house would be impure only by his testimony. But if one believes him in this one also must believe him that he did not touch and therefore the house is pure.
184 *Ps.* 122:3. The Babli 26a quotes another verse.
185 All of Israel are presumed to strictly observe all rules of purity.
186 *Ps.* 122:4, the holidays of pilgrimage.

(fol. 78c) **משנה ז**: הַפּוֹתֵחַ אֶת חָבִיתוֹ וְהַמַּתְחִיל בְּעִסָּתוֹ עַל גַּב הָרֶגֶל. רִבִּי יְהוּדָה אוֹמֵר יִגְמוֹר. וַחֲכָמִים אוֹמְרִים לֹא יִגְמוֹר. מִשֶּׁעָבַר הָרֶגֶל הָיוּ מַעֲבִירִין עַל טַהֲרַת עֲזָרָה. עָבַר הָרֶגֶל בְּיוֹם שִׁישִּׁי לֹא הָיוּ מַעֲבִירִין מִפְּנֵי כְבוֹד הַשַּׁבָּת. רִבִּי יְהוּדָה אוֹמֵר אַף לֹא בְּיוֹם חֲמִישִׁי שֶׁאֵין הַכֹּהֲנִים פְּנוּיִים:

Mishnah 7: If one[187] opens a barrel, or one starts to sell his dough, on the holiday, Rebbi Jehudah says, he may finish, but the Sages say, he may not finish. After the holiday one proclaims the purity of the courtyard[188]. If the holiday was over on a Friday one did not go over it because of the honor of the Sabbath[189]. Rebbi Jehudah says, also not if the holiday was over on Thursday since the priests are not free[190].

187 A fellow grocer selling wine or a fellow baker selling dough to vulgars on the holiday. On the holiday itself the touch of the vulgar does not make impure. For R. Jehudah therefore at the end of the holiday everything is pure but for the Sages the impurity only is suspended during the holiday but re-appears after the holiday if the remainders of wine or dough are offered for sale.
188 One alerts the Cohanim and Levites that following the Sages, all utensils which were used during the holiday must be purified by immersion in a *miqweh* after the holiday.
189 So not to interfere with the preparations for the Sabbath.
190 On the holiday an enormous amount of ashes collected on the altar which has to be removed on the first day after the end of the holiday. There would be no manpower for the purifying of the courtyards.

(79d line 9) **הלכה ז**: רִבִּי חֲנַנְיָה בְשֵׁם רִבִּי יוֹחָנָן. הִתִּירוּ סוֹפוֹ מִפְּנֵי תְחִילָּתוֹ. שֶׁאִם אוֹמֵר אַתְּ לוֹ שֶׁלֹּא יִגְמוֹר אַף הוּא אֵינוֹ פוֹתֵחַ. וְלֹא יִפְתַּח. אַף הוּא מְמַעֵט בְּשִׂמְחַת הָרֶגֶל.

רִבִּי שְׁמוּאֵל בַּר נַחְמָן בְּשֵׁם רִבִּי יוֹנָתָן. מַה פְּלִיגִין. בְּחָבִית שְׁלַיַין. אֲבָל בְּחָבִית שֶׁלְשֶׁמֶן כָּל־עַמָא מוֹדֵיי שֶׁאֵינָהּ גּוֹמְרָהּ. כֵּיצַד הוּא עוֹשָׂהּ. תַּנֵּי רִבִּי חִיָּיה. שׁוֹפְכָהּ. תַּנֵּי בַּר קַפָּרָה. שׁוֹבְרָהּ. וְהָא תַּנָא רִבִּי חֲלַפְתָּא בֶּן שָׁאוּל. מַנִּיחָהּ לָרֶגֶל הַבָּא.

רִבִּי סִימוֹן בְּשֵׁם רִבִּי יְהוֹשֻׁעַ בֶּן לֵוִי. יוֹם טוֹב שֶׁחָל לִהְיוֹת בְּעֶרֶב שַׁבָּת אוֹכֵל אַף תִּשְׁבּוֹת הָרֶגֶל כָּרֶגֶל. אָמַר רִבִּי זְעוּרָה. מַתְנִיתָהּ אֲמָרָה כֵן. עֶרֶב פֶּסַח כַּפֶּסַח. וְיוֹם טָבוֹחַ כַּעֲצֶרֶת. אָמַר רִבִּי חֲנַנְיָה. אוֹף אֲנָן תַּנִּינָן דְּרָבָא. רִבִּי יְהוּדָה אוֹמֵר אַף לֹא בְּיוֹם חֲמִישִׁי שֶׁאֵין הַכֹּהֲנִים פְּנוּיִים:

Halakhah 7: Rebbi Ḥananiah in the name of Rebbi Joḥanan: They permitted its end because of its beginning. Since if you would tell him that he may not finish he would not open[191]. Let him not open! Then he diminishes the enjoyment of the holiday.

Rebbi Samuel bar Naḥman in the name of Rebbi Joḥanan: Where do they disagree? About a wine barrel. But about an oil barrel everybody agrees that he does not finish. What does he do? Rebbi Ḥiyya stated, he pours it out. Bar Qappara stated, he breaks it. However Rebbi Ḥalaphta ben Shaul stated, he leaves it for the next holiday[192].

Rebbi Simon in the name of Rebbi Joshua ben Levi: If a holiday falls on a Friday, one eats making Sabbath after the holiday like the holiday[193]. Rebbi Ze`ira said, a *baraita* states this: The eve of Passover is like Passover[194], the day of slaughter[195] is like Pentecost. Rebbi Ḥananiah said, we also stated more than this: "Rebbi Jehudah says, also not if the holiday was over on Thursday since the priests are not free[196]."

191 If the grocer is not sure that he may sell the entire contents of a new barrel, nobody would expect him to supply wine or oil towards the end of the holiday.

192 R. Ḥalaphta ben Shaul is a contemporary of R. Ḥiyya and Bar Qappara. His statement is the only one agreeing with R. Joḥanan's statement since oil in contrast to wine may be kept in open barrels for a greater amount of time. Therefore his statement must be practice. R. Ḥiyya's statement seems impractical since he eliminates the now impure oil but retains the impure barrel, whereas Bar Qappara sees to it that the barrel is purified by breaking it.

193 The reference is to the last day of a holiday. If that day is a Friday, on the following Sabbath by necessity one eats the food of the holiday. Therefore on this Sabbath the vulgar still must be considered as a fellow and his touch does not cause impurity.

194 Since the *Pesaḥ* sacrifice on the 14th of Nisan follows holiday rules.

195 The day following the one-day festival of Pentecost, when the pilgrims bring all sacrifices which cannot be brought on the holiday itself. Therefore the day must have

the status of the holiday itself to allow full participation of all Jews.

196 For R. Jehudah the Friday following a holiday of Thursday always has the status of the holiday which by the argument of Note 193 implies that the following Sabbath also has the same status.

(fol. 78c) **משנה ח**: כֵּיצַד מַעֲבִירִין עַל טַהֲרַת הָעֲזָרָה. מַטְבִּילִין אֶת הַכֵּלִים שֶׁהָיוּ בַּמִּקְדָּשׁ. הָיוּ לָהֶן שְׁנַיִים וּשְׁלִישִׁים שֶׁאִם נִטְמְאוּ הָרִאשׁוֹנִים יָבִיאוּ שְׁנַיִים תַּחְתֵּיהֶן. כָּל־הַכֵּלִים שֶׁהָיוּ בַּמִּקְדָּשׁ טְעוּנִין טְבִילָה חוּץ מִמִּזְבַּח הַזָּהָב וּמִזְבַּח הַנְּחֹשֶׁת מִפְּנֵי שֶׁהֵן כַּקַּרְקַע דִּבְרֵי רִבִּי אֱלִיעֶזֶר. וַחֲכָמִים אוֹמְרִים מִפְּנֵי שֶׁהֵן מְצוּפִּין:

Mishnah 8: How does one proclaim the purity of the courtyard[188]? One immerses all vessels in the Temple[197]. There were seconds and thirds, that in case the first ones became impure one would bring the seconds in their place. All vessels in the Temple need immersion except the golden altar and the copper altar since they are like soil[198], the words of Rebbi Eliezer, but the Sages are saying, because they are plated[199].

197 After the end of the holiday. The Mishnah in the Babli makes it clear that the purification is because of the impurity of the vulgar which only was suspended, not eliminated during the holiday. Since the Mishnah in the printed Yerushalmi is not from the ms. on which the text of the Halakhah is based, one cannot infer too much from differences in the text of the Mishnah. However, since the Halakhah strictly follows the text of the Mishnah here and its first paragraph makes it clear that the reason for the purification is that one suspects that in the throng of holiday traffic a vessel might have become impure by biblical standards it is clear that the Yerushalmi does not accept the argument of the Babli. This supports the thesis that the picture of relations between Pharisees and non-Pharisees given in the Babli cannot be accepted as historical fact; cf. Introduction to Tractate Demay.

198 And therefore not susceptible to impurity.

199 Therefore one never touches the altar itself but only the cover which cannot transmit impurity to the altar.

(79d line 19) **הלכה ח**: וְכֵלִים טְעוּנִין טְבִילָה. אָמַר רִבִּי בָּא. אֲנִי אוֹמֵר. שֶׁמָּא שֶׁהָיָה שָׁם אֶחָד מִן הַכֵּלִים שֶׁלֹּא הוּזָּה. מֵעַתָּה נָחוֹשׁ לְכוּלָּן. אָמַר רִבִּי בּוּן בַּר חִייָה. אֲנִי אוֹמֵר. שֶׁהָיָה שָׁם אֶחָד מִן הַכֹּהֲנִים שֶׁיָּצָא לְדַבֵּר עִם הָאִשָּׁה עַל עִיסְקֵי קִינָּהּ וְנִתְזָה צִיּנוֹרָה שֶׁלְּרוֹק מִתּוֹךְ פִּיהָ עַל בְּגָדָיו

וּטְמֵאתוֹ. מֵעַתָּה נָחוּשׁ לְכוּלָם. תִּיפְתָּר בְּשֶׁנִּיטְמָא בְסָפֵק מַשְׁקִין. תַּמָּן תַּנִּינָן. סְפֵק מַשְׁקִין לְטַמֵּא טָמֵא. וּלְטַמֵּא טָהוֹר. תַּמָּן בִּתְרוּמָה וְכָאן בַּקּוֹדֶשׁ. חוֹמֶר הוּא בַקּוֹדֶשׁ.

Halakhah 8: Do vessels need immersion? Rebbi Abba said, I am saying that possibly one of the vessels there was not sprinkled upon[200]. Then should we not suspect all of them[201]? Rebbi Abun bar Ḥiyya said, I am saying that there was one of the Cohanim who left to speak with a woman about her nest and a drop of spittle fell on his clothing from her mouth and made him impure[202]. Then should we not suspect all of them? Explain it if it became impure by fluids of uncertain status[203]. There we have stated[204]: "Fluids of uncertain status, to become impure they are impure, to make impure they are pure[205]." There about heave, here about *sancta*. One is restrictive for *sancta*.

200 While the expression "sprinkled upon" refers to water with the ashes of the Red Cow needed to purify the impurity of the dead, clearly here it cannot refer to a procedure that extends for a week but is taken as general expression for purifying biblical impurity. However, if the immersion is for biblical impurity, the vessel returns to a status of purity only after the following sundown. Then the question arises, how was the Temple service performed for the remainder of the day of immersion if there were no pure vessels available? The answer is given in the Mishnah, that there were reserve vessels available which had not been used during the holiday.

201 The answer given in the preceding Note seems to be invalid since one refers to pre-existing biblical impurity. Then the second and third vessels should also be immersed and not only after a holiday but every day of the year. While the second objection may answered that daily immersion clearly is impractical, the first objection remains unanswered.

202 A woman after childbirth or after an extended period of menstrual impurity regains her right to participate in *sacra* only by a sacrifice of a couple of birds, a "nest". These sacrifices have to be brought after the woman was purified by immersion in a way which shields the Cohanim (Mishnah *Šeqalim* 6:8), here one refers to a Cohen who counsels a woman still impure as *zavah*, whose body fluids are primary sources of biblical impurities, on the ways of purification.

203 Which are impure in the first degree by rabbinical convention only. Then it is reasonable to restrict the general immersion to holidays since at all other days precautions can be taken that such a case does not occur in the Temple.

204 Mishnah *Taharot* 4:9. The Mishnah seems to imply that the case envisaged by R. Abun bar Hiyya cannot occur since possible rabbinic impurity does not cause certain impurity of implements known to be pure.

(79d line 26) תַּנֵּי. שׁוּלְחָן שֶׁנִּיטְמָא מַטְבִּילִין אוֹתוֹ בִּזְמַנּוֹ אֲפִילוּ בַּשַּׁבָּת. דִּבְרֵי רַבִּי מֵאִיר. וַחֲכָמִים אוֹמְרִים. מִיָּד. אַשְׁכַּחַת אֲמַר. עַל דַּעְתֵּיהּ דְּרַבִּי מֵאִיר. מְטַמֵּא שְׁנֵי לְחָמִים. עַל דַּעְתּוֹן דְּרַבָּנָן אֵינוֹ מְטַמֵּא אֶלָּא לֶחֶם אֶחָד בִּלְבָד. אָמַר רִבִּי יַעֲקֹב בַּר סוֹסִי קוֹמֵי רִבִּי יוֹסֵה. וַאֲפִילוּ עַל דַּעְתֵּיהּ דְּרַבִּי מֵאִיר אֵינוֹ מְטַמֵּא אֶלָּא לֶחֶם אֶחָד בִּלְבָד. תִּיפְתָּר שֶׁנִּיטְמָא בִסְפֵק מַשְׁקִין. פַּעַם אַחַת הִטְבִּילוּ אֶת הַמְּנוֹרָה. אָמְרוּ צְדוּקִים. רְאוּ פְרוּשִׁים מַטְבִּילִין גַּלְגַּל חַמָּה.

It was stated[205]: "If the table became impure one immerses it at its time, even on the Sabbath, the words of Rebbi Meïr. But the Sages are saying, immediately."[206] You find to say, in Rebbi Meïr's opinion it makes two breads impure; in the rabbis' opinion it only makes one bread impure[207]. Rebbi Jacob bar Sosai said before Rebbi Yose, even according to Rebbi Meïr it makes only one bread impure. Explain it if it became impure by fluids of questionable status[208]. "Once they immersed the candelabrum. The Sadducees said, look the Pharisees immerse the ball of the sun.[205,209]"

205 Tosephta 3:35.

206 The table in the Sanctuary is movable, therefore it is an implement and subject to impurity, e. g., by contact with a dead reptile. In the case of biblical impurity it should be impossible to return it to its place before sundown; this is R. Meïr's position. The Sages require that it be returned immediately, as soon as it is no longer impure even if it is not yet pure, since the verse requires that the shew-bread be "always" on the table, i. e., every day and certainly at sundown and sunrise.

207 The biblically impure table makes the bread it touches biblically impure. For the rabbis the higher degrees of impurity are rabbinic (or rather, conventional), to be disregarded in the Sanctuary. For R. Meïr one accepts at least one degree of conventional impurity (but not all three additional ones.)

208 If the impurity of the table from the start was not clearly biblical, R. Meïr accepts the rabbis' point of view.

209 They object to conventional extensions of the notions of impurity.

(79d line 32) תַּמָּן תַּנִּינָן. נִכְנְסוּ לְלִשְׁכַּת הַכֵּלִים וְהוֹצִיאוּ מִשָּׁם תִּשְׁעִים וּשְׁלֹשָׁה כְלֵי כֶסֶף וּכְלֵי זָהָב. רִבִּי שְׁמוּאֵל בַּר נַחְמָן בְּשֵׁם רִבִּי יוֹנָתָן. כְּנֶגֶד תִּשְׁעִים וְשָׁלֹשׁ אַזְכָּרוֹת שֶׁכָּתוּב בְּפָרָשַׁת חַגַּי וּזְכַרְיָה וּמַלְאָכִי. אָמַר רִבִּי חוּנָה. חִישַּׁבְתִּים וְאֵינָן אֶלָּא שְׁמוֹנִים וְשָׁלֹשׁ. כְּנֶגֶד שְׁמוֹנִים וְשָׁלֹשׁ חוֹתָמוֹת שֶׁכָּתוּב בָּעֲזָרָה שֶׁהָיָה כָּל־אֶחָד וְאֶחָד מְיַיחֵד שְׁמוֹ שֶׁלְהַקָּדוֹשׁ בָּרוּךְ הוּא וְחוֹתֵם. אִית דְּבָעֵי מֵימַר. כְּיוֹם מְרוּבֶּה שֶׁלְּתָמִיד כְּנֶגֶד שְׁלֹשָׁה עָשָׂר פָּרִים וְאַרְבָּעָה עָשָׂר כְּבָשִׂים וְאֵילִים שְׁנַיִם וְשָׂעִיר אֶחָד.

There we have stated[210]: "They entered the storage room of the vessels and brought out 93 silver and gold vessels." Rebbi Samuel bar Naḥman in the name of Rebbi Jonathan: Corresponding to the 93 Names written in the Chapters of Haggai, Zacharia, and Malachi[211]. Rebbi Huna said, I computed them and they are only 83, corresponding to the 83 signatures written in Ezra[212] where each of them declared the Unity of the Name of the Holy One, praise to Him, and signed. Some want to say, corresponding to the day when the daily sacrifices were the most, corresponding to thirteen bulls, fourteen sheep, two rams, and one goat[213].

210 Mishnah *Tamid* 3:4.
211 "Name" usually is reserved for the Tetragrammaton. Here certainly "Zacharia" should be deleted since his text contains 132 times the Tetragrammaton. The count is correct if one considers only Haggai and Malachi and also allows Elohim as a Name.
212 Those mentioned in Nehemiah 10.
213 All 93 vessels are only needed on the first day of Tabernacles.

(79d line 39) רִבִּי שִׁילֹה דִכְפַר תַּמָּרתָה בְּשֵׁם רִבִּי יוֹחָנָן. טַעֲמֵיהּ דְּרִבִּי לִיעֶזֶר וְצִפִּיתָ אֹתוֹ זָהָב טָהוֹר וגו'. הַתּוֹרָה קָרָאת אוֹתוֹ קַרְקַע. עַד כְּדוֹן מִזְבַּח הַזָּהָב. מִזְבַּח הָעוֹלָה מְנַיִין. וְדִין הוּא. מָה אִם מִזְבַּח הַזָּהָב שֶׁהוּא אַמָּה עַל אַמָּה אַתְּ אָמַר קַרְקַע. מִזְבַּח הָעוֹלָה שֶׁהוּא חָמֵשׁ עַל חָמֵשׁ לֹא כָל־שֶׁכֵּן. אִית דְּבָעֵי מֵימַר. רָבוּעַ רָבוּעַ. מַה כָּאן קַרְקַע אַף כָּאן קַרְקַע. אָמַר רִבִּי הִילָא. טַעֲמוֹן דְּרַבָּנָן. הַמִּזְבֵּחַ עֵץ שָׁלוֹשׁ אַמּוֹת גּוֹבַהּ וגו'. הַתּוֹרָה קָרָאת אוֹתוֹ מִיטַלְטֵל. עַד כְּדוֹן מִזְבַּח הָעוֹלָה. מִזְבַּח הַזָּהָב מְנַיִין. וְדִין הוּא. מָה אִם מִזְבַּח הָעוֹלָה שֶׁהוּא חָמֵשׁ עַל חָמֵשׁ אַתְּ אָמַר מִיטַלְטֵל. מִזְבַּח הַזָּהָב שֶׁהוּא אַמָּה עַל אַמָּה לֹא כָל־שֶׁכֵּן. אִית דְּבָעֵי מֵימַר. רָבוּעַ רָבוּעַ. מַה כָּאן מִיטַלְטֵל אַף כָּאן מִיטַלְטֵל. וַחֲכָמִים אוֹמְרִים. מִפְּנֵי שֶׁהֵן מְצוּפִין. לֹא צִיפּוּי שֶׁהוּא עוֹמֵד מַחֲמָתוֹ הוּא. לֹא כֵן אָמַר רִבִּי שִׁמְעוֹן בֶּן לָקִישׁ בְּשֵׁם רִבִּי הוֹשַׁעְיָה. כְּעוֹבִי דִּינַר גּוֹרְדִּיָינוֹ הָיָה בּוֹ. אָמַר רִבִּי לָא. לִמְלַכְתּוֹ אֵינוֹ עוֹמֵד מַחֲמָתוֹ הוּא. וְאַתְיָיא כַּיי דְּאָמַר רִבִּי שִׁמְעוֹן בֶּן לָקִישׁ. וְעָשִׂיתָ מִזְבֵּחַ מִקְטַר קְטוֹרֶת אֵין כָּתוּב כָּאן אֶלָּא מַקְטֵר קְטוֹרֶת. הַמִּזְבֵּחַ הָיָה מַקְטִיר אֶת הַקְּטוֹרֶת. וִיהֵא כְטַבְלָה עֲשׂוּיָה לֵילֵךְ וּלְהַנִּיחַ. לֹא כֵן אָמַר רִבִּי אַמִּי בְּשֵׁם רִבִּי שִׁמְעוֹן בֶּן לָקִישׁ. הַשּׁוּלְחָן לָמָּה טָמֵא. לֹא מִפְּנֵי שֶׁמּוֹצִיאִין אוֹתוֹ וּמַרְאִין אוֹתוֹ לְעוֹלֵי רְגָלִים. וְזֶה לֹא בִּמְקוֹמוֹ הוּא עוֹמֵד. אַף זֶה שִׁימֵּשׁ כְּלִי בַּמִּקְדָּשׁ. וִיהֵא טָהוֹר. וְלָמָּה טָמֵא. אָמַר רִבִּי מָנָא. כַּיי דְּתַנִּינָן תַּמָּן. שָׁלֹשׁ מַשְׁפְּלוֹת הֵן. אָמַר רִבִּי זְעוּרָה. מִפְּנֵי שֶׁמִּשְׁתַּמְּשִׁין בּוֹ עַל גַּב חֲבִילֵיהּ. וְכָאן מִפְּנֵי שֶׁמִּשְׁתַּמְּשִׁין בּוֹ עַל גַּב חֲבִילָיו.

Rebbi Shiloh from Kefar-Tamarta in the name of Rebbi Johanan: The reason of Rebbi Eliezer: *And you shall cover it with pure gold*[214], etc. The Torah called it real estate[215]. So far the golden altar. From where the altar of the elevation sacrifices? It is a logical argument. Since the golden altar which is one cubit square is called real estate, the altar of elevation sacrifices which is five cubits square not so much more? Some want to say, *square, square*[216]. Since here it is real estate, also there it is real estate. Rebbi Hila said, the reason of the rabbis[217], *the altar is of wood, three cubits its height*[218], etc. The Torah called it movable[219]. So far the altar of the elevation sacrifices. From where the golden altar? It is a logical argument. Since the the altar of the elevation sacrifices which is five cubit square is called soil, the golden altar which is one cubit square not so much more? Some want to say, *square, square*. Since here it is movable, also there it is movable. "But the Sages say, because they are covered." But is it not cover which stands because of it[220]? Did not Rebbi Simeon ben Laqish say in the name of Rebbi Hoshaia: Its thickness was that of a Gordian denar[221] Rebbi La said, for its purpose it does not stand because of it[222]. This parallels what Rebbi Simeon ben Laqish said, *you shall make an altar for incense smoke*[223] is not written here but *burning incense*; the altar was burning the incense[224]. But is it not like a table[224a] made to be moved and deposited? Does not Rebbi Immi say in the name of Rebbi Simeon ben Laqish: why is the table impure[225]? Not because one was removing it and showing it to the pilgrims[226]? But this one remains in its place. It also served as a vessel in the Sanctuary. Then it should be pure, why is it impure[225]? Rebbi Mana said, as what we have stated there,[227] "there are three baskets[228]". Rebbi Ze`ira said, because one uses it for its bales; so also here one uses it for its bales[229].

214 *Ex.* 30:3.

215 Since the Torah mentions its roof and its walls, it is described as a house.

216 *Ex.* 30:3 (the golden altar), 27:1 (the brass altar).

217 These rabbis are not mentioned in the Mishnah. The argument is that the Sages mentioned in the Mishnah could use R. Eliezer's argument in the inverse direction to establish their rule.

218 *Ez.* 41:22. The altar there is called "table", a movable implement.

219 In the Torah both altars are movable, to be carried travelling in the desert.

220 If the cover could not stand alone it cannot be separated from the implement it covers which is a rectangular box of wood, enclosing a volume and therefore susceptible of impurity.

221 The only honest gold denar minted during the military anarchy (in the 240's by Gordianus III.) The implication is that the gold cover could stand by itself; the objection cannot be sustained.

222 The previous argument can be reinforced; the gold is the essential carrier of the altar and the wood is ancillary.

223 *Ex.* 30:1.

224 No fire was used on the golden top of the altar (which if used would have melted the top in no time). The golden top transformed the incense into smoke.

224a Latin *tabula*.

225 In all this arguments, "pure" means "not susceptible to impurity" and "impure" "able to become impure".

226 The table was not fixed; it cannot be considered a fixed part of the building. In addition, the rim around the table makes it a container which is "impure". But once a permanent Temple was built, the altars are fixed and should be "pure" as fixtures of the building.

227 Mishnah *Kelim* 24:9.

228 A basket for manure may become impure by body fluids, a box for straw only becomes impure by the impurity of the dead, a cover for camels is pure.

229 Since the Mishnah classifies the baskets by their use, also here the altar has to be classified by the "impure" incense.

Introduction to Tractate Mo`ed Qaṭan

The Tractate also is known as *Mašqin*, from the first word of the first Mishnah, since the title "Mo`ed Qaṭan", minor holiday, is appropriate only for the first two Chapters. The topic is the rules for the intermediate days of Passover and Tabernacles which in the biblical text are designated as holidays of pilgrimage for which Temple ceremonies are specified in *Lev.*, sacrifices in *Num.*, and an obligation to celebrate the holidays in joy in *Deut*. The emphasis in the Tractate is on the interpretation of "celebrating the holiday in joy." The rabbinic rules are that agricultural and other gainful or professional work is permitted only if its omission would cause loss, except that day workers public works may be hired on holidays since this produces income to the poor and keeps costs down for the public. In addition, in order to force people to enter the holiday period well groomed, one forbids most grooming on the intermediate days. The exceptions are stated at the start of the third Chapter and since similar restrictions apply to mourners, the remainder of the Chapter is devoted to an exposition of burial and mourning rites.

מועד קטן פרק ראשון משקין

(fol. 80a) **משנה א**: מַשְׁקִין בֵּית הַשְּׁלָחִין בַּמּוֹעֵד וּבַשְּׁבִיעִית בֵּין מִמַּעְיָין שֶׁיּוֹצֵא בַּתְּחִילָּה בֵּין מִמַּעְיָין שֶׁאֵין יוֹצֵא בַּתְּחִילָּה. אֲבָל לֹא מִמֵּי גְשָׁמִים וְלֹא מִמֵּי קִילוֹן. וְאֵין עוֹשִׂין עוּגִיּוֹת לַגְּפָנִים: רִבִּי אֶלְעָזָר בֶּן עֲזַרְיָה אוֹמֵר אֵין עוֹשִׂין אֶת הָאַמָּה בַּתְּחִילָּה בַּמּוֹעֵד וּבַשְּׁבִיעִית וַחֲכָמִים אוֹמְרִים עוֹשִׂין אֶת הָאַמָּה בַּתְּחִילָּה בַּשְּׁבִיעִית וּמְתַקְּנִין אֶת הַמְקוּלְקֶלֶת בַּמּוֹעֵד. וּמְתַקְּנִין אֶת קִילְקוּלֵי הַמַּיִם שֶׁבִּרְשׁוּת הָרַבִּים וְחוֹטְטִין אוֹתָן. וּמְתַקְּנִין אֶת הַדְּרָכִים וְאֶת הָרְחוֹבוֹת וְאֶת מִקְווֹת הַמַּיִם וְעוֹשִׂין כָּל־צוֹרְכֵי הָרַבִּים וּמְצַיְינִין אֶת הַקְּבָרוֹת וְיוֹצְאִין אַף עַל הַכִּלְאַיִם:

Mishnah 1: One waters irrigated plots on the holiday[1] and in the Sabbatical year both from a well which flows newly[2] and from a well which does not flow newly, but neither from rain water nor from pumped water[3], nor does one make beds for vines[4]. Rebbi Eleazar ben Azariah says, one does not make new water canals on the holiday or in the Sabbatical year but the Sages are saying that one makes new water canals in the Sabbatical year[5] and one fixes the broken ones on the holiday and one repairs all defects in the public water system and cleans it[6]. [7]Also one repairs the roads, and the streets, and water pools, and one looks after all public needs, and marks the graves, and also goes to inspect for *kilaim*.

1 In this Tractate, "holiday" always means "intermediate days of Passover or Tabernacles." While there is no verse forbidding work on these days, by rabbinic custom only agricultural work necessary to avoid losses and not involving excessive effort is permitted.

2 Even though there is some work involved in guiding the waters of a new source to the plots.

3 Greek κήλων "pump-handle". Pumping water for intensive agriculture would be excessive work on a holiday.

4 Walled circular depressions around vines for purposes of irrigation. They may be serviced but not made anew.

5 Since this is construction rather than agricultural work, it is permitted in the Sabbatical but forbidden on the holiday.

6 As the Babli explains, since commercial building activities are forbidden on the holiday, hiring people for public works helps the poor to find work and helps the public by keeping the wages low since there is no competition from the private sector.

7 The following is repeated from Mishnah *Šeqalim* 1:1, Notes 4-8.

(80a line 40) מַשְׁקִין בֵּית הַשְּׁלָחִין כול'. נִיחָא מַעְיָין שֶׁלֹּא יָצָא כַתְּחִילָה. מַעְיָין שֶׁיּוֹצֵא כַתְּחִילָה. וְלֹא טָרִיחַ הוּא. אֶלָּא כְרִבִּי מֵאִיר. דְּרִבִּי מֵאִיר אָמַר. מַשְׁקִין מִמֶּנּוּ אֲפִילוּ שְׂדֵה בֵית הַבַּעַל. אָמַר רִבִּי יוֹסֵי. דִּבְרֵי הַכֹּל כְּשֶׁהָיָה אֶחָד וְנַעֲשָׂה שְׁנַיִם אוֹ שֶׁהָיוּ מֵימָיו מוּעָטִין וְנִתְבָּרְכוּ. וְתַנֵּי כֵן. מַעְיָין שֶׁיָּצָא כַתְּחִילָה מַשְׁקִין מִמֶּנּוּ אֲפִילוּ שְׂדֵה בֵית הַבַּעַל. דִּבְרֵי רִבִּי מֵאִיר. וַחֲכָמִים אוֹמְרִים. אֵין מַשְׁקִין מִמֶּנּוּ אֶלָּא שְׂדֵה בֵית הַשְּׁלָחִין שֶׁחֲרֵבָה. עַל דַּעְתֵּיהּ דְּרִבִּי מֵאִיר מַשְׁקִין מִמֶּנּוּ דָּבָר שֶׁאֵינוֹ אָבֵד. וְדָבָר שֶׁהוּא טָרִיחַ. עַל דַּעְתּוֹן דְּרַבָּנָן אֵין מַשְׁקִין מִמֶּנּוּ אֶלָּא דָבָר שֶׁהוּא אָבֵד וּבִלְבַד דָּבָר שֶׁאֵינוֹ טָרִיחַ. אָבֵד וְטָרִיחַ מָה אֱמְרִי בָהּ רַבָּנָן. נִישְׁמְעִינָהּ מִן הָדָא. כָּל־שֶׁהִיא פְסֵידָה וְחוֹלֶכֶת זוֹ הִיא בֵּית הַשְּׁלָחִין. עָמְדָה מִלְהַכְחִישׁ זוֹ בֵּית הַבַּעַל. מַחֲלוֹקֶת דְּרִבִּי מֵאִיר וַחֲכָמִים. עַד כַּמָּה תִשְׁהֵא וְתֵיעָשֶׂה בֵּית הַשְּׁלָחִין. עַד כְּדֵי שֶׁתִּשְׁהֵא שְׁנַיִם שְׁלֹשָׁה יָמִים קוֹדֶם לָרֶגֶל. נִישְׁמְעִינָהּ מִן הָדָא. קַבְרַיי נְגַב קוֹמֵי מוֹעֲדָא תְּלָתָא יוֹמִין. חָזַר בְּמוֹעֲדָא. אָתָא עוֹבְדָא קוֹמֵי רַב חוּנָה וְאָמַר. אִילֵּין דְּאַכְחֲשִׁין יִשְׁתְּיָין. אִילֵּין דְּלָא אַכְחַשִׁין לָא יִשְׁתְּיָין. רִבִּי יוֹנָה וְרִבִּי יוֹסֵי הוֹרוֹן בְּהָדָא מְקֵרֶת דְּצִילַיָיא דַּהֲוָות זְרִיעָה סְעָרִין מֵיחַצְדִינּוּן בְּמוֹעֲדָא דְּלָא יִפְקְעוֹן וְיֵיבְדוּן.

"One waters irrigated plots," etc. One understands a well which does not flow newly. A well which flows newly? Is that not requiring effort[8]? But it follows Rebbi Meïr, as Rebbi Meïr says, one uses it to irrigate even a field depending on rain water[9]. Rebbi Yose said, it is the opinion of everybody if it was one and became two or its waters were few and it was blessed[10]. We have stated thus[11]: "From a well which flowed newly one irrigates even a field depending on rain water, the words of Rebbi Meïr; but the Sages are saying one uses it to irrigate only an irrigated plot which dried up[10]." In the opinion of Rebbi Meïr one irrigates from it something not in danger of loss and something requiring effort. In the opinion of the rabbis one irrigates from it only something in danger of loss and only if not requiring effort. What do the rabbis say if there is danger of loss but it requires effort[12]? Let us hear from the following: Anything which is continuously losing value is an irrigated plot[13]. When it stopped weakening it is a field depending on rain water; the disagreement between Rebbi Meïr and the Sages[14]. How long does it have to be irrigated to become an irrigated field? Only if was irrigated two, three days before the holiday? Let us hear from the following: The Qabray[15] dried up three days before the holiday, and it came back on the holiday. The case came before Rav Huna who said, those weakened shall be irrigated, those not weakened may not be irrigated[16]. Rebbi Jonah and Rebbi Yose instructed about that cool shadowy place which was sown with barley that it should be cut on the holiday to avoid their cracking and being lost[17].

8   Since the water has to be directed to the desired spot, a bed has to be dug for the stream. This may involve more work than compatible with the idea of a holiday. (Differently in the Babli, 2a.)

9   The general rule is that agricultural work is forbidden unless needed to avoid loss. A new well is a precious source; to waste its water would be great loss. Since the water is not yet channelled, it may be directed to any place desired.

A field not irrigated depends on rain water. The expression *bet habba`al* really is idolatrous since *Ba`al*, like the Greek Zeus, is rain (considered the god of rain).

10   In this case also no new bed has to be constructed.

11   Tosephta 1:1, Babli 2a.

12   This case is not covered by the Tosephta.

13   Even a field used in extensive agriculture becomes one of intensive culture if it needs additional water to save the crop.

14   R. Meïr but not the Sages would allow additional irrigation.

15   An otherwise unidentified Iraqi brook.

16   A direct application of the rule spelled out before, following the Sages. In addition, it shows that anything happened more than 3 days before the holiday is disregarded, answering the question.

17   They extend the rule which turns extensive into intensive agriculture to all cases, not only the supply of water.

(80a line 66) נִיחָא מֵי קֵילוֹן. מֵי גְשָׁמִים. אָמַר רִבִּי יוֹחָנָן. גְּזְרוּ מֵי גְשָׁמִים מִפְּנֵי שֶׁהֵן כְּמֵי קֵילוֹן. רִבִּי בִּיסְנָא בְשֵׁם רִבִּי לָא. לֹא שָׁנוּ אֶלָּא בַּמּוֹעֵד. הָא בַּשְּׁבִיעִית מוּתָּר. מַה בֵּין שְׁבִיעִית מַה בֵּין מוֹעֵד. שְׁבִיעִית עַל יְדֵי שֶׁהִיא מוּתֶּרֶת בַּמְּלָאכָה הִתִּירוּ בֵּין דָּבָר שֶׁהוּא טָרִיחַ בֵּין דָּבָר שֶׁאֵינוּ טָרִיחַ. מוֹעֵד עַל יְדֵי שֶׁהוּא אָסוּר בַּמְּלָאכָה לֹא הִתִּירוּ אֶלָּא דָּבָר שֶׁהוּא אָבֵד וּבִלְבַד דָּבָר שֶׁאֵינוּ טָרַח. וְאִית דְּבָעֵי מִישְׁמְעִינָהּ מִן הָדָא. שְׁבִיעִית עַל יְדֵי שֶׁזְּמַנָּהּ מְרוּבָּה הִתִּירוּ. מוֹעֵד עַל יְדֵי שֶׁזְּמַנּוֹ קָצוֹר אָסְרוּ. אוֹתָן שִׁבְעַת יָמִים הָאַחֲרוֹנִים לֹא מִסְתַּבְּרָא מֵיעַבְדִינּוּן כְּשִׁבְעַת יְמֵי הָרֶגֶל וְיִהְיוּ אֲסוּרִין.

6 אותן G | אותי ימים G | הימים מסתברא G | מסתברה מיעבדינון G | מעבדנון   7 אסורין G | אסורים

One understands pumped water. Rain water? Rebbi Joḥanan said, they decided about rain water because it is like pumped water[18]. Rebbi Bisna in the name of Rebbi La: They stated this only on a holiday; therefore in the Sabbatical it is permitted. [19]What is the difference between Sabbatical and holiday? In the Sabbatical when work is permitted they permitted both activities requiring effort and activities not requiring effort. On a holiday when work is forbidden they only permitted to avoid loss and only activities not requiring effort. Some want to understand it from the following: In the

Sabbatical which is extended they permitted, on a holiday which is short they forbade. [20]Then these last seven days should be compared to the seven days of a holiday and be forbidden[21].

18 Babli 4a.
19 There is a close parallel to this text in *Ševi`it* 2:10 (Notes 107-109).
20 From here on to almost the end of the Tractate there are Genizah fragments edited by L. Ginzberg (G).

21 The last seven days of the Sabbatical then should be treated like intermediate days of a holiday in these matters. Since this is nowhere stated, the second argument is rejected.

(80a line 75) רִבִּי יִרְמְיָה בָעֵי. מֵי תַמְצִיוֹת שֶׁלֹּא פָּסְקוּ מָה הֵן. נִישְׁמְעִינָהּ מִן הָדָא. אִילּוּ הֵן מֵי תַמְצִיוֹת. כָּל־זְמַן שֶׁהַגְּשָׁמִים יוֹרְדִין וְהֶהָרִים בּוֹצְצִין. פָּסְקוּ גְשָׁמִים אַף עַל פִּי שֶׁהֶהָרִים בּוֹצְצִין הֲרֵי הֵן כְּמֵי תַמְצִיוֹת. פָּסְקוּ מִלִּהְיוֹת בּוֹצְצִין הֲרֵי הֵן כְּמֵי גְבִים. עַד אֵיכָן. חִייָה בַר בּוּן בְּשֵׁם רִבִּי יוֹחָנָן. עַד כְּדֵי שֶׁתִּפְרַח חֲבֵרִית. רִבִּי לְעָזָר בֵּירִבִּי יוֹסֵי בְּשֵׁם רִבִּי תַנְחוּם בֵּירִבִּי חִייָה. עַד כְּדֵי שֶׁיֵּיעָשׂוּ כְרַכְלֵי הָאַוְוז. רִבִּי יִרְמְיָה בָעֵי. פְּרָחָה חֲבֵרִית וְלֹא פָּסְקוּ. לְמַפְרֵיעוֹ הוּא נַעֲשָׂה כְמַעְיָין אוֹ מִכָּן וָלְבָא. לֵיי דָא מִילָה. הִטְבִּיל בּוֹ מַחְטִים וְצִינּוֹרוֹת. אִין תֵּימַר. לְמַפְרֵיעוֹ הוּא נַעֲשָׂה מַעְיָין. טָהֲרוּ. אִין תֵּימַר. מִכָּן וָלְבָא. לֹא טָהֲרוּ. רִבִּי לְעָזָר בֵּירִבִּי יוֹסֵי שָׁאַל. אִילֵּין אַגְטַרְגַּייָא מָה אַתְּ עָבִיד לוֹן. כְּמֵי קִילּוֹן אוֹ אֵינָן כְּמֵי קִילּוֹן. בְּרֵיכָה שֶׁנִּתְמַלְּאֵת מִן הַמַּעְיָין וְהִפְסִיק הַמַּעְיָין מִתּוֹכָהּ מָהוּ לְהַשְׁקוֹת מִמֶּנָּה. נִישְׁמְעִינָהּ מִן הָדָא. אֲבָל אֵין מַשְׁקִין לֹא מִמֵּי הַגְּשָׁמִים וְלֹא מִמֵּי הַקִּילּוֹן. מָה אֲנָן קַיָּימִין. אִם בְּשָׁעָה שֶׁהַגְּשָׁמִים יוֹרְדִין. וַהֲלֹא כְמוּשְׁקִין לַיָּם הַגָּדוֹל הֵן. אֶלָּא כִי נָן קַיָּימִין בְּשָׁעָה שֶׁפָּסְקוּ גְשָׁמִים. אִם בְּשָׁעָה שֶׁפָּסְקוּ גְשָׁמִים לֹא כִבְרֵיכָה שֶׁנִּתְמַלְּאֵת מִן הַמַּעְיָין וְהִפְסִיק הַמַּעְיָין מִתּוֹכָהּ הִיא. וְאַתְּ אָמַר. אֵין מַשְׁקִין מִמֶּנָּה. הָדָא אָמְרָה. בְּרֵיכָה שֶׁנִּתְמַלְּאֵת מִן הַמַּעְיָין וְהִפְסִיק הַמַּעְיָין מִתּוֹכָהּ אֵין מַשְׁקִין מִמֶּנָּה. בְּרֵיכָה שֶׁנִּתְמַלְּאֵת מִן הַקִּילּוֹן וְהִמְשִׁיךְ הַמַּעְיָין לְתוֹכָהּ מָהוּ לְהַשְׁקוֹת מִמֶּנָּה. נִישְׁמְעִינָהּ מִן הָדָא. שְׂדֵה בֵית הַשְּׁלָחִין שֶׁנִּיטּוֹפָהּ לְתוֹךְ שְׂדֵה בֵית הַשְּׁלָחִין אַחֶרֶת מַשְׁקִין מִמֶּנָּה. אָמַר רִבִּי יִרְמְיָה וְעוֹדָהּ מְנַטֶּפֶת. וְכִי מַחֲמַת הַנִּיטּוּף הִיא יְכוֹלָה לְהַשְׁקוֹת. לֹא מַחֲמַת עַצְמָהּ שֶׁהִיא מְלֵיאָה. וְאַתְּ אָמַר. מַשְׁקִין מִמֶּנָּה. הָדָא אָמְרָה. בְּרֵיכָה שֶׁנִּתְמַלְּאֵת מִן הַקִּילּוֹן וְהִמְשִׁיךְ הַמַּעְיָין לְתוֹכָהּ מַשְׁקִין מִמֶּנָּה. וְתַנֵּי שְׁמוּאֵל כֵּן. הַפּוֹסְקוֹן וְהַבְּרֵיכָה שֶׁמִּילְּאָן קוֹדֶם לָרֶגֶל לֹא יַשְׁקֶה מֵהֶן בָּרֶגֶל. אִם הָיְתָה אַמַּת הַמַּיִם עוֹבֶרֶת בֵּינֵיהֶן מַשְׁקֶה מֵהֶן וְאֵינוֹ נִמְנָע.

1 מה הן G | מהן נישמעינה G | משמענה הדא G | הדה 2 תמצית G | תמציות יורדין G | יורדים בוצצין G | בוצצים שההרים G | שהרים בוצצין G | בוצצים 3 תמציות G | תמציות בוצצין G | בוצצים גביים G | גוויים 4 שתפרח G | שתיפרח חברית חברית G | חברית 5 חברית G | הברית כמעיין G | מעין 6 ליי דא G לידיה מילה G | מלה וצינורות G | וצינוריות אין G | אן הוא G | - 7 אין G | אן ולבא G | ולבה אגרגייא G | גטרגטייא 8 עביד G | עבד

Rebbi Jeremiah asked, what is the status of uninterrupted rest-water[22]? Let us hear from the following[23]: "What is rest-water? All the time that it rains and the mountains are muddy[24]; after the rain stopped and the mountains still are muddy it is rest-water. When they are no longer muddy it is like cistern water." How far? Hiyya bar Abun[25] in the name of Rebbi Johanan: Until the soft soil[26] produces flowers. Rebbi Eleazar ben Rebbi Yose in the name of Rebbi Tanhum ben Rebbi Hiyya: Until they become like goose feet[27]. Rebbi Jeremiah asked: If the soft soil produced flowers before it stopped? Is it considered like a source[28] retroactively or only for the future? In which respect? If he immersed in it needles and hooks[29]. If you are saying that retroactively it is considered like a source they are pure, only for the the future they are impure. Rebbi Eleazar ben Rebbi Yose asked, how do you treat these waterfalls[30]? Like pumped water or not like pumped water? May one irrigate from a pond which was filled from a well, but water supply from the well stopped? Let us hear from the following: "but one irrigates neither from rain water nor from pumped water[3]." Where do we hold? If in a time when it rains, is it not as if irrigating the ocean[31]? But we must hold in the time when the rain stopped. If it is in the time when the rain stopped, is this not like a pond which was filled from a well, but water supply from the well stopped? Since you are saying that one does not irrigate from it this implies that one does not irrigate from a pond which was filled from a well, but water supply from the well stopped[31]. May one irrigate from a pond which was filled with pumped water but one channelled well water into it[32]? Let us hear from the following: One irrigates from an irrigated field which drips into another irrigated field. Rebbi Jeremiah said, as long as it drips. Is one able to irrigate because of the dripping, is it not rather because it is full? This implies that one irrigates from a pond which was filled with pumped water but one channelled well water into it. Samuel stated thus: One does not irrigate on a holiday from pools[32] and ponds which were filled before the holiday. But one irrigates without hesitation if a water channel passes through them.

22 Water which is caused by rain but at the time of use it does not rain.

23 Tosephta *Miqwaot* 1:13.

24 This is rain water, of restricted use for *miqwaot*.

25 Usually he is called R. Hiyya; the reason for the omission of his title and the addition of his patronymic are a riddle.

26 Translation following G, reading the word as Arabic ברה.

27 That single drops are spread out like the impressions of goose feet.

28 Which purifies everything immersed in it.
29 Crotchet needles. These are small and can be immersed in water too shallow to be used to immerse larger items but still part of a connected body of water measuring 40 *seah*.
30 Latin *cataracta*, explanation of Arukh, completely justified by the reading of G.

31 This and the following arguments can be summarized simply by stating that the original source of the water in the pond is irrelevant. Using the water for irrigation on a holiday is permitted if the pond is replenished by a permitted source and forbidden if replenished by a forbidden source. Babli 4a.
32 Latin *piscina*.

(80b line 22) וְאֵין עוֹשִׂין עוּגִיּוֹת לַגְּפָנִים: אֵילּוּ הֵן עוּגִיּוֹת אֵילוּ הֵן הַבָּדִידִין שֶׁבְּעִיקְּרֵי אֵילָנוֹת. כָּיי דְתַנִּינָן תַּמָּן. יַד הַבָּדִיד אַרְבָּעָה.

"Nor does one make beds for vines⁴." The beds are furrows around the roots of the trees, as we have stated there³³, "the handle of the spade is four {handbreadths}³⁵."

33 Mishnah *Kelim* 29:7.
34 The word בדיד denotes both the spade and the ditch excavated by it; Babli 4b.

(Otherwise one could read the word as "insulating wall" retaining the water around the root of the tree.)

(80b line 24) **הלכה ב**: תַּמָּן תַּנִּינָן. רִבִּי אֶלְעָזָר בֶּן עֲזַרְיָה אוֹסֵר עַד שֶׁיַּעֲמִיק שְׁלֹשָׁה אוֹ עַד שֶׁיַּגְבִּיהַּ שְׁלֹשָׁה אוֹ עַד שֶׁיִּתֵּן עַל הַסֶּלַע: פָּתַר לָהּ תְּרֵין פִּתְרִין. בְּשֶׁהָיָה לוֹ דָבָר מְמוּעָט בְּתוֹךְ בֵּיתוֹ מֵעֶרֶב שְׁבִיעִית וְהוּא מְבַקֵּשׁ לְהוֹצִיאוֹ בְּתוֹךְ שָׂדֵהוּ בַּשְּׁבִיעִית הֲרֵי זֶה מוֹסִיף עָלָיו וְהוֹלֵךְ מִשֶּׁיִּפָּסְקוּ עוֹבְרֵי עֲבֵירָה. רִבִּי לְעָזָר בֶּן עֲזַרְיָה אוֹסֵר. מַה טַעֲמָא דְרִבִּי לְעָזָר בֶּן עֲזַרְיָה. שֶׁמָּא לֹא יִמְצָא לוֹ זֶבֶל וְנִמְצָא מְזַבֵּל אֶת אוֹתוֹ הַמָּקוֹם. כַּמָּה דְרִבִּי יוֹסֵי אָמַר. אֵין זֶבֶל מָצוּי. כֵּן רִבִּי לְעָזָר בֶּן עֲזַרְיָה אָמַר. אֵין זֶבֶל מָצוּאי. פָּתַר לָהּ פָּתֵר חוֹרָן. בְּשֶׁהָיָה לוֹ דָבָר מְמוּעָט בְּתוֹךְ בֵּיתוֹ בְעֶרֶב שְׁבִיעִית וְהוּא מְבַקֵּשׁ לְהוֹצִיאוֹ לְתוֹךְ שָׂדֵהוּ בַּשְּׁבִיעִית הֲרֵי זֶה מוֹסִיף וְהוֹלֵךְ מִשֶּׁיִּפָּסְקוּ עוֹבְרֵי עֲבֵירָה. רִבִּי לְעָזָר בֶּן עֲזַרְיָה אוֹסֵר. מַה טַעֲמָא דְרִבִּי לְעָזָר בֶּן עֲזַרְיָה. שֶׁמָּא לֹא יִמְצָא לוֹ זֶבֶל וְנִמְצָא מְזַבֵּל אֶת אוֹתוֹ הַמָּקוֹם. וְלֹא כְבָר הוּא מְזוּבָּל מֵעֶרֶב שְׁבִיעִית. רִבִּי יִרְמְיָה רִבִּי בּוּן בַּר חִייָה בְשֵׁם רִבִּי בָּא בַּר מָמָל. מִפְּנֵי מַרְאִית הָעַיִן. עַד שִׁיּוֹצִיא עֶשֶׂר מַשְׁפְּלוֹת כְּאַחַת. וְלֵית לְרַבָּנָן מִפְּנֵי מַרְאִית הָעַיִן. אָמַר רִבִּי אִידִי דְחוּטְרָא. סָלוֹ וּמַגְרֵיפוֹ מוֹכִיחִין עָלָיו שֶׁהוּא עוֹשֶׂה אַשְׁפָּה. רִבִּי יוֹסֵי בֵּירִבִּי בּוּן אָמַר אִילֵּין שְׁמוּעָתָא דְּהָכָא דְתַנִּינָן תַּמָּן. רִבִּי אֶלְעָזָר בֶּן עֲזַרְיָה אוֹמֵר. אֵין עוֹשִׁין אֶת הָאַמָּה כַּתְּחִילָּה בַּמּוֹעֵד וּבַשְּׁבִיעִית. אָמַר רִבִּי יִרְמְיָה. מִפְּנֵי שֶׁהוּא מַכְשִׁיר אֶת צְדָדֶיהָ לַזְּרִיעָה. רִבִּי יִרְמְיָה רִבִּי בּוּן בַּר חִייָה בְשֵׁם רִבִּי בָּא בַּר מָמָל. מִפְּנֵי מַרְאִית הָעַיִן. הֲוֹון בָּעֵיי מֵימַר. מָאן דְּאָמַר תַּמָּן מִפְּנֵי מַרְאִית הָעַיִן. וְכָא מַרְאִית הָעַיִן. מָאן דְּאָמַר תַּמָּן. מִפְּנֵי שֶׁהוּא מַכְשִׁיר אֶת צְדָדֶיהָ לַזְּרִיעָה.

וָכָא מָה אִית לֵיהּ. לֵית לָךְ אֶלָּא כְהָדָא. שֶׁמָּא לֹא יִמָּצֵא לוֹ זֶבֶל וְנִמְצָא מְזַבֵּל אֶת אוֹתוֹ הַמָּקוֹם. מַה נָּפַק מִן בֵּינֵיהוֹן. חָפַר לַעֲשׂוֹת אַמָּה שֶׁלְבִּנְיָין. הֲווֹן בָּעֵיי מֵימַר. מָאן דְּאָמַר תַּמָּן מִפְּנֵי מַרְאִית הָעַיִן. וָכָא מִפְּנֵי מַרְאִית הָעַיִן. מָאן דְּאָמַר תַּמָּן. מִפְּנֵי שֶׁהוּא מַכְשִׁיר אֶת צְדָדֶיהָ לַזְּרִיעָה. הֲרֵי אֵינוֹ מַכְשִׁיר אֶת צְדָדֶיהָ לַזְּרִיעָה. הַכֹּל מוֹדִין שֶׁאִם הָיָה לוֹ שָׁם אֲבָנִים אוֹ צְרוֹרוֹת אוֹ סִיד אוֹ גִיפְסָס מוּתָּר.

[35]**Halakhah 2**: There, we have stated[36]: "Rebbi Eleazar ben Azariah forbids unless he raises or lowers by three {hand-breadths} or puts it on a rock.[37]" [38]One may give two explanations. If he had a small amount{of manure} in his house from before the Sabbatical and he wants to transport it to his field during the Sabbatical, he may continuously add to it after the sinning sinners[39] stopped. Rebbi Eleazar ben Azariah forbids it. What is the reason of Rebbi Eleazar ben Azariah? Maybe there will be no more manure and it turns out that he fertilizes that place. It turns out that Rebbi Eleazar ben Azariah parallels Rebbi Yose. Just as Rebbi Yose says[40], manure is not easily found, so Rebbi Eleazar ben Azariah says, manure is not easily found. One may give another explanation: If he had a small amount{of manure} in his house from before the Sabbatical and he wants to transport it to his field during the Sabbatical, he may continuously add to it after the sinning sinners stopped. Rebbi Eleazar ben Azariah forbids it. What is the reason of Rebbi Eleazar ben Azariah? Maybe there will be no more manure and it turns out that he fertilizes that place. Is it not already fertilized from before the Sabbatical[41]? Rebbi Jeremiah, Rebbi Abun bar Hiyya in the name of Rebbi Abba bar Mamal: because of the bad impression, unless he transports ten boxes together[42]. Do the rabbis not care about bad impressions? Rebbi Idi said his stick, his basket, and his shovel prove that he intends to make a dungheap. Rebbi Yose ben Rebbi Abun applied these traditions from here, as we have stated: "Rebbi Eleazar ben Azariah says, one does not make new water canals on the holiday or in the Sabbatical year." Rebbi Jeremiah[43] said, because he would prepare its banks to be sown. Rebbi Jeremiah, Rebbi Abun bar Hiyya in the name of Rebbi Abba bar Mamal: because of the bad impression. They wanted to say, the one who says there "because of the bad impression" also here "because of the bad impression". The one who says there "because he would prepare its banks to be sown", what would you have

here? The only answer would be, "maybe there will be no more manure and it turns out that he fertilizes that place." What is the difference between them? If he dug a water canal for a building. They wanted to say that the one who said there "because of the bad impression" also here "because of the bad impression". The one who says here "because he would prepare its banks to be sown", clearly here its banks will not be prepared to be sown. Everybody agrees that if he assembled there stones, pebbles, lime, or cement[44] it is permitted.

35 This corresponds to the division of Mishnaiot in the Babli where the second part of Mishnah 1 is formulated as separate Mishnah.

36 Mishnah Ševi`it 3:2.

37 While in the Sabbatical it is forbidden to work to ameliorate the fields, it is permitted to assemble dungheaps on or close to the fields to be used after the end of the Sabbatical. In Mishnaiot Ševi`it 3:1-2 there are differences of opinion on whether it is necessary to clearly separate the dungheaps from the fields and how this is to be done.

38 From here to the end of the paragraph the text is copied from a text of Ševi`it close to, but separate from, the text there, as shown later when the Mishnah here is quoted as "there".

39 A misreading of עוֹבְדֵי עֲבוֹדָה "agricultural workers" in the Ševi`it text. The agricultural workers will stop at the end of the harvest of the year preceding the Sabbatical.

40 His position in Mishnah Ševi`it 3:1 may be interpreted in this way.

41 Since the addition is permitted only at a place already used as dungheap before the start of the Sabbatical.

42 Then everybody sees that the intent is to built a dungheap, not immediate use as manure.

43 With the text in Ševi`it one has to read "R. Ze`ira" since in the next sentence R. Jeremiah is quoted accepting another opinion.

44 Greek γύψος.

(80b line 54) וּמְתַקְּנִין אֶת הַמְּקוּלְקֶלֶת בַּמּוֹעֵד. דָּבָר שֶׁהוּא לְצוֹרֶךְ הַמּוֹעֵד. אֲבָל דָּבָר שֶׁאֵינוֹ לְצוֹרֶךְ הַמּוֹעֵד אָסוּר. בְּשֶׁלְיָחִיד אֲבָל בְּשֶׁלְרַבִּים אֲפִילוּ דָּבָר שֶׁאֵינוֹ לְצוֹרֶךְ הַמּוֹעֵד מוּתָּר. כְּהָדָא דְּבָנֵי דְסָכּוּתָא אִיתְפָּחֲתַת בְּמוֹעֲדָא וּשְׁרָא לוֹן רַבִּי אַבָּהוּ מְעַבְדִינָהּ בְּמוֹעֲדָא. בְּטָרִיחַ וְכֵיוָנוֹ לָא סָבְרִינָן מֵימַר וּבְלְבַד שֶׁלֹּא וְכַוֵּין אֶת מְלַאכְתּוֹ בַּמּוֹעֵד. אָמְרִין. אִין לָא מִתְעַבְדָּא כְּדוֹן לָא מִתְעַבְדָּא עוֹד. אַיָּירָא דְצִיפּוֹרִין אִיתְפָּחֲתִין בְּמוֹעֲדָא. חֲבֵרַיָּיא סָבְרִין מֵימַר שָׁרֵי מִן הָדָא. וּמְתַקְּנִין אֶת קִילְקוּלֵי הַמַּיִם. אָמַר רַבִּי פִּינְחָס. לֹא אָסַר רַבִּי יִרְמְיָה אֶלָּא מִשֶּׁם הִילְכַת הַפַּטִּישׁ. בֵּית עֶלְמָא דְּבַר מִקְטְיָא אִיתְפָּחַת בְּמוֹעֲדָא. רַב חוּנָה סָבַר מֵימַר שָׁרֵי מִן הָדָא. וְעוֹשִׂין כָּל־צוֹרְכֵי הָרַבִּים. אָמַר לֵיהּ רַבִּי מָנָא. וְלָא תַּנֵּי רַבִּי שְׁמוּאֵל. אֶלָּא לִהְיוֹת שָׁפִין אֶת סִדְקֵיהֶן.

5 הדא A | הדה   6 קילקולי A | כל כלי   משם A | משום   הילכות הפטיש A | חלב הפשט   7 מקטיא A | מקטיא

קטיא | A איתפחת | A איתפתת רב חונה סבר | A סבר רב הונא הדא | A הדה 8 ולא AS ולית ר' | A -
סדקיהן | A סידקיהן

"One fixes the broken ones on the holiday." If it is for the needs of the holiday, but anything not for the needs of the holiday is forbidden for an individual, however for the public even not for the needs of the holiday it is permitted[45]. As the following[46]: the baths of Sakuta were damaged on the holiday and Rebbi Abbahu permitted them to be repaired on the holiday. If it needs exertion and he planned it, we would not say so, only if he did not intend his work for the holiday[47]. They said, if it is not done now it never will be done. [48]The cauldron of Sepphoris was damaged on the holiday. The colleagues wanted to say that it is permitted from the following, "one repairs all defects in the public water system." Rebbi Phineas said, Rebbi Jeremiah only forbade because of the rules of the hammer[49]. The cemetery of Bar Meqatia was damaged on the holiday. Rav Huna was of the opinion that it is permitted from the following: "and one looks after all public needs." Rebbi Mana told him, but did not Rebbi[50] Samuel state, "only to smooth its fissures[51]."

45 Babli 5a.
46 Parallels to these examples are in the Babli, 4b-5a.
47 Even for public works.
48 From here on there exists a parallel text from remainders of an Ashkenazic text edited by Jacob Suzman, *Kobez al-Yad* 12 (A).

49 Since the High Priest Johanan forbade the use of hammers on the intermediate days of a holiday, *Ma`aser Šeni* 5:9.
50 The title is omitted in A. Either one reads Rav Huna, Samuel, and Rebbi Mana I, or Rebbi Huna, Rebbi Samuel, and Rebbi Mana II.
51 One may repair but not rebuild.

(80b line 65) וְחוֹטְטִין אוֹתָן. גֵּרְפִין אוֹתָן. כַּיי דְתַנִּינָן תַּמָּן. הַחוֹטֵט בַּצִּנּוֹר לְקַבֵּל צְרוֹרוֹת.

" And cleans it." One cleans it, as we have stated there[52], "he who cleans a pipe to get pebbles."

52 Mishnah *Miqwaot* 4:3.

(80b line 66) וְעוֹשִׂין כָּל־צוֹרְכֵי הָרַבִּים. אֵילּוּ הֵן צוֹרְכֵי הָרַבִּים. דָּנִין דִּינֵי מָמוֹנוֹת וְדִינֵי נְפָשׁוֹת דִּינֵי מַכּוֹת. וּפוֹדִין אֶת הַשְּׁבוּיִין וְעַרָכִים וַחֲרָמִים וְהֶקְדֵּישׁוֹת וּמַשְׁקִין אֶת הַסּוֹטָה וְשׂוֹרְפִין אֶת הַפָּרָה וְעוֹרְפִין עֶגְלָה עֲרוּפָה וְרוֹצְעִין עֶבֶד עִבְרִי וּמְטַהֲרִין אֶת הַמְצוֹרָע וּמְפָרְקִין אֶת הַמִּנְעָל מֵעַל גַּבֵּי הָאִימוּם אֲבָל לֹא מַחֲזִירִין אוֹתוֹ.

2 ופודין | A ופודים וערכים | A וערכין הסוטה | A השוטה 3 ורוצעין | A ורוצעים ומטהרין | A ומטהרים
4 אותו | A אותן

וּמְצַיְּינִין עַל הַקְּבָרוֹת. וְלֹא כְבָר צִיְּינוּ מֵאֲדָר. תִּיפְתָּר שֶׁיָּרַד שֶׁטֶף שֶׁלְגְּשָׁמִים וּשְׁטָפוֹ.

וְיוֹצְאִין אַף עַל הַכִּלְאָיִם: לֹא כְבָר יָצְאוּ בָאֲדָר. תִּיפְתָּר שֶׁהָיְתָה הַשָּׁנָה אֲפִילָה וְאֵין הַצְּמָחִים נִיכָּרִין.

וּמְנַיִין לְצִיּוּן. רִבִּי בֶרֶכְיָה רִבִּי יַעֲקֹב בַּר בַּת יַעֲקֹב בְּשֵׁם רִבִּי חוּנְיָיה דִּבְרַת חַוָּרָן. רִבִּי יוֹסֵה אָמַר לָהּ רִבִּי יַעֲקֹב בַּר אָחָא בְּשֵׁם רִבִּי חוּנְיָיה דִּבְרַת חַוָּרָן רִבִּי חִזְקִיָּה רִבִּי עוּזִּיאֵל בְּרֵיהּ דְּרִבִּי חוּנְיָיה דִּבְרַת חַוָּרָן. וְטָמֵא טָמֵא יִקְרָא. כְּדֵי שֶׁתְּהֵא טוּמְאָה קוֹרְאָה לוֹ בְּפִיהָ וְאוֹמֶרֶת לוֹ. פְּרוֹשׁ. רִבִּי לָא בְשֵׁם רִבִּי שְׁמוּאֵל בַּר נַחְמָן. וְעָבְרוּ הָעוֹבְרִים בָּאָרֶץ וְרָאָה עֶצֶם אָדָם וּבָנָה אֶצְלוֹ צִיּוּן. מִיכָן שֶׁמְּצַיְּינִין עַל הָעֲצָמוֹת. אָדָם. מִיכָן שֶׁמְּצַיְּינִין עַל הַשִּׁזְרָה וְעַל הַגּוּלְגּוֹלֶת. וּבָנָה. מִיכָן שֶׁמְּצַיְּינִין עַל גַּבֵּי אֶבֶן קְבוּעָה. אִם אוֹמֵר אַתְּ עַל גַּבֵּי אֶבֶן תְּלוּשָׁה. אַף הִיא הוֹלֶכֶת וּמְטַמֵּא בְמָקוֹם אַחֵר. אֶצְלוֹ. בִּמְקוֹם טַהֲרָה. צִיּוּן. מִיכָן לְצִיּוּן. וּמָצָא אֶבֶן אַחַת מְצוּיֶּינֶת. אַף עַל פִּי שֶׁאֵין מְקַיְּימִין כֵּן הַמַּאֲהִיל עָלֶיהָ טָמֵא. אֲנִי אוֹמֵר. מֵת קַמְצוּץ וְהָיָה נָתוּן תַּחְתֶּיהָ. הָיוּ שְׁתַּיִם. הַמַּאֲהִיל עֲלֵיהֶן טָהוֹר וּבֵינֵיהֶן טָמֵא. אִם הָיָה חָרוּשׁ בֵּינְתַּיִם הֲרֵי הֵן כִּיחִידִיּוֹת. בֵּינֵיהֶן טָהוֹר וּסְבִיבוֹתֵיהֶן טָמֵא. תַּנֵּי. אֵין מְצַיְּינִין עַל הַבָּשָׂר שֶׁמָּא נִתְאַכֵּל הַבָּשָׂר. רִבִּי יוּסְטָא בַּר שׁוּנֶם בְּעָא קוֹמֵי רִבִּי מָנָא. וְלֹא נִמְצָא מְטַמֵּא טַהֲרוֹת לְמַפְרֵעַ. אָמַר לֵיהּ. מוּטָב שֶׁיִּתְקַלְקְלוּ בוֹ לְשָׁעָה וְאַל יִתְקַלְקְלוּ בוֹ לְעוֹלָם.

[53]"And one looks after all public needs." [54]"The following are the public needs: One judges civil suits, and capital crimes, and cases of flogging, and one redeems kidnap victims, and valuations, and bans, and dedications, and one lets the suspected adulteress drink, and burns the Cow, and one breaks the neck of the calf whose neck was to be broken, and one pierces the ear of a Hebrew slave, and one purifies the sufferer from skin disease, and removes the shoe from the block but one may not return it."

"One marks the graves." Were they not already marked in Adar? Explain it if there was a flood caused by rain which rinsed it off[64].

"And also one goes to inspect for *kilaim*." Did they not already go in Adar? Explain it if the year was late and the plants not recognizable.

[55]From where about marks? Rebbi Berekhiah, Rebbi Jacob the son of the daughter of Jacob, in the name of Rebbi Onias from Hauran. Rebbi Yose said it, Rebbi Jacob bar Aha in the name of Rebbi Onias from Hauran. Rebbi Hizqiah, Rebbi Uziel the son of Rebbi Onias from Hauran in the name of Rebbi Onias from Hauran: *impure, impure, he shall call out*[56]; the impurity itself has to call out and say to you: go away! Rebbi Hila in the name of

Rebbi Samuel bar Naḥman: *The emissaries shall crisscross the land; if one sees a bone of a human he builds a sign near it*[57] *A bone*, from here that one makes signs for bones. *A human*, from here that one makes signs for spine and skull. *He builds*, from here that one makes signs on fixed stones. If you say on loose ones, it would move and make other places impure. *Near it*, on a place of purity. *A sign*, from here the marks.

[58]If one found a single marked stone, even though one should not keep it so, if somebody forms a tent over it he is impure; I say a marked corpse was under it. If there were two, he who forms a tent over any one of them is pure; between them he is impure. If between them was a ploughed strip they are single stones, between them the area is pure and around them impure.

It was stated[59]: "One does not mark flesh, for perhaps it will decompose." Rebbi Justus bar Shunem asked before Rebbi Mana: Will that not cause pure food to be retroactively made impure? He said to him, it is better that these should become unusable for a limited time than that {the place} become unusable forever.

53   From here to the end of the Halakhah the text is copied in *Šeqalim* 1:1, Notes 55-75. The origin of the text is here, since most of the following has no relevance for the topic of *Šeqalim*.

54   Tosephta 2:11.

55   This text in addition is in *Ma`aser Šeni* 5:1, :Notes 17-25) and *Sotah* 9:1 (Notes 29-31). Babli *Mo`ed Qatan* 6a. The biblical roots for the duty of the authorities to mark the places of graves with taxpayers' money.

56   *Lev.* 13:46.

57   *Ez.* 39:15.

58   Tosephta *Šeqalim* 1:5.

59   Tosephta *Šeqalim* 1:5.

(fol. 80a) **משנה ב**: רִבִּי אֱלִיעֶזֶר בֶּן יַעֲקֹב אוֹמֵר מוֹשְׁכִין אֶת הַמַּיִם מֵאִילָן לְאִילָן אֲבָל לֹא יַשְׁקֶה אֶת כָּל־הַשָּׂדֶה כּוּלָּהּ. זְרָעִים שֶׁלֹּא שָׁתוּ לִפְנֵי הַמּוֹעֵד לֹא יַשְׁקֵם בַּמּוֹעֵד. וַחֲכָמִים מַתִּירִין בָּזֶה וּבָזֶה: צָדִין אֶת הָאִישׁוּת וְאֶת הָעַכְבָּרִים בִּשְׂדֵה הָאִילָן וּבִשְׂדֵה הַלָּבָן כְּדַרְכּוֹ בַּמּוֹעֵד וּבַשְּׁבִיעִית. רִבִּי יְהוּדָה אוֹמֵר בִּשְׂדֵה הָאִילָן כְּדַרְכּוֹ וּבִשְׂדֵה הַלָּבָן שֶׁלֹּא כְדַרְכּוֹ. וּמְקָרִין אֶת הַפִּירְצָה בַּמּוֹעֵד וּבַשְּׁבִיעִית בּוֹנֶה כְּדַרְכּוֹ:

Mishnah 2: Rebbi Eliezer ben Jacob says, one draws water from tree to tree, but he should not water the entire orchard. Produce which was not irrigated before the holiday he may not irrigate during the holiday. However, the Sages permit in both cases[60]. One may catch the mole[61] and rats from an orchard or a white field[62] normally[63] on the holiday or in the Sabbatical; Rebbi Jehudah says from an orchard normally but from a white field with a change. One mends[64] a breach on the holiday; but in the Sabbatical he builds normally.

60 One may irrigate an entire orchard tree by tree and irrigate any produce grown in intensive culture, since otherwise the farmer would incur substantial loss. However the water must be led from one tree to the next by a narrow channel, to avoid irrigating the entire surface area of the orchard.

61 And any other pest damaging the roots of plants.

62 A field used for growing grain in extensive agriculture.

63 Without any change of week-day practices.

64 A breach in a separating wall may be fixed by filling it with stones, but the stones may not be fixed with mortar.

(80c line 11) **הלכה ג**: רִבִּי מָנָא אָמַר לָהּ סְתָם. רִבִּי אָבוּן בְּשֵׁם שְׁמוּאֵל. בִּסְתָם חֲלוּקִים. מָה אֲנָן קַייָמִין. אִם בִּמְרוּוָחִין דִּבְרֵי הַכֹּל אָסוּר. אִם בִּרְצוּפִין דִּבְרֵי הַכֹּל מוּתָּר. אֶלָּא כִי אֲנָן קַייָמִין בִּנְטוּעִין מַטָּע עֶשֶׂר לְבֵית סְאָה. רִבִּי לִיעֶזֶר בֶּן יַעֲקֹב עָבַד לוֹן כִּמְרוּוָחִין. וְרַבָּנָן עָבְדִין לוֹן כִּרְצוּפִין. הָא רַבָּנָן אָמְרֵי. בִּמְרוּוָחִין אָסוּר לְהַשְׁקוֹת. מָהוּ לְהַמְשִׁיךְ. נֵילַף הָדָא דְרַבָּנָן מִן דְּרִבִּי לִיעֶזֶר בֶּן יַעֲקֹב. כַּמָּה דְרִבִּי לִיעֶזֶר בֶּן יַעֲקֹב אָמַר. בִּמְרוּוָחִין אָסוּר לְהַשְׁקוֹת וּמוּתָּר לְהַמְשִׁיךְ. כֵּן רַבָּנָן אָמְרֵי. בִּמְרוּוָחִין אָסוּר לְהַשְׁקוֹת וּמוּתָּר מֵימַר. וְלֹא כֵן סָבְרִינָן מֵימַר. בִּמְרוּוָחִין דִּבְרֵי הַכֹּל אָסוּר. וְהֵן עָפָר לָבָן לֹא כִמְרוּוָחִין הוּא. אֶלָּא כָאן בַּשְּׁבִיעִית וְכָאן בַּמּוֹעֵד. מַה בֵּין שְׁבִיעִית מַה בֵּין מוֹעֵד. שְׁבִיעִית עַל יְדֵי שֶׁהִיא מוּתֶּרֶת בַּמְּלָאכָה הִתִּירוּ בֵּין דָּבָר שֶׁהוּא טָרִיחַ בֵּין דָּבָר שֶׁאֵינוֹ טָרִיחַ. מוֹעֵד עַל יְדֵי שֶׁהוּא אָסוּר בַּמְּלָאכָה לֹא הִתִּירוּ אֶלָּא דָבָר שֶׁהוּא אָבֵד וּבִלְבַד דָּבָר שֶׁאֵינוֹ טָרִיחַ. וְאִית דְּבָעֵי מֵימַר נִישְׁמְעִינָהּ מִן הָדָא. שְׁבִיעִית עַל יְדֵי שֶׁזְּמַנָּהּ מְרוּבָּה הִתִּירוּ. מוֹעֵד עַל יְדֵי שֶׁזְּמַנּוֹ קָצוּר אָסוּר. אוֹתָן שִׁבְעַת יָמִים הָאַחֲרוֹנִים לֹא מִסְתַּבְּרָא מֵיעַבְדִּינּוֹן כְּשִׁבְעַת יְמֵי הָרֶגֶל וְיִהְיוּ אֲסוּרִין. אַשְׁכַּח תַּנֵּי. מַרְבִּיצִין בְּעָפָר לָבָן בַּשְּׁבִיעִית אֲבָל לֹא בַּמּוֹעֵד.

1 אבון | ש אבין חלוקים | ש חולקין   2 אנן | ש נן רבנן | G רבנן   4 רבנן אמרי | ש רבניו אמריו   6 רבנן אמרי | ש רבנין אמריו   במרווחין אסור להשקות ומותר להמשיך | ש מותר להמשיך ואסור להשקות ולא | ש לא   8 מותרת | ש מותר   9 טריח | ש טורח שהוא אסור | ש שאסור   10 טריח | ש טורח   11 האחרונים | ש אחרות   12 - | Aש דברי ר' שמעון. ור' אליעזר בן יעקב אוסר

Halakhah 3: [65]Rebbi Mana said it anonymously, Rebbi Abun in the name of Samuel. They disagree anonymously[66]. Where are we holding? If they are widely spaced everybody agrees that it is forbidden. If they are tightly planted everybody agrees that it is permitted[67]. But we deal with the case that they are planted ten to a *bet seah*. Rebbi Eliezer ben Jacob treats it as widely spaced, the rabbis treat it as tightly planted. So the rabbis said, if widely spaced it is forbidden to irrigate[68]; may one continue[69]? Let us learn the opinion of the rabbis from that of Rebbi Eliezer ben Jacob. Just as Rebbi Eliezer ben Jacob says, it is forbidden to irrigate but permitted to continue, so the rabbis say that it is forbidden to irrigate but permitted to continue. Did we not think that according to everybody if they are widely spaced it is forbidden; but is white dust[70] not as if widely spaced? But here it is the Sabbatical, there the holiday. [71]What is the difference between Sabbatical and holiday? In the Sabbatical when work is permitted they permitted both activities requiring effort and activities not requiring effort. On a holiday when work is forbidden they only permitted to avoid loss and only activities not requiring effort. Some want to understand it from the following: In the Sabbatical which is extended they permitted, on a holiday which is short they forbade. [20]Then these last seven days should be compared to the seven days of a holiday and be forbidden[21]. It was found stated: "One may sprinkle with water on white dust during the Sabbatical year but not during the holiday[72], <the words of Rebbi Simeon. Rebbi Eliezer ben Jacob forbids.>[73]"

65 This text is copied from *Ševi'it* 2:10 (Notes 102-109). In G, the text is replaced by a Note: "One repeats up to 'forbidden'."

66 Since the Mishnah is in the name of R. Eliezer ben Jacob, not anonymous, it follows that the majority, whose opinion is disregarded, must disagree.

67 An orchard is widely spaced if the rules of *Kilaim* would permit to plant crops in the space between the trees; tightly planted if this is not possible. The border between the two cases are 10 saplings planted on a *bet se'ah*, 2'500 square cubits (Mishnah *Kilaim* 5:1).

68 Irrigate the entire orchard at the same time.

69 Water the depression around one tree and then let the water flow in a narrow channel to the next tree, to avoid watering possible growing areas of vegetables.

70 The earth of a "white field".

71 Copied from Halakhah 1, Notes 19-21.

72 Babli 6b.

73 Added from *Ševi'it* and A.

(80c line 28) וַחֲכָמִים מַתִּירִין בָּזֶה וּבָזֶה: מָהוּ בָּזֶה וּבָזֶה: בֵּין שֶׁשָּׁתוּ קוֹדֶם לְרֶגֶל בֵּין שֶׁלֹּא שָׁתוּ קוֹדֶם לְרֶגֶל. אֶלָּא כָאן בָּאִילָן כָּאן בִּזְרָעִים.

"However, the Sages permit in both cases." What means "in both cases"? Whether it was irrigated before the holiday or was not irrigated before the holiday? But both for tree and for vegetable.

(80c line 30) **הלכה ד**: אֵישׁוּת זוֹ חוּלְדָּה. אַף עַל פִּי שֶׁאֵין רְאָיָיה בַדָּבָר זֵיכֶר לַדָּבָר. נֵפֶל אֵשֶׁת בַּל־חָזוּ שָׁמֶשׁ:

נִיחָא בִשְׂדֵה הָאִילָן. בִּשְׂדֵה הַלָּבָן. אֶלָּא בִשְׂדֵה הַלָּבָן שֶׁהִיא סְמוּכָה לִשְׂדֵה הָאִילָן. כְּדַרְכּוּ. צָד בִּמְצוּדָה. שֶׁלֹּא כְדַרְכּוּ. תּוֹחֵב בַּשְּׁפוּד וּמַכֶּה בַקַּרְדוֹם וּמְרַדֵּד אֶת הָאֲדָמָה תַחְתֶּיהָ. תַּנֵּי. מַחֲרִיבִין חוּרְרֵי הַנְּמָלִים בַּמּוֹעֵד. כֵּיצַד הוּא עוֹשֶׂה. רַבָּן שִׁמְעוֹן בֶּן גַּמְלִיאֵל אוֹמֵר. נוֹטֵל מֵאִילוּ וְנוֹתֵן בְּצַד אִילוּ וְהֵן מְחַנְּקִין אִילוּ אֶת אִילוּ. וְהוּא שֶׁתְּהֵא אַמַּת הַמַּיִם עוֹבֶרֶת בֵּינֵיהֶן.

Halakhah 4: *Eshut* is the mole. Even though it is no proof, it is an indication: *Like a still-born mole, Never seeing the sun*[74]!

One understands a mole; a white field[75]? But a white field next to an orchard.

"Normally", catching using a trap. "With a change", he sticks on a spear, hits with an axe, or flattens the earth under it. It was stated[76]: "One destroys ant hills on the holiday. How does one do it? Rabban Simeon ben Gamliel says, he takes from one and puts them next to another and they will kill one another," but only is a water canal in between.

74 *Ps.* 58:9.
75 Moles will damage the roots of trees but the roots of grain are too short to be damaged by them. There seems not to be any damage done by moles in a grain field.
76 Babli 6b, Tosephta 1:5.

(80c line 37) וּמְקָרִין אֶת הַפִּירְצָה בַּמּוֹעֵד. אֶבֶן עַל גַּבֵּי אֶבֶן וּצְרוֹר עַל גַּבֵּי צְרוֹר. וּבַשְּׁבִיעִית בּוֹנֶה כְּדַרְכּוּ. אֶבֶן עַל גַּבֵּי צְרוֹר וּצְרוֹר עַל גַּבֵּי אֶבֶן. וּבְפִירְצָה שֶׁאֵינָהּ סָנָה אֶת הֶעָפָר. אֲבָל פִּירְצָה שֶׁהִיא הָיְתָה סָנָה אֶת הֶעָפָר אָסוּר לְגוֹדְרָהּ בַּשְּׁבִיעִית. וְתַנֵּי כֵן. כָּל־פִּירְצָה שֶׁהִיא סָנָה אֶת הֶעָפָר אָסוּר לְגוֹדְרָהּ בַּשְּׁבִיעִית. וְשֶׁאֵינָהּ סָנָה אֶת הֶעָפָר מוּתָּר לְגוֹדְרָהּ בַּשְּׁבִיעִית. בְּשֶׁאֵינָהּ מַכְשֶׁלֶת אֶת הָרַבִּים. אֲבָל אִם מַכְשֶׁלֶת הָרַבִּים אַף עַל פִּי שֶׁהִיא סָנָה אֶת הֶעָפָר מוּתָּר לְגוֹדְרָהּ בַּשְּׁבִיעִית. כְּהָדָא. אִם הָיָה כּוֹתְלוֹ גוֹהֶה סוֹתְרוֹ וּבוֹנֵהוּ. וְיִסְתּוֹר וְלֹא יִבְנֶהוּ. רִבִּי חֲנַנְיָה בְשֵׁם רִבִּי יוֹחָנָן. הִתִּירוּ סוֹפוֹ מִפְּנֵי תְחִילָּתוֹ. שֶׁאִם אוֹמֵר אַתְּ לוֹ שֶׁלֹּא יִבְנֶה אַף הוּא אֵינוּ סוֹתְרוֹ וְנִמְצָא בָא לִידֵי סַכָּנָה.

1 ומקרין G | ומקרים 2 סנה A | שגה 3 היתה | -G 6 כהדא A | כהדא 7 או' את A | אמ'

"One mends a breach on the holiday," stone on stone and pebble on pebble; "but in the Sabbatical he builds normally," stone on pebble and pebble on stone[77]. Only a breach which is not surrounded by dust[78]. But it is forbidden to mend a breach which is surrounded by dust in the Sabbatical year. It was stated such: In the Sabbatical year it is forbidden to fence in any breach which is surrounded by dust; but it is permitted fence in any breach which is not surrounded by dust, unless it represents a danger to the public. But if it represents a danger to the public even though it is surrounded by dust it may be fenced in in the Sabbatical year. As the following[79]: "If his wall was sloping one tears it down and rebuilds." Could he not tear down and not build? Rebbi Ḥanania in the name of Rebbi Joḥanan: They permitted the end because of the beginning. For if you tell him not to build he will not tear down and create a danger.

77 Differently in the Babli, 7a.
78 If the opening is closed by earth to a reasonable height.
79 Babli 7a, Tosephta 1:7.

(fol. 80a) **משנה ג**: רִבִּי מֵאִיר אוֹמֵר רוֹאִין אֶת הַנְּגָעִים לְהָקֵל אֲבָל לֹא לְהַחֲמִיר. וַחֲכָמִים אוֹמְרִים לֹא לְהָקֵל וְלֹא לְהַחֲמִיר. וְעוֹד אָמַר רִבִּי מֵאִיר מְלַקֵּט אָדָם עַצְמוֹת אָבִיו וְאִמּוֹ מִפְּנֵי שֶׁשִּׂמְחָה הִיא לוֹ. רִבִּי יוֹסֵי אוֹמֵר אֵבֶל הוּא לוֹ. וְלֹא יְעוֹרֵר עַל מֵתוֹ וְלֹא יַסְפִּידֶנּוּ קוֹדֶם לָרֶגֶל שְׁלֹשִׁים יוֹם: אֵין חוֹפְרִין כּוּכִין וּקְבָרוֹת בַּמּוֹעֵד. אֲבָל מְחַנְּכִים אֶת הַכּוּכִין וְעוֹשִׂין נִבְרֶכֶת וְאָרוֹן עִם הַמֵּת בֶּחָצֵר. רִבִּי יְהוּדָה אוֹסֵר אֶלָּא אִם כֵּן יֵשׁ עִמּוֹ נְסָרִים:

Mishnah 3: Rebbi Meïr says, one inspects skin-disease[80] to alleviate but not to restrict; but the Sages say, neither to alleviate nor to restrict. Rebbi Meïr also said, a person may collect his father's or mother's bones because it is an occasion of joy[81]. Rebbi Yose says, it is an occasion of mourning. Thirty days before the holiday one should neither memorialize nor eulogize his deceased[82]. One does not dig niches[83] and graves[84] on the holiday but one may ready them for use. One makes a temporary grave[85] and a coffin for the deceased in the courtyard; Rebbi Jehudah forbids unless he has boards ready[86].

80 The purity status of a person afflicted with skin disease, while depending on the form of the disease, becomes active only by the declaration of a Cohen inspecting the

appearance of the diseased skin (*Lev.* 13-14). In many cases, a sufferer is declared provisionally impure for a period of observation, one or two weeks. R. Meïr permits the Cohen to inspect the disease on the intermediate days of a holiday if he notes that the inspection will result in freeing the sufferer from his impurity, but not if the inspection will declare the sufferer impure in a severe way. The Sages do not allow any inspection.

81 It is part of the traditional belief that sinners are punished in the World to Come only as long as some of their flesh exists. Therefore it was the custom to bury the dead either without any coffin or in a coffin not hermetically closed to hasten the decay of the flesh and then rebury the bones in an ossuary frequently deposited in a niche in a large burial cave. R. Yose holds the more popular opinion that the collection of bones is a mourning rite; only the deposition of the ossuary in a cave is occasion to celebrate the pain-free existence of his parents in the World to Come.

82 Since if this is well executed, the sorrow and pain awakened will diminish his ability to rejoice on the holiday.

83 For ossuaries.

84 Burial caves.

85 To be used until the flesh has disappeared.

86 He holds that while making the coffin is permitted on the intermediate days, sawing trees or logs to prepare boards to be used is not justified.

(80c line 47) **הלכה ה**: תַּמָּן תַּנֵּינָן. בַּהֶרֶת כַּגְּרִיס וּפָסֶת כַּגְּרִיס [וְנוֹלַד לַפִּסְיוֹן מִחְיָה אוֹ שֵׂעָר לָבָן] וְהֶלְכָה לָהּ הָאוֹם. רִבִּי עֲקִיבָה מְטַמֵּא. וַחֲכָמִים אוֹמְרִים תֵּירָאֶה כַתְּחִילָּה. הָא רִבִּי עֲקִיבָה מְטַמֵּא וּמַחֲלִיט. וְרַבָּנָן אָמְרֵי. תֵּירָאֶה בַתְּחִילָּה מַחֲלִיטִין. וּמָה בֵינֵיהוֹן. רִבִּי יוֹחָנָן אָמַר. עֶרֶב הָרֶגֶל בֵּינֵיהוֹן. רִבִּי עֲקִיבָה אוֹמֵר. הֵי קַדְמְיָיתָא וְאֵין אַתְּ נִזְקָק לוֹ לֹא לְהָקֵל וְלֹא לְהַחְמִיר. וְרַבָּנָן אָמְרֵי. חוֹרֵי הִיא וְאַתְּ פּוֹטְרוֹ מִן הָרִאשׁוֹנָה. וְהֵיידָא הִיא שֶׁלֹּא לְהַחְמִיר שֶׁאֵין אַתְּ נִזְקָק לוֹ לַשְּׁנִיָּיה לֹא לְהָקֵל וְלֹא לְהַחְמִיר. רִבִּי יוֹסֵה בְשֵׁם רִבִּי אֲחָא. אַתְיָיא דִיחִידָיָיא דְהָכָא כְסתַמָּא דְתַמָּן וְדִיחִידָיָיא דְתַמָּן כְּסתָמָא דְהָכָא. אַתְיָיא דִיחִידָיָיא דְהָכָא כְסתַמָּא דְתַמָּן. רִבִּי עֲקִיבָה אוֹמֵר. הִיא קַדְמְיָיתָא וְאֵין אַתְּ נִזְקָק לוֹ לֹא לְהָקֵל וְלֹא לְהַחְמִיר. וְדִיחִידָיָיא דְתַמָּן כְּסתַמָּא דְהָכָא. וְרַבָּנִין אָמְרֵי. חוֹרֵי הִיא וְאַתְּ פּוֹטְרוֹ מִן הָרִאשׁוֹנָה. וְתַנֵּינָן הָכָא. רִבִּי מֵאִיר אוֹמֵר רוֹאִין אֶת הַנְּגָעִים בַּתְּחִילָּה לְהָקֵל אֲבָל לֹא לְהַחְמִיר. רִבִּי יוֹסֵי בֵּירִבִּי בּוּן בְּשֵׁם רִבִּי אֲחָא. בֵּין דִּיחִידָיָיא דְהָכָא בֵין דְּרַבָּנָן דְּהָכָא מוֹדֵיי לְרַבָּנָן דְּתַמָּן דְּהָקֵל אֲבָל לֹא לְהַחְמִיר. תַּמָּן בְּשֶׁהֶלְכָה לָהּ הָאוֹם. בְּרַם הָכָא בְּשֶׁהֶלְכוּ לָהֶם הַסִּימָנִין וְהָאוֹם קַיֶּימֶת. אָמַר רִבִּי. נִרְאִין דִּבְרֵי רִבִּי יוֹסֵי בְמוּסְגַּר וְדִבְרֵי רִבִּי מֵאִיר בְּמוּחְלָט. רִבִּי זְעוּרָה אָמַר. יְמֵי הָרֶגֶל בֵּינֵיהוֹן. רִבִּי עֲקִיבָה אוֹמֵר. הִיא קַדְמִייתָא וְהוּא נִכְנָס לָעֲזָרָה. וְרַבָּנִין אָמְרֵי. חוֹרֵי הִיא וְאֵינוֹ נִכְנָס לָעֲזָרָה. הָא רִבִּי עֲקִיבָה מְטַמֵּא וּמַחֲלִיט. וְרַבָּנָן אָמְרֵי. תֵּירָאֶה כַתְּחִילָּה מַחֲלִיטִין. וּמָה בֵינֵיהוֹן. (עֶרֶב הָיָה לוֹ שָׁמוֹעַ פָּטוּר מִפִּי כֹהֵן שָׁעָה אַחַת.) שְׁמוּאֵל אָמַר. פְּרִיחָה בֵּינֵיהוֹן. רִבִּי עֲקִיבָה אוֹמֵר. הִיא קַדְמִייתָא בְּפוֹרֵחַ מִן הַטָּמֵא טָהוֹר. וְרַבָּנִין אָמְרֵי. חוֹרֵי הִיא. בְּפוֹרֵחַ מִן הַטָּהוֹר טָמֵא. וְאָמְרוּן בְּשֵׁם

שְׁמוּאֵל. פְּרִיחָה וּשְׁחִין הַמּוֹרָד בֵּינֵיהוֹן. רִבִּי עֲקִיבָה אוֹמֵר. הִיא קַדְמִיָּיתָא בְּפוֹרֵחַ מִן הַטָּמֵא טָהוֹר. וְרַבָּנִין אָמְרֵי. חוֹרֵי הִיא. בְּפוֹרֵחַ מִן הַטָּהוֹר טָמֵא. בְּגִין דְּהִיא חוֹרֵי. הָא אֵין הִיא הִיא טָהוֹר. וְאַתְיָיא כַיי דְּאָמַר רִבִּי שִׁמְעוֹן בֶּן לָקִישׁ. דְּאִיתְפַּלְגוּן. פֶּרְחָה בוֹ בִשְׁחִין הַמּוֹרָד. רִבִּי יוֹחָנָן אָמַר טָהוֹר. רִבִּי שִׁמְעוֹן בֶּן לָקִישׁ אָמַר. טָמֵא.

Halakhah 5: There, we have stated[87]: "A white spot in the size of a grit[88] and it spread in the size of a grit [and in the spread appeared a healthy spot or a white hair][89] but the original disappeared. Rebbi Aqiba declares him impure, but the Sages are saying, it should be seen as a new case[90]." Therefore, Rebbi Aqiba declares him impure absolutely[91]. But the rabbis are saying, it should be seen as a new case as absolutely {impure}. What is the difference between them? Rebbi Johanan said, holiday eve is between them. Rebbi Aqiba says that this is the former case and you do not deal with him neither to alleviate nor to restrict[92]. But the rabbis are saying that this is a new case and you free him from the first one. And this is "not to restrict" that you should not deal with the second case neither to alleviate nor to restrict[93]. Rebbi Yose in the name of Rebbi Aha, it turns out that the single opinion here parallels the anonymous opinion there and the single opinion there parallels the anonymous opinion here. The single opinion here parallels the anonymous opinion there: Rebbi Aqiba says that this is the former case and you do not deal with him neither to alleviate nor to restrict[94]. And the single opinion there parallels the anonymous opinion here: The rabbis are saying that this is a new case and you free him from the first one. And we have stated here, "Rebbi Meïr says, one inspects skin-disease[80] to alleviate but not to restrict" Rebbi Yose ben Rebbi Abun in the name of Rebbi Aha: Either following the single opinion here or the rabbis here the rabbis there agree to alleviate but not to restrict[95]. There, if the original disappeared, but here, if the indications {of impurity} disappeared and the original remains[96]. "Rebbi said, the opinion of Rebbi Yose is reasonable for one in quarantine and the opinion of Rebbi Meïr if he is absolutely {impure}[97]." Rebbi Ze`ira said, they disagree about the holiday itself. Rebbi Aqiba says that this is the former case; could he enter the Temple courtyard? But the rabbis are saying, this is a new case; could he not enter the Temple courtyard[98]? Therefore, Rebbi Aqiba declares him impure absolutely. But the rabbis are saying, it should be seen as a new case to become absolute. What is between them? (It will be sweet for him to hear a temporary release from the mouth of the Cohen.)[99] Samuel said, they disagree about expansion[100]. Rebbi Aqiba says that this is the former case and the expansion of impurity is pure. But the rabbis are saying that this is a new case and the expansion of purity is impure. One said in Samuel's name, expansion and treatment-resistant scabies[101] is between them. Rebbi Aqiba says that this is the former case and the expansion of impurity is pure. But the rabbis are saying that this is a new case and the expansion of purity is impure. Because it is another case. Therefore otherwise it would be pure. It parallels what Rebbi Simeon ben Laqish said when they differed, if it developed treatment-resistant scabies, Rebbi Johanan said pure, Rebbi Simeon ben Laqish said impure[102].

87 Mishnah *Nega`im* 4:10.

88 The minimum size of a spot which triggers the impurity of skin-disease, determined to be (36 hair-widths)^2 (*Ma`serot* 5:7 Note 127).

89 Corrector's addition from the Mishnah, to explain the argument; not in A.

90 The rules of a white spot are in *Lev.* 13:9-17. The white spot causes impurity if either a white hair grows in it or it surrounds a spot of healthy skin. The Mishnah describes a case where a white spot without these signs was declared pure, but then grew and in the additional white area grew a white hair while the original spot disappeared. Since the new area also is of a size which by itself would trigger impurity there is no doubt that the individual is impure. The only difference between R. Aqiba and the majority is whether one has an old case turning impure or a new case of original impurity.

91 The impurity of skin-disease is tentative if the individual has to be quarantined for one or two weeks, and is absolute if there is no doubt about the impure state. The main difference is that the person declared absolutely impure when healed needs an elaborate ceremony of reparation to be re-admitted to the Sanctuary and *sancta*.

92 Since the person is pure on holiday eve and becomes impure not by the physical facts on his body but only by a pronouncement of a Cohen, if the Cohen is told to refuse to inspect skin disease on holiday eve the person will be able to celebrate the holiday with his family while otherwise he would not only be impure but also forbidden to dwell inside any walled city of the Holy Land.

93 For the rabbis he only is told not to inspect if the outcome would be a declaration of impurity; he is invited to inspect healed sufferers from skin disease to re-integrate them into society.

94 A quotes here the appropriate portion of the Mishnah, a text not necessary for the understanding but preferable to maintain the parallelism between one case and the other.

95 The Mishnah in *Nega`im* gives no

indication whatsoever how skin disease has to be treated on a holiday.

96 The dispute between the majority and R. Meïr is only in the case that the signs of impurity disappeared and the Cohen would pronounce him pure after a superficial look, whereas it is understood without question that the detailed examination required for a pronouncement of impurity is not conducted on a holiday.

97 Tosephta 1:8, Babli 7a, where it is explained that the opinion attributed to the Sages in our Mishnah is R. Yose's statement. In both Babylonian texts the attributions by Rebbi are switched.

98 The classical commentaries all emend the text but this is now precluded by the fact that the text is faithfully copied in A. One has to read the text as rhetorical questions which should be raised in neither case.

99 Text deleted by the editor of the Venice text and therefore missing in all printed editions, but confirmed by A.

According to the Sages, if the earlier white spot was one which required quarantine (*Lev.* 13:18-23) a declaration of purity, even if then followed by a declaration of absolute impurity because of the new case, might be welcome news which would be precluded by R. Aqiba.

100 Samuel imagines a different background for the Mishnah. If originally the whiteness covered most but not all of the skin, growth which makes all of the skin white (or the parts required for this in rabbinic tradition) eliminates the impurity. But if there was no impurity because of the total whiteness of the skin, appearance of healthy skin creates impurity. (Mishnah *Nega`im* 8:1, *Sifra Tazria` Pereq* 3[7]).

101 In judging the white spots, skin covered by scabies is not taken into consideration. Therefore the status of a white spot developing near a region of treatment-resistant scabies will change if at last the scabies is healed since expansion into that region now generates impurity which it did not do earlier.

102 If the entire skin was white including the region of scabies and then the scabies was healed, for R. Johanan it is pure since the place of the scabies was not counted and therefore now the whiteness expands from a state of impurity which causes purity, but for R. Simeon ben Laqish the person was pure if all skin not subject to scabies was white and now it is an expansion from pure status and as such impure.

(80c line 73) וְעוֹד אָמַר רִבִּי מֵאִיר. מְלַקֵּט אָדָם עַצְמוֹת אָבִיו וְאִמּוֹ מִפְּנֵי שֶׁשִּׂמְחָה הִיא לוֹ. בָּרִאשׁוֹנָה הָיוּ קוֹבְרִין אוֹתָן בְּמַהֲמוֹרוֹת. נִתְאַכֵּל הַבָּשָׂר הָיוּ מְלַקְּטִין אוֹתָן וְקוֹבְרִין אוֹתָן בָּאֲרָזִים. אוֹתוֹ הַיּוֹם הָיָה מִתְאַבֵּל וּלְמָחָר הָיָה שָׂמֵחַ. לוֹמַר שֶׁנִּינוּחוּ אֲבוֹתָיו מִן הַדִּין.

Rebbi Meïr also said, a person may collect his father's or mother's bones because it is an occasion of joy[81]. [103]In earlier times, they were burying them in ditches. When the flesh had rotted away, they collected them and buried them in cedar wood. On the day itself he was mourning, the day after he was happy, implying that his parents were at rest from judgment.

103 From *Sanhedrin* 6:12, Notes 146-148.

(80d line 1) תַּנֵּי. הַמַּעֲבִיר אָרוֹן מִמָּקוֹם לְמָקוֹם אֵין בּוֹ מִשּׁוּם לִיקוּט עֲצָמוֹת. אָמַר רִבִּי אָחָא. הָדָא דַתְּ אָמַר בְּאָרוֹן שֶׁלְּאֶבֶן. אֲבָל בְּאָרוֹן שֶׁלְעֵץ יֵשׁ בּוֹ מִשּׁוּם לִיקוּט עֲצָמוֹת. אָמַר לֵיהּ רִבִּי יוֹסֵי. וַאֲפִילוּ תֵימַר בְּאָרוֹן שֶׁלְעֵץ אֵין בּוֹ מִשּׁוּם לִיקוּט עֲצָמוֹת. אֵי זֶהוּ לִיקוּט עֲצָמוֹת. מַעֲבִירָן בָּאֶפִּיקַרְסִין מִמָּקוֹם לְמָקוֹם. וְתַנֵּי כֵן. לִיקוּט עֲצָמוֹת מְלַקֵּט עֶצֶם עֶצֶם מִשֶּׁיִּתְאַכֵּל הַבָּשָׂר. רִבִּי חַגַּי בְשֵׁם רִבִּי זְעוּרָה. לִיקוּטֵי עֲצָמוֹת כִּשְׁמוּעָן. תַּנֵּי. אֵין שְׁמוּעָה לְלִיקוּטֵי עֲצָמוֹת. אָמַר רִבִּי חַגַּי. וְהוּא שֶׁשָּׁמַע לְמָחָר. אֲבָל אִם שָׁמַע בּוֹ בַיּוֹם יֵשׁ שְׁמוּעָה לְלִיקוּטֵי עֲצָמוֹת. וְיֵשׁ שִׁיעוּר לְלִיקוּטֵי עֲצָמוֹת. תַּנָּא נִיקוּמַכַי קוֹמֵי רִבִּי זְעוּרָה. אֵין שִׁיעוּר לְלִיקוּט עֲצָמוֹת. כְּהָדָא רִבִּי מָנָא הוֹרֵי לְרִבִּי הִלֵּל דְּכִיפְרָא לִקְרוֹעַ וּלְהִתְאַבֵּל כְּרִבִּי אָחָא. שֶׁלֹּא לְהִיטַּמְאוֹת כְּרִבִּי יוֹסֵי. תַּנֵּי. לִיקוּטֵי עֲצָמוֹת אֵין אוֹמְרִין עֲלֵיהֶן קִינִים וָנָהִי. אֵין אוֹמְרִין עֲלֵיהֶן לֹא בִרְכַת אֲבֵלִים וְלֹא תַנְחוּמֵי אֲבֵלִים. אֵילוּ הֵן בִּרְכַת אֲבֵלִים.¹⁰⁴ מַה שֶׁהֵן אוֹמְרִים בַּשּׁוּרָה. תַּנֵּי. אֲבָל אוֹמְרִין עֲלֵיהֶן דְּבָרִים. מָהוּ דְבָרִים. רַבָּנָן¹⁰⁵ אָמְרֵי. קִילוּסִין.

¹⁰⁶It was stated: If a person transports a casket from place to place the rules of collecting bones do not apply. Rebbi Aḥa said, that only is about a stone sarcophagus. But to a wooden casket the rules of collecting bones do apply. Rebbi Yose said, even to a wooden casket the rules of collecting bones do not apply. When is there collecting bones? If one transports them in a striped garment from place to place. And it was stated thus: In collecting bones one collects them bone by bone after the flesh has decomposed. Rebbi Ḥaggai in the name of Rebbi Ze`ira: Collecting bones {is} what it means. It was stated: There is no information about collecting bones. Rebbi Ḥaggai said, that is if he was informed the next day. But on the day itself there is information about collecting bones. Is there a minimum for collecting bones? Nikomachos stated before Rebbi Ze`ira: There is no minimum about collecting bones. About this, Rebbi Mana instructed Rebbi Hillel from Kifra to tear and mourn following Rebbi Aḥa but not to defile himself following Rebbi Yose. It was stated: When collecting bones one does not recite lamentations and dirges; one recites neither the blessings for mourners nor the consolations for mourners. These are blessings for mourners: <what is recited in the synagogue. These are consolations of mourners,>¹⁰⁴ what is said in the row. It was stated: But one says words. What are words? The rabbis <of Caesarea>¹⁰⁵ are saying, eulogies.

104 A adds (from the text in *Pesahim*): מה
דקיסרין.

105 A adds (from the text in *Pesahim*): שהן אומרי׳ בבית הכנסת. אילו הן תנחומי אבלי׳ (p. 68).

106 The text is from *Pesahim* 8:8 (Notes 136-143).

(80d line 14) לֹא יְעוֹרֵר אָדָם עַל מֵתוֹ. אֵי זֶהוּ הָעֵירוּר. מַזְכִּירָתוֹ בֵּין הַמֵּתִים. וְלֹא יַסְפִּידֶנּוּ. אֵי זֶהוּ הֶסְפֵּד. שֶׁהוּא עוֹשֶׂה לוֹ הֶסְפֵּד בִּפְנֵי עַצְמוֹ. הָדָא דַתְּ אָמַר בְּיָשָׁן. אֲבָל בְּחָדָשׁ מוּתָּר. אֵי זֶהוּ חָדָשׁ וְאֵי זֶהוּ יָשָׁן. חָדָשׁ בְּתוֹךְ שְׁלֹשִׁים יוֹם. יָשָׁן לְאַחַר שְׁלֹשִׁים יוֹם. תַּנֵּי. לֹא תָעוֹרֵר אִשָּׁה לְיִוְיָתָהּ בְּמוֹעֵד. רִבִּי נַחְמָן בְּשֵׁם רִבִּי מָנָא אָמַר. לְוִיָתָהּ כְּמָה דְתֵימַר הָעֲתִידִים עוֹרֵר לִוְיָתָן׃ תַּנֵּי. לֹא יִשָּׂא אָדָם אִשָּׁה שֶׁיֵּשׁ לָהּ בָּנִים אֲפִילוּ בַקֶּבֶר. אָמַר רִבִּי יָסָא. מִפְּנֵי מַעֲשֶׂה שֶׁאֵירַע.

"A person should neither memorialize," what is memorializing? Mentioning him among the dead. "Nor eulogize his deceased," what is eulogy? He arranged an eulogy for him alone. That you are saying, for old ones, but for new ones it is permitted. What is new and what is old? New within thirty days, old after thirty days. It was stated, a woman shall not memorialize her consort on the holiday. Rebbi Nahman in the name of Rebbi Mana said, her consort, as one says *those who assist in stating their affliction*[107]. It was stated: A man should not marry a woman who has sons, even in the grave. Rebbi Yasa said, because of what happened[108].

107 *Job* 3:8, translation of Saadia Gaon based on this Yerushalmi (ed. Y. Qafeh, p. 42).

108 A adds the story from the Babli 8a.

(8d line 21) **הלכה ו**: אֵי זֶהוּ חִינּוּךְ קְבָרוֹת. רִבִּי יוֹסֵי בַּר נוֹהֲרַיי אָמַר. סָדוֹ בַסִּיד. רַב חִסְדָּא אָמַר. אִם הָיָה אָרוֹךְ מְקַצְּרוֹ. רִבִּי יְהוֹשֻׁעַ בֶּן לֵוִי אָמַר. מַאֲרִיךְ בּוֹ מִצַּד אֶחָד וּמַרְחִיב בּוֹ מִצַּד אֶחָד. תַּנֵּי רִבִּי חִייָה. מַאֲרִיךְ בּוֹ וּמַרְחִיב בּוֹ בֵּין מִצַּד אֶחָד בֵּין מִשְּׁנֵי צְדָדִין. וְעוֹשִׂין נִבְרֶכֶת בַּמּוֹעֵד. זֶה הַבְּקִיעַ. כָּל־שֶׁהוּא תוֹשָׁב נִקְרָא בְּקִיעַ. וְאָרוֹן עִם הַמֵּת בֶּחָצֵר. הָדָא דַתְּ אָמַר בְּמֵת שֶׁאֵינוֹ מְפוּרְסָם. אֲבָל בְּמֵת שֶׁהוּא מְפוּרְסָם עוֹשִׂין לוֹ אָרוֹן אֲפִילוּ בַשּׁוּק. כַּד דְּמַךְ רִבִּי חֲנַנְיָה חַבְרוֹן דְּרַבָּנִין עַבְדוֹן לֵיהּ אָרוֹן בַּשּׁוּקָא. הַכֹּל מוֹדִין שֶׁלֹּא יָקוֹץ לוֹ אֲרָזִים. וְדִכְוָתָהּ לֹא יַחְצוֹב לוֹ אֲבָנִים. הָיוּ חֲצוּבוֹת. תִּפְלוּגְתָּא דְּרִבִּי יְהוּדָה וְרַבָּנָן.

Halakhah 6: What is readying a grave? Rebbi Yose ben Nehorai said, one whitewashes it with lime. Rav Hisda said, if it was long he shortens it. Rebbi Joshua ben Levi said, he enlarges it at one side and widens it at another side. Rebbi Hiyya stated, "he enlarges and widens it whether on one side or at two sides[109]."

"On the holiday one makes a temporary grave," "this is a cleavage.[110]" Everything flat is called cleavage[111].

"And a coffin for the deceased in the courtyard;" this is what you are saying about a deceased who is not famous. But for a famous deceased one makes a coffin even in public. When Rebbi Ḥanina the colleague of the rabbis expired they made him a coffin in public. Everybody agrees that one may not cut down cedars for him, and similarly not quarry stones for him[112]. If they had been quarried[113], the disagreement between Rebbi Jehudah and the rabbis.

109 Tosephta 1:9, Babli 8b. One may do what is necessary as long as one does not start digging a new grave.
110 Tosephta 1:9, Babli 8b.
111 As long it is not done professionally.

112 Creating materials for work is never permitted on the holiday.
113 But not ready for use without further smoothing, etc.

(fol. 80a) **משנה ד**: אֵין נוֹשְׂאִין נָשִׁים בַּמּוֹעֵד לֹא בְתוּלוֹת וְלֹא אַלְמָנוֹת, וְלֹא מְיַבְּמִין מִפְּנֵי שֶׁשִּׂמְחָה הִיא לוֹ. אֲבָל מַחֲזִיר אֶת גְּרוּשָׁתוֹ. וְעוֹשָׂה אִשָּׁה תַּכְשִׁיטֶיהָ בַּמּוֹעֵד.

Mishnah 4: One does not marry women on a holiday, neither virgins nor widows, nor does one enter into levirate marriage, because it is a joy for him[114]. But he may take back his divorcee, and a woman does adorn herself[115] on the holiday.

114 Since there is a biblical commandment to enjoy the holiday, no competing causes of joy should be procured on the holiday. But remarrying his divorcee will increase his conventional enjoyment of the holiday.
115 By make-up. manicure, pedicure, etc.

(80d line 30) **הלכה ז**: אֵין נוֹשְׂאִין נָשִׁים בַּמּוֹעֵד. שִׁמְעוֹן בַּר בָּא בְשֵׁם רִבִּי יוֹחָנָן. מִפְּנֵי בִיטוּל פְּרִיָּיה וְרִבְיָיה. בְּעוֹן קוֹמֵי רִבִּי יָסָה. הָעֶבֶד מָהוּ שֶׁיִּשָּׂא בַמּוֹעֵד. אֲמַר לוֹן. נִישְׁמְעִינָהּ מִן הָדָא. מִי שֶׁחֶצְיוֹ עֶבֶד וְחֶצְיוֹ בֶּן חוֹרִין. וְאָמַר שִׁמְעוֹן בַּר בָּא בְשֵׁם רִבִּי יוֹחָנָן. מִפְּנֵי בִיטוּל פְּרִיָּיה וְרִבְיָיה. הָדָא אָמְרָה שֶׁהָעֶבֶד מְצוּוֶה עַל פְּרִיָּיה וְרִבְיָיה. וְכָל־שֶׁהוּא מְצוּוֶה עַל פְּרִיָּיה וְרִבְיָיה אָסוּר לוֹ לִישָׂא בַמּוֹעֵד.

Halakhah 7: [116]Simeon bar Abba in the name of Rebbi Joḥanan: Because of refraining from being fruitful and increase[117]. They asked before Rebbi Yose[118]: May a slave marry a woman on a holiday[119]? He told them, let us hear from the following: "One who is half a slave and half a free man." And Rebbi Simeon bar Abba said in the name of Rebbi Joḥanan: Because of refraining from being fruitful and increase. This implies that a slave is commanded to be fruitful and multiply and anybody commanded to be fruitful and multiply is forbidden to marry on a holiday[120]

116 There is a parallel in *Gittin* 4:5, Notes 144-148.

117 For him the prohibition of weddings on the intermediate days of a holiday is purely rabbinical, so that people should not refrain from marrying during the rest of the year in order to save money.

118 Following the text in *Gittin*, rather than the text here, "Yasa", a contemporary of R. Joḥanan.

119 The question is difficult to understand since the slave cannot marry as long as he is a slave but is a full Jew subject to all Jewish laws the moment he is manumitted. Maybe the question is about a slave manumitted on the holiday.

120 Even if in this case the marriage has to be postponed for a few days. Tosaphot *Hagiga* 2b, *Gittin* 41b, point out that in a certain sense a male slave cannot fulfill the commandment to be fruitful because he cannot have any family relationship with his biological children.

(80d line 36) רִבִּי אִילָא רִבִּי לְעָזָר בְּשֵׁם רִבִּי חֲנִינָה. עַל שֵׁם שֶׁאֵין מְעָרְבִין שִׂמְחָה בְּשִׂמְחָה. רִבִּי לָא שָׁמַע לָהּ מִן הָדָא כִּי | חֲנוּכַּת הַמִּזְבֵּחַ עָשׂוּ שִׁבְעַת יָמִים וְהֶחָג שִׁבְעַת יָמִים: רִבִּי יַעֲקֹב בַּר אָחָא שָׁמַע לָהּ מִן הָדָא מַלֵּא שְׁבוּעַ זֹאת. רִבִּי אַבָּהוּ בְּשֵׁם רִבִּי לְעָזָר. מִפְּנֵי הַטּוֹרַח. תַּנֵּי אֲבָל מִתְכַּוֵּין הוּא וְנוֹשֵׂא מֵעֶרֶב הָרֶגֶל. לֵית הָדָא פְלִיגָא עַל רִבִּי לְעָזָר. לֵית הָדָא פְלִינָא עַל רִבִּי יוֹחָנָן. וַאֲפִילוּ עַל רִבִּי חֲנִינָה לֵית הִיא פְלִיגָא. אָמַר רִבִּי בָּא. עָלַת כַּלְתָא נָפְקַת טְרחוּתָא.

1 אילא G | לא G 2 הדא G | הדה G (always) ר' | G - 3 זאת G | זות ואתנה לך גם את זאת 4 מתכוין G | מיתכוון פליגא G | פליגה (always) 5 כלתא G | כלתה טרחותא G | טרחותה

Rebbi Ila, Rebbi Eleazar in the name of Rebbi Ḥanina: Because one does not mix one joy with another joy. Rebbi La understood it from the following[121]: *For they celebrated the initiation of the altar for seven days and the holiday*[122] *for seven days.* Rebbi Jacob bar Aḥa understood it from the following[123]: *finish the week of this one.* Rebbi Abbahu in the name of Rebbi Eleazar: Because of the exertion. It was stated: But one may plan and marry on the eve of a holiday. This does not disagree with Rebbi Eleazar[124]; this does not disagree with Rebbi Johanan[125]. And even with Rebbi Hanina it does not disagree[126]. Rebbi Abba said, when the bride enters the exertion leaves[127].

121 *1Chr.* 7:9.
122 Tabernacles.
123 *Gen.* 29:27.
124 Who forbids on a holiday because of the extra exertion a wedding implies, since the wedding is held before the holiday.
125 Who forbids putting off weddings at least for people who have not yet procreated.
126 Who prohibits mixing one joy with another joy, since the main joy of the seven days of the wedding week is the first day.
127 This proves that the *baraita* does not disagree with R. Hanina. Once the bride enters the wedding chamber after the wedding, the attendants and caterers are no longer needed. Babli 8b.

(80d line 43) אֲבָל מַחֲזִיר הוּא אֶת גְּרוּשָׁתוֹ. מִפְּנֵי (שֶׁשִּׂמְחָה) [שֶׁאֵינָהּ שִׂמְחָה] הִיא לוֹ. הָדָא דַתְּ אָמַר מִן הַנִּישּׂוּאִין. אֲבָל מִן הָאֵירוּסִין אָסוּר.

1 ששמחה G | שהוא שמחה הדא G | הדה   2 הנישואין G | הנישואים האירוסין G | הארוסים

"But he may take back his divorcee," because it is [no][128] joy for him. This you are saying after marriage, but after preliminary marriage it is forbidden.

128 Distortion by the editor of the Venice edition who misunderstood the text. Remarrying his divorcee with whom he had lived is joyful for the man since it relieves him from the thought that he was stupid in divorcing her, but marrying a woman with whom he never lived is a new experience which would compete with the enjoyment of the holiday.

(80d line 45) וְעוֹשָׂה אִשָּׁה תַּכְשִׁיטֶיהָ בַּמּוֹעֵד. וְאֵילוּ הֵן תַּכְשִׁיטֵי אִשָּׁה. גּוֹדֶלֶת וְכוֹחֶלֶת וּפוֹקֶסֶת וְנוֹטֶלֶת אֶת שְׂעָרָהּ וְאֶת צִיפָּרְנֶיהָ וּמַעֲבֶרֶת כְּלִי חָדָשׁ עַל פָּנֶיהָ. אָמַר רִבִּי יוּדָן אָבוֹי דְּרִבִּי מַתַּנְיָה בְּלָשׁוֹן נָקִי הִיא מַתְנִיתָה.

1 את שערה G | סערה ואת G -   2 ציפרניה G | וצפורניה היא G | הוא

"A woman does adorn herself on the holiday." [129]The following are women's adornments: She braids, and puts on kohl, and combs her hair, and removes hair and fingernails, and moves a grating[130] instrument over her face. Rebbi Yudan the father of Rebbi Mattaniah said, the *baraita* is in clean language[131].

129 Babli 9b.
130 The commentators all read חרש "clay" for חדש "new" in the text. I do not know why a clay instrument should be used. It

seems much more that it is a depilatory instrument, and the word is Arabic חדש "grating".

131 Using "face" for "genitals, *mons veneris*".

(fol. 80a) **משנה ה**: רִבִּי יְהוּדָה אוֹמֵר לֹא תָסוּד מִפְּנֵי שֶׁנִּוּוּל הוּא לָהּ:

Mishnah 5: Rebbi Jehudah says, she may not use lime[132] because it disfigures her.

132 They used to use lime as a depilatory on the face which at the same time irritated the skin and thereby increased the blood flow to made gave more color to the cheeks. The beauty treatment described was applied mainly to single girls to make them more marriageable.

(80d line 47) רִבִּי יְהוּדָה אוֹמֵר לֹא תָסוּד מִפְּנֵי שֶׁנִּוּוּל הוּא לָהּ: תְּרֵין אֲמוֹרִין רִבִּי חֲנַנְיָה וְרִבִּי מָנָא. חַד אָמַר. בְּסִיד שֶׁהִיא מַתֶּרְתוֹ בְתוֹךְ הַמּוֹעֵד נֶחְלְקוּ. אֲבָל בְּסִיד שֶׁהִיא מַתֶּרְתוֹ לְאַחַר הַמּוֹעֵד דִּבְרֵי הַכֹּל אָסוּר. וְחוֹרָנָה אָמַר. בְּסִיד שֶׁהִיא מַתֶּרְתוֹ לְאַחַר הַמּוֹעֵד נֶחְלְקוּ. אֲבָל בְּסִיד שֶׁהִיא מַתֶּרְתוֹ בְתוֹךְ הַמּוֹעֵד דִּבְרֵי הַכֹּל מוּתָּר. וְלֹא יָדְעִין מָאן אָמַר דָּא וּמָאן אָמַר דָּא. מִן מַה דְאָמַר רִבִּי חֲנִינָה רִבִּי יָסָא בְשֵׁם רִבִּי יוֹחָנָן. וְרִבִּי יוּדָה כְדַעְתֵּיהּ. כְּמָה דְרִבִּי יוּדָה אָמַר תַּמָּן. צָרַת שָׁעָה צָרָה. כֵּן הוּא אָמַר הָכָא. נִיווּל שָׁעָה נִיווּל. הֲוֵי דוּ אָמַר. בְּסִיד שֶׁהוּא מַתֶּרְתוֹ בְתוֹךְ הַמּוֹעֵד נֶחְלְקוּ. אֲבָל בְּסִיד שֶׁהִיא מַתֶּרְתוֹ לְאַחַר הַמּוֹעֵד דִּבְרֵי הַכֹּל אָסוּר.

"Rebbi Jehudah says, she may not use lime because it disfigures her." [133]Two Amoraim, Rebbi Hanina and Rebbi Mana[134]. One said, they disagreed about lime which she removed on the holiday[135], but lime which she removes after the holiday everybody agrees that it is forbidden[136]. But the other says, they disagreed about lime which she removes after the holiday. But lime which she removes during the holiday everybody agrees that it is permitted. We did not know who said what. From what R. Hanina, Rebbi Yasa said in the name of Rebbi Johanan, Rebbi Jehudah is consistent: just as Rebbi Jehudah said there, temporary pain is pain[137], so he says here, temporary disfiguration is disfiguration. This implies that they disagreed about lime which she removed on the holiday, but lime which she removes after the holiday is forbidden.

133 *Avodah zarah* 1:1, Notes 48-52; Babli 9b.
134 R. Mana I.
135 To be beautiful on the final day of the holiday.
136 As a misuse of the holiday.

137 In Mishnah *Avodah zarah* 1:1.

(fol. 80a) **משנה ה**: הַהֶדְיוֹט תּוֹפֵר כְּדַרְכּוֹ וְהָאוּמָן מְכַלֵּב. וּמְסָרְגִין אֶת הַמִּטּוֹת רִבִּי יוֹסֵי אוֹמֵר אַף מְמַתְּחִין:

Mishnah 5: The individual[138] sews normally but the professional staples[139]. And one makes a lattice for couches[140]; Rebbi Yose says also one tightens[141].

138 Greek 'ιδιώτης, used for any person not specially trained in a trade.

139 He must work somewhat unprofessionally, as explained in the Halakhah.

140 The mattress of a couch was supported by a lattice of ropes. Even though stringing the ropes turns a frame into a couch, it is permitted to do so on the intermediate days of the holiday.

141 If the ropes become somewhat loose, one may tighten them on the holiday to make the couch more enjoyable even though it still would be usable without tightening.

(80d line 57) **הלכה ח**: דְּבֵית רִבִּי יַנַּאי אֲמָרוּ. כְּדַרְכּוֹ מְמַלֵּא אֶת הַמַּחַט. מְכַלֵּב אַחַת אַחַת. רִבִּי יוֹחָנָן אָמַר. כְּדַרְכּוֹ אַחַת אַחַת. מְכַלֵּב מַפְסִיעַ. מַתְנִיתָהּ מְסַיְּיעָא לְרִבִּי יוֹחָנָן. הָרוֹצְעָנִין מַכְלִיבִין בַּמּוֹעֵד. אִין תֵּימַר אַחַת אַחַת. כָּךְ הִיא אוּמְנוּתָן. אֶלָּא כִי נָן קַיָּימִין בְּמַפְסִיעַ. אֵי זֶהוּ הֶדְיוֹט וְאֵי זֶהוּ אוּמָן. אָמַר רִבִּי יוֹסֵי בֶּן חֲנִינָה. כָּל־שֶׁהוּא מְזַוֵּיג אֶת הָאוֹמָרִיּוֹת זֶהוּ אוּמָן. וְכָל־שֶׁאֵינוֹ מְזַוֵּיג אֶת הָאוֹמָרִיּוֹת זֶה הוּא הֶדְיוֹט. אָמַר רִבִּי סִימוֹן. בְּתוֹפֵר כִּיסִין כִּיסִין הִיא מַתְנִיתָהּ.

Halakhah 8: In the House of Rebbi Yannai they said, "normally", he fills his needle. "Staples", stitch by stitch[142]. Rebbi Johanan said, "normally", stitch by stitch. "Staples", he jumps[143]. A *baraita* supports Rebbi Johanan: The cobblers are stapling on the holiday. If you would say stitch by stitch, that is what they are doing professionally. But we must hold that they sew irregularly. Who is an individual and who is a professional? Rebbi Yose ben Hanina said, one who matches seams is a professional, but any who does not match seams is an individual[144]. Rebbi Simon said, the Mishnah refers to those who sew pockets[145].

142 The unprofessional may fully use the thread in his needle; the professional has to take a new thread for every stitch. Nothing is said about the quality of the sewing.

143 The unprofessional may do his best on the holiday; the professional may not sew in

professional quality. Nothing is said about the quantity of the thread.
144 Babli 10a.

145 There are no seams to be matched. R. Yose ben Ḥanina's criterion is insufficient.

(80d line 63) מְמַתְּחִין. רִבִּי יָסָא אָמַר. אִיתְפַּלְגוּן חִזְקִיָּה וְרִבִּי יוֹחָנָן. חִזְקִיָּה אָמַר. סֵירוּג. שְׁתִי וָעֵרֶב. מִיתּוּחַ. אוֹ שְׁתִי אוֹ עֵרֶב. רִבִּי יוֹחָנָן אָמַר. סֵירוּג. אוֹ שְׁתִי אוֹ עֵרֶב. מִיתּוּחַ. הָיְתָה רָפָה מְמַתְּחָהּ. אָמַר רִבִּי חִייָה בַּר בָּא. הַכֹּל מוֹדִין בְּסֵירוּג שֶׁהוּא שְׁתִי וָעֵרֶב. מַה פְּלִיגִין. בְּמִיתּוּחַ. חִזְקִיָּה אָמַר. אוֹ שְׁתִי אוֹ עֵרֶב. רִבִּי יוֹחָנָן אָמַר. אִם הָיְתָה רָפָה מְמַתְּחָהּ. רִבִּי יָסָא הוֹרֵי לִשְׁמוּאֵל בַּר חֲנִינָה. סֵירוּג. שְׁתִי וָעֵרֶב. וְלָא יָדְעִין אִי כְהָדָא דְחִזְקִיָּה וְאִין כְּהָדָא דְרִבִּי חִייָה בַּר בָּא דִּבְרֵי הַכֹּל. אָמַר רִבִּי בּוּן בַּר חִייָה קוֹמֵי רִבִּי זְעוּרָה. מַתְנִיתָהּ אֳמָרָה כֵן. סֵירוּג. שְׁתִי וָעֵרֶב. דְּתַגִּינָן תַּמָּן. הַחֶבֶל מֵאֵימָתַי הוּא חִיבּוּר לַמִּיטָה. מִשֶּׁיְּסָרֵג בָּהּ שְׁלֹשָׁה בָתִּים. אִית לָךְ מֵימַר. שְׁתִי וְלֹא עֵרֶב אוֹ עֵרֶב וְלֹא שְׁתִי. מָהוּ לְהַעֲרִיב וּלְסָרֵג.

רַב הוֹשַׁעְיָה אִית לֵיהּ קֶמַח וְטָחַן חִטִּין. רִבִּי זְעוּרָה אָמַר לְרִבִּי יוֹנָה. פּוּק זְבוֹן לוֹן שִׁיחוֹרִין לְדוּכְנָהּ. אָמַר לֵיהּ. אִית לוֹן פִּילְחָה דְמוֹעֲדָא. וְאִיקְפַּד עֲלוֹי.

1 רב | G ר׳   2 פילחה | G פלחה   עלוי | G עלויי

"One tightens." [146]Rebbi Yasa said, Ḥizqiah and Rebbi Joḥanan disagree. Ḥisqiah said: making a lattice, warp and woof; tightening, either warp or woof. Rebbi Joḥanan said: making a lattice, either warp or woof; tightening, if it is loose he tightens it. Rebbi Hiyya bar Abba said, everybody agrees that making a lattice means warp and woof. Where do they disagree? About tightening. Ḥisqiah said: either warp or woof; Rebbi Joḥanan said: if it is loose he tightens it. Rebbi Yasa instructed Samuel bar Ḥanina that "making a lattice" means warp and woof. We do not know whether this follows Ḥizqiah or it follows Rebbi Hiyya bar Abba and everybody's opinion. Rebbi Abun bar Hiyya said before Rebbi Ze`ira: a Mishnah says so that making a lattice means warp and woof, as we have stated there[147], "when is the rope connected to the bed[148]? If he plaited three boxes." Could you say warp without woof or woof without warp? Could one pitch woof and make a lattice?

Rav Hoshaia had flour but he ground wheat[149]. Rebbi Ze`ira said to Rebbi Jonah[150]: go out and buy us black ones[151] to pound. He said to him, do we have a holiday grindstone? He was offended by him[151].

146 Babli 10a a different version of the entire argument
147 Mishnah *Kelim* 19:1.

148 That impurity is transferred from one to the other.
149 Even though he did not need new flour

for the holiday. It is permitted to grind food on the intermediate days without restriction. Babli 12b.

150 Student of R. Ze`ira.

151 Traditionally interpreted as a kind of black peas.

152 That the student dared to reject the teacher's ruling.

(fol. 80a) **משנה ו**: מַעֲמִידִין תַּנוּר וְכִירַיִם בַּמּוֹעֵד. רַבִּי יְהוּדָה אוֹמֵר אֵין מְכַבְּשִׁין אֶת הָרֵיחַיִם בַּתְּחִילָה: עוֹשִׂין מַעֲקֶה לַגַּג וְלַמִּרְפֶּסֶת מַעֲשֶׂה הֶדְיוֹט אֲבָל לֹא מַעֲשֶׂה אוּמָּן. שָׁפִין אֶת הַסְּדָקִין וּמַעֲגִּילִין אוֹתָן בַּמַּעֲגִילָה בַּיָּד וּבָרֶגֶל אֲבָל לֹא בַּמַּחְלָצַיִם.

Mishnah 6: One installs an oven and a stove[153] on the holiday. Rebbi Jehudah says, one does not roughen millstones initially on the holiday[154]. One makes a railing for the roof or the balustrade unprofessionally but not professionally[155]. One smooths the fissures[156] and works them with a roller[157], with hand, or with foot, but not with a spatula.

153 On the intermediate days one may bring a new oven and fix it on the ground with mortar.

154 Since smooth stones do not grind, millstones must be rough. To turn a smooth stone into a millstone is hard professional work. But remaking a millstone in use is permitted.

155 Since having a railing at dangerous places is a biblical commandment, emergency repairs can be made, to be made permanent after the holiday. The balustrade gives access to the apartments on the upper floor of a multi-family house.

156 One makes fissures of the roof disappear by filling with mortar.

157 Any round implement can be used as a roller to flatten the mortar.

(80d line 75) **הלכה ט**: תָּנֵא רִבִּי חֲלַפְתָּא בַּר שָׁאוּל. וּבִלְבַד שֶׁלֹּא יְגָדֲרֶנּוּ כַּתְּחִילָה. תַּנֵּי. תַּנּוּר וְכִירַיִם חֲדָשִׁים אֵין סָכִין אוֹתָן בַּשֶּׁמֶן וְאֵין טוֹלִין אוֹתָן בְּמַטְלִית וְאֵין חוֹסְמִין אוֹתָן בְּצוֹנִין בִּשְׁבִיל שֶׁיִּתְחַסְּמוּ. וְאִם בִּשְׁבִיל לִשְׁפּוֹת עֲלֵיהֶן אֶת הַקְּדֵירָה מוּתָּר. וְתַנֵּי כֵן. תַּנּוּר וְכִירַיִם חֲדָשִׁים הֲרֵי הֵן כְּכָל־הַכֵּלִים הַמִּיטַּלְטְלִין בֶּחָצֵר. רִבִּי יוּדָן בֵּירִבִּי יִשְׁמָעֵאל הוֹרֵי מִדּוֹחַק לְהָבִיא כִירָה חֲדָשָׁה מִבֵּית הָאוּמָּן לִשְׁפּוֹת עָלֶיהָ אֶת הַקְּדֵירָה כַּתְּחִילָה בְּיוֹם טוֹב.

1 חלפתא G | חלפתה בר G | בן 2 סכין G | סכים אותן G | אותם G | טולין טולים אותן G | חוסמין אותן | G חוסמים אותם בצונין G | בצונים 3 שיתחסמו G | שייתחסמו ואם G | אם לשפות G | לישפות 4 המיטלטלין G | המוטלטלים הורי G | אורי

Halakhah 9: Rebbi Ḥalaphta bar Shaul stated, only that it not be newly formed on the holiday[158]. It was stated: A new oven or stove one does neither soak with oil nor patch with a strip nor wash down with cold water to close its pores[159]. But in order to actually cook a pot on it this is permitted. And it was stated thus: New oven or stove are like all implements which are moved in a courtyard. Rebbi Yudan ben Rebbi Ismael instructed in an emergency to bring a new stove from the house of the potter to newly cook on it on the full holiday[160].

158 Babli 11a. Yerushalmi גדר is the same as Babli גדל by an change of liquids.

159 All these activities are the end of the production of the clay stove, not the start of its use which only is using it to cook a dish. Babli *Yom Ṭov (Beṣah)* 34a.

160 On the full holiday, not only on the intermediate days.

(fol. 80a) **משנה ז**: הַצִּיר וְהַצִּנּוֹר וְהַקּוֹרָה וְהַמַּנְעוּל וְהַמַּפְתֵּחַ שֶׁנִּשְׁבְּרוּ מְתַקְּנָן בַּמּוֹעֵד וּבִלְבַד שֶׁלֹּא יְכַוֵּין מְלַאכְתּוֹ בַּמּוֹעֵד. כְּבָשִׁין שֶׁהוּא יָכוֹל לֶאֱכוֹל מֵהֶן בַּמּוֹעֵד כּוֹבְשָׁן:

Mishnah 7: A hinge, and a pipe, and a beam, and a lock, and a key which were broken one fixes on the holiday on condition that he not plan his work[161] for the holiday. Any preserves of which one can eat on the holiday[162] one makes.

161 If they are broken before the start of the holiday one has to try to fix them before the start of the holiday.

162 Even if only a small part will be consumed on the holiday.

(81a line 6) **הלכה י**: לְגַג שְׁלֹשָׁה וּלְמִרְפֶּסֶת עֲשָׂרָה. שָׁפִין אֶת הַסְּדָקִין. תַּנֵּי רִבִּי חִיָּיה. הַשָּׁף שָׁף בְּרֶגֶל וְהַמְּעַגֵּל מְעַגֵּל בַּיָּד. מַתְנִיתָן בְּמַעֲגִילָה קְטַנָּה. וּמַה דְּתַנֵּי רִבִּי חִיָּיה בְּמַעֲגִילָה גְדוֹלָה.

1 שלשה G | שלושה   2 והמעגל G | המעגל   3 דתני G | תני

Halakhah 10: [163]For the roof three, for the balustrade ten {hand-widths}[164].

"One smooths the fissures." Rebbi Ḥiyya stated, he who smooths, smooths with his foot; he who uses a roller smooths with the hand. Our Mishnah is about a small roller, but what Rebbi Ḥiyya stated is about a large roller[165].

163 Discussion of the second part of Mishnah 6.
164 The height of railings provisionally installed on a holiday.
165 The Mishnah allows to control the roller both with hand or foot. The *baraita* which requires control by hand refers to a roller which cannot be controlled by foot. The Babli 11a interprets this as meaning that no roller is used at all but the action of a roller imitated by hand or foot. This cannot be read into the Yerushalmi.

(81a line 9) הַצִּיר וְהַצִּנּוֹר וְהַקּוֹרָה וְהַמַּנְעוּל וְהַמַּפְתֵּחַ שֶׁנִּשְׁבְּרוּ מְתַקְּנָן בַּמּוֹעֵד וּבִלְבַד שֶׁלֹּא יְכַוֵּין אֶת מְלַאכְתּוֹ בַּמּוֹעֵד. כְּהָדָא רִבִּי מָנָא אִיתְבַּר עוּקָא דְסוּלָמֵיהּ. שָׁאַל לְרִבִּי יוֹנָה אָבוֹי וְשָׁרָא לֵיהּ. אֲפִילוּ כֵן אָמַר לֵיהּ. פּוּק חֲמֵי חַד סָב וּסְמוֹךְ עֲלוֹי. נְפַק וְאַשְׁכַּח רִבִּי בּוּן בַּר כַּהֲנָא. וּשְׁאַל לֵיהּ וְשָׁרָא לֵיהּ.

2 כהדא G | כהדה איתבר עוקא דסולמיה G | אתבר עוקה דסולמה אבוי G | אביי ושרא G | ושרה 3 ליה G | לה כהנא G | כהנה 4 ושרא ליה G | ושרה

"A hinge, and a pipe, and a beam, and a lock, and a key which were broken one fixes on the holiday on condition that he not plan his work[161] for the holiday." As the following: Rebbi Mana's ladder's depression broke[166]. He asked his father Rebbi Jonah who permitted it. Nevertheless he told him, go out and find an Elder and rely on him[167]. He went out and found Rebbi Abun bar Cahana who permitted to him.

166 The stairs on which one mounted from the ground floor to the first floor of his house were fixed in a depression in the ground floor, whose wooden casing broke on the holiday.
167 While there was no doubt that the repairs were permitted on the intermediate days of the holiday and he was the Chief Rabbi, he did not want to appear lenient to his own family.

(81a line 13) וְכָל־כְּבָשִׁים שֶׁהוּא יָכוֹל לוֹכַל מֵהֶן בַּמּוֹעֵד כּוֹבְשָׁן׃ הָא כְבָשִׁין שֶׁאֵינוֹ יָכוֹל לוֹכַל מֵהֶן בַּמּוֹעֵד לֹא. אָמַר רִבִּי בָּא. הָדָא דַתְּ אָמַר בְּשֶׁאֵינָן אֲבוּדִין. אֲבָל אִם הָיָה דָבָר אָבֵד מוּתָּר. תַּנֵי. לֹא יְהֵא יוֹצֵא וּמְלַקֵּט עֲשָׂבִים וּמוֹכְרָן בַּשּׁוּק שֶׁאֵין דַּרְכּוּ לוֹכַל מֵהֶן בַּמּוֹעֵד. אָמַר רַב הוֹשַׁעְיָה. אִם אוֹמֵר אַתְּ כֵּן נִמְצֵאתָה מַתִּיר אֶת הָאוּמָּנוּת בַּמּוֹעֵד. לֹא כֵן אָמַר רִבִּי בָּא. הָדָא דַתְּ אָמַר בְּשֶׁאֵינָן אֲבִידִין. אֲבָל אִם הָיָה דָבָר אָבֵד מוּתָּר. מַתְנִיתָהּ בְּשֶׁלְּקָטָן בָּרֶגֶל. מַה דְּאָמַר רִבִּי בָּא. בְּשֶׁלְּקָטָן מֵעֶרֶב הָרֶגֶל.

"Any preserves of which one can eat on the holiday[162] one makes." Therefore not preserves of which one cannot eat on the holiday. Rebbi Abba said, this you are saying if they would not spoil. But things apt to spoil are permitted[168]. It was stated: One may not go out and collect[169] greenery which is not usually eaten on the holiday and sell it on the market. Rav Hoshaia said, if you would say so you would permit professional work on the holiday. But did not Rebbi Abba say, this you are saying if they would not spoil; but things apt to spoil are permitted[170]? The *baraita* if he collected it on the holiday; what Rebbi Abba said if he collected it on the eve of the holiday[171].

168 Any foodstuff which is in danger to spoil may be preserved on the intermediate days of the holiday.
169 Harvest from the soil.
170 If the vegetables which will spoil quickly may be preserved, why can they not be sold to be eaten, even if out of season?
171 Anything harvested legitimately may be preserved, but nothing harvested on the holiday itself falls under this rule. Cf. Babli 11a.

מי שהפך פרק שני מועד קטן

(fol. 81a) **משנה א**: מִי שֶׁהָפַךְ אֶת זֵיתָיו וְאֵירְעוֹ אֵבֶל אוֹ אוֹנֶס אוֹ שֶׁהִטְעוּהוּ פּוֹעֲלִין טוֹעֵן קוֹרָה רִאשׁוֹנָה וּמַנִּיחָהּ לְאַחַר הַמּוֹעֵד דִּבְרֵי רִבִּי יְהוּדָה. רִבִּי יוֹסֵי אוֹמֵר זוֹלֵף וְגוֹמֵר כְּדַרְכּוֹ׃

Mishnah 1: If one turned his olives over[1] and mourning or an emergency happened to him[2], or he was mislead[3], loads the crossbar a first time and leaves it until after the holiday[4], the words of Rebbi Jehudah. Rebbi Yose says, he removes the fluid, and finishes as usual[5].

1 He started treating the olives in a vat before emptying them into the olive press in order to soften them to release their oil. There is a danger that the harvest will spoil if the pressing is delayed.

2 By circumstances beyond his control he was prevented from pressing the olives before the start of the holiday.

3 He hired workers who did not show up.

4 On the holiday he may load the olives into the press and apply the usual pressure by covering the olives with a plank which is held down by a crossbar. Then the extra virgin olive oil will flow out but nothing more. According to R. Jehudah (who usually presents the opinion of R. Eliezer) that is all he may do; he may have to lose the later pressings.

5 If the delay was not the fault of the oil producer, he may press all the oil from the harvest, clean up, and plug the vessels in which the oil is stored.

(81a line 48) מִי שֶׁהָפַךְ אֶת זֵיתָיו כול'. אֲנַן תַּנִּינָן. מִי שֶׁהָפַךְ אֶת זֵיתָיו. תַּנֵּי רִבִּי חִייָה. מִי שֶׁהָיוּ זֵיתָיו הֲפוּכִין וּשְׁנוּיִין. מַתְנִיתָן צְרִיכָה לְרִבִּי חִייָה וּדְרִבִּי חִייָה צְרִיכָה לְמַתְנִיתָן.

Text of Scribe

אִילּוּ תַּנִּינָן וְלָא תַּנָא רִבִּי חִייָה הֲוֵיהוֹן אֲמָרִין. לָא אֲמָרָן אֶלָּא מִי שֶׁהֲפָכָן וּשְׁנָייָן. אֲבָל אִם הֲפָכָן פַּעַם אַחַת דִּבְרֵי הַכֹּל אָסוּר. הֲוֵי צוֹרְכָה לְמַתְנִיתֵיהּ דְּרִבִּי חִייָה. אוֹ אִילּוּ תַּנָא רִבִּי חִייָה וְלָא תַּנִּינָן אֲנָן. הֲוֵיהוֹן אֲמָרִין. לָא אֲמָרָן אֶלָּא מִי שֶׁהֲפָכָן פַּעַם אַחַת. אֲבָל אִם הֲפָכָן וּשְׁנָייָן דִּבְרֵי הַכֹּל מוּתָּר. הֲוֵי צוֹרְכָא לְמַתְנִיתָן וְצוֹרְכָא לְמַתְנִיתָא דְּרִבִּי חִייָה.

Text of Venice editor

אִילּוּ תַּנִּינָן וְלָא תַּנָא רִבִּי חִייָה הֲוֵייָנָא אֲמָרִין. לָא אֲמָרָן אֶלָּא מִי שֶׁהֲפָכָן פַּעַם אַחַת. אֲבָל אִם הֲפָכָן וּשְׁנָייָן דִּבְרֵי הַכֹּל מוּתָּר. הֲוֵי צוֹרְכָה לְמַתְנִיתֵיהּ דְּרִבִּי חִייָה. אוֹ אִילּוּ תַּנָא רִבִּי חִייָה וְלָא תַּנִּינָן אֲנָן. הֲוֵיהוֹן אֲמָרִין. לָא אֲמָרָן אֶלָּא מִי שֶׁהֲפָכָן וּשְׁנָייָן. אֲבָל אִם הֲפָכָן פַּעַם אַחַת דִּבְרֵי הַכֹּל אָסוּר. הֲוֵי צוֹרְכָא לְמַתְנִיתָן וְצוֹרְכָא לְמַתְנִיתָא דְּרִבִּי חִייָה.

"If one turned his olives over," etc. We stated, "if one turned his olives over." Rebbi Ḥiyya stated, he whose olives were turned over repeatedly[6]. Our Mishnah needs the statement of Rebbi Ḥiyya, and the statement of Rebbi Ḥiyya needs our Mishnah.

Text of Scribe

[7]If we had stated but Rebbi Ḥiyya had not stated, we would have said, we only said if he repeatedly had turned them over, but if he turned then over once everybody agrees that it is forbidden. Therefore our Mishnah needs the statement of Rebbi Ḥiyya. Or if Rebbi Ḥiyya had stated but not we, we would have said that we only said if he turned them over once. But if he repeatedly turned them over, everybody agrees that it is permitted. Therefore there is need for our Mishnah and need for the *baraita* of Rebbi Ḥiyya.

Text of Venice editor

If we had stated but Rebbi Ḥiyya had not stated, we would have said, we only said if he had turned them over only once, but if he turned then over repeatedly everybody[8] agrees that it is permitted. Therefore our Mishnah needs the statement of Rebbi Ḥiyya. Or if Rebbi Ḥiyya had stated but not we, we would have said that we only said if he turned them over repeatedly. But if he turned them over only once, everybody agrees that it is forbidden. Therefore there is need for our Mishnah and need for the *baraita* of Rebbi Ḥiyya.

6 Under these circumstances also he notes the disagreement of RR. Jehudah and Yose.
7 It is clear that this text reads our Mishnah as R. Ḥiyya's and R. Ḥiyya's text as that of the Mishnah. The Venice text is logically correct.
8 R. Jehudah in that case could have been presumed to agree with R. Yose. R. Ḥiyya states that he did not.

(81a line 55) אָמַר רִבִּי פִינְחָס בֵּירִבִּי זַכָּיי. מַתְנִיתָן בָּעֲטִינִים. מַה דְתַנֵּי רִבִּי חִייָה בְּגַרְגְּרִים. רַבָּנִן דְּקַיְסָרִין אָמְרִין. מַתְנִיתָן כְּרִבִּי יוּדָה. וּמַה דְתַנֵּי רִבִּי חִייָה כְּרִבִּי יוֹסֵה. רִבִּי יוּדָה אוֹמֵר. יָאבֵד דָּבָר מְמוּעָט וְאַל יָאבֵד דָּבָר מְרוּבֶּה. רִבִּי יוֹסֵה אוֹמֵר. אַל יָאבֵד דָּבָר כָּל־עִיקָר.
1 בעטינים G | בעטנים   2 רבנן | רבנין אמרין G | אמר או׳ | G אמ׳   3 יאבד G | יאביד   מרובה G | מרובא   יאבד G | יאביד

Rebbi Phineas ben Rebbi Zakkai said, our Mishnah is about macerated ones, what Rebbi Ḥiyya stated is about berries[9]. The rabbis of Caesarea are saying, the Mishnah follows Rebbi Jehudah, what Rebbi Hiyya stated follows Rebbi Yose[10]. Rebbi Jehudah said, small amounts may be lost so large amounts would not be lost; Rebbi Yose says, nothing at all shall be lost.

9   He holds that R. Jehudah permits to load the olives into the press only if the oil started to flow out. Therefore if the olives are already in a state where oil is flowing he agrees that they belong into the press but not if their skins are intact. When the berries have been turned over several times they are macerated.

10   One cannot say that either of the texts follows one rabbi since both mention both authorities. But the Mishnah emphasizes the position of Rebbi Jehudah who permits only marginal activities to avoid large losses and the *baraita* emphasizes the point of view of R. Yose that every loss of edibles has to be prevented.

(81a line 59) רִבִּי יוּדָה בַּר פָּזִי בְּשֵׁם רִבִּי יוֹחָנָן. כְּשֵׁם שֶׁהֵן חֲלוּקִין כָּאן כָּךְ הֵן חֲלוּקִין בְּהִילְכוֹת אֵבֶל. דְּתַנֵּי. אֵילּוּ דְבָרִים שֶׁעוֹשִׂין לָאָבֵל בִּימֵי אֶבְלוֹ. דּוֹרְכִין אֶת עֲבָטוֹ. וְזוֹלְפִין אֶת יֵינוֹ. וְגָפִין אֶת חָבִיּוֹתָיו. וְזֵיתָיו הֲפוּכִין וּשְׁנוּיִין טוֹחֲנָן כְּדַרְכָּן. וּמַשְׁקִין בֵּית הַשַּׁלְחִין שֶׁלּוֹ בְּשֶׁהִגִּיעַ זְמַנּוֹ לִשְׁתּוֹת. וְזוֹרְעִין אֶת נִירוֹ פִּשְׁתָּן בָּרְבִיעָה. דִּבְרֵי רִבִּי יוּדָה. אָמְרוּ לוֹ. אִם אֵינָהּ נִזְרַעַת פִּשְׁתָּן תִּזָּרַע מִין אַחֵר. אִם אֵינָהּ נִזְרַעַת בְּשַׁבָּת זוֹ תִּזָּרַע בְּשַׁבָּת אֲחֶרֶת. מָנוּ אָמְרוּ לוֹ. רִבִּי יוֹסֵה. מִחְלְפָה שִׁיטָתֵיהּ דְּרִבִּי יוּדָה. תַּמָּן הוּא אָמַר. יֹאבַד דָּבָר מְמוּעָט וְאַל יֹאבַד דָּבָר מְרוּבֶּה. וְכָא אָמַר הָכֵין. שַׁנְיָא הִיא. תַּמָּן שֶׁדַּרְכּוֹ לְהֵעָרִים. וְכָל־שֶׁכֵּן מִחְלְפָה שִׁיטָתֵיהּ דְּרִבִּי יוּדָה. מָה אִית תַּמָּן שֶׁדַּרְכּוֹ לְהֵעָרִים אַתְּ אָמַר מוּתָּר. כָּאן שֶׁאֵין דַּרְכּוֹ לְהֵעָרִים לֹא כָל־שֶׁכֵּן. אָמַר רִבִּי חִינָּנָא. מָנוּ אָמְרוּ לוֹ. חֲכָמִים. שֶׁהֵן בְּשִׁיטַת רִבִּי יוּדָה בַּמּוֹעֵד.

1 חלוקין | G חלוקים (2) | בהילכות | G בהלכות   2 אבל | G אביל   שעושין | G שעושים   דורכין | G דורכים   וזולפין | G וזולפים   וגפין | G וגפים   3 את חביותיו | G חביּיותיו   ושנויין | G ושניים   ומשקין | G ומשקים   השלחין | G השלחים   בשהגיע | G משהגיע   זמנו | G זמן   4 לשתות | G לישתות   וזורעין | G וזורעים את   נירו | G ניריו   נזרעת | G ניזרעת (2)   6 אמ' | G מר   מרובה | G מרובא   וכא | G וכה   7 אמ' הכין | G מר הכן וכל | G כל   שיטתיה | G שטתה   8 כאן | G כן   9 בשיטת | G כשיטת

Rebbi Jehudah bar Pazi in the name of Rebbi Johanan: Just as they[11] differ here they differ in the rules of mourning. As it was stated[12]: The following things one does for the mourner in his mourning period. One presses his vat, and stirs his wine, and plugs his amphoras, and his repeatedly turned olives one grinds as usual[13], and one waters his irrigated fields if it is time for them to be irrigated[14], and one sows his field flax at the start of the rainy season[15], the words of Rebbi Jehudah. They told him, if it is not sown with flax it can be sown with another kind; if it was not sown in this week it can be sown in another week[16]. Who is "they told him"? Rebbi Yose[17]. The argument of Rebbi Jehudah seems inverted. There he said, small amounts may be lost so large amounts not be lost, and here he says so? There is a difference since there he is wont to be tricky[18]. So much more the argument of Rebbi Jehudah seems inverted, since there where he is wont to be tricky he says it is permitted, here where he is not wont to be tricky, not so much more? Rebbi Ḥinnena said, who is "they told him"? The Sages following Rebbi Jehudah's argument for the holiday[19].

11 R. Jehudah and R. Yose, referring to the week following the burial when the mourner is prohibited gainful work.
12 Babli 11b.
13 After they have been pressed, to recoup the remaining oil (of lesser quality.)
14 If his fields are allotted a certain time spot in the public water system, not using the water would cause major loss. While on the holiday he irrigates himself, in his week of mourning this has to be done by third parties.
15 Since if not seeded at that time the flax harvest would be lost.
16 Even though the other crop may be of lesser value. In the corresponding case for the holidays, this seems to correspond more to R. Jehudah's position than to R. Yose's.
17 Since he is the only known dissenter from R. Jehudah's opinion.
18 Nobody plans to do work during the mourning week whereas the Mishnah is full of warnings not to plan work for the holiday week.
19 The statement of R. Joḥanan is disproved and R. Jehudah's statement for holiday and mourning week are not identical.

(fol. 81a) **משנה ב:** וְכֵן מִי שֶׁהָיָה יֵינוֹ בְּתוֹךְ הַבּוֹר וְאֵירְעוֹ אֵבֶל אוֹ אוֹנֶס אוֹ שֶׁהִטְעוּהוּ זוֹלֵף וְגוֹמֵר וְגָף כְּדַרְכּוֹ דִּבְרֵי רִבִּי יוֹסֵי. רִבִּי יְהוּדָה אוֹמֵר עוֹשֶׂה לוֹ לִימוּדִים בִּשְׁבִיל שֶׁלֹּא יַחְמִיץ:

Mishnah 2: Similarly, if his wine was in the cistern and mourning or an emergency happened to him[2], or he was mislead[3], he may stir and treat and plug normally, the words of Rebbi Yose. Rebbi Jehudah says, he makes planks for it so it should not turn into vinegar[20].

20 Since R. Yose permits to plug the wine amphoras he clearly allows to draw the wine from the cistern, filter out the yeast, and store the wine. R. Jehudah only allows to stop the action of the yeast in the cistern, not to remove the wine.

(81a line 71) **הלכה ב**: אָמַר רִבִּי זְעוּרָה. לֹא אָמַר אֶלָּא וְכֵן מִי שֶׁהָיָה יֵינוֹ בְּתוֹךְ הַבּוֹר. הָא כַּתְּחִילָה אָסוּר. מָה אֲנָן קַייָמִין. אִם בְּשֶׁהִגִּיעַ זְמַנּוֹ לִבְצוֹר וְלֹא בָצַר הוּא חָטָא עַל נַפְשֵׁיהּ. אִם בְּשֶׁלֹּא הִגִּיעַ זְמַנּוֹ לִבְצוֹר יְכִיל הֲוָה קָאִים. אֶלָּא כִּי נָן קַייָמִין בְּשֶׁהִגִּיעַ זְמַנּוֹ לִבְצוֹר הֲוָה סָבוּר דּוּ יְכִיל קַיָּים וְלֹא קָם. כְּהָדָא רִבִּי שִׁמְעוֹן בֵּירִבִּי יַנַּיי קָטַף כַּרְמֵיהּ בְּמוֹעֲדָא. חֲמוֹנֵיהּ כָּל-עַמָּא וְקַטְפוּן בַּתְרֵיהּ בְּשַׁתָּא חוֹרִיתָא שֶׁבְקֵיהּ וַיָּבָשׁ. יָלְפוּן מְקַלְקַלְתָּא וּמִתְקַנְתָּא לֹא יָלְפוּן.

Halakhah 2: Rebbi Ze`ira said, it only says "if his wine was in the cistern." Therefore to start is forbidden. Where do we hold? If it was time to harvest the grapes and he did not harvest, he caused the damage to himself. If it was not time for the grape harvest, what could he have done? But we must hold that the time for the grape harvest arrived and he thought that he could finish but he could not. As the following[21]: Rebbi Simeon ben Rebbi Yannai harvested his vineyard on the holiday. Everybody saw him and harvested after him. In another year[22] he left it and it dried up. They are learning the wrong behavior but are not learning the correct behavior.

רַב חִייָה בַּר אַשִׁי בְּשֵׁם רַב. הוֹחָרָא שָׁרִי מֵיעַבְדִּינָהּ בְּמוֹעֲדָא לָצוּד בּוֹ דָגִים בַּמּוֹעֵד. רַב יְהוּדָה הוֹרֵי בְּאִילֵּין מָהוֹלַיָּיא שָׁרִי מֵיעַבְדִּינָן בְּמוֹעֲדָא לְצוֹרֶךְ הַמּוֹעֵד. רִבִּי אַמִּי הוֹרֵי בְּאִילֵּין פּוּמְפַּיָּיא שָׁרִי מֵיעַבְדִּינָן בְּמוֹעֲדָא לְצוֹרֶךְ הַמּוֹעֵד. רַבָּנָן דְּקַיְסָרִין אָמְרֵי. מַסִּיקִין לַפְסִין וּקְדֵירוֹת לְצוֹרֶךְ הַמּוֹעֵד. שְׁמוּאֵל אָמַר. זָפְתִין גַּרְבָּא וְלֹא זָפְתִין כּוּזְתָא. זָפְתִין גַּרְבָּא. דְּזִיפְתָא דְּקַדְקֵירָא. וְלֹא זָפְתִין כּוּזְתָא. דְּזִיפְתָא גְּלִידָא. אִית דִּמְחַלְּפִין. זָפְתִין כּוּזְתָא וְלֹא זָפְתִין גַּרְבָּא. זָפְתִין כּוּזְתָא. דְּהִיא לְשָׁעָה. וְלֹא זָפְתִין גַּרְבָּא. שֶׁהִיא לִשְׁחוּת.

Rav Ḥiyya bar Ashi in the name of Rav: One is permitted to knit a net on the holiday to catch fish on the holiday. Rav Jehudah instructed that sieves may be made on the holiday for the needs of the holiday. Rebbi Immi instructed that *pompa*[23] may be made on the holiday for the needs of the holiday. The rabbis of Caesarea are saying, one fires pans and pots[24] for the needs of the holiday. Samuel said, one pitches barrels but one does not pitch pitchers. One pitches barrels since the pitch is thin; one does not pitch pitchers since the pitch is glazed. Some do switch: one pitches pitchers but one does not pitch barrels[24]. One pitches pitchers since this is for immediate use; one does not pitch barrels, since this is for storage.

21 Babli 12b.
22 Not the following year, but the first year in which Tabernacles was the time of grape harvest.
23 An unidentified utensil.
24 Since ceramic ware must be fired before

use, these are not implements at the start of the holiday.. 24 Babli 12a.

(fol. 81a) **משנה ג**: מַכְנִיס אָדָם פֵּירוֹתָיו מִפְּנֵי הַגַּנָּבִים וְשׁוֹלֶה פִּשְׁתָּנוֹ מִן הַמִּשְׁרָה בִּשְׁבִיל שֶׁלֹּא תֹאבַד וּבִלְבַד שֶׁלֹּא יְכַוֵּין אֶת מְלַאכְתּוֹ בַּמּוֹעֵד. וְכוּלָּן אִם כִּוְּנוּ אֶת מְלַאכְתָּן בַּמּוֹעֵד יֹאבֵדוּ:

Mishnah 3: A person may haul in his produce[25] because of thieves and remove his flax from the steeping[26] to avoid spoiling on condition that he not plan his work on the holiday. In all cases if they planned their work for the holiday it should spoil.

25 Which may mean harvesting or removing his standing sheaves from the field.

26 A necessary procedure to obtain the fibers from the stalks.

(81b line 10) **הלכה ג**: וּדְלָא כְרִבִּי יוּדָה. דְּרִבִּי יוּדָה אָמַר. יוֹשֵׁב וְשׁוֹמֵר. רִבִּי יַעֲקֹב בַּר אֲחָא בְּשֵׁם רַבָּנָן. פְּרַגְמַטְיָא אֲבֵדָה שָׁרֵי מְטַלְטְלָתָהּ בַּמּוֹעֲדָא. רִבִּי יַעֲקֹב בַּר אֲחָא בְּשֵׁם רִבִּי יָסָא. הָדָא שְׁיָירְתָּא שָׁרֵי מִיזְבּוֹן מִינָהּ בְּמוֹעֲדָא. הֲוָה יָדַע דַּשְׁיָירְתָּא מֵעוּל וּמֵיזְלָא עִיבִידְתֵּיהּ. אָמַר רִבִּי מָנָא. אִין יָדַע דְּלֹא(א) מִיזְבַּן וְהוּא פְּחַת מִן אַגְרָא יַזְבִּין. [אֲמַר רִבִּי יוֹסֵי בַּר בּוּן. אַגְרָא וְקַרְנָא קֶרֶן הוּא. אִין יָדַע דְּלָא מַזְבֵּין וְהוּא פְּחַת מִן קַרְנָא יַזְבִּין. וְאִי לָא לָא יַזְבִּין.] רִבִּי יוֹנָה וְרִבִּי יוֹסֵה הוֹרוֹן בְּהָדֵין לְסוֹטָה שָׁרֵי מְזַבַּנְתֵּיהּ בְּמוֹעֲדָא לְצוֹרֶךְ הַמּוֹעֵד. רִבִּי יִצְחָק בֵּירִבִּי לָעְזֵר מִפַּקַּד לְרִבִּי הוֹשַׁעְיָה בֵּירִבִּי שַׁמַּי דַּהֲוָה פָרוֹשׁ. אִין אַתְּ יָדַע דְּאַתְּ מַזְבֵּן וְאִילְפָא מוּרְכָּא לָךְ וְאַתְּ אֲתֵי (מִסְתֵּי) [מִשְׁתֵּי] גַּבָּן זְבִין. וְאִילָּא לָא תַזְבִּין. רִבִּי יוֹנָה בּוֹצְרַיָּה הֲוָה לֵיהּ סִפְרָן. שְׁאַל לְרִבִּי הוּנָא. מַחוּ מְזַבְּנָתוֹן בְּמוֹעֲדָא. אָמַר לֵיהּ. מַחְדֵּי אַתְּ מוֹעֲדָא שְׁתֵי אַתְּ קוֹנְדִּיטוֹן.

6 הורון G | אורון מזבנתיה G | מזבנתה במועדא G | במועדה 7 שמי G | שמיי אין G | אן ואילפא מורכא G | ואלפה מורכה 8 זבין G | זבן ואילא G | ואן לא תזבין G | תזבן בוצריה G | בוצרייה ספרן G | ספרין 9 הונא G | חונה במועדא G | במועדה מועדא G | מועדה

Halakhah 3: And not following Rebbi Jehudah, since Rebbi Jehudah said, he sits and watches[27]. Rebbi Jacob bar Aḥa in the name of the rabbis: merchandise[27a] in danger of spoilage may be moved[28] on the holiday. Rebbi Jacob bar Aḥa in the name of Rebbi Yasa: it is permitted to buy from a caravan on the intermediate days of a holiday[29], if he knows that the caravan comes and depresses the prices. Rebbi Mana said, if he knows that not buying would depress his earnings he may buy; otherwise he may not buy. [Rebbi Yose bar Abun said, earnings and capital are capital. If he knows that not buying would depress his capital he may buy; if not he may not buy.][30] Rebbi Jonah and Rebbi Yose instructed in the matter of fine tissues[31] that one may buy them on the holiday to be used on he holiday. Rebbi Isaac ben Rebbi Eleazar commanded to Rebbi Hoshaia ben Rebbi Shammai who was coming from a ship: Sell if you know that if you are selling the ship will wait for you when you come to drink with us[31]; otherwise do not sell. Rebbi Jonah from Bostra had books. He asked Rebbi Huna, may I sell them on the holiday? He told him, enjoy the holiday, drink spiced wine[32].

27 He forbids transporting anything not connected with use on holiday; he prefers that the farmer spend his holiday on the field guarding it rather than permitting agricultural activities without direct connection to the holiday.

27a Greek πραγματεία.

28 Moved to a safe place for sale after the holiday.

29 This will involve a major business transaction not connected to the enjoyment of the holiday.

30 Addition of the editor of the Venice *editio princeps*; source unknown.

31 Cf. *Šabbat* 4, Note 45.

32 Latin *conditum (vinum)*. Some of the proceeds must be spent on extra holiday expenses.

(81b line 22) רִבִּי חֲנַנְיָה חַבְרֵין דְּרַבָּנִין אָמַר. פְּרַגְמַטְיָא נִגְבֵּית מִנִּכְסֵי יְתוֹמִין קַטַּנִּים. הַוֹוֹן בָּעֵיי מֵימַר. בְּשֶׁיֵּשׁ עֵדִים. הָא אִם אֵין עֵדִים יוֹדְעִין לֹא. רַבָּנָן דְּקֵיסָרִין בְּשֵׁם רִבִּי לָא. לָכֵן צְרִיכָה בְּשֶׁיֵּשׁ עֵדִים יוֹדְעִין. הָא אִם אֵין עֵדִים יוֹדְעִין נַעֲשִׂית דְּפִיקָדוֹן. [כָּךְ אָנוּ אוֹמְרִים] פִּיקָדוֹן לֹא יִנָּבֶה מִנִּכְסֵי יְתוֹמִין קַטַּנִּים. מַה בֵינוֹ לַמִּלְוֶה. מִלְוָה נִיתְנָה לְהוֹצָאָה. וְזֶה לֹא נִיתַּן לְהוֹצָאָה.

1 חבריין G | חברון פרגמטיא G | פרגמטיה יתומין G | יתומים קטנים G | קטנין   2 בשיש G | בשייש עדים G | עדים יודעים   יודעין לא G | ידעים לה רבנן | רבניו לא G | אלא לכן G | לכן למן   3 בשיש עדים יודעין G | בשייש עדים יודעים ידעין G | ידעים כך G | כך   4 ייגבה G | יגבא יתומין G | יתומים למלוה G | למלווה מלוה G | מלווה ניתן G | ניתנה

Rebbi Ḥananiah the colleague of the rabbis said, merchandize is foreclosed from the property of orphans[33]. They wanted to say, if there are witnesses; therefore not if there are no witnesses. The Rabbis of Caesarea in the name of Rebbi La: It is necessary that witnesses know since if there are no witnesses who know it is treated as a deposit. [So we are saying,][34] a deposit is not forclosed from the property of minor orphans. What is the difference from a loan? A loan is given to be spent, but this was not given to be spent³⁵.

33 Since the rules of merchandize in emergency situations are discussed, another rule is mentioned of the same category. Merchandize given in commission can be retrieved from minor heirs even though most other claims must be frozen until the defendants come of age and are able to dispute outsiders' claims.

34 Addition of the Venice editor, confirmed by G.

35 *Qiddušin* 2:1 (Note 78), Babli 47a.

(81b line 27) אָמַר רִבִּי בָּא בַּר מָמָל. אִילּוּ הָיָה לִי מִי שֶׁיִּימָנֶה עַמִּי הִיתַּרְתִּי בְּשַׂר בְּכוֹר לְהִישָּׁקֵל בְּלִיטְרָא וְהִיתַּרְתִּי שֶׁיִּהוּ עוֹשִׂין מְלָאכָה בְחוֹלוֹ שֶׁלְמּוֹעֵד. כְּלוּם אָסְרוּ בְּשַׂר בְּכוֹר לְהִישָּׁקֵל בְּלִיטְרָא לֹא כְדֵי שֶׁיִּהוּ מוֹכְרִין אוֹתוֹ בְזוֹל. וְהֵן מַעֲרִימִין עָלָיו וּמוֹכְרִין אוֹתוֹ בְּיוֹקֶר. כְּלוּם אָסְרוּ לַעֲשׂוֹת מְלָאכָה בְחוֹלוֹ שֶׁלְמוֹעֵד אֶלָּא כְדֵי שֶׁיִּהוּ אוֹכְלִין וְשׁוֹתִין וִיגִיעִין בַּתּוֹרָה. וְאִינּוּן אֲכָלִין וְשָׁתִין וּפָחֲזִין.

אָמַר רִבִּי יוֹחָנָן. אִם הִזְכִּירוּךְ לְבוּלֵי יְהִיה בַּעַל גְּבוּלָךְ. אָמַר רִבִּי יוֹחָנָן. קְבְלִין לָרָשׁוּת לְהִיפָּטֵר מִבּוּלֵי. אָמַר רִבִּי יוֹחָנָן. לוֹוִין בְּרִיבִּית לַחֲבוּרַת מִצְוָה וּלְקִידּוּשׁ הַחוֹדָשׁ. רִבִּי יוֹחָנָן בְּצַפְרָא הֲוָה נְחַת לִכְנִישְׁתָּא וְהֲוָה מְלַקֵּט פֵּירוּרִין וַאֲכָל וַאֲמַר. יְהֵא חָלְקִי עִם אִילֵּין דַּאֲכָלוּן הָכָא רוּמְשִׁית.

Rebbi Abba bar Mamal said, If there were somebody who would vote with me, I would permit to sell firstling meat by the pound³⁶ and I would permit to work on the intermediate days of the holiday³⁷. They only forbade to sell firstling meat by the pound so it should be sold cheaply³⁸; but they are tricky about it and selling it dearly. They only forbade to work on the intermediate days of the holiday so they should eat, and drink, and exert themselves in Torah; but they eat, and drink, and behave wantonly.

³⁹Rebbi Joḥanan said, if you were nominated for the city council, may the Jordan be the master of your border⁴⁰. Rebbi Joḥanan said, one complains to the government to be freed from the city council⁴¹. Rebbi Joḥanan said, one borrows against interest for a company of obligation and the sanctification of the month. Rebbi Joḥanan used to go to the assembly hall in the morning⁴², collect the crumbs, and eat them, saying: May my part be with those who ate here in the evening.

36 Mishnah *Bekhorot* 5:1.

37 The prohibition has no explicit biblical basis.

38 This is clearly the thrust of the Mishnah. Even though the biblical text repeatedly declares the defective firstling as intrinsically profane, its meat is sold at premium prices because of its connection with *sancta*.

39 This paragraph is a slight reformulation of a paragraph in *Sanhedrin* 8:2 (Notes 32-35). It refers to the implication of the earlier parts of this Halakhah that one only is permitted to earn money on the intermediate days of a holiday in order to have more money to spend on festive meals.

40 Since the Roman government never allowed local taxes, it appointed rich people to the council (βουλή); these had to provide public services at their own expense. To avoid such an onerous *leiturgia*, one is permitted to leave the Land of Israel.

41 While in general one should avoid contact with Roman imperial officials, it is permitted to file complaints to make oneself undesirable, so as not to be considered for a council appointment.

42 Before he became a member of the body fixing the calendar.

(fol. 81a) **משנה ד**: אֵין לוֹקְחִין בָּתִּים עֲבָדִים וּבְהֵמָה אֶלָּא לְצוֹרֶךְ הַמּוֹעֵד אוֹ לְצוֹרֶךְ הַמּוֹכֵר שֶׁאֵין לוֹ מַה יֹּאכַל. אֵין מְפַנִּין מִבַּיִת לְבַיִת אֲבָל מְפַנֶּה הוּא לַחֲצֵרוֹ מִפְּנֵי שֶׁשִּׂמְחָה הִיא לוֹ. אֵין מְבִיאִין כֵּלִים מִבֵּית הָאוּמָּן וְאִם חוֹשֵׁשׁ לָהֶן מְפַנָּן לְחָצֵר אַחֶרֶת:

Mishnah 4: One only buys[43] houses, slaves, animals, or stones, for the needs of the holiday or for the needs of the seller who otherwise would not have anything to eat. One does not evacuate from place to place[44], but he may evacuate into his own courtyard[45] since this causes him joy. One does not bring vessels from the potter's house[46]; but if he[47] is afraid for them he evacuates them into another courtyard.

43 From Jews.
44 Both of which are the owner's property.
45 Moving his own movable property into his own real estate is permitted without restrictions.
46 Except in cases of need as stated in Chapter 1, Note 160.
47 The potter is afraid of thieves.

(81b line 37) **הלכה ד**: נִיחָא כּוּלְּהוֹן. אֲבָנִים. כְּהָדָא. אִם הָיָה כּוֹתְלוֹ גּוֹחֶה סוֹתְרוֹ וּבוֹנֵהוּ. וְיִסְתּוֹר וְלֹא יְבְנֶה. רְבִּי חֲנַנְיָה בְשֵׁם רְבִּי יוֹחָנָן. הִתִּירוּ סוֹפוֹ מִפְּנֵי תְחִילָּתוֹ. שֶׁאִם אוֹמֵר אַתְּ לוֹ שֶׁלֹּא יִבְנֶה אַף הוּא אֵינוֹ סוֹתְרוֹ. וְנִמְצָא בָא לִידֵי סַכָּנָה.

Halakhah 4: One understands all of them. Stones[48]? As the following[99]: "If his wall was sloping one tears it down and rebuilds." Could he not tear down and not build? Rebbi Hanania in the name of Rebbi Johanan: They permitted the end because of the beginning. For if you tell him not to build he will not tear down and create a danger.

48 One understands the mention in the Mishnah of all items except stones (which are not mentioned in the Babylonian Mishnah).

49 Chapter 1, Note 79.

(81b line 41) רִבִּי יְהוֹשֻׁעַ בֶּן לֵוִי שָׁאַל לְרִבִּי שִׁמְעוֹן בֶּן לָקִישׁ. מָהוּ לִיקַּח בָּתִּים מִן הַגּוֹי. אָמַר לֵיהּ. אֵימַת רִבִּי שָׁאַל. בַּשַּׁבָּת. תַּנֵּי. בַּשַּׁבָּת מוּתָּר. כֵּיצַד הוּא עוֹשֶׂה. מַרְאֶה לוֹ כִּיסִין שֶׁלְדִינָרִין וְהַגּוֹי חוֹתֵם וּמַעֲלֶה לְאַרְכָיִים. שֶׁכֵּן מָצָאנוּ שֶׁלֹּא נִכְבְּשָׁה אֶלָּא יְרִיחוֹ אֶלָּא בַשַּׁבָּת. דִּכְתִיב כֹּה תַעֲשֶׂה שֵׁשֶׁת יָמִים. וּכְתִיב וּבַיּוֹם הַשְּׁבִיעִי תָּסוֹבּוּ אֶת־הָעִיר שֶׁבַע פְּעָמִים. וּכְתִיב עַד רִדְתָּהּ. אֲפִילוּ בַשַּׁבָּת.

Rebbi Joshua ben Levi asked Rebbi Simeon ben Laqish[50]: may one buy houses from a Gentile? He said to him, about when does the Rabbi ask? On the Sabbath. It was stated: One the Sabbath it is permitted. How does one do it[51] He shows him wallets full of denars and the Gentile signs and files it with the Archives[52]. Since so we find that Jericho was only conquered on the Sabbath, as it is written[53], *so you shall do during six days.* And it is written[54], *and on the Seventh Day you shall circle the city seven times.* And it is written[55], *until it is conquered,* even on the Sabbath[56].

50 The teacher asking the student to examine him.
\51 Babli *Bava qamma* 80b. The rabbinic prohibition of instructing a Gentile to do acts forbidden to a Jew on the Sabbath is never intended to hinder Jews from acquiring real estate in the Holy Land.
52 Latin *archivum*, the registry of deeds.
53 *Jos.* 6:3.
54 *Jos.* 6:4.
55 *Deut.* 20:20.
56 *Šabbat* Chapter 1 (Note 396), Babli 19a; *Sifry Deut.* 203.204; Tosephta *Eruvin* 3:7, an interpretation attributed to Roman (post-Hasmonean) times.

(81b line 46) הֲרֵי שֶׁאֵין לוֹ מַה יֹאכַל קוֹצֵר וּמְעַמֵּר וְדָשׁ וּבִלְבַד שֶׁלֹּא יָדוּשׁ בְּפָרָה. בִּמְסַפֵּק לְיָחִיד. אֲבָל בִּמְסַפֵּק לָרַבִּים דָּשׁ אֲפִילוּ בְּפָרָה.

"If he has nothing to eat he harvests, and forms sheaves, and threshes, on condition that he not thresh with cattle.[57]" That if he supplies for a single person. But supplies for the public he even threshes with cattle.

אֵין מְפַנִּין מִדִּירָה נָאָה לְדִירָה נָאָה וְלֹא מִדִּירָה (נָאָה) [כְּעוּרָה] לְדִירָה כְּאוּרָה וְלֹא מִדִּירָה כְּאוּרָה לְדִירָה נָאָה. אֵין צוֹרֶךְ לוֹמַר מִדִּירָה נָאָה לְדִירָה כְּאוּרָה. וּבְתוֹךְ שֶׁלּוֹ אֲפִילוּ מִדִּירָה נָאָה לְדִירָה כְּאוּרָה. שִׂמְחָה לָאָדָם בְּשָׁעָה שֶׁהוּא דָר בְּתוֹךְ שֶׁלּוֹ.

One does not evacuate from a beautiful dwelling to a beautiful dwelling, nor from a (beautiful) [ugly] dwelling to an ugly dwelling, nor from an ugly dwelling to a beautiful dwelling; not to mention from a beautiful dwelling to an ugly dwelling. But if it is his own property, even from a beautiful dwelling to an ugly dwelling; it is a joy for a person to dwell in his own.

אֵין מְפַנִּין אֶת הַמֵּת וְאֶת הָעֲצָמוֹת מִקֶּבֶר מְכוּבָּד לִמְכוּבָּד וְלֹא מִבָּזוּי לְבָזוּי וְלֹא מִבָּזוּי לִמְכוּבָּד. אֵין צוֹרֶךְ לוֹמַר מִן הַמְכוּבָּד לַבָּזוּי. וּבְתוֹךְ שֶׁלּוֹ אֲפִילוּ מִן הַמְכוּבָּד לַבָּזוּי. עָרֵב הוּא לָאָדָם שֶׁהוּא נִינוֹחַ אֵצֶל אֲבוֹתָיו.

2 לבזויי G | לבזויי (2) ערב G | ערב

One evacuates the dead or bones[58] neither from an honored grave to an honored one, nor from a contemptible one to a contemptible, nor from a contemptible to an honored one. But if it is his own property, even from an honored to a contemptible; it is sweet for a person to rest with his forefathers.

57 Babli 12b, Tosephta 1:11.   58 At any time.

(81b line 54) אֵין מְבִיאִין כֵּלִים מִבֵּית הָאוּמָּן. הָדָא אֲמְרָה. פְּרַגְמַטְיָא אָבֵדָה שָׁרֵי מְטַלְטְלָתָא בְּמוֹעֲדָא.

הדה אמרה פרגמטיה אבידה שרי מטלטלתה במועדה

"One does not bring vessels from the potter's house." This implies, merchandise in danger of spoilage may be moved[28] on the holiday.

(fol. 81a) **משנה ה**: מְחַפִּין אֶת הַקְּצִיעוֹת בַּקַּשׁ. רִבִּי יְהוּדָה אוֹמֵר אַף מְעַבִּין. מוֹכְרֵי פֵירוֹת כְּסוּת וְכֵלִים מוֹכְרִין בְּצִנְעָה לְצוֹרֶךְ הַמּוֹעֵד. הַצַּיָּידִין וְהַדַּשּׁוֹשׁוֹת וְהַגָּרוֹסוֹת עוֹשִׂין בְּצִנְעָה לְצוֹרֶךְ הַמּוֹעֵד. רִבִּי יוֹסֵי אוֹמֵר הֵם הֶחֱמִירוּ עַל עַצְמָן:

Mishnah 5: One covers cut figs with straw[59]; Rebbi Jehudah says, also one thickens[60]. The sellers of produce, clothing, and vessels, sell privately for holiday needs. Hunters, grain splitters and farina millers do their work privately on the holiday. Rebbi Yose said, they restricted themselves[61].

59 Figs spread out on the roof to dry into either dried figs or fig cakes, to protect them from birds.
60 If it is necessary to put the drying figs on top of one another to produce fig cakes.
61 These professions were exempted from rabbinic restrictions of their work since their products are necessary for the enjoyment of the holiday, but they preferred to declare a general holiday for themselves.

(81b line 56) **הלכה ה**: כֵּינֵי מַתְנִיתָה מְעַבִּין. רִבִּי יְהוּדָה אוֹמֵר. יְאַבֵּד דָּבָר מְמוּעָט וְאַל יְאַבֵּד דָּבָר מְרוּבֶּה. רִבִּי יוֹסֵה אוֹמֵר. אַל יְאַבֵּד דָּבָר כָּל־עִיקָּר. כַּהֲנָא אָמַר. אִית מִילִין בְּמוֹעֵד דְּקַשְׁיִין מִן אֲהִילוּת וּמִן נְגָעִים. תַּמָּן אָמַר רַב יִרְמְיָה בְּשֵׁם רַב. פּוֹרְסִין מַחֲצֶלֶת עַל גַּבֵּי שִׁיפּוּף בַּשַּׁבָּת. וָכָא הוּא אָמַר הָכֵין. רַבָּנָן דְּקַיְסָרִין בְּשֵׁם רִבִּי יַעֲקֹב בַּר אָחָא. לִתוֹלֵשׁ מִן הַקַּרְקַע בֵּינֵיהוֹן. רַבָּנָן אָמְרֵי. קוֹצֵר וּמְעַבֶּה. רִבִּי יוּדָה אוֹמֵר. לֹא יִקְצוֹר אֶלָּא יְעַבֶּה.

1 מעבין | G מעבים יהודה | G ידה 2 מרובה | G מרובא כהנא | G כהנה מילין | G מילן דקשיין | G קשיין 3 פורסין | G פורסים שיפוף | G שיפוף כולו לבינים 4 וכא | G וכה אמ' | G מר הכין | G הכן רבנן | G רבנין (2) לתולש | G ליתולש 5 ומעבה | G ומעבא יעבה | G יעבא

Halakhah 5: So is the Mishnah: one thickens[62]; Rebbi Jehudah said, small amounts may be lost so large amounts not be lost; Rebbi Yose says, nothing at all shall be lost[63]. Cahana said, there are things in holidays more difficult than "tent coverings" and "skin diseases"[64]. There, Rav Jeremiah said in the name of Rav, one spreads a mat over rows <of any bricks> on the Sabbath[65]. And here he says so? The rabbis of Caesarea in the name of Rebbi Jacob bar Aḥa: To pluck from the ground is between them. The rabbis are saying, he plucks and thickens[66]. Rebbi Jehudah says, he may not pluck but may thicken[67].

62 One does not read "also", which would make R. Jehudah more lenient than the anonymous majority (identified with R. Yose) which must be supposed to be more lenient than R. Jehudah.
63 Quoted from Halakhah 1, Note 30.
64 It is more difficult to understand R. Jehudah's switch from restrictive to lenient than many hidden inferences from biblical rules contained in Tractates *Ahilut* and *Nega`im* in the Sixth Order of the Mishnah.
65 Quoted from *Šabbat* 4, Note 39. If there is no problem of covering building material on the Sabbath, covering potential food on the holidays should be no problem at all and would not need a mention in the Mishnah, not to speak of R. Jehudah's switch. The <added text> is from G and the text in *Šabbat*.
66 The rabbis permit to pluck straw from the field on the intermediate days of the holiday in order to cover drying figs.
67 R. Jehudah forbids plucking straw, he only permits thickening. Once the Mishnah is corrected as in Note 62 there is no problem; he is restrictive.

(81b line 62) קִיבְּלוּ עֲלֵיהֶן חַרְמֵי טִיבֶּרְיָה וּדְשׁוֹשֵׁי עַכּוֹ וּגְרוֹסֵי צִיפּוֹרִין שֶׁלֹּא לַעֲשׂוֹת מְלָאכָה בְחוֹלוֹ שֶׁלְמוֹעֵד. נִיחָא גְרוֹסֵי צִיפּוֹרִין דְּשׁוֹשֵׁי עַכּוֹ. חַרְמֵי טִיבֶּרְיָה וְאֵינָן מְמַעֲטִין בְּשִׂמְחַת הָרֶגֶל. צָד הוּא בְחַכָּה צָד הוּא בְמִכְמוֹרֶת. אֲפִילוּ כֵן אֵינָן מְמַעֲטִין בְּשִׂמְחַת הָרֶגֶל. רִבִּי אִימִּי מֵיקַל לוֹן שֶׁהֵן מְמַעֲטִין בְּשִׂמְחַת הָרֶגֶל.

[68]The net-fishermen of Tiberias, and the grain splitters of Acco, and the farina millers of Sepphoris, accepted not to work on the intermediate days of a holiday. One understands the farina millers of Sepphoris, and the grain splitters of Acco. The net-fishers of Tiberias, do they not diminish the enjoyment of the holiday? He may fish with a hook; he may fish with a stationary net. Even so, do they not diminish the enjoyment of the holiday? Rebbi Immi cursed them because they diminish the enjoyment of the holiday[69].

68 This is from *Pesahim* 4:1, Notes 43-47.
69 And the rules of the guild would not permit the individual to supply his neighbors.

מועד קטן פרק שלישי ואילו מגלחין

(fol. 81c) **משנה א**: וְאֵילוּ מְגַלְּחִין בַּמּוֹעֵד הַבָּא מִמְּדִינַת הַיָּם וּמִבֵּית הַשִּׁבְיָה וְהַיּוֹצֵא מִבֵּית הָאֲסוּרִים וּמְנֻדֶּה שֶׁהִתִּירוּ לוֹ חֲכָמִים. וְכֵן מִי שֶׁנִּשְׁאַל לֶחָכָם וְהוּתַּר וְהַנָּזִיר וְהַמְצוֹרָע מִטּוּמְאָתוֹ לְטַהֲרָתוֹ:

Mishnah 1: And the following shave[1] on the holiday: He who comes from overseas[2], or from being kidnapped[3], or leaves jail[4], and one whose excommunication was lifted by the Sages[5], and also who asked the Sages and was permitted[6], and the *nazir*[7], and the sufferer from skin disease between his impurity and his purity[8].

1 While in biblical Hebrew this means to shave off the hair completely, in the Mishnah this usually means "grooming to get a haircut, to trim the beard," unless applied to biblical rules. As explained in the Halakhah, getting a haircut is not forbidden intrinsically on the holiday; it is forbidden by custom so everybody should enter the holiday decently groomed.

2 Coming off a long trip (including a caravan trip).

3 By Gentiles.

4 Even when jailed by a Jewish authority.

5 Since rabbinic excommunications are lifted only if the person excommunicated followed the rabbinic rules about excommunications which forbid grooming, if the excommunication is lifted on the holiday grooming is necessary.

6 He made a vow which included not grooming and had the vow voided by a rabbi.

7 At the end of his period of *nezirut* he is obligated by biblical law to cut his hair. If the period ends during the holiday, the biblical law has to be followed.

8 He has to shave off all his hair as part of his purification ritual; described in *Lev.* 14:8.

(81c line 39) וְאֵילוּ מְגַלְּחִין בַּמּוֹעֵד הַבָּא מִמְּדִינַת הַיָּם וּמִבֵּית הַשִּׁבְיָה וְהַיּוֹצֵא מִבֵּית הָאֲסוּרִין. הָא שְׁאָר כָּל־בְּנֵי אָדָם אֲסוּרִין. אָמַר רִבִּי סִימוֹן. גָּזְרוּ עֲלֵיהֶן שֶׁלֹּא יִיכָּנְסוּ לָרֶגֶל מְנוּוָלִין. תַּמָּן תַּנִּינָן. אַנְשֵׁי מִשְׁמָר וְאַנְשֵׁי מַעֲמָד אֲסוּרִין מִלְּסַפֵּר וּמִלְּכַבֵּס. וּבַחֲמִישִׁי מוּתָּרִין מִפְּנֵי כְבוֹד הַשַּׁבָּת: הָא שְׁאָר כָּל־הַיָּמִים אֲסוּרִין. רִבִּי יוֹסֵה רִבִּי אַבָּהוּ בְשֵׁם רִבִּי יוֹחָנָן רִבִּי אָבוּן בְּשֵׁם חִזְקִיָּה. גָּזְרוּ עֲלֵיהֶן שֶׁלֹּא יִיכָּנְסוּ לְשַׁבָּתָן מְנוּוָלִין.

1 השבייה G השיבה | 2 אסורין G אסורים עליהן G עליהם ייכנסו G יכנסו | 3 ואנשי G אנשי אסורין G אסורים מותרין G מותרים | 4 הימים G היימים אבהו G אבהוא אבון ר' בון G בון ר' יסא

⁹"**And the following shave on the holiday: He who comes from overseas, or from being kidnapped, or leaves jail.**" Therefore all other people are forbidden? Rebbi Simon said, they decreed about them so they should not enter the holiday badly groomed¹⁰. There, we have stated¹¹: "The people of the watch and those of the bystanders are forbidden to shave and to wash their garments, but on Thursday they are permitted because of the honor of the Sabbath." Therefore on all other days they are forbidden? Rebbi Yose, Rebbi Abbahu in the name of Rebbi Johanan; Rebbi Abun, <Rebbi Yasa>¹² in the name of Hizqiah: They decreed about them so they should not enter their week badly groomed.

9 This text is re-written from a text in *Ta`aniot* 2:12, Notes 185-189.
10 Babli 14a.
11 Mishnah *Ta`aniot* 2:13.
12 Added from *Ta`aniot* and G.

(81c line 44) תַּנֵּי בְשֵׁם רִבִּי יוּדָה. הַבָּא מִמְּדִינַת הַיָּם אָסוּר לוֹ לְגַלֵּחַ. רִבִּי יוּדָה כְדַעְתֵּיהּ. דְּרִבִּי יוּדָה אָמַר. אָסוּר לְפָרֵשׁ לַיָּם הַגָּדוֹל. מֵעַתָּה כֹהֵן שֶׁיָּצָא חוּץ לָאָרֶץ וְיָצָא שֶׁלֹּא בִרְצוֹן חֲכָמִים יְהֵא אָסוּר לוֹ לְגַלֵּחַ. חַד כֹּהֵן אֲתָא לְגַבֵּי רִבִּי חֲנִינָה. אָמַר לֵיהּ. מָהוּ לָצֵאת לְצוּר לַעֲשׂוֹת דְּבַר מִצְוָה לַחֲלוֹץ אוֹ לְיַיבֵּם. אָמַר לֵיהּ. אָחִיו שֶׁלְאוֹתוֹ הָאִישׁ יָצָא. בָּרוּךְ הַמָּקוֹם שֶׁנְּגָפוֹ. וְאַתְּ מְבַקֵּשׁ לַעֲשׂוֹת כְּיוֹצֵא בוֹ. אִית דְּבָעֵי מֵימַר. הָכֵין אָמַר לֵיהּ. אָחִיו שֶׁלְאוֹתוֹ הָאִישׁ הִנִּיחַ חֵיק אִמּוֹ וְחִיבֵּק חֵיק נָכְרִיָּה. וּבָרוּךְ שֶׁנְּגָפוֹ. וְאַתְּ מְבַקֵּשׁ לַעֲשׂוֹת כְּיוֹצֵא בוֹ. שִׁמְעוֹן בַּר בָּא אֲתָא לְגַבֵּי רִבִּי חֲנִינָה. אָמַר לֵיהּ. כְּתוֹב לִי חָדָא אִיגְּרָא דְּאִיקָר נֵיפּוֹק לְפַרְנָסָתִי לְאַרְעָא בָרַיְיתָא. אָמַר לוֹ. לְמָחָר אֲנִי הוֹלֵךְ אֵצֶל אֲבוֹתֶיךָ. יְהוּ אוֹמְרִים לִי. נְטִיעָה אַחַת שֶׁלְחֶמְדָּה לָנוּ בְּאֶרֶץ יִשְׂרָאֵל הִיתַּרְתָּהּ לָהּ לָצֵאת לְחוּץ לָאָרֶץ.

It was stated in the name of Rebbi Jehudah: Shaving is forbidden to someone who comes from overseas. Rebbi Jehudah follows his own opinion since Rebbi Jehudah said, it is forbidden to sail on the ocean¹³. Then a Cohen who left for outside the Land and left against the will of the Sages should be forbidden to shave. A Cohen came to Rebbi Hanina. He said to him, may one leave for Tyre for as religious obligation, to give *halisah* or to enter levirate marriage¹⁴? He answered him, this man's brother left; praised be the Omnipresent Who smote him. And you want to do what he did. Some want to say, so he spoke to him: This man's brother disdained his mother's bosom and embraced another's bosom, and you want to do what he did. Simeon bar

Abba[15] came to Rebbi Hanina and asked him to write a letter of recommendation so he could leave for his sustenance outside the Land. He said to him, tomorrow I shall go to your forefathers; they would say to me, one desirable plant we had in the Land of Israel and you permitted it to leave the Land.

13 Babli 14a.
14 He wanted to go there since his brother left a childless widow who had to be married by him or receive *haliṣah*. In the parallel in the Babli (*Ket.* 111a) the brother dies in Khusistan, clearly outside the Land. Tyre is outside the rabbinic Land of Israel.
15 Originally a Babylonian.

(81c line 56) וְהַיּוֹצֵא מִבֵּית הָאֲסוּרִין. הֲוֵינָן סָבְרִין מֵימַר. בְּשֶׁהָיָה חָבוּשׁ אֵצֶל הַגּוֹיִם. אֲבָל אִם הָיָה חָבוּשׁ אֵצֶל יִשְׂרָאֵל לֹא. אָתָא מֵימַר לָךְ. וַאֲפִילוּ חָבוּשׁ אֵצֶל יִשְׂרָאֵל. אֵינוֹ עָרֵב לְאָדָם לְגַלֵּחַ בְּבֵית הָאֲסוּרִין.

"Or he leaves jail." We thought to say, if he was jailed by Gentiles, but not if he was jailed by Jews. He comes to inform you, even if he was jailed by Jews. It is not agreeable to a person to groom in jail[16].

16 Quoted by Tosaphot 13b *s. v.* והיוצא.

(81c line 59) וְהַמְנוּדֶּה שֶׁהִתִּירוּ לוֹ חֲכָמִים. מָה אֲנָן קַיָּימִין. אִם בְּשֶׁהִתִּירוּ לוֹ קוֹדֶם לְרֶגֶל יְגַלֵּחַ. אִם בְּשֶׁלֹּא הִתִּירוּ לוֹ קוֹדֶם לְרֶגֶל אַל יְגַלֵּחַ. אֶלָּא כִּי אֲנָן קַיָּימִין בְּשֶׁהִתִּירוּ לוֹ קוֹדֶם לְרֶגֶל וְחָל יוֹם שְׁלֹשִׁים שֶׁלּוֹ לִהְיוֹת בָּרֶגֶל. שֶׁאֵין נִידּוּי פָּחוּת מִשְּׁלֹשִׁים. וְאֵין נְזִיפָה פָּחוּת מִשִּׁבְעַת יָמִים. אֵין נִידּוּי פָּחוּת מִשְּׁלֹשִׁים יוֹם. עַד | חוֹדֶשׁ יָמִים עַד אֲשֶׁר־יֵצֵא מֵאַפְּכֶם. וְאֵין נְזִיפָה פָּחוּתָה מִשִּׁבְעָה יָמִים. הֲלֹא תִכָּלֵם שִׁבְעַת יָמִים. רִבִּי הֲוָה מוֹקֵר לְבַר אֶלְעָשָׂה. אָמַר לֵיהּ בַּר קַפָּרָא. כָּל־עַמָּא שְׁאָלִין לְרִבִּי וְאַתְּ לֵית אַתְּ שָׁאַל לֵיהּ. אָמַר לֵיהּ. מָה נִישְׁאוֹל. אָמַר לֵיהּ. שְׁאוֹל. מִשָּׁמַיִם נִשְׁקָפָה. הוֹמִיָּה בְיַרְכְּתֵי בֵיתָהּ. מְפַחֶדֶת כָּל־בַּעֲלֵי כְנָפַיִם. רָאוּהָ נְעָרִים וְנֶחְבָּאוּ. וִישִׁישִׁים קָמוּ עָמָדוּ: הַנֵּס יֹאמַר הוּ הוּ. וְהַנִּלְכָּד נִלְכַּד בַּעֲוֹנוֹ. הָפַךְ רִבִּי וְחַמְתֵּיהּ גָּחִיךְ. אָמַר רִבִּי. אֵינִי מַכִּירָךְ זָקֵן. וְיָדַע דְּלֵית הוּא מִתְמַנְּייָא בְּיוֹמוֹי.

1 שהתירו G | שהיתירו בשהתירו G | בשהיתירו 2 התירו G | היתירו בהתירו G | בשהיתירו 3 שלשים | שלשים G שלושים G | להיות להיות G | ליהיות 4 משלשים G | משלושים 5 תכלם G | תיכלם ליה G | לה קפרא G | קפרה 6 עמא G | עמא נישאול G | נשאול נשאל ליה G | לה נשאל G | נישקפה הומיה G | הומייה כנפים | כנפיים G 8 בעונו G | בעוונו וחמתיה גחיך G | וחמתה בידה 9 מתמנייא G | מתמני

"And one whose excommunication was lifted by the Sages." Where are we holding? If they lifted it before the holiday, he should have shaved. If they did not lift it before the holiday, he may not shave. But we hold that they lifted it before the holiday and his thirtieth day fell during the holiday, since no excommunication is less than thirty days[17] and no rebuke is less than seven days[18]. No excommunication is less than thirty days, *up to a month of days, until it will come out of your noses*[19]. And no rebuke is less than seven days, *let her be locked away for seven days*[20]. Rebbi honored Ben Elasa[21]. Bar Qappara said to him, everybody is asking Rebbi, only you are not asking Rebbi. He asked him, what to ask? He said to him, ask[22]: "From Heaven she looks down, she is busy in her house; boys see her and hide[23], *old men rise and stand*. The one who flees says, ho, ho, and the one caught is caught in his sin." Rebbi turned around[24] and saw him laughing. Rebbi said, I do not know you, old man. He understood that he would not be ordained during his lifetime[25].

17 An excommunication has to be observed for 30 days even if lifted quickly (but not if it was annulled) Babli 16a.
18 A student reprimanded by his teacher may not show himself for 7 days.
19 *Num.* 11:20.
20 *Num.* 12:14.
21 A very rich but totally ignorant family with whom he had relations by marriage.
22 A riddle.
23 A variation of *Job* 29:8; the next clause is a direct quote.
24 He recognized Bar Qappara's poetic style.
25 Babli 17a, bottom.

(81c line 71) בִּיקְשׁוּ לְנַדּוֹת אֶת רִבִּי מֵאִיר. אָמַר לָהֶן. אֵינִי שׁוֹמֵעַ לָכֶם עַד שֶׁתֹּאמְרוּ לִי אֶת מִי מְנַדִּין וְעַל מַה מְנַדִּין וְעַל כַּמָּה דְבָרִים מְנַדִּין.

2 מנדין G | מנדים (3) ועל G | ועד

בִּיקְשׁוּ לְנַדּוֹת אֶת רִבִּי לִיעֶזֶר. אֲמָרִין. מָאן אֲזַל מוֹדַע לֵיהּ. אָמַר רִבִּי עֲקִיבָה. אֲנָא אֲזַל מוֹדַע לֵיהּ. אֲתָא לְגַבֵּיהּ אֲמַר לֵיהּ. רִבִּי רִבִּי. חֲבֵירָיךְ מְנַדִּין לָךְ. נְסִתֵּיהּ נְפַק לֵיהּ לְבָרָא אָמַר. חָרוּבִיתָא חָרוּבִיתָא. אִין הֲלָכָה כְדִבְרֵיהֶם אִתְעֲוֹקְרִין. וְלָא אִיתְעֲקֶרֶת. אִין הֲלָכָה כְדִבְרַיי אִתְעֲוֹקְרִין. וְאִיתְעֲקֶרֶת. אִין הֲלָכָה כְדִבְרֵיהֶן חוֹזְרִין. וְלָא חָזְרַת. אִין הֲלָכָה כְדִבְרַיי חוֹזְרִין. וְחָזְרַת. כָּל־הָדֵין שְׁבָחָא וְלֵית הֲלָכָה כְרִבִּי אֱלִיעֶזֶר. אָמַר רִבִּי חֲנִינָה. מִשְׁנִיתָנָה לֹא נִיתְנָה אֶלָּא אַחֲרֵי רַבִּים לְהַטּוֹת. [וְלֵית רִבִּי אֱלִיעֶזֶר יָדַע שֶׁאַחֲרֵי רַבִּים לְהַטּוֹת:] לֹא הִקְפִּיד אֶלָּא עַל יְדֵי שֶׁשָּׂרְפוּ טַהֲרוֹתָיו בְּפָנָיו. תַּמָּן תַּנִּינָן. חִיתְּכוֹ חוּלְיוֹת וְנָתַן חוֹל בֵּין חוּלְיָא לְחוּלְיָא, רִבִּי לִיעֶזֶר מְטַהֵר וַחֲכָמִים מְטַמְּאִין. זֶה תַּנּוּרוֹ שֶׁלְחַכִינַּיי. אָמַר רִבִּי יִרְמְיָה. כָּךְ גָּדוֹל נַעֲשָׂה בְּאוֹתוֹ הַיּוֹם. כָּל־מָקוֹם שֶׁהָיְתָה עֵינוֹ שֶׁלְרִבִּי לִיעֶזֶר מַבֶּטֶת הָיָה נִשְׂרָף. וְלֹא עוֹד אֶלָּא אֲפִילוּ חִיטָּה אַחַת חֶצְיָהּ נִשְׂרָף וְחֶצְיָהּ לֹא נִשְׂרָף. וְהָיוּ עָמוּדֵי בֵּית הַוָּעַד מְרוֹפָפִין. אָמַר לָהֶן רִבִּי יְהוֹשֻׁעַ. אִם חֲבֵרִים מִתְלַחֲמִים אַתֶּם מָה אִיכְפַּת לָכֶם. וְיָצְאָה בַת קוֹל וְאָמְרָה. הֲלָכָה כֶאֱלִיעֶזֶר בְּנִי. אָמַר רִבִּי יְהוֹשֻׁעַ. לֹא בַשָּׁמַיִם הִיא. רִבִּי קְרִיסְפִּי רִבִּי יוֹחָנָן בְּשֵׁם רִבִּי. אִם יֹאמַר לִי אָדָם. כָּךְ שָׁנָה רִבִּי

לִיעֵזֶר. שׁוֹנֶה אֲנִי כִּדְבָרָיו. אֶלָּא דְּתַנָּאָא מְחַלְפִין. חַד זְמַן הֲוָה עֲבַר בַּשּׁוּקָא וַחֲמַת חָדָא אִיתָּא סְחוֹתָהּ דְּבֵייתָא וּטְלָקַת וְנָפְלָת גּוֹ רֵישֵׁיהּ. אֲמַר. דּוֹמֶה שֶׁהַיּוֹם חֲבֵירַיי מְקָרְבִין אוֹתִי. דִּכְתִיב מֵאַשְׁפּוֹת יָרִים אֶבְיוֹן:

They wanted to excommunicate Rebbi Meïr[26]. He said to them, I do not listen to you unless you tell me whom one excommunicates, why one excommunicates, and how many reasons there are to excommunicate[27].

[28]They wanted to excommunicate Rebbi Eliezer. They said, who will go and inform him? Rebbi Aqiba said, I shall go and inform him. He went to him and said to him, my teacher, my teacher[29], your colleagues are excommunicating you. He took him outside, saying: Carob tree, carob tree, if practice has to follow their words, be uprooted. It was not uprooted. If practice has to follow my words, be uprooted. It was uprooted. If practice has to follow their words, turn back. It did not turn back. If practice has to follow my words, turn back. It turned back. All these extraordinary happenings and practice do not follow Rebbi Eliezer. Rebbi Hanina said, when it was given, it also was given *to follow the majority opinion*[30]. [Did Rebbi Eliezer not know that practice has to follow the majority opinion?][31] He was offended only because they burned his food prepared in purity in his presence[32]. There we have stated[33]: "If it was cut into strips and sand was placed between any two strips, Rebbi Eliezer declares pure[34] but the Sages declare impure. This is the Hakhinai oven." Rebbi Jeremiah said, a big itching was happening on that day: Everything on which Rebbi Eliezer gazed was burned[35]. Not only that, but a grain of wheat might have been half burned and half not burned, and the walls of the house of assembly were weakened. Rebbi Joshua said to them, if colleagues are fighting, what does this concern you? There came an unembodied voice and said, practice follows My son Eliezer. Rebbi Joshua said, *it is not in Heaven*[36]. Rebbi Crispus, Rebbi Johanan in the name of Rebbi: If a person would say to me, that is how Rebbi Eliezer stated, I am stating following his words since the Tannaïm switch[37]. Once he was walking in public and he saw a woman when sweeping her house throwing it out, it fell on his head. He said, it seems that today my colleagues are befriending me, for it is written: *He lifts the downtrodden from the dung heap*[38].

26 Probably because in many cases he ruled against common practice and he did not make a big effort to explain his reasons to rabbis who were not his students.

27 And they were dependent on him to formulate these rules.

28 Babli *Bava meṣia`* 59b.

29 Nobody else wanted to go since they knew that R. Eliezer's rage would be deadly. R. Aqiba declared himself R. Eliezer's student, insulating himself from the leaders of the preceding generation who pronounced the excommunication.

30 *Ex.* 23:2. This declares rabbinic consensus to be superior to prophetic inspiration. This claim of rabbinic authority to override the will of Heaven is the mirror image of Jesus's claim (*Matth.* 12:8) that the prophet (Son of Man) is master over biblical laws.

31 Addition by the Venice editor, justified by G where one reads רבים . . . . . ולית ר' ליעז. להטות.

32 This follows the story in the Babli that R. Eliezer was excommunicated in his presence.

33 Mishnah *Kelim* 5:10.

34 In Mishnah *Kelim*, "pure" always means "impervious to impurity"; "impure" means "susceptible to impurity". Since every strip of pottery is not a vessel and the connections between the strips are not permanent, the entire oven is not an implement and therefore pure. The Sages argue that since the oven is usable as described it is an implement and impure.

35 This describes the antique theory of vision, that the image in the eye is formed by rays emanated from the eye and scanning the objects.

36 *Deut.* 30:12.

37 If a statement consistent with our practice is ascribed to R. Eliezer it need not be rejected since one may assume that it was ascribed to him in error.

38 *Ps.* 113:7. The Babli holds that R. Eliezer's excommunication was lifted only at his death.

(81d line 16) רִבִּי יְהוֹשֻׁעַ בֶּן לֵוִי שָׁלַח בָּתַר חַד בַּר נַשׁ תְּלָתָה זִימְנִין וְלָא אֲתָא. שָׁלַח אֲמַר לֵיהּ. אִילוּלֵי דְלָא חֲרָמִית בַּר נַשׁ מִן יוֹמוֹי הֲוִינָא מְחָרֵם לְהַהוּא גּוּבְרָא. שֶׁעַל עֶשְׂרִים וְאַרְבָּעָה דְבָרִים מְנַדִּין וְזֶה אֶחָד מֵהֶן. וְכֹל אֲשֶׁר לֹא־יָבוֹא לִשְׁלֹשֶׁת הַיָּמִים כַּעֲצַת הַשָּׂרִים וְהַזְּקֵנִים יָחֳרַם כָּל־רְכוּשׁוֹ וְהוּא יִבָּדֵל מִקְּהַל הַגּוֹלָה: אָמַר רִבִּי יִצְחָק בֵּירִבִּי לְעָזָר. אִית סַגִּין מִינְהוֹן מְבַדְּרָן בְּמַתְנִיתָא. תַּמָּן תַּנִּינָן. שָׁלַח לוֹ שִׁמְעוֹן בֶּן שָׁטַח אָמַר לוֹ צָרִיךְ אַתָּה לְנַדּוֹת. שֶׁאִילוּ נִגְזְרָה גְזֵירָה כְּשֵׁם שֶׁנִּגְזְרָה בִּימֵי אֵלִיָּהוּ [לֹא נִמְצֵאת מֵבִיא אֶת הָרַבִּים לִידֵי חִלּוּל הַשֵּׁם. שֶׁכָּל־הַמֵּבִיא אֶת הָרַבִּים לִידֵי חִלּוּל הַשֵּׁם צָרִיךְ נִידּוּי. תַּמָּן תַּנִּינָן. שָׁלַח לוֹ רַבָּן גַּמְלִיאֵל אִם מְעַכֵּב אַתָּה אֶת הָרַבִּים נִמְצֵאתָ מַכְשִׁילָן לֶעָתִיד לָבוֹא.] לֹא נִמְצֵאת מְעַכֵּב אֶת הָרַבִּים מִלַּעֲשׂוֹת מִצְוָה. שֶׁכָּל־הַמְעַכֵּב אֶת הָרַבִּים לַעֲשׂוֹת דְּבַר מִצְוָה צָרִיךְ נִידּוּי.

Rebbi Joshua ben Levi sent for a man three times[38a] but he did not come. He sent, saying to him, if I had not ever excommunicated a person, I would have excommunicated this man since for 24 reasons one excommunicates and this is one of them: *The entire property of anybody who will not come within three days following the council of ministers and Elders shall be confiscated and he shall be separated from the community of the Diaspora*[39]. Rebbi Isaac ben Rebbi Eleazar said, there are many more of these dispersed in the Mishnah[40]. There, we have stated[41]: "Simeon ben Shatah sent to him and told him, you should be excommunicated." [42]For if there had been a decision made as it was decided in the days of Elijah, [would you not have caused a desecration of the Name in public? And everybody who causes a public desecration of the Name must be excommunicated. There, we have stated[43]: Rabban Gamliel sent to him, if you hinder the public you will create a future stumbling block for the public;][44] would not prevent the public from performing a meritorious act? And any who would hinder the public from performing a meritorious act must be excommunicated.

38a Summons to appear in rabbinic court.

39 *Ezra* 10:8.

40 The rules, together with most of procedural law, never were completely fixed. Babli *Berakhot* 19a.

41 Mishnah *Ta`aniot* 3:8.

42 Copied from *Ta`aniot* 3:8, Notes 106-108.

43 Added from *Ta`aniot* by the Venice editor.

44 Mishnah *Roš Haššanah* 1:6.

(81d line 27) תַּנֵּי. אָמַר רִבִּי יוֹסֵי. תּוֹדַס אִישׁ רוֹמִי הִנְהִיג אֶת אַנְשֵׁי רוֹמִי שֶׁיִּהוּ אוֹכְלִין גְּדָיִים מְקוּלָסִין בְּלֵילֵי פְסָחִים. שָׁלְחוּ חֲכָמִים וְאָמְרוּ לוֹ. אִילוּלֵי שֶׁאַתְּ תּוֹדַס לֹא הָיִינוּ מְנַדִּין אוֹתָךְ. וּמָהוּ תּוֹדַס. אָמַר רִבִּי חֲנַנְיָה. דַּהֲוָה מְשַׁלַּח פַּרְנָסַתְהוֹן דְּרַבָּנָן. לֹא נִמְצֵאתָה מֵבִיא אֶת הָרַבִּים לִידֵי אֲכִילַת קֳדָשִׁים בַּחוּץ. שֶׁכָּל־הַמֵּבִיא אֶת הָרַבִּים לִידֵי אֲכִילַת קֳדָשִׁים בַּחוּץ צָרִיךְ נִידּוּי.

[45]It was stated: Rebbi Yose said, Theudas of Rome led the people of Rome to eat helmeted kid-goat in the Passover nights. the Sages sent and said to him, if you were not Theudas, would we not put you in the ban? Who was Theudas? Rebbi Hananiah said, because he was providing for the rabbis. Are you not causing the public to eat *sancta* outside the Temple? And anybody causing the public to eat *sancta* outside the Temple has to be put in the ban.

45 Copied from *Pesahim* 7:1, Note 24.

(81d line 32) תַּמָּן תַּנִּינָן. אֶת מִי נִידּוּ. אֶלְעָזָר בֶּן הַנָּד שֶׁפִּיקְפֵּק בְּטָהֳרַת הַיָּדַיִם. הָדָא אָמְרָה. הַמְפַקְפֵּק בְּדָבָר אֲפִילוּ מִדִּבְרֵי סוֹפְרִים צָרִיךְ נִידּוּי. תַּמָּן תַּנִּינָן. דִּכְמָה הִשְׁקוּהָ. מָהוּ דִּכְמָה.

דִּכְוָותָהּ. נִידּוּהוּ וָמֵת בְּנִידּוּיוֹ וְסָקְלוּ בֵית דִּין אֲרוֹנוֹ. לְלַמֶּדְךָ שֶׁכָּל־הַמְנוּדֶּה וּמֵת סוֹקְלִין אֲרוֹנוֹ׃ הָדָא אָמְרָה. הַמְבַזֶּה זָקֵן אֲפִילוּ לְאַחַר מִיתָה צָרִיךְ נִידּוּי. בְּיוֹמוֹי דְּרִבִּי זְעוּרָה הֲווֹן מְרַחֲקִין וּמְקָרְבִין. אָמַר לָהֶן [רִבִּי] לָא. הַשְׁתָּא מְרַחֲקִין וְהַשְׁתָּא מְקָרְבִין. אָמַר רִבִּי יוֹסֵה. חָזְרוּ וְנִמְנוּ. לִכְשֶׁיַּחֲזוֹר בּוֹ יְהוּ מְקָרְבִין אוֹתוֹ.

There, we have stated[46]: "Whom did they excommunicate? Eleazar ben Hannad who questioned the purity of hands[47]." This implies that one who questions even one of the words of the Sopherim[48] needs excommunication. There, we have stated: "They[49] let her drink *dikma*." What is *dikma*? An imitation[50]. "They excommunicated him, he died in his excommunication, and the Court stoned his coffin. To teach you that one stones the coffin of anybody dying in his excommunication." This implies that anybody insulting an Elder, even after his death, needs to be excommunicated[51]. In the days of Rebbi Ze`ira they were excommunicating and readmitting[52]. (He said to them, no.) [Rebbi La said to them:] Now one excommunicates and now one readmits? They took up the matter and voted, when he changes his opinion one readmits them[53].

46 Mishnah *Idiut* 5:6.
47 The secondary impurity of hands which is purely rabbinical and whose rules cannot be harmonized with biblical rules of impurity. It seems that he denied the impurity of hands of people whose body was not impure.
48 Non-biblical but pre-rabbinic.
49 Aqabia ben Mehallalel denied that a freedwoman could be subject to the *sotah* ritual and held that Shemaya and Abtalyon, the heads of a Synhedrion in early Roman times, staged an imitation ritual for a freedwoman suspected of infidelity. One may assume that this is influenced by the Roman prejudice against *libertinae*. Babli *Berakhot* 19a.
50 Parsing the word as Aramaic דְּ־כְמָה "which is like it."
51 Since he insulted the memory of Shamaya and Abtalyon.
52 In the days of rising Christianity they tried to follow the received rules of excommunication but blunt its effects by immediately cancelling the act.
53 They decided that it was better not to re-admit christianizing Jews.

(81d line 39) הַמְנוּדֶּה לָרַב מְנוּדֶּה לַתַּלְמִיד. הַמְנוּדֶּה לַתַּלְמִיד אֵינוֹ מְנוּדֶּה לָרַב. הַמְנוּדֶּה לְאַב בֵּית דִּין מְנוּדֶּה לֶחָכָם. הַמְנוּדֶּה לֶחָכָם אֵינוֹ מְנוּדֶּה לְאַב בֵּית דִּין. הַמְנוּדֶּה לַנָּשִׂיא מְנוּדֶּה לְכָל־אָדָם. עַד כְּדוֹן חָכָם שֶׁנִּידָּה. וַאֲפִילוּ חָבֵר שֶׁנִּידָּה. נִישְׁמְעִינָהּ מִן הָדָא. הָדָא אַמְתָא מִן דְּבַר פָּטָא הֲוָת עָבְרָה קוֹמֵי חָדָא כְנִישְׁתָּא. חֲמַת חַד סְפַר מָחֵי לְחַד מֵיינוּק יְתִיר מִן צוֹרְכֵיהּ.

אֲמָרָה לֵיהּ. יְחֲוֵי הַהוּא גּוּבְרָא מֵחֲרָם. אֲתָא שְׁאַל לְרִבִּי אֲחָא. אֲמַר לֵיהּ. צָרִיךְ אַתְּ חֲשַׁשׁ עַל נַפְשָׁךְ. הָדָא אֲמָרָה. הָעוֹשֶׂה דָבָר שֶׁלֹּא כְשׁוּרָה צָרִיךְ נִידּוּי. רִבִּי שִׁמְעוֹן בֶּן לָקִישׁ הֲוָה מְעַיְּינֵי תְּיָינִין בְּבַרְבַּרִית. אָתוֹן לִיסְטַיָּא וְגָנְבוּן מִינְהוֹן בַּלַּיְלְיָא. וּבְסוֹפָא אַרְגֵּשׁ בְּהוֹן. אֲמַר לוֹן. לִיהֲוֹן אִילֵּין עַמָּא מֵחֲרָמִין. אֲמָרוּן לֵיהּ. יֵיא הַהוּא גּוּבְרָא מֵחֲרָם. חָשׁ עַל נַפְשֵׁיהּ. אֲמַר. מָמוֹן אִינּוּן חַיָּיבִין לִי. דִּילְמָא נַפְשָׁן. נְפַק בֶּרֵי בַּתְרֵיהוֹן. אֲמַר לוֹן. שָׁרוּן לִי. אֲמָרוּן לֵיהּ. שָׁרֵי לוֹן וַנַן שָׁרֵיי לָךְ. הָדָא אֲמָרָה. הַמְנַדֶּה אֶת מִי שֶׁאֵינוֹ צָרִיךְ וְנִידָּה אוֹתוֹ נִידּוּיוֹ נִידּוּי.

One who is excommunicated by the teacher is excommunicated for the student; excommunicated by the student is not excommunicated for the teacher[54]. One who is excommunicated by the chief judge[55] is excommunicated for the rabbi; excommunicated by the rabbi is not excommunicated for the chief judge. One who is excommunicated by the patriarch is excommunicated for everybody[54]. So far if an ordained rabbi excommunicated; even a fellow? Let us hear from the following[56]: A slave woman of Bar Pata passed by a synagogue. She saw a Bible teacher who hit a child more than necessary. He said to him, this man has to be put in the ban. He went and asked Rebbi Aḥa who told him, you have to worry about yourself[57]. This implies that a person who does something unbecoming needs to be excommunicated. Rebbi Simeon ben Laqish was looking after figs at Barbarit[58]. Robbers came and stole from them during the night. At the end he noticed them. He said to them, these people shall be excommunicated. They said to him, this person shall be excommunicated. He was worried about himself. He said, they owe me money; maybe souls[59]? He went out after them, said to them: permit me. They said to him, if you permit us we shall permit you. This implies that if somebody excommunicated somebody unnecessarily and he in turn excommunicated him, his excommunication is excommunication[59].

54 Babli 17a. It means that the student has to treat him as excommunicated, but the community at large does not have to take notice unless the excommunication was proclaimed by an authority accepted by all of the community.

55 The Chief Judge of the Patriarch's Court (or of the Head of the Diaspora's Court in Babylonia).

56 Babli 17a.

57 He himself has to follow the rabbinic rules for the excommunicated for the next 30 days.

58 A place identified by some as Barbalissus in Asia Minor.

59 He causes them to sin if they do not

follow the rules of the excommunicated. This means that he himself is guilty of "putting a stone in the path of the blind."
60 Babli 17a. As long as a ban is not proclaimed by a competent court in due form, the intended offender has the right to impose the same ban on the proclaimer, even if he be the local rabbi. In the Medieval responsa literature this is mentioned as *aderabba*.

(81d line 53) מִי מַתִּיר. לֹא כֵן תַּנֵּי. מֵת אֶחָד מִמְּנַדָּיו אֵין מַתִּירִין לוֹ. אָמַר רִבִּי יְהוֹשֻׁעַ בֶּן לֵוִי. הָדָא דַתְּ אָמַר בְּשֶׁאֵין שָׁם נָשִׂיא. אֲבָל אִם יֵשׁ שָׁם נָשִׂיא הַנָּשִׂיא מַתִּיר. רִבִּי יַעֲקֹב בַּר אָחָא בְּשֵׁם רִבִּי בָּא בַּר מָמָל. מַעֲשֶׂה בְּאֶחָד שֶׁמֵּת אֶחָד מִמְּנַדָּיו וְלֹא הִתִּירוּ לוֹ. וְלֹא כֵן אָמַר רִבִּי יְהוֹשֻׁעַ בֶּן לֵוִי. הָדָא דַתְּ אָמַר בְּשֶׁאֵין שָׁם נָשִׂיא. אֲבָל אִם יֵשׁ שָׁם נָשִׂיא הַנָּשִׂיא מַתִּיר. וְקָמַת מַה דְּאָמַר רִבִּי יַעֲקֹב בַּר אָחָא בְּשֵׁם רִבִּי בָּא בַּר מָמָל. בְּשֶׁלֹּא חָזַר בּוֹ. רִבִּי יַעֲקֹב בַּר אַבַּיֵי בְּשֵׁם רַב שֵׁשֶׁת. נִמְנוּ בְאוּשָׁא שֶׁלֹּא לִנְדּוֹת זָקֵן. וַאֲתִייָא כַּיי דְּאָמַר רִבִּי שְׁמוּאֵל בְּשֵׁם רִבִּי אַבָּהוּ. זָקֵן שֶׁאֵירַע בּוֹ דָּבָר אֵינוֹ מוֹרִידִין אוֹתוֹ מִגְּדוּלָּתוֹ אֶלָּא אוֹמְרִים לוֹ. הִיכָּבֵד וְשֵׁב בְּבֵיתֶךָ. רִבִּי יַעֲקֹב בַּר אַבַּיֵי בְּשֵׁם רִבִּי אָחָא. זָקֵן שֶׁשָּׁכַח תַּלְמוּדוֹ מַחֲמַת אוֹנְסוֹ נוֹהֲגִין בּוֹ קְדוּשַּׁת אָרוֹן. רִבִּי אָחָא רִבִּי תַּנְחוּם רִבִּי חִייָה בְּשֵׁם רִבִּי יוֹחָנָן. זָקֵן שֶׁנִּידָּה לְצוֹרֶךְ עַצְמוֹ אֲפִילוּ כַהֲלָכָה אֵין נִידּוּיוֹ נִידּוּי.

Who permits[61]? Did we not state, if one of the excommunicators died one may not permit him[62]? Rebbi Joshua ben Levi said, this you are saying in the absence of a Patriarch. But if there is a Patriarch, the Patriarch permits[63]. Rebbi Jacob bar Aḥa in the name of Rebbi Abba bar Mamal: It happened that one of the excommunicators died and they did not permit him. Did not Rebbi Joshua ben Levi say, this you are saying in the absence of a Patriarch, but if there is a Patriarch, the Patriarch permits? What Rebbi Jacob bar Aḥa in the name of Rebbi Abba bar Mamal said is confirmed if he did not reform[64]. Rebbi Jacob bat Abbay in the name of Rav Sheshet: At Usha[65] they voted not to excommunicate an ordained rabbi. This parallels what Rebbi Samuel said in the name of Rebbi Abbahu: One does not strip an ordained rabbi who is guilty of something of his title but tells him, *respect yourself and sit in your house*[66]. Rebbi Jacob bat Abbay in the name of Rebbi Aḥa: One treats an ordained rabbi who forgot his learning by an act of God with the holiness of the Ark[67]. Rebbi Aḥa, Rebbi Tanḥum, Rebbi Ḥiyya in the name of Rebbi Joḥanan: Excommunication by an ordained rabbi who excommunicated for his personal benefit is no excommunication[68].

61 An excommunication proclaimed by a competent court, which does not expire automatically after 30 days.
62 Babli 16a, somewhat different.

558   MO'ED QATAN CHAPTER THREE

63 Babli 17a.
64 If there is no legal basis for excommunication any competent court can revoke it.
65 Where rabbinic Judaism (as far as it differs from its predecessor, Pharisaic Judaism) was organized after the end of the Hadrianic persecutions.
66 *2K.* 14:10. An overriding authority has

to forbid him to act as Rabbi. Babli 17a.
67 As the Babli explains, *Berakhot* 8b, the Ark contained both the second whole and the first broken tablets. Therefore the broken mind of the Sage has to be treated with the reverence due to his earlier whole mind.
68 The opposite is noted (but not recommended) in the Babli, 17a.

(81b line 65) בְּיוֹמוֹי דְּרִבִּי יִרְמִיָה אֲתַת עֲקָא עַל טִיבֶּרְיָיאֵי. שְׁלַח בָּעֵי מְנַרְתָּא דְּכַסְפָּא גַּבֵּי רִבִּי יַעֲקֹב בֵּירִבִּי בּוּן. שְׁלַח אֲמַר לֵיהּ. עַדַּיִין לֹא שָׁב יִרְמִיָה מֵרָעָתוֹ. וּבִיקֵּשׁ לְנַדּוֹתוֹ. וַהֲוָה רִבִּי חִייָה בְּרֵיהּ דְּרִבִּי יִצְחָק עֲטוּשְׁיָיא יָתִיב תַּמָּן. אֲמַר לֵיהּ. שָׁמַעְתִּי שֶׁאֵין מְנַדִּין זָקֵן אֶלָּא אִם כֵּן עָשָׂה כְיָרָבְעָם בֶּן נְבָט וַחֲבֵירָיו. אֲמַר לֵיהּ. דִּכְמָה הַשְׁקוּהָ. וּכְיָרָבְעָם בֶּן נְבָט וַחֲבֵירָיו עָשָׂה. וְנִדּוּן אִילֵּין לָאִילֵּין. וְחָשׁוּן אִילֵּין עַל אִילֵּין וְצָרְכוּן מִשְׁתַּרְיָיא אִילֵּין מִן אִילֵּין.

In the days of Rebbi Jeremiah there came a calamity on the Tiberians. He sent and demanded a silver candelabrum from Rebbi Jacob ben Rebbi Abun[69]. He sent to tell him, Jeremiah still does not change from his evil ways[70]. He wanted to excommunicate him. Rebbi Hiyya ben Rebbi Isaac from Atoshia was sitting there. He said to him, I heard that one may excommunicate an ordained rabbi only if he acted like Jerobeam ben Nebat and his colleagues. He answered, "They[49] let her drink *dikma*." Did he act like Jerobeam ben Nebat and his colleagues? They excommunicated one another, worried one about the other, and needed permission from one another[71].

69 As contribution to the expenses of the community.
70 Since he holds that ordained rabbis are exempt from community taxes.
71 This shows that the rules stated earlier

are guidelines rather than laws, and that in any case the target of an excommunication has to see to it that it be lifted even if he disputes its legality.

(81d line 71) וְכֵן מִי שֶׁנִּשְׁאַל לְחָכָם וְהוּתַּר. מָה אֲנָן קַייָמִין. אִם בְּשֶׁנִּשְׁאַל קוֹדֶם לָרֶגֶל יִגָּלַח. אִם בְּשֶׁלֹּא נִשְׁאַל קוֹדֶם לָרֶגֶל לֹא יִגָּלַח. אֶלָּא כִּי אֲנָן קַייָמִין בְּשֶׁנִּשְׁאַל קוֹדֶם לָרֶגֶל וְלֹא מָצְאוּ פֶּתַח לְנַדְּרוֹ אֶלָּא בָרֶגֶל. כְּהָדָא. רִבִּי שִׁמְעוֹן בֵּירִבִּי לֹא מָצְאוּ פֶּתַח לְנַדְרוֹ עַד שֶׁבָּא אֶחָד מִזִּקְנֵי הַגָּלִיל. וְאִית דְּאָמְרֵי רִבִּי שִׁמְעוֹן בֶּן אֶלְעָזָר הֲוָה. וַהֲוָה נָסִיב לֵיהּ מִן הָכָא וּמֵקִים לֵיהּ הָכָא. נָסִיב לֵיהּ מִן הָכָא וּמֵקִים לֵיהּ הָכָא. עַד דְּאָקִימְיֵהּ גּוּ שִׁימְשָׁא מַפְלֵי מְאָנוֹי. אָמְרוּן לֵיהּ. אִילּוּ הֲוִיתָה יָדַע דְּהָדֵין סַבָּא עָבַד לָךְ הָכֵין נָדַר הֲוֵיתָה. אָמַר לוֹן. לָא. וְשָׁרוֹן לֵיהּ. וְלֵיהּ אָמְרִין.

הָדָא מְנָן לָךְ. אֲמַר לוֹן. מְשָׁרֵת מֵאִיר הָיִיתִי בִּבְרִיחוֹ שְׁנַיִם. וְיֵשׁ אוֹמְרִים. מַקְלוֹ שֶׁלְרִבִּי מֵאִיר הָיְתָה בְיָדוֹ וְהִיא הָיְתָה מְלַמְּדַתּוֹ דַעַת.

"And also who asked the Sages and was permitted[6]." Where do we hold? If he asked before the holiday he should shave; if he did not ask before the holiday he should not shave. But we hold in case that he asked before the holiday and they found an opening only on the holiday[72]. As the following: [73]They did not find an opening for Rebbi Simeon ben Rebbi until one of the Sages of Galilee came; some say, he was Rebbi Simeon ben Eleazar. He took him from one place and put him in another, he took him from one place and put him in another until finally he put him into the sun and told him to check his garments for fleas. They said to him, if you had known that this old man would treat you in such a way, would you have made the vow? He said, No. They permitted him. They asked, from where do you have this? He said to them, I was Meïr's servant when he fled the second time, but some say that Rebbi Meïr's staff was in his hand and it taught him knowledge.

72 The rabbi may invalidate a vow only after the person making the vow conceded that had he considered a certain consequence of the vow beforehand, he never would have made the vow. This is known as "opening (to regretting the vow)." Differently Babli 17b.

73 The following is copied (partially completed by the Venice editor) in *Nedarim* 9:1, Notes 29-31. Babli *Nedarim* 22b.

(82a line 6) תַּנֵּי. כָּל־אֵילּוּ שֶׁאֲמָרוּ. מְגַלְּחִין לְגַלֵּחַ בְּתוֹךְ שְׁלֹשִׁים יוֹם שֶׁלְּאֵבֶל. אִית תַּנָּיֵי תַּנֵּי. אָסוּר. [וְאִית תַּנָּיֵי תַּנֵּי. מוּתָּר.] אָמַר רַב חִסְדָּא. מָאן דְּאָמַר. מוּתָּר. בְּשֶׁיֵּשׁ שָׁם רֶגֶל. מָאן דְּאָמַר. אָסוּר. בְּשֶׁאֵין שָׁם רֶגֶל. מַתְנִיתָה פְּלִיגָא עַל רַב חִסְדָּא. הֲרֵי שֶׁתְּכָפוּהוּ אֲבֵלָיו זֶה אַחַר זֶה הֲרֵי זֶה מֵיקַל בַּסַּכִּין וּבַמִּסְפֶּרֶת אֲבָל לֹא בַמִּסְפָּרַיִים. וְיֵיעָשֶׂה אֵבֶל הַשֵּׁינִי אֵצֶל הָרִאשׁוֹן כְּמִי שֶׁהוּא אָנוּס וְיָנִיחַ. הֲוֵי לֹא אִתְאָמְרַת אֶלָּא מִפְּנֵי כְבוֹד הָרֶגֶל. רִבִּי שְׁמוּאֵל בַּר רַב יִצְחָק בָּעֵי. נִיחָא בְתוֹךְ שִׁבְעָה. בְּתוֹךְ שְׁלֹשִׁים. הָתִיב רִבִּי חֲנַנְיָה חַבְרוֹן דְּרַבָּנָן. וְהָא תַאנֵי. אִילּוּ דְבָרִים שֶׁאֵבֶל אָסוּר בָּהֶן כָּל־שִׁבְעָה. אִם בְּתוֹךְ שְׁלֹשִׁים הוּא אָסוּר בְּתוֹךְ שִׁבְעָה לֹא כָל־שֶׁכֵּן. לֹא אִיתְאָמְרַת אֶלָּא בְשֶׁתְּכָפוּהוּ אֲבֵלִים. הָדָא אָמְרָה שֶׁהוּא מוּתָּר. אָמַר רִבִּי מַתַּנְיָה. מָאן דְּאָמַר. אָסוּר. כְּדַרְכּוֹ בַּמִּסְפָּרַיִים.

[74]It was stated: All these for whom they said that they shave on a holiday are permitted to shave during the thirty days of mourning[75]. There are Tannaim who state, forbidden. [There are Tannaim who state, permitted.] Rav Ḥisda said, he who said permitted, if there happened to be a holiday; he

who said forbidden, if there was no holiday. A *baraita* disagrees with Rav Hisda. If his mournings immediately followed one another he can lighten with a knife or coarse shears but not with scissors. But the second mourning relative to the first should be considered as an act of God and he should be permitted[76]. Therefore it only was said for the honor of the holiday. Rebbi Samuel bar Rav Isaac asked, one understands the first Seven days. Within Thirty? Rebbi Ḥanania the colleague of the rabbis asked: Did we not state, these are the matters which are forbidden to the mourner during all Seven[77]? If he would be forbidden during Thirty days, within Seven not so much more? It could not have been said except if mournings immediately followed one another. Does this imply that he is permitted[78]? Rebbi Mattania said, he who said "forbidden", as usual with scissors.

74 Parallels to the arguments here are in the Babli, 17b.

75 The rules of mourning require abstention from all gainful work for 7 days, as well a abstention from grooming of all sorts. Work and some grooming are permitted during the following 23 days.

76 Since the *baraita* implies that this is not so, the rules of holidays are not transferable to those of mourning.

77 Since the prohibition of mourning is separately stated for the first seven days of mourning, the same rules cannot apply for the remainder of the 30 days.

78 But the general practice is not to shave for 30 days. Therefore one has to accept R. Mattania's answer, that emergency shavings are permitted during the 30 day period following the holiday rules.

(82a line 18) שָׂפָם וּנְטִילַת צִפּוֹרְנַיִם. אִית תַּנָּיֵי תַּנֵּי. בָּרֶגֶל מוּתָּר וּבָאֲבֵל אָסוּר. אִית תַּנָּיֵי תַּנֵּי. בָּרֶגֶל אָסוּר וּבָאֲבֵל מוּתָּר. מָאן דְּאָמַר. בָּרֶגֶל מוּתָּר. בְּשֶׁיֵּשׁ שָׁם רֶגֶל. וּבָאֲבֵל אָסוּר. בְּשֶׁאֵין שָׁם רֶגֶל. מָאן דְּאָמַר. בָּרֶגֶל אָסוּר. בְּשֶׁיֵּשׁ שָׁם הַעֲרָמָה. בָּאֲבֵל מוּתָּר. בְּשֶׁאֵין שָׁם הַעֲרָמָה. רַב חִייָה בַּר אָשִׁי בְּשֵׁם רַב. הֲלָכָה כְדִבְרֵי מִי שֶׁהוּא מֵיקַל כָּאן וְכָאן. רִבִּי שִׁמְעוֹן בַּר אַבָּא בְּשֵׁם רִבִּי יְהוֹשֻׁעַ בֶּן לֵוִי. הֲלָכָה כְדִבְרֵי מִי שֶׁהוּא מֵיקַל בְּהִילְכוֹת אָבֵל. רַב אָמַר. שָׂפָם כִּנְטִילַת צִפּוֹרְנַיִם לְכָל־דָּבָר. אָמַר רִבִּי יִרְמְיָה. וּבִלְבַד בְּנוֹטוֹת. רִבִּי יִצְחָק בַּר נַחְמָן בְּשֵׁם רִבִּי חֲנִינָה. זוּג בָּא לִפְנֵי רִבִּי בְּשָׂפָם וּנְטִילַת צִפּוֹרְנַיִם וְהִתִּיר לָהֶם רִבִּי. רִבִּי סִימוֹן בְּשֵׁם רִבִּי חֲנִינָה. שְׁנֵי זוּגוֹת הָיוּ. אֶחָד מֵעֲמָתָן וְאֶחָד מִיַּד עָלָה. אֶחָד׳ בְּשָׂפָם וְאֶחָד בִּנְטִילַת צִפּוֹרְנַיִם. וְהִתִּיר לָהֶן רִבִּי. כְּהָדָא רִבִּי שְׁמוּאֵל בַּר אַבָּא דָמִחְכַת אַחְתֵּיהּ וַהֲוָה יָתִיב מַצְמֵי טַרְפוֹי. סָלַק רִבִּי לְעָזָר לְגַבֵּיהּ וְלָא כְסִיתוֹן. סָלַק רִבִּי נָתָן בַּר אַבָּא לְגַבֵּיהּ וְכַסִּיתוֹן. אָמַר לֵיהּ. מִן קוֹמוֹי רִבִּי לְעָזָר לָא כְסִיתִינוּן. וּמִן קוֹמוֹי אַתְּ מְכַסֵּי לוֹן. אָמַר לֵיהּ. וּמַה אַתְּ סָבַר. דְּאַתְּ חָבִיב עָלַי כְּרִבִּי לְעָזָר.

Mustachios[79] and cutting fingernails. There are Tannaim who state, permitted on a holiday and forbidden in mourning. There are Tannaim who state, forbidden on a holiday and permitted in mourning[80]. He who said permitted on a holiday, if there happens to be a holiday; and forbidden in mourning, if there is no holiday. He who said forbidden on a holiday, if it involves trickery[81]; and permitted in mourning, without trickery. Rav Hiyya bar Ashi in the name of Rav: practice follows him who is lenient at both occasions. Rebbi Simeon bar Abba in the name of Rebbi Joshua ben Levi: practice follows him who is lenient in the rules of mourning[82]. Rav said, the lips follow cutting fingernails in all respects. Rebbi Jeremiah said, only if they interfere[83]. Rebbi Isaac bar Nahman in the name of Rebbi Hanina: A pair came before Rebbi about lips and cutting fingernails and Rebbi permitted it to them. Rebbi Simon in the name of Rebbi Hanina: There were two pairs, one from Amatheh[84] and one from Yedid-Aleh, one about lips and one about cutting fingernails, and Rebbi permitted to them. As the following. The sister of Rebbi Samuel bar Abba died and he was sitting cutting his fingernails. Rebbi Eleazar visited him and he did not cover them. Rebbi Nathan bar Abba visited him and he was covering them[85]. He said to him, you did not cover them in front of Rebbi Eleazar; but in front of me you are covering them? He answered him, do you think that you are as dear to me as Rebbi Eleazar[86]?

79 Trimming them.
80 Babli 17b.
81 When with some effort he could have done it before the start of the holiday.
82 Babli 18a and many other occasions. In G: ר׳ יעקב בר .... שמעון בר אבא.
83 If the hairs of the mustachio interfere with eating. Babli 18a.
84 In the Babli 18a, Hamath.
85 Not knowing whether his visitor knew that cutting fingernails in the mourning period was permitted.
86 There was no danger that R. Eleazar would misinterpret current practice.

(fol. 81c) **משנה ב**: וְאֵילוּ מְכַבְּסִין בַּמּוֹעֵד הַבָּא מִמְּדִינַת הַיָּם וּמִבֵּית הַשִּׁבְיָיה. וְהַיּוֹצֵא מִבֵּית הָאֲסוּרִין. וְהַמְנוּדֶּה שֶׁהִתִּירוּ לוֹ חֲכָמִים. וְכֵן מִי שֶׁנִּשְׁאַל לְחָכָם וְהוּתָּר. מִטְפְּחוֹת הַיָּדַיִם וּמִטְפְּחוֹת הַסְּפָרִים וּמִטְפְּחוֹת הַסְּפָג. וְכָל־הָעוֹלִין מִטּוּמְאָה לְטַהֲרָה הֲרֵי אֵילוּ מוּתָּרִין וּשְׁאָר כָּל־אָדָם אֲסוּרִין:

Mishnah 2: And the following may wash[87] on the holiday: He who comes from overseas[2], or from being kidnapped[3], or leaves jail[4], and one whose excommunication was lifted by the Sages[5], and also who asked the Sages and was permitted[6]. Hand towels, and barber's cloths, and body towels, and all who ascend from impurity to purity[89] are permitted to wash, but anybody else is forbidden.

87 Professionally wash.
88 For most of them are biblically required to wash their garments (immersing them in a *miqweh*.)

(82a line 33) **הלכה ב**: תַּנֵּי. בַּלְנָרֵי נָשִׁים מוּתָּר לְכַבְּסָן בַּמּוֹעֵד. הִיא בַּלְנָרֵי נָשִׁים הִיא בַּלְנָרֵי אֲנָשִׁים. מָהוּ בַּלְנָרֵי נָשִׁים. רַבָּנָן דְּקֵיסָרִין אָמְרֵי. אַנְטִינִיָּיא. רִבִּי אַבָּהוּ בְּשֵׁם רִבִּי יוֹחָנָן. מִי שֶׁאֵין לוֹ אֶלָּא חָלוּק אֶחָד מוּתָּר לְכַבְּסוֹ בַּמּוֹעֵד. אָמַר רִבִּי יוֹסֵה בֵּירְבִּי בּוּן. וּבִלְחוֹד תְּרֵיי. דְּיֵחָא שְׁלַח חַד וְלָבַשׁ חַד. בָּעוּן קוֹמֵי רִבִּי יוֹסֵה. בִּגְדֵי קְטַנִּים מַהֶן. אָמַר לוֹן. כְּמִי שֶׁאֵין לוֹ אֶלָּא חָלוּק אֶחָד. בָּעוּן קוֹמוֹי. תַּנִּינָן. אֵין קוֹרְעִין וְלֹא חוֹלְצִין וְאֵין מַבְרִין אֶלָּא קְרוֹבָיו שֶׁלְמֵת. הָוַת מַטְלְתֵיהּ זְעִירָא וּקְרִיבוֹי בָּעָן מֵיעוֹל לְגַבֵּיהּ. מָהוּ דְּיַתְבוּן פַּלְגוֹן מִן לְגֵיו וּפַלְגוֹן מִן לְבַר. אָמַר לוֹן. יַעֲלוּן פַּלְגוֹן יוֹמָא דֵין וּפַלְגוֹן לְמָחָר. אָמַר רִבִּי מָנָא. הֵן דַּהֲוֵינָן סָבְרִין דּוּ מְקַלְּלָה חָמַר.

Halakhah 2: It was stated: It is permitted to wash women's bath cloths on the holiday. Women's bath cloths have the same status as men's bath cloths. What are women's bath cloths? The rabbis of Caesarea are saying, 'οθόνιον[89]. Rebbi Abbahu in the name of Rebbi Joḥanan: A person who only has one garment may wash it on the holiday[90]. Rebbi Yose ben Rebbi Abun said, this means two, that he may give one to be washed and wear one. They asked before Rebbi Yose, what is the status of small children's garments? He said to them, like one who only has one garment. They asked before him: We have stated[91], "only the relatives of the deceased may tear their clothes, take off their shoes, and accept the consolation meal.[92]" If his strip was small and his relatives want to come to him, may half of them sit inside and half outside? He said to them, half of them should come today and half tomorrow. Rebbi Mana said, there we[93] had thought that he was going to be lenient, but he was restrictive.

89 "Fine linen".
90 Babli 18a.
91 Mishnah 3:7.

92 The first meal after the burial may not be prepared by the mourners themselves but must be brought to them by others; it should

be consumed at the place of the closest relative.

93 The students of R. Yose like himself.

(82a line 43) תַּנֵי. מִטְפְּחוֹת סַפָּרִים אֵין מְכַבְּסִין אוֹתָן בְּמֵי רַגְלַיִם. אֲבָל מְכַבְּסִין אוֹתָן בְּנֶתֶר וּבוֹרִית מִפְּנֵי הַכָּבוֹד.

It was stated: One does not wash barbers' cloths with urine, but one washes them with soda and soap, out of respect[94].

94 Since they will be used on human bodies.

(fol. 81c) **משנה ג**: וְאֵילּוּ כּוֹתְבִין בַּמּוֹעֵד קִידּוּשֵׁי נָשִׁים גִּטִּין וְשׁוֹבָרִין דְּיַּיתִּיקֵי מַתָּנָה וּפְרוֹזְבּוּלִין אִיגְּרוֹת שׁוּם וְאִיגְּרוֹת מָזוֹן שִׁטְרֵי חֲלִיצָה וּמֵיאוּנִין וּשְׁטָרֵי בֵרוּרִין וּגְזֵירוֹת בֵּית דִּין וְאִיגְּרוֹת שֶׁל רְשׁוּת:

Mishnah 3: And the following one writes on the holiday: Preliminary marriage documents of women[95], bills of divorce, and receipts[96], wills[97], gifts[98], *prozbol*[99], letters of estimation[100], and letters of provisions[101], documents of *haliṣah*[102], and repudiation[103], and documents of selections[104], and court decisions, and private letters.

95 While one may not marry on the holiday, there is no restriction on preliminary marriages which prohibit the woman to any other man.
96 Acknowledgement of the divorcee that she received all the monies due to her upon divorce.
97 Greek διαθήκη.
98 Gift documents executed by a healthy person.
99 The document which turns a private debt into a court document and therefore makes the debt enforceable after a Sabbatical year.

100 Written estimations of the value of real estate in court proceedings.
101 Court authorization for the guardian to use an estate's property for the support of a widow or an absentee husband's property for the support of his wife.
102 Evidence of the execution of the ritual which eliminates levirate marriage.
103 Evidence of repudiation of a marriage by a minor girl who had been married off by mother or brothers after her father's death.
104 Agreement which constitutes a panel of arbitration.

(82a line 45) **הלכה ג**: וְאֵינוֹ מֵיצַר. אָמַר רִבִּי זְעוּרָה. מִכֵּיוָן שֶׁנָּתַן דַּעְתּוֹ לְגָרֵשׁ אֵינוֹ מֵיצַר.

וְשׁוֹבָרִים. אִימוֹלוֹגִין. אִיגְרוֹת שׁוּם. שׁוּם הַיְתוֹמִים. אִיגְרוֹת מָזוֹן. מְזוּנוֹת אַלְמָנָה. שְׁטָרֵי חֲלִיצָה. אֵילוּ הֵן שְׁטָרֵי חֲלִיצָה. תַּמָּן אָמְרִין. דְּקָרְבַת קוֹדְמֵינָא וְשָׁרַת סִיָּנֵיהּ מְעִילוֹי רִיגְלֵיהּ דְּיְמִינָא וְרָקַת קוֹדְמֵינָא רוֹקָא דְּמִתְחֲזֵי עַל אַרְעָא וְאָמְרַת. כָּכָה יֵעָשֶׂה לָאִישׁ אֲשֶׁר לֹא־יִבְנֶה אֶת־בֵּית אָחִיו: וְשִׁטְרֵי מֵיאוּנִין. אֵילוּ הֵן שְׁטָרֵי מֵיאוּנִין. לָא רְעֵינָא לֵיהּ לָא שְׁוֵיָינָא לֵיהּ. לָא צָבִינָא לְאִיתְנַסְבָא לֵיהּ. וּשְׁטָרֵי בֵרוּרִין. רִבִּי יוֹחָנָן אָמַר. קוֹמְפְּרוֹמִיסִין. זֶה בוֹרֵר לוֹ אֶחָד וְזֶה בוֹרֵר לוֹ אֶחָד. וּגְזֵירוֹת בֵּית דִּין. אֵילוּ גִיזְרֵי דִינִין. וְאִיגְּרוֹת שֶׁל רְשׁוּת. זוֹ שְׁאִילַת שָׁלוֹם.

Halakhah 3: Is he not sorry[105]? Rebbi Ze`ira said, since he decided to divorce he is not sorry.

"And receipts," documents of consent[106]. "Letters of estimation," estimation for orphans. "Letters of provisions," support of a widow. "Documents of *ḥaliṣah*." The following are documents of *ḥaliṣah*. There[107], they are saying: That she appeared before us and removed his shoe from his right foot and spat before us visible spittle on the ground and said, *so shall be done to a man who will not build his brother's house*[108]. "And documents of repudiation." The following are documents of repudiation[109]: I do not want him, I do not find him worthy, and I have no desire to be married to him. "And documents of selections." Rebbi Joḥanan said, *compromissa;* each party selects one[110]. "And court decisions," Decisions of lawsuits. "And private letters," greetings.

105 This questions why divorce is permitted on a holiday. Is this not an occasion which contradicts the spirit of the holiday?
106 Greek ὁμολογία, "consent". A joint declaration of payor and payee that the debt is extinguished.
107 Babylonia. The Babylonian text is rather longer, Babli *Yebamot* 39b.
108 *Deut.* 25:9.
109 Babli *Yebamot* 107b.
110 Babli *Bava batra* 168a.

(fol. 81c) **משנה ד**: אֵין כּוֹתְבִין שְׁטָרֵי חוֹב בַּמּוֹעֵד. אִם אֵינוֹ מַאֲמִינוֹ אוֹ שֶׁאֵין לוֹ מַה יֹּאכַל הֲרֵי זֶה יִכְתּוֹב. אֵין כּוֹתְבִין סְפָרִים תְּפִילִּין וּמְזוּזוֹת בַּמּוֹעֵד וְאֵין מַגִּיהִין אוֹת אַחַת אֲפִלּוּ בְּסֵפֶר הָעֲזָרָה. רִבִּי יְהוּדָה אוֹמֵר כּוֹתֵב הוּא אָדָם תְּפִילִּין וּמְזוּזוֹת לְעַצְמוֹ וְטוֹוֶה לְעַצְמוֹ תְּכֵלֶת לְצִיצִית:

Mishnah 4: One does not write debt documents on the holiday, but if he does not trust him or if he has nothing to eat, he shall write[111]. One does not write Torah scrolls, *tefillin*[112] and *mezuzzot*[113] on the holiday; also one does not correct even a single letter in the Temple Courtyard Scroll[114]. Rebbi Jehudah says, a person may write *tefillin* and *mezuzzot* for himself[115], and spin for himself the blue string for his *ṣiṣit*[116].

111 While one does not write commercial or investment documents, if it is necessary to provide one of the parties involved with support for the enjoyment of the holiday one has to write. The rabbinic prohibition of writing may not be an obstacle to fulfilling the biblical obligation to enjoy the holiday.
112 To be worn on head and arm, *Ex.* 13:9,16.
113 To be placed on the doorposts, *Deut.* 6:9, 11:20.
114 In the Babli: "In the Ezra scroll".
115 Since *tefillin* are required to be worn on the intermediate days of the holiday and *mezuzot* are an obligation every day.
116 The blue thread which distinguishes Jewish garments from other 3rd Millennium BCE Semitic garb; *Num*. 15:38. This also is an obligation not suspended during the holiday.

(82a line 54) **הלכה ד**: אֵין כּוֹתְבִין שִׁטְרֵי אֲרָסִיּוֹת וְקַבְּלָנוּת בַּמּוֹעֵד. הַשָּׁם שָׁם כְּדַרְכּוֹ. וּבִלְבַד שֶׁלֹּא יָמוּד וְשֶׁלֹּא יִשְׁקוֹל וְלֹא יִמְנֶה. וּמְקַבְּלִין קִיבּוֹלֶת בַּמּוֹעֵד לַעֲשׂוֹתָהּ לְאַחַר הַמּוֹעֵד. וְאֵין מְקַבְּלִין קִיבּוֹלֶת לַעֲשׂוֹתָהּ בְּתוֹךְ הַמּוֹעֵד. הַשָּׁם שָׁם כְּדַרְכּוֹ וּבִלְבַד שֶׁלֹּא יָמוּד וְשֶׁלֹּא יִשְׁקוֹל וְלֹא יִמְנֶה.

אָמַר רִבִּי יִרְמְיָה. אִם אֵינוֹ מַאֲמִינוֹ לַלֹּוֶה. אוֹ שֶׁאֵין לוֹ מַה יֹּאכַל לַלֹּבְקָר. אָמַר לוֹ רִבִּי יוֹסֵי. אִם אוֹמֵר אַתְּ כֵּן נִמְצֵאתָהּ מַתִּיר אֶת הָאוּמָנוּת בַּמּוֹעֵד. אֶלָּא אִם אֵינוֹ מַאֲמִינוֹ לַמִּלְוֶה שֶׁעֲבָרָה. אוֹ שֶׁאֵין לוֹ מַה יֹּאכַל לַמִּלְוֶה הַבָּאָה.

חַד בַּר נָשׁ אוֹבַד תְּפִילּוֹי בְּמוֹעֲדָא. אֲתָא לְגַבֵּי רִבִּי חֲנַנְאֵל וּשְׁלָחֵיהּ לְגַבֵּי רִבִּי אַבָּא בַּר נָתָן. אָמַר לֵיהּ. הַב לֵיהּ תְּפִילָךְ וְזִיל כְּתוֹב לָךְ. אָמַר לֵיהּ רַב. אִיזִיל כְּתוֹב לֵיהּ. מַתְנִיתָהּ פְּלִיגָא עַל רַב. כּוֹתֵב הוּא אָדָם תְּפִילִין וּמְזוּזָה לְעַצְמוֹ. הָא לְאַחֵר לֹא. פָּתַר לָהּ בְּכוֹתֵב לְהַנִּיחַ.

Halakhah 4: "One does not write documents for sharecroppers[117] or contractorship[118] on the holiday. The appraiser appraises normally on condition that he neither measure nor weigh nor count." "But one accepts contractorship on the holiday on condition that it be executed after the holiday; one does not accept contractorship on the holiday on condition that it be executed on the holiday. The appraiser appraises normally on condition that he neither measure not weigh nor count."[119]

Rebbi Jeremiah said, "if he does not trust him," the debtor, "or if he has nothing to eat," the scribe. Rebbi Yose said to him, if you would say so you would permit professional work on the holiday[120]. But "if he does not trust him," about the past loan, "or if he has nothing to eat," about the future loan.

A man lost his *tefillin* on the holiday. He came to Rebbi Ḥananel who sent him to Rebbi Abba bar Nathan. He said to him[121], give him your *tefillin* and go, write for yourself. Rav said to him, go and write for him[122]. The Mishnah disagrees with Rav: "a person may write *tefillin* and *mezuzot* for himself[115]," therefore not for others. He explains it: writing for supply[123].

117 Since agricultural work is forbidden on the holiday, there is no need for such a contract on the holiday.

118 The contractor is paid for the finished work; he works on his own time. The lessor of the contract does not tell when or how to do his work.

119 *Baraitot* similar to Tosephta 2:3,5. Babli 12a.

120 Cf. Chapter 1, Note 169.

121 R. Ḥananel directed the scribe R. Abba bar Nathan to give away his own *tefillin* and write himself new ones following R. Jehudah.

122 If practice follows R. Jehudah then it is not necessary to use a trick to follow his rule, but *tefillin* needed of the holiday may be written on the holiday. Babli 19a. There the name correctly is *Rav* Ḥananel.

123 To be sold later. At the moment of writing he has no customer waitimg.

(82a line 64) וְטוֹוָה עַל יְרֵיכוֹ תְּכֵלֶת לְצִיצִיתוֹ. רַב יְהוּדָה בְּשֵׁם שְׁמוּאֵל רִבִּי אַבָּהוּ בְּשֵׁם רִבִּי יוֹחָנָן. טוֹוָה אֲפִילוּ בַּפֶּלֶךְ. רַב אָמַר. טוֹוָה בַּפֶּלֶךְ. בֵּין לוֹ בֵּין לְאַחֵר. מַתְנִיתָה פְלִיגָא עַל רַב. וְטוֹוָה עַל יְרֵיכוֹ תְּכֵלֶת לְצִיצִיתוֹ. פָּתַר לָהּ בְּטוֹוָה לְהָנִיחַ.

"And spins on his hip the blue string for his *ṣiṣit*[124]." Rav Jehudah in the name of Samuel, Rebbi Abbahu in the name of Rebbi Joḥanan: he spins even using a spindle[125]. Rav said, he spins using a spindle both for himself or for others. The Mishnah disagrees with Rav: "and spins on his hip the blue string for his *ṣiṣit*;" therefore not for others. He explains it: spinning for supply[123].

124 This version of the Mishnah is identical with that quoted in the Babli.

125 Babli 19a. P:ractice is more lenient than even R. Jehudah.

(fol. 81c) **משנה ה**: הַקּוֹבֵר אֶת מֵתוֹ שְׁלֹשֶׁת יָמִים קוֹדֶם לָרֶגֶל בָּטְלוּ מִמֶּנּוּ גְּזֵירַת שִׁבְעָה. שְׁמוֹנַת יָמִים קוֹדֶם לָרֶגֶל בָּטְלוּ מִמֶּנּוּ גְּזֵירַת שְׁלֹשִׁים מִפְּנֵי שֶׁאָמְרוּ שַׁבָּת עוֹלָה וְאֵינָהּ מַפְסֶקֶת רְגָלִים מַפְסִיקִין וְאֵינָן עוֹלִין:

Mishnah 5: The decree of Seven is cancelled for him who buried his dead three days before the holiday[126]. Eight days before the holiday, the decree of Thirty is cancelled for him[127], since they said, Sabbath is counted but does not interrupt, holidays interrupt but are not counted[128].

126 The rules of post-exilic Judaism as formulated by Ezra and his successors require a strict mourning period of seven days where grooming and gainful work are prohibited, followed by another 23 days of lesser mourning where there are no restrictions of work. Except for father and mother there are no talmudic mourning rites after 30 days. If a holiday falls into the first mourning week it eliminates the remaining restrictions of the first 7 days. The mourner then still is required to observe the next 23 days of lesser mourning.

127 If at least one day of the lesser mourning period was observed, the following holiday eliminates all mourning rites.

128 While mourning is forbidden on the Sabbath, it is counted as if mourning had been observed but it does not eliminate any of the traditional mourning periods. A holiday stops the mourning, but in case of the holiday occurring during the first week the holiday week does not diminish the required lesser mourning period following the end of the holiday.

(82a line 67) **הלכה ה**: גְּזֵירַת שִׁבְעָה. סַנְדָּל וְסַפָּג. גְּזֵירַת שְׁלֹשִׁים. אִיחוּי וְגִיהוּץ וְתִגְלַחַת. אֵי זֶהוּ גִיהוּץ. כְּלֵי צֶמֶר מְגוּהָצִין חֲדָשִׁים. וּכְלֵי פִשְׁתָּן מְגוּהָצִין לְבָנִים. רִבִּי חֶלְבּוֹ רַב חוּנָה בְשֵׁם רַב. חָל יוֹם שְׁמִינִי שֶׁלּוֹ לִהְיוֹת בַּשַּׁבָּת מְגַלֵּחַ עֶרֶב שַׁבָּת. הֵיךְ אֶיפְשָׁר. תִּיפְתָּר שֶׁגְּרָרַתּוּ חַיָּה וְנִתְיָיאֲשׁוּ מִלְּבַקֵּשׁ. וְתַנֵּי כֵן. הֲרֵי מִי שֶׁגְּרָרַתּוּ חַיָּה. מֵאֵימָתַי מוֹנִין לוֹ. מִשֶּׁנִּתְיָיאֲשׁוּ מִלְּבַקֵּשׁ. מְצָאוּהוּ אֵיבָרִים אֵיבָרִים. מוֹנִין לוֹ מִשֶּׁיִּמָּצֵא רֹאשׁוֹ וְרוּבּוֹ. רִבִּי יְהוּדָה אוֹמֵר. הַשִּׁזְרָה וְהַגּוּלְגּוֹלֶת רוּבּוֹ. אָמַר רִבִּי אָבוּן. תִּיפְתָּר שֶׁנִּסְתַּם הַגּוֹלֵל עֶרֶב שַׁבָּת עִם חֲשֵׁיכָה. הֵיךְ אֶיפְשָׁר. אָמַר רִבִּי אָחָא. תִּיפְתָּר שֶׁסְּתָמוֹ גּוֹי. אִית בָּעֵי מֵימַר שֶׁבָּאַת לוֹ שְׁמוּעָה קְרוֹבָה בַשַּׁבָּת.

Halakhah 5: "The decree of seven", sandal and soap[129]. "The decree of thirty," mending, and pressing, and shaving[130]. What is pressing? New pressed woolen garments, and pressed white linen garments[131].

Rebbi Ḥelbo, Rav Ḥuna in the name of Rav: If his eighth day fell on a Sabbath, he shaves on Friday[132]. How is this possible[133]? Explain it if he had been dragged away by a wild animal and they gave up hope to look after him[134]. It was stated thus: When do you start to count for somebody who was dragged away by a wild animal? When they gave up hope to look after him. If they found separate limbs of him one counts when his head and most of his body had been found. Rebbi Jehudah says, spine and skull form the majority. Rebbi Abun said, explain it that the cover plate[135] was laid Friday evening at the start of darkness. How is this possible? Rebbi Aḥa said, explain it if it was closed by a Gentile. Some wanted to say that he received a current notice[136] on the Sabbath.

129 The items forbidden to use during the seven days of intense mourning. The reading and meaning of ספן is questionable but in the absence of parallels it is impossible to guess anything better.

130 Before the burial, the near relatives have to tear their clothing. These tears cannot be mended before the end of the 30 day mourning period. Pressing is ironing under pressure using starch. For shaving, cf. Note 1.

131 Pressing is only forbidden if it makes garments ready for an appearance in society.

132 Since shaving is permitted only at the end of the 30 day period, one has to explain that the Sabbath was the eve of a holiday (explicit in Babli 17b). Then the holiday eliminates the remainder of the 30 day mourning period; if it were a weekday the mourner would have to shave. To underline the importance of the Sabbath, one permits to shave on Friday.

133 If the eighth day is a Sabbath then the first day was a Sabbath. But burials are forbidden on the Sabbath and the mourning period only starts with the close of the burial ceremony.

134 And this could have been on the Sabbath if the family then decided not to go out again on Sunday.

135 Which signals the start of the mourning period. This can happen to everybody.

136 A person who was not informed of the death of a close relative has to observe all mourning rituals if he is informed within the first 30 days; this is called "current notice". If the news reaches him later, "an out of date notice", he only has to observe a short period of symbolic mourning. Also this is an explanation not dependent on the rare case of a person eaten by an wild beast.

(82a line 75)   רִבִּי אַמִּי הֲוָה לֵיהּ עוֹבְדָא וְגִילַּח יוֹם שְׁלֹשִׁים. [וְאֶחָד רִבִּי] הֲוָה לֵיהּ עוֹבְדָא וְגִילַּח יוֹם שְׁלֹשִׁים וְאֶחָד. אָמַר רִבִּי זְרִיקוֹ. מִן מַתְנִיתָן יָלֵף לָהּ רִבִּי אַמִּי. דְּתַנֵּינַן תַּמָּן. מִי שֶׁנָּזַר שְׁתֵּי נְזִירִיּוֹת מְגַלֵּחַ אֶת הָרִאשׁוֹנָה יוֹם שְׁלֹשִׁים וְאֶחָד וְאֶת הַשְּׁנִייָה יוֹם שִׁשִּׁים וְאֶחָד. אָמַר רִבִּי יוֹסֵי. תַּמָּן לְשֶׁעָבַר וְהָכָא כַּתְּחִילָּה. רִבִּי יִרְמְיָה הוֹרֵי לְרִבִּי יִצְחָק עַטוֹשִׁיָּיא. וְאִית דְּאָמְרֵי. לְרִבִּי חִייָה בְּרֵיהּ דְּרִבִּי יִצְחָק עַטוֹשִׁיָּא. לְגַלֵּחַ יוֹם שְׁלֹשִׁים מִן מַתְנִיתָן. שְׁמוֹנַת יָמִים קוֹדֶם לָרֶגֶל בָּטְלוּ מִמֶּנּוּ גְּזֵירַת שְׁלֹשִׁים. הִיא שְׁמִינִי הִיא שְׁלֹשִׁים. אָמַר רִבִּי יוֹסֵה. שַׁנְייָא הִיא תַּמָּן שֶׁמִּפְּנֵי כְבוֹד הָרֶגֶל הִתִּירוּ. תֵּדַע לָךְ שֶׁהִיא כֵן. דְּאָמַר רִבִּי חֶלְבּוֹ רַב חוּנָה בְשֵׁם רַב. חָל יוֹם שְׁמִינִי שֶׁלּוֹ לִהְיוֹת

בַּשַּׁבָּת מְגַלֵּחַ עֶרֶב שַׁבָּת. אִין תֵּימַר שֶׁלֹּא מִפְּנֵי הָרֶגֶל הִתִּירוּ. מֵעַתָּה אֲפִילוּ חָל יוֹם שְׁלֹשִׁים שֶׁלּוֹ לִהְיוֹת בַּשַּׁבָּת מְגַלֵּחַ עֶרֶב שַׁבָּת. וְעוֹד מִן הָדָא דְּתַנֵּי. עַל כָּל־הַמֵּתִים הוּא שׁוֹלֵל לְאַחַר שִׁבְעָה וּמְאַחֶה לְאַחַר שְׁלֹשִׁים. וְיִשְׁלוֹל יוֹם שִׁבְעָה וִיאַחֶה יוֹם שְׁלֹשִׁים. אָמַר רִבִּי חַגַּי. דִּיהֲוָה שְׁמַעְתָּא כֵן וּשְׁמַעְתָּא כֵן.

1 אמי | ז אימי [ואחד רני] היה | ז והוה   2 זריקן | ז זריקא אמי | ז אימי   4 והכא | ז וכא כתחילה | ז לכתחילה לר' | ז לרב   5 בריה דר' | ז בר רב עטושייא | A -   מתניתן A מתניתין קודם לרגל | ז -   6 שמיני | ז שמינית A שמונים שלשים | ז יום ל' יוסה | Az יוסי שנייא A שמייה שמפני A מפני כבוד | ז [כבוד]   7 שהיא כן | ז -   דאמ' | ז דמר   רב חונה בשם רב | ז בר חונה בשם ר' יוחנן A רב הונה בשם רב שמיני | ז שמונה שלו | A -   9 ערב | ז בערב הדא A הדה   דתני | ז דאמ' ר' יוחנן הוא | ז כולן   10 לאחר | A ליום ויאחה | A וישלש חגי | Az חגי דיחיה | A דיהבה שמעתא | ז שמועתא A שני עתה   11 שמעתא | ז שמועתא ושמעתה רב | A ר'

תַּנֵּי. זוֹ דִּבְרֵי אַבָּא שָׁאוּל. רַב יְהוּדָה בְשֵׁם שְׁמוּאֵל רִבִּי אַבָּהוּ בְשֵׁם רִבִּי יוֹחָנָן. הֲלָכָה כְאַבָּא שָׁאוּל. וְתַנֵּי כֵן. הֲלָכָה כִדְבָרָיו. רִבִּי בָּא בְשֵׁם רַב. דִּבְרֵי אַבָּא שָׁאוּל בֵּין יָמִים בֵּין גְּזֵירוֹת בָּטְלוּ. אֲבָל דִּבְרֵי חֲכָמִים יָמִים בָּטְלוּ .גְּזֵירוֹת לֹא בָּטְלוּ. מַה בֵּינֵיהוֹן. רַב חוּנָה אָמַר. עֶרֶב הָרֶגֶל בֵּינֵיהוֹן. אִם גִּילַּח עֶרֶב הָרֶגֶל יְגַלַּח אַחַר הָרֶגֶל. אִם לֹא גִּילַּח עֶרֶב הָרֶגֶל לֹא יְגַלַּח אַחַר הָרֶגֶל. רִבִּי יוֹחָנָן אָמַר. אַף עַל פִּי שֶׁלֹּא גִּילַּח עֶרֶב הָרֶגֶל יְגַלַּח אַחַר הָרֶגֶל. רִבִּי לְעָזֶר הוֹרֵי לְרִבִּי שִׁמְעוֹן בַּר בָּא לְגַלֵּחַ לְאַחַר הָרֶגֶל. וְלֹא יָדְעִין אִי כְּהָדָא דְאַבָּא שָׁאוּל וְאִין כְּהָדָא דְרַבָּנָן דִּבְרֵי הַכֹּל.

2 ר' בא | A רבא   3 ימים בטלו גזירות לא בטלו | A גזירות בטלו ימים לא בטלו חונה | A הונא   4 ביניהון | A ביניהם אם לא . . . אחר הרגל | A אם לאו לא   5 לעזר | A אליע'   6 לר' שמעון | A לשמעון   7 לאחר | A אחר כהדא | A כהדה   (2) ואין | A אי

[137]Something happened to Rebbi Immi and he shaved on the 30th day. Something happened [to one rabbi] and he shaved on the 31st day[138]. Rebbi Zeriqan said, Rebbi Immi learned this from our Mishnah, as we have stated there[139]: "If somebody vowed two *neziriot*[140], he shaves for the first on the 31st day, for the second on the 61st day." Rebbi Yose said, there after it happened, here from the start[141]. Rebbi Jeremiah instructed Rebbi Isaac from Aṭoshia, and some say, Rav Ḥiyya ben Rebbi Isaac from Aṭoshia, to shave on the 30th day, following the Mishnah: "Eight days, the decree of 30 days is waived for him." The eighth has the same status as the 30th day[142]. Rebbi Yose said, there is a difference; there they permitted in order to honor the holiday. You should know this, since Rebbi Ḥelbo, Rav Huna said in the name of Rav: If his eighth day fell on the Sabbath, he shaves Friday. If you say that they did permit not in order to honor the holiday, then even if his 30th day falls on the Sabbath, he should shave Sabbath eve[143]. In addition, from what was stated[144]: "For all deceased he stitches together after seven days and mends after 30." Why should he not stitch on the seventh day and mend on

the 30th day¹⁴⁵? Rebbi Haggai said, this has been transmitted in this way and that has been transmitted in that way¹⁴⁶.

It was stated¹⁴⁷: These are the words of Abba Shaul. Rav Jehudah in the name of Samuel, Rebbi Abbahu in the name of Rebbi Johanan: Practice follows Abba Shaul¹⁴⁷. Rebbi Abba in the name of Rav: The word of Abba Shaul: both days and decrees are cancelled. But the words of the Sages: the days are cancelled but the decrees are not cancelled¹⁴⁸. What is the difference between them? Rav Huna said, the eve of a holiday is between them¹⁴⁹. If he shaved before the holiday he may shave after the holiday. If he did not shave before the holiday he may not shave after the holiday. Rebbi Johanan said, even if he did not shave before the holiday he may shave after the holiday. Rebbi Eleazar instructed Rebbi Simeon bar Abba to shave after the holiday, but we do not know whether following Abba Shaul or following the consensus of the rabbis¹⁵⁰.

137 This paragraph is copied from *Nazir* 3:1 (Notes 7-16,ו).

138 The editor's insert declares the question of the first day when shaving is permitted to be open, different authorities following different rules. The text in *Nazir* and the scribe's text here note that R, Immi himself was inconsistent in this matter. S. Lieberman (*Tarbiz* 3) accepts the editor's addition as genuine (but more likely would be חד בירבי). The only certain statement is that the Venice text is not a genuine version of the Yerushalmi.

139 Mishnah *Nazir* 3:2.

140 If somebody declares himself a *nazir* without indicating the duration of his vow, it is automatically interpreted to mean that he is *nazir* for 30 days. If the 30th day could not possibly be a day for shaving, he should be able to shave only on the 62nd day. Therefore if the rabbinic rules for mourning are modelled on the biblical of the *nazir*, the Mishnah gives support both for the 30th and the 31st as days of shaving by the mourner.

141 R. Yose criticizes R. Immi. The Mishnah requires the *nazir* to shave on his 31st day; it only legitimizes shaving on the 30th after the fact. But R. Immi shaved on the 30th on his own initiative. R. Zeriqan seems to hold that what is acceptable after the fact in biblical rules is permitted from the start in rabbinic usage.

142 The argument here goes as follows: If the 8th day of mourning was holiday eve, the mourner can shave in the afternoon in preparation for the holiday. The time elapsed from dawn to the afternoon is counted as a full day for him. Therefore, the person who shaves on the 30th day can nevertheless count the entire 30th day as being part of his mourning period.

143 Nobody permits shaving on the 29th day.

144 Babli 22b. In the Babli and in *Nazir*

this is an Amoraic statement.

145 For the seven-day period, the mourner is required to wear the garment torn before the burial. He can stitch together the tear after the end of the seven-day period (after 30 days for father or mother) and invisibly mend it after thirty days (never mending invisibly for father or mother.) Why does one not allow stitching or mending on the last day of a period if "part of the day is counted as a whole day"?

146 Since one tradition is in from the school of Rav and the other (in the formulation of *Nazir*) of the school of R. Joḥanan, the two formulations of old (pre-)tannaitic traditions do not have to be coherent.

147 Babli 19b.

148 Babli 19a. The question remains whether the text of A reproduces the Babli or whether the scribe's text is the genuine Yerushalmi text.

149 As explained in the text (and accepted by the Babli): If the mourner uses the leniency offered to him to shave before the holiday, the decree of 30 days is abolished for him. But if he does not shave, he demonstrates that he does not accept the leniency and therefore the holiday does not eliminate the decree for him.

150 While we know the ruling to follow in this particular case we do not know what is the logical basis and therefore are handicapped in applying this rule to different situations.

(82b line 21) רִבִּי לְעָזֶר הוֹרִי לְשִׁמְעוֹן בַּר בָּא. הָרֶגֶל עוֹלֶה לְמִנְיָין שְׁלֹשִׁים. אָמַר רִבִּי יוֹסֵי. אַשְׁכְּחוֹן תַּלְתִּין קוֹדְמִין לְשִׁבְעָה. הַקּוֹבֵר אֶת מֵתוֹ שְׁלֹשָׁה יָמִים קוֹדֶם לָרֶגֶל בָּטְלוּ מִמֶּנּוּ גְּזֵירַת שִׁבְעָה. לֹא אָמַר אֶלָּא שְׁלֹשָׁה. הָא שְׁנַיִם לֹא. הָדָא דַתְּ אָמַר בֵּינוֹ לְבֵין עַצְמוֹ. אֲבָל הָרַבִּים אֵין הָרַבִּים מִתְעַסְּקִין עִמּוֹ. וְתַנֵּי כֵן. הַקּוֹבֵר אֶת מֵתוֹ שְׁלֹשָׁה יָמִים בְּתוֹךְ הָרֶגֶל מוֹנֶה שִׁבְעָה לְאַחַר הָרֶגֶל. שְׁלֹשָׁה יָמִים הָרִאשׁוֹנִים הָרַבִּים מִתְעַסְּקִין עִמּוֹ. אַרְבָּעָה הַיָּמִים הָאַחֲרוֹנִים אֵין הָרַבִּים מִתְעַסְּקִין עִמּוֹ. וּמְלֶאכְתּוֹ נַעֲשִׂית בַּאֲחֵרִים. וַעֲבָדָיו וּבְהֶמְתּוֹ עוֹשִׂין בְּצִינְעָה בְּמָקוֹם אַחֵר. מָהוּ לְהַרְאוֹת לוֹ פָּנִים. רִבִּי יַעֲקֹב בַּר אִידִי בְּשֵׁם רִבִּי חֲנִינָה. וַהֲלֹא אָמְרוּ. אֵין אָבֵל בַּשַּׁבָּת. מִפְּנֵי מַה אָמְרוּ לְהַרְאוֹת לוֹ פָּנִים. לֹא מִפְּנֵי הַכָּבוֹד. וְהָכָא מִפְּנֵי הַכָּבוֹד. וְדִכְוָותָהּ. יוֹם אֶחָד לִפְנֵי הָרֶגֶל בָּטְלוּ מִמֶּנּוּ גְּזֵירַת שְׁנַיִם.

1 למניין שלשים A | ממניין שלשים יום   2 קודמין A | קודם   3 הא שנים A | ראשונים   הדא A | הדה דת |
דאת A   5-6 ארבעה...עמו   6 נעשית A | נעשת   7 חנינה A | חנינא

Rebbi Eleazar instructed Simeon bar Abba: the holiday is counted in the count of thirty[151]. Rebbi Yose said, we find that thirty precede seven[152]: "The decree of seven is cancelled for him who buried his dead three days before the holiday." He only said three, therefore not two. That is what you are saying, in private; but the public does not occupy themselves with him[153]. It was stated this way[154]: One who buried his dead three days during the holiday counts seven after the holiday. During the first three days the public occupies themselves with him[155]; the last four days the public do not occupy themselves with him. His work is done by others and his slaves and animals work in privacy at other places. Does one visit him? Rebbi Jacob bar Idi in the name of Rebbi Ḥanina: Did they not say that there is no mourning on the Sabbath? Why did they say that one visits him? Not to honor? So here to honor. Similarly, one day before the holiday cancels the decree of two[156].

151 If the burial was shortly before the start of the holiday, so that no mourning in the style of the first seven days was possible, then the seven days have to be observed after the holiday but nevertheless the count of 30 starts immediately and after the end of the 7 day period only 14 days of reduced mourning have to be observed. Babli 20a.

152 The same is true if the burial is in the holiday week; the count of 30 starts immediately but the 7 are observed only after the end of the holiday.

153 Since there was public mourning before the holiday, there is none afterwards.

154 Babli 20a.

155 Since there was no public mourning during the holiday there is after the holiday, but since it is deferred, the public recognition is reduced.

156 Since there were no two days of mourning, the full seven days with public participation have to be observed after the holiday. All these rules were abolished in 5th Cent. Babylonian practice, a Century after work on the Yerushalmi had ceased, when the holiday was held to remove the decree of seven if at least one hour of mourning was observed before the start of the holiday; Babli 20a.

(82b line 32) אָבֵל בַּיּוֹם הָרִאשׁוֹן אֵינוֹ נוֹתֵן תְּפִילִּין. בַּיּוֹם הַשֵּׁינִי הוּא נוֹתֵן תְּפִילִּין. אִם בָּאוּ פָּנִים חֲדָשׁוֹת חוֹלְצָן כָּל־שִׁבְעָה. דִּבְרֵי רִבִּי לִיעֶזֶר. רִבִּי יְהוֹשֻׁעַ אוֹמֵר. בַּיּוֹם הָרִאשׁוֹן וּבַיּוֹם הַשֵּׁינִי אֵינוֹ נוֹתֵן תְּפִילִּין. בַּשְּׁלִישִׁי הוּא נוֹתֵן תְּפִילִּין. אִם בָּאוּ פָּנִים חֲדָשׁוֹת אֵינוֹ חוֹלְצָן. אִם בַּיּוֹם הַשֵּׁינִי אֵינוֹ נוֹתֵן תְּפִילִּין. צוֹרְכָה מֵימַר מִי שֶׁמֵּתוֹ מוּטָּל לְפָנָיו. אֶלָּא בְגִין דְּתַנָּא דָא תַּנָּא דָא. רִבִּי זְעוּרָה מַר עוּקְבָן בְּשֵׁם שְׁמוּאֵל. רִבִּי זְעוּרָה רַב יִרְמִיָה בְּשֵׁם רַב. הֲלָכָה כְּרִבִּי לִיעֶזֶר בִּנְתִינָה וּכְרִבִּי יְהוֹשֻׁעַ בַּחֲלִיצָה. רִבִּי זְעוּרָה בָּעֵי. אִם נָתַן בַּיּוֹם הַשֵּׁינִי כְּרִבִּי לִיעֶזֶר מָהוּ שֶׁיַּעֲשֶׂה רִבִּי לִיעֶזֶר כְּרִבִּי יְהוֹשֻׁעַ שֶׁלֹּא לַחֲלוֹץ. אָמַר רִבִּי יוֹסֵי בֵּירִבִּי בּוּן. וְכֵינִי. אִם נָתַן בַּיּוֹם הַשֵּׁינִי כְּרִבִּי לִיעֶזֶר נַעֲשָׂה רִבִּי לִיעֶזֶר כְּרִבִּי יְהוֹשֻׁעַ שֶׁלֹּא לַחֲלוֹץ. אֵין כֵּינִי נֹאמַר. הֲלָכָה כְּרִבִּי לִיעֶזֶר.

[157]A mourner may not put on *tefillin* on the first day; on the second day he puts on *tefillin* and when new faces appear during the seven days of mourning he takes them off; these are the words of Rebbi Eliezer. Rebbi Joshua says: On the first and second days he does not put on *tefillin*; on the third day he puts on *tefillin* and if new faces come he does not take them off[158]. If he does

not put on *tefillin* even on the second day, why is it necessary to mention[159] "anyone whose dead is lying before him"? Because he stated the one he stated the other[160]. Rebbi Ze`ira, Mar Uqban in the name of Samuel; Rebbi Ze`ira, Rav Jeremiah in the name of Rav: Practice follows Rebbi Eliezer in putting on and Rebbi Joshua in taking off. Rebbi Ze`ira inquired: If he put them on on the second day, following Rebbi Eliezer, would Rebbi Eliezer act like Rebbi Joshua, not to take them off? Rebbi Yose bar Abun said: Is it so that Rebbi Eliezer would act like Rebbi Joshua, not to take them off? If it were so, we should say "practice follows Rebbi Eliezer."

157 This text appears also in *Berakhot* 3:1 (Notes 5-9). While it clearly is a commentary on Mishnah *Berakhot* 3:1, the manuscript text there is copied from here.

158 Babli 21a (with attributions switched). All authorities in all sources agree that a mourner may not put on *tefillin* the entire first day of mourning, even if the burial was conducted in the preceding night. So there is no connection between *tefillin* and the necessity to attend the burial.

159 In Mishnah *Berakhot* 3:1 which rules that before the burial the family members do not recite *Shema`* nor put on *tefillin*.

160 Since it is necessary to mention that he is free from reciting *Shema`* (and from prayer, whether that is stated in the Mishnah or not), the mention of *tefillin* is added as a memory aid in the orally transmitted Mishnah.

(82b line 42) הֲרֵי שֶׁאֵין לוֹ מַה לּוֹכַל. בַּיּוֹם הָרִאשׁוֹן וּבַשֵּׁנִי אֵינוֹ עוֹשֶׂה מְלָאכָה. בַּשְּׁלִישִׁי הוּא עוֹשֶׂה בְצִינְעָה. אֲבָל אָמְרוּ. תָּבוֹא מְאֵירָה לִשְׁכֵינָיו שֶׁהִצְרִיכוּהוּ לְכַךְ. בַּר קַפָּרָא אָמַר. אֲפִילוּ בַשְּׁלִישִׁי לֹא יַעֲשֶׂה כָל־עִיקָר. בַּר קַפָּרָא כְּדַעְתֵּיהּ. דְּבַר קַפָּרָא אָמַר. אֵין תּוֹקְפוֹ שֶׁלְאֵבֶל אֶלָּא עַד שְׁלֹשָׁה יָמִים. רִבִּי אַבָּא בְּרֵיהּ דְּרִבִּי פַּפֵּי רִבִּי יְהוֹשֻׁעַ דְּסִיכְנִין בְּשֵׁם רִבִּי לֵוִי. כָּל־תְּלָתָא יוֹמִין נַפְשָׁא טַיֵּיסָא עַל גּוּפָא. סְבִירָה דְּהִיא חֲזָרָה לְגַבֵּיהּ. כֵּיוָן דְּהִיא חַמְיָיא דְּאִישְׁתַּנֵּי זִיוֵיהוֹן דְּאַפּוֹי הִיא שָׁבְקָא לֵיהּ וְאָזְלָה לָהּ. לְאַחַר שְׁלֹשָׁה יָמִים הַכֶּרֶס נִבְקַעַת עַל פָּנָיו וְאוֹמֶרֶת לָהּ. הֵא [לָךְ] מַה שֶׁגְּזַלְתָּה וְחָמַסְתָּה וְנָתַתָּה בִי. רִבִּי חַגַּי בְּשֵׁם רִבִּי יֹאשִׁיָּה מַיְיתֵי לָהּ מִן הָכָא. וְזֵרִיתִי פֶרֶשׁ עַל־פְּנֵיכֶם וַאֲפִילוּ פֶּרֶשׁ חַגֵּיכֶם. בְּאוֹתָהּ שָׁעָה אַךְ־בְּשָׂרוֹ עָלָיו יִכְאָב וְנַפְשׁוֹ עָלָיו תֶּאֱבָל: אֲרִיסָיו וַחֲכִירָיו וְקַבְּלָיו הֲרֵי אֵילוּ עוֹשִׂין. אִיכָּרָיו וְסַפָּנָיו וְגַמָּלָיו אֵינָן עוֹשִׂין. רִבִּי יְהוֹשֻׁעַ בֶּן לֵוִי אָמַר. הָיְתָה לוֹ פָרָה מְנַמֶּלֶת בָּעִיר הֲרֵי זֶה עוֹשֶׂה. אָמַר לֵיהּ רִבִּי יוֹסֵה. הָדָא דַתְּ אָמַר בָּהוּא דְחַיָּיב לֵיהּ. הָא בַתְּחִילָּה אָסוּר.

4 שלשה ימים A | שלשים יום פפי A | מני יהושע A | יהושע 5 טייסא A | שייסא דהיא חמייא A | דחמיא 6 שלשה ימים A | שלשימים 7 יאשיה A | יאשיהו הכא A | הדה 8 ואפילו A - | 9 וקבליו A | וקבלית יהושע A | יהושע 10 מגמלת A | מגמלה הדא A | הדה דת A | דאת 11 בתחילה A | לכתחילה

If he has nothing to eat, he cannot work on the first and second days. On the third day he works in privacy; but they said, a curse should come over his neighbors who forced him to this. Bar Qappara said, also on the third day he should not work anything[161]. Bar Qappara follows his own opinion, since bar Qappara said the force of mourning is only up to three days. Rebbi Abba the son of Rebbi Pappai, Rebbi Joshua from Sikhnin in the name of Rebbi Levi: For three days the soul hovers over the body, thinking that she will return to it. When she sees that the looks of his face change, she abandons it and leaves. After three days the belly breaks open in front of his face and says to it, here [you have] what you robbed, and you wronged, and put into me[162]. Rebbi Haggai in the name of Rebbi Joshia brought it from here: *I shall scatter excrement on your faces,* even *excrement of your holidays*[163]. At that moment, *but his body will hurt him and his soul mourn for him*[164]. His sharecroppers, and his tenants, and his contractors do work[165]; his agricultural workers, and his mariners, and his camel drivers do not work[166]. Rebbi Joshua ben Levi said, if he had a cow associated[167] in town, she works. Rebbi Yose said to him, this you are saying about one under contract; therefore not to start[168].

161 Babli 21b. The Babli puts the burden on the communal welfare fund.
162 Babli *Šabbat* 151b. *Gen. rabba* 100(7).
163 *Mal.* 2:3.
164 *Job* 14:22, Babli *Šabbat* 152b.
165 They are independent contractors.
166 These are paid wages.

167 Arabic גמל "to be united, collected." The cow is under contract to work with another owner's cow as a pair, drawing a plough or a cart.
168 Existing contracts are to be honored but the mourner may not enter into new contracts.

(82b line 56) שְׁנֵי אַחִין שְׁנֵי שׁוּתָפִין שְׁנֵי טַבָּחִים שְׁנֵי חֶנְוָנִים שֶׁאֵירַע לְאֶחָד מֵהֶן דָּבָר הֲרֵי אֵילוּ נוֹעֲלִין אֶת חָנוּתָן. (חֲבֵירָיו וּפוֹעֲלָיו) [נַחֲמָרָיו וּפוֹעֲלָיו] עוֹשִׂין בְּצִינְעָה בְּמָקוֹם אַחֵר.
2 ופועלין A | ופועליו בצינעה A | בצינעא במקום אחר A -

Two brothers, two partners, two butchers, two grocers, if there happened something to one of them[169] they lock their store but (his colleagues and the workers) [his donkey drivers and his workers][170] work in privacy at another place[171].

169 The death of a close relative.
170 Alteration by the Venice editor, to be deleted.
171 The last words missing in A, probably

correctly. There is no reason why they could not serve their customers inside the locked store.

(82b line 57) אֲבָל כָּל־זְמַן שֶׁמֵּתוֹ מוּטָל לְפָנָיו אוֹכֵל אֵצֶל חֲבֵירוֹ. אֵין לוֹ חָבֵר אוֹכֵל בְּבַיִת אַחֵר. אֵין לוֹ בַיִת אַחֵר עוֹשֶׂה מְחִיצָה וְאוֹכֵל. אִם אֵינוֹ יָכוֹל לַעֲשׂוֹת מְחִיצָה הוֹפֵךְ אֶת פָּנָיו כְּנֶגֶד הַכּוֹתֶל וְאוֹכֵל. וְאֵינוֹ לֹא מֵיסֵב וְאוֹכֵל. וְלֹא אוֹכֵל כָּל־צוֹרְכוֹ. וְלֹא שׁוֹתֶה כָל־צוֹרְכוֹ. וְלֹא אוֹכֵל בָּשָׂר וְלֹא שׁוֹתֶה יַיִן. וְאֵין מְזַמְּנִין עָלָיו. וְאִם בֵּירַךְ אֵין עוֹנִין אַחֲרָיו אָמֵן. וַאֲחֵרִים שֶׁבֵּירְכוּ אֵינוֹ עוֹנֶה אַחֲרֵיהֶן אָמֵן. בַּמֶּה דְבָרִים אֲמוּרִים. בַּחוֹל. אֲבָל בַּשַּׁבָּת מֵיסֵב וְאוֹכֵל. וְאוֹכֵל כָּל־צוֹרְכוֹ. וְשׁוֹתֶה כָל־צוֹרְכוֹ. וְאוֹכֵל בָּשָׂר וְשׁוֹתֶה יַיִן. וּמְזַמְּנִין עָלָיו. וְאִם בֵּירַךְ עוֹנִין אַחֲרָיו אָמֵן. וַאֲחֵרִים שֶׁבֵּירְכוּ עוֹנֶה אַחֲרֵיהֶן אָמֵן. אָמַר רַבָּן שִׁמְעוֹן בֶּן גַּמְלִיאֵל. הוֹאִיל וְהִיתַּרְתָּה לוֹ אֶת כָּל־אֵילּוּ חַיְּיבֵיהוּ בִּשְׁאַר מִצְוֹתֶיהָ שֶׁלַּתּוֹרָה. חַיֵּי שָׁעָה הִיתַּרְתָּה לוֹ חַיֵּי עוֹלָם לֹא כָל־שֶׁכֵּן. רִבִּי יוּדָה בַּר פָּזִי בְשֵׁם רִבִּי יְהוֹשֻׁעַ בֶּן לֵוִי. הֲלָכָה כְרַבָּן שִׁמְעוֹן בֶּן גַּמְלִיאֵל. נִמְסַר לָרַבִּים אוֹכֵל בָּשָׂר וְשׁוֹתֶה יַיִן. נִמְסַר לַכַּתָּפִים כְּמִי שֶׁנִּמְסַר לָרַבִּים.

1 אין A | ב ואם אין 2 אין A | ואם אין A | ב ואם 3 ואינו לא | ב ולא צורכו A | צורכיו 4 עליו A | - ואחרים שבירכו אינו A | ואם בירכו אחרים אין 5 בחול A | שחל בחול ב הדא דתטמ' בחול בשבת A | חל בשבת 6 ומזמנין A | מזמנין 7 עונה A | עוניו והיתרתה | ב והתרתי 8 מצותיה A | מצוותה חיי | ב אם חיי היתרתה | ב התרת

[172] All the time that his deceased is lying before him, he eats at his neighbor's. If he has no neighbor, he eats in another room. If he has no other room, he makes a wall of separation and eats. If he is unable to make a wall of separation, he turns his face towards the wall and eats. He does not eat reclining; he does neither eat nor drink his fill. He eats neither meat nor drinks wine. One does not allow him to participate in a group to say Grace. If he recited Grace, one does not answer "amen" after him. If others recited Grace, he does not answer "amen". That is on weekdays. But on the Sabbath, he does eat reclining; he eats meat and drinks wine, eats and drinks his fill. One lets him participate in a group to say Grace. If he recited Grace, one does answer "amen" after him. If others recited Grace, he answers "amen". Rabban Simeon ben Gamliel[173] said: Because you allowed all of these, oblige him for all other obligations of the Torah[174]. If you permitted him temporary life, so much more eternal life. Rebbi Judah ben Pazi in the name of Rebbi Joshua ben Levi: Practice follows Rabban Simeon ben Gamliel. If he was handed over to the public, he may eat meat and drink wine[175]. If he was handed over to the carriers[176] it is as if he was handed to the public.

172 The text is from *Berakhot* 3:1 (Notes 42-47, **ב**); the *baraita* is also in *Semahot* X. Babli *Berakhot* 17b.

173 In the Babli sources: Rabban Gamliel, a source of lesser authority.

174 And sexual relations with his pure wife are biblical obligations for any married man.

175 If the corpse was handed over to the public corporation handling burials, the "holy companionship", the dead is no longer "lying before the family members" and they may eat and drink.

176 To be delivered to the burial corporation.

(82b line 71) אֲבָל בַּשַּׁבָּת הָרִאשׁוֹנָה אֵינוֹ הוֹלֵךְ לְבֵית הַכְּנֶסֶת. בַּשְּׁנִיָּיה הוֹלֵךְ לְבֵית הַכְּנֶסֶת וְאֵינוֹ יוֹשֵׁב בִּמְקוֹמוֹ. בַּשְּׁלִישִׁית יוֹשֵׁב בִּמְקוֹמוֹ וְאֵינוֹ מְדַבֵּר. בָּרְבִיעִית שָׁוֶה לְכָל־אָדָם. רִבִּי יְהוּדָה אוֹמֵר. אֵיפְשָׁר לוֹמַר בַּשַּׁבָּת הָרִאשׁוֹנָה שֶׁהָרַבִּים מִתְעַסְּקִין עִמּוֹ. אֶלָּא הַשְּׁנִיָּיה הִיא הָרִאשׁוֹנָה. הַשְּׁלִישִׁית הִיא הַשְּׁנִיָּיה. הָרְבִיעִית הִיא הַשְּׁלִישִׁית. רִבִּי שִׁמְעוֹן אוֹמֵר. אֲבָל בַּשַּׁבָּת הָרִאשׁוֹנָה הוֹלֵךְ לְבֵית הַכְּנֶסֶת וְאֵינוֹ יוֹשֵׁב בִּמְקוֹמוֹ. בַּשְּׁנִיָּיה יוֹשֵׁב בִּמְקוֹמוֹ וְאֵינוֹ מְדַבֵּר. בַּשְּׁלִישִׁית שָׁוֶה לְכָל־אָדָם. רִבִּי יְהוֹשֻׁעַ בֶּן לֵוִי אָמַר. הֲלָכָה כְדִבְרֵי מִי שֶׁהוּא מוֹסִיף יָמִים.

The mourner does not go to the synagogue on the first Sabbath. On the second he goes but does not sit in his place. On the third he sits in his place and does not talk. On the fourth he is equal to everybody. Rebbi Jehudah says, it is impossible to speak of the first Sabbath since the public cares for him, but the second is the first, the third is the second, the fourth is the third. Rebbi Simeon says, the mourner goes to the synagogue on the first Sabbath but does not sit on his place. On the second he sits on his place and does not talk. On the third he is equal to everybody[177]. Rebbi Joshua ben Levi said, practice follows him who adds days[178].

177 Babli 23a; *Semahot* X. The opinion ascribed here to R. Simeon is not mentioned in the Babli sources.

178 It is not known what this means. If one follows the rule that in matters of mourning practice follows the lenient opinion, it means that one follows R. Simeon who increases the days where there is no difference between the mourner and the other congregants (Babli 22a). If practice should follow the opinion that the mourner should observe a maximum of days not behaving like the other congregants, one has to follow the opinion ascribed here to R. Jehudah. The statement is quoted by Tosaphot 23a (top line) without explanation.

(82c line 3) הֲרֵי שֶׁבָּא וּמָצָא אָבֵל בְּתוֹךְ בֵּיתוֹ. בַּשֵּׁינִי וּבַשְּׁלִישִׁי מַשְׁלִים עִמָּהֶן. בָּרְבִיעִי מוֹנֶה לְעַצְמוֹ. רִבִּי שִׁמְעוֹן אוֹמֵר. אֲפִילוּ (בַּשִּׁישִׁי) [בָּרְבִיעִי] מַשְׁלִים עִמָּהֶן. רִבִּי יְהוֹשֻׁעַ בֶּן לֵוִי אָמַר. הֲלָכָה כְרִבִּי שִׁמְעוֹן בְּשֶׁאֵינוֹ גָדוֹל מִשְׁפָּחָה. אֲבָל אִם הָיָה גָדוֹל מִשְׁפָּחָה מוֹנֶה לְעַצְמוֹ. כְּהָדָא

HALAKHAH 5   577

רִבִּי מָנָא הוֹרֵי לְרִבִּי אַרְמֵנִייָא. מִכֵּיוָן שֶׁאַתְּ גְּדוֹל מִשְׁפָּחָה מְנֵה לְעַצְמָךְ. בְּשֶׁלֹּא הוּרְאוּ לוֹ רוֹב פָּנִים. אֲבָל אִם הוּרְאוּ לוֹ רוֹב פָּנִים נוֹטְלוֹ לַמֶּרְחָץ. כְּהָדָא רַב הוּנָא הוֹרֵי לַאֲחוֹי דְּרִבִּי יְהוּדָה בַּר זַבְדִּי. מִכֵּיוָן שֶׁהוּרְאוּ לוֹ רוֹב פָּנִים נוֹטְלוֹ לַמֶּרְחָץ.

3 לעצמו A | עצמו   כהדא A | כהזה   4 מנא A | מני   ארמנייא A | יעקב בארמנייא   בשלא A | הדה דתמר דשלא   הוראו A | הראו   5 הוראו A | הראו   רב A | ר'   6 שהוראו לו A | דהוו ליה

If he came and found mourning in his house. On the second or third {day}[179] he finishes with them. On the fourth he counts by himself. Rebbi Simeon says, even on the (sixth) [fourth][180] he finishes with them. Rebbi Joshua ben Levi said, practice follows Rebbi Simeon if he was not the head of the family. But the head of the family counts by himself. As the following: Rebbi Mana instructed Rebbi <Jacob in>[181] Armenia: since you are the head of the family, count by yourself. <This you are saying> if he did not see most of the people. But if most of the people were seen by him one takes him to the bath house[182]. As the following: Rav <Rebbi>[183] Huna instructed the brother of Rebbi Jehudah bar Zavdi, since most of the people were seen by him, take him to the bath house.

179 If the person who was unaware of the death arrived on the 2nd or 3rd day of mourning.
180 In the absence of parallel sources there is no reason to prefer the Venice editor's version over that of the scribe.
181 Addition from A.
182 Visiting the mourner is a meritorious deed. If the majority of the congregation came to pay their respects to the head of the family he would not have to sit alone without purpose. Since washing in a thermal bath is forbidden during the first seven days of mourning, this is a public demonstration that the late comer is following the rules of the remainder of his family.
183 Reasons of chronology force the adoption of <A>'s text.

(82c line 9) הֲרֵי שֶׁמּוֹלִיכִין אוֹתוֹ מִמָּקוֹם לְמָקוֹם. כְּגוֹן אִילֵּין דְּקָבְרִין בְּבֵית שָׁרַיי. אִית תַּנָּיֵי תַנֵּי. אִילּוּ שֶׁכָּן מוֹנִין מִשֶּׁיָּצָא הַמֵּת. וְאִילּוּ שֶׁשָּׁם מוֹנִין מִשֶּׁיֵּסָּתֵם הַגּוֹלֵל. אִית תַּנָּיֵי תַנֵּי. אִילּוּ וְאִילּוּ מוֹנִין מִשֶּׁיֵּסָּתֵם הַגּוֹלֵל. רִבִּי סִימוֹן בְּשֵׁם רִבִּי יְהוֹשֻׁעַ בֶּן לֵוִי. הַכֹּל הוֹלֵךְ אַחַר גְּדוֹל הַמִּשְׁפָּחָה. רִבִּי יַעֲקֹב בַּר אָחָא בְּשֵׁם רִבִּי אַסִי. לְחוֹמְרִין. מָהוּ חוֹמְרִין. אִם הָיָה גְּדוֹל הַמִּשְׁפָּחָה כָּאן. אִילּוּ כָּאן מוֹנִין מִשֶּׁיָּצָא הַמֵּת וְאִילּוּ שֶׁשָּׁם מוֹנִין מִשֶּׁיֵּסָּתֵם הַגּוֹלֵל. אִם הָיָה גְּדוֹל הַמִּשְׁפָּחָה שָׁם. אִילּוּ וְאִילּוּ מוֹנִין מִשֶּׁיֵּסָּתֵם הַגּוֹלֵל. כְּהָדָא. גַּמְלִיאֵל זוּגָא דָמְכַת אַחְתֵּיהּ. סְלַק הִילֵּל אַחְוֵוהּ עִימֵּיהּ. אָמַר לֵיהּ רִבִּי מָנָא. מִכֵּיוָן שֶׁאַתְּ גְּדוֹל מִשְׁפָּחָה כַּד תְּהֵא סָלַק גַּב אָחוּךְ הֲוֵי שָׁלַף סַנְדְּלָךְ.

4 לחומאין A | לחומארים   (2) 6 זוגא A | זווגא

In case one carries him from place to place, as those who bury in Bet-Shearim. There are Tannaim who state, those here count[184] from when the deceased left; those there count from when the cover plate[135] was laid. There are Tannim who state, these and those count from when the cover plate was laid. Rebbi Simon in the name of Rebbi Joshua ben Levi: Everything goes after the head of the family. Rebbi Jacon bar Aḥa in the name of Rebbi Assi[185]: As restriction. What means "as restriction"? If the head of the family was here, those here count from when the deceased left; those there count from when the cover plate was laid. If the head of the family is there, these and those count from when the cover plate was laid. As the following: The sister of Gamaliel the twin died. His brother Hillel came down to him. Rebbi Mana said to him, since you are the head of the family, when you come down to your brother take off your shoes[186].

184 The seven days of mourning.
185 He usually is referred to as R. Yasa. In the quote in Tosaphot 22b (s.v. מהדריתו) "R. Yose".
186 In the quote in Tosaphot (Note 185) a more intelligible reading: "Since there is a head of family". Gamaliel was the head of family; his brother starts mourning (and counting) when he enters his brother's house.

(82c line 19) הֲרֵי שֶׁמְפַנִּין אוֹתוֹ מִקֶּבֶר לְקֶבֶר. אִית תַּנָּיֵי תַנֵּי. מִשֶׁיִּיסָּתֵם הַגּוֹלֵל הָרִאשׁוֹן. אִית תַּנָּיֵי תַנֵּי. מִשֶׁיִּיסָּתֵם הַגּוֹלֵל הַשֵּׁינִי. רִבִּי יוֹנָה הֲוָה לֵיהּ עוֹבְדָה. שָׁאַל לְרִבִּי חֲנַנְיָה חֲבֵרוֹן דְּרַבָּנָן. אָמַר לֵיהּ. מִשֶׁיִּיסָּתֵם הַגּוֹלֵל הָרִאשׁוֹן. רִבִּי יִרְמְיָה הֲוָה לֵיהּ עוֹבְדָא. שָׁאַל לְרִבִּי זְעוּרָה. שָׁאַל רִבִּי זְעוּרָה לְרִבִּי אַמִּי. אָמַר לֵיהּ. מִשֶׁיִּיסָּתֵם הַגּוֹלֵל הַשֵּׁינִי. אֲתָא לְגַבֵּיהּ. אָמַר לֵיהּ. לְחוּמְרָא חוֹרִי לָךְ. רִבִּי יוֹנָה וְרִבִּי יוֹסֵה תְּרֵיהוֹן אֲמָרִין. הָדָא דְתֹ אָמַר. בְּתוֹךְ שִׁבְעָה. אֲבָל לְאַחַר שִׁבְעָה כְּבָר עָבַר הָאֵבֶל. בְּשֶׁנֶּתְנוּ דַעְתָּן לְפַנּוֹתוֹ. אֲבָל אִם לֹא נָתַן דַּעְתּוֹ לְפַנּוֹתוֹ מִשֶׁיִּיסָּתֵם הַגּוֹלֵל הָרִאשׁוֹן. כְּהָדָא. (גמלייל) [גַּמְלִיאֵל] דִּיקוֹנְתַּיָּה קָבְרוּנֵיהּ בּוּרְסָאֵי גַּבּוֹן. בָּתַר תְּלָתָא יוֹמִין אִימְלְכוֹן מְחַזְרָא יָתֵיהּ. אֲתוֹן וּשְׁאָלוֹן לְרִבִּי סִימוֹן. אָמַר לוֹן רִבִּי סִימוֹן בְּשֵׁם רִבִּי יְהוֹשֻׁעַ בֶּן לֵוִי. מִכֵּיוָן שֶׁלֹא נָתְתֶם דַּעְתְּכֶם לַפַנּוֹתוֹ מִשֶׁיִּיסָּתֵם הַגּוֹלֵל הָרִאשׁוֹן. יֵשׁוּעַ אֲחוֹי דְדוֹרַיי הֲוָה לֵיהּ עוֹבְדָא. אֲתָא שְׁאַל לְרִבִּי אַבָּהוּ. אָמַר לֵיהּ. מִשֶׁיִּיסָּתֵם הַגּוֹלֵל הַשֵּׁינִי. אָמַר לֵיהּ רִבִּי יַעֲקֹב בַּר אָחָא. עִמָּךְ הָיִיתִי וּשְׁאַלְתִּינָהּ לְרִבִּי אֲבוּדְמָא דְמִן חֵיפָה. אָמַר. מִשֶׁיִּיסָּתֵם הַגּוֹלֵל הָרִאשׁוֹן. אָמַר לֵיהּ. אֲנָא לָא שְׁמָעִית. אִין שָׁמַעַתְּ פּוּק וְהוֹרִי.

If they moved him from one grave to another[187]. There are Tannaim who state, from the moment[188] the first cover plate was laid. There are Tannaim who state, from the moment the second cover plate was laid. A case happened to Rebbi Jonah. He asked Rebbi Hananiah the colleague of the rabbis, who said to him, from the moment the first cover plate was laid. A case happened to Rebbi Jeremiah. He asked Rebbi Ze`ira; Rebbi Ze`ira asked Rebbi Immi[189]. He said to him, from the moment the second cover plate was laid. He came to him; he said to him, he instructed you by a restriction. Rebbi Jonah and Rebbi Yose both say, this you are saying within the Seven {days}. But after Seven mourning already passed[189]. If they intended it from the start. But if there was no intent from the start to remove him, from the moment the first cover plate was laid. As the following: The people of Bursa buried Gamliel from Yakontia with them. After three days they changed their mind to return him. They went and asked Rebbi Simon. Rebbi Simon said to them in the name of Rebbi Joshua ben Levi: Since you had no intention to remove him, from the moment the first cover plate was laid. A case happened to Jesua the brother of Dorai. He came to ask Rebbi Abbahu who told him, from the moment the second cover plate was laid. Rebbi Jacob bar Aḥa said to him, I was with you when we asked this from Rebbi Eudaimon from Haifa who said, from the moment the first cover plate was laid. He told him, I did not hear. If you heard, go out and instruct.

187 For some reason it was necessary to move the corpse to another grave. This was possible since every burial was considered temporary until the bones could be collected in an ossuary and deposited in a burial cave.

188 One starts the seven days of formal mourning.

189 All persons mentioned are Babylonian.

(82c line 34) מְנַיָין לָאֵבֶל מִן הַתּוֹרָה שִׁבְעָה. וַיַּעַשׂ לְאָבִיו אֵבֶל שִׁבְעַת יָמִים: וּלְמֵידִין דָּבָר קוֹדֶם לְמַתַּן תּוֹרָה. רִבִּי יַעֲקֹב בַּר אֲחָא בְּשֵׁם רִבִּי זְעוּרָא שָׁמַע לָהּ מִן הָדָא. וּפֶתַח אֹהֶל מוֹעֵד תֵּשְׁבוּ יוֹמָם וָלַיְלָה שִׁבְעַת יָמִים וּשְׁמַרְתֶּם אֶת־מִשְׁמֶרֶת מִשְׁכַּן יְיָ. כְּשֵׁם שֶׁשִּׁימֵּר הַקָּדוֹשׁ בָּרוּךְ הוּא עַל עוֹלָמוֹ שִׁבְעָה. כַּךְ אַתֶּם שַׁמְּרוּ עַל אֲחִיכֶם שִׁבְעָה. וּמְנַיָין שֶׁשִּׁימֵּר הַקָּדוֹשׁ בָּרוּךְ הוּא עַל עוֹלָמוֹ שִׁבְעָה. וַיְהִי לְשִׁבְעַת הַיָּמִים וּמֵי הַמַּבּוּל הָיוּ עַל־הָאָרֶץ. וּמִתְאַבְּלִין קוֹדֶם שֶׁיָּמוּת הַמֵּת. אֶלָּא בָשָׂר וָדָם שֶׁאֵינוֹ יוֹדֵעַ מַה עָתִיד לִהְיוֹת אֵינוֹ מִתְאַבֵּל עַד שֶׁיָּמוּת הַמֵּת. אֲבָל הַקָּדוֹשׁ בָּרוּךְ הוּא שֶׁהוּא יוֹדֵעַ מַה עָתִיד לִהְיוֹת שִׁימֵּר עַל עוֹלָמוֹ תְּחִילָּה. אִית דְּבָעֵי מֵימַר. אֵילּוּ שִׁבְעַת יְמֵי אֶבְלוֹ שֶׁלִּמְתוּשֶׁלַח הַצַּדִּיק. אָמַר רִבִּי הוֹשַׁעְיָה. כִּי־שֶׁמֶן מִשְׁחַת יְיָ עֲלֵיכֶם. כְּשֵׁם שֶׁנִּתְרַוִּויתֶם בְּשֶׁמֶן הַמִּשְׁחָה כָּל־שִׁבְעָה. כַּךְ אַתֶּם שַׁמְּרוּ עַל אֲחִיכֶם כָּל־שִׁבְעָה. רִבִּי אַבָּהוּ בְּשֵׁם רִבִּי יוֹחָנָן. אַל־נָא תְהִי כַמֵּת. תִּסְגֵּר. מַה יְמֵי הַמֵּת שִׁבְעָה אַף יְמֵי הֶסְגֵּר שִׁבְעָה. חַד בַּרְבִּי אֲמַר הָדָא דְרִבִּי יוֹחָנָן קוֹמֵי דְרִבִּי שִׁמְעוֹן בֶּן לָקִישׁ וְלֹא קִיבֵּל עֲלוֹי. אֲמַר. הָכָא עֲבַד לָהּ לְהֶסְגֵּר. וְהָכָא עֲבַד לָהּ

לְהֶחְלַט. דְּאָמַר רִבִּי יוֹחָנָן בְּשֵׁם רִבִּי יַנַּאי. אַל־נָא תְהִי כַּמֵּת. מַה יְמֵי הַמֵּת אֵינָן עוֹלִין. אַף יְמֵי הֶחְלַט אֵינָן עוֹלִין. רִבִּי יִרְמְיָה וְרִבִּי חִייָה בְּשֵׁם רִבִּי שִׁמְעוֹן בֶּן לָקִישׁ. רִבִּי אַבָּהוּ רִבִּי יוֹסֵי בֶן חֲנִינָה בְּשֵׁם רִבִּי שִׁמְעוֹן בֶּן לָקִישׁ. וַיִּתְּמּוּ יְמֵי בְכִי אֲבֶל מֹשֶׁה: יְמֵי שִׁבְעָה. בְּכֵי שְׁנַיִם. אֲבֶל שְׁלשִׁים. וְאִית דִּמְחַלְּפִין. יְמֵי שְׁנַיִם. בְּכֵי שִׁבְעָה. אֲבֶל שְׁלשִׁים. רִבִּי יוֹסֵה רִבִּי חִייָה בְּשֵׁם רִבִּי שִׁמְעוֹן בֶּן לָקִישׁ. רִבִּי יוֹנָה וְרִבִּי חִייָה וְרִבִּי שִׁמְעוֹן בֶּן לָקִישׁ בְּשֵׁם רִבִּי יוּדָן נְשִׂייָא. וְהָפַכְתִּי חַגֵּיכֶם לְאָבֶל. מַה יְמֵי הֶחַג שִׁבְעָה. אַף יְמֵי הָאָבֶל שִׁבְעָה. אָמַר רִבִּי אַמִּי לְרִבִּי חִייָה בַּר בָּא. אוֹ מַה יְמֵי הֶחַג שְׁמוֹנָה. אַף יְמֵי הָאֵבֶל שְׁמוֹנָה. אָמַר לֵיהּ. שְׁמִינִי רֶגֶל בִּפְנֵי עַצְמוֹ הוּא. אוֹ מַה הָעֲצֶרֶת יוֹם אֶחָד. אַף הָאֵבֶל יוֹם אֶחָד. אָמַר לֵיהּ. מִיכַּן לַשְׁמוּעָה רְחוֹקָה. וְתַנֵּי כֵן. שְׁמוּעָה קְרוֹבָה יֶשׁ לָהּ שִׁבְעָה וּשְׁלשִׁים. וּרְחוֹקָה אֵין לָהּ שִׁבְעָה וּשְׁלשִׁים.

From where in the Torah that mourning is seven {days}? *He organized seven days of mourning for his father*[190]. Can you infer anything from before the giving of the Torah[191]? Rebbi Jacob bar Aḥa in the name of Rebbi Ze'ira understood it from the following: *At the door of the Tent of Meeting you shall sit day and night for seven days, and keep the watch of the Eternal's sanctuary*[192]. Just as the Holy One, praise to Him, watched over His World for seven {days}, so you shall watch for your brothers for seven {days}. And from where that the Holy One, praise to Him, watched over His World for seven {days}? *It was after seven days that the Deluge came over the world*[193]. May one mourn before the dying person dies? Only flesh and blood who do not know what will be in the future do not mourn until the dying person dies. But the Holy One, praise to Him, Who knows what will be in the future did first watch for His world. Some want to say, these are the seven days of mourning for Methusela the Just[194]. Rebbi Hoshaia said, *for the Eternal's anointing oil is on you*[195]. Just as you were anointed with the anointing oil all of seven, so watch for your brothers all of seven. Rebbi Abbahu in the name of Rebbi Joḥanan: *please let her not be like the dead*[196]. *She shall be locked away*[197]. Just as the day of isolation for the dead are seven, so the days of quarantine are seven. One student reported this from Rebbi Joḥanan before Rebbi Simeon ben Laqish, who did not accept it. He said, here he[198] uses it for isolation, but there he uses it for making absolute, as Rebbi Joḥanan said in the name of Rebbi Yannai, *please let her not be like the dead*: just as the days of the dead are not counted, so the days of being absolute are not counted[199]. Rebbi Jeremiah and Rebbi Ḥiyya in the name of Rebbi Simeon ben Laqish; Rebbi Abbahu, Rebbi Yose ben Ḥanina in the name of Rebbi Simeon ben Laqish: *the days of crying of the mourning for Moses ended*[200]. "The days", seven. "Of crying", two. "Mourning", thirty[201]. Some switch, "the days", two, "of crying", seven, "mourning", thirty. Rebbi Yose, Rebbi Ḥiyya, and Rebbi Simeon ben Laqish in the name of Rebbi Judah the Patriarch: *I shall turn your holiday into mourning*[202]. Since the days of Tabernacles are seven, also the days of mourning are seven. Rebbi Immi said to Rebbi Ḥiyya bar Abba: Maybe since the days of Tabernacles are eight[203], also the days of mourning are eight? He answered him, the eighth day is a separate holiday[204] Or since Pentecost is one day, also mourning is one day? He answered him, from here about a deferred information[205]. And it was stated such: Current information requires Seven and Thirty. Deferred information does not require Seven and Thirty.

190 Gen. 50:10.
191 And in any case the mourning organized by Josef could not have followed Jewish rules.
192 *Ex.* 8:35, quoted incorrectly.
193 Gen. 7:10. Gen. rabba 32(10).
194 Gen. rabba 32(10), Babli *Sanhedrin* 108b. Methusela had Lemekh when he was 187, Lemekh had Noe when he was 182, and the Flood was in Noe's year 600, which was Methusela's year 969, the year of his death.
195 *Lev.* 10:7.
196 *Num.* 12:12.
197 *Num.* 12:14.
198 R. Joḥanan accepts two contradictory explanations of one and the same verse.
199 Since a *nazir* must be pure, a vow of *nazir* made when the person either was impure in the impurity of the dead or having been declared absolutely impure in the impurity of skin disease is suspended until the person becomes pure. Only then may he start counting the thirty days of his vow. Babli *Nazir* 56a.
200 *Deut.* 34:8. Gen. rabba 100(7).
201 The duration of standard mourning.
202 *Am.* 8:10. There is no proof from the Torah.
203 And חג, biblically "holiday of pilgrimage", in Mishnaic Hebrew means "Tabernacles." Babli 20a.
204 *Ḥagigah* 1:6, Note 151.
205 When a relative is informed of a death long after it occurred and he has to observe some signs of mourning at that time only. Babli 20a.

(82c line 60) אֵית תַּנָּיֵי תַנֵּי. שְׁמוּעָה קְרוֹבָה בְּתוֹךְ שְׁלֹשִׁים. וּרְחוֹקָה לְאַחַר שְׁלֹשִׁים. אֵית תַּנָּיֵי תַנֵּי. שְׁמוּעָה קְרוֹבָה בְּתוֹךְ שְׁנֵים עָשָׂר חוֹדֶשׁ. וּרְחוֹקָה לְאַחַר שְׁנֵים עָשָׂר חוֹדֶשׁ. רִבִּי אַבָּהוּ בְּשֵׁם רִבִּי יוֹחָנָן. הֲלָכָה כְּדִבְרֵי מִי שֶׁהוּא אוֹמֵר. שְׁמוּעָה קְרוֹבָה בְּתוֹךְ שְׁלֹשִׁים וּרְחוֹקָה לְאַחַר שְׁלֹשִׁים.

Some Tannaim state: Recent information is within thirty {days}, and deferred after thirty. Some Tannaim state: Recent information is within twelve months, and deferred after twelve month. Rebbi Abbahu in the name of Rebbi Joḥanan: Practice follows the words of him who says, recent information is within thirty {days}, and deferred after thirty[206].

206 Babli 20a. The formulation in the Yerushalmi shows that it doubts the name attributions given as certain in the Babli.

(82c line 65) הֲרֵי שֶׁשָּׁמַע שֶׁמֵּת לוֹ מֵת בָּרֶגֶל. לֹא הִסְפִּיקוּ יְמֵי הָרֶגֶל לָצֵאת עַד שֶׁשָּׁלְמוּ לוֹ שְׁלֹשִׁים. חֲבֶרַיָּא אָמְרֵי. מִכֵּיוָן שֶׁשָּׁמַע בְּתוֹךְ שְׁלֹשִׁים מוֹנֶה שִׁבְעָה לְאַחַר שְׁלֹשִׁים. אָמַר לוֹן רִבִּי יוֹסֵי. מִכֵּיוָן שֶׁשָּׁמַע בְּשָׁעָה שֶׁאֵינוֹ יָכוֹל לְהִתְאַבֵּל כְּמִי שֶׁשָּׁמַע לְאַחַר שְׁלֹשִׁים. [ו]אֵין לוֹ אֶלָּא יוֹם אֶחָד בִּלְבַד. רִבִּי אִידִי דְקַיְסָרִין בְּשֵׁם רִבִּי יוֹחָנָן. בָּאת לוֹ שְׁמוּעָה קְרוֹבָה בַשַּׁבָּת. קוֹרֵעַ לְמָחָר וּמִתְאַבֵּל. אָמַר רִבִּי חֲנַנְיָה. אֵינוּ מִתְאַבֵּל. אָמַר לֵיהּ רִבִּי מָנָא. וְיֵשׁ קְרִיעָה בְלֹא אֵיבוּל. שֶׁכֵּן עַל אָבִיו וְעַל אִמּוֹ אֲפִילוּ לְאַחַר כַּמָּה חַיָּב לִקְרוֹעַ. רִבִּי אַבָּהוּ בְּשֵׁם רִבִּי יוֹחָנָן. אֲפִילוּ טְפֵילָה לַטְפֵילָה אָסוּר בְּתִגְלַחַת. כְּהָדָא רִבִּי מָנָא הֲוָה בְקִיסָרִין. שָׁמַע דִּדְמָךְ בַּר בְּרֵיהּ וַאֲזַל וְסָפַד. אָמְרוּן לֵיהּ. לֹא כֵן אַלְפָן רִבִּי. אֲפִילוּ טְפֵילָה לַטְפֵילָה אָסוּר בְּתִגְלַחַת. אָמַר לוֹן. בְּאִינּוּן דַּהֲווֹן גַּבֵּיהּ. אֲנָן לָא הֲוֵינָן גַּבֵּיהּ. רִבִּי אֲבוּדַּמִי בַּר טוֹבִי בְּשֵׁם רִבִּי אַבָּהוּ. וַאֲפִילוּ טְפֵילָה לַטְפֵילָה חַיָּב לִקְרוֹעַ. דְּאָמַר רִבִּי אַבָּהוּ. הָאֲנָק | דּוֹם מִיכָּן שֶׁהוּא צָרִיךְ לִצְוָוחַ. מֵתִים אֵבֶל לֹא־תַעֲשֶׂה. מִיכָּן שֶׁהוּא צָרִיךְ לְהִתְאַבֵּל. פְּאֵרְךָ חֲבוֹשׁ עָלֶיךָ. אִית דְּבָאֵי מֵימַר. אֵילּוּ הַתְּפִילִין. אִית דְּבָאֵי מֵימַר. זֶה הַגִּיהוּץ. מָאן דְּאָמַר. אֵילּוּ הַתְּפִילִין. אִי מַה תְּפִילִּין לִשְׁנֵי יָמִים. אַף הָאֵבֶל לִשְׁנֵי יָמִים. מָאן דְּאָמַר. זֶה הַגִּיהוּץ. אִי מַה הַגִּיהוּץ שְׁלֹשִׁים יוֹם. אַף הָאֵבֶל שְׁלֹשִׁים. וּנְעָלֶיךָ תָּשִׂים בְּרַגְלֶיךָ. מִיכָּן שֶׁהוּא אָסוּר בִּנְעִילַת הַסַּנְדָּל. וְלֹא תַעְטֶה עַל־שָׂפָם. מִיכָּן שֶׁהוּא צָרִיךְ לְכַסּוֹת אֶת פִּיו. וְלֶחֶם אֲנָשִׁים לֹא תֹאכֵל: מִיכָּן שֶׁהַקְּטַנִּים הוֹלְכִין אֵצֶל הַגְּדוֹלִים. וּמְנַיִין שֶׁהַגְּדוֹלִים הוֹלְכִין אֵצֶל הַקְּטַנִּים. אָמַר רִבִּי שְׁמוּאֵל בַּר רַב יִצְחָק. כָּתוּב כִּי־כָה | אָמַר יי אַל־תָּבוֹא בֵית מַרְזֵחַ וג׳.

If he was informed on the holiday about the death of a relative but the Thirty[207] were completed before the end of the holiday. The colleagues are saying, since he was informed within the Thirty, he counts Seven[208] after the Thirty. Rebbi Yose said to them, since he heard at a moment where he could not mourn it is as if he was informed after Thirty(;) [and] he observes only one day[209]. Rabbi Idi of Caesarea in the name of Rebbi Joḥanan: If he received recent information on the Sabbath, he tears {his garment} the next day and mourns[210]. Rebbi Ḥanania said, he does not mourn[211]. Rebbi Mana said to him, is there tearing without mourning? Since for his father or his mother even after a length of time he is obligated to tear[212]. Rebbi Abbahu in the name of Rebbi Johanan: Even as derivative of a derivative[213] he is forbidden to shave. As the following: Rebbi Mana was in Caesarea. He heard that his grandson had died, and he went and eulogized[214]. They said to him, did the Rabbi not teach us, even as derivative of a derivative he is forbidden to shave? He said to them, those who were with him[215]. We were not there. Rebbi Eudaimon bar Tobi in the name of Rebbi Abbahu: even as derivative of a derivative he is obligated to tear, as Rebbi Abbahu said, *groan silently*[216], from here that he has to cry. *Do not arrange mourning for the dead*, from here that he has to mourn. *Your splendor put on yourself*, some want to say, these are *tefillin*. Some want to say, this is pressing[217]. He who says these are *tefillin*; just as *tefillin* refer to two days, also mourning two days? He who says this is pressing; just as pressing is for thirty days, also mourning thirty days[218]? *Put your shoes on your feet*, from here that he is forbidden wearing shoes. *And do not cover your mustache*, from here that he has to cover his mouth. Could he cover it from below? Rav Hisda said, so they should not say, he has a mouth-ache. *And do not eat men's bread*, from here that the smaller ones go to the greater ones[219]. And from where that the greater ones go to the smaller ones? Rebbi Samuel bar Rav Isaac said, it is written[220]: *For so says the Eternal, do not go to a funeral repast*[221], etc.

207 The 30 days after the burial, when all mourning ends except for father and mother.

208 He has to observe the strict Seven days of mourning for himself even though the other members of the family have stopped even the minor mourning rites of the Thirty.

209 Babli 20b.

210 Since as a general principle the Sabbath, while it is a day without mourning, is counted as one of the Seven or Thirty days. Therefore if the last day of the Thirty was a Sabbath, the information is recent and he has to act on it immediately after the end of the Sabbath.

211 By the principle just explained, his not mourning on the Sabbath must be counted as mourning and he ends mourning at the end of the Sabbath with the family. But since he would have to rend his garments, he has to make up after the Sabbath.

212 This is R. Hanania's answer to R. Mana. Rejected by the Babli, 20a/b.

213 A person either not directly involved or a more distant relative.

214 It seems that instead of ספד "to eulogize" one has to read ספר "was groomed" as printed in more recent editions of the Yerushalmi.

215 A bystander present at the time of death has to tear his clothes. Babli 15a.

216 *Ez.* 24:17. Since Ezechiel was commanded not to mourn at the death of his wife, the list of things he is forbidden is the list of things every other mourner is obliged to follow. Babli 15a.

217 Wearing freshly pressed garments.

218 The list in Ezechiel is a general guideline, not a legal document.

219 The Prophet, who is an important personality, is forbidden to accept the meal of consolation offered him by common people.

220 *Jer.* 16:5.

221 Same argument as in Note 219, in the inverse direction.

(82d line 11) תַּנֵּי. אֵילוּ דְבָרִים שֶׁאָבֵל אָסוּר בָּהֶן כָּל־שִׁבְעָה. בִּרְחִיצָה בְסִיכָה בִנְעִילַת הַסַּנְדָּל וּבְתַשְׁמִישׁ הַמִּיטָה מְלַסְפֵּר וּמְלְכַבֵּס מִלְּקְרוֹת בַּתּוֹרָה וּמִלְשְׁנוֹת מִדְרָשׁ הֲלָכוֹת וְהַגָּדוֹת מִשְׁאֵילַת שָׁלוֹם וּמִלַּעֲשׂוֹת מְלָאכָה. מָאן תַּנָא. אֲבָל אָסוּר בִּרְחִיצָה כָּל־שִׁבְעָה. רִבִּי נָתָן. רִבִּי אִמִּי הֲוָה לֵיהּ עוֹבְדָא. שָׁאַל לְרִבִּי חִייָה בַּר בָּא וְהוֹרִי לֵיהּ כָּל־שִׁבְעָה כְרִבִּי נָתָן. רִבִּי יוֹסֵי הֲוָה לֵיהּ עוֹבְדָא. שְׁלַח לְרִבִּי בָּא בַר כֹּהֵן. אָמַר לֵיהּ. וְלֹא כֵן אַלְפָן רִבִּי. רִבִּי אִמִּי הֲוָה לֵיהּ עוֹבְדָא. וְשָׁאַל לְרִבִּי שִׁמְעוֹן בֶּן לָקִישׁ וְהוֹרִי לֵיהּ כָּל־שִׁבְעָה כְרִבִּי נָתָן. אָמַר לֵיהּ. וְדִילְמָא תְּרֵין עוֹבְדִין אִינּוּן. אֲנַן אָמְרִין לָהּ עַל דְּרִבִּי חִייָה בַּר אַבָּא וְאַתּוּן אָמְרִין לָהּ עַל דְּרִבִּי שִׁמְעוֹן בֶּן לָקִישׁ. וְעוֹד מִן הָדָא. רִבִּי חָמָא אֲבוֹי דְּרַב הוֹשַׁעְיָה הֲוָה לֵיהּ עוֹבְדָא. שָׁאַל לְרַבָּנָן וְאַסְרִין. רִבִּי יוֹסֵה בָעֵי. הֵיידָן רַבָּנָן. רַבָּנָן דְּהָכָא [אוֹ] רַבָּנָן מִדְּרוֹמָא. אִין תֵּימַר רַבָּנָן דְּהָכָא. נִיחָא. אִין תֵּימַר רַבָּנָן דִּדְרוֹמָא. וְרַבְרְבַיָּיא קוֹמוֹי וְהוּא שָׁאִיל לִזְעִירַיָּיא. אִין תֵּימַר רַבָּנָן דְּהָכָא. נִיחָא. אִין תֵּימַר רַבָּנָן דִּדְרוֹמָא. אַתּוּן שָׁרְיָין וְאֵינּוּן אָסְרִין. דְּתַנֵּי. מָקוֹם שֶׁנָּהֲגוּ לִרְחוֹץ אַחַר הַמִּיטָה מַרְחִיצִין. וּבְדָרוֹם מַרְחִיצִין. אָמַר רִבִּי יוֹסֵה בֵּירִבִּי בּוּן. מִי שֶׁהוּא מַתִּיר אֶת הָרְחִיצָה עוֹשֶׂה אוֹתָהּ כַּאֲכִילָה וּשְׁתִייָה. הָדָא דְאַתְּ מַר בִּרְחִיצָה שֶׁהִיא שֶׁלְּתַּעֲנוּג. אֲבָל בִּרְחִיצָה שֶׁאֵינָהּ שֶׁלְּתַּעֲנוּג מוּתָּר. שְׁמוּאֵל בַּר אַבָּא עָלוּ בוֹ חַטָטִין. אָתוֹן וּשְׁאָלוּן לְרִבִּי יָסָא. מָהוּ דְיַסְחֵי. אָמַר לוֹן. וְאִין לָא סָחֵי מַיִית הוּא. אִין כֵּינִי אֲפִילוּ בְתִשְׁעָה בְאָב. אִין כֵּינִי אֲפִילוּ בְיוֹם הַכִּיפּוּרִים. רִבִּי יוֹסֵי בֶּן חֲנִינָה רָאוּ אוֹתוֹ טוֹבֵל. אִין לְקֵירוּיָיו לָא יָדְעִין וְאִין לְהַקֵּר גּוּפוֹ שֶׁאֵין רְחִיצַת צוֹנִין רְחִיצָה לָא יָדְעִין. הוֹרֵי רִבִּי בָּא בַר כֹּהֵן כָּהֵן תִּנְיָינָא.

4 חייא | B חייא יוסה | B יוסי   5 שלח | B ושאל -   6 לר' שמעון בן | B לריש כל שבעה כר' נתן | B כר' נתן כל שבעה   עובדין | G עובדה איגון | G הנון   7 לה | B ליה - G - | חייה | B חייא אבא G בא לה | B ליה   דר' שמעון בן | B דריש הדא | G הדה   8 חמא G חמה   הושעיה | B אושעיא עובדא G עובדה   שאל G שאיל ואסרין | G ואסרון יוסה | B יוסי   הידן | B איידן G היידון   9 דהכא | G דהכה   [או] | B או G - מדרומא | B דרומייא G דרומייה הכא | G דהכה ניחא | G ניחה   דדרומא | B דרומייא G דרומייה   10 רברבייא | G רברבייה   לזעירייא | G לזעירייה אין תימר ... ניחא | B -   דדרומא | B דרומייא G דדרומה   11 אתון | G אינון   12 יוסה ביר' בון | B יוסי ביר' אבון   הרחיצה | B הרחיצה הזאת   הדא דאת מר | B הדא דתימר G הדתמר   13 שמואל | B שמואל | כהדא שמואל G כהדא שמואל אבא | G אבה   14 ושאלון | B שיילון G שאלון   מהו | G מהוא   דיסחי | B דייסחי   ואין לא סחי | B דלא יסחי G - | בעי G כני (2)   15 בן חנינה | B בר' חנינא   16 לקירויוי | B לקירויי   לקירויו | G לקיר   להקיר צונין | G צונים בר כהן | G - | 17 כהן | G כהחן תניא G תניה

It was stated: The following are forbidden to the mourner all Seven {days}: Washing, anointing, wearing shoes, sexual relations, grooming, washing clothes, reading in the Torah, studying Midrash[222a], practices, and homiletics, greeting, and working.

[222]Who stated that the mourner is forbidden to take a bath during the entire Seven? Rebbi Nathan. Something happened[223] to Rebbi Immi; he asked Rebbi Hiyya bar Abba[224] who instructed him "all Seven days following Rebbi Nathan". Something happened to Rebbi Yose; he sent to Rebbi Abba bar Cohen[225] who said to him: Rebbi, did you not so teach us that something happened to Rebbi Immi, he asked Rebbi Simeon ben Laqish who instructed him "all Seven following Rebbi Nathan". He said to him, maybe these were two separate incidents, we say it in the name of Rebbi Hiyya bar Abba, you say it in the name of Rebbi Simeon ben Laqish[226]. And also from the following: Something happened to Rebbi Hama, father of Rav Hoshaya, he asked the rabbis and they forbade it. Rebbi Yose asked, which rabbis? The rabbis here or the rabbis in the South? If you say the rabbis of here, it is fine. If you would say the rabbis from the South, would he have asked minor authorities when greater ones were available to him? If you say the rabbis of the South, we would allow[227] and they would forbid, as we have stated: "At a place where it is customary to bathe after a funeral[228], one may bathe; in the South one bathes." Rebbi Yose ben Rebbi Abun said: He who permits that bath makes it like eating and drinking. That means, about a bath for pleasure. But a bath that is not for pleasure is permitted. Samuel bar Abba developed scab. They came and asked Rebbi Yasa, what is the rule, may he bathe? He said to them: If he does not bathe, would he not die[229]? If he needs it, even on the Ninth of Av. If he needs it, even on Yom Kippur[230]. They saw Rebbi Yose, son of Rebbi Hanina, immersing himself. They did not know whether it was for his emission[231], they did not know whether it was to cool down because bathing in cold water is not called bathing[232]. Rebbi Abba bar Cohen instructed following this statement[233].

222a The derivation of a consistent corpus of rules and laws from biblical verses. "Torah" here includes all of the Hebrew Bible.

222 This text is copied in *Berakhot* 2:7 (Notes277-293,ב).

223 A close relative died.
224 He did not want to permit himself to bathe, so he asked a colleague (and sometimes student).
225 The reasonable text is **ב**: He sent R. Abba bar Cohen (a very minor figure) to R. Aha, person of stature almost equal to R. Yose himself.
226 It is not known whether these are two different decisions by two different authorities, in which case they constitute precedent to be followed, or one decision reported in different ways and open to discussion.
227 One has to follow the reading common to G (which restarts here) and **ב**: They permit and they forbid, in which case none of their statements can serve as precedent.

228 In the interpretation of Nahmanides (*Writings*, ed. Chavel, p. 175-176) this is not a general permission to bathe during the Seven days but only a sanitary prescription strictly referring to the aftermath of the burial.
229 In case of scab this is a hyperbola but it means that all medically indicated ablutions are permitted during the Seven days.
230 Even though the standards of medical necessity are different in the various cases.
231 An involuntary emission of semen which pollutes and requires immersion in a *miqweh*.
232 For the rules of mourning only warm baths are prohibited.
233 That cold bathing is permitted during the Seven. Babli *Ta`anit* 13a,13b.

(82d line 35) הוֹרֵי רִבִּי אָחָא בַּבָּא מִן הַדֶּרֶךְ וְהָיוּ רַגְלָיו קֵיהוֹת עָלָיו שֶׁמּוּתָּר לְהַרְחִיצָם בַּמָּיִם. תַּנֵּי. אָבֵל וּמְנוּדֶּה שֶׁהָיוּ מְהַלְּכִין בַּדֶּרֶךְ מוּתָּרִין בִּנְעִילַת הַסַּנְדָּל. לִכְשֶׁיָּבוֹאוּ לָעִיר יַחֲלוֹצוּ. וְכֵן בְּתִשְׁעָה בְאָב וְכֵן בְּתַעֲנִית צִיבּוּר. תַּנֵּי. מְקוֹם שֶׁנָּהֲגוּ לִשְׁאוֹל בְּשָׁלוֹם אֲבֵילִים בַּשַּׁבָּת שׁוֹאֲלִין. וּבַדָּרוֹם שׁוֹאֲלִין. רִבִּי הוֹשַׁעְיָה רַבָּא אֲזַל לְחַד אֲתָר. חָמָא אֲבֵילַיָּיא בְּשׁוּבְתָא וּשְׁאַל בּוֹן. אֲמַר. אֲנִי אֵינִי יוֹדֵעַ מִנְהַג מְקוֹמְכֶם. אֶלָּא שָׁלוֹם עֲלֵיכֶם כְּמִנְהַג מְקוֹמֵינוּ. רִבִּי יוֹסֵי בֵּירְבִּי חֲלַפְתָּא הֲוָה מְשַׁבַּח בְּיִרְבִּי מֵאִיר קוֹמֵי צִיפּוֹרָאֵי. אָדָם גָּדוֹל אָדָם קָדוֹשׁ אָדָם צָנוּעַ. חַד זְמַן חָמָא אֲבֵילַיָּיא וּשְׁאַל בּוֹן. אֲמָרִין לֵיהּ. רִבִּי. אָהֲנוּ דְאַתְּ מַתְנֵי שְׁבָחֵיהּ. אֲמַר לוֹן. מָה עֲבַד. אֲמָרוּ לֵיהּ. חָמָא אֲבֵילַיָּיא בְּשׁוּבְתָא וּשְׁאַל בּוֹן. אֲמַר לוֹן. בָּעֲיֵי אַתּוּן מֵידַע מָהוּ חֵיילֵיהּ. בָּא לְהוֹדִיעֵינוּ שֶׁאֵין אֵבֶל בַּשַּׁבָּת. דִּכְתִיב בִּרְכַּת י'י הִיא תַעֲשִׁיר. זוֹ בִּרְכַּת שַׁבָּת. וְלֹא־יוֹסִף עֶצֶב עִמָּהּ׃ זוֹ אֲבֵילוּת. כְּמָה דַתְּ אֲמַר נֶעֱצַב הַמֶּלֶךְ עַל־בְּנוֹ׃

1 להרחיצם | **ב** להרחיצן G לרחצם   2 הסנדל G סנדל לכשיבואו G וכשיבואו לעיר | **ב** אל העיר   3 מקום | **ב** במקום בשבת G בשלום | G - 4 | כהדה חמא | **ב** וחזה G חמה אביליייא | **ב** אביליא G אבילייה ושאל | **ב** ושאיל לון | G**ב** בון אמ' | **ב** אמ' לון   6 ביר' | **ב** בדר' ציפוראיי | G**ב** ציפוראי אבילייא | G אבילייה בשובתה   7 לון | **ב** בון אהנו | **ב** אהן עבד | **ב** עיסקיה G עסקיה   8 בעיי | **ב** בעאי להודיענו | **ב** להודיעכם   9 דכת' | **ב** הדא היא דכת'   10 דת אמר | **ב** דתימ'

Rebbi Aha instructed about him who comes from the road and his feet ache that he is permitted to wash them with water[234]. It has been stated: "A mourner and one excommunicated are permitted to wear sandals on a trip.

When they come to town they should remove them. The same holds for the Ninth of Av and public fasts[235]." It is stated: "At a place where one is used to greet mourners on the Sabbath one may do so. In the South one does greet[236]." [237]The great Rebbi Hoshaya went to some place, saw there mourners on the Sabbath and greeted them. He said to them: "I do not know the custom of your place, but be greeted according to the custom of our place." Rebbi Yose, son of Rebbi Ḥalaphta[238], praised Rebbi Meïr before the people of Sepphoris: A great, holy, and meek man. At some time, he saw mourners on the Sabbath and greeted them. They said to him: Is that the one whose praise you proclaim? He said to them, what did he do? They said to him, he saw mourners on the Sabbath and greeted them. He said to them: you have to recognize his strength; he comes to make you aware that there is no mourning on the Sabbath[239]. That is what is written[240]: *The Eternal's blessing makes rich*, that is the blessing of Sabbath, *He will not add grief to it*, that is mourning, as it is said[241]: *The king is grieving about his son.*

234 This is permitted in all cases as a medical necessity.

235 Public fast days in times of draught. Babli 15b.

236 The questionable "greeting" includes a phrase similar to the one prescribed in the Babli" "It is Sabbath where one may not console but consolation soon may come to you."

237 *Gen. rabba* 100(7).

238 He is the Tanna usually referred to simply as "R. Yose."

239 He and R. Meïr induced the people in Galilee to adopt the custom of the South (i. e., Lydda and its surroundings) to allow mentions of consolation on the Sabbath. Babli 24a.

240 *Prov.* 10:22.

241 *2S.* 19:3.

(82d line 47) שְׁמוּאֵל אָמַר. פח"ז חוֹבָה. נת"ר רְשׁוּת. פְּרִיעַת רֹאשׁ חֲזִירַת קֶרַע זְקִיפַת הַמִּיטָה חוֹבָה. נְעִילַת סַנְדָּל תַּשְׁמִישׁ הַמִּיטָה רְחִיצָה רְשׁוּת. חַד תַּלְמִיד מִן דִּשְׁמוּאֵל שִׁימֵּשׁ מִיטָתוֹ. שָׁמַע שְׁמוּאֵל וְאִיקְפַּד עָלָיו וָמִית. אָמַר. לַהֲלָכָה אִיתְאֲמָרַת. דִּילְמָא לְמַעֲשֶׂה. רַב אָמַר. ח"ז חוֹבָה. פ"ן רְשׁוּת. חֲזִירַת קֶרַע זְקִיפַת הַמִּיטָה חוֹבָה. פְּרִיעַת רֹאשׁ נְעִילַת סַנְדָּל רְשׁוּת. תְּרֵין בְּנוֹי דְרַבִּי נָפְקוּן. חַד רֵישֵׁיהּ מְגַלֵּי וּשְׁלִיחַ סַנְדָּלוֹי. חַד רֵישֵׁיהּ מְכַסֵּי וּלְבִישׁ סַנְדָּלוֹי. רִבִּי יוֹנָה סְלַק לְגַבֵּי רִבִּי גוּרְיוֹן. נְפַק לְגַבֵּיהּ לְבִישׁ סַנְדָּלוֹי. אֲמַר לֵיהּ. מָה אַתְּ סְבַר דִּיַלְפִינָן עוֹבְדָא מִמָּךְ. לָא יַלְפִין עוֹבְדָא מִן בַּר נָשׁ זְעִיר.

Samuel said, PHZ are obligatory, NTR meritorious[242]. Uncovering the head, turning around the tear[243], turning the couch upright[244], are obligatory. Wearing shoes, sexual relations, washing[245], are meritorious. A student of Samuel had sexual relations. Samuel heard, was offended by him, and he died. He said, this was said as legal rule; maybe to be acted on? Rav said, HZ are obligatory, PN meritorious. Turning around the tear, turning the bed upright, are obligatory; uncovering the head, wearing shoes, are meritorious. Two of Rebbi's sons went out, one with his head uncovered having taken off his shoes; the other with his head covered wearing shoes[246]. Rebbi Jonah went up to Rebbi Gorion, who came out to him wearing shoes. He said to him, what are you thinking? That one will adopt action from you[247]? One does not learn action from an unimportant personality.

242 Babli 24a.
243 One has to wear the kaftan which was torn in honor of the deceased for the entire week (except the Sabbath) but after the funeral the tear should not be seen.
244 So it cannot be used.
245 These three items are to be read in the negative: Not wearing shoes, not having sexual relations, not bathing.

246 This proves that Rebbi did not insist in his own family that particular rules should be followed. The case shows that it was not done that a person of rank would be seen in public without having his head wrapped in a kefiyah.
247 To change the general practice in Galilee not to wear shoes during the Seven days of mourning.

(82c line 56) וּמִלְקְרוֹת בַּתּוֹרָה. אָמַר רִבִּי יוֹחָנָן. וְאֵין וְאֵין־דּוּבֵר אֵלָיו דָּבָר. וַאֲפִילוּ דָבָר שֶׁלַּתּוֹרָה. אָמַר לֵיהּ רִבִּי שִׁמְעוֹן בֶּן לָקִישׁ. כָּל־גַּרְמֵיהּ אִילּוּ תַנָּא לֹא הֲוָה מַיְית. מַאי כְדוֹן. כַּיֵי דָמַר רִבִּי יוּדָה בַּר פָּזִי בְשֵׁם רִבִּי יוֹחָנָן. בְּשֶׁלֹּא הָיוּ יוֹדְעִין בַּמָּה לִפְתּוֹחַ לוֹ. אִם בְּגוּפוֹ אִם בְּמָמוֹנוֹ אִם בְּנֶפֶשׁ בָּנָיו וּבְנוֹתָיו. חַד תַּלְמִיד מִן דְּרַב חִסְדָּא אִיבְּאַשׁ. שְׁלַח לֵיהּ תְּרֵין תַּלְמִידִין דְּיִיתְנוּן עִמֵּיהּ. אִיתְעֲבִיד קוֹמֵיהוֹן כְּמִין חִיוֵי וְאַפְסְקוּן וּדְמָךְ. חַד תַּלְמִיד מִן דְּבַר פְּדָיָה אִיבְּאַשׁ. שְׁלַח לֵיהּ תְּרֵין תַּלְמִידִין דְּיִיתְנוּן עִמֵּיהּ. אִיתְעֲבִיד קוֹמֵיהוֹן כְּמִין (כוֹסְבָּא) [כּוֹכְבָא] וְאַפְסְקוּן וּדְמָךְ. תַּנֵּי. אֲבָל שׁוֹנֶה הוּא בְּמָקוֹם שֶׁאֵינוֹ רָגִיל. כְּהָדָא רִבִּי יָסָא הֲוָה לֵיהּ עוֹבְדָא. שְׁלַח לֵיהּ רִבִּי יוֹחָנָן תְּרֵין תַּלְמִידִין דְּיִיתְנוּן עִמֵּיהּ. אֵין מִשּׁוּם דְּשָׁרֵי לָא יְדַעִין. וְאֵין מִשּׁוּם דְּלָא רָגִיל לָא יְדַעִין. וְרִבִּי יָסָא לֹא רָגִיל. אֶלָּא כְגוֹן אִילֵּין מִילֵּיהוֹן דְּרַבָּנָן דְּבַר נַשׁ מִישְׁתָּאִיל בְּהוֹן וְקַיָּים לֵיהּ כְּמָאן דְּלָא רָגִיל. רִבִּי יוֹסֵי בַּר פֵּיטְרָס חָמוֹי דְּרִבִּי יְהוֹשֻׁעַ בֶּן לֵוִי קַדְמָייָא הֲוָה לֵיהּ עוֹבְדָא. שְׁלַח לֵיהּ בַּר קַפָּרָא תְּרֵין תַּלְמִידִין דְּיִיתְנוּן עִמֵּיהּ. אֵין דְּשָׁרֵי לָא יְדַעִין. וְאֵין מִשּׁוּם שֶׁהָיָה לָהוּט אַחַר הַתּוֹרָה לָא יְדַעִין. וְתַנֵּי כֵן. אִם הָיָה לָהוּט אַחַר הַתּוֹרָה מוּתָּר.

"Reading in the Torah." Rebbi Johanan said, *nobody was saying anything to him*[248], not even a word from the Torah. Rebbi Simeon ben Laqish said to him, he himself would not have died if he had stated[249]. What about it? As Rebbi Jehudah bar Pazi said in the name of Rebbi Johanan, because they[250] were at a loss how to start with him, whether about his body, or his money, or the souls of his sons and daughters. A student of Rav Hisda became sick. He sent him two students to study with him. He turned before them into a kind of snake; they interrupted and he died[251]. A student of Bar Pedaya became sick. He sent him two students to study with him. He turned before them into a kind of (oil cake) [a star][252]; they interrupted and he died. It was stated: But he may study a subject not familiar to him. As the following: Something happened to Rebbi Yasa[253]. Rebbi Johanan sent him two students to study with him. If because it is permitted we do not know; or if because it was a subject not familiar to him we do not know. What was not familiar to Rebbi Yasa[254]? But for example rabbinic decisions people are asked about and it is for him as if not familiar[255]. Something happened to Rebbi Yose bar Petrus the first father-in-law of Rebbi Joshua ben Levi. Bar Qappara sent him two students to study with him. If because it is permitted we do not know; or if because he was ardent for words of the Torah we do not know. And it was stated thus: If he was ardent for words of the Torah it is permitted.

248 *Job* 2:13.

249 Since a person who studies continuously cannot be touched by the Angel of Death. Babli 24a.

250 Job's companions.

251 If the Angel of Death is commanded to take the soul of a certain person who is studying permanently, he has to create a diversion which leads to an interruption of study. Babli 24a.

252 The Venice editor replaced the hapax כוסבא by the familiar כוכבא "star" which in the situation is most unlikely. One may read כוסבא as Arabic *kisba* "oil cake".

253 A close relative died.

254 Since R. Yasa was an overriding authority, he must be assumed to be conversant with all talmudic subjects.

255 Decisions by others which might disagree with his own views.

(84d line 71) עַל כָּל־דָּבָר הָאָמוּר בַּתּוֹרָה כֹּהֵן מִיטַמֵּא יִשְׂרָאֵל מִתְאַבֵּל. הוֹסִיפוּ עֲלֵיהֶם אָחִיו וַאֲחוֹתוֹ מֵאִמּוֹ וַאֲחוֹתוֹ הַנְּשׂוּאָה מִתְאַבֵּל וְאוֹנֵן אֲבָל לֹא מִיטַמֵּא. אֲרוּסָתוֹ לֹא מִתְאַבֵּל וְלֹא אוֹנֵן וְלֹא מִיטַמֵּא. תַּנֵּי. כָּל־שֶׁמִּתְאַבְּלִין עָלָיו מִתְאַבְּלִין עִמּוֹ. רַב דָּמְכַת אַחְתֵּיהּ. וּפְקִיד לִחְיָיה בְּרֵיהּ.

אָמַר לֵיהּ. כַּד תֵּי סָלִיק לְגַבַּיי הֲוֵי שְׁלַח סָנְדָּלָךְ. רִבִּי מָנָא הֲווֹן בְּנוֹיי דְּרִבִּי חֲנִינָה אֲחוֹי מֵייתִין. אֲתוֹן וּשְׁאָלוּן לְרִבִּי יוֹסֵי. מַהוּ לִכְפּוֹת אֶת הַמִּיטָה. אָמַר לוֹן. לֹא צָרִיךְ. מַהוּ לִישָׁן עַל גַּבֵּי מִיטָה כְּפוּיָה. אָמַר לוֹן. לֹא צָרִיךְ. מַהוּ לִקְרוֹת אֶת שְׁמַע וּלְהִתְפַּלֵּל. אָמַר לוֹן. נִשְׁמְעִינָהּ מִן הָדָא. הֲרֵי שֶׁהָיָה עָסוּק עִם הַמֵּת בַּקֶּבֶר וְהִגִּיעָה עוֹנַת קְרִיַת שְׁמַע. פּוֹרֵשׁ לִמְקוֹם טַהֲרָה וְלוֹבֵשׁ אֶת תְּפִילָיו וְקוֹרֵא קְרִיַת שְׁמַע וּמִתְפַּלֵּל.

In any case mentioned in the Torah[226] for whom a Cohen defiles himself an Israel mourns. They added to these his maternal brother and sister[227] and his married sister; he mourns and is in deep mourning but would not[228] defile himself. For his preliminarily wedded wife[229] he neither mourns nor is a deep mourner nor defiles himself. It was stated: About any one would mourn one joins in the mourning[230]. Rav's sister died. He commanded to his son Ḥiyya, when you will visit us, take off your shoes. The sons of Rebbi Ḥanina the brother of Rebbi Mana, died. They came and asked Rebbi Yose, does one have to overturn the bed? He told them, it is unnecessary. Does one have to sleep on an overturned bed? He told them, it is unnecessary[231]. What about reading the *Shema`* and praying? He told them, let us understand from the following: If he was occupied for corpse digging a grave and the time for reading the *Shema`* and praying arrived, he moves to a place of purity, puts on his *tefillin*, reads the *Shema`* and prays[232].

226 *Lev.* 22:2-3. Babli 20b.
227 Since biblically the "family" is restricted to paternal relatives.
228 If he were a Cohen.
229 With whom he never lived.
230 If A would have to mourn if B died and B has to mourn for a relative for whom A does not have to mourn, nevertheless in B's presence A has to follow the rules of mourning.
231 Since this is not in the principal mourner's presence.
232 Babli *Berakhot* 14b. The statement about the grave-digger implies that A's obligations are undiminished but may not be fulfilled in B's presence.

(83a line 5) מֵאֵימָתַי כּוֹפִין אֶת הַמִּיטוֹת. מִשֶּׁיָּצָא הַמֵּת מִפֶּתַח הֶחָצֵר. דִּבְרֵי רִבִּי לִיעֶזֶר. וְרִבִּי יְהוֹשֻׁעַ אוֹמֵר. מִשֶּׁיִּסְתְּמֵם הַגּוֹלָל. וּכְשֶׁמֵּת רַבָּן גַּמְלִיאֵל כֵּיוָן שֶׁיָּצָא מִפֶּתַח הֶחָצֵר אָמַר רִבִּי לִיעֶזֶר לַתַּלְמִידִים. כְּפוּ אֶת הַמִּיטוֹת. וּכְשֶׁנִּסְתַּם הַגּוֹלָל אָמַר רִבִּי יְהוֹשֻׁעַ לַתַּלְמִידִים. כְּפוּ אֶת הַמִּיטוֹת. אָמְרוּ לוֹ. כְּבָר כָּפִינוּם עַל פִּי זָקֵן. בְּעֶרֶב שַׁבָּת הוּא זוֹקֵף אֶת מִיטוֹתָיו. בְּמוֹצָאֵי שַׁבָּת הוּא כוֹפָן. תַּנֵּי. דַּרְגֵּשׁ נִזְקֶפֶת וְאֵינָהּ נִכְפֵּית. רִבִּי שִׁמְעוֹן בֶּן אֶלְעָזָר אוֹמֵר. שׁוֹמֵט אֶת

HALAKHAH 5

הַקְלַמְנְטָרִין שֶׁלָּהּ וְדַיּוֹ. רִבִּי יוֹסֵה בְשֵׁם רִבִּי יְהוֹשֻׁעַ בֶּן לֵוִי. הֲלָכָה כְרִבִּי שִׁמְעוֹן בֶּן אֶלְעָזָר. רִבִּי יַעֲקֹב בַּר אָחָא בְשֵׁם רִבִּי יָסָא. מִיטָה שֶׁנְּקְלִיטֶיהָ עוֹלִין וְיוֹרְדִין עִמָּהּ שׁוֹמְטָן וְדַיּוֹ.

1 ליעזר | ב אליעזר   2 ליעזר | ב אליעזר   3 לתלמידים | ב לתלמידיו | ב לתלמידים | ב -   4 זקן | ב הזקן
מיטותיו | בס מיטותו   5 ניכפית | ב ניכפת   6 הקלמנטרין | ב קלבינטרין נ קלונטרין קלונטרין ודייו | ב ודיו   7 יסא |
ב יוסי נ איסי   שנקליטיה | ב שניקליטה עמה | נ בו שומטן | נ שומטו

[233]When does one overturn the couches? From the moment when the dead left the gate of the courtyard, the words of Rebbi Eliezer. But Rebbi Joshua says, from when the cover plate was laid on the grave[234]. And when Rabban Gamliel died, after he left the gate of the courtyard, Rebbi Eliezer said to the students: Overturn the couches. And when the cover plate was laid on the grave, Rebbi Joshua said to the students: Overturn the couches. They said to him: We already did turn them over on the orders of the old man. Friday evening he rights his couch, at the end of Sabbat he overturns them. It was stated: A dargesh is put upright[235] and is not turned over. Rebbi Simeon ben Eleazar says, he removes its qlmnṭryn[235] and that is enough[236]. Rebbi Yose in the name of Rebbi Joshua ben Levi: practice follows Rebbi Simeon ben Eleazar. Rebbi Jacob bar Aḥa in the name of Rebbi Yasa, a couch whose posts are upright[237] and removed together with it, he takes them off and that is enough.

233 This and the next two paragraphs are copied in *Berakhot* 3:1 (Notes 16-41,ב) and partially in *Nedarim* 7:5(ג).

234 Babli *Sanhedrin* 47b.

235 Most commentators (Babli *Sanhedrin* 20a, *Nedarim* 56a) explain that the *dargesh* is lifted to stand either on its front end or its foot end. But already Rosh (Rabbenu Asher ben Yeḥiel, 14th Century in Mayence and Toledo) has shown in his commentary to Babli *Nedarim* that this explanation is impossible and that the statement must mean: it is left standing as is. The other commentators are influenced by the version of the Babli.

235 The spelling and, therefore, the meaning of the word are uncertain. The Babylonian equivalent (27a) is קרביטין which according to Z. Frankel is Byzantine Greek κραββατάριον "accessories to the bed." [Cf. κράββατος "couch, mattress"; Latin *grabatus*, from Macedonian κράβατος "low couch, camp bed" (E. G.).]

236 There is a question whether the anonymous Tanna requires more or less than Rebbi Simeon ben Eleazar. The quote in Semahot XI reads: "A surrounding *dargesh* is not turned over. Rebbi Simeon ben Eleazar says, he removes the accessories and leaves it as is." In this formulation, Rebbi Simeon ben Eleazar explains that while the *dargesh* is not turned over, some sign of mourning has to be made. It seems that this is also the explanation here, that Rebbi

Simeon ben Eleazar adds a certain requirement to the first statement.
237 Τα 'ανάκλιτα, "things to lean on";
according to both Rashi and Arukh the two posts over which the mosquito screen was hung.

(83a line 14) אֵי־זוֹ הִיא מִיטָה וְאֵי־זוֹ הִיא דַּרְגֵּשׁ. אָמַר רַבִּי יִרְמִיָה. כָּל־שֶׁמְסָרְגִין עַל גּוּפָהּ זוֹ הִיא מִיטָה. וְכָל־שֶׁאֵין מְסָרְגִין עַל גּוּפָהּ זוֹ הִיא דַּרְגֵּשׁ. הַמִּיטָה וְהָעֲרִיסָה מִשֶּׁיְשׁוּפֵם בְּעוֹר הַדָּג. אִם מְסָרֵג הוּא עַל גּוּפָהּ לְאֵי זֶה דָּבָר הוּא שָׁפָהּ. אָמַר רַבִּי לְעָזָר. תִּיפְתַּר בְּאִילֵּין עַרְסָתָא קַיְסָרִיָתָא דְּאִית לָהּ נִיקְבוֹ.

2 זו היא | **ב** זהו   מיטה | **ב** המיטה | **נ** ושאין המיטה | **נ** מיטה   והעריסה | **ב** והערסה **נ** וערסיה   אם מסרג | **נ** ומסרג   לעזר | **ב** אלעזר   4 ערסתא | **נ** ערסייתא | **ב** ערסייתא   לה | **ב** להן   ניקבן | **ב** נקבין **ב** נוקבין   3

What is a couch and what is a dargesh? Rebbi Jeremiah[238] said, one that one plaits[30] on its body is a couch and one that one does not plait on its body[239] is a dargesh. But have we not stated[240] "Bed and crib after he rubs them with fish skin[241]" If he plaits on its body, why does he rub[242]? Rebbi Eleazar said, explain it with those Caesarean cribs that have holes[243].

238 In Babli *Sanhedrin* 20a/b this appears in the name of Rebbi Jeremiah in the name of Rebbi Johanan.

239 The couch has a frame and instead of a box spring it has length- and crosswise strips that are plaited together.

240 Mishnah *Kelim* 16:1.

241 This Mishnah deals with the moment when a wooden implement is finished. Wood in itself cannot become ritually impure but wooden vessels and implements can. The moment when a wooden bed frame is finished so that it can become ritually unclean is the moment when it can be delivered by the carpenter to the customer, after it is polished with the classical equivalent of sand paper.

242 If the entire frame is covered by the strips forming the base of the bed, who cares how the wooden frame looks?

243 The strips are not wound around the frame but go through the holes in the frame, leaving half of it exposed.

(83a line 19) וּמִנַּיִין לִכְפִיַּית הַמִּיטוֹת. רִבִּי קְרִיסְפִּי בְּשֵׁם רִבִּי יוֹחָנָן. וַיֵּשְׁבוּ אִתּוֹ לָאָרֶץ. עַל הָאָרֶץ אֵין כָּתוּב כָּאן אֶלָּא וַיֵּשְׁבוּ אִתּוֹ לָאָרֶץ. אֶלָּא דָּבָר שֶׁהוּא סָמוּךְ לָאָרֶץ. מִכָּן שֶׁהָיוּ יְשֵׁנִין עַל מִיטוֹת כְּפוּיוֹת. בַּר קַפָּרָא אָמַר. אֵיקוֹנִין אַחַת טוֹבָה הָיְתָה לִי בְתוֹךְ בֵּיתָךְ וּגְרַמְתָּנִי לְכְפוֹתָהּ. אַף אַתְּ כְּפֵה מִטָּתָךְ. וְאִית דְּמַפְקִין לִישָׁנָא. יְכָפֶּה הַסַּרְסוּר. רִבִּי יוֹנָה וְרִבִּי יוֹסֵה תְּרֵיהוֹן בְּשֵׁם רִבִּי שִׁמְעוֹן בֶּן לָקִישׁ. חַד אָמַר. מִפְּנֵי מָה הוּא יָשֵׁן עַל מִיטָה כְּפוּיָה. כְּדֵי שֶׁיְּהֵא נֵיעוֹר בַּלַּיְלָה וְנִזְכָּר שֶׁהוּא אָבֵל. וְחוֹרָנָה אָמַר. מִתּוֹךְ שֶׁהוּא יָשֵׁן עַל גַּבֵּי מִיטָה כְּפוּיָה הוּא נֵיעוֹר בַּלַּיְלָה וְנִזְכָּר שֶׁהוּא אָבֵל.

1 ומניין | **ב** מניין   המיטות | **ב** המיטה   2 אלא | **ב** -   3 כפויות | **ב** כפויות היתה | **ב** היה   לכפותה | **ב** לכופפה   4 תריהון | **ב** תרויהון   5 ניעור | **ב** נועור   6 גבי | **ב** -

HALAKHAH 5

From where the overturning of beds[244]? Rebbi Crispus in the name of Rebbi Johanan: *They sat with him towards the ground*[245]. It does not say here "on the ground" but *they sat with him towards the ground,* on something close to the ground. It follows that they were sleeping on overturned couches[246]. Bar Qappara said: A beautiful form[247] I had in your house and you caused me to overturn it, you also overturn your bed! Some quote it by the expression "overturn the agent![248]" Rebbi Jonah and Rebbi Yose, both in the name of Rebbi Simeon ben Laqish. One said, why does he sleep on an overturned coach? So that he should wake up in the night and realize that he is a mourner. The other one said, since he sleeps on an overturned bed he wakes up in the night and realizes that he is a mourner.

244 Levi Ginzberg noted correctly that all the sermons here point only to the overturning of beds on which one sleeps, not couches on which one sits

245 *Job* 2:13.

246 Since the friends were sitting with Job for seven days and seven nights they must have slept "towards the ground."

247 Greek εἰκών.

248 Bar Qappara holds that people die because of the sins of their relatives. This is appropriate only for children since nobody below the age of 20 is liable before the Heavenly Court. The agent is the bed on which one not only sleeps but also has sex. Hence the couch is the agent which produces the birth of a new baby.

(83a line 27) אָמַר. אֵינִי כוֹפֶה אֶת הַמִּיטָה. הֲרֵי אֲנִי יָשֵׁן עַל גַּבֵּי הַסַּפְסָל. אֵין שׁוֹמְעִין לוֹ. מִפְּנֵי שֶׁאָמַר. אֵינִי כוֹפֶה אֶת הַמִּיטָה. אֲבָל אִם אָמַר. הֲרֵי אֲנִי כוֹפֶה אֶת הַמִּיטָה. שׁוֹמְעִין לוֹ. מַתְנִיתָהּ לֹא אֲמָרָה כֵן אֶלָּא וּכְשֶׁמַּבְרִין אוֹתוֹ כָּל־הָעָם מְסוּבִּין עַל הָאָרֶץ וְהוּא מֵיסֵב עַל הַסַּפְסָל. בְּכֹהֵן גָּבוֹל. הָא בְכֹהֵן הֶדְיוֹט לֹא. וּבְרַבִּים. הָא בְיָחִיד לֹא. וְלָא עָבְדִין כֵּן.

If he said, I do not overturn my bed but I shall sleep on the footstool[249] one does not listen to him. Because he said, I do not overturn my bed. But if he said, I am overturning my bed, one listens to him[250]. The Mishnah does not say so but[251]: "If one brings him the first meal[252], the people sit in a circle on the ground and he sits in their circle on a footstool." The High Priest, therefore not a common priest. In public, therefore not in private. But one does not act on this[253].

249 Latin *subsellium*. Probably the vocalization should be סַפְסָל.

250 If he overturned the bed he may sleep anywhere. Babli 27a

251 Mishnah *Sanhedrin* 2:1.
252 Mourners are not permitted to prepare their own first meal after the burial. The people who bring them the food are supposed to eat with them. This is an Amoraïc statement in the Babli (27b) but is implied as an ancient custom in 2S. 3:35, *Ez.* 24:17.

(83a line 32) כְּפִיַּית הַמִּיטוֹת פְּעָמִים עוֹשֶׂה שִׁשָּׁה חֲמִשָּׁה אַרְבָּעָה שְׁלֹשָׁה. בְּעֶרֶב שַׁבָּת שִׁשָּׁה. בְּעֶרֶב שַׁבָּת עִם דִּימְדּוּמֵי חַמָּה חֲמִשָּׁה. יוֹם טוֹב לְאַחַר שַׁבָּת אַרְבָּעָה. שְׁנֵי יָמִים טוֹבִים שֶׁלְּרֹאשׁ הַשָּׁנָה שְׁלֹשָׁה. חַד תַּלְמִיד מִן דְּרִבִּי מָנָא הוֹרִי לְחַד מִן קְרִיבוֹי דִּנְשִׂיָּיא. מִשֶּׁהוּא זוֹקְפָהּ שׁוּב אֵינוֹ כוֹפָהּ. כַּמָּה יָמִים הָיָה לוֹ. רִבִּי יַעֲקֹב בַּר אָחָא בְּשֵׁם רִבִּי יָסָא. שְׁנֵי יָמִים הָיָה לוֹ. רִבִּי בָּא רִבִּי אִמִּי רִבִּי יַעֲקֹב בַּר זַבְדִּי בְּשֵׁם רִבִּי יִצְחָק. שְׁלֹשָׁה. רִבִּי חִינְנָא בַּר פָּפָּא הוֹרִי לִכְפוֹתָהּ אֲפִילוּ יוֹם אֶחָד. וְאִיתְחֲמֵי לֵיהּ יַעַן כִּי מָרִיתָ. תַּנֵּי. הַדָּר בְּפוּנְדָּק אֵין מְחַיְּיבִין אוֹתוֹ לִכְפוֹת. דְּלָא יְהַוּוֹן אָמְרִין. חָרָשׁ הוּא.

Overturning the beds sometimes is for six, five, four, three {days}. On Friday, six[253]. On Friday before sundown, five[254]. A holiday after the Sabbath, four[255]. The two days of New Year, three[256]. A student of Rebbi Mana[257] instructed a relative of the Patriarch: after he uprights it he does not have to overturn again. How many days did he do it[258]? Rebbi Jacob bar Aḥa in the name of Rebbi Yasa: He did it for two days. Rebbi Abba, Rebbi Immi, Rebbi Jacob bar Zavdi in the name of Rebbi Isaac: three. Rebbi Ḥinena bar Pappus instructed to overturn it even for one day; but he saw in his dream *because you rebelled*[259]. It was stated: One who stays in an inn[260] does not have to overturn, so they should not say that he is a sorcerer.

253 If the burial was on Friday and no beds were overturned before the Sabbath, the obligation starts only at the end of the Sabbath and continues in the following week.
254 If beds were overturned on Friday even though they have to be put back in order for the Sabbath it is counted as one day and only five have to be observed in the following week.
255 If the holiday were on the Sabbath it would have eliminated all mourning rites of the Seven days. But since it follows the Sabbath it does not eliminate but is counted as a day of the Seven.
256 Same argument as the preceding one, again assuming that the burial was on Friday preceding and the first day of the New Year is on Sunday, a case excluded in the computed calendar.
257 R. Mana I.
258 Later practice denies the Tosephta (2:9) that beds have to be overturned after the Sabbath (cf. above, Note 233) if they had been overturned at least two days before the Sabbath. Babli 20a.
259 *1K.* 13:21. The instruction has to be retracted.

260 Greek πανδόκιον. In the quote by Tosaphot 21a (s.v. אלו) "a guest", even if not in a public inn.

(83a line 41) הֲרֵי שֶׁמֵּת חָמִיו אוֹ חֲמוֹתוֹ אוֹ אֶחָד מִקְרוֹבֵי אִשְׁתּוֹ אֵינוֹ כוֹפָהּ לֹא לִכְחוֹל וְלֹא לִפְקוֹס אֶלָּא נוֹהֵג עִמָּהּ כְּדֶרֶךְ שֶׁהִיא נוֹהֶגֶת. וְכֵן הִיא שֶׁמֵּת חָמִיהָ אוֹ חֲמוֹתָהּ אוֹ אֶחָד מִקְרוֹבֵי בַעֲלָהּ אֵינָהּ לֹא כוֹחֶלֶת וְלֹא פוֹקֶסֶת אֶלָּא נוֹהֶגֶת עִמּוֹ כְּדֶרֶךְ שֶׁהוּא נוֹהֵג. שְׁמוּאֵל אָמַר. לֹא שָׁנוּ אֶלָּא חָמִיו אוֹ חֲמוֹתוֹ. הָא אֶחָד כָּל־הַקְּרוֹבִים לֹא. רִבִּי בָּא בַר כֹּהֵן אָמַר קוֹמֵי רִבִּי יוֹסֵי רִבִּי יוּדָה בַּר פָּזִי בְשֵׁם רִבִּי יוֹחָנָן. בְּדָר עִמּוֹ. קָם רִבִּי יוֹסֵי עִם רִבִּי יוּדָה בַּר פָּזִי. אָמַר לֵיהּ. אַתָּה שְׁמַעְתָּ מִן אָבוּךְ הָדָא מִילְתָא. אָמַר לֵיהּ. אַבָּא לָא הֲוָה אָמַר כֵּן. אֶלָּא אֲחוֹי דְּאִיתְּתֵיהּ דְּבַר נְחֶמְיָה מִית. אָתוֹן וּשְׁאָלוֹן לֵיהּ. מָהוּ לִכְפּוֹת אֶת הַמִּיטָה. אָמַר לוֹן. לֹא צָרִיךְ. מָהוּ לִקְרוֹת אֶת שְׁמַע וּלְהִתְפַּלֵּל. אָמַר לֵיהּ. נִשְׁמְעִינָהּ מִן הָדָא. הֲרֵי שֶׁהָיָה עָסוּק עִם הַמֵּת בַּקֶּבֶר וְהִגִּיעָה עוֹנַת קִרְיַת שְׁמַע. הֲרֵי זֶה פּוֹרֵשׁ לְמָקוֹם טַהֳרָה וְלוֹבֵשׁ אֶת תְּפִילָּיו וְקוֹרֵא קִרְיַת שְׁמַע וּמִתְפַּלֵּל.

If his father-in-law or his mother-in-law or one of his wife's relatives died, he cannot force her neither to put on kohl, nor make-up[261] but behaves with her just as she behaves[262]. And so he, if her father-in-law or her mother-in-law or one of her husband's relatives died, puts on neither kohl nor make-up but behaves with him just as he behaves. Samuel said, they said this only about his father-in-law or his mother-in-law[263]. Rebbi Abba bar Cohen said before Rebbi Yose: Rebbi Judah bar Pazi in the name of Rebbi Johanan: If he dwells with him[264]. Rebbi Yose met Rebbi Judah bar Pazi. He asked him, did you hear this from your father? He said to him, my father did not say so. In fact, the brother of Bar Nehemiah's wife died. They came and asked him, does one have to overturn the bed? He told them, it is unnecessary. What about reading the *Shema*` and praying? He told them, let us understand from the following: If he was occupied digging a grave for a corpse and the time for reading the *Shema*` and praying arrived, he moves to a place of purity, puts on his *tefillin*, reads the *Shema*` and prays[232].

261 Greek φῦκος, Latin *fucus*.
262 Babli 20b.
263 But not for other relatives is he obliged to overturn his bed and observe the mourning rites even in her absence. In his mourning wife's presence the rules were explained already, Notes 231-232, as stated later in the paragraph..
264 It is not clear who dwells with whom. Since the authenticity of the statement is denied, the exact meaning is unimportant.

(83a line 53) מִפְּנֵי שֶׁאָמְרוּ שַׁבָּת עוֹלָה וְאֵינָהּ מַפְסֶקֶת וְהָרְגָלִים מַפְסִיקִין וְאֵינָן עוֹלִין: רִבִּי סִימוֹן בְּשֵׁם רִבִּי יוֹחָנָן. שֶׁהוּא מוּתָּר בְּתַשְׁמִישׁ הַמִּיטָה. קָם רִבִּי יִרְמִיָה עִם רִבִּי יוּדָה בֵּירִבִּי סִימוֹן. אָמַר לֵיהּ. הָכֵין (מן) [אָמְרִין] כָּל־תַּלְמִידוֹי דְרִבִּי יוֹחָנָן. לָא שְׁמַע בַּר נַשׁ מִינֵּיהּ הָדָא מִילְתָא אֶלָא אָבוּךְ אָמַר לֵיהּ רִבִּי יַעֲקֹב. אִין דְּאִיתְאַמְרַת לָא אִיתְאַמְרַת אֶלָא מִן אִילֵּין מִילַיָיא דְּהָכֵין הָכֵין. מִילְתֵיהּ דְּרִבִּי יְהוֹשֻׁעַ בֶּן לֵוִי אָמְרָה. שֶׁהוּא אָסוּר בְּתַשְׁמִישׁ הַמִּיטָה. דְּאָמַר רִבִּי סִימוֹן בְּשֵׁם רִבִּי יְהוֹשֻׁעַ בֶּן לֵוִי. וַהֲלֹא אָמְרוּ. אֵין אֵבֶל בָּרֶגֶל. אֶלָא שֶׁהָרַבִּים נוֹהֲגִין בּוֹ בְצִינְעָה. מָהוּ בְצִינְעָה. שֶׁהוּא אָסוּר בְּתַשְׁמִישׁ הַמִּיטָה. הֲתִיבוּן. הֲרֵי הָרֶגֶל הֲרֵי הוּא אָסוּר בְּתַשְׁמִישׁ הַמִּיטָה וְאֵינוֹ עוֹלֶה. אַף הַשַּׁבָּת הוֹאִיל וְהִיא אֲסוּרָה בְתַשְׁמִישׁ הַמִּיטָה לֹא תַעֲלֶה. אָמַר רִבִּי בָּא. אֵיפְשַׁר לְשִׁבְעָה בְלֹא רֶגֶל. אֲבָל אֵי אֶיפְשַׁר לְשִׁבְעָה בְלֹא שַׁבָּת.

"Since they said, Sabbath is counted but does not interrupt, holidays interrupt but are not counted[128]." Rebbi Simon in the name of Rebbi Joḥanan: Because he is permitted sexual relations[265]. Rebbi Jeremiah met Rebbi Judah ben Rebbi Simon. He said to him, (is that from) [so say][266] all students of Rebbi Joḥanan? Nobody heard this from him except your father[267]. Rebbi Jacob said to him, if it was said, it only was said as one of the questionable statements[268]. The word of Rebbi Joshua ben Levi implies that he is forbidden sexual relations. As Rebbi Simon said in the name of Rebbi Joshua ben Levi[269], even though they said that there is no mourning on a holiday, the public observe it in private. What means in private? That he is forbidden sexual relations. They objected: Since on a holiday he is forbidden sexual relations and it does not count, the Sabbath where he is forbidden sexual relations should not count. Rebbi Abba said, it is possible to have Seven without a holiday[270]; it is impossible to have Seven without a Sabbath.

265 On a holiday.

266 The scribe's text in parentheses is superior.

267 Who was not a regular student of R. Joḥanan.

268 As noted later, sexual relations are forbidden *de facto* but not *de jure*.

269 R. Simon's statements in the name of his teacher R. Joshua ben Levi are authoritative. The Babli 24a brings it in the name of Rebbi Joḥanan.

270 A very infrequent event does not lead to general rules.

(fol. 81c) **משנה ו**: רִבִּי אֱלִיעֶזֶר אוֹמֵר מִשֶּׁחָרַב בֵּית הַמִּקְדָּשׁ עֲצֶרֶת כַּשַּׁבָּת. רַבָּן גַּמְלִיאֵל אוֹמֵר רֹאשׁ הַשָּׁנָה וְיוֹם הַכִּפּוּרִים כָּרְגָלִים. וַחֲכָמִים אוֹמְרִים לֹא כְדִבְרֵי זֶה וְלֹא כְדִבְרֵי זֶה אֶלָּא עֲצֶרֶת כָּרְגָלִים רֹאשׁ הַשָּׁנָה וְיוֹם הַכִּפּוּרִים כַּשַּׁבָּת:

Mishnah 6: Rebbi Eliezer says, since the Temple was destroyed Pentecost is like Sabbath[271]. Rabban Gamliel says, New Year's Day and the Day of Atonement are like holidays[272]. But the Sages are saying not like the words of either one but Pentecost is like holidays[273], New Year's Day and the Day of Atonement are like Sabbath[274].

271 When the Temple existed, the entire week starting with Pentecost was festive occasion for holiday sacrifices. Without a Temple Pentecost is just one day like the Sabbath.
272 New Year's Day is under the rules of holidays. The Day of Atonement goes by the rules of the Sabbath but in contrast to the Sabbath no infraction is a capital crime.
273 It is a full holiday in all Pentateuchal lists of these.
273 They are solemn occasions without biblical commandment to enjoy.

(83a line 64) **הלכה ו**: דְּבֵית רִבִּי יַנַּאי אָמְרֵי. עֲצֶרֶת עוֹלָה שִׁבְעָה כָּרְגָלִים. בָּעוּן קוֹמֵי רִבִּי יוֹסֵה. שְׁלֹשָׁה לִפְנֵי עֲצֶרֶת וַעֲצֶרֶת שִׁבְעָה הֲרֵי עֲשָׂרָה. אֶלָּא שְׁלֹשָׁה לִפְנֵי עֲצֶרֶת שִׁבְעָה. וַעֲצֶרֶת שִׁבְעָה הֲרֵי אַרְבָּעָה עָשָׂר. אָמַר רִבִּי יוֹסֵי בֵּירִבִּי. וְכֵינִי. יוֹם אֶחָד לִפְנֵי עֲצֶרֶת מוֹנֶה חֲמִשָּׁה. לְאַחַר הָעֲצֶרֶת מוֹנֶה אַרְבָּעָה. שְׁלֹשָׁה בָּטְלוּ מִמֶּנּוּ גְּזֵירוֹת שִׁבְעָה.

Halakhah 6: They said in the House of Rebbi Yannai: Pentecost is counted as seven like holidays. They asked before Rebbi Yose: Three preceding Pentecost, and Pentecost seven, is that ten? Or three preceding Pentecost are seven, and Pentecost seven, they are fourteen[274]? Rebbi Yose the important one said, one day preceding Pentecost is counted five, two days after Pentecost are counted as four. Three, the decree of Seven is cancelled[275].

274 The Mishnah states that the Seven days of mourning are stopped by Pentecost and are not to be resumed after the holiday. The question now is how does this influence the count of Thirty days?
275 Since Mishnah 5 states that the holiday is not counted for the Thirty, neither is Pentecost. All its influence is to stop the count of Seven. Babli 24b.

(83a line 69) תַּנֵּי. אֵין מַרְאִין פָּנִים לֹא בְּרֹאשׁ הַשָּׁנָה וְלֹא בְּיוֹם הַכִּיפּוּרִים. אָמַר רִבִּי שְׁמוּאֵל בַּר רַב יִצְחָק. יוֹם הַכִּיפּוּרִים שֶׁחָל לִהְיוֹת בַּשַּׁבָּת מַרְאִין בּוֹ פָּנִים. כְּהָדָא רִבִּי חִזְקִיָּה הֲוָה לֵיהּ

עוֹבְדָא. סְלָקוּן רַבָּנָן לְגַבֵּי מָרְאִין פָּנִים מֵיחֲמָיָא לֵיהּ אַפִּין בְּצוֹמָא רַבָּא. אֲמַר לוֹן. כְּלוּם אָמְרוּ אֵין מָרְאִין פָּנִים לֹא בְרֹאשׁ הַשָּׁנָה וְלֹא בְיוֹם הַכִּיפּוּרִים לֹא מִפְּנֵי הַתְּפִילָה. שַׁנְיָיא הִיא יוֹם הַכִּיפּוּרִים שֶׁחָל לִהְיוֹת בַּשַּׁבָּת. שַׁנְיָיא הִיא יוֹם הַכִּיפּוּרִים שֶׁחָל לִהְיוֹת בַּחוֹל.

It was stated: One makes no consolation visits on New Year's Day and the Day of Atonement. Rebbi Samuel bar Rav Isaac said, one makes consolation visits on the Day of Atonement which falls on a Sabbath. As the following: Something happened to Rebbi Ḥizqiah. The rabbis came to pay him a consolation visit on the Day of Atonement. He said to them, did they not say that one makes no consolation visits on New Year's Day and the Day of Atonement? Not because of prayer? There is a difference, concerning the Day of Atonement which falls on a Sabbath; there is a difference, concerning the Day of Atonement which falls on a weekday.

משנה ז: אֵין קוֹרְעִין וְלֹא חוֹלְצִין וְאֵין מַבְרִין אֶלָּא קְרוֹבָיו שֶׁל מֵת. וְאֵין מַבְרִין אֶלָּא עַל מִטּוֹת זְקוּפוֹת וְאֵין מוֹלִיכִין לְבֵית הָאָבֵל לֹא בְּטַבְלָא וְלֹא בָאִסְקוּטְלָא וְלֹא בְקָנוֹן אֶלָּא בְסָלִּים. וְאֵין אוֹמְרִים בִּרְכַּת אֲבֵלִים בַּמּוֹעֵד אֲבָל עוֹמְדִין בַּשּׁוּרָה וּמְנַחֲמִין וּפוֹטְרִין אֶת הָרַבִּים: (fol. 81c)

Mishnah 7: Only the relatives of the deceased tear their clothes, or take them off[276], or are brought the first meal[277]. One receives the first meal only on upright standing couches[278]. Also one carries the first meal to the mourner's house neither on a tablet[279], nor in a bowl[280], nor in a reed basket[281]; only in sacks[282]. On the holiday one does not recite the blessing of the mourners[283], but one stands in a row, consoles, and dismisses the public[284].

276 It used to be that male mourners were sitting with bare shoulders.

277 On a holiday; whereas on weekdays those close to the deceased also could show their mourning. The first meal cannot be prepared by the mourners themselves at any time.

278 In contrast to weekdays when overturned couches are the standard.

279 Latin *tabula*.

280 Latin *scutella*.

281 Greek κανοῦν.

282 Since the poor have only sacks, they should not be excluded from the meritorious act of providing the first meal.

283 In the cemetery all burial ceremonies are omitted.

284 When leaving the cemetery the public forms two rows between which the mourners leave while the public tells that

the All-Merciful may console them among the mourners of Zion and Jerusalem. In contrast to weekdays the public is dismissed at the cemetery and the mourners return to their house unaccompanied.

(83a line 76) **הלכה ז**: אֵין קוֹרְעִין וְלֹא חוֹלְצִין וְאֵין מַבְרִין אֶלָּא קְרוֹבָיו שֶׁל מֵת. אָמַר רִבִּי יִרְמְיָה. וּבִלְבָד קְרוֹבִים שֶׁהֵן רְאוּיִין לְהִתְאַבֵּל. כְּהָדָא דְתַנֵּי. חָכָם שֶׁמֵּת [הַכֹּל] קְרוֹבָיו וַאֲפִילוּ קְרוֹבִים שֶׁאֵינָן רְאוּיִין לְהִתְאַבֵּל. כְּהָדָא רִבִּי אָבוּן דְּמָךְ בְּמוֹעֲדָא וְלֹא גָמַל לוֹ רִבִּי מָנָא חֶסֶד. וַהֲווֹן צִיפּוֹרָאֵי אֲמְרִין. עַד מָוֶת שְׂנָא. בָּתַר מוֹעֲדָא עֲבַד לֵיהּ אִיקְרֵיהּ. עָאֵל וְאָמַר קוֹמֵיהוֹן כְּהָדָא דְתַנֵּי. חָכָם שֶׁמֵּת הַכֹּל קְרוֹבָיו. בְּאִינּוּן דַּהֲווֹן גַּבֵּיהּ. אֲנַן לָא הֲוִינָן גַּבֵּיהּ.

3 במועדא G | במועדה   4 מועדא G | מועדה   ליה G | לה

Halakhah 7: "Only the relatives of the deceased tear their clothes, or take them off, or are brought the first meal. Rebbi Jeremiah said, only relatives who have to mourn[285]. As this which was stated: If a Sage dies [all] are his relatives, even relatives who do not have to mourn. As the following: Rebbi Abun died on a holiday and Rebbi Mana did not participate in mourning. The Sepphoreans said, he hates him even in death. After the holiday he eulogized him. He preached and said in front of them, as was stated: If a Sage dies all are his relatives, referring to those who were present. We were not present[286].

285 As enumerated in Halakhah 5, Notes 226 ff.

286 And therefore prevented from mourning on the holiday.

(83b line 6) הַקּוֹרֵעַ מִן הַמִּלָּל וּמִן הַשָּׁלָל וּמִן הָרְדִיד אֵינוֹ קֶרַע. מִיָּן הָאִיחוּי הֲרֵי זֶה קֶרַע. אֵי זֶהוּ אִיחוּי. אָמַר רִבִּי אַחָא. כָּל־שֶׁאֵין מְקוֹמוֹ נִיכָּר.

עֲשָׂרָה קְרָעִים אֲסוּרִין בְּאִיחוּי. הַקּוֹרֵעַ עַל אָבִיו. וְעַל אִמּוֹ. וְעַל רַבּוֹ שֶׁלִּימְּדוֹ חָכְמָה. וְעַל הַנָּשִׂיא. וְעַל אַב בֵּית דִּין. וְעַל שְׁמוּעוֹת הָרָעוֹת. וְעַל קִלְלַת הַשֵּׁם. וְעַל שְׂרֵיפַת תּוֹרָה. וְעַל יְרוּשָׁלַם. וְעַל בֵּית הַמִּקְדָּשׁ.

1 באיחוי G | ביאחוי

עַל אָבִיו וְעַל אִמּוֹ וְעַל רַבּוֹ שֶׁלִּימְּדוֹ חָכְמָה מִנַּיִין. וֶאֱלִישָׁע רֹאֶה וְהוּא מְצַעֵק אָבִי | אָבִי רֶכֶב יִשְׂרָאֵל וּפָרָשָׁיו. רִבִּי מַתּוּן בְּעָא קוֹמֵי רִבִּי יוֹחָנָן. וּמֵאֱלִישָׁע אָנוּ לְמֵידִין תּוֹרָה. אָמַר לֵיהּ. מַתּוּן מַתּוּן. מַה הַמֵּת מִשֶּׁהוּא מִסְתַּלֵּק עוֹד אֵינוּ רוֹאֵהוּ. כָּךְ זֶה מִשֶּׁנִּסְתַּלֵּק עוֹד לֹא רָאָהוּ. כְּשֵׁם שֶׁקּוֹרְעִין עַל הַחֲכָמִים כָּךְ קוֹרְעִין עַל תַּלְמִידֵיהֶן. חִזְקִיָּה אָמַר. אֵי זֶהוּ תַלְמִיד חָכָם. כָּל־שֶׁשָּׁנָה הֲלָכוֹת וְעַד תּוֹרָה. אָמַר לֵיהּ רִבִּי יוֹסֵה. הָדָא דַתְּ אָמַר בָּרִאשׁוֹנָה. אֲבָל עַכְשָׁיו אֲפִילוּ הֲלָכוֹת. רִבִּי אַבָּהוּ בְשֵׁם רִבִּי יוֹחָנָן. כָּל־שֶׁהוּא מְבַטֵּל עֲסָקָיו מִפְּנֵי מִשְׁנָתוֹ. תַּנֵּי. כָּל־שֶׁשּׁוֹאֲלִין אוֹתוֹ וְהוּא

מֵשִׁיב. אָמַר רִבִּי הוֹשַׁעְיָה. כְּגוֹן אֲנָן דְּרַבְּבִינָן מַשְׁגְּחִינָן עֲלֵינָן וַאֲנָן מְתִיבִין לוֹן. אָמַר רִבִּי בָּא בַּר
מָמָל. כָּל־שֶׁהוּא יוֹדֵעַ לְבָאֵר מִשְׁנָתוֹ. וַאֲנָן אֲפִילוּ רַבְּבִינָן לָא חַכְמִין מְבָאֲרָה מַתְנִיתָן.

1 מניין G | מניי 3 משהוא G | מישהוא משנסתלק G | ...נסתלק 4 שקורעין G | שקורעים חכם G
חכמין 5 יוסה G | 2 יוסי 7 ר' G | רב משגחינן | 2 משגחין לון | 2 לו 8 יודע G | יודיע ואנן G | ונן
מתניתן G | מתניתון

He who tears the seam or the inner seam or the shawl, it is no tear[287]. From mending it is a tear. What is mending? Rebbi Aḥa said, any whose place is not recognizable.

Ten tears may not be mended artistically: He who tears for his father, and for his mother, and for his teacher who taught him wisdom, and for the Patriarch, and for the Chief Judge, and because of bad news, and because of blasphemy, and because of burning Torah, and for Jerusalem, and for the Temple[288].

For his father, and for his mother, and for his teacher who taught him wisdom, from where? *And Elisa saw, and he cried 'my father, my father, chariot of Israel and its charioteers'*[289]. Rebbi Mattun asked before Rebbi Joḥanan: May one infer instruction from Elisa[290]? He said to him Mattun, Mattun, just as a dead person from the moment he is deceased cannot see him, so also from the moment he disappeared he did not see him. In the same way one tears for the Sages so one tears for their students. Who is a student of the Sages[291]? Ḥizqiah said, any who has studied practices up to the Torah[292]. Rebbi Yose said to him, that you are saying for earlier ones. But today only practices[293]. Rebbi Abbahu in the name of Rebbi Joḥanan: Any who neglects his business for his learning. It was stated: Any whom one asks and he answers. Rebbi Hoshaia said, for example, we, since our instructors supervise us and we answer them[294]. Rebbi Abba bar Mamal said, any who can explain his Mishnah. But as relates to us, even our teachers are not wise to explain our Mishnah[295].

287 Rending one's clothes is valid only if the tissue itself is torn. Babli 26b.

288 Babli 26a, *Semahot* 9.

289 *2K.* 2:12. The verse ends: *he got hold of his garments and tore them into two tears.*

290 Since Eliahu did not die, nothing should be inferred from Elisha's actions. Babli 26a, *Sanhedrin* 60b.

291 Qualified that the public should mourn for him. From here on to the end of the Tractate the text is written twice by the scribe. The second text is only partial, the remainder has been filled in by the corrector. The scribe's second text is noted

"2" in the variant readings; the corrector's mostly has been disregarded.

292 For any rabbinic or biblical rule he can explain the origin and its development.

293 It is enough that he knows all the rules.

294 The *baraita* could have been interpreted to mean that a Student of the Sages must be able to answer any question in rabbinic learning. This is now qualified that he only has to pass the examinations which qualify for ordination.

295 He denies that the rules of Students of the Sages apply to anybody nowadays.

(83b line 21) אֵי זֶהוּ רַבּוֹ. כָּל־שֶׁפָּתַח לוֹ תְחִילָה. דִּבְרֵי רִבִּי מֵאִיר. רִבִּי יְהוּדָה אוֹמֵר. כָּל־שֶׁרוֹב תַּלְמוּדוֹ מִמֶּנוּ. רִבִּי יוֹסֵה אוֹמֵר. כָּל־שֶׁהֵאִיר עֵינָיו בְּמִשְׁנָתוֹ. וּמַה הֵאִיר עֵינָיו בְּמִשְׁנָתוֹ. רִבִּי אַבָּהוּ בְשֵׁם רִבִּי יוֹחָנָן. הֲלָכָה כְּמִי שֶׁהוּא אוֹמֵר. כָּל־שֶׁרוֹב תַּלְמוּדוֹ מִמֶּנוּ. וְלָמָּה לֹא אָמַר כְּרִבִּי יְהוּדָה. אִית תַּנָּיֵי תַּנֵּי וּמְחַלֵּף. רִבִּי אֶלְעָזָר קָרַע עַל שֶׁפָּתַח לוֹ תְחִילָה. שְׁמוּאֵל חָלַץ עַל שֶׁהֵאִיר עֵינָיו בְּמִשְׁנָתוֹ. וּמַה הֵאִיר עֵינָיו בְּמִשְׁנָתוֹ. אָמַר רִבִּי יוֹסֵי בֵּירִבִּי בּוּן. בִּשְׁנֵי מַפְתֵּיחוֹת. אֶחָד יוֹרֵד לַאֲמַת הַשֶּׁחִי וְאֶחָד פּוֹתֵחַ כֵּיוָן: מָהוּ אֶחָד יוֹרֵד לַאֲמַת הַשֶּׁחִי. שֶׁהָיָה שׁוֹחֶה אַמָּה עַד שֶׁלֹּא יִפְתַּח.

1 כל שפתח לו תחילה | G רבו שלימדו מקרא ומשנה יהודה | G יודה   2 ומה האיר עיניו במשנתו | GC אפילו דבר אחד

296"Who is his teacher? The one who taught him first[297], the words of Rebbi Meïr. Rebbi Jehudah said, the one from whom he received most of his instruction. Rebbi Yose said, anyone who explained a Mishnah to him.[298]" What means, who explained a Mishnah to him?[299] Rebbi Abbahu came in the name of Rebbi Joḥanan: Practice follows him who said, the one from whom he received most of his instruction. Why did he not explain that this follows Rebbi Jehudah? There are Tannaïm who state it switched[300]. Rebbi Eleazar tore his garment for his first teacher. Samuel took off {his shoes} for one who had explained a Mishnah to him[301]. What Mishnah did he explain to him? Rebbi Yose ben Rebbi Abun said, "There are two keys. For one he has to go down to his arm-pit and one opens straight.[302]" What means "for one he has to go down to his arm-pit"? He had to lower his hand under his arm-pit until it could be opened[303].

296 A very similar text is *Horaiot* 3:4, Notes 251ff., *Bava mesia`* 3:13, Notes 136-145.

297 Text of G: His teacher who taught him Scripture and Mishnah, the elementary school teacher.

298 Tosephta *Horaiot* 2:5, *Bava mesia`* 2:30.

299 Reading of G and corrector: "even in only one subject."

300 The name tradition in the Tosephta is not certain.
301 As a sign of mourning.
302 Mishnah *Tamid* 3:6.
303 The doors of the Temple Hall could be opened only from the inside. When the door was locked, a Cohen entered from a small side door which led to a guard room. The lock of this side door was hidden; the Cohen had to take the key, lower his entire arm to the arm-pit behind the partition wall and only then could insert the key. *Tamid* 30b.

(83b line 29) עַל הַנָּשִׂיא וְעַל בֵּית דִּין וְעַל שְׁמוּעוֹת הָרָעוֹת מְנַיָּין. וַיַּחֲזֵק דָּוִד בִּבְגָדָיו וַיִּקְרָעֵם וגו'. וַיִּסְפְּדוּ וַיִּבְכּוּ וַיָּצוּמוּ עַד־הָעָרֶב עַל־שָׁאוּל. זֶה הַנָּשִׂיא. וְעַל־יְהוֹנָתָן בְּנוֹ. זֶה אַב בֵּית דִּין. וְעַל־עַם יְיָ וְעַל־בֵּית יִשְׂרָאֵל כִּי נָפְלוּ בֶחָרֶב. אִילּוּ שְׁמוּעוֹת הָרָעוֹת.

From where for the Patriarch, and for the Chief Judge, and because of bad news? *David grasped his garments and tore them*[304], etc. [305]*They eulogized, and cried, and fasted for Saul*, that is the Patriarch, *And for his son Jonathan*, that is the Chief Judge, *and about the Eternal's people and the House of Israel, for they fell by the sword*; these are bad news[306].

304 *2K.* 1:11.
305 *2K.* 1:12.
306 This is the definition of bad news for which one has to mourn. Babli 26a.

(83b line 33) עַל קִלְלַת הַשֵּׁם מְנַיָּין. וַיְהִי כִּשְׁמוֹעַ הַמֶּלֶךְ חִזְקִיָּהוּ אֶת דִּבְרֵי רַב שָׁקֵה וַיִּקְרַע אֶת־בְּגָדָיו. מָהוּ לִקְרוֹעַ עַל קִלְלַת הַגּוֹי. מָאן דְּאָמַר. רַב שָׁקֵה גּוֹי הָיָה. קוֹרְעִין. וּמָאן דְּאָמַר. יְהוּדִי הָיָה. אֵין קוֹרְעִין. תַּנֵּי רִבִּי הוֹשַׁעְיָה. אֶחָד שֶׁשָּׁמַע קִלְלַת הַשֵּׁם מִיִּשְׂרָאֵל וְאֶחָד שֶׁשָּׁמַע קִלְלַת הַשֵּׁם מִן הַגּוֹי חַיָּיב לִקְרוֹעַ. מַה טַעֲמָא. הִנֵּה יְיָ אֱלֹהֵי כָּל־[בָּשָׂר] הֲמִמֶּנִּי יִפָּלֵא כָּל־דָּבָר׃

For blasphemy, from where?[307] *When king Hezekias heard the words of Rab Šake, he rent his garment*[308]. Does one have to rent for a Gentile's blasphemy? According to him who said that Rab Šake was a Gentile, one rends. According to him who said that Rab Šake was a Jew, one does not rend[309]. Rebbi Hoshaia stated: Both one who heard blasphemy from an Israel or one who heard blasphemy from a Gentile have to rent their garment. What is the reason? *Since I am the Eternal, God over all [flesh], should anything be extraordinary to me*[310]?

מָהוּ לִקְרוֹעַ בַּזְּמַן הַזֶּה. רִבִּי יוֹסֵה רִבִּי יִרְמְיָה בְשֵׁם רִבִּי יוֹחָנָן. מִשֶּׁרָבוּ הַגּוּדְפָנִים פָּסְקוּ מִלִּקְרוֹעַ. מָהוּ לִקְרוֹעַ עַל הַכִּינּוּיִים. נִשְׁמְעִינָהּ מִן הָדָא. רִבִּי שִׁמְעוֹן בֶּן לָקִישׁ הֲוָה מְהַלֵּךְ בָּאִיסְרָטָא. פָּגַע בֵּיהּ חַד כּוּתַי וַהֲוָה מְגַדֵּף וְהוּא קָרַע. מְגַדֵּף וְהוּא קָרַע. נְחַת לֵיהּ מִן

חַמְרָא וִיהַב לֵיהּ מַרְתּוּקָא גוֹ לִיבֵּיהּ. אֲמַר לֵיהּ. רָשָׁע. אִית לְאִימָּךְ מָאנִין מְסַפְּקָא לִי. הָדָא
אֲמְרָה שֶׁקּוֹרְעִין עַל הַכִּינּוּיִין וְשֶׁקּוֹרְעִין בַּזְּמַן הַזֶּה.

Does one rend his garment nowadays[310]? Rebbi Yose, Rebbi Jeremiah in the name of Rebbi Johanan[312]: When blasphemers proliferated, they stopped rending[313]. Does one rend for substitute names today? Let us hear from the following: Rebbi Simeon ben Laqish was travelling on the highway. He met a Samaritan who was repeatedly blaspheming, and he was rending. He dismounted from the donkey and gave him a blow on his heart saying to him: Criminal! Does your mother have garments to supply me with? This implies that one rends for substitute names[314] and rends his garments at the present time.

307 Why does one have to rend his garment when he hears blasphemy since this obligation is not mentioned in the Torah?
308 *2K.* 19:1. Since the king heard the blasphemy from his ministers, it proves that one has to rend his garment even if he hears it indirectly. Babli *Sanhedrin* 69a.
309 On the one hand, it is not likely that a high official of the king of Assyria was not an Assyrian. On the other hand, why should a high Assyrian official be able to speak Hebrew unless he was a Jewish apostate? *Sanhedrin* 7:1, Note 231; Babli *Sanhedrin* 60a. M. Cogan and H. Tadmor, *II Kings*, The Anchor Bible vol. 11 (1988) p. 230.

310 *Jer.* 32:26.
311 Since the pronunciation of the Name is unknown, an obligation to rend one's garments would imply that it applies to substitutes of the Name. The paragraph has a parallel in *Sanhedrin* 7:1, Notes 233-235.
312 Compared to *Sanhedrin*, the chain of transmission is much shortened.
313 The same statement in the Babli *Sanhedrin* 60a in the name of R. Hiyya (bar Abba). The implication is that the status of substitute names is the same as that of the Name.
314 Disagreeing with R. Johanan.

(83b line 44) עַל שְׂרֵיפַת הַתּוֹרָה מְנַיִין. וַיְהִי | כִּקְרוֹא יְהוּדִי שָׁלֹשׁ דְּלָתוֹת וְאַרְבָּעָה. מָהוּ שָׁלֹשׁ
דְּלָתוֹת וְאַרְבָּעָה. תְּלַת אַרְבַּע פְּסִיקָן. כֵּיוָן שֶׁהִגִּיעוּ לְפָסוּק הַחֲמִישִׁי כִּי־יְ"יָ הוֹגָהּ עַל רֹב־פְּשָׁעֶיהָ
מִיַּד יִקְרָעֶהָ בְּתַעַר הַסּוֹפֵר וְהַשְׁלֵךְ וגו'. וְלֹא פָחֲדוּ וְלֹא קָרְעוּ אֶת־בִּגְדֵיהֶם.

Because of burning Torah from where? *It was when Yehudi read three or four stanzas*[315]. What means "*three or four stanzas*"? Three or four verses. When he came to the fifth verse[316], *for the Eternal afflicted her for the magnitude of her sins*, immediately *he cut it off with a scribe's knife and threw it*, etc. *But they showed no fear nor tore their garments*[317].

315 *Jer.* 36:23.
316 *Thr.* 1:5. Traditionally the scroll cut into pieces and burned by King Yehoyakim was a first version of *Threni*.
317 *Jer.* 36:24. Since the ministers are chastised for not tearing their garments it follows that there was an obligation to do so. It also follows that "Torah" includes all of the Hebrew Scriptures.

(83b line 48) הָרוֹאֶה תַלְמִיד חָכָם שֶׁמֵּת כְּרוֹאֶה סֵפֶר תּוֹרָה שֶׁנִּשְׂרָף. אָמַר רִבִּי אַבָּהוּ. יָבֹא עָלַי אִם טָעַמְתִּי כְלוּם כָּל־אוֹתוֹ הַיּוֹם. רִבִּי יוֹנָה הֲוָה בְצוֹר. שָׁמַע דִּדְמַךְ בְּרֵיהּ דְּרִבִּי אַבָּהוּ. אַף עַל גַּב דְּאָכַל וְשָׁתָה מַיָּא אַסְקֵיהּ צוֹם כָּל־הַהוּא יוֹמָא. רִבִּי בָּא וְרִבִּי הוּנָא בַּר חִיָּיה הֲווֹן יְתִיבִין. אָתַת נַעֲמִיתָא וְחַטְפַת תְּפִילוֹי דְּהוּנָא בַּר חִיָּיה. צָדָהּ רִבִּי בָּא וְחָנְקָהּ. אָמַר לֵיהּ רִבִּי הוּנָא בַּר חִיָּיה עוֹד מְעַט וְהָיִינוּ בָאִים לִידֵי שְׂרֵיפַת תּוֹרָה. אָמַר לֵיהּ. וַעֲדַיִין אַתְּ לְזוֹ. כֵּן אָמַר רַב יִרְמְיָה בְּשֵׁם רַב. אֵין קוֹרְעִין אֶלָּא עַל סֵפֶר תּוֹרָה שֶׁשְּׂרָפוֹ מֶלֶךְ יִשְׂרָאֵל בִּזְרוֹעַ. כְּגוֹן יְהוֹיָקִים בֶּן יֹאשִׁיָּהוּ מֶלֶךְ יְהוּדָה וַחֲבֵירָיו. עוּלָא בִּירִיָּיא רִבִּי לַעְזָר בְּשֵׁם רִבִּי חֲנִינָה. הָרוֹאֶה סֵפֶר תּוֹרָה שֶׁנִּשְׂרָף חַיָּיב לִקְרוֹעַ עַל הַגְּוִיל בִּפְנֵי עַצְמוֹ וְעַל הַכְּתָב בִּפְנֵי עַצְמוֹ. מַה טַעֲמָא. אַחֲרֵי | שְׂרֹף הַמֶּלֶךְ אֶת־הַמְּגִילָה וְאֶת־הַדְּבָרִים. אֶת־הַמְּגִילָה זֶה הַגְּוִיל. וְאֶת־הַדְּבָרִים זֶה הַכְּתָב.

He who sees a dead scholar is like him who sees a Torah scroll burned. Rebbi Abbahu said, it should come over me if I tasted anything that whole day[318]. Rebbi Jonah was in Tyre. He heard that Rebbi Abbahu's son had died. Even though he had eaten and drunk water he kept it as fast day that whole day[319]. Rebbi Abba and Rebbi Huna bar Ḥiyya were sitting. An ostrich came and snatched Rebbi Huna bar Ḥiyya's *tefillin*. Rebbi Abba caught it and strangled it. Rebbi Huna bar Ḥiyya said to him, we almost came to burning the Torah. He said to him, do you still hold this? So said Rav Jeremiah in the name of Rav: One only rends his garment for a Torah scroll which an Israelite king burned forcibly, as e. g. Yehoyakim ben Josia the King of Judah[320]. Ulla from Bireh, Rebbi Eleazar in the name of Rebbi Ḥanina: He who sees a Torah scroll burned has to rend his garment separately for the parchment and for the writing. What is the reason? *After the king's burning of the scroll and the words*[321]. *The scroll,* this is the parchment. *And the words,* that is the writing[322].

318 When he buries a fellow scholar.
319 On fasting only part of the day cf. *Nedarim* 8:1 Note 20.
320 Some of whose ministers tried to talk him out of burning the scroll, *Jer.* 36:25. Babli 26a.
321 *Jer.* 36:27.
322 Babli 26a.

(83b line 60) רִבִּי בֶּרֶכְיָה רִבִּי חֶלְבּוֹ עוּלָא בִירִייָא רִבִּי לְעָזָר בְּשֵׁם רִבִּי חֲנִינָה. עָתִיד הַקָּדוֹשׁ בָּרוּךְ הוּא לַעֲשׂוֹת רֹאשׁ חוֹלָה לַצַּדִּיקִים לֶעָתִיד לָבוֹא. מַה טַעַם. שִׁיתוּ לִיבְּכֶם לְחֵילָה. לְחוֹלָה כְתִיב. וְהַצַּדִּיקִים מַרְאִין אוֹתוֹ בְּאֶצְבַּע וְאוֹמְרִים. כִּי זֶה | אֱלֹהִים אֱלֹהֵינוּ עוֹלָם וָעֶד הוּא יְנַהֲגֵנוּ עֲלָמוּת: עֲלָמוּת בַּעֲלִימוּת. עֲלָמוּת בְּזָרִיזוּת. עֲלָמוּת. כְּאִלֵּין עוֹלִימָתָא. תִּירְגֵּם עֲקִילַס. אַתָּנָא־סִייָא. עוֹלָם שֶׁאֵין בּוֹ מָוֶת. וְהַצַּדִּיקִים מַרְאִין בּוֹ בְּאֶצְבַּע וְאוֹמְרִים. כִּי זֶה | אֱלֹהִים אֱלֹהֵינוּ עוֹלָם וָעֶד הוּא יְנַהֲגֵנוּ עֲלָמוּת: הוּא יְנַהֲגֵנוּ בָּעוֹלָם הַזֶּה. הוּא יְנַהֲגֵנוּ לֶעָתִיד לָבוֹא.

Rebbi Berekhia, Rebbi Ḥelbo, Ulla from Bireh, Rebbi Eleazar in the name of Rebbi Hanina[323]: In the future the Holy One, praise to Him, will lead a circular dance for the Just ones. What is the reason? *Put your hearts to the walls*[324], it is written "to its circular dance.[325]" And the Just one will point with their finger and say, *Truly, He is GOD, our Power, Forever; He will lead us beyond death*[326]! *Almut*, in strength; *almut*, in agility. *Almut*, like these girls. Akilas translated 'αθανασία, a world without death. And the Just one will point with their finger and say, *Truly, He is GOD, our Power, Forever; He will lead us beyond death!* He will lead us in this world, He will lead us in the future[327].

323 Copied in *Megillah* 3:2, Shortened in the Babli, *Ta`anit* 31a, Midrash *Ps.*, *Ps.* 48[5].
324 *Ps.* 48:14.
325 This reading is not found in masoretic texts.
326 *Ps.* 48:15.
326 "Lead us in worlds" is the translation of LXX.

(83b line 68) וְעַל יְרוּשָׁלַם וְעַל בֵּית הַמִּקְדָּשׁ. וַיָּבוֹאוּ אֲנָשִׁים מִשְּׁכֶם וּמִשִּׁלֹה וּמִשֹּׁמְרוֹן שְׁמוֹנָה אֲנָשִׁים מְגוּלְּחֵי זָקָן וּקְרוּעֵי בְגָדִים. אֶחָד שֶׁשָּׁמַע שֶׁחֶרְבָה יְרוּשָׁלַם וְאֶחָד הָרוֹאֶה אֶת יְרוּשָׁלַיִם בְּחוּרְבָּנָהּ חַיָּיב לִקְרוֹעַ. הָרוֹאֶה אֶת יְרוּשָׁלַם מִן הַצּוֹפִים חַיָּיב לִקְרוֹעַ. אִית תַּנָּיֵי תַנֵּי. מוֹסִיף עַל הַקֶּרַע. אִית תַּנָּיֵי תַנֵּי. תְּחִילַת הַקֶּרַע טֶפַח וְתוֹסַפְתּוֹ כָּל־שֶׁהוּא. אִית תַּנָּיֵי תַנֵּי. תְּחִילַת הַקֶּרַע טֶפַח וְתוֹסַפְתּוֹ שָׁלֹשׁ אֶצְבָּעוֹת. רִבִּי יוֹסֵה רִבִּי יִרְמְיָה בְּשֵׁם רִבִּי חִייָא בַּר בָּא רִבִּי חִזְקִיָּה רִבִּי יִרְמְיָה בְּשֵׁם רִבִּי יוֹחָנָן. הֲלָכָה כְמִי שֶׁהוּא אוֹמֵר. תְּחִילַת הַקֶּרַע טֶפַח וְתוֹסַפְתּוֹ כָּל־שֶׁהוּא.

"And for Jerusalem, and for the Temple." *There came men from Sichem and from Shilo and from Samaria, eight men with shaved beards and torn garments,* the first tear is one hand-breadth, the addition anything[327]. One who was informed that Jerusalem was destroyed like one who sees Jerusalem in its destruction has to tear. He who sees Jerusalem from Mount Scopus has to tear[328]. There are Tannaim who state, he adds to the tear. There are Tannaim who state, the first tear is one hand-breadth, the addition anything[329]. There are Tannaim who state, the first tear is one hand-breadth, the addition three finger-breadths. Rebbi Yose, Rebbi Jeremiah in the name of Rebbi Hiyya bar Abba; Rebbi Hizkiah, Rebbi Jeremiah in the name of Rebbi Johanan: Practice follows him who said, the first tear is one hand-breadth, the addition anything.

327 *Jer.* 41:5. Babli 26a.
328 Babli 26a.

329 Not nothing but possibly less than the smallest unit of measurement in use.

(83b line 76) מָהוּ לְהַבְדִּיל קְנֵה שָׂפָה. רִבִּי יִרְמְיָה רִבִּי חִייָה בְשֵׁם רִבִּי שִׁמְעוֹן בֶּן לָקִיש. וַיַּחֲזֵק דָּוִד. אֵין חֲזָקָה פָּחוּת מִטֶּפַח. וַיִּקְרָעֵם. רִבִּי סִימוֹן בְּשֵׁם רִבִּי יְהוֹשֻׁעַ בֶּן לֵוִי. מִיכָּן שֶׁהוּא צָרִיךְ לְהַבְדִּיל קְנֵה שָׂפָה. מֵת לוֹ מֵת קוֹרֵעַ. מֵת לוֹ מֵת אַחֵר אֲפִילוּ שֶׁשָּׁמַע עַל אָבִיו וְעַל אִמּוֹ וְעַל רַבּוֹ שֶׁלִּימְּדוֹ חָכְמָה קוֹרֵעַ קֶרַע אֶחָד לְכוּלָן. רִבִּי יְהוּדָה בֶן תֵּימָא אוֹמֵר. קוֹרֵעַ עַל זֶה בִפְנֵי עַצְמוֹ וְעַל זֶה בִפְנֵי עַצְמוֹ וּבִלְבַד שֶׁלֹּא יַעֲשֶׂה עַל אָבִיו וְעַל אִמּוֹ תוֹסֶפֶת. וְלָא דָא הִיא קַדְמִייָתָא. אֶלָּא שֶׁלֹּא יוֹסִיף לֹא עַל שֶׁלְאָבִיו וְלֹא עַל שֶׁלְאִמּוֹ. רִבִּי חֶלְבּוֹ וְרַב מַתָּנָה יוֹסֵי בַּר מְנִישָׁא בְשֵׁם רַב. הֲלָכָה כְּרִבִּי יְהוּדָה בֶן תֵּימָא. מֵת לוֹ מֵת קוֹרֵעַ. מֵת לוֹ מֵת אַחֵר מוֹסִיף עַל הַקֶּרַע וְקוֹרֵעַ. עַד אֵיכָן. אָמַר רִבִּי חֲנִינָה. עַד שֶׁהוּא מַגִּיעַ עַד טִיבּוּרוֹ. תַּנָּא חַד סָב קוֹמֵי רִבִּי זְעוּרָה. אֲפִילוּ נִתְמַנֶּה לוֹ בְגֶד כָּל־שִׁבְעָה חַייָב לִקְרוֹעַ. אָמַר לֵיהּ רִבִּי זְעוּרָה. הָדָא דְתֵימַר בִּשְׁאָר הַקְּרוֹבִים. אֲבָל עַל אָבִיו וְעַל אִמּוֹ אֲפִילוּ לְאַחַר שִׁבְעָה חַייָב לִקְרוֹעַ. מֵת לוֹ מֵת קוֹרֵעַ. מֵת לוֹ מֵת אַחֵר מַרְחִיק שָׁלֹשׁ אֶצְבָּעוֹת וְקוֹרֵעַ. שֶׁלְמוֹ מִלְּפָנָיו מַתְחִיל מֵאַחֲרָיו. שֶׁלְמוֹ מִלְּמַעֲלָן מַתְחִיל מִלְּמַטָּן. שֶׁלְמוֹ אֵילוּ וָאֵילוּ. רִבִּי חִייָה בְּרֵיהּ דְּרִבִּי אָדָא דְיָפוֹ אָמַר. נַעֲשָׂה כְּפוֹחֵחַ.

Does one have to sever the trim[330]? Rebbi Jeremiah, Rebbi Hiyya in the name of Rebbi Simeon ben Laqish: *David grasped*[304]. There is no grasping less than a hand-breadth[331]. *And tore them*, Rebbi Simon in the name of Rebbi Joshua ben Levi: From here that he has to sever the trim[332]. If a relative died, he rends. If another relative died, even if he heard about his father or his mother, or his teacher who taught him wisdom, he rends one tear for all of them. Rebbi Jehudah ben Tema says, he rends for each one separately, only that he shall not make that for his father or his mother as an addition. Is that not the first {statement}[333]? But he may not add to that for his father or his mother. Rebbi Helbo and Rav Mattana, Yose ben Manisha in the name of Rav: Practice follows Rebbi Jehudah ben Tema. If a relative died, he rends. If another relative died, he adds to the tear and rends. How far? Rebbi Hanina said, until he reaches to his navel. An old man stated before Rebbi Ze`ira:

Even if he receives another garment during all the Seven he is obligated to rend[334]. Rebbi Ze`ira said to him, this you are saying about other relatives. But for his father and his mother even after the Seven he is required to rend. If a relative died, he rends. If another relative died, he moves three finger-widths and rends. If the front is full he starts in the back. If the upper part is full he starts with the bottom part[335]. If both of them are full, Rebbi Ḥiyya the son of Rebbi Ada from Yafo says, he became shabby[336].

330 The double seem which forms the end of the garment at his neck. Rending of garments in mourning starts at the neck.
331 Babli 22b.
332 In the Babli 26b this is required only for father or mother.
333 Since R. Jehudah ben Tema only requires that for every deceased there should be a separate action of rending, not that a new tear should be started at the rim of the garment.
334 He is not permitted to wear a whole garment during the Seven days of mourning.
335 Babli 26b.
336 Since in shabby clothing he is not permitted to lead in prayer, he has to get another garment and rend it.

(83c line 17) רִבִּי חִינְנָא בַּר פַּפָּא סָלַק גַּבֵּי רִבִּי תַנְחוּם בֵּירִבִּי חִייָה. נָפַק לְגַבֵּיהּ לְבִיש סְנָטִירְיהּ. מָהוּ סְנָטְרֵיהּ. מָאנִין דְּלָא חֲפִיתִין. אֲמַר לֵיהּ. הָדָא מְנָן לָךְ. אֲמַר לֵיהּ. הָכֵין הֲוָה רִבִּי סִימוֹן רִבִּי עֲבַד. אֲמַר לֵיהּ. הִתְפַּלֵּל עָלֵינוּ. אֲמַר לֵיהּ. יִסּוּג תּוּרְעָתָךְ. שֶׁכָּל־אוֹתָהּ הַשָּׁנָה הַדִּין מָתוּחַ כְּנֶגֶד הַמִּשְׁפָּחָה. דְּאָמַר רִבִּי יוֹחָנָן. כָּל־שִׁבְעָה הַחֶרֶב שְׁלוּפָה. עַד שְׁלשִׁים הִיא רוֹפֶפֶת. לְאַחַר שְׁנֵים עָשָׂר חוֹדֶשׁ הִיא חוֹזֶרֶת לִתַעֲרָהּ. לְמָה הַדָּבָר דּוֹמֶה. לִכְיפָה שֶׁלְאֲבָנִים. כֵּיוָן שֶׁנִּתְרַעְרְעָה אַחַת מֵהֶן נִתְרַעֲרְעוּ כּוּלָן. וְאָמַר רִבִּי לְעָזָר. אִם נוֹלַד בֶּן זָכָר בְּאוֹתָהּ הַמִּשְׁפָּחָה נִתְרַפְּאת כָּל־אוֹתָהּ הַמִּשְׁפָּחָה.

Rebbi Ḥinena bar Pappus went to visit Rebbi Tanḥum ben Rebbi Ḥiyya[337]. He went out to him in dishonorable garb[338]. What is dishonorable garb? Garments which are short-sleeved. He said to him, from where do you have this[339]? He said to him, so acted my teacher Rebbi Simon. He said to him, pray for me[340]. He said, may your breach be fenced in. For all of this year judgment is directed towards this family, as Rebbi Joḥanan said[341]: All Seven the sword is drawn. Up to Thirty it wavers. After twelve months it returns to its sheath. To what can this be likened? To a stone cupola. If one becomes loose, all are loose. But Rebbi Eleazar aid, if a male child was born to this family, the entire family is healed.

337 To make a consolation visit to a mourner.
338 The consensus of all dictionaries following Buxtorf is: "senatorial", which is most inappropriate. I am reading the word as Arabic شنطر "to dishonor".
339 To wear not only a garment which is torn but one which is inappropriate to be worn by a person to whom respect is due.
340 The mourner asked the visitor.
341 Babli 27b, text and Tosaphot מכאן.

(83c line 25) מְנַיִין שֶׁאָבֵל חַיָּב לִקְרוֹעַ מְעוֹמָד. דִּכְתִיב וַיָּקָם אִיּוֹב וַיִּקְרַע אֶת־מְעִילוֹ וַיָּגָז אֶת־רֹאשׁוֹ. רִבִּי יוּדָה בַּר פָּזִי בְשֵׁם רִבִּי יוֹחָנָן. מִיכָּן שֶׁאָבֵל צָרִיךְ לִקְרוֹעַ מְעוֹמָד. כְּדָאָמַר רִבִּי יוֹחָנָן הוֹרִי רִבִּי יָסָא לִשְׁלוֹל לְמָחָר. כַּד דְּמַךְ רִבִּי יָסָא הוֹרִי רִבִּי חִייָה בַּר בָּא לִנְעוֹל בּוֹ בַיּוֹם. אָמַר רִבִּי זְעוּרָה. וְלָא פְלִיגִין. מָאן דְּאָמַר. יִשְׁלוֹל לְמָחָר. יִנְעוֹל לְמָחָר. וּמָאן דְּאָמַר. יִנְעוֹל בּוֹ בַיּוֹם. יִשְׁלוֹל בּוֹ בַיּוֹם.

From where that the mourner has to rend while standing? As it is written, *Job rose, rent his coat, and shore his head*[342]. Rebbi Judah bar Pazi in the name of Rebbi Joḥanan: From here that the mourner has to rend while standing[343]. As Rebbi Joḥanan said[344], Rebbi Yasa instructed to patch up the next day[345]. When Rebbi Yasa died, Rebbi Ḥiyya bar Abba instructed to wear shoes on the same day. Rebbi Ze`ira said, they do not disagree[346]. He who says to patch up the next day, one shall wear shoes the next day. He who says to wear shoes today one patches the same day.

342 *Job* 1:20.
343 Babli 20b, bottom.
344 This text is impossible since R. Yasa (Assi) was a student of R. Joḥanan. Qorban Haedah emends to: "When R. Joḥanan died." This emendation is possible.
345 The students who are mourners who are not required to keep the Seven days.
346 While they disagree whether a mourner who is not a close relative has to show the signs of his mourning the entire day of the funeral or only to the end of the funeral services, they agree that wearing leather shoes and patching up the tear in the garment go together.

(83c line 30) אָמְרוּ לוֹ. מֵת רְאוּבֵן. וְקָרַע. וְאַחַר כָּךְ אָמְרוּ לוֹ. שִׁמְעוֹן הָיָה. כְּבָר יָצָא יְדֵי קִירְעוֹ. אָמְרוּ לוֹ. מֵת רְאוּבֵן. וְקָרַע. וְאַחַר כָּךְ אָמְרוּ לוֹ. קַיָּים הָיָה וָמֵת. אִית תַּנָּיֵי תַנֵּי. יָצָא יְדֵי קִירְעוֹ. אִית תַּנָּיֵי תַנֵּי. לֹא יָצָא יְדֵי קִירְעוֹ. מָאן דְּאָמַר. יָצָא יְדֵי קִירְעוֹ. כְּבָר קָרַע. מָאן דְּאָמַר. לֹא יָצָא יְדֵי קִירְעוֹ. וַהֲרֵי עַל חַי קָרַע. וְעוֹד מִן הָדָא דְתַנֵּי. קָרַע וְחָזְרָה בוֹ נְשָׁמָה. אִם עַל אָתָר אֵינוֹ צָרִיךְ לִקְרוֹעַ. אִם לְאַחַר זְמָן צָרִיךְ לִקְרוֹעַ. כַּמָּה הוּא עַל אָתָר. כְּדֵי דִיבּוּר. כַּמָּה

הוּא כְּדֵי דִיבּוּר. רִבִּי סִימוֹן בְּשֵׁם רִבִּי יְהוֹשֻׁעַ בֶּן לֵוִי. כְּדֵי שְׁאֵילַת שָׁלוֹם בֵּין אָדָם לַחֲבֵירוֹ. אַבָּא בַּר בַּר חָנָה בְשֵׁם רִבִּי יוֹחָנָן. כְּדֵי שְׁאֵילַת שָׁלוֹם בֵּין הָרַב לַתַּלְמִיד וְיֹאמַר לוֹ. שָׁלוֹם עָלֶיךָ רִבִּי.

5 כמה | ב וכמה (2)

They told him, Reuben died, and he rent. After that they said to him, it was Simeon[347]. He already fulfilled his obligation tearing. They told him, Reuben died, and he rent. After that they said to him, he was alive but then died. There are Tannaim who state, he fulfilled his obligation tearing. There are Tannaim who state, he did not fulfill his obligation tearing. He who said, he fulfilled his obligation tearing; already he rent. He who said, he did not fulfill his obligation tearing, did he not rent about a living person? Furthermore, from what was stated: [348]He rent but then his soul returned. If immediately, he does not have to rend. If after a delay he has to rend. What is immediately? The time for speech. What is the time for speech? Rebbi Simon in the name of Rebbi Joshua ben Levi: up to a greeting from one person to another. Abba bar bar Hana in the name of Rebbi Johanan: up to a greeting from a student to his teacher, that he would say: "peace be with you, my teacher."

347 And both are his close relatives for whom he has to rend his garment.
348 From here to the end of the Halakhah the text is copied from *Berakhot* 2:1 (Notes 49ff.,ב) For the present text, Babli *Nedarim* 87a; *Bava qamma* 73b.

83c line 40) רִבִּי יוֹחָנָן הֲוָה מִסְתַּמִּיךְ עַל רִבִּי יַעֲקֹב בַּר אִידִי וַהֲוָה רִבִּי לְעָזָר חָמֵי לֵיהּ וּמִיטַּמֵּר מִן קוֹמוֹי. אָמַר. הָא תַּרְתֵּין מִילִין הָדֵין בַּבְלַיָּיא עֲבַד לִי. חָדָא דְלָא שָׁאַל בִּשְׁלָמִי. וְחָדָא דְלָא אֲמַר שְׁמוּעֲתָא מִן שְׁמִי. אֲמַר לֵיהּ. כֵּן אִינּוּן נַהֲגִין גַּבּוֹן. זְעֵירָא לָא שָׁאַל בִּשְׁלָמֵיהּ דְּרַבָּא. דְּאִינּוּן מְקַיְּימִין רָאוּנִי נְעָרִים וְנֶחְבָּאוּ וְישִׁישִׁים קָמוּ עָמָדוּ. מִי מְהַלְּכִין חָמֵי לֵיהּ חַד בֵּית מִדְרָשׁ. אֲמַר לֵיהּ. הָכֵין הֲוָה רִבִּי מֵאִיר יָתֵיב וְדָרַשׁ וַאֲמַר שְׁמוּעֲתָא מִן שְׁמֵיהּ דְּרִבִּי יִשְׁמָעֵאל וְלָא אֲמַר שְׁמוּעֲתָא מִן שְׁמֵיהּ דְּרִבִּי עֲקִיבָה. אֲמַר לֵיהּ. כָּל־עַמָּא יָדְעִין דְּרִבִּי מֵאִיר תַּלְמִידֵיהּ דְּרִבִּי עֲקִיבָה. אֲמַר לֵיהּ. וְכָל־עַמָּא יָדְעִין דְּרִבִּי לְעָזָר תַּלְמִידֵיהּ דְּרִבִּי יוֹחָנָן. וּמַהוּ מֵיעֲבוֹר קוֹמֵי אַדוּרֵי צַלְמָא. אֲמַר לֵיהּ. וּמָה אַתְּ פְּלִיג לֵיהּ אוֹקָר. עֲבוֹר קוֹמוֹי וְאַסְמֵי עֵינוּיי. אֲמַר לֵיהּ. יָאוּת רִבִּי לְעָזָר עֲבַד לָךְ דְּלָא עֲבַר קוֹמָךְ. אֲמַר לֵיהּ. רִבִּי יַעֲקֹב בַּר אִידִי. יוֹדֵעַ אַתְּ לְפַיֵּיס. וְרִבִּי יוֹחָנָן בָּעֵי דְּיֵימְרוּן שְׁמוּעֲתָא מִן שְׁמֵיהּ. אַף דָּוִד בִּיקֵּשׁ עָלֶיהָ רַחֲמִים. אָמַר אָגוּרָה בְאָהָלְךָ עוֹלָמִים. רִבִּי פִּינְחָס רִבִּי יִרְמְיָה בְשֵׁם רִבִּי יוֹחָנָן. וְכִי עָלַת עַל לֵב דָּוִד שֶׁהוּא חָיָה לְעוֹלָמִים. אֶלָּא כָּךְ אָמַר. אֶזְכֶּה שֶׁיִּהוּ דְבָרַיי נֶאֱמָרִין בְּבָתֵּי כְנֵסִיּוֹת וּבְבָתֵּי מִדְרָשׁוֹת. וּמָה אֲנִים לֵיהּ. בַּר טִירָא אֲמַר. הָאוֹמֵר שְׁמוּעָה מִשֵּׁם אוֹמְרָהּ שִׂפְתוֹתָיו רוֹחֲשׁוֹת בַּקֶּבֶר. מַה טַעֲמָא. דּוֹבֵב שִׂפְתֵי יְשֵׁנִים. כְּכוֹמֶר זֶה שֶׁלָעֲנָבִים

שֶׁהוּא זָב מֵאֵילָיו. רִבִּי חִינְנָא בַּר פָּפָא וְרִבִּי סִימוֹן. חַד אָמַר. כָּהֵן דְּשָׁתֵי קוֹנְדִיטוֹן. וְחָרָנָה אָמַר. כָּהֵן דְּשָׁתֵי חָמַר עָתִּיק. אַף עַל גַּב דְּהוּא שָׁתֵי לֵיהּ טַעֲמֵיהּ בְּפוּמֵיהּ.

1 לעזר | ב [אלעזר]   2 קומוי | ב קדמוי תרתין | ב תרתיי עבד לי | ב עביד בי בשלמי | 3 מן שמי | ב משמי גבון | ב גביהן דרבא | ב דרובה   4 וישישים קמו עמדו | ב - ליה G | ב לה מדרש | ב המדרש   5 ליה - G | הכין G | הכה ב הכא יתיב G | יתב ודרש | ב דרש שמועתא G | שמועתה   6 שמועתא G שמועתה שמיה G | שמה ידעין G | ידעון תלמידתיה | ב תלמידו   7 וכל | ב כולי לעזר | ב אלעזר ומהו G א' לה מהיא ב מיהו מיעבור G | מעבור אדורי | ב אהדורי צלמא | ב צילמא   8 ליה G | לה את פליג ב איתפליג ליה - G | אוקר | ב אוקיר G איקר עינויי G | עינויי ב עיניה ליה G | לה יאות ר' לעזר | ב ר' אלעזר [יאות]   9 לך G | בך ב - קומך | בG קומיך ליה בG | - ר' | ב - יודע G | יודעא דיימרון G | דיאמרון   10 שמועתא | בG שמועתה שמיה G | שמה דוד G | דויד רחמים G | רחמיי   11 לב דוד G | דויד חייה לעולמים | ב חי לעולם כך אמ' | בG אמר דויד   12 כנסיות G | כנסיית אנים | ב הנייא בר טירא G | בר נזירה ב לוי בר נזירא האי' | בG כל האומר   13 שפתותיו | G סיפתותיי בקבר | G עימו בקבר שפתי | G שיפתי ככמר | G ככמר זה G הזה   14 חיננא G חננה ב חנגא כהן | ב כהדין קונדיטון | G קונדיטון   15 כהין | ב כהדין ליה G | לה טעמיה בפומיה | G טעמה בפומה

[349] Rebbi Joḥanan was leaning on Rebbi Jacob bar Idi when Rebbi Eleazar saw him and hid himself before him. He said, these two things this Babylonian does to me: First, that he does not greet me, and second, that he does not teach the traditions in my name. He said to him, thus they behave among themselves; the younger one does not greet the older since they observe *Boys see me and hide themselves, and old people rose and stood*[350]. As they were walking, he saw a Bet Midrash. He[351] said to him: Here Rebbi Meïr sat and reported traditions in the name of Rebbi Ismael but he never reported traditions in the name of Rebbi Aqiba. He[352] answered: Everybody knows that Rebbi Meïr was the student of Rebbi Aqiba. He[351] retorted, everybody knows that Rebbi Eleazar is the student of Rebbi Joḥanan. May one pass by the water statue? He[352] said to him, do you want to honor it? Pass it by and blind its eyes! He[351] said to him, Rebbi Eleazar did well that he did not pass before you. He[352] said to him: Rebbi Jacob bar Idi, you know how to pacify. But Rebbi Joḥanan required that traditions should be reported in his name. Also David begged for divine mercy in this respect, *may I dwell in Your tent forever*[353]! Rebbi Phineas, Rebbi Jeremiah, in the name of Rebbi Joḥanan; Could David think of living forever? Rather, David meant: May I have the merit that my words will be mentioned in my name in synagogues and houses of study. What profit does he have from this[354]? The son of Tira[355] said: If someone mentions a tradition in the name of its author, the latter's lips whisper with him in the grave. What is the reason? *Dripping from the lips of*

the sleeping ones[356]. Like that bunch of grapes which drips by itself. Rebbi Ḥinena bar Pappus and Rebbi Simon, one said, like one who drinks spiced wine[357], the other said, like one who drinks old wine, even though he consumed it, its taste remains in his mouth.

349 This and the next paragraph have no relevance for the topic under discussion; they are included since together with the preceding paragraph they formed a unit for transmission both here and in *Berakhot* 2:1 (Notes 53-64).
350 *Job.* 21:8.
351 R. Jacob bar Idi.
352 R. Johanan.

353 *Ps.* 61:5.
354 Translated following the text in *Berakhot*. The word אנים used here seems to be a corruption.
355 With the other two sources read: "Ben Nezira"; ט is a scribal error for נ.
356 *Cant.* 7:10.
357 Latin *conditum (vinum)*.

(83c line 60) וְאֵין דּוֹר שֶׁאֵין בּוֹ לֵיצָנִים. וּמֶה הָיוּ פָּרִיצֵי הַדּוֹר עוֹשִׂין. הָיוּ מְהַלְּכִין אֵצֶל חַלּוֹנוֹתָיו שֶׁלְדָוִד וְאוֹמְרִים. דָּוִד. אֵימָתַי יִבָּנֶה בֵית הַמִּקְדָּשׁ. אֵימָתַי בֵּית יי׳ נֵלֵךְ. וְהוּא אוֹמֵר. אַף עַל פִּי שֶׁהֵן מִתְכַּוְונִין לְהַכְעִיסֵינִי יָבוֹא עָלַי שֶׁאֲנִי שָׂמֵחַ בְּלִבִּי. שָׂמַחְתִּי בְּאוֹמְרִים לִי בֵּית יי׳ נֵלֵךְ: וְהָיָה כִּי־מָלְאוּ יָמֶיךָ לָלֶכֶת עִם־אֲבוֹתֶיךָ. אָמַר רִבִּי שְׁמוּאֵל בַּר נַחְמָן. אָמַר הַקָּדוֹשׁ בָּרוּךְ הוּא לְדָוִד. יָמִים מְלֵיאִים אֲנִי מוֹנֶה לָךְ. אֵין אֲנִי מוֹנֶה לָךְ יָמִים חֲסֵירִים. כְּלוּם שְׁלֹמֹה בְנָךְ בּוֹנֶה בֵית הַמִּקְדָּשׁ לֹא לְהַקְרִיב בְּתוֹכוֹ קָרְבָּנוֹת. חָבִיב עָלַי מִשְׁפָּט וּצְדָקָה שֶׁאַתְּ עוֹשֶׂה יוֹתֵר מִן הַקָּרְבָּנוֹת. מַה טַעַם. עֲשֹׂה צְדָקָה וּמִשְׁפָּט נִבְחָר לַיי׳ מִזָּבַח:

1 ליצנים | ב ליצניו ומה | ב מה פריצי | G פרוצי עושין | G עושים מהלכין | ב הולכין G הולכים 2 שלדוד G | (ש)לדויד ואומ׳ | G ואומ׳ לו דוד | G דויד אימתי | G אימתיי (2) יבנה | ב ייבנה 3 שהן מתכוונין | ב שמתכוונין G מתכוונים | G - (מ)ה טעמה | G | ימלאו G מלאו 4 מלאו G ימלאו ללכת עם אבותיך | ב - נחמן | ב נחמני 5 לדוד | G דויד אין אני | ב איני 6 בתוכו | ב בו עלי | G עליי שאת | ב שאתה יותר | G יתר 7 מה | ב ומה טעם | G טעמה

There is no generation without scoffers. What did the hooligans of that generation do? They went to David's windows and said to him: David, when will the Temple be built, when will we go to the Eternal's house[358]? But he said, even though they intend to enrage me, it comes over me that I am happy, *I enjoy it when they say to me: let us go to the Lord's house*[359]. *When your days will be complete to go to your fathers*[360]; Rebbi Samuel bar Nahman said, the Holy One, praise to Him, said to David: `I am counting full days for you, I am not counting missing days for you[361]. Will not your son Solomon build the Temple to sacrifice? Law and justice that you are upholding is more to my liking than sacrifices.' What is the reason? *Upholding justice and law is preferred by the Eternal to sacrifice*[362].

358 Knowing that he could not build it.
359 *Ps.* 122:1.
360 *1Chr.* 17:11. The quote in *Berakhot* is influenced by *2S.* 7:12.
361 This is one of the blessings bestowed on Israel at Sinai (*Ex.* 23:26) that the Just will live complete years, as in fact Moses died on his 120th birthday. The actual age of David is never mentioned.
362 *Pr.* 21:3.

(fol. 81c) **משנה ח**: אֵין מַנִּיחִין אֶת הַמִּטָּה בָּרְחוֹב שֶׁלֹּא לְהַרְגִּיל אֶת הַהֶסְפֵּד. וְלֹא שֶׁל נָשִׁים לְעוֹלָם מִפְּנֵי הַכָּבוֹד. נָשִׁים בַּמּוֹעֵד מְעַנּוֹת אֲבָל לֹא מְטַפְּחוֹת. רִבִּי יִשְׁמָעֵאל אוֹמֵר הַסְּמוּכוֹת לַמִּטָּה מְטַפְּחוֹת:

1 המיטה G המטה | להרגיל G להרבות ההספד G הספד   2 מענות G במענות | למיטה G למטה

Mishnah 8: One does not put down the bier on the plaza, not to force a eulogy[363], nor that of women ever for reason of honor[364]. Women on a holiday wail in chorus but do not clap hands[365]. Rebbi Ismael says, those close to the bier clap hands.

363 On weekdays the bier is put down at places where there is space to accommodate the crowd to be repeatedly addressed by a eulogizer. Eulogies are forbidden on the holiday; in order not to bring the attendees to expect a eulogy one carries the bier directly to the cemetery.
364 It is considered insulting to a woman to make her the object of a public spectacle.
365 According to Rashi this means they clap with their hands; others explain that they clap hands on hands or hands on hips.

(83d line 9) **הלכה ח**: עַל־כָּל הַמֵּתִים הוּא דּוֹחֶה בַּמִּיטָה וְאֵינוֹ מַרְבֶּה בָעֲסָקָיו. עַל אָבִיו וְעַל אִמּוֹ מַרְבֶּה בָעֲסָקָיו וְאֵינוֹ דוֹחֶה בַּמִּיטָה. אִם הָיָה שְׁעַת דּוֹחַק אוֹ עוֹנַת גְּשָׁמִים אֲפִילוּ עַל אָבִיו וְעַל אִמּוֹ מַרְבֶּה בָעֲסָקָיו וְאֵינוֹ דוֹחֶה בַּמִּיטָה. שֶׁכָּל־הַמַּרְבֶּה בָעֲסָקָיו עַל אָבִיו וְעַל אִמּוֹ הֲרֵי זֶה מְשׁוּבָּח.

1 במיטה G במטה   בעסקיו G בעסקו   2 בעסקיו G בעסקו   3 בעסקיו G במטה
(2)   במיטה G במטה   על G של (2)

עַל כָּל־הַמֵּתִים אֵינוֹ מַבְדִּיל קָנֶה שָׂפָה אֶלָּא עַל אָבִיו וְעַל אִמּוֹ. דִּבְרֵי רִבִּי מֵאִיר. רִבִּי יְהוּדָה אוֹמֵר. כָּל־קֶרַע שֶׁאֵינוֹ מַבְדִּיל קָנֶה שָׂפָה הֲרֵי זֶה קֶרַע שֶׁלְּתִיפְלוּת. רִבִּי יוֹחָנָן פְּלִיג עִם רִבִּי יוּדָה בְּתַרְתֵּיי. רִבִּי יוֹחָנָן שָׁמַע דְּרִבִּי חֲנִינָה תְּשִׁישׁ. סָלַק בָּעֵי מְבַקְּרָתֵיהּ. גּוּ אִיסְרַטָה שָׁמַע שְׁמַע דִּדְמָךְ. נְחַת מִן חַמָרֵיהּ וַאֲפִיק מָאנָא דְטַבְיָיא דְשׁוּבַתָּא וּבְזָעָן. כַּיי דְתַנִּינָן תַּמָּן. כֹּהֵן גָּדוֹל פּוֹרֵם מִלְּמַטָּן

וְהֶחָדְיוֹט מִלְמַעֲלָן. רִבִּי לָעֶזֶר בְּשֵׁם כַּהֲנָא. לְמַעֲלָן. לְמַעֲלָן מִקָּנֶה שָׂפָה. לְמַטָּן. לְמַטָּן מִקָּנֶה שָׂפָה. רִבִּי יוֹחָנָן אָמַר. לְמַטָּן מַמָּשׁ. וְאָתְיָא דְרִבִּי לָעֶזֶר בְּשֵׁם כַּהֲנָא כְּרִבִּי יוּדָה. אִין כְּרִבִּי יוּדָה לֹא יִפְרוֹם כָּל־עִיקָּר. מַאי כְדוֹן. חוֹמֶר הוּא בְכֹהֵן גָּדוֹל שֶׁהוּא מַבְדִּיל קָנֶה שָׂפָה.

1 ועל אמו | G ואמו   2 עם ר' | G על דר'

[366]For all deceased he pushes the bier and minimizes the activities[367]; for his father and his mother he maximizes the activities and does not push the bier. If it was a time of emergence or the rainy season, even for his father and his mother he maximizes the activities and does not push the bier[368], since everybody who maximizes the activities for his father and his mother is praiseworthy.

[369]For no deceased one he rends the trim except for father and mother, the words of Rebbi Meïr. Rebbi Jehudah says, any tear which does not completely sever the trim is a frivolous tear. Rebbi Johanan disagrees with Rebbi Jehudah in two things. Rebbi Johanan heard that Rebbi Hanina was weak. He was going up to visit him. On the road he heard that he had died. He descended from his donkey, took out the good Sabbath garment, and tore it. As we have stated there[370]: "The High Priest rends his garment below, the common priest above." Rebbi Eleazar in the name of Cahana: On top, high starting with the seam, below, low starting with the seam. Rebbi Johanan said, really low. Rebbi Eleazar in the name of Cahana follows Rebbi Jehudah. If following Rebbi Jehudah, he should not tear at all! How about this? It is a stringency for the High Priest that he shall sever the seam completely[371].

366 The Halakhah is a continuation of the preceding one; Mishnah 8 is not discussed.
367 To have the deceased buried as quickly as possible, which is beneficial to the deceased.
368 In *Semahot* 9 (and the corrector's text here) "minimizes, pushes". But in the scribe's text "does not maximize" was written and the negation then deleted. Together with the evidence of G this prevents amending the text.
369 The following paragraph is a re-writing of one in *Sanhedrin* 2:1 (Notes 31-38) and *Horaiot* 3:6 (Notes 200-202). About rending the trim around the neck, see Notes 330 ff.
370 Mishnah *Horaiot* 3:6.
371 Meaning that it is a stringency for the High Priest that he is forbidden to sever the seam completely. The High Priest is forbidden to let his hair grow or tear his clothes (*Lev.* 21:10). R. Meïr interprets the verse to mean that in mourning he may not tear his garment in the way other people do The Mishnah is R. Meïr's. It is obvious that one speaks here of the High Priest's personal belonging, not his robes of office,

which may not be torn (*Ex.* 28:32,29:23). The point is made that *Lev.* 21:10 does not use the frequently used verb קרע "to tear" but the infrequent פרם "to tear in little pieces". This is interpreted in *Sifra Emor Parashah* 2(3) to mean that the High Priest is not totally forbidden to rend his garments, only he may not do what everybody does. If he rends it, it may only be at the bottom, where few people will notice, and it may not be deep. Horaiot 12b.

(83d line 23) עַל־כָּל הַמֵּתִים הוּא שׁוֹלֵל לְאַחַר שִׁבְעָה וּמְאַחֶה לְאַחַר שְׁלשִׁים. עַל אָבִיו וְעַל אִמּוֹ אֵינוֹ מְאַחֶה עוֹלָמִית. תַּנֵּי בְשֵׁם רִבִּי נָתָן. הָאִשָּׁה שׁוֹלֶלֶת מִיַּד וּמְאַחָה לְאַחַר שְׁלשִׁים. עַל אָבִיהָ וְעַל אִמָּהּ אֵינוֹ מְאַחָה עוֹלָמִית. אֵי זֶהוּ אִיחוּי. כְּאָרִיג. הַסּוּלָּם וְהַקֻּפֵּשׁ אֵין מְעַכְּבִין.

עַל־כָּל הַמֵּתִים אֵינוֹ קוֹרֵעַ אֶלָּא הָעֶלְיוֹן בִּלְבָד. עַל אָבִיו וְעַל אִמּוֹ אֲפִילוּ עֲשָׂרָה זֶה עַל גַּבֵּי זֶה. אֵין אָפִיקָרְסִין מְעַכֶּבֶת. הָאִשָּׁה אֵינָהּ קוֹרַעַת אֶלָּא הָעֶלְיוֹן בִּלְבָד. תַּנֵּי. רִבִּי שִׁמְעוֹן בֶּן אֶלְעָזָר אוֹמֵר. הָאִשָּׁה קוֹרַעַת אֶת הַפְּנִימִי וְהוֹפַכְתּוֹ לַאֲחוֹרֶיהָ וְחוֹזֶרֶת וְקוֹרַעַת אֶת הַשְּׁאָר.

עַל־כָּל הַמֵּתִים הוּא אָסוּר בְּגִיהוּץ עַד שְׁלשִׁים. עַל אָבִיו וְעַל אִמּוֹ עַד שְׁנֵים עָשָׂר חוֹדֶשׁ. אֵי זֶהוּ גִיהוּץ. כְּלֵי צֶמֶר מְגוֹהָצִין חֲדָשִׁים וּכְלֵי פִשְׁתָּן מְגוֹהָצִין לְבָנִים.

עַל־כָּל הַמֵּתִים הוּא אָסוּר בְּתִגְלַחַת עַד שְׁלשִׁים. עַל אָבִיו וְעַל אִמּוֹ עַד שֶׁיְּשַׁלַּח פֶּרַע אוֹ עַד שֶׁיִּגְעֲרוּ בוֹ קְרוֹבָיו. רִבִּי שְׁמוּאֵל בַּר אֲבוּדְמִי דָּמְכַת אִימֵּיהּ קוֹמֵי מוֹעֲדָא תְּמָנְיָא יוֹמִין. אֲתָא שְׁאַל לְרִבִּי מָנָא. אֲמַר לֵיהּ. כָּל־דָּבָר שֶׁהוּא תָּלוּי בְּשִׁבְעָה וּשְׁלשִׁים הָרֶגֶל מַפְסִיק. בְּרַם הָכָא עַד שֶׁיְּשַׁלַּח פֶּרַע אוֹ עַד שֶׁיִּגְעֲרוּ בוֹ חֲבֵירָיו.

2 שיגערו G | שייגערו קרוביו G | חבי קרובי[372] - | G כהדה אבודרמי G | אבודמא אימיה | G אמה מועדא G | מועדה תמניא G | תלתה אתא G | אתה 3 ליה G | לה 11 הכא G | הכה

For all deceased he stitches together after Seven and mends after Thirty[144]. For his father or his mother he never mends. It was stated in the name of Rebbi Nathan: A woman stitches together immediately and mends after Thirty {days}; for her father and her mother she never mends[373]. What is mending? Like fabric.[374] The ladder[375] and the *qepeš*[376] do not obstruct[377].

For all deceased he rends the uppermost {garment} only. For his father or his mother even ten on top of the other. The head cover[378] does not obstruct. A woman rends only the uppermost. It was stated: Rebbi Simeon ben Eleazar says, a woman rends the undergarment, turns it around, and rends the remainder[379].

For all deceased he is forbidden ironing up to Thirty. For his father and his mother all of twelve months. What is ironing? Ironed new woolen garments and ironed white linen garments[380].

For all deceased he cannot shave until after Thirty; for his father and his mother until it becomes wild growth or until his relatives complain[381]. <As the following:>[382] The mother of Rebbi Samuel ben Eudaimon died eight[383] days before the holiday. He came to ask Rebbi Mana who told him, anything dependent on Seven and Thirty is interrupted by the holiday. But here, until it becomes wild growth or until his colleagues complain.

372 The scribe started to write "his colleagues", the version quoted at the end of the paragraph and then changed his mind and wrote "his relatives" as in the ms., without deleting the half-written word.
373 Babli 26b.
374 The mended piece looks like new fabric.
375 An outer garment made of strips, looking like a ladder. Since it does not cover anything there is no need to rend it.
375 A *hapax*; no traditional meaning is known. Since it appears in one sentence with a "ladder garment", one may conjecture that this also is a garment which does not cover anything but its strips are both horizontal and vertical: Arabic قفع "make

in shape of a net."
377 If it is not torn, no rules are violated.
378 The Kafiyya, Greek 'επικάρσιον "striped garment".
379 Babli 26b.
380 These look like new when properly ironed and therefore are forbidden. Babli 22b.
381 Babli 22b.
382 Inserted from G.
383 In G: 3. In the text the question is about the influence of the holiday on the observance of the Thirty. In the text of G it is about the Seven; but since shaving is forbidden in the Thirty there would be no reason to ask. Therefore the manuscript text is preferable to that of G.

(83d line 38) עַל־כָּל הַמֵּתִים אֵינוֹ מְגַלֵּחַ אֶת לִבּוֹ אֶלָּא עַל אָבִיו וְעַל אִמּוֹ. דִּבְרֵי רַבִּי מֵאִיר. רַבִּי שְׁמוּאֵל בְּשֵׁם רִבִּי אֲבְדּוּמִי בַּר תַּנְחוּם. מִפְּנֵי שֶׁבְּטֵלָה מִמֶּנּוּ מִצְוַת כָּבֵד.

1 המתים G | המיתים   2 אבדומי G | אבודמא   מצות G | מצוות

עַל־כָּל הַמֵּתִים הוּא אָסוּר לֵילֵךְ בִּסְחוֹרָה עַד שְׁלֹשִׁים יוֹם. עַל אָבִיו וְעַל אִמּוֹ עַד שֶׁיִּגְעֲרוּ בוֹ חֲבֵירָיו וְיֹאמְרוּ לוֹ. צֵא עִמָּנוּ.

1 לילך G | ללך   בסחורה G | לסחורה   שיגערו G | שייגערו

עַל־כָּל הַמֵּתִים הוּא אָסוּר לֵילֵךְ בִּסְעוּדָה עַד שְׁלֹשִׁים יוֹם. עַל אָבִיו וְעַל אִמּוֹ עַד שְׁנֵים עָשָׂר חוֹדֶשׁ. אִם הָיְתָה חֲבוּרַת מִצְוָה אוֹ קִידּוּשׁ הַחוֹדֶשׁ <מוּתָּר>.

<הֲרֵי> שֶׁהָיָה מַחֲלִיף בְּגָדִים כָּל־שִׁבְעָה חַיָּיב לִקְרוֹעַ אֶת כּוּלָן. רִבִּי חִייָה רַבָּה וְרִבִּי חָמָא אֲבוּי דְּרִבִּי הוֹשַׁעְיָה תְּרֵיהוֹן אָמְרִין. כּוּלְּהוֹן אֲסוּרִין בְּאִיחוּי. בַּר קַפָּרָא אָמַר. אֵין לָךְ אָסוּר בְּאִיחוּי אֶלָּא יוֹם הָרִאשׁוֹן בִּלְבַד. אָמַר רִבִּי חוּנָה. פְּלָגָא אַחֶרֶת בֵּינֵיהוֹן. מָאן דָּמַר. כּוּלְּהוֹן אֲסוּרִין בְּאִיחוּי. עוֹשֶׂה שְׁאָר הַיָּמִים כְּיוֹם הָרִאשׁוֹן. אֲפִילוּ יֵשׁ עָלָיו כַּמָּה בְגָדִים חַיָּיב לִקְרוֹעַ אֶת

כּוּלָן. מָאן דָּמַר. אֵין לָךְ אָסוּר בָּאִיחוּי אֶלָּא יוֹם הָרִאשׁוֹן בִּלְבָד. עוֹשֶׂה שְׁאָר הַיָּמִים תּוֹסֶפֶת. אֲפִילוּ יֵשׁ עָלָיו כַּמָּה בְגָדִים אֵינוֹ קוֹרֵעַ אֶלָּא אֶת הָעֶלְיוֹן בִּלְבָד.

1 לקרוע G | לקרע כולן G | כולם חמא G | חמה   2 כולהון G | אסורין G | אסורים באיחוי G | באחוי אין G | אן   3 באיחוי G | באחוי חונה G | חנה פלגא G | פלגה כולהון G | כולהם   4 לקרע G | לקרע   5 כולן G | כולם בלבד G | - עושה G | -   6 אפילו יש עליו כמה בגדים G | -.

For no deceased he does bare his heart except for his father and his mother, the words of Rebbi Meïr. Rebbi Samuel in the name of Rebbi Eudaimon bar Tanḥum: Because the commandment "honor" became inactive for him.

For all deceased he is forbidden to peddle merchandise all Thirty days. For his father and his mother until his colleagues criticize him and say, go out with us[384].

For all deceased he is forbidden to go to a dinner all Thirty days; for his father and his mother up to twelve months. If it was a religious assembly or the Sanctification of a month <it is permitted.>[385]

<If he was>[385] exchanging garments all the Seven he is obligated to rend all of them[386]. The Great Rebbi Ḥiyya and Rebbi Ḥama the father of Rebbi Hoshaia both say, all of them are forbidden to mend. Bar Qappara says, only the one of the first day is forbidden to mend. Rebbi Huna[387] said, there is another disagreement between them. He who says, all of them are forbidden to mend, makes the following days like the first day. Even if he wears several garments, he has to rend all of them.

Text of the Leiden scribe

He who says, only the one of the first day is forbidden to mend, makes the other days supplement. Even if he wears several garments, he rends only the outermost.

Text of the Genizah scribe

For him who says, only the one of the first day is forbidden to mend, the other days are supplement; he rends only the outermost.

384 Babli 22a/b.
385 Unreadable in the manuscript, added from G (and the Venice print).
386 Babli 24a.
387 In G: R. Hinena.

משנה ט: (fol. 81c) וּבְרָאשֵׁי חֳדָשִׁים בַּחֲנוּכָּה וּבְפוּרִים מְעַנּוֹת וּמְטַפְּחוֹת. בָּזֶה וּבָזֶה אֲבָל לֹא מְקוֹנְנוֹת. נִקְבַּר הַמֵּת לֹא מְעַנּוֹת וְלֹא מְטַפְּחוֹת. אֵיזֶהוּ הָעִינּוּי שֶׁכּוּלָּן עוֹנוֹת כְּאַחַת. וְקִינָה שֶׁאַחַת מְדַבֶּרֶת וְכוּלָּן עוֹנוֹת אַחֲרֶיהָ שֶׁנֶּאֱמַר וְלַמֵּדְנָה בְנֹתֵיכֶם נֶהִי וְאִשָּׁה רְעוּתָהּ קִינָה. אֲבָל לֶעָתִיד לָבוֹא מָהוּ אוֹמֵר בִּלַּע הַמָּוֶת לָנֶצַח וּמָחָה יי אֱלֹהִים דִּמְעָה מֵעַל כָּל פָּנִים וגו׳:

1 ובראשי G | בראשי   בחנוכה G | ובחנוכה   אבל G | -   2 איזהו G | איזה הוא   וקינה G | קינה   3-4 אבל .. וגו׳ | G -.

Mishnah 9: On New Moons, Ḥanukkah and Purim[388] they wail in chorus and clap their hands, but in neither case they recite dirges. After the deceased was buried they neither wail in chorus nor clap their hands. What is wailing in chorus? They all recite together. A dirge, if one speaks and all repeat after her, as it is said[389], *and teach your daughters wailing and a woman her friend dirge.* [390]But in the Future World what does it say[391]? *He swallowed up Death forever, and the Eternal, God, wiped tears from all faces*, etc.

388 Which are holidays but on a much lower level than the intermediate days of biblical holidays.

389 *Jer.* 9:19.
390 Missing in G.
391 *Is.* 25:5.

(83d line) **הלכה ט**: רִבִּי תַּנְחוּם בַּר עִילַּיי דְּמָךְ בַּחֲנוּכְתָּא. רִבִּי דּוֹסָא דְּמָךְ בְּרֵישׁ יַרְחָא דְּנִיסָן. עֲבָדִין לֵיהּ אִיבְרַיָּיא. סָבְרִין מֵימַר. מִן דַּעְתּוֹן דְּרַבָּנָן. וּבָדְקוּן וְאַשְׁכְּחוּן דְּלָא מִן דַּעְתּוֹן דְּרַבָּנָן. רִבִּי קְרוֹסְפֵּי דְּמָךְ בְּמוֹעֲדָא וְעָבְדוּן לֵיהּ אִיבְרַיָּיא. סָבְרִין מֵימַר. מִן דַּעְתֵּיהּ דְּרִבִּי אִמִּי. וּבָדְקוּן וְאַשְׁכְּחוּן דְּלָא מִן דַּעְתֵּיהּ דְּרִבִּי אִמִּי. רִבִּי חֶלְבּוֹ רִבִּי בָּא בַּר זַבְדָּא בְּשֵׁם רַב. אֲפִילוּ לְשָׁעָה. מִן הָדָא וַתָּמָת שָׁם מִרְיָם וַתִּקָּבֵר שָׁם: וַאֲנָן חֲמֵי רַבָּנָן עֲנִייָן בְּדִיבּוּרָא. אָמַר רִבִּי יִרְמְיָה. חֲבֵירִים זְרִיזִין הֵן וְאֵינָן בָּאִין לִידֵי הֶסְפֵּד.

1 בחנוכתא G | בחנוכתה   דוסא G | דוסה   בריש ירחא G | בראש ירחה   דניסן G | ניסן   2 עבדין ליה איברייא G | עבדון לון אבריה   דעתון G | דעתהון (2)   דרבן G | דרבנין (2)   3 קרוספי G | קריספא   במועדא G | במעדה   ועבדון G | עבדון   איברייא G | אבריה   דעתיה G | דעתה   4 דעתיה G | דעתה   5 הדא G | הדה   ענייין G | עני   בדיבורא G | בדבורה   6 באין G | באים

Rebbi Tanḥum bar Illai expired on Ḥanukkah. Rebbi Dosa expired on the New Month of Nisan. They made them[392] outside[393]. They thought, with the agreement of the rabbis. They investigated and found, not with the agreement of the rabbis. Rebbi Crispus expired on the holiday. They made him outside. They thought, with the agreement of Rebbi Immi. They investigated and found, not with the agreement of Rebbi Immi. Rebbi Ḥelbo, Rebbi Abba bar Zavda in the name of Rav: Even momentarily[394], from this[395]: *And Miriam died there and was buried there.* But we see that the rabbis repeat the words[396]. Rebbi Jeremiah said, the colleagues are careful and they will not deliver eulogies.

392 Translated following G.

393 The common translation is: "They prepared them the first meal after the burial", סְעוּדַת הַבְרָאָה. In that sense אבריה would be *hapax*; its meaning not confirmable from other sources. Since the requirement that the first meal after the burial not be prepared by the mourners themselves nowhere is qualified that it would apply only on weekdays, the translation is unconvincing. It seems much better to stay with the common meaning of איבריא "outside" (root בר). The funerals were organized that the wailing women, mentioned in the Mishnah, performed outside, in the street, on the way to the cemetery. This is frowned upon because it invited the delivery of public eulogies. The implication is that public eulogies are not to be held on New Months, Hanukkah, and Purim, even though this is not stated in the Mishnah. However if they happen, the rabbinate is not required to intervene, since in the cases mentioned here the displeasure of the rabbis only was discovered after the fact.

394 On the minor holidays mentioned in the Mishnah one does not stop the funeral procession on the way to the cemetery even momentarily.

395 *Num.* 20:1; Babli 28a. The verse is interpreted in *Seder Olam* to imply that Miriam died on the 1st of Nisan and was buried immediately (in the author's edition Chap. 9, first sentence, and commentary).

(line 59 83d) תַּנֵּי. אֵין מוֹלִיכִין חֲלִילִין לְבֵית הָאָבֵל . אֲבָל מוֹלִיכִין חֲלִילִין לְבֵית הַשִּׂמְחָה וּלְבֵית הַמִּשְׁתֶּה.

1 מוליכין | G מוליכים (2) חלילין | G חלילים (2) השמחה | G שמחה   2 המשתה | G משתה

It was stated[396]: One does not bring flutes the the house of the mourner[397], but one brings to a festivity[398] and a wedding feast[399].

396 Tosephta 2:17.

397 Playing mourning dirges on instruments would be "going in the ways of the Emorites", a pagan ritual.

398 Any private festivity, as described in Plato's *Symposion*.

399 Either this refers to New Moon etc., or to a wedding on the eve of a major holiday when the main festivity is during the intermediate days of the holiday.

Indices

Sigla

Parallel Texts from Yerushalmi Tractates

Bikkurim	א	Megillah	מ
Berakhot	ב,ב	Nedarim	נ
Genizah excerpts	ג	Sotah	ס
Demay	ד	Avodah zarah	ע
Roš Haššanah	ה	Peah	פ
Nazir	ו	Mo'ed Qatan 1	ק
Hagigah	ח	Mo'ed Qatan 2	ר,2
Gittin	ט	Ševi'it	ש
Yebamot	י	Terumot	ת
Ketubot	כ		

Manuscript texts and early prints

Ashkenazi Text edited by Sussman	A	Scribe of Leiden ms. ( )	S
Corrector [ ]	C	Addition from Genizah text	< >
Genizah Text edited by Ginzberg	G	Translator's addition	{ }
Rome Manuscript of *Zera`im*	R		

Index of Biblical Quotations

Gen. 1:1	433	8:16	41,42,50	22:2	69	48:5	185
1:2	417,433	8:19	41,42,50	22:13	61,69		
1:6	147	9:3	267	22:14	69	Ex. 2:23	15
1:9	147	9:27	237	27:15	266	4:11	428
1:14	147,433	10:2	237	27:22	168	5:1	391
1:20	147,433	10:3	237	27:28	8	8:35	581
1:24	433	10:4	237	27:29	255	12:12	266
1:28	181,208	10:18	237	29:27	527	12:15	283
2:4	421,433	11:1	237	30:10	581	12:16	444
2:6	53,98	15:13	15	35:11	185	12:18	283
4:4	267	17:14	382	35:22	368	12:20	283
6:18	41,42,50	18:27	48	37:7	428	12:48	156
6:19	267	20:13	253	42:5	355	13:9	249,365
7:10	581	21:12	69	43:34	396	14:13,14	21
7:14	267	21:19	175	48:16	61	15:26	299

15:32	431	9:1	317	15:38	565	16:17	399	
16:25	18	9:22	122	15:41	244	17:18	239	
17:14	216	10:7	581	19:9	453	20:9	253	
18:1	271	11:34	475	19:18,19	301	20:20	544	
18:12	271	11:36	409	20:1	618	21:5	122	
19:9	98	12:3	301	21:24	175	22:6	366	
22:28	487	13:6	235	23:19	56	22:7	427	
23:2	553	13:13	234	24:17	168	25:8	378	
23:11	175	13:46	235,514	25:9	102	25:9	378,564	
23:14	376	14:2	235	28:2	134	26:13	30	
23:15	393	14:3	235	28:7	275	26:14	39	
23:16	209,446	14:9	235	29:1	303	28:21	103	
23:17	380,383	16:2	49	29:36	402	30:12	553	
23:35	346	16:32	264	30:2	406	31:11	379	
24:5	142,271	17:13	173	30:3	406	31:12	378	
24:13	155	18:5	161	35:32	363	32:2	53	
24:16	155	18:21	366	35:33	98	32:3	346	
27:10	239	19:2	355	36:7,8	185	32:6	245	
28:40	379	19:32	338			32:11	421	
29:38	448	22:2,3	590	Deut.2:16	102	32:30	169	
30:1	501	22:15	38	3:5	193	33:12	279	
30:3	501	23:21	446	4:11	427	33:15	279	
30:37	267	22:32	355	4:31	173	33:26	142	
32:1,7	156	23:4	303	4:32	429	33:27	417	
32:11	56	23:21	209	4:35	380	34:8	581	
32:14	56	23:41	401	4:44	218	34:12	156	
32:17,18	156	23:44	331	5:5	339			
32:19	156	25:29	194	5:19	218			
32:25	369	27:18	25	6:6	287	Jos.6:3,4	544	
32:35	369	27:34	218	6:8	247	7:9,10	72	
34:17	464			7:14	255	8:30	277	
34:20	388, 377,	Num.3:13	266	8:10	346	12:3	193	
	393	6:22	122,370	9:10	340	16:6	279	
34:27	340, 411	6:24	122	9:17	156	19:15	196	
38:23	61	8:19	136	10:12	14	19:33	196	
39:33	278	8:25	123	10:17	336	19:35	193	
		10:8	263	11:14	134	22:22	244	
		10:10	264	11:16	98			
Lev. 3:9	278	10:11	162	11:21	244	Jud. 6:25	277	
4:3	342	10:20	162	12:5	386	17:18	253	
4:17	49	10:33	162	12:6	386,395	18:31	253	
4:21	49	10:35	317	12:8	273,275	19:21	262	
6:2	271	11:20	551	12:9	284	20:48	196	
6:12	258	12:12	581	12:13	275,280	21:18	185	
6:23	272	12:14	551,581	14:24	396			
7:11	271	13:25	162	16:6	275	1Sam. 1:12	123	
7:14	278	13:31	164	16:10	396	1:22	123	
7:19	481	13:32	163	16:14	383,398	1:25	278	
7:30	304	13:33	163	16:15	398	2:10	61	
7:38	303	14:1	162	16:16	134	2:27	18	

3:20	418	21:13	175	24:2	157,160	20:2	58
4:4	281	23:13	102	24:78	173	28:6	66
6:19	175,195	25:5	61	26:1,2	160	29:3	60
7:6	72	26:4	431	32:21	160	31:19	428
7:9	277	26:19	8	39:15	514	31:21	429
8:17	277	26:21	56	41:22	501	35:10	59
9:13	346	27:3	28			36:8	144
9:24	277	30:15	14	Hos.2:13	180	42:8	26
12:17	44	43:14	18	6:2	3	45:3	240
14:33	278	48:13	433	8:12	411	45:14	260
20:27	149	51:16	144	9:1	321	48:14	297,605
28:15	418	52:3	14	Joel 1:18	54	48:15	297,605
		54:9	111	2:13	46,55	58:9	517
2Sam.3:35	594	55:10	27	2:15	35	59:8	517
19:3	587	58:5	53	2:16	35,49	60:12	168
19:10	321	60:22	14	2:23	19,22	61:5	611
		65:24	66,115	Am. 4:7	97	62:10	44,178
1K. 5:2	182	66:1	437	4:12	243	68:5	431
8:3	74			4:13	417	68:6	44
8:37	66	Jer. 1:11	160	5:15	418	68:7	178
13:21	594	2:35	73	8:10	574	68:36	336
17:1	8	3:2	98	Jona 3:8	54	78:60	278
17:20	8	5:30	105	3:10	46	78:67	278
18:1	8	6:29	317	Micha 5:6	8	81:11	105
18:36	74,275	9:9	176	7:3	53	90:3	437
18:37	74,107	9:11	404	Hab. 3:6	218	91:15	47
18:39	102	9:19	617	Nah. 3:9	133	95:7	18
21:13	253	11:16	164	Zeph. 2:1	51	95:11	406
		12:8	284	2:3	418	101:2	117
2K.		12:9	284	Hag. 1:8	49	102:26	433
1:11,12	602	14:1	66	2:9	285	104:6	398
2:12	600	16:5	584	Sach. 2:9	64	106:44	15
8:4	312	30:6	431	3:2	175	107:6	63
14:10	558	30:7	14	8:16	144	109:12	427
17:3	185	32:18	336	8:19	156	110:3,4	8
19:1	603	32:23	404	9:12	239	113:7	553
22:16	338	32:26	602	9:13	18	113:1	255,287
25:3	160	35:16	150	9:14	69	114:1	287
25:8	181	36:18	343	10:1	96,98	115:1	287
25:9	312	36:23	604	11:17	169	116:1	287
		36:24	604	Mal.2:3	574	116:15	422
Is. 1:15	122	36:25	604	3:16	218	118:16	255
5:1	464	39:2	160			118:20	303
6:14	267	41:2	157			118:27	287
12:6	68	41:5	606	Ps. 2:1	58	118:28	287
12:33	290	49:38	18	4:2	74	122:1	612
13:5	55	50:25	55	11:3	36	122:3,4	495
14:5	266			16:11	420	126:1	109
21:11	16,18	Ez. 7:9	140	17:15	52	127:10	404
21:12	18	7:16	140	19:8	359	130:1	243

132:1	431	24:8	551	6:1	295	7:8	150	
132:14	284	28:17	427	8:9	287	7:10	150	
135:7	98,118	28:25	25	9:1	190,301	7:11	150	
136:6	398	30:3	42	9:10	198	7:13	150	
145:19	112	30:28	105	9:19	193,198,	7:20	150	
147:17	398	36:27	25		294	7:38	150	
148:3	398	37:6	417	9:21	220	8:5	336	
		37:11	113	9:22	190,191,	8:6	336	
Prov. 3:1	332	42:10	427		198,206	8:8	343	
5:18	243	42:12	427	9:26	292,295	9:5	77	
7:20	14			9:27	189,287	9:32	336	
10:1	114	Cant. 1:4	423	9:28	191,198,	11:35	196	
10:7	153,321	3:11	183		218,297	13:15	175	
10:22	587	4:16	271	9:29	216,218,			
14:23	123	7:10	611		295	1Chr.7:9	527	
15:4	16			9:30	191	8:12	196	
17:5	171	Ruth 3:14	427	9:31	189,218	9:20	261	
17:21	114			9:32	292	9:22	138	
21:3	612	Thr. 1:2	162	10:2	218,295	17:11	612	
23:23	191	1:5	605			24:4	137	
23:28	112	2:2	168	Dan.2:18	147	24:6	137	
25:2	429	3:16	182	5:8	239	24:15	137	
25:14	98	3:18	171	8:2	18	27:1	134	
25:16	422	3:29	418	9:4	336	28:12	191	
		3:41	50	10:12	93	28:19	191	
Job 1:20	608	3:51	169	12:7	14	29:21	444	
2:13	589,593							
3:14	427	Eccl. 1:10	340,411			2Chr. 7:14	52	
3:8	524	1:15	400	Ezra 2:6	150	12:6	51	
8:7	321	3:2	243	2:8	150	21:22	321	
12:6	102	4:9	181,208	2:9	150	24:20	173	
14:22	574	4:17	243	2:15	150	29:28	168	
15:9	349	5:5	422	2:30	150	30:27	164	
15:18	369	7:8	427	2:35	150			
15:19	369	12:14	418	2:36	130	Sirach		
20:4	429			4:7	239	3:21,22	428	
21:8	611	Esth. 2:5	292	8:23	147	38:1	105	
22:18	113	2:6	334	9:28	199			
22:29	113	3:1	292			Matth. 12:8	553	
22:30	113	3:7	220	Neh. 7:39	139			

Index of Talmudical Quotations

Babylonian Talmud

Berakhot		4a	373	3a	297,343	8b	98,147
8a	354	6a	218	4a	196,298	10a	12,29
8b	558	17a	465	4b	191,202	11a	42
9b	58	17b	466	5a	204,205	12a	33,207
14b	590	18b	481	5b	198	13a	586
17b	576	50b	404	6b	193,220,222	13b	35,586
19a	554,555	87b	156,176	7a	215,218	14a	35,107
25a	311	90b	301	7b	215	14b	11
27b	130,133	98a	381	8a	230	15b	48,49
28b	58,59	104a	269	9a	251	16a	47,48,49,50, 54,58
29a	61			10a	278		
31a	11	Yoma		13b	219	16b	57,74,77
31b	102	6a	301	16b	191,334	18a	82
32b	123	9a	285	17a	287	19b	93,95
33b	111,367	12b	259	18a	287,290	20b	115
35b	134	21b	49	18b	296,343	22a	105
48b	171,346	35b	172	19a	292,294,295, 296	22b	111
59a	23	47a	260			23a	111
		69b	336	19b	247,340	25b	24,26,102
Šabbat		72b	261	20a	296	26b	120
17a	264	73a	263	21b	144,343,347	27a	138
19a	544	75a	163	22a	144,360	27b	147
24a	124	77b	7	22b	72	28a	152
24b	124	80a	394	23a	144,352	28b	160
28b	365	80b	218	23b	355	29a	18,63,163, 165, 181
63a	252	87a	301	24b	121,365		
87a	156	88a	41	25a	367,368	29b	177
104a	218,250			25b	370	30b	185
108a	244,248,249	Sukkah		26a	311,313	31a	171,185, 186, 297,605
115b	288	5a	252	27a	317		
118b	18,269	52b	102	28a	324		
121a	301			28b	324	Mo'ed Qatan	
134a	224	Roš Haššanah		29a	404	2a	506
137a	383	6a	230	30a	328	4a	507
151b	574	11b	23	31a	329	4b	509
152b	574	16b	52	31b	332,335	5a	512
		18b	86,157	32a	249	6a	514
		19b	86			6b	517
Eruvin				Taanit		7a	518
6a	296	Yom Tov (Beṣah)		2b	4	8a	524
22a	55	34a	532	3b	10	8b	525
41a	91			4b	12,20	9b	405,527
		Megillah		6a	23	10a	530
Pesahim		2a	189,193,198	6b	25	11a	532,534

11b	538	14b	420,422	Nazir		60b	600
12a	566	15a	421,422	23b	404	69a	603
12b	531,539,545	15b	423	56a	581	94b	174
14a	549,550	16a	431			105a	54,404
15a	584	16b	435	Gittin		108a	42
15b	90,587	17a	447	57a	168	108b	581
16a	558	17b	209,447	57b	173		
16b	112	18b	452,456	60a	317	Horaiot	
17a	551,556,557,558	19a	456	60b	339,340	10b	404
		19b	456			12b	614
17b	559,560,561,568	20a	470	Qiddušin			
		21a	462	33b	338	Ševuot	
18a	561,562	22b	465,469	47a	572	35b	252,253
18b	44	23a	469				
19a	566	23b	472			Avodah Zarah	
19b	571	24a	481	Bava Qamma		7a	88
20a	572,581,582,594	24b	484	50a	55	25a	278
		25a	493,495	73b	609	36b	260
20b	583,590,595	25b	492	80b	544		
21a	573			82a	199,348		
21b	574			102a	88	Zevaḥim	
22a	576	Yebamot				99a	486
22b	607,615,616	39b	564	Bava Mesi`a		111a	275
23a	575	42b	88	28a	111	115b	267
24a	587,588,589,595,616	72b	386	58b	117	116a	271
		90b	440	59b	553	116b	267
24b	597	102b	40	78b	206	117a	271
26a	600,602,605,606			85b	343	118a	278,280
		Ketubot		102a	373	118b	279,280,284
26b	600,607,615	28a	352	107b	51	119a	278,281
27b	608	34b	227			120a	277,278
28a	618	103b	140	Bava Batra			
30b	608	111a	550	9a	53	Menaḥot	
				13b	248	7a	474
Hagigah		Sotah		14a	248	29b	239,240,246
2a	381,382	2a	178	60b	51	30a	248
2b	526	22b	404	168a	564	30b	244
3a	378	27a	42			32a	245
4a	380,383	29b	481	Sanhedrin		32b	372
4b	386	38a	122	4b	382	33a	240
5b	418	40b	77	18a	51	33b	372
6a	380			19a	51,349	35a	365
6b	271	Nedarim		20a	592	44a	373
7a	393	32a	559	21b	238	64b	157
8a	394	33a	229	22a	178	72a	306
8b	394	37b	343	46a	440		
9a	381	61a	222	47b	591	Bekhorot	
10a	406	63a	23	48a	315	36b	408
11b	416,429	78b	408	54b	416		
12b	417	87a	609	60a	603		

Temurah		6a	318	Ḥulin			
14b	275	11a	136	31b	302	Niddah	
16b	218	11b	165	33b	450	11b	88
28b	277	15b	16	35a	477	67b	301
		16b	404	35b	459		
Arakhin				81b	227		
2b	382			139a	230		

Parallel texts in Yerushalmi

Taaniot Chapter One

Berakhot 5:2	page 8	Note 22
Šeqalim 6:2	22	119
Berakhot 9:3	24	130
Avodah zarah 3:6	28	147
Yoma 8:1	37	200
Maaser Šeni 2:1	38	208
Šabbat 9	38	208
Ketubot 1:1	44	249
Yom Tov 5:2	44	249

Taaniot Chapter Two

Berakhot 4:3	58	82
Berakhot 4:3	65	118
Berakhot 1:8	67	124
Moed Qatan 3:1	80	194
Megillah 1:6	81	194
Megillah 1:5	82	194
Yebamot 4:11	86	226

Taaniot Chapter Three

Demay 1:3	95	10
Qiddušin 4:1	98	26
Berakhot 9:7	108	92
Nedarim 8:1	115	125
Pesaḥim 5:7	118	137

Taaniot Chapter Four

Megillah 4:8	121	15
Berakhot 4:1	123	31
Megillah 3:6	128	57
Pesaḥim 4:1	135	79
Berakhot 4:1	157	222
Yom Tov 5:2	178	352
Ketubot 1:1	178	352
Megillah 1:6	181	370

Megillah Chapter One

Taaniot 4:6	page 208	Note 131
Šeqalim 4:1	208	131
Taaniot 4:9	209	132
Taaniot 2:13-14	211	145
Šeqalim 1:1	222	184
Yom Tov 5:2	223	193
Yom Tov 5:2	224	196,202
Ketubot 3:1	226	203
Terumot 7:1	226	203
Nedarim 4:1	229	224
Roš Haššanah 1:1	230	227
Sukkah 3:12	255	403
Horaiot 3:3	257	411
Yoma 1:1	258	425

Megillah Chapter Two

Ševiit 9:1	290	26
Berakhot 2:1	291	31
Berakhot 2:4	299	83
Terumot 1:2	299	83
Roš Haššanah 1:10	308	138

Megillah Chapter Three

Berakhot 3:5	311	9
Yoma 3;6	314	24
Taaniot 4:1	328	111
Taaniot 4:2	330	120

Megillah Chapter Four

Peah 1:6	340	16
Hagigah 1:8	340	16
Berakhot 5:4	342	23
Bikkurim 3:5	342	29
Berakhot 7:1	346	45
Taaniot 4:3	350	73

Ketubot 1:1	page 355	Note 100
Ketubot 11:6	358	116
Berakhot 5:4	359	121
Soṭah 7:6	361	129
Yoma 7:1	361	129
Taaniot 4:1	364	148
Berakhot 5:3	367	162

Ḥagigah Chapter One

Terumot 1:2	378	10
Yebamot 12:5	378	10
Yebamot 8:1	382	38
Šabbat 19	382	38
Peah 1:1	393	90
Sukkah	398	127
Pesaḥim 3:7	405	150
Nedarim	408	166
Peah 2:6	410	183
Megillah 4:1	411	189

Ḥagigah Chapter Two

Sanhedrin 6:5	436	119
Yom Tov 2:4	441	137

Ḥagigah Chapter Three

Soṭah 5:2	480	101
Eruvin 9:4	491	160

Moed Qatan Chapter One

Ševiit 2:10	page 507	Note 19
Šeqalim 1:1	514	53
Ševiit 2:10	516	65
Pesaḥim 8:8	524	106
Gittin 4:5	526	116
Avodah zarah 1:1	528	133

Moed Qatan Chapter Two

Pesaḥim 4:1	547	68

Moed Qatan Chapter Three

Taaniot 2:12	549	9
Taaniot 3:8	554	42
Nedarim 9:1	559	73
Nazir 3:1	570	137
Berakhot 3:1	573	157
Berakhot 3:1	576	172
Berakhot 2:7	585	220
Berakhot 3:1	591	233
Nedarim 7:5	591	233
Horaiot 3:4	601	296
Megillah 3:2	605	323
Berakhot 2:1	609	348
Horaiot 3:6	613	369
Sanhedrin 2:1	613	369

Mishnah

Idiut 5:6	264, 555	Hulin 2:5	478	5:10	553	2:8	452
7:7	221	Bekhorot 5:1	542	8:10	484	7:6	495
8:1	472	Arakhin 9:5	194	15:6	465	7:8	495
8:4	465	9:6	196	16:1	592	8:9	489
Avot 1:2	144	Tamid 1:3	309	16:7	315	Miqwaot 4:3	512
2:8	420	3:4	500	19:1	530	7:6	456
		3:6	601	24:9	502	8:5	462
Zevaḥim 1:1	275	5:5	472	25:7	467	Niddah 10:6	486
1:3	133	7:3	309	29:7	501	10:7	486
12:1	486	Middot 2:5	185	Parah 5:3	491	Yadayim 2:4	450
14:4	266	Qinnim 1:1	230	11:5	452, 477	3:2	482
Menaḥot 3:3	474	2:5	388	Zavim 2:2	232	Uqeṣin 3:5	491
8:3	488			Negaʿim 4:10	521		
10:4	309	Kelim 1:8	386	Ṭahorot 2:2	477		

Tosephta

Berakhot 3:25	59	2:9	103	1:4	391	2:17	618
2:19	311	3:1	120	2:1	420		
3:20	342	3:6	151	2:7	429	Sotah 7:13	210
5:5	143	3:7	152	3:2	456	7:15	210
		3:8	153	3:6	469		
Yoma 4:5	37,41	3:10	181	3:8	481	Horaiot 2:3	257
Šeqalim 1:5	514	3:12	44	3:10	481	2:5	601
Sukkah 4:17	402	Megillah 1:1	193	3:12	484		
Taaniot 1:2	28	1:2	202	3:16	481	Zevahim 13:1	267
1:3	23	1:5	206	3:35	499	13:15	275
1:4	26	1:6	222	Mo`ed Qatan		Menahot 3:30	372
1:6	33	1:7	223	1:5	516	Hulin 10:16	427
1:10	74	2:5	338,343	1:7	518		
1:11	77	2:12	313	1:8	521	Kelim Bava batra	
2:2	80	2:18	324	1:9	525	1:2-3	470
2:5	86	3:10	335	1:11	545	3:9	465
2:6	86,87	3:13	352	2:3	566	Miqwaot 1:13	568
2:7	91	3:34	370	2:5	566	Taharot 1:6	450
2:8	95	Hagigah 1:1	382,386	2:11	514	Yadayim 1:5	452

Midrashim

Mekhilta dR. Ismael 18, 71,346,380,385,386
Mekhilta dR. Simeon b. Yohai 71,283
Megillat Taanit 108,209
Sifra 235,258,302,402, 409,481,522,614
Sifry 18,39,264,383,398 474,544
Seder Olam 123,176,262 284,285,328,618
Gen. r. 24,26,28,36,42, 48,52,53,69,98,130,142, 334,355,428,429,431, 433,574,581

Ex. r. 18
Lev. r. 69,178,420,433
Num. r. 56,98,266
Cant. r. 18,168
Thr. r. 50,168,172,175, 182,185,404
Eccl. r. 52,140,427
Ruth r. 427
Tanhuma 52,56,58,175, 261
Tanhuma Buber 52
Avot dR. Nathan A 377
Midrash Samuel 73,98, 433
Midrash Psalms 18,69,

73,297,655
Midrash Prov. 218
Pesiqta rabbati 130
Pesiqta dR. Cahana
Soferim 248,249,332, 333,334,363,374
Semahot 576,591,600, 613
Yalqut Šimony 105,171, 175
Jonathan 73
Pseudo-Jonathan 71, 366,367

Author Index

Alfassi	339,363	Driver, S. R.	73	Fleischer, E.	68
Cogan, M.	602	Ehrlich, A. B.	73	Geiger, A.	250
Dikduke Sopherim 90,		Elbogen, I	8	Ginzberg, L.	36, 59,
	215,306,488	Epstein, J. N.	89		130,507

Goldstein, N. 216	Lisowski, G. 346	Rashba 218,242,293
Grätz, H. 260,321	Maimonides 210,218,	Rashbam 412
Herschler, M. 190	232,349,353	Rashi 349,353,363,377,
Isaya II of Trani 293	Meïri 190,293	488,612
Jehudah Hallevi 218	Mendelssohn, M. 218	Rosh 591
Josephus 196,260	Nachmanides 216,586	Shulhan Arukh 180
Kutscher, E. 250,422	Nathanson, S. 215	Sussman, J. 41,512
Liebermann, S. 239, 250,296,404,569	Or Zarua 179	Tadmor, H. 602
	Qafeh, Y. 524	

Index of Greek, Latin, Arabic, and Hebrew Words

’αθανασία	605	μέλαθρον	453	macellum	391
’ανάκλιτα	592	νάρθηξ	8	mulus	95,373
’αναλογεῖον	315	‘ομολογία	564	paenula	409
’ανθύπατος	321	οὐ’σία	171	parum	106
’αρχεον	218	πανδόκιον	595	piscina	509
’άρχων	171	παντόκακος	31	saltuarius	404
’ασθενής	40	παρά	290	scutella	598
’αυτονομία	193	παράκλητος	4	subsellium	315,593
βαβούλια	31	πίναξ	418	tabula	502,598
βίος	431	πολύπους	386	uncia	156
βουλευτής	171	πραγματεία	541	vellum	315
γύργαθος	462	σάβανον	360		
γύψος	511	σημεῖον	3,160	גמל	574
δήλωμα	50	στρατιά	168	טוא	279
διαθήκη	563	συμφωνία	244	כסבא	509
διφθέρα	289,411	συνηγορία	69	כסף	171
διαθήκη	8	τιμή	31	כרת	508
διπλωματάριον	72	‘υποπόδιον	433	סכף	171
εἰκών	593	φῦκος	595	סרק	30
’επικάρσιον	615	χάλκανθος	289	פס	391
θέατρον	31	χάραξ	16,188	שנטר	608
θέρμος	91	ψυκτήρ	472	קפץ	615
’ιδιώτης	45,486,529	’ωνή	171	קרמיז	24
’ισάτις	364				
κανοῦν	598	carruca	84	אזכרה	59
κέντρον	334	cataracta	509	אחר	422
κήλων	504	collare	336	ערך	53
κλιντήρ	315	compendiarium	323	פשש	391
κοντός	84	conditum	541,611	רבע	26
κόστος	491	delatores	321		
κράββατος	591	fucus	595		
λάγηνος	215	impilia	40		
λοπάς	230,433	lagena	215		

Subject Index

Acacia wood 36
Accepting rabbinic rules 571
Adar, dating in 222
Additions, insignificant 414
Aderabba 557
Aelia Capitolina, founding of 153
Akylas the proselyte 418
Altar wood 149
Amen Amen 368
Amidah, text 60,63
Animal tithe 397
Anointing oil 50,255
Antoninus 269
Appraisals 357
Appraisals, reduction 357
Ark, movable 46
Ascending to Heaven 56
Ashes, on head 46
Atbash encryption 114
Atbash rule for holidays 200

Barbalissus 556
Bastard, marriage of 228
Bible, paragraphs 245
Breaking tablets, date 155
Brother's virgin wife 228
Burial customs 519
Bystanders 78,134

Calendar, computed 45, 200
Caligula 161
Cave as *miqweh* 456
Chaos 418
Charity money, sanctity 318
Childless woman 181
Children, liability for 377
Cleanly people 465
Cohen barred from sancta 486
Cold bathing 586
Commandments, number 273
Confession, on sacrifice 304
Correcting text 241,242
Crawling animals 50
Criminal torts 226,228
Dargesh 591
Date of Metuselah's death 581
Day of Atonement, sacrifices 361
Deaf-and-dumb, legal status 299
Deaf-mute child 380
Dealing on holiday 540
Death of Miriam 618
Debts to Temple 388
Decisions to be reasoned 413
Dew, praying for 8
Discipline of heave 452
Disciplining rabbis 558
Disqualification 477
Disregarding judicial rules 439
Divine modes 56
Drinking as eating 39

Edom-Rome 16
Eight Verses 332
Eighth Day of Tabernacles 401,402
Eleazar watches 138.
Elementary education, obligatory 404
Elijah's altar 74
Elisha ben Abuya legend 422,427
Enjoyment of meat 391
Epidemic 103
Equal cut 346
Esoteric teachings 422
Esther scroll, as legal text 191
Esther scroll, in suburbs 193
Esther scroll, in Tiberias 194
Esther scroll, reading dates 188,197,215
Esther scroll, status 204
Excommunication, duration 551,555
Excommunication, to be lifted 558
Exempt fluids 465

Fast days, regular 34
Fasting on Friday 89,91
Fasting on Sabbath 115
Fellow grocer 496
Final *mem* 239
Finger holes 461
Flesh 383,422
Flour sacrifces, impurity 475
Flour sacrifices 474
Four Readings 326
Friend of the Synagogue 269

Garlic 349
Gate of Heaven 124
Golden calf, punishment for 156
Gordian denar 501
Gossip a sin 16
Grain blight 106
Great *Hallel* 117

Hallel 303
Heretic predestination 366
Heretic sects 365
Hermaphrodite 382
Hermeneutical rules 346
High Priest, invested 255
High Priest, mourning 613
Holiday burial 598
Holidays, rabbinic 87
Holy pious 33
Holy sinners 30
Holy spirit 191
Homiletics not prescriptive

412
Homosexuality, active and
  passive   416
Hypocrite as blasphemer
                         415

Ignorant congregation   352
Immersion, of woman   301
Immersion, unintentional
                         302
Impounding by court   554
Impure land   488
Impurities of gonorrhea
                    231,232
Impurities of skin disease
                    231,234
Impurity not by touch   453
Impurity of hands   448,449
Impurity, by place   484
Impurity, by support   457
Impurity, day-by-day   298
Impurity, of body fluids
                460,470,484
Impurity, of childbirth 486,
                         498
Impurity, of skin disease
                519,521,522
Impurity, of toddlers   384
Impurity, stages of   386
Impurity, stages   459
Inclusion-exclusion   356
Institution of Ezra   348
Intercalary month   221
Intercalation,
  announcement   221
Interpreting Mishnah   88

Jerusalem, prayer for   64
Joy, obligatory   396,398
Judaism, abstract   218
Judaism, historic   218

Khalkis, city   86
Kilaim in orchard   516

Leather shoes   37,40
Letters as numbers   50
Letters encrypted   321
Levites' song   164
Lifting vows   559

Locative as nominative 250
LXX changes in text   251

Marriage, preordained 44,
                         178
Masoretic text   142
Mezuzza, calligraphic 244
Mezuzzah, place   372
Minimal lengths   421
Minimum value,
  reinterpretation   394
Minimum value, rabbinic
                         393
Minor holiday   504
Minor holiday, work   506
Mishnah, final edition 204
Mixing sources of money
                         394
Mourner's meal   355,562,
                         594
Mourning periods 567,570,
                         581
Mourning, current notice
                         568
Mourning, late notice   568
Mourning, rules of   560
Mourning, shortened   572

Names not to be erased 252
Names, prefixed and
  suffixed   252
Nest of birds   172
Netherworld   8
New Moon meal   206
New Years, Day, start   309
Nineveh   11
Noahide sacrifices   271

Obulus   389
Omer, counting   305
Omer, cutting   304
Onias Circle Drawer   109
Onias's fast   108
Oral law, divisions   340
Ordination   140
Ordination, rabbinic   409
Overturning beds   594

Paleo-Hebrew *waw*   239
Pantokaka   30

Paragraph, closed   245
Paragraph, open   245
Parsing sentences   343
Partial obligation   381
Partially deaf   379
Pentecost on Friday   444
Pentecost, meaning 155,
                         329
Pentecost, week of   205
Pentecostal week   597
Personal obligation   405
Pharisaic leadership   434
Place selected by Eternal
                         265
Pledges, changes in   206
Plural and singular   386
Plural, undetermined   379
Power of rains   3
Prayer against Sectarians
                          76
Prayer text   14
Prayer, Galilean rite   68
Prayer, instituted   67
Prayer, lead by blind   67
Prayer, public private   72
Prayer, repeated   12
Prayers, evening   130
Prayers, five daily   130
Praying immovably   10
Prebends on slaughter-day
                         447
Priest of doubtful
  legitimacy   259
Priest, anointed for war
                256,261,263
Priestly calendar   138
Priestly clans   78
Priestly watches   78,80
Priestly watches, localities
                         164
Priestly watches, Second
  Temple   139
Promise to Heaven   388
Prophets, scrolling   358
Prophets, translation   358
Prozbol   563
Psalms, numbering   58
Pseudo-Jonathan   15
Punishing non-crimes   440
Pure and impure   553

INDICES

Purification sacrifice, of
   deceased   388
Purification sacrifices,
   location   273
Purification   480
Purifying Temple 495,497,
                           499
Purifying vessels   461
Purim gifts to poor   206
Purim in intercalation 215
Purim meal   206
Purim, Torah reading 144
Purity by intention 454,456
Purity, impurity   384

Qonam   313
Quorum   355

Rabbinic over prophetic
                           553
Rain, praying for 3,10,12
Rain, useful   24
Raqqat   194
Reader, badly dressed 363
Reader, of Prophets   352
Readers, multiple 342,347
Reading curses   332
Reading, Palestinian rule
                           325
Readings, holiday   329
Rent clothing   586,607
Reserve vessels   498
Rest and Inheritance 284
Reward not guaranteed
                           418
Roman pound   182

Sacrifice of appearance 389
Sacrifice, personal   377
Scribal errors, maximum
                           246
Scroll of Fasts   81
Scroll sewn   247
Scroll, benedictions   343

Scroll, column size   244
Scroll, number of lines 246
Scroll, read by minor 298,
                           300
Scroll, read in Greek 288
Scroll, reading for
   another's benefit 294
Second *Pesah*   381
Senile sage   558
Septimius Severus   169
Septuagint   142
Sexless turned out male
                           381
Shema Pronouncing 299
Shema Reading   352,363
Simeon ben Shetah legend
                           439
Sinar   349
Son of Man   56
Song Mosis   333
Songs, writing of   333
Space, time created   415
Splitting verses   360
Stories of teh Golden Calf
                           369
Study precedes action 405
Study prevents death 589
Study, benediction   347
Synagogue board,   318
Synagogue, as shortcut 324

Tabernacles, readings 210
Table of Noahide peoples
                           237
Targum, canonical 339,343
Targum, improvised 342
Targum, status of   240
Tearing clothing   568
Tefillin knots   247
Tefillin making   248
Tefillin   236
Temple service, stopping
                           297
Temple site forever   265

Temple tax, replacement
                           219
Tevul Yom   450
Tineius Rufus   177
Tirion   84
Tithe declaration   378
Torah reading   145
Torah reading, date   199
Torah, benediction   348
Torah, original script 238,
                           250
Torah, scrolling   361
Town board   318
Trading prebends   451
Triclinium   143

Unetanne Toqef   54
Ursicinus   317

Vessel, combining 469,472
Voiding vows   408
Vows and obligations 400
Vulgar in Fellow's house
                           495
Vulgar workers   489,493
Vulgar   456

Wailing women   618
Washing garments   562
Washing hands for sancta
                           482
Water libation   73
Weaving the lulav   4
White mules   95
Wimpel   310,317
Witness to death   584
Women studying Torah
                           377
Wooden box, pure   172
Writing *he*   239
Writing on leather   249
Writing verses   321

www.ingramcontent.com/pod-product-compliance
Lightning Source LLC
Chambersburg PA
CBHW021412300426
44114CB00010B/471